Of Children

Of Children

AN INTRODUCTION TO

CHILD DEVELOPMENT

EIGHTH EDITION

GUY R. LEFRANÇOIS
UNIVERSITY OF ALBERTA

Wadsworth Publishing Company

An International Thomson Publishing Company

Belmont • Albany • Bonn • Boston • Cincinnati • Detroit
London • Madrid • Melbourne • Mexico City • New York
Paris • San Francisco • Singapore • Tokyo • Toronto • Washington

Editor: Sabra Horne

Editorial Assistants: Kate Peltier, Janet Hansen

Production Editors: Angela Mann, Cathy Linberg

Managing Designer: Ann Butler

Print Buyer: Karen Hunt

Art Editor: Bobbie Broyer

Permissions Editor: Jeanne Bosschart

Cover and Interior Designer:
  Seventeenth Street Studios

Copy Editor: Alan Titche

Photo Researcher: Photosynthesis

Cover Illustrator: Laurie Anderson

Compositor: Thompson Type

Printer: Quebecor Printing Book Group/Hawkins

**Library of Congress
Cataloging-in-Publication Data**
Lefrançois, Guy R.
  Of children : an introduction to child
development / Guy R. Lefrançois. — 8th ed.
     p.   cm.
  Includes bibliographical references and index.
  ISBN 0-534-21936-5
  1. Child development.   I. Title.
RJ131.L38   1994
305.23'1—dc20   94-30151

For more information,
contact Wadsworth Publishing Company:

Wadsworth Publishing Company
10 Davis Drive
Belmont, California 94002, USA

International Thomson Publishing Europe
Berkshire House 168-173
High Holborn
London, WC1V 7AA, England

Thomas Nelson Australia
102 Dodds Street
South Melbourne 3205
Victoria, Australia

Nelson Canada
1120 Birchmount Road
Scarborough, Ontario
Canada M1K 5G4

International Thomson Editores
Campos Eliseos 385, Piso 7
Col. Polanco
11560 México D.F. México

International Thomson Publishing GmbH
Königswinterer Strasse 418
53227 Bonn, Germany

International Thomson Publishing Asia
221 Henderson Road
#05-10 Henderson Building
Singapore 0315

International Thomson Publishing Japan
Hirakawacho Kyowa Building, 3F
2-2-1 Hirakawacho
Chiyoda-ku, Tokyo 102, Japan

1976

1982

1985

1991

This book is
affectionately
dedicated to
Laurier,
Claire,
Rémi,
and Elizabeth,
beautiful children,
and to all things beautiful.

Brief contents

one   the beginning

CHAPTER 1   STUDYING THE CHILD   3

CHAPTER 2   THEORIES OF
             DEVELOPMENT   41

two   biological beginnings

CHAPTER 3   GENETICS AND CONTEXT 101

CHAPTER 4   PRENATAL DEVELOPMENT
             AND BIRTH   145

three infancy

CHAPTER 5   PHYSICAL AND
             COGNITIVE DEVELOPMENT
             IN INFANCY   193

CHAPTER 6   SOCIAL DEVELOPMENT
             IN INFANCY   243

four   early childhood

CHAPTER 7   PHYSICAL AND COGNITIVE
             DEVELOPMENT IN EARLY
             CHILDHOOD   293

CHAPTER 8   SOCIAL DEVELOPMENT
             IN EARLY CHILDHOOD   343

five   middle childhood

CHAPTER 9   PHYSICAL AND COGNITIVE
             DEVELOPMENT IN MIDDLE
             CHILDHOOD   391

CHAPTER 10   SOCIAL DEVELOPMENT IN
             MIDDLE CHILDHOOD   443

six   adolescence

CHAPTER 11   PHYSICAL AND COGNITIVE
             DEVELOPMENT IN
             ADOLESCENCE   499

CHAPTER 12   SOCIAL DEVELOPMENT
             IN ADOLESCENCE   543

seven epilogue

CHAPTER 13   THE END   601

etailed contents

one   the beginning

CHAPTER I   STUDYING THE CHILD   3

How This Text Explores Growing Up   5
    Some Definitions   6
Changing Attitudes Toward Children   7
    Snapshot 1: Childbirth in Medieval Europe   8
    Snapshot 2: Begging and Stealing in
      Eighteenth-Century Europe   9
    Snapshot 3: Child Abandonment in
      Eighteenth-Century Europe   9
    Snapshot 4: Child Labor in
      Nineteenth-Century Europe   9
    Snapshot 5: The Developing World Today   10
    Snapshot 6: The Industrialized World
      Today   11
    Why Look at History?   13
Children's Rights   14
    Establishing the Rights of Children   14
    Disregard of Children's Rights in
      the Third World   16
The Study of Children   20
    Early Observers of Children   20
    Later Observers of Children   21
    The Study of Children Today   22
Recurring Questions in Developmental Psychology   22
Basic Beliefs Concerning Human Development   23
Methods of Studying Children   24
    Observations   24
    Experiments   26
    Correlational Studies   28
    Longitudinal and Cross-Sectional Research   30
    Dealing with Sources of Variation   31
Evaluating Developmental Research   33
    Sampling   33
    Ecological and Cross-Cultural Validity   34
    Memory   35
    Subject Honesty   35
    Experimenter Bias   35
    Subject Bias   35
Main Points   37
Focus Questions: Applications   38
Study Terms   39
Further Readings   39

CHAPTER 2   THEORIES OF DEVELOPMENT   41

Theory and Science   44
    Functions of Theories   44
    Developing Theories   44
    Evaluating Theories   45
    Facts and Expectations   45
    Characteristics of Good Theories   45
Models in Child Development   46
    Machine Models and Organism Models   46
    A Contextual or Ecological Model   47
Psychoanalytic Approaches: Freud   48
    Basic Freudian Ideas   49
    Three Levels of Human Personality   50
    Psychosexual Stages in Human
      Development   52
    Defense Mechanisms   54
    Freudian Theory in Review   54
Psychoanalytic Approaches: Erikson   56
    Psychosocial Stages in Human
      Development   56
    Erikson's Theory in Review   59
Havighurst's Developmental Tasks   59
Behavioristic Approaches   61
    Overview of Behavioristic Approaches   61
    Classical Conditioning   62
    Operant Conditioning   64
    Behavioristic Approaches in Review   67
Social Cognitive Theory   68
    The Processes of Observational Learning   68
    Manifestations of Observational Learning   69
    Self-Efficacy Judgments   70
    Social Cognitive Theory in Review   74
A Cognitive Approach: Piaget   74
    Basic Concepts in Cognitive Development   75
    The Stages of Cognitive Development   76
    Piaget's Theory in Review   78
Biological and Ecological Approaches   79
    Ethology and Bowlby's Attachment
      Theory   79
    Bowlby's Theory in Review   82
    Sociobiology   83
    Vygotsky's Cultural-Historical Approach   84
    Vygotsky's Theory in Review   86

Bronfenbrenner's Ecological
Systems Theory 87
Humanistic Approaches 91
Maslow's Humanistic Need Theory 92
Humanism in Review 93
A Final Word About Theories 93
Main Points 95
Focus Questions: Applications 96
Study Terms 97
Further Readings 98

two   biological beginnings

CHAPTER 3   GENETICS AND CONTEXT 101

Feral Children 103
The Interaction of Genetics and Context 105
What Is Interaction? 105
How Genes and Environment Interact 106
Basic Concepts of Heredity 107
Ovum, Sperm, and Conception 107
Proteins 108
DNA 108
Chromosomes 108
Sex Chromosomes 109
Genes and Their Function 109
Genotype and Phenotype 111
Reaction Range and Canalization 113
Molecular Genetics 114
Genetic Defects 115
Defects Resulting from Genetically Related
Parents 115
Huntington's Disease 117
Sickle-Cell Anemia 117
PKU 118
Other Genetic Defects 119
Chromosomal Disorders 120
Down Syndrome 120
Abnormalities of the Sex Chromosomes 122
Identifying and Dealing with Genetic Risk 124
Prenatal Diagnosis 124
Treating Genetic Disorders 126
Genetic Counseling 126
Genetics and the Future 128
Studying Gene-Context Interaction 130
Historical Family Studies 130
Animal Studies 131
Intervention Studies 133
Studies of Twins 134

Studies of Adopted Children 136
An Illustration of Gene-Context
Interaction 138
The Continuing Nature-Nurture Controversy 139
Main Points 140
Focus Questions: Applications 142
Study Terms 142
Further Readings 143

CHAPTER 4   PRENATAL DEVELOPMENT
AND BIRTH   145

Conception 147
Detecting Pregnancy 147
Stages of Prenatal Development 148
Stage of the Fertilized Ovum 148
The Embryo Stage 150
Fetal Period 151
Factors Affecting Prenatal Development 153
Prescription Drug Use 154
Exposure to Chemicals 156
Nicotine Intake 157
Caffeine Consumption 157
Alcohol Consumption 157
Substance Abuse 158
Maternal Health 160
Maternal Emotions and Stress 161
Maternal Age 165
Maternal Nutrition 166
Social Class 168
Rh(D) Immunization 168
Childbirth 170
The Initiation of Childbirth 173
Classifications of Birth Status 174
Stages of Labor 175
Cesarean Delivery 177
Neonatal Scales 178
The Mother's Experience: Prepared
Childbirth 179
The Child's Experience 181
Prematurity 182
Causes of Prematurity 182
Effects of Prematurity 183
Prevention of Prematurity 185
Care of Premature Infants 185
A Reassuring Note 186
Main Points 186
Focus Questions: Applications 188
Study Terms 188
Further Readings 189

three infancy

CHAPTER 5 PHYSICAL AND COGNITIVE DEVELOPMENT IN INFANCY   193

Blueprint for a Neonate   195

Nutrition, Health, and Physical Growth in Infancy   197

The Breast Versus Bottle Controversy   197

Nutrition and Brain Development   200

Physical Growth in Infancy   200

Sudden Infant Death Syndrome   202

Behavior in Newborns   205

The Orienting Response   205

Reflexes   206

Motor Development in Infants   207

Perceptual Development in Infants   209

Vision   209

Hearing   214

Smell, Taste, and Touch   216

Cognitive Development in Infants   217

Memory in Infants   217

Basic Piagetian Ideas on Infancy   219

The Object Concept   220

Sensorimotor Development in Infants   222

Imitation in Infancy   226

Language and Communication   227

A Definition of Language   228

Elements of Language   230

Language Development in Infants   231

Achievements in the Prespeech Stage   231

The Beginnings of Verbal Communication   232

Infants' First Sounds   233

The Sentencelike Word (Holophrase)   235

Two-Word Sentences   235

From Sensation to Representation   237

Main Points   238

Focus Questions: Applications   240

Study Terms   240

Further Readings   241

CHAPTER 6 SOCIAL DEVELOPMENT IN INFANCY   243

The Family Context   245

Child Development as an Interactional Process   245

How Personal Characteristics Affect Interactions   246

A Triadic Model of Child Development   247

How Babies Affect Parents and Vice Versa   247

Infant States   248

States of the "Average" Infant   249

Do Infants Dream?   250

Behaviors as Indicators of Infants' Emotions   250

Crying   251

Smiling and Laughing   251

Wariness and Fear   252

Regulation of Emotions in Infancy   255

Temperament   256

Types of Temperament Among Infants   256

The Implications of Infants' Temperament   258

Cultural Context and Temperament   259

Attachment in Infants   261

Studying Attachment   262

Mother-Infant Bonding   262

Stages of Attachment   265

Types of Attachment   267

The Implications of Attachment   268

Fathers and Infant Attachment   270

Separation Anxiety and Fear of Strangers   271

Fear of Strangers   272

The Effects of Culture on Separation Anxiety   272

Individual Differences in Separation Anxiety   273

Can Children Be Prepared for Separation?   273

The Role of Attachment to Inanimate Objects   273

Long-Term Separation and Deprivation   274

Infant Daycare   276

The Effects of Parenting on Infants' Development   278

Early Gender-Role Influences   279

The Origins and Effects of Gender Typing   279

Exceptionality in Infants   280

Motor Skill Disorders   282

Epilepsy   284

Other Physical Problems   284

Autistic Disorder   285

The Whole Infant   286

Main Points   286

Focus Questions: Applications   288

Study Terms   288

Further Readings   288

four   early childhood

CHAPTER 7   PHYSICAL AND COGNITIVE
DEVELOPMENT IN EARLY
CHILDHOOD   293

Children and Magical Thinking   295
Physical Growth in Early Childhood   295
Motor Development   298
    Assessing Motor Development   300
    The Relationship Between Motor and
    Cognitive Development   301
Cognitive Development: Memory in Preschoolers   301
    Incidental Mnemonics   302
    Memory Strategies of Preschoolers   303
Cognitive Development in Preschoolers: Piaget's View   305
    Preconceptual Thinking   305
    Intuitive Thinking   307
    Replications of Piaget's Work   309
    Cognitive Achievements of Preschoolers   312
Preschool Education   314
    Preschool Education Elsewhere   315
    Nursery Schools   316
    Compensatory Preschool Programs   316
    Kindergartens   317
    Effective Preschool Education:
    The Family Context   319
Language and the Preschooler   320
    Language in Infancy   322
    Multiple-Word Sentences   323
    More Complex Grammatical Changes   324
    Adultlike Structures   324
Explanations of Language Development   326
    The Role of Early Experience
    in Language Development   326
    The Role of Parents as Teachers
    of Language   326
    The Role of Biology in Language
    Development   329
Bilingualism and a Changing Language Context   330
    Transitional Bilingualism   330
    The Psychological Effects of Bilingualism   331
    Bilingualism in Today's Schools   334
    Nonstandard Languages   335
Speech and Language Problems in Early Childhood   336
The Relation of Language and Thought   337
Language Is for Communicating and Conversing   338
Main Points   339
Focus Questions: Applications   341

Study Terms   341
Further Readings   341

CHAPTER 8   SOCIAL DEVELOPMENT
IN EARLY CHILDHOOD   343

The Socialization of Emotions   345
    Interpreting Emotions   345
    Regulating Emotions   347
    Expressing Emotions   347
Theories of Social Development   348
    Erikson's Psychosocial Stages   348
    Social Imitation   350
Play   353
    Functions of Play   353
    Types of Play   354
    The Implications of Imagination   356
    Social Play   358
Gender Roles in Early Childhood   361
    Gender Schemas   362
    Assuming Gender Identity   362
    Gender Differences   363
The Contemporary Family   365
    Parenting Young Children   367
    Do Parents Make a Measurable
    Difference? 369
    Learning to Parent   371
Family Composition   372
    Birth Order   372
    Family Size   373
    Social Class and Related Factors   373
One-Parent Families   374
    General Effects of Loss of a Parent   374
    Developmental Effects of Divorce   374
    Sex-Related Effects of Divorce   376
    Contextual Effects of Divorce   376
    Why Divorce Has Negative Effects   376
    Some Conclusions   377
    A Final Word   379
Children in Stepfamilies   380
    Possible Problems in Stepfamilies   380
    The Positive Side of Stepfamilies   381
Childcare Outside the Home   381
    General Effects of Childcare   382
    Research on the Quality of Childcare   383
    Finding Quality Childcare   383
Main Points   384
Focus Questions: Applications   386
Study Terms   386
Further Readings   387

five middle childhood

CHAPTER 9   PHYSICAL AND COGNITIVE DEVELOPMENT IN MIDDLE CHILDHOOD   391

Middle Childhood Defined   393

Physical Development   393
Growth   393
Nutrition and Health   395
Motor Development   397
Some Physical and Sensory Problems   398
The Physically Gifted   400

Intellectual Development: Piaget's View   400
The Conservations   401
Can Conservation Be Accelerated?   405
Classes, Seriation, and Number   405
Summary of Concrete Operations   407

Children as Information Processors   407
Types of Memory   409
Memory Processes   411
Schemata and Scripts: A Model of Long-Term Memory   412
Developmental Changes in Memory   413

Metacognition and Metamemory   414
Motivation and Self-Efficacy in Learning   415
Cultural Differences in Learning Strategies   416
The Use of Cognitive Strategies   416

Intelligence   417
What Is Intelligence?   418
Measuring Intelligence   419
Developmental Changes in IQ   421
Misconceptions About and Misuses of IQ   422
The Usefulness of Intelligence Tests   423

Intellectual Exceptionality   424
Mental Retardation   424
Learning Disabilities   426
Intellectual Giftedness   430
Creativity   430
Trends and Controversies in Special Education   437

The Magical Child   439

Main Points   439

Focus Questions: Applications   441

Study Terms   441

Further Readings   442

CHAPTER 10   SOCIAL DEVELOPMENT IN MIDDLE CHILDHOOD   443

Social Cognition   445
The Development of Social Cognition   445
Theories of Mind   445

Self-Worth   448
Some Definitions   448
Theoretical Approaches to Self-Worth   448
Measuring and Investigating Self-Worth   449

The Influence of Friends and Peers   452
Children's Views of Friendship   452
Dimensions of Childhood Friendships   453
Peer Groups   455
Parents and Peers   455
Sociometric Status   459
Functions of Peers   460

The Role of the School   461
Schooling and IQ   461
Teachers' Expectations   462
Self-Expectations   463

The Effects of Television   465
Children's Viewing Patterns   465
What Children Comprehend   466
Violence and Aggression   466
Positive Effects   471
Why Is Television Influential?   472
Rock Videos, VCRs, and Video Games   473
A Summary of Television Issues   474

Violence in the Family   474
The Case Against Punishment   475
The Case for Punishment   475
Kinds of Punishment   476
Child Maltreatment   476
The Nature of Child Abuse and Neglect   479
The Consequences of Maltreatment   481
The Abusive Family Context   483
What Can Be Done?   485

Socioemotional Exceptionality   486
Prevalence and Causes   486
Attention-Deficit Hyperactivity Disorder   487
Other Behavior Disorders   489
Stress in Childhood   490
Socioemotional Giftedness   492

Main Points   492

Focus Questions: Applications   495

Study Terms   495

Further Readings   495

six   adolescence

CHAPTER 11   PHYSICAL AND COGNITIVE
              DEVELOPMENT IN
              ADOLESCENCE   499

A Period of Transitions   501
        Transitions in Preindustrial Societies   501
        Transitions in Industrialized Societies   502
Physical Changes of Adolescence   504
        Puberty   504
        Pubescence   505
        Physical Changes   506
        Early and Late Maturation   508
        Physical Concerns of Adolescents   510
Nutrition During Adolescence   511
        Obesity   511
        Anorexia Nervosa   512
        Bulimia Nervosa   516
Intellectual Development in Adolescence   518
        Piaget's View: Formal Operations   518
        An Information-Processing View   521
Adolescent Egocentrism   523
        The Imaginary Audience   524
        The Personal Fable   526
        Reckless Behavior   526
Moral Development in Adolescence   528
        Behaving Morally   529
        Morality as an Understanding of Justice   529
        Piaget's Approach to Morality   530
        Kohlberg's Stages of Morality   531
        The Generality of Kohlberg's Stages   533
        Gilligan's Approach: Gender Differences
          in Morality   535
        Implications of Research on Moral
          Development   537
Main Points   539
Focus Questions: Applications   541
Study Terms   541
Further Readings   541

CHAPTER 12   SOCIAL DEVELOPMENT
              IN ADOLESCENCE   543

The Self   545
        The Self in Adolescence   546
        A Measure of Self-Image   546
        Sturm und Drang? 549
        Developmental Changes in Notions
          of Self   551

        Some Origins of Self-Worth   552
        Identity   553
Social Development in Context   556
        Parenting Adolescents   557
        Peer Groups   558
Gender Roles in Adolescence   562
        Gender-Role Stereotypes   562
        Gender Differences   563
Sex   566
        Sexual Beliefs and Behavior   566
        Adolescent Pregnancy   569
        Homosexuality   574
        Sexually Transmitted Diseases   574
The Turmoil Topics   577
        Delinquency   577
        Adolescent Gangs   580
        Drugs   581
        Suicide   590
Another Note   594
Main Points   594
Focus Questions: Applications   596
Study Terms   596
Further Readings   597

seven   epilogue

CHAPTER 13   THE END   601

A Summary   603
        Chapter 1   603
        Chapter 2   603
        Chapter 3   603
        Chapter 4   604
        Chapters 5 and 6   604
        Chapters 7 and 8   604
        Chapters 9 and 10   604
        Chapters 11 and 12   604
        Of "Average Children" and
          of Other Children   605
Other Views   605
        Humanism   606
        Existentialism   607

Glossary   610
References   627
Acknowledgments   671
Author Index   673
Subject Index   682

Thematic contents

TOPIC	CHAPTER	PAGE	SECTION HEADING
Cognitive development	5	193	whole chapter (infancy)
	7	293	whole chapter (early childhood)
	9	391	whole chapter (middle childhood)
	11	499	whole chapter (adolescence)
Exceptionality	3	115	Genetic Defects
		120	Chromosomal Disorders
	4	153	Factors Affecting Prenatal Development
	6	280	Exceptionality in Infants
	9	424	Intellectual Exceptionality
	10	486	Socioemotional Exceptionality
The family context	2	79	Biological and Ecological Approaches
	3	130	Studying Gene-Context Interactions
	6	245	The Family Context
		261	Attachment in Infants
		278	The Effects of Parenting on Infants' Development
	8	365	The Contemporary Family
		372	Family Composition
		374	One-Parent Families
	10	452	The Influence of Friends and Peers
		474	Violence in the Family
	12	545	The Self
		556	Social Development in Context
Gender roles	6	279	Early Gender-Role Influences
	8	361	Gender Roles in Early Childhood
	12	562	Gender Roles in Adolescence
Genetics and context	3	101	whole chapter
History and methods	1	3	whole chapter
Intelligence	9	417	Intelligence
Language development	5	227	Language and Communication
		228	A Definition of Language
		231	Language Development in Infants
	7	320	Language and the Preschooler
		326	Explanations of Language Development

TOPIC	CHAPTER	PAGE	SECTION HEADING
		330	Bilingualism and a Changing Language Context
		336	Speech and Language Problems in Early Childhood
		337	The Relation of Language and Thought
Memory	5	217	Memory in Infants
	7	301	Cognitive Development: Memory in Preschoolers
	9	407	Children as Information Processors
Morality	2	68	Social Cognitive Theory
	8	345	The Socialization of Emotions
	10	474	Violence in the Family
	11	528	Moral Development in Adolescence
	12	577	The Turmoil Topics
Physical Development	5	197	Nutrition, Health, and Physical Growth in Infancy
		207	Motor Development in Infants
	7	295	Physical Growth in Early Childhood
		298	Motor Development
	9	393	Physical Development
	11	504	Physical Changes of Adolescence
		511	Nutrition During Adolescence
Piaget	2	74	A Cognitive Approach: Piaget
	7	305	Cognitive Development in Preschoolers: Piaget's View
	9	400	Intellectual Development: Piaget's View
	11	518	Intellectual Development in Adolescence
Play	8	353	Play
Prenatal Development	4	145	whole chapter
School and childcare	6	276	Infant Daycare
	7	314	Preschool Education
	8	381	Childcare Outside the Home
	10	461	The Role of the School
Social Development	6	243	whole chapter (infancy)
	8	343	whole chapter (early childhood)
	10	443	whole chapter (middle childhood)
	12	543	whole chapter (adolescence)
Television	10	465	The Effects of Television
Theories	2	41	whole chapter

A VISUAL GUIDE TO

Of Children

Dear Reader,

This, as you know, is the Eighth Edition of the book I first wrote more than two decades ago. At that time, I tried to tell you why I had written it as it was then. I remember saying that I didn't want to clutter your mind with trivia; that because you are bright and enthusiastic, I should try not to give you too many things to forget without also giving you something to remember. I've tried to keep these things in mind while writing this Eighth Edition.

It wasn't easy because in some ways, the study of child development has become more complex rather than simpler. We have even more theories now, more findings, more speculation, more controversy. As a result, children don't fit any more neatly between the covers of a book today than they did in the first edition. We are still forced to dissect and analyze the mythical "average child." And there is always the danger that the real non-average child may be lost in the process. So, in this book I stop every once in a while to remind you—and myself—that this book is of children.

Of Children is an introductory textbook in child development. It deals with physical, social, emotional, and intellectual development from infancy to adolescence. My goal is to present the most important and useful information about children simply and clearly, to communicate how fascinating the subject of child development can be and also how provocative, challenging, and sometimes controversial.

On the following five pages, you will be guided through a number of important features designed to make this book an effective learning experience, as well as some specific revisions to this Eighth Edition that reflect many vital factors affecting the study of child development today.

eatures of this book worth learning about—

At the beginning of each chapter—

FOCUS QUESTIONS

introduce readers to the chapter by
identifying some of the main ideas
to be covered.

OUTLINES

indicate the order and relationships
of topics within each chapter.

VIGNETTES

introduce the chapter with
a personal, relevant story.

focus questions

WHAT IS THE LIKELY OUTCOME OF A
CHILD BEING RAISED BY A CHICKEN?
A WOLF? ALONE IN AN ATTIC?

WHAT ARE THE MARVELS AND THE
MYSTERIES OF WHAT OUR ELDERS
CALLED THE BIRDS AND BEES?

WHAT ARE THE MOST COMMON
GENETIC DEFECTS AND PROBLEMS?

HOW CAN WE DIAGNOSE GENETIC
PROBLEMS?

WHAT CAN WE DO ABOUT THEM?

WHAT IS THE NATURE-NURTURE
CONTROVERSY?

outline

FERAL CHILDREN

THE INTERACTION OF GENETICS
AND CONTEXT
  What is Interaction?
  How Genes and Environment
    Interact

BASIC CONCEPTS OF HEREDITY
  Ovum, Sperm, and Conception
  Proteins
  DNA
  Chromosomes
  Sex Chromosomes
  Genes and Their Function
  Genotype and Phenotype
  Reaction Range and Canalization
  Molecular Genetics

GENETIC DEFECTS
  Defects Resulting from Genetically
    Related Parents
  Huntington's Disease
  Sickle-Cell Anemia
  PKU
  Other Genetic Defects

CHROMOSOMAL DISORDERS
  Down Syndrome
  Abnormalities of the Sex
    Chromosomes

IDENTIFYING AND DEALING WITH
GENETIC RISK
  Prenatal Diagnosis
  Treating Genetic Disorders
  Genetic Counseling
  Genetics and the Future

STUDYING GENE-CONTEXT
INTERACTION
  Historical Family Studies
  Animal Studies
  Intervention Studies
  Studies of Twins
  Studies of Adopted Children
  An Illustration of Gene-Context
    Interaction

THE CONTINUING NATURE-
NURTURE CONTROVERSY

MAIN POINTS

FOCUS QUESTIONS: APPLICATIONS

STUDY TERMS

FURTHER READINGS

W

hen I was little and misbehaved, my
parents would sometimes threaten to put me
out with the chickens if I didn't smarten up. The
threat might not have been very effective had it
not been for the tragic tale of Robert Edward
Cuttingham, whom we knew as "Chicken."

We all knew the story, how his parents had
left him too long and too often with the chickens so that his brain and his habits grew up
chickenlike rather than human. Rumor was he
always slept in the chicken coop during the
summer, that he came indoors only when it got
so cold the water froze on the river. They said,
too, that he slept perched on a railing and that
when he awoke in the morning he'd crow as
loud and long as any rooster. John George Scott,
who lived up in the hills behind the Cuttingham
farm, said he heard him lots of times and saw
him quite often, walking all crouched over, his
arms dragging at his sides, darting around with
his head bobbing back and forth, looking for
seeds and stuff on the ground.

I thought I saw him once, too, when I was
out setting rabbit snares—not real clearly,
more like a shadow or a streak in the woods,
moving low and close to the ground and making a strange chirping kind of noise. I told
everybody about it, maybe exaggerating just a
little, describing how he came up to me, twisting his head from side to side, looking at me
with his beady eyes, not stopping until he was
no more than three feet away. "Then," I said,
"he turned his head and looked at me with just
one eye, just like a real chicken." We had great
fun that afternoon running along the

Throughout the book—

"AT A GLANCE" SECTIONS

that consist of highly current data reflecting some important feature of life for North American children. Most chapters include one or more such sections, designed to make an impact through their relevance, brevity, and graphic illustration.

"IN OTHER CONTEXTS"

boxed inserts in each chapter that present factual third-person accounts of children in other cultures. Each box concludes with a brief "To Think About" section posing questions underlining the context-bound nature of our beliefs about children. Such critical questions not only encourage interaction with the text material, but provide an excellent basis for classroom or seminar discussion.

FLEXIBLE USAGE—

While readers will find that the organization of this book is chronological (major sections deal with infancy, childhood, and adolescence, in order), each section contains all major topics in the study of child development. Accordingly, it is simple to rearrange chapters to conform to a topic approach using the detailed thematic table of contents included on pages xiii–xiv.

---

at a **G** **lance** **economic characteristics of mother-only families**

i n 1991, nearly three-fourths of U.S. children under 18 lived with both parents. Of these, nearly 47 million children (71.8 percent) lived in families that owned rather than rented their homes. Of the 2 million children who lived with their fathers only, more than half (51.4 percent) lived in owned homes. In contrast, only about one-third (32.8 percent) of the 14.6 million children living with mothers only were living in owned homes. Moreover, income in these mother-only homes was dramatically lower than in two-parent or father-only homes.

f **igure 8.5**

(bottom left) Median income of two-parent, father-only, and mother-only U.S. families, 1991. The median is the midpoint; half the families in each category earn more than the median and half earn less. Source: Adapted from U.S. Bureau of the Census (1992), p. 452.

f **igure 8.6**

(bottom right) Percentage of two-parent and mother-only U.S. families in various income brackets, 1991. Source: Adapted from U.S. Bureau of the Census (1992), p. 54.

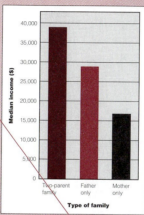

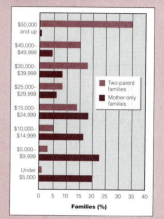

---

in other **C** **ontexts** **a !Kung woman's first child**

W hen she felt the contractions were sufficiently strong and frequent, Sanya, a woman of the !Kung, hunter-gatherers of the Kalahari, rose silently from her bed. She didn't awaken her husband—or even her parents, although they, too, slept in the same hut. Among the !Kung, a marriage is not considered consummated before the birth of a child; until then, the couple lives with the wife's parents. This would be Sanya's first child.

For a moment, Sanya thought she might awaken her mother; the first birth is sometimes assisted by the mother. But !Kung women are strong and independent, and Sanya scarcely hesitated. Alone, she walked out into the veld, smelling the rich earth smells

walk back to the village and the women would massage her back while her husband, using his walking stick, would draw a fine line in the sand.

erased all traces of the delivery, burying the stained grasses and carefully marking the spot with a stick so that no man would accidentally step on it and lose his sexual potency or his hunting skills.

Quickly, she hurried home. Tonight there would be a feast and a dance for the new baby.

To Think About: To what extent might the pain and fear sometimes associated with childbirth be influenced by cultural expectations? Can you think of other reactions and expectations that are typical in your cultural group—and that you therefore assume to be "natural" but that might be quite different elsewhere?

To Read: Goldsmith, J. (1990a). Childbirth wisdom: From the world's

ILLUSTRATIONS

are used to reinforce a variety of text material (in the form of tables, charts, and graphs). Because subjects surrounding child development are often substantially data-driven, they can often be better understood when they are explained visually.

VIVID PHOTOS
. . . TIMELY EXAMPLES

that complement text discussions, are used to illustrate developmental concepts and theories and to reflect some of the current realities of child development today.

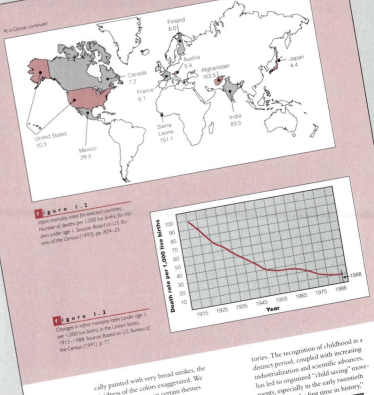

At a Glance, continued

figure 1.2
Infant mortality rates for selected countries. Number of deaths per 1,000 live births, for children under age 1. Source: Based on U.S. Bureau of the Census (1992), pp. 824–25.

figure 1.3
Changes in infant mortality rates (under age 1, per 1,000 live births) in the United States, 1915–1988. Source: Based on U.S. Bureau of the Census (1991), p. 77.

cally painted with very broad strokes, the vividness of the colors exaggerated. We tend to concentrate on certain themes and ignore what doesn't fit.

In today's industrialized world we no longer abandon children for fear they will

tories. The recognition of childhood as a distinct period, coupled with increasing industrialization and scientific advances, has led to organized "child saving" movements, especially in the early twentieth century. "For the first time in history,"

and, at the end of each chapter—

MAIN POINTS

provide an excellent means for quick review by providing brief synopses of the chapter's highlights.

FOCUS QUESTIONS: APPLICATIONS

restate the focus questions, found at the beginning of each chapter, into a wide variety of applied questions and projects, many requiring systematic observations of children and library research.

STUDY TERMS

are listed in order of appearance (along with their page references). Such terms and concepts are also found boldfaced within the chapter.

FURTHER READINGS

provide leads on up-to-date sources of information to assist with independent study or with research papers.

And, at the end of the book—

*A **Glossary** of the terms presented in boldface throughout the text.*

---

ponder whether the questions posed by any developmental research project are important—whether the answers obtained really matter in our understanding of children.

CHILDREN'S RIGHTS

4. The legal rights of children in today's industrialized societies are primarily rights of protection (to adequate medical and educational care, to affection and love, to a peaceful environment, to the opportunity to develop) rather than adult rights of choice that entail adult responsibilities. In the developing world, children's most basic rights are often ignored. In many of these areas, formal education is substandard or nonexistent, and physical and mental abuse of children is common.

PIONEERS IN CHILD STUDY

5. Among early pioneers of the scientific study of children were John Locke (*tabula rasa*) and Jean-Jacques Rousseau ("noble savage"). Later pioneers included Charles Darwin (baby biography; evolution), G. Stanley Hall ("ontogeny recapitulates phylogeny"), and John B. Watson (we become what we are as a function of our experiences).

main points

THIS TEXT

1. Development, the process whereby children adapt to their environment, includes maturation (genetically programmed unfolding), growth (quantitative changes), and learning (changes due to experience).

CHANGING ATTITUDES TOWARD CHILDREN

2. There is evidence that in medieval times children were considered miniature adults whose presence in the family did not engender strong feelings of parental attachment, perhaps

---

STUDYING CHILDREN

7. Naturalistic (nonintrusive) observations of children include diary descriptions (regular descriptions of interesting events), specimen descriptions (continuous sequences of behavior), event sampling (recordings of predetermined behaviors), and time sampling (recordings during predetermined time intervals). Nonnaturalistic observations may be clinical (questionnaires or interviews) or experimental.

8. In an experiment, an investigator randomly assigns subjects to groups and controls independent variables to determine whether they affect dependent variables (outcomes). Correlational studies look at relationships among variables.

9. Child development studies can be longitudinal studies, which compare the same children at different periods in their lives, or cross-sectional studies, which compare different children at the same time.

10. One way of separating effects due to cohorts (groups of people born during same time span) and to age is to use sequences of samples

menter bias, ecological validity, and other factors. Truth, here as elsewhere, is relative.

focus questions: applications

■ What is this book about?
1. Define the key terms listed in the "Study Terms" section.

■ How have attitudes toward children changed? Why are they important?
2. Compare medieval attitudes toward children as reflected in sports such as, say, "baby tossing", with North American attitudes today. Compare these attitudes with those reflected in instances of wartime atrocities against children (child beatings, starvation, rape, murder, and so on).

■ What are the rights of children? The responsibilities of parents and nations?
3. When, if ever, should the state interfere in the home vis-a-vis the care and upbringing of children?

■ What are the most basic questions and beliefs in the study of...
4. ...

---

study terms

psychology 6
developmental psychology 6
growth 6
maturation 6
learning 6
development 6
infancy 9
baby tossing 14
nature-nurture controversy 23
stages 23
naturalistic observations 24
diary description 24
specimen description 25
time sampling 25
event sampling 25
nonnaturalistic observation 25
experiment 26
variable 26
independent variable 26
dependent variable 26
hypothesis 26
experimental group 26
control group 26
dyad 27
blind procedure 27
correlation 29
correlational study 29
longitudinal study 30

further readings

Fascinating descriptions of changes in the status of children throughout history are provided by:

Aries, P. (1962). *Centuries of childhood: A social history of family life* (R. Baldick, trans.). New York: Alfred A. Knopf. (Originally published 1960.)

Kessen, W. (1965). *The child.* New York: John Wiley.

A booklet containing all the Children's Rights articles of the U.N.'s Convention on the Rights of the Child can be obtained free from:

United Nations Children's Fund
UNICEF House, H-9F
United Nations Plaza
New York, NY 10017
telephone: (212) 326-7072

The following collection of articles is a practical discussion of the rights of children, the responsibilities of parents, guardians, and nations with respect to children, and legal recourses available to children and their parents:

Westman, J. C. (1991). Introduction. In J. C. Westman (ed.), *Who speaks for the children?* Sarasota, Fla.: Professional Resource Exchange, Inc.

and, for additional support:

Available to instructors:
an Instructor's Resource Manual (written by the author) with transparency masters, sample course outlines, detailed lecture outlines, ideas for lecture introductions, crossword puzzles for students, and a wide variety of highly current lecture-enriching material—much of it cross-cultural or applied; a comprehensive Test Bank (also available in electronic form, providing the option of customizing exams); free videos from Penn State University's Behavioral Sciences collection (ask your ITP Higher Education sales rep for details).

Available to students:
a complete Study Guide containing chapter summaries, plus a range of exercises and self-tests to help you gauge your progress and prepare for exams.

This *Eighth Edition recognizes more clearly than its predecessors the importance of the contexts (relationships) within which we develop. It makes greater use of cross-cultural research, and it is more sensitive to the fact that our increasingly multicultural societies don't provide all children with the same experiences or opportunities. As a result, our conclusions don't always apply to all children everywhere.*

In this Eighth Edition, you will find many things about which we had scarcely begun to dream in the seventh edition:

■ *Amazing new discoveries in the field of genetics that have astounding implications for controlling human reproduction and remedying genetic defects*

■ *Medical advances that almost guarantee the survival of infants so premature they would unquestionably have died at the time of the first edition*

■ *A new recognition of the capabilities of infants and preschoolers, evident in their invention of intuitive theories of mind*

■ *The proliferation of new environmental hazards—including chemicals, drugs, and various pollutants—that sometimes have serious consequences for the unborn (and the long-born)*

■ *The increasing importance of other languages and other cultures in societies in which "minorities" are rapidly becoming majorities*

■ *The continuing effects of changing social trends relating to drug use, divorce, gender issues, nonfamily infant and childcare, teen pregnancy, violence on television, computers, and so on.*

Of Children deals with all this and much more. . . .

Thank you to

- Dick Greenberg, my first editor, who was among the first to glimpse the wolf and who gave it one dickens of a wallop.

- Ken King, my second editor, whose help with the next four editions kept the wolf in his secret places.

- Suzanna Brabant, my next editor, who thought maybe the wolf could be tamed—but didn't.

- Sabra Horne, my current editor, who fears no wolves.

- Kate Peltier and Janet Hansen, editorial assistants; Angela Mann and Cathy Linberg, production editors; Ann Butler, managing designer; Alan Titche, copy editor; Bobbie Broyer, art editor; and Jeanne Bosschart, permissions editor.

- George Semb, who prepared the Study Guide and Test Items, and who, when I took him into the wilderness, saw only one mangy fox, no bears, and especially no wolves.

- A legion of Wadsworth reps, past and current, without whose efforts the wolf would not be so lean.

- My maternal grandmother, with whom I lived in early adolescence, who taught me to stew a rabbit, leaving bits out there for the wolves.

- The many reviewers of the previous seven editions, whose influence is still apparent in these pages.

- The reviewers of this eighth edition, to whom I am very grateful for their more recent influences:

Leonard Abbeduto, University of Wisconsin, Madison; Armin Arndt, Eastern Washington University; James Batts, Eastern Kentucky University; Shirley Cassara, Bunker Hill Community College; Dixie Ruth Crase, Memphis State University; Derl Keen, Fresno City College; Mary Monfort, University of Central Oklahoma; Merlyn Mondol, Saginaw Valley State University; Virginia Monroe, University of South Dakota; Paul Roodin, Sate University of New York at Oswego; Bernard Rosenthal, Western Connecticut State University; and Tirzah Schutzengel, Bergen Community College.

My hope that you will enjoy this book and learn from it remains unchanged, as does my conviction that each is necessary for the other.

Yours,

Edmonton, Alberta
1994

one

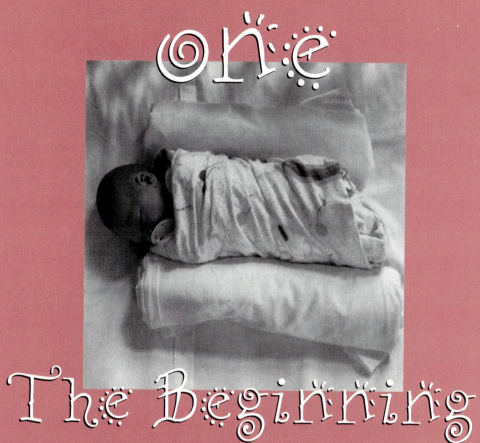

The Beginning

Grown-ups love figures.
Antoine de Saint-Exupéry, The Little Prince

*W*hen you tell them that you have made a new friend," Antoine de Saint-Exupéry continues, "they never ask you any questions about essential matters." They never say, "What does his voice sound like? What games does he love best? Does he collect butterflies?" Instead, they demand: "How old is he? How many brothers has he? How much money does his father make?" Only from these figures do they think they have learned anything about him.

Grown-up that it is, science, too, asks questions that are impersonal and objective. It asks, "How do average 4 year olds think?" "How can they be made to understand reality?" "In what ways must they change to be more like adults?" It seldom asks questions like "What does Marilyn feel about rainbows?" "What does Cindy know of spiders and sugar and silver strings?" "Why does Robert sometimes cry in the middle of the night?"

As is made clear in the two chapters that make up Part I, the science that studies children deals with *average* children. But we always have to keep in mind that there is no average child. The concept is an invention made necessary by our need to make sense of children.

In this text, especially in "In Other Contexts" inserts, we pause often to remind ourselves of that fact—and to notice, as well, that Marilyn sings when she sees rainbows, and that Cindy has dreamt the magic that binds spiders and sugar and silver strings. And we ask, too, what it is that makes Robert cry.

1

Studying the Child

Child! Do not throw this book about;
Refrain from the unholy pleasure
Of cutting all the pictures out!
Preserve it as your chiefest treasure.
Hilaire Belloc, Bad Child's Book of Beasts

focus questions

WHAT IS THIS BOOK ABOUT?

HOW HAVE ATTITUDES TOWARD CHILDREN CHANGED? WHY ARE THESE ATTITUDES IMPORTANT?

WHAT ARE THE RIGHTS OF CHILDREN? THE RESPONSIBILITIES OF PARENTS AND SOCIETIES?

WHAT ARE THE MOST BASIC QUESTIONS AND BELIEFS IN THE STUDY OF CHILDREN?

HOW DO WE STUDY CHILDREN?

HOW RELIABLE ARE OUR CONCLUSIONS?

outline

HOW THIS TEXT EXPLORES GROWING UP

Some Definitions

CHANGING ATTITUDES TOWARD CHILDREN

Snapshot 1: Childbirth in Medieval Europe
Snapshot 2: Begging and Stealing in Eighteenth-Century Europe
Snapshot 3: Child Abandonment in Eighteenth-Century Europe
Snapshot 4: Child Labor in Nineteenth-Century Europe
Snapshot 5: The Developing World Today
Snapshot 6: The Industrialized World Today
Why Look at History?

CHILDREN'S RIGHTS

What are the Rights of Children?
Disregard of Children's Rights in the Third World

THE STUDY OF CHILDREN

Early Observers of Children
Later Observers of Children
The Study of Children Today

RECURRING QUESTIONS IN DEVELOPMENTAL PSYCHOLOGY

BASIC BELIEFS CONCERNING HUMAN DEVELOPMENT

METHODS OF STUDYING CHILDREN

Observations
Experiments
Correlational Studies
Longitudinal and Cross-Sectional Research
Dealing with Sources of Variation

EVALUATING DEVELOPMENTAL RESEARCH

Sampling
Ecological and Cross-Cultural Validity
Memory
Subject Honesty
Experimenter Bias
Subject Bias

MAIN POINTS

FOCUS QUESTIONS: APPLICATIONS

STUDY TERMS

FURTHER READINGS

*J*ason was one of Marie's kindergarten kids. He was a solemn little guy, wide-eyed and earnest, and dead serious about most things.

During circle time in Marie's kindergarten, children share things. Once, when it was Jason's turn, he brought to class something nobody there had ever seen before: a live black widow spider. He had gotten it from an uncle who lives near Medicine Hat. "Where my uncle's house is," he proudly told the class, "there's things that can kill you, like snakes and black widows."

It was a very large female black widow spider; the entire class crowded in to have a closer look. "Just the lady ones can kill you," Jason explained. "See the red thing on its belly? That means it can kill you if it wants. My uncle got bit by one and he nearly died."

"Is there anything else you want to say about the spider before we put it away?" Marie asked. "Oh yes," Jason announced solemnly. "My uncle keeps my aunt under his bed."

There were gasps of amazement; nobody laughed.

"Why?" they asked Jason. He shrugged. "He does, you know," he answered.

"No," someone said, more in wonder than in disbelief.

"Really. I heard her," said Jason.

"But not really," Marie said. "It's just a joke, Jason. Nobody keeps anybody under their bed."

"My uncle does," said Jason. "He really does."

He's such a solemn little child, so honest, so serious. What if … what if his uncle really? … Shouldn't someone do something?

"Let's go to Medicine Hat," I said to Marie, "and look under the bed; it's only a six-hour drive." We didn't go. But later that week there were parent-teacher interviews at Marie's school, and Jason's mother came. Marie mentioned the spider, said how excited the class was to see it, how well-informed Jason was. This was all by way of sneaking in the question, "Jason's uncle doesn't really keep an aunt under his bed, does he, heh, heh?"

He didn't. But for some reason he didn't want Jason and his sister to go under the bed, so he told them that's where their aunt was. And whenever they went to look, he projected his voice and croaked in a high-pitched tone, "If you come any closer, little children, I'll bloody eat you!"

So they didn't go any closer and nothing bloody ate them.

how this text explores growing up

Y ou and I are grown up; we're not scared of things under the bed, are we? Unlike little children, we know very well that there's nothing under the bed; we can look if we want to and nothing will eat us. You can't fool us just by projecting your voice. We recognize lies and we know that magic isn't real and we know there are some things people don't do. Don't we?

Little children don't know these things. Part of growing up is learning them—learning what to expect; becoming familiar with what's out there; sorting fact from fancy, reality from wishes, tears from laughter.

Describing and explaining differences among infants, children, adolescents, and adults is mostly what this text is about.

Of Children is divided into seven parts (see Table 1.1). Part I is an introduction: It explains what developmental psychology is and how psychologists study children, and it introduces some of the most important theories used to explain developmental change. The first chapter in Part II deals with our genetic origins; the second looks at systematic changes that occur from conception through birth and at important influences on the unborn child. Parts III through VI look at physical, intellectual (cognitive), and emotional changes and processes during each of the major pre-adult periods: infancy (birth to age 2); early childhood (2 to 6 or 7); middle childhood (6 or 7 to 11 or 12); and adolescence (11 or 12 to 19 or 20). Part VII is simply an ending.

table 1.1

Organization of Of Children

PART	AGES	CHAPTERS
I The Beginning	—	1 Studying the Child 2 Theories of Development
II Biological Beginnings	—	3 Genetics and Context 4 Prenatal Development and Birth
III Infancy	Birth to 2 years	5 Physical and Cognitive Development 6 Social Development
IV Early Childhood	2 to 6 or 7	7 Physical and Cognitive Development 8 Social Development
V Middle Childhood	6 or 7 to 11 or 12	9 Physical and Cognitive Development 10 Social Development
VI Adolescence	11 or 12 to 19 or 20	11 Physical and Cognitive Development 12 Social Development
VII Epilogue		13 The End

some definitions

Psychology* is a general term for the science that studies human behavior and thought. **Developmental psychology** is the division of psychology that is concerned specifically with changes that occur over time and with the processes and influences that account for these changes. In other words, *development* refers to changes in behavior with the passage of time. The task of the developmental psychologist is twofold: to describe changes and to discover their underlying causes. A third, closely related task is to advance theories that organize and interpret observations and that are also useful for making predictions.

Three important concepts in the study of children are *growth, maturation,* and *learning.* To develop is to grow, to mature, and to learn.

Growth ordinarily refers to physical changes. These are mainly quantitative changes because they involve addition

*Boldfaced terms are defined in the Glossary in the back of the book.

rather than transformation. Changes such as increasing height or enlargement of the nose are examples of growth.

Maturation describes changes that are more closely related to heredity than to a child's environment. Sexual unfolding during pubescence is an example of maturation. Although these changes follow a genetically programmed timetable, in almost all aspects of human development maturation and learning interact. Learning to walk, for example, requires not only that the child's physical strength and muscular coordination be sufficiently mature but also that there be an opportunity to practice the different skills involved.

Learning involves changes that result from experience rather than simply from a maturational process. All changes in behavior resulting from experience are examples of learning, provided these changes are not simply the temporary effects of drugs or fatigue.

In summary, **development** is the total process whereby individuals adapt to their environment, and because we adapt by growing, maturing, and learning, all

t able 1.2

Important definitions

Psychology	*The science that studies human thought and behavior*
Developmental psychology	*Division of psychology concerned with changes that occur over time and with the processes and influences that account for these changes*
Development involves:	
Growth	*Physical changes; primarily quantitative*
Maturation	*Naturally unfolding changes, relatively independent of the environment (for example, pubescence—the changes of adolescence that lead to sexual maturity)*
Learning	*Relatively permanent changes in behavior that result from experience (rather than from maturation, fatigue, or drugs)*

these processes are aspects of development. (See Table 1.2.) The main difference between learning and development is that learning is concerned with immediate, short-term adaptation, whereas development refers to gradual adaptation over a period of years. Accordingly, the subject of developmental psychology is the human from conception to death (although in this text we don't deal with the entire life span but stop instead somewhere in adolescence). Developmental psychology undertakes two important tasks: observing children and their progress in adapting to the world, and trying to explain that adaptation.

changing attitudes toward children

The attitudes toward children reflected in this text are warm, positive, sympathetic, concerned—all the good things we think of as characteristic of our enlightened, twentieth-century attitudes toward children. It has not always been so. In fact, even today it isn't always and everywhere entirely so, as the following snapshots of children show.

These historical snapshots are important not so much for what they tell us about the lives of children (although that, too, is interesting and important in its own right), but more because they emphasize the extent to which we are products of our particular social, cultural, and historical realities. In today's jargon, we are products of our *contexts*. So, to understand the lives of children, we need to know something of their contexts—that is, something of their families, their schools, the economic and political realities of their days, their place in history and in culture. It's a point that is repeated often in this text, and that is emphasized in the "In Other Contexts" inserts. These deal with the lives of children whose contexts are not the average North American or European context.

We should note at the outset that historical snapshots are not always very accurate. For one thing, there are few records of what life might have been like before the "print cultures"—those societies that regularly produce written artifacts. For another, what records there are aren't always very reliable. For example, Hampsten (1991) reports that the impressions we have of what life might have been like in North America for children of the first European settlers on the Great Plains vary greatly depending on whether they are based on people's own recollections or on more objective descriptions. "The stories we tell ourselves are the ones we are likely to want to believe," says Hampsten (p. 4). As a result, settlers' children tend to remember their growing-up

What we know of how children were regarded and treated in the past is often based on highly unreliable records, such as mothers' diaries, school regulations, the laws and judgments of the courts—even paintings such as this in which artists tended to portray children as miniature adults.

experiences as far more positive than they actually were, and autobiographies make poor sources of scientific information. When Hampsten looked at contemporaneous letters and diaries describing the lives of children, usually written by their mothers, she found that life on the frontier was difficult, lonely, and often extremely dangerous.

Similarly, when Aries (1962) attempted to uncover what the lives of medieval European children were like, he was forced to put together fragments gathered from many sources: historical paintings, school and university regulations, and Doctor Heroard's description of the upbringing of the French king Louis XIII. The result is a dramatic—and maybe not entirely accurate—account of conditions and attitudes that seem quite different from ours.

snapshot 1: childbirth in medieval europe

Aries (1962) describes a mother who has just given birth to her fifth child. She is depressed; now there is one more mouth to feed, one more body to clothe and look after. There had not been enough to go around before. What will it be like now? A neighbor consoles her: "Before they are old enough to bother you," she says, "you will have lost half of them, or perhaps all of them" (p. 38).

What do we see in this snapshot? By today's standards we see a callous attitude toward children reflected in the notion that children's deaths are somehow preferable to the burdens of caring for them. The logical inference is that the mother's emotional attachment to her children did not compare with the emotional links that bind mother and child today, because if you are not strongly attached to the child, there is little need to worry that it might suffer or die.

snapshot 2: begging and stealing in eighteenth-century europe

Historical accounts of the lives of eighteenth-century European children are often shocking descriptions of abuse and cruelty—perhaps because, like today, the most flagrant and horrible abuses are the most sensational and the most likely to have been recorded. In 1761, for example, the British courts sentenced one Anne Martin to two years in Newgate prison. Her crime? She habitually poked out the eyes of the children she took begging with her; it increased their incomes—and hers.

Aha, you say, the courts did offer some protection to children! True, but it was skimpy protection indeed. As Pinchbeck and Hewitt (1973) point out, Anne Martin's case was unusual in that the children whose eyes she removed weren't her own. Had they been her own children, it's likely that no one would have paid any attention because parents could generally treat their own children any way they wanted!

Nor were the courts above severely punishing children for infractions of laws. Siegel and White (1982) report the case of a 7-year-old girl who stole a petticoat; surely not that terrible a crime. Still, she was brought to trial, convicted, sentenced—and hanged!

snapshot 3: child abandonment in eighteenth-century europe

Eighteenth-century European attitudes toward children were reflected not only in the ways children were treated by the courts, but also in the ways children were treated by their parents. In the crowded and disease-riddled slums of eighteenth-century European cities, thousands of parents, ignorant of all but the most primitive birth control methods, bore children whom they promptly abandoned in the streets or on the doorsteps of churches and orphanages. Foundling homes sprang up all over Europe in an attempt to care for these children, but the majority died in **infancy** (before the age of 2 years). Kessen (1965) reports that of 10,272 infants admitted to one foundling home in Dublin in the last quarter of the eighteenth century, only 45 survived. (Indeed, before 1700, even if a child were not abandoned its chances of surviving till the age of 5 were less than one in two; most died of diseases, including the plague.)

The high mortality rate of abandoned children was not restricted to eighteenth-century Europe but was characteristic on the other side of the Atlantic as well, even into the nineteenth century. It seems that with few exceptions, children in infant homes (asylums) in the United States before 1915 died before the age of 2 (Bakwin, 1949).

snapshot 4: child labor in nineteenth-century europe

The nineteenth century brought some improvement in the status of children in Europe and abandonments decreased drastically, at least partly because of children's increasing economic value as workers. In thousands of factories and mines, children as young as 5 or 6 years, male and female, worked 10 hours a day or more at grueling labor in conditions so hazardous that many became ill and died (Kessen, 1965). At that time, children were employed extensively in the coal mines of the British countryside. Most of these mines were underground, and the tunnels that led to the workings were often no more than 28 inches high, were poorly ventilated, and were sometimes filled with 3 or 4 inches of water. Children were particularly valuable in the coal mines because they were small enough to crawl through these tiny tunnels, dragging baskets loaded with coal behind them by means of a "girdle and chain." The seventh earl of Shaftesbury (his name was Anthony Ashley Cooper) described the blisters and the wounds that resulted from this device, the illnesses that children suffered in the mines, the physical and mental abuse, and the beatings. He begged the British House of Commons to pass a bill that would establish the minimum age for employment of males in the coal mines at 13 and that would completely prohibit the employment of females underground. Following considerable debate and in spite of strong opposition, a bill prohibiting females from working underground was passed. However, many members were convinced that children whose fathers were miners were more likely to profit from an education in the mines than from a "reading" education; as long as they had reached the age of 10, boys could continue to be employed in the mines.

Conditions in North America were, in some instances, not vastly different from those that prevailed in parts of Europe. Children were employed in great numbers in factories and cotton mills, in fields, and in shops.

snapshot 5: the developing world today

The twentieth century, too, has had its share of ignorance, of cruelty, of needless pain and suffering. Sixty-eight of the world's developing nations have mortality rates for children under age 5 (called "under five mortality rates," abbreviated U5MR) greater than 71 per 1,000 children born alive—a rate many times higher than is common in developed countries (Grant, 1992). In, Afghanistan, for example, about 163 infants of every 1,000 born alive subsequently die before age 1, a rate 16 times higher than that of the United States or Canada (U.S. Bureau of the Census, 1992). (See "At a Glance: Infant Survival.") The United Nations reports that some 4,500 infants die each day from measles, tetanus, and whooping cough, and another 7,000 from diarrheal dehydration (Grant, 1992). Pneumonia adds significantly to this total, and starvation more than doubles it. As a result, even in 1990 more than 30,000 children died each day from preventable causes (*Le monde au chevet de l'enfance menacée*, 1990). That's about 10 million preventable child deaths a year, almost 2 million of them from vaccine-preventable diseases (Figure 1.1).

We tend to idealize childhood as a happy, carefree prelude to a more care-filled adulthood. But for a long period of our recent past, children were highly prized—and exploited—for their economic value in mines and factories, on farms, and in various work camps—as was the case in this early twentieth-century cotton mill in Georgia.

*I*n many parts of the world, infant mortality—defined as deaths before the age of 1 year—exceeds 100 for every 1,000 live births. The vast majority of these infants die of preventable causes such as measles or diarrheal dehydration. At the turn of the twentieth century, infant mortality rates in the United States and Canada were also about 100 per 1,000, but they have now been reduced to about 10 or fewer per 1,000. Infant mortality rates in the United States are more than twice as high for blacks (17.7 per 1,000) than for whites (8.2 per 1,000).

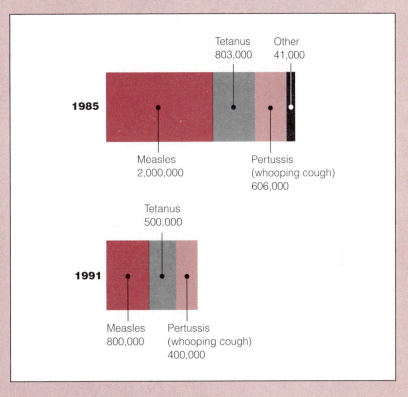

figure 1.1

Changes in estimated number of deaths in children under age 5 from vaccine-preventable diseases. Information is based on the report of the Expanded Programme on Immunizations, Global Advisory Group Meeting, UNICEF, Copenhagen, November 1985 and August 1991. Sources: Grant (1986), The state of the world's children: 1986. New York: Oxford University Press, p. 3, and Grant (1992), The state of the world's children: 1992. New York: Oxford University Press, p. 12.

continued

snapshot 6: the industrialized world today

Obviously, not all children were murdered in those very dark ages we call antiquity. Nor were all children of the Middle Ages abandoned or ignored until they died and then buried in the back yard or in the garden. Europe's children in the eighteenth and nineteenth centuries weren't all thrown into the coal mines, and North America's children weren't all driven into the cotton fields and textile factories. Even then, the majority of parents were probably loving and caring. Historical accounts are typi-

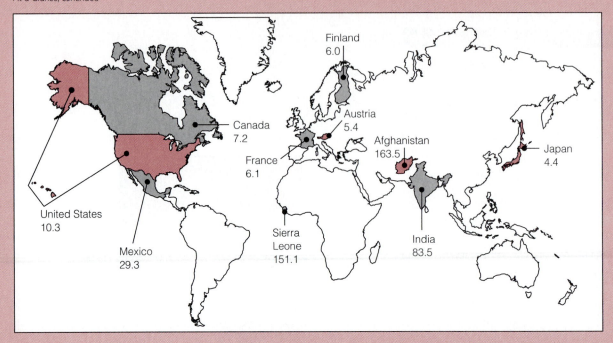

f igure 1.2

Infant mortality rates for selected countries. Number of deaths per 1,000 live births, for children under age 1. Source: Based on U.S. Bureau of the Census (1992), pp. 824–25.

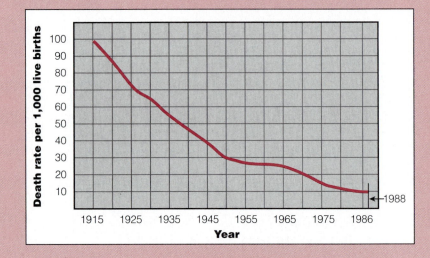

f igure 1.3

Changes in infant mortality rates (under age 1, per 1,000 live births) in the United States, 1915–1988. Source: Based on U.S. Bureau of the Census (1991), p. 77.

cally painted with very broad strokes, the vividness of the colors exaggerated. We tend to concentrate on certain themes and ignore what doesn't fit.

In today's industrialized world we no longer abandon children for fear they will prove too much of an economic burden; nor do we send them into mines and fac-tories. The recognition of childhood as a distinct period, coupled with increasing industrialization and scientific advances, has led to organized "child saving" move-ments, especially in the early twentieth century. "For the first time in history," writes Culbertson (1991), "children were accorded basic rights as individuals to preservation of health and life, education, freedom from working in the adult labor force, and protection within the judicial system" (p. 8). (Children's rights are discussed in more detail later in this chapter.)

This does not mean that all is perfect with the children of the industrialized world. There have been dramatic social changes in recent decades. For example, the percentage of never-married 20- to 24-year-old women increased from 30 in 1960 to 64 in 1991 (U.S. Bureau of the Census, 1992). In addition, divorce rates have increased dramatically in recent decades, so that close to half of all children spend an average of six years in a one-parent family. In 90 percent of these families, the mother is the single parent (U.S. Bureau of the Census, 1992). Coupled with this, demographic (population) changes have resulted in smaller families, reduced birthrates, more childless couples, and greater proportions of young adults (resulting from previous increases in birthrates) and elderly people (resulting from medical advances). Another important change, the effects of which are discussed in detail in Chapter 10, is associated with the role of television in people's lives, especially children's.

Some observers argue that the net effect of these changes is that recent decades are less child-centered than had been anticipated. In fact, says Bullock (1993), childhood may be a terribly lonely and often frightening experience for many. Among other things, childhood in our times brings with it a high probability of being looked after by a series of strangers, most likely outside the child's home. It includes, as well, the probability of losing a father or a mother for much of the time of growing up—or at least of losing some of their interest and attention, and perhaps some of their affection as well. Childhood now brings the possibility of major adjustments if one or the other of

the parents remarries, particularly if step-siblings are brought into the family.

There was a time, not very long ago, when the things that most children feared were highly predictable: pain, death, spinach, darkness, and things that go bump in the night. Recent decades have added some new fears: concerns over whether or not parents will divorce, fears related to being left alone, and fears associated with the likelihood of having to make new adjustments (Packard, 1983).

But lest this paint too bleak a picture, realize that the challenges and the changes of recent decades don't overwhelm all children and are not always a source of loneliness or despair. For many children, the times may present a challenge that results in strength rather than in weakness. Keep in mind, too, that these changes have few effects on the lives of many children.

why look at history?

These brief, historical snapshots are included here not so that you might be either horrified at the inhumanity of your species or proud of your apparent enlightenment. Rather, they are meant to illustrate how attitudes toward children reflect culture and history. The importance of a child's context is underlined often in this text—for example, in the boxes entitled "In Other Contexts."

In a sense, we are all a little like the children described in these boxes; none of us is the typical, average child of which this text speaks. Not only is each of us the product of an absolutely unique assortment of genetic material (unless we have an identical twin), but we are also products of experiences that are influenced more than a little by the social-cultural contexts of our lives.

Ponder, for example, how different your life might have been had *you* been born in medieval times.

children's rights

n medieval times, one of the sports by which the gentry amused themselves was **baby tossing**—the practice of throwing infants from one gamesman to another. One of the unlucky babies was King Henry IV's infant brother, who was killed when he fell while being tossed from window to window (deMause, 1974).

Throughout history, children have died not only in sport but for other causes, too. Had you lived in Massachusetts in 1646, you would not have had to put up with unruly offspring. Say you had a son who wouldn't listen to you, who was making your life miserable. All you would have had to do was drag him before a magistrate, establish that here was a stubborn and rebellious kid, and, as long as he was 16 or more, they'd put him to death for you! That was the law (Westman, 1991b).

By the twentieth century, the once-absolute control that parents and various agencies had over the lives of children had been weakened considerably. Yet it was still possible for parents and teachers to get rid of troublesome children. Farleger (1977) reports numerous instances in which children were "voluntarily" committed to mental institutions, often only because they presented problems for others ("voluntarily" because parents and guardians simply "volunteered" them). Until recently, such children had no legal recourse, no matter how badly they felt they had been treated.

Clearly, the world has not always treated its children very well—and still doesn't do so universally. But, says deMause (1975), we are at the threshold of a deep-seated, helping attitude toward children (see Table 1.3), as reflected in the efforts of various advocacy groups to establish the rights of children and to make society responsible for ensuring that these rights are safeguarded. Parents no longer have absolute jurisdiction and control over their children. Increasingly, major court decisions favor children who feel they have been wronged.

Evidence of increasing concern about the rights of children is apparent not only in court decisions but also in the adoption of ethical principles to guide research concerning children (published by the Society for Research in Child Development; Ethical standards for research with children, 1973). These principles recognize that research is unethical when a child is coerced into participating, when a child is exposed to stress or other potentially damaging conditions, when a child's privacy is invaded, and so on. The principles specify that permission of parents and children alike must be obtained before conducting child research. Furthermore, consent must be "informed" in the sense that all are fully aware of any aspect of the research that might affect their willingness to participate.

establishing the rights of children

A United Nations convention on the rights of the child held in 1989 culminated in the formulation of an extensive charter of children's rights. In September 1990, summit meetings on children's rights led to the signing by 105 nations of a Charter of Children's Rights (Balke, 1992). As of March 1992, 135 nations had signed this charter, and 126 of these nations had prepared or were preparing programs to implement its provisions (Bäckström, 1992). Among other things, the provisions of the charter include a child's right to:

- adequate medical care

- adequate nutrition

- affection, love, and understanding

t **able 1.3**

Six historical trends in treatment of children

Antiquity	*Little evidence of strong parental attachment; occasional infanticide socially acceptable*
Middle Ages	*Poverty and emotional indifference led to widespread abandonment of infants; very high infant mortality rates*
Renaissance	*Ambivalent attitude toward children*
Eighteenth century	*Industrialization contributed to widespread use of children as manual laborers in factories, mines, fields, shops, and so on*
Nineteenth century	*Child labor continued to flourish; beginnings of important medical and educational changes*
Twentieth century	*Child-centered, especially in the industrialized world; concern with the rights and plights of children, but still many instances of abuse, starvation, exploitation, and unnecessary mortality*

■ education

■ the opportunity for play and recreation

■ special care if required

■ a peaceful environment

■ the opportunity to develop individual abilities

These are birthrights, says the U.S. National Committee for the Rights of the Child (Turgi, 1992). Other birthrights include:

■ protection from abuse, neglect, and exploitation

■ protection under the law

■ freedom from discrimination based on race, sex, religious beliefs, and age

As Caldwell (1989) notes, the rights of children are geared toward providing optimal, growth-fostering conditions for them. In general, they are rights of *protection* rather than rights of *choice*; that is, children must be protected from the dangers to which their immaturity exposes them, and their access to a growth-fostering environment must be safeguarded. According to Saidla (1992), treating children as mini-adults is a misuse of the concept of children's rights. In many instances, children lack the matur-

Note: Although these trends and attitudes are descriptive of some cultures and of some families during the periods in question, they sometimes were not very widespread. Clearly, although infanticide might once have been acceptable under some circumstances, no society permitted all its infants to be killed. Similarly, even at the height of child labor exploitation in the eighteenth century, there were many well-cared-for children who played and went to school and had carefree childhoods in loving homes.
Source: Based in part on deMause (1975).

ity and the knowledge required for making the best choices in their own lives. My 16-year-old has the right to adequate nutrition, medical care, and education, but, understandably, he does not have the right to make all his own nutritional, educational, and medical choices. Many of those choices are his parents' responsibility. We might not be able to convince him that he should eat his spinach because it is good for him, but we can at least point him toward school each morning carrying a well-balanced lunch (and a pocketful of coins that he can exchange for his own nutritional choices).

This does not mean, of course, that children have no responsibilities. As Caldwell (1989) points out, society expects its children to assimilate dominant cultural values and eventually foster the continuation of the culture. In addition,

society expects its children to take advantage of their rights and the opportunities provided for them—that they will mature and learn. (See Figure 1.4 for a summary of the relationships among the rights and responsibilities of parents, society, and children; Figure 1.5 for a look at child poverty; and "In Other Contexts: Children of War" for examples of horrendous violations of children's rights.)

disregard of children's rights in the third world

As we have seen, more than 30,000 of the world's children die each day of vaccine-preventable diseases, diarrheal dehydration, and starvation (Grant, 1992). At a theoretical level, solutions for these social crimes are simple and technically possible: Vaccine-preventable diseases require immunization;

nutrition-related suffering and dying can be relieved through a redistribution of vast surpluses of food; and the incidence of diarrheal infection can be lessened through sanitation, and its effects can be countered through oral rehydration therapy (ORT). (ORT involves an attempt to increase the infected child's fluid intake and replace essential salts. ORT solutions can be made by dissolving specially prepared mixtures in water, or they can be made from salts, sugar, or rice powder dissolved in the correct proportions.) Further, the effects of each of these causes of infant and child death—vaccine-preventable diseases, diarrheal infection, and poor nutrition—can be lessened enormously through something as simple as breast-feeding. Incidence of diarrhea among breast-fed infants is far lower than among bottle-fed infants (Breast milk prevents disease, 1984). In addition, breast milk provides infants with a degree of immunity to various other diseases and provides them with nutritious food under hygienic conditions (David & David, 1984). (Clearly, these arguments for breast-feeding are somewhat less relevant in developed societies in which malnutrition, poor sanitation, and gastrointestinal infections are less common.)

Not surprisingly, one of the important factors in infant mortality is the mother's education. There is, according to Levine

continued on page 20

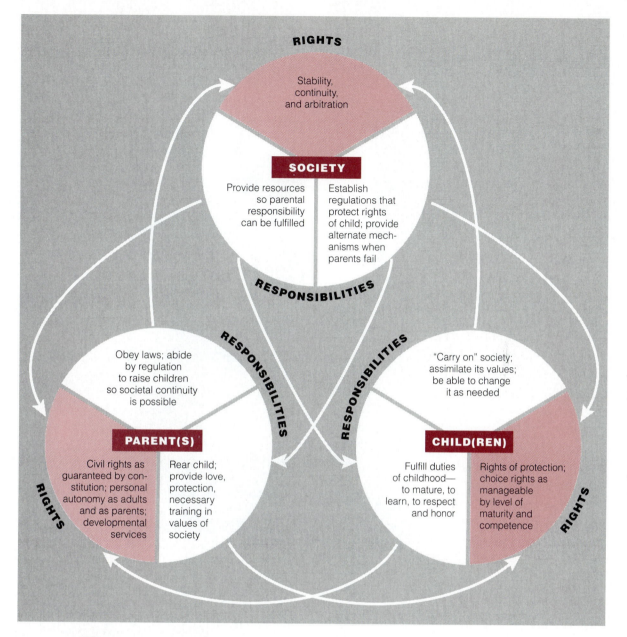

RIGHTS

Stability,
continuity,
and arbitration

SOCIETY

Provide resources
so parental
responsibility
can be fulfilled

Establish
regulations that
protect rights
of child; provide
alternate mech-
anisms when
parents fail

RESPONSIBILITIES

RESPONSIBILITIES

RESPONSIBILITIES

Obey laws; abide
by regulation
to raise children
so societal continuity
is possible

"Carry on" society;
assimilate its values;
be able to change
it as needed

PARENT(S)

Civil rights as
guaranteed by con-
stitution; personal
autonomy as adults
and as parents;
developmental
services

Rear child;
provide love,
protection,
necessary
training in
values of
society

CHILD(REN)

Fulfill duties
of childhood—
to mature, to
learn, to respect
and honor

Rights of protection;
choice rights as
manageable
by level of
maturity and
competence

RIGHTS

RIGHTS

f igure 1.4

Caldwell's triadic model of the rights and re-
sponsibilities of parents, children, and society in
relation to each other. Source: Caldwell, B. M.
(1980). "Balancing children's rights and par-
ents' rights." In R. Haskins & J. J. Gallagher
(Eds.), Care and education of young children
in America: Policy, politics and social science.
Norwood, NJ: Ablex, p. 37. Reprinted by per-
mission of the publisher.

N ot only do children have a right to be protected from harm, proclaims the United Nations, but their right to access to a growth-fostering environment must also be safeguarded. Children's rights include the right to adequate medical care, nutrition, education, and special care if required—and the right to a peaceful environment and to affection, love, and understanding. But even in one of the wealthiest and most child-centered of the world's nations, millions of children are poor. Strangely, although the proportion of Americans over age 65 living in poverty declined from 24.6 to 12.2 percent between 1970 and 1990, during that same period the proportion of American children below the poverty level increased from 14.9 to 19.9 percent. About 12.7 million children in the United States live in poverty.

f igure 1.5

Children living in poverty in the United States. These figures include only children under 18 who live at home. Source: Adapted from U.S. Bureau of the Census (1992), p. 456.

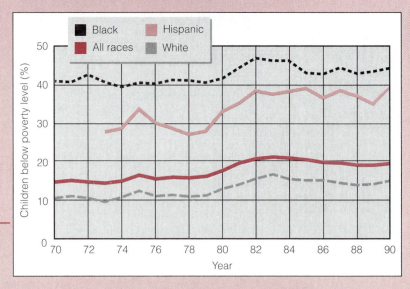

Nahariya, Israel. *In April, four terrorists came by sea, looking for victims. Finally they found the apartment Danny and Semadar Haran shared with Einat, their 5-year-old daughter, and Yael, their 2-year-old son. They found Danny first, took him to the beach, and shot him dead. Then they found Einat and smashed her head on a rock, killing her too. Yael, hiding with Semadar in a small utility room, began to cry; the mother clamped her hand tightly over his mouth—too tightly. He suffocated (Rosenblatt, 1984).*

Sarajevo, Bosnia. *Raujl Davidovich ran across an opening where the skating rink, Zetra, once stood. Here, only 10 years earlier, the Winter Olympics had brought promise of peace and cooperation; now Kosevo Stadium is littered with fresh graves. It wasn't Raujl's lucky day. Although he had survived the crossing many times during the two years of relentless war, today a sniper's bullet tore into his chest, smashing him down hard. In a blur of pain and fear, he slid across the frozen ground, coming to rest against the corpse of an old woman. He wouldn't even have noticed the corpse otherwise. "It doesn't hurt all that much," he thought. It was his last thought (War Crimes, 1994).*

In medieval times, victims of war were almost invariably soldiers. Even during World War I, more than 95 per-

cent of all casualties were armed personnel. But by World War II, almost half of all casualties were civilian. Fifty years later, the world's 40-odd wars typically kill about four civilians for every armed fighter—most of them women and children (Grant, 1992).

To Think About Enormous numbers of Irish children, of Palestinian and Israeli children, of Bosnian and Croatian and Serbian children, of Nicaraguan and Guatemalan and Salvadoran children, have lost parents, siblings, friends. How do you suppose this might affect their attitudes toward violence and war? Toward attachment and love? Toward life itself?

A Task How many instances of violations of children's rights can you discover in a single issue of your local newspaper?

In the days of more "civilized" wars, soldiers tried to kill other soldiers only; rarely did grown-up civilians, let alone children, get in the way. Even as recently as during World War I, almost all casualties were armed personnel. Now about three of every four casualties of the more than three dozen ongoing "wars" are civilians, the majority of them children.

To Read The UNICEF report edited by D. Harland (1989): Children on the front line: The impact of apartheid, destabilization and warfare on children in Southern and South Africa. New York: United Nations Children's Fund.

(1987), a growing consensus that schooling for females can be a direct cause of reductions both in birthrates and in infant death rates. An analysis of information collected by the World Bank from some 99 different third-world countries shows a very strong relationship between the proportion of a country's females enrolled in primary schools and infant mortality rates some 22 years later (Caldwell, 1986). These data reveal that even incomplete primary schooling often leads to smaller families and to the loss of fewer children, even when sanitation, nutrition, and medical attention have not improved noticeably.

Sadly, in most developing countries, fewer than 50 percent of all children enroll in primary schools. Even at this level, dropout rates are extremely high, quality of education is very low, and the relative cost of education is high (Tsang, 1988). As Grant (1986) points out, "it is the poor, those whose need is greatest, who have the least surplus of resources—of money, time, energy, health, knowledge, and confidence—to invest in improvements. That is the catch-22 of poverty . . . and so the cycle goes on" (p. 41).

But the cycle needn't go on forever, for nutrition, education, immunization, and medical care can break it. The cost? *Le Monde (Le monde au chevet de . . . ,* 1990) reports a UNICEF estimate that an expenditure of 2.5 billion dollars per year through this decade would save the lives of some 50 million children—and that expenditure is roughly what the major cigarette manufacturers spend worldwide each year on advertising!

the study of children

The study of children is a relatively recent enterprise, closely tied both to the social changes that occurred in seventeenth- and eighteenth-century attitudes toward children and to intellectual movements reflected in the writings of philosophers and early scientists. In addition, advances in biology and medicine and the increasing availability of elementary education contributed significantly to the development of child psychology.

early observers of children

Closely associated with these intellectual movements were people such as the British philosopher John Locke and the French philosopher Jean-Jacques Rousseau.

JOHN LOCKE

Locke, writing in the late seventeenth century, argued that a child is basically a rational creature, born with a mind that is like a blank slate (*tabula rasa*). At first there is nothing on it, but experience changes that. Thus the child described by Locke is a passive recipient of knowledge, information, and habits and is highly responsive to rewards and punishments. In Locke's (1699) words, "If you take away the Rod on one hand, and these little Encouragements which they are taken with, on the other, How then (will you say) shall Children be govern'd? Remove Hope and Fear, and there is an end of all Discipline."

JEAN-JACQUES ROUSSEAU

Rousseau's child, described in his book *Emile* (1762), is a direct contrast to the child described by Locke. Rousseau's child is active and inquiring. Furthermore, this child is not a "blank slate"—neither good nor bad until the rewards and punishments of experience exert their influence—but rather innately good—a "noble savage." Rousseau insists that if children were allowed to develop in their own fashion, untainted by the corruption and evil in the world, they would certainly be good when grown: "God makes all things good; man meddles with them and they become evil."

Although both Locke and Rousseau are closely associated with the beginning of the study of children, their ideas led to very different conceptions of childhood. Locke's description of the child as a passive creature, molded by the rewards and punishments of experience, has a close parallel to descriptions of development in learning theory, particularly as exemplified in the works of B. F. Skinner and Albert Bandura (described in Chapter 2). Rousseau's view of an active, exploring child developing through deliberate interaction with the environment finds an important place in the work of Jean Piaget (also described in Chapter 2).

later observers of children

Although the science of child psychology owes much to early "child philosophers" such as Rousseau and Locke, its beginnings are usually attributed to the first systematic observations and written accounts of children, such as William Preyer's (1882) detailed observations of his own children and Charles Darwin's (1877) biography of his son (Cairns & Valsiner, 1984).

G. STANLEY HALL

Hard on the heels of these European pioneers followed the American, G. Stanley Hall (1891), who became the first president of the American Psycho-

logical Association. Hall was profoundly influenced by Charles Darwin's theory of evolution. "Ontogeny recapitulates phylogeny," he informed his colleagues, summarizing in one short phrase his conviction that the development of a single individual in a species parallels the evolution of the entire species (an idea now largely discredited). As evidence for this theory, Hall described the evolution of children's interests in games, noting how these games seem to correspond to the evolution of human occupations and lifestyles. Notice, insisted Hall, how a child is, in sequence, interested in games corresponding to each of the following: an arboreal existence (for example, climbing on chairs and tables); a cave-dwelling existence (crawling into small spaces, making tiny shelters with old blankets); a pastoral existence (playing with animals); an agricultural existence (tending flowers and plants); and finally an industrial existence (playing with vehicles).

Hall pioneered the use of the questionnaire as a tool for studying children, questioning them at great length in an attempt to discover something of their behavior and their thoughts. Often, too, he presented his questionnaires to adults to try to get them to remember what they had felt and thought as children. Always, he tabulated, summed, averaged, and

Children's games, G. Stanley Hall insisted, parallel different stages in the evolution of humans. The play of the children shown here, he might have said, corresponds to the period in human history when humans lived in hollows under trees and in caves. This "theory of recapitulation" is now largely discredited.

compared the results of his question-naires, a true pioneer of the application of scientific procedures and principles to the study of human development.

JOHN B. WATSON

Another American pioneer of child psychology was John B. Watson (1914), who introduced an experimental, learning theory-based approach to the study of development. His influence, as well as that of Skinner, shaped a model that came to dominate child study through the early part of the twentieth century. This model looked for the causes of developmental change among the rewards and punishments of the environment and viewed the child as the passive recipient of these influences.

The contributions of Watson and Skinner, along with other important contributors to the study of children such as Sigmund Freud, Erik Erikson, and Jean Piaget, are discussed in Chapter 2, which deals with theories of development.

the study of children today

Economic and social changes have done much to change our attitudes toward children. Advances in medicine and hygiene have saved many children from early deaths and made it less traumatic for us to love them. Legislation has begun to grant them legal rights and protection from various forms of abuse. Children, for most people in our society, are no longer either an economic burden or a necessity. We, and they, have the advantage of a wealthier and perhaps kinder age. As a result, today's industrialized societies can aptly be described as child-centered (deMause, 1975).

In this child-centered age, we study children for a variety of reasons, not least because we want to understand how we become what we are. Our hope is that with greater understanding, we will be better able to ensure the development of happy, productive, healthy individuals. It should not be surprising, then, to find that child psychology is a highly applied field in the sense that it is directed toward practical as well as theoretical concerns. The questions that have traditionally seemed most important address the welfare of children. Accordingly, child psychologists have directly investigated questions relating to instruction, discipline and behavior problems, emotional disorders, perceptual problems, language acquisition, social development, morality, and a variety of other topics that are important to teachers, nurses, counselors, physicians, child welfare professionals, clergy, and parents.

To simplify, our study of developmental processes is intended to provide us with information about (1) the sorts of behaviors we might expect from children at different ages, (2) the optimal experiences for children at different developmental levels, and (3) the nature of developmental problems and the best treatments for them.

recurring questions in developmental psychology

A number of important questions have served as recurring themes in developmental psychology and have guided much of its research and theorizing. The question explored by Locke and Rousseau is one of them:

■ Is it best to view the child as an active, exploring organism, discovering or inventing meaning for the world, as Rousseau argued?

■ Or is it more useful to emphasize, as did Locke, the effects of rewards and punishments on a more passive recipient?

Most developmental psychologists today do not adhere to one or the other point of view so passionately as did Rousseau and Locke. Rather, the predominant view is of an active, exploring child deliberately attempting to create meaning out of the world (Rousseau's view) while recognizing the important influence of reward and punishment (Locke's view).

■ What are the relative effects of genetics and of environments on the developmental process?

This question has been the source of one of the main controversies in psychology: the **nature–nurture controversy**. Extreme points of view on this issue maintain either that the environment is solely responsible for whatever children become (nurture) or that genetic background (nature) determines the outcome of the developmental process. Although neither of these extreme positions is completely valid, the issue continues to be debated and is discussed in detail in Chapter 3.

■ Is development a continuous, relatively uninterrupted process, or does it consist of separate stages?

As is true for most of the recurring questions in human development, there is no simple answer. **Stages** in developmental psychology are defined as separate, sequential, age-based steps in the development of abilities, understanding, or competencies. Many important developmental theories are stage theories (for example, those of Piaget or Freud). But, as we see in Chapter 2, it has been difficult to identify abilities or competencies that invariably develop in a fixed, predictable sequence, and appear at a predetermined age. We don't develop like caterpillars— cocoon to butterfly to egg to caterpillar to cocoon to butterfly, each stage undeniably different from the one that precedes or follows it. Nevertheless, stage theories are useful in organizing the facts of human development and in helping us understand and talk about them.

basic beliefs concerning human development

None of these issues has been completely resolved. Perhaps they cannot be, and perhaps history will show that they were not particularly important in any case. What is important, however, is to keep in mind that what we think and say about children—indeed, the questions we ask and sometimes the answers we are prepared to accept—are strongly influenced by our assumptions and beliefs. Among them are the following:

■ Children are actively exploring and are engaged in trying to create meaning; they are not simply the passive recipients of external forces, responding blindly to the rewards and punishments that life provides and ingesting information as it is provided.

■ The causes of development are to be found in the interaction of environmental and genetic forces, rather than in their separate effects.

■ Development occurs in a specific historical and cultural context (that is, in a specific environment) and is profoundly influenced by the interaction between a person's characteristics and properties of the environment.

■ Some common threads appear to run through the developmental paths that different individuals take. These commonalities allow developmental psychologists to describe developmental stages or phases and to make generalizations.

■ At the same time, there are pronounced differences among individuals, even among those having very similar contexts and genetic histories. The differences become even greater when context and genetic history are more dissimilar.

■ Change is what human development is all about. The quest to describe and understand changes that occur with age and experience is based on the belief that some of the personal and environmental factors that influence change, and some of the processes involved, are identifiable and their effects predictable.

methods of studying children

t is unfortunate that in trying to make sense of the mind and emotions of infants, we can no longer remember what it was like to be an infant. Nor can infants tell us in words. As a result, much of what we know of the private lives of preverbal children is based on inferences we make. However, these inferences are based not on speculation, inspiration, or the prejudices of grandparents, but on careful, controlled, and replicable observations.

If you want to study children, you might observe natural events, such as children playing in a playground, or you might collect information on less naturally occurring events, such as controlled experiments or interviews of children. In addition, your research might be either longitudinal (following the same subjects over a long period of time) or cross-sectional (using a sample of subjects of different ages at one point in time). Of course, these research strategies are not mutually exclusive; your study of development might simultaneously be both experimental *and* longitudinal *or* cross-sectional. The following sections describe each of these approaches.

observations

Observation is the basis of all science, and thus the study of children always begins with observation. Researchers use two types of observation: naturalistic and nonnaturalistic.

NATURALISTIC OBSERVATION

Naturalistic observation occurs when children are observed without interference in natural (rather than contrived) situations—for example, on the playground or in school. Psychologists who observe children and write **diary descriptions** of their behavior (sequential descriptions of behavior at predetermined intervals) are using naturalistic observation. Similarly, psychologists who

Naturalistic observations of children involve as little interference with ongoing activities as possible and occur in "natural" environments such as playgrounds, homes, or schools.

table 1.4

Naturalistic methods of observing children

METHOD	DESCRIPTION	MAIN USES	EXAMPLE
Diary description	Fairly regular (often daily or weekly) descriptions of important events and changes	Detecting and understanding major changes and developmental sequences	Investigator makes occasional, dated notes of child's interesting language expressions
Specimen description	Detailed description of sequences of behavior, detailing all aspects of behavior	Studying individual children in depth; not restricted to only one or two predetermined characteristics	Investigator videotapes sequences of child's behavior for later analysis
Time sampling	Behaviors are recorded intermittently during short but regular time periods	Detecting and assessing changes in specific behaviors over time	Investigator records what child is doing during 30-second spans, once every 30 minutes
Event sampling	Specific behaviors (events) are recorded during the observational period; other behaviors are ignored	Understanding the nature and frequency of specific behaviors (events)	Investigator notes each time child bangs her head on the wall

Source: Based in part on Wright, 1960

describe continuous sequences of behavior (**specimen descriptions**), behaviors observed during specified time intervals (**time sampling**), or specific behaviors only (**event sampling**) are also using naturalistic observation (Wright, 1960; see Table 1.4). Note that in each of these methods, children's behavior remains unaffected by the observation.

Time sampling specifies when observations will be made; event sampling specifies the behavior that will be observed. Time and event sampling are often used together. For example, in a study of children's playground behavior, an investigator might use a checklist to record instances of specific behaviors such as laughing, yelling, fighting, or cooperating (*event* sampling); each child might also be observed for those same specific behaviors for five-minute periods at two-hour intervals (*time* sampling).

NONNATURALISTIC OBSERVATION

In **nonnaturalistic observations**, the investigation affects children's behavior. Nonnaturalistic observations are sometimes termed *clinical* if they involve the use of interviews or questionnaires. When investigators attempt to manipulate or change a child's environment, the resulting studies are called experimental. Experiments are described in the next section.

In practice, the methods child development researchers use are determined by the questions they want to answer. Some questions can best be answered by one approach; others, by another. And some questions, of course, lend themselves to more than one approach. If you are interested in knowing whether children have more affection for cats than for dogs, you might simply compare the number of children who have dogs with the number who have cats (naturalistic observation). Alternately, you might ask a sample of children which they like best (interview technique). Or you might arrange for different children, alone and in groups, to meet different cats and dogs—also alone and in groups (experimental approach)—and assess the children's reactions (perhaps through simple visual observation, or perhaps by measuring their heart rates and other physiological functions).

Note that each of these approaches might lead to somewhat different answers for the same questions. Even if there are more cats than dogs in the homes of your subjects—many parents think cats are less demanding—children might really like dogs better. And maybe, even if they do like dogs better, more would be afraid of dogs than of cats because strange dogs are somewhat more frightening than strange cats. Thus an important point to keep in mind as you evaluate some of the studies described in this text is that answers are sometimes partly a function of the research methods; the conclusions might have been different had the investigation been different.

In many cases, the study of children involves a combination of methods rather than any single method. For example, because experiments typically require observations, interviews and questionnaires are often part of experiments.

experiments

The **experiment** is science's most powerful tool for gathering useful observations. An experiment is distinguished from other observations in that it requires the systematic manipulation of some aspect of a situation to detect and measure the effects of that manipulation. In an experiment, the observer controls certain **variables** (characteristics that can vary)—called **independent variables**—to investigate their effect, or lack of effect, on other variables, termed **dependent variables**. For example, in an experiment to investigate the relationship between two teaching methods and the development of language skills, the experimenter can manipulate (control) the variable "teaching method" by using

teaching method A with one group of students and method B with a second group. In addition, if we are to have faith in the results of the experiment, subjects must be randomly assigned to the two methods to guard against the possibility that students in one group might have some systematic language-acquisition advantage over students in the other group.

In this illustration, "teaching method" is the independent variable; it is under the experimenter's control. The various measures of the subjects' language skills are dependent variables. The experimenter's **hypothesis** (scientific prediction) is that the independent variable (teaching method) will affect the dependent variables (language skills).

Experimental procedures often use experimental groups and control groups. **Experimental groups** are ordinarily made up of subjects who are treated in some special way. The object is usually to discover whether the special treatment (independent variable) has a predictable effect on some outcome (dependent variable). To ensure that any changes in the dependent variable are in fact due to the treatment, it is often necessary to use a second group—the **control group** (also called *no treatment group*)—for comparison. This second group must be as similar as possible to the experimental group in all relevant ways except that it does not experience the special treatment. The effect of the treatment is then assessed by comparing the two groups with respect to some outcome (dependent variable) after the experimental group has been given the treatment.★

It is important to recognize that the results of experiments can be believed

---

★This is only one of a large variety of experimental designs that are used in psychological research. For others, see Ray and Ravizza (1985).

with confidence only when those results have been replicated—that is, when the same outcome can be observed in repetitions of the same experiment. Replication is science's only reliable method for determining causes and effects, for science puts little credence on things that happen only once.

AN EXAMPLE OF AN EXPERIMENT

An example of the use of experiments to investigate some ideas concerning emotions may be helpful here. According to a theory of emotions developed by Carroll Izard (1977), expressions of emotion by one member of a **dyad** (two interacting people) can bring about similar emotions in the other member. The theory also argues that feelings are powerful human motivators that can lead to predictable kinds of behaviors. For example, emotions associated with interest might lead to exploration, play, learning, or other sorts of approach behaviors; in contrast, sadness typically leads to a slowing or cessation of exploration or play or to other kinds of avoidance behaviors.

Considerable evidence has been gathered to support and clarify this theory with respect to adults and children. However, relatively little has been done with infants, partly because of difficulties involved in identifying and measuring infants' emotions.

In an experiment conducted by Termine and Izard (1988), 36 nine-month-old infants were brought into a laboratory on two separate occasions (nonnaturalistic observation). On each occasion they were placed in a high chair directly in front of their mothers, and their behaviors and facial expressions, as well as those of their mothers, were videotaped for later analysis. In one experimental manipulation, mothers were instructed to express sadness both orally and facially. They were asked to recall a

sad incident and to talk about it, and they were instructed in the basic components of a sad face (for example, turning down the corners of the mouth). After two minutes of sad expression and vocalization, an experimenter entered and presented the infant with four sets of toys, all of which were removed some three minutes later. During this period, mothers were reminded at 30-second intervals, via earphones, to continue to look sad and to occasionally say something sad like, "I feel so sad today."

In a second experimental manipulation, the same infants were brought into an identical situation, except that this time the mothers were instructed to sound and look joyful. Half the infants were exposed to the sad situation first; the other half, to the joy situation first.

This experiment permits a comparison of the effects of two sets of independent variables (sad or joyful facial expressions and vocalizations) on a set of dependent variables having to do with infants' responses to their mothers. Three separate hypotheses (scientific predictions) were examined: (1) Infants would show more joy in the joy situation and more sadness in the sad condition, (2) infants would look at their mothers less in the sad condition (an avoidance behavior) and more in the joy situation (an approach behavior), and (3) infants would play more in the joy situation than in the sad condition.

Measures of infants' emotions, of the extent to which they looked at their mothers, and of their play behavior were obtained by having two trained observers analyze videotapes of each experimental session. It is especially important to note that a **blind procedure** was used; that is, the observers, working independently, were unaware of the experimental condition to which each infant had been exposed. As explained in a subsequent

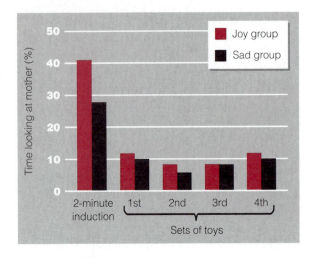
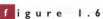

f igure 1.6

Infants' responses to their mothers' expressions of joy and sadness. Source: *Based on Termine and Izard (1988), p. 226.*

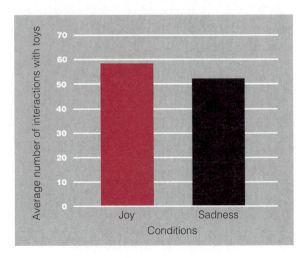

f igure 1.7

Average (mean) frequency of play interactions with toys in joy and sadness conditions. Play includes mouthing, manipulation, and naming. Source: *Based on Termine and Izard (1988), p. 277.*

section of this chapter, this procedure is an important safeguard against the possibility that the observer's expectations might affect experimental outcomes.

Analysis of the results supported the investigators' principal expectations. First, infants in the joy situation expressed significantly more joy; those in the sad condition, more sadness. Also, infants in the sad condition also displayed more anger, perhaps because, as Termine and Izard (1988) suggest, anger and sadness are related emotions.

Second, as shown in Figure 1.6, infants in the sad condition looked at their mothers significantly less during the initial two minutes, during which time the mother was actively attempting to induce an emotional state. After the presentation of the toys, infants in both groups looked at their mothers only very briefly. Finally, infants in the joy situation played more with the toys than did infants in the sad condition (Figure 1.7).

A single experiment does not *prove* anything. In fact, a whole battery of related experiments is not likely to prove

very much either; absolute proof is a rare luxury in science. Still, experiments such as this, carefully controlled and replicated, are, as we have noted, science's only reliable way of investigating cause-and-effect relationships. They are science's best source of information, the foundation for its most logical and useful conclusions. But in many situations experiments are not possible or would be quite unethical. In some of these situations, correlational studies might be used.

correlational studies

Many studies of child development proceed as follows: Researchers decide to investigate the sources (causes) of specific characteristics in a group of children; children with these characteristics are identified; a comparison group of otherwise-similar children without these characteristics is also identified. An attempt is next made to obtain historical information about these children (for example, home environment, presence or absence of a father, intelligence, presence of similar characteristics in biological ancestors, and so on). Researchers then compare the two groups with respect to these historical variables. In the end, either a relationship—a **correlation**★—will be found to exist between specific historical variables and present characteristics, or no relationship will be found.

Largely through **correlational studies** such as these, research has established relationships between socioeconomic variables such as poverty and delinquency, or between the personality characteristics of parents and children. Many such studies, sometimes termed *retrospective*, are described in this text. They are called retrospective because they try to identify relationships by looking back at a child's history (*retro* means backward) to see how factors in the child's past are related to present behavior.

CORRELATION DOES NOT PROVE CAUSATION

One caution is extremely important here. One of the most common errors in interpreting research results arises from the apparently logical (but false) assumption that if two events are correlated, one *causes* the other. It might be possible to demonstrate, for example, that in many areas there is a strong positive correlation between the number of police personnel in a city and the number of criminal arrests among students; the more police officers, the more arrests of students. Should we conclude that there is something about police officers that causes criminal behavior among students?

By the same token, if we find that measures of home background (socioeconomic indicators such as family income, parental education, and so on) are correlated with school achievement, can we conclude that parental income and education *cause* high or low achievement? No. At best, correlational studies show relationships or their absence; they do not establish causation.

Even though correlational studies cannot establish that one thing causes another, it is nevertheless true that the presence of a correlation is a necessary condition for inferring causality. However, a correlation alone is not a sufficient condition. If, as my grandmother believed, it is true that having freckles causes people to have violent tempers, then there must be a correlation between presence of freckles and bad tempers. If there is no such correlation, then my grandmother is dead wrong: Freckles do not cause bad tempers. Unfortunately, however, even if this correlation exists and is very strong, she might still be wrong. Freckles might simply be the work of the same fairies who mischievously hand out uncontrollable tempers—or they might be nothing more than genetic accidents in my grandmother's sample.

So, identifying a correlation between two things is necessary if we are to determine whether one causes the other, but a correlational relationship is still not proof of a causal relationship, although a carefully controlled experiment might strongly suggest causality.

These comments do not mean that correlational studies should be avoided and that only experiments should be conducted. Not only are correlational studies often highly informative (when interpreted cautiously), but experiments are often impossible for practical or ethical reasons. Consider, for example, an experiment designed to investigate the effects of poverty on young children. Such an experiment would require that

---

★A correlation is a mathematical measure of strength of relationship. It is usually expressed as a number ranging from +1.00 (a perfect positive relationship; as one variable increases, so does the other), through 0 (no relationship), to −1.00 (a perfect inverse relationship; as one variable increases, the other decreases).

investigators assign randomly selected children to precisely defined conditions of wealth or poverty at a critical stage in their lives and that these children be examined and compared later—hardly an ethical undertaking.

longitudinal and cross-sectional research

There are two approaches to studying human development: longitudinal and cross-sectional. A **longitudinal study** observes the same subjects over a period of time; a **cross-sectional study** compares different subjects at different developmental levels at the same time. For example, there are two ways of investigating the rules of different games played by 2 year olds and 6 year olds. One way is to observe a group of 2-year-old children at play, and then four years later observe the same children again. This is the longitudinal approach, which, for these purposes, is more time-consuming than necessary. The same results could be obtained by simultaneously observing several groups of 2- and 6-year-old children and then comparing them directly.

Cross-sectional and longitudinal approaches are both essential for studying human development. Each has some strenghts, and some weaknesses and limitations as well. For some questions, a longitudinal approach is necessary despite the fact that it is time-consuming. If investigators want to discover whether intelligence test scores change with age or remain stable, they must do this by observing the same children at different times; this question cannot be answered using a cross-sectional approach. A cross-sectional approach cannot give us information about changes that occur over time within a single individual because it looks at each individual only once.

Among the problems associated with longitudinal research are its higher cost, the fact that instruments and methods may become outdated before completion, the possibility that some of the research questions will be answered in some other way before the project is finished, and the tremendous amount of time that is sometimes required. Often an experiment must be designed to continue beyond the lifetime of a single investigator (or team of investigators). This is the case with the Terman study of giftedness, which began in the early 1920s and continues today (Terman et al., 1925). This kind of study encounters an additional problem related to subject mortality. The death of subjects not only reduces the size of samples but may also bias the results. If, for example, individuals of a certain personality type die younger than do others, a longitudinal assessment of personality change might reveal some significant changes with old age when such change is, in fact, not the case. As a purely hypothetical illustration, if aggressive people die before those who are nonaggressive, we might be led to believe that people become less aggressive as they age.

One of the most serious limitations of longitudinal studies is that they usually assume that currently valid measures will be equally valid in the future. This problem is particularly evident in longitudinal studies of vocabulary growth, intelligence, and related variables for which rapidly changing conditions may significantly affect the appropriateness of measures used.

Cross-sectional studies sometimes suffer from a similar problem, stemming from their assumption that children now at one age level are comparable to children at that age level at another time. With respect to intelligence, for example,

A longitudinal study of development follows the same subjects over a period of time. It is highly useful for providing information about changes that occur within individuals over time. However, longitudinal studies can be highly time-consuming and therefore very expensive.

drastic improvements in educational experiences and in exposure to television can affect children over a period of time to the extent that measures of intelligence obtained at one time cannot meaningfully be compared with measures obtained some years earlier.

It should be noted that many of the problems associated with longitudinal research (for example, subject mortality, higher cost, greater time requirement, changing contexts in the lives of subjects) apply only to longer-term research. But not all longitudinal research is long-term. For example, longitudinal studies of infant development might span only weeks, or perhaps only days or hours. However,

because human development spans a huge spread of years, much of our longitudinal research necessarily is long-term.

Table 1.5 summarizes the various methods used to study children.

dealing with sources of variation

Cross-sectional and longitudinal studies look at three separate sources of variation: (1) changes related to *age*, (2) influences related to *time* of testing, and (3) the influence of *cohort*. Of these, influences due to the cohort are especially confounding.

A **cohort** is a group of individuals who have in common the fact that they

chapter 1 31 studying the child

t able 1.5

Methods of studying children

Observation	The basis of all science. Observation is naturalistic *when children are observed without interference in natural rather than contrived situations. Naturalistic observation may involve time or event sampling, diary descriptions, or specimen descriptions (see Table 1.4). Nonnaturalistic observation may be clinical when it involves structured interviews or questionnaires.*
Experiment	*Science's most powerful means of gathering observations. Experiments involve systematic attempts to manipulate the environment to observe the effects of specific independent variables on given dependent variables.*
Correlational study	*A look at relationships between two (or more) variables. A correlation exists when changes in one variable are accompanied by systematic changes in another (for example, during childhood, increasing age is correlated positively with increasing strength). The existence of a correlation is necessary but insufficient for inferring causality.*
Longitudinal study	*A study in which the same subjects are followed over a period of time.*
Cross-sectional study	*A study in which subjects of different ages are studied at one point in time.*

were born within the same time period. The "1970 cohort" includes all individuals who were born during 1970; the "December 1970" cohort includes all individuals born during December 1970; and the "cohort of the eighth decade in the twentieth century" includes all individuals born in the 10-year period between January 1, 1970 and December 31, 1979. A cohort is therefore of a specific initial size and composition. It does not normally increase in size, but rather typically decreases as members die until it has completely disappeared. Its composition also gradually changes in other ways. Because men die sooner than women, the male-female ratio of a cohort usually changes over time. Similarly, racial composition might also change as a result of different mortality rates.

What is most important for the developmental psychologist is not so much that individuals of a single cohort are of the same age, but that they may be subject to a variety of experiences that are very different from those to which members of other cohorts are exposed. For example, my grandmother's cohort dates

to the turn of the twentieth century and includes people who were born into a world without electricity, television, computers, and airline travel. These rather obvious cohort-related influences might be important in attempting to understand why an 8 year old in 1978 might be quite different from an 8 year old in either 2028 or 1928. Less obvious cohort-related influences also include changes in medical practices (including the widespread use of a variety of inoculations), in nutrition, in leisure-time activities, in work roles, in morality, and so on. Because of these influences, cohorts that are scarcely separated in time might turn out to be very different in some important ways.

One of the most serious problems that developmental researchers must face is the difficulty of separating the effects of age, time, and cohort. Often these sources of variation cannot be distinguished. In a cross-sectional design it may be impossible to determine whether differences between two age groups are age-related, or whether they are due to generational factors because two different

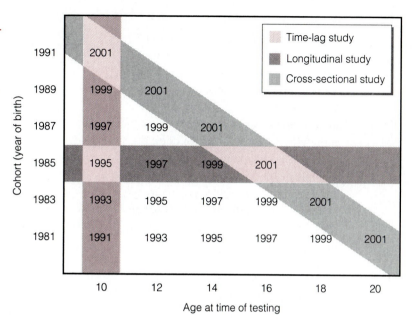

f igure 1.8

Schematic representation of three research designs. Years inside the figure indicate time of testing. Vertical columns represent possible time-lag studies (different cohorts; different times of measurement; same ages). Horizontal rows represent possible longitudinal studies (same cohort measured at different times). Diagonals represent possible cross-sectional studies (different cohorts examined at one point in time).

cohorts are being examined. In a simple longitudinal study it may be impossible to separate the effects of time of testing from those of age. In addition, generalizations derived from a longitudinal study might be applicable only to the specific cohort under investigation.

One way of overcoming these important research problems is to use what are termed *sequential designs* (Schaie, 1965). Essentially, these studies involve taking series of samples at different times of measurement. One well-known sequential design is the **time-lag study** in which different cohorts are compared at different times. For example, a time-lag study might compare 10 year olds in 1995 with 10 year olds in 1997, 1999, and 2001 (see Figure 1.8). Because subjects are of the same age when tested but were born in different years, they belong to different cohorts. Consequently, observed differences among the groups might reveal important cohort-related influences.

evaluating developmental research

Truth in psychology, as in most disciplines, is relative. The validity of research conclusions can seldom be judged as absolutely right or wrong, but must instead be evaluated in terms of how useful, clear, consistent, and generalizable they are. Of all these, perhaps **generalizability** is most important. Too often, results of a specific research project apply only to the situation in which they were obtained; they cannot be generalized to other, similar situations. The value of conclusions that can't be generalized is limited.

sampling

Research in psychology seeks to reach conclusions that are generalizable to entire populations—that is, to entire collections of individuals (or objects, or situations) with similar characteristics.

For example, the entire collection of North American fifth-grade children defines a population; all left-handed, brown-eyed 4 year olds make up another population. In most cases, the populations that are of interest to a researcher are too large to be investigated in their entirety. What the investigator does, instead, is select from this larger population a sample that is carefully chosen to be representative of the entire population.

For example, if the object is to obtain valid information about the moral beliefs and behaviors of American children, a sample (a portion) of American children is interviewed. But if the results are to be generalizable, the sample cannot comprise subjects from San Francisco or Boston alone. Rather, subjects must represent all major geographical areas in the nation. In addition, care must be taken to ensure that all nationalities, major religious groups, socioeconomic levels, occupations, and ages are represented in proportions similar to those in the entire population. One of the simplest and most effective ways of ensuring this is to select subjects at random from the entire population.

ecological and cross-cultural validity

There is a large body of research that indicates that Japanese students perform better than American students on measures of mathematics achievement (see, for example, Westbury, Ethington, Sosniak, & Baker, 1993). Several conclusions can be based on this observation: Japanese students are more intelligent—or at least more capable in mathematics; the Japanese school system is more effective than the U.S. school system; or both.

Are any of these conclusions valid? No, says Westbury (1992). A more careful analysis of the data suggests that the

nese mathematics curriculum fits the tests used in the study more closely than does the U.S. curriculum, giving Japanese students an unfair advantage. When students are compared only on what they have been taught, American students do about as well as the Japanese.*

A similar situation exists when comparing children from different cultures— or even when comparing children within single multicultural nations. We can never be certain whether observed differences reflect real differences (in underlying capacities, for example), or whether they result from the influences of different environments (ecologies). For example, according to Stevenson (see Coulter, 1993), the finding that Japanese (and Taiwanese) students do better than North American students in mathematics may also be due to a combination of the following facts: North American students spend about 20 hours per week with friends, whereas Japanese and Taiwanese students spend closer to 10; more than 75 percent of North American students but fewer than 40 percent of Asian students are dating; and 60 percent of North American students but only 20 percent of Asian students have jobs.

The fact that children from different cultures often perform differently on various tests and in different situations underlines the importance of asking two questions: (1) Are the tests and assessment procedures we're using suitable for different cultures? and (2) What might be the underlying causes of observed differences? Conclusions based on research conducted only with North American

---

*It's worth noting that not all researchers agree with Westbury's conclusions. Some, like Baker (1993), argue that even when American students are tested on only what they have been taught, they still do more poorly. There is currently considerable controversy concerning whether there are real differences between American and Japanese children in mathematics achievement—and much disagreement concerning the reasons for any differences that might exist.

Children from different cultures sometimes perform very differently on various tests, a fact whose meaning is often completely unclear. Researchers need to ask not only whether the tests are suitable for different cultures, but also what some of the other causes of observed differences might be. Conclusions based on research conducted with only one cultural group cannot easily be generalized to other groups.

samples may not be valid in Western Europe or in third-world countries. Similarly, research conducted only with white middle-class subjects in North America should not be generalized to the entire population.

memory

When Hampsten (1991) studied the diaries and letters of American pioneer women, she found that life had been harsh and difficult for their children. Most children had to work hard at very young ages, many were exposed to a variety of physical dangers, and many died

or were maimed. But when as adults they wrote accounts of their childhoods, they described all the happy experiences and few of the bad times. Autobiographical memory, claim Brewin, Andrews, and Gotlib (1993), is highly unreliable, and thus researchers who use people's recollections to understand the past must take into consideration the possibility of unintentional distortions.

subject honesty

Researchers must also consider whether subjects might distort the facts intentionally, especially when personal matters are being researched. Comparisons of adolescent sexual behavior today with behavior characteristic of adolescents several generations ago are typically unreliable, mainly for this reason. Given prevailing attitudes toward sexual behavior, it is not unreasonable to suppose that today's adolescents are more likely to be honest about sexual behavior than the adolescents of the 1920s might have been.

experimenter bias

Some research indicates that investigators sometimes unconsciously bias their observations to conform to their expectations. One effective means of guarding against experimenter bias is the **double-blind procedure**. This technique requires simply that experimenters, examiners, and subjects remain unaware of either the expected outcomes of the research or of the assignment of subjects to experimental or control groups.

subject bias

Subject bias may also affect the outcomes of an experiment. In a highly publicized experiment, two psychologists

(Roethlisberger & Dickson, 1939) compared ways to increase productivity among workers in the Hawthorne plant of the Western Electric Company in Chicago. In successive experiments, the workers were subjected to shorter working periods, longer working periods, better lighting conditions, poorer lighting conditions, long periods of rest, short periods of rest, work incentives such as bonuses, and a variety of other conditions. Under most of these conditions, productivity apparently increased, an observation that led to the conclusion that if subjects are aware that they are members of an experimental group, performance may improve simply because of that fact.

Although the **Hawthorne effect,** as it is now called, is usually accepted as fact in social science research, its existence has not been well established—in spite of the experiments just described. Following a careful reexamination of the original experiments and interviews with some of the people involved at that time, Rice (1982) found little evidence of a Hawthorne effect. He reports that productivity did not increase in many of the experiments, but that later reports of the study usually concentrated on only one experiment in which there was some eas-

ily explained improvement over the five-year course of the study. Adair, Sharpe, and Huynh (1989) analyzed 86 studies for the presence of a Hawthorne effect and concluded that in most research, this effect is rare or trivial.

When we consider all these aspects of research, it's clear that we must be careful when interpreting the results of developmental research. Among the important questions to ask are these:

- Is the sample representative of the population to which the research is generalized?

- Can the results be applied to other groups within the culture or to other cultures, or are they specific to this environment—to this ecological reality?

- Do the observations rely on the memory and honesty of the subjects? Are the observations objective and replicable?

- Has the possibility of experimenter or subject bias been taken into consideration?

Table 1.6 summarizes the criteria for evaluating developmental research.

And then, of course, it's important to

---

table 1.6

Checklist for evaluating the usefulness, clarity, logical consistency, and generalizability of developmental research

Sampling	*Is the sample a good representation of the population to which the observations and conclusions are meant to apply?*
Ecosystem	*Is there something special or unique about the social, cultural, or historical context in which observations are made? Do the characteristics of the context in interaction with the characteristics of the individuals reduce the generalizability of the findings?*
Subject Memory	*Must the investigation rely on human memories? Has the possibility of systematic or random distortion been taken into account?*
Subject Honesty	*Does the validity of the observations depend on the honesty of subjects? Do they have a reason to consciously or unconsciously distort facts?*
Experimenter or Subject Bias	*Is there a possibility that experimenters' or subjects' expectations have influenced observations?*

ponder whether the questions posed by any developmental research project are important—whether the answers obtained really matter in our understanding *of children.*

main points

THIS TEXT

1. Development, the process whereby children adapt to their environment, includes maturation (genetically programmed unfolding), growth (quantitative changes), and learning (changes due to experience).

CHANGING ATTITUDES TOWARD CHILDREN

2. There is evidence that in medieval times children were considered miniature adults whose presence in the family did not engender strong feelings of parental attachment, perhaps because infant mortality was very high. During the eighteenth and nineteenth centuries, child labor flourished and childrearing practices were often harsh. The twentieth century has brought increasing concern with the social, physical, and intellectual welfare of children, especially in the industrialized world. However, in many nonindustrialized, underdeveloped areas of the world, millions of children die each year—primarily from malnutrition, vaccine-preventable causes such as measles and tetanus, and diarrheal dehydration.

3. Lower birthrates, greater numbers of childless couples, delayed marriages, increasing numbers of one-parent families, and the impact of television have altered the experience of childhood.

CHILDREN'S RIGHTS

4. The legal rights of children in today's industrialized societies are primarily rights of protection (to adequate medical and educational care, to affection and love, to a peaceful environment, to the opportunity to develop) rather than adult rights of choice that entail adult responsibilities. In the developing world, children's most basic rights are often ignored. In many of these areas, formal education is substandard or nonexistent, and physical and mental abuse of children is common.

PIONEERS IN CHILD STUDY

5. Among early pioneers of the scientific study of children were John Locke (*tabula rasa*) and Jean-Jacques Rousseau ("noble savage"). Later pioneers included Charles Darwin (baby biography; evolution), G. Stanley Hall ("ontogeny recapitulates phylogeny"), and John B. Watson (we become what we are as a function of our experiences).

RECURRING QUESTIONS AND BELIEFS

6. Recurring questions in human development ask about the relative influence of heredity and environment, whether development is continuous or occurs in discrete stages, and whether we should view children as primarily active or passive. Common basic beliefs are that a child is active and creates meaning, that causes of development are complex interactions between the environment and specific characteristics of an individual, and that in spite of marked individual differences, there are some commonalities in the developmental patterns of different individuals.

STUDYING CHILDREN

7. Naturalistic (nonintrusive) observations of children include diary descriptions (regular descriptions of interesting events), specimen descriptions (continuous sequences of behavior), event sampling (recordings of predetermined behaviors), and time sampling (recordings during predetermined time intervals). Nonnaturalistic observations may be clinical (questionnaires or interviews) or experimental.

8. In an experiment, an investigator randomly assigns subjects to groups and controls independent variables to determine whether they affect dependent variables (outcomes). Correlational studies look at relationships among variables.

9. Child development studies can be longitudinal studies, which compare the same children at different periods in their lives, or cross-sectional studies, which compare different children at the same time.

10. One way of separating effects due to cohorts (groups of people born during same time span) and to age is to use sequences of samples, thus permitting different combinations of longitudinal, cross-sectional, and time-lag studies. In a *time-lag study*, different cohorts are compared at different times (for instance, 7 year olds in 1991 are compared with 7 year olds in 1995, 1999, and 2003).

EVALUATING RESEARCH

11. The value and generalizability of research results are subject to the influences of sample representativeness, subject memory and honesty, experi-

menter bias, ecological validity, and other factors. Truth, here as elsewhere, is relative.

focus questions: applications

■ What is this book about?
1. Define the key terms listed in the "Study Terms" section.

■ How have attitudes toward children changed? Why are they important?
2. Compare medieval attitudes toward children as reflected in sports such as, say, "baby tossing", with North American attitudes today. Compare these attitudes with those reflected in instances of wartime atrocities against children (child beatings, starvation, rape, murder, and so on).

■ What are the rights of children? The responsibilities of parents and nations?
3. When, if ever, should the state interfere in the home vis-a-vis the care and upbringing of children?

■ What are the most basic questions and beliefs in the study of children?
4. What are your *personal* beliefs about the most important influences in development? On what evidence are these beliefs based?

■ How do we study children?
5. Ask a simple, specific, important question about the development of children. How might you find an answer for your question?

■ How reliable are our conclusions?
6. Referring to question 5, how would you evaluate your answer?

study terms

psychology 6
developmental psychology 6
growth 6
maturation 6
learning 6
development 6
infancy 9
baby tossing 14
nature-nurture controversy 23
stages 23
naturalistic observations 24
diary description 24
specimen description 25
time sampling 25
event sampling 25
nonnaturalistic observation 25
experiment 26
variable 26
independent variable 26
dependent variable 26
hypothesis 26
experimental group 26
control group 26
dyad 27
blind procedure 27
correlation 29
correlational study 29
longitudinal study 30
cross-sectional study 30
cohort 31
time-lag study 33
generalizability 33
double-blind procedure 35
Hawthorne effect 36

further readings

Fascinating descriptions of changes in the status of children throughout history are provided by:

Aries, P. (1962). *Centuries of childhood: A social history of family life* (R. Baldick, trans.). New York: Alfred A. Knopf. (Originally published 1960.)

Kessen, W. (1965). *The child*. New York: John Wiley.

A booklet containing all the Children's Rights articles of the U.N.'s Convention on the Rights of the Child can be obtained free from:

United Nations Children's Fund
UNICEF House, H-9F
United Nations Plaza
New York, NY 10017
telephone: (212) 326-7072

The following collection of articles is a practical discussion of the rights of children, the responsibilities of parents, guardians, and nations with respect to children, and legal recourses available to children and their parents:

Westman, J. C. (1991). Introduction. In J. C. Westman (ed.), *Who speaks for the children?* Sarasota, Fla.: Professional Resource Exchange, Inc.

Not everyone believes that science is the only, or even the best, way of knowing. For a provocative and sometimes challenging view of science and our conception of reality, see:

Pearce, J. C. (1971). *The crack in the cosmic egg*. New York: Fawcett.

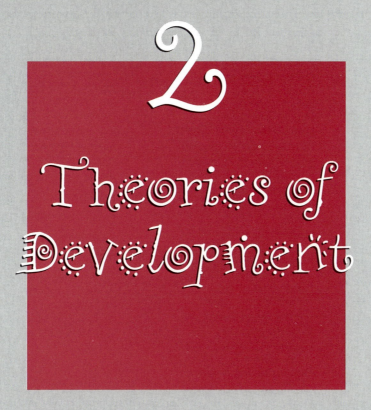

2

Theories of Development

A belief is not true because it is useful.
Henri-Frederic Amiel, Journal

focus questions

WHAT'S IN A THEORY? WHAT'S A THEORY FOR? HOW CAN YOU TELL WHETHER A THEORY IS A GOOD ONE?

HOW DOES FREUDIAN PSYCHOANALYSIS RELATE TO CHILD DEVELOPMENT?

WHAT ARE THE PRINCIPAL ASSUMPTIONS AND EXPLANATIONS OF BEHAVIORISM?

DO CHILDREN LEARN THROUGH IMITATION?

WHAT ARE THE BASIC IDEAS UNDERLYING PIAGET'S THEORY?

WHAT ARE SOME OF THE ROLES OF BIOLOGY AND CULTURE IN CHILD DEVELOPMENT?

outline

THEORY AND SCIENCE

Functions of Theories
Developing Theories
Evaluating Theories
Facts and Expectations
Characteristics of Good Theories

MODELS IN CHILD DEVELOPMENT

Machine Models and Organism Models
A Contextual or Ecological Model

PSYCHOANALYTIC APPROACHES: FREUD

Basic Freudian Ideas
Three Levels of Human Personality
Psychosexual Stages in Human Development
Defense Mechanisms
Freudian Theory in Review

PSYCHOANALYTIC APPROACHES: ERIKSON

Psychosocial Stages in Human Development
Erikson's Theory in Review

HAVIGHURST'S DEVELOPMENTAL TASKS

BEHAVIORISTIC APPROACHES

Overview of Behavioristic Approaches
Classical Conditioning
Operant Conditioning
Behavioristic Approaches in Review

SOCIAL COGNITIVE THEORY

The Processes of Observational Learning
Manifestations of Observational Learning
Self-Efficacy Judgments
Social Cognitive Theory in Review

A COGNITIVE APPROACH: PIAGET

Basic Concepts in Cognitive Development
The Stages of Cognitive Development
Piaget's Theory in Review

BIOLOGICAL AND ECOLOGICAL APPROACHES

Ethology and Bowlby's Attachment Theory
Bowlby's Theory in Review
Sociobiology

Vygotsky's Cultural-Historical Approach
Vygotsky's Theory in Review
Bronfenbrenner's Ecological Systems Theory

HUMANISTIC APPROACHES

Maslow's Humanistic Need Theory
Humanism in Review

A FINAL WORD ABOUT THEORIES

MAIN POINTS

FOCUS QUESTIONS: APPLICATIONS

STUDY TERMS

FURTHER READINGS

Even now I still have some difficulty reacting appropriately to the term theory. It's an awesome term; sometimes it frightens me. This is a reaction conditioned by long hours in my grandmother's kitchen, where she would repeatedly stop my ramblings with, "Yes, but that's just theory. Have you looked at the facts?" And then she would tell me what the facts were; they usually contradicted my "theory."

I might, to this day, have remained convinced that facts and theory are completely different, and that theory is what one resorts to only when the facts are unknown, had it not been for my grandmother's theory of wastes. (My cousins and I were less polite then; we called it Grandma's _____ theory.)

We had been sitting on the porch one June evening, she knitting and I dreaming, both of us gazing out over the garden—a fine garden with potatoes only two hills to a pail and carrots big as my arm. Interrupting my dreams of fantastic future glories, I commented on the excellence of my grandmother's garden, being careful to observe that Tremblay's potatoes were never so large or plentiful and that his carrots were like shoestrings next to hers.

"It's the horse manure," she said matter-of-factly. The word she used—merde—is somewhat less offensive in French than its counterpart in English.

"He uses manure too," I said, always ready to contradict the old lady.

"Cow manure."

"Cow manure? It's manure, too. Why shouldn't his garden be as good? He's got a lot of it."

"I have a theory about that," said my grandmother. I saw my chance, and I jumped right in.

"A theory?" Politely, of course. "But facts, Grandma. We should speak of facts, not theory."

"The facts," she informed me calmly, "are that I have a far better garden than Tremblay, that I use horse manure, and that he uses cow manure."

And the theory, as she explained in detail, simply accounted for the facts: It explained why horse manure favors potatoes and carrots; why small chicken droppings invigorate cabbages; why flattened and dried patties of cow dung excite flowers. It is not a simple theory; nor is it likely of much interest to you, sophisticated as you are. But for my grandmother, a proud woman—proud of her favored potatoes and carrots, her invigorated cabbages, her excited flowers—it was of considerable interest.

theory and science

And for me, it was a lesson in theory—a lesson that I now pass on. A theory need not be an exotic collection of obscure pronouncements; nor does it substitute for facts in the absence of the latter. In its simplest sense, a **theory** is no more than an explanation of facts. As Thomas (1992) puts it, specifically with respect to theories of child development, to theorize is to suggest "(1) which facts are most important for understanding children and (2) what sorts of relationships among the facts are most significant for producing this understanding" (p. 4).

functions of theories

Put another way, a theory is a collection of related statements intended to organize and explain observations. Explanation is important because if we can explain something, we might also be able to predict certain outcomes. If my grandmother understands why specific manures affect certain crops in given ways, she can not only predict these effects but also exercise a high degree of control over her garden (barring such acts of God as severe storms, locust infestations, or small boys chasing cats among the turnips).

Similarly, if a theory explains why it is that some children are happy and others are not, then it should be possible, given relevant facts, to predict which children will be happy. Also, if the circumstances affecting happiness are under our control, it should also be possible to bring happiness to saddened lives. Thus theories may have very practical aspects. At the same time, they are one of science's primary guides for doing research. In large part, it is a theory—sometimes crude, sometimes elegant and refined—that tells a re-

searcher where to, say, look for a cure for cancer, what the cure will look like when it is found, and how it might be used. In the same way, psychology's theories tell a researcher where and how to look for personality or intellectual change in the course of development. They suggest as well what some of the causes of change might be and how change may be brought about.

developing theories

Theories are seldom handed to philosophers and scientists carved in pieces of rock—or even written on pieces of paper. They arise, instead, from observations that are assumed to be factual and that are important enough to require explanation. Because they arise from observations, and because what different individuals choose to observe (that is, what they consider to be important and in need of explanation) may vary a great deal, there are many different theories in most areas of research.

The types of observations on which scientific theories are based are seldom of the kind that were of such intimate interest to my grandmother. Science, if nothing else, insists on a kind of objectivity, precision, and **replicability** (repeatability) that would have been difficult in my grandmother's garden. We can accurately say, in fact, that science is less a collection of methods than an attitude. The classic "scientific method" (statement of problem, prediction, materials and methods, observations, conclusions) is simply a means of ensuring that observations are made under sufficiently controlled circumstances that they could be made by anyone else—that, in short, they can be replicated and confirmed. The attitude that characterizes science's search for explanation emphasizes the replicability of observations and demands precision in measuring and observing; hence the importance of the research methods described in Chapter 1. Clearly, if the facts on which a theory is based are themselves suspect, the theory is not likely to be very useful.

evaluating theories

Why, you might ask, must there be a variety of theories if a theory is simply an explanation of facts? Some of the reasons have already been mentioned. First, different theories may be used to explain quite different facts. And even very general theories of development—those that attempt to explain all of development—are not all based on the same observations; that is, theorists select the observations that require explanation. Furthermore, given the same set of observations, not all theorists will arrive at the same sets of explanations. Finally, fact (or truth) is no more obvious in developmental psychology than it is elsewhere. Our observations are often more or less accurate depending on the precision of our measurements, they are often relevant only in specific circumstances and sometimes for specific individuals, and they are colored by our expectations—in other words, by our theories and our assumptions.

facts and expectations

"We do not discover scientific facts," Scarr (1985) explains; "we invent them" (p. 499). Nor do we always generalize appropriately, and it is on generalizations that our theories are based.

As a clear example of how expectations color observations, Hunt (1961) reports how, in the seventeenth century, a man named Joseph DeAromati noticed that it's possible to see parts of plants in bulbs or in seeds. This observation led

him to conclude that plants are fully formed in the seed, a conclusion that was quickly generalized to humans, leading to the theory of *preformationism*. In essence, this theory maintained that if your eyes were good enough to see the detail inside a sperm or an egg, you would see a fully formed but stunningly miniature little human—a sort of extreme human bonsai. There arose a heated controversy between the *animalculits*, who were certain the complete little person would be found inside the sperm, and the *ovists*, who thought it far more likely the little person would be inside the egg (the ovum).

Then Antonie van Leeuwenhoek invented the microscope, which should have resolved the controversy once and for all. "The little person is inside the homunculus," said a prominent scientist named Hartsoeker, peering through his microscope. "I've seen it." And to prove he had, he drew it.

Even with microscopes and the best of intentions, we sometimes see what isn't there at all. Imagine how much poorer is our sight when our microscopes are not so strong.

characteristics of good theories

We cannot easily determine whether a theory is right or wrong—whether it is accurate and truthful or not. But we can evaluate it in other ways, most of which concern its usefulness. In other words, theories need not be accurate explanations of selected observations; they can be nothing more than useful attempts to explain important things. And two theories that present different explanations for the same observations might both be useful—or useless. Sometimes the differences result from the fact that the theories present different levels of analyses, are based on different assumptions, or emphasize different aspects of human functioning.

Thomas (1992) suggests a number of criteria that might be used to judge the "goodness" of a theory of child development. A theory is better, says Thomas, if it (1) accurately reflects the facts, (2) is expressed in a clearly understandable way, (3) is useful for predicting future events as well as explaining past ones, (4) can be applied in a practical sense (that is, has real value for counselors, teachers, pediatricians, and so on), (5) is consistent within itself rather than self-contradictory, (6) is not based on a great number of assumptions (unproven beliefs), (7) stimulates new research and discovery, and (8) explains development in ways that make sense.

models in child development

Imagine this problem: Your instructor brings into class a small thing inside a larger glass thing. You don't know what this small thing is. Your task is to decide what would be the best way to discover all you can about it. Think about the problem for a moment before reading on.

Is there enough information in the previous paragraph for you to make some reasonably intelligent suggestions? Consider now what your suggestions might be had I written: "Your instructor has brought into class a small animal inside a glass jar," or "Your instructor has brought into class a small piece of machinery inside a glass box," or again, "Your instructor has brought into class a strange new fruit in a glass container." Why is the task of investigating the object so much easier in the last three cases? Simply because you've been given information that allows you to classify the object in terms of something about whose properties and

functioning you already know a great deal. You have, in your view of the world, a mental **model**, or pattern, of what animals, fruits, and machines are like.

Psychologists investigating human development are, in some ways, in the same position as a student presented with a "thing." If we had no prior conceptions about people, it would be difficult to know which questions would be the best ones to ask. But we do have prior beliefs based on our experiences and our culture, which, says Kelley (1992), influence our scientific propositions. What we do, in effect, is look at development in terms of something that's more familiar. We begin with a metaphor, a comparison. We say this is like that, and thus it might work in the same way as that. The "that" serves as our model.

machine models and organism models

In developmental psychology, two basic models underlie many of our theories: the organismic model and the mechanistic model (Fischer & Silvern, 1985). The **organismic model** assumes that it is useful to view people as though they were like active organisms; the **mechanistic model** assumes that it is more useful to view people as though they were like machines. In the first instance, the model is primarily *active*; in the second, the model is *reactive*.

These underlying models are very important in the development of theories. In effect, they suggest what a theorist will investigate and what the resulting theory will look like. An organismic view (Piaget's, for example) describes development as a process resulting from self-initiated activities and looks for regularities in behavior to understand the wholeness and unity of the organism. In contrast, a mechanistic view (early behaviorism, for example) describes development as a process resulting from reactions to external events and searches for the machinelike predictability that might result given sufficient knowledge about how the machine reacts to external forces.

But much of development is not highly linear and predictable, contends Steenbarger (1991). Rather, it is profoundly influenced by the situations in which people find themselves; it reflects continually changing *interactions* between individuals and their environments. Put another way, human development reflects the influence of context (Kleinginna & Kleinginna, 1988).

Children are profoundly influenced by the people and the things with which they interact daily (as well as by broader aspects of their contexts). In turn, they, too, affect their environments. The contextual model emphasizes the importance of things like family, school, peers, siblings, and other important aspects of the social and physical environment.

a contextual or ecological model

The **contextual** (or *ecological*) **model** emphasizes the role of society, culture, and family and recognizes the importance of both the historical period in which the individual develops and events that are unique to the individual (Bronfenbrenner, 1989).

The contextual model shares characteristics of both the organismic and mechanistic models. It is organismic in that it sees development as the product of organism-environment interaction and because it looks for universal principles that might be useful for describing development (Lerner, 1985). It is mechanistic in that it is concerned with the influence of the environment on the developing organism.

OPEN AND CLOSED SYSTEMS

One of the important characteristics of a contextual model is that it is based on an **open systems** view of human development (Bertalanffy, 1950). An *open*

system is one that depends on interaction (in contrast to a *closed system*, which is completely predictable and totally unaffected by its environment). Thus an open system is constantly open to change; it is fundamentally dependent on its context and adapts continually as a function of interacting with its context. Accordingly, in an open system it is impossible to predict precisely what the final adaptation will be.

According to Valsiner (1987), all biological, psychological, and social systems are open systems. Hence all developmental research should ideally be based on models that take into consideration interaction between a person's characteristics and characteristics of the environment.

ECOLOGICAL SYSTEMS THEORY

The contextual or ecological model is exemplified in Bronfenbrenner's *ecological systems theory* and in Vygotsky's *social-cognitive theory*, both described later in this chapter. It is also the model that is most apparent throughout this text, which, with Bronfenbrenner, views development as the progressive adaptation of active, growing human beings to changing environments. Our emphasis is on understanding development as an interactive process involving individuals with different characteristics in a range of different ecological systems or contexts. Hence the emphasis on the importance of family, school, peers, siblings, and other significant aspects of context. Throughout this text, contextual influences on development are dramatically illustrated in "In Other Contexts" boxes, which explore the lives and characteristics of children from other cultures (or from subgroups within our own cultures).

You might ask, at this point, whether one of these three models—the mechanistic, the organismic, or the contextual/ecological—is correct and, by implication, the others incorrect. But the question is irrelevant because models are simply metaphors—implied comparisons. Models direct our research and shape our beliefs and our theories—and perhaps our textbooks too—but we should not judge them as either correct or incorrect. We might as well ask whether the verse "The moon was a ghostly galleon, tossed upon cloudy seas" is more accurate than "That orbed maiden with white fire laden, Whom mortals call the moon." Metaphors are either apt and useful or clumsy and useless. We might judge our poetic metaphors in terms of the images and feelings they evoke; we can judge our scientific metaphors only in terms of their usefulness.

Table 2.1 summarizes these three metaphors (models). The remainder of this chapter describes seven major groups of developmental theories. (For those who prefer to see an overview first, these groups of theories are summarized in Table 2.12 on page 94). Note how each reflects the influence of one or more of the basic underlying metaphors.

psychoanalytic approaches: Freud

Sigmund Freud's psychoanalytic theory reflects an organismic approach in its basic assumption that the most important causes of human behavior and personality are deep-seated, usually unconscious forces within individuals. Freud believed that these forces, some of which lead to conflict between desires and conscience, are at the root of mental disorders. Hence therapists (psychoanalysts) can help restore mental health, argued Freud, by helping patients understand unconscious drives and resulting conflicts. Among the techniques that he found most useful for this—techniques that soon became part of standard psychoanalytic procedure—were free association; the analysis of dreams and of the unintended use of words and expressions (popularly referred to as *Freudian slips*), both of which were assumed to reflect unconscious desires or fears; hypnosis; and painstaking analysis of childhood experiences, especially those of a sexual or traumatic (intensely frightening) nature.

Not surprisingly, the principal usefulness of Freudian psychoanalytic theory has been for treating mental disorder. However, much of the theory is developmental. Even though the most important beliefs of psychoanalytic theory are no longer an important part of current developmental theories, their historical importance and their influence on the thinking of later theorists justifies their inclusion here. The following sections present a brief account of this incredibly complex, sometimes bewildering, but always fascinating view of the development and machinations of human personality.

While reading about Freud, it is worth keeping in mind that his theory is very much a product of the Victorian era in which it was developed—an era that by today's standards was one of extreme sex-

Characteristics of the three basic models in developmental psychology

	MODEL		
	ORGANISMIC	**MECHANISTIC**	**ECOLOGICAL**
Metaphor	*People as biological organisms*	*People as machines*	*People as plastic, strong, resilient, and adaptive*
Perception of person	*Sees individual as active, self-directed*	*Sees individual as reactive to environment*	*Sees individual as active and reactive*
Developmental process	*Tends toward final adult stage, describable in terms of logical characteristics of adult thought*	*Described in terms of learning and problem solving; no clearly described end goal*	*Involves universal principles influenced by an individual's specific social, historical, and personal context*
Theories	*Age-related stage theories emphasizing similarities of thought at each level*	*Theories emphasizing the continuity of development*	*Theories emphasizing the interaction of age, historical variables, important life events, culture, and other aspects of context with individual characteristics*
Emphasis	*Attention to similarities*	*Attention to individual differences*	*Attention to similarities; recognition of context- and person-related differences*
Theorists	*Piaget; Freud*	*Early behaviorists*	*Bronfenbrenner; Vygotsky; Bandura and contemporary behaviorists*

ual repression and masculine domination. These cultural factors greatly influenced Freud's theory and are reflected in both the importance he gave sexual motives and behaviors and the masculine orientation of the theory. Much of what Freud initially thought about development applied primarily to male children—and to females only as a sometimes very hasty and incomplete afterthought (Gilligan, 1982).

basic freudian ideas

One of the most fundamental of Freudian ideas is the notion that human behavior—and consequently the direction that personality development takes—is driven by two powerful tendencies: the urge to survive and the urge to procreate (Roazen, 1975). Because the urge to survive is not usually threatened by our environments (the

Freud's theory was profoundly influenced by the male-dominated, sexually repressive beliefs and customs of the Victorian era in which he lived. Paintings and photographs of Freud's era often depict the family very formally, with the stern-faced father typically in a position of command.

Freudian term for environment is *reality*), it is of secondary importance. But the urge to procreate is constantly being discouraged and even prevented by reality, and this accounts for the tremendous importance of sexuality in Freud's description of human development.

Sexuality is a very broad term in Freud's writings. It means not only activities that are clearly associated with sex but all other activities that may be linked with body pleasure, however remotely (for example, behaviors such as thumb sucking or smoking). Sexual urges are sufficiently important in Freud's system that they are given a special term: *libido*. The **libido** is the source of energy for sexual urges; accordingly, the urges themselves are referred to as libidinal urges, even though satisfaction of sexual impulses need not involve the sexual regions of the body.

three levels of human personality

Freud describes the sequential development of three levels of personality: id, ego, and superego.

ID

The newborn infant has a simple, undeveloped personality consisting solely of primitive, unlearned urges that will be a lifetime source of what Freud called psychic energy, the urges and desires that account for behavior. Freud's label for the child's earliest personality is **id**. The urges that define id are primarily sexual.

The Freudian infant is all instincts (unlearned tendencies) and reflexes, a bundle of unbridled psychic energy seeking almost desperately to satisfy urges that are based on a need to survive and to procreate. An infant has no idea of what is possible or impossible, no sense of reality, no conscience, no internal moral rules that govern conduct. The most powerful urge at this stage is to seek immediate satisfaction of impulses. A child who is hungry does not wait; now is the time for the nipple and the sucking!

EGO

Almost from birth, a child's instinctual urges collide with reality. The hunger urge (linked with survival) cannot always be satisfied immediately. The reality of the situation is that the mother is often occupied elsewhere, and the infant's satisfaction must be delayed or denied. Similarly, the child eventually learns that defecation cannot occur anywhere and at any time; parental demands conflict with the child's impulses. This constant conflict between id impulses and reality develops the second level of personality, the **ego**.

The ego grows out of a realization of what is possible and what is not; it is the rational level of human personality. It develops as a result of a child's experiences, and it comes to include the realization that delaying gratification is often a desirable thing, that long-term goals sometimes require the denial of short-term

goals. Although the id wants immediate gratification, the ego channels these desires in the most profitable direction for the individual. Note that the levels of personality represented by the id and the ego are not in opposition. They work together toward the same goal: satisfying the needs and urges of the individual.

SUPEREGO

The third level of personality—labeled the **superego**—sets itself up in opposition to the first two. The term *superego* refers to the moral aspects of personality. Like the ego, the superego develops from contact with reality, but it is more concerned with social than physical reality. The development of the superego (or conscience) does not occur until early childhood. Freud assumed that it resulted mainly from identifying with parents, especially with the same-sex parent. To identify, said Freud, is to attempt to become like others—to adopt their values and beliefs as well as their behaviors. By identifying with their parents, children learn the religious and cultural rules that govern their parents' behaviors; these rules then become part of a child's superego. Because many religious, social, and cultural rules oppose the urges of the id, the superego and the id are generally in conflict. Freud assumed that this conflict accounts for much deviant behavior.

In summary, Freud's theory describes three levels of personality: the id, the ego, and the superego (Figure 2.1). The id is the source of psychic energy deriving from instincts of survival and procreation. The ego is reality-oriented and intervenes between the id and the superego to maintain a balance between the id's urges and the superego's rules. It is as though the id were continually saying, "I want that almond torte right now; I want to be caressed immediately; I want that Ferrari

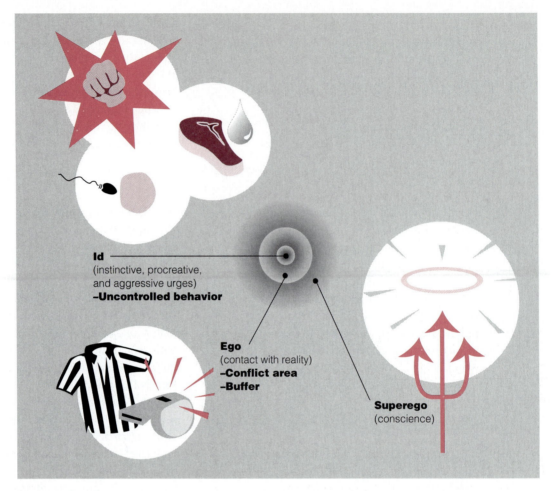

Id
(instinctive, procreative,
and aggressive urges)
–Uncontrolled behavior

Ego
(contact with reality)
–Conflict area
–Buffer

Superego
(conscience)

f **igure 2.1**

The Freudian conception of the three levels of personality: id, ego, and superego. The id, consisting of instinctual urges, develops first; the ego and the superego (conscience) develop later. In normal personality development, the ego acts as a buffer between the id and superego, which are in conflict with each other. Personality disorders may arise from unrestricted conflict when the ego fails to mediate successfully.

today; I want to punch that guy's lights out," while the superego chides, "Don't you dare; deny your desires; thou shalt not steal; fighting is a sin." And the ego, seated between these warring forces, attempts calmly to make peace: "Have you considered eating only at mealtime and with some moderation? Why don't you wait 'til you get married? Take a bus if you can't have a Ferrari. As for that idiot, let the courts handle it. You can watch. How would that be?" (See Figure 2.2.)

psychosexual stages in human development

Freud's account of the development of the three levels of personality is a description of **psychosexual development**. Stages in psychosexual development are distinguishable by the objects or activities necessary for the satisfaction of urges during that stage; the labels for each stage reflect changes in matters of sexual satisfaction as the child matures (see Table 2.2).

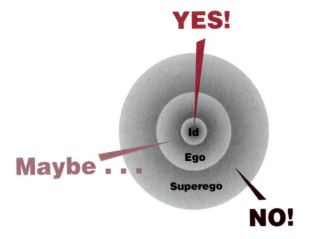

YES!

Maybe . . .

Id

Ego

Superego

NO!

f i g u r e **2 . 2**

In a simplified sense, the id is basic urges. It says "Yes, more food, more sex, more more . . ." to all impulses. The superego reflects rules and regulations of society and of religion: "No, control your desires! Moderate! Sex is only for making babies!" The ego tries to mediate: "Maybe, let's see what we can work out. Maybe we can substitute something else for sex? Maybe we can do it secretly!"

THE ORAL STAGE

The **oral stage** lasts through most of infancy (approximately to the age of 18 months). It is characterized by the infant's preoccupation with the mouth and with sucking. During this first stage, a child's personality consists mainly of id. Children constantly seek to satisfy their urges and are incapable of deliberately delaying gratification.

THE ANAL STAGE

Toward the end of the first year, the area of sexual gratification begins shifting gradually from the oral region to the anal region. According to Freud, in the early part of the **anal stage** a child derives pleasure from bowel movements. Later in this stage the child acquires control of sphincter muscles and may then get considerable pleasure from withholding bowel movements to increase anal sensation. Both of these behaviors oppose the

mother's wishes. As a result of these conflicts, the child begins to develop an ego—a sense of reality, an awareness that some things are possible whereas others are not, coupled with the ability to delay gratification to some extent.

THE PHALLIC STAGE

The third stage, which lasts roughly from ages 2 to 6, is labeled the **phallic stage** because the zone of sexuality has now shifted from the anal to the genital region and because the phallus (the male genital) is of primary importance in the sexuality of girls as well as boys. Whereas gratification had been obtained earlier by sucking or by expelling or withholding feces, children now often masturbate (manipulate their **genitalia**).

According to Freud, normal development now takes the male child through the **Oedipus complex**, when his increasing awareness of the sexual meanings of his genital area leads him to desire his mother (and to unconsciously wish to replace his father). For girls at 4 to 6 years, there is the **Electra complex**, in which a girl's sexual feelings for her father lead her to become jealous of her mother.

THE LATENCY STAGE

The resolution of the Oedipus complex marks the transition from the phallic stage to the period of sexual **latency** that follows (from age 6 to 11). This period is marked by a loss of sexual interest in the opposite-sex parent and a continued **identification** with the same-sex parent. The process of identification is very important in Freud's system because it not only involves attempts to behave like the parent with whom the child is identifying but also implies attempting to be like the object of identification in terms of beliefs and values. In this way, a child begins to develop a superego. Note that identification, like many other significant phe-

table 2.2

Freud's stages of psychosexual development

STAGE	APPROXIMATE AGES	CHARACTERISTICS
Oral	0–18 months	Sources of pleasure include sucking, biting, swallowing, playing with lips; preoccupation with immediate gratification of impulses; id is dominant
Anal	18 months to 2 or 3 years	Sources of sexual gratification include defecation and urination, as well as retaining feces; id and ego
Phallic	2 or 3 to 6 years	Child becomes concerned with genitals; source of sexual pleasure involves manipulating genitals; period of Oedipus or Electra complex; id, ego, and superego
Latency	6–11 years	Loss of interest in sexual gratification; identification with same-sex parent; id, ego, and superego
Genital	11 years and older	Concern with adult modes of sexual pleasure, barring fixations or regressions.

nomena described by Freud, is largely an *unconscious* rather than a conscious process.

THE GENITAL STAGE

Following this lengthy period of sexual neutrality, a child enters the stage of adult sexuality, the **genital stage** (at around age 11), and begins to establish heterosexual attachments. Also during this last developmental stage, the superego (conscience), which has previously been very rigid, becomes progressively more flexible.

defense mechanisms

An overview of Freud's theories would be incomplete without a consideration of **defense mechanisms**—the irrational and sometimes unhealthy methods some people use to compensate for their inability to satisfy the demands of the id and to overcome the anxiety that accompanies the continual struggle between the id and the superego (A. Freud, 1946). Defense mechanisms are invented by the ego in its role as mediator between the id and the superego; they are the ego's attempt to establish peace between the two so that the personality can continue to operate in an apparently healthy manner. Defense mechanisms are especially important for understanding disturbed personalities, although they are not at all uncommon in the lives of those who have no clearly recognizable disturbances. It is only when people rely on them excessively that defense mechanisms become unhealthy. (See Table 2.3 for examples of common defense mechanisms.)

freudian theory in review

Freud paints a dark and often cynical picture of human nature: Primitive forces over which we have no control drive us relentlessly toward the satisfaction of instinctual urges and bring us into repeated conflict with reality. From the very moment of birth, our most basic selves—our ids—react with anxiety and fear. We fear that our overpowering urges to survive

table 2.3

Some common freudian defense mechanisms

MECHANISM	EXAMPLE
Displacement: *Undesirable emotions are directed toward a different object*	*A man who is angry at his wife kicks his dog*
Reaction formation: *Behavior is the opposite of the individual's actual feelings*	*A woman who loves an unobtainable man behaves as though she dislikes him*
Intellectualization: *Behavior is stripped of its emotional meaning*	*A man who loves his aunt too dearly treats her with extreme consideration, kindness, and devotion but convinces himself that he is motivated by duty and not by love*
Projection: *People attribute their own undesirable feelings or inclinations to others*	*A person who is extremely jealous of his brother believes it is his brother who feels that way toward him*
Denial: *Reality is distorted to make it conform to the individual's wishes*	*A heavy smoker who is unable to give up the habit decides that there is no substantial evidence linking nicotine with human diseases*
Repression: *Unpleasant experiences are stored deep in the subconscious mind and become inaccessible to waking memory*	*A child who is sexually abused remembers nothing of the experience*

(and eventually to procreate) will not be satisfied, and we suffer from the anxiety accompanying that fear. According to Freud, this trauma of birth leads to all our adult anxieties.

Hofer (1981) describes Freud's theory as one of the most comprehensive and influential of all human psychological theories. It has had tremendous influence on our attitudes toward children and child-rearing. More than anyone else, Freud was responsible for making parents realize how important the experiences of the early years can be. The importance of Freudian theory is not limited to its direct effects on parents, educators, physicians, and others but includes its tremendous influence on the development of other theories (such as those of Erikson and John Bowlby). However, many of Freud's students and followers have not accepted Freudian theory entirely.

Freud's theory is clearly weak from a scientific point of view, based as it is on a limited number of observations collected by a single individual (Freud himself) and not being subjected to any rigorous analysis. Further, it uses complex terms and concepts in confusing and ambiguous ways, it leads to contradictory predictions, and it places excessive emphasis on sexual and aggressive impulses (Rothstein, 1980).

In spite of these criticisms, Freud's work still stands as an immensely rich basis for thinking about and understanding human personality. In summarizing the contributions of psychoanalysis, Kegan (1982) notes that it remains the single most important guide for mental health practitioners in clinics and in hospitals. Ironically, however, its status in academic psychology is considerably more tarnished. In contrast, although theories such as Piaget's cognitivism are an ongoing source of debate and research in academic circles, they have remarkably little influence on the application of psychology in the real world.

psychoanalytic approaches: Erikson

Freud's influence can be found among the many theories developed by some of his followers. Perhaps the most important of these for understanding human development is the theory advanced by Erik Erikson (1956, 1959, 1961, 1968). It draws heavily from Freud's work, but also departs from it in several important ways.

Recall that Freud's primary emphasis was on the role of sexuality (libido) and on the importance of conflicts involving different levels of personality (id, ego, superego). In contrast, Erikson downplays the role of sexuality and of psychodynamic conflicts and instead emphasizes the importance of children's social environment. His theory is a theory of **psychosocial development** rather than of psychosexual development.

A second departure from Freudian theory is Erikson's concern with the development of a healthy ego (or **identity**, in Erikson's words) rather than with the resolution of powerful internal conflicts.

psychosocial stages in human development

Erikson describes eight stages of human development, the first five of which span infancy, childhood, and adolescence. (The final three describe maturity.) Each of Erikson's stages involves a basic conflict brought about primarily by children's need to adapt to the social environment. Resolution of this conflict results in the development of a sense of competence. Although Erikson's first five stages closely parallel Freud's psychosexual stages in terms of ages, his descriptions and emphases are quite different. Erikson's first five stages are summarized in Table 2.4 and are described in more detail next.

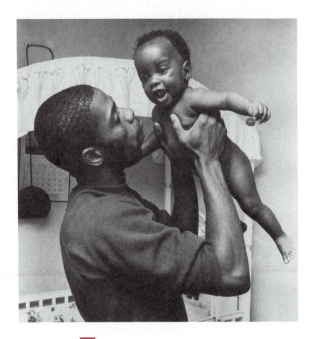

One of an infant's first important tasks, says Erikson, is to develop a sense of trust.

TRUST VERSUS MISTRUST

One of the most basic components of a healthy personality is a sense of trust. This sense of trust toward oneself and toward others develops in the first year of life (Erikson, 1959). Infants are initially faced with a fundamental conflict between mistrust of a world about which very little is known and an inclination to develop a trusting attitude toward that world.

The most important person in an infant's life at this stage is the primary caregiver—usually the mother. Successful resolution of the conflict between trust and mistrust depends largely on the infant's relationship with this caregiver, and on the gradual realization that the world is predictable, safe, and loving. According to Erikson, if the world is unpredictable and the caregiver rejecting, the infant may grow up to be mistrustful and anxious.

table 2.4

The first five of Erikson's eight psychosocial stages

ERIKSON'S PSYCHOSOCIAL STAGES	CORRESPONDING FREUDIAN PSYCHOSEXUAL STAGES	PRINCIPAL DEVELOPMENTAL TASKS	IMPORTANT INFLUENCES FOR POSITIVE DEVELOPMENTAL OUTCOME
Trust vs. mistrust	Oral (0–18 months)	Developing sufficient trust in the world to explore it	Mother; warm, loving interaction
Autonomy vs. shame and doubt	Anal (18 months to 2 or 3 years)	Developing feeling of control over behavior; realizing that intentions can be acted out	Supportive parents; imitation
Initiative vs. guilt	Phallic (2 or 3 to 6 years)	Developing a sense of self through identification with parents and a sense of responsibility for one's own actions	Supportive parents; identification
Industry vs. inferiority	Latency (6–11 years)	Developing a sense of self-worth through interaction with peers	Schools and teachers; learning and education; encouragement
Identity vs. identity diffusion	Genital (11 years and older)	Developing a strong sense of identity—of ego (self); selecting among various potential selves	Peers and role models; social pressure

Source: Based in part on Erikson (1959).

AUTONOMY VERSUS SHAME AND DOUBT

During this stage, corresponding to Freud's anal stage, children begin to realize they are authors of their own actions. With the recognition that they can carry out some of the behaviors they intend, children develop a sense of autonomy. However, this autonomy is threatened by children's inclination not to accept responsibility for their own actions, but instead to return to the comfort and security that characterized the first stage—an inclination that gives rise to feelings of shame and doubt (Erikson, 1961).

If children are to successfully resolve this conflict and develop a sense of autonomy, it is important that parents encourage attempts to explore and that they provide opportunities for independence. Overprotectiveness can lead to doubt and uncertainty in dealing with the world later. What the child needs, according to Erikson (1959), is a balance between parental firmness and flexibility.

INITIATIVE VERSUS GUILT

By the age of 4 or 5, children have resolved the crisis of autonomy. In short, they have discovered that they are somebody; during the next stage they must discover who it is that they are (Erikson, 1959). True to his Freudian orientation, Erikson assumes that children try to discover who they are by attempting to be like their parents. During this stage they establish a wider physical environment, made possible by their greater freedom of movement. Their language development is sufficiently advanced for them to ask questions, understand answers, and also imagine all sorts of possibilities. In fact, says Erikson (1959), they can now imagine things that frighten them.

With their increasing exploration of the environment, children develop a sense of initiative. Not only are they autonomous, but they are also responsible for their behavior. Because the central process involved in resolving the initiative-versus-guilt conflict is one of identification, parents and family continue to be the most important influences in a child's development. It is important for them to encourage young children's sense of initiative and to nurture a sense of responsibility.

INDUSTRY VERSUS INFERIORITY

The fourth developmental stage, corresponding to Freud's latency stage, is marked by children's increasing need to interact with and be accepted by peers. It now becomes crucial for children to discover that their selves, their identities, are significant; that they can do things; in short, that they are competent. Children now avail themselves of all opportunities to learn those things they think are of importance to their culture, hoping that by so doing they will become someone. This is the source of their rising need for accomplishment through industrious behavior. Although this stage corresponds to Freud's period of latency, Erikson points out clearly that the only sense in which a child may be considered "latent" is in terms of the formation of heterosexual attachments. In all other ways, children are much too active to be deemed "latent."

Successful resolution of this stage's conflict depends to a large extent on the responses of significant social agencies—especially schools and teachers—to children's efforts. If the child's work is continually demeaned and seldom praised, the outcome may be a lasting sense of inferiority.

IDENTITY VERSUS IDENTITY DIFFUSION

Erikson's fifth developmental stage, corresponding to Freud's genital period and spanning adolescence, involves the development of a strong sense of identity, which implies the development of a strong ego—hence Erikson's expression, *ego identity.* The crisis implicit in this stage concerns a conflict between a strong sense of self and the diffusion of self-concepts.

At a simple level, the formation of an identity appears to involve arriving at a notion, not so much of who one is but rather of who one can be—in other words, of developing one of several potential selves. The source of conflict lies in the various possibilities open to children—possibilities that are magnified by the variety of cultural models in the environment. Conflict and doubt over choice of identity lead to what Erikson terms *identity diffusion.* It is as though adolescents are torn between early acceptance of a clearly defined self and the dissipation of their energies as they experiment with a variety of roles. One of the primary functions of adolescence is to serve as a period during which the child need not make a final decision concerning self (as a moratorium, in Erikson's words). The development of identity during adolescence is discussed in Chapter 12.

ADULT STAGES

Erikson's description of development does not end with adolescence but continues throughout the entire life span. He describes three additional psychosocial conflicts that occur during adulthood and old age and require new competencies and adjustments. The first of these, *intimacy and solidarity versus isolation,* relates to the need to develop intimate relationships with others (as opposed to being isolated) and is especially important for marriage and parenthood. The second, *generativity versus self-absorption,* describes a need to assume social, work, and community responsibilities that will be beneficial to others (that will be generative), rather than remaining absorbed in self. The third, *integrity versus despair,* concerns facing the inevitability of death and the need to realize that life has meaning—that we should not despair because its end is imminent.

Erikson's theory in review

Erikson's theory is variously referred to as a theory of the life cycle, of ego psychology, of psychosocial development, or as a psychoanalytically oriented theory concerned mainly with the development of healthy personality. He describes development in terms of a series of crises through which individuals progress. Each of these crises involves a conflict between new abilities or attitudes and inclinations that oppose them. Resolution of conflict results in the development of a sense of competence with respect to a specific capability that is primarily social; hence the concept of psychosocial development. The resolution of conflicts is never perfected during one developmental phase but continues through succeeding stages; hence the concept of life cycle. Perhaps the most crucial crisis involves the development of a strong sense of identity; hence the concept of ego psychology.

We should note that although Erikson assigns ages to each of these psychosocial stages, the ages do little more than provide a very general guide. This is especially true during adulthood, when important social, physical, and emotional events such as retirement, children leaving home, illness, and death occur at widely varying ages and sometimes in a totally unpredictable sequence. Some of the important social and physical changes of childhood are more predictable; hence the ages assigned to the psychosocial crises of childhood are more accurate.

Erikson's theory, like Freud's, does not lend itself well to experimental validation. What Erikson's theory provides is a very general framework for describing and interpreting some of the major changes that occur in the human life span. Its usefulness rests largely in the insights that may result from examining the lives of individuals within the context of the theory.

Havighurst's developmental tasks

Another stage theory that describes development in terms of tasks that must be sequentially mastered was proposed by Robert Havighurst (1972, 1979).

Developmental tasks are requirements placed on individuals by their societies—and by themselves—as they progress through life. In Havighurst's (1972) words, "A developmental task is a task which arises at or about a certain period in the life of the individual, successful achievement of which leads to his happiness and to success with later tasks, while failure leads to unhappiness in the individual, disapproval by the society, and difficulty with later tasks" (p. 2).

Developmental tasks begin with the simple and essential requirements of infancy: learning to eat solid foods, to walk, eventually to talk. They progress to a wide range of socially important achievements—learning to tell right from wrong, adopting a gender role, learning to get along with peers—and culminate in the requirements of old age: learning to adjust to changing physical powers and social circumstances and learning to accept the inevitability of dying.

t a b l e   2 . 5

Havighurst's developmental tasks

PERIOD	DEVELOPMENTAL TASKS
Infancy and early childhood (birth through preschool period)	1. *Achieving physiological rhythms in sleeping and eating* 2. *Learning to take solid foods* 3. *Beginning to relate emotionally to parents and siblings* 4. *Learning to talk* 5. *Learning to control elimination of body wastes* 6. *Learning to walk* 7. *Learning to distinguish right from wrong* 8. *Learning sex differences and sexual modesty*
Middle childhood (the elementary school period)	1. *Learning skills necessary for physical games* 2. *Building a positive self-concept* 3. *Adopting an appropriate masculine or feminine role* 4. *Learning to get along with peers* 5. *Developing values, a sense of morality, a conscience* 6. *Becoming personally independent; weakening family ties* 7. *Developing basic reading, writing, and arithmetic skills* 8. *Developing an understanding of the self and the world*
Adolescence	1. *Developing conceptual and problem-solving skills* 2. *Achieving mature relationships with male and female peers* 3. *Developing an ethical system to guide behavior* 4. *Striving toward socially responsible behavior* 5. *Accepting the changing physique and using the body effectively* 6. *Preparing for an economically viable career* 7. *Achieving emotional independence from parents* 8. *Preparing for marriage and family life*
Young adulthood	1. *Courting and selecting a mate* 2. *Learning to live happily with partner* 3. *Starting a family and assuming parent role* 4. *Rearing children* 5. *Assuming home management responsibilities* 6. *Beginning career or occupation* 7. *Assuming appropriate civic responsibilities* 8. *Establishing a social network*
Middle adulthood	1. *Assisting children in transition from home to world* 2. *Developing adult leisure activities* 3. *Relating to spouse as a person* 4. *Reaching adult social and civic responsibility* 5. *Maintaining satisfactory career performance* 6. *Adjusting to physiological changes of middle age* 7. *Adjusting to aging parents*
Old age	1. *Adjusting to physical changes* 2. *Adjusting to retirement and to changes in income* 3. *Establishing satisfactory living arrangements* 4. *Learning to live with spouse in retirement* 5. *Adjusting to death of spouse* 6. *Forming affiliations with aging peers* 7. *Adopting flexible social roles*

Based on Havighurst, 1972, 1979.

Developmental tasks provide a rough but often highly useful index of developmental maturity and adjustment. In a sense they tell us whether a child is ready for school, a young adult for marriage, an older adult for retirement.

Some of the most important of Havighurst's developmental tasks are listed in Table 2.5. Note that these are culture-specific; they apply primarily to Western societies (Havighurst, 1982). In other contexts, this list might be very different.

behavioristic approaches

reud and Erikson's psychoanalytic approaches have a number of important things in common: First, they are *developmental theories* (they are concerned with changes that occur in individuals over time); second, they are *stage theories* (development consists of progression through sequential stages); and third, they make important assumptions concerning the biological (inherited) aspects of behavior and personality.

overview of behavioristic approaches

Behavioristic approaches do not share any of these characteristics to any important extent. They make few assumptions about biological predispositions (and certainly none about *unconscious* forces), and they do not describe sequential stages of increasing capabilities and competencies.

BASIC ASSUMPTIONS OF BEHAVIORISM

Behaviorism, as the term implies, focuses on immediate behavior. It is especially concerned with relationships between experience and behavior, and consequently it makes extensive use of concepts such as reinforcement and punishment, which describe how behavior may be encouraged or discouraged.

Several fundamental assumptions underlie behavioristic approaches to development (also referred to as *learning theory approaches*). Most important among these is the belief that behavior is reducible to responses or actions that can be observed, measured, and analyzed. The label *behaviorism* derives from the behaviorist's concern with responses (behaviors).

Another important behavioristic assumption is the belief that responses are a function of reinforcement (usually **rewards**) and punishment. Accordingly, the main goals of behavioristic theorists have been to discover the rules that govern relationships between stimuli (conditions that lead to behavior) and responses, and to learn how responses can be controlled through the administration of rewards and punishments.

UNDERLYING MODEL IN BEHAVIORISM

Note that many of these assumptions are also assumptions of the mechanistic model, which views the child as more passive than active. According to this model, experiences and circumstances—especially those that are reinforced or punished—are among the most important factors in shaping the course of our development. In some ways, this model asserts that our behavior is like the functioning of a machine. As long as we understand how the machine works, we are in a position to predict its actions, given sufficient knowledge of the immediate circumstances. The goal of the behavioristic theorist is to understand the human machine so well that with sufficient knowledge of past functioning and of immediate circumstances, it would be possible to predict behavior accurately and, in some instances, to control it as well.

The behavioristic approach is not only somewhat mechanistic, but is also fundamentally contextualist in its emphasis on the importance of environmental influences (see Bijou, 1989). The rewards and punishments that are the causes and consequences of behavior are, in fact, context.

EARLY PIONEERS OF BEHAVIORISM

The behavioristic approach was introduced into American psychology through the work of John B. Watson and B. F. Skinner and led to a dramatic upheaval in psychology, the effects of which are still being felt (Cairns, 1983). Both theorists believed strongly in the importance of the environment as the principal force in shaping development. Both believed that development could be understood through an analysis of specific behaviors, the circumstances leading to them, and their consequences. Watson is associated with a learning theory based on a model of **classical conditioning**; Skinner developed a model of **operant conditioning**. **Conditioning** refers to a simple kind of learning whereby certain behaviors are affected by the environment, becoming more or less probable and predictable. Classical and operant conditioning are described and illustrated in the following sections.

classical conditioning

Among the early contributors to modern knowledge about human learning was the Russian psychologist Ivan Pavlov. While doing research with dogs, Pavlov (1927) noticed that the older and more experienced animals in his laboratory began to salivate when they saw their keeper approaching. Because none of the dogs had ever tasted the keeper, Pavlov reasoned that they were salivating not because they expected to eat him, but because they had formed some sort

Rewards and punishments, behaviorism insists, shape our behaviors. If the cat purrs or feels nice or moves in interesting ways when Philomena reaches for him, she is likely to reach again. But if her reach actually becomes a grab and a yank and the cat scratches her, she might be less likely to reach next time.

of **association**, or link, between the sight of the keeper and the presentation of food. This observation led Pavlov to a series of investigations of a simple form of learning called classical conditioning (see Figure 2.3).

The psychology of learning has its own language for the stimuli and responses of classical conditioning. The stimulus that is part of the original stimulus-response link (the reflex) is the **unconditioned stimulus** (US). Food in the mouths of Pavlov's dogs is an unconditioned stimulus; it leads to a response without any new learning. The stimulus that is originally neutral but comes to be effective through repeated pairing with the unconditioned stimulus is called the conditioning or **conditioned stimulus** (CS). In the well-known Pavlovian ex-

figure 2.3

Classical conditioning. In (1), an unconditioned stimulus leads to an unconditioned response, whereas in (2) a conditioning stimulus does not lead to the same response. In (3), the unconditioned stimulus is paired with the conditioning stimulus a number of times so that eventually the conditioning stimulus alone elicits the original response, as in (4).

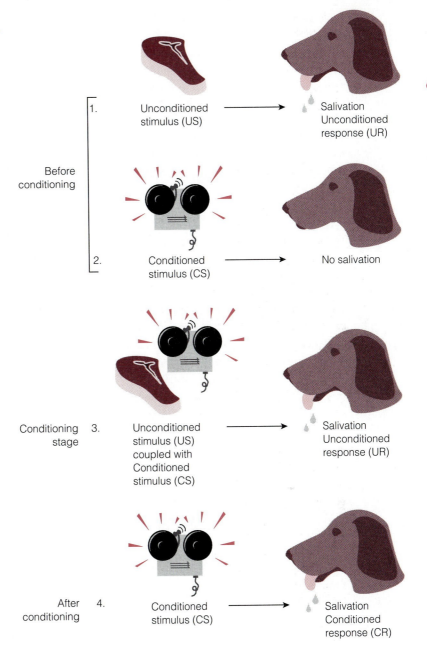

Before conditioning

1. Unconditioned stimulus (US) → Salivation Unconditioned response (UR)

2. Conditioned stimulus (CS) → No salivation

Conditioning stage

3. Unconditioned stimulus (US) coupled with Conditioned stimulus (CS) → Salivation Unconditioned response (UR)

After conditioning

4. Conditioned stimulus (CS) → Salivation Conditioned response (CR)

periment shown in Figure 2.3, the bell or buzzer is a conditioned stimulus. Eventually, it gives rise to responses similar to those originally made only for unconditioned stimuli. Corresponding responses are termed the **unconditioned response** (UR) or the **conditioned response** (CR), depending on whether

they occur in response to the unconditioned or the conditioned stimulus. Salivating in response to a buzzer is a conditioned response.

In a demonstration of classical conditioning of emotional responses in children, Watson and Rayner (1920) conditioned an 11-month-old infant,

Little Albert, to fear a white rat. They did this simply by making a loud noise (an unconditioned fear-inducing stimulus) and showing Albert the rat at the same time (conditioned stimulus). After repeating the procedure seven times, all they had to do was show Albert the rat and he would begin to whimper and try to crawl away. (Unfortunately, Little Albert was taken away from the hospital before Watson could cure him, as a conditioning procedure could have been used for that as well; Jones, Albert, & Watson, 1974.)

Although Watson and Rayner's experiment with Little Albert is more systematic than most situations in which we acquire emotional responses, the results can be generalized. There is considerable evidence that emotional reactions do transfer from one situation to another. People who react with fear to the sound of a dentist's drill are not fearful because the sound of the drill has caused them pain in the past. But the sound of the drill (a conditioned stimulus) may have been associated with pain and now elicits related reactions. Similarly, children who dislike their teacher and who react negatively to the teacher's presence may eventually react negatively to classrooms, to school-related activities, to voices that sound like the teacher's, to adults who resemble her or him, to students who look like other students in the class, to pencils, and so on.

operant conditioning

A classical conditioning model like Pavlov's is sometimes useful for explaining the learning of simple behaviors that occur in response to specific stimuli. But as Skinner (1953, 1957, 1961) pointed out, many human behaviors are not **elicited responses** evoked by obvious stim-

uli, but appear instead to be **emitted responses** produced by the organism, for whatever reason. In Skinner's terms, an emitted behavior is an **operant**; an elicited response is a **respondent**. His major work is an attempt to explain how operants are learned.

The simplest explanation of operant conditioning is that the consequences of a response determine how likely it is to be repeated. Behaviors that are reinforced tend to be repeated; those that are not reinforced are less likely to be repeated (see Figure 2.4). This is very different from saying that learning will occur as a function of the pairing of stimuli, regardless of a behavior's consequences. Clearly, when Little Albert reacted with fear to the rat, it was not because his fear responses led to pleasant consequences, but because the rat was paired with some other fear-producing situation.

REINFORCEMENT AND PUNISHMENT

That which increases the probability of a response occurring is said to be reinforcing. A **reinforcer** is the stimulus that reinforces; **reinforcement** is the *effect* of a reinforcer. **Negative reinforcement** is one kind of reinforcement; **positive reinforcement** is the other. Both positive and negative reinforcement increase the probability of a response occurring. The difference between the two is that positive reinforcement is effective as a result of the addition of a reward to a situation after a behavior has occurred, whereas negative reinforcement is effective through the removal of an unpleasant stimulus. A simple way of remembering the difference is to remember that positive reinforcement involves a reward for behavior, whereas negative reinforcement involves relief from something unpleasant.

Unfortunately, real-life situations are more complicated than this black-and-

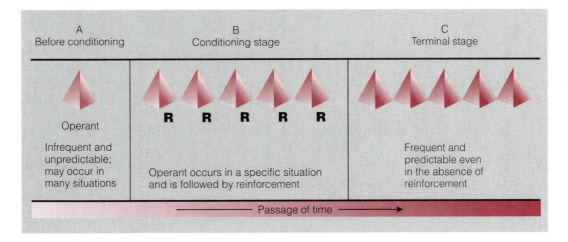

figure 2.4

Schematic model of operant conditioning. In (A), the operant behavior alone is not rewarded. In (B), conditioning begins. The operant behavior takes place by chance; it is immediately reinforced. It occurs again, by chance or deliberately, and the reinforcement is repeated. As the timeline in the figure shows, repetition becomes more and more frequent as the learner catches on. Eventually, the operant behavior continues even without reinforcement at the terminal stage (C).

white terminology suggests. Subjective judgments such as "pleasant" and "unpleasant," although they aid our understanding, are misleading. Reinforcement and punishment have to do with *effects* rather than perceived pleasantness. Whereas reinforcement, whether positive or negative, serves to make a response more likely, punishment does not. Thus a parent or teacher who keeps "punishing" a child but who observes that the punished behavior becomes more rather than less frequent may well be reinforcing that behavior—or something (or someone?) else is. Similarly, sometimes a teacher's praise of a student's behavior leads to a drastic reduction of that behavior. Reinforcement? No, by definition this is **punishment**. The important point is that pleasantness and unpleasantness are subjective; in contrast, reinforcement and punishment are objective phenomena defined in terms of increases or decreases in the frequency of behavior.

There are several kinds of punishment. The kind we usually first think of involves an unpleasant consequence, like being beaten with a hickory stick. Another kind of punishment involves taking away something that is pleasant, such as being prevented from watching television (called a *time-out procedure*), or having to give up something desirable like money or privileges (called *response-cost* punishment). Another possibility, of course, is that the behavior will have no consequences and will simply stop occurring (a phenomenon termed **extinction**).

Distinctions among the various kinds of reinforcement and punishment are illustrated in Figure 2.5. As the illustration makes clear, both may involve stimuli with pleasant or unpleasant effects, but whether these stimuli are added to or removed from the situation determines whether they are reinforcing or punishing. It is worth emphasizing again that both reinforcement and punishment are defined by their effects. Many types of reinforcers, some of which are described in Table 2.6, can be used systematically in childrearing and in the classroom.

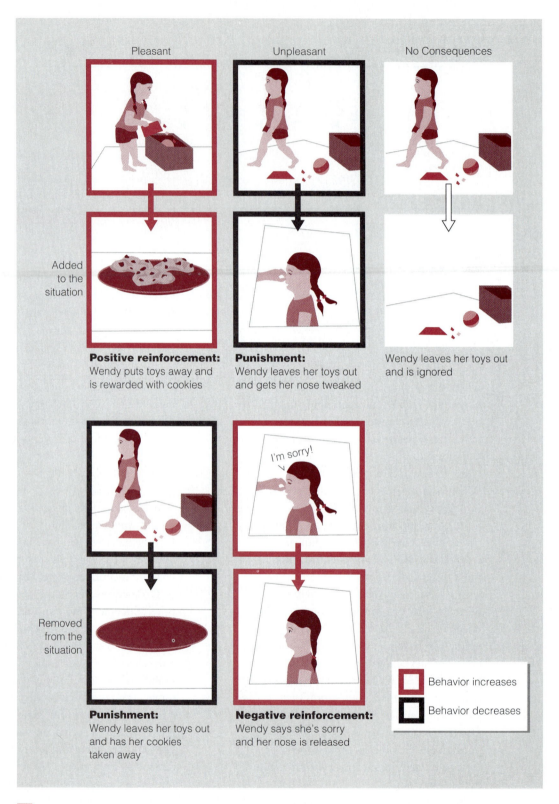

Pleasant | Unpleasant | No Consequences

Added to the situation

Positive reinforcement: Wendy puts toys away and is rewarded with cookies

Punishment: Wendy leaves her toys out and gets her nose tweaked

Wendy leaves her toys out and is ignored

I'm sorry!

Removed from the situation

Punishment: Wendy leaves her toys out and has her cookies taken away

Negative reinforcement: Wendy says she's sorry and her nose is released

Behavior increases

Behavior decreases

f **igure   2.5**

The combination of applications of stimuli and stimulus effects that define reinforcement, punishment, and extinction.

t **a b l e** **2 . 6**

Examples of classes of reinforcers

REINFORCERS	EXAMPLES
Consumables	Candy, drinks, chocolates, fruit
Manipulatables	Toys, games, puzzles
Visual and auditory stimuli	Bells, buzzers, smiling puppets, green lights
Social stimuli	Praise, a pat on the back, a smile, applause
Token reinforcers	Coins, counters, points, or other tokens that can be exchanged for other reinforcers
Premack principle	Activities that occur frequently— and that are presumably pleasant (reading; watching television)—can be used to reinforce other, less frequently occurring activities (studying)

Sources: Bijou and Sturges (1959), Premack (1965).

behavioristic approaches in review

Learning theory explanations of human development emphasize the role of the environment in shaping our personalities and behaviors. Unlike psychoanalytic approaches, they are not concerned with psychodynamic conflicts and other hidden causes of behavior; and unlike the more cognitive approaches, which we discuss next, they do not often pay much attention to concepts such as understanding and knowing. Instead, they focus on the role of reinforcement and punishment and on the extent to which behavior can be shaped by its consequences.

One of the main criticisms of these approaches is that they are poorly suited to explaining higher mental processes— thinking, feeling, analyzing, problem solving, evaluating, and so on. Their emphasis and their principal usefulness concern actual behavior rather than conceptual processes.

A second criticism of behavioristic approaches is that by emphasizing the machinelike qualities of human functioning, they rob us of what we consider most human—namely, our ability to think and imagine, and our ability (real or imagined) to exercise significant control over our own behavior. Critics have claimed that in its attempts to reduce behavior to observable stimuli and responses, behaviorism dehumanizes us.

Although these criticisms may be reasonable and fair with respect to older and more extreme interpretations of behaviorism, they are less pertinent for more recent positions. Bijou (1989), for example, notes that whereas Watson's theory describes an essentially passive organism, today's behaviorism sees the individual "as always being in an interactive relationship with the environment" (p. 68). In his words, the individual is "adjustive" rather than simply "reactive." However, Bijou's contemporary behaviorist does not view our ability to think, to imagine, or to feel as a cause of behavior. Bijou labels these cognitive activities *implicit interactions.* The primary concern of the behaviorist is not so much these implicit— hence, unobservable—interactions as it is the more observable interactions between stimuli and responses. Bijou cautions, however, that insofar as the contemporary behaviorist views people as adjustive rather than simply reactive, the environment is given a less important role in determining behavior. The causes of behavior, he claims, are not found in the environment alone, but rather in all the factors that are involved in a person's interactions, including history of past interactions.

On a more positive note, Skinner's theory, says Travis (1992), reflects that he was not only a scientist, a psychologist, and a philosopher, but also a poet. Operant theory continues to have a tremendous influence not only in theory and research but also in practical applications. Behavioristic approaches to development are sometimes very useful not only for understanding developmental change, but also for controlling it. The deliberate application of conditioning principles to change behavior (termed **behavior modification**) has proven extremely useful in a variety of settings, including the classroom and psychotherapy.

Theories, we should remember, are inventions whose purpose is to simplify, to explain, and sometimes to predict. Unlike orthodox views of traditional religions, they need not be accepted or rejected in their entirety. Elements from different theories can sometimes be combined to produce new theories—new insights—that go far beyond the original theories. A case in point is Albert Bandura's social cognitive theory, which in some ways serves as a transition between behaviorism and cognitivism.

social cognitive theory

At one level, Bandura's theory is a behavioristic theory of imitation based on the assumption that much important learning involves various models that act as social influences on children. At another level, it is a cognitive theory that gives an important role to children's ability to symbolize—that is, to reason, to imagine, to ferret out cause-and-effect relationships, to anticipate the outcomes of behavior. There is no doubt, Bandura (1977) assures us, that reinforcement controls much of our behavior, but it does not control us blindly. Its effects depend largely on our awareness of the relationship between our behavior and its outcomes. As Bruner (1985) points out, reinforcement often occurs a long time after the behavior it follows, as happens, for example, when you study for an

examination. In such cases, it is not reinforcement (or the possibility of punishment) that affects behavior directly so much as it is your ability to anticipate the consequences of behavior.

Bandura's social learning theory—a theory of **observational learning** (or **imitation**)—can be summarized simply as follows:

■ Much human learning and behavior is a function of observing the behavior of others or of symbolic models such as fictional characters and television or folk heroes.

■ Imitation is often reinforced.

■ Observational learning can therefore be explained largely through operant conditioning principles.

the processes of observational learning

Bandura (1977) emphasizes that the effects of models are largely due to their informative function. From observing models we learn not only how to do certain things, but also what the consequences of our behaviors are likely to be. Accordingly, there are four distinct processes involved in observational learning.

ATTENTIONAL PROCESSES

First there are *attentional processes*. Children are not likely to learn very much from a model if they pay no attention to important aspects of that model's behavior. Whether or not they attend, Bandura informs us, depends a great deal on the value of the model's behavior. (Is it important for the observer to be able to swear like that? Throw a ball in that way? Cock his head in just that fashion?) In the same way, behavior that is not very distinctive, that occurs only rarely, or that is complex and difficult to perform is less likely to be attended to.

RETENTIONAL PROCESSES

Children must not only attend, but must also be able to remember. This, explains Bandura, implies being able to represent mentally the behavior to be imitated, either in words or images.

MOTOR REPRODUCTION PROCESSES

In order to imitate, an observer must be able to translate into an actual sequence of behavior what has been attended to and retained (represented mentally). This might require certain motor and physical capabilities, or their development, as well as the ability to monitor and correct ongoing behavior.

MOTIVATIONAL PROCESSES

Finally, in observational learning, as in all learning, there must be relevant *motivational processes*; that is, in the absence of appropriate motivation (reasons for behavior), many behaviors that are observed and potentially learned will not be performed. In this connection, learning theorists make an important distinction between acquisition and performance. Much is acquired (learned, in other words) but does not become part of behavior (is not performed).

Models do not all have the same influence on children. Children are most likely to imitate people who are important to them and with whom they identify (such as parents, siblings, and close friends); similarly, they are most likely to imitate behaviors that are highly valued.

manifestations of observational learning

A model may be an actual (perhaps very ordinary) person whose behavior serves as a guide, a blueprint, an inspiration for somebody else; a model might also be **symbolic**. Symbolic models include things like book characters, oral or written instructions, pictures, mental images, cartoon or film characters, television actors, and so on. Nor are models always examples of more advanced skills and competencies displayed by older people, as might be the case when children imitate adults. Hanna and Meltzoff (1993) report that even young toddlers imitate and learn from each other.

Bandura and Walters (1963) describe three different effects of imitation on learning in children: the modeling effect, inhibitory-disinhibitory effects, and the eliciting effect.

THE MODELING EFFECT

The **modeling effect** is the learning of novel behavior and is illustrated in the learning of some aspects of language. That Eskimo children learn Eskimo rather than Greek is evidence that they model the language that surrounds them. (There is much more than imitation involved in language learning; see Chapter 5.)

THE INHIBITORY-DISINHIBITORY EFFECTS

The effects of imitation are also found in the **inhibitory effect** (the suppression of deviant behavior) and the **disinhibitory effect** (the appearance of previously suppressed deviant behavior). These effects are usually the result of either punishment of or reward to the model for engaging in deviant behavior. Consider the case of a highly moral teenager whose friends have recently begun to use marijuana. The behavior is deviant by the teen's own standards, but the amount of reinforcement (in terms of social prestige, acceptance by the group, and so on) that others appear to derive from using the drug may *disinhibit* this behavior in the teen. There is really no new learning involved, as in modeling, but merely the disinhibition of previously suppressed behavior. If this teenager later observes that members of her peer group are punished by the law, parents, or school authorities, or if they experience ill effects from the drug, the teen might suddenly stop using marijuana. Again, there is no new learning involved, although there is a change in behavior resulting from the influence of models; thus this change illustrates the inhibitory effect.

THE ELICITING EFFECT

A third effect of imitation is the **eliciting effect**, in which an observer's behavior is neither identical to a model's behavior, nor deviant, nor novel, but is simply related to it. It is as though the model's behavior suggests some response to the observer and therefore *elicits* that response. A child "acting up" in school may elicit misbehavior in his classmates; they may not imitate his behavior precisely, but may simply engage in the same general type of behavior or misbehavior.

The three effects of imitation are summarized in Table 2.7.

t able 2 . 7	
Three effects of imitation	
Modeling	Acquiring new behavior as a result of observing a model
Inhibitory-Disinhibitory	Ceasing or starting some deviant behavior as a result of seeing a model punished or rewarded for similar behavior
Eliciting	Engaging in behavior related to that of a model

self-efficacy judgments

Psychological theories are not often static, unchanging things—unless the theorist has lost interest, moved on to other things, or died. And even then, if the theory is at all compelling or important, there will be others who will ponder it, who will try to change its shape to fit new facts, to answer new questions, to respond to new interests.

Albert Bandura's theory is a good example. His early ideas stemmed very directly from a behavioristic orientation, and thus his imitation-based theory of social learning attempts to explain the complex effects of modeling in terms of rewards and punishments, either actual or anticipated. But his more recent writings are concerned as much or more with the effects of *anticipating*, of *imagining* the consequences of a behavior. There is little room for imagining among the objective, observable, and measurable stimuli, responses, and reinforcement schedules of the behaviorist. In short, Bandura's social-learning theory has become progressively more *cognitive* (more concerned with *knowing, understanding, thinking*, and other mental processes). It gives an increasingly important role to the *informative* function of models. It is what the observer imagines and anticipates that is most important in learning through imitation.

Bandura's most recent research and theorizing has taken yet another turn, one that is even more clearly cognitive (Bandura, 1986, 1993; Evans, 1989). It concerns what is termed **self-referent thought**—thought that has to do with our selves, with our own mental processes. Among other things, self-referent thought deals with our estimates of our abilities, with our notions about how capable and effective we are in our dealings with the world and with others. A very specific term has been coined to describe our estimates of our own effectiveness: **self-efficacy**.

In a nutshell, efficacy means competence in dealing with the environment. The most efficacious people are those who can most effectively deal with a variety of situations, even when these situations are ambiguous or highly stressful. Thus self-efficacy has two separate but related components: the skills that are required for the successful performance of a behavior and an individual's beliefs about personal effectiveness. From a psychological point of view, it is not so much the skills component that is important, but rather a person's own evaluations of personal efficacy.

IMPLICATIONS OF SELF-EFFICACY JUDGMENTS

Among the most important of all the different aspects of self-knowledge, Bandura insists, is our conception of personal efficacy. This is so because our judgments about our personal effectiveness are extremely important determiners of what we do and don't do. In fact, in some situations, self-efficacy may be a better predictor of behavior than relevant skills are (Schunk, 1984). Under most circumstances, children (and adults, too) do not seek out and undertake activities in which they expect to perform badly. "Efficacy beliefs," says Bandura (1993), "in-

fluence how people feel, think, motivate themselves, and behave." (p. 118)

Judgments of personal efficacy affect not only our choices of activities and settings, but also the amount of effort we are willing to put out when faced with difficulties. The stronger our beliefs about our efficacy, the more likely we are to persist and the greater will be the effort expended. But if our notions of self-efficacy are not very favorable, we may abandon difficult activities after very little effort and time.

Finally, perceived self-efficacy influences our thoughts and emotions. Those who judge that their effectiveness is low are more likely to evaluate their behaviors negatively and to see themselves as being inadequate.

SOURCES OF INFLUENCE ON EFFICACY JUDGMENTS

Judgments of personal efficacy, Bandura (1986) suggests, are influenced by four sources. The first is the direct effects of individuals' behavior. Whether we succeed or not must surely have some effect on our estimates of how efficacious we are. However, inferences of self-efficacy are not always completely predictable; that is, the individual who is mostly successful does not invariably arrive at highly positive judgments of self-efficacy, nor does lack of success always correspond to negative judgments. As Weiner (1980a) points out, there are different factors to which we can attribute success or lack of success. Some of these, like ability and effort, are under personal control and reflect directly on the efficacy of the individual. Others, such as luck or the difficulty of the task, are not under personal control and do not, therefore, have very direct implications for judgments of self-efficacy.

Some individuals are more likely than others to attribute the outcomes of their behaviors to factors over which they have control. Dweck (1975) refers to these people as *mastery-oriented*. Others are more likely to attribute their failures and successes to luck or to the difficulty of the task. Dweck describes these individuals as being characterized by *helplessness* rather than by a mastery orientation.

One source of influence for judgments of personal efficacy, then, are personal accomplishments, especially individual attributions concerning the causes underlying these accomplishments. A second influence is vicarious (secondhand); it comes from observing the performance of others. Even as children we arrive at notions of how effective we are partly on the basis of comparisons we make between ourselves and others. And, as Bandura (1981) suggests, the most informative comparisons we can make are those that involve others whose performance is similar to ours. A 12 year old who demolishes his 6-year-old brother in a game of skill and intelligence learns very little about his personal effectiveness. Similarly, if he, in turn, is blown away by his father, he may not have learned much more—except, perhaps, a touch of humility.

A third source of influence on self-judgments, Bandura (1986) argues, is persuasion. "You can do it, Guy. I know you can. Sing for us. We love the way you sing." (This is a totally fanciful illustration; even dumb animals dislike the way I sing.) Persuasion, depending on the characteristics of the persuader and on the relationship between persuader and "persuadee," can sometimes change an individual's self-efficacy judgments and lead that person either to attempt things that would not otherwise be attempted or not to attempt them: "Guy, they're just flattering you. *Please* don't sing."

The fourth source of influence on self-efficacy judgments is a person's level of **arousal**. The word *arousal* can have a lot of meanings; in this context, its most important meaning has to do with intensity of an immediate emotional reaction. Situations that produce very high arousal are shocking, sudden, frightening, intensely exciting, deeply moving—in short, situations that lead to profound positive or negative emotions. High arousal can significantly affect self-judgments in either direction. For example, extreme fear might conceivably lead to specific judgments of high or low efficacy. A mountain climber might, because of fear that threatens to turn his legs to jelly, decide that he is not capable of completing a climb. In contrast, a mother who finds her child trapped beneath an overturned automobile might, in a sudden surge of emotion, believe that she is capable of lifting the vehicle off the child.

At a less extreme level, whether arousal has positive or negative effects on an individual's self-judgments may depend largely on experiences the individual has had in situations of high or low arousal. Some people find that moderately high arousal helps their performance; others react in the opposite way. For example, the trepidation that precedes speaking in public may be seen as helpful by some speakers and as highly negative by others.

In summary, four separate sources of influence can affect an individual's judgments of self-efficacy (see Table 2.8). Bandura calls these sources *enactive* (based on the outcome of the individual's own actions), *vicarious* (based on comparisons between the person's performance and the performance of others), *persuasory* (the result of persuasion), and *emotive* (the result of arousal or emotion).

DEVELOPMENT OF SELF-EFFICACY

Not long ago my oldest son said something that surprised and alarmed

t able 2.8

Four sources of influence on self-efficacy judgments

SOURCES OF INFLUENCE	EXAMPLES OF INFORMATION THAT MIGHT LEAD JOAN TO ARRIVE AT POSITIVE ESTIMATES OF HER PERSONAL EFFICACY
Enactive	She receives an A in mathematics.
Vicarious	She learns that Ronald studied hard but only got a B.
Persuasory	Her teacher tells her she can probably win a scholarship if she tries.
Emotive	She becomes intensely involved before taking a test and feels exhilarated afterwards.

me. We were talking about the various foolish things each of us had done when we were very young. "Do you remember that house we had on the farm?" he asked. "Well, I used to think I'd be able to fly from the upstairs window if I held a really clean sheet over my head like Superman's cape. And I almost tried it one day. I looked all over the house, but I didn't know where the clean sheets were and I thought Mom would be mad if I took one off the bed and I wasn't sure it would work with a dirty sheet. So I didn't jump."

Young children don't have very good notions of their personal capabilities. Their self-judgment, and their corresponding self-guidance, is less than perfect. As a result, without external controls they, like my son, would often be in danger of severely hurting themselves. Instead of imposing on themselves the internal self-judgment, "*I* can't do that," they require the external judgment, "*You* can't do that."

The sense of personal control over behavior that is essential for judgments of personal efficacy begins to develop very early in infancy. Some of its roots lie in

an infant's discovery that looking at the mother makes her look back in return; that smiling or crying draws her attention; that waving a hand makes her smile. Later, as infants begin to move around freely, they begin to learn more about the effects of their behaviors—and also more about their *effectiveness* as behavers. Language provides them with a means to analyze and think about themselves, and a means to symbolize and anticipate the consequences of their behaviors.

In a child's early stages, Bandura (1986) informs us, the most important source of information for the development of self-referential thought is the family. Soon, however, peers begin to increase in importance. Now the behavior of others, as well as their responses to our behavior, is factored into our personal estimates of our efficacy. Eventually schools, too, exert their powerful influences. Teachers tell us a great deal about how well we can do things—or how badly. So, too, do the responses of our classmates, and the responses of our parents to the evidence we bring home of our worth in school, of our intelligence, of our ability to do the things that teachers require in ways that please them.

And so it continues throughout life. In adolescence we are faced with new tasks, new challenges—as we are, too, throughout adulthood and into old age. At every step these new challenges require new competencies and new behaviors—and new judgments of personal effectiveness.

Among the judgments of efficacy that are perhaps most important to an individual at all stages of life are those that concern the ability to capture the attention, interest, and affection of others. As Kegan (1982) argues, we strive to *mean* something. We want people to pay attention to us; to like us; to want to be with us, listen to us, and do things with us. Put another way, we need to feel that we are

Efficacy refers to a person's effectiveness in dealing with the world; self-efficacy relates to judgments of personal effectiveness. One of the most important self-efficacy judgments for happiness has to do with beliefs about the ability to attract the attention, the affection, and the friendship of others.

capable of eliciting these feelings on the part of others—that we are *socially effective*. Hence the central role of self-efficacy judgments in our lives and in our happiness.

social cognitive theory in review

In some important ways, Bandura's social cognitive theory bridges the gap between behavioristic theories, which try to explain development entirely in terms of observable, nonmental events like stimuli and responses, and cognitive positions, which are mainly concerned with mental events. Thus this theory is based on the notion that certain social behaviors (notably, imitative behaviors) are reinforced in various ways and are therefore more likely to recur. At the same time, it recognizes the power of our ability to imagine the consequences of our actions. It is our *anticipation* of the taste of the ice cream that hurries us to the store, not just a blind reaction to external stimulation.

Bandura's theory is a striking example of how theories need not be static, unchanging things, of how they can change

with new information and new beliefs. Thus his recent writings deal with self-efficacy and are concerned with how what we think, feel, and do is profoundly influenced by our judgments of our personal effectiveness.

Although the theory provides a useful way of looking some aspects of development, especially at social motivation, it is not a comprehensive theory meant to account for most of the important observations in human development; Jean Piaget's theory of cognitive development is.

a cognitive approach: Piaget

sychoanalytic theorists are concerned primarily with personality development; behavioristic theorists emphasize behavior and its consequences; a third group of theorists focus on the intellectual (cognitive) development of children.

Cognition is the art or faculty of knowing. Cognitive theorists are concerned with *how* we know—that is,

All the world's a stage,
And all the men and women merely players;
They have their exits and their entrances,
And one man in his time plays many parts,
His acts being seven ages.
—William Shakespeare, As you like it (act 2, scene 7)

In Shakespeare's account there are seven major acts in our plays—and, we might add, many small scenes in each. Together these scenes weave the patterns that color the chronology of human development.

At first, the infant,
Mewling and puking in the nurse's arms.

But mewling and puking is not all there is to the first of our ages. Although an infant is moved more easily to tears than a child—and a child more easily than an adult—there is much laughter too in those early years.

Then the whining schoolboy, with his satchel
And shining morning face, creeping like snail
Unwillingly to school.

Not so. Many race and laugh their way to school—
even boys.

And then the lover,
Sighing like furnace . . .

Or maybe just eating popcorn and lying around and
falling in love on the way to adulthood.

Then a soldier,
Full of strange oaths and bearded like the pard. . . .
And then the justice,
In fair round belly . . .
Full of wise saws. . . .
The sixth age shifts
Into the lean and slippered pantaloon,
With spectacles on nose and pouch on side. . . .

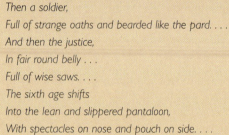

But not all soldiers are "full of strange oaths and bearded like the pard." Some are just children playing the games of childhood; others are children playing the more desperate games of adulthood. And, sadly, some must face sorrows far bigger than their years as they glimpse the

Last scene of all,
That ends this strange eventful history,
 . . . mere oblivion,
Sans teeth, sans eyes, sans taste, sans everything.

with how we obtain, process, and use information.

The most widely cited and most influential of all theories of cognitive development is Piaget's (Stanton, 1993). Important aspects of his theory are introduced briefly in the following sections. More specific details of the theory, and the contributions of other approaches to cognitive development, are discussed in subsequent chapters (Chapters 5, 7, 9, and 11) that deal chronologically with children's intellectual development.

---

basic concepts in cognitive development

Piaget was trained as a biologist rather than as a psychologist. Consistent with his early training, he began his study of children by posing two of the most fundamental questions of biology: (1) What is it that enables organisms to adapt to their environments and survive? and (2) What is the most useful way of classifying living organisms? He rephrased these questions and applied them to the development of children: (1) What are the characteristics and capabilities of children that allow them to adapt to their environments? and (2) What is the most useful way of classifying or ordering child development? Piaget's answers for these two questions, developed over an extraordinarily prolific career spanning more than six decades (he died in 1980 at the age of 84), are the basis for his theory and the topics we explore next.

ASSIMILATION AND ACCOMMODATION LEAD TO ADAPTATION

The newborn infant that Piaget describes is in many ways a helpless little organism, unaware that the world out there is real, lacking any storehouse of thoughts with which to reason or any capacity for intentional behaviors, and having only a few simple reflexes. But infants are much more than this. They are also remarkable little sensing machines that seem to be naturally predisposed to acquiring and processing a tremendous amount of information. They continually seek out and respond to stimulation. As a result, the sucking, reaching, grasping, and other reflexes that are present at birth become more complex, more coordinated, and eventually purposeful. The process by which this occurs is *adaptation*. And to answer the first of the questions of biology as simply as possible, **assimilation** and **accommodation** are the processes that make adaptation possible.

Assimilation involves responding to situations with activities or knowledge that have already been learned or that were present at birth. For example, an infant is born with the capability to suck—what Piaget calls a sucking **scheme** (sometimes used interchangeably with **schema**; plural: **schemata**). The sucking scheme allows the infant to assimilate a nipple to the behavior of sucking. Similarly, a child who has learned the rules of addition can assimilate a problem such as 2 + 2 (can respond appropriately in terms of previous learning). Often, however, our understanding of the world is insufficient to deal with the current situation. The newborn's sucking schema is adequate for ordinary nipples but does not work quite as well for fingers and toes; the preschooler's understanding of numbers is sufficient for keeping track of toys but is inadequate for impressing kindergarten teachers. The changes in information and behavior that are thus required define accommodation. In short, assimilation involves reacting on the basis of previous learning and understanding; accommodation involves a change in understanding. And the interplay of assimilation and accommodation

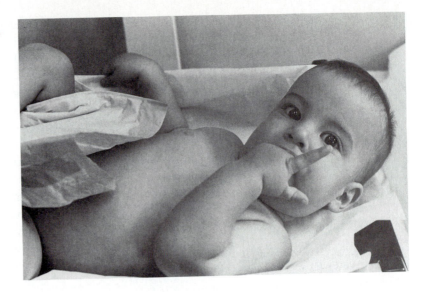

First is the nipple, a bulbous thing that, from birth, infants know what to do with—in Piaget's terms, they can assimilate to the activity of sucking. But even a well-practiced activity (Piaget calls it a schema) like sucking a nipple needs to be changed if it is also to accommodate fingers—and sometimes even toes or entire hands. Assimilation and accommodation are the two drivers of cognitive growth.

leads to adaptation. (See Chapter 5 for further illustrations of these concepts.)

DEVELOPMENT CAN BE ORDERED IN STAGES

The second of Piaget's questions seeks the most useful way of organizing and classifying child development. Piaget's answer is found in his description of the stages through which each child passes. There are four major stages in this description, each marked by the child's strikingly different perceptions of the world and different adaptations to it. Each stage is the product of learning that occurred in earlier stages, and each is a preparation for the next stage.

Note that although Piaget's theory is most easily explained and understood in terms of stages, he nevertheless viewed development as a continuous process of successive changes. Development does not consist of abrupt, clearly recognizable changes like steps on a stairway; it is more like a gradual (if unevenly sloped) incline.

Although cognitive development moves along relatively smoothly, it is simpler and more useful to divide it into stages. Doing so allows us to compare behaviors and capabilities that are characteristic of different levels, and sometimes it leads to discoveries about the processes underlying change. Note, too, that the ages Piaget assigned to each stage are simply averages reflecting the behaviors of upper-middle-class Swiss children through the middle of the twentieth century. Children from different cultural contexts and with different characteristics sometimes pass through these stages much earlier or much later than Piaget's norms would suggest.

the stages of cognitive development

Piaget's major stages of cognitive development are summarized in Table 2.9 and are briefly discussed next. (These subjects are covered in greater detail in Chapters 5, 7, 9, and 11.)

Piaget's stages of cognitive development

STAGE	APPROPRIATE AGE	SOME MAJOR CHARACTERISTICS
Sensorimotor period	0–2 years	Intelligence in action; world of the here and now; no language, no thought, no notion of objective reality at beginning of stage
Preoperational thinking	2–7 years	Egocentric thought; reason dominated by perception; intuitive rather than logical solutions; inability to conserve
Concrete operations	7 to 11 or 12 years	Ability to conserve; logic of classes and relations; understanding of numbers; thinking bound to concrete objects and events; development of reversibility in thought
Formal operations	11 or 12 to 14 or 15 years	Complete generality of thought; propositional thinking; ability to deal with the hypothetical; development of strong idealism

Note: Each of these characteristics is detailed in the appropriate sections of Chapters 5, 7, 9, and 11.

SENSORIMOTOR PERIOD

Piaget labeled the first two years of life the **sensorimotor period**, so called because during this time children understand the world largely through immediate action and sensation. For infants, the world exists here and now; it is real only when it is being acted on and sensed. When the ball is no longer being touched, looked at, or chewed, it doesn't exist. It isn't until toward the end of the second year that children finally realize that objects have a permanence and an identity of their own—that they continue to exist when they are not in view. By then, children have also begun to acquire language and are progressing rapidly from a sensorimotor to a more cognitive intelligence.

PREOPERATIONAL THINKING

Following the acquisition of language, children enter the period of **preoperational thought** (ages 2 to 7). At this stage, says Piaget, children rely exces-sively on perception rather than on logic. The famous so-called "conservation experiments" illustrate this well. In one of these experiments, children are presented with two glasses that contain equal amounts of water. The experimenter then pours the contents of one glass into a tall, thin tube—or, alternately, into a wide, shallow dish. The child is then asked whether each of the containers still has the same amount of water or whether one container has more than the other. Preoperational children, relying on the appearance of the two containers, almost invariably say that the tall tube has more because it is higher (or less because it is thinner)—or that the shallow dish has more because it is "fatter" (or less because it is shorter). Even when they realize that the water could be poured back into its original container so that both glasses would again appear equal, preoperational children continue to rely on perception (on actual appearance) rather than on reasoning. (See Chapter 7 for more details.)

CONCRETE OPERATIONS

The major acquisition in the next period of development (ages 7 to 11 or 12) is the ability to think in terms of **concrete operations**. An operation is a thought—what Piaget called an internalized action. In this sense, it is a mental action or, more precisely, an operation performed on ideas according to certain rules of logic. These rules of logic permit the concrete operational child to scoff at the ridiculous simplicity of a conservation problem: Of course there is the same amount of water in both containers because none has been added or taken away, because one misleading dimension is compensated for by the other (it is taller but thinner), and because the act of pouring the water from one container to the other can be reversed to prove that the quantity of water has not changed. Concrete operational children are capable of this kind of logic, but it is a logic that is tied to real, concrete objects and events. They are still unable to reason logically about hypothetical situations or events and cannot go from the real to the merely possible or from the possible to the actual. Thought is bound to the real (concrete) world; hence concrete operations (see Chapter 9).

FORMAL OPERATIONS

When children finally free themselves from the restrictions that once bound them to the concrete world, they enter the last stage of cognitive development—**formal operations**, characterized by the ability to manipulate abstract ideas—beginning about age 11 or 12. Piaget believed that during this stage children's thought has the *potential* of becoming as logical as it will ever be. Note the emphasis on the word *potential*; many of us remain strangers to the deductive logic of formal operations throughout our lives.

However, as Ricco (1993) argues, the logic of formal operations is a logic concerned with hypothetical states of affairs; for many of life's problems, other forms of logic—especially those dealing with meaning—are more appropriate. Piaget recognized this, and in some of his latest writings he discusses a formal operations logic of meanings (see Piaget & Garcia, 1991).

Piaget's theory in review

Child development, in Piaget's view, is best described as the emergence of progressively more logical forms of thought—that is, as the development of ways of thinking that become increasingly more effective in freeing children from the present and allowing them to use powerful symbol systems to understand and manipulate the environment. According to his theory, the major characteristics of thinking in each of the four developmental stages influence all aspects of children's understanding of the world, including their notion of space, time, numbers, reality, causality, and so on.

A theory such as Piaget's is considerably easier to evaluate objectively than are the psychoanalytic approaches. It makes very specific predictions about how average children function intellectually at different age levels, and an enormous number of these predictions have been tested by researchers. In general, this body of research confirms many of Piaget's initial findings, especially about the order of stages, although it is clear that the ages at which different children reach specific stages can vary considerably (Stanton, 1993).

Evidence suggests that Piaget underestimated the information-processing capabilities of infants and young children (Wellman & Gelman, 1992). However, this is due less to weaknesses in the theory than to Piaget's lack of tools and instruments with sufficient sensitivity to detect infants' cognitive capacities. Recent studies of infants' responsiveness to stimulation often make use of sophisticated instruments that measure changes in heart and respiration rate, movements of the eyeballs, changes in pupil size, brainwave activity, and so on—all devices not available to Piaget in the 1920s and 1930s.

Some critics argue that Piaget overestimated the importance of motor activity in infants' cognitive development and underplayed the importance of perception, most especially of visual perception (Bullinger, 1985). Others criticize Piaget because his theory says relatively little about individual differences among children, about the factors that might account for these differences, or about what can be done to promote intellectual development. In addition, the language and concepts of the theory are sometimes difficult, and it is not always clear that terms such as *assimilation* and *accommodation* add significantly to our understanding of human behavior.

One additional weakness of Piaget's theory is that it assumes that development ceases with adolescence. Although Piaget recognized that the abilities that characterize formal operations, the final developmental stage, are not always achieved during adolescence (or even in adulthood), he described no further developmental stages—as have a number of others, including Erikson and, more recently, Arlin (1975) and Basseches (1984).

In spite of these criticisms, Piagetian theory has clearly been the most dominant cognitive developmental theory of this century, and it continues to have a profound influence on current research and practice.

biological and ecological approaches

iological approaches to understanding human development emphasize the importance of innate, predetermined behavior patterns or tendencies. These approaches often stem from research conducted with nonhuman animals, in which genetic influences are sometimes more readily apparent than among humans.

Ecological approaches emphasize the importance of individuals' context—hence the importance of the environment. But for contemporary ecological theorists, it is not so much the context as the interaction between a person's characteristics and specific characteristics of the environment that is important. As Urie Bronfenbrenner (1989) insists, the most useful ecologically oriented model is one that jointly considers the person and the context and looks for processes to explain changes in development—hence the term *process-person-context model*.

The following sections look at John Bowlby's biologically based theory of attachment; at sociobiology, which attempts to uncover the biological basis of social behaviors; and at Bronfenbrenner's ecological systems theory, which emphasizes the importance of the accommodation between changing human beings and changing aspects of their environments.

ethology and Bowlby's attachment theory

The role of biology (of heredity) in determining animal behavior has long been accepted. I accept without question that my brother's Chesapeake Bay retriever is reasonably adept at sniffing out certain potent-smelling birds precisely because she is a Chesapeake. I would not expect the same behavior of Tigger, our prematurely retired cat. Even if Tigger's and the Chesapeake's early experiences had been identical, I still would not expect Tigger to enjoy walking at my heels or to drool at the prospect of a cold swim in a reedy pond. We know that many of the behaviors and habits characteristic of an individual of some nonhuman species are not acquired solely as a function of experience. A moth doesn't fly into a flame because it has learned to do so; dead moths don't fly. We can therefore assume that the attraction light has for a moth, like the overpowering urge of a Canada goose to fly south in the fall or a salmon to swim upriver, is the result of inherited tendencies.

Are we, in at least some ways, like moths and salmon? If so, what are our flames, our rivers?

ETHOLOGY

Ethologists (scientists whose principal concern is **ethology**, the study of behavior in natural situations) think that yes, we are just a little like moths. And al-though the flames that entice us might be less obvious than those that attract the moth, they are perhaps no less powerful.

Lorenz's (1952) study of imprinting in ducks and geese was among the first to draw parallels between animal and human behavior. **Imprinting** is the tendency of newly hatched geese (or chickens, ducks, and some other birds) to follow the first moving object they see shortly after hatching—during a **critical period**, so called because exposure to the same moving object (a releaser) before or after this period does not ordinarily result in the appearance of the same imprinted behavior (Figure 2.6).

Imprinting among newly hatched birds clearly has survival value. A gosling's chances of survival are far better if it, along with all its fellow goslings, follows its mother. Of course, the gosling does not follow the mother because it is aware of a genetic relationship between this big bird and itself; it follows her simply because she happened to be the first moving object it saw during the critical few hours following hatching. Ethologists have repeatedly demonstrated that if

Imprinting among birds clearly has survival value, even when it is directed toward an experimenter such as Konrad Lorenz. Bowlby suggests that attachment between infant and mother may have a similar genetic underpinning.

some other object such as a balloon were to replace the mother goose, the young gosling would quite happily follow it instead. When Lorenz substituted himself for the mother goose, the young goslings followed him much as they would have their mother.

The critical period is all-important. Newly hatched geese or chickens that are not exposed to a moving object during this critical period fail to become imprinted and subsequently will not follow their mothers. Similarly, a lamb that is removed from its mother after birth and not brought back for a week or more does not ordinarily show any evidence of attachment to her. Perhaps even more striking, ewes do not appear to be attached to their lambs under these circumstances and will sometimes butt them out of the way if they insist on coming too close (Thorpe, 1963).

BOWLBY'S ATTACHMENT THEORY

Although the search for imprinted behaviors among humans has not led to the discovery of behaviors as obvious as "following" among geese, some theorists argue that ethologists' emphasis on observation and on genetic contributions to behavior are important, especially when an individual's social relationships are also taken into account (Hinde, 1989). Other theorists, such as Bowlby (1979, 1980, 1982), suggest that there are important parallels between the findings of ethologists and the development of attachment between mother and infant. Bowlby's research with young infants indicates that we have a natural (inherited)

figure 2.6

A model of imprinting. Under appropriate environmental conditions, exposure to a releaser during the critical period leads to imprinting, which is manifested in predictable behaviors. Imprinting does not occur in the absence of a releaser or if the releaser is presented too early or too late.

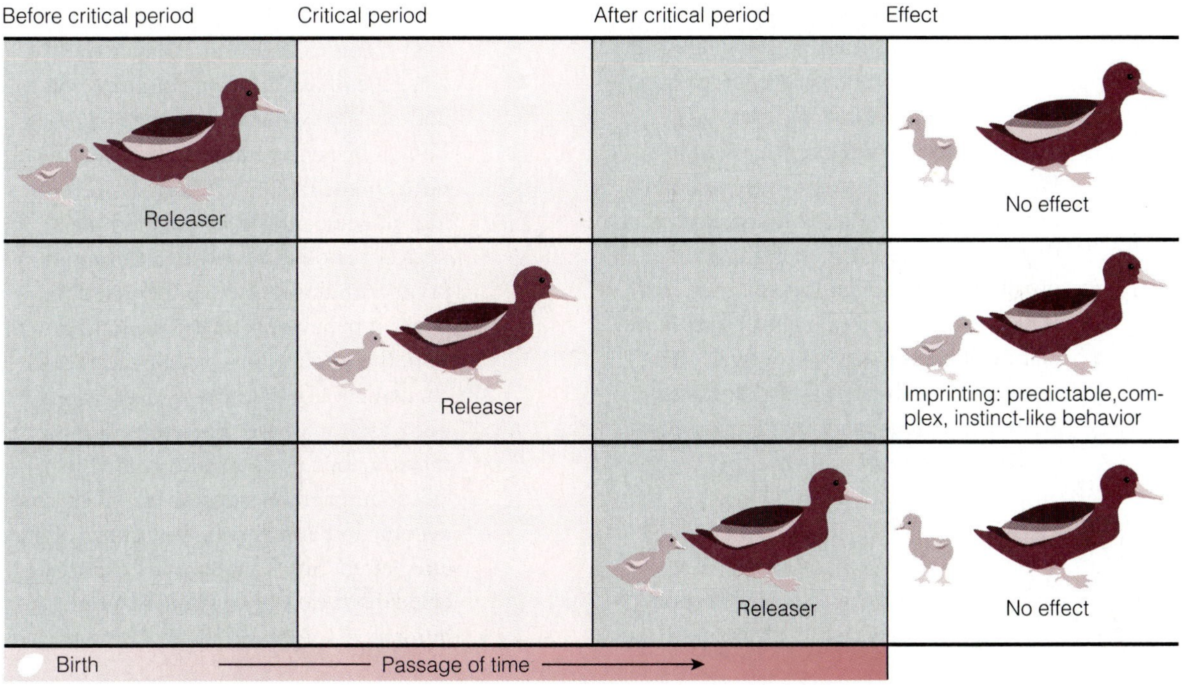

tendency to form emotional bonds with our mothers or with some other permanent caregiver. Such bonds, Bowlby argues, would clearly have been important for an infant's survival in a less civilized age. The need for bonds is evident in an infant's attempts to maintain physical contact, to cling, and to stay in visual contact with the mother (Bowlby, 1979). It is evident as well in the effects of separating mother and infant—effects that are marked, in Bowlby's (1979) words, by "emotional distress and personality disturbance, including anxiety, anger, depression, and emotional detachment" (p. 127).

Although researchers have not identified specific critical periods during which a mother or other caregiver must be present for an infant to form strong attachment bonds, many speak of a **sensitive period**, which, according to Bowlby, spans the first six months of life. Although attachment behaviors (clinging, looking) tend to be directed indiscriminately toward anyone in the early months, by the age of 6 months, infants who have been given the opportunity to do so will have formed strong bonds with their mother. Abrupt disruptions of these bonds after the age of 6 months can be extremely distressing (see Chapter 6). However, in the normal course of development, the bonds become less intense as the child matures. Although the mother usually remains the dominant figure until well into the third year of life, by then the child will experience progressively less anxiety during her temporary absences and will have begun to form important attachments to others.

Bowlby's theory in review

Bowlby's ethological theory provides an intriguing biological explanation for mother-infant attachment. However, critics point out that he has overemphasized the role of the mother and neglected that of the father. But as Ainsworth (1979) notes, Bowlby has focused on the role of the mother primarily because she is typically the principal caregiver. In the absence of the mother, the father or some other caregiver may substitute for her.

A more serious criticism of Bowlby's theory attacks his belief that failure to form strong attachments during infancy subsequently causes adjustment problems and difficulties in establishing loving relationships as an adult. If this were inevitably true, children raised without contact with their mothers for prolonged periods (in institutions, or even in day-care centers or foster homes) should experience problems. But this is often not the case. When home-raised infants are compared with those raised in day-care centers, they are not very different—although, as Clarke-Stewart (1989) notes, day-care infants are more likely to avoid their mothers after separation and to be insecurely attached.

It seems clear that the concepts and language of animal imprinting are not entirely appropriate for understanding human behavior. Human attachment is not as predictable a behavior as "following" in geese; nor is there as definite a critical period during which the appropriate stimulus must be presented if the relevant behavior is to appear. In addition, the implications of not forming an attachment bond with a primary caregiver early in life are not as clear for an infant as for a gosling. The gosling that fails to imprint on its mother is likely to become lost and perish; our infants often fare better. (See Chapter 6 for a more detailed discussion of attachment among humans.)

Another group of theorists interested in applying knowledge of biology (more specifically, of genetics and evolution) to an understanding of human development and behavior are the sociobiologists. Sociobiologists argue that science has neglected the role of heredity in determining many of the behaviors that we attribute to our environments and upbringing. **Sociobiology** is defined as "the systematic study of the biological basis of all social behavior" (Wilson, 1975, p. 4). Its single most striking—and most controversial belief—is that human social behavior is the product of a lengthy evolutionary history and is therefore genetically based. Among other things, sociobiologists explain altruistic behavior (helping, self-sacrificing) in terms of the evolutionary concept of survival. Nature, as Dawkins (1976) points out, is indifferent to the individual except insofar as the survival of the individual contributes to the survival of a group of individuals with related genes. The fundamental unit in the Darwinian law of survival of the fittest is the gene (or, more precisely, the DNA material that defines the gene's hereditary characteristics). Thus altruism makes evolutionary sense only when an altruistic act increases the probability of survival of some genetic material that is closely related to the altruist's genetic material. In Wilson's (1975) terms, "the ruling principle [is] the maximum average survival and fertility of the group as a whole" (p. 107). In the same way that it makes adaptive sense for a honeybee to sting an invader in the act of protecting her hive, even though she must then die, it also makes sense for a human being to be altruistic even if doing so lessens that individual's probability of surviving, provided that it increases the probability that others with related genes will survive as a result. As John Haldane (a British biologist) reportedly put it, "I would gladly lay down my life for two brothers or eight cousins" (Hofer, 1981, p. 20). It is in this sense that the "maximum average survival" of the group is improved.

In much the same way that altruism might be explained by reference to the "selfishness" of genes (it is, after all, genetic material that survives), sociobiological theory can be used to explain maternal love, sexual mores, aggression, spitefulness—indeed, contend its proponents, the entire range of human social behaviors.

SOCIOBIOLOGY IN REVIEW

Not surprisingly, sociobiological theory has provoked considerable controversy and negative reaction. Critics have been quick to point out that the theory is highly speculative and is based on a handful of assumptions that have not been tested and that are probably untestable in any case (Eckland, 1977). As Mazur (1977) notes, the theory assumes that behaviors occur because they increase the genetic survival of a group (or the probability that genetic material will survive). But how do we know this is so? Because the behavior occurred. And why did the behavior occur? Because it increases average genetic survival. Such circular reasoning offers no hope of proof. To validate the theory, it would be necessary to establish the presence of "altruistic" genes by some means unrelated to the behaviors these genes are intended to explain. This has yet to be accomplished.

This does not mean that genetics is therefore irrelevant to understanding human behavior. In fact, as is made clear in Chapter 3, our genes are fundamentally involved in everything we do. What it does mean is that science has not yet succeeded in showing that there are specific genes, or combinations of genes, that directly cause specific individual behaviors. The fundamental error in sociobiological theory concerns level of explanation. Evolutionary theory, the basis of sociobiology, is designed to explain variation in species or related groups of species (Plomin, 1987); it can rarely predict an individual's behaviors.

Ethologists (and sociobiologists) emphasize the importance of biological or genetic contributions to development; ecologically oriented theorists stress the importance of culture or context. However, the differences between ethological and ecological positions have to do more with different emphases than with different beliefs. Most theorists accept that both ecological (cultural or environmental) influences and biological tendencies determine human development. In Hinde's (1989) words, "the futility of a dichotomy between the biological and social aspects of human nature is now generally recognized."

Two theories that emphasize the influence of culture on development are those of Vygotsky and Bronfenbrenner.

Vygotsky's cultural-historical approach

The Russian psychologist Lev Vygotsky was a major force in Soviet psychology by the time he was 28; that was in 1924. Sadly, 10 years later he died of tuberculosis, but many of his ideas, old as they are now, still seem fresh and important.

Among the most central of Vygotsky's ideas is the belief that human development is fundamentally different from the development of animals. Why? Because humans can use tools and symbols; as a result, they create cultures, and cultures

have a vitality, a life of their own. They grow and change and exert a very powerful influence on their members. They determine the end result of competent development—the sorts of things that its members must learn, the ways they should think, the things they are most likely to believe. As Bronfenbrenner (1989) puts it, we are not only culture-producing beings, but also culture-produced.

There are several underlying themes that run through Vygotsky's theory. One, just mentioned, concerns the centrality of culture in human development; a second deals with the functions of language; and a third relates to children's relationship with the environment—a relationship Vygotsky described as the *zone of proximal development* (Kozulin, 1990). We next look at each of these themes briefly.

THE CENTRALITY OF CULTURE

Culture, Vygotsky insists, is what most clearly separates us from animals. Culture is the manifestation of our ability to think and to invent symbol systems (Vygotsky, 1986). It permits humans to have a history, and perhaps a future as well.

There is an important distinction, says Vygotsky, between *elementary* mental functions and *higher* mental functions. Elementary functions are our natural, unlearned capacities. They are evident in a newborn's ability to attend to human sounds and to discriminate among them, and they are apparent in its ability to remember the smell of its mother, or in the capacity to goo and gurgle and to scream and cry. In time, however, these elementary capacities are gradually transformed into higher mental functions—that is, they change from natural, unlearned functions to more sophisticated, learned behaviors and capacities. This transformation, which is absolutely fundamental to human development, is made possible through children's interactions with their culture and, most important, through social interaction with adults and competent peers. As Abecassis (1993) puts it, "For Vygotsky, biology alone cannot explain the development of higher mental functions; it is necessary to add culture" (p. 48). And one of the most important features of culture is language.

THE ROLE OF LANGUAGE

Language, after all, is what makes thinking possible, Vygotsky insists (see Wertsch, 1985). During the preverbal stage of development, children's intelligence is much like that of, say, an ape. It is purely natural, purely practical—*elementary*, in other words. But language changes all that.

Vygotsky describes three forms of language that develop sequentially; each has different functions (see Table 2.10). The first, **social** (or external) **speech**, is common until around the age of 3. It is the most primitive form of speech, and its function is largely to control the behavior of others (as in, "I want candy!") or to express simple concepts. Through the early part of this stage, Vygotsky contends, thinking and language develop separately.

The second stage, egocentric speech, dominates children's lives approximately between ages 3 and 7. This type of speech is a sort of bridge between the social speech of the preceding period and the more **internal** (inner) **speech** of the next period. Egocentric speech often serves to control children's own behavior, but may be spoken out loud. For example, young children often talk to themselves as they are trying to do something: "Push. Okay, now turn. Turn. Tu . . . push. . . ."

In the third stage, inner speech develops. This is our private self-talk—what James (1890) called our stream of con-

t a b l e 2.10

Vygotsky's conception of the role of language

STAGE	APPROXIMATE AGES	FUNCTION
Social (external) speech	To age 3	Controls the behavior of others; expresses simple thoughts and emotions
Egocentric speech	3–7 years	Bridge between external and inner speech; serves to control own behavior, but may be spoken out loud
Inner speech	Age 7 onward	Self-talk; makes possible the direction of our thinking and our behavior; involved in all higher mental functioning

sciousness. According to Vygotsky, inner speech is what makes thought possible. It is the basis of all higher mental functioning.

ZONE OF PROXIMAL DEVELOPMENT

Language is a cultural invention. It is one of the most important ways in which context, children's culture, influences and shapes the course of development. For Vygotsky, development is a function of the interaction between culture and children's basic biological capacities and maturational timetables. But, insisted Vygotsky, it is the environmental context (the culture) that is most important, not biological maturation (Valsiner, 1987). Development (or growth) takes place when environmental opportunities and demands are appropriate for the child. In

Development (or growth), says Vygotsky, requires that the demands of the environment be at an appropriate level for children—in his words, that they be within the zone of proximal development. Demands that are too trivial can be wasteful; those that are beyond a child's capabilities (say with peer or parental help) are ineffective.

a sense, culture *instructs* the child in the ways of development. But the instruction is effective only if the child's biological maturation and current developmental level are sufficiently advanced. For every child, says Vygotsky, there is a zone of proximal development—a sort of potential for development. In his words, the **zone of proximal development** is "the distance between the actual developmental level as determined by independent problem solving and the level of potential development as determined through problem solving under adult guidance or in collaboration with peers" (Vygotsky, 1978, p. 86). Demands that are beyond children's capacities—in other words,

that are beyond their zone of proximal development—are ineffective in promoting growth; similarly, demands that are too simple are wasteful.

Vygotsky's theory in review

In summary, Vygotsky's theory describes development as a social process. Cognitive development, claims Vygotsky, results from interactions of a child with adults and more competent peers. By participating *jointly* in various activities, children develop and practice cognitive skills that were initially beyond their abilities, but fall within their *zone of potential development* (Gordon & Armour-Thomas, 1991).

Vygotsky's theory underscores the role of culture, and especially that of its most important invention, language. As Tudge and Winterhoff (1993) note, Vygotsky believed that development is a social process assisted by adults and more competent peers. For Vygotsky, the driving force in development is found in the demands and requirements of the culture. In contrast, Piaget's child is more solitary, working alone to discover and create meaning. The driving force in this system is cognitive uncertainty and contradiction (*disequilibrium* is Piaget's term). And Bandura's child learns through social imitation; the driving force is a need to learn through observation. Although these analyses are somewhat oversimplified, they capture the most obvious features of each of these three theories.

One of Vygotsky's most important contributions is his recognition of the importance of culture in shaping children's development. And although the concepts of culture and language as determiners of development are perhaps too vague to be of immediate practical value to child-care specialists, teachers, or even psychologists, they are absolutely fundamental to our understanding of the complexity and variety of the human experience. The *average* children of which our textbooks speak are always average only in *their* culture. It is largely to remind ourselves of this that every chapter of this text includes one or more "Of Other Children" boxes.

Another theory that also emphasizes the importance of context-person interaction is Bronfenbrenner's ecological systems theory.

Bronfenbrenner's ecological systems theory

Psychological, biological, and social systems are *open* systems; this means that their existence depends on interaction and that they are constantly subject to change as a function of interaction. The Piagetian infant, born with a small number of reflexes, adapts and changes as a function of interacting with the environment—as a result of assimilating and accommodating, to use Piaget's terms. It is infant-environment interaction that results in the notion that objects are permanent, that symbols represent, that quantities can be added and subtracted, that there is a fine and elegant logic that governs physics and chemistry.

Bronfrenbrenner refers to the interaction of the individual with the environment as the *ecology of human development* (also the title of his 1979 book). Here is how he expressed the cornerstone of his theory:

> *The ecology of human development is the scientific study of the progressive, mutual accommodation, through the life course, between an active, growing human being, and the changing properties of the immediate settings in which the developing person lives, as this process is affected by the relations between these settings, and by the larger contexts in which the settings are embedded. (Bronfenbrenner, 1989, p. 188).*

The emphasis in this theory is on understanding development as an interactive function of the person and the environment. Hence Bronfenbrenner's model has three components: the person, the context in which behavior occurs, and the processes that account for developmental change. It is, in Bronfenbrenner's words, a *process-person-context* model, and development is simply the processes through which ". . . properties of the person and the environment interact to produce constancy and change in the characteristics of the person . . ." (p. 191).

THE IMPORTANCE OF CONTEXTS

One of the basic principles of Bronfenbrenner's ecological systems theory is that differences in intellectual performance among groups are a function of interactions with different cultures (or subcultures) that are characterized by different types of cognitive processes. It follows that a person's cognitive competence is always culturally relative. A very intelligent, well-adapted bushman of the Cameroon jungle would not necessarily function very intelligently in downtown Chicago—but then a Chicago lawyer might quickly lose his bearings (and perhaps his marbles) in the Cameroon jungle.

Not only are we influenced by our contexts, but we also influence them in turn. If infant Ronald cries more than is polite or expected, he may change some significant aspects of the environment with which he interacts. His mother may come running sooner than she otherwise would; his nurse might become more irritable, more impatient; his father might pay more, or less, attention to him; his siblings might openly resent his intrusion in the family; even the dog might be annoyed. And each of these changing aspects of context might, in turn, alter Ronald's behavior. That his mother runs to soothe him might encourage him to cry even more. But now, perhaps his mother senses what is happening and comes more slowly, more reluctantly, and again the interaction changes. Thus the mother's personality and her beliefs about childrearing interact with Ronald's personality and his behavior in a constantly changing, *open ecological system*. There is always an interplay between a person's characteristics and those of the environment, says Bronfenbrenner (1989): "The one cannot be defined without reference to the other" (p. 225). He also makes the point that some characteristics (termed *developmentally instigative*) are more important than others in influencing contexts. Temperament, low birth weight, physical characteristics such as size or appearance, age, sex, race, developmental handicaps, and many other factors tend to provoke important reactions—hence changes—in context, which in turn affect the individual.

DIMENSIONS OF CONTEXT

Bronfenbrenner describes four different levels of context in which a developing child interacts. From nearest (most proximal) to most remote, these are the *microsystem*, the *mesosystem*, the *exosystem*, and the *macrosystem* (see Table 2.11).

■ **The microsystem**. Interactions that occur at an immediate, face-to-face level define the microsystem. The complex patterns of behaviors, roles, and relationships within the home, the school, the peer group, the workplace, the playground, and so on are the microsystem component of an individual's ecological system. The interaction of Ronald's crying with the

t a b l e   2.11

Levels of context in Bronfenbrenner's ecological (open) system theory

Microsystem	Child in immediate, face-to-face interaction
Mesosystem	Relationships between two or more microsystems
Exosystem	Linkages and relationships between two or more settings, one of which does not include the child
Macrosystem	The totality of all other systems, evident in the beliefs, the options, the life-styles, the values, and the mores of a culture or subculture

behaviors of mother, father, siblings, and dog illustrates what is meant by a microsystem: Everybody in a microsystem influences everybody else.

■ **The mesosystem**. In turn, microsystems may influence each other in important ways. For example, how Ronald's mother treats him may be influenced by her interactions with his father. Perhaps she is less likely to be gentle and loving with her son if she has just had an argument with her husband. Similarly, how Ronald interacts with his sister, Nan, may reflect how his mother interacts with Nan. Interactions between elements of the microsystem that include the developing person define what is meant by the mesosystem.

■ **The exosystem**. The home does not exist in isolation. How parents treat children is influenced by schools, by teachers, perhaps by the church, and by employers and friends. In short, it is influenced by all of the relationships that exist between members of a child's microsystem and others. For example, interactions between Ronald and his father may be influenced by the father's relationships with his colleagues or his fishing buddies. Interactions between an element of the microsystem that ordinarily includes the developing child and an element of the wider context that does not include the child define the exosystem.

■ **The macrosystem**. All the interactive systems—micro-, meso-, and exo-systems—that characterize cultures (or subcultures) define the macrosystem. Macrosystems are describable in terms of beliefs, values, customary ways of doing things, expected behaviors, social roles, status assignments, life-styles, religions, and so on, as these are reflected in interactions among systems. In Bronfenbrenner's (1989) words, the macrosystem "may be thought of as a societal blueprint for a particular culture, subculture, or other broader social context" (p. 228).

Macrosystems can change over time, and sometimes these changes are very significant for a developing individual. For example, within the last few decades of the twentieth century there have been profound changes in family employment patterns (from one to two wage earners), in family structure (from two- to one-parent families), in childrearing styles (from home-rearing to other child-care options), in age of marriage (from younger to older), in age of childbearing (also from younger to older), and in range of expected school attendance (from quasi-compulsory kindergarten to quasi-expected postsecondary). Clearly, many of these macrosystem changes directly affect the microsystems of which a child is a functional part—the family, the home, the school.

For an illustration of how contexts are shaped by cultural expectations and beliefs, and of how important they can be in the life of a developing child, see "In Other Contexts: Ellen De Luca, The Fat Girl."

BRONFENBRENNER'S ECOLOGICAL SYSTEMS THEORY IN REVIEW

Although most contemporary developmental theorists pay lip service to the importance of taking context, person, and interaction into account, many researchers continue to operate within one of the two models that have dominated much of our thought and research. One model says that the causes of developmental change are to be found primarily within the individual; the other insists that the individual's environment is a more important cause of change. It's the old nature-nurture debate (about which we say more in Chapter 3).

The model that underlies our thinking is tremendously important to our research and our conclusions. One model says that if Johnny turns out to be an unmanageable scoundrel, we should look for the cause and the explanation in his temperament and his personality characteristics; the other says we should look to his environment. But neither of these models says that we should look at how Johnny's characteristics influence his environment, and at how, in turn, his environment influences him. Neither insists that the cause is to be found in the progressive changes in the *interactions* that take place between Johnny and his alcoholic mother, his overworked and indifferent teachers, or his peers (the microsystem). Neither suggests that the aborted affair between Johnny's father and his kindergarten teacher is of consequence (the mesosystem). Neither is concerned with interactions that might have occurred between Johnny's mother and her employer, leading to a reduction in

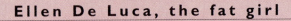

Her name was Ellen De Luca. But I never thought of her with a name until the day I made her cry," says Jeff of the girl who arrived at his first high school ceramics class at the same time as he did (Sachs, 1984). The girl was easily twice as wide as Jeff, so he had to stand back and let her through first. "What a butt!" said the guy behind him.

The fat girl moved off to a corner, away from the others, and Jeff promptly fell in love with Norma, a slim, beautiful blond, the kind of girl, he says, "I had been dreaming about ever since I started dreaming about girls."

In the class, the beautiful Norma threw exquisite pots and vases; fat Ellen's were as clumsy and ugly as she was. She kept bumping into things, breaking pottery, slamming doors— and also watching Jeff, wistfully catching him kissing Norma or rubbing her back. But he didn't even know Ellen's name, noticing only how big she was as she waddled down the aisles, or how she would sometimes eat two cheeseburgers in the school cafeteria and then maybe as many as six chocolate

bars. And she threw the wrappers under the table. Fat and sloppy.

"Somebody should tell her," said Jeff. "Tell her what?"

"That she'd do herself and the rest of us a big favor if she'd go bust up another class. It's a real drag having her around."

The fat girl, standing alone and unobserved behind Jeff, heard every word. Crying, she turned and shuffled away. Next day, and the next, and the one after that, she didn't return to class. In the end, Jeff went to her home and tried to apologize, but Ellen de Luca would hear none of it. "I'm going to kill myself," she said.

"I didn't mean it, Ellen. Honestly," Jeff insisted.

"It's everybody else too." she answered. "Nobody likes me. I'm going to kill myself."

To Think About: Norma and Ellen share many important aspects of context: They attend the same school and classes, they know many of the same people, and their families live in the same neighborhoods and have similar lives and values. What is it that makes

The "average" child, who is typically the subject of most child development studies and textbooks, shares many aspects of life's important realities with other "average" children. But there are many children whose contexts are far less "average."

their lives so different? Can you think of other situations in which cultural rules and expectations interact with people's characteristics to determine important aspects of context?

Based on Sachs, M. (1984). The fat girl. New York: Dutton.

her pay and chronic, irrepressible disgruntlement (the exosystem). Neither asks the researcher to look at how society's encouragement of the changing structure of the family affect Johnny's well-being (the macrosystem). That neither model asks these questions is a weakness of some of our traditional approaches to understanding child development; that Bronfenbrenner's ecological systems theory does is among its strengths.

But it is one of its weaknesses as well. Explanations based on ecological systems theory require the analysis of an almost infinite number of highly complex interactions. Identifying these interactions; observing and quantifying them; sorting out relationships among them; teasing out reciprocal influences between individuals and their micro-, meso-, and exosystems; and determining how changing cultural values and options impinge on the individual—all these are difficult tasks. But perhaps if we mull them over long enough, we may find that they are not impossible tasks to achieve. Bronfenbrenner's ecological systems theory at least suggests where we should begin.

humanistic approaches

Had I spoken of Piaget or Freud, of Skinner or sociobiology, of ethology or ecology, in my grandmother's kitchen, the old lady would have listened politely. She was always polite. But in the end she would probably have said, "That's theory. It's all very nice, but what about Frank?" Why Frank? Simply because he was a unique child. And although there is little doubt that Freud, Skinner, and Piaget might each have had something very intelligent, and perhaps even useful, to say about Frank's habits of stealing chicken eggs, writing poetry, and danc-

ing little jigs in mudholes, they would have been hard-pressed to convince my grandmother that they knew more about Frank than she did. My grandmother was a **humanist**.

Humanistic psychologists concern themselves with the uniqueness of the individual child. A basic humanistic belief is that it is impossible to describe the environment, much less a child, in a truly meaningful way because what constitutes the important features of the environment varies among individuals—a view labeled **phenomenology**. What phenomenology emphasizes is the importance of each person's view of the world and of themselves. To understand the behavior of children, this view says, we must try to perceive the world as they see it—from the perspective of their knowledge, their experiences, and their goals and aspirations (Rogers, 1951). This orientation does not imply that it is impossible to understand human nature or human behavior generally; it does imply, however, that a general understanding of human behavior may not tell us very much about the behavior of any one child. As we noted earlier, an individual child is not an average; there is no average child.

Because humanism recognizes more clearly than other positions that there is no average child, this orientation does not easily lead to theories that are both highly specific and widely applicable. But it does suggest an attitude toward children and toward development that is of tremendous potential value to those concerned with the welfare of children. Humanistic orientations tend to personalize (to humanize) our attitudes toward children; they restore some of the dynamism of the developmental process that our more static and complex theories might otherwise remove.

Maslow's humanistic need theory

A well-known humanistic theory is that of Abraham Maslow (1970). His main concern was with the development of the healthy personality.

We are moved by two hierarchical systems of needs, Maslow informs us. The **basic needs** are physiological (food, drink) and psychological (security, love,

esteem); the **metaneeds** are higher-level needs. Metaneeds show themselves in our desire to know, in our appreciation of truth and beauty, and in our tendencies toward growth and fulfillment—qualities termed **self-actualization** (Figure 2.7). The basic needs are also labeled *deficiency needs* because, when they are not satisfied, we try to remedy what we lack. For example, hunger represents a deficiency

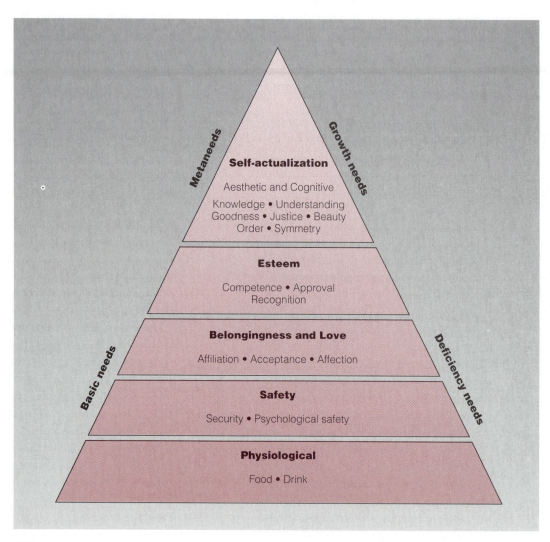

f igure 2.7

Maslow's hierarchy of needs. Lower-level needs are always attended to first, claims the theory; only after these are reasonably well satisfied is the individual driven by the higher-level, growth needs.

that can be satisfied by eating. Similarly, the metaneeds are termed *growth needs* because activities that relate to them don't fulfill a lack but instead lead to growth.

Our needs are hierarchically arranged, says Maslow, in the sense that the metaneeds will not be attended to unless the basic needs have been reasonably well satisfied; that is, we pay attention to beauty, truth, and the development of our potential when we are no longer hungry and unloved (at least not terribly so).

The most important of Maslow's metaneeds is self-actualization. Maslow (1970) suggests that self-actualization is characterized by absence of "neurosis, psychopathic personality, psychosis, or strong tendencies in these directions" (p. 150). On the more positive side, he claims that self-actualized people "may be loosely described as [making] full use and exploitation of talents, capacities, potentialities, etc." (p. 150). Using this loose definition, Maslow's examination of 3,000 college students revealed only one person he considered to be actualized (although there were several dozen "potentials").

humanism in review

One way to look at self-actualization is as a process that guides the direction of development, rather than as a state that we can attain. The view that children are directed by a need to become (to actualize) and that the process of actualization is essentially positive and self-directed presents a subtle but important contrast to the more mechanistic, more passive, and less inner-directed theories we have considered so far.

Critics have been quick to point out that humanism does not present a scientific theory in the sense that, say, behaviorism does. Instead, it presents a general description of the human condition, a description that is viewed by some as too vague and unreliable to contribute much to the development of psychology as a science. Humanists counter by pointing out that science is only one way of knowing, that there is value in the insights provided by more subjective approaches.

Among the most important contributions of the humanistic approach are its recognition of the importance of the self and its emphasis on the uniqueness of each child. Although humanistic theory does not address well the specifics of the developmental process, it might in the end serve to explain facts that are not easily accounted for by other theories. (See Chapter 13 for more about humanism.)

a final word about theories

We began this chapter by insisting that facts and theories are not worlds apart in terms of "truthfulness"—that theories are intended to be explanations of facts. From these explanations, scientists strive for understanding, for the ability to predict, and sometimes for control. But theories do more than explain facts. As Thomas (1992) notes, they suggest which facts we should look at. In effect, they guide our invention of "facts" and give them meaning (Scarr, 1985). Theories lead us to accept certain things as true—specifically, those things that fit our beliefs and expectations. By the same token, theories also lead us to ignore contradictory or apparently irrelevant observations.

Table 2.12 summarizes the approaches to developmental theory discussed in this chapter. History, as is so often its custom, may one day inform us about the fruitfulness of these approaches.

t able 2.12

table 2.12

Approaches to developmental theory

APPROACH	REPRESENTATIVE THEORIST(S)	MAJOR ASSUMPTIONS (THEORETICAL BELIEFS)	KEY TERMS
Psychoanalytic	Freud	Individual is motivated by instinctual urges that are primarily sexual and aggressive.	Id, ego, superego, psychosexual development
	Erikson	Child progresses through developmental stages by resolving conflicts that arise from a need to adapt to the sociocultural environment.	Competence, social environment, developmental tasks, psychosocial development
Descriptive	Havighurst	Development consists of mastering a sequence of tasks imposed on the individual by self and society	Developmental task, culture-specific
Behavioristic	Watson; Skinner	Changes in behavior are a function of reinforcement and punishment.	Reinforcement, punishment, stimuli, responses
Social cognitive	Bandura	Observational learning leads to developmental change; our ability to symbolize and to anticipate the consequences of our behavior is fundamental, as are our estimates of our self-efficacy.	Imitation, model, eliciting effect, self-efficacy
Cognitive	Piaget	Child develops cognitive skills through active interaction with the environment.	Stages, assimilation, accommodation, adaptation, schema
Biological	Bowlby; Wilson	Social behaviors have a biological basis understandable in evolutionary terms. The formation of attachment bonds is one example.	Attachment bonds, biological fitness, survival value, altruistic genes, sensitive period
Ecological systems	Vygotsky; Bronfenbrenner	The ecology of development is the study of accommodations between a person and the environment (culture), taking the changing characteristics of each into account.	Culture, language, open systems, ecology, microsystem, mesosystem, exosystem, macrosystem
Humanistic	Maslow	All individuals are unique but strive toward the fullest development of their potential.	Self, positive growth, metaneeds, self-actualization.

main points

THEORY, SCIENCE, AND MODELS

1. A theory is a collection of statements intended to organize and explain observations. Theories should reflect "facts," be understandable, and be useful for both predicting events and explaining the past. Models are metaphors that underlie theories. Mechanistic models emphasize our machine-like predictability; organismic models emphasize the active, exploring nature of children; and contextual models underline the influence of historical variables and culture.

PSYCHOANALYTIC APPROACHES: FREUD AND ERIKSON

2. Freud's theory assumes that among the important causes of behavior are deep-seated, unconscious forces that can be discovered through dream analysis, hypnosis, free association, and the analysis of childhood experiences. Chief among these forces are sexual urges (*libido*), which define the first level of personality, the *id*. The second level is the *ego* (reality-based and typically in conflict with the id); the third is the *superego* (conscience; social and cultural taboos).

3. Freud describes five developmental stages (oral, anal, phallic, latency, and genital) differentiated from each other in terms of the areas of a child's body that are the main source of sexual gratification at the time. Erikson's psychosocial theory of child development describes conflict-driven progress through stages that require increasing social competence (*trust versus mistrust, autonomy versus shame*

and doubt, initiative versus guilt, industry versus inferiority, and *identity versus identity diffusion*).

HAVIGHURST'S DEVELOPMENTAL TASKS

4. Havighurst describes development in terms of a sequence of age-related requirements placed on children by society. These tasks provide a rough index of developmental maturity.

BEHAVIORISTIC APPROACHES

5. Behavioristic theories focus on children's immediate behavior and on the environmental forces that affect it. In classical conditioning, repeated pairing of stimulus or response events leads to learning. In operant conditioning, the probability of a response occurring changes as a function of its consequences (positive and negative reinforcers increase the probability of a response occurring; punishment does not).

BANDURA'S SOCIAL COGNITIVE APPROACH

6. Bandura describes four observational learning (imitation) processes relating to paying attention, remembering, being able to perform, and being motivated to do so. Through imitation, children learn new responses (the *modeling effect*); they suppress or engage in deviant responses (the *inhibitory or disinhibitory effect*); or they are encouraged to do things related to the behavior of a model (the *eliciting effect*).

7. *Self-efficacy* refers to judgments about personal effectiveness. These judgments are important in determining what we do and don't do, the amount of effort we expend, and our

feelings about ourselves. Judgments of self-efficacy are based on our behavior (enactive); on comparisons between ourselves and others (vicarious); on the effects of others persuading us (persuasory); and on our level of arousal (emotive).

PIAGET'S COGNITIVE APPROACH

8. Piaget's biologically based theory of cognitive development describes adaptation through assimilation (using activities that are already in children's repertoire) and accommodation (changing activities to conform to environmental demands). Development is described in four major stages: sensorimotor (world of here and now; intelligence in action); preoperational (egocentric thought; perception-dominated; intuitive rather than logical); concrete operations (more logical but tied to real objects and events); and formal operations (potentially logical thought; hypothetical, idealistic reasoning).

BIOLOGICAL AND ECOLOGICAL APPROACHES

9. Biological approaches to development look at the role of biology (heredity); ecological approaches emphasize the importance of interaction in changing contexts. Ethologists are biologically oriented scientists who study behavior in natural situations. Bowlby uses principles of ethology (specifically, of imprinting) to explain the development and importance of the attachment bonds that form between mothers (or other principal caregivers) and their infants.

10. Sociobiology argues for the biological basis of social behavior and attempts to explain such behaviors—

for example, altruism—in terms of their group survival value.

11. Vygotsky's cultural-historical approach emphasizes the importance of culture, especially language. The zone of proximal growth, an expression of Vygotsky's belief in the interdependence of development and environment, is a child's potential for development in a given context.

12. Bronfenbrenner's ecological systems theory looks at the interaction between the growing child and environmental contexts. It describes four levels of context: the *microsystem* (the child in face-to-face interaction); the *mesosystem* (interactions among elements of the child's microsystem); the *exosystem* (interactions between one of the child's microsystems and another context with which the child does not ordinarily interact); and the *macrosystem* (the totality of all contexts relevant to the child's life).

HUMANISTIC APPROACHES

13. Humanistic theory is concerned with uniqueness and human potential (self-actualization). Maslow describes two sets of needs that motivate us: *deficiency* (basic) *needs*, which are psychological (safety, esteem, love) and physical (food, drink); and *metaneeds* (growth needs), such as the need to *self-actualize*.

focus questions: applications

■ What's in a theory? What's a theory for? How can you tell whether a theory is a good one?
1. What would an ideal theory of child development tell us?

■ How does Freudian psychoanalysis relate to child development?

2. Can you identify examples of children's behavior that illustrate each of Freud's psychosexual stages? Or Erikson's psychosocial stages?

■ What are the principal assumptions and explanations of behaviorism?

3. Devise a classroom procedure that applies some of the principles of conditioning theory for either teaching a specific lesson or reducing a behavior problem.

■ Do children learn through imitation?

4. Observe children with a view to identifying examples of each of the three principal effects of imitation.

■ What are the basic ideas underlying Piaget's theory?

5. Illustrate the twin processes of assimilation and accommodation in a child's behavior.

■ What are some of the roles of biology and culture in development?

6. Identify the most important characteristics of the type of culture you think would be best for fostering optimal human development. Or do you believe culture makes little difference—that we would be what we are no matter what?

study terms

theory 44
replicability 44
model 46
organismic model 46
mechanistic model 46
contextual model 47
open systems 47
libido 50
id 51

ego 51
superego 51
psychosexual development 52
oral stage 53
anal stage 53
phallic stage 53
genitalia 53
Oedipus complex 53
Electra complex 53
latency 53
identification 53
genital stage 54
defense mechanisms 54
psychosocial development 56
identity 56
behaviorism 61
reward 61
classical conditioning 62
operant conditioning 62
conditioning 62
association 62
unconditioned stimulus 62
conditioned stimulus 62
unconditioned response 63
conditioned response 63
elicited responses 64
emitted responses 64
operant 64
respondent 64
reinforcer 64
reinforcement 64
negative reinforcement 64
positive reinforcement 64
punishment 65
extinction 65
behavior modification 68
observational learning 68
imitation 68
symbolic 69
modeling effect 69
inhibitory effect 70
disinhibitory effect 70
eliciting effect 70
self-referent thought 71
self-efficacy 71
arousal 72
cognition 74

assimilation 75
accommodation 75
scheme 75
schema 75
schemata 75
sensorimotor period 75
preoperational thought 75
concrete operations 78
formal operations 78
ethology 80
imprinting 80
critical period 80
sensitive period 82
sociobiology 83
social speech 85
internal speech 85
zone of proximal development 86
microsystem 88
mesosystem 88
exosystem 88
macrosystem 89
humanist 91
phenomenology 91
basic needs 92
metaneeds 92
self-actualization 92

further readings

Because Freud, Erikson, and Piaget were voluminous writers, it is often easier, and sometimes more valuable, to use secondary sources for information about their theories. The following are especially useful starting points:

Baldwin, A. L. (1980). *Theories of child development* (2nd ed.). New York: John Wiley.

Thomas, R. M. (1992). *Comparing theories of child development* (3rd ed.). Belmont, Calif.: Wadsworth.

Wadsworth, B. J. (1989). *Piaget's theory of cognitive and affective development* (4th ed.). New York: Longman.

two

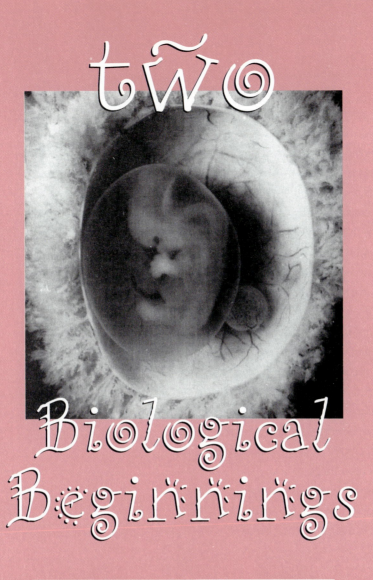

Biological Beginnings

I'm afraid you've got bad eggs, Mr. Jones.
Oh no, my lord, I assure you! Parts of it are excellent!
Punch, 1895

That's what you and I were in the beginning—an egg. Not a big, oval chicken egg such as Mr. Jones had on his plate; instead, a microscopic egg—and, of course, a sperm, even tinier. Of the millions that began the journey, this was the only sperm to finish, the only one to butt its tiny head hard enough, long enough, to succeed in penetrating that tough eggshell.

Those were our biological beginnings, you and I.

But what if we had a bad egg? Or a bad sperm, for that matter? Is that possible?

As we'll see in the next two chapters, science says that yes, it's sometimes possible for an egg or a sperm to be defective. And it's possible, too, for what started out as a good egg to be spoiled by drugs or bad nutrition or radiation or other things.

But most of the time we can, like Mr. Jones, claim that our eggs—or at least some parts of them—are most excellent!

3

Genetics and Context

Men's natures are alike; it is their habits that carry them far apart.
Confucius, Analects

focus questions

WHAT IS THE LIKELY OUTCOME OF A CHILD BEING RAISED BY A CHICKEN? A WOLF? ALONE IN AN ATTIC?

WHAT ARE THE MARVELS AND THE MYSTERIES OF WHAT OUR ELDERS CALLED THE BIRDS AND BEES?

WHAT ARE THE MOST COMMON GENETIC DEFECTS AND PROBLEMS?

HOW CAN WE DIAGNOSE GENETIC PROBLEMS?

WHAT CAN WE DO ABOUT THEM?

WHAT IS THE NATURE-NURTURE CONTROVERSY?

outline

FERAL CHILDREN

THE INTERACTION OF GENETICS AND CONTEXT
What Is Interaction?
How Genes and Environment Interact

BASIC CONCEPTS OF HEREDITY
Ovum, Sperm, and Conception
Proteins
DNA
Chromosomes
Sex Chromosomes
Genes and Their Function
Genotype and Phenotype
Reaction Range and Canalization
Molecular Genetics

GENETIC DEFECTS
Defects Resulting from Genetically Related Parents
Huntington's Disease
Sickle-Cell Anemia
PKU
Other Genetic Defects

CHROMOSOMAL DISORDERS
Down Syndrome
Abnormalities of the Sex Chromosomes

IDENTIFYING AND DEALING WITH GENETIC RISK
Prenatal Diagnosis
Treating Genetic Disorders
Genetic Counseling
Genetics and the Future

STUDYING GENE-CONTEXT INTERACTION
Historical Family Studies
Animal Studies
Intervention Studies
Studies of Twins
Studies of Adopted Children
An Illustration of Gene-Context Interaction

THE CONTINUING NATURE-NURTURE CONTROVERSY

MAIN POINTS

FOCUS QUESTIONS: APPLICATIONS

STUDY TERMS

FURTHER READINGS

When I was little and misbehaved, my parents would sometimes threaten to put me out with the chickens if I didn't smarten up. The threat might not have been very effective had it not been for the tragic tale of Robert Edward Cuttingham, whom we knew as "Chicken."

We all knew the story, how his parents had left him too long and too often with the chickens so that his brain and his habits grew up chickenlike rather than human. Rumor was he always slept in the chicken coop during the summer, that he came indoors only when it got so cold the water froze on the river. They said, too, that he slept perched on a railing and that when he awoke in the morning he'd crow as loud and long as any rooster. John George Scott, who lived up in the hills behind the Cuttingham farm, said he heard him lots of times and saw him quite often, walking all crouched over, his arms dragging at his sides, darting around with his head bobbing back and forth, looking for seeds and stuff on the ground.

I thought I saw him once, too, when I was out setting rabbit snares—not real clearly, more like a shadow or a streak in the woods, moving low and close to the ground and making a strange chirping kind of noise. I told everybody about it, maybe exaggerating just a little, describing how he came up to me, twisting his head from side to side, looking at me with his beady eyes, not stopping until he was no more than three feet away. "Then," I said, "he turned his head and looked at me with just one eye, just like a real chicken." We had great fun that afternoon running along the *lake, flapping our arms and crowing like demented roosters.*

But deep down we were all just a little scared that if we behaved badly enough our parents would carry out their threats and we'd wind up just like the chicken boy.

feral children

In those days, we didn't even know any of the other stories, of which there are many, of children abandoned by their parents and brought up by wolves or wild dogs or tigers. Singh and Zingg (1942) describe 30 of these stories, 30 cases of **feral children** (wild children) like "chicken-boy." One is that of Amala and Kamala, two children reportedly dug out of a wolf's den in Northern India. They had supposedly been abandoned as infants and raised by a she-wolf. When they were dragged from the den, claim Singh and Zingg, they were as wild as any wolf. And when they had been tamed somewhat, they continued to scurry about on all fours, growling at people, refusing cooked food, gnawing on bones, and devouring raw meat. Eventually they languished and died.

But maybe we shouldn't take these stories too seriously; the evidence is not very convincing. In fact, Dennis (1941, 1951) claims he couldn't find a single *documented* case of a child actually having been raised by a wild animal. The evidence, he says, is based solely on reports of children who apparently were found with animals or in animal lairs. The identity of these children usually has been unknown, so the length of time they spent in isolation can only be guessed; and in no case has anyone actually observed them with their supposed "adoptive parents." Dennis suggests that it is likely that the so-called "wild children" were initially brain-damaged or otherwise retarded, and that this might explain why they were abandoned by their parents in the first place.

But the literature has since reported several stories of abandoned children that are more believable. One is the story of

Although there are no fully documented cases of children actually being raised by animals, some children have been neglected by parents and raised in almost total isolation. Such cases can provide researchers with important information about the interaction of heredity and environment, and about critical periods for learning things such as language.

Genie—a less dramatic story, perhaps, but no less sad. Unlike Amala and Kamala, Genie was not abandoned in the wilds. Instead, at the age of 20 months she was abandoned in a small upstairs bedroom in her own home. Except for brief periods when she was still a toddler, Genie would not leave her room from the age of 20 months to 13½ years.

Genie's room was barren and completely unfurnished, save for a small crib entirely covered with wire mesh and an infant potty. She was left in this room, day after day, alone and naked except for a sturdy leather harness strapped to her body and fastened to the potty so that she was forced to sit on it for hours at a time. At night, when she was not forgotten and left on the potty, she would be stuffed into a sleeping bag, specially made to restrain her like a straitjacket, and placed inside the crib, completely imprisoned within the wire mesh. Sometimes her father or, more rarely, her brother, would come in and feed her—almost always either baby food, soupy cereal, or a soft-boiled egg. Her father insisted that contact with her be minimal and that no one speak to her, so feeding times were extremely rushed; whoever fed her simply stuffed as much food as possible into her mouth. If she spit some of it out, her face would be rubbed in it. And if she cried or whimpered or made some other noise, perhaps with her potty or her crib, her father would come in and beat her with a stick. He never spoke to her, either; instead, he pretended he was a dog, barking and growling at her and sometimes scratching her with his fingernails. If he just wanted to threaten her, he would stand outside her door and make his most vicious dog noises.

When Genie was 13½ years old, following an especially violent fight with the father, the mother finally took her and left. Shortly after that, Genie was discovered, charges were filed against the parents, and Genie was admitted to a hospital. Genie's father committed suicide on the day he was to be brought to trial. Although Genie made some progress, her language and social development remained far below normal (see Curtiss, 1977, and Rymer, 1993, for more complete details).

the interaction of genetics and context

From a psychological point of view, Genie's story is important because it provides evidence relevant to the heredity-environment issue. Simply stated, the issue concerns the relative contributions of our genes (**heredity**, or "nature") on the one hand, and of our experiences (**environment**, or "nurture") on the other. If the question were simply one of determining which of these two forces is responsible for this characteristic or that characteristic—or for a certain percentage of this characteristic and a different

percentage of that—stories about Genie and other abandoned children would provide us with useful information. We would assume that whatever characteristics these children share with others who are brought up in more "normal" environments result from genetic influences, and that whatever "human" characteristics they failed to develop we should attribute to environmental forces. Thus we might separate the relative contributions of each to human development.

But the issue is not quite so simple, and both the questions psychologists ask and the answers they accept have changed dramatically over the years. Sternberg (1991) points out that in the 1960s, psychology accepted the idea that the reason why some children were more intelligent than others was that they had inherited more "intelligence" from their parents. However, by the 1970s, many had come to believe that intelligence is determined mainly by a child's experiences. The 1980s brought the conviction that both heredity and environment are important, but not as isolated forces—that rather it is the **interaction** between the two that is important. In Gottlieb's (1992) words:

> *The cause of development—what makes development happen—is the relationship of the two components, not the components themselves. Genes in themselves cannot cause development any more than stimulation in itself can cause development."*
> (p. 161)

what is interaction?

There are at least two different points of view with respect to what is meant by the interaction of heredity and environment (Overton, 1973): the additive model and the interactive model. The *additive* model assumes that heredity accounts for a certain percentage of the variation in a characteristic, environment for the remainder. This is the model that has governed the research and speculation of people such as Jensen (1968), who argues that approximately 80 percent of the variation in measured intelligence is accounted for by genetic factors; the remaining 20 percent is influenced by the environment. The *interactive model*, currently the more favored of the two models, argues that heredity and environment do not influence development in a linear, additive way, but interact instead. And the interaction is not always simple and highly predictable.

Consider a relationship as simple as that of water and temperature. We know that water and temperature can interact to form ice; but can we understand the hardness of ice, its taste, its effect on our skin, solely by understanding temperature and water? Is it not true that steam can also result from the interaction of water and temperature? We recognize that the interaction is more complex, but it still appears to be linear and predictable: More heat eventually equals steam; less heat eventually equals ice. Even here, however, the interaction is not quite as simple as we might think. With changes in air pressure, the interaction of water and temperature change. Now more or less heat is required for the same effect.

So, too, with genetics, context, and human behavior; interaction is not a simple additive affair. Relative contributions of heredity and environment may change with a person's age, may be different in different environments, and may vary from one individual to another.

how genes and environment interact

Quite apart from their interactive role in influencing developmental outcomes, genes and environment can influence each other directly (Lerner, 1991, 1993).

What we know of evolution makes it clear that those gene combinations that underlie adaptive behaviors are more likely to survive in our gene pools; those that are maladaptive have a poorer chance of surviving. Thus does the environment influence genes.

It is perhaps not so obvious, but no less true, that genes can also influence environment. For example, a study of 700 pairs of twins reported by Plomin (1989) provides strong evidence of a close relationship between genetic influence and measures of environmental factors. This relationship, Plomin argues, may come from two sources: First, parental characteristics that are themselves genetically influenced might determine important aspects of a child's environment. For example, parents with high IQs might provide more books for their children, might enroll them in a variety of courses, might take them on safaris, and so on. Second, children's characteristics that are genetically influenced might have a direct bearing on their environments. For example, parents might provide different experiences (hence different environments) for children with high IQs.

The story of Genie provides one example of the complexity of gene-environment interaction, specifically in the area of language development. It seems obvious that the acquisition of language is made possible by our genes. Not only have we been endowed with vocal cords, tongues, mouths, ears, brains, and other structures that make the production and the identification of speech sounds possible, but we also seem to be predisposed to acquire language early in our lives. Genie, who was not exposed to language during this sensitive early period (roughly, the early preschool years), had not learned to speak or to understand others. When she was later exposed to a normal language environment, as well as to direct language tuition, she managed to develop a small vocabulary and to acquire a limited and uncertain grasp of elementary language-production rules. But, as Curtiss (1977) points out, her development of language was far from normal.

As we saw in Chapter 2, Bronfenbrenner's ecological systems theory is based squarely on the notion that the characteristics of both the person *and* the context must be taken into account. We return to the ecology of human genetics and human contexts later in this chapter; first we take a look at the basic concepts of heredity.

basic concepts of heredity

The mechanics of heredity are complex and sometimes bewildering. But they can be simplified.

ovum, sperm, and conception

Human life begins with **conception**, the joining of the mother's **egg cell (ovum)** and the father's **sperm cell**. For new life to occur, this union is necessary; and because two people of opposite sexes are involved, it ordinarily requires a physical union between a male and a female as well—ordinarily, but not always.*

★*Conception* is also possible with **artificial insemination**, typically a clinical procedure wherein the father's sperm is introduced directly into the mother (sometimes using anonymous donor sperm, in which case the identity of the biological father may never be known). Another possibility involves inserting an ovum from a donor into a woman whose Fallopian tubes are blocked. Still another possibility involves conception completely outside the mother's body, either in another woman's body or in vitro (literally meaning "in glass"). The fertilized egg is then implanted in the mother to develop as it normally would. Surrogate mothering, in which one woman bears a child for another, is another possibility, as are fertility drugs, whose effects are typically to stimulate increased production of mature ova. None of these procedures is a certain solution for all childless couples, and none is a cure for the causes of childlessness. But when successful, they do remove the symptom: childlessness.

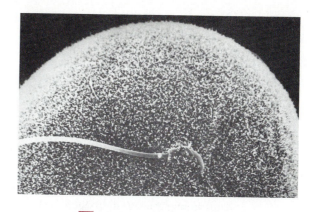

Conception, the biological beginning, occurs when a sperm cell succeeds in penetrating an ovum's relatively tough outer shell. The 23 chromosomes of which it is composed then unite with the ovum's 23 chromosomes to form the 23 pairs of chromosomes that compose an individual's entire genetic complement.

A single ovum is released by a mature and healthy woman usually once every 28 days (ordinarily between the 10th and the 18th day of her menstrual cycle). Sometimes two or more eggs released at once are fertilized, or a single fertilized egg divides, thus making possible multiple births.

Interestingly, all of a woman's ova are present in her **ovaries** at birth—perhaps as many as a million of them. They are primitive and immature, and more than half of them atrophy before puberty (the beginning of sexual maturity). Of those that remain, approximately 400 will mature and be released between puberty and menopause (cessation of menstruation). In contrast, a man produces sperm at the rate of several billion a month (200 to 300 million every four days or so) and usually continues to produce them from puberty until death.

The ovum is the largest cell in the human body—approximately 0.15 millimeters in diameter, about half the size of each period on this page. The sperm cell, by contrast, is one of the smallest cells in the body, 0.005 millimeters in diameter. The tail of each sperm cell, which is fully

12 times longer than the main part of the cell to which it is attached, enables the sperm to swim toward the ovum.

The egg cell and the sperm cell, called **gametes**, are the immediate origins of new life. Not only do they give rise to the development of a new human, but they also carry the instructions or blueprints that constitute that individual's genetic inheritance. **Genetics**, the science that studies heredity, is a complex field that is among the fastest growing of all modern disciplines. (To try to simplify it accurately in only a few pages is somewhat presumptuous. But as we have little choice, we will strive for clarity, if not for completeness.)

proteins

The basis of the living, functioning cells of which we are composed can be reduced to complicated molecules called **proteins**, which in turn are made up of different amino acids, of which 20 different kinds are known (Emery & Mueller, 1992). Amino acids are arranged in a vast number of combinations and sequences that determine the nature and function of a protein. And the number of possible combinations is astronomical. Consider that as few as the 26 letters that make up the English alphabet can be sequenced to generate new combination of sentences, paragraphs, chapters, even books—virtually indefinitely.

dna

These crucial combinations and sequences of amino acids are determined by a special code contained in a molecule called **deoxyribonucleic acid (DNA)**. This molecule has a structure resembling a spiral staircase, called a **double helix** (see Figure 3.1), in which pairs of substances are arranged in a huge variety of

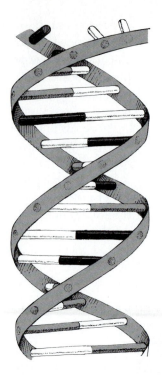

f **i g u r e   3 . 1**

DNA molecules are arranged in sequences of pairs in a spiraling, double-helix structure. Genes, the units of heredity, can be thought of as locations or addresses on a segment of DNA molecule.

sequences. In effect, the sequence of the pairs is the genetic code that determines our heredity.

chromosomes

We have two kinds of cells in our body: **sex cells** (ova or sperm) and body cells (called **somatic cells**). All normal body cells contain identical genetic information; that is, all have the same assortment of DNA molecules—the same genetic code. These DNA molecules are located on rodlike structures called **chromosomes**. Every human body cell has 23 pairs of these chromosomes. Each of us inherited one member of each pair of chromosomes from our mother and the corresponding member of each pair from our father—in other words, 23 chromosomes from each of our parents (46 chromosomes total). The division of body cells involves what is called **mitosis**, a process that results in genetically identical cells.

Unlike somatic cells, each mature sex cell (sperm and ovum) contains 23 chromosomes rather than 23 pairs. This is because the gametes (sex cells) result from a special kind of cell division termed **meiosis**, which results in daughter cells that have only half the number of chromosomes of the parent cell.

When chromosome pairs in the parent cell divide to form mature sperm (in males) or ova (in females), they do so randomly; that is, individual members of chromosome pairs wind up in any of a mind-boggling number of different possible combinations. And because there are two parents involved, the total number of different individuals that can result from a single human mating is some almost meaningless number larger than 60 trillion.*

So should we be amazed that we are so much like our parents and siblings? Not really. You see, in these over 60 trillion theoretically possible combinations there is a vast amount of redundant information, much of which is absolutely fundamental to our humanity. That information codes for, among other things, a single head, two eyes, a brain with a marvelously developed cortex, limbs, digits, and on and on.

But genetics, the science of heredity, deals less with our sameness than with our variability. It is concerned with the chemistry and the biology that account for differences among individuals of the same species.

*And this figure does not even take into account the fact that during meiosis, segments of chromosomes sometimes cross over and exchange places, thereby increasing the number of possible combinations astronomically.

sex chromosomes

Of the 23 chromosomes contained in each sperm and each ovum, one, termed the **sex chromosome**, determines whether the offspring is male or female. (The other 22 chromosomes are called **autosomes**.) As shown in Figure 3.2, the father produces two types of sperm, one type with a larger sex chromosome labeled X and one type with a smaller sex chromosome labeled Y. If the sperm that fertilizes the ovum contains an X chromosome, the offspring will be a girl; if the sperm cell contains a Y chromosome, the result will be a boy. Because the mother produces only X chromosomes, it is accurate to say that only the father's sperm can determine the sex of the offspring (a fact of which Henry VIII was unaware when he disposed of his wives for failing to give him sons).

The ratio of males to females at birth is about 105 to 100 (U.S. Bureau of the Census, 1992). But males are more susceptible to various illnesses and diseases so that, by the age of 5, there are almost as many girls as boys. By age 75, women outnumber men by about 2 to 1.

genes and their function

The units of heredity carried by the chromosomes are called **genes**. Some of our 23 chromosomes contain between 50,000 and 100,000 genes; others, especially the sex chromosomes, contain far fewer (Friedman et al., 1992). These genes, either in pairs or in complex combinations of pairs, determine our potential for inherited characteristics.

There are, for example, pairs of genes that correspond to eye color, hair characteristics, and virtually every other physical characteristic of an individual. In addition, other combinations of genes appear to be related to personality char-

f **igure 3.2**

This figure illustrates a crucial fact of which Henry VIII was unaware: Only the male sex cell, the sperm, can contain either an X or a Y sex chromosome; the ovum always contains only the X chromosome. Because an XY pairing determines that the offspring will be male (XX is female), the "failure" of Henry's wives to produce sons was really his fault.

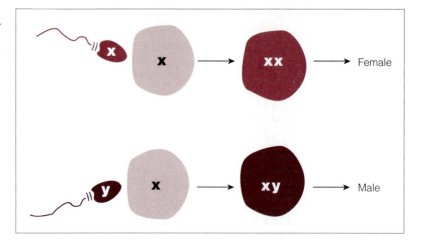

acteristics such as intelligence—although the ways in which genes affect personality are not as obvious or as easily measured as the ways in which they affect physical characteristics.

Some cases of alcoholism, too, may be genetically related.* But the story with respect to alcoholism is still not entirely clear. Certainly, there is no evidence that genes *determine* alcoholism. But it does seem likely that in at least some cases, genes predispose certain individuals to alcoholism. Given certain environmental conditions (availability of alcohol; social values that encourage alcohol consumption), these individuals are more likely to become alcoholics.

*There are at least three lines of evidence to suggest this: We know that children of alcoholics are about four times more likely to be alcoholics than are members of the general population; studies of twins have found very high concordance rates for alcoholism (*high concordance* means that when one twin has a specific characteristic, the probability is high that the other will also); and certain racial groups appear to be more prone to alcoholism, whereas others are less likely to become alcoholic.

Although environmental influences (social and cultural factors and family habits and values, for example) may account for some of the higher incidence of alcoholism for some people, a fourth source of evidence is even more convincing: There appear to be detectable, biologically based differences between alcoholic-prone and "normal" individuals. Differences have been found with respect to certain liver enzymes involved in metabolizing alcohol (Emery & Mueller, 1992), and with respect to specific brain receptors that might be associated with responses to alcohol (Blum et al., 1990).

Among many other characteristics known to be largely determined, or at least influenced, by genes are a variety of disorders, illnesses, and defects, including some forms of blindness and baldness, hemophilia, and Down syndrome. Some of these conditions are discussed later in this chapter.

Genes are arranged in corresponding pairs on chromosomes, one gene being inherited from each parent. From studies of animals and plants (particularly fruit flies and peas), as well as from observations of humans and other animals, scientists have discovered that one of the pair may be *dominant* over the other. When a **dominant gene** is paired with a corresponding **recessive gene**, the characteristics corresponding to the dominant gene will appear in the individual. We know, for example, that the gene for normally pigmented skin is dominant over the gene for albinism (unpigmented skin). Hence an individual who inherits a gene for normal skin from one parent and one for albinism from the other will nevertheless have pigmented skin. A true albino (completely unpigmented skin) inherited a recessive gene for unpigmented skin from each parent. It follows as well that two albino parents will inevi-

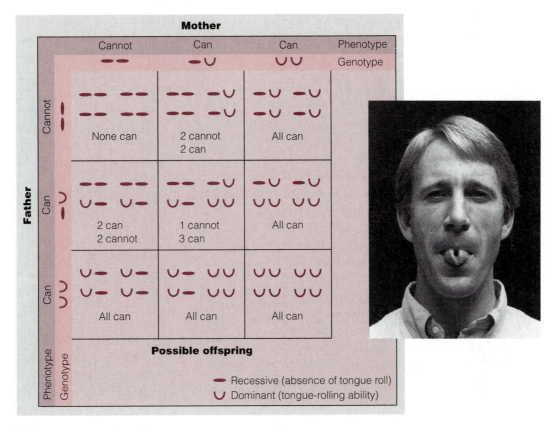

f i g u r e   3 . 3

Can you roll your tongue as shown? Because tongue-rolling ability is determined by a dominant gene, if you can roll your tongue, then either your mother or your father can, because one of them must have the dominant gene for tongue rolling. If you cannot, one or both of them might still be able to roll their tongues. All possibilities are shown in the figure.

tably produce albino children. Figure 3.3 illustrates another characteristic related to the presence of a dominant gene: the ability to roll the tongue in a particular way.

If human genetics were limited to the effects of single pairs of genes and their dominance or recessiveness, genetics would be relatively simple. In fact, however, many characteristics are a function of an undetermined number of pairs of genes acting in combination. In addition, genes are seldom completely dominant or recessive under all circumstances. Some genes appear to be dominant over a specific gene but recessive with respect to another. Furthermore, the DNA of which genes consist occasionally under-

goes *mutations*—changes that may be brought about through X rays, chemicals such as mustard gas, some drugs, or other causes.

genotype and phenotype

Your genetic makeup is your **genotype;** it consists of all the genes you have inherited from your parents. Your manifested characteristics are your **phenotype**, which can often be observed (color of hair, for example). Genotype is hidden and typically must be inferred from phenotype, although it can sometimes be determined through an examination of the matter of which genes are composed.

It's possible to make accurate inferences about genotype for characteristics determined by recessive genes, but not for those determined by dominant genes. Normally, for example, the gene for brown eyes is dominant over that for blue eyes. Therefore we can infer that individuals whose phenotype (manifested characteristics) includes blue eyes must have two recessive genes for blue eyes (genotype). On the other hand, we can't be certain about the genotype for brown-eyed individuals because they might have either two dominant genes for brown eyes or a dominant gene for brown eyes and a recessive gene for blue eyes (see Figure 3.4).

The effects of genotype on phenotype are not quite so simple as the eye-color illustration implies. In fact, most human characteristics, including eye color, are usually polygenic, the result of combinations of genes. The effects of polygenetic determination are not either/or (for example, either blue or brown), but include a whole range of possibilities. Thus it is that individuals are not simply blue or brown-eyed, but can also have eyes that are green or hazel or blue-green, or any variety of other shades.

According to Plomin (1987), three conclusions summarize the relationship between genotype (inherited genetic structure) and phenotype (manifested characteristics):

■ First, it is clear that genotypic differences lead to phenotypic differences. People whose parents are blue-eyed are far more likely to be blue-eyed than those whose parents are dark-eyed.

■ Second, characteristics that are influenced by more than one gene tend not to be dichotomous (either/or) but are distributed in a manner that approximates what is referred to as the **normal curve** (a bell-shaped curve in which the majority of cases cluster near the average, with fewer and fewer cases occurring farther and farther from the average). For example, height is influenced by genetic makeup, but most people aren't extremely tall or extremely short; instead, most are average, with few people at the farthest extremes.

■ The environment also has important effects on manifested characteristics. Height reflects not only genetic influences but also environmental conditions such as nutrition and health.

f i g u r e   3 . 4

Phenotype (manifested characteristics) is influenced by genotype (genetic makeup). But genotype cannot always be inferred from phenotype. A brown-eyed person might have two genes for brown eyes or just one, with a recessive gene for blue eyes.

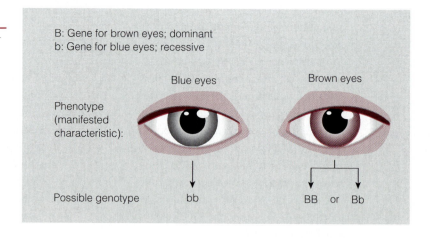

B: Gene for brown eyes; dominant
b: Gene for blue eyes; recessive

Blue eyes   Brown eyes

Phenotype
(manifested
characteristic):

Possible genotype   bb   BB   or   Bb

For some characteristics, a person's environment makes a great deal of difference (in language learning, for example); for others, it makes little apparent difference (for eye color, for example). That is, some manifested characteristics seem to correspond much more closely to underlying genetic material than do others. These characteristics, which are less affected by environmental forces, are said to reflect a higher degree of **canalization** (Waddington, 1975). For characteristics that are not highly canalized, phenotype may be very different from what might have been predicted on the basis of genetic makeup alone. Eye color is a highly canalized characteristic; it typically corresponds to genotype and is unaffected by environment. In contrast, many complex intellectual abilities (the ability to learn several languages, for example) do not appear to be highly canalized but are highly affected by experience. In evolutionary terms, canalization may be seen as a genetic tendency toward a predictable regularity that ensures that individuals of one species will be much more similar than dissimilar.

THE EPIGENETIC LANDSCAPE

Figure 3.5 presents Waddington's (1975) *epigentic landscape*, an analogy he uses to illustrate the relationship of genetic and environmental forces in development. In this model, genetic forces are represented by the valleys and contours that run down the landscape; the tilt of the landscape represents environmental forces; and the ball represents some characteristic of the developing organism. Where the ball ends up represents the final state of that characteristic.

The analogy makes several important points. First, shifts (different tilts) in the environment can change the ball's path and dramatically affect the final outcome; second, for highly canalized traits (deeper channels), far greater environmental forces (changes in tilt) will be needed to influence the final outcome; and third, subtle environmental forces are more likely to affect the course of development early (at the top of the figure) rather than late in development (at the bottom of the figure, where all channels are deeper).

REACTION RANGE

Even for highly canalized characteristics, phenotype (manifested charac-

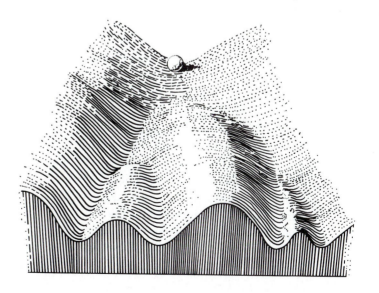

teristics) seldom results only from predetermined genetic influences, but is usually influenced by environmental factors as well; that is, **epigenesis**, the unfolding of genetically influenced characteristics, is brought about by the interaction of genes and environment. In a sense, it is as though genetic influences (genotypes) make possible a range of different outcomes, some more probable than others. As these genetic influences interact with environmental forces, the outcomes become manifest (phenotypic).

Gottesman (1974) introduces the concept of **reaction range** to illustrate this interaction. Simply stated, the reaction range for a particular characteristic includes all the possible outcomes for that characteristic given variations in the nature and timing of environmental influences. Take, as an example, the case of height, which is at least partly determined by genetics. Although Robert's genes might be such that his most probable adult height will be 6 feet, given exceptional nutrition and exercise, Robert might end up being 6 feet 8 inches tall and a star basketball player. On the other hand, given inadequate nutrition and early ill-health, Robert might end up being only 5 feet 6 inches. Thus does the environment interact with genotype to determine which of the many possible outcomes—that is, which *reaction* from the *range* of all possible reactions—will be manifested.

The existence of a reaction range for any given characteristic makes it possible for the same genotype to give rise to very different outcomes (different phenotypes). By the same token, highly similar phenotypes need not reflect identical genotypes. One of the important tasks of the psychologist is to determine the nature and timing of experiences that are most likely to have a beneficial influence on phenotype.

molecular genetics

Mendelian genetics, named after Gregor Mendel, the nineteenth-century Austrian monk who first discovered the secrets of genes, makes inferences about the dominance and recessiveness of genes largely by looking at the characteristics of parents and of offspring. In contrast, **molecular genetics** studies heredity by looking at the actual structures of genes. The techniques of molecular genetics make it possible to examine chromosomes directly, to look at sequences of DNA molecules, to identify their specific chemical components, and to locate chemical segments that correspond to genes.

How is this done? Among the important techniques that have come out of molecular genetics is the use of certain enzymes that essentially cut sequences of DNA apart (see Wingerson, 1990). When two individuals have identical DNA sequences, the length of the resulting fragments will be identical; but if the sequences are different, the resulting fragments will be of different lengths (called *restriction fragment length polymorphisms*, or RFLP's). Thus RFLP's (pronounced "riff-lips") allow geneticists to identify the genes on specific chromosomes that are associated with the presence or absence of some observable characteristic. These genes, termed **marker genes**, are common to the general population; they are normally found in all individuals (Emery & Mueller, 1992).

Marker genes have now been discovered for all chromosomes, and they continue to be discovered at the rate of two or more a month. Some examples are marker genes for Huntington's disease and for some forms of schizophrenia (Loehlin, Willerman, & Horn, 1988), and for manic-depression (Egeland et al., 1987).

For traits that result from the effects of a large number of genes, it's possible to use a large number of RFLP's to begin to sort out genetic contributions. The approach is complex but extremely promising. It offers the possibility not only of discovering the location and composition of DNA sequences that underlie human traits and genetic defects, but perhaps also of correcting defective genes—or, at the very least, of identifying their presence early, perhaps even before conception.

By the early 1990s, more than 2,000 genes had been identified and assigned to specific locations, but more than 95 percent of our genes remain unmapped (Friedman et al., 1992). The goal of a massive federally funded genetics project now underway in the United States is to provide eventually a complete genetic map of the human being—a map of what is termed the *genome*, the complete set of genetic instructions contained in our cells (Bishop & Waldholz, 1990).

The implications of success in this endeavor are staggering. Correcting genetic defects might be possible, and so could accurately predicting the outcome of different gene pairings. What comes next? Does medicine play God? Do governments engineer genes to produce the kinds of people they want? Do chromosomal tests become mandatory? Do such tests become part of who we are, like our Social Security numbers?

genetic defects

In addition to their role in determining the course of normal development and in assuring that we are more alike than different, genes are also sometimes responsible for certain diseases and defects. In most cases, these disorders are linked with recessive rather than dominant genes. The reason for this is simple: Any abnormality that is linked with a domi-

nant gene will always be manifested in all individuals with that gene and will have relatively little chance of being passed on to offspring (particularly if it leads to early death). In contrast, abnormalities that are linked to recessive genes will be manifested only in individuals who have inherited a recessive gene from both of their parents. Many individuals may be carriers of a single recessive gene for some abnormality, without manifesting the abnormality. Their offspring will, likewise, not manifest the abnormality unless both parents carry the relevant recessive gene and each passes it on to the offspring.

defects resulting from genetically related parents

The risk of genetic disorders among the children of genetically related parents is considerably higher than for children whose parents are not related: If genetic disorders linked to a recessive gene are present in a family, matings among family members will have a higher probability of producing offspring with a pair of the recessive genes (or groups of genes) in question. In contrast, if a member of this family who is a carrier of the recessive gene mates with someone outside the family who does not carry the gene, there is only one chance in four that any one offspring will inherit the gene and no chance that this offspring will manifest the disorder (because the gene is recessive). Thus continued matings between individuals who are not genetically related may, over several generations, eventually succeed in eradicating or greatly reducing the prevalence of the recessive gene in question. By the same token, continued matings between family members might lead to a proliferation of the gene and a corresponding increase in the manifestation of the disorder it un-

Hemophilia-A is a sex-linked recessive genetic disorder. Males who carry the recessive gene on their X chromosome are always affected: Their blood-clotting mechanisms don't work properly, and they run the risk of dying from untreated bruises, cuts, or internal bleeding. Females who carry the recessive gene on one X chromosome typically also have the normal dominant gene on the other X chromosome; thus they don't suffer from the disease, but they can pass the defective gene on to their children. Many members of the royal families of nineteenth-century Europe carried the gene. Queen Victoria of England was a carrier, and so were two of her daughters (Figure 3.6).

f i g u r e   3 . 6

Descendants of Queen Victoria, showing female carriers and affected males.

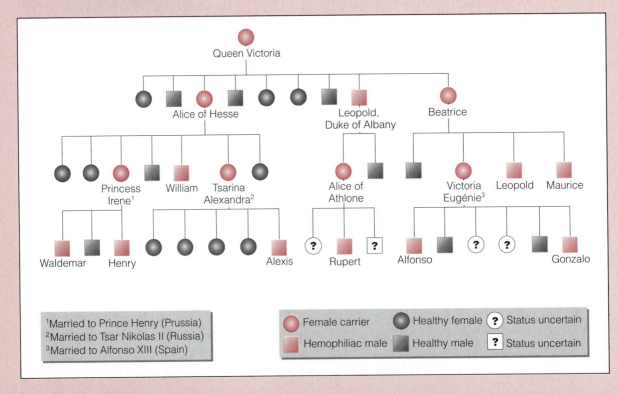

¹Married to Prince Henry (Prussia)
²Married to Tsar Nikolas II (Russia)
³Married to Alfonso XIII (Spain)

Female carrier   Healthy female   **?** Status uncertain
Hemophiliac male   Healthy male   **?** Status uncertain

derlies (see "At A Glance: Hemophilia Among European Royalty" and Figure 3.6).

Huntington's disease

Most very serious or fatal genetic disorders, as just noted, are linked to recessive genes; if they were associated with dominant genes, all carriers would be affected and would either die before having children or would be aware of the risks involved and refrain from parenthood. One exception to this general rule, however, is **Huntington's disease** (also called Huntington's chorea), a disease that is both fatal and associated with a dominant gene. The disorder is still present because it does not ordinarily manifest itself until the age of 30 or 40. When it does appear, it leads to rapid neurological deterioration and eventual death.

Until recently there was no way of determining whether an individual carried the dominant gene for Huntington's disease. Thus people whose grandparents, parents, uncles and aunts, or siblings had cases of Huntington's could only wait to discover whether the disease would eventually strike them too. Now, however, using the RLFP technology described earlier, geneticists have succeeded in locating the gene for the disorder, making it possible to determine relatively accurately the probability that an individual will be affected (Hayden, 1992). However, because Huntington's disease is still incurable—and fatal—many individuals who might be carriers of the gene prefer not to be screened. A survey by Jacopini et al. (1992) found that fewer than half of those who knew they were at risk intended to take advantage of the screening available to them. However, as for other genetically based disorders, there exists the possibility of eventually being able to replace this defective DNA sequence with a normal gene.

sickle-cell anemia

Sickle-cell anemia is a genetic disorder linked to a recessive gene (Figure 3.7). In the United States, approximately 10 percent of all African-Americans, and a much lower proportion of whites, carry the recessive gene for sickle-cell anemia (Snyder, Freifelder, & Hartl, 1985). These 10 percent are **heterozygous** for this gene (having one normal and one abnormal gene); another 0.25 percent of the African-American population are **homozygous** recessive individuals (carrying two defective genes). Effects of the defective gene are clearly apparent in abnormally shaped red blood cells (sickle-shaped, rather than circular), which multiply with lack of oxygen (Figure 3.8). Sickle-shaped cells tend to clot together and thus carry even less oxygen, thereby

figure 3.7

Sickle-cell anemia is linked to a recessive gene. In this illustration, parents are heterozygous (each possesses both the normal gene, which is dominant, and the sickle-cell gene, which is recessive) and therefore neither parent suffers from the disease. As shown, there is a 1 in 4 chance that the offspring of such parents will inherit two defective genes and suffer from the disease.

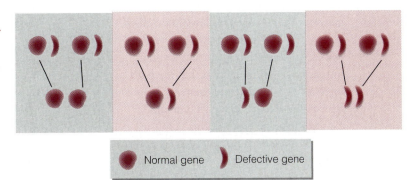

Normal gene   Defective gene

The slide shows normal, oxygenated red blood cells (circular), and abnormal, sickle-shaped cells (flattened and curved).

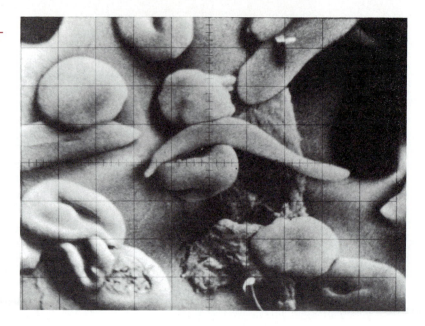

increasing in number and reducing oxygen still more. Individuals who are homozygous recessive for this gene often die in childhood or are severely ill throughout life; those who are heterozygous for the gene are ordinarily healthy except in conditions of low oxygen such as at high altitudes; there they may become quite ill, indicating that the normal gene is not completely dominant.

The fact that sickle-cell anemia is so common among blacks, particularly in Central African coastal areas (40 percent heterozygous and 4 percent homozygous recessive), would, on the surface, appear to be a contradiction of evolutionary theory; we would expect the presence of the sickle-cell gene to have disappeared over generations. However, following the discovery that individuals who are heterozygous for sickle-cell trait are also resistant to malaria, it becomes clear that the high incidence of this defective gene in malaria-prone areas is, in fact, a dramatic example of ongoing evolution. Not surprisingly, incidence of the disease is now decreasing among African-Americans.

p k u

Phenylketonuria (PKU) is a genetic defect associated with the presence of two recessive genes. In individuals suffering from this disease, the liver enzyme responsible for breaking down the amino acid phenylalanine into usable substances (tyrosine, skin pigments, and neurotransmitters) is absent or inactive. Infants who inherit two recessive genes for PKU appear normal at birth, but with the continued ingestion of phenylalanine (which makes up about 5 percent of ingested protein by weight) their nervous system deteriorates irreversibly, and they become increasingly mentally retarded. Fortunately, however, PKU is easily detected at birth, and its onset can be prevented by providing children with diets low in phenylalanine from infancy (Friedman et al., 1992). Here, then, is a disorder that is clearly genetic, but that does not become manifest until the occurrence of specific environmental events (ingestion of phenylalanine). Furthermore, in the absence of these environmental influences (that is, given a diet low in phenyl-alanine), the individual's genotype (presence of relevant recessive genes) will not be reflected in the phenotype (manifested characteristics).

other genetic defects

There are many other genetic defects; in fact, several thousand have now been identified and catalogued (Friedman, Dill, & Hayden, 1992). Some of these, like Huntington's disease, are associated with a dominant gene; others, like sickle-cell anemia, result from the presence of two recessive genes. Still others are multifactorial: They result from genetic factors in combination with either prenatal or postnatal exposure to environmental factors, such as the ingestion of phenylalanine by individuals who carry the genes for PKU.

TAY-SACHS DISEASE

Another disorder caused by a recessive gene is **Tay-Sachs disease**, an enzyme disorder that results in the brain's inability to break down certain fats. Eventually these build up, preventing neural transmission and leading to the degeneration of brain cells. Affected individuals commonly die before the age of three. Although the gene for Tay-Sachs disease can be detected, the disease cannot yet be prevented or cured.

MUSCULAR DYSTROPHY (MD)

A degenerative muscular disorder of which there are various forms, **muscular dystrophy (MD)**, is often linked to a recessive gene or is multifactorial. It usually involves an inability to walk and may lead to death. Some forms of MD (for example, *Duchenne/Becker MD*) can be detected in fetuses by genetic screening. In addition, parents can be tested to arrive at an estimate of the probability that their

offspring will be affected (Cortada, Milsark, & Richards, 1990).

NEURAL TUBE DEFECTS

Among the most common congenital malformations are **neural tube defects**, which occur at a rate of 1 for every 500 to 1,000 births (Miller et al., 1990). Neural tube defects may take the form of *spina bifida*, in which the spine remains open at the bottom, or of *anencephaly*, in which portions of the skull and brain are absent. Such defects often lead to severe retardation or death. Although genetically linked, the causes of these defects are multifactorial. They generally develop very early in pregnancy (as early as the first week) and can be detected by means of an **AFP test**—a standard test conducted at about the 13th week of pregnancy to ascertain the level of *alpha-fetoprotein* in the mother's blood. If this substance is present in higher-than-normal concentrations, additional tests such as ultrasound or fetoscopy (described later) are performed to determine whether or not there is a neural tube defect. In some jurisdictions, AFP screening is routine or even mandatory (as are tests for PKU).

DIABETES MELLITUS

Some forms of **diabetes**, an insulin-deficiency disease, are associated with recessive genes, as well as with other factors. Children born to mothers with diabetes mellitus have a 2 to 3 times higher risk of birth defects, which can include limb deformities, cardiac problems, neural tube defects, and other problems (Friedman, 1992).

NONMEDICAL CONDITIONS

In addition to the several thousand known medical conditions that are clearly genetically linked, there is increasing evidence of a genetic basis for at least some manifestations of emotional and behavior problems such as alcoholism, depression, anorexia nervosa, infantile autism, and schizophrenia (Loehlin et al., 1988). For some of these conditions, specific marker genes have been located. However, their causes are usually multifactorial; accordingly, they are highly susceptible to environmental influence.

chromosomal disorders

Genetic defects are linked to specific recessive or dominant genes, or to a combination of genes; they may also be related to certain environmental conditions. **Chromosomal disorders**, on the other hand, are associated not with specific genes but with errors in chromosomes. Many of these errors result from improper divisions and recombinations during meiosis.

down syndrome

Down syndrome is the most common chromosomal birth defect. About 1 out of every 680 live births has Down syndrome, but about twice that many fetuses are affected by the condition, approximately half resulting in spontaneous miscarriages during the first third of pregnancy (Dill & McGillivray, 1992).

Some children with Down syndrome have characteristic loose folds of skin over the corners of the eyes, producing an Oriental appearance; hence the now uncommon label *mongolism*. Also, mental retardation is common among children with Down syndrome, and their language development is often retarded. Not all children are equally affected.

Most cases of Down syndrome are due to failure of the 21st pair of chromosomes to separate during meiosis (a phenomenon termed *nondisjunction*). Hence the resulting gamete (sex cell) has an extra copy

The most common chromosomal birth defect is Down syndrome (trisomy 21), which is far more common among children of older mothers. Possible manifestations of Down syndrome include Oriental facial characteristics (hence the no-longer-used term mongolism) and slower mental development. Symptoms vary considerably in severity.

of the 21st chromosome. When this gamete (sex cell) is combined with the other gamete during fertilization, the zygote (fertilized egg) has an extra 21st chromosome (thus the alternative medical label, **trisomy 21**). A smaller number of cases are due to *translocation* of chromosome 21 material to another chromosome (Emery, 1984).

DOWN SYNDROME AND MOTHER'S AGE

Because nondisjunction of the 21st chromosome typically occurs during meiosis of the ovum rather than of the sperm, Down syndrome is usually associated with the mother rather than the father. Increased probability of producing a child with Down syndrome is closely associated with the age of the mother, with the incidence ranging from 1 in 1,420 for women in their early 20s to about 1 in 30 for women aged 45 (Dill & McGillivray, 1992; see Figure 3.9). The age of the father also appears to be linked with a higher incidence of Down syndrome, with men ages 50 to 55 having a 20 to 30 percent greater chance of fathering children with Down syndrome (Erickson & Bjerkedal, 1981). In these instances, disjunction failure would usually occur during meiosis of the sperm, rather than of the egg.

f **i g u r e   3 . 9**

The probability of Down syndrome and other chromosome abnormalities in newborns increases dramatically with the age of the mother. Source: Based on Friedman (1992).

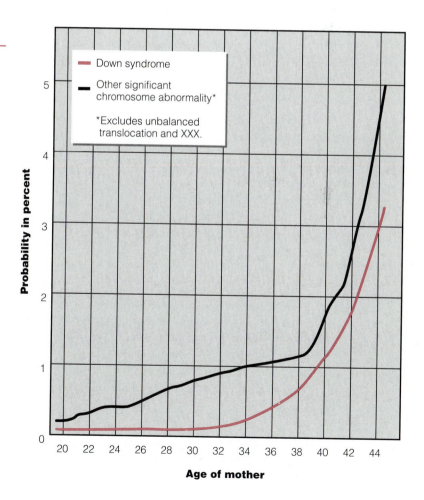

Because medical science knows precisely what the genetic cause of Down syndrome is, it is possible to detect its presence in the fetus before birth. Procedures for doing so are discussed later in this chapter.

DOWN SYNDROME AND ALZHEIMER'S DISEASE

The extra 21st chromosome that is present in Down syndrome has led to an important discovery with respect to **Alzheimer's disease**, some forms of which appear to be inherited ("Test can predict . . . ," 1993). Alzheimer's is a disease of later life (usually appearing between ages 40 and 80) whose principal symptoms include progressive loss of memory and eventual deterioration of brain function leading to death. Physiologically, it involves a tangling and plaquing of nerve fibers. These plaques are composed primarily of *amyloid filaments.* Investigators noticed that middle-aged individuals with Down syndrome typically display the same development of amyloid filaments as Alzheimer's patients. Further research revealed that the gene that underlies the production of amyloid is located on the 21st chromosome (Goldgaber et al., 1987). It appears that, at least in some cases, Alzheimer's may result from a defective gene on the 21st chromosome.

abnormalities of the sex chromosomes

A number of chromosomal defects involve the sex chromosomes. Some involve the absence of a chromosome; others involve the presence of an extra chromosome.

TURNER'S SYNDROME

Turner's syndrome affects 1 out of 2,500 female children (Dill & McGilliv-ray, 1992). These children are born with a missing sex chromosome, a condition given the shorthand notation 45,X (or 45, XO).* Most such children are aborted spontaneously; those that survive typically have underdeveloped secondary sexual characteristics, although this is not evident until puberty. Possible signs of the disorder include (1) swelling in the extremities that disappears with age, leaving loose folds of skin (webbing), particularly in the neck region, fingers, and toes, and (2) short stature. Mental ability is usually normal. Injections of the female sex hormone estrogen before puberty are sometimes helpful in bringing about greater sexual maturation, although Turner's syndrome females are sterile (Emery & Mueller, 1992).

KLINEFELTER'S SYNDROME

Another chromosomal aberration linked to a sex chromosome involves the presence of an extra X chromosome in a male child (47, XXY) and is called **Klinefelter's syndrome**. It is considerably more common than Turner's syndrome (1 out of 1,000 males; Dill & McGillivray, 1992) and is marked by the presence of both male and female secondary sexual characteristics. Children suffering from this disorder typically have small, undeveloped testicles, more highly developed breasts than is common among boys, high-pitched voices, and little or no facial hair after puberty. Therapy with the male sex hormone testosterone is often effective in improving the development of masculine characteristics and in increasing sex drive (Johnson et al., 1970). Without therapy, many children suffering from Klinefelter's syndrome remain infertile throughout life. Also, incidence of

*The number indicates the total number of chromosomes; the letters refer to the sex chromosomes present. Thus a normal male is denoted 46,XY.

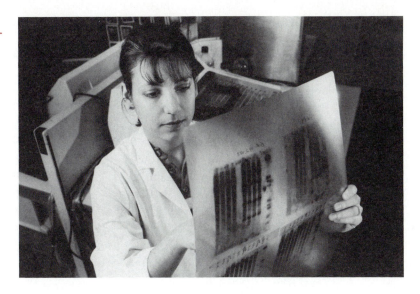

Mapping of fetal chromosomes enables researchers to identify disorders linked directly to the presence or absence of known genes; mapping of parental chromosomes sometimes makes it possible to determine the probability that their offspring will inherit specific characteristics.

schizophrenia is higher among Klinefelter's children (Friedman & McGillivray, 1992).

XYY MALES

Males with an extra Y chromosome (47, XYY), sometimes referred to as "super males" because of the extra Y chromosome, are characteristically tall; sometimes they are also of lower than average intelligence. Some research has linked this syndrome with criminality, but the conclusion remains tentative and premature (Emery & Mueller, 1992). However, XYY males are often less mature and more impulsive than normal.

FRAGILE X SYNDROME

Fragile X syndrome is the most common cause of *inherited* mental retardation (Wolf-Schein, 1992). Note that Down syndrome, which accounts for more cases of mental retardation, is not inherited in the sense that corresponding genes are transmitted from parents to children; it results instead from an abnormality in how chromosomes divide.

In fragile X syndrome, the X chromosome is abnormally compressed or even

broken. Although the condition can also occur in females, it is far more common among males and is one of the reasons why there are more mentally retarded males than females in the general population (Zigler & Hodapp, 1991). Interestingly, about 70 percent of females with fragile X syndrome are of normal intelligence; this is the case for only about 20 percent of affected males (Dill & McGillivray, 1992). In addition, about 12 percent of autistic children have this syndrome (Wolf-Schein, 1992).

Unlike Down syndrome, in which mental retardation is typically apparent very early in life, fragile X individuals often manifest no symptoms of retardation until puberty (Silverstein & Johnston, 1990). Between the years of 10 and 15, however, there is frequently a marked decline in intellectual functioning.

OTHER SEX-LINKED DEFECTS

Fragile X syndrome is a *sex-linked* defect; the genes that underlie its manifestation are located on the X chromosome. This chromosome is also the site for genes relating to various other defects, such as night-blindness, baldness, and hemophilia. Each of these defects is associated with recessive genes, and each, like fragile X syndrome, is more often manifested among males than females. Why? Simply because females who inherit the defective gene on one of their two X chromosomes often have the corresponding *normal* gene on the other chromosome. As a result, they are *carriers* of the defective gene, but they do not manifest it (because it is recessive). Males, on the other hand, have only one X chromosome; the other sex chromosome is a Y. In many cases, the normal dominant gene that would counter the effect of the recessive gene for one of these disorders is not present on the Y chromosome. Accordingly, males manifest conditions such as hereditary baldness and fragile X syndrome far more often than do females. Yet the gene is passed on from mother to son—not from father to son—because it is the father who always passes on a Y chromosome to his sons, and the mother who always passes on the X chromosome.

identifying and dealing with genetic risk

Medical advances, coupled with improved nutrition, have greatly reduced the number of infectious diseases and nutritional deficiencies for which children are hospitalized (Emery & Mueller, 1992). Now, about 1 in 20 children admitted to hospitals suffer from problems that are at least partly genetic in origin.

For disorders that are linked directly to the presence or absence of known genes, it is sometimes possible to identify affected children before birth. For other disorders whose origins are only partly genetic or for which the genetic contributions are complex and not completely known, it is nevertheless often possible to determine the *probability* that a child will be affected.

prenatal diagnosis

Fetal diagnosis is the assessment of aspects of the condition of the unborn. There are six principal techniques for fetal diagnosis: amniocentesis, chorionic villus sampling (CVS), ultrasound, fetoscopy, radiography, and preimplantation diagnosis.

AMNIOCENTESIS

In **amniocentesis**, a hollow needle is inserted into the amniotic fluid surrounding the fetus, allowing a physician to obtain 15 to 20 ml of fluid. This fluid contains fetal cells, which are then examined to reveal the absence of chromosomes or the presence of extra chromosomes. In addition, the blood type of the fetus and the chemical composition of the amniotic fluid may be determined, which may provide evidence of other diseases that might affect the unborn child. Because the procedure involves a slight risk of infection and leads to miscarriages in from 0.5 to 1 percent of cases, it is commonly used only when the pregnant woman is older and when there is a probability of fetal abnormality or other complications. Amniocentesis is not usually performed until the 15th to 17th week of pregnancy (Gilmore & Aitken, 1989).

One of the most common uses of amniocentesis has been for the detection of trisomy 21 (Down syndrome). Because of the moderate risks associated with the procedure, and because incidence of trisomy 21 increases dramatically with age (see Figure 3.9), the procedure is most commonly used when the mother is 35 or older or when a younger mother is known to be at risk. However, because about 95 percent of pregnant women are under 35, initial screening by age alone misses about 80 percent of Down syndrome fetuses (Kloza, 1990).

Fortunately, there is now another way of identifying women who are at higher risk of bearing a child with Down syndrome. Specifically, it has been discovered that the level of *alpha-fetoprotein* (AFP) in the pregnant woman's blood is significantly lower than normal. (Recall that AFP levels are routinely assessed to detect the likelihood of neural tube defects, with higher than normal levels indicating a higher probability of problems.) Thus AFP tests, claims Kloza (1990), can significantly increase detection of Down syndrome babies among younger mothers.

CHORIONIC VILLUS SAMPLING (CVS)

Chorionic villus sampling (CVS, or chorion biopsy) is another medical procedure for obtaining and examining fetal cells. In CVS, a plastic tube is inserted through the vagina (or a fine needle through the abdomen) to obtain a sample of the chorion (Liu, 1991). The chorion is a precursor of the placenta and contains the same genetic information as the fetus. The advantage of a chorion biopsy over amniocentesis is that it can be performed as early as seven weeks after conception. Also, because it provides enough fetal cells, chromosomal examination can usually be performed the same day (Young, 1991). (Amniocentesis, on the other hand, requires a two- to three-week period of tissue culture.) If the results lead to a decision to terminate the pregnancy, this can be accomplished more simply and more safely in the first trimester of pregnancy. (Amniocentesis does not provide results until well into the second trimester of pregnancy.)

Chorion biopsy procedures are somewhat more experimental than amniocen-

tesis and carry a slightly higher risk of complications—loss of the fetus in about 3 to 4 percent of cases (Gilmore & Aitken, 1989).

ULTRASOUND

Ultrasound (sometimes called sonogram) uses sound waves to provide an image of a fetus. It is among the least harmful and least traumatic of techniques currently available, and is also the method of choice for demonstrating that a fetus is alive. In addition, it is the most exact means for estimating fetal age, detecting the position of the fetus, discerning changes in fetal position, detecting multiple pregnancies, and identifying a variety of growth disorders and malformations. Ultrasound images of the fetus in "real time" make it possible to see the beginnings of fetal activity, including behaviors such as thumb sucking. They also allow the physician to examine bone structure, to assess length of bones, to determine relationships among the size of various body structures, and even to count fingers and toes. Ultrasound is always used with amniocentesis or CVS to guide the physician, but is not a substitute for these procedures because it cannot provide samples of fetal cells.

FETOSCOPY

Fetoscopy is a surgical procedure that allows the physician to see the fetus by means of instruments inserted through the vagina. It is used mainly to obtain samples of tissues from the fetus itself, the most important being blood. Fetoscopy can furnish the physician with important information about the status of the fetus, especially when there is a possibility of disorders such as hemophilia (Golbus, 1982; Rodeck, 1982). However, it carries higher risks than amniocentesis—about a 3 to 5 percent higher probability of miscarriage (Emery & Mueller, 1992).

RADIOGRAPHY

Some inherited disorders and malformations can be diagnosed through **radiography**—that is, by means of X rays of the fetus. However, because of the possibility that X rays may harm the fetus, sonograms are used instead whenever possible.

PREIMPLANTATION DIAGNOSIS

All the fetal diagnostic techniques discussed so far can be carried out only after the fetus has begun to develop. However, it is now possible to determine the chromosomal structure of the fetus *before* the fertilized egg has implanted. One way of doing this is to remove a mature egg and fertilize it with the father's sperm (in-vitro fertilization) (Emery & Mueller, 1992). The zygote is allowed to multiply to the eight-cell stage, and then a single cell is removed and examined for the presence of specific genetic disorders—all within a matter of hours. Removal of a single cell apparently does not affect subsequent development. If no defects are found, the zygote can then be implanted in the uterus.

Preimplantation diagnosis brings with it the great advantage that it can identify problems before a therapeutic abortion would otherwise be necessary. However, its use is still limited to a handful of advanced, highly specialized medical centers.

treating genetic disorders

Not all genetically based disorders are equally serious. Many can be treated and controlled; some can be cured. For example, the effects of PKU, as previously noted, can be prevented through diet. And in Chapter 4 we see how the effects of Rh incompatibility in the fetus, once a usually fatal condition, can be prevented through inoculation of the mother or re-

versed through blood transfusions. For other conditions, it is sometimes possible to replace deficient enzymes, proteins, vitamins, or other substances (the use of insulin to control diabetes, for example). Similarly, various drugs or even surgery may be used to control and sometimes to cure genetic diseases (cancer, for example).

Emery and Mueller (1992) suggest that in addition to these (and other) medical treatments, there are several other possible though not yet proven treatments. One involves the use of clones (identical copies) of normal genes to replace those that are defective; another is the use of viruses or even of antibiotics to eradicate bacteria or other agents involved in the development of genetically linked diseases.

genetic counseling

Although prenatal (and preimplantation) diagnosis, along with techniques for monitoring changes in the mother, provide powerful tools for detecting potential problems, there are many genetically based problems that cannot always be detected with absolute certainty. In many cases, however, it's possible to estimate the probability of a given outcome. In such cases, parents and physicians may be faced with difficult decisions involving serious ethical questions. In these situations, genetic counseling offers a needed service.

Genetic counseling is a branch of medicine and of psychology that attempts to provide counsel to physicians and parents. Such counseling typically strives to assess the probability of a defect's occurrence, its likely seriousness, the extent to which it can be treated or even reversed, and the best courses of action to follow once a decision has been made about whether or not to have a child. In many instances, genetic counseling takes place before conception and takes into account the age and health of the mother and the presence of genetic abnormalities in the mother's and father's families. In other cases, genetic counseling occurs after conception (see Table 3.1).

In spite of the availability of genetic counseling in a number of medical, research, university, and community centers, there is still a relatively widespread lack of knowledge about such counseling on the part of physicians and potential clients alike. In addition, psychological

t **able 3.1**

Probability of some common genetic defects

GENETIC DEFECT	INCIDENCE (PER 100 POPULATION)	SEX RATIO (M:F)	NORMAL PARENTS HAVING A SECOND AFFECTED CHILD (%)	AFFECTED PARENT HAVING AN AFFECTED CHILD (%)	AFFECTED PARENT HAVING A SECOND AFFECTED CHILD (%)
Asthma	3–4	1:1	10	26	—*
Cerebral palsy	.2	3:2	1	—	—
Cleft palate only	.04	2:3	2	7	15
Cleft lip and/or cleft palate	.1	3:2	4	4	10
Club foot	.1	2:1	3	3	10
Congenital heart disease (all types)	.5	1:1	1–4	1–4	10
Diabetes mellitus (juvenile, insulin-dependent)	.2	1:1	6	1–2	—
Dislocation of hip	.7	1:6	6	12	36
Epilepsy ("idiopathic")	.5	1:1	5	5	10
Hydrocephalus	.005	1:1	3	—	—
Manic-depressive psychosis	.4	2:3	10–15	10–15	—
Mental retardation (of unknown cause)	.3–.5	1:1	3–5	10	20
Profound childhood deafness	.1	1:1	10	8	—
Schizophrenia	1–2	1:1	10	16	—
Spina bifida (neural tube defect)	.3	2:3	5	4	—
Tracheo-esophageal fistula	.03	1:1	1	1	—

*— means no data available
Source: Adapted from A. E. Emery & R. F. Mueller, *Elements of medical genetics* (8th ed.). Edinburgh and London: Churchill-Livingstone, 1992. Used by permission.

barriers such as fear, social stigma, religious values, and financial considerations can limit the use of genetic counseling and reduce its effectiveness even when it is available.

Prenatal diagnosis can also present some potential for abuse. (See "In Other Contexts: Chang Yu-ju, An Only Child.) In the Ganxiao district of Hubei Province in northern China, as elsewhere in China, parents take tremendous pride in male children. Accordingly, government regulations limiting parents to a single child have led to the widespread killing of baby girls. In addition, many parents are having the sex of the fetus determined before birth so that female fetuses can be aborted. As a result, by 1983 there were as many as five boys for every girl under the age of 5 in Ganxiao district ("China fears sexual imbalance," 1983).

genetics and the future

Genetic counseling has traditionally been limited to advising prospective parents about the likelihood of their having a child with a given problem and providing them with information about their options. And the options have typically consisted of deciding to try to conceive or not to, or of deciding to have a therapeutic abortion or not to. It may be different in the very near future.

We now appear to be on the threshold of a new age. Almost daily there are new discoveries in genetics. Scientists are now able to detect genetic weaknesses, as well as strengths, from the very earliest moments of life. Our mushrooming knowledge of cell biology at the molecular level is opening new doors into the vast and almost uncharted world of genetic engineering. Science is breaking the genetic code; it's learning to read the messages that direct the arrangements of the amino acids that, in turn, define the structure

and function of the protein molecules that are the fundamental units of our biological lives. Science has begun to experiment with ways of altering genetic messages, of rewriting the code either to enhance the possibilities implicit in our genes or to correct errors. Using recombinant DNA techniques, scientists can use bacteria to reproduce sequences of genetic material. The results include new medications, new refining and manufacturing processes, new products, even new lives.

Pergament (1990) suggests that the following developments are possible, perhaps even highly probable, in the twenty-first century:

- By 2001 it will be possible to separate X- and Y-bearing sperm, to inactivate one or the other, and therefore to select the sex of children before conception.

- By 2002 science will have discovered how to preserve mature ova, which can then be stored and used for reproduction in future generations.

- Using technologies of robotics, computers, and genetic engineering, by 2003 the analysis of chromosomes will be simple and accurate.

- The human genome will have been completely mapped by 2005, so that by 2010 it will be possible to analyze genetic makeup before implantation and, using in-vitro fertilization, to ensure the genetic health of the zygote.

- By 2020 gene scanners will permit detailed analyses of all chromosomes, not only in the egg and sperm, but also in human tissue (kidneys, eyes, bladder, and so on) to detect anomalies and mutations.

- And by 2050, says Pergament, the artificial womb will have been per-

Chang Yu-ju is the first, and only, son of a Chinese family living in an industrial town just west of Beijing. On the wall of his parents' house hangs a contract they have signed with the local health station. The contract is a promise that they will have only one child. The state thanks them for their promise; more than that, it helps them keep their promise and rewards them for doing so.

The state helps them by providing free sex education and advice, free contraceptives, free sterilization for both men and women, even a free contraceptive pill for men that has been available since 1970 (Liljeström, 1982). The state helps them as well with praise, good examples, and many posters extolling the virtues of one-child families.

The state rewards them in material ways as well. Yu-ju's parents received a bonus when he was born; parents of subsequent children get no such bonuses. In addition, they will receive a monthly supplement until Yu-ju reaches the age of 14. Had they been peasants, they would have been given an additional allotment of land (twice as much as usual) for their personal use. Instead, when Yu-ju was born his mother received additional maternity leave, and the family was given larger living quarters.

Yu-ju, too, will be rewarded for being the first child. He'll receive priority for entry into nursery schools, hospitals, even universities. In fact, many hospitals have special beds reserved for first children, both to ensure that they will be well cared-for and to minimize the risk that parents might be left childless should they lose their only one. Nor will Yu-ju ever be forced to work in the country if he doesn't want to.

Occasionally the state bends the rules to accommodate conditions in remote rural areas. Thus, it might allot several hundred "second" children to be distributed among a rural town's couples. Also, couples who have a handicapped child might be permitted to have another child, as would be two people who remarry, even if each has previously had a child.

Some Results of One-Child-Only Policies:

Although these policies are not universally applied in China, they have resulted in a dramatic decline in population growth (from 2.3 percent per year between 1965 and 1980 to 1.3 percent between 1980 and 1990). In addition, under-5 mortality rates have dropped from 203 per 1,000 in 1960 to 42 per 1,000 in 1990, with complete immunization rates of more than 98 percent (Grant, 1992).

Another result of these policies is a sometimes alarming increase in the ratio of male to female children in areas where prenatal diagnosis allows parents to determine the sex of the child and to arrange for the abortion of fe-

Chinese government policies that reward parents for having only one child and that punish them for having more than one are reflected in a dramatic decline in population growth and in a large reduction in mortality rates among children under 5. They are also seen in a tremendous imbalance between male and female children because parents, anxious to have a son, often terminate pregnancies when the fetus has been identified as female.

male fetuses ("China fears sexual imbalance," 1983). Although Mao Tse Tung insisted that "girls are just as good as boys," not everyone truly believes this is so.

To Think About: What are some of the possible implications of growing up an only male child under these circumstances? Of growing up an only female child?

fected. It will then be possible to take long-preserved ova and sperm, join them in vitro, and let the artificial womb take over.

Important ethical issues are involved here. Some concern the potential dangers of experiments that can, theoretically, produce new forms of life, the consequences of which cannot really be imagined because the nature of that life may be unknown before its creation.

Other issues concern the morality of altering genetic codes, the ethics of decisions relating to creating or ending life, the legality and morality of surrogate mothering and artificial insemination, maybe even the very definition of life. Perhaps by 2050 these issues will have become more important than the science that gave them birth, and another new discipline will have arisen to deal with them.

But we have not yet reached the year 2050, and we continue to struggle with questions whose answers are not at all clear. Although we know vastly more now than we did even 10 years ago, there is still much about our beginnings that we do not understand.

studying gene-context interaction

enesis refers to the beginning; it refers, as well, to development or unfolding. Our genes are aptly named: They clearly are our beginnings. But they are more than simply beginnings; in interaction with our contexts, they are also involved in guiding our development. "Genes do not by themselves produce structural or functional characteristics," says Lerner (1991, p. 27). Instead, they *interact* with context to produce change.

Earlier we looked at Waddington's epigenetic landscape. The most important point this analogy makes is this: All genetically influenced characteristics, whether or not they are highly canalized (highly probable), can be influenced by context. Waddington's analogy of canalization, say Turkheimer and Gottesman (1991), emphasizes the interdependence of genes and experiences. The current emphasis in genetic research is on finding out how context and genes work together. Keep in mind that genetic and environmental forces do not compete; rather, they work together to increase the individual's adaptation (Cairns, Gariépy, & Hood, 1990).

historical family studies

One way to investigate gene-context interaction is to look at differences and similarities among members of a family. Why? Simply because family members share genes. As Plomin (1987) points out, there is 100 percent genetic similarity between identical twins, approximately 50 percent similarity among siblings who share both parents, and somewhere around 25 percent similarity among siblings who share only one parent. In actuality, however, what is called *assortative mating*—the tendency of mates to select each other on the basis of similarity—increases genetic relatedness even more.

It is the high degree of genetic relatedness among family members that led Francis Galton, Charles Darwin's cousin, to conclude that intelligence is largely hereditary. He had noticed that most of England's outstanding scientists came from just a few families. But this isn't very good research, surely. Even if Galton's observations were entirely accurate, they don't prove his point because it could be argued, for example, that the reason these families produced outstanding scientists was simply that they provided their children environments that led to the development of genius. Still, Galton was convinced of the heritability of intelligence, and he argued that parents should be selected for favorable genetic characteristics—a practice termed **eugenics**.

animal studies

Gene-environment interactions can sometimes be studied more easily with animals than with humans. First, certain anatomical measurements are sometimes possible with animals but not with humans (brain dissections, for example). Second, animals' environments can be controlled far more completely than can humans' environments (in terms of environmental stimulation, food, social contacts, and so on). Third, animal matings can be controlled precisely, and many generations can be produced and studied over shorter periods of time.

Still, there are some serious limitations of animal studies, not the least of which is the difficulty of generalizing findings from animals to humans. Because this text is about children, we mention rats and other animals only in passing.

BREEDING ANIMALS FOR INTELLIGENCE

Animal studies have demonstrated that it is possible to breed different strains of the same species that are predictably different in some identifiable characteristics. For example, in only a few generations mice can be bred for aggression, emotionality, or preference for alcohol, and rats can be bred for intelligence (see Figure 3.10). In much the same way, various "personality" characteristics have been developed in different breeds of dogs: fierceness and fighting ability in pit bull terriers, vigilance in German shepherds, and obstinacy and contrariness in the Lefrançois hound.

GENE-CONTEXT INTERACTION IN ANIMALS

But even in rats, dogs, and other non-human animals, genetics by itself tells little of the story. Consider, for example, the case of the song thrush, which thrives on eating snails. This bird uses its beak to grab the snail's foot and smashes the snail's shell against a rock by means of a rapid, sideways motion of its head, back and forth, back and forth (Weisfeld, 1982). This appears to be a genetically influenced behavior because the European blackbird, a close relative of the song thrush that also eats snails, doesn't seem to be able to learn the same shell-smashing behavior. But it is also an environmentally influenced behavior because the young song thrush doesn't instinctively know how to smash a snail shell; it learns to do so largely by trial-and-error during a critical period early in its life. If it's not given an opportunity to learn during this critical period, it goes through life never knowing how to eat a snail the way other song thrushes do it.

What investigations such as these illustrate most clearly is the complexity of gene-environment interaction, even for behaviors we might assume to be entirely genetically based. In addition, animal studies suggest that behaviors that have important adaptive functions become more probable through succeeding generations. Because these behaviors concern biological adaptation and the survival and propagation of species, they are typically related to feeding, rest, defense, reproduction, or elimination (Weisfeld, 1982).

GENE-DETERMINED BEHAVIORS IN HUMANS?

Are there similar, genetically ordained behaviors among humans? Some researchers think so. These behaviors, they argue, are common to all members of

An approximate representation of Tryon's (1940) successful attempt to breed maze-bright (intelligent) and maze-dull (dumb) rats. He kept track of how many errors rats made as they learned to run a maze and then mated the fastest learners with other bright rats and the slowest learners with other dull rats. After only 18 generations, there was no longer any overlap between the groups. The dullest rats among the bright group had become brighter than the smartest of the dull group. (Based on Tryon, 1940, p. 113).

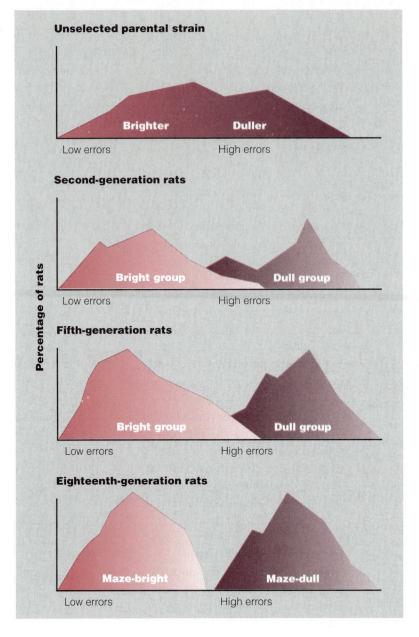

the species—and hence to all human cultures. In addition, they occur in the absence of experiences that might otherwise explain their acquisition. Weisfeld (1982) suggests that these genet-ically programmed behaviors might in-clude such things as infants' distress at being separated from their mother or other caregiver (more about this in Chapter 6); the tendency of mothers in all cultures to hold their infants on the left side, whether or not they are right-handed; various facial expressions that have identical meanings everywhere (such as the human smile, which occurs in blind as well as in sighted infants); and human vocalizations, which are initially identical in deaf and in hearing infants.

f **igure 3.11**

Comparisons between Mountain children and one contrast group on some measures of intelligence.

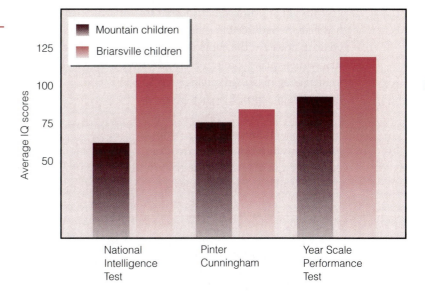

intervention studies

Another way of studying gene-environment interactions is to *intervene* either by depriving individuals of certain experiences or by enriching their environment. Outcomes can then be assessed to determine the effects of the experiences (or the lack thereof).

THE SHERMAN AND KEY STUDY

In a classical intervention study, Sherman and Key (1932) compared the intelligence test scores of groups of isolated children (Mountain children) with those of a control group in a socially more typical environment (Briarsville children). The Mountain children had been exposed to very little schooling, lived in homes with little (if any) reading material, and had almost no contact with the outside world. The Briarsville children had been exposed to normal schooling and had access to the wider culture through newspapers and other contacts. Not surprisingly, Briarsville children performed significantly better than the Mountain children on different measures of intelligence (see Figure 3.11).

Sherman and Key argue that these differences reflect the effects of the environment. But that isn't the only possible explanation. We don't know, for example, whether the parents of these children were comparable in terms of intelligence; none were tested. It's possible that the parents who chose to isolate themselves in the mountains were less intelligent than those who stayed closer to the cultural mainstream. It's also possible that they were more intelligent. And it's possible as well that the test was biased in favor of the Briarsville children.

PROJECT HEAD START

Project Head Start is a massive, federally funded U.S. program designed to alleviate some of the possible disadvantages of being born and raised in homes that are less advantaged economically, socially, and intellectually. There have been more than 2,000 different Head Start programs (Zigler & Freedman, 1987). Many of these lasted only a few hours a day, and many did not expose children to systematic, well-thought out experiences. Not surprisingly, some evaluations of Head Start have concluded that intelligence is perhaps not as plastic and malleable as had been hoped (see Lazar et al., 1982). In general, however, the evidence suggests that higher-quality programs are effective in increasing measured intelligence, and that children exposed to such programs often do better in subjects such as mathematics. In addition, there are usually improvements in measures that are more difficult to quantify, such as social functioning (Zigler & Freedman, 1987).

studies of twins

"If I had any desire to lead a life of indolent ease," Gould (1981) tells us, "I would wish to be an identical twin, separated at birth from my brother and raised in a different social class. We could hire ourselves out to a host of social scientists and practically name our fee. For we would be exceedingly rare representatives of the only really adequate natural experiment for separating genetic from environmental effects in humans" (p. 234).

Why is this so? Because identical twins are genetically identical; they result from the splitting of a single fertilized ovum (zygote). This segmentation results in two zygotes with an identical genetic makeup, producing **identical (monozygotic) twins**. The other type of twins, **fraternal (dizygotic) twins**, results from the fertilization of two different egg cells by two different sperm cells. This is possible only when the mother's ovaries simultaneously release more than one egg and results in twins who are no more alike genetically than ordinary **siblings**. Unfortunately for researchers, the incidence of twins is relatively low—approximately 1 in every 86 births. Furthermore, identical twins are much rarer than fraternal twins—about 1 in every 300 births in North America. The precise causes of twin birth are not known, although it appears that there is a hereditary factor be-

cause twins are found more often in some families than others. Also, older parents are more likely to have twins than are younger parents (Ernst & Angst, 1983).

STUDIES OF INTELLIGENCE

Many studies of twins have looked at correlations for intelligence test scores. Recall from Chapter 1 that a correlation coefficient is a measure of strength of relationship, usually expressed as a number ranging from -1 to $+1$ (see Figure 3.12). A high *positive* correlation— say, $+0.75$ to $+1.00$—means that if one twin has a low intelligence test score, the other twin is likely also to have a low score (or both are likely to have high or mediocre scores). A high *negative* correlation means that a low score for one would be associated with a high score for the other.

In general, the median correlation coefficient for intelligence test scores for identical twins is above $+0.80$, whereas that for fraternal twins is below $+0.60$ (Bouchard & McGue, 1981). If members of identical and fraternal twin pairs have had similar environments, these correlations may be interpreted as evidence that measured intelligence is influenced by heredity. With decreasing genetic similarity there is a corresponding decrease in the correlation in intelligence scores; the correlation for cousins is less than that for twins. This, too, is evidence of the influence of heredity.

But these data also support the belief that contexts influence measured intelligence. Because most sets of identical twins have more similar environments than do cousins or siblings, the higher correlations between various intelligence measures for identical twins may be due at least in part to their more nearly identical environments. And the difference between identical twins reared together and those reared apart is additional

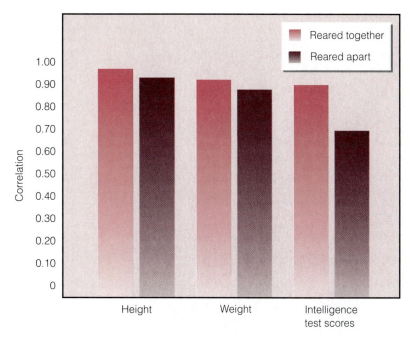

figure 3.12

Correlation indicates the extent to which two measures vary together. A correlation at or near 0 indicates no relationship; measures at or near +1 or −1 indicate nearly perfect relationships. That the intelligence test scores of identical twins reared together correlate at around .9 means that if one member of a twin pair has a high (or low) measured IQ, the other likely will have a high (or low) IQ as well. A high negative correlation would mean that if one score were high, the corresponding score would be low.

evidence that environment influences development. Median correlations of intelligence test scores of identical twins raised together and apart were +0.85 and +0.67, respectively. Because these twins are genetically identical, environmental forces are clearly important. It is also revealing that as identical twins grow up, their phenotypes (manifested characteristics) become less similar while their genotypes remain identical. It seems that the interaction of these identical genotypes with somewhat different contexts leads to progressively more dissimilar developmental outcomes (McCartney, Bernieri, & Harris, 1990).

STUDIES OF PERSONALITY

Studies of twins also provide evidence that a host of personality characteristics are strongly influenced by genetic factors in interaction with context (Plomin, 1989). In an Australian survey of 3,810 pairs of adult identical and fraternal twins, for example, Martin and Jardine (1986) found higher correlations for personality characteristics such as anxi-

ety, depression, conservatism, and introversion/extroversion for identical twins. Similar results have also been reported in a survey of American adult twins (Pogue-Geile & Rose, 1985).

Perhaps more striking is evidence that various types of mental disorders appear to have a genetic basis. For example, Gottesman and Shields (1982) examined 28 pairs of identical twins and reported 42 percent concordance for schizophrenia (that is, of all members of twin pairs who were schizophrenic, 42 percent had a schizophrenic twin). The concordance between members of 34 pairs of fraternal twins was only 9 percent.

Studies of adopted children and of mental disorders among related family members also confirm the finding that some forms of schizophrenia, as well as manic depression, have a genetic component (see Loehlin, Willerman, & Horn, 1988). Similarly, as noted earlier, heredity is often involved in the onset of alcoholism and may also be implicated in such disorders as Alzheimer's disease and infantile autism.

studies of adopted children

When it is possible to obtain information about both biological and adoptive parents, and about natural and adopted children, studies of adopted children permit a wide range of comparisons that make it easier to untangle the interaction of genes and context.

In the Texas Adoption Project, which began in 1973, investigators have had access to data that include physical as well as cognitive measures of the adopted children's biological mothers (and sometimes fathers as well), the adopted children themselves, the adoptive parents, and the adoptive parents' biological children in the adoptive home (Horn, 1983; Willerman, 1979; Loehlin, 1985). This study thus makes it possible to look at correlations in which the members of a pair have common genes but different environments (adopted children and their biological mothers), in which members of a pair share an environment but are genetically unrelated (adopted children and their adoptive parents), and in which there is some commonality of both genes and the environment (adoptive parents and their biological children).

Some of the results of the Texas Adoption Project—those concerning IQ—are summarized in Figure 3.13. What is most striking about these findings is that the correlations between adopted children and their biological mothers are higher than those between the adopted children and their adoptive parents. Also, the correlation between adopted children and their biological mothers is about the same as that between adoptive parents and their own children, in spite of the fact that the adopted children, unlike the biological

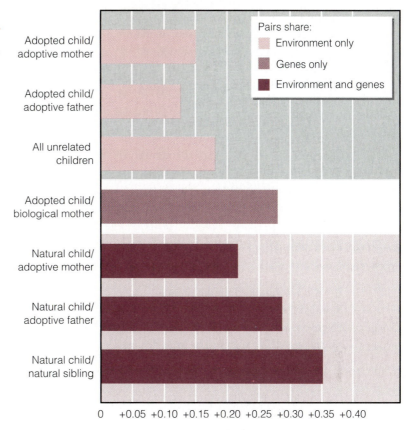

f **igure 3.13**

IQ correlations from the Texas Adoption Project.
Source: *Data from J. M. Horn, The Texas Adoption Project,* Child Development, *1983, 54,
268–275. Reprinted by permission of The Society for Research in Child Development, Inc.*

children, are not raised by their own
mothers. Eysenck and Kamin (1981)
claim that this is strong evidence that genetics is the principal determinant of variation in intelligence. We should note,
however, that these correlations are very
low—they do not by themselves account
for very much variation in intelligence.
But as geneticists would be quick to
point out, the degree of genetic relatedness between a child and a biological parent is not nearly as high as that between
siblings, and is even less than that between identical twins.

Several other studies of adopted children, many of them using longitudinal
designs, have begun to contribute significantly to our knowledge of the ways in
which heredity and environment interact

to determine changes during the course
of development. One of the Minnesota
Adoption Studies, for example, found
that black children adopted into white
homes performed as well on IQ tests as
the biological children in the adoptive
homes (Scarr & Weinberg, 1983). These
black children adopted into white homes
also had higher average intelligence test
scores than their biological parents. Significantly, however, their measured intelligence was more closely related to that of
their biological than their adoptive parents. What this means is that if the biological parents were ranked according
to measured IQ and then their children
were ranked in the same way, the correspondence between the two rankings
would be high (the correlation would be

high). Put simply, variations in measured intelligence are more easily explained in terms of genetics than environment (Plomin, 1989).

So, how do we evaluate the nature-nurture question? According to Lerner (1993), to insist that nature can be separated from nurture violates the facts as we know them. The only logical conclusion is that the causes of human variation are to be found in interactions among our genes and our contexts.

an illustration of gene-context interaction

A dramatic illustration of gene-context interaction is found in Elder, Nguyen, and Caspi's (1985) analysis of the lives of 167 children who lived during the Great Depression in the 1930s, a time of severe economic hardships for both parents and children. Fathers seemed to be most affected, perhaps because they often lost their jobs and their ability to look after their families. As a result, says Elder (1979), some fathers became more punitive and more exploitive; others became more rejecting and indifferent. In contrast, mothers, for whom loss of the husband's job would be an economic but not a personal blow, seemed relatively unaffected, and their relationships with their children changed little.

These changes, notes Elder, were especially difficult for adolescents, whose relationships with parents changed in systematic ways (Elder et al., 1985). Boys' perceptions of the power and attractiveness of their fathers tended to decline, whereas the influence of the boys' peers increased. Interestingly, however, adolescent boys did not appear to suffer in terms of confidence, aspirations, and positive self-concept. In contrast, girls tended to lower their aspirations and their self-esteem and to experience increased

moodiness and unhappiness. These negative effects, claims Elder, were linked not so much to economic hardships as to the rejecting behavior of the fathers. And, in general, the negative effects were more serious for girls than for boys. But what is most striking is that the least attractive girls suffered most. In Elder, Nguyen and Caspi's (1985) words, "If girls were unattractive, family hardship accentuated fathers' overly demanding, exploitive behavior . . . [but] only when girls were rated as unattractive" (p. 371). In fact, in some cases economic hardship actually increased the extent to which fathers were warm and supportive of their *attractive* daughters, sacrificing and going out of their way to provide for them.

Related to this, a large number of studies have found that on average, teachers judge physically attractive students to be more socially skillful, more likely to achieve, and even more intelligent (see Ritts, Patterson, & Tubbs, 1992).

The lesson to be learned from studies such as these is clear: If we are to understand the development and the lives of people, it is essential that we take into account the contexts in which they are born and live. In Bronfenbrenner's terms, we need to look at the microsystem (in this study, the adolescent in interaction with father, mother, and peers); the mesosystem (family interactions with school or with adolescents' workplaces); the exosystem (the father's changed relationship with his work setting); and the macrosystem (the dramatic social and economic changes of the Great Depression). An ecological approach to understanding development emphasizes not only the importance of the interactions that define children's ecological systems, but underscores as well the importance of the characteristics of individuals and settings in interaction. And it provides a framework for beginning to understand how characteristics that have a strong genetic basis (physical appearance, for example) can influence interactions in systems that are also influenced by environmental factors (such as economic conditions, for instance).

the continuing nature-nurture controversy

When Snyderman and Rothman (1987) questioned 1,020 American psychologists, they found that most believed that intelligence is inherited to a significant degree. This, of course, does not contradict the fact that all human characteristics are influenced by the interaction of genes and changing contexts.

So what is the controversy? Essentially, it's still the same old nurture-nature question—the question of whether certain traits are influenced primarily by heredity or only by the environment, the question of how important each is. It's a controversy that stems from an extreme and often emotional belief that all of us are—or at least should be—equal. And if we are equal, then it cannot be that Frances has an assortment of genes highly likely to lead to charm, intelligence, and grace while Francis starts his life with an assortment of genes that propel him blindly toward stupidity or schizophrenia.

Or can it? Science suggests that yes, our genes are different and yes, we have different probabilities of reaching certain outcomes. But science also tells us that, in Gottlieb's (1992) words: ". . . the persistence of the nature-nurture dichotomy reflects an inadequate understanding of the relations among heredity, development, and evolution . . ." (p. 137).

Science also tells us that genes, by themselves, determine little. They simply underlie potential, making some outcomes more probable than others. Even in the face of highly probable (highly canalized) outcomes, environmental forces can lead to surprising and wonderful things.

That is the essence of Gottesman's (1974) concept of reaction range (discussed earlier). Reaction range is the range of possibilities implicit in our genes. It includes all the outcomes possible for any particular characteristic, given variations in the timing and nature of environmental influences.

What the concept of reaction range recognizes is our plasticity (or adaptability), which is one of our most fundamental characteristics. As Lerner (1987) notes, it is as though our genetic makeup, our biology, sets a range of possible outcomes. Ultimately, it is the complex interplay between our contexts and our characteristics that gradually shapes our developmental paths.

How important is it if we are males in a culture that favors males; if we are members of a minority group in settings that discriminate against minority groups; if we are professors in environments that heap respect on academics, or if we are blue-eyed or brown, or tall or short, or weak or strong, or quick or slow? The meanings of each of these can be understood only in its context.

Stern (1956) simplified the concept of human plasticity. In Stern's hypothesis (Figure 3.14), plasticity is likened to the stretchability of a rubber band:

> *The genetic endowment in respect to any one trait has been compared to a rubber band and the trait itself to the length which the rubber band assumes when it is stretched by outside forces. Different people initially may have been given different lengths of unstretched endowment, but the natural forces of the environment may have stretched their expression to equal length, or led to differ-*

figure 3.14

The Stern hypothesis, an example of gene-environment interaction. Individuals with different inherited potentials for intellectual development can manifest a wide range of measured intelligence as a function of environment-gene interaction.

Inherited potential

Environment	Genes for low intelligence	Genes for high intelligence
Poor	Very dull	Dull or average
Average	Dull	Quite intelligent
Excellent	Average or quite intelligent	Genius

ences in attained length sometimes corresponding to their innate differences and at other times in reverse of the relation. (p. 53)

Put more simply, some of us were born with short unstretched bands (limited inherited potential for intelligence), others with longer bands. Some environments stretch bands a lot; others hardly stretch them at all. Long bands, of course, stretch more easily.

Do highly demanding environments break bands? Do old bands become frayed and brittle? Do bands stretch more easily when new? Unfortunately, analogies are simply comparisons; they provide no logical answers for questions like these.

main points

GENETICS AND CONTEXT IN INTERACTION

1. We tend to think of our genes as being within us, and of contexts as being outside of us, each separate from the other. But each changes as a function of the other. Developments made possible by our genes (for ex-

ample, language) nevertheless depend on context (for instance, our not being abandoned). Thus genes and contexts interact to determine the course and outcomes of human development. (Their combined influence is interactive rather than additive.)

BASIC CONCEPTS OF HEREDITY

2. The basis of biological life are the protein molecules whose function is determined by the arrangement of the 20 known amino acids of which they are composed. In turn, arrangements of the amino acids are determined by a special genetic code contained in sequences of deoxyribonucleic acid (DNA) molecules located on rodlike structures called chromosomes. The hereditary basis of life resides in the egg (ovum) and the sperm cell, each of which contains 23 chromosomes, half the number of chromosomes found in ordinary human body cells (23 pairs). In the chromosomes are the carriers of heredity, the genes.

3. The presence of a Y chromosome in the fertilized egg determines that the

offspring will be male; two X chromosomes produce a female. Only the male can produce a Y chromosome, whereas both females and males produce X chromosomes.

4. Genes, in pairs or in combinations of pairs, interact with the environment to determine the potential for certain characteristics. Genetic makeup is *genotype*; *phenotype* refers to manifested characteristics. Manifested characteristics (phenotype) that usually correspond closely to underlying genetic makeup (genotype) are said to be highly canalized. *Reaction range* refers to the range of possibilities implicit in genotype. Marker genes are specific segments of DNA that are associated with some identifiable characteristic.

GENETIC DEFECTS

5. Many genetic defects are associated with recessive genes and will therefore not be manifested unless the individual inherits the genes (or gene combinations) from both parents. Such defects include Huntington's chorea (associated with a dominant gene; usually a fatal neurological disorder not manifested until later in life); sickle-cell anemia (a blood disorder); PKU (a metabolic disorder leading to mental retardation but preventable through diet); and other conditions such as Tay-Sachs disease, muscular dystrophy, some forms of diabetes, and neural tube defects.

CHROMOSOMAL DISORDERS

6. Chromosomal disorders result from errors in chromosomes rather than from defective genes. Chromosomal abnormalities include Down syndrome, which results from an extra chromosome 21; Turner's syndrome, which affects girls only and is linked to an absent sex chromosome (XO rather than XX); XYY syndrome, which affects men only; Klinefelter's syndrome, in which men have an extra X chromosome (XXY); and fragile X syndrome (also linked with mental retardation).

GENETIC RISK

7. Many genetic abnormalities and fetal diseases can be detected before birth by several means: amniocentesis (analysis of amniotic fluid withdrawn through a needle), chorionic villus sampling (CVS; analysis of a sample of the chorion), fetoscopy (a surgical procedure used to obtain fetal blood or skin samples), ultrasound (use of sonar techniques to detect physical characteristics as well as fetal movement), radiography (X rays), or preimplantation diagnosis (examination of zygote cells before implantation in the uterus).

8. High genetic risk frequently presents alternatives other than therapeutic abortion, including drugs, enzymes, surgical procedures, blood transfusions, surgery, dietary control, and various other procedures to prevent, alleviate, or cure genetically influenced conditions. Genetic counseling advises parents about the probabilities (or the certainty) of genetically based problems, about available options, and about the most likely outcomes.

STUDIES OF GENE-CONTEXT INTERACTION

9. Animal studies indicate that there are sometimes complex behaviors in animals that are highly influenced by genes but will nevertheless not be learned in the absence of appropriate experiences. It isn't clear whether humans manifest similar behaviors.

10. Studies of isolated children and intervention studies (often conducted in preschool settings) indicate that early experiences can have long-lasting influences on children. Also, the fact that identical twins reared together are more similar than those reared apart corroborates these findings. However, with greater genetic relatedness, individuals usually resemble each other more closely, a finding that illustrates the importance of genetics (as do studies in which animals are deliberately bred to display specific qualities such as maze-brightness.)

11. Studies of adopted children typically report higher (though modest) correlations between biological mothers and their children than between adopted children and adoptive parents.

12. Elder's study of the differential effects of the Great Depression on the lives of attractive and less attractive girls illustrates how biology (attractiveness) and the environment can interact to influence development. It is useful to emphasize the plasticity rather than the limits implicit in our genes.

focus questions: applications

■ What is the likely outcome of a child being raised by a chicken? A wolf? Alone in an attic?

1. Would a fully documented case of a feral child tell us anything important? What? Why?

■ What are the marvels and the mysteries of what our elders call the birds and bees?

2. What are the basic, biological mechanics involved?

■ What are the most common genetic defects and problems?

3. How serious are these from a biological, evolutionary point of view? Why?

■ How can we diagnose genetic problems?

4. What are the most important purposes of genetic diagnosis?

■ What can we do about genetic problems?

5. What are some of the implications of increasing knowledge about, and ability to alter, genetic messages.

■ What is the nature-nurture controversy?

6. So what is it about? Is it an important controversy? Why?

study terms

feral children 103
heredity 105
environment 105
interaction 105
conception 107
egg cell (ovum) 107
sperm cell 107
artificial insemination 107
ovaries 107
gametes 108
genetics 108
proteins 108
deoxyribonucleic acid (DNA) 108
double helix 108
sex cells 108
somatic cells 108
chromosomes 108
mitosis 109
meiosis 109
sex chromosome 109
autosomes 109
genes 109
dominant gene 110
recessive gene 110

genotype 111

phenotype 111

normal curve 112

canalization 113

epigenesis 114

reaction range 114

Mendelian genetics 114

molecular genetics 114

marker genes 114

Huntington's disease 117

heterozygous 117

homozygous 117

phenylketonuria (PKU) 118

Tay-Sachs disease 119

muscular dystrophy (MD) 119

neural tube defects 119

AFP test 119

diabetes 119

chromosomal disorders 120

Down syndrome 120

trisomy 21 121

Alzheimer's disease 122

Turner's syndrome 122

Kleinfelter's syndrome 122

fragile X syndrome 123

amniocentesis 124

chorionic villus sampling 125

ultrasound 125

fetoscopy 125

radiography 126

eugenics 131

identical (monozygotic) twins 134

fraternal (dizygotic) twins 134

siblings 134

further readings

For fascinating, tragic, and contemporary accounts of an abandoned child, see:

Curtiss, S. (1977). *Genie: A psycholinguistic study of a modern-day wild child.* New York: Academic Press.

Rymer, R. (1993). *Genie: A scientific tragedy.* New York: Harper Perennial.

A comprehensive summary of current research on the heritability of intelligence, personality characteristics, and psychopathologies such as schizophrenia, alcoholism, and Alzheimer's disease is the following:

Loehlin, J. C., Willerman, L., & Horn, J. M. (1988). Human behavior genetics. *Annual Review of Psychology, 39,* 101–133.

For those interested in the details of heredity, see:

Emery, A. E., & Mueller, R. F. (1992). *Elements of medical genetics* (8th ed.). Edinburgh & London: Churchill Livingstone.

Friedman, J. M., Dill, F. J., Hayden, M. R., & McGillivray, B. C. (1992). *Genetics.* Baltimore: Williams & Wilkins.

The next two books are highly recommended journalistic accounts of progress in one of the most exciting research frontiers of this decade:

Wingerson, L. (1990). *Mapping our genes: The genome project and the future of medicine.* New York: Dutton.

Bishop, J. E., & Waldholz, M. (1990). *Genome: The story of the most astonishing scientific adventure of our time—the attempt to map all the genes in the human body.* New York: Simon & Schuster.

Useful references in the rapidly changing fields of prenatal diagnosis and genetic counseling include:

Whittle, M. J., & Connor, J. M. (Eds.). (1989). *Prenatal diagnosis in obstetric practice.* Boston: Blackwell Scientific Publications.

Liu, D. T. (Ed.). (1991). *A practical guide to chorion villus sampling.* New York: Oxford University Press.

Fine, B. A., Gettig, E., Greendale, K., Leopold, B., & Paul, N. W. (Eds.). (l990). *Strategies in genetic counseling: Reproductive genetics and new technologies.* White Plains, N.Y.: March of Dimes Birth Defects Foundation.

Evers-Kiebooms, G., Fryns, J. P., Cassiman, J. J., & Van den Berghe, H. (Eds.). (1992). *Psychosocial aspects of genetic counseling.* New York: John Wiley.

Stephen Jay Gould gives a fascinating account of the history of mental measurement and a strong indictment of past and sometimes current beliefs about IQ and its heritability in his aptly titled book:

Gould, S. J. (1981). *The mismeasure of man.* New York: W. W. Norton.

Our genes are not simply limits; they are potential. They make possible our uniqueness and our flexibility. The following collection explores the potential implicit in our adaptability:

Gallagher, J. J., & Ramey, C. T. (Eds.). (1987). *The malleability of children.* Baltimore: Brookes.

4

Prenatal Development and Birth

Take her up tenderly,
Lift her with care;
Fashioned so slenderly,
Young, and so fair!
Thomas Hood, The Bridge of Sighs

focus questions

HOW EARLY CAN PREGNANCY RELIABLY BE DETECTED?

HOW DOES A FETUS GROW?

WHAT SORTS OF THINGS CAN HARM OR NURTURE A FETUS'S DEVELOPMENT?

HOW ARE INFANTS DELIVERED HERE AND ELSEWHERE?

outline

CONCEPTION

DETECTING PREGNANCY

STAGES OF PRENATAL DEVELOPMENT
Stage of the Fertilized Ovum
The Embryo Stage
The Fetal Period

FACTORS AFFECTING PRENATAL DEVELOPMENT
Prescription Drug Use
Exposure to Chemicals
Nicotine Intake
Caffeine Consumption
Alcohol Consumption
Substance Abuse
Maternal Health
Maternal Emotions and Stress
Maternal Age
Maternal Nutrition
Social Class
Rh(D) Immunization

CHILDBIRTH
The Initiation of Childbirth
Classifications of Birth Status
Stages of Labor
Cesarean Delivery
Neonatal Scales
The Mother's Experience: Prepared Childbirth
The Child's Experience

PREMATURITY
Causes of Prematurity
Effects of Prematurity
Prevention of Prematurity
Care of Premature Infants

A REASSURING NOTE

MAIN POINTS

FOCUS QUESTIONS: APPLICATIONS

STUDY TERMS

FURTHER READINGS

I remember very clearly when my older brother, Maurice, made me ask our mother about the birds and the bees. "Ask mom where babies come from," he insisted. "Ask her. Come on, ask her."

In those days such questions were a big deal, which I didn't know at the time. So, not because I was especially curious but because I was determined even then not to be a wimp, I asked the question.

"So where do babies come from, maman?" (in French, of course, that being the only language I then knew).

"Quoi?" said she (meaning "What the @##%!@ are you asking now?"), although even with my undeveloped intelligence I knew she had heard every word—which I repeated in any case.

"You'd better have a talk with your father," she finally answered.

"What did mom say?" asked Maurice.

"Ask dad," said I. Which I would surely have forgotten to do had Maurice not reminded me.

"Where do babies come from?" I asked my papa who, cigarette dangling precariously from the lower right corner of his mouth, mumbled, "Ask your mother."

"She said ask you."

"Well then, try your grandmother."

I didn't really intend to but, again, Maurice reminded me.

"Grandmère," says I, "about babies …"

"Ah yes," said she, dragging me out into the turnips so that she could point out a pair of mating dragonflies—surely as titillating a sight as I have ever seen.

"The heat's on them," she said by way of

preface; then, by way of explanation, "That means they're gonna have little ones."

I tried to explain the whole thing to Maurice, but he had heard a different explanation. And he remained convinced that there is more to these matters than is revealed by the sight of a pair of dragonflies clutching each other on a May morning in what cannot be anything but ecstasy.

Later, I discovered he was right, that there were secrets yet to be uncovered. That's what this chapter is about: the rest of the secrets.

conception

t all begins with conception, when an egg (ovum) is fertilized by a sperm cell. The resulting zygote, containing the individual's entire genetic endowment in the arrangement of the DNA molecules that make up its 23 pairs of chromosomes, is the biological beginning of life. Normally, all changes that take place in this cell's development will result from the interaction of genetic predispositions with the environment, both before and after birth. As noted in Chapter 3, it is difficult to separate these two effects; they are not, in fact, separate and additive, but combined and interactive. Nevertheless, it is possible to isolate and describe the effects of specific experiences at certain times and under certain circumstances. For example, during prenatal development, some drugs and chemicals and other environmental conditions can have markedly harmful effects on the fetus. This chapter looks at some of these possible effects as it traces the normal course of prenatal development from conception through birth.

detecting pregnancy

rospective parents often find it useful to be able to detect **pregnancy** well in advance of the birth of the baby. In the absence of chemical tests or a medical examination, there are few certain signs of pregnancy before the later stages of **prenatal development**. However, there are some less certain signs, which can include cessation of menses (menstruation), morning sickness, changes in the breasts, and quickening (fetal motion). Most of these symptoms do not occur very early in pregnancy. Cessation of **menses** is not usually noticed until at least two weeks of pregnancy have passed because conception ordinarily occurs approximately two weeks after the last menstrual period. Nor is this a certain sign of pregnancy; many other factors may cause it. Morning sickness, although it affects approximately two-thirds of all pregnant women, does not ordinarily begin until about two weeks after the missed period and can easily be mistaken for some other ailment. During the early stages the breasts frequently enlarge and become slightly painful, and the aureoles darken. Because these symptoms are highly subjective, they are quite unreliable. **Quickening**, the movement of the fetus in the womb, is not usually noticed by the mother until the fourth or fifth month, and by then most women have realized for some time that they are pregnant.

In addition to these probable indications of pregnancy, there are some more positive signs, such as the fetal heartbeat, which can be heard with the aid of a stethoscope. Similarly, fetal movements can be detected by feeling the abdomen or sometimes simply by observing it. X rays and ultrasound are two other methods of ascertaining the presence of a fetus.

Several decades ago, the surest early medical test of pregnancy required the aid of a rabbit, a frog, a mouse, or some other poor creature. Fortunately for the rabbits and mice, who always had to be killed to complete the test, chemical pregnancy tests are now widely available, even in kit form for in-home use. These kits detect changes in a woman's urine through a chemical reaction and are effective as early as two weeks after conception. Positive indications in early pregnancy tests are highly reliable. Negative readings are less accurate, however, and should be followed by a second test a week or so later if the menstrual period has still not begun.

stages of prenatal development

The **gestation period** (the time between conception and birth) varies considerably for different species: Cows take about as long as people; elephants need 600 days; dogs come to term in approximately 63 days, rabbits in 31.

The human gestation period is usually calculated in lunar months, each month consisting of 28 days; hence a typical pregnancy lasts 10 lunar months or 280 days, when these days are counted from the onset of the last menstrual period, as they usually are. However, the actual gestation period is approximately 266 days because fertilization usually cannot occur until 12 to 14 days later, when ovulation takes place.

The American College of Obstetrics and Gynecology has standardized the terminology used to describe prenatal development by identifying three developmental stages with clear time boundaries (Table 4.1). The **fertilized ovum stage** (also called the **germinal stage**) begins at fertilization and ends two weeks later, shortly after implantation in the uterus. (The fertilized ovum is also called a **zygote**.) The **embryo stage** follows and terminates at the end of the eighth week. The final stage, the **fetus**, lasts from the end of the second lunar month until the birth of the baby.

stage of the fertilized ovum

Fertilization usually occurs in a woman's **Fallopian tubes**, each of which links an ovary to the **uterus** (Figure 4.1). Fertilization results from the invasion of the tubes by sperm cells, one of which successfully penetrates the outer covering of the ovum and unites with it. It is estimated that the male must ejaculate 20

t a b l e   4 . 1

Stages of gestation (prenatal development)

STAGE	DESCRIPTION
Fertilized ovum	Also termed the germinal stage, or the period of the zygote; begins at fertilization and ends two weeks later, after implantation of the zygote (fertilized egg) in the uterine wall. Still microscopic.
Embryo	From end of second to end of eighth week of intrauterine development. During this stage most of the important morphological (pertaining to form) changes occur. Teratogens (influences that cause malformations and defects) are most influential during this period. At the end of this period, the embryo is close to 2 inches (4.5 cm) long and weighs about ⅔ ounce (19 grams).
Fetus	From the end of eighth week until birth. Accelerating growth occurs toward the end of this period.

f i g u r e   4 . 1

Fertilization and implantation. At (1), many millions of sperm cells have entered the vagina and are finding their way into the uterus. At (2), some of these sperm are moving up the Fallopian tube (there is a similar tube on the other side) toward the ovum. At (3), fertilization occurs. The fertilized ovum drifts down the tube, dividing and forming new cells as it goes, until it implants in the wall of the uterus (4) by the seventh or eighth day after fertilization.

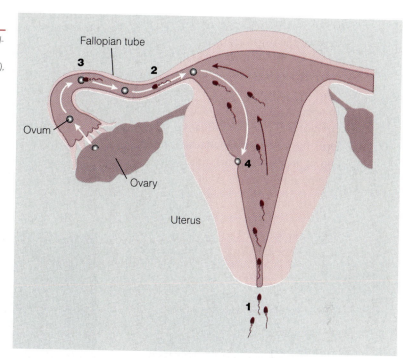

million or more sperm cells if one is to succeed in reaching and fertilizing the egg. Once a single sperm has penetrated the ovum's outer shell, the egg then becomes impenetrable to other sperm. From that moment a human child begins to form, but it will be approximately 266 days before this individual is finally born.

After fertilization, the ovum is carried toward the uterus by currents in the Fal-

lopian tubes, a process requiring between five and nine days. Cell divisions occur during this time, so that the fertilized ovum, which initially consisted of a single egg cell and a single sperm cell, now contains about 125 cells (Handyside, 1991). It is hardly larger at the end of the first week than it was at the time of fertilization, mainly because the cells of which it consists are considerably smaller than they originally were. This is not surprising because the ovum has received no nourishment from any source other than itself. After about one week or so, the ovum is ready to implant itself in the uterine wall. At this stage, many potential pregnancies terminate due to implantation failure.

The ovum facilitates implantation by secreting certain enzymes and producing tiny, tentaclelike growths, called villi, that implant themselves in the lining of the uterus to obtain nutrients from blood vessels. This is the beginning of the **placenta**—the organ that, while keeping the blood of the mother and of the fetus separate, allows nutrients to pass to the fetus and waste materials to be removed. In time, the placenta and the fetus are connected by the **umbilical cord**, a long, thick cord that is attached at one end to the placenta and at the other to what will be the child's navel. The umbilical cord consists of two arteries and one large vein and will eventually be approximately 20 inches (50 cm) long. It contains no nerve cells, so that there is no connection between the mother's nervous system and that of the child **in utero** (in the uterus). Note that the placenta serves as a link between mother and fetus, whereas the umbilical cord links the fetus to the placenta.

the embryo stage

The embryo stage, beginning at the end of the second week of pregnancy, follows implantation of the fertilized ovum in the wall of the uterus. The normal course of physiological development in the embryonic and fetal stages is highly predictable and regular (Figure 4.2).

figure 4.2

The fertilized ovum at (a) three days after conception, and the fetus (b) at 15 weeks.

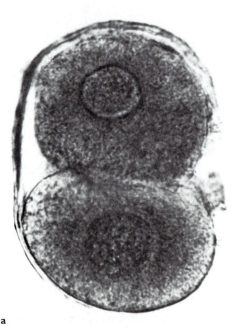

a

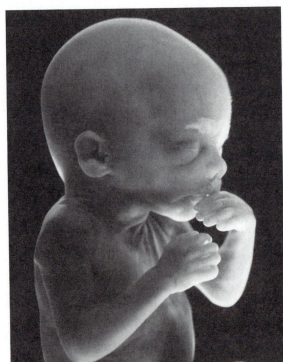

b

At the beginning of this stage, the embryo is still only a fraction of an inch long and weighs much less than an ounce. Despite its tiny size, not only has cell differentiation into future skin cells, nerves, bone, and other body tissue begun, but the rudiments of eyes, ears, and nose have also begun to appear. In addition, some of the internal organs are beginning to develop. In fact, by the end of the first lunar month, a primitive heart is already beating. By the end of the second lunar month, the embryo is between 1½ and 2 inches (3.8 and 5 cm) long and weighs close to two-thirds of an ounce (19 gm). All the organs are now present, the whole mass has assumed the curled shape characteristic of the fetus, and the embryo is clearly recognizable as human. Arm and leg buds have appeared and begun to grow, resembling short, awkward paddles. External genitalia (sex organs) have also appeared.

the fetal period

By the end of the eighth week of pregnancy, which marks the beginning of the fetal period, the absolute mass of the fetus is still quite unimpressive. By the end of the third lunar month (10 weeks of pregnancy), it may reach a length of 3 inches (7.5 cm) but will still weigh less than an ounce (20 gm). The head of the fetus is one-third of its entire length; this will have changed to one-fourth by the end of the sixth lunar month and to slightly less than that at birth (see Table 4.2 and Figures 4.3 and 4.4).

During the third month of pregnancy, the fetus is sufficiently developed that if it is aborted it can make breathing movements and give evidence of both a primitive **sucking reflex** and the **Babinski reflex** (the infant's tendency to fan its toes when tickled on the soles of its feet)

table 4.2

Prenatal developmental events, by lunar month

LUNAR MONTH	DEVELOPMENTAL EVENTS
1	Cell differentiation into those that will be bones, nerves, or other cells
2	All organs present; leg buds and external genitalia just appearing; capable of primitive breathing movements and sucking; bones forming, organs differentiated
3	
4	
5	Fetal movement (quickening); lanugo appears
6–7	Heartbeat clearly discernible; eyelids present
8–10	All major changes have now occurred; development is largely a matter of increasing weight and length

if stimulated appropriately. However, the fetus will have no chance of survival if born at this stage of development.

During the fourth lunar month of pregnancy, the fetus grows to a length of 6 inches (16 cm) and weighs approximately 4 ounces (113 gm). The bones have begun to form, all organs are clearly differentiated, and there may even be evidence of some **intrauterine** (within the uterus) movement. During the fifth month a downy covering, called **lanugo**, begins to grow over most of the fetus's body. This covering is usually shed during the seventh month but is occasionally still present at birth. The fetus weighs approximately 11 ounces (311 gm) and may have reached a length of 10 inches (25 cm) by the end of the fifth lunar month.

Toward the end of the sixth month, it is possible to palpate (feel by touch) the fetus through the mother's abdomen. The heartbeat, already discernible in the fifth month, is now much clearer. The eyelids have now separated so that the fetus can open and close its eyes. It is approximately a foot (30 cm) long and

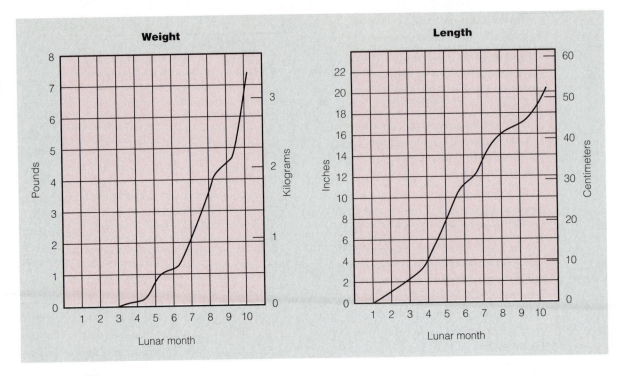

Weight

Length

Pounds

Kilograms

Inches

Centimeters

Lunar month

Lunar month

igure 4.3

*Approximate weight and length of the fetus at the end
of each lunar month of prenatal development.*

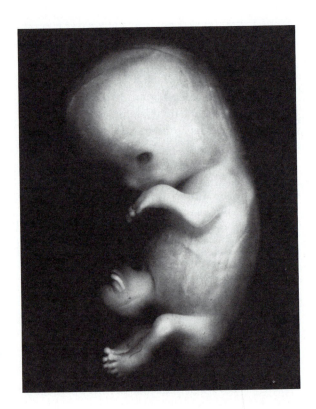

igure 4.4

*The fetus at 48 days, late in the embryonic stage. At this
stage all organs are already present, the heart is beating,
and limbs and external genitalia have appeared.*

weighs close to 20 ounces (567 gm). If born now, it would have some chance of surviving in a modern hospital with sophisticated care to compensate for the immaturity of its digestive and respiratory systems.

The fetus's growth in size and weight becomes more dramatic in the last few months of the final stage. Brain development is also particularly crucial during the last three months of pregnancy, as it will continue to be after birth, especially for the first two years of life. The unborn child's sensitivity to malnutrition is assumed to be related to neurological growth during the late stages of fetal development. This sensitivity is sometimes evident in lower developmental scores during infancy and impaired mental functioning among children born to malnourished mothers (Lewin, 1975).

Most of the physical changes that occur after the seventh month are quantitative (Table 4.2). It is now a matter of sheer physical growth: from 15 inches and 2.6 pounds (38 cm; 1,180 gm) in the seventh month, to 16 inches and 4 pounds (41 cm; 1,816 gm) in the eighth month, to 17.5 inches and 4.7 pounds (44 cm; 2,133 gm) in the ninth month, and to 20 inches and 7.5 pounds (50 cm; 3,405 gm) at the end of the tenth month.

Two terms that are sometimes used to describe the general pattern of fetal development are **proximodistal** and **cephalocaudal**. Literally, these terms mean "from near to far" and "from the head to the tail," respectively. They refer to the fact that among the first aspects of the fetus to develop are the head and internal organs; the last are the limbs and digits.

After approximately 266 days of intrauterine development, most fetuses are ready to be born, although some appear to be ready earlier and some later. But before we look at birth, we turn to a discussion of the factors that may be important to the normal or abnormal development of the fetus.

factors affecting prenatal development

There are two classes of influences that cause malformations and physical defects in the fetus. **Teratogens** affect the embryo or fetus directly (from *teras*, the Greek word for "monster," so called because such substances were thought to be capable of producing monsters—and can in fact produce monstrous deformities). Among the most common teratogens are various maternal illnesses, drugs, chemicals, and minerals. Note that the effects of teratogens are *not* passed on from one generation to another.

In contrast, the effects of **mutagens** can be transmitted from one generation to another because mutagens cause changes in genetic material that can lead to malformations and defects. Radiation is a well known mutagen. Thus, deafness caused by a mutated gene (resulting from exposure to a mutagen such as radiation, for example) may be passed on to offspring; deafness caused by a virus (such as the teratogenic cytomegalovirus) will not be.

It is important to note at the outset that the effects of many teratogens often depend on a variety of factors, both environmental and genetic. That is, the occurrence and severity of a defect associated with a particular teratogen are often determined by a fetus's genetic background, the timing of the exposure, and the stresses that might result from the additional presence of other teratogens—not to mention the moderating effects of other positive external influences. Accordingly, the effects of any given teratogen can vary widely from one fetus to another.

Because it is clearly unethical to use human subjects in controlled investigations of chemical substances whose effects may be injurious to the fetus, our information about the effects of drugs on the fetus is often based on studies of animals or on observations of human infants under poorly controlled conditions. Generalizing results from studies of animals to humans in the case of prenatal exposure to drugs presents an additional problem, because certain drugs have dramatically different effects on members of different animal species as well as on children relative to adults (Friedman, 1992). Also, normal adult doses of a drug might well represent huge doses for a fetus weighing only ounces, particularly if the drug crosses the placental barrier easily.

FREQUENCY OF DRUG USE

The frequency of prescription (rather than recreational) drug use by pregnant women and the variety of drugs they consume is not known. Heinonen, Slone, and Shapiro (1983) gathered data on more than 50,000 pregnant women in the United States and calculated that the average number of different prescription drugs taken during pregnancy was 3.8. In addition, an estimated 75 percent of pregnant women take a variety of non-prescription drugs such as analgesics (painkillers such as headache tablets) and cough or cold preparations (Rayburn et al., 1982). However, there are indications that extent of drug use by pregnant women—and the problem of overprescribing by the medical profession as well—may be declining due to increasing awareness of the possibly harmful effects of some drugs on the fetus. More recent studies report that as many as 90 percent of mothers in the United States claim not to have taken any drug during pregnancy (see Whittle & Rubin, 1989).

SOME TERATOGENIC DRUGS

Among the better-known teratogens are thalidomide, which causes severe physical changes in the embryo; quinine, which is associated with congenital deafness; barbiturates and other painkillers, which reduce the body's oxygen supply, resulting in varying degrees of brain damage; and various anesthetics that appear to cross the placental barrier easily and rapidly and cause depression of fetal respiration and decreased responsiveness in the fetus (Schardein, 1985).

Among nonprescription drugs that may also have negative effects on the fetus is aspirin, which may increase the tendency to bleed in both mother and fetus (Stockman, 1990) and which is clearly linked with physical deformities among experimental animals (Vórhees & Mollnow, 1987). Also, megadoses of vitamins C, D, A, K, and B_6 have been linked with birth defects (Scher & Dix, 1983).

The prescription drugs mentioned in this section are only a few of the drugs that are known to be harmful to the fetus. There are many others that do not seem to have any immediate negative effects, but whose long-term effects are still unclear. **Diethylstilbestrol (DES)**, for example, is a drug that was heavily prescribed during the 1940s and 1950s for women who were at risk for spontaneous abortions. Not until several decades later did medical researchers discover a link between DES use by pregnant women and vaginal cancer among females subsequently born to these women. Because the effect occurs so long after taking the drug and because it is manifested in only a small percentage of the offspring, it is extremely difficult to detect. For this reason, many medical practitioners discourage the use of any prescription drugs by pregnant women unless absolutely necessary.

IMPORTANCE OF TIMING OF DRUG INTAKE

The most serious structural changes (physical deformities and abnormalities) that are sometimes associated with drug intake or with other factors such as maternal malnutrition are most likely to occur during the embryonic stage of development. After this stage, the fetus's basic structure has already been formed and is not as vulnerable to external influences (see Figure 4.5). Also, during the first two weeks after conception the fertilized ovum is thought to be highly resistant to the influence of teratogens—or if the embryo is affected, it is likely to be aborted (Friedman, 1992). In fact, about 30 to 40 percent of all potential pregnancies are lost before they are recognized—that is, in the first two weeks (Simpson, 1991).

f i g u r e   4 . 5

The most serious structural defects in prenatal development are most likely to occur in the first eight weeks, although teratogens can have serious consequences throughout gestation.

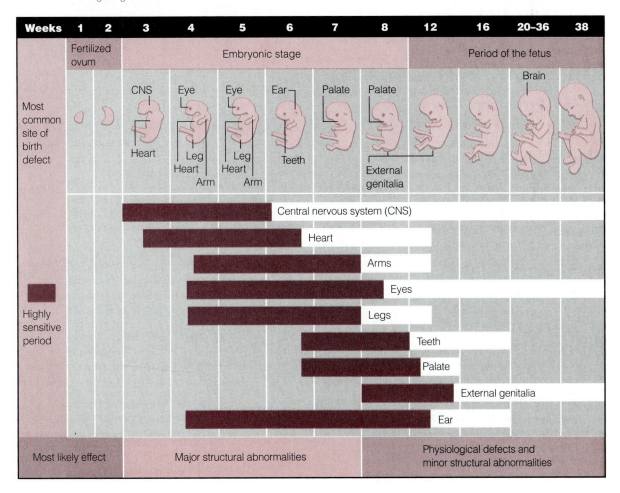

exposure to chemicals

The effects of chemicals on mother and fetus are very difficult to ascertain, partly because the effects of many chemicals are sometimes too subtle and not sufficiently widespread to be easily noticed. It is also the case that there are so many chemicals in our environments that it is almost impossible to separate their individual effects from one another (Elkington, 1986). There are more than 60,000 chemicals currently in use in North America, and several thousand new chemicals are introduced each year (Sloan, Shapiro, & Mitchell, 1980). Although the majority of these are "contained" in one way or another—that is, they do not find their way into our air, our water, or our food—and are considered essentially harmless, we are exposed to others on a daily basis in the form of water, air, or food pollutants, or as toxic wastes of various kinds. Unfortunately, their ultimate effects on our lives or on the lives of those not yet born are not fully understood.

MERCURY

We do know, however, that the ingestion of mercury by expectant mothers may result in severe retardation and physical deformities in their children. Although mercury occurs naturally in some areas, it is most often problematic as an industrial waste. It is also sometimes used to treat seed grains. Its effects received worldwide attention following the births of a large number of severely deformed and retarded infants in Minimata Bay, Japan. The deformities were traced to the presence of high levels of mercury in the fish that inhabitants of this community consumed in great quantities; the mercury was, in this case, an industrial waste.

The effects of mercury are now known as Minimata disease.

PCBS AND RELATED HYDROCARBONS

Other chemicals that are known to be harmful include a range of hydrocarbons that are used as herbicides or insecticides. These hydrocarbons include dioxin and PCB, both of which appear to be associated with a higher incidence of miscarriage and with physical deformities (Jacobson & Jacobson, 1990). Agent Orange, a chemical widely used to defoliate trees during the Vietnam War, is a dioxin-like chemical that has also been linked with fetal abnormalities and death.

In addition to the chemicals known to be harmful to the fetus, there are many toxic chemicals whose effects on fetal development are unknown, although we know how they affect children and adults. Lead is one example. It is present in some fuel emissions, in some paints, in certain metal products, and elsewhere. It accumulates slowly in the body; and when it reaches sufficiently high concentrations, it can lead to serious physical and mental problems in children and adults (Weisskopf, 1987).

HOW COMMON ARE THESE CHEMICALS?

We might want to think that terrible things happen only to other people, to strangers who live in faraway places, but such is not the case. They happen where I am and where you are. When, in the spring of 1986, the nuclear reactor in Chernobyl, Ukraine, spewed radioactive particles into the air, their presence could be felt and measured in Norway, in Poland, in France, and yes, even in North America. And we know that radiation is an extremely powerful mutagen and that relatively low levels can lead to abortion, stillbirths, and physical abnormalities.

And we know, too, that today's highly industrialized environments are loaded with synthetic substances and potentially harmful chemicals. But, says Tierney (1988), perhaps we have overemphasized the danger of many of these synthetic carcinogens (cancer-causing agents). Fortunately, only relatively rarely are we exposed to them in sufficient doses or over a long enough period that they either affect our health measurably or become teratogens for the unborn.

nicotine intake

The harmful effects of smoking on the smoker and the effects of "secondhand" smoke on the nonsmoker have been well documented. Some of its effects on the fetus also seem clear.

The U.S. Surgeon General, following an extensive review of the literature on cigarette smoking during pregnancy, summarized some of its most important and consistent effects (U.S. Department of Health & Human Services, 1981). Cigarette smoking, the Surgeon General concludes, (1) is linked with a higher probability of placental problems in which the placenta becomes detached from the uterine wall, often leading to fetal death or stillbirth; (2) is associated with significantly lower birthweight, which, in turn, is associated with a higher probability of subsequent complications; (3) is linked with a higher risk of miscarriage and fetal death; and (4) is related to a higher incidence of early childhood respiratory infections and diseases. In brief, cigarette smoking is clearly harmful not only to the mother, but also to the fetus and placenta.

Although smoking during pregnancy has decreased since the 1960s, almost one-third of pregnant women smoked in 1987 (Food and Nutrition Board, 1990). Those with less education were most likely to smoke.

caffeine consumption

The effects of caffeine on the fetus remain somewhat unclear, perhaps because the effects are different for different individuals and because they do not appear to be very dramatic (Food and Nutrition Board, 1990). Nevertheless, large doses of caffeine given to pregnant rats have been associated with birth defects in their offspring. And some research indicates that the probability of premature delivery is somewhat higher among mothers who consume higher levels of caffeine (Jacobson et al., 1985). However, current evidence suggests that caffeine is not a human teratogen, although very high consumption might be toxic for the fetus (Brendt & Beckman, 1990).

alcohol consumption

Alcohol consumption by pregnant women may be associated with premature birth and with various defects in their offspring. The classical collection of alcohol-related effects in the newborn is labeled **fetal alcohol syndrome** (Streissguth, Barr, & Martin, 1983). The major features of FAS are central nervous system problems sometimes manifested in mental retardation, retarded physical growth, and cranial and facial malformations. These malformations typically include a low forehead, widely spaced eyes, a short nose, a long upper lip, and absence of a marked infranasal depression (the typical depression in the center of the upper lip, extending upward toward the nose) (Abel, 1984).

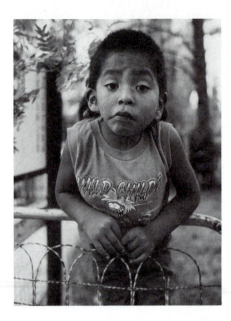

Fetal alcohol syndrome, most often apparent in central nervous system problems including mental retardation, may also be evident in facial and cranial malformations, including widely spaced eyes, low forehead, long upper lip, and absence of distinct infranasal depression.

With humans it is problematic to conduct the types of experiments that would allow researchers to determine precisely the amounts of alcohol and the timing of intake that result in these effects. Nor is it possible to separate completely the effects of alcohol from those of other drugs that might accompany alcohol use, or from the effects of malnutrition, also a possible corollary of alcohol use. However, a number of studies have looked at FAS among animals and have found, to no one's great surprise, that injections of ethanol (drinking alcohol) in pregnant mice quite readily produce what appears to be FAS in their offspring. Not only are these offspring less likely be born alive, but many of them also display facial and skull deformations highly similar to those characteristic of FAS children (Rosett & Sander, 1979).

The current consensus is that even in small amounts, alcohol may be harmful to the fetus, although it may not necessarily lead to fetal alcohol syndrome. Accordingly, some researchers speak of "fetal alcohol effects" rather than of FAS. For example, one study compared the effects of heavy drinking (four or more drinks a day) with the effects of more moderate drinking (two to four drinks a day) and with those of lighter drinking (fewer than two drinks a day) (Streissguth et al., 1980). Some of the symptoms associated with FAS were found in 19 percent of the children born to mothers in the first group, 11 percent of those in the second, and only 2 percent of those in the third.

The evidence is not all in, and the conclusions are still tentative. However, in summarizing the effects of alcohol on the developing fetus, Brendt and Beckman (1990) conclude that consuming six drinks or more of alcohol per day constitutes a high risk, but that fewer than two drinks per day is not likely to lead to fetal alcohol syndrome. And Graham (1985) suggests that binge drinking may be especially harmful to the fetus in the early stages of pregnancy, and that it might be associated with neural tube defects.

Given these findings, corroborated by a large number of other investigations, it should come as no surprise that an increasing number of medical practitioners recommend that pregnant women refrain completely from alcohol use. In Friedman's (1992) words, "No safe level of maternal drinking during pregnancy has been established" (p. 117).

substance abuse

As we have seen, various prescription and nonprescription drugs used for medicinal purposes can harm the developing fetus, as can various legal recreational drugs such as alcohol, nicotine, and caffeine. In addition, many illegal recreational drugs—narcotics, LSD, marijuana, and cocaine—can also affect a fetus adversely.

NARCOTICS

Babies born to narcotics addicts are themselves addicted, and they subsequently suffer a clearly recognizable withdrawal (labeled the **neonatal abstinence syndrome**). Its symptoms may include tremors, restlessness, hyperactive reflexes, high-pitched cries, vomiting, fevers, sweating, rapid respiration, seizures, and sometimes death (Chasnoff, 1986). Often these symptoms don't reach a peak until the infant is 3 or 4 days old. Some physicians recommend methadone maintenance in low doses for the mother during the later stages of pregnancy and then gradual weaning of the infant from methadone after birth (Iennarella, Chisum, & Bianchi, 1986).

In addition to their addictive effects evident in the neonatal abstinence syndrome, the use of narcotics has also been linked with prematurity and low birthweight, and with behavior problems such as hyperactivity (Kolata, 1978).

LSD

The effects on human fetuses of maternal use of substances such as LSD remain somewhat unclear. Although research with pregnant monkeys who were given LSD found chromosomal damage in the mothers and a high rate of stillbirths and early deaths among infants (Kato, 1970), these findings cannot easily be corroborated with humans. As Bolton (1983) points out, mothers who have used LSD have also typically drunk alcohol as well, and may also have used other drugs. In addition, many of them receive

little prenatal medical care, some suffer from drug-related illnesses and diseases, and many have severely deficient diets. The causes of fetal and birth problems among this group of mothers cannot easily be identified.

MARIJUANA

There is some uncertainty about the effects of marijuana as well (Food and Nutrition Board, 1990). Fried's (1986) investigation of 700 pregnant women, about 4 percent of whom were heavy or moderate users of marijuana, found no differences between marijuana users and nonusers with respect to rate of miscarriages, birth complications, or physical anomalies at birth. The study did find, however, that the gestational period was an average of 1.1 weeks shorter for heavy users. In addition, newborns whose mothers were regular heavy marijuana smokers exhibited more tremors and more intense startle reactions, and they were less responsive to a light directed at their eyes. However, tests of motor and cognitive functioning do not ordinarily reveal any differences between infants of marijuana users and nonusers.

Friedman (1992) includes marijuana (and LSD as well) among the substances that have not been *proven* to be teratogenic in humans.

COCAINE

Two more recent and perhaps increasingly common drugs abused by pregnant women are cocaine and crack. (Crack is easily manufactured from cocaine, is less expensive, and has far more intense and immediate effects than cocaine used more conventionally; see Chapter 12.) Cocaine addiction is reportedly about five times more common than heroin addiction in the United States. Some reports claim it has reached "epidemic proportions" (Food and Nutrition Board, 1990). However, estimates of illegal drug use are seldom very reliable.

Once thought to be relatively harmless, cocaine is now considered not only highly addictive, but also potentially very harmful to the unborn. Like most mood-altering drugs, it crosses the placental barrier easily. And because it is fat-soluble, it remains in the placenta and in amniotic fluid, where, notes Mullin (1992), the fetus ingests it over and over again. A dose of cocaine lasts about 48 hours in the adult; in the fetus it may last four or five days (Brody, 1988).

Infants born to cocaine and crack users manifest more startle reactions and more tremors than children of nonusers (Chasnoff, Burns, Schnoll, & Burns, 1985). They are also more likely to manifest disturbances in sleep patterns, feeding difficulties, diarrhea, fever, and increased irritability. On average, they are smaller and may show evidence of growth retardation (for example, delayed age of developing visual and auditory orientation, of pulling up to a sitting position, and of standing) (Mullin, 1992). And not only are they more likely to be stillborn or to abort spontaneously (Rosenak, Diamant, Yaffe, & Hornstein, 1990), but they are about 10 times more likely to die of sudden infant death syndrome (SIDS, described in Chapter 5) (Chasnoff, 1986/1987).

maternal health

A wide range of diseases and infections are also known to affect the fetus. The best known is probably rubella (German measles); others are syphilis, gonorrhea, and poliomyelitis, each of which can cause mental deficiency, blindness, deafness, or miscarriages. Cretinism (subnormal mental development, undeveloped bones, a protruding abdomen, and rough, coarse skin) may be related to a thyroid malfunction in the mother or to an iodine deficiency in her diet. If the deficiency is not too extreme, it can sometimes be alleviated in the child through continuous medication after birth.

DIABETES

Diabetes is a maternal condition that can have serious consequences for the fetus (Hare, 1989). Before the discovery of insulin, fetal and maternal death was very common. Now, however, mortality rates among diabetic mothers are about the same as those among nonpregnant diabetic women. And with timely diagnosis and proper medical management, fetal deaths are generally below 5 percent (Coustan, 1990). Management involves careful monitoring of mother and fetus to assess and control sugar levels (glycemic control). Simple self-monitoring procedures are available for in-home use.

Although fetal death as a complication of maternal diabetes has been greatly reduced, the rate of birth defects among these infants is still 2 to 4 times higher. The most common defects include limb, heart, and neural tube defects (Friedman & McGillivray, 1992). Most of these birth defects result from influences that occur early in pregnancy—hence the importance of careful monitoring from the outset.

HERPES INFECTIONS

Herpes simplex type 2 (genital herpes) is the most common of all sexually transmitted diseases; it can have serious effects on the fetus, particularly if the mother's infection is active at the time of delivery. The probability that infants will contract the virus during birth is extremely high—40 to 60 percent (Eden et al., 1990). In addition, evidence suggests that as many as 50 percent of mothers suffering from active herpes infections give birth prematurely (Babson et al., 1980). Because the newborn does not possess many of the immunities that are common among older children and adults, the herpes virus may attack the infant's internal organs, leading to visual or nervous system problems or death in about 50 percent of cases (Eden et al., 1990). As a result, infants born to mothers infected with herpes virus are often delivered through cesarean section to prevent infection.

Another form of herpes virus, **cytomegalovirus**, affects the salivary glands and can also be passed on to the fetus during birth. It is one of the main *infectious* causes of mental retardation, and also an important cause of deafness.

AIDS

Acquired immune deficiency syndrome (AIDS) is another sexually transmitted disease that is of considerable current concern. First reported in the United States in 1981, the disease remains incurable and thus ultimately fatal. In 1991, more than 43,000 new cases of AIDS were reported in the United States (U.S. Bureau of the Census, 1992). Estimates were that worldwide, more than 1 million women would be infected in 1993. And the prognosis is that virtually all will eventually die from resulting complications. By the year 2000, about 4 million women will have died ("AIDS will kill . . . ," 1993.) And in the United States in 1991, eight times more men than women were diagnosed as being positive for infection with the virus that causes AIDS.

AIDS is transmitted through the exchange of body fluids, primarily through blood/blood exchange or through semen/blood exchange. Accordingly, transmission occurs mainly through anal intercourse (because of the thinness of rectal tissues, which frequently tear during intercourse), through blood transfusions involving infected blood, and through the communal use of hypodermic syringes. Not surprisingly, AIDS is most common among homosexual males and among intravenous drug users but is also increasing among heterosexual men and women (see Chapter 12 for more information).

Most infants and children acquire AIDS directly from their mothers through blood exchange in the uterus or during birth. The risk of transmission from infected mother to fetus ranges from 35 percent to 60 percent (Trofatter, 1990). Prognosis for an infected newborn is poor (see "At A Glance: Pediatric AIDS Mortality," Figure 4.6), but with the combined use of AZT and antibiotics beginning soon after birth, about one-third of infected children are surviving 8 to 10 years or even longer (AIDS kids beat odds against survival," 1994).

Clearly, high-risk women (current or past intravenous drug users and those whose sexual partner(s) include bisexual males and/or men who have been or are intravenous drug users) should be tested for antibodies for the AIDS virus before considering pregnancy.

The effects of many of the factors affecting prenatal development are listed in Table 4.3, page 164.

maternal emotions and stress

A once-common folk belief was that the mother's emotional states could be communicated directly to her unborn child. If the pregnant woman worried

*A*cquired immune de-
ficiency syndrome
(AIDS) is a fatal dis-
ease transmitted
through the exchange of body fluids.
Most cases of pediatric (childhood)
AIDS are transmitted directly from
mother to fetus. In later childhood,
AIDS is acquired primarily through
blood transfusions and is consequently
rarer. With increasing sexual activity
after adolescence, incidence of AIDS
rises dramatically. Male AIDS cases
outnumbered female cases by a factor
of almost 10 to 1 in 1991.

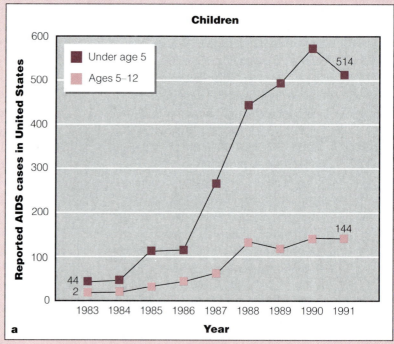

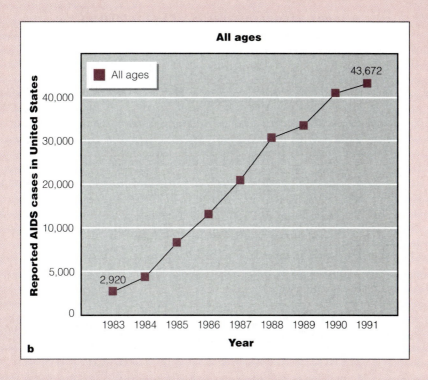

All ages

b

f **i g u r e   4 . 6**

(a, b) Rising number of AIDS cases in the United States, 1983 to 1991. Source: Adapted from U.S. Bureau of the Census (1992), p. 125.

too much, her child would be born with a frown; if she had a particularly traumatic experience, it would mark the infant, perhaps for life; if she were frightened by a rabbit, the result might be a child with a harelip. Accordingly, she must try to be happy and have pleasant experiences so that the child could be born free of natative influences.

Most of these beliefs about pregnancy are simply tales. However, because of the close relationship between the mother and the fetus, a number of investigators have pursued the idea that stimuli affecting her will also have some effect on the fetus, however indirect.

There is some evidence that intense maternal emotions affect fetuses. Mothers who are anxious during much of their pregnancy frequently have infants who are more irritable and more hyperactive and have more feeding problems. This is especially true if the mother experiences long-term stress rather than isolated episodes (Spezzano, 1981). One prevalent theory is that an anxious mother's chemi-

table 4.3

Influences on the fetus

AGENT	SOME REPORTED EFFECTS OR ASSOCIATIONS
Alcohol	Fetal alcohol syndrome; intrauterine growth retardation; microcephaly; mental retardation
Nicotine	Placental lesions; intrauterine growth retardation; increased mortality
Street drugs	Fetal and pregnancy complications sometimes leading to death; no reported association with malformations
Caffeine	Not likely to be a teratogen, although excess consumption may be toxic
Aspirin	Heavy use associated with lowered birthrate; no increase in malformation
Tetracycline	Tooth and bone staining if exposed during last two-thirds of pregnancy
Vitamin A	Urogenital anomalies associated with massive doses; ear malformations; neural tube defects; cleft palate; facial abnormalities
Vitamin D	Heart defects; facial malformation; mental retardation
Thalidomide	Limb reduction defects; anomalies of external ears, kidneys, and heart
Diethylstilbestrol (DES)	Anomalies of cervix and uterus; higher risk of cervical cancer
Methylmercury	Minamata disease; cerebral palsy; microcephaly; mental retardation; blindness; death
Lithium carbonate	Heart and blood vessel defects; neural tube defects
Polychlorinated biphenyls	Cola-colored children; gum, nail, and groin pigmentation; can affect offspring for up to 4 years after maternal exposure
Radiation	Microcephaly; mental retardation; eye anomalies; visceral malformations
Iodine deficiency	Hypothyroidism or goiter; neurological damage
Maternal starvation	Intrauterine growth retardation; central nervous system anomalies; fetal death
Mechanical (constraint in womb)	Defects involving limb development and position; neural tube, lip, palate, or abdominal defects
Diabetes	Malformations involving internal organs; caudal dysplasia
Rubella	Mental retardation; deafness; cardiovascular malformations; cataracts

Source: Based on R. L. Brendt & D. A. Beckman. (1990). Teratology. In R. D. Eden, F. H. Boehm, & M. Haire (Eds.), *Assessment and care of the fetus: Physiological, clinical, and medicolegal principles* (Table 17-4, pp. 227–28). Norwalk, Conn.: Appleton & Lange. Reprinted by permission of the publisher.

cal balance affects her unborn child physiologically and therefore, indirectly, psychologically.

These findings are highly tentative. Not only is it extremely difficult to arrive at valid and useful measures of emotional states in mother and infant, but it is also often impossible to control a variety of other factors that might be related. For example, some of the factors sometimes associated with high maternal stress (poverty, inadequate diet, medical problems) might also be associated with fetal problems. Hence conclusive statements about the influence of maternal emotional states on the unborn are not warranted.

A mother's age can also be related to the well-being of the fetus. Infants of both older and younger mothers are sometimes at a disadvantage.

OLDER MOTHERS

We know, as was pointed out in Chapter 3, that the incidence of trisomy 21 (Down syndrome) is about 40 times higher for women over age 40 than for women aged 20. We know, as well, that the probability of fathering a child with Down syndrome is 20 to 30 percent higher for fathers over the age of 55. Fragile X syndrome is also more common with increasing maternal age, as are Klinefelter's syndrome and trisomy 18 (associated with neural tube defects, congenital heart disease, growth retardation, and other problems) (Hsu, 1986).

However, perhaps in part due to the availability of procedures such as CVS or amniocentesis (see Chapter 3 for an explanation of these procedures) that make it possible to determine the presence of a number of chromosomal abnormalities and other defects or diseases prenatally, increasing numbers of women (and men) are making the decision to have a family later. Kopp and Kaler (1989) point out that the greatest increase in fertility rates in recent years has been among women in their early 30s. However, fewer than 7 percent of all births occur to women over the age of 35 (Drugan, Johnson, & Evans, 1990).

In spite of the association between the mother's age and some chromosomal abnormalities, modern health care makes it possible for many women to deliver healthy, full-term babies at ages that would have entailed much greater risk a few decades ago. In fact, when Spellacy, Miller, and Winegar (1986) compared outcomes for 511 pregnancies of women over 40 with more than 26,000 pregnancies of women between ages 20 and 30, they found that age posed little risk when factors such as cigarette smoking and maternal weight were taken into account.

TEENAGE MOTHERS

Birthrates among teenage mothers remain very high relative to the rest of the population. In fact, in 1988, 12.5 percent of all births were to mothers aged 15 to 19 (U.S. Bureau of the Census, 1992). The teenage birthrate in the United States is among the highest in the world, approximately 17 times higher than in Japan and 3 times higher than in the former Soviet Union (Davis & Harris, 1982).

Children born to younger teenage mothers are often at a physical, emotional, and intellectual disadvantage relative to children born to older mothers. There are more miscarriages, premature births, and stillbirths among teenage mothers, and surviving infants are more often the targets of abuse and neglect. Their developmental scores on various measures are often retarded (Smith, Weinman, & Malinak, 1984), and incidence of low birthweight is about 3 times higher for teenage mothers (National Center for Health Statistics, 1987).

As Lamb and Elster (1985) point out, however, much of this research fails to take into account the social circumstances of teenage parenthood—the poverty and the lack of social, educational, and medical assistance. In retrospect, it seems that it is not the age of the teenage parent that is the important factor, but the health care available to the mother both before and after the birth of her child. All other things being equal and unless she is very young (below age 15), if a teenage mother and her infant receive the same

North American teenage pregnancy rates are very high (about 1 in every 8 births in the United States). Largely because of lack of medical assistance and poorer nutrition, these mothers are at greater risk for miscarriage, prematurity, and stillbirths, and their surviving infants are more often retarded and more likely to suffer abuse and neglect.

medical attention as an older mother, the health and developmental status of her infant will be normal (McCormick, Shapiro, & Starfield, 1984).

But all other things are not often equal for teenage mothers. And they will not be equal, argues Grow (1979), unless various agencies provide comprehensive services for teenage parents who keep their children. In the absence of such services, the economic and social conditions under which the majority of teenage mothers are forced to live, the emotional stresses that accompany these conditions, and the demands of pregnancy and of childrearing present serious disadvantages. (See Chapter 12 for a more detailed discussion of teenage pregnancy.)

maternal nutrition

Infant size at birth, which is related to maternal nutrition, is one of the key determinants of survival and health ("Nutrition during pregnancy," 1990).

EFFECTS OF SERIOUS MALNUTRITION

During the German siege of Leningrad in World War II, many Russians lived near starvation in bitterly cold, unheated homes. Many died. But perhaps most striking, in one clinic that had seen an average of 3,867 births a year for the preceding three years, only 493 infants were born in 1942 (Shanklin & Hoden, 1979). Most of these babies were born in the first half of the year and had been conceived before the famine was at its height; only 79 were born in the second half of the year. In addition to this dramatic decline in birthrate, there were also great increases in amenorrhea (cessation of menstruation, which, incidentally, is not uncommon among anorexic women), low levels of fertility, and an increase in miscarriages.

EFFECTS OF LESS SERIOUS MALNUTRITION

There is little doubt that starvation, and extreme malnutrition, can have serious negative consequences for the fetus. But investigating the effects of less dramatic forms of malnutrition is difficult. Investigators can't always separate the effects of malnutrition from the effects of other factors that often accompany malnutrition (poor sanitation, poor medical care, drug use, and so on). Effects sometimes attributed solely to malnutrition might also, at least in part, be related to these other factors. In addition, malnutrition is seldom limited to the prenatal period but usually continues into infancy and even childhood. As Stein et al. (1975) note, perhaps the most plausible conclusion is that the effects of malnutrition are a complex interaction of the severity and nature of deprivation, its timing, and its duration. It is not improbable, as Lewin (1975) suggests, that long-term intellectual deficits may result from malnutrition that begins before birth and continues for some time afterward, and it is possible that some of the short-term effects associated with prenatal malnutrition are reversible given adequate nourishment after birth.

NUTRITIONAL REQUIREMENTS DURING PREGNANCY

During pregnancy, the mother's energy requirements and her metabolism change. The presence of a growing fetus means that the mother requires some-

where between 10 and 15 percent more calories. And metabolic changes include an increased synthesis of protein, which is important for the formation of the placenta and enlargement of the uterus; a reduction in carbohydrate consumption, the effect of which is to provide sufficient glucose for the fetus; and increased storage of fat to satisfy the mother's energy requirements (Chez & Chervenak, 1990).

Not only must pregnant women increase protein intake, but there is also an increased need for important minerals (for example, calcium, magnesium, iron, and zinc) and vitamins (mainly B_6, D, and E). Recommended dietary allowances for pregnant women range from 25 to 50 percent above those for nonpregnant women (*Recommended Dietary Allowances*, 1980).

Research indicates that *average* intake of these nutrients is often less than recommended for American women (Food and Nutrition Board, 1990). Hence current medical advice emphasizes that what the woman eats is more important than how much. With respect to fetal brain growth, protein appears to be among the most important ingredients of a good diet. In studies of both humans and rats in which expectant mothers had protein-deficient diets, the offspring developed fewer brain cells or performed more poorly on subsequent tests of intellectual performance (McKay et al., 1978).

OPTIMAL WEIGHT GAIN DURING PREGNANCY

Current medical advice contradicts the long-held belief that women should be careful to minimize weight gain during pregnancy. Infant mortality rates are often lower in countries where pregnant women gain significantly more weight than do pregnant women in the United States or Canada. Maternal weight gain leads to higher fetal weight and reduces the risk of illness and infection. Accord-

During pregnancy, protein and mineral needs increase greatly, as does need for caloric intake (by about 10 to 15 percent). Current recommended weight gain during pregnancy for an initially average-weight woman is 25 to 35 pounds; for women who are initially underweight, it is even higher.

ingly, doctors who once cautioned women to limit their weight gain to about 10 pounds now suggest that the optimal weight gain for a woman who begins pregnancy at an average weight is somewhere between 25 and 35 pounds (11.5 to 16 kg) (Chez & Chervenak, 1990); it is even higher for women who are initially underweight. For women who are initially overweight, recommended gains are correspondingly lower (15–25 lbs; 7–11.5 kg) ("Nutrition

during pregnancy," 1990). Total recommended weight gain for women carrying twins is 35 to 45 pounds (16–20.5 kg).

Unfortunately, this medical advice is probably most relevant to those least likely to be exposed to it and least able to take advantage of it. Malnutrition and starvation, seldom a deliberate choice, are important issues and responsibilities for our social consciences.

social class

The greatest single cause of infant death is premature birth. Prematurity is among the most direct causes of cerebral palsy and various mental defects. The causes most closely responsible for premature births are social rather than medical.

These facts are important and well documented (Kopp & Parmelee, 1979). Although social class does not explain anything by itself, the high correlation between low social class and higher incidence of premature birth suggests that the living conditions and associated emotional and health consequences of poverty are not conducive to the production of healthy full-term babies (Baker & Mednick, 1984). There is little doubt that prenatal care of mothers who live in poverty is not often comparable to that afforded middle-class mothers; nor is postnatal health care. General diet, protein intake, and mineral and vitamin intake are frequently significantly inferior among women of poverty; the effects of these factors are often the consequences of an infant's being born poor.

Rh(D) immunization

There is a particular quality of blood in Rhesus monkeys that is often, but not always, present in human blood. Because this factor was first discovered in Rhesus monkeys, it is called the Rh (or Rhesus) factor. Individuals who have this factor are Rh-positive; those who don't are Rh-negative.

A specific component of the Rh blood group, labeled D, is especially important for the pregnant mother and her fetus. Introduction of Rh(D)-positive blood into an individual who is Rh(D)-negative leads to the formation of antibodies to counteract the D factor—a process termed *immunization* (Bowman, 1990). If these antibodies are then introduced into an individual with Rh(D)-positive blood, they attack that person's blood cells, causing a depletion of oxygen and, in the absence of medical intervention, death.

Unfortunately, this situation can occur in the fetus (termed *fetal erythroblastosis*) when the fetus has Rh(D)-positive blood and the mother is Rh(D)-negative. Because the Rh factor is a dominant genetic trait, this situation can occur only when the father is Rh(D)-positive and the mother is Rh(D)-negative. If blood from the fetus gets into the mother's bloodstream—termed *transplacental hemorrhage*—the mother's blood will begin to produce antibodies. These are usually not produced early enough or in sufficient quantities to affect the first child, but subsequent fetuses may be affected.

Transplacental hemorrhage occurs in approximately 50 percent of all pregnant women, either during pregnancy or immediately after birth (Knuppel & Angel, 1990). Hence the chances of Rh(D) immunization are very high—if, of course, the mother is Rh(D)-negative and the father Rh(D)-positive. At one time, this condition was always fatal. Now, however, it is possible for a physician to monitor antibody levels in the mother's blood, determining when levels are high enough to endanger the fetus. At this point, there are several alternatives. If the fetus is suffi-

ciently advanced (32 or 33 weeks, for example), labor might be induced or a cesarean delivery performed, and the infant given a complete blood transfusion immediately (Bowman, 1990). If the fetus is not sufficiently advanced, a blood transfusion may be performed in utero.

Fortunately, this type of medical intervention is not often necessary since the development of *Rhogam* (Rh Immune Globulin or RhlG) in 1968. Rhogam contains *passive* antibodies that prevent the formation of additional antibodies.

It has become routine for physicians to ascertain whether a pregnant woman is Rh(D)-negative and whether she is at risk of Rh(D) immunization; this information should be gathered at the time of the first prenatal visit. Bowman (1990) suggests that husbands or partners of Rh(D)-negative women should then be screened as well. If they too are Rh(D)-negative, there is little chance of fetal erythroblastosis. However, because of the possibility of an extramarital conception, mothers who are Rh(D)-negative and their fetuses should be monitored closely throughout pregnancy.

When an expecting mother is at risk of immunization (that is, she is Rh(D)-negative and the father is Rh(D)-positive), Rhogam is sometimes administered during the seventh month of gestation, even though the incidence of immunization before delivery is low (approximately 2 percent). Current medical guidelines are that all such women be administered Rhogam within no more than 72 hours of delivery, as soon as it has been determined that the fetus is Rh(D)-positive and that she is therefore at risk of Rh(D) immunization. Similarly, Rhogam should be administered in the event of the abortion or miscarriage of an Rh(D)-positive fetus if the mother is Rh(D)-negative. The drug must be administered after the termination of every Rh(D)-positive

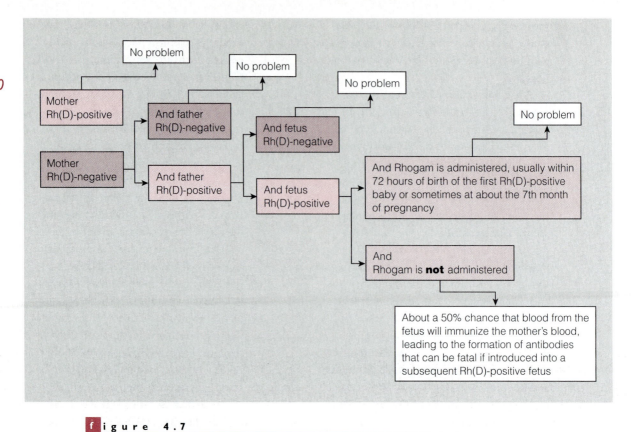

Rh(D) immunization flowchart. Immunization occurs when the Rh(D) factor is introduced into an Rh(D)-negative mother's blood, leading to the formation of antibodies that, if they are later introduced into the bloodstream of an Rh(D)-positive fetus, attack the fetus's blood cells in a potentially fatal condition termed fetal erythroblastosis. *An injection of the drug Rhogam can prevent this condition.*

pregnancy. (See Figure 4.7 for a an Rh(D) decision flowchart.)

childbirth

hildbirth is something that happens almost 4 million times a year in the United States—although fertility rates (proportion of women having children) have declined in the United States (see Figure 4.8 in "At A Glance: Births and Deaths in the United States").

Birth in today's industrialized nations is largely considered a medical procedure. Doctors and other medical personnel work to ensure the safety of the newborn as well as the safety and comfort of the

mother. They have at their command techniques and procedures to induce labor, to accelerate it, to delay it, even to stop it if necessary. They can administer drugs to lessen the mother's pain, perform blood transfusions on the infant, or deliver through cesarean section. They can even decide to allow a normally proceeding birth to continue without medical intervention.

Elsewhere, and in earlier times, people's experiences of birth were different. It occurred in birthing huts, in fields, in forests or, perhaps most often, in homes. These "primitive" (or perhaps "more natural") births were sometimes a solitary experience; sometimes there were

I n 1960, when the baby boom was nearing its peak, almost 4.3 million babies were born in the United States. And only 1.7 million people died, leaving a natural population increase of about 2.6 million. Numbers of births dropped below 4 million in the 1970s. In spite of a substantial increase in total population, number of births have remained fairly constant at between 3.5 and slightly more than 4 million since 1980. This means that fertility rate (number of births per 1,000 population) has dropped, partly because of more effective contraception and partly as a result of changed attitudes toward conception and childbearing.

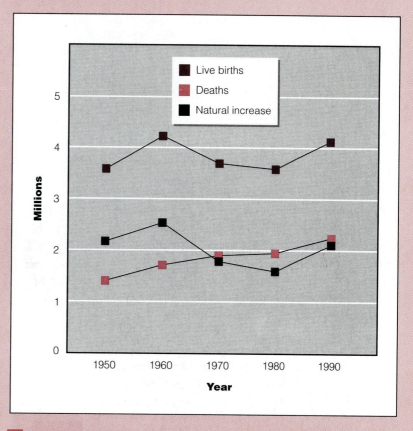

f igure 4.8

Births and deaths in the United States, 1950–1990. Source: Based on U.S. Bureau of the Census (1992), p. 65.

midwives, healers, or other attendants. In general, it was believed to be far simpler, shorter, and less painful than birth often is today. Goldsmith (1990a) quotes a nineteenth-century traveler who had been trekking with the Guiana women of South America: "When on the march an Indian is taken with labor, she just steps aside, is delivered, wraps up the baby with the afterbirth and runs in haste after the others" (p. 22). (See "In Other Contexts: A !Kung Woman's First Child.")

But we know too that in earlier times birth was often a tragic experience: Infant mortality was high, and the death of the mother too was not uncommon. A century ago, more than 100 of every 1,000 infants died; that number has now

hen she felt the contractions were sufficiently strong and frequent, Sanyo, a woman of the !Kung, hunter-gatherers of the Kalahari, rose silently from her bed. She didn't awaken her husband—or even her parents, although they, too, slept in the same hut. Among the !Kung, a marriage is not considered consummated before the birth of a child; until then, the couple lives with the wife's parents. This would be Sanyo's first child.

For a moment, Sanyo thought she might awaken her mother; the first birth is sometimes assisted by the mother. But !Kung women are strong and independent, and Sanyo scarcely hesitated. Alone, she walked out into the veld, smelling the rich earth smells of the land, the excitement of another dawn. Silently, she gathered handfuls of sedges and grasses, laying them in a soft bed at the foot of a tree. Then she leaned back against the tree, caught up in the mounting sensations of the contractions, excited that she, too, would soon be a mother, anticipating the pride with which she would walk back to the village, carrying her newborn.

Did Sanyo sense any fear, even a twinge of apprehension? No. She knew that some births were longer than others, that some were sometimes difficult. If hers were like that, she would

walk back to the village and the women would massage her back while her husband, using his walking stick, would draw a fine line in the sand, straight away from the hut, out through the village and beyond, praying all the while: "Come out, come out, come to the village, everyone is waiting for you" (Fried & Fried, 1980, p. 29).

Sanyo had no need for mother or husband. When she sensed the baby's head emerging, she squatted over the grassy mound, delivering it easily onto the soft bed. A girl! She, like all first-born girls, would be named for her father's mother.

Sanyo wiped the baby clean with the grasses, cut the umbilical cord with a stick, wrapped the baby in the blanket she had brought, and quickly

erased all traces of the delivery, burying the stained grasses and carefully marking the spot with a stick so that no man would accidentally step on it and lose his sexual potency or his hunting skills.

Quickly, she hurried home. Tonight there would be a feast and a dance for the new baby.

To Think About: To what extent might the pain and fear sometimes associated with childbirth be influenced by cultural expectations? Can you think of other reactions and expectations that are typical in your cultural group—and that you therefore assume to be "natural" but that might be quite different elsewhere?

To Read: Goldsmith, J. (1990a). Childbirth wisdom: From the world's oldest societies. Brookline, Mass.: East-West Health Books. Also see the book upon which this account is based: Fried, M. N., & Fried, M. H. (1980). Four rituals in eight cultures. New York: W. W. Norton.

been reduced by almost 90 percent (U.S. Department of Health and Human Services, 1989). The decline in infant mortality rates is due not only to medical advances, but also to improved sanitation and a consequent reduction in maternal and infant infections. Through the Middle Ages, high risk of death during childbirth (or of subsequent infections) made childbearing a relatively dangerous undertaking. Even as recently as 1960, of every 100,000 women giving birth in the United States, an average of 37 died (75 percent of these were nonwhites). By 1989, maternal mortality rates had been cut by more than 80 percent (still twice as high for black as for white mothers). In the same period, infant death rates were more than halved, from 26 per 1000 live births to less than 8 (see Figure 4.9).

Surprisingly, what causes the childbirth process to begin remains almost as much of a mystery today as it has always been. Hippocrates, writing some 2,400 years ago, thought he knew. The child starts the whole process, he informed his readers. When the fetus has grown too big, there simply isn't enough nourishment available, so it becomes agitated, it kicks around and moves its arms, and it ruptures the membranes that hold it in. And then it forces its way out, head first because the head part is heavier than the bottom part (see Liggins, 1988).

Hippocrates was wrong, although many people believed his speculation right into the eighteenth century. We now know that even dead fetuses may go

f igure   4 . 9

Declining maternal and infant mortality rates from delivery and complications of pregnancy and childbirth, 1960 to 1989. Source: U.S. Bureau of the Census (1990), p. 77.

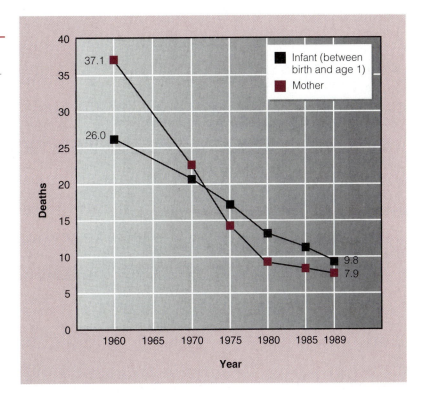

through the process of **labor**—the process whereby the fetus, the placenta, and other membranes are separated from the woman's body and expelled—which would not be possible if they were responsible for initiating it.

There have been many other theories over the years, but, as Liggins (1988) concludes, we still don't have "the final chapter of the 2,000-year-old search for the cause of labor" (p. 387). But even though we don't know its cause, we do understand a lot about the process.

classifications of birth status

The physical status of the child has traditionally been classified according to the length of time spent in gestation and by weight (see Figure 4.10). A fetus expelled before the 20th week and weighing less than 500 grams (about 1 pound) is termed an **abortion** (sometimes called a *miscarriage*). A fetus delivered between the 20th and 28th week and weighing between 500 and 999 grams (between 1 and 2 pounds) is an **immature birth**. At one time, immature births invariably died; the majority still do, most of them from respiratory failure. But with modern medical procedures, an increasing number survive, some born as much as four months prematurely and weighing as little as 750 grams (1½ pounds) or less.

The birth of a baby between the 29th and the 36th weeks is called a **premature birth**, provided the child weighs between 1,000 and 2,499 grams (between 2 and 5½ pounds). Complications are more common if the child weighs less than 1,500 grams. A few decades ago, only 20 percent of premature infants in the 1,000 to 1,500 gram range (2 to 2½-pounds) survived; now between 90 and 95 percent survive ("Preemies' diet seen key to progress," 1988).

A **mature birth** occurs between the 37th and the 42nd weeks and results in an

f **igure 4.10**

Classifications of the newborn.

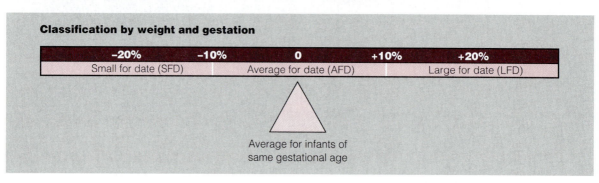

Classification by length of time in gestation

Week	18	20	22	24	26	28	30	32	34	36	38	40	42	44
Classification	Abortion		Immature				Premature				Mature			Postmature
Avg. weight (lbs.)	Under 1		1–2				2–5½				At least 5½			
	(500g)		(500–999g)				(1,000–2,499g)				(2,500g)			

Classification by weight and gestation

−20%	−10%	0	+10%	+20%
Small for date (SFD)		Average for date (AFD)		Large for date (LFD)

Average for infants of same gestational age

infant weighting over 2,500 grams (5½ pounds). A late delivery is called a **post-mature birth**.

All newborns, regardless of whether they are premature, are also classified as small-for-date (SFD) when they weigh less than 90 percent of the weight of newborns of the same gestational age; as large-for-date (LFD) when they weigh above the 90th percentile (that is, in the top 10 percent); or as average-for-date (AFD) (see Figure 4.10).

Medically, it's important to distinguish between prematurity and being small-for-date because the implications of being small-for-date may be more serious than the implications of being simply premature. The premature but average-for-date infant has been developing at a normal rate and, unless very premature, may suffer no negative consequences. However, the small-for-date infant, regardless of gestational age, has been developing less rapidly than normal. The most common causes of growth retardation are chromosomal abnormalities, maternal infections and diseases, and maternal substance use (like smoking). As we saw, each of these can have serious negative consequences for a fetus.

stages of labor

Labor usually begins gradually and proceeds through three stages. That there are exceptions to the normal process has been substantiated by numerous fathers who were caught unaware, taxi drivers who drove too slowly, pilots who did not quite make it, and many others for whom nature would not wait. Although physicians can induce labor, as we saw, the precise natural cause of the beginning of labor remains unknown. Yet labor begins, more often than not, at the prescribed time.

STAGE 1: DILATION

The first stage of labor is the longest, lasting an average of 12 hours but varying greatly in length. Generally, labor is longest and most difficult for a woman's first delivery.

The first stage consists of initially mild contractions that are usually spaced quite far apart (like butterflies in my stomach, said one woman). Contractions become more painful and last considerably longer toward the end of the first stage of birth (like a bear cub in my guts, said another).

In the first stage, the **cervix** (the opening to the uterus) dilates to allow passage of the baby from the uterus, down through the birth canal, and eventually into the world. Contractions are involuntary and exert a downward pressure on the fetus as well as a distending force on the cervix. If the **amniotic sac** (the sac filled with amniotic fluid in which the fetus develops) is still intact, it absorbs much of the pressure in the early stages and transmits some of the force of the contractions to the neck of the cervix. However, if the sac has ruptured or bursts in the early stages of labor, the baby's head will rest directly on the pelvic structure and cervix, serving as a sort of wedge.

STAGE 2: DELIVERY

The second stage of birth, **delivery**, begins when the cervix is sufficiently dilated. It starts with the baby's head emerging (in a normal delivery) at the cervical opening and ends with the birth of the child (Figure 4.11). The second stage usually lasts no more than an hour and often ends in a few minutes. The fetus ordinarily presents itself head first and can usually be born without the intervention of a physician. On occasion, however, complications arise that require some sort of intervention. For example,

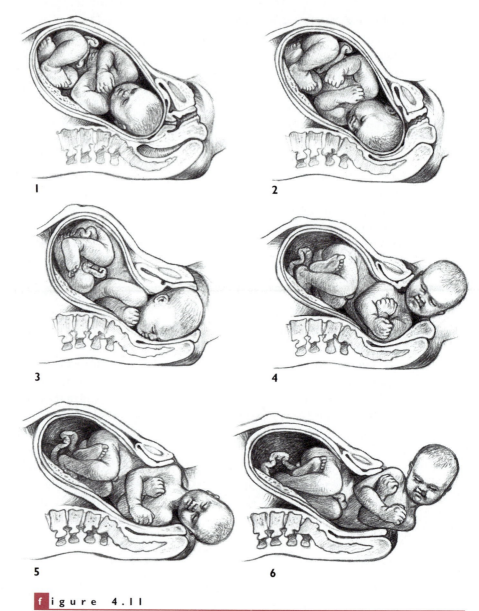

1

2

3

4

5

6

figure 4.11

These cross-sections show the normal presentation and delivery of a baby. The first stage (illustrations 1 and 2) lasts an average of 12 hours and terminates with sufficient dilation of the cervix (the opening to the womb) so that the actual delivery can begin (stage 2; illustrations 3–6). The second stage seldom lasts more than an hour. The third stage is the delivery of the afterbirth (the placenta and other membranes).

the head of the fetus may be too large for the opening provided by the mother. In such a case the physician may make a small incision in the vaginal outlet (an **episiotomy**), which is sutured after the baby is born. Complications can also arise from abnormal presentations of the fetus: **breech** (buttocks first), **transverse** (crosswise), or a variety of other possible positions. Some of these can be corrected before birth by turning the fetus manually in the uterus (**version**). Sometimes the fetus is delivered just as it presents itself.

Toward the end of the delivery stage, the attending physician or nurse severs the neonate's umbilical cord; places silver nitrate or antibiotic drops in its eyes to guard against gonococcal infection; and checks to see that its breathing, muscle tone, coloration, and reflexive activity are normal. Following this, the physician assists in the third and final stage of birth and evaluates the condition of the **neonate**, or newborn, perhaps by means of the Apgar scale (discussed later in this chapter).

STAGE 3: THE AFTERBIRTH

In the third stage, the **afterbirth**—the placenta and other membranes—is expelled. This process usually takes less than five minutes and seldom more than 15. The physician examines the afterbirth carefully to ensure that all of it has been expelled. If it is incomplete, surgical procedures (frequently **dilation and curettage**, or **D & C**—a scraping of the uterus) may be performed to remove remaining portions. At the end of the third stage of labor, the uterus should contract and remain contracted. It is sometimes necessary to massage the abdominal area or administer various drugs to stimulate contraction and to guard against the danger of postpartum (after birth) hemorrhage.

cesarean delivery

In an increasing number of instances, medical intervention bypasses these three stages of birth through cesarean deliveries, which constitute almost one-third of all births in the United States (see Figure 4.12 in "At A Glance: Cesarean Delivery in the United States"). In such cases, birth is accomplished by making an incision through the mother's abdomen and uterus and removing the baby. Lieberman (1987) suggests that cesareans are most often indicated when the mother's labor

fails to progress, if previous cesareans have been performed, when the fetus is in a breech presentation, or if the physician detects signs of fetal distress. Cesarean deliveries are ordinarily undertaken before the onset of labor, but they can also be performed after labor has begun.

Although cesarean deliveries have clearly saved the lives of many mothers and infants and alleviated much pain and suffering, the rapid increase in the proportion of cesarean births relative to nonsurgical births has been a source of some concern (deRegt et al, 1986). Although much of this increase clearly results from dramatic improvements in the physicians' ability to monitor the fetus during labor, critics assert that not all Cesarean deliveries are necessary. When unnecessary, such surgery presents potential disadvantages and dangers not inherent in a routine delivery, including greater medical risk to the mother, a longer recovery period, and higher risk of infection. In addition, the use of anesthetics during surgery may depress neonatal responsiveness and may be related to the occasional respiratory problems of infants delivered by cesarean section. This problem may be compounded by the fact that infants delivered surgically do not normally experience the surge of hormones that is common among infants during normal labor. Among other things, these hormones stimulate respiratory and cardiac activity (Lagercrantz & Slotkin, 1986).

Lieberman (1987) reports that a number of hospitals have succeeded in dramatically reducing rates of cesarean deliveries without any increase in fetal or maternal problems. This is accomplished largely by reviewing the need for a cesarean delivery in cases in which they might simply have been done routinely, as sometimes happens for breech births, twins, or patients who have had previous cesareans.

Cesarean section deliveries in the United States have quadrupled in frequency since 1970 (see Figure 4.12). Not surprisingly, the highest rates are for women in older age groups. Although cesarean deliveries have clearly saved the lives of many mothers and infants, some critics argue that they are used too frequently. Although the procedure is routine and low-risk, it entails a somewhat higher risk of infection, medical problems for the mother, and respiratory problems among infants.

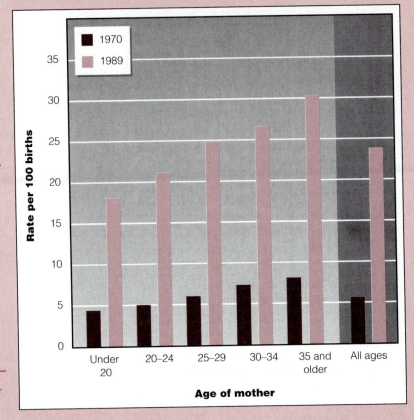

f igure 4.12

Changes in rate of cesareans by age, 1970–1989 (per 100 births). Source: U.S. Bureau of the Census, 1992, p. 67.

neonatal scales

In almost all North American hospitals it is routine to evaluate the condition of newborns by means of the Apgar scale. The scale, shown in Table 4.4, is almost self-explanatory. Infants receive scores (0, 1, or 2) according to whether or not each of five appropriate signs—*a*ppearance (color), *p*ulse (heart rate), *g*rimace (reflex irritability), *a*ctivity (muscle tone), and *r*espiration—is present. Maximum score is 10; average score is usually 7 or better;

a score of 4 or less indicates that the neonate must be given special care immediately. The Apgar evaluation is administered at least twice: at one minute after birth and at five minutes after birth (and sometimes at 10 minutes after birth). Five- and 10-minute scores are often higher than one-minute scores.

A second important scale for assessing the condition of a newborn infant is the Brazelton Neonatal Behavioral Assessment Scale (Brazelton, 1973). Like the Apgar scale, it can be used to detect

t a b l e 4 . 4

The Apgar scale

SCORE	APPEARANCE	PULSE	REFLEX IRRITABILITY (GRIMACE)	MUSCLE TONE (ACTIVITY)	RESPIRATION
0	Blue, pale	Absent	No response	Flaccid, limp	Absent
1	Body pink, extremities blue	Less than 100 beats per minute	Grimace	Weak; baby inactive	Irregular, slow
2	Entirely pink	Over 100 beats per minute	Coughing, sneezing, crying	Strong; baby active	Good; baby crying

problems immediately after birth. In addition, it provides useful indicators of both central nervous system maturity and social behavior. The Brazelton scale involves evaluation of 26 specific behaviors, including reaction to light, to cuddling, to voices, and to a pinprick; it also includes the strength of various reflexes. The scale is particularly useful in identifying infants who might be prone to later psychological problems (Als et al., 1979). For example, parents of infants who are less responsive to cuddling and to other social stimulation might be alerted to this from the very beginning and might be able to compensate by providing the infant with more loving contact than might otherwise have been the case.

the mother's experience: prepared childbirth

The preceding discussion of the delivery of a human child is admittedly clinical and perhaps a little like the cold, antiseptic hospitals in which most North American babies are born: It fails to uncover and transmit the magic of the process. We can recapture some of the wonders, however, by looking more closely at mothers' experiences of childbirth. In preparation for this discussion, I spoke with several women whose experi-

ence qualified them to make subjective comments more valid than those my imagination might supply.

"What's it like, having a baby?" I asked.

"It's a piece of cake," my first expert assured me in her characteristic, cliché-ridden way. "It's as easy as rolling off a log."

"It hurts like ★!@#!" my second expert insisted, in her typically profane manner. "It's a hell of a big log!"

Combining these impressions, a slightly less than absolutely clear picture of the situation emerges.

The inexperienced mother sometimes approaches birth with some degree of apprehension; there is often some pain associated with childbirth. However, advocates of **natural childbirth** (also called *prepared childbirth*) claim that through a regimen of prenatal exercises and adequate psychological preparation, many women experience relatively painless childbirths.

Natural childbirth, a phrase coined by a British physician, Grantly Dick-Read (1972), refers to the process of having a child without anesthetics. The Dick-Read process involves physical exercises, relaxation exercises, and psychological preparation for the arrival of the child, all directed toward delivery in which pain-

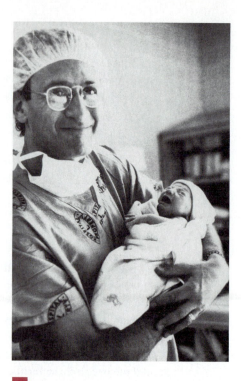

Birth culminates in a staggering change in an infant's environment—from an all-providing, temperature-controlled, dark, quiet, and cushioned world to the ever-changing lights and noises, fluctuating temperatures, smells and tastes, textures, and movements of the outside world. And now, too, the infant must breathe for itself.

killers are unnecessary. Natural childbirth is based on the assumption that alleviating the fear of pain, together with training in relaxation, will result in less pain.

THE LAMAZE AND LEBOYER METHODS

Two popular methods of prepared childbirth are the Lamaze and the Leboyer techniques. The Lamaze (1972) method teaches expectant mothers a variety of breathing and relaxation exercises. These are practiced repeatedly, often with the assistance of the father, until they become so habitual that they will be used almost "naturally" during the actual process of birth.

The Leboyer method is concerned more with the delivery of the infant than with advance preparation of the mother. Leboyer (1975) advocates delivering the baby in a softly lit room, immersing the infant almost immediately in a lukewarm bath, often for a relatively long time, and then placing the baby directly on the mother's abdomen. These procedures are designed to ease the infant's transition from the womb to the world; thus the need for soft lights that do not contrast as harshly with the darkness of the womb as does conventional delivery-room lighting, and for a lukewarm bath to approximate the feeling of being supported by amniotic fluid. Leboyer claims that his procedures eliminate much of the shock of birth and result in better-adjusted individuals. Critics suggest that birth in dimly lit surroundings might contribute to the physician's failing to notice important signs of distress or injury and that the dangers of infection are greater under these circumstances than they are when more conventional hospital practices are used.

HOSPITALS OR HOMES, DOCTORS OR MIDWIVES?

Not only are many mothers choosing to have their babies by natural means, but many are also deciding where birth will occur. For some, home is that choice; others choose hospital birthing rooms—a homier and more comfortable alternative than a conventional operating or delivery room—or hospital family suites where father and other siblings can actually stay. Although most North American births still occur in hospitals, length of hospitalization is considerably shorter than it once was (often only a matter of hours).

Traditionally, in countries such as Great Britain the majority of births were attended to by midwives rather than by physicians, a practice less common in North America (Sagov et al., 1984). However, with the medicalization of birth, the use of midwives has declined, even in Europe, and their role has changed. An increasing number of births are attended to by physicians, and when midwives are used, they are often part of a medical team. Their role on that team has also declined dramatically in importance (Robinson, 1989). In many cases, midwives are used primarily as receptionists or to do routine tasks like weighing pregnant women and taking urine samples.

THE USE OF MEDICATION IN CHILDBIRTH

For one mother, childbirth may be quite painful; for another it may be a slightly painful but intensely rewarding and satisfying experience. Although the amount of pain can be controlled to some extent with anesthetics, the intensity of the immediate emotional reward will also be dulled by the drugs. In addition, sedatives given to the mother may affect the infant. Children delivered without sedatives are frequently more alert, more responsive to the environment, and better able to cope with immediate environmental demands (Brazelton, Nugent, & Lester, 1987). In short, they may have a slight initial advantage, the long-range implications of which are unclear.

POSTPARTUM DEPRESSION

As many as 10 percent of all women suffer from depression after giving birth (Campbell & Cohn, 1991). It isn't clear whether this **postpartum depression** is due to hormonal changes, to the effects of sedating drugs that might have been used in labor, to disruptions in life-style, or to other factors (Dalton, 1989). Unfortunately, depressed mothers may be a risk factor for newborns, especially if their depression leads them to neglect or reject their babies.

The prognosis for postpartum depression is excellent, with most cases improving quickly with time and disappearing completely within a year (Campbell & Cohn, 1991).

---

the child's experience

How do children, the heroes of this text, react to the process of birth? They are likely indifferent to the process, because they cannot reason about it, cannot compare it with other more or less pleasant states, can do nothing deliberately to alter it, and will not even remember it. But consider the incredibly dramatic difference that birth makes. Up to now, the child has been living in a completely friendly and supportive environment. Receiving nourishment, getting oxygen, eliminating wastes—everything has been accomplished without effort. The uterus has been kept at exactly the right temperature, the danger of bacterial infection has been relatively insignificant, and there have been no psychological threats—so far as we know. Now, at birth, the child is suddenly exposed to new physiological and perhaps psychological dangers. Once mucus is cleared from its mouth and throat, the newborn must breathe unassisted for the first time. As soon as the umbilical cord ceases to pulsate, it is unceremoniously clipped an inch or two above the abdomen and tied off with a clamp. And the child is now completely separate—singularly dependent and helpless, to be sure, but no longer a physiological parasite on the mother.

PHYSICAL DANGERS OF BIRTH

Birth is not without danger for the newborn. Injuries, including brain damage, sometimes occur during the birth of a child, often resulting from the tremendous pressure exerted on the head during birth—especially if labor is long and if the amniotic sac has been broken early, in which case the head, in a normal presentation, has been repeatedly pressed against the slowly dilating cervix. In addition, the infant must pass through an opening so small that deformation of the head often results. (For most infants the head usually assumes a more normal appearance within a few days.)

An additional source of pressure on the child's head may be **forceps**, clamp-like instruments sometimes used during delivery. Although the fetus's head can withstand considerable pressure, the danger of such pressure is that it may rupture blood vessels and cause hemorrhaging. In severe cases, death may result; otherwise, brain damage may result from **anoxia** because cranial hemorrhage can restrict the supply of oxygen to the brain.

Anoxia can also result if the umbilical cord becomes lodged between the fetus's body and the birth canal, disrupting the flow of oxygen through the cord (a situation referred to as **prolapsed cord**). Anoxia may be related to impaired neurological, psychological, and motor functioning associated with brain damage. Most studies of this condition have suffered from the difficulty of determining the actual contribution of anoxia to behaviors later observed in infants and children. Because other complications of birth may have caused the anoxia in the first place, it is difficult to tell whether the complication itself or the resulting anoxia is the crucial variable.

PSYCHOLOGICAL BIRTH TRAUMA

In addition to the physiological **trauma**, or shock, that accompanies birth, there is a remote possibility of psychological trauma. Rank's (1929) theory of the trauma of birth maintains that the sudden change from a comfortable, relatively passive existence to the cold and demanding world creates great anxiety for a newborn child, who is plagued forever after by a desire to return to the womb. Evidence of this unconscious desire is supposedly found in the position assumed by many children and adults while sleeping or in times of stress—the characteristic curled "fetal position." However, there is no substantial evidence to support the theory of psychological birth trauma.

prematurity

rematurity is defined by a short gestation period (36 weeks or less) and low birthweight (small-for-date, or SFD—less than 90 percent of average weight for term, usually less than 2,500 grams (or 5½ pounds). It is one of the more serious possible complications of birth, affecting approximately 10 percent of all infants born in the United States. Incidence of prematurity is considerably higher in some other countries (Crowley, 1983).

causes of prematurity

Even though we do not know the precise causes of premature delivery (Creasy, 1990), a number of factors are related to its occurrence (see Table 4.5), including poverty, malnutrition, mother's age, smoking, and other drug use, all of which are implicated in other infant disadvantages (Creasy, 1988). Note, however, that factors such as social class and race have no inherent explanatory value. Certainly, neither causes prematurity any more than they cause the environmental conditions of poverty, ill health, and lower socioeconomic opportunity with which they are often associated (see "At A Glance: Birthweight and Prenatal Influences").

Other related factors include various illnesses in the mother during pregnancy. In addition, infants from multiple births are more frequently premature than are infants from single births. Finally, a number of infants are preterm in the absence of any of these negative influences and in spite of excellent maternal care, nutrition, and health.

effects of prematurity

One of the most obvious possible effects of prematurity is death. Indeed, only a few decades ago the likelihood of death for a premature infant weighing between 2,000 and 2,500 grams (4½ and 5½ pounds) was approximately six times greater than for an infant weighing 3,000 grams (6 pounds, 10 ounces) or more. Now, however, the majority of premature infants weighing 2,000 grams (4½ pounds) or more survive. In fact, more than 90 percent of infants who weigh as little as 1,000 to 1,500 grams survive (Goldsmith, 1990b). Most of these preterm infants spend the first two to three months of their lives in intensive care nurseries, often in incubators (also called *isolettes*) (Harrison, 1985). Chances of survival decrease 10 to 15 percent for each 100 grams below 1,000 grams. (Goldsmith, 1990b). However, half or more of neonates who weigh less than 1,250 grams suffer adverse consequences; one-third or more suffer from severe physical or mental handicaps (Beckwith & Rodning, 1991).

Other possible effects of prematurity and/or of prolonged hospitalization following birth include lower intelligence, a higher incidence of cerebral palsy, and general developmental retardation. These effects, of course, are not found among all preterm babies and are progressively less likely for infants who are least prema-

t a b l e   4.5
Factors associated with higher risk of prematurity
MAJOR FACTORS
Multiple gestation
DES exposure
Uterine anomaly
Cervix dilated more than 1 cm at 32 weeks
Two previous second-trimester abortions
Previous preterm delivery
Previous labor during preterm, with term delivery
Abdominal surgery during pregnancy
Uterine irritability
MINOR FACTORS
Febrile (fever) illness
Bleeding after 12 weeks
More than 10 cigarettes per day
One previous second-trimester abortion
More than two previous first-trimester abortions

Based on R. H. Holbrook Jr., R. K. Laros Jr., & R. K. Creasy (1988), Evaluation of a risk-scoring system for prediction of preterm labor. *American Journal of Perinatology* 6, 62.

ture and who weigh the most at birth. For example, in studies of premature identical twins, the heavier of the twins tends to have higher measures of intelligence (Churchill, 1965). Among preterm infants who weigh 2,000 or more grams, subsequent complications are relatively rare.

In view of these rather alarming findings, and given the highly likely relationship between nutrition and prematurity, probably a great deal can be done for unborn children and their mothers through programs of education, nutrition, and housing. But it should also be pointed out that not all premature infants suffer noticeable disadvantages relative to their mature peers.

*P*rematurity and low birthweight are among the most
serious complications of
birth. Low birthweight may
contribute to infant death or general
developmental retardation, including
lower intelligence. Factors implicated in
low birthweight include smoking and
use of other drugs, maternal age, and
inadequate nutrition and prenatal care.
The relationship of social class and
race to low birthweight and prematurity is probably due primarily to other
associated factors such as poorer nutrition and prenatal care.

f igure 4.13

*The relationship of race to low birthweight (less
than or equal to 5 lb., 8 oz. (2,500 gm) for
1960 and 1970; less than 5 lb., 8 oz. (2,500
gm) for 1980, 1987, and 1989). Source: U.S.
Bureau of the Census (1990), p. 66.*

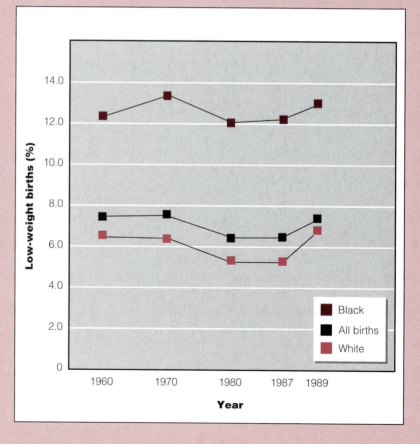

prevention of prematurity

"We still aren't fully aware of all the events that occur to elicit this [birthing] reaction," says Dr. David Olson (quoted in "Shortening the time . . . ,"1993, p. 4). If we were, he adds, we might be able to figure out how to prevent premature delivery. At present, all we can do is try to identify women who appear to be at greater risk. This can't be done with certainty because the precise causes of premature delivery are not always known. However, it's possible to estimate degree of risk given knowledge of a woman's status with respect to the factors listed in Table 4.5. It's also possible to monitor uterine activity and sometimes to detect an increase in activity before the onset of preterm labor.

There are a number of different approaches to preventing preterm labor, including bedrest, avoiding sexual intercourse, the use of antibiotics and other drugs, and suturing the cervix. None of these has been clearly proven to be effective, although there is some evidence that each might sometimes be helpful (Goldsmith, 1990b).

care of premature infants

Premature infants born in the 23rd to 25th week of pregnancy have a 50 percent survival rate; 85 percent of those born between the 26th and 28th week survive ("Shortening the time . . . ." 1993). Nor is prematurity inevitably linked with physical, psychological, or neurological inferiority. With adequate care, many premature infants fare as well as full-term infants.

NUTRITION AND MEDICAL CARE

What are the dimensions of that care? First they include advances in medical knowledge and technology. Ventilators,

for example, make possible the survival of infants whose hearts and lungs are not sufficiently developed to work on their own; so does intravenous feeding with what is termed *total parenteral nutrition* (TPN). The contents of this nutrition are especially important because they substitute for nutrients that the infant would ordinarily have received as a fetus. Certain fatty acids appear to be crucially involved in brain growth and neuron development during the last trimester of pregnancy—roughly the period of intrauterine growth that a 27-week preterm infant would miss ("Preemies' diet seen key to progress," 1988). Accordingly, premature infants' nutrition must include these nutrients at the appropriate time and in the appropriate form. Not surprisingly, hospital care of premature infants is sometimes enormously expensive ("Shortening the time . . . ," 1993).

PSYCHOLOGICAL CARE

In addition to important medical advances in the care of premature infants, a tremendous amount of research in the past 20 years has investigated the possibility that at least some of the adverse psychological consequences of prematurity might be due to the lack of stimulation the preterm infant receives in an intensive care nursery—or, perhaps more accurately, the inappropriateness of the stimulation.

Scarr-Salapatek and Williams (1973) compared two groups of premature infants. The first group was treated in the conventional manner; that is, the infants were kept in isolettes with a minimum of human contact. This practice is premised on the belief that premature infants are particularly susceptible to infection and are highly vulnerable once infected. The second group was also kept in isolettes, but these infants were taken out for feeding and were talked to and fondled by their nurses. In addition, their isolettes were decorated with mobiles, and in follow-up visits after they had left the hospital they were given numerous toys to take home. It is highly significant that by the age of 1 these infants were heavier than infants in the control group and scored higher on developmental scales.

Harrison (1985) summarizes 24 studies that have evaluated various forms of "supplemental" stimulation for preterm infants. Some investigated the effects of tactile stimulation (stroking, holding); others looked at auditory stimulation (taped recordings of the mother's voice, for example), vestibulary stimulation (oscillating hammock or waterbed), gustatory stimulation (pacifier), or, as in the Scarr-Salapatek and Williams study, multimodal stimulation. The studies support the conclusion that additional stimulation of preterm infants is beneficial to their development. Positive effects include greater weight gains, shorter hospital stays, greater responsiveness, and higher developmental scores on various measures. The evidence is clear that the traditional hands-off treatment once given most premature infants is not the best form of care for them.

a reassuring note

t is often very disturbing for nonmedical people to consult medical journals and textbooks in search of explanations for their various ailments. Inevitably they discover that they have all the symptoms for some vicious infection or exotic disease. So if you happen to be pregnant at this moment or are contemplating pregnancy, you might find yourself a little apprehensive. I draw this to your attention only to emphasize that by most accounts pregnancy and delivery are positive experiences. The intrauterine world of the unborn infant is less threatening and less

dangerous than our world. In most cases, when a fetus comes to term, the probability that the child will be normal and healthy far outweighs the likelihood that it will suffer any of the defects or abnormalities described in this chapter. After all, pregnancy and birth are natural processes that are at least as old as the human race.

main points

DETECTING PREGNANCY

1. Early signs of pregnancy are not always clear, but simple urine tests can be performed very early in pregnancy—at home or by physicians. The gestation period for humans is about nine calendar months (10 lunar months, or 280 days, beginning from the onset of the last menses).

STAGES OF PRENATAL DEVELOPMENT

2. Prenatal physiological development occurs in three stages: During weeks 1 and 2, the *fertilized ovum* moves down the fallopian tube and implants itself in the uterine wall; between weeks 3 and 8 after conception, the *embryo*, including all major organs, develops; from week 9 to birth, the *fetus* grows mainly in size and weight and develops neurologically.

FACTORS AFFECTING PRENATAL DEVELOPMENT

3. A wide range of prescription drugs can act as teratogens (including thalidomide, associated with underdeveloped or absent limbs, and DES, linked with higher incidence of cervical cancer among female offspring.) Harmful chemicals include mercury (Minimata disease), hydrocarbon compounds like dioxin and PCB

(higher incidence of spontaneous abortions and physical deformities), and lead (serious physical and mental problems in children and adults).

4. Cigarette smoking increases fetal heart rate and activity and is associated with significant retardation of fetal growth, much higher incidence of premature births, smaller birthweights, higher probability of placental problems, higher risk of miscarriage and fetal death, and higher incidence of childhood respiratory diseases.

5. Alcohol consumption may lead to fetal alcohol syndrome (FAS), symptoms of which may include mental retardation, retarded physical growth, and characteristic cranial and facial malformations (low forehead, widely spaced eyes, short nose, long upper lip, absence of a marked infranasal depression). Infants born to narcotics addicts are themselves usually addicted at birth (neonatal abstinence syndrome). Infants of cocaine users are more likely to abort, be stillborn, die of SIDS, or suffer from behavioral problems later in childhood.

6. Diseases such as rubella, syphilis, gonorrhea, and diabetes can lead to mental deficiency, blindness, deafness, or fetal death. Herpes can be transmitted to the fetus during birth and can lead to serious complications, including death (it can be prevented through a cesarean delivery). AIDS can also be transmitted from mother to fetus (35 to 60 percent probability) and is fatal.

7. For older mothers there is a higher probability of some chromosomal defects (trisomy 21; trisomies 13 and 18; Klinefelter's syndrome; fragile X syndrome). Infants born to teenage mothers are at higher risk of physical, emotional, and intellectual disadvantage (more miscarriages, premature births, and stillbirths, and more emotional and physical abuse among those who survive)—usually because of the less advantageous social and medical circumstances of teenage parenthood.

8. Maternal malnutrition, often associated with poverty, may lead to higher fetal mortality, lower fertility, and poorer brain development. In the absence of medical intervention (injections of Rhogam), mothers who are negative for the Rh blood factor would be at risk of giving birth to infants suffering from fetal erythroblastosis when the father is Rh(D)-positive.

CHILDBIRTH

9. Birth (ordinarily 266 days after conception) occurs in three stages: *labor* (dilation of the cervix in preparation for delivery; 9 to 12 hours), *delivery* (usually accomplished within an hour); and *afterbirth* (expulsion of the placenta and other membranes, lasting several minutes). Natural, or prepared, childbirth refers to the preparation for and process of having a child without anesthetics.

10. Newborns are routinely evaluated at birth by means of the Apgar scale— a scale that looks at their *a*ppearance (color), *p*ulse (heart rate), *g*rimace (reflex irritability), *a*ctivity (muscle tone), and *r*espiration (respiratory effort).

PREMATURITY

11. Prematurity appears to be linked to social class variables such as diet and poorer medical attention, the age of

the mother, smoking, drugs, multiple gestations, and previous history of preterm deliveries. Its most apparent effects are the greater possibility of death, physical defects, hyperkinesis, and impaired mental functioning. Medical advances have made it possible for over 90 percent of premature infants weighing as little as 1,000 to 1,500 grams (2.2 to 3.3 pounds) to survive. The severity of possible medical consequences of prematurity has been significantly ameliorated by medical advances.

focus questions: applications

■ How early can pregnancy be reliably detected?
1. What are some of the advantages of early detection?

■ How does a fetus grow?
2. Describe the major changes that occur during each of the three stages of prenatal development.

■ What sorts of things can harm or aid the fetus's development?
3. Using library resources, write a brief summary of recent research dealing with the consequences of mother's age, drug use, or nutrition on the fetus.

■ How are infants delivered here and elsewhere?
4. To impress your professor with your dedication and enthusiasm, arrange to attend the birth of an elephant, a giraffe, or some other animal (zoos, veterinarians, farmers, and pet owners might be helpful). Compare this animal birth with a human birth.

study terms

pregnancy 147
prenatal development 147
menses 147
quickening 148
gestation period 148
fertilized ovum stage 148
germinal stage 148
zygote 148
embryo stage 148
fetus 148
fertilization 148
Fallopian tubes 148
uterus 148
placenta 150
umbilical cord 150
in utero 150
sucking reflex 151
Babinski reflex 151
intrauterine 151
lanugo 151
proximodistal 153
cephalocaudal 153
teratogens 153
mutagens 153
diethylsilbestrol (DES) 154
fetal alcohol syndrome 157
neonatal abstinence syndrome 159
cytomagalovirus 161
acquired immune deficiency syndrome (AIDS) 161
birth 170
labor 174
abortion 174
immature birth 174
premature birth 174
mature birth 174
postmature birth 175
cervix 175
amnionic sac 175
delivery 175
episiotomy 176
breech 176

transverse 176

version 176

neonate 177

afterbirth 177

dilation and curettage (D&C) 177

natural childbirth 179

postpartum depression 181

forceps 182

anoxia 182

prolapsed cord 182

trauma 182

further readings

The first of the following collections examines the effects of maternal addiction on the fetus; the second considers the effects of other teratogens and of maternal illness and disease. The third book explores the clinical effects of alcohol:

Chasnoff, I. J. (Ed.). (1986). *Drug use in pregnancy: Mother and child.* Boston, Mass.: MTP Press.

Whittle, M. J., & Connor, J. M. (Eds.). (1989). *Prenatal diagnosis in obstetric practice.* Boston: Blackwell Scientific Publications.

Abel, E. L. (1984). *Fetal alcohol syndrome and fetal alcohol effects.* New York: Plenum Press.

The following book is a massive collection of detailed medical information on the factors that influence prenatal development (including drugs, diseases, and genes) and on the various possible medical interventions:

R. D. Eden, F. H. Boehm, & M. Haire, (Eds.). (1990). *Assessment and care of the fetus: Physiological, clinical, and medicolegal principles.* Norwalk, Conn.: Appleton & Lange.

AIDS is a topic of considerable current interest—and misinformation. Long's book provides clear answers to 100 of the most common questions asked about AIDS. Anderson's little booklet deals most specifically with AIDS among children:

Long, R. E. (1987). *AIDS* (The Reference Shelf, Vol. 59, No. 3). New York: H. W. Wilson.

Anderson, G. R. (1986). *Children and AIDS: The challenge for child welfare.* Washington, D. C.: Child Welfare League of America, Inc.

Those interested in an account of birth in primitive tribes throughout the world might consult:

Goldsmith, J. (1990). *Childbirth wisdom: From the world's oldest societies.* Brookline, Mass.: East-West Health Books.

The following is a detailed discussion of nutrition and weight gain for pregnant women:

Food and Nutrition Board. (1990). *Nutrition during pregnancy.* Washington, D.C.: National Academy Press.

Those interested in alternative approaches to childbirth are referred to the originators of some of the more popular approaches:

Dick-Read, G. (1972). *Childbirth without fear: The original approach to natural childbirth* (4th ed.). (H. Wessel & H. F. Ellis, Eds.). New York: Harper & Row.

Lamaze, F. (1972). *Painless childbirth: The Lamaze method.* New York: Pocket Books.

Leboyer, F. (1975). *Birth without violence.* New York: Random House.

three

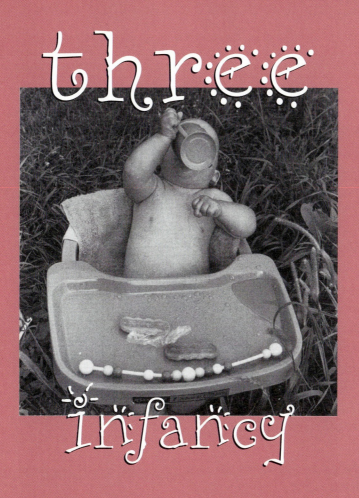

infancy

His lordship says he will turn it over in what he is pleased to
call his mind.
Richard Bethell (Baron Westbury), Life of Westbury

*W*hat do you suppose does go on in his lordship's mind? Do you think that in the very beginning, our infant lord pauses to ponder problems of quantum physics or Boolean algebra?

Not likely. You see, the world is an amazing and bewildering place for his lordship because he is totally unfamiliar with it. Much of the business of growing up is a matter of becoming familiar with things. That is mostly what occupies the first two years of life: becoming familiar with breasts and bottles, with cups and cats, with doors and dragons; learning when to cry, when to be afraid, when to laugh and smile; learning about mothers and fathers, and about strangers too; and learning to speak. This is what the next two chapters are about.

While reading these chapters, keep in mind that his little lordship is a real person; he is far more than just a compilation of science's hard-earned facts and speculations. Try to remember—or at least to imagine—some of the feelings of being an infant. Is the world bewildering and frightening? Exciting and marvelous? Astonishing and delightful?

5

Physical and Cognitive Development in Infancy

"There's no use trying," she said: "One can't believe impossible things."
"I dare say you haven't had much practice," said the Queen.
"When I was your age, I always did it for half an hour a day.
Why sometimes I've believed as many as six impossible things before breakfast."
Lewis Carroll, Alice Through the Looking-Glass

focus questions

HOW IMPORTANT IS NUTRITION FOR NEONATES?

WHAT ARE SOME IMPORTANT CHARACTERISTICS OF NEONATES?

WHAT CAN NEWBORNS SEE? HEAR? SMELL? TASTE? FEEL?

DO NEWBORNS HAVE THOUGHTS?

HOW CAN INFANTS MANAGE TO LEARN SOMETHING AS COMPLICATED AS A LANGUAGE?

outline

BLUEPRINT FOR A NEONATE

NUTRITION, HEALTH, AND PHYSICAL GROWTH IN INFANCY

The Breast Versus Bottle Controversy
Nutrition and Brain Development
Physical Growth in Infancy
Sudden Infant Death Syndrome

BEHAVIOR IN NEWBORNS

The Orienting Response
Reflexes

MOTOR DEVELOPMENT IN INFANTS

PERCEPTUAL DEVELOPMENT IN INFANTS

Vision
Hearing
Smell, Taste, and Touch

COGNITIVE DEVELOPMENT IN INFANTS

Memory in Infants
Basic Piagetian Ideas on Infancy
The Object Concept
Sensorimotor Development in Infants
Imitation in Infancy

LANGUAGE AND COMMUNICATION

A Definition of Language
Elements of Language

LANGUAGE DEVELOPMENT IN INFANTS

Achievements in the Prespeech Stage
The Beginnings of Verbal Communication
Infants' First Sounds
The Sentencelike Word (Holophrase)
Two-Word Sentences
From Sensation to Representation

MAIN POINTS

FOCUS QUESTIONS: APPLICATIONS

STUDY TERMS

FURTHER READINGS

W here I lived, up there in Northern Saskatchewan, there were no doctors or hospitals close by—and no easy way to get to them in any case. So pretty well everybody was born right at home.

I too was born at home. I assume the affair took place in the little bedroom with the one small window that looked out over the prairie toward the hills to the south. On that hot June day the air would have been alive with the buzzing of insects; and the dog, who was to become my best friend, would have been sleeping on the porch.

I remember nothing of my birth, but I was reminded of it as I worked my way through the previous chapter. In Goldsmith's (1990a) Childbirth Wisdom, I read how normal pregnancies and births in preindustrial tribes involve little stress and little disruption in daily routines. "The vast majority of Tlinget women," she quotes an observer of this Alaskan tribe, "suffer very little and some not at all when their children are born. They have been known to give birth while sleeping" (p. 23). Another, speaking of the Modoc Indians, writes "the squaw … suffers but an hour or even less" (p. 23).

I don't know if that's the way it was with my mother. But I remember that one August morning when I was 7 they sent three of my siblings and me to Delisle's, where we played in the barn loft, climbing into the rafters and jumping down into the new hay over and over, until some time in mid-afternoon my father came for us.

"Come see your new sister," said he. Which we did. I can still see her in my mind's eye, *fresh-born, her skull flattened a little on one side, her skin mottled blue and red, her eyes screwed shut, little fists clenched, wailing in shrieks. And I remember saying, like a 7 year old can, "Gawwd, she's so ugly. Look at her, will you!"*

blueprint for a neonate

Neonates—newborns—are often like that, or worse if they haven't been cleaned up yet and they still have remnants of their stay in the womb clinging to them. Often, too, their features are deformed from the pressures of passing through the birth canal.

Newborns are remarkably helpless creatures. They have little physical and motor control, and, unlike the young of many animals, they would not survive very long if left on their own.

What is it like to be a newborn? Does the world *mean* anything? Does the newborn have primitive ideas, budding concepts, some sort of pattern or blueprint that will govern its intellectual growth? What does it feel? Is there joy in the beating of its little heart? Is it capable of ecstasy? Does sadness drive its cries? Does purpose inform its movements?

These are not easy questions to answer. In fact, it will take us the remainder of this chapter, and most of the next, to consider the answers that science (and sometimes good sense) has begun to provide.

Let's start first with the bare bones of an answer. Imagine for a moment that you've been asked to design an organism that begins life in as primitive a condition as a neonate—that is, with as little physical and motor control as an infant has and with as unsophisticated an understanding of self and world. But you must design this organism in such a way that within two years it will be able to walk, talk, recognize its grandmother, ride a tricycle, and laugh and sing.

So what do you do? You program it for change. And because you're clever, you pay particular attention to change of three types: biological, intellectual, and social. Biologically, you design a creature

Some anthropologists believe that normal pregnancies and births in preindustrial tribes were much like births typically are among animals—that they involved little stress and little disruption in daily routines.

traordinary amount of information (see Flavell, 1985). You program it so that it will process this information regardless of whether it receives any immediate and tangible reward (such as food or a caress) for doing so. You provide it with an information-processing system that is automatically geared toward focusing on the most informative aspects of the environment. Accordingly, your little organism reacts strongly to surprise and novelty; it searches out the unexpected; it develops ways of organizing the information it gathers; it is programmed to invent concepts and ideas.

Socially, you program into the organism a wide range of emotions to serve as motives for many of the things it does. They lead it to establish complex relationships with other organisms of the same species (and sometimes with members of other species). Socially, you program the organism to be gregarious, to love, to try eventually to spread its seed and contribute to the survival of its species—perhaps, as well, to defend things that might be related to its survival and to that of others of its kind.

And as a crowning achievement in your design of this creature you pretune it to attend to speech; you wire it so that it is capable of inventing language.

Our bare-bones answer to the question "What is a neonate?" is this: A neonate is a self-driven little sensing machine designed to mature and grow physically in a predetermined way, programmed as an extraordinarily capable information-processing system, endowed with powerful emotions and gregarious tendencies, and prewired to develop language.

In this chapter we look at the newborn's growth and behavior, at motor development, and at perceptual and cognitive development. In the next chapter we look at infants' social relationships and attachments and at personality in in-

that is capable of converting raw proteins, carbohydrates, minerals and vitamins, and other foodstuffs into nutrients. And you program the effects of these nutrients into a sequence of biological growth and maturation that will, among other things, eventually lead to the organism's control of its movements. And because you are something of a poet, you put some grace, some exuberance, into those young movements.

Intellectually, you program your little organism to process an absolutely ex-

fants. These two chapters cover *infancy*, a period that lasts from the first few weeks of life to the age of 2.

nutrition, health, and physical growth in infancy

Newborns are almost completely helpless physically. They can't move to new places; they have no way of ensuring that their environments are neither too cold nor too warm; they can't clean themselves; they have no protection against wild dogs, vultures, or one-eyed cats. They can't even find food unless it is put under their very noses. Once they find it, though, they suck. Sucking is one of those primitive reflexes present at birth in virtually all mammals.

the breast versus bottle controversy

The sucking reflex is what ensures an infant's survival. It may seem strange, then, that, in Kessen's (1965) words, " . . . the most persistent single note in the history of the child is the reluctance of mothers to suckle their babies" (p. 1).

It seems that for many years a battle has been waged on this issue. On the one side have been the many physicians and philosophers who have insisted that mothers should breast-feed their own infants. Their arguments are varied. Some have invoked nature: Breastfeeding is natural, they reason. All animals do it; therefore, human mothers should too. Others have argued that breast milk is best for children simply because "it became accustomed to it in the mother's womb" (S. de St. Marthe, 1797, quoted in Kessen, 1965, p. 2). Others have appealed to religion and duty: "The mother's breast is an infant's birthright and suckling a sacred duty, to neglect which is prejudicial to the mother and fatal to the child" (Davis,

1817, quoted in Kessen, 1965, p. 3). There have been some, too, who have reasoned that maternal qualities might somehow be transmitted through breast milk. Especially to be guarded against was the milk of foster mothers of dubious virtue and morality, for "Who then, unless he be blind, does not see that babies imbibe, along with the alien milk of the foster mother, morals different from those of their parents?" (Comenius, 1633; quoted in Kessen, 1965, p. 3).

On the other side of this battle have been mothers who, for one reason or another, have been reluctant to breast-feed their infants. Their arguments are generally more personal and more private, and their numbers have varied through history, growing through certain decades and lessening again through others.

There is still a conflict—a breast versus bottle controversy—although most mothers see the issue as largely a matter of personal choice. The choice is sometimes made on the basis of convenience. It is simply not convenient for many working mothers to breast-feed their infants, just as it is not convenient for women who carry their infants into the fields to also carry bottles with them.

At other times, the choice is made on the basis of current fashion. For example, through much of the early part of the twentieth century, breast-feeding declined in popularity in North America, so that by the early 1970s fewer than 1 mother in 4 breast-fed their infants. But in the past several decades, breast-feeding has again increased in popularity (Eiger & Olds, 1987). One survey reports that 83 percent of women in one Canadian city breast-fed their infants (Kuzyk, 1993). (See Figures 5.1 and 5.2 in "At A Glance: Changes in Breast-Feeding Patterns.")

What do physicians now recommend? Pretty much what they have recom-

Throughout history, philosophers, psychologists, religious leaders, physicians, and nurses have typically been in favor of breast-feeding; some mothers have not. Ultimately, the choice is a personal one. Breast-feeding may be especially important in nonindustrialized countries, where its wholesale abandonment contributes to a high incidence of infant death due to diarrheal dehydration (often linked with contaminated water used to make infant formula), to infants' lack of immunity to infections and disease (some immunity is transmitted to infants through mother's milk), or to general undernutrition. There has been a dramatic increase in breast-feeding in the United States in recent years, especially among more highly educated mothers.

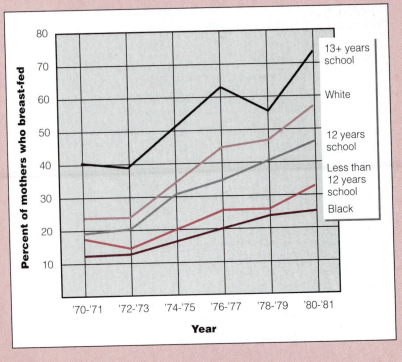

figure 5.1

Increases in breast-feeding for U.S. women by race and education, 1970–1981. Based on U.S. Bureau of the Census, 1988, p. 64.

mended all along: When possible, mothers should breast-feed their infants (Lieberman, 1987). But breast-feeding advocates' reasons have changed. They no longer appeal to notions of maternal duty or infants' sacred rights; nor do they argue that morals are transmitted via mother's milk. They advocate breast-feeding because mothers's milk, science tells us, *is* the best of foods for most newborns. As Lieberman (1987) puts it, it is "species specific" and even infant-specific. It contains just about the right combination of nutrients, the right proportion of fats and calories, the almost-perfect assortment of minerals and vitamins. Furthermore, it is easier for infants to digest than cow's milk, and less likely to lead to allergic reactions. And one additional benefit is that it provides infants with a measure of immunity against infections and diseases, and especially against diarrhea, which, as we saw in Chapter 1, is one of the principal causes of infant mortality in the developing world. Accordingly, the World Health Organization strongly recommends advising women in developing countries to return to breast-feeding where this practice has been abandoned. In addition, they advocate discouraging

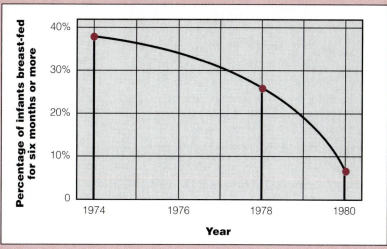

f **i g u r e   5 . 2**

*Decline in breast-feeding, Sao Paulo, Brazil,
1974–1980. Information is from a report by
the International Union of Nutrition Scientists,
Ad Hoc Task Force on Rethinking Infant Nutrition Policies, March 1982. Source: Published for
UNICEF in James P. Grant, Executive Director
of the United Nations Children's Fund (1986).
The state of the world's children: 1986. New
York: Oxford University Press, p. 25.*

the distribution of infant formula. Not only is formula sometimes mixed with unsanitary water, often leading directly to infant diarrhea, but where money is scarce, formula is often in short supply. As a result it is sometimes diluted too much, thereby compounding malnutrition problems.

In spite of these compelling arguments for breast-feeding, it would be misleading not to emphasize that in much of the industrialized world, where sanitation and nutrition are excellent, bottle-fed infants thrive every bit as well as those who are breast-fed. In addition, it is worth noting

that breast milk is affected by the mother's intake of food and drugs, as well as by chemicals to which she is exposed. Alcohol, nicotine, barbiturates, stimulants such as caffeine, sedatives, and prescription drugs can each have an effect on breast-fed infants. Clearly, there are circumstances under which an infant might fare much better with cow's milk or goat's milk.

It's true that bottle-feeding does not provide infants exactly the same kind of contact as breast-feeding. And, as is discussed in Chapter 6, close contact between infants and their caregivers is important for their physical and psychological well-being. But bottle-feeding can provide for much the same kind of contact. Furthermore, it also makes it possible for fathers and infants to share the close contact of feeding times. And that, too, might have its advantages.

nutrition and brain development

The newborn's central nervous system is functionally immature at birth. Although the brain is relatively large (approximately one-quarter the size of the rest of the body, compared with an adult ratio of about 1 to 8), much of it is not yet functioning (except for the brain stem, which is involved in activities such as breathing, sleeping, and temperature control). Activity in the association areas of the brain (the cortex, where most brain-wave activity occurs in adults) increases during the first months of life, becoming common by the age of 7 months (Chugani & Phelps, 1986).

Optimal brain development appears to be influenced by two important factors. One is sensory stimulation. Evidence from experiments with animals suggests that exposure to sights and sounds is crucial for normal development of the visual and auditory areas of the brain (Hubel & Wiesel, 1970). Similarly, evidence from studies of children indicates that experiences are important for intellectual development.

The other important factor in development of the brain is nutrition. Protein is especially important to normal brain development, both during the prenatal period and in the first year or so of life (Lewin, 1975). Iron deficiencies may also be implicated in poorer mental development (Pollitt, Haas, & Levitsky, 1989).

Although *severe* malnutrition can lead to poor mental development, the often-quoted conclusion that *moderate* malnu-

trition leads to lower IQ and retarded mental development is overstated and premature, claims Ricciuti (1991). Similarly, the belief that these effects can be prevented or perhaps even reversed through improved nutrition and various nutritional supplements is more a statement of social policy than of scientific fact. Poor nutrition, Ricciuti explains, is only one facet of a collection of conditions that often accompany poverty— conditions such as poor sanitation, poor medical care, limited intellectual stimulation, and disease. According to Ricciuti (1991), "There is essentially no evidence of a direct influence on mental development, apart from the influence of the social and environmental conditions typically associated with endemic under-nutrition either in the family or in the larger social environment" (p. 62).

The point here is not that malnutrition has no harmful effects on mental development; severe malnutrition can clearly be detrimental. However, we cannot say the same of *moderate* malnutrition because of the difficulty of separating its effects from the effects of other facets of poverty. Hence, as Ricciuti (1991) suggests, social programs should be directed toward improving poor children's developmental environments (in homes, day-care centers, and schools), rather than simply improving their diets.

physical growth in infancy

Physical growth in infancy is relatively predictable given adequate nourishment. However, because of our different genetic programs, identical nourishment will not make all infants exactly the same at all ages. Average physical development during infancy is shown in Figures 5.3 and 5.4. Note that these are median, or mid-point, values. What this means is that 50 percent of all infants of a given

f. **i g u r e 5 . 3**

Height at the 50th percentile for U.S. infants, birth to 24 months. Source: Adapted from Health Department, Milwaukee, Wisconsin; based on data by H. C. Stuart and H. V. Meredith, prepared for use in the Children's Medical Center, Boston. Used by permission of the Milwaukee Health Department.

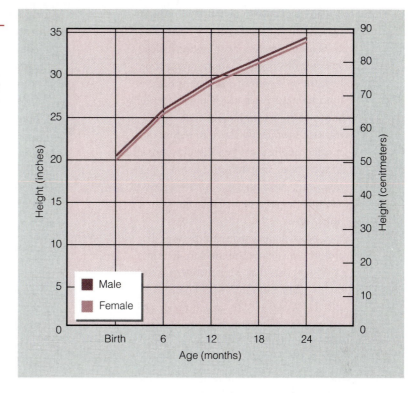

f. **i g u r e 5 . 4**

Weight at the 50th percentile for U.S. infants, birth to 24 months. Source: Adapted from Health Department, Milwaukee, Wisconsin; based on data by H. C. Stuart and H. V. Meredith, prepared for use in the Children's Medical Center, Boston. Used by permission of the Milwaukee Health Department.

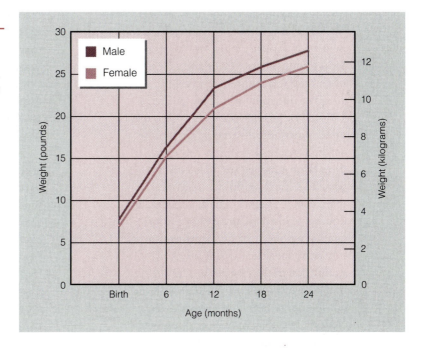

age are expected to be taller than the indicated measurement, and 50 percent will be shorter. There is nothing intrinsically valuable or "normal" about being at or near these "norms"; conversely, there is nothing negative about being moderately above or below the norm. Only when an infant is *significantly* above or below the median might there be cause for concern. In such cases, as Jelliffe and Jelliffe (1990) point out, monitoring an infant's growth can then be used as an early sign of malnutrition.

Unfortunately, many of the world's children *are* below the median. Lozoff (1989) reports that 86 percent of all children are born in third-world countries, and the World Health Organization estimates that well over half of them suffer from malnutrition. Most serious is protein undernutrition, which, as we saw, may have long-term negative effects not only on physical growth, but also on cognitive functioning. Remember, however, that these effects cannot be attributed to malnutrition alone, but are likely due to a combination of factors related to poverty. Not surprisingly, several long-term studies indicate that these effects often cannot be entirely reversed by adequate nutrition later in life (Galler, 1984). One possible reason for this is that undernourished infants tend to become apathetic and listless and to withdraw from environmental and social stimulation. The effects of this withdrawal are often compounded by the fact that many undernourished infants are born into families with little or no formal education and experience a serious lack of stimulation in the first place. The effects of these circumstances, together with the possible contribution of protein deficiency to less than optimal development of brain cells, may constitute a significant developmental disadvantage.

Lozoff (1989) suggests that although adequate nutrition in later life is clearly

necessary if the effects of early undernutrition are to be countered, improved nutrition alone is not sufficient. There is some hope that programs designed to assist mothers in providing emotional and cognitive stimulation for their children may be helpful. However, prevention through the provision of adequate nutrition in the first place is clearly the most effective approach to solving this serious worldwide problem. It may, in the long term, also be the most economical.

sudden infant death syndrome

One of our local newspapers recently ran the story of a 3-month-old infant who had apparently been vigorous and healthy, but who had been found lifeless in his crib one morning. Police described the death as "suspicious" and were investigating.

Several days later, the newspaper again reported on this death. Medical authorities had determined that the infant had died of **sudden infant death syndrome (SIDS)**, sometimes popularly referred to as "crib death" or "cot death," and all suspicions had been abandoned. In fact, however, a diagnosis of sudden infant death syndrome is really not a diagnosis at all; it is an admission that the cause of death is unknown.

This mysterious cause of infant death accounts for approximately 1.4 deaths for every 1,000 live births. This makes SIDS the leading cause of death of infants between the ages of 1 month and 1 year, excluding other inclusive categories like "congenital anomalies" (see Figure 5.5 in "At A Glance: Infant Mortality in the United States"). It accounts for somewhere between 10,000 and 20,000 deaths per year in the United States alone.

First formally defined in 1969, SIDS is simply "the sudden and unexpected death of an infant who has seemed well, or almost well, and whose death remains

Almost 10 of every 1,000 infants born in Canada and the United States die before the age of 1. Infant mortality in Canada is somewhat lower than in the United States: 7.9 compared with 10.0 in 1988. The difference is due largely to higher infant mortality among blacks and other races in the United States. The majority of infant mortalities occur before the end of the first month and are due to abnormalities that are congenital (present at birth; often associated with immaturity). For those who die later, the mysterious and unexplained condition labeled sudden infant death syndrome *is the leading cause of death.*

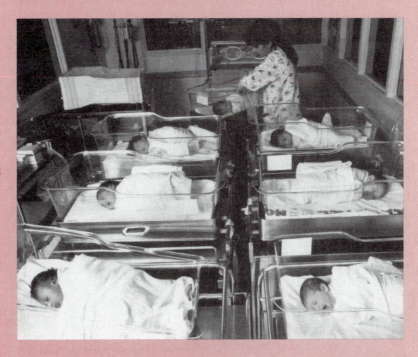

figure 5.5

Some leading causes of death before the age of 1 in the United States, 1989. Source: Adapted from U.S. Bureau of the Census (1992), p. 81.

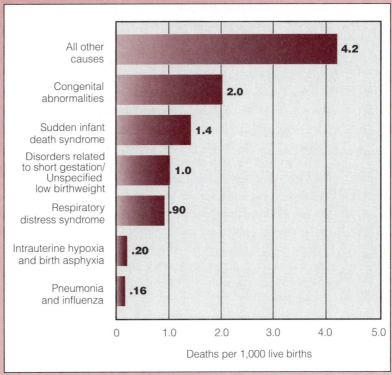

Deaths per 1,000 live births

unexplained [later]" (Valdes-Dapena, 1991, p. 3). In spite of considerable on-going research, SIDS can neither be predicted nor prevented. In Valdes-Dapena's words, "SIDS presents as the sudden, unexpected, and unexplained death of an infant. We really know little more than that about it, for certain" (p. 11).

Although the cause of SIDS is unknown, SIDS victims share some characteristics. The most common of these, surprisingly, is age. SIDS occurs during a far narrower age span than almost all diseases. Specifically, it is extremely rare in the first several weeks of life, peaks between 2 and 4 months, falls rapidly to age 6 months, and then declines more slowly until the age of 1. SIDS deaths are uncommon (fewer than 5 percent of the total) after the age of 1 (Hillman, 1991).

Other than age, there are a number of nonspecific risk factors for SIDS. One is sex, with males accounting for about 60 percent of cases. In addition, there is some evidence that SIDS is more common among lower socioeconomic groups, and that the risk is somewhat higher for younger mothers and for mothers who have had many children in close succession (Hillman, 1991). Also, SIDS may be slightly more probable among infants whose siblings have been victims, among infants born prematurely, and among those who have recently suffered from upper respiratory infections.

Other occasional correlates of SIDS include lower Apgar scores at birth, abnormal crying, an abnormal Moro reflex (defined later in this chapter), variable heart rate and jitteriness, mothers who smoke excessively, mothers who had more difficulties during pregnancy, and abnormal sucking behavior (Burns & Lipsitt, 1991).

There is some speculation, as well, that maturation of the brain may be delayed or abnormal in some SIDS victims.

Thus SIDS has sometimes been associated with **apnea**, a temporary cessation of breathing that generally causes the person to wake up. Burns and Lipsitt (1991) and Hunt (1991) suggest that SIDS may result from an infant's inability to *learn* the voluntary behaviors that eventually replace defensive breathing reflexes. "There is a critical at-risk period for all infants when reflexive defensive responses have faded, but voluntary defensive responses are not yet sufficiently strong," says Hunt (1991, p. 185). Young infants reflexively stick out their tongues when a piece of plastic is put over their mouths. If the object is not dislodged, they typically move their heads from side to side; and if that doesn't work, they swing their arms toward their faces. Eventually these behaviors are replaced by more voluntary behaviors. Perhaps SIDS victims have not learned these voluntary behaviors because of behavioral or neurological problems linked with a slow-to-mature nervous system.

On occasion, parents become aware that something is wrong and are able to revive their infant before death occurs. Some of these infants, termed "near misses for SIDS," have been studied in attempts to discover either the causes of SIDS or the combination of factors that might be most useful for identifying at-risk infants. Duffty and Bryan (1982) studied 72 "near-miss" infants, as well as 52 other infants who were siblings of SIDS victims. Parents of these children were taught resuscitation techniques and how to use a monitor designed to detect cessation of breathing.

Among the 72 "near-miss" infants, 31 experienced prolonged apnea while being monitored at home, and 14 of these infants required "vigorous stimulation" for revival on at least one occasion. Among the 52 siblings of SIDS victims, 16 had at least one episode and 7 required "vigorous" intervention. One died in spite of the fact that the mother, a trained nurse, had initially been able to revive the infant.

It's important to emphasize that in many SIDS cases apnea does not appear to be involved, and that a monitor can neither predict the occurrence of SIDS nor, of course, prevent it. The use of a monitor, suggests Ranney (1991), may add stress in an already stressful household, especially when, as is not uncommon, the machine emits false alarms, further terrifying parents. At the same time, use of a monitor for at-risk children might reassure parents that they are doing everything they can to ensure their child's survival.

SIDS remains unexpected, unexplained, not preventable and, by definition, fatal. It occurs throughout the world and appears to have existed many centuries ago, although it would not have been as easily recognized or considered as important because infant mortality from other causes was so high (Valdes-Dapena, 1991).

None of the factors sometimes associated with SIDS has been shown to *cause* it. Many SIDS victims are apparently thriving infants who seem to be completely normal and healthy, and who simply die, usually silently in their cribs at night. Small wonder that physicians and parents remain baffled and saddened.

behavior in newborns

ne of the serious problems that researchers of early infancy face is the scarcity of behaviors to observe and upon which to base conclusions. Clearly, very young infants cannot be asked to explain their behaviors or their feelings; nor can they be given instructions about how to behave in experimental situations. How, then, can investigators determine whether an infant is curious,

interested, bored, or confused? How do we know when and if learning has occurred?

the orienting response

Part of the answer lies in a group of subtle, sometimes barely perceptible behaviors that have played an important role in experimental child psychology. These behaviors are collectively labeled the *orienting response*. Defined simply, the **orienting response** is our tendency (and that of other animals) to respond to new stimulation by becoming more alert—that is, by attending or *orienting* to it. It is, as Berg and Berg (1987) put it, a "mechanism that enhances the processing of information in all sensory systems" (p. 268).

In animals such as dogs and cats, the orienting response is clear. On hearing a new sound, for example, a dog will pause and its ears may perk up and turn slightly toward the sound; its attitude says, in effect, "What the heck was that?" The human infant may not respond so obviously, but distinct and measurable changes take place; these in combination define the human orienting response. The changes include alterations in pupil size, acceleration or deceleration of heart rate, changes in the conductivity of the skin to electricity (*galvanic skin response*, or GSR; also termed *electrodermal response*), and other physiological changes that are observable by using sensitive instruments.

The value of the orienting response to child psychologists is that it can be used as an indication of attention, because it occurs only in response to a novel stimulation to which a child is then attending. It can also be used as an indication of learning because it stops when the stimulation is no longer novel. When an infant has learned a stimulus (when it has become familiar), the orienting reaction will no longer take place. This decrease in the orienting reaction is termed *habituation*.

In a study by Moffitt (1971), heart rates of infants ages 5 to 6 months were monitored while they heard a repetitive tape recording of the sound *gah*. When infants first heard this sound, their heart rates slowed dramatically, a clear indication of an orienting response (Clarkson & Berg, 1983). But with continued repetition of the sound (spoken by the same voice, in the same tone, at the same volume), infants quickly habituated to the stimulus and heart rates rapidly returned to normal. Suddenly, with no break in inflection, tone, or volume, the tape recording changed: It said *bah* instead of *gah*. Heart rates decelerated dramatically and immediately. The conclusion? Five- to 6-month-old infants are able to tell the difference between sounds as similar as *bah* and *gah*. So even though infants can't *tell* us whether *"mother"* sounds the same as *"father,"* whether blue looks the same as red, or whether salt tastes the same as sugar, we can turn to the orienting response and to other subtle behaviors for our answers.

reflexes

Most of a newborn's responses are reflexive—that is, they don't require learning and can easily be elicited in a normal child by presenting the appropriate stimulus. Although neonates may engage in some nonreflexive activity, it is unlikely that they engage in any *deliberate* activity. Although generalized behaviors such as squirming, waving the arms, and kicking are sometimes too complex and too spontaneous to be classified as reflexes, they don't appear to be intentional (White, 1985).

Probably the best known reflex of newborns is the sucking reflex. It is easily produced by placing an object in a child's mouth. The **head-turning reflex** (also called the rooting reflex) is related to sucking and can be elicited by stroking a baby's cheek or the corner of the mouth. This reflex is evident in breast-fed babies, who turn readily toward the nipple when the breast touches their cheek. Other **vegetative reflexes** (related to eating) include swallowing, hiccuping, sneezing, and vomiting; each can be elicited by the appropriate nourishment-related stimulation.

Some common motor reflexes in newborns have no apparent survival value today but might have been useful in humanity's early history. These reflexes include the startle reaction: throwing out the arms and feet symmetrically and then pulling them back toward the center of the body (also called the **Moro reflex**). Some have speculated that this reflex might be important for tree-dwelling primate infants. If they suddenly fall but throw out their arms and legs while so doing, they might be lucky enough to catch a branch and save themselves. The Moro reflex is sometimes useful in diagnosing brain damage because it is frequently present later in life among people with impaired motor function. In normal infants it ordinarily disappears with the development of the brain and increasing control over motor actions (Hall & Oppenheim, 1987).

Other reflexes that disappear with time are the Babinski reflex, the typical fanning of the toes when an infant is tickled in the middle of the soles of the feet; the **palmar reflex** (also called the Darwinian or grasping reflex), which is sometimes sufficiently pronounced that a neonate can be raised completely off a bed when grasping an adult's finger in each hand; the swimming reflex, which occurs when a baby is balanced horizontally on its stomach; and the stepping reflex, which occurs when an infant is held vertically with its feet lightly touching a surface. Table 5.1 lists some common reflexes of newborns.

An infant's reflexive behaviors are not always entirely rigid, unmodifiable reactions to external conditions. It's true that by definition a reflex is a simple, unlearned, and largely uncontrollable response to a specific stimulus—when the nipple is in the mouth, the infant sucks. But two things are noteworthy here: First, very early an infant begins to exercise a limited degree of control over some of the circumstances that lead to reflexive behaviors. When not hungry, an infant may avert its head or purse its lips tightly, thus avoiding the stimulation that might lead to the sucking response. Second, also beginning very early in life, an infant is capable of modifying some reflexive responses, including sucking. Sucking, Sameroff (1968) informs us, consists of at least two components: the squeezing pressure applied along the sides of the nipple and the negative pressure (suction) applied to the tip of the nipple.

In an intriguing study, Sameroff (1988) designed a nipple that could not only record the different pressures applied to the nipple (squeezing pressure and suction at the tip), but could also be controlled so that it would deliver nutrients under specific conditions. For example, nutrients might be delivered to an infant only as a function of suction at the tip, or it might be delivered only as a function of squeezing pressure. When Sameroff used his apparatus with 30 infants as young as 2 days old, he discovered that, even at this young age, infants were already able to adapt their sucking behavior in response to consequences. When nutrients re-

t a b l e 5.1

Some reflexive behaviors of newborns

REFLEX	STIMULUS
Sucking	Object in the mouth
Head turning	Stroking the cheek or the corner of the mouth
Swallowing	Food in the mouth
Sneezing	Irritation in the nasal passages
Moro reflex	Sudden loud noise
Babinski reflex	Tickling the middle of the soles
Toe grasp	Tickling the soles just below the toes
Palmar grasp	Placing object in the hand
Swimming reflex	Infant horizontal, supported by abdomen
Stepping reflex	Infant vertical, feet lightly touching flat surface

sulted from squeezing the nipple hard between the tongue and the palate, that is exactly what the infant did; when it resulted from suction created by negative pressure in the mouth, infants sucked rather than squeezed.

The human organism—programmed to process information, to learn, to change—is capable of change very early.

motor development in infants

The changes infants go through during the first two years of life, say Hazen and Lockman (1989), are more profound than any that will occur during the remainder of their lives. Within this brief period, initially helpless and completely dependent infants learn to move and explore, to recognize recurring features of the world, to solve practical problems, and to represent symbolically and to communicate.

The normal sequence of motor development in infancy is highly predictable — although major developments occur at different ages for different children. At the age of about 8 months, this urchin can pull herself to a standing position. But it will be some time yet before she can crawl over the barricade.

There is a close link between **motor development** (the development of control over physical actions) and intellectual development. An infant's ability to manipulate and explore makes possible the discovery of the properties of physical objects, such as their permanence and their location in space. These discoveries, in turn, are related to the infant's growing ability to *reason* about objects and develop concepts (ideas) (Bertenthal & Campos, 1990)—hence Piaget's (1954) label, *sensorimotor*, to describe development in the first two years of life.

The order in which children acquire motor skills is highly predictable, although the ages at which these skills appear can vary considerably. Tables of developmental **norms**, such as that represented by the Denver Developmental Screening Test, are sometimes useful for assessing a child's progress. However, as always, there is no "average" child.

The normal sequence of motor development reflects the two developmental principles mentioned in Chapter 4. First, development is *cephalocaudal* in that it proceeds from the head toward the feet. For example, infants can control eye movements and raise the head before acquiring control over the extremities. Recall that fetal development proceeds in the same manner: The head, eyes, and internal organs develop in the embryo before the appearance of the limbs.

Second, development is *proximodistal*: it proceeds in an inward-outward direction. For example, internal organs mature and function before the (more external) limbs develop. Similarly, children acquire control over parts of the body closest to the center before they can control the extremities. Thus they can control gross motor movements before hand or finger movements.

The sequence of early motor development probably reflects some sort of genetically influenced timetable. However, an infant's context can dramatically influence both the ages at which different motor skills are acquired and their quality. Gerber (1958) reports an investigation of 300 Ugandan infants who, a mere two days after birth (all home deliveries without anesthetics), could sit upright, heads held high, with only slight support of the elbows—a feat that most American children cannot accomplish until close to the age of 2 months (Bayley, 1969). And all 300 Ugandan children were expert crawlers before they were 2 months old!

perceptual development in infants

ur existence as human beings depends largely on our ability to make sense of the world and of our selves. The struggle to discover what things are and what they mean begins in infancy and depends on three closely related processes: sensation, perception, and conceptualization.

Sensation is the effect when physical stimuli are translated into neural impulses (which can then be transmitted to the brain and interpreted). Thus sensation depends on the activity of one or more of our specialized sense organs—eyes, ears, and taste buds, for example.

In its simplest sense, **perception** is the brain's interpretation of sensation. Thus wavelengths corresponding to the color red affect our retinas in specific ways, causing electrical activity in our optic nerve. When this activity reaches the part of our brain that deals with vision, we *perceive* the color in question. That we can now *think* about the color red, compare it to other colors, or make some decision based on it is a function of the third process, **conceptualization**.

To summarize, sensation is primarily a physiological process dependent on the senses (the effect of light waves on the retina of the eye), and perception is the effect of sensation (the recognition that this is a red light). Conceptualization (the realization that because this is a red light, I should stop) is a more cognitive, or intellectual, process.

vision

For years researchers assumed that newborns had poorly developed vision with little ability to detect form, patterns, or movements. One of the reasons for this relates to problems in doing research with infants, who can't communicate directly the effects of sensory experience. But with the development of increasingly sensitive instruments to detect subtle changes in an infant's behavior, earlier preconceptions are being replaced—although there still are difficulties with infants as research subjects (see Figure 5.6 in "At A Glance: Infants as Research Subjects").

VISION AT BIRTH

How well can an infant see? Is the world fuzzy and blurred, or is it crisp and clear? Is it 20/20, or better or worse? How can we find out?

Researchers' estimates of infant **visual acuity** may vary considerably because of the different methods used to assess vision. As a result, a small controversy clouds the field (see Norcia & Tyler, 1985). However, a number of important things are clear.

First, infants are far from blind at birth, although some of their visual world may be somewhat fuzzy and blurred. Second, there is a three- to fourfold improvement in an infant's visual acuity between birth and the age of 1 year (Aslin & Smith, 1988). In fact, by the age of 6 months, an infant's visual acuity may be close to that of a normal adult. And third, a newborn's visual accommodation is more limited than that of adults. It appears that newborns focus most accurately at a distance of approximately 12 inches (30 cm) (Banks, 1980). Significantly, that is about the distance of a mother's face when she is feeding her infant. This is but one of the ways in which neonates appear to be programmed to perceive important aspects of the environment.

COLOR AND MOVEMENT

Although no one has determined exactly when color vision is first present in

Young infants, especially newborns, are not always very good research subjects. When Fantz (1963) wanted to see how newborns reacted to visual stimulation, one of the most important conditions for selecting subjects was whether they kept their eyes open long enough to be shown the stimuli. And when Meltzoff and Moore (1989) investigated newborns' ability to imitate, only 40 of 93 infants completed the eight-minute test session, even though the researchers chose only infants who showed no signs of hunger and remained alert for at least five minutes before the testing. The remaining 53 infants either fell asleep, cried, had spitting or choking fits, or had a bowel movement.

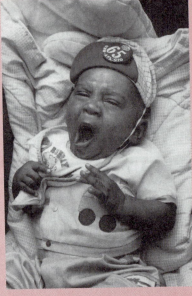

f **i g u r e   5 . 6**

Difficulties in testing infants. Only 40 of 93 infants, ages 13.37–67.33 hours, completed an eight-minute test session. Testing of the remaining 53 infants had to be abandoned for the reasons shown. Source: Meltzoff and Moore, 1989, pp. 954–962.

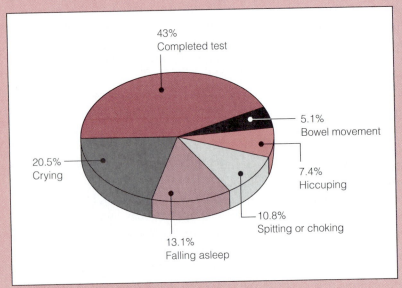

infants, we do know that it is well developed by 2 to 4 months (Bornstein, 1979; Fagan, 1974). By the age of 4 months, infants even show a preference for certain colors, such as pure reds and blues (Bornstein & Marks, 1982).

Pupillary reflexes—changes in the size of the pupil caused by changes in the brightness of visual stimulation—demonstrate that neonates are sensitive to light intensity. Also, eye movements indicate that an infant is capable of visually following a slowly moving object within a few days of birth and is sensitive to patterns and contours as early as two days after birth (Fantz, 1965). There is evidence as well that although infants less than 2 months of age can perceive high-

f **igure   5.7**

Use of the glass-covered visual cliff indicates that depth perception is developed at a very young age in humans and other animals. At left, an infant refuses to cross over even after receiving tactile assurance that the "cliff" is in fact a solid surface. At right, a goat exhibits a similar reaction—although, unlike a human infant, it can jump to the other side. Goats show this response at the tender age of 1 day.

contrast contours (or edges), they cannot yet perceive relationships among different contours or forms (Pipp & Haith, 1984).

DEPTH PERCEPTION

In addition to perceiving color, movement, and form and to demonstrating preferences for these, young infants can also perceive depth. In Gibson and Walk's (1960) "visual cliff" studies, a heavy sheet of glass was positioned over a checkered surface; half of this surface was flush with the glass and half was some three feet lower (see Figure 5.7). An adult standing or sitting on the glass can plainly see a dropoff or cliff where the patterned surface falls away from the glass. So can goats who, at the age of only 1 day, avoid the deep side, either going around it or

jumping over it when they can. So too can infants, who, when they are old enough to crawl, typically refuse to cross the deep part, even when their mothers call them from the other side. Thus perception of depth is present at least from the time that the infant can crawl.

For a number of years, a test for depth perception before an infant could crawl seemed impossible. The refinement of physiological measures, however, has made it possible to look at changes in heart rate when infants who cannot crawl are simply moved from the shallow to the deep side of the visual cliff apparatus. Interestingly, Bertenthal and Campos (1990) report that infants who have not yet learned to crawl do *not* normally show much evidence of fear when lowered onto the deep side—that is, their heart rates do not accelerate significantly. Hence either fear of falling is learned rather than innate, or these infants simply do not yet perceive depth. These authors argue that they perceive depth but have not yet learned to fear it. Through self-locomotion, infants eventually develop the *visual-vestibular* sense essential to maintaining equilibrium (and related to fear of falling). In addition, locomotion requires them to develop skills of visual attention if they are to avoid colliding with objects; it allows them as well to learn about dangers associated with height, perhaps from parental reactions as they approach stairs or stand on chairs.

VISUAL PREFERENCES

As we saw, if the time spent looking at colors is an indication of preference, very young infants prefer reds and blues. It's possible, but perhaps not likely, that they really don't prefer these colors at all, but are simply puzzled or intrigued by them. This possibility has led researchers to investigate infants' visual preferences.

In one well-known study of infants' visual preference, 18 infants, ranging in age from 10 hours to 5 days, were shown six circular stimulus patterns of different complexity, the most complex being a human face (Fantz, 1963). In diminishing order of complexity, the other stimuli included concentric circles, newsprint, and three circles of different solid colors. Figure 5.8 shows the percentage of total time spent by subjects looking at each of the figures. That the face was looked at for a significantly higher proportion of total time indicates not only that infants can discriminate among the various figures, but also that they prefer faces—or perhaps that they prefer complexity.

Morton and Johnson (1991) also suggest that infants are born with some innate knowledge about faces that allows them to recognize and be attracted to them. There is evidence, for example, that by the second day of life they already prefer their mother's face (Masi & Scott, 1983). However, as Leon (1992) points out, studies of infants' reactions to their mother's face have generally provided the infant with the sound of the mother's voice, and sometimes with her smell as well. Thus it isn't clear that infants actually prefer the *sight* of the mother rather than her smell or the sound of her voice.

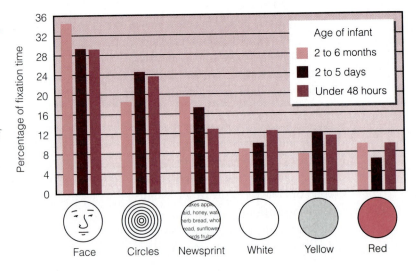

f i g u r e 5 . 8

Relative percentage of time infants looked at six circular visual stimuli. The graph depicts infants' preference for the human face and for more complex stimuli. Source: Based on data in Robert L. Fantz, Pattern vision in newborn infants, Science, 1963, 140, 296–297. Copyright 1963 by the American Association for the Advancement of Science. Used by permission of the American Association for the Advancement of Science and the author.

Infants not only recognize faces, but seem to prefer certain kinds of faces over others—and that may be very important. Langlois, Roggman, and Rieser-Danner (1990) exposed 60 1-year-old infants to an experimenter wearing either of two professionally constructed, highly realistic masks—one attractive and one unattractive. Infants' responses to each were markedly different: In the presence of the attractively masked person they withdrew far less, played more, and generally showed more signs of positive emotions. Even at the age of 1, infants apparently prefer attractive people and react more positively to them.

In a related study, Langlois et al. (1991) presented 1-year-old infants with attractive or unattractive dolls. Again, infants preferred the attractive dolls, playing with them significantly longer than with the unattractive dolls. And in further studies, infants as young as 6 months seem to prefer faces judged attractive, whether the faces were male or female, younger or older, or black or white (Langlois et al., 1991).

Why? Perhaps, suggest Langlois et al. (1991), because attractiveness is a sort of facial "averageness." Faces created by averaging and digitizing facial features are judged highly attractive (Langlois & Roggman, 1990). Faces that are unusual may be interesting, but "average" faces are more clearly representative manifestations of the ideal human gene pool. People with average, and therefore attractive, faces are less likely to carry genes that might be harmful.

The significance of these findings is twofold. First, it had long been thought that attractiveness is a learned and culturally determined quality, and that young infants would not likely have been exposed to enough models or to enough value judgments to have developed preferences. But this does not appear to be

the case. Second, if infants *prefer* attractive faces, where does that leave ugly parents, grandparents, or brothers and sisters? Or even strangers? Recall the finding of Elder et al. (1985) that attractive daughters were better treated by their fathers during the Great Depression in the 1930s (see Chapter 3). Are attractive fathers and mothers treated differently by their children? If so, what might the implications be for the ecological systems defined by the family?

RULES OF VISUAL PERCEPTION

Earlier in this chapter you were asked to consider the problem of designing a newborn so that it would become more sophisticated as a 2 year old, and eventually as a 12 year old, a 42 year old, a 92 year old. In designing this little organism, we considered that, among other things, you would have to program it to become an extraordinarily capable information-processing system tuned to detect and respond to the most important features of the environment, and predisposed, as well, to make sense of these features.

Does what we know about an infant's visual system conform to our design requirements? Haith (1980) says yes. Infants, he informs us, do not respond to the visual world in a simple, reflexive manner, response following stimulus in predictable mechanical fashion. Instead, infants behave as though preprogrammed to follow specific rules geared to maximizing information. After all, acquiring information is the purpose of looking.

So how do infants look? Haith's research using infrared lights bounced off infants' corneas to reveal movements of their eyes produced the following important results.

First, contrary to what we might have expected, infants move their eyes even when there's no light, scanning the darkness in a highly controlled manner, using small movements appropriate for finding shadows, edges, spots. When viewing a uniformly lit but unpatterned field, their eye movements are broader sweeping movements suitable for discovering bolder contours. It seems clear that from birth, visual scanning patterns are not simply under the control of external stimuli (after all, scanning occurs in darkness as well as in light) but are internally controlled. It is as though infants, true to our speculative design, are preprogrammed to obtain information.

Second, newborns actually *look* at stimuli. They position their eyeballs so that a maximum amount of visual information falls on the *fovea*—the part of the retina that has the highest concentration of visual cells. It's as though the infant's scanning rules are designed to maximize stimulation—and, consequently, to maximize information.

Third, when a newborn looks at a simple stimulus (such as a vertical or horizontal line), the eyes cross back and forth repeatedly over the edges of the stimulus. The effect is to maintain a high level of neural firing in the visual cells.

Haith concludes that there appears to be a single important principle that governs a newborn's visual activity: Maximize neural firing. It is a built-in (endogenous) principle that assures that the newborn's visual activity will lead to the greatest possible amount of information—a vital feature for an organism that must be an outstanding information-processing system. This principle—maximize neural firing—is manifested in the following list of babies' visual rules (Haith, 1980, p. 96):

- Rule 1. If awake and alert and the light is not too bright, open eyes.

- Rule 2. If in darkness, maintain a controlled, detailed search.

- Rule 3. If in light with no form, search for edges using broad, jerky sweeps of the field.

- Rule 4. If an edge is found, terminate the broad scan and stay in the general vicinity of that edge. Try to implement eye movements that cross the edge. If such eye movements are not possible in the region of the edge (as is the case for edges too distant from the center of the field), scan for other edges.

This view of an infant's visual perception as rule-governed and information-oriented, rather than as stimulus-bound, is a dramatic departure from psychology's traditional approach to these matters—a departure that is evident in many other areas of child study as well. Today's infant—and child—is no longer merely a passive recipient of external influences, but has become active, exploring, information-seeking.

Happily, vision is not the infant's only source of information.

hearing

Dogs, bears, cats, and many other animals are deaf at birth; the human neonate is not. In fact, the ear is fully grown and potentially functional a few months *before* birth. But just how well a newborn hears is still a matter of some debate, much of which arises because the results of investigations are often confounded by marked variations in how different infants respond to sounds. Also, various indicators of sensitivity (changes in heart rate, respiration rate, EEG activity, electrical conductivity of the skin, and the more obvious indicators of attention such as blinking, turning, or startling) have been used in different studies and have sometimes led to contradictory conclusions.

SOUND SENSITIVITY IN NEONATES

Most investigations indicate that neonates are only slightly less sensitive than adults to sound intensity (loudness, measured in decibels; see Figure 5.9). Neonates' average hearing threshold falls somewhere between 20 and 30 decibels (or even higher, depending on the criteria and measures used) (Acredolo & Hake, 1982); that of a normal adult is at 0 decibels. The difference is not very significant because even a quiet conversation is usually above these thresholds (60 or more decibels).

Investigations of infants' responsiveness to frequency (high or low pitch) have yielded somewhat inconsistent results partly because of the criteria used, and partly because subjects of different ages have been studied (Aslin, 1987). Studies of older infants usually show that sensitivity to higher frequencies increases with age (Trehub et al., 1991), and the general conclusion that infants (as opposed to newborns) are more sensitive to higher frequencies is widely accepted. Some researchers suggest that the common tendency of adults to raise the pitch of their

f i g u r e   5 . 9

Decibel values of some ordinary sounds. Compared with adults, neonates are only slightly less sensitive to sound intensity. Source: Lefrançois (1983).

Source of sound	Decibel value	
Electric guitars in rock concerts	125	
Loudest woman in 1973 British shouting contest		
Hammering on steel plate 2 feet away	115	Pain threshold for humans
Loudest man in 1973 British shouting contest		
	105	
Riveter 35 feet away		
Subway train	95	
Pneumatic drill at 10 feet		Possible hearing damage
	85	with prolonged exposure
	75	
Noisiest spot at Niagara Falls		
Ordinary conversation at 3 feet	65	
Department store shopping		
	55	
Quiet automobile 10 or more feet away		
	45	
Night noises in a city		
	35	
		Neonate hearing threshold
Quiet garden in London	25	
Average whisper at 4 feet		
	15	
Rustle of leaves in gentle breeze		Adult hearing threshold:
Quiet whisper 5 feet away	5	arbitrary value for point below
	0	which an acoustic wave at
		1,000 Hz will not be heard
Butterfly at 6 feet		
Butter slowly melting		

The hearing threshold for normal adults is arbitrarily given a value of zero decibels. The rustling of nearby leaves in a gentle breeze might be around 7 or 10 decibels; a running car motor at 10 feet is at about 55 decibels. The newborn's hearing threshold appears to be between 25 and 35 decibels.

voices when speaking to infants or young children is the result of an unconscious recognition of children's greater sensitivity to higher frequencies (Fogel, 1984).

VOICE DISCRIMINATION IN INFANTS

Amazingly, it appears that an infant as young as 3 days is able to discriminate among different voices and seems to prefer the sound of its mother's voice. In a study in which systematic changes in an infant's sucking were reinforced with the sound of a woman reading a book, the infant responded to its mother's voice but not to voices of other women (DeCasper & Fifer, 1980). Have newborns, in the

mere space of three days, learned to tell the difference between their mothers' voices and the voices of others? Have they developed a reliable preference for their mothers' voices so soon? DeCasper and Fifer think this unlikely. They suggest that these findings are evidence that a fetus can hear sounds while in the uterus and can distinguish among them. Moreover, if these findings and this interpretation are correct, they provide evidence of learning in utero (Aslin, Pisoni, & Jusczyk, 1983).

In summary, newborns are sensitive to a wide range of sounds and seem particularly sensitive to sounds that fall within the frequency range of the human voice, almost as though their systems were pretuned to normal speech frequencies (Eisenberg, 1976).

smell, taste, and touch

How sensitive are neonates to odors, tastes, and touch. Do they have to learn these things?

Apparently not. Within hours of birth, infants will attempt to turn their faces away when exposed to a strong and unpleasant smell like ammonia (Lipsitt, Engen, & Kaye, 1963). And their facial expressions are distinctly different when they are exposed to the smell of vanilla and to that of raw fish (Steiner, 1979). Like many adults, they like the smell of raw fish less than that of vanilla. Similarly, they smack their lips when sweet things are placed on their tongues. They pucker their mouths in response to sour tastes, and open them for bitter tastes (Steiner, 1979). It seems that the ability to taste and smell is present at birth and does not depend on experience. Even at the age of 1 day, infants can differentiate among various types of solutions and among concentrations of sweetener. Almost invariably, they prefer any of these sweeteners to plain water. And contrary to what we might have been led to believe about the natural wisdom of the body, they prefer sweetened water to milk (Desor, Maller, & Greene, 1978).

What about sensitivity to pain? Early investigations had concluded that neonates are remarkably insensitive to much of the stimulation that children and adults would find quite painful (McGraw, 1943). Circumcision doesn't really hurt boy babies, they assured us. But they (whoever *they* are) were probably at least partly wrong. Babies do holler when circumcised! And more recent research has not established that the neonate is initially insensitive to pain, although there is some indication that pain sensitivity increases over the first few days of life (Haith, 1986). Nor is there any substantial evidence of sex differences in sensitivity to touch. Studies that have used items from the Brazelton Newborn Behavioral Assessment Scale (NBAS) have found strong evidence of touch sensitivity in neonates, with no discernible difference between the sexes. The relevant item in the NBAS involves placing a cloth over the infant's face. Even at the age of 2 hours, newborns usually respond with strong and abrupt movements that would ordinarily remove the cloth.

Neonates are remarkably alert and well suited to their environments. They can hear, see, and smell; they can turn in the direction of food, suck, swallow, digest, and eliminate; they can respond physically to a small range of stimuli; and they can cry and vomit. Still, they are singularly helpless creatures who would surely die if the environment did not include adults intimately concerned with their survival. There is much they need to learn, much with which they must become familiar, before they can stand on their own two feet—not only physically, but cognitively as well.

cognitive development in infants

For a long time, Maya Pines (1966) tells us, psychology neglected the infant's mind as though everyone knew that babies didn't really have minds or if they did, they wouldn't be very important in any case at this stage of development. But our views have changed. "Babies are very competent," says Bower (1989). "They are set to use whatever information we give them" (p. ix).

As far back as 1920, Piaget had begun to map the course of children's intellectual development. Piaget's story of the growth of children's minds tells of their growing awareness of the world in which they live, and of their discovery or invention of ways of interacting with this world. It is a complex and fascinating story, but it is not the whole story; there are other theories of cognitive development, other explanations of how we come to know. Some of these theories are labeled *information-processing approaches*. They look at what is involved in memory: deriving information, abstracting, sorting, organizing, analyzing, and retrieving, for example. We look at memory processes in infants before we turn to Piaget's theory of cognitive development.

memory in infants

If neonates, ignorant and helpless as they are at birth, are ever to reach the level of competence of the 2 year old, there is much that they must learn and remember: what is edible and what isn't; how to get from here to there, or from there to here; how to ask for things; how to hold a cup; how to get people's interest and attention; and much more.

A neonate's memory is not nearly as efficient and powerful as yours or mine.

In fact, a number of researchers have concluded that an infant's memory is very weak and is more often measured in minutes or hours rather than in days or months (Lipsitt, 1982). Clearly, however, from the very beginning infants must have some ability to learn and remember. This primitive ability will eventually develop into the type of memory that is characteristic of the 2 year old, the 40 year old, the 90 year old.

One of the most common ways of investigating infants' memory is to use components of the orienting response described earlier. For example, researchers might look at an infant's response to a single photograph (or other stimulus) presented on two different occasions. If the infant remembers something about the photograph, heart rate would not be expected to change in the same way as it might when the infant is presented with a completely new photograph.

A second approach is simply to look at how long it takes for an infant to habituate (become accustomed) to a stimulus. Habituation might be revealed in patterns of eye movements (the infant stops looking at the stimulus) or, again, in changes in components of the orienting response such as respiration or heart rate.

A third measure of an infant's memory involves behavior. For example, Rovee-Collier and her associates (1980) taught 3-month-old infants to make a mobile turn by moving their feet (each infant's foot was fastened to a lever that, when moved, caused the mobile to move). Infants remembered the procedure several weeks later.

Using measures such as these, investigators have found that even newborns have memories. True, they are not very elaborate memories, but they are a beginning. Within days of birth, for example, newborns are able to recognize their mothers' smell (Macfarlane, 1975) and

to discriminate among different speech sounds (Rovee-Collier, 1987)—clear evidence of memory.

In one study, Swain, Zelazo, and Clifton (1993) had 1-day-old newborns listen to a word and then monitored them as they turned their heads toward the sound. Within a short period of time, these infants habituated (learned) the word and stopped turning. One day later, half of these infants were again exposed to the same word; the other half heard a different word. Again, all infants initially oriented to the word, turning their heads toward it. But those who were exposed to the same word both days habituated significantly more rapidly than those who heard a new word—clear evidence that they remembered something of the word.

Still, evidence suggests that an infant's memory for most things appears to be of relatively short duration. For example, young infants who are conditioned to associate a puff of air with a tone, or a feeding schedule with a bell, may remember from one day to the next, perhaps for 6 or 10 days. But without any reminders in the interim, all evidence of memory is likely to be gone within a few days (Rovee-Collier, 1987).

DEVELOPMENTAL PHASES IN INFANTS' MEMORY

Perlmutter (1980) describes three sequential phases in the development of memory in infants. In the first phase, an infant's memory seems to be largely a matter of neurons firing when a new stimulus is presented and stopping with habituation. As the infant becomes more familiar with the stimulus (that is, learns and remembers), the period before habituation becomes shorter.

The second phase, which begins at around 3 months, is related to the infant's growing ability to accomplish intended actions. Infants now actively look and search; they begin to reach, even to grasp; they explore; and they recognize things and people. Recognition is a sure sign of memory.

In the third phase, by the age of 8 or so months, infant memories have become much more like our own in that they are more abstract and more symbolic. They remember classes of things like fuzzy objects and big people and pets and building blocks and beets.

Memory in adults and in older children is greatly facilitated by certain strategies, the most important of which are *organization, grouping*, and *elaboration*. Although infants do not systematically use any of these strategies, 2 year olds already have some notions about what memory is and understand mental-event terms such as *remember, think, know*, and *pretend*. When asked to remember something, they pay attention and they try to remember. These actions, says Wellman (1988), are strategies in their own right.

There is a great gulf between the immature memory of the week-old child who can demonstrate a vague recollection of a familiar smell or sound, and that of the 1-year-old who mistakenly yells "Dada" when he sees a stranger's familiar-looking back in the supermarket. There is also a vast difference between this 1 year old's memory and the memory of a 12 year old, whose intellectual strategies permit mental feats of which the 1 year old cannot yet even dream. (See Chapter 7 for more information about memory.)

---

basic piagetian ideas on infancy

An infant's world, says Jean Piaget, is a world of *the here and now*. It's a world that makes sense when the infant looks at it, hears it, touches it, smells it, or tastes it. The infant does not have concepts in the sense that we think of them—no store of

memories or hopes or dreams, no fund of information with which to think.

But what neonates have are the sensory systems and the cognitive inclinations that make them into a self-reinforcing, information-processing organism. When Piaget describes infants, he speaks of organisms that continually seek out and respond to stimulation and that, by so doing, gradually build up a repertoire of behaviors and capabilities.

At first an infant's behaviors are limited mainly to the simple reflexes with which it is born; but in time these behaviors become more elaborate and more coordinated with one another. The process by which this occurs is **adaptation**, and the complementary processes that make adaptation possible are **assimilation** and **accommodation** (see Chapter 2).

To review briefly, assimilation and accommodation are highly active processes whereby an individual searches out, selects, and responds to information, the end result of which is the actual *construction* of knowledge. Imagine, for example, a young child walking on a windblown beach, stooping now and again to pick up pebbles and toss them onto the water. In Piaget's view, there is a **schema** involved here—a sort of mental or cognitive representation—that corresponds to the child's knowledge of the suitability of pebbles as objects to be thrown upon the waves, as well as other schemata that concern the activities involved in bending, retrieving, and throwing. The pebbles are, in a sense, being assimilated to appropriate schemata; they are understood and used in terms of the child's previous knowledge.

Imagine, now, that the child bends to retrieve another pebble but finds, instead, that she has picked up a wallet. The wallet is clearly not a pebble, and perhaps it should not be responded to in the same way. But still, why not? The "throwing things on the big waves" schema is readily available and momentarily preferred, and so the wallet too is assimilated to the throwing schema. The child tries to hurl it toward the water, but the new object's heaviness is surprising and the child's throwing motion inadequate, and the wallet fails to reach the surf. Now, when she picks it up again, she doesn't hurl it in quite the same way. She holds it in two hands, grasps it tightly with her pudgy little fingers, and pushes hard with her little legs as she throws. In Piaget's terms, she has accommodated to the characteristics of this object that make it different from the pebbles she has been throwing.

To simplify these sometimes difficult concepts, to assimilate is to respond in terms of preexisting information. It often involves ignoring some aspects of the situation to make it conform to aspects of the mental system. In contrast, to accommodate is to respond to external characteristics and to make changes in the mental system as a result.

The process by which balance between accommodation and assimilation is maintained is labeled **equilibration**. At one extreme, if an infant always assimilated but never accommodated, there would be no change in schemata (mental structure), no change in behavior. Everything would be assimilated to the sucking schema, the grasping schema, the looking schema (that is, everything would be sucked or grasped or simply looked at). Such a state of disequilibrium would result in little adaptation and little cognitive growth. At the other extreme, if everything were accommodated and not assimilated, schemata—and behavior—would be in a constant state of flux: First the nipple would be sucked, then it would be chewed, now pinched, then swatted. Again, such an extreme state

of disequilibrium would result in little adaptation.

Equilibration, says Piaget, is an internal tendency that governs the balance between assimilation and accommodation and that accounts for the *construction* of knowledge; that is, it accounts for adaptation and cognitive growth throughout development.

Equilibration is but one of four forces that shape development (Piaget, 1961). Another is *maturation*, a sort of biologically determined unfolding of potential. Maturation—or biology—does not determine cognitive growth but is related to the unfolding of potential. A third factor is *active experience*, a child's interaction with the world. The fourth is *social interaction*, which helps a child develop ideas about things, about people, and about the self.

These four factors—active experience, maturation, equilibration, and social interaction—are the cornerstones of Piaget's basic theory. To summarize the theory in one sentence, cognitive growth results from assimilation and accommodation, governed by a need to achieve and maintain equilibrium, and occurring through active experience and social interaction broadly related to unfolding maturation.

It is a large mouthful conceptually; perhaps we can chew on it a little more in the next section.

the object concept

An infant's world is a "blooming, buzzing mass of confusion," William James (1890) informed us more than a century ago, with the assumption that at first sensations like colors, sounds, smells, and tastes would all be indistinct and blurred. In those years, psychologists believed that a neonate's senses don't function at birth, or function very poorly. As we saw earlier, they were wrong: Children see colors, movements, and shapes almost from birth, they can detect *and remember* odors, and they can hear even before they are born.

Still, James was at least partly correct. Why? Because infants don't realize that objects exist out there, that they are real and continue to exist even when they're not being seen, felt, or heard. According to Piaget, in an infant's world of the here and now, there are no permanent objects. The nipple exists when the infant sees, touches, or sucks it; when it can't be sensed, it doesn't exist. Imagine what the world would be like, suggest Wellman and Gelman (1992), if we thought objects disappeared and reappeared—that is, if we had no concept of *objective objects*. This **object concept**, they explain, is absolutely fundamental to our reasoning about the world; our very conception of the world demands that objects be real, out there, substantive, and independent of us. There is no "out there" for infants; they must discover the permanence and objectivity of objects for themselves. This discovery is one of the truly great achievements of infancy.

How do children discover that objects are real and permanent? The processes are not clearly understood, but it seems evident that experiencing and exploring the real world are an important part of the process. In a series of investigations, Stambak et al. (1989) videotaped young infants' responses to different objects, such as nesting cups or hollow cubes or rods. Analysis of these videotapes reveals that even very young infants organize their behaviors in systematic ways, that their exploration is not simply the random exercising of behaviors. Thus, some infants typically banged different objects

with a rod; some explored the insides of the hollow cubes with their fingers, or with their hands if the cubes were large enough. In a sense, it is as though infants have already begun to invent questions and problems and to devise little experiments to find the answers. In a series of naturalistic observations reported by Sinclair et al. (1989), infants often spent the entire 20-minute observation session coming back to the same idea.

Not only does the exploration of objects by young infants become increasingly systematic with advancing age, but it also involves more varied activities. As Rochat (1989) puts it, exploration becomes increasingly multimodal between the ages of 2 and 5 months. Initially, for example, exploration is mainly visual or oral; later, it also becomes manual. By the age of 3 or 4 months, most infants use both mouth and hands to explore. And, significantly, type of manipulation depends more and more on the objects being explored. Some things are more easily understood, more meaningful, when held in both hands, licked, drooled on, and gummed emphatically.

To investigate infants' understanding of objects, Piaget (1954) showed children an attractive object and then hid it from view. If the object exists only when infants perceive it, reasoned Piaget, they will make no effort to look for it when they can't see it *even if they actually saw it being hidden.* When children begin to look for an object they can no longer see, this is definite evidence that they can imagine it—that they know the thing still exists.

Piaget found that in their earliest stage, children do not respond to the object once it is removed; next, they search for the object, but only where they last saw it; and finally, they know that objects continue to exist and look for them in a variety of places. This final stage, claims Piaget, occurs at about age 18 months.

Some subsequent investigations of the development of the object concept indicate that the age of acquisition is perhaps younger than Piaget suggests. For example, Bower (1971, 1977) used the orienting response of very young infants to determine whether an object ceases to exist when it is removed from sight. In one study, an infant is shown a ball, and then a screen is moved between the infant and the ball; a few seconds later the screen is removed. In some trials, the ball is still there; in others it has been taken away. When infants do not yet have object permanence, they should not be surprised that the ball is gone. But they would be surprised (as indicated by changes in heart rate) to see it gone if they expected it to be there—if, in other words, they had acquired notions of object permanence. Bower's main finding is that infants as young as 3 weeks of age seem to have some notion of object permanence, *providing the object is hidden from view for only a few seconds*. When the object is hidden for longer (15 seconds, as opposed to 1½ seconds), infants at this age all show surprise when the ball is still present after the screen is removed.

In a related study, Baillargeon (1987) found that infants as young as 3½ months seemed to have some primitive notions about the solidity of objects. When one object was moved through a space that should have been occupied by another object, they seemed surprised (if the fact that they looked longer at that impossible situation than at another comparable but possible situation can be interpreted as surprise).

Do such findings mean that Piaget was wrong? Do infants have a notion of the permanence and independent identity of objects a long time before the age of

18 months? Probably. What the studies clearly indicate is that under the proper circumstances, infants appear to have a short-lived recollection of absent objects. In addition, infants as young as 3 or 4 months have begun to understand that objects are solid and stationary (Baillargeon, 1992). However, it will still be a long time before an infant now 3 weeks old will deliberately search for an object that has not been present just recently (Bower, 1989).

sensorimotor development in infants

Piaget believed that children's understanding of the world throughout most of infancy is determined by the activities they can perform on it and by their perceptions of it—hence his label *sensorimotor*. Table 5.2 summarizes Piaget's stages of intellectual development from birth through adolescence. Piaget simplifies infants' cognitive development during the sensorimotor period by dividing it into six substages, summarized in Table 5.3 and described next.

EXERCISING REFLEXES (BIRTH–1 MONTH)

During the first month, infants spend much of their waking time exercising the abilities with which they are born: They suck, look, grasp, and cry. In addition to their obvious survival functions, these activities have an important cognitive function. By repeatedly performing these activities, an infant eventually develops control over them and begins to gain control over aspects of the environment. By the end of the first month, infants are quite proficient at reaching and grasping,

t**able 5.2**

Piaget's stages of cognitive development

STAGE	APPROXIMATE AGE	MAJOR CHARACTERISTICS
Sensorimotor	0–2 years	Motoric intelligence; world of the here and now; no language, no thought in early stages; no notion of objective reality
Preoperational*	2–7 years	Egocentric thought
Preconceptual	2–4 years	Reason dominated by perception
Intuitive	4–7 years	Intuitive rather than logical solutions; inability to conserve
Concrete operations†	7 to 11 or 12 years	Ability to conserve; logic of classes and relations; understanding of numbers; thinking bound to the concrete; development of reversibility in thought
Formal operations‡	11 or 12 to 14 or 15 years	Complete generality of thought; propositional thinking; ability to deal with the hypothetical; development of strong idealism

*Discussed in Chapter 7.
†Discussed in Chapter 9.
‡Discussed in Chapter 11.

t able 5.3

The six substages of sensorimotor development

SUBSTAGE AND APPROXIMATE AGE (IN MONTHS)	PRINCIPAL CHARACTERISTICS
Exercising reflexes (0–1)	Simple, unlearned behaviors (schemata) such as sucking and looking are practiced and become more deliberate.
Primary circular reactions (1–4)	Activities that center on the infant's body and that give rise to pleasant sensations (thumb sucking, for example) are repeated.
Secondary circular reactions (4–8)	Activities that do not center on the child's body but lead to interesting sights or sounds (repeatedly moving a mobile, for example) are repeated.
Purposeful coordinations (8–12)	Separate schemata (such as the ability to look at an object and reach for it) become coordinated; familiar people and objects are recognized; primitive understanding of causality begins, implicit in the use of signs to anticipate events.
Tertiary circular reactions (12–18)	Repetition with variation (repeating a sound with a number of deliberate changes, for example) is experimented with.
Mental representation (18–24)	Transition between sensorimotor intelligence and a more cognitive intelligence is made; activity is internalized so that its consequences can be anticipated before its actual performance; language becomes increasingly important in cognitive development.

as well as at looking and sucking. However, they still have trouble putting different actions together (coordinating their behavior) to obtain a single goal. For example, infants presented with a visually appealing object can look at it but cannot reach toward it. The ability to look at an object and to continue looking at it when it moves (or when the child moves) precedes the ability to direct the hand toward the object (Provine & Westerman, 1979). Deliberately reaching and grasping is a complex activity that depends on the purposeful coordination of looking schemes, reaching schemes, and grasping schemes. This coordination is not usually apparent until after 3 to 5 months (Von Hofsten & Lindhagen, 1979).

PRIMARY CIRCULAR REACTIONS (1–4 MONTHS)

Early in infancy, children engage in many repetitive behaviors (thumb sucking, for example) called **primary circular reactions**—reflexive responses that serve as stimuli for their own repetition. For example, if an infant accidentally gets a hand or a finger into its mouth, this triggers the sucking response, which results in the sensation of the hand in the mouth. That sensation leads to a repetition of the response, which leads to a repetition of the sensation, which leads to a repetition of the response. This circle of action is called *primary* because it involves the infant's own body.

Despite the infant's ability at this substage to acquire new behaviors (new adaptations through accommodation to different stimulation), these new behaviors come about accidentally and always involve the child's body. Interaction with the world is still highly one-sided; it is still a world of the here and now, a world that exists and has meaning when it is doing something to the child or when the child is doing something to it.

SECONDARY CIRCULAR REACTIONS (4–8 MONTHS)

During the third substage, **secondary circular reactions** appear. Like primary circular reactions, they are circular because the responses stimulate their own repetition; but because they deal with objects in the environment rather than only with the infant's body, they are called *secondary*. Six-month-old infants engage in many secondary circular reactions. They accidentally do something that is interesting or amusing and then repeat it again and again. By kicking, Piaget's infant son caused a row of dolls dangling above his bassinet to dance. The boy stopped and watched the dolls. Eventually, he repeated the kicking, perhaps not *intending* to make the dolls move, but probably because they had stopped moving and no longer attracted his attention. As he kicked, the dolls moved again, and again he paused to look at them. In a very short time he was repeating the behavior over and over— a circular reaction.

This behavior, which Piaget described as "behavior designed to make interesting sights and sounds last," is especially important because it signals the beginning of intention. In Frye's (1991) words, these are behaviors in which infants "knowingly employ means to goals" (p. 15).

PURPOSEFUL COORDINATIONS (8–12 MONTHS)

The development of intention becomes even more apparent when, in the fourth substage, infants acquire the ability to coordinate previously unrelated behaviors to achieve some desired goal. They can now look at an object, reach for it, grasp it, and bring it to the mouth *with the intention* of sucking it.

During this substage infants also begin to recognize familiar objects and people—which explains why they may now become upset when a parent leaves or when a stranger appears (see Chapter 6).

At this time, too, an infant begins to use signs to anticipate events: Daddy putting on his jacket is a sign that he is leaving. Understanding that certain events are signs that some other event is likely to occur is closely related to the ability to understand causality. For the young infant, whose logic is not always as perfect as yours or mine, the sign itself is often interpreted as the cause. A child who realizes that Daddy will be leaving when he puts on his jacket *knows* that the cause of leaving is putting on the jacket—just as the cause of going to bed is taking a bath or putting on pajamas.

TERTIARY CIRCULAR REACTIONS (12–18 MONTHS)

In the fifth substage, infants begin to modify their repetitive behaviors *deliberately* to see what the effects will be. Rayna, Sinclair, and Stambak (1989) observed this **tertiary circular reaction** in the behavior of a 15-month-old girl whose current preoccupation was with breaking objects. Breaking something often seemed to lead to a repetition of the behavior (hence a circular response), but with deliberate variation (hence tertiary; recall that primary and secondary reactions are repetitive, with only occasional accidental variations). For example, in one session she picked up a ball of clay, scratched at it until a piece came off, examined the piece, and then repeated the procedure several times, each time examining the clay on her finger. Next she noticed a ball of cotton, picked it up, and pulled it into two halves; then she pulled one of the halves into two more pieces, and so on, again and again. Similarly, in another session a 15-month-old boy who had been tearing apart bits of clay happened across a piece of spaghetti, pressed it to the floor, broke it, picked up the

largest piece, broke it again, and repeated the process a number of times. Once finished, he attempted to break a short plastic stick and then a pipe cleaner; finally, he tore a sheet of paper into tiny bits.

The most important feature of tertiary circular reactions is that they are repetitive behaviors deliberately undertaken to see what their effects will be; that is, they are explorations.

MENTAL REPRESENTATION (18 MONTHS–2 YEARS)

Toward the end of the sensorimotor period, infants begin to make a transition from a motoric intelligence to a progressively more cognitive intelligence. During this final substage of the sensorimotor period, infants demonstrate that they have begun to learn to represent objects and events mentally. They can now occasionally combine these representations to arrive at mental solutions for problems, and they are now able to anticipate the consequences of many of their activities before actually executing them. Their behavior is consequently no longer restricted to trial and error, but makes use of mental representation as well. In Piaget's terms, it is as though the child can now begin to internalize (represent mentally) actions and their consequences without in fact having to carry them out.

Piaget illustrates this growing ability to internalize actions before their execution by describing his daughter's behavior when she was given a partly open matchbox containing a small thimble. Because the opening was too small for her to withdraw the thimble, she had to open the box first. A younger infant would simply grope at the box, attempting clumsily to remove the thimble. But Piaget's daughter, then 22 months, appeared instead to be considering the problem. She opened and closed her mouth repeatedly as if displaying internal thought processes. Finally, she placed her finger directly into the box's partial opening, opened it, and removed the thimble.

The ability to conceptualize the environment is also reflected in infants' mushrooming language development, which, according to Piaget, is greatly facilitated by their imitative behavior.

imitation in infancy

In the earliest stages of imitation, infants are able to imitate objects, activities, or people that are immediately present. Stick your tongue out in front of a 3 month old, and a tongue is likely to be stuck right back out at you.

Can newborns imitate? Yes, say a number of researchers. At a mere 2 weeks of age, infants are already able to imitate simple things like an adult sticking out the tongue or opening the mouth wide (Meltzoff & Moore, 1983, 1989). In fact, infants can imitate within one hour of birth, insists Reissland (1988), who looked at imitation among 12 newborns who had been delivered without complications and without drugs and who were thus awake and alert. Models (the experimenters or their assistants) bent over the infants and either widened their lips or pursed them. The results? Infants moved their lips in accordance with lip movements of the models significantly more often than at variance with them.

But maybe these infants aren't really imitating, suggest Kaitz et al. (1988), who looked at imitation among infants ages 10 to 51 hours. They studied infants' ability to imitate both facial expressions (happy, sad, or surprised) and tongue protrusion. Again, infants seemed to demonstrate modeling of tongue protrusion, but when they were shown happy, sad, or surprised faces, their behaviors did not seem to be directly imitative. Although

they often responded by either opening or pursing their mouths, which of the two they did seemed not to depend on whether the model was happy, sad, or surprised. The conclusion? Perhaps infants do not truly imitate these facial gestures, but instead simply manifest a generalized, almost reflexive response.

Masters (1979) and Jacobson and Kagan (1979) also suggest that young infants, and especially neonates, are *not* actually imitating when they stick out their tongue or purse their lips in apparent response to a model doing the same thing. They argue that these behaviors are largely reflexive, related to feeding, and simply released by the nearness of the model rather than being an actual imitation.

Meltzoff and Moore (1989) disagree. In their study, they exposed 40 infants, ages 16 to 67 hours, to models who either protruded their tongues or shook their heads. Gestures lasted for one minute, followed by a one-minute interval during which the model adopted an expressionless, "passive" face. Each gesture and passive-face sequence was repeated once (total testing time: eight minutes). Infants were equally able to imitate head shaking—a nonvegetative behavior—and tongue protrusion. Furthermore, during the passive-face interludes, some continued to imitate the behavior they had previously seen. Melzoff and Moore (1989) argue that the evidence supports the conclusion that infants have a general ability to match certain adult behaviors. However, they note that imitative behavior in newborns is not completely automatic and easily triggered, and that it is more easily brought about for certain behaviors than for others. They suggest, too, that the inborn capacity to match the behaviors of others may be very important for social and cognitive development.

ACHIEVEMENTS OF IMITATION IN INFANCY

There are at least three different kinds of learning that imitation makes possible for infants, claim Hay, Stimson, and Castle (1991). First, infants learn about *places* by following people around, in much the same way that young kittens and other animals learn places by following. When given the opportunity, infants readily follow their mothers into unfamiliar surroundings. Often, too, they will follow strangers. And even more often, they will follow a moving toy (Hay, 1981). Significantly, once they have followed a leader, they are more likely to go back and explore on their own. Second, imitation facilitates certain familiar social behaviors such as sharing toys. When experimenters (or parents, or siblings) play "give and take" games with infants, infants are subsequently more likely to want to give toys to others. Third, infants learn new social behaviors by observing them in others. (See "In Other Contexts: Saliswa, An African Child.")

DEFERRED IMITATION

Many of a very young infant's imitative behaviors don't continue when the model is no longer present. The infant is initially capable of imitating only when the model is there, or within a very short period of time thereafter. Piaget (1951) suggested that **deferred imitation**—the ability to imitate something or someone no longer present—is not likely to occur before the age of 9 to 12 months. When 2-year-old Amanda dresses up in her mother's shoes and struts in front of a mirror in the absence of her mother, she is practicing deferred imitation.

In one study of deferred imitation, Meltzoff (1988) arranged for a group of 14-month-old infants to observe a model performing six different actions with six different objects. Some of the actions were clearly novel for the infants and would not occur in the course of their daily activities. Following these training sessions, the objects were removed immediately, before the infants had any opportunity to interact with them. When the infants were presented with the same six objects a full week later, they showed considerable evidence of precise imitative behavior.

Deferred imitation is very important for the cognitive development of an infant, depending, as it does, on the infant's ability to represent mentally and to remember. In much the same way, associating a name with an object not immediately present requires representing the object mentally. Hence deferred imitation is one of the important abilities that underlies the acquisition of language.

language and communication

espite its tremendous power, **language** is not essential for **communication** (the transmission of messages). Animals that don't have language can nevertheless communicate danger. White-tailed deer wave their tails; pronghorn antelope bristle their rump patches; ground squirrels whistle. Some of these signals communicate danger to other members of the same species; others such as the flag-waving of the white-tailed deer, may also be examples of cross-species communication (Alcock, 1984). There is evidence that this behavior might not only signal danger to other deer, but might also serve as a signal to predators. It says, in effect, "I've seen you, so forget it." And the wolf, who is the deer's main predator in many areas, reads the signal. He knows he can't ordinarily catch a healthy deer in a prolonged chase, so he

In ethnographic literature about African peoples," writes Reynolds (1989), "reference is often made to 'the African child' as if such a composite creature exists" (p. 2). We make the same mistake in psychology even while we constantly deny the reality of the composite average.

Saliswa is not just an average African child. She is one of many Xhosa children who, in 1980, lived in an urban squatter settlement about 20 miles (33 kilometers) from the center of Cape Town, South Africa. Saliswa, then 2, lived in a shack built of discarded panels of corrugated metal, framed with scraps of lumber, lined with bits of paper and plastic, and having a cardboard floor.

Major day-to-day problems in Saliswa's settlement involve getting water; staying warm in winter and cool enough in summer; getting access to schools, hospitals, shops, and "crèches" (child-care facilities); and managing to cook on paraffin stoves without burning the house down. "We sleep on our graves," said one of Saliswa's neighbors (Reynolds, 1989, p. 20).

There are other, perhaps even more serious, problems. For years, the Xhosas lived under the heel of South Africa's apartheid policies. The shacks they built in the sand were considered illegal; often they were torn down or burnt before their eyes. Parents were imprisoned for being in "white man's territory." Children were beaten or sometimes killed; their lives were surrounded by violence. (Yet, notes Reynolds (1989), there was remarkably little violence in either their interactions with each other or their games). Educational opportunities were highly limited, future mobility and career opportunities almost nonexistent. (With the recent free elections in South Africa, these Apartheid policies may now be history.)

Like Saliswa, more than 300 million of the world's children live in squatter's settlements, most of them in the poorest of third-world countries. And al-

lies down and licks his chops, or he seeks other prey. Thus his reading of signals—his literacy—allows him to save his energy.

Communication between humans and other animals also occurs. An animal trainer who instructs his dog to roll over is communicating with the animal (at least when the dog obeys, and perhaps even when the dog does not obey). And the dog who walks to his empty dish, looks at his master, and then begins to growl is not only dangerous but is also communicating very effectively. This communication, however, is a far cry from that made possible by language. The parrot who can say "Polly wants a cracker" is not only boringly conventional but is also probably incapable of saying "A cracker wants Polly, heh, heh" with the intention of conveying a different meaning.

---

a definition of language

The parrot merely mimics; it does not communicate. It cannot deliberately rearrange sounds according to established rules to say what it means. It does not know language.

Language is *the use of arbitrary sounds, with accepted referents, that can be arranged in different sequences to convey different meanings.* This definition includes what Brown

though more than 90 percent of all children in the developing world now start school, fewer than two-thirds reach fourth grade (Grant, 1992).

Strikingly, military expenditures have increased by more than 5 percent over the past two decades in six of the poorest countries in Africa (Uganda, Burkina, Tanzania, Kenya, Liberia, and Malawi); during this same period, welfare expenditures have declined in each of these countries, sometimes by as much as 50 percent. In 1990, each spent about five times more on their militaries than on social programs (Grant, 1992).

To Think About: *What impact do you suppose Saliswa's context might have on her fantasies? Her dreams? Her play? Her intellectual development?*

To Read: *R. O. Ohuche and B. Otaalam's (1981)* The African child and *his environment (Pergamon Press) summarizes a large number of studies that have looked at children's environments in 13 countries of sub-Saharan Africa.*

(1973) describes as the three essential characteristics of language: displacement, meaning, and productiveness.

Language involves *displacement* because it makes possible the representation of objects and events that are not immediate—that are displaced—in both time and space. "The moon was a ghostly galleon," we can say, "tossed upon cloudy seas." Yet neither ghosts nor galleons, nor even moons nor seas, need be where we can touch them or see them. Indeed, what you and I can speak of need not even be where anybody has ever seen or touched them. We can speak of green blurbs and hypodrives in Scurrilian space vessels and other fantastic things that live only in our imaginations. There is virtually no limit to how far language can be displaced from the things it represents.

One of the primary functions of language is the communication of **meaning**. Although **psycholinguists**—those who study the relationship between language and human functioning—do not always agree about the best definition for meaning, we in our ordinary conversations tend to agree much more than disagree. Indeed, it is because you and I have similar meanings for words and sentences that we can communicate as we are now doing.

The third characteristic of language, **productiveness**, means that, given a

Language is not always necessary for communication.

There are four basic components of language: **phonology, semantics, syntax**, and **pragmatics**. Each is essential for effective communication via language.

Phonology refers to the **phonemes** or sounds of a language. A phoneme is the simplest unit of language and is nothing more complex than a single sound such as that represented by a consonant or word. There are 45 phonemes in the English language.

Phonemes can be combined to form **morphemes**, which are the units of *meaning* in language. Morphemes may be made up of sounds such as *ing* or *ed*—word endings that affect the meanings of words—or of whole words. Children cannot produce morphemes until they can first pronounce the phonemes. Simply making the sound is not enough; they must be able to make it when they intend to do so, and they must also be able to combine morphemes in meaningful combinations.

Organizing words into meaningful sentence units requires an intuitive knowledge of *syntax*, or grammar, the set of rules governing the combinations of words that will be meaningful and correct for the speakers of that language.

As children practice and master sounds (phonemes), meanings (semantics), and grammatical rules (syntax), they must also learn a large number of unspoken rules and conventions governing conversation (Bates, 1976). Put another way, they must learn the *pragmatics* of language. An implicit knowledge of pragmatics is what tells children when and how they should speak. It includes countless rules and practices governing manners of expression, intonation, accents, and all the other subtle variations that give different

handful of words, a set of mutually accepted rules about how they can be combined, and agreement about the significance of the various pauses, intonations, and other characteristics of speech, we can produce meanings forever. Language presents so many possibilities for meaningful combinations that almost every day of your life you will say something that no one else has ever said in exactly the same way. Language makes you creative.

meanings to the same morphemes and that might vary appreciably from one context to another. For example, that parents use shorter sentences, speak in higher-pitched voices, and use more concrete names and fewer abstractions when speaking with young children than with other adults is a function of their knowledge of pragmatics.

Phonology, semantics, syntax, and pragmatics are the elements of language. Most of us acquired these elements in an amazingly painless, effective, and efficient way without really being conscious of what we were doing.

language development in infants

Early studies of how children acquire language often concentrated on counting how many words children had in their vocabularies at a given age. Psychologists soon found that children's passive vocabularies (their comprehension) far exceeded their active vocabularies (their production of speech); that is, in the early stages of language learning children can usually understand many more words than they can use in their own speech. And before they use words in speech, many children also develop a wide range of communicative gestures (Bates et al., 1989).

A second way of approaching early language development is by examining the quality of the language acquired, rather than by estimating vocabulary size at different ages. Today's linguists treat the developing child as a fellow linguist; they examine the progression of children's knowledge of each of the elements of language, not only to learn how a child acquires the ability to use language, but also to learn more about language itself.

For convenience, language learning is often divided into two main stages: the prespeech stage and the speech stage. In the prespeech stage, meaningful speech sounds are gradually developed; in the speech stage a child progresses from sounds to words, grammar, and pragmatics. The prespeech stage lasts from birth to about the end of the first year (or the early part of the second) and ends with the appearance of single words.

achievements in the prespeech stage

During the prespeech stage, children engage in three different speech-related behaviors: They cry (sometimes a great deal), coo, and gurgle; they develop a repertoire of gestures, many of which are intended to communicate desires; and they practice **babbling**—the production of single sounds.

Two critical achievements of this period generally occur between the ages of 9 and 13 months (Bates 1976). The first is marked by the appearance of the intention to communicate and is evident in signals and gestures that clearly have meaning for both infant and caregiver. Squirming and gazing intently at the milk bottle are pragmatic (effective) ways of saying to mama, "If I don't get that bottle soon, I'm gonna holler!"

The second important achievement is the discovery of symbols—that things have names (Bates, 1976). This should not be confused with the simple ability to represent. As Mandler (1984) makes clear, there are two kinds of representation. *Simple representation* involves nothing more complex than memory. All that is in memory is represented. In this sense, a newborn's ability to suck involves representation. But this type of representation is far from *symbolic representation*, which defines semanticity (meaning) and is essential for language. Symbolic representation begins with the infant's discovery that things can be named—can be symbolized with sounds. Ultimately, children learn to speak so they can communicate, Rice (1989) tells us. Thus they can achieve important social goals.

---

the beginnings of verbal communication

Research dealing with the origins of language has been particularly interested in the pragmatics and semantics of infants' first gestures and sounds (Bates et al., 1981; Terrace, 1985). Researchers believe that the ability to use and understand words grows out of a complex series of interactions between infant and parents. These interactions, referred to collectively by Bruner (1983), as the language acquisition support system (LASS), involve things like learning how to make eye contact, how to direct attention through eye movements and gestures, and how to take turns.

TURN-TAKING

Knowing when and how to take turns is basic to adult conversation. When we have conversations, we wait for the signals that tell us it's our turn, and we give others their signals—well, most of us do; there are some who simply shout a little louder. Most of us have learned the rules that govern turn-taking without really knowing that we have learned them, and without, in most cases, being able to verbalize them. As Duncan and Fiske (1977) inform us, there are a handful of signals that tell us when we may speak and by which we tell others that it is their turn. These signals include an upward or downward change of pitch at the end of an utterance, the completion of a gram-

matical clause, a drawl on the last syllable, or the termination of a gesture. These are among the signals that children must learn if they are eventually to converse in socially acceptable ways.

Amazingly, children seem to have a relatively sophisticated awareness of turn-taking signals at very young ages. In one investigation, Mayer and Tronick (1985) found that even at the age of 2 months, infants and their mothers are already taking turns. They videotaped 10 mothers and their infants in face-to-face interaction when the infants were 2, 3, and 5 months old. Analyses of videotapes revealed that not only did infants rarely vocalize (other than for occasional "fussy" vocalizations) when their mothers were speaking, but they seemed to understand the mother's turn-taking signals. They responded not only to head and hand movements, but also to changes in intonation at the ends of utterances, to terminal drawls, and to the completion of grammatical clauses. Accordingly, they cooed and smiled mostly during the mother's pauses. Mothers, for their part, modified the number of turn-taking signals they gave according to the child's responsiveness. This is very much what adults do. As Duncan and Fiske (1977) note, although a single turn-taking cue is often sufficient for smooth transitions in adult conversations, quite often more than one cue is given. The more cues given, the more likely it is that the listener will take a turn.

USE OF GESTURES

Even before they have begun to use words, infants have typically developed a repertoire of gestures that are clearly meaningful for both infants and caregivers. One of the most common of these gestures, notes Bretherton (1991), is the gaze. Infants use gazing not only to indicate what they want, but to direct other people's attention. And they typically alternate the gaze between the desired object and the person whose attention they are trying to direct, as if to confirm that the message is being received. If the person doesn't respond as desired, Bretherton explains, the infant may intensify the gaze or combine it with other gestures like pointing or making noise.

infants' first sounds

Communicating through language depends on sounds—on the ability of infants to discriminate among them and on the ability to produce them.

SOUND DISCRIMINATION

There is some evidence that infants have a built-in capacity to discriminate among sounds. Recall, for example, Moffitt's (1971) experiment described earlier in this chapter in which the heart rates of 5- and 6-month-old infants were monitored while they were exposed to taped recordings of the sounds *bah* and *gah*. Changes in heart rate whenever the sound changed indicated that these infants could tell the difference between them.

Some sounds may be more difficult to tell apart than others. For example, infants have trouble telling *sa* from *za*, but they can much more easily discriminate between *sa* and *fa* or *va* and *sa* (Eilers & Minifie, 1975). With language experience, however, children are eventually able to discriminate reliably among all these sounds. In some cases, however, if the sounds are not part of their language, they may experience difficulty discriminating among them even as adults—as is the case for the sounds *la* and *ra* for a native Japanese speaker, for example (Miyawaki et al., 1975).

SOUND PRODUCTION

Discriminating among sounds is one aspect of early language learning; producing intended sounds is the other. It starts with the crying, cooing, and eventual babbling of an infant. Eventually it progresses to a word, and then beyond.

Infants as young as 3 weeks old produce three kinds of sounds, reports Legerstee (1991). There are the longer, *melodic* sounds characterized by variable pitch; *vocalic* sounds, which are short, more nasal bursts characterized by relatively uniform pitch; and *emotional* sounds such as laughing, crying, and fussing.

One of the remarkable things about infants' early sounds is that their emission is context-dependent. In a longitudinal investigation of eight infants ages 3 to 25 weeks, Legerstee (1991) found that melodic sounds typically occur when mothers are conversing with their infants; that vocalic sounds are more common with unresponsive adults; and that emotional sounds occur far more often in contexts involving other people than in situations in which the infant is interacting with an inanimate object such as a doll.

It was long believed that all the sounds of every language in the world are uttered in the babbling of an infant—even in the babbling of deaf infants. This belief leads directly to the conclusion that the ability to produce speech sounds is innate, a conclusion that does not appear to be entirely true. For example, although the first sounds uttered by deaf infants are very similar to those of hearing children, their later vocalizations are typically quite different. These first sounds, say Eilers and Oller (1988), are precursors to the form of babbling in which infants finally utter well-formed syllables with clearly articulated consonants and vowels—a stage that does not occur until some time between 7 and 10 months. Before then, infants make unarticulated noises: They coo, squeal, growl, whisper, and yell. And although it might be possible to discern many sounds that resemble those found in the world's 5,000 or so languages in these early sounds, infants' utterances remain unsystematic and do not obey the laws of syllables (requiring clarity and a complete vowel of adequate duration).

Infants' first sounds are "soft sounds," notes Bijou (1989b), but eventually infants gain control over their sound-producing apparatus. Also, they discover that producing sounds is "fun," as is evident in the fact that contented infants may spend hours in solitary babbling without any prompting. As a result, by the age of 10 months, most hearing children babble clearly, systematically, and repetitively. Deaf children do not reach this stage until later. "It cannot be maintained," say Eilers & Oller (1988), "that babbling is independent of hearing" (p. 23).

Certain sounds appear in the babbling of almost all infants, but many other sounds are almost never heard, even though they are important parts of some languages. The most common sounds that infants babble are the easiest ones given the anatomical structure of their vocal apparatus: consonants such as b's, d's, w's, and m's (described by linguists as *stop, glide,* or *nasal* consonants). Thus words like "mama," "papa," and "dada" are among the simplest for virtually all infants. In fact, there are some who believe that "mama" and "papa" are common to an astounding number of the world's languages precisely because they are among the first systematic sounds infants babble. In many of these languages, says Ingram (1991), "'Mama' emerges as a general request for the fulfillment of

some need, while 'papa' is a more descriptive term for parents" (p. 711).

Not surprisingly, then, "mama" or "papa" is the first clearly recognizable word spoken by many infants. However, it is seldom easy to determine when infants say their first word.

Many infants repeat a sound such as *bah* many times before it becomes associated with an object. The point at which sounds like *bah* cease to be babbles and become words ("ball," for example) is unclear but has usually occurred by the age of 1 year. Infants' first words are often created by repeating two identical sounds, such as in "mama," "dada," or "bye bye."

The appearance of the first word is rapidly followed by new words that the child practices incessantly. Most of an English-speaking child's first words are nouns—simple names for simple things, usually objects or people that are part of the here and now: "dog," "mama," "banket" (blanket), or "yefant" (elephant). Verbs, adjectives, adverbs, and prepositions are acquired primarily in the order listed here, with the greatest difficulty usually being the use of pronouns, especially the pronoun "I" (Boyd, 1976).

But before they learn words, infants have begun to show signs that they understand much more than they can say—words that are not yet part of their active vocabulary, even some entire sentences. "Stick out your tongue," she is told by a proud parent, and she sticks out her tongue. "Show Daddy your hand," and she shows it. "Can you wink?" Sure can (two eyes, though).

For convenience, the learning of language is described in terms of six sequential stages (Wood, 1981). The first of these, the prespeech stage (see Table 5.4), lasts until approximately age 1. It consists of the crying, the cooing, and the bab-

table 5.4

Stages in children's development of language

STAGE OF DEVELOPMENT	NATURE OF DEVELOPMENT	SAMPLE UTTERANCES
1. Prespeech (before age 1)	Crying, cooing, babbling.	"Waaah," "dadadada."
2. Sentencelike word (holophrase) (by 12 months)	The word is combined with nonverbal cues (gestures and inflections).	"Mommy." (meaning: "Would you please come here, mother.")
3. Two-word sentences (duos) (by 18 months)	Modifiers are joined to topic words to form declarative, interrogative, negative, and imperative structures.	"Pretty baby." (declarative) "Where Daddy?" (interrogative) "No play." (negative) "More milk!" (imperative)
4. Multiple-word sentences (by 2 to 2½ years)	Both a subject and predicate are included in the sentence types. Grammatical morphemes are used to change meanings ("-ing" or "-ed," for example).	"She's a pretty baby." (declarative) "Where Daddy is?" (interrogative) "I no can play." (negative) "I want more milk!" (imperative) "I running." "I runned."
5. More complex grammatical changes and word categories (between 2½ and 4 years)	Elements are added, embedded, and permuted within sentences. Word classes (nouns, verbs, and prepositions) are subdivided. Clauses are put together.	"Read it, my book." (conjunction) "Where is Daddy?" (embedding) "I can't play." (permutation) "I would like some milk." (use of "some" with mass noun) "Take me to the store." (use of preposition of place)
6. Adultlike structures (after 4 years)	Complex structural distinctions made, as with "ask-tell" and "promise."	"Ask what time it is." "He promised to help her."

Source: Based in part on Barbara S. Wood, (1981). *Children and communication: Verbal and nonverbal language development* (2nd ed.), p. 142. © 1981. Reprinted by permission of Prentice-Hall, Inc., Englewood Cliffs, New Jersey.

bling just described. The next two stages—that of the sentencelike word and the two-word sentence—are described in the following sections. The remaining three stages are detailed in Chapter 7.

the sentencelike word (holophrase)

Some time after the sixth month (usually around age 1), children utter their first meaningful word. This word's meaning is seldom limited to one event, action, or person but often means something that an adult would require an entire sentence to communicate; hence the term *holophrase*.

McNeill (1970) suggests that children's knowledge of grammar is innate—that they have notions of grammar long before they arrive at an understanding of how to express different grammatical forms in adultlike ways. Thus although most holophrases are nouns, they are not used simply for naming. When a child says "milk," he might mean, "There is the milk." He might also mean, "Give me some milk," "I'm thirsty," "I want you to hold me," "Go buy some milk," or "Are you going to do that to the cow again?"

two-word sentences

Not surprisingly, the progression of speech development is from one word to two (roughly by the age of 18 months), and later to more than two. There does

By the age of 2, children can name all the familiar people and things they encounter; they can use adjectives and adverbs; and they can ask questions and answer simple questions. But there is still much learning and practicing to do, for which naming and counting things like sheep can be very useful.

not appear to be a three-word stage following this two-word stage, but rather a multiword stage in which sentences range in length from two to perhaps five or more words (Brown, 1973).

BABY TALK

Children continue to acquire words during their second year, but the number of syllables they can use is limited. Many of their words are one- or two-syllable words, which often repeat the same syllable in different combinations ("mommy," "daddy," "baby," "seepy" [sleepy], "horsy," "doggy"). Even when it is incorrect to do so, a child may repeat the syllable in a one-syllable word, as in "car car" or "kiss kiss."

In an attempt to communicate with children on their level, parents sometimes exaggerate the errors committed by their infants. The result is occasionally something like, "Wou my itsy bitsy witta baby come to momsy womsy?" But there is no evidence that parental (or grandparental) models of this type hamper the rapid and

correct acquisition of language. In the early stages, the warmth of the interaction may be more important than the nature of the language used.

The transition from holophrases to two-word sentences generally occurs around 18 months. Bloom (1973) suggests that this process begins slowly with the relatively hesitant combining of familiar words, but that the use of two-word sentences increases very rapidly once a child begins to understand the number of meanings that can be so conveyed. Speech at this stage is sometimes described as being *telegraphic* because it eliminates many parts of speech while still managing to convey meanings. "Dog allgone" is a two-word utterance "telegraphed" from the lengthier adult equivalent, "The dog is not here now."

EARLY GRAMMAR

Whether precise grammatical functions can be accurately assigned to these two-word utterances is a matter of some debate. The functions of the words "fish" and "eat" in the two-word utterance "fish eat" are, in fact, dependent on the intended meaning. But because children use neither number agreement (for example, "fish eats" to mean "the fish eats" and "fish eat" to mean "I eat fish") nor order ("eat fish" versus "fish eat") to signal meaning, psycholinguists can never be certain that children at this stage are aware of grammatical functions (Clark & Clark, 1977).

By the age of 2, infants have reached the point at which they can name all the familiar objects and people in their environment. Moreover, they can now combine words into meaningful sentencelike units. They can also use adjectives and adverbs, questions, and simple negatives and affirmatives; and they have begun to learn a variety of subtle and implicit rules governing intonation, inflection, and the conventions that guide conversations.

But there is much more yet to be learned; there remain three stages in our six-stage description of the sequence of language acquisition. The story of that sequence continues in Chapter 7.

from sensation to representation

The word *infant* derives from the Latin *infans*, meaning "without speech." And, in fact, throughout much of the period we call *infancy*, a child is without speech. As noted earlier, the world of the newborn is a world of the here and now, a world populated only by those objects and feelings that are immediately perceived, a world that cannot be represented symbolically but can only be acted on and felt. But an infant's capacities to act and to feel are far more impressive than we have long believed—perhaps even more impressive than most of us still believe (see Pearce, 1977; Pines, 1982).

Although the term *sensorimotor* describes well the predominant relationship between infant and world, it does not describe the most important cognitive achievements of the first two years of life. Some of these achievements are listed in Table 5.5. By the time a child is 2, the world no longer exists only in the immediate, sensible present. Objects have achieved a permanence and an identity that no longer depend solely on the

table 5.5

Average ages for mental development in infants

MONTH	ACTIVITY
0.2	Regards person momentarily, responding either to speech or to movements
0.7	Eyes follow moving person
0.7	Makes definite response to speaking voice
1.5	Smiles or laughs in response to another person's speaking to and smiling at child
2.0	Visually recognizes mother; expression changes when infant sees mother bending over to talk to child
2.6	Manipulates red ring placed in child's hand or grasped by child
3.8	Carries red ring to mouth during free play
3.8	Inspects own hands
4.1	Reaches for cube, even if not actually touching it
5.1	Laughs or shows pleasure when held and played with
5.8	Lifts cup with handle
6.0	Looks for spoon that has fallen
9.1	Responds to verbal request not accompanied by gesture
12.0	Turns pages of book, even if effort is clumsy
14.2	Says two words meaningfully (approximations all right if clear)
20.6	Puts two or more words denoting two concepts into one sentence or phrase.

Source: Adapted from Bayley Scales of Infant Development by N. Bayley, 1969. Reproduced by permission. Copyright © 1969 by The Psychological Corporation, San Antonio, Texas. All rights reserved.

By the age of 5 or 6 months, infants smile and laugh when held and played with.

child's activities; there is a dawning understanding of cause-and-effect relationships; language is rapidly exercising a profound effect on cognitive development. These achievements, together with children's recognition of their own identities—their selves—represent a dramatic transition from a quasi-animalistic existence to the world of thought and emotions as we know it. But although it is a dramatic transition, at least in its import, it is neither sudden nor startling. Those who follow the lives of individual children closely (and daily) never see the transition from sensorimotor intelligence to preoperational thought. It happens suddenly and irrevocably on the second birthday only in textbooks. Real life is less well organized.

main points

NUTRITION, HEALTH, AND PHYSICAL GROWTH IN INFANCY

1. Breast milk is among the most easily digested foods for infants and is useful in guarding against the possibility of illness and disease, especially diar-

rhea in developing countries. Optimal brain development in early infancy is influenced by nutrition (especially protein intake) and stimulation. Severe malnutrition may have harmful consequences.

2. Sudden infant death syndrome (SIDS) accounts for the unexpected and largely unexplainable death of between 1 and 2 out of every 1,000 apparently healthy infants. It is slightly more common among males, rarely occurs before 2 weeks or after 6 months, and is sometimes associated with a mild upper-respiratory infection or with sleep apnea (a sleep disorder involving sudden cessation of breathing).

BEHAVIOR IN NEWBORNS

3. A neonate's behaviors consist mainly of reflexes: the orienting response (an alerting response useful as a measure of attention and learning); the sucking reflex; the Moro (startling) reflex; the Babinski reflex (fanning and curling the toes); the palmar (grasping) reflex; and the swimming, stepping, swallowing, and sneezing reflexes. Many of these disappear with brain development and the achievement of voluntary control over movements.

MOTOR DEVELOPMENT IN INFANTS

4. Although there is wide individual variation in the ages at which motor capabilities are attained, the sequence appears to be similar among most infants.

PERCEPTUAL DEVELOPMENT IN INFANTS

5. Sensation is primarily a physiological process; perception is our interpreta-

tion of sensation. Depth perception, response to patterns, and the ability to recognize colors are well developed in newborns. An infant's sight seems to be governed by a need to maximize information and is governed by certain visual rules.

6. Neonates are only slightly less sensitive than adults to sound intensity (loudness). Sensitivity to higher frequencies increases with age. Infants appear to recognize and prefer their mother's voice at ages as young as 3 days. Almost from birth, infants prefer pleasant odors and sweet tastes. They appear to be sensitive to touch (and to pain) within a few hours of birth.

COGNITIVE DEVELOPMENT IN INFANTS

7. A neonate's memory is not as efficient, as powerful, or as long-term as that of older children or adults. By the age of 8 months, neonates' memories have become more abstract.

8. In Piaget's theory, cognitive growth results from the interplay of assimilation (responding based on preexisting information and well-practiced capabilities) and accommodation (adapting behavior to the demands of the situation). Equilibration is the governing force that strives to balance assimilation and accommodation.

9. Piaget's six substages of the sensorimotor period are exercising reflexes (0–1 month); primary circular reactions (repetitive self-centered behaviors; 1–4 months); secondary circular reactions (repetitive environment-centered behaviors; 4–8 months); purposeful coordinations (the coordination of activities in

goal-oriented behaviors, discovery of object concept; 8–12 months); tertiary circular reactions (exploration through deliberately modifying repetitive behaviors; 12–18 months); and mental representation (gradual transition to a more symbolic intelligence; 18–24 months).

10. There is increased frequency of behaviors like tongue protrusion following exposure to a model, even in neonates. These apparently imitative behaviors are not easily triggered and are probably limited to a handful of behaviors. Deferred imitation is seen by the age of 9 to 12 months, depends on the ability to represent mentally and to remember, and is therefore important in cognitive development.

LANGUAGE AND COMMUNICATION

11. Language is characterized by displacement (allows remote events to be represented), meaningfulness (has significance), and productiveness (allows the generation of an unlimited number of meaningful combinations). Its four basic elements are phonology (sounds), semantics (meanings of words), syntax (grammar or rules that govern relationships among parts of speech), and pragmatics (rules and conventions concerning how and when to speak).

12. Infants as young as 2 months of age have a relatively sophisticated awareness of turn-taking signals ordinarily used in conversation. There is some evidence that infants have a built-in capacity to discriminate among certain sounds, and they are able to produce a large variety of sounds in t' babbling; however, some sounds

more common than others among all infants, and some sounds are rarely uttered. Babbling becomes systematic by ages 7 to 10 months.

13. Two important achievements of the prespeech stage are the development of the intention to communicate and the discovery of symbols—the realization that things have names. The first word usually appears by the end of the first year and is often sentence-like in nature (a holophrase). Two-word sentences appear around the age of 18 months. These are telegraphic, condensing considerable information into two words.

focus questions: applications

■ How important is nutrition for a newborn?
1. As a class project, organize a breast versus bottle debate.

■ What are some important characteristics of neonates?
2. Evolution, we are told, is a poor engineer. Try *your* hand at designing the human organism. Start with something as ignorant as a newborn. What kinds of capabilities and propensities would you design into a newborn? How do these compare with what is actually there?

■ What can a newborn see? Hear? Smell? Taste? Feel?
3. An infant's world is a blooming, buzzing mass of confusion, thought William James. Is it?

■ Do newborns have thoughts?
4. What sorts of thoughts, if any, do you suppose a newborn would have? What changes would you expect in the first year?

■ How can an infant manage to learn something as complicated as a language?
5. Why are theories based on imitation not entirely adequate explanations for language learning?

study terms

sudden infant death syndrome (SIDS) 202
apnea 204
orienting response 205
head-turning reflex 206
vegetative reflexes 206
Moro reflex 206
palmar reflex 206
motor development 208
norms 208
sensation 209
perception 209
conceptualization 209
visual acuity 209
pupillary reflexes 210
adaptation 219
assimilation 219
accommodation 219
schema 219
equilibration 220
object concept 221
primary circular reactions 224
secondary circular reactions 224
tertiary circular reactions 225
deferred imitation 227
language 227
communication 227
meaning 229
psycholinguists 229
productiveness 229
phonology 230
semantics 230
syntax 230

pragmatics 230
phonemes 230
morphemes 230
babbling 233

further readings

The following two sources are simple, non-technical descriptions of development in infancy. They offer many practical suggestions that might be useful for parents interested in understanding and promoting the intellectual development of their infants:

Devine, M. (1991). *Baby talk: The art of communicating with infants and toddlers.* New York: Plenum Press.

White, B. L. (1985). *The first three years of life* (rev. ed.). Englewood Cliffs, N.J.: Prentice-Hall.

A clear, useful account of Piaget's writings is:

Wadsworth, B. J. (1989). *Piaget's theory of cognitive and affective development* (4th ed.). New York: Longman.

Guidelines and norms for monitoring physical growth in young children are detailed in:

Jelliffe, D. B., & Jelliffe, E. F. (1990). *Growth monitoring and promotion in young children: Guidelines for the selection of methods and training techniques.* New York: Oxford University Press.

The following collection presents a detailed and current overview of what is known about SIDS:

Corr, C. A., Fuller, H., Barnickol, C. A., & Corr, D. M. (Eds.). (1991). *Sudden infant death syndrome: Who can help and how.* New York: Springer.

The major premise of the following captivating and sometimes disturbing book is that we have grossly underestimated infants' intellectual capacities and that, worse still, we damage and even destroy much of that capacity:

Pearce, J. C. (1977). *Magical child: Rediscovering nature's plan for our children.* New York: Bantam Books.

An outstandingly clear and well-written account of cognitive development that examines Piaget's theories in considerable detail is:

Flavell, J. H. (1985). *Cognitive development* (2nd ed.). Englewood Cliffs, N.J.: Prentice-Hall.

6

Social Development in Infancy

When the first baby laughed for the first time, the laugh broke into a thousand pieces and they all went skipping about, and that was the beginning of fairies.
James Matthew Barrie, Peter Pan

focus questions

HOW DO INFANTS INFLUENCE CAREGIVERS?

ARE ALL INFANTS BASICALLY THE SAME IN TERMS OF EMOTIONAL REACTIONS AND PERSONALITY?

ARE MOTHER-INFANT BONDS "NATURAL" AND UNLEARNED?

WHAT ARE THE CONSEQUENCES OF SEPARATING INFANTS FROM THEIR CAREGIVERS?

HOW DO THE TERMS *AVERAGE, NORMAL,* AND *EXCEPTIONAL* RELATE TO EACH OTHER?

outline

THE FAMILY CONTEXT
Child Development as an Interactional Process
How Personal Characteristics Affect Interactions
A Triadic Model of Child Development
How Babies Affect Parents and Vice Versa

INFANT STATES
States of the "Average" Infant
Do Infants Dream?

BEHAVIORS AS INDICATORS OF INFANTS' EMOTIONS
Crying
Smiling and Laughing
Wariness and Fear
Regulation of Emotions in Infancy

TEMPERAMENT
Types of Temperament Among Infants
The Implications of Infants' Temperament
Cultural Context and Temperament

ATTACHMENT IN INFANTS
Studying Attachment
Mother-Infant Bonding
Stages of Attachment
Types of Attachment
The Implications of Attachment
Fathers and Infant Attachment

SEPARATION ANXIETY AND FEAR OF STRANGERS
Fear of Strangers
The Effects of Culture on Separation Anxiety
Individual Differences in Separation Anxiety
Can Children Be Prepared for Separation?
The Role of Attachment to Inanimate Objects
Long-Term Separation and Deprivation

INFANT DAYCARE

THE EFFECTS OF PARENTING ON INFANTS' DEVELOPMENT
Early Gender-Role Influences
The Origins and Effects of Gender Typing

EXCEPTIONALITY IN INFANTS
Motor Skill Disorders
Epilepsy
Other Physical Problems
Autistic Disorder

THE WHOLE INFANT

MAIN POINTS

FOCUS QUESTIONS: APPLICATIONS

STUDY TERMS

FURTHER READINGS

I*nfancy and early childhood were a time of great joy for typical Eskimo children. It was as though their parents realized that after these first few carefree years, life would be harsh and cruel. There will be enough suffering later, the old ones would say. Let the little ones amuse themselves while they are still unaware of what is to come.*

And if the little Eskimo boy decides he will be a great hunter and he wishes to go hunting right now, his father will rouse himself from his bed of caribou hides and fashion him a bow—with all the seriousness with which he would fashion his own bow. And when it is done, the boy may go out into the barrens with words of encouragement echoing in his ears. And if he is successful and kills a bird, he will be praised as the mightiest of hunters. But if he is not successful, he will be teased as would any grown-up hunter. Because if he wants to act grown-up, he will be allowed to in every way.

Mowat (1952) once asked an Eskimo father, Ootek, why he never spanked his children, even when they behaved in the most exasperating manner. Ootek was astounded at the question; he found it so difficult to understand that Mowat had to rephrase it several ways. And when he finally understood, he became quite angry.

"Who but a madman would raise his hand against blood of his blood," he roared. "Who but a madman would, in his man's strength, stoop to strike against the weakness of a child? Be sure that I am not mad, nor yet is Howmik [his wife] afflicted with madness" (p. 141).

the family context

Some of us might occasionally strike our children—or almost certainly raise our voices to them. Yet not all of us are mad, or at least not certifiably so. We—Ootek and us—are simply products of different cultures.

So, too, are our children. A young Eskimo might expect to be treated with adultlike respect if he announces that he will now go and track the caribou herd. But my neighbor's 4 year old, Peter, hardly expects his parents to say, "Yeah, have a nice trip, then, Pete" when he informs them he's going to be a truck driver like his father, and can he take the truck to the store right now.

To understand what it's like to be a child, it's essential to know which child, when, and where; that is, we need to know something of the child's ecology. And to understand the lives of infants, we need to ask about interactions in the family because, in most cases, the family defines the most important aspects of the child's context.

child development as an interactional process

Throughout much of child psychology's brief history, the main emphasis has been on how parents affect their offspring. Although it's apparent that infants and children also affect parents' lives, these effects have not been considered important for the infants and children themselves. After all, child psychology is about children, not about parents.

Not so, ecological and culturally based theories such as Bronfenbrenner's and Vygotsky's inform us: Influence in development is interactional; it does not flow only one way. Not only do infants and children affect their parents, but these effects are often instrumental in changing how parents, in turn, affect their children. As an illustration, consider Louis, an especially difficult infant who cries a lot, refuses his mother's breast unpredictably, and soils his diaper at awkward times and with a wolfish grin, as if to say, "There, that'll teach ya!" His mother, in turn, is easily annoyed, impatient, highly emotional, and given to temper tantrums. Sara, on the other hand, is a dream of a baby. She sleeps regularly, seldom cries, loves her mother's breast, and soils her diaper only at regular intervals, always very politely with an apologetic little grimace, as if to say, "Phugh and Yuk! I sure hate to have to do that!" Sara's mother is a calm, enthusiastic, patient parent who is absolutely delighted with her infant.

In Bronfenbrenner's terms, the ecology—the interactions—will be very different in each of these two microsystems. After all, the characteristics of Louis, Sara, and their mothers are very different; the interactions between parent and child are not likely to be very similar.

how personal characteristics affect interactions

A wide range of infant and parental characteristics are important in determining an infant's developmental context. The infant's temperament is clearly important. Parents interact differently with *difficult* as opposed to *easy* infants. (These characteristics are described later in this chapter.) And, of course, how parents interact with their children depends partly on their own characteristics (such as patience or irritability).

Physical appearance may also influence how parents interact with children—and perhaps how children interact with their parents. Recall how some fathers treated their attractive daughters

more favorably than their less attractive daughters during the Great Depression.

And the infant's sex is important—as is the parent's sex. It appears that in general (but with many important exceptions) fathers engage in more physically exciting, stimulating play with infants than do mothers. They hold them primarily to play with them (Hodapp and Mueller, 1982). In contrast, mothers hold them for nurturant, caregiving reasons—and to play as well. Also, infants' responses to parents differ according to the sex of the parent. Fathers appear to elicit more positive emotions from their infants during play than do mothers. And perhaps most important, there appears to be a subtle fostering of sex-role differentiation involved in these early parent-infant interactions, especially after the infant has reached the age of 1. There is evidence that after that age, fathers tend to interact more with sons than with daughters. At about that time, it appears that sons begin to prefer their fathers: They approach and touch them more, and they ask more often to be picked up by them. Similarly, there is a tendency, though somewhat less strong, for girls to show greater preference for their mothers (Lamb, 1980).

Discovering the nature of these interactions and influences is not simple; interpreting them is even more difficult. Do fathers and mothers treat sons and daughters differently because of sex-related differences in infant behaviors and interests? Or do differences in the behaviors and interests of infants result from how their parents interact with them? Or both?

Questions such as these have led to some important changes in how researchers view the influence of the family on the developing child. Traditionally, the analysis has examined two-person or dyadic relationships: for example, mother-infant, father-infant, or infant-sibling.

This model, useful though it continues to be, has one major shortcoming: It fails to take into consideration both the complexity of the majority of the families into which infants are born and the great variety of indirect effects that parents and families can have on infants. Our prevailing models have been *dyadic* and psychological, whereas alternative models proposed by individuals such as Parke (1979) and Belsky (1981) are *triadic* and partly sociological.

a triadic model of child development

This new family-based triadic model differs from the traditional dyadic model in several ways. First, it suggests that far more influences are at work on an infant than just a mother on the one hand and a father on the other. There is also a family, a social unit made up of husband and wife (as opposed to just father and mother) and characterized by a marital relationship—hence the triad of child-parent-family.

Second, the model suggests that many complex influences other than the obvious parent-infant links may come into play. Belsky (1981) refers to these as "second-order" effects. Some possible second-order effects include the influence that a father might have on a mother, which might then cause her to interact differently with their infant; the relationship that the mother has with the infant, which might influence the way the father interacts with the infant; the influence that the infant's arrival (or temperament) has on the marital relationship and the consequent effects on parenting; and the influence of economic changes. Note that these second-order effects are what Bronfenbrenner (1989) labeled the meso-, exo-, and macrosystems.

This view suggests new lines of research and new interpretations of older

The reciprocal relationships between each parent and child, as well as the relationships between parents (and among siblings, parents, and other important people in the child's environment) are all important influences in a child's development. Even as parents affect children, so too do children affect parents.

research. It emphasizes the dynamic nature of the parenting unit and the fact that this unit is more than just mother and father. It reaffirms that even as parents influence children, so too do infants influence parents; and it goes even further in pointing out that the influence extends to more than two individuals; it includes an entire complex of relationships, including those with grandparents and other relatives. As Levitt, Guacci, and Coffman (1993) demonstrate, infants can form attachment relationships with many people, even those who initially were strangers.

how babies affect parents and vice versa

What does research tell us about these relationships and their reciprocal effects? Perhaps not as much as we would like to know, because many of the results remain unclear or contradictory. To summarize briefly, Belsky (1981) reviews research indicating that the birth of an infant often changes the marital relationship, sometimes increasing stress and discord, sometimes having the opposite effect; that discordant and conflict-ridden marital relationships may contribute to the development of antisocial behavior in children; that highly supportive marital relationships are related to caregiving skills with young infants; that the birth of an infant might make a good marriage better but is less likely to make a bad one good; and that among the most important qualities of parenting are sensitive mothering (attentiveness, warmth, responsiveness, and stimulation) and involved fathering (doing things with infants, including caregiving and playing).

But, as Belsky points out, "we still know very little about the direct influence of the child on marital relations and even less about the reverse process of influence" (p. 17). The adoption of a contextual/ecological model may increase our understanding considerably.

infant states

When discussing the characteristics of infants, we sometimes assume that all "normal" infants are pretty much the same; that all react in similar, predictable ways; and that individual differences observed in older children are not very apparent in very young infants. In fact, however, individual differences are detectable very shortly after birth, are consistent, and are related to differences evident later in life. Infants who are unperturbed by unfamiliar situations, say Kagan and Snidman (1991), are likely to become sociable, outgoing, fearless 10 year olds. The label used for consistent, identifiable differences among infants is *temperament* (discussed later in this chapter). Infant temperament is sometimes apparent in **infant state**, the general condition of an infant.

Wolff (1966) presents a simple classification of infant states: regular (deep) sleep, irregular (or disturbed) sleep, drowsiness, alert inactivity, and focused activity (see Table 6.1). Additional states may sometimes be detected using physio-

---

table 6.1

States reflecting infant's responsiveness to environment

STATE	DESCRIPTION	RESPONSIVENESS
Regular (deep) sleep	Largely motionless, eyes closed, breathing regular	No response to mild stimuli
Irregular sleep	Twitching motions, eyes closed, breathing irregular	Sounds or bright light can elicit grimace or smile
Drowsiness	Moderately active state, precedes or follows sleep, eyes may be closed or open	Responsive to stimuli
Alert inactivity	Relative inactivity, eyes open, breathing more rapid than in regular sleep, examining environment	Highly responsive; maintains examination of world
Focused activity (includes crying)	High activity, eyes open, low alertness, rapid breathing	Low responsiveness to stimuli

Source: Wolff (1969).

logical measures or more refined observational criteria. Wolff (1959) distinguishes between deep sleep and irregular sleep largely by heart and respiration rate. Similarly, he distinguishes between alert inactivity and focused activity by spontaneous changes in the infant's alert responsiveness. Crying can be considered an inflexibly focused activity.

---

states of the ''average'' infant

Infants vary considerably in the amount of time spent in each state. Brown (1964) studied states in six babies. Although this group of babies, on average, spent approximately one-third of their time asleep, one slept almost twice that much (56 percent of the time). One child was in an alert state only 4 percent of the time; another, 37 percent of the time. One infant cried 39 percent of the time; another, only 17 percent of the time. Additional evidence of striking individual differences among these babies is that one infant responded to 86 percent of all auditory stimuli, whether they occurred randomly or were presented to her, regardless of her state. A low-intensity noise would cause her to open her eyes when in a state of apparently deep sleep.

Given these tremendous individual differences, knowledge of the "average" newborn's daily states is perhaps not too revealing. Hutt, Lenard, and Prechtl (1969) have found that this hypothetical infant sleeps between 75 and 80 percent of the time and that three-quarters of this time is spent in irregular sleep. The "average" newborn is drowsy or alert perhaps two or three hours of the day and engages in more intense, focused activity (such as feeding or crying) for another hour or two.

Although the "average" neonate sleeps as much as 75 or 80 percent of the time,

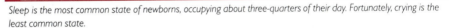

Sleep is the most common state of newborns, occupying about three-quarters of their day. Fortunately, crying is the least common state.

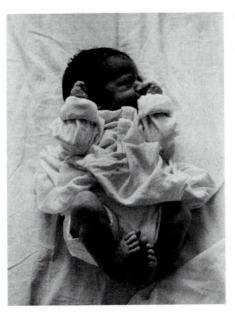
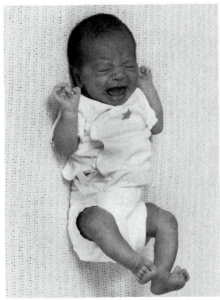

for most young infants periods of sleep are relatively short and are interspersed with many brief periods of wakefulness. With increasing age, infants sleep somewhat less in total but for longer periods of time.

do infants dream?

It isn't clear whether infants dream while they sleep; they can't tell us. However, an extremely high proportion of an infant's sleeping time (as much as 50 percent) is characterized by **rapid eye movement (REM) sleep**, and we know that, in children and adults at least, most dreams occur during REM sleep (Dement, 1974). The amount of REM sleep declines gradually during infancy; by the age of 2 years, approximately 25 percent of an infant's sleep is of the REM variety—very similar to adults' average of 20 to 23 percent (Roffwarg, Muzio, & Dement, 1966).

Note that the concept of infant state refers to an infant's alertness; that is, infant state simply takes into account whether an infant is sleeping, drowsy, alert, or crying. As we saw, however, infants differ in terms of the amount of time they characteristically spend in each of these states. These differences may, in fact, reflect basic, genetically influenced differences in temperament (or personality). They may also reflect the influence of different environments. Both of these possibilities are examined in more detail in our discussion of temperament later in this chapter.

behaviors as indicators of infants' emotions

Emotions are abstract, notes Beckwith (1991): "The emotions of one person cannot be directly perceived by another" (p. 78). This makes it difficult to investigate emotions, especially in infants, who are still incapable of communicating their feelings in language more sophisticated than gurgles, wails, grunts, sighs, sobs, and belches. And situations that adults ordinarily interpret as emotion-producing cannot always be assumed to be emotion-related for infants. Still, we can see infants smile and laugh, and we can hear them cry. And from these behaviors, we can make inferences about what they might be feeling.

Beginning with the pioneering work of J. B. Watson (1914), a number of psychologists have assumed that infants are capable of reflexive emotional responses from birth. Watson identified three distinct emotional responses of a neonate: fear, rage, and love. He assumed that each of these was a reflex and could therefore be elicited by a specific stimulus. Rage was thought to result from being confined or from having movements restricted; fear, from a loud noise or from being dropped suddenly; and love, from being stroked or fondled. Sherman and Sherman (1929) later suggested that whenever investigators thought a child was reacting emotionally in response to a particular stimulation, they were subjectively interpreting the infant's behavior in terms of adult and personal predispositions. In other words, adults might be inferring motives and emotions with no valid basis for doing so.

More recently, theorists such as Izard and Malatesta (1987) suggest that human facial expressions reveal a number of distinct emotions, including interest (or general excitement), joy, surprise, distress, anger, disgust, contempt, fear, shame, and guilt. They suggest as well that the facial expressions of infants indicate that they may be capable of most of these feelings (Termine & Izard, 1988). Furthermore, some infants may have a distinct tendency to respond predictably in some situations, at least with respect to anger or sadness (Collins & Gunnar, 1990).

It is extremely difficult to separate such closely related emotions as joy and surprise (or distress, anger, and disgust, or shame and guilt). Accordingly, much of the research on infants' emotions has looked at *behaviors* such as crying, smiling, and fear reactions. We look briefly at each of these behaviors before considering infants' temperaments and attachments.

crying

Wolff (1969) analyzed tape recordings of infants crying and identified four distinct cries that he interprets as expressions of different emotions.

The most frequent cry is called the *rhythmic cry*. It is the type of cry to which most infants eventually revert after initially engaging in another type of crying. Most experienced parents apparently recognize their infant's rhythmic cries and typically interpret them as meaning that there is nothing seriously wrong.

The *angry cry* is characterized by its protracted loudness and results from more air being forced through the vocal cords. It, too, does not fool an experienced mother.

A third distinguishable cry, says Wolff, is that of pain. An infant's *pain cry* is characterized by a long wail followed by a period of breath holding.

Finally, there is the *hunger cry*. Gustafson and Harris (1990) report that most mothers respond quickly to hunger cries or to cries of pain and that they readily discriminate between the two, although more mothers seem to be more sensitive to the general distress level of their infant than to the cause of the distress. Interestingly, first-time parents tend to respond to infant crying sooner than parents who have more than one child. And mothers are more likely to be attentive than are fathers (Donate-Bartfield & Passman, 1985).

The meanings of an infant's cries are apparently not universal. Isabell and McKee (1980) observe that in many primitive cultures in which a child is carried about constantly by the mother, mother-infant communication can occur through physical contact. In these cultures, there appears to be little need for the vocal signals of distress that we have come to expect from our infants. For instance, among indigenous tribes in the northern Andes, infant crying is extremely rare and is invariably interpreted as a sign of illness. Why else would a warm, well-fed, and constantly embraced infant cry?

smiling and laughing

Smiling, a universal phenomenon among human cultures, is a fleeting response in a warm, well-fed infant and appears to occur as early as 2 to 12 hours after delivery (Wolff, 1963). This early smile involves the lower part of the face, not the upper cheeks and eyes, and is described as a reflex smile rather than a true social smile.

HOW INFANTS LEARN TO SMILE

In the weeks and months following birth, infants smile in response to an ever-widening range of sights and sounds. The social smile occurs first in response to a human voice (by the third week). By the age of 3½ months, infants smile more in response to familiar than unfamiliar faces (Gewirtz, 1965).

Gewirtz identified three stages in the development of smiling. The first phase, *spontaneous or reflex smiling*, occurs in the absence of readily identifiable stimuli and is often, though perhaps incorrectly, attributed to "gas pains." *Social smiling*, the second phase, takes place initially in response to auditory and visual stimuli that are social in nature—that is, related to other humans. Finally, a child displays the *selective social smile*, common among children and adults. It occurs in response to social stimuli that the child can identify as familiar. With the appearance of the selective social smile, children smile less often in response to an unfamiliar voice or face and display more withdrawal behavior and other signs of anxiety in the presence of strangers. (More about stranger anxiety in a later section of this chapter.)

Hodapp and Mueller (1982) note that the development of smiling in infants follows the same general pattern as the development of crying. Initially, infants smile and cry in response to internal states, primarily gastric disturbances. They use the term *endogenous* (related to internal states) to describe these smiles and cries. With the passage of time, however, infants become more responsive to external stimulation, and both crying and smiling become more *exogenous* (responsive to external stimuli). By the age of 4 or 5 weeks, many infants will interrupt their feeding to smile when they hear their mother's voice. Similarly, crying now occurs in response to external sources of frustration, such as having a pacifier presented and then taken away. In brief, the early development of these behaviors follows an internal to external progression. Whereas the first instances of smiling and crying might be considered to be primarily physiological, within a short period of time cognitive elements (such as are involved in recognizing a voice, a face, or an object) are clearly involved.

FIRST LAUGHTER

At about 4 months, infants begin to laugh in addition to smiling. At first, laughter is most likely to occur in response to physical stimulation such as tickling; later, infants laugh in response to more social and eventually more cogni-

tive situations—seeing other children laughing, for example (Sroufe & Wunsch, 1972).

Although the function of laughter in infants has never been very clear, perhaps because it has not been investigated very much, Sroufe and Waters (1976) suggest that it probably serves to release tension. Fear, by contrast, signifies a continued buildup of tension.

SMILES AFFECT RELATIONSHIPS

Smiling and laughing are central in parent-child interaction. From parents' smiles and strokes, infants learn that they are loved and important; and parents, too, look for smiles and other nonverbal gestures in their infants as evidence that they are themselves worthwhile and loved.

The bidirectionality of parent-child influence can be seen in a variety of situations. An infant's fretting and crying trigger soothing behavior in the mother: rocking, singing, talking quietly, and so on (Lewis & Lee-Painter, 1974). In turn, the mother's soothing behavior quiets the infant. Perhaps the infant's quiet behavior now leads to a mutual gaze. Has the infant learned to be quiet and loving in response to the mother's soothing behavior? Or has the mother learned to be soothing in response to the infant's crying?

And what about fear? Does it, like crying and smiling, stem initially from internal conditions? Or is it always a response to the environment?

wariness and fear

Some years ago I went to a Halloween costume party. As part of my "costume," I attempted to grow a beard. After a number of months, I had succeeded in covering most of my face with hair. The remainder of my costume required little effort or imagination. Shortly after the party, I shaved off all my whiskers. When I walked out of the bathroom clean-shaven, my 1-year-old daughter took one look at me and burst into tears. Although I was initially taken aback, my daughter's reaction should not have been unexpected; we know that young children often react to the unexpected with fear.

WHAT DO INFANTS FEAR?

Fear, argued Watson and Rayner (1920), is an infant's unlearned response to loud noises and sudden loss of support. Later, some infants come to fear a wide range of stimuli; others remain relatively unperturbed in the face of environmental changes. Fear of heights appears to be almost universal in infants by the age of 13 to 18 months and is present in more than 20 percent of all children by the age of 7 months (Scarr & Salapatek, 1970). Fear of strangers is not ordinarily seen before the age of 6 months and becomes most common by 2 years. Other situations that may evoke fear in an infant typically involve some unexpected change. For example, a Jack-in-the-box may be frightening; so might an experimenter or parent wearing a mask—or a newly shaven one. In addition, separation from the mother is frightening for some infants, as are sounds presented in irregular fashion. As Hinde (1983) notes, it seems that as certain objects and people become familiar, infants begin to react with fear to strangers and to unfamiliar objects.

BRONSON'S LONGITUDINAL STUDY OF INFANTS' FEARS

One of the classical studies of the roots of fear in infancy is Bronson's (1972) longitudinal study of wariness, an emotion somewhere between mild discomfort or distress and outright fear. The study involved observing 16 male and 16 female infants at the ages of 3, 4, 6½, and 9 months, videotaping all sessions, and analyzing them in detail later. In addition, parents were interviewed.

Details of the observation sessions varied depending on the infants' ages. At 3 and 4 months, infants were observed lying on their backs in their cribs while they were presented with a number of novel objects, such as a paper parasol being opened and closed and a mobile over their cribs. In addition, an adult male "stranger" leaned over the crib, smiled slightly at the infant, and asked the infant to smile, using the infant's name repeatedly. This episode lasted for approximately one minute, unless the infant smiled broadly and repeatedly or began to cry.

At the age of 6½ months, infants were observed as they sat upright in an infant seat, their mother within view, while a hidden experimenter pushed a number of novel objects in front of the infant (such as a box that emitted random beeps). During the observation, a male "stranger" squatted in front of the infant and spoke quietly for one minute unless, again, the child cried or smiled continuously. At the end of the observation session, the stranger picked up the infant unless his presence had already elicited crying.

Observations at the age of 9 months took place with the baby on the floor and again involved the beeping object and the stranger. In this final observation, the stranger placed the infant on his knee for approximately one minute, unless the infant had cried or smiled repeatedly earlier.

Examination of videotapes led to the development of a sequence of categories for classifying infant reactions ranging from smiling with delight (repeated

table 6.2

Categories for describing infant reactions

SCALE POINT	CATEGORY DESCRIPTION	CRITERION BEHAVIORS FOR EACH AGE		
		3 AND 4 MONTHS	6½ MONTHS	9 MONTHS
1	Smiled with delight	Wiggled or vocalized as smiled	Repeated broad smiles or smiles with sounds of pleasure	
2	Smiled		Smiled more than once, but not broadly	
3	Neutral		Predominantly blank expression and no vocalization	
4	Uneasy	Severe frown or puckering of chin	Frowned or sounded unhappy (or, on pickup, turned body away)	Frowned, sounded unhappy, or crawled to mother (or, on pickup, squirmed or turned body away)
5	Cried		Cried or whimpered	

Source: Adapted from G. W. Bronson, Infants' reactions to unfamiliar persons and novel objects. *Monographs of the Society for Research in Child Development,* 1972, 37, No. 3. © The Society for Research in Child Development, Inc. Used by permission.

smile), through smiling (a less broad, discontinuous smile), a neutral reaction (blank expression without vocalization), uneasiness (frowning, vocalizing, squirming, or trying to crawl away), and crying (Table 6.2).

Bronson's first finding was that the most prevalent class of responses for 3- and 4-month-old infants is smiling rather than being uneasy or crying. By the age of 6½ months, however, there is increasing evidence of wariness; and by 9 months, evidence of *learned* fears. These findings corroborate those of many other researchers, indicating that infants are not likely to display marked stranger anxiety until after the age of 6 months.

Second, maternal behavior affects the development of wariness in infants. Bronson classified mothers according to maternal behavior. At one extreme are mothers who seem especially good at recognizing infants' moods and needs, who respond sensitively, and who appear to enjoy interacting with their infants. At the other extreme are those who seem quite indifferent to infants' needs and moods, whose interactions with infants appear more routine and less enjoyable, and who often limit interaction to essential tasks such as feeding, bathing, and diaper changing. For some reason, these two styles of mothering appear to be far more crucial for male infants. Boys of mothers in the first group (sensitive and so on) were less likely to be afraid of strangers and of novel objects. In this study, as in an earlier Bronson (1971) study, style of mothering did not appear to be as important for female infants.

Third, at all ages objects are far less potent than strangers in bringing about wariness or fear. By the age of 9 months, a number of infants had reacted with fear to strangers and seemed to have learned to associate specific features of a person with fear (beards or white smocks, for example). Similarly, wariness of novel objects was very rare before 9 months. By that age, mothers reported a number of instances in which many of the infants responded with fear to something other than a strange person. Situations or objects that make loud noises or move suddenly (vacuum cleaners or a Jack-in-the-box, for example) are most likely to bring about fear reactions in infants.

Fourth, an infant's *temperament* (discussed next) is related to the likelihood of being wary or afraid. In Bronson's study, the most wary infants were the most highly *reactive*—that is, the ones who cried most, were easily distressed (say, at bath time), were startled most easily, or blinked when presented with novel stimulation.

WHY INFANTS ARE SOMETIMES AFRAID

Why are infants sometimes wary and sometimes not? Bronson's data suggest that the reason lies in innate temperament interacting with various experiences. The relationship of age to the development of fear may at least partly reflect the fact that certain experiences are unlikely to occur (or occur less frequently) at earlier ages, and that the meanings of some experiences depend on an infant's level of understanding. Clearly, a stranger is not a stranger until a familiar person can be recognized as familiar.

But why should some strangers and some novel objects elicit fear? One plausible explanation is Hebb's (1966) suggestion that infants develop certain expectations about their world and that violations of these expectations (*incongruence* is Hebb's term) may lead to fear—which might well be why my infant daughter burst into tears. . . .

regulation of emotions in infancy

When you or I find ourselves in a frightening situation, when our hearts race and our knees turn to jelly, we do something to control or *regulate* our emotions. Perhaps we play cognitive games with ourselves: We might tell ourselves that we have nothing to be afraid of, that we are such wonderful surgeons or public speakers or students that we will perform marvelously. Or we might change the situation so that it isn't frightening anymore, perhaps by avoiding it.

There is a temptation to think that infants are not capable of this sort of control of emotions—that if they are frightened, all they can do is cry, and that if they are delighted, then, like little robots, they must smile. We sometimes think of them as responding almost blindly to the stimulation that the world provides willy-nilly for them.

We are wrong; they are not nearly so helpless. Beginning very early in life, infants are capable of what Gianino and Tronick (1988) label *self-directed* and *other-directed regulatory behaviors*. These behaviors are designed to regulate, or control, their emotions.

As an example, Tronick (1989) describes a peek-a-boo game between a mother and her infant. In this little episode, the infant turns away from the mother just before the "peek" and begins to suck on his thumb, staring blankly into space. The mother sits back. Within a few seconds the infant turns to the mother, pulls out his thumb, and contorts his body; his expression is clearly interested. The mother smiles, moves closer, and says "Oh, now you're back!" The infant smiles and coos. Shortly, he goes back to sucking his thumb. But again, after a few seconds, he turns to the mother once more and smiles.

The infant in this instance seems to be attempting to control the mother's behavior. This *other-directed* regulatory behavior is evident in how he turns back to the mother, how he coos and smiles, how he tries to make her do things that he finds exciting. In effect, he is controlling her behavior and, by the same token, exercising control over his own emotions. And when things become too exciting, too emotional, he can regulate his emotions by turning away from his mother. Now he distracts himself by sucking his thumb and by staring into space—evidence of *self-directed* regulatory behavior.

Tronick (1989) argues that the many emotion-regulating behaviors in which infants engage are evidence that infants' behavior is goal-directed. When an emotional state is negative, infants turn their faces, suck their thumbs, stare at something neutral or pleasant; the goal is clearly to avoid the situation and to reduce the emotion. But when the emotional state is positive, the infant smiles, looks, reaches; the goal now is to maintain or heighten the emotion. Thus does the infant begin to learn not only how to regulate emotions, but also how to communicate them. (See Chapter 8 for a more detailed discussion of the early socialization of emotions.)

temperament

When psychologists speak of differences in the customary ways of reacting and behaving that differentiate adults from each other, they generally speak of personality differences. The term *personality* includes all of the abilities, predispositions, habits, and other characteristics that make each of us different. A cluster of related characteristics is called a *trait* (Wiggins & Pincus, 1992).

When psychologists speak of differences among infants, they don't often use the term *personality* because it is somewhat too global for the characteristics of young infants; it implies a degree of learning that has not yet had time to occur. Instead, psychologists speak of infant **temperament**, or characteristic emotional responses. Clusters of related temperament characteristics are labeled *types*.

One important difference between *temperament* and *personality* is that temperament is assumed to have a primarily genetic basis (Chess & Thomas, 1989a), whereas personality develops through interaction with the environment. Accordingly, Buss and Plomin (1985) define temperament as "inherited personality traits present in early childhood" (p. 84). Thus a child is born with a certain temperament rather than with a certain personality. We see this temperament in the prevailing moods or the states we discussed earlier (crying, for example). The personality that later develops is an outgrowth of interaction between innate temperament and environmental influences (Carey, 1989).

types of temperament among infants

In the classical studies of infants' temperament, known as the New York Longitudinal Study (NYLS), Thomas, Chess, and Birch (1968, 1970; Thomas and Chess, 1977, 1981) studied 141 children from 85 highly educated, professional families. The main goals of the study were to develop ways of identifying infants' temperaments and to examine the relationship between temperament and later adjustment. The principal data-gathering techniques used in early stages of the study were regular, structured interviews with parents and direct observations of the infants themselves. In later phases of the NYLS, a variety of testing, interview, and observational approaches was used.

Analysis of the NYLS data suggests at least nine different characteristics that are easily observed in infants (particularly after the infant is 2 or 3 months of age) (see Table 6.3) and on which they can be rated as being high, medium, or low. Furthermore, certain infants seem to have remarkably similar patterns of characteristics. These patterns fall into three distinct types of infant that parents seem to recognize readily. *Difficult* infants are characterized by irregularity (lack of rhythmicity) in such things as eating, sleeping, and toilet functions; withdrawal from unfamiliar situations; slow adaptation to change; and intense (as well as negative) moods. In contrast, *easy* infants are characterized by high rhythmicity (regularity in eating, sleeping, and so on), high approach tendencies in novel situations, high adaptability to change, and a preponderance of positive moods as well as low or moderate intensity of reaction. *Slow to warm up* infants are characterized by low activity level, high initial withdrawal from the unfamiliar, slow adaptation to change, greater negativity in mood, and a moderate or low intensity of reaction (Table 6.4). Of the original 141 children in the NYLS, 65 percent could be classified as belonging to one of these three temperament types (40 percent *easy*; 15 percent *difficult*; 10 percent *slow to warm up*); the remaining 35 percent displayed varying mixtures of the nine temperament characteristics.

There are many different ways of classifying infants' temperament (see Bates, 1989). For example, Buss and Plomin (1985) suggest that it might be useful to classify infants on three main dimensions: emotionality, activity, and sociability (termed the EAS approach). *Emotionality* refers to the ease with which an infant becomes aroused, especially in situations that might lead to fear or anger. *Activity*

---

t a b l e 6 . 3

Nine temperament characteristics of infants

1. *Level and extent of motor activity*
2. *Rhythmicity (regularity of functions such as eating, sleeping, and eliminating)*
3. *Withdrawal or approach in new situations*
4. *Adaptability to change in the environment*
5. *Sensitivity to stimuli*
6. *Intensity (energy level) of responses*
7. *General mood or disposition (cheerful, cranky, friendly, and so on)*
8. *Distractibility (how easily infant may be distracted from ongoing activities)*
9. *Attention span and persistence in ongoing activities*

---

refers to an infant's customary "vigor and tempo" in actual behavior. And *sociability* has to do with an infant's tendency to approach or avoid others.

Another approach to temperament is more physiological (Strelau, 1989). It relates to Pavlov's observation that some individuals have more *excited* nervous systems than others, that their physiological reactions to stimulation are more intense. Hence differences in physiological reactions such as brain wave activity, heart rate, or motor responses may underlie differences in temperament. For example, Stifter and Fox (1990) showed that measures of heart-rate variability are closely related to infants' reactivity in the first year of life. And Kagan and Snidman (1991) found that infants who have a tendency to avoid unfamiliar events cried more easily and displayed lower levels of motor activity, in contrast with those who like to approach the unfamiliar. "This implies but does not prove," say Kagan and Snidman (1991), "that variation in the excitability of brain areas that

table 6.4

Infants' temperaments

Temperament	Description
Easy	Regularity in eating and sleeping (high rhythmicity); high approach tendencies in novel situations; high adaptability to change; preponderance of positive moods; low or moderate intensity of responses
Difficult	Irregularity in eating and sleeping (low rhythmicity); withdrawal in novel situations; slow adaptation to change; preponderance of negative moods; high intensity of reactions to stimulation
Slow to warm up	Low activity level; high initial withdrawal from unfamiliar; slow adaptation to change; somewhat negative mood; moderate or low intensity of reaction to stimulation
Varying mixtures; unclassified	

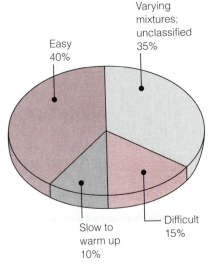

Easy 40%

Varying mixtures; unclassified 35%

Difficult 15%

Slow to warm up 10%

Approximate percentage of infants with each temperament

Note: Thomas and Chess (1981) caution that these three types do not exhaust all possibilities. In addition, although it is sometimes convenient to classify infants in these ways, there are wide ranges of behaviors within each category. *Easy* children don't all react the same way to the same situations; nor do all *difficult* children. Furthermore, some 35 percent of all infants appear not to fit into any of these categories.

Source: Based on classifications used by Thomas, Chess, and Birch (1968, 1970) and Thomas and Chess (1981) in the New York Longitudinal Study (NYLS).

mediate motor activity and crying participates in the actualization of the temperamental categories" (p. 856).

the implications of infants' temperament

"An infant's temperament," say Kagan and Snidman (1991), "renders some outcomes very likely, some moderately likely, and some unlikely—although not impossible—depending on experience" (p. 856).

TEMPERAMENT AND SUBSEQUENT BEHAVIOR

Specifically, the temperament they label *uninhibited to the unfamiliar*, which is characterized by a tendency to approach in strange situations, is likely to lead to spontaneous, fearless, outgoing youngsters. In contrast, infants who are markedly inhibited in the face of the unfamiliar are likely to continue to be timid at the age of 8 years.

In a long-term followup of infants in the Thomas and Chess (1981) study, researchers found that infants of *difficult* temperament were more likely to manifest problems requiring psychiatric attention. Of the 42 children (out of a sample of 141) who had such problems, 70 percent had been classified as *difficult* infants, and only 18 percent as *easy*.

Similarly, Kagan and Snidman's (1991) followup of infants through the first two years of life found remarkable consistency in their temperaments, which they attribute to the biological basis of temperament.

DIFFERENT TEMPERAMENTS MAY REQUIRE DIFFERENT PARENTING

But this does not mean, caution Kagan and Snidman (1991), that genetically influenced aspects of temperament inevitably determine our personalities, that our contexts are of no importance. In fact, knowing something of an infant's temperament may be very useful in allowing us to alter contexts in beneficial ways. Thomas, Chess, and Korn (1982) suggest, for example, that *easy* children, because of their high adaptability, will respond well to a variety of parenting styles (such as permissive or authoritarian). In contrast, a more *difficult* infant may require more careful parenting. Because these children adapt more slowly and respond less well to novelty and change, they require consistent and patient parents. Also, given their more intense and more negative moods, they are not likely to react well to either highly authoritarian or highly permissive parents.

The contribution of temperament to an infant's development, and its relationship to the behavior of parents, presents yet another example of the extent to which parent-child influences are bidirectional. Consider, for example, the case of Pat an *easy* child who adapts readily to change, smiles a lot, is rhythmic in feeding and sleeping routines, responds well to parents and to strangers, and, perhaps

most important, appears to be happy. Parents react with pleasure to such a child, note Thomas and Chess (1981). They feel responsible for what Pat is; they think of themselves as wonderful parents. They smile and laugh as they tend to their little child, who smiles right back at them. They gaze at each other, and everything they say and do with Pat says, "You're wonderful!"

But Fran does not smile so much, cries more, eats and sleeps irregularly, is timid in the face of the unfamiliar, and whines and fusses much of the time. Hence Fran's social progress seems slower than Pat's, and the message Fran's parent's receive does not say, "You're wonderful, dear parent." Nope. Instead it says, "As a parent, you're just so-so," or worse yet, "As a parent, you're just plain lousy."

Not all parents will read the same message in the same situation, of course. Nor will all react in the same way. The nature of the interaction depends on *parents'* characteristics as much as on those of their infants. But there are some parents who will feel anxious and guilty about their *difficult* or *slow-to-warm* infant—some who will try too hard to change the infant or who will silently give up and, perhaps without even knowing it, begin an insidious process of rejection.

---

cultural context and temperament

Chess and Thomas (1989b) make the important point that although temperament has a biological basis, it is constantly changing as a result of child-context interaction. Consequently, developmental outcomes are not always easy to predict. The infant who is initially *difficult* may become an adolescent whose charm, grace, and other good qualities make a parent puff up with pride; and the infant who is initially *easy* may, it's true, become a thoroughly reprehensible, adolescent—or worse.

Understanding the relationship between temperament and developmental outcomes requires taking into account interactions between the infant and both the immediate context (the *microsystem* in Bronfenbrenner's ecological model) and the wider culture context (the *macrosystem*). deVries and Sameroff's (1984) study of infant temperament among three African tribes provides an illustration. The tribes studied were the Kikuyu, a relatively modern, wage-earning tribe who view infants as vulnerable, toilet train

them later than other tribes, expect them to develop motor skills later, and distribute childcare responsibilities among a number of groups and individuals; the Digo, a farming and fishing tribe with a leisurely life-style, who monitor their infants closely and expect a high level of motor and social development, even at the age of 3 months; and the Masai, a pastoral tribe who live in small mud huts, who suffer from more illness and disease, and who breast-feed their infants for two or more years and carry them everywhere with them.

Temperaments among these three tribes, claim deVries and Sameroff, reflect cultural factors. Thus, ratings for the

Early experiences can play an important part in determining a child's temperament. The fact that Masai mothers are in close contact with their babies, often breast-feeding them until they are 2 or 3, may help explain why their infants are good-natured and have regular eating and sleeping habits.

Masai and Digo were generally more positive, with more infants classed as *easy* than as *difficult*. Also, Digo infants, raised in a more leisurely context, were characterized by less rhythmicity—that is, less adherence to routine.

deVries and Sameroff (1984) assumed that *difficult* infants would be at higher risk of subsequent problems than *easy* infants, as is often the case in North American cultures. And this was, in fact, the case in two of the tribes, but not for the Masai. deVries (1989) reports that when the Masai were revisited between four and six months later, things were far better for the *difficult* infants. In fact, mortality was much higher among the *easy* infants. Why?

There had been a serious drought in the region, deVries explains, and many infants had died or suffered from malnutrition and disease. That the *difficult* infants had been least likely to die, speculates deVries, was probably because they cried more when they were frustrated and hungry, and thus succeeded more often in being fed. Thus a particular environmental characteristic "fit" better with the *difficult* temperament—a temperament that, under most circumstances in our culture, seldom "fits" as well as the *easy* temperament.

In Lerner et al.'s (1986) terms, the optimal situation is one in which there is high *goodness-of-fit* between infant and context. This situation exists when external demands and expectations are compatible with the infant's basic temperament—that is, with the infant's inclinations and customary ways of doing things. Conversely, there is a poor fit when the infant's temperament is not in accord with environmental demands.

For example, Fran (who, you may recall, is a *difficult* infant) reacts loudly and impatiently to frustration. Fran's father is distressed and annoyed at this behavior because he expects and wants Fran to be more like Pat. There is a poor fit here, and the result is conflict and strain in Fran's family.

Difficult temperaments do not always lead to poor fit; nor do *easy* temperaments always result in high goodness-of-fit. Goodness-of-fit would be higher than expected, for example, if Fran's father took pride in his child's lustiness, independence, and aggressiveness. And if *easy* Pat's parents were afraid that their child might not cope well in what they think is a dog-eat-dog world, goodness-of-fit between Pat's temperament and context might be unexpectedly poor. Here, as elsewhere, we need to consider the characteristics of the person *in interaction with* characteristics of the context.

attachment in infants

Among the most important interactions in the early life of infants are those involving parent–infant attachment.

Infants have two principal tasks, say Greenspan and Lieberman (1989). The first task is a biological one: to achieve a balance between what the organism needs and what it assimilates, a balance termed *homeostasis*. In this context, homeostasis is maintained when the infant is not too hungry, thirsty, cold, or hot. Maintaining homeostasis is greatly facilitated by infants' increasing ability to regulate or control their behavior as they interact with their environment.

The second task, very closely related to maintaining homeostasis, involves forming an attachment—generally with a principal caregiver to begin with, later with other individuals in the immediate environment (the microsystem). "Neonates must form a bond with their mothers," explains Leon (1992), "if they are to receive the sustenance, protection, and comfort they require to grow and develop" (p. 377).

studying attachment

Attachment is a powerful emotional bond that is not easily defined, for an infant cannot describe it for us. Hence measurements of infants' attachment are always indirect. Investigators observe how an infant behaves toward a person (or a thing, such as a blanket, for instance): crying, smiling, clinging, avoiding, holding, and so on. They focus on the infant's behavior in unfamiliar situations, on physical contact between infants and caregivers, on the infant's reaction when caregivers leave.

One of the problems in such studies is that it is not possible to conduct controlled investigations that would illustrate clearly the effects of attachment bonds— or of rupturing these bonds. Human infants cannot ethically be removed from their mothers at critical times in their lives, perhaps for different periods of time, to determine what the effects of doing so might be. However, this has been done with infant monkeys. In various experiments, infant monkeys have been deprived of their mothers and raised with wire or cloth-covered monkey surrogates (Harlow, 1959), or even with dogs (Mason & Kenney, 1974). Under these circumstances, most infant monkeys form strong attachments to the surrogate, be it a wire or a cloth model (see Figure 6.1 in "At A Glance: Mother-Deprived Monkeys"). However, these little monkeys, deprived of their mothers at birth, often don't fare as well when they become adults. Unfortunately, these studies don't necessarily tell us very much about human infants—and, according to

Ainsworth (1984), perhaps not very much about infant monkeys either.

mother-infant bonding

Mother-infant bonding describes the formation of an emotional or attachment bond between mother and infant. Although the term *bond* is often used as though it were synonymous with *attachment*, mother-infant bonding refers primarily to the very early, biologically based attachment that a mother develops for her infant. Attachment is a more general term that includes the host of positive emotions that link parents and children, and other people as well.

BONDING AMONG NONHUMAN SPECIES

The term *bond* in this context is defined in much the same way as it is by ethologists (those who study animal behavior in natural settings)—that is, as a largely hereditary (hence biologically based) link that a mother forms for her offspring under appropriate circumstances. Among nonhuman species these "appropriate circumstances" generally involve nothing more complicated than the mother being exposed to her infant during some critical period that begins at birth and lasts for a short time thereafter. In the absence of appropriate experiences during this critical period, bonding failure occurs. When newborn lambs are taken from their mothers at birth and not returned to them for a week or more, the mothers refuse to accept them as their own (Thorpe, 1963). If the youngsters get in the way, the ewes simply butt them aside! The mothers have failed to bond to their infants. Does it follow that mothers whose infants are taken away at birth, perhaps because they require intensive care or simply because it is hospital routine, will not bond with these infants?

nfant monkeys who are raised in isolation subsequently experience serious developmental problems, often manifested in an inability to achieve sexual relations. Female monkeys raised under such conditions who then have infants of their own will often reject them. But when the mothers of infant monkeys are replaced with a substitute, infants typically form a strong attachment to the substitute. Research that has compared infant monkeys' attachment to cloth-covered and wire mother substitutes indicates that quality of physical contact is especially important for monkeys.

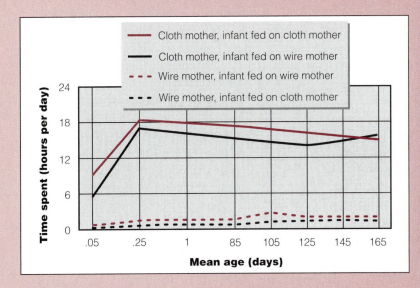

f igure 6.1

Amount of time spent by infant monkeys on cloth and wire surrogate mothers. The results show a strong preference for the cloth mother regardless of whether the infant was fed on the wire model or on the cloth model. Source: From Harry F. Harlow, Love in infant monkeys, Scientific American, 1959, 200, 68–74. Copyright 1959 by Scientific American, Inc. All rights reserved. Used by permission.

The infant monkey remains on the terry cloth mother even though he must stretch to the wire model in order to feed.

BONDING FAILURE AMONG HUMANS

As we saw in Chapter 2, theorists such as Bowlby (1958) and Klaus and Kennell (1983) think that might be the case. They maintain that although there is a biological predisposition toward the formation of this bond, it does not exist automatically as soon as the child is born—hence the importance of close contact and interaction with an infant from the earliest moments after birth. They suggest, as well, that the failure to establish a strong mother-infant bond is detrimental to the future adjustment and emotional health of the child and may be related to such things as child abuse or growth failure (a physical/psychological condition also known as "failure to thrive").

Failure to thrive (FTT) is a condition in which an apparently normal infant fails to gain weight, falling in the process into the bottom 3 percent of normal standards. Abramson (1991) reports significantly more expressions of negative emotion among these infants. In addition, the condition is marked by listlessness, loss of appetite, illness, and, in its more extreme manifestations, even death. Researchers such as Bowlby (1940) and Spitz (1945) first noticed this condition among institutionalized infants and attributed it to lack of mothering. Because of this, FTT is also called *maternal deprivation syndrome*.

BONDING MECHANISMS

Theorists such as Bowlby argue that because of the importance of the mother–infant bond, there must be powerful genetic predispositions that ensure its formation. Clearly, no emotional bond links an infant to its mother immediately at birth. A neonate taken from its mother and given to another will surely never know the difference unless, of course, the facts are disclosed later.

But that a bond does form with the primary caregiver(s) is also clear. Wellman and Gelman (1992) point out that infants have certain biological *preadaptations* that facilitate the development of this bond. These include perceptual biases such as an infant's built-in visual accommodation for a distance of approximately 8 to 10 inches (about the distance to the caregiver's face during feeding); a young infant's apparent preference for human faces; and a sensitivity and responsiveness to human voices.

Infants also have some reflexive response tendencies that seem especially designed for social interaction. Like the young of most mammals, infants root and

suck, and they also cling. One of the functions of these reflexes is to ensure that the infant obtains nourishment and survives. But more than this, feeding is among the first important social interactions between caretaker and infant. In almost all cultures, note Fogel, Toda, and Kawai (1988), feeding leads to the mutual gaze, which is highly significant in the development of attachment.

Schaffer (1984) also suggests that certain biological rhythms are geared to social interaction. Some, like those expressed in the infant states of waking and sleeping, are modifiable and eventually become attuned to the mother's cycles of waking and sleeping. Others, like the rhythms apparent in sucking behavior, seem to contain many of the elements of a dialogue and may underlie the learning of the turn-taking rules that are a fundamental part of conversations. It seems that infants suck in organized and relatively predictable patterns—short bursts of activity followed by pauses (Kaye, 1977). And the mother appears to be unconsciously attuned to these rhythms, adjusting her behaviors to those of the infant. During the sucking bursts, she is typically quiet; but during the pauses, she jiggles or strokes the infant, or talks to it.

All of this, says Bowlby (1958), is evidence that there are powerful biological forces directing both mother and infant toward mutual attachment. Attachment would have had particularly important survival value at a time when physical survival was threatened by the "hissing serpents and dragons of Eden" (Sagan, 1977).

IMPORTANCE OF BONDING

Historically, one of the important functions of infants' distress at being separated from the mother was that it served to keep her close (Oatley & Jenkins,

1992)—perhaps to protect them from wild beasts.

But now dragons and serpents no longer lurk so blatantly in our forests—or parking lots. But, say Klaus and Kennell (1983), there is nevertheless a critical period very early in our lives during which we *must* have contact with our mothers so that a bond may form. Bonding failure, they claim, can have serious negative consequences later.

The evidence? Klaus et al. (1972) randomly selected a group of 28 low-income mothers and gave half of them both "extended" contact with their infants immediately after birth (one hour of the first two hours following birth) and five additional hours of contact with their infants on each of the first three days following birth. The remaining 14 mothers, serving as a control group, had contact with their infants according to hospital routine—that is, mainly at regular feeding times.

Follow-up interviews and filmed observations of mothers and infants one month later indicated that mothers in the extended-contact group were more attached to their infants, showed more concern for them, and expressed considerably more interest in them. These mothers fondled their babies more, engaged in more verbal interaction with them, and spent more time in mutual gazing. And when the infants were aged 1 and 2, there were still significant differences between extended-contact and control group mothers, not only in attachment but in verbal interaction as well (Ringler et al., 1975). Other research indicates that extended contact between mother and infant immediately following birth may be manifested in closer mother-infant attachment, in physical development (greater weight gains), and in higher measured intelligence (see Kennell, Trause, & Klaus, 1975).

Should we conclude that there is a critical period early in the lives of neonates during which contact with the mother (or perhaps some other important caregiver) is critical? Perhaps not. Many subsequent studies have not found clear evidence of harmful effects of early infant-mother separation (see, for example, Schaffer, 1984). The evidence of a critical period and of lasting harmful effects of "bonding failure" is totally unconvincing, claims Goldberg (1983).

It seems plausible, Wasserman (1980) argues, that the formation of attachments is sufficiently important to human development that the infant and mother can take advantage of other opportunities for bonding without harmful consequences. Furthermore, the assumption that limited contact with infants immediately after birth—a common practice in many hospitals—may lead to "bonding failure" and subsequent health and adjustment problems has not been supported. In a careful investigation, Egeland and Vaughn (1981) found no greater incidence of abuse, child neglect, illness, or adjustment problems among children who had been separated from their mothers for several weeks immediately after birth.

This does not mean, of course, that early contact between parents and infants is not highly desirable, or that maternal rejection and neglect are irrelevant. That is clearly not the case. But the importance of a "crucial" few hours immediately after birth has not been established.

stages of attachment

According to ethologists such as Bowlby, the reason for infant attachment seems clear. After all, an infant's very survival demands a solicitous caregiver. What better way to ensure that the caregiver will be there when needed than to

table 6.5

Sequential phases in the development of infant attachment

PHASE	APPROXIMATE AGE	IMPORTANT BEHAVIORS
Preattachment	First month	Crying, smiling, rooting, clinging, sucking, looking at; movements synchronized with adult speech; discrimination of mother's voice
Attachment in the making	Into second half of first year	Singling out objects of primary attachment; selective social smile, directed more toward attachment object/person than toward the unfamiliar
Clear-cut attachment	Second half of first year	Continued use of behaviors designed to draw attention—smiling, crying, squirming; use of newly developed locomotor skills to approach attachment object/person
Goal-corrected attachment	Second year	Begins to adopt mother's point of view and to make inferences about mother's behavior; manipulation of mother's behavior in more subtle ways following gradual recognition of cause-and-effect relationships

Source: Based on Bowlby (1969).

program into the human gene pool powerful parent-infant attachment tendencies? However, nature does not program the attachment itself; rather, attachment develops later. Nor do the infant's genes limit attachment to the biological mother and/or father.

Bowlby (1969) describes four phases in the development of an infant's attachment (Table 6.5). Through each of these phases, the infant's behavior seems to be guided by a single overriding principle: *Keep the attachment object close.* In most cases, that attachment object is the mother.

PREATTACHMENT

The first phase, *preattachment*, spans the first few weeks of life. From the very beginning infants seem predisposed to identify and respond to stimulation from other people, especially from mothers. From very shortly after birth, infants will often move their bodies in synchrony with adult human speech, but not in synchrony with disconnected vowel sounds or even rhythmic tapping sounds (Con-

don & Sander, 1974). Also, within the first month of life, not only are infants able to discriminate their mother's voice from that of other women, but they also show marked preference for their mother's voice (DeCasper & Fifer, 1980).

ATTACHMENT IN THE MAKING

During the second phase, *attachment in the making*, there is growing emphasis on behaviors that promote contact with important adults—for example, crying, smiling, sucking, rooting, clinging, and looking at and following with the eyes. The second phase culminates in clearly identifiable attachment sometime during the second half of the first year of life. Now infants manifest the *selective social smile*—the smile that occurs in recognition of familiar faces. At the same time, smiling in response to unfamiliar faces becomes less common.

CLEAR-CUT ATTACHMENT

The third phase, *clear-cut attachment*, becomes evident with an infant's development of locomotor abilities. Now in-

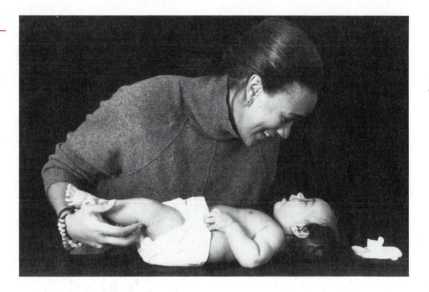

Mutual gazing is among the earliest forms of mother-infant interaction and appears to be very important in the formation of emotional bonds. It benefits an infant by keeping the object of its attachment close.

fants are able to do far more than simply attract the mother's or father's attention through smiling, crying, reaching, and so on; they can crawl over and grab a leg; they can climb up and wrap themselves around a neck; they can cling to the strings that hang from the rear of old-fashioned, pre-Velcro aprons.

GOAL-CORRECTED ATTACHMENT

Some time in the second year, Bowlby informs us, infants enter a phase of *goal-corrected attachment*. Infants have now developed notions of self and others as being separate and permanent and have begun to understand something of the point of view of others. Gradually it becomes possible for infants to make inferences about the effects of their behaviors, and of their parents' behaviors as well, and it becomes possible to affect the behavior of parents in ways more subtle than crying, smiling, yelling, or toddling over and grabbing hold.

Ainsworth (1973) makes the important point that one of the major functions of an infant's early behavior is not only to foster and maintain a high degree of attachment, but also to permit exploration of the environment. For this reason, the infant must strike a balance between proximity-seeking behavior and exploratory behavior. At the same time, it is important that it maintain a sense of security about the environment and about the attachment. Thus Ainsworth speaks of two related concepts that motivate much of what infants do: the *attachment-exploration balance* and the *secure-base* phenomenon. It is noteworthy that in the absence of the mother (or some other important attachment object/person), many infants will cease exploratory behavior. Others are less likely to do so; their attachments seem to be different.

types of attachment

How do you determine whether, to whom, and how strongly an infant is attached? One way is Ainsworth et al.'s (1978) *strange situation* procedure, a sequence of the following events, each of which lasts approximately three minutes:

1. Mother and baby enter a room.

2. Mother puts baby down; stranger enters, speaks with mother, and shows baby a toy; mother leaves.

3. If baby cries, stranger attempts to comfort it; if baby is passive, stranger attempts to interest it in the toy.

4. Mother returns, pauses in doorway; stranger leaves; mother leaves.

5. Baby is alone.

6. Stranger comes back.

7. Mother returns; stranger leaves.

What the strange situation provides is a way of assessing attachment under stress. It permits researchers to ascertain an infant's anxiety or security under these circumstances. When Ainsworth and her associates placed 1-year-old infants in the strange situation, they discovered attachment behaviors that sorted themselves into three categories.

Securely attached infants use the mother as a base for exploration. They go about freely and play in the room, but they often reestablish contact, either by looking at the mother, interacting verbally with her, or returning to her. When the mother leaves, these infants are upset and often stop their exploration. During the reunion events they greet the mother warmly and try to reestablish physical contact or some sort of interaction with her. Securely attached infants manifest few, if any, negative reactions toward their mothers during reunion.

In contrast, *anxious infants* display significant negative behavior toward the mother during reunion events. Some of these infants, **avoidant infants**, either ignore the mother's return or actively avoid contact with her, sometimes by looking away, sometimes by pushing her away physically. Interestingly, they rarely cry when the mother leaves.

A second group of anxious infants, **ambivalent infants**, are very upset when the mother leaves. Their behavior is apparent evidence of strong attachment. Strangely, however, they often display anger when the mother returns. The anger is sometimes very subtle; for example, they might push the mother away even when they appear to want to be held (hence the ambivalence).

The majority of infants in Ainsworth's research—approximately two-thirds of them—can be classified as securely attached; approximately one-fifth are avoidant and the remainder, ambivalent (see Table 6.6).

the implications of attachment

Patterns of attachment appear to reflect relatively stable qualities. Waters (1978) reports, for example, that there is little change in classification between the ages of 12 and 18 months. However, this is not the case when there are major changes in an infant's context, such as somebody leaving or dying (Waters, Hay, & Richters, 1986).

Infants who are mistreated often display marked instability of attachment; they are also more likely to be insecurely attached (Schneider-Rosen et al., 1985). Interestingly, when these children are removed from their homes to escape abuse, they tend to establish with foster caregivers the same sorts of anxious attachments they had in their original homes. Reassuringly, however, the more sensitive the new caregiver is, the more likely the infant is to form secure attachments (Howes & Segal, 1993).

LONG-TERM EFFECTS OF ATTACHMENT

There is mounting evidence that securely attached infants—who, as we noted, are in the majority in North

table 6.6

Types of infant attachment

Attachment classification	Common behavior when mother leaves or returns
Secure	Use mother as a base from which to explore; upset when she leaves; greet her return positively and reestablish physical contact
Insecure or Anxious Avoidant	Rarely cry when mother leaves; ignore mother when she returns or actively avoid her, sometimes pushing her away or pointedly not looking at her
Ambivalent	Very upset when mother leaves; often angry when she returns; may push her away while seeking proximity (hence ambivalence)

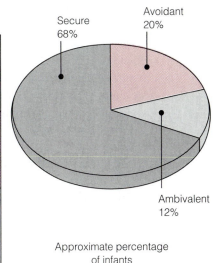

Secure 68%
Avoidant 20%
Ambivalent 12%

Approximate percentage of infants

Source: Based on Bowlby (1969).

American cultures—fare better in the long term (in these cultures). These infants are often more competent, better problem solvers, more independent, more curious, and perhaps more resilient. In one study, children who experienced high levels of support from their mothers (which is closely related to secure attachment) fared significantly better in kindergarten (Pianta & Ball, 1993). In contrast, insecurely attached infants are somewhat more likely to be overly dependent and to experience problems in school (see Collins & Gunnar, 1990).

IMPLICATIONS OF ATTACHMENT IN OTHER CULTURES

Clearly, attachments are a function of interactions. Furthermore, the nature of these interactions, as well as their outcomes, is influenced by the characteristics of both infant and caregiver (or other significant people in the child's context).

Hence the importance of the family—and of the culture in which the family is embedded—because it, too, influences childrearing practices and attitudes toward children. Our North American macrosystem is relatively child-centered; it emphasizes the rights of children and encourages parents to provide physically and psychologically safe environments. It should not be surprising that more than two-thirds of infants appear to be securely attached; perhaps it should be surprising that as many as one-third are not!

Elsewhere in the world, different cultures reflect different values, and sometimes childrearing practices and attitudes toward children are quite different. In some of these cultures, insecurely attached infants are far more common than in North America (for example, western Germany, Japan, and Israel; see Sagi, Ijzendoorn, & Koren-Karie, 1991).

CAN ATTACHMENT STYLES BE CHANGED?

Whether parents should attempt to change their infants' predominant patterns of attachment—and whether they would be very effective in trying to—are important questions. Unfortunately, they are also very difficult questions. What seems clear is that it is important to provide all infants with an opportunity to develop attachments that will provide them with the security they need to engage in the exploration of a bewildering, exciting, and sometimes frightening world. Those opportunities are not always found only in the form of a mother; grandparents, siblings, uncles, and aunts can also be important. So can fathers.

fathers and infant attachment

Our culture's traditional views of the family and of parental roles have typically focused on the importance of the mother in the early social development of the infant; the father's role has often been ignored. Many of our developmental theories (Freud's, for example) argue that the father becomes important after the age of 2 or 3. Further, because many theories have viewed infants as largely incompetent—as passive and as moved by primitive physiological needs rather than by a need to discover and to know—neither parent has been seen as playing a very important role other than as a caregiver.

Some of these traditional values are still the norm in many of the world's cultures. For example, Ho (1987) reports that in China, looking after the young is still largely a mother's function; the father's role is more that of a disciplinarian. There, traditional values emphasize filial devotion and respect—that is, children,

especially sons, are taught to respect and obey their fathers (and grandfathers). Recently, however, there appears to have been a dramatic decline in some of these values. At the same time, fathers have begun to involve themselves more in childrearing.

In North America, too, important changes are rapidly altering our conception of the father's role. These changes include an increasing number of "father-assisted" childbirths, in which the father often has an opportunity to interact with the infant as early as the mother does. In addition, changing work patterns and changing male-female responsibilities in the home have done a great deal to revise the role of the father vis-à-vis the infant. As Lamb and Elster (1985) note, mothers continue to be extremely important to infants, but they are not unique; fathers and other caregivers are also tremendously important. In fact, it seems that newborns and young infants may form attachments with fathers that are almost as strong as those with mothers (Collins & Gunnar, 1990).

Fathers are as competent and as important as mothers in a caregiving role, conclude Collins and Gunnar (1990) after summarizing the research on father-infant attachment. But there are some systematic differences between mother-infant and father-infant interactions.

Most obvious, fathers spend more time in play interactions with their infants; mothers spend more time in nurturant roles (feeding, bathing, changing). As a result, some infants—especially males—display more *affiliative behaviors* toward fathers than toward mothers (Lamb, 1980). Affiliative behaviors demonstrate a social relationship that stops short of being attachment. Evidence of affiliation includes smiling, looking at, laughing, and giving; evidence of attachment might include seeking to be close, clinging, wanting to be picked up, putting the head in the lap, snuggling, and so on.

In a study of 20 infants, Lamb (1980) found that fathers fared extremely well in the attachment and affiliation their infants displayed toward them. For younger infants (7 to 13 months), there was no difference in the amount of attachment behavior directed toward mother or father, although both were the object of far more attachment behavior than was a stranger. However, fathers were recipients of more affiliative behaviors (smiling, looking at, vocalizing, laughing, and giving) than were mothers. For older infants (15 to 24 months), fathers continued to have more affiliative behaviors directed toward them and were now also the objects of more attachment behaviors (seeking proximity, touching, approaching, wanting to be held). The differences between mothers and fathers in amount of affiliative and attachment behavior directed toward them by their infants was minimal, however. In fact, boys displayed most of these behaviors toward their fathers; girls were somewhat less predictable.

It appears that infants (especially males) begin to affiliate with their fathers at a very young age, when given the opportunity to do so (Lamb et al., 1983). Lamb suggests that here, at age 2, is evidence of the beginning of same-sex modeling. Fathers interact (touching and verbalizing) more with sons than with daughters, and with firstborns more than with subsequent children. Interestingly, in an unfamiliar situation the departure of both the father and the mother is followed by signs of distress, whereas the departure of a stranger leads to an increase in play behavior (Kotelchuck, 1976).

Young infants, especially boys, show more affiliative behaviors toward their fathers than their mothers—behaviors such as smiling, laughing, looking at, and giving. Attachment behaviors toward each are very similar—behaviors such as approaching, touching, wanting to be held.

separation anxiety and fear of strangers

Some infants are profoundly uneasy in the absence of a mother or father or in the presence of strangers; others are not. Looking at infants' reactions in these situations is one of the ways in which psychology investigates parent-child attachment. One group of studies, well illustrated by Ainsworth's strange situation, deals with the effects of very short-term separations and attempts to measure what is called *separation protest*. A second type of study looks at the consequences of long-term separation such as might result from divorce or the death of a parent. A third group of studies explores parent-child attachment by looking at the reactions of infants to strangers. If Jamaal's behavior is identical toward all adults, it is unlikely that he has formed a strong, specific attachment to his mother or father. However, if he reacts with fear in the presence of strangers, he has at least learned to equate the presence of his parents with comfort and security.

fear of strangers

Fear of strangers occurs in many infants, but not usually before the age of 9 months (Eckerman & Whatley, 1975). That fear develops at all may result from the fact that once children have become familiar with their environment—can recognize it—they develop certain expectations of the likelihood of events. The appearance of the unexpected is incongruous with infants' expectations and leads to anxiety. This explanation is what Hebb (1966) labels the *incongruity hypothesis.*

One test of the incongruity hypothesis is provided by Schaffer's (1966) investigation of the onset of fear in children. Schaffer looked at how social interaction variables (like maternal availability, number of siblings, or exposure to strangers) were related to infants' responses when confronted with strangers. He found that only two of these factors were related to fear of strangers: number of siblings in the home and exposure to strangers. Infants who are in contact with the largest number of people (strangers and siblings) are less likely to manifest fear, will react with the least amount of fear, and will stop being afraid of strangers at an earlier age. This finding is consistent with the incongruity hypothesis because early

exposure to a wide variety of strangers would necessarily eliminate (or at least reduce) incongruity associated with the presence of a stranger.

the effects of culture on separation anxiety

In this connection, it is worth noting that childrearing styles vary widely within North American cultures; these variations might have implications for the development of attachment behaviors and stranger anxiety. Jackson (1993), for example, points out that African-American childrearing makes far wider use of *multiple caregiving* than is the norm among whites. As a result, African-American infants may develop quite different attachment patterns with primary caregivers. These cultural differences, says Jackson, must be taken into consideration when designing infant attachment studies.

Additional corroboration of the incongruity hypothesis is provided by Kagan's (1976) investigations of the development of separation protest in four different cultural settings outside the United States: Latino families in Guatemala; Indian families, also in Guatemala; kibbutzim families in Israel; and Bushmen families in the Kalahari Desert. In all these groups, separation protest and fear of strangers was minimal before the age of 9 months, peaked between 12 and 15 months, and then declined. Kagan argues that the fact that separation anxiety becomes evident at about the same age in all infants is evidence that it is closely related to some maturational factors. He suggests that these factors are cognitive (related to mental processes, such as thinking and remembering) and that they relate specifically to an infant's ability to make inferences about the meaning and consequences of a parent's departure (or a stranger's appearance).

individual differences in separation anxiety

Not all infants react the same way to the departure of a parent or the arrival of a stranger. In one study, Jacobson and Wille (1984) studied the reactions of 93 children, aged 15 to 18 months, to brief periods of separation from their mothers. They found that previous separation experience was closely related to the amount of distress the children manifested, but the relationship was curvilinear; that is, distress did not increase in linear fashion with increasing separation experiences, but declined with moderate exposure to separation. Specifically, children who had experienced moderate amounts of maternal separation were best able to cope with the absence of their mothers; it was as though they had learned that the separation would only be temporary. Those who had experienced either very little or a great deal of separation were the most distressed—perhaps because they had had either too little opportunity to learn about separation or had learned that separations would be frequent or prolonged.

can children be prepared for separation?

Trying to prepare young preschoolers in advance for an upcoming separation from their mothers doesn't always work as intended. Adams and Passman (1983) had one group of mothers of 2- to 2½-year-old children discuss their upcoming departure for three days preceding the event; a second group of mothers did not prepare their children in advance. And, at the time of departure, some of the moth-ers in both groups provided a brief explanation of their departure and then either left immediately or lingered for one minute; others left as they normally would.

Amazingly, children who had not been prepared in advance showed *less* distress after the mother's departure than children whose mothers had discussed their departure during the previous three days. And those whose mothers did not linger after explaining they were leaving also showed less distress than those whose mothers lingered for 60 seconds. One possible explanation, argue Adams and Passman, is that the lengthy preparation actually teaches children to become alarmed. In the same way, lingering just before departure may teach the child that displaying anxiety might serve to delay the departure (Adams & Passman, 1981).

It follows from these studies that children who are most likely to be free of strong anxiety either at their mother's (or father's, or other caregiver's) absence or in the presence of strangers have many siblings, have been exposed to strangers frequently, have mothers who normally leave without lingering, and have been separated from the mother moderately often. There is evidence, too, that mothers whose parenting is *secure* (rather than dismissing or preoccupied) have infants who are more comfortable with separation (Crowell & Feldman, 1991).

the role of attachment to inanimate objects

Children who are attached to some inanimate object like a blanket or a teddy bear may also be very comfortable with separation. No less than half of all middle-class American children show strong attachments to inanimate objects, the two most common of which are, not surprisingly, blankets (60 percent of children) and pacifiers (66 percent; Passman & Halonen, 1979). Attachments to pacifiers lessen by age 2, but those to blankets remain high throughout most of the preschool period.

In one study, Passman and Weisberg (1975) compared the effectiveness of mothers and blankets in reducing a child's anxiety in a strange situation. They found that as long as their blankets were close by, children who were attached to their blankets played and explored as much and displayed no more anxiety than children who were not attached to blankets but whose mothers were present. In fact, children who were attached to their blankets played and explored more than children who lacked the presence of a mother, a favorite toy, or a blanket.

Related studies (Passman, 1974, 1977) have found that a blanket is as effective as the mother in a learning situation for children who are attached to their blankets. In situations of higher stress (high arousal), however, the mother becomes more effective than a blanket in reducing anxiety (Passman, 1976; Passman & Adams, 1982). In play situations, pacifiers (Halonen & Passman, 1978), color films of mothers (Passman & Erck, 1978), black and white videotapes of mothers (Adams & Passman, 1979), and even Polaroid photographs of mothers (Passman & Longeway, 1982) are sometimes as effective as the actual presence of mothers.

Winnicott (1971) refers to objects such as teddy bears and blankets as **transitional objects** because they become the focus of children's affection and attention while they are in transition between a state of high dependence on the parent and the development of a more independent self. According to this view, the development of self requires separation from the parent and **individuation**—the recognition of one's own individuality (Harter, 1983). The process of separating

and becoming independent gives rise to anxiety; the blanket or the teddy bear serves to comfort children.

In North American cultures, attachment to blankets, teddy bears, pacifiers, and other inanimate objects seems to be normal in the sense that a majority of children manifest these attachments. But, some parents worry, are children who are attached to these inanimate, nonsocial objects perhaps more insecure, less well adjusted, than children whose attachments are more social?

Not likely, says Passman (1987). In a study of 108 preschoolers, he found little relationship between attachment to blankets and general fearfulness. "Blanket-attached children," he concludes, "are thus neither more insecure nor more secure than are others" (p. 829).

So if you are anxious and cannot bring your mother with you, do bring your blanket . . . or whatever.

long-term separation and deprivation

Spitz (1945, 1954) and Bowlby (1940, 1953) were among the first to describe the harmful consequences of parent-child separation. Spitz (1945), reporting the fate of institutionalized children, claimed that they had significantly higher mortality rates, that they were retarded in physical development, and that their emotional development was so severely thwarted by lack of mothering that they frequently withdrew, became depressed, and sometimes died as a result. In effect, what he described was FTT (failure to thrive, described earlier).

The effects of separation are highly dependent on the age at which infants are separated from parents. Separation before the age of 6 months usually does not have the same consequences as later separation (Casler, 1961). Children separated from their parents after the age of 6 months are already likely to have formed a strong attachment to them. Any harmful effects of separation may result from rupturing this attachment bond, rather than from the child's deprivation of a parent. If children are separated from their mothers before becoming strongly attached to them, we might expect that separation will not be as traumatic.

Yarrow and Goodwin (1973) studied 70 adopted children between birth and 16 months of age. All these children were in foster homes before adoption, and all appeared to have had normal environments both before and after adoption. The aim of this study was to discover the effects on infants of separation from a parent figure. Because children were adopted at various ages, it was also possible to examine differences in their reactions as a function of age.

Not surprisingly, reactions were least apparent for children adopted while under 3 months of age. This finding is consistent with the observation that before this age children have not formed any strong attachments. Only nine children were adopted before the age of 3 months, however; the remainder were placed at ages ranging from 3 to 16 months. Only 15 percent of all the children were completely free of all disturbances; the remainder showed disturbances of differing severity (Tables 6.7 and 6.8). These disturbances were most obvious in infants' sleeping schedules and were also evident in feeding behaviors, social reactions (withdrawal, for example), and emotional behavior (crying). Disruptions in social

t a b l e   6 . 7

Immediate impact of long-term mother-child separation on infants ages 3 to 16 months

IMPACT	PERCENTAGE
No disturbances	15
Mild disturbances	36
Moderate disturbances	23
Severe disturbances	20
Extreme disturbances	6

Source: Based on data provided by Yarrow and Goodwin (1973).

The adverse effects of long-term separation from parents is closely related to an infant's age. Effects are seldom seen in infants younger than 3 months; they are almost universal in infants separated from parents after the age of 9 months. Some of these effects may include disruptions of sleeping schedules, feeding problems, social withdrawal, crying, and increased fear of strangers.

table 6.8

Severity of reaction to maternal separation acording to age

AGE	SLIGHT OR NO REACTION	MODERATELY SEVERE TO VERY SEVERE REACTION
Less than 3 months	100%	0
3–4 months	60	40
4–5 months	28	72
6 months	9	91
9 months	0	100

Source: Based on data provided by Yarrow and Goodwin (1973).

reactions included decreased social responsiveness, increased stranger anxiety, and specific disturbances in interactions with the new mother evident in feeding difficulties, colic, digestive upsets, and most strikingly, physical rejection of the new mother or excessive clinging to her. In addition, developmental scores were lower in 56 percent of the cases following adoption.

Apparently, separation from the mother or mother-figure has an adverse effect on many significant aspects of infants' development. Hence, the permanent loss of a parent, as happens through death or sometimes through divorce, can have serious negative consequences for infants—and for older children as well (see Chapter 8). What about regular but temporary loss of parental contact, as happens in many forms of childcare?

infant daycare

More than one out of every two North American preschool children is now in daycare (Hayes et al., 1990). And, with increasing numbers of mothers going back to work within weeks of childbirth, the fastest growing type of daycare facility is infant daycare (see Figures 6.2 and 6.3 in "At A Glance: Work-

ing Moms and Childcare"). Given what we know about the importance of caregiver-infant interaction and attachment, questions relating to the effects of daycare on the social, emotional, and intellectual development of infants become critically important. (See Chapter 8 for a discussion of the effects of daycare on older children.)

Gamble and Zigler (1986) summarize a large body of research that has looked at the effects of daycare on infants' attachment to parents and on different aspects of social behavior. An important goal of this research has been to determine whether daycare can either prevent the formation of attachments between parent and infant or can redirect attachment toward a different caregiver. Reassuringly, all available evidence suggests not.

It seems that infants' primary attachment to parents can be established in a wide variety of circumstances and is highly resistant to disruption. Konner (1982) reports that it occurs in societies as disparate as that of the !Kung, in which infants are in immediate contact with their mothers 24 hours a day, and in Israeli kibbutzim, where infants have contact with their mothers for only a short period each afternoon and on weekends.

Still, even though daycare does not, in general, appear to disrupt parent-infant

ince 1975 there has been a dramatic increase in the number of working mothers with children. Legislation in Canada makes it illegal to dismiss an employee because of pregnancy and grants mothers a 17-week maternity leave with full unemployment benefits and guarantee of employment at the end of that period. As a result, increasing numbers of women are returning to work within a year of giving birth. In addition, increasing numbers of employers are providing childcare benefits, sponsoring daycare facilities, promoting job-sharing arrangements, or allowing mothers to work at home.

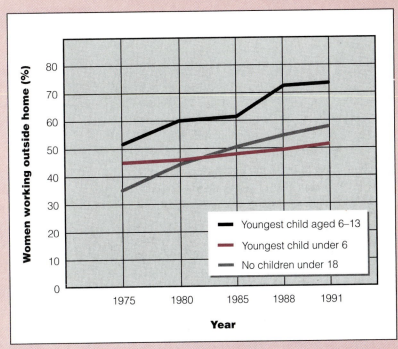

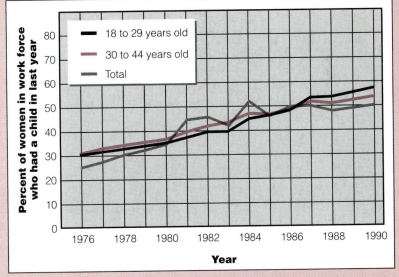

f igure 6.2

(top) Increase in percentage of mothers who live with husbands and work outside the home. Note by comparison that growth in employment is far more modest for wives without minor children at home. Source: Adapted from U.S. Bureau of the Census (1992), p. 388.

f igure 6.3

(bottom) Changes in percentages of women who enter the work force within one year of giving birth (1977–1979 data extrapolated). Source: U.S. Bureau of the Census, 1992, p. 71.

attachment bonds, there is evidence that repeated short-term separation from the mother might lead to the development of what Ainsworth labeled anxious or insecure attachment rather than secure attachment (Belsky & Rovine, 1988). For example, in summarizing studies on infant daycare, Clarke-Stewart (1989) draws two principal conclusions: First, the evidence suggests a somewhat higher probability that daycare infants will avoid their mothers after separation, that they will be insecurely attached; and second, these children are sometimes less obedient subsequently and may be more aggressive with their peers. Similarly, Vaughn, Gove, and Egeland (1980) found a high proportion of insecurely attached infants among those whose mothers had returned to work before they had reached the age of 1. They suggest that this effect might result in part from the mother's emotional unavailability and physical absence, and that this unavailability might alter the quality of mother-infant interaction.

But, warns Bowman (1993), the conclusion that infant daycare might lead to anxious attachments is misleading. It fails to take into account *quality* of daycare. When daycare does have apparently detrimental effects on infants, these effects are often associated with *poorer quality* daycare. In contrast, it has been shown repeatedly that *high-quality* daycare programs not only have no negative effects but may actually facilitate social development (Field et al., 1988). High-quality care is characterized by a well-trained staff, a low ratio of infants to caregivers, and supportive families. (See Chapter 8 for a more detailed discussion of the characteristics of high-quality daycare.)

We should hasten to point out, too, that some infants seem far less vulnerable than others to the stresses of separation from their mothers (Egeland & Sroufe,

1981). By the same token, some may be more vulnerable. Studies reviewed by Gamble and Zigler (1986) suggest that boys are more often vulnerable than girls.

the effects of parenting on infants' development

In the same way as quality of infant daycare can have measurable effects on children, so too can quality of parenting. Following a review of research that has looked at the effects of parents on infants, Belsky, Lerner, and Spanier (1984) describe six important dimensions of parenting: attentiveness, physical contact, verbal stimulation, material stimulation, responsive care, and restrictiveness. The first five of these dimensions have positive effects on infants' social, emotional, and intellectual well-being; the sixth is more negative. That is, parents who are attentive to their children (for example, look at them more); who touch them, play with them, cradle and rock them; who speak to them and provide them with objects to look at, to touch, to taste, to smell; and who are responsive to their cries and to their other signals of distress, amusement, interest, or amazement are more likely to have intellectually advanced and emotionally well-adjusted infants. Parents who are restrictive in that they verbally and physically limit infants' freedom to explore may, to some extent, influence their infants' intellectual development negatively.

In summary, Belsky et al. (1984) point out that parents most likely to promote optimal cognitive development during infancy are those who serve as, or give children access to, the greatest sources of stimulation (speaking, holding, touching, responding to, providing toys, and so on); those who are restrictive—that is, those who limit the amount of stimulation to which infants are exposed—are likely to have an opposite effect. (See Chapter 8 for further discussion of parenting styles.)

In general, children rate their mothers and fathers differently with respect to important dimensions of parenting such as warmth and control. In China, says Ho (1987), mothers look after children, whereas fathers discipline them. Perhaps it isn't surprising that Berndt et al. (1993) found that Chinese children (as well as children from Taiwan and Hong Kong) see their mothers as warmer and less controlling than their fathers.

Interestingly, children in Western societies express very similar views of their parents (Collins & Russell, 1991). No matter how involved fathers are in child-rearing, mothers are typically seen as more affectionate, warmer, and less strict. This is not surprising given that mothers are the ones who feed, wash, and clothe children—in other words, the ones who nurture them (Hodapp and Mueller, 1982). In contrast, fathers typically either play with them or discipline them.

early gender-role influences

There is a tendency for fathers to interact more—and differently—with sons, even when they are infants. Thus, even in these earliest parent-infant interactions, the child's sex has begun to make a difference.

Sex differences in attitudes and behaviors are evident in gender roles (or sex roles). **Gender roles** are the particular combinations of attitudes, behaviors, and personality characteristics that a culture considers appropriate for an individual's anatomical sex—in other words, those characteristics considered masculine or feminine. **Gender typing** describes the processes by which boys and girls learn masculine and feminine roles.

Although it might be tempting to think that masculinity and femininity are primarily the products of genetically ordained physiological and hormonal differences between males and females, evidence suggests that this is only partly the case. In some cultures, certain behaviors that we might consider feminine are expected of men and are therefore masculine; at the same time, the aggressiveness and dominance that we think of as masculine characterize women (see Chapter 10 for more details). Clearly, cultures and families have a great deal to do with the eventual gender roles of their children.

the origins and effects of gender typing

The assigning of gender roles begins at the very beginning—or even before, when parents wonder, "Hey, should we take a chance and paint the room blue? But, shoot, it might be a girl! Maybe we'd better stay with something neutral like desert tan, and we can add the blue or the pink later."

When an infant is born, the attending physician or midwife doesn't say, "Holy jeepers! It's a beautiful *baby*!" No. The key word is not *baby*; it's *boy* or *girl*. The simple anatomical fact of being a boy or a girl tells mother and father and all the significant others what to think and how to react. The knowledge that it's a "boy" or "girl" even colors the parents' perceptions. When Rubin, Provenzano, and Luria (1974) asked 30 parents to describe their day-old infants as they would to a relative or a close friend, without any hesitation they spoke of their alert, strong, well-coordinated, firm, and hardy sons, and of their fine-featured, soft, and delicate daughters. Yet these parents, especially the fathers (who were most guilty of exaggerating the sex-appropriate characteristics of their sons), had scarcely had any opportunity to interact with and get to know their infants. And hospital records clearly indicated that these male and female infants were indistinguishable in terms of weight, muscle tone, activity, responsiveness, and so on.

But many parents waste little time making their new infants sexually distinct: They color the boy-infants blue, the girl-infants pink. Because of the connotations associated with these colors, they emphasize long-established sexual stereotypes. And in much the same way, the names parents give their infants reinforce their sometimes unconscious beliefs about male-female differences. Kasof (1993), for example, shows how male names (such as John or Michael) are seen as more attractive, more intellectually competent, and stronger. In contrast, many female names (Edith, for example) carry connotations of being less attractive, more old-fashioned, and less able.

We are a little like the Mundugumor of New Guinea, suggests Pogrebin (1980). The Mundugumor believed that a variety of signs could be used at birth to predict what an individual would become. For example, they were convinced that only those infants whose umbilical cords were wound around their necks at birth stood any chance of becoming great artists. Amazingly, they were correct! All Mundugumor artists whose talents were accepted as outstanding had, in fact, been born with their umbilical cords twisted around their necks.

But our fortune-telling is not so primitive—or is it? We know it's ridiculous to think that the position of the umbilical cord is of any consequence. Instead, we look for an appendage between the legs of our infants. To a considerable extent, its presence or absence tells us how to interact with them, what sorts of toys they are most likely to enjoy, what their personalities should be. The anatomical fea-

tures that determine sex also allow us to predict whether an infant will grow up to be strong and alert and aggressive, or weaker, more delicate, more sensitive, more emotional. And surprisingly often, our predictions are every bit as accurate as those of the Mundugumor. (We will consider the development of gender role differences again in Chapters 8 and 12.) In some parts of the world, an infant's anatomy can even be a matter of life or death (see "In Other Contexts: Indira's Sister").

exceptionality in infants

This text deals mainly with the physical, intellectual, and social development of the "average person" from conception until death. It is worth repeating, however, that there is no average person, that "average" is simply a useful mathematical invention. If we had no "average person" about whom to speak, we would have to speak instead of individuals. And there are so many different ones—more than 5 billion now—that the task would be absolutely overwhelming.

Still, we need to keep in mind that our average is a fiction and that the individual—Robert, Shannon, Jennifer, David—is our reality and our main concern. We need to keep in mind, too, that some of these individuals depart so dramatically from our average—are so *exceptional*—that they are worthy of study in their own right.

Exceptionality is a two-sided concept: There are, on the one hand, children who are exceptionally gifted; on the other, there are those who have an exceptional lack of normal abilities and competence. Furthermore, exceptionality is found in each of the three major areas of human development: physical,

indira's sister was never named; her story is very short. She was born in a little hut on a windswept and barren plain in Northern India. When the midwife held her up, her mother felt a small twinge of sadness when she couldn't find the appendage between her legs that would have saved her life. Her father shrugged and walked away; there was no need for words, no need to explain what everyone knew must be done. There was already one girl in the family: Indira. Indira had been allowed to live, but the cost of keeping her would be high. Boys run around or ride their ponies covered only in a short rag, or even naked, but girls must always be dressed in an expensive sari. And girls eat, too, though they don't need to be given as much as boys. And then there is the matter of the dowry. Such a price for having a girl!

There are different ways of killing an infant. The one Indira's mother chose is quite common: She stuffed rice into the newborn's mouth and nose and held a pillow tight against its face until the struggles stopped.

"Will you bury it," she asked Indira tiredly, "so the dogs don't find it?"

Although on average women survive longer than men in all of the world's developed countries, the opposite is occasionally the case in developing countries. In India, Pakistan, and Bangladesh, in parts of which infanticide is still practiced, more than a million female infants die each year simply because they are female. In certain provinces of Northern China, thousands of fetuses are surgically aborted because they are female.

In most of the developing world, insists Grant (1992), there is an apartheid based on gender. In these countries, it is women who clean the house, cook the meals, care for the children, carry water and fuel, and look after the old and the sick. It is also women who grow most of the food in developing countries. In return, women get less food, less education, less training, less income, and less protection.

"Employment rights, social security rights, legal rights, property rights, and even civil and political liberties," writes Grant (1992), "are all likely to depend upon the one, cruel chromosome" (p. 57). In the same way, access to education is far more limited for females than for males.

To Think About: What are the probable implications of granting equal educational opportunity to girls in developing countries? How might this affect their care of children? Are Indira's views of life and death, of what it means to be male or female, likely to resemble yours?

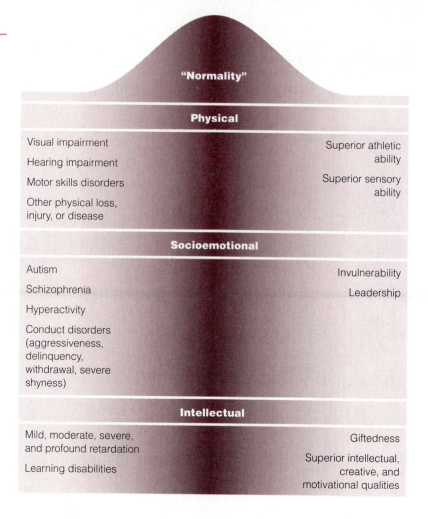

"Normality"

Physical

Visual impairment	Superior athletic ability
Hearing impairment	Superior sensory ability
Motor skills disorders	
Other physical loss, injury, or disease	

Socioemotional

Autism	Invulnerability
Schizophrenia	Leadership
Hyperactivity	
Conduct disorders (aggressiveness, delinquency, withdrawal, severe shyness)	

Intellectual

Mild, moderate, severe, and profound retardation	Giftedness
Learning disabilities	Superior intellectual, creative, and motivational qualities

socioemotional and intellectual (see Figure 6.4).

In this section we deal briefly with some of the most common manifestations of physical and socioemotional exceptionality in infancy. In Chapter 9 we look at physical and intellectual exceptionality in childhood, and in Chapter 10 we discuss socioemotional exceptionality in older children.

motor skill disorders

Not all children learn to walk or tie their shoes, or dance as expected; some experience *developmental delays* in acquiring motor skills.

CEREBRAL PALSY

Cerebral palsy, also labeled *significant developmental motor disability*, is a collection of symptoms (a syndrome) that includes motor problems and may also include psychological problems, convulsions, or behavior disorders (Abroms & Panagakos, 1980). It was originally known as *Little's disease* after the surgeon who first described it, but is, in fact, not a disease. It varies in severity from being so mild that it is virtually undetectable, to paralysis.

Cerebral palsy is most often a congenital disease—that is, it is present at birth in more than two-thirds of all cases (Verhaaren & Connor, 1981). It is generally

t a b l e   6 . 9

Categories of cerebral palsy (classified by body functioning)*

Ataxia	Manifested in balance problems and an uncertain walk. Affects approximately one out of four people with cerebral palsy.
Spasticity	Characterized by loss of control over voluntary muscles. Movements tend to be jerky and uncontrolled. Some symptoms in two out of five cerebral palsy victims.
Athetosis	Marked by trembling, drooling, facial gestures, and other involuntary and purposeless muscle activity (fluttering of the hands, for instance, in contrast to the rigid, jerky movements of spasticity). Often affects speech as well. Frequently found in combination with spasticity. Affects one out of five cerebral palsy individuals.
Tremors	Involves shaky movements, most often of the hands, sometimes visible only when the individual is voluntarily attempting to do something. Involves less extensive movement than athetosis or spasticity.
Rigidity	Caused by strong opposing tension of flexor and extensor muscles, resulting in fixed and rigid bodily postures (sometimes referred to as lead-pipe cerebral palsy).
Mixed	Involves a combination of characteristics descriptive of one or more of the common classifications. Most cerebral palsy victims fall within this category, although the majority are described in terms of their most predominant combination of characteristics.

*Note: It should be emphasized that the effects of cerebral palsy are sometimes so mild as to be undetectable. At other times they are serious enough to cause death in infancy.

associated with brain damage, although the damage is often mild and nonspecific. Sometimes it results from *anoxia* (lack of oxygen during the birth process, or before or after birth). It can also result from either maternal infection and disease or postnatal brain injury sometimes resulting from diseases such as meningitis or encephalitis.

Estimates of the prevalence of cerebral palsy are imprecise because many of the milder cases are not reported and because there is no "cure" for the condition. Estimates cited by Abroms and Panagakos (1980) vary from 1.63 to 7.5 cases for every 1,000 live births.

One of the most common signs of cerebral palsy is spasticity (inability to move voluntarily) in one or more limbs (see Table 6.9). Such motor impairments are sometimes so severe that it is difficult to assess a child's intellectual ability. As a result, it was often assumed that intellectual deficits were common among those suffering from cerebral palsy. However, more recent evidence suggests that fewer than half of cerebral palsy victims are mentally retarded (Erickson, 1987).

DEVELOPMENTAL COORDINATION DISORDERS

There are motor skills disorders that are not associated with brain damage or cerebral palsy. These are often evident in delayed development among children, many of whom also have other developmental disorders, such as mental retardation, autism, or even attention-deficit disorders (Deuel, 1992). These disorders may be apparent in difficulties in *learning* motor tasks such as walking, running, skipping, tying shoes, and so on; they

Cerebral palsy is a motor disorder that can be so mild as to be almost undetectable, or so severe that it can be evident in paralysis. Although many victims of cerebral palsy are mentally retarded, more than half are not. A positive self-image and acceptance by others are especially important for children with cerebral palsy and other motor skill disorders.

may also be apparent in difficulties in *carrying-out* motor activities. A common label for these problems is *developmental coordination disorder*.

According to the *Diagnostic and Statistical Manual of Mental Disorders* (DSM-III-R) of the American Psychiatric Association, a developmental coordination disorder exists when (1) a person's performance of activities requiring motor coordination (such as crawling, walking, sitting, handwriting, sports) is markedly below what would be expected for the person's age, (2) the disturbance interferes with academic achievement or activities of daily living, and (3) the disturbance is not due to a known physical disorder (such as cerebral palsy) (American Psychiatric Association, 1987).

epilepsy

Epilepsy is essentially a seizure disorder of unknown causes. Seizures involve abnormal electrical activity in the brain. The more serious forms of epilepsy (sometimes termed *grand mal*, as opposed to *petit mal*) can often be controlled with drugs. Petit mal seizures, which last only between 1 and 30 seconds, are seen in a "momentary absentness" of a child and are often accompanied by rhythmic, fluttering movements of both eyelids (Abroms & Panagakos, 1980). These seizures may occur very often and are sometimes interpreted by parents or teachers as a sign that the student is deliberately not paying attention. Modern medication can successfully prevent the occurrence of petit mal seizures in more then 80 percent of cases (Love & Walthall, 1977). In more than 70 percent of all cases, petit mal seizures cease altogether by age 18 (Nealis, 1983).

other physical problems

A large number of other physical problems sometimes require special education or services. These include diseases and conditions such as muscular dystrophy, cancer, asthma, diabetes, the absence of one or more limbs, and paralysis, to name but a few. Some are congenital, some result from infections and diseases acquired after birth, and others result from accidents of various kinds. Many cases are associated with serious emotional and social problems, which are often related to difficulties children experience in being accepted by others and in developing a positive self-concept. Hence a great deal of what special education programs, parents, and therapists can do for physically exceptional children relates to their emotional and social well-being.

autistic disorder

Tim was an apparently normal, healthy child, the second child born to a couple in their early 20s. He was an *easy* infant who cried very little and who, in fact, appeared most content when left alone. His mother later recalled that he didn't smile as a young infant and that he didn't appear to recognize her. Still, he progressed apparently normally through his first year and learned to walk at the young age of 9 months, displaying advanced motor development by tripping or falling less often than most toddlers do.

But at the age of 2, he had still not learned to speak. An examination showed his hearing to be normal. His parents hoped he would be a "late bloomer." But even at the age of 3, Tim still did not respond to his parents' speech. In addition, he had developed few social skills, and he engaged in unusual and repetitive behaviors, such as spinning the wheels of his toy car or sitting and rocking his body endlessly.

Tim's condition is rare; its prevalence is probably far less than 1 in 100,000 (Werry, 1972). It is what is labeled **autistic disorder**, a disorder described by the American Psychiatric Association (1987) as a *pervasive developmental disorder.*

Autistic disorder is apparent mainly in infants' failure to develop normal communication skills. Its other features include a lack of normal responsiveness to other people, bizarre responses to aspects of the environment, and a pattern of developmental delays (Fong & Wilgosh, 1992). Among its major symptoms, the

APA (1987) lists (1) severe and consistent impairment in social relationships (for example, inappropriate emotional responses, lack of awareness of feelings of others, abnormal social play, inability to make friends), (2) significant impairment in verbal and nonverbal communication (for example, absence of babbling, lack of facial expressiveness, absence of imaginative activity as in "make-believe" games, abnormal speech production, inability to initiate or maintain a conversation), and (3) markedly restricted range of interests and behaviors (for example, stereotyped movements like spinning or head banging, persistent preoccupation with parts of objects like repeatedly smelling or feeling something, serious distress over trivial changes in environment, unreasonable insistence on routines, and preoccupation with one activity).

Although autistic disorder usually manifests itself before the age of 3, it sometimes develops later (Mesibov & Van Bourgondien, 1992). The most common treatment is to use tranquilizers and antipsychotic drugs. Although there is little evidence that these substances are very effective in alleviating the condition, they are useful in making patients more manageable. Psychotherapy (psychoanalysis, for example) has not proven very effective, although some forms of behavior therapies (based on conditioning theories described in Chapter 2) beginning early in the child's life and sustained over a long period of time are sometimes helpful (see Erickson, 1987). But, as Erickson notes, none of these therapies, including the behavior therapies, is very likely to make autistic children act normally.

Follow-up studies of children diagnosed as having autistic disorder have not given much reason for optimism. Combining several long-term studies that looked at these children between 5 and 10 years after initial diagnosis, DeMyer et al. (1973) found that only 1 to 2 percent of them had recovered sufficiently that they could be classed as normal. Another 5 to 15 percent were almost normal, 16 to 25 percent could be classed as "fair," and more than half were in poor condition. Not surprisingly, the prognosis is best for those who succeed in developing language skills.

the whole infant

There is something frustrating about pigeonholing developing infants into such psychologically convenient descriptive categories as capabilities, physical development, motor development, socioemotional development, and intellectual development. We lose sight of the infant in our sometimes-confused array of beliefs, findings, tentative conclusions, convincing arguments, and suggestions.

The average infant of which we speak is hypothetical. And although it's true that many infants are very close to the hypothetical average when they are 1 month old, fewer are still average at the age of 2 months, even fewer at 6 months, and by the age of 1 year, almost none. By the time a child becomes as old as you or I, the average individual will no longer exist but will appear only in the overly simplified theories of the social scientist, or in the files of the market researcher who wants to know what the "average" person is wearing this spring.

Each person is an integrated whole whose intellect, emotions, and physical being all interact. Each part is linked with and dependent on every other part of the living organism. But if we try to describe a child in that way, the sheer complexity of the task might overwhelm us.

So we continue to speak of the isolated forces that affect human development as though they existed apart from the integrated, whole child. But it bears repeating that our divisions, although necessary, are artificial and sometimes misleading.

main points

THE FAMILY CONTEXT

1. To understand infancy, it's necessary to ask about interactions within the family as well as in the larger context, keeping in mind that influences are bidirectional (infants affect parents too), involve a variety of individuals and relationships, and are strongly influenced by the characteristics of both parents and infants.

INFANT STATES AND EMOTIONS

2. Infant states include regular sleep (no responsiveness to stimuli), irregular sleep (stimuli can elicit smile or grimace, twitching motions), drowsiness, alert inactivity (eyes open, examining environment), and focused activity (including crying, high anxiety, eyes open, low alertness, rapid breathing, low responsiveness to stimuli). They reflect basic individual differences very early in life.

3. Infants' facial expressions and other behaviors suggest that they feel various emotions. These behaviors include smiling (the true social smile is uncommon before 3 weeks), laughing, fear in response to loud noises (fear of strangers is not common before the age of 6 months, when children recognize familiar and unfamiliar people).

TEMPERAMENT

4. One classification of basic temperaments includes *difficult* infants (with-

drawal from the unfamiliar, slow adaptation to change, negative moods), *easy* infants (high adaptability, high approach tendencies), and *slow to warm up* infants (low activity level, high withdrawal, slow adaptation, more negative moods). "Goodness-of-fit" between infants' temperaments and environmental demands may affect developmental outcomes. In our cultures, some *difficult* infants may run a higher risk of behavior and emotional problems than do *easy* children.

ATTACHMENT IN INFANTS

5. Bonding refers to the biologically based processes by which mother and infant form attachment links. Attachment appears important to the healthy development and adjustment of infants (although there is no critical period during which this bonding must occur; nor can it occur only with the mother).

6. Bowlby identifies four attachment phases: *preattachment* (first month; crying, smiling, clinging, sucking, responding to caregiver's voice); *attachment in the making* (into second half of first year; selective social smile); *clear-cut attachment* (after 6 months; use of newly developing motor skills to approach attachment object); and *goal-corrected attachment* (second year; more subtle manipulation of attachment person's behavior).

SEPARATION ANXIETY AND FEAR OF STRANGERS

7. Ainsworth's research describes *securely attached* infants (use mother as a base from which to explore; are upset when she leaves; react positively and attempt to reestablish contact when

she returns) and *anxiously* or *insecurely attached* infants, who may be *avoidant* (rarely cry when mother leaves; ignore or avoid her when she returns) or *ambivalent* (are very upset when mother leaves; often angry when she returns; seek proximity while attempting to avoid mother, sometimes by pushing her away).

8. Infants appear to become equally attached to their mothers and fathers when given the opportunity to do so but display more affiliative (let's be friends) behaviors toward their fathers. Fear of strangers occurs in many infants (after age 6 months) but is less pronounced in those who have been exposed to more people. *Transitional objects* such as blankets and teddy bears are sometimes as effective as a parent in reducing anxiety in some stressful situations.

9. Long-term separation from parents may have harmful effects on infants, particularly after 6 months of age but seldom before 3 months. However, high-quality infant daycare does not appear either to disrupt parent-infant bonds or to prevent their formation and has no consistent negative effects.

EFFECTS OF PARENTING ON INFANTS' DEVELOPMENT

10. Important positive dimensions of parenting include attentiveness, physical contact, verbal stimulation, material stimulation, and responsive care; restrictiveness is more negative. From the very beginning, parents often exert a subtle influence on the gender-typing of their infants.

EXCEPTIONALITY IN INFANTS

11. Exceptionality has both positive and negative dimensions. Exceptional

children are those who require special education and related services to realize their full human potential. Exceptionalities include physical and motor problems in infancy (for example, *motor skill disorders* such as cerebral palsy and *developmental coordination disorder*, epilepsy, various diseases, congenital physical problems, and physical problems resulting from accidents).

12. Autistic disorder is a rare but very serious early form of emotional disorder marked by failure to develop communication skills or normal social relationships, as well as by bizarre responses to aspects of the environment. It is seldom "cured" but is often treated with drugs.

focus questions: applications

■ How do infants influence caregivers?

1. Write up a case illustration of reciprocal caregiver(s)-infant influence.

■ Are all infants basically the same in terms of emotional reactions and personality?

2. Arrange to observe two or three infants (perhaps in an infant day-care center) using one of the observation techniques described in Table 1.4. Look for evidence of temperamental differences. Write up your observations.

■ Are caregiver-infant bonds "natural" and unlearned?

3. In your opinion, what does the widespread attachment of children to inanimate objects such as blankets suggest about the source and importance of caregiver-infant bonds?

■ What are the consequences of separating infants from their caregivers?

4. Write a term paper on the effects of parental death on children of different ages.

■ How do the terms *average, normal,* and *exceptional* relate to each other?

5. Give examples of each term with respect to infants, referring to physical, socioemotional, and intellectual development.

study terms

infant state 248
rapid eye movement (REM) sleep 250
temperament 256
mother-infant bonding 262
failure to thrive (FTT) 264
securely attached infants 268
avoidant infants 268
ambivalent infants 268
individuation 274
transitional objects 274
gender roles 279
gender typing 279
exceptionality 280
autistic disorder 285

further readings

Valsiner's collection of articles is an excellent illustration of how developmental psychologists are taking into account the influence of cultural, historical, and family systems on developmental outcomes:

Valsiner, J. (Ed.). (1989). *Child development in cultural context.* Lewiston, N.Y.: Hogrefe and Huber.

A good summary of research on temperament in infants is:

Kohnstamm, G. A. Bates, J. E., & Rothbart, M. K. (Eds.). (1989). *Tem-*

perament in Childhood. New York: John Wiley.

In the following book, Bowlby examines mother-infant interaction with special emphasis on the development of attachment:

Bowlby, J. (1982). *Attachment and loss* (Vol. 1). New York: Basic Books.

An important view of mother-infant bonding is presented in:

Klaus, M. H., & Kennell, J. H. (1983). *Bonding: The beginnings of parent-infant attachment* (Rev. ed.). St. Louis: C. V. Mosby. (Originally published as *Maternal-infant bonding.*)

There is not enough childcare in North America; nor is there enough quality childcare, says Angela Browne Miller in the first of the following three books. The other two detail changes in North American society today that are having an important impact on the lives of infants:

Browne Miller, A. (1990). *The day care dilemma.* New York: Plenum Press.

Hernandez, D. J., & Myers, D. E. (1993). *America's children: Resources from family, government, and the economy.* New York: Sage.

Hayes, C. D., Palmer, J. L., & Zaslow, M. J. (Eds.). (1990). *Who cares for America's children? Child care policy for the 1990's.* Washington, D. C.: National Academy Press.

Pogrebin's book is a provocative analysis of the role parents play in gender typing their infants:

Pogrebin, L. C. (1980). *Growing up free: Raising your child in the 80's.* New York: McGraw-Hill.

four

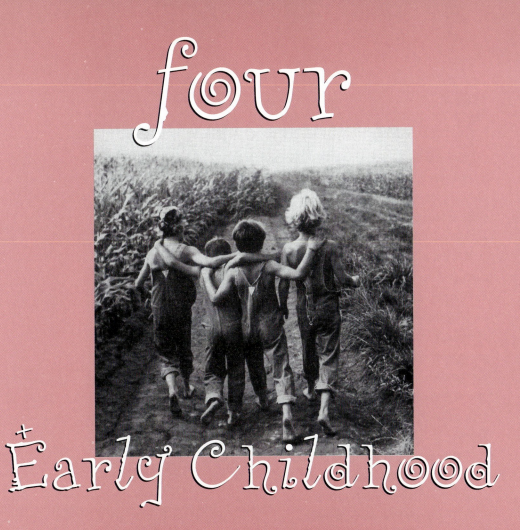

Early Childhood

Bliss was it in that dawn to be alive,
But to be young was very heaven.
William Wordsworth, A Poet's Epitaph

i f to be young is "very heaven," does it follow that to be old is hell? What is it that the young lose as they age? Now that you are older, do you remember what you might have lost? Do you think it was innocence?

Perhaps, but it was surely ignorance too, because there is a dramatic shedding of ignorance in the years from 2 to 6. In those years there are astounding strides in the acquisition of language, and in the ability to think clearly and logically and to deal with complex things like numbers. There are stunning advances, as well, in the ability to interpret the emotions of others and to control the expression of feelings.

And there are some wonderful developments in the ability to stretch the imagination, to understand magical things, to play....

Do you remember how you played?

Maybe that is what the old forget that makes life less like heaven.

7

Physical and Cognitive Development in Early Childhood

Childhood is measured out by sounds and smells
And sights, before the dark of reason grows.
John Betjeman, "Summoned by Bells"

focus questions

WHAT SORTS OF PARALLELS EXIST BETWEEN MOTOR AND COGNITIVE DEVELOPMENT?

HOW DOES PIAGET DESCRIBE COGNITIVE DEVELOPMENT IN EARLY CHILDHOOD?

WHAT ARE SOME OF THE EFFECTS OF PRESCHOOL EDUCATION?

HOW DO YOUNG CHILDREN LEARN LANGUAGE?

IS KNOWING A SECOND LANGUAGE GOOD, BAD, OR IRRELEVANT FOR COGNITIVE DEVELOPMENT?

outline

CHILDREN AND MAGICAL THINKING

PHYSICAL GROWTH IN EARLY CHILDHOOD

MOTOR DEVELOPMENT
Assessing Motor Development
The Relationship Between Motor and Cognitive Development

COGNITIVE DEVELOPMENT: MEMORY IN PRESCHOOLERS
Incidental Mnemonics
Memory Strategies of Preschoolers

COGNITIVE DEVELOPMENT IN PRESCHOOLERS: PIAGET'S VIEW
Preconceptual Thinking
Intuitive Thinking
Replications of Piaget's Work
Cognitive Achievements of Preschoolers

PRESCHOOL EDUCATION
Preschool Education Elsewhere
Nursery Schools
Compensatory Preschool Programs
Kindergartens
Effective Preschool Education: The Family Context

LANGUAGE AND THE PRESCHOOLER
Language in Infancy
Multiple-Word Sentences
More Complex Grammatical Changes
Adultlike Structures

EXPLANATIONS OF LANGUAGE DEVELOPMENT
The Role of Early Experience in Language Development
The Role of Parents as Teachers of Language
The Role of Biology in Language Development

BILINGUALISM AND A CHANGING LANGUAGE CONTEXT
Transitional Bilingualism
The Psychological Effects of Bilingualism
Bilingualism in Today's Schools
Nonstandard Languages

SPEECH AND LANGUAGE PROBLEMS IN EARLY CHILDHOOD

THE RELATION OF LANGUAGE AND THOUGHT

LANGUAGE IS FOR COMMUNICATING AND CONVERSING

MAIN POINTS

FOCUS QUESTIONS: APPLICATIONS

STUDY TERMS

FURTHER READINGS

At Harry's place on Thanksgiving, we sat around a table laden with what would surely have passed for a grand feast in medieval times. And as we filled our plates, Harry tried to impress upon his 4- and 6-year-old sons the many things for which they should be thankful. He spoke to them of pioneers and pilgrims in savage days, when there were neither roads nor streets, neither theaters nor stores.

"If they needed a loaf of bread or some meat, they couldn't just go and buy it," Harry explained.

"There was no stores?" the younger one asked, not yet willing to believe in a world that primitive. "Not even for candy?"

"No stores at all," Harry assured him. "They had to grow and make all their food."

"Gardens!" the older one shouted. "They had gardens."

"Good!" Harry beamed. "They had gardens. Now, if you were a pilgrim and you had to grow all your own food, and you could never go to the store to get anything, what would you plant in your garden?"

"Corn!" the older one said.

"Good!"

"And peas!"

"Right! And what would you plant?" Harry asked the younger boy.

"Potatoes!" he answered, cleverly glancing at his plate.

"Good! Anything else? What else would you plant?"

The younger boy examined his plate carefully.

"I'd plant turkeys next," he announced solemnly.

children and magical thinking

The mind of a 4 year old is sometimes wonderfully inventive; it isn't limited by the rules that constrain our thoughts. The thinking of 4 year olds, as Pearce (1977) put it, is magical; it does not always need to be checked against reality. In these early years, thinking is wishful and fantastic. It somehow assumes that reality can be changed by a thought. Thus it is that a magic spell can produce a witch or a princess, a silver thread or a pot of gold; a dream can be real, and perhaps reality too can be a dream; and a wish can make a race car of a stone, a cave of a small corner, a giant sailing ship of a discarded matchbox.

But, Pearce tells us, we do not gladly accept—perhaps we do not even understand—the magical child. Our approach to children and our research ask instead: "How can the child be made to attend to reality? Or how can we make the child abandon magical thinking?" (p. xv).

Perhaps we should try to understand more, and control and change less.

In this chapter we examine the early development of thinking and the growth of language. But first, we look at physical growth and motor development of children ages 2 to 6.

physical growth in early childhood

A comparison of the 6 year old with the 2 year old offers some idea of the phenomenal changes that take place during the preschool years. Still, the changes that occur from birth to the end of a child's second year are probably even more striking. Figures 7.1 and 7.2 trace the physical development of boys and girls from ages 2 to 6. Comparing these data with those in Figures 5.3 and 5.4 reveals that there is a dramatic deceleration in growth rates after infancy, especially in height. In fact, the average

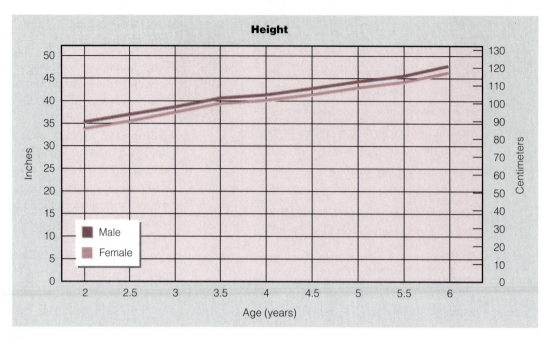

f **igure 7.1**

Height at the 50th percentile for U.S. children ages 2 to 6. Source: Adapted from the Health Department, Milwaukee, Wisconsin; based on data by H. C. Stuart and H. V. Meredith, prepared for use in Children's Medical Center, Boston. Used by permission of the Milwaukee Health Department.

f **igure 7.2**

Weight at the 50th percentile for U.S. children ages 2 to 6. Source: Adapted from the Health Department, Milwaukee, Wisconsin; based on data by H. C. Stuart and H. V. Meredith, prepared for use in Children's Medical Center, Boston. Used by permission of the Milwaukee Health Department.

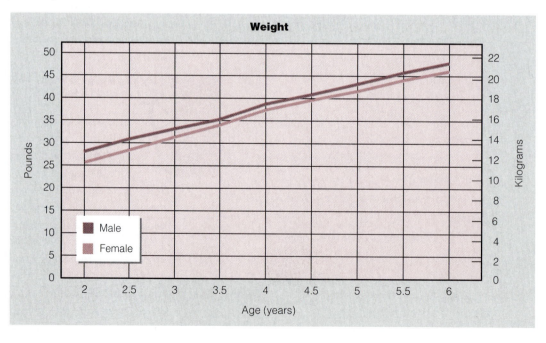

rate of weight gain for children is greater during the first year than it is for any year between the ages of 2 and 6.

Different growth rates for different parts of the body help explain some of the changes that occur between the ages of 2 and 6. The thick layers of fat that give 1-year-old children their babyish appearance begin to disappear slowly during the second year of life and continue to recede gradually. Because these tissues grow much more slowly than other tissues, by the time children have reached age 6 their layers of fat are less than half as thick as they were at age 1. Partly because of this change, they begin to look more like adults.

Other changes, as well, account for the gradual transition from the appearance of infancy to the appearance of young boyhood or girlhood. Not only does the relative amount of fatty tissue change during the preschool years, but its distribution also changes as a result of the more rapid growth of bone and muscle. The squat appearance of infants is explained by the fact that their waists are usually as large as their hips or chests. Six-year-old children, by contrast, have begun to develop waists that are smaller than their shoulders and hips. This be-

comes even more evident in early adolescence.

The relatively larger waists of infants are due not only to layers of fat but also to the size of the internal organs, many of which grow at a much more rapid rate than other parts of the body. Given space limitations between children's pelvis and diaphragm, their abdomens often protrude. This condition changes as they grow in height during the preschool years.

Other aspects of body proportions that account for the different appearance of 6 year olds include changes in the ratio of head to body size (shown in Figure 7.3). The head of a 2-month-old fetus is approximately half the length of the entire body; at birth, it is closer to one-fourth the size of the rest of the body; and by the age of 6, it is close to one-eighth the size, only a short step removed from the head-to-body ratio of 1 to 10 that is typical of adults. Thus from the age of 2 to 6 the head changes from approximately one-fifth to one-eighth of total body size, a significant enough change to be noticeable. Because of this, and because of changes in the distribution of fat and in the space that the child now has for internal organs, the 6 year old looks remark-

figure 7.3

Changes in form and proportion of the human body during fetal and postnatal life. Reproduced with permission from Jensen et al., Biology. Belmont, Calif.: Wadsworth, 1979, p. 233.

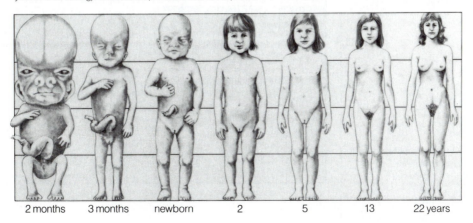

| 2 months | 3 months | newborn | 2 | 5 | 13 | 22 years |

ably like an adult; the 2 year old looks more like a typical baby.

Note that this general description of preschoolers' physical development describes conditions in the developed world, where most children are adequately nourished and cared for. That is not the case for most of the world's children (Grant, 1992). In addition, even with the best currently available care and nutrition, many preschoolers suffer from various health problems as they grow up (see Figure 7.4 in "At A Glance: Preschoolers' Health Problems").

motor development

Learning to walk is an infant's most significant motor achievement, and it has extremely important social and cognitive implications. Infants who can walk (or at least crawl) can not only

at a Glance   preschoolers' health problems

Most preschoolers occasionally suffer from illness or injury serious enough to require medical attention or to keep them home at least one day (Figure 7.4). In fact, only 2 or 3 of every 100 preschoolers will not have an upper-respiratory infection at least once (a cold, for example), and almost one-third will suffer some physical injury. Between ages 5 and 17, the rates for all common health problems decline—except for injuries and other respiratory problems. At all ages except after 65, rate of injuries is higher for males than females.

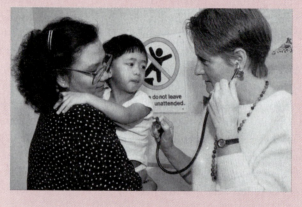

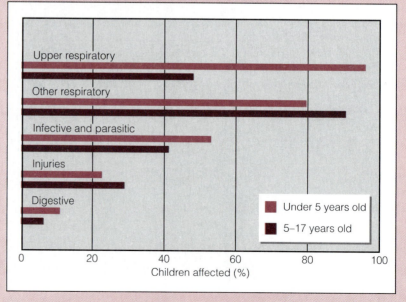

figure 7.4

Preschoolers' and older children's susceptibility to injury and illness. The graph shows the percentage of children who will be affected at least once by the indicated condition. Source: Adapted from U.S. Bureau of the Census (1992), p. 126.

approach those to whom they are attached, but they can also leave them to explore places they would otherwise see only from somebody's arms or by looking over the edge of some wheeled baby vehicle. Self-locomotion facilitates the process of becoming familiar with the world.

At the same time that they learn to walk, infants also practice and eventually learn to coordinate other motor activities, so that by age 2 they are remarkably adept at picking up objects, stacking blocks, unlacing shoes, and a host of other actions. The close relationship between motor and cognitive development during early childhood is evident in Jean Piaget's theory. It is through actual experience and activity with objects that children learn about the properties of objects, and about sorting, classifying, and counting—all of which are basic for continued intellectual development.

In early childhood, children continue to progress in motor development, their locomotion becoming more certain as they lose the characteristic wide-footed stance of the toddler (from 18 months to 2½ years). As their equilibrium stabilizes and their feet move closer together, their arms and hands also move closer to their bodies. They no longer need as wide a stance to maintain their balance—nor do they always need to keep their arms out

as if they were perpetually walking a rail. Still, they fall far more often than you or I (but it doesn't hurt so much).

As their walking improves, infants also acquire the ability to climb stairs standing upright and completely unassisted. And eventually they learn to hop with two feet and to skip.

Preschoolers also develop a variety of other motor skills that are closely related to increasing control and coordination of fine-muscle movements. Among these are the skills required for tracing geometric figures or for copying them freehand. Gesell (1925), whose work maps out in detail the sequential progression of children's motor development, reports that before age 2 children are usually incapable of copying a circle or a horizontal line, although a 2 or 3 year old can do so quite easily. By the age of 4, children can also copy a square and a rectangle but are unable to copy a diamond (see Figure 7.5).

As Broderick (1986) points out, successfully copying geometric figures is not simply a fine-motor task; it also requires important perceptual and cognitive abilities. For example, visual abilities are involved in perceiving the shape to be copied and in comparing it with the child's own drawing; cognitive abilities come into play when the child successfully interprets the requirements of the

figure 7.5

Usual order of difficulty, with very approximate ages, for copying simple geometric designs reasonably well. Because of the close relationship between motor and intellectual development in early childhood, many intelligence tests for young children include tasks such as these.

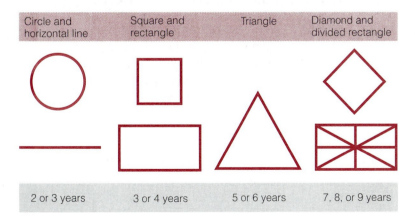

Circle and horizontal line	Square and rectangle	Triangle	Diamond and divided rectangle
2 or 3 years	3 or 4 years	5 or 6 years	7, 8, or 9 years

task, plans an approach, and evaluates its execution, sometimes modifying and correcting; and, of course, fine-motor abilities are involved in carrying out the task.

Children as young as 1 or 2 can easily discriminate among different geometric forms, says Broderick (1986), but they cannot copy them. In an investigation of the drawing skills of 80 children, she found that although 5 and 6 year olds can draw recognizable squares, they cannot draw diamonds. Although what they draw is usually clearly recognizable as a diamond, the figures are often oriented many degrees to one side or the other. Strangely, even 12 year olds and adults experience difficulty with diamonds. For example, adults often make highly noticeable errors in angularity—that is, opposing angles of the diamonds are sometimes quite different from each other, although not nearly as different as those drawn by younger children.

Given the close relationship between motor and cognitive development in early childhood and the highly predictable sequence for learning to copy geometric figures, it is not surprising that many intelligence tests (for example, the Stanford-Binet and the Wechsler) include such items.

---

assessing motor development

All parents are concerned about the developmental progress of their children. They feel proud of their offsprings' accomplishments and are sometimes distressed and worried when their children do not develop as rapidly as they expect—or as rapidly as someone else's children.

Here, as in all areas of human development, there are no absolute norms, no definite, preestablished levels of performance that must be reached by certain ages. Our definitions of what is normal are inexact. Still, psychology and human biology provide us with indications of what we might expect, and this information provides benchmarks against which to evaluate our children—if we must.

A variety of different scales of infant and child development can be used for these purposes. As we saw, there are neonatal scales with which to assess the physiological and neurological condition of newborns (for example, the Brazelton Neonatal Behavioral Assessment Scale, or the APGAR). There are also scales to assess motor and mental development in infancy (for example, the Bayley Scales of Infant Development). And there are developmental scales that span infancy and childhood (for example, the Denver Developmental Screening Test, or the Gesell Developmental Schedules). Each of these instruments typically provides simple tasks that can be presented to infants or children or describes observations that can be made. Each also provides specific tables of norms describing what sorts of behaviors can be expected at different ages.

The Denver Developmental Screening Test, for example, was initially designed primarily to permit identification of infants and children suffering from developmental delays (Frankenburg et al., 1981). It has subsequently been revised and restandardized for various ethnic groups, and it is now known as the Denver II (Denver Developmental Materials, 1990). It provides age norms corresponding to the levels at which 25, 50, 75, and 90 percent of children are expected to demonstrate a given capability. Four different areas are examined by the test: language, personal-social, fine-motor, and gross-motor. A child is considered to be developmentally delayed when incapable of a task of which 90 percent of children of the same age are capable. Isolated developmental delays are not considered serious, but when a child is delayed on two or more tasks and in more than one area, further assessment may be required.

the relationship between motor and cognitive development

A child's physical and motor development are closely related; the acquisition of many skills depends on development of the required musculature and on control of these muscles.

The relationship of physical development to other areas of development is sometimes not so obvious, although no less real. For example, a child's play, particularly with peers, is often influenced by motor skills because various aptitudes are called for in different games. A child who is still incapable of jumping with both feet is not likely to be invited by older children to join in a game of jump rope; a child who cannot grasp marbles skillfully may be left out of the game. Conversely, the child who is precocious in physical and motor development is likely to be the first one chosen to participate in games—indeed, may be the one to initiate them. Clearly, then, physical and motor development have an important influence on children's social development; game playing is one important means of socialization (more about this in Chapter 8).

As we have seen, the relationship between motor and intellectual development in a child's early years is one of the most fundamental aspects of Piaget's theory. The infant's world of the "here and now" is a world that has meaning only in action. An object exists only when the infant looks at it; its meaning is what can be done with it now. But as the infant gains control over fine- and gross-motor movements, it becomes possible to go to an object, look behind it, pick it up, explore it. These seemingly simple but initially impossible acts open up an entirely new world of cognitions.

So it continues throughout early childhood. A young child's increasing refinement of control over motor movements (see Table 7.1), and an ever-growing store of experiences with real objects, leads gradually to an intellectual (cognitive) understanding of some of the properties of things. It leads as well to an understanding of abstractions, such as the principles that govern the use of numbers, the formation of classes, or the abstraction of a host of other concepts. These are some of the subjects we look at next.

cognitive development: memory in preschoolers

We don't expect preschool children, much less infants, to be completely logical. We are seldom surprised when 3 year olds insist loudly that a small cat, identical in appearance to their small cat, must surely be theirs; we are not shocked when a 4 year old fails to realize that there really aren't more candies in his sister's dish just because they're all spread out; we express little dismay when a 2½ year old calls a duck a chicken. For some reason, these instances of prelogical thinking simply amuse us; they are what we expect of young children.

But we would be surprised if older children continued to insist on calling all shaggy-looking pigs "doggie"; if they refused to believe that 6 ounces of soft

t able 7.1

Physical abilities of children ages 2 to 5

AT 2 YEARS BEGINS TO	AT 3 YEARS BEGINS TO	AT 4 YEARS BEGINS TO	AT 5 YEARS BEGINS TO
Walk	*Jump and hop on one foot*	*Run, jump, and climb with close adult supervision*	*Gain good body control*
Run			*Throw and catch a ball, climb, jump, skip with good coordination*
Actively explore his environment	*Climb stairs by alternating feet on each stair*	*Dress self using buttons, zippers, laces, and so on*	
Sit in a chair without support	*Dress and undress self somewhat*	*Use more sophisticated eating utensils such as knives to cut meat or spread butter*	*Coordinate movements to music*
Climb stairs with help (both feet on each stair)	*Walk a reasonably straight path on floor*		*Put on snowpants, boots, and tie shoes*
	Walk on balance beam		*Skip*
Build block towers	*Ride a tricycle*	*Walk on balance beam with ease*	*Jump rope*
Feed self with fork and spoon	*Stand on one foot for a short time*	*Walk down stairs alone*	*Walk in a straight line*
Stand on balance beam	*Catch large balls*	*Bounce and catch ball*	*Ride a two-wheel bike*
Throw ball	*Hop*	*Push/pull wagon*	*Roller skate*
Catch	*Gallop*	*Cut, following lines*	*Fold paper*
Jump	*Kick a ball*	*Copy figure X*	*Reproduce alphabet and numbers*
Push and pull	*Hit a ball*	*Print first name*	
Hang on bar	*Paste*		*Trace*
Slide	*String beads*		
	Cut paper with scissors		
	Copy figures 0 and +		

Source: From G. W. Maxim (1993). *The very young* (4th ed.). Columbus, Ohio: Merrill, p. 80. Reprinted by permission of Merrill, an imprint of Macmillan Publishing Company. Copyright © 1993 by Merrill Publishing.

drink in a glass is the same amount as 6 ounces in a bottle; or if they thought they could increase the mass of a wad of gum simply by stringing it out and wrapping it around their ears. We expect some intellectual (cognitive) differences between preschoolers and older children.

Between birth and the end of the early childhood period (around age 6), children learn and remember an overwhelming assortment of things: the identities of people and animals; the locations of things; numbers, letters, and songs; and thousands of words and all sorts of complex rules for putting them together.

From the very beginning children clearly have some ability to learn and to remember. But, as we saw in Chapter 5, neonates' memories are very brief. The effects of simple conditioning procedures sometimes last only hours, or perhaps a day. Still, an infant is not long confused about whether this is her mother's voice, or her face. Recognition of things like voices and faces is a certain sign of memory. But there are some important differences between the memories of infants and those of adults. Chief among them is the fact that infants do not deliberately and systematically organize, group, or elaborate material to remember it—and these three activities are the most important memory strategies of adults and older children.

incidental mnemonics

A number of researchers argue that preschoolers rarely use systematic strategies for remembering. Most of what preschoolers remember is the result of what Wellman (1988) calls **incidental mnemonics**. Incidental mnemonics are not deliberate; hence they are not really strategies. They are what happens when someone pays attention, for whatever reason, and later remembers, or what happens when someone is exposed to the same thing often enough that it becomes familiar and known. Remembering, in these cases, is not the result of a deliberate and systematic attempt to elaborate or to rehearse, but is, in a sense, involuntary (or *incidental*).

We know that incidental mnemonics underlie much of preschoolers' learning. Because these are incidental and involuntary processes, and because there is little evidence of adultlike strategies such as deliberately rehearsing or organizing, researchers have assumed that memory strategies develop only in later childhood. According to Wellman (1988), the available evidence suggests that this is wrong. Although preschoolers do use deliberate strategies to help them remember, two things are noteworthy about these strategies: (1) They seldom involve deliberate reorganization or elaboration, or even rehearsal, and (2) many of preschoolers' mnemonic strategies are faulty in the sense that they are misused and often do not lead to an improvement in memory.

memory strategies of preschoolers

That preschoolers deliberately use memory strategies seems clear from a number of different studies. For example, Wellman (1988) asked 3 year olds to bury a toy in a sandbox before leaving the room with the experimenter. Some of the children were asked to remember where they had buried the toy; others were asked if there was anything they would like to do before leaving, but were given no instructions about remembering the toy's location.

Strikingly, half the children who had been instructed to remember the toy's location *marked* it by placing a mound over the object, by marking the sand, or sometimes by placing another toy on top of it; only 20 percent of the no-instructions group did likewise (Figure 7.6).

Marking the toy's location is an intelligent and effective strategy. As we noted, however, many of the preschooler's memory strategies are not so effective. Heisel and Retter (1981) asked 3- and 5-year-old youngsters to hide an object in one of 196 separate containers arranged in a large 14 by 14 matrix and instructed some of them to remember where they had hidden the object. Significantly, many of the children in both age groups used memory strategies when they had been instructed to remember. The strategies used by the 5 year olds were often very effective—namely, hiding the object in one of the corner locations because they could be remembered and relocated very easily. But what is perhaps most striking is that the 3 year olds' strategies, while every bit as consistent as those of the older children, were often very ineffective. Almost half of these 3 year olds tried to hide the object in the same location on every trial, thus demonstrating that they were using a systematic strategy; but the location was typically somewhere near the center of the array. As a result, when they were later asked to find the object these children fared almost as poorly as those who had not used any strategy.

The overuse of an inappropriate memory strategy is one of the most common mistakes made by young children trying to remember, says Wellman (1988). An important developmental change in memory strategies is a gradual reduction in the use of faulty strategies

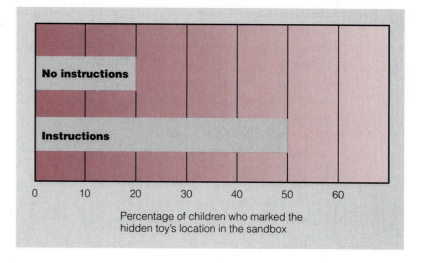

Of 3 year olds asked to hide a toy in a sand-box, half who were asked to try to remember where the toy was hidden (the instructions group) marked its location; only 20 percent of the no-instructions group did likewise. Pre-schoolers may be capable of using simple memory strategies, but often do not do so spontaneously.

No instructions

Instructions

0   10   20   30   40   50   60

Percentage of children who marked the hidden toy's location in the sandbox

and an increase in more effective strate-gies. Effective strategies increase dramati-cally in elementary school.

A preschooler's increasing ability to re-member results in part from increasing familiarity with things and events. For example, Saarnio (1993) showed that the more familiar preschoolers were with certain scenes, the better they were able to remember objects in the scenes.

The development of memory skills may also depend on social interaction. Recall from Chapter 2 that Vygotsky (1977) argues that a child's learning pro-cess is guided by interaction with adults or more advanced peers. When Harris and Hamidullah (1993) asked mothers to teach their 4 year olds to remember dif-ferent things (like the names of four car-toon characters or the location of animals in a zoo), the mothers spontaneously used strategies. The most common strat-egy used was rehearsal (repeating and having children repeat). In addition, many mothers combined these verbal re-hearsal strategies with nonverbal strate-gies such as pointing out cues (like spots on the cartoon dog, whose name was Spotty the Dog).

Ornstein, Baker-Ward, and Naus (1988) summarize the progression of

children's development of memory strat-egies in the following five stages:

1. In the beginning, young children don't deliberately use strategies to remember.

2. Preschoolers may occasionally use strategies, but these efforts don't al-ways result in memory improvement.

3. In the early elementary school years, children use somewhat more effective strategies but are often distracted by irrelevant information.

4. Later, strategies become increasingly effective and are applied in a variety of settings.

5. Finally, as a result of repeated practice with memory strategies, their use be-comes habitual and automatic.

In summary, preschoolers are clearly able to remember. But in most cases, memory results not from the deliberate use of memory strategies, but from *incidental mnemonics*—for example, pay-ing attention to something or being ex-posed to it more than once. In contrast, elementary-school children often delib-erately use memory strategies.

table **7.2**

Piaget's stages of cognitive development

STAGE	APPROXIMATE AGE	SOME MAJOR CHARACTERISTICS
Sensorimotor	0–2 years	Motoric intelligence World of the here and now No language, no thought in early stages No notion of objective reality

Preoperational
    Preconceptual
    Intuitive
	2–7 years
	2–4 years
	4–7 years
		Egocentric thought
		Reason dominated by perception
		Intuitive rather than logical solutions
		Inability to conserve

Concrete operations	7 to 11 or 12 years	Ability to conserve Logic of classes and relations Understanding of numbers Thinking bound to the concrete Development of reversibility in thought
Formal operations	11 or 12 to 14 or 15 years	Complete generality of thought Propositional thinking Ability to deal with the hypothetical Development of strong idealism

One of the important differences between older memorizers and preschoolers is that older children have acquired some understanding of the processes involved in learning and remembering. They have developed intuitive notions of themselves as information processors capable of applying strategies and of monitoring and changing them as required. In the current jargon, they have developed some of the skills involved in **metamemory** (defined as the knowledge that children have about the processes involved in remembering) (Borkowski, Milstead, & Hale, 1988). (More about the memories of older children in Chapter 9).

cognitive development in preschoolers: Piaget's view

n Chapter 5 we looked at the **sensorimotor period** of infancy—Piaget's first major stage of intellectual development, so called because an infant's intelligence involves immediate sensation and percep-

tion. The next major stage, spanning the preschool years, involves **preoperational thought**.

In Piaget's theory, an operation is a thought characterized by some specific logical properties; it is a logical thought. When Robert believes he has more gum when he rolls it into a fat ball and less when he spreads it out like a thin pancake on his sister's pillow, he is demonstrating preoperational (or prelogical) thinking. His thinking is not yet characterized by **reversibility**; that is, he doesn't yet understand either the possibility or the implications of *undoing* an action mentally.

Piaget divides the preoperational period (ages 2 to about 7 years) into two subperiods. The first, lasting from 2 to 4, is termed **preconceptual**; the second, from 4 to 7, is called *intuitive* (Table 7.2).

preconceptual thinking

As we saw, young infants' intelligence is initially rooted in sensation and action,

Between the ages of 2 and 4, children begin to classify objects they encounter by noting their characteristics. At first, through what Piaget labels transductive reasoning, this girl might conclude that here are a whole bunch of dogs—a sort of preconcept. Eventually, however, long tails, hooves, and snorting noises will help her identify these as horses.

but toward the end of the second year, and especially with the advent of language, infants begin to symbolize. Now they can represent their actions mentally and anticipate consequences before the action actually occurs. Also, they have begun to develop some understanding of causes—of actions as means to ends.

PRECONCEPTS

As children begin to symbolize they develop the ability both to internalize objects and events in the environment and to relate them by their common properties. Thus they develop **concepts**. But these concepts are not as complete and logical as adults' and are therefore referred to as **preconcepts**.

Despite their incompleteness, preconcepts nevertheless enable children to

make simple classifications necessary for identifying various things. Thus children recognize an adult because they have a budding concept that tells them that an adult is whatever walks on two legs, is very tall, and speaks in a gruff voice. By noting their characteristics, children can identify dogs, birds, elephants, and houses. What children frequently cannot do, however, is distinguish among different individuals belonging to the same species. Piaget (1951) illustrates this with his son, Laurent, who one day pointed out a snail to his father as they were walking. Several minutes later they came upon another snail, and the child exclaimed that here again was *the* snail. The child's failure to recognize that similar objects can belong to the same class and still be different objects—that is, that they can retain an identity of their own—is an example of a preconcept. A related example is the preschooler who steadfastly continues to believe in Santa Claus, even after seeing 10 different Santas on the same day. For the child they are all identical (Lefrançois, 1967).

There are two other striking features of children's reasoning processes during the preconceptual period, evident in *transductive reasoning* and *syncretic reasoning*.

TRANSDUCTIVE REASONING

Transduction can be contrasted with the two main types of logical reasoning: deduction and induction. To deduce is to go from the general to the particular. For example, from my knowledge that mammals give birth to live young, I might deduce that a specific mammal such as a three-toed sloth gives birth to tiny live sloths. In contrast, to induce is to go from specific examples to a broader generalization. After observing a number of barn swallows build nests of a mixture of mud and a cementlike type of saliva, I might generalize that all (or most) barn swallows build similar nests.

Transductive reasoning makes inferences from one particular to another—that is, from one instance to another—often because of superficial similarities. It is very much like inductive reasoning except that it is based on a single case rather than many. If I find that one red-headed person has a particularly charming personality, I might transduce that all red-headed people will also be charming. Transductive reasoning can occasionally—and somewhat accidentally—lead to a correct inference; it can also lead to totally incorrect conclusions. Consider the following example:

A flies; B flies; therefore B is A.

Clearly, if A is a bird and B is also a bird, then A is a B and vice versa. However, if A is a plane and B is a bird, the same reasoning process leads to an incorrect conclusion. Thus it is that a young preschooler can unashamedly insist that cats are dogs and chickens are turkeys.

SYNCRETIC REASONING

Preschoolers' classification behavior is also marked by the use of **syncretic reasoning**, in which different objects are grouped according to the child's limited and frequently changing rules. For example, a 2-year-old child who is placed in front of a table bearing a number of objects of different kinds and colors and who is asked to group objects that go together might reason something like this: The blue truck goes with the red truck because they both are trucks, and this thing goes with them because it's blue and that truck is blue. Here's a ball and here's a marble and they go together, and here's a crayon that's yellow like the ball, so it goes with them too.

The important point is that preschoolers' classification rules change constantly; they see little reason to use the same rule consistently. We adults, whose thinking is not so magical, do not have the same luxury.

intuitive thinking

The period of **intuitive thinking** begins at about age 4 and ends at approximately 7. It is labeled *intuitive* because although children solve many problems correctly, they do not always do so using logic. During this period their thinking is said to be intuitive, egocentric, perception-dominated, and characterized by classification errors.

In one of Piaget's problems designed to explore intuitive thinking, three balls are shown to a child and then inserted into a cardboard tube so that the child can no longer see them. The balls are blue, red, and yellow. At first, when the tube is held vertically, the child knows clearly which ball is on top. Then the tube is turned a half rotation (180 degrees), and the child is asked which ball is now at the top. Alternatively, it may be turned a full rotation, one and one-half turns, two turns, and so on. Piaget found that as long as preschoolers could continue to "imagine" (keep track of) the position of the balls inside the tube, they could answer correctly, but they could not arrive at a rule about the relationship between odd and even numbers of turns or half turns and the location of the balls. They solved the problem through *intuitive* mental images rather than logical reasoning.

CLASSIFICATION PROBLEMS OF PRESCHOOLERS

Preschoolers' difficulties with class inclusion are easily demonstrated in experiments in which children are shown a collection of objects made up of two subclasses—for example, a handful of wooden beads of which 15 are brown and five are blue. The subject is asked what the objects are. "Wooden beads," says the child. The experimenter then divides the beads into subclasses, brown and blue, and asks whether there are more brown beads or more wooden beads. The trick is obvious, you say? Not to a child at this stage of development. "There's more brown beads," the child replies, as though breaking down a class into its subparts destroys the parent class.

PRESCHOOLER EGOCENTRICITY

In one Piaget study, a girl doll and a boy doll are suspended side by side on a piece of string in plain view of a child. The experimenter, holding one end of the string in each hand, steps behind a screen so that the dolls are hidden from the child's view. The child is asked to predict which of the dolls will appear first if the experimenter moves the string toward the right. Let us assume that the boy doll appears first. The experimenter then hides the dolls again and repeats the same question: "Which of the dolls will come out first if they are moved to the same side again?" The procedure is repeated several times regardless of whether the child answers correctly. A normally intelligent child will answer correctly for every early trial. What happens in later trials is striking: The child eventually makes the opposite and clearly incorrect prediction! If asked why, one of the more common answers is that it is not fair that the same doll comes out first every time; now it is the other doll's turn. Children inject their own values, their own sense of justice, into the experimental situation, demonstrating their egocentric thought processes. The term **egocentric** is not derogatory but simply points out an excessive reliance on the thinker's individual point of view coupled with a corresponding inability to be objective.

Egocentric thought is further demonstrated by preschoolers' inability to imagine what a mountain looks like when seen from another point of view—for example, from the top or bottom or another side. It is apparent too in what Piaget terms egocentric speech, the characteristic self-talk of budding young linguists who repeat words and sounds to themselves—much as young prelingual infants might babble, but using real words. Egocentricity abounds as well in the conversations of young children in which speakers pay little attention to their listeners or to other speakers, except that they sometimes take turns in delivering their little pronouncements:

Geoff: It's a black one.

Jason: I have to go home soon.

Geoff: I'm going to find a red one.

Jason: I'm thirsty.

Geoff: I don't like black ones.

A conversation? No: More a *collective monologue,* according to Piaget. But real conversations, which require the nonego-centric ability to adopt another's point of view, are not far behind (and are discussed later in this chapter).

PRESCHOOLERS' RELIANCE ON PERCEPTION

Preschoolers' perceptions also dominate thinking, as is easily shown in Piaget's **conservation** problems (see Chapter 9). In a typical conservation-of-mass problem, for example, a child is shown two identical balls of modeling clay (or similar substance) and acknowledges that there is the same amount of clay in each. One of the balls is then either flattened into a thin pancake, broken into small pieces, rolled into a long snake, or otherwise deformed. The child now believes that the altered shape(s) contains either more or less clay, depending on its appearance. Preoperational children rely on actual perception of the object rather than on any of the logical rules that will later govern thinking (for example, nothing has been added to or taken away from the clay, and so it must still contain an identical amount). Figure 7.7 illustrates simple tasks that can be used to demonstrate some of the important prelogical characteristics of preschoolers' thought processes.

replications of Piaget's work

An increasing number of researchers, sometimes referred to as neo-Piagetians, no longer consider it appropriate to refer to preschool children as "prelogical." Preschoolers' logic may not be as advanced as yours or mind, and there may be something to be learned by contrasting it with a more advanced logic, but it is, nevertheless, a logic that is worthy of study in its own right.

The term *neo-Piagetian* is a collective word for developmental theorists whose research stems from a Piagetian tradition, but who have gone beyond where Piaget stopped. It includes all those who continue to replicate his work, and in a loose sense, those who ponder his questions and his answers.

Literally hundreds of studies have been conducted to investigate Piaget's view of children's progression through stages of cognitive development. With a few exceptions, most have found that the sequence described by Piaget is valid, not only in European and North American countries, but in many other parts of the world as well. For example, when Opper (1977) looked at the classification abilities of preoperational children in Thailand and Malaysia, she found that they, like Piaget's subjects, believed that a bouquet consisting of seven roses and two orchids contained "more roses than flowers." Other cross-cultural research is in general agreement that the sequence described by Piaget is cross-culturally valid (Dasen, 1977). However, some evidence shows that Piaget's estimates of the ages of attainment are, in effect, underestimates for some North American and European children on specific tasks. This evidence typically comes from experiments that attempt to make it simpler for children to demonstrate knowledge of the concept or ability in question. Some of these studies, for example, concern Piaget's "mountain" problems, which illustrates children's egocentricity (inability to adopt someone else's point of view).

In this study, children observed three mountains of unequal height set on top of a table. They were allowed to walk

Preconceptual period: 2–4 years	Preconceptual	Similar objects are assumed to be identical.
	Transductive	Reasoning from particular to particular.
		A dog (is furry, likes balls) (is furry, likes balls, must also be a dog)
	Syncretic	Groupings according to idiosyncretic and changing criteria.
		"Put those that go together on the table."
Intuitive period: 4–7 years	Intuitive	Tube is rotated; child must predict order of balls, but cannot do so unless the rotations are so few that they can be "imagined."
	Perception-dominated	Child admits two balls of clay are "the same" in A. In B, where one has been flattened, child thinks amount has been changed.
		A B 1 2 1 2
	Egocentric	Boy and girl dolls are behind screen. They are always brought out on the same side so that the boy always appears first. Child eventually predicts the other doll should be first: "It's her turn."
	Prone to errors of classification	Child realizes some flowers are daisies, fewer are tulips, but answers "Daisies" to the question: "Are there more flowers or more daisies?"

f i g u r e   7 . 7

Tasks and experiments concerned with preoperational thought

around the display to become familiar with all sides of the mountains. Later they sat on one side of the table, a doll was placed on the other side, and they were asked to select photographs representing the doll's point of view. Piaget found that children in the preoperational period usually indicated that the doll would see the same things they themselves saw, a finding that he interpreted as evidence of egocentricity.

When Piaget's mountain task is made simpler, children sometimes respond quite differently. Liben (1975) asked preschoolers to describe what a white card would look like from both their and the experimenter's point of view under a number of different conditions involving wearing colored glasses. In one condition, for example, the experimenter would wear green-tinted glasses and the children, no glasses. A correct, nonegocentric response in this case would be

that the card would look green to the experimenter. Liben found that almost half the 3 year olds answered correctly, and most of the older children had no difficulty with the questions. Similarly, when Hughes (reported in Donaldson, 1978) presented preschoolers with a situation in which they had to determine whether a "police officer" could see a doll from a vantage point quite different from the child's, subjects had little difficulty determining what the officer's point of view would actually be (see Figure 7.8).

Do these studies mean that Piaget's conclusions about preoperational children's egocentricity are invalid? The answer is no. Donaldson (1978) points out that all these studies present children with problems that are really very different from the problem of the mountains. A child who can accurately predict whether a police officer can see into an area when the officer is on the opposite side of the

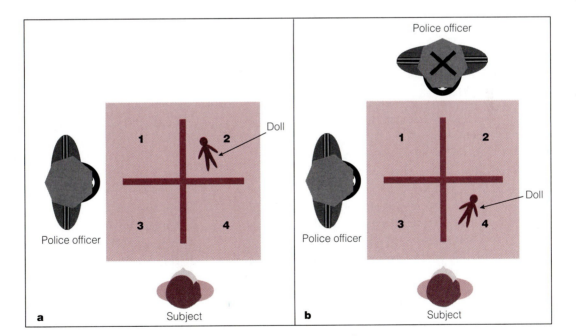

f igure 7.8

Arrangement for the Hughes experiment. (a) Subjects had to determine whether a doll hidden in 1, 2, 3, or 4 could be seen by the police officer at left. (b) In a later part of the experiment, a second police officer was placed at X. The child then had to decide where the doll would have to be hidden so as not to be seen by either officer. Preschoolers had little trouble answering correctly.

table from the child should not be expected to be able to describe what the physical array would look like to the officer. Among other things, doing so would require that the child be able to reverse left and right (in other words, that the child realize that the officer's left is the child's right)—a task that is sometimes difficult even for adults, as those of us who have occasionally been surprised by our movements in mirrors can testify.

What these and related studies most clearly point out is that egocentricity and other characteristics of children's thinking are far more complex than had been suspected. Indeed, they are far more complex than Piaget himself had suspected, and it is only recently that neo-Piagetians have begun to explore that complexity. The most striking thing about these recent investigations is their emphasis on what preoperational children *can* do, rather than on what they *cannot* do. As Flavell (1985) notes, it is now inappropriate and misleading to think of a preschool child's mind as preoperational or pre-conceptual.

cognitive achievements of preschoolers

Among the most significant cognitive advances that occur during the preschool years are symbolic representation, classification, and number concepts.

SYMBOLIC REPRESENTATION

First, there are monumental advances in a child's ability to represent the world symbolically. According to Fischer and Silvern's (1985) summary of neo-Piagetian research, this level, which they label *representations*, first emerges between the ages of 18 and 24 months. Accordingly, the ability to represent has its roots in sensorimotor development and is probably most evident in language.

CLASSIFICATION

A second major class of achievements during the preschool period is described by Fischer and Silvern (1985) as *relations of a few representations*. These capabilities appear around the age of 4 to 5 years and are evident in children's ability to solve problems that require understanding relationships among different ideas. For example, when Smith (1979) asked 4 year olds questions of the type, "A basenji is a kind of dog but not a poodle. Is a basenji an animal?" many answered correctly. Similarly, many had no difficulty with questions of the form, "An abalone is a kind of food but not a plant. Is an abalone a vegetable?" These are class-inclusion questions; they require at least some knowledge of class membership (animals include dogs; nonplants are not included among vegetables). They depend on the child's ability to relate concepts.

NUMBER CONCEPTS

Also included among abilities that fall within *relations of a few representations* is preschoolers' remarkable understanding of numbers. There are few preschoolers who cannot count objects and who do not understand that six jellybeans is more than four. Indeed, most will tell you without prompting that six is exactly two more than four, or that if you had seven jellybeans to begin with and your little brother ate five of them, you would have only two left. Children *invent* their own solutions for problems of this kind, claims Aubrey (1993). As a result, they come to school with a wide range of competencies, not all of which are always taken into account by the school curriculum.

Gelman (1982; Gelman & Gallistel, 1978) identifies two kinds of knowledge about numbers that appear during the preschool period. First there are *number abstraction skills* that give children an understanding of numerosity—of how many things there are in a collection of, say, snails in one's pockets. Second, there are *numerical reasoning principles* that allow children to reason about or predict the outcome of certain simple numerical operations, such as adding to or taking from.

Gelman identifies five principles that allow us to count. We take them completely for granted in spite of the fact that they are remarkably complex and wonderfully logical. And, amazingly, preschoolers *discover* these principles and actually use them in ways far more logical than we had expected.

The *one-on-one principle* says that if you are to count something, you must assign a single number to each item and you must include every item in your assignment, but no item can be assigned more than one number.

The *stable order principle* requires that the assignment of numbers to items be sequential, successive, and nonarbitrary; that is, the correct order for counting is always one, two, three, and never one, three, two. Of course, the neophyte counter may indulge in certain idiosyncrasies, may distort the conventional sequence or invent a brand new one, as in, "One, two, free, eleben, twenty!" What is remarkable, however, is that children who invent such a sequence will often use it repeatedly, in stable order.

The *cardinal principle* says that the last number assigned to the last item in a collection describes the *numerosity* of that collection. Gelman (1982) points out that many children as young as 2½ or 3 years old appear to understand this principle even when they are still incapable of verbalizing it. For example, some children will successfully count five objects (say, flamingos), but will then be uncertain about what to answer when the examiner asks, "How many pink flamingos are

Not all preschoolers are as gifted as this little urchin; but most can tell you without hesitation that if you had seven jellybeans to begin with and your little brother ate five of them, you would have only two left. This 4 year old doing premath homework might even be able to name the mathematical operation involved. Piaget is sometimes criticized for having focused too much on what preschoolers cannot do—and too little on the remarkable cognitive achievements of children during this period.

there in the pail?" But when a puppet subsequently counts out the flamingos— "One flamingo, two flamingos, three . . . , four . . . , five flamingos!"—and then announces, "There are four flamingos!" children may spot the error immediately.

The three counting principles just described explain how to count; a fourth, the *abstraction principle,* relates to what can be counted. It says, in effect, that anything can be counted: yuppies, puppies, and guppies; ponies and baloneys; hops, skips, and jumps. Four year olds behave as though they are completely aware of this. If you ask them how many things there are in the car, they may count people and books, dogs and steering wheels, ignition keys, and various other gidgets and gadgets. They know, intuitively and brilliantly, that objects do not have to belong to the same class to be countable—that countability is an abstraction that belongs to everything.

Finally, the *order irrelevance principle* states that the order in which items are counted does not matter, that to successfully count the three animals in the garage requires only the assignment of a number, in correct sequence, once to each of the items. The horse can be one, the hedgehog two, and the toad three; or the toad can be one, the horse two, the hedgehog three. In one of Gelman's studies, a puppet leads the child to count objects in different orders, and then exclaims, "I tricked you. I made you make them all number one!" But children are seldom confused by this procedure. It is as though, with the understanding of the counting principles, there comes an understanding that numbers do not belong to objects or events—that they are abstractions that can be applied to all events, subject only to the logical rules that give them meaning.

Number abstraction and numerical reasoning skills are important and complex cognitive abilities that illustrate dramatically some of the achievements of preschoolers. These achievements stand in sharp contrast to Piaget's view of the deficits in preoperational thought (Gold, 1986).

As Gelman (1978) notes, our preoccupation with what preschool children cannot do has blinded us to their achievements. Research has only recently begun to pay attention to the fact that preschoolers are not egocentric in all situations, have considerable understanding of numbers, and can classify and make logical inferences under a variety of circumstances. Also, as we have known for some time but have not always emphasized, their language development is nothing short of phenomenal. In short, preschoolers are a tremendous cognitive distance from sensorimotor children.

Can their capabilities be influenced through preschool education? Should they be?

preschool education

These questions concerning preschool education are a source of considerable current debate. On one side of the debate are people such as Elkind (1987), who fears that so fearlessly and relentless do we push our children toward competence that *the hurried child* misses much of childhood, and Sigel (1987), who deplores the *hothouse* atmosphere of many early childhood programs. There are a number of misconceptions about preschool education, say Canning and Lyon (1991). One is the assumption that children *need* to be given experiences not provided in most homes; another is the belief that structured experiences (such as learning to play the violin as a toddler, or being taught a second language) will inevitably have a beneficial effect on a child's development in general. This "myth of early experience," write Canning and Lyon (1991), has led us to forget that "the adult's role in preschool environments should be to provide appropriate play opportunities and be available to children" (p. 2).

On the other side of the debate are people such as Doman (1984) and Eastman and Barr (1985), who reason that preschool children can benefit tremendously from formal academic instruction. Even infants can be—and, according to

Doman, should be—taught basic reading skills. Accordingly, there has been a strong trend toward providing progressively more structured educational programs at the preschool level. This trend, says Rescorlo (1991), stems from psychology's emphasis on the importance of early experience, a perception of decline in achievement of North American students relative to other groups (for example, the Japanese), and parents' desire for their children to be the best.

There is no simple and clear resolution for this debate, which may be one reason why there are so many different forms of preschool education programs. Some are distinct; they are describable in terms of specific principles and procedures. The majority, however, are highly eclectic. They include kindergartens, nurseries, preschools, playschools, intervention programs, compensatory education programs, and day-care centers (day-care is discussed in Chapter 8). They are found in schools and homes, in church basements and community centers, in parks and shopping malls, in universities and technical schools, even in office build-

ings. Their offerings are a varied mixture dictated in part by the ages of their charges, the resources available, the wishes of parents, the restrictions and mandates of local laws and regulations, and the inclinations and capabilities of instructors and caregivers.

preschool education elsewhere

When cars stop at busy intersections in Manila and Quezon City in the Philippines, says Tsuchiyama (1992), children rush out to sell things or to beg for money. "They are called 'street children,'" he writes. "They have dropped out of school. . . . [T]hey sleep on the roadside" (p. 56).

In the Philippines, almost 20 percent of children ages 6 to 11 are not enrolled in school; one-third of all children don't graduate from fourth grade. Similarly, in Africa and in most other developing countries, fewer than 50 percent of all children attend primary schools; many drop out before they finish (Grant, 1992). And in most of the world's poorer countries, only a tiny percentage—those from rich families—have access to preschool education.

But in North America and much of Europe, children have free (even compulsory) access not only to elementary and high schools, but also to a tremendous assortment of preschools, including nursery schools, compensatory preschool programs, and kindergartens.

nursery schools

For many years nursery schools were among the most prevalent form of preschool education. They typically take in very young preschoolers and emphasize social and emotional development. Their principal activities consist of games, dancing, singing, listening to stories, and so on—many of the functions that are also performed by good day-care facilities. Clarke-Stewart (1984) reports that children who attend nursery schools are, on the average, more self-reliant, more outgoing, more spontaneous, and more confident than comparable children who do not attend nursery school.

compensatory preschool programs

Compensatory preschool programs are designed to make up for initial deficits in children. The best known and most massive compensatory education program ever undertaken in the United States was project Head Start, which began in 1964 and was conceived as part of that country's "war on poverty." The program allocated large amounts of funds to the creation of eight-week summer programs for children from disadvantaged backgrounds. Almost three decades later, the Head Start budget has grown to almost $3 billion, and almost 800,000 preschoolers are enrolled in the program ("Bush calls for unprecedented increase . . . ," 1992).

Because of the variety of approaches used in these projects, it has been difficult to assess their effectiveness. Many early studies indicated that children enrolled in Head Start programs continued to be inferior to more advantaged children who had not been exposed to such programs, and critics were quick to conclude that huge amounts of money had been squandered in poorly planned, poorly executed, and basically ineffective programs (Bronfenbrenner, 1977b). However, subsequent research has sometimes found quite dramatic improvements resulting from Head Start programs. Lee, Brooks-Gunn and Schnur (1988) note that earlier researchers often failed to look at initial differences between groups exposed to Head Start and comparison groups. When they found that disadvantaged groups were still disadvantaged *after* the programs, they concluded that the programs had not worked. A study of 969 subjects conducted by Lee and associates (1988) found that although Head Start programs did not eliminate the difference between Head Start children and comparison groups, they reduced it.

Following a review of various studies of Head Start programs, Haskins (1989) concludes that there is no doubt that such programs have an immediate, positive impact on children, although the long-term effects are neither as pronounced nor as clear. However, the best forms of preschool education may produce detectable long-term benefits in "life success measures"—such as, for example, reductions in teen age pregnancy, delinquency, unemployment, and reliance on welfare assistance.

What are these "best" forms of preschool intervention? It depends, of course, on what the goals are. If we measure success in terms of preparation for academic tasks, the most effective forms of intervention are typically highly specific, "model" approaches (Haskins, 1989). Such programs are usually based on identifiable theories and characterized by well-formulated approaches and carefully developed materials. Among the better-known model approaches that have sometimes been used as Head Start programs (or in other nursery school or kindergarten programs) are the Direct Instruction Approach and the Montessori Method.

DIRECT INSTRUCTION

The *direct instruction approach*, initiated by Bereiter and Engelmann (1966), presents a sharp contrast to the traditional approach of most kindergartens and nursery schools. Instead of being primarily child-centered and emphasizing social and emotional development, it is instructor-centered and emphasizes the teaching of skills and concepts. Instructional methods are highly structured and involve *telling* children and *asking* them to repeat, alone or in unison. It teaches reading, language, and arithmetic. Not surprisingly, it has shown some marked positive results in these areas.

Direct instruction has its critics, however. Some people fear that such approaches place too much emphasis on learning basics, on repetition, on drill, and on success. They argue that the high-pressure, achievement-oriented principles that underlie direct instruction violate our fundamental belief in the rights of children to play, to enjoy, to dream, and to make magical, nonrealistic things.

THE MONTESSORI METHOD

The *Montessori method*, which dates back to the turn of the twentieth century (Montessori, 1912), is another highly structured approach to preschool education. It was initially developed for use with mentally retarded children but has proven to be effective and popular as a general program. Unlike most preschool programs, it is designed for use in elementary and high schools as well.

One of the distinctive features of the Montessori method is the use of specially developed materials for teaching sense discriminations (how to differentiate among related stimuli such as sounds or colors). Montessori believed that all learning stems from sense perception and can therefore be improved by training the senses. Perhaps the best known of her materials are large letters of the alphabet, covered with sandpaper, that are used to teach children to read. The prescribed teaching method requires not only that children look at the letters, but that they also trace their shapes with their finger tips, saying the sound of the letter and getting a tactile sensation of it at the same time. (See Figure 7.9 for some other examples of Montessori materials.)

Evaluations of Montessori programs have generally been quite positive, in spite of the criticism that such programs, given their highly structured nature, might stifle a child's creativity. For example, a study of the long-term effects of preschool programs found that the highest achievers in grades six, seven, and eight were males who had been exposed to a preschool Montessori program (Miller & Bizzell, 1983).

kindergartens

Not long ago, kindergartens were usually considered an optional preschool program. Now, a majority of North American children attend kindergartens, most of which are housed in regular schools, funded in the same manner as

Solid geometrical insets

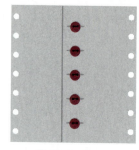

Lacing frame

Buttoning frame

Sound boxes

The tower   The broad stair

A   B   C

Plane geometric inserts (made of metal)
A. Tracing negative area
B. Tracing positive area
C. Use of colored crayons (left to right)

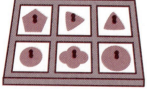
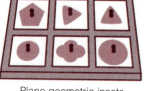

Plane geometric insets

Sandpaper boards

Plane geometric forms
(in three series)

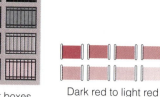

Color boxes   Dark red to light red

Some traditional Montessori materials. Some are designed to promote sense discrimination (for example, the sound or the color boxes; the sandpaper boards); some, to encourage the development of motor skills (the lacing and buttoning frames); some, the use of precise fine-motor movements (the geometric insets, which are best grasped with the finger tips and are also used for tracing).

schools, and staffed by teachers whose certification requirements are the same as those who teach at more advanced levels. In many ways, kindergartens are part of regular school. Many no longer simply prepare children for the first-grade tasks of learning to read and write and count; they actually engage in the business of teaching these things (if the children don't already know them). One of the big differences between kindergarten and regular schools, in most (but no longer all) jurisdictions, is that kindergartners can go home at lunch time and stay there the rest of the afternoon, or they can stay home all morning and go to school only in the afternoon.

But perhaps we are *hurrying* our children too much, Elkind (1981a) warns. Perhaps we should let them slow down and be children, play and dream, and do magical things that don't require knowing how to read and write and count things in perfect sequence.

Not only are we hurrying our children, says Elkind (1987), but many parents are also *miseducating* them. These parents are "Gold Medal" parents whose burning ambition is to produce a star basketball or hockey player, a world-class gymnast, a violin prodigy. Or they are "College Degree" parents whose babies are destined for Harvard or MIT. For these parents, children have become symbols of parental ambitions and proof of parental success.

We must strike a balance, Elkind (1981a) urges, between the *spoiled* child, who remains a child too long, and the *hurried* child, who does not remain a child long enough and whose life might be plagued by ". . . a fear of failure—of not achieving fast enough or high enough" (p. xii). The description of a kindergarten in China in "In Other Contexts: Wai Wong's Kindergarten" provides some perspective in this matter.

Numerous researchers insist that the essential requirement for an effective intervention program is to take into account the family as a childrearing unit and to provide conditions that will ameliorate a negative home environment (see, for example, McCartney & Howley, 1992). Accordingly, health, nutrition, housing, and employment must be raised to adequate levels if intervention programs are be effective. And parents need to be involved directly in the program, although how they are involved is also critical (White, Taylor, & Moss, 1992).

Bronfenbrenner (1977b) describes a sequential, five-stage strategy for intervention. It begins before parenthood (*Stage 1: Preparation for Parenthood*), and its goal is to give schoolchildren adequate information about the care of children and the nutritional and health requirements of pregnant women. The second stage (*Stage 2: Before Children Come*) involves taking steps to ensure that the family into which a child will be born will provide adequate shelter, food, and economic security. The third stage (*Stage 3: The First Three Years of Life*) is concerned with the establishment of emotional bonds between parents and children through caregiving activities and other interactions. Not until the fourth stage (*Stage 4: Ages 4 Through 6*) does intervention in the form of a preschool program begin. Bronfenbrenner suggests that this program be cognitively oriented and that it involve parents directly. Nor does intervention cease when children enter first grade. In the fifth stage (*Stage 5: Ages 6 through 12*), parents are encouraged to become highly involved in school activities. However, for many parents who work outside the home, becoming involved in school activities may be very

Wai Wong attends East-is-Red Kindergarten in Canton, China. Today the children have been told there will be visitors. Lei has been given the honor of watching the door.

"They're coming," shouts Lei, and everyone stops their work and applauds loudly, calling out several times in unison Ni hao anti, the traditional greeting meaning "Hello uncles and aunts."

The visitors, a delegation of American and Canadian early childhood educators, enter amid smiles of welcome. But almost immediately, everyone in the class turns back to their work. And during the course of the next hour, the teacher directs the students in a series of lessons, demonstrations, games, and songs not dramatically different from what might be seen in a North American kindergarten. Nevertheless, delegation members notice some differences. First, the room seems stark, lit with two naked lightbulbs, the walls painted white, the floor made of stone. The simplicity of the physical plant, the visitors later discover, is not uncommon in much of China, although many preschools are brighter, more cheerfully decorated, and better equipped (Kessen, 1975). In contrast, unlike the adults in the community, who all seem to be dressed in the same drab, colorless clothes, the children are dressed in brightly colored clothing, and the girls, like Wai Wong, have bright ribbons in their hair.

But what strikes the delegation most is the eagerness of the children, their willingness to learn, their attentiveness, their laughter, their apparent happiness. "Not once during the whole morning," writes Sparkes (1990) of a visit to a similar preschool, "was there a tearful eye, a noncompliant behavior, or an aggressive interaction" (p. 21).

The delegation wonders, and asks why things are thus. Sometimes people are puzzled at their questions. Physical punishment is extremely rare in modern China; child abuse is almost unheard of (Korbin, 1981). "See the tree," says one teacher, pointing to a picture on the wall of a tree in glorious bloom. Such pictures are found in most preschools in China. The rows of blossoms indicate how well the children live up to the school's demands for four expressions of "beauty": beauty of the mind,

difficult. (See "At A Glance: Working Mothers and Preschool Children" for information on the number of preschoolers' mothers who work.)

language and the preschooler

More than three decades ago, psychologist Kevin Hayes and his wife Catherine tried to teach a chimpanzee to speak (Hayes & Hayes, 1951). They had reasoned that if any animal other than humans were ever to succeed in learning a language, a close biological relative like the chimpanzee would be the most likely candidate. But they failed miserably. It seems that the chimpanzee's vocal apparatus simply does not lend itself to *speaking* a language.

Some years later, a succession of researchers undertook to teach chimpanzees a different form of language: American Sign Language. Its big advantage is that it would not require chimpanzees (or gorillas) to make sounds, but simply to make gestures. A number of these researchers reported what seemed like remarkable success (for example,

beauty of language, beauty of behavior, and beauty of the environment (Norén Björn, 1982). To quarrel, to disobey, to refuse to cooperate—these would not be "beauty."

Another teacher emphasizes the unity, the cooperativeness, the socialism upon which Chinese society today is based. The rules are clear: The individual is subordinate to the organization; the minority is subordinate to the majority; the lower level is subordinate to the higher; and all is subordinate to the Central Committee (Liljeström, 1982). The rules are seen not as a form of oppression, but as a rational and sensible social system.

China, the delegation is repeatedly told, is not what it used to be. You would look in vain, now, for the children you would have seen at the turn of the twentieth century, "lice-ridden children... children with distended stomachs and spindly arms and legs... children who had been purposely deformed by beggars... children covered with horrible sores... children cast into

the streets to beg and forage in the garbage bins for subsistence" (Korbin, 1981, p. 167).

Children are our most prized possession, the Chinese insist. They treat them accordingly.

To Think About: Quick sketches such as these "In Other Contexts" inserts often mislead: They cannot deal with exceptions; nor can they provide the detail that is necessary for a more complete and accurate understanding. How would your quick sketch of a North American preschool compare with that of Wai Wong's school? What do the apparent differences and similarities tell us about cultures? About genetics?

Premack & Premack, 1972; Fouts, 1987). However, critics quickly insisted that none of the chimpanzees involved had actually learned a language. Detailed examinations of videotapes of "sign-speaking" chimpanzees seemed to indicate that what they had learned was simply to imitate—to associate a symbol or gesture with food, or to use some movement or gesture to make some demand associated with reinforcement (see, for example, Terrace, 1985). But the debate is by no means over, and researchers continue to report the development of "communicative" or "conversational"

competence among various nonhuman primates (see, for example, Greenfield & Savage-Rumbaugh, 1993).

Still, when language is defined as *the use of arbitrary sounds with established and accepted referents, either real or abstract, that can be arranged in sequence to convey different meanings*, it is still, as far as we know, uniquely human.

Children learn language so that they can communicate better. To understand language, say Bloom et al. (1988), we must take into consideration that it is an *intentional* behavior. The intention to express thoughts and to understand the

In 1991, 53 percent of U.S. children between the ages of 3 and 5 who lived at home with their mothers had mothers who were employed outside the home. In fact, more than half of all new mothers go back to work within one year of giving birth (U.S. Bureau of the Census, 1992). The number one reason for going back to work is financial need; career development and personal enjoyment are also important reasons (Volling & Belsky, 1993). Of the more than 11 million U.S. children ages 3 to 5 in 1991, over 6 million were in nursery schools and kindergartens. Only 14 percent of the 5 year olds were not enrolled in preprimary schools.

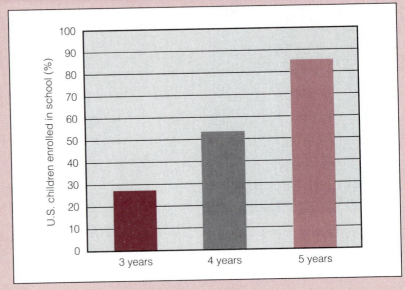

figure **7.10**

Preprimary school enrollment, 1991, for U.S. children ages 3 to 5. Source: Adapted from U.S. Bureau of the Census (1992), p. 147.

---

thoughts of others is the motive that leads a child to learn words and grammatical constructions.

language in infancy

In Chapter 5 we noted that infants seem remarkably well prepared to learn language. And parents, for their part, play the role of teacher, unconsciously "fine-tuning" their verbal interactions to a level appropriate for their infant.

The first three stages of language development in Wood's (1981) six-stage description (Table 7.3) span infancy. The first, the prespeech stage, lasts until around age 1 and is characterized by a transition from crying, gurgling, cooing, and babbling to the utterance of meaningful speech sounds.

table 7.3

Stages in children's development of language

STAGE OF DEVELOPMENT	NATURE OF DEVELOPMENT	SAMPLE UTTERANCES
1. Prespeech (before age 1)	Crying, cooing, babbling.	"Waaah," "dadadada."
2. Sentencelike word (holophrase) (by 12 months)	The word is combined with nonverbal cues (gestures and inflections).	"Mommy." (meaning: "Would you please come here, mother.")
3. Two-word sentences (duos) (by 18 months)	Modifiers are joined to topic words to form declarative, interrogative, negative, and imperative structures.	"Pretty baby." (declarative) "Where Daddy?" (interrogative) "No play." (negative) "More milk!" (imperative)
4. Multiple-word sentences (by 2 to 2½ years)	Both a subject and predicate are included in the sentence types. Grammatical morphemes ("-ing" or "-ed," for example) are used to change meanings.	"She's a pretty baby." (declarative) "Where Daddy is?" (interrogative) "I no can play." (negative) "I want more milk!" (imperative) "I running." "I runned."
5. More complex grammatical changes and word categories (between 2½ and 4 years)	Elements are added, embedded, and permuted within sentences. Word classes (nouns, verbs, and prepositions) are subdivided. Clauses are put together.	"Read it, my book." (conjunction) "Where is Daddy?" (embedding) "I can't play." (permutation) "I would like some milk." (use of "some" with mass noun) "Take me to the store." (use of preposition of place)
6. Adultlike structures (after 4 years)	Complex structural distinctions made, as with "ask-tell" and "promise."	"Ask what time it is." "He promised to help her."

Source: Based in part on Barbara S. Wood, (1981). *Children and communication: Verbal and nonverbal language development* (2nd ed.), p. 142. © 1981. Reprinted by permission of Prentice-Hall, Inc., Englewood Cliffs, New Jersey.

The second stage, that of the sentencelike word, appears around age 1. It involves the use of words with a repertoire of gestures, cries, and inflections, all to communicate meaning.

The third stage involves the use of two-word sentences (duos) and is evident by the age of 18 months. Increasing language sophistication now makes it possible for children to combine words with different modifiers to ask questions, make declarations, express denial, or issue commands (see Chapter 5 for more details).

The story continues here with a discussion of the remaining three stages.

multiple-word sentences

In time, children move from two-word combinations to multiple-word sentences. This typically occurs around the age of 2 to 2½. "Allgone dog" becomes "Dog is gone" and eventually "The dog is gone" or My dog is gone."

Note that the transition to multiple-word sentences does not mean that *all* expressions before this stage are limited to two or fewer words. In fact, many children use three- and four-word utterances very early in their development of language. Woods's point is that these earlier multiple-word combinations seldom use complete subjects and predicates and are less complete grammatically.

Although children's speech continues to be somewhat telegraphic, children now make increasing use of morphemes to express meaning (Brown, 1973). Recall that morphemes are the smallest units of meaning in language. They include all words, as well as grammatical endings such as "-ed" and "-ing," suffixes, prefixes, articles, and so on. The use of grammatical morphemes, for example, is what allows the child to transform the verbs *go* to *going*, *jump* to *jumped*, *eat* to *eated*, and *do* to *doed*.

Children's speech is often highly inventive. Carlson and Anisfeld (1969) report the case of a 29-month-old boy who manipulated phonemes in songs and rhymes. To the tune "The bear went over the mountain," he sang "Da de de doder da doundin"; and for "I've been working on the railroad," he sang "I pin purkin' on a pail poad." Another example of inventiveness in language occurred in the speech of my daughter Claire who, when about 3 and having learned that "pitch black" was very black, insisted that other things can be "pitch clean," "pitch empty," or "pitch big."

Other examples of inventiveness in early language are found in the words children create as they reinvent the grammatical rules of their language and discover the meanings of its many morphemes. "Daddy unpickmeup," insisted my youngest linguist, squirming to be put down. "You already feeded me."

more complex grammatical changes

Between the ages of 2½ and 3 or 4, children begin to acquire some of the more complex aspects of syntax (grammar). In particular, they develop the ability to make meaningful transformations, typically of one of three forms: *conjunction*, *embedding*, and *permutation* (Wood,

1981). Simple conjunction is illustrated by the addition or combination of the two sentences "Where?" and "We go" to form a third sentence, "Where we go?" Embedding is inserting. For example, the word "no" may be embedded in the sentence "I eat" to form a sentence with quite a different meaning: "I no eat." Permutation is altering the order of words in sentences to change their meaning. Initially, children make use of intonation rather than permutation. For example, the sentence "I can go" may be a simple declaration when the "I" or the "can" is emphasized but becomes a question when "go" is uttered with rising intonation. A simple permutation from "I can go" to "Can I go?" achieves the same meaning with much less ambiguity.

As children begin to show an understanding of various adult-accepted rules for transforming sentences, they also behave as though they had an implicit understanding of the grammatical function of various words and phrases. They use nouns as nouns and not as verbs, adjectives are no longer treated as verbs, and nouns are further categorized as plural or singular. Evidence of children's understanding of this type of categorization is evident in their appropriate use of both verbs and such determiners as "that," "the," "those," and "these." For example, the child will now say "That box is empty"; an earlier error might have taken the form of "This boxes is empty." (See "At A Glance: Speech at Age 4 Years, 6 Months" for an example of the use of invented sounds in one preschooler's language.)

adultlike structures

The further refinement and elaboration of speech requires mastery of countless subtle and intricate grammatical rules

Language development in the preschool period is almost explosive, so rapidly do children's vocabularies grow and the sophistication of their grammar improve. Rémi's story at 4½—with accompanying art—displays imagination and verbal skills far in advance of a 2 year old's.

added detail:
look at those elbows + knees

The Story of the Gas Station
(as told by Rémi—4 Years, 6 Months—with his Legos)

I'm going to fill up with regular. *Vrooooom.*

Thanks. *Vrr-rrr-rrr.*

I'm coming to fill it with regular. *Whtttt-taah.*

SMASH!!

Broken car now. They crashed into each other.

I want to oil my car.

Oh. Oh. I have a flat tire. I need some air.

Phhh. Phhh. Phhh.

Tchuuu.

I'm stuck. He broke the house down. He needs a new tire.

Neeowrr. Neeowrr.

WOWEE! He got a flat tire.

I need unleaded gas.

Tchuu. Schewww.

The end.

that we all use unconsciously. Some of these rules govern the arrangement of words in meaningful expressions; they specify what is (and is not) grammatically acceptable and meaningful. They tell us that "the fat mosquito" is a correctly structured phrase, but "Fat the mosquito" is not (although "Fat, the mosquito" might be). Other rules permit us to transform phrases or to combine them to create a variety of meaningful statements. Thus there are rules that allow us to transform a passive sentence into an active one ("The dog was bitten by the man" to "The man bit the dog") or a negative to a positive ("I did not go" to "I went"). Much of this learning occurs in the first elementary grades.

explanations of language development

Each of us uses language as if we had a relatively complete understanding of a tremendous range of grammatical rules. Yet, as Bereiter (1991) notes, unless we are taught these rules formally, we can't explain them. In fact, linguists have not yet been able to work out a complete set of consistent and valid rules even for a single language.

The remarkable thing is that, in an amazingly short time, young children acquire a working knowledge of a very complex system of rules. How?

There are two principal classes of explanations for the development of language. One emphasizes the role of experience (learning); the other emphasizes the importance of biology (hereditary predispositions). Current evidence suggests that biology and experience are both important but that each, by itself, does not present an entirely adequate explanation.

the role of early experience in language development

There is an overwhelming amount of learning involved in making the transition from the first meaningful sound to the fluent conversations of the 6 year old. Yet most children accomplish this learning apparently effortlessly and in much the same sequence across different cultures. "Children learn language," says Rice (1989), "as a means of talking about what they know so they can accomplish social goals important to them" (p. 153).

Strangely, however, adults who were initially without language (because of isolation, for example) do not fare as well. Recall Genie, the abandoned child described in Chapter 3. As a child she had been exposed to almost no language models (her father barked and growled at her), and although she was rescued at the age of 13½, attempts to teach her to speak were not very successful. Similarly, adults who try to acquire a second language usually experience more difficulty doing so than do young children; and even if they are successful, their pronunciation will typically be characterized by a variety of errors that would not be found among those who learned the language at a younger age. There appears to be a sensitive period early in life when learning one or more languages is easiest.

the role of parents as teachers of language

That children acquire the speech patterns, idioms, accents, and other language characteristics of the people around them makes it clear that learning is centrally involved in language acquisition. Parents and other caregivers play an important role as language models: They provide children with verbal and nonverbal models of correct language and of the subtle rules governing conversations and the communication of messages. Put another way, they provide models of the pragmatics, semantics, syntax, and phonology of language. In addition, parents also serve as important dispensers of reinforcement for the child's verbalizations.

In Chapter 5 we spoke of the bidirectionality of parent-child influence, noting that what a caregiver does influences the infant and that, no less true, what the infant does influences the caregiver. We see evidence of bidirectionality of influence in the development of language as well (Bruner, 1977, 1978; Stern et al., 1983). An infant's level of language comprehension and use appears to have subtle but marked effects on the behavior of parents. Bruner (1978) refers to a fine-tuning theory of mother-infant interaction ("mother" because she is more often the principal caregiver than is the father). His observations of mothers and their children led him to conclude that virtually all mothers alter their speech patterns according to the understanding of their children. It is as though the mother becomes a teacher, not because she consciously intends to be one, but because she "fine-tunes" her responses and behaviors to the immediate demands of her child. Furthermore, there is a consistency and regularity in the mother's altered speech patterns. One mother typically used four sequential types of statements when "reading" to her young son. First she would say "Look"—an attention-getting utterance. Next she would pose a standard question—"What is that?"—pause, and then provide a label: "It's an X." Finally, following the child's response, she would say, "That's right." Additional evidence of "fine-tuning" occurred whenever the child responded earlier in the sequence.

If, for example, he said "Truck" as soon as the page turned, the mother would go immediately to her final response: "That's right."

THE USE OF MOTHERESE (CHILD-DIRECTED LANGUAGE)

In later stages of language development, the role of the mother as sensitive, fine-tuned teacher becomes even more apparent. Boyd (1976) notes that the language mothers use when talking to their children—sometimes called **motherese** (or *child-directed language*)—is quite different from what they would normally use when speaking with adults. Motherese is a good example of pragmatics in language; the mother adjusts her speech to the requirements of the situation. Thus, mothers tend to use simpler, shorter, and more repetitive utterances. In other words, they *reduce* (by simplifying and repeating). On other occasions, mothers *expand* the child's expressions. A child might say, "Daddy gone," to which the mother might reply, "Yes, Daddy is gone." Moerk (1991) points out that most expansions are corrections, and that corrections of this kind are especially important in early language learning.

Studies of motherese in different languages have typically found that the most important features of mother-to-infant speech appear to be universal. For example, Grieser and Kuhl (1988) found this to be true even in Mandarin Chinese, which is very different from English in that it is *tonal* (inflection and intonation are far more meaningful). Mothers' speech in Mandarin Chinese also tends to be grammatically and semantically simpler and pitched at a higher frequency.

There are other, perhaps more subtle, ways in which the speech of a mother (or other caregivers, and even siblings) is influenced by the presence of infants.

child—an expectation that is confirmed by research (Rice, 1989).

Some children are fast language learners; others are much slower. For example, one study found a difference of 30 months between the fastest and the slowest learners among a sample of 128 3½ year olds (Wells, 1985). One of the differences between the fastest and the slowest learners may be the extent and quality of the motherese to which they are exposed. Hampson and Nelson (1993) videotaped a sample of 45 toddlers and analysed their speech and that of their mothers. They found that the mothers of the most linguistically advanced children used a higher percentage of object names in their speech, and fewer commands. Similarly, Furrow, Nelson, and Benedict (1979) report evidence that the shorter sentences, uncomplicated grammars, and absence of pronouns and complex verb tenses of motherese contribute positively to language development.

In summary, there is growing evidence that the mother (or father) plays a crucial role in the development of language and that this role goes well beyond providing a suitable model of the family's language. Unconsciously, parents modify their speech and become teachers—perhaps far better teachers than they could possibly be trained to be. As Moskowitz (1978) observes, the level of a mother's language usage appears to remain relatively constant at a stage very close to six months in advance of the child's level. From birth, there is an "interpersonal synchrony" between mother and infant (Schaffer, Collis, & Parsons, 1977); re-

Moskowitz (1978) describes the typical speech of caregivers as simpler, higher pitched, characterized by exaggerated intonation, made up of shorter sentences, and consisting of a higher than normal percentage of questions. In addition, the speech of caregivers vis-à-vis their infants is almost always centered on the present and only seldom on the past or future, almost as though they knew, as did Piaget, that the young infant's world is a world of the here and now. Accordingly, as Goodwin (1980) suggests, we would expect that most of the child's first words would deal with things that are immediate, directly perceivable, and important to the

search has scarcely begun to explore the nature and dimensions of this synchrony.

LANGUAGE ACQUISITION IN MISTREATED CHILDREN

Additional evidence of the importance of parent-infant interaction in language development is found in studies of mistreated children. Early evidence seemed to indicate that as many as 20 percent of abused children were delayed in language development (see, for example, Johnson & Morse, 1968). This finding is somewhat difficult to explain: Why should abuse, in and of itself, impede the normal development of language? More recent research, however, reveals that it is not so much *abuse* as *neglect* that is the important factor (Allen & Wasserman, 1985). Now the explanation is clearer. Abuse is typically defined as involving such actions as attacking, hitting, shoving, and beating, whereas neglect involves disregard of safety, inadequate nutrition, and inattention to health needs. In other words, the abusive parent physically hurts the child; the neglectful parent ignores the child. Physical abuse, if it does not also involve absence of verbal interaction with a caregiver, would not be expected to be manifested in retarded language development. In contrast, neglect, which would typically include the absence of frequent and sustained caregiver-infant interaction, would be expected to affect the acquisition of language skills.

Sadly, many abused children are also neglected, and vice versa. Of 61 mistreated children that Allen and Oliver (1982) studied, 17 were neglected only, 13 were abused but not neglected, and the remaining 31 were both abused and neglected. These researchers found that language development in the neglected children was significantly retarded, whereas that of the abused children was not.

the role of biology in language development

In spite of the important role that experience plays in the development of language, it does not offer a complete explanation for many aspects of language learning.

EVIDENCE FOR A BIOLOGICAL INFLUENCE

Evidence of a biological influence on language acquisition may be found in the similarities among the earliest speech sounds of infants from very different backgrounds; in the ease and rapidity with which children learn language; in the fact that children make only a fraction of the mistakes they might be expected to make if they were learning primarily through reinforcement, imitation, and trial and error; and in the observation that many of the mistakes children make are not imitative but appear instead to result from the incorrect application of rules that are themselves correct and useful.

ARE HUMANS PREPROGRAMMED FOR LANGUAGE LEARNING?

In the beginning, children of deaf parents babble like other children—although not as clearly, systematically, or repetitively as hearing children (Eilers & Oller, 1988). It is almost as though biology preprograms humans for language acquisition, claims Lenneberg (1969). Subsequently, children acquire grammatical rules in an astoundingly short period of time, in a sense *inventing* the language and *creating* errors based on their invention of rules (rather than on imitation).

These observations have given rise to a number of biological theories to explain language learning, including Chomsky's (1957, 1965) theory of LAD (language acquisition device) and Nelson's (1989) RELM (the rare event learning mechanism). What LAD and RELM have in common is that they attempt to account for infants' apparent predisposition for acquiring language by making the assumption that we are born with some special language-learning capacity. Children behave as though they were prewired for grammar, says Chomsky. How else are we to explain the fact that they make so few errors while learning syntax?

But LAD and RELM are really not explanations at all; they are simply metaphors. Infants behave as though they have at their command a range of cognitive skills, of language-related predispositions, and from this observation we might infer that there must be some innate neurological prewiring at birth. But as Rice (1989) observes, there is no satisfactory explanation of how these things work. Metaphors are not mechanisms; they are simply analogies.

bilingualism and a changing language context

In 1982, almost 75 percent of schoolchildren in the United States were white, approximately 10 percent were Hispanic, and the remainder included a varied mixture of ethnic groups. Projections suggest that by the year 2020, the proportion of white school-age Americans will have dropped to about 50 percent, and that of the Hispanic group will have increased to around 25 percent. The remainder will be blacks (about 16.5 percent) and other races (Pallas, Natriello, & McDill, 1989). In California, the "minority" has already become the "majority," notes Garcia (1993): 52 percent of students currently belong to "minority" categories. And

by 2020, 70 percent of beginning first-grade students will belong to nonwhite groups.

These changing demographics are due partly to lower birthrates among white families (15.0 per 1,000 population in 1989) than among blacks (23.1 per 1,000 in 1989) and other races (22.0 per 1,000 in 1989) (U.S. Bureau of the Census, 1992). In addition, immigration rates are much higher for nonwhites.

The educational implications of these changes are considerable. In 1982, most schoolchildren spoke English, the dominant, standard, majority language. Will that still be the case in 2020? (See Figures 7.11 and 7.12 in "At A Glance: The Effects of Changing Demographics on Education.")

transitional bilingualism

For most children whose early environment includes two languages, learning a second language does not appear to be much more complicated than learning to ride a bicycle. In the end, however, for most individuals there is a dominant or preferred language. Few individuals become what Diaz (1983) calls *balanced bilinguals*—people who are equally fluent and comfortable in both languages.

Although children can easily learn two or more languages, one of the dangers is that a child's skills in the less valued language will deteriorate over time. This is especially true in North American societies, in which the dominant language is highly reinforced but second languages often are not. As Pease-Alvarez and Hakuta (1992) put it, "Don't worry about English; they are all learning it; instead, if you are going to worry, worry about the lost potential in the attrition of the second language" (p. 5). In fact, note Hakuta and D'Andrea (1992), in many instances the bilingualism that has characterized parts of North America has been purely "transitional": Within three or four generations, the native language is completely replaced by the dominant English language.

the psychological effects of bilingualism

There are two views with respect to the psychological effects of bilingualism. One maintains that children have a limited amount of cognitive space available for language and that learning two or more languages places such a strain on cognitive capacity that the individual suffers. According to this view, the second language competes with the first and, in the end, the individual is not as proficient in either language as the monolingual individual. This competitive view is based in part on early studies of bilingualism, which often concluded that bilingual children were handicapped. Not only did they perform less well on measures of ability (such as intelligence tests), but they also tended to do less well in either language.

The second view maintains that there is no competition among languages and no clear limitation of the cognitive resources necessary for language learning. This view is based on research that indicates that "all other things being equal, higher degrees of bilingualism are associated with higher levels of cognitive attainment" (Hakuta & Garcia, 1989, p. 375).

Which view is correct? The simple answer is that either may be at least partly correct, depending on the individual and the context. *Subtractive bilingualism* is the term coined by Lambert (1975) to describe the negative influence of a second language. *Additive bilingualism* describes situations in which learning a second language has a positive influence on the first.

Research indicates that for some minority group children (whose first language is a minority language), learning a second language may be a subtractive experience. But for those whose first language is the dominant, majority language, learning a second language is more often an additive experience (Cummins & Swain, 1986).

SUBTRACTIVE BILINGUALISM

Learning a second language for children who are members of a distinct minority group (such as French-speaking children in Canada and Spanish-speaking children in the United States) may be subtractive in the sense that they become progressively less functional and fluent in their first language as their language skills improve in the second (Pease-Alvarez & Hakuta, 1992). This does not happen because learning the second language actually interferes with learning or remembering the first, but for one of several other reasons. One is that the majority language (the second language in this case) is usually the dominant language in the media and in the community. As a result, the minority language receives little support and reinforcement outside the home. Consequently, it tends to be used in less valued social roles and milieus (Landry, 1987).

A second explanation for the occasionally negative (subtractive) effect of learning the dominant language as a second language is that use of the minority language in the home is sometimes discouraged by parents or by the children themselves.

And third, the minority language spoken in the home is sometimes not a very good model of that language; it is often characterized by idiom and colloquialism, by vocabulary impoverishment, by improper grammar, and by idiosyncratic

n 1982, nearly 75 percent of U.S. schoolchildren were white, and the dominant language was clearly standard English. But in some American states such as California, more than half of current school children have a language other than English as their first language. That percentage is expected to reach 70 within two decades—at which time it is expected that fewer than half of all schoolchildren in major urban schools throughout the United States will speak English as a first language. This will have important implications for education.

Part of the reason for these changing demographics is a much lower birthrate among white families (17.4 per 1,000 population in 1970; 15.0 in 1989) than among blacks (25.3 per 1,000 in 1970; 23.1 in 1989) and

other races (26.1 per 1,000 in 1970; 22.0 in 1989). In addition, net immigration rates continue to be much higher for races other than whites.

pronunciation (Carey, 1987). And if it is not part of the children's schooling, they are unlikely to read or write in it. Thus they may develop a relatively high level of oral proficiency in the minority language while developing little competency in reading or writing it. For all of these reasons, competence in the minority language suffers, and the bilingual experience becomes subtractive.

ADDITIVE BILINGUALISM

However, learning a second language for children whose first language is the majority language appears to be largely an additive experience. Such is the case, for example, for many English-speaking children enrolled in French immersion programs in Canada and in Spanish immersion programs in the United States. The evidence seems clear that these pro-

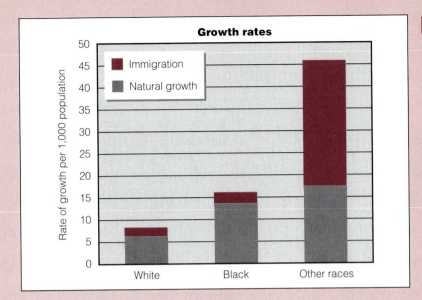

f **igure 7.11**

Rate of annual population growth from natural increases and immigration for three U.S. groups, 1989. Source: Adapted from U.S. Bureau of the Census (1992), p. 14.

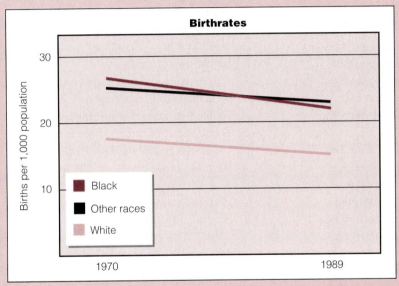

f **igure 7.12**

Birthrates for three U.S. groups, 1970–1989. Source: Adapted from U.S. Bureau of the Census (1992), p. 14.

grams can be very successful in developing linguistic skills, and in contributing to general academic achievement as well (Garcia, 1993). Although most students who go through immersion schooling don't develop as high a proficiency level as native speakers, their language deficiencies don't seem to interfere with their use of the second language. In addition, these students typically achieve at least as well in academic subjects and on measures of social and cognitive development as comparable students in conventional English programs. And within one year of receiving English instruction, their performance on measures of English literacy is as good as that of monolingual English students (Genesee, 1985).

So, do languages compete so that learning two or more languages is a subtractive experience, or does learning a second language have a generally positive influence? The answer is that although one language may suffer as a second is being learned, it is not because competition exists between the two, but more often because social conditions reduce the value of one language and provide a poor model of the language, or even actively discourage its use. The current view is that a second language does not interfere with the first; in fact, level of proficiency and rate of learning of the second language is closely related to proficiency in the first (Hakuta & Garcia, 1989).

A staggering amount of research has been conducted on the effects of bilingual programs, says Cziko (1992), but the conclusions are neither clear nor simple. One of the problems, as Lam (1992) notes, is that some programs are exemplary, whereas others are not; some teachers are more effective than others; and some students learn more easily than others.

Bilingual programs, argue Cummins and Swain (1986), can be a positive experience for minority- and majority-group children alike. Not only does a good bilingual program develop functional proficiency in a second language, but it can also strengthen skills in the first language. Immersion programs are likely to provide an additive experience for children whose first language is the majority language, for these children already have a high level of proficiency in their native language. However, for minority-group children, instruction should occur primarily in the minority language, and the majority language should be learned as a second language. French-speaking minority children whose schooling is primarily in French, with English as a second language, not only maintain and improve their French far more than those schooled primarily in English, but they

also perform as well in English (Cummins, 1986).

bilingualism in today's schools

North American societies have been multilingual and multicultural from the very beginning—although education has more often been unilingual. This has often posed problems for students and teachers—problems that, Brisk (1991) notes, were traditionally viewed as problems with *students* rather than with the educational system. As a result, in most cases schools accepted no responsibility for any problems a minority-language child might experience. Teachers simply assumed that the problem would rectify itself with exposure to traditional schooling. If it didn't . . . well, too bad, students would simply have to fail.

The current emphasis in education is for schools to accept responsibility for problems related to minority-languages. A common educational response is to establish a bilingual or English-as-a-second language (ESL) program. The main purpose of these programs has been to prepare students to fit into the traditional, English-only school curriculum (Brisk, 1991).

There are different opinions about the best way of teaching English as a second language. Some argue that it is better to teach and strengthen the native language first to develop a high level of proficiency in it before teaching English. Others recommend immersing students in an English environment from the very beginning with as little use as possible of the native language. These recommendations have given rise to at least six different types of bilingual programs in schools (Lam, 1992).

Brisk (1991) argues that as our societies become increasingly multilingual and multicultural, schools must become more responsive to the needs of students. What schools should be focused on, say Collett and Serrano (1992), is becoming truly *inclusive*—that is, truly multicultural. Schools should not simply admit students from different backgrounds and then try to make them all the same by preparing them to fit into a traditional English-only curriculum. Serafini (1991) argues that recognizing and encouraging diversity in schools, and valuing competence in languages other than English, may do much to reduce racism.

It would be astounding were we all to agree. We don't. In the United States, powerful and highly vocal groups of *English-only* advocates argue that English should be designated the official language—as it has now been in at least 18 states (Padilla, 1991). Many English-only (or English First, or U.S. English) members are strongly opposed to publicly funded bilingual education. In contrast, groups such as *English Plus* advocate expanding bilingual programs for adults and children alike.

The debate is tense, notes McGroarty (1992), even though in the United States bilingual education is mandated by law. U.S. courts have ruled that putting all children in English classrooms regardless of their language and cultural background does not amount to treating all children equally. In Canada, the right to instruction in both official languages is guaranteed in some provinces but not in others. Most notably, Quebec's Bill 101 tends to entrench the use of French only in all public sectors in the province of Quebec (Padilla, 1991).

---

nonstandard languages

Some of the issues relevant to bilingualism are also relevant to what are termed **nonstandard languages**, which are variations (different dialects) of the dominant language. The dominant language, which most of us understand, read, and speak, is the **standard language**. It is viewed as correct and acceptable and serves as a standard against which to judge other dialects of the language.

The most common nonstandard dialect in the United States is Black English, which is spoken by an estimated 60 to 70 percent of African-Americans (Garcia, 1993). Other common dialects include the English sometimes spoken by Hispanic-Americans or by French Canadians.

We often assume that the frequent schooling problems of children less proficient in standard English has to do with their language. Bernstein (1958, 1961), for example, argues that the reason for this is that nonstandard forms of English, (he labeled them **restricted language codes**) are in many ways inferior to standard forms (labeled **elaborated language codes**). Elaborated language is grammatically correct, complex, and precise; restricted language is simple, grammatically incorrect, uses a limited vocabulary, and often resorts to gestures to make a point (Table 7.4). It is little wonder, Bernstein argued, that children whose homes are characterized by restricted language codes are often at a disadvantage in school. For the first time in their lives, they are required to use increasingly precise and grammatically correct language. They almost invariably begin by performing less well than those who have had more mainstream early language experiences. Before they can catch up, they often find themselves so far behind that they may feel it is hardly worth trying.

There is evidence to suggest, however, that Bernstein's view might not be the best explanation for the poorer performance of children who don't speak the

t able 7.4

Hypothetical examples of restricted and elaborated language codes

RESTRICTED

Mother: Clean your feet.
Child: Why for?
Mother: 'Cause.
Child: 'Cause what?
Mother: I said it, is why for.
Child: Ain't dirty.

ELABORATED

Mother: Please wipe your feet, Sam. On the mat.
Child: Why do I have to?
Mother: Because you'll track mud all over the floor if you don't. I can see mud on your soles.
Child: Not if I walk fast on my tiptoes, I won't track.
Mother: (Laughing) You little scoundrel. You'd have to walk on your hands.

standard form of the majority language. Children may do less well in school not so much because the nonstandard language is less complex, less sophisticated, and less grammatical, but rather because the language is *different*. Because instruction in school occurs in the standard language and because achievement is measured in that language, these children are clearly at a disadvantage, no matter how sophisticated their nonstandard language skills may be (Harrison, 1985).

In addition, notes Garcia (1993), children whose dialect is noticeably different tend to be judged inferior by teachers and other students. Their poorer performance may then be partly a result of a negative self-fulfilling prophecy.

What, then, can be done to enhance a child's sophistication in the standard language? What should be done? Should anything be done?

Here, as elsewhere, asking the questions is easier than getting clear answers. Cummins (1986) argues that minority-group children should be instructed in their minority language, with the majority language presented as a second lan-

guage. Seymour (1971) makes the same recommendations vis-à-vis black children who use a nonstandard dialect: He suggests that schools should encourage the use of the nonstandard dialect at least part of the time. Others argue that because most commerce outside school takes place in the majority language, those who know only other dialects of that language will be at the same disadvantage outside school as they are in it.

So the questions remain.

speech and language problems in early childhood

We assume that by the time children reach school age, their language skills will be sufficient for them to understand and follow instructions, express interests and wants, tell stories, ask questions, carry on conversations—in short, communicate. Sadly, that is not always the case.

There are a number of different language and speech problems, each of which can vary tremendously in seriousness (see, for example, Schiefelbusch & McCormick, 1981). At one extreme are children who, because of severe mental retardation, neurological damage or disease, mental disorders such as autism, or deafness, are essentially nonverbal. Their communication might consist of a few gestures or signs.

There are other children whose speech is largely incomprehensible, sometimes because conceptual development is so poor that thought sequences seem illogical and speech becomes largely nonsensical, and sometimes because of speech production problems like those reflected in poor articulation, voice control problems, and stuttering.

And there are children whose language development is less advanced than normal, perhaps because of mild mental retardation or because of a learning disability reflected in language deficits. The predominant view is that these children don't learn different language forms or acquire language differently; their skills simply develop more slowly. Some of these children are of normal or above-normal intelligence and have no deficits other than their problems with language. However, because of our schools' predominantly verbal teaching and testing methods, many of these children are viewed as intellectually handicapped, and their language problems may be interpreted as the result of inferior ability rather than as the cause of poor achievement.

It is not clear what causes language problems in the absence of other handicaps. Although an impoverished and unstimulating home context may sometimes be implicated, in some cases children of apparently normal intelligence from advantaged backgrounds experience significant developmental delays or language impairments (Rice, 1989).

Speech problems and delayed language development are most common among children who have some other handicap—that is, retarded children and others suffering from motor, neurological, or mental disorders. They are relatively uncommon among the majority of children.

the relation of language and thought

The significance of language acquisition for children is in many ways obvious. Not only does language allow children to direct the behavior of others according to their wishes (as when they ask for something), but it also provides a means for acquiring information that would otherwise be inaccessible (as when they ask questions, listen to stories, or watch television). In addition, there is considerable evidence that language is closely involved in logical thought processes, although the exact relationship between thinking and language remains unclear.

One extreme position, the Whorfian, maintains that language is essential for thinking (Whorf, 1941, 1956). This position is based on the assumption that all thinking is verbal and that thought is therefore limited to what is made possible by language.

In contrast, psychologists such as Piaget and Vygotsky argue that thought often precedes language. Piaget (1923), for example, points out that the development of certain logical concepts often precedes the learning of words and phrases corresponding to those concepts. Words such as "bigger," "smaller," "farther," and so on do not appear to be understood until the concepts they represent are themselves understood.

Both Vygotsky and Piaget argue that language and thought first develop independently. Thus, there is considerable evidence of what we consider to be thought among preverbal children and nonhuman animals. But after the age of 2, language and thought become more closely related. After that age, thought becomes increasingly verbal, and the use of language allows children to control behavior.

Vygotsky's view, described in Chapter 2, holds that speech has three separate forms, each with different functions. *Social speech* is directed toward others to control their behavior or to express simple thoughts and emotions. *Egocentric speech* (common between ages 3 and 7) is a form of self-talk, spoken out loud, that serves to control the child's own behavior. And *inner speech* is self-talk that provides a means for directing our thinking

Some psychologists argue that thought precedes language, that children often don't learn or understand certain words or expressions before they understand the logical concepts that underlie them. For example, children don't usually develop words to express "all gone" until they have mastered the concept of object permanence.

and our behavior. (See Table 2.10 in Chapter 2.) It is, according to Vygotsky, the source of all our higher mental functioning (Vygotsky, 1986; Wertsch, 1985).

There are two forms of the Wharfian hypothesis. The strongest form argues that thought *depends on* language and will not occur in its absence. The weaker version maintains that language *influences* thinking.

To accept the more extreme position would be to assert that people who are prelinguistically deaf and who have not learned an alternate communication system cannot think. We would also have to believe that prelinguistic infants cannot think and that thought among children

who have begun to develop language is restricted to subjects and ideas for which the thinker has appropriate language. And we would have to believe that, say, cats cannot think.

We don't believe all these things. So we accept the position that thought can occur in the absence of language. At the same time, research and good sense inform us that our sophisticated thought processes are inextricably bound with language—as are our belief systems, our values, our worldviews (Hunt & Agnoli, 1991). So convinced are we of this that attempts to bring about difficult social changes often begin with attempts to change language. Antiracist and antisexist movements are a case in point. In the first edition of this text, it was acceptable to use masculine pronouns as though all children, all psychologists, and, indeed, all significant people, were male. Speaking of one of Blaise Pascal's *Pensées*, for example, I wrote: "one of the paradoxes of human existence is that despite man's great intelligence it is impossible for him to know where he came from or where he is going" (Lefrançois, 1973, p. 351). That this type of chauvinistic sexism is no longer acceptable in our language may eventually be reflected in its eradication from our thoughts and from those of our children.

language is for communicating and conversing

Language is more than a collection of sounds whose combinations refer to objects and actions and whose expression conveys our meanings. And it is more than a way of thinking and expressing our thoughts. Language is the means by which we draw information from past generations, record our own small contributions, and pass them on to generations that will come later. It is the great binding force of all cultures.

But infants, newly learning language, are not concerned with its great cultural contributions. Their first interest is in communicating, and the first communications are simple assertions ("that dog"; "see daddy"; "my ball") or requests ("milk!"; "more candy"). The second concern is with conversation.

A conversation is an exchange typically involving two or more people (although some people do talk to themselves—and answer themselves as well). It is generally verbal, although it can consist of a combination of gestures and verbalization, or it can consist entirely of gestures, as is the case of ASL (American Sign Language). Genuine conversational exchanges begin around age 2. Initially, they are highly telegraphic, as is the child's speech; there aren't many variations possible when your sentences are limited to a single word. A short excerpt from an intelligent conversation with one of my children illustrates this:

Him: Fish.

Me: Fish?

Him: Fish!

Me: Fish? Fish swim.

Him: Fish! Fish! (The conversation becomes more complex.)

Me: There are fish in the lake. (An original thought, meant to stimulate creativity.)

Him: Fish. (Pointing, this time, in the general direction of the lake, I think.)

From such primitive, repetitive conversation, children progress to more complex expressions and begin to learn the importance of subtle cues of intonation, accentuation of words, rhythm of sentences, tone, and accompanying ges-tures. They learn, as well, about the implicit agreements that govern our conversations—the well-accepted rules that determine who shall speak and when, whether interruptions are permissible and how they should occur, what information must be included if we are to be understood, and what we can assume is already known.

Thus, more or less, do infants progress from a sound to a word, from one word to two, from an expression to a conversation, from a conversation to a book. . . .

main points

PHYSICAL GROWTH AND MOTOR DEVELOPMENT

1. There is a gradual slowing of physical growth after infancy. Also, parts of the body grow at different rates (the head grows more slowly, for example) so that 6 year olds look more like an adult than do 2 year olds.

2. Learning to walk and to coordinate motor activities (such as those involved in tracing geometric designs) are important motor achievements of the preschool period. Physical and motor development may be assessed using measures such as the Denver Developmental Screening Test.

COGNITIVE DEVELOPMENT

3. The younger preschooler's memory often makes use of incidental mnemonics (paying attention) rather than of deliberate strategies such as organizing. Older preschoolers may use more deliberate strategies, many of them learned through social interaction with mothers or peers.

4. The two substages of Piaget's pre-operational period are the precon-

ceptual (ages 2 to 4; marked by errors of classification, transductive reasoning, and syncretic reasoning) and the intuitive (4 to 7; marked by egocentricity, class-inclusion problems, and reliance on perception). Replications of Piaget's work have often confirmed the sequence he describes but sometimes find specific competencies at younger ages.

PRESCHOOL EDUCATION

5. Preschool education programs include nursery schools, day-care centers, and compensatory programs such as Head Start, direct instruction, and the Montessori method. High-quality programs have positive effects. Kindergartens are often compulsory in North America but are rare and elitist in developing countries. Some critics fear that emphasis on formal instruction at the preschool level *hurries* children needlessly and robs them of their childhood.

LANGUAGE AND THE PRESCHOOLER

6. Language is the use of arbitrary sounds with established referents that can be arranged in sequence to convey meaning. During the preschool period a child goes from two-word expressions to multiple word sentences that make extensive use of grammatical morphemes such as "-ing" and "-ed" to convey meaning. More complex sentences and adult-like grammatical structures are usually present by age 4.

7. Experience—especially interactions with a caregiver—plays a crucial role in early language learning. Mothers typically adjust their speech (use motherese, with its higher intona-

tions, shorter sentences, more repetition, and simpler concepts), fine-tuning it to a level about 6 months in advance of their infants. Neglected children are sometimes retarded in language development, probably because of more limited verbal interaction with a caregiver.

8. The role of biology in language learning is evident in the fact that the earliest speech sounds of all infants are highly similar, and that children make relatively few imitative errors in learning a language. It is also evident in the remarkable speed with which children learn grammar.

9. In North America, and especially in the United States, minority languages are rapidly become majority languages in schools. Learning two languages does not appear to be a very difficult task for young children. Learning a second language later in life may be more difficult and may be a *subtractive* experience if the first language is not highly valued or reinforced. For most children who learn a second language after the first is well established and for whom the first language is highly reinforced and widely used, learning a second language is an *additive* (positive) experience.

10. Children who speak nonstandard dialects are often at a disadvantage because of the fact that schoolwork and commerce in the community are generally in the standard dialect. Some children experience language problems ranging from complete absence of speech and comprehension to minor articulation and voice problems (often related to mental retardation, neurological damage or disease, mental disorders such as autism, or deafness).

11. A strong version of the Whorfian hypothesis maintains that language is necessary for thought; a weaker version holds that language influences thinking. Piaget and Vygotsky maintain that thought and language are initially separate (prelinguistic children can think) but become progressively more closely related. Vygotsky describes three stages in language development: *social speech* (to age 3; speech used to control others); *egocentric speech* (3 to 7; speech used to control own behavior, but often spoken out loud); and *inner speech* (7 to adulthood; private self-talk).

focus questions: applications

■ What sorts of parallels exist between motor and cognitive development?

1. What sorts of motor skills might be used as indicators of developmental progress in early childhood?

■ How does Piaget describe cognitive development in early childhood?

2. Provide a specific, original, example of preconceptual thinking. Of intuitive thinking.

■ What are some of the effects of preschool education?

3. Arrange to observe a preschool in action.

■ How do young children learn language?

4. When you observe your preschool, focus on children's language usage, looking for instances of language errors and problems, as well as for examples of especially advanced language usage.

■ Is knowing a second language good, bad, or irrelevant for cognitive development?

5. As a term-paper project, use library resources to examine the proposition that knowing a second language is generally beneficial.

study terms

incidental mnemonics 303
metamemory 305
sensorimotor period 305
preoperational thought 305
reversibility 305
preconceptual 305
concepts 306
preconcepts 306
transductive reasoning 307
syncretic reasoning 307
intuitive thinking 307
egocentric 308
conservation 309
motherese 327
nonstandard languages 335
standard language 335
restricted language codes 335
elaborated language codes 335

further readings

A simple, layperson's description of physical growth, play, parenting, and preschools can be found in:

Lee, C. (1990). *The growth and development of children* (4th ed.). New York: Longman.

The collection cited next contains a number of good articles dealing with some of the topics in this chapter:

Okagaki, L., & Sternberg, R. J. (Eds.). (1991). *Directors of development: Influences on the development of children's thinking.* Hillsdale, N.J.: Lawrence Erlbaum.

A good summary of Piaget's theory is provided by:

Wadsworth, B. J. (1989). *Piaget's theory of cognitive and affective development* (4th ed.). New York: Longman.

Language development is described in more detail in:

Wood, B. S. (1981). *Children and communication: Verbal and nonverbal language development* (2nd ed.). Englewood Cliffs, N.J.: Prentice-Hall.

Berko-Gleason, J. (Ed.). (1989). *The development of language* (2nd ed.). Columbus, Ohio: Charles E. Merrill.

The following book is a fascinating collection of papers dealing with language and thought in both animals and humans:

Greenberg, G., & Tobach, E. (1987). *Cognition, language, and consciousness: Integrative levels.* Hillsdale, N.J.: Lawrence Erlbaum.

8

Social Development in Early Childhood

Whoever is delighted in solitude is either a Wilde Beast,
or a God.
Francis Bacon, Essay 27: Of Friendship

focus questions

WHAT DO PRESCHOOLERS UNDERSTAND OF WHAT OTHERS FEEL?

OF WHAT IMPORTANCE IS PLAY IN CHILDHOOD?

TO WHAT EXTENT ARE MASCULINITY AND FEMININITY DETERMINED BY OUR GENES?

WHAT DIFFERENCES DOES PARENTING MAKE? FAMILY SIZE? POSITION IN THE FAMILY?

HOW SIGNIFICANT IS THE LOSS OF A PARENT?

IS OUT-OF-HOME CHILDCARE AS GOOD AS AT-HOME CARE BY PARENTS?

outline

THE SOCIALIZATION OF EMOTIONS
Interpreting Emotions
Regulating Emotions
Expressing Emotions

THEORIES OF SOCIAL DEVELOPMENT
Erikson's Psychosocial Stages
Social Imitation

PLAY
Functions of Play
Types of Play
The Implications of Imagination
Social Play

GENDER ROLES IN EARLY CHILDHOOD
Gender Schemas
Assuming Gender Identity
Gender Differences

THE CONTEMPORARY FAMILY
Parenting Young Children
Do Parents Make a Measurable Difference?
Learning to Parent

FAMILY COMPOSITION
Birth Order
Family Size
Social Class and Related Factors

ONE-PARENT FAMILIES
General Effects of Loss of a Parent
Developmental Effects of Divorce
Sex-Related Effects of Divorce
Contextual Effects of Divorce
Why Divorce Has Negative Effects
Some Conclusions
A Final Word

CHILDREN IN STEPFAMILIES
Possible Problems in Stepfamilies
The Positive Side of Stepfamilies

CHILDCARE OUTSIDE THE HOME
General Effects of Childcare
Research on the Quality of Childcare
Finding Quality Childcare

MAIN POINTS

FOCUS QUESTIONS: APPLICATIONS

STUDY TERMS

FURTHER READINGS

W hen Ronald, one of my little nephews, had his third birthday, I made him cry twice.

The first time was when I gave him a model of a yellow Volkswagen Beetle as a birthday present, nicely wrapped in purple paper covered with pictures of tiny pink ponies. Ronald loves horses, and I had briefly considered getting him one for his birthday. But my sister said she wouldn't be especially happy with that idea because she doesn't like horses in her house. So I gave Ronald the pony paper instead, and as he was ripping it off the Beetle I said, "It's a horse. I got you a tiny baby horse!"

It was a joke and some of the adults laughed . . . and Ronald got terribly excited. But when he saw the yellow Volkswagen, his lip began to quiver and his eyes filled with tears.

"Your uncle didn't mean a real horse," his mother explained, but it wasn't the right thing to say; he ran to her and buried his face in her lap, sobbing. I would rather have been somewhere else.

He recovered quickly, and I tried to make it up to him when I left. "Uncle Guy's going to Alaska," I said. "Do you want to come?" He nodded solemnly. We all laughed. Nice, joke, huh?

"You want to come?" He nodded again and reached out for me to pick him up, which I did. "Let's go," I said. He nodded vigorously. I held him for a while longer. "Heh, heh," I said. Pretty funny.

"Let's go," he said.

"Heh, heh," I repeated. "You can't really come. When you're older."

He looked at me for a long moment, as if trying to understand. Then his lip began to quiver again.

When I left, he was sobbing in his mother's arms.

wished I had bought him a horse, because if I had, he would not have cried (although his mother might have).

You see, young children don't always know what is real and what isn't; they can't always tell the difference between a jest and a promise. Nor, of course, can we, but we are much better at it than they are. In addition, young children do not have the fine control adults have over their emotions or over the expression of those emotions. They are more easily moved to tears—and to laughter. Put another way, their emotions are not completely socialized.

The socialization of emotions involves at least three things: learning to interpret emotions; achieving some control over them; and learning when, where, and how displaying them is appropriate and expected.

interpreting emotions

One of the important things that happens during infancy is that children gradually discover that they are *selves*—that they are separate and individual, and that they are capable of feelings (Kopp & Brownell, 1991). Along with the recognition of the self as separate comes the realization that others, too, are separate and permanent and also capable of feelings.

Emotions are generally defined as the *feeling* or *affective* component of human behavior. As Oatley (1992) puts it, emotions are really *communications,* to oneself and to others, that relate to the occurrence of events concerning important goals. Thus Ronald's expressions of sorrow communicate that a specific event (receiving a toy car) signals failure to achieve an important goal (getting a horse). In much the same way, our expressions of joy signal events relating to reaching (or anticipating reaching) our goals.

INTERPRETING FACIAL EXPRESSIONS

Initially infants do not know how to interpret the feelings of others. Facial expressions of joy or sadness, for example, are meaningless for a 1-month-old infant. But some time between the ages of 3 and 6 months, there appears a growing recognition not only that others are capable of emotional reactions, but that these can be inferred from expressions and from behavior (Oster et al., 1989). By the age of 9 months to a year, infants in ambiguous situations actively search other people's faces as though looking for a clue that might guide their own behavior. When they see others crying, they are likely to feel sad, perhaps even to cry. And if others laugh and are happy, they too are more likely to be joyful (Termine & Izard, 1988).

During the preschool years, children's ability to make inferences about other people's emotions, and to interpret their own emotions, appears to be global and relatively imprecise. When Brown et al. (1991) asked preschoolers how they would feel following a story event associated with happiness, sadness, or anger, they typically responded in terms of an intense emotion. And when, later in the story, an event occurred that would lead to a lessening of the emotion, preschoolers often thought they would feel a *different* emotion. If they had been sad earlier, now they would be happy. Strikingly, it seldom occurred to them that they might be *more* or *less* sad or happy. In contrast, older children in the same study often thought they would feel a different degree of the same emotion.

If specifically asked to describe what they think someone else is feeling, preschoolers might infer that someone feels "good" or "bad" because they are crying or laughing. They don't yet look for underlying causes upon which to base inferences. It is not until later childhood, or even adolescence, that children spontaneously analyze others' emotions, trying to sort them out and understand their causes (Hughes, Tingle, & Sawin, 1981).

INTERPRETING DECEPTION

Early in the preschool period, children cannot readily tell the difference between emotions that are real and those that are a pretense. Thus, if someone falls but jumps up and "laughs it off" in embarrassment, 2 year olds are likely to conclude that the person is happy, but 5 year olds interpret the situation more accurately, realizing that a person who laughs after falling is pretending.

Harris and Gross (1988) speculate that children probably discover that some expressions of emotion are false when they begin to realize that they are themselves able to mislead others about their own emotions. When 3-year-old Ronald plays hide-and-seek with his sister, she always wins. All she has to do is say, "Where are you, Ronald? Are you in the bedroom?" and Ronald yells from behind the couch, "No way, I'm not in the bedroom." He cannot deceive his sister any more than could the 3 year olds in a study by Sodian (1991), who were asked to mislead a competitor in a game by pointing to the container that *did not* contain an object. Invariably, these 3 year olds were unable to conceal the information; they insisted on pointing at the correct container.

It isn't until about age 4, claim Ruffman et al. (1993), that children begin to understand that deceiving others involves getting them to *believe* things that are false. In one of their experiments, for example, they had a story character, John, put on another character's (Katy's) much-too-large shoes to steal a piece of chocolate. The shoes left huge footprints in flour leading to the chocolate. Although the 3 year olds understood clearly that the huge footprints were associated with Katy, they nevertheless predicted that a third character, Mr. Bubbly, would believe that John—not Katy—had stolen the chocolate. After all, John *was* the thief.

regulating emotions

We saw in Chapter 6 that even very young infants can do things to control the emotions they feel. For example, a frightened infant might close his eyes, suck his thumb, or bury his face in his mother's lap—examples of what Gianino and Tronick (1988) call *self-directed regulatory behaviors.* Alternately, infants might push away the frightening thing—an example of *other-directed regulatory behaviors.*

Preschoolers, with their expanding mobility and rapidly developing cognitive and social skills, become increasingly adept both at avoiding situations that lead to negative emotions and at seeking out and maintaining emotions associated with good feelings. But, somewhat like infants, their control of emotions is *situational* and *behavioral* rather than cognitive. When they hear the ice-cream man's bell, they run excitedly to get mother—or money; when the frightening part of a story comes, they close their eyes and cover their ears. In Brown et al.'s (1991) investigation in which children were questioned following emotion-related events in stories, the younger children saw emotions as being situation-specific: To change a feeling, one need only change the situation. Monica is sad because she has lost a toy. "But," she predicts, "I will be happy when I go to bed." Why? "Because I wouldn't have to look for it."

In contrast, older children's control of emotions is more cognitive. One way of not feeling sad about a lost toy, the older child insists, is not to think about it, or

to think a happy thought. Most of us are more like older than younger children. We can't just go to bed.

expressing emotions

It has begun to embarrass 3-year-old Ronald to cry in front of me—and even more to cry in front of strangers. But it doesn't bother him very much to cry in front of his mother or his sister. Ronald has begun to learn what researchers refer to as *display rules.*

One aspect of display rules has to do with learning when and how it's appropriate to display certain emotions; another deals with understanding the emotional expressions (emotional displays) of others. Part of display rule learning involves discovering that expressed emotion does not always correspond to underlying emotion. Even young children are able to smile when they lie, or pretend it doesn't hurt when it would be embarrassing to cry.

It's not clear how preschoolers learn simple display rules, such as the rule that says that if you don't like a gift, you should hide your disappointment. When Cole (1986) filmed 3- to 4-year-old girls opening a disappointing gift either alone or in front of the giver, she found highly noticeable differences between the facial displays in the two situations. Although the girls' disappointment was clear when they opened the gift alone, most of them covered their feelings with smiles when the giver was present. What is interesting, however, was that these girls were unaware of their deception. It seems that preschoolers learn to control their emotional expression before they realize the effects of their behavior on others.

Lewis, Sullivan, and Vasen (1987) report that although older preschoolers attempt to control their emotional displays, they are successful with only a limited number of emotions. They continue to

Preschoolers do not control their expression of emotions as well as or as carefully as do adults. When it hurts, it embarrasses them little to cry. And when it's funny, it is simple to laugh without restraint.

cry and laugh more easily than we do. But even as adults, we are not always able to hide our feelings. If someone gives us a dollar when we fully expected a hundred, we might find it very difficult to smile, even though our socialization is far more advanced than that of children.

theories of social development

ocialization is the process by which children learn behaviors that are appropriate for people of their sex and age. As children are socialized, they acquire the traditions, beliefs, values, and customs of their groups. It is the means by which they learn the rules of membership in a society—rules like how and when to display emotion.

Socialization is clearly defined and determined by cultural context. There are countless examples: North American audiences clap their hands, cheer, and whistle when they are pleased; European audiences whistle when they are displeased. Japanese men bow when they meet each other; Americans shake hands. Thus what is learned might vary a great deal depending on the context, a fact that makes the "average child" even more of a myth. But the processes by which socialization occurs are highly similar among different cultural groups.

Erikson's psychosocial stages

As we saw in Chapter 2, an important theory of social development is Erik Erikson's, which describes children's devel-

To become autonomous, says Erikson, children must explore and be independent—and parents must provide children with opportunities to do so. Overprotection can lead to doubt and uncertainty. Yet there is clearly a need to continue to protect; not all trees are for climbing.

opment in terms of a series of stages, each of which is characterized by conflicting tendencies or desires, and each of which requires the attainment of some new competence. The theory clearly emphasizes social development (hence the label *psychosocial development*).

The first three of Erikson's psychosocial stages span the years from birth to around the end of the preschool period. To review briefly, the first, *trust versus mistrust,* lasts through most of infancy. The important task in this stage is to develop sufficient trust in the world to be able to go out and begin exploring it actively. Throughout this period, the most important influence in an infant's life is clearly

the principal caregiver(s)—often, though by no means always, the mother.

The second stage, *autonomy versus shame and doubt,* spans the first year or so of the preschool period. At this time, children begin to discover that they are responsible for their own actions, a discovery that is closely linked with the development of intentionality. The child's developing autonomy depends on opportunities to explore and to be independent, says Erikson (1959). Hence the need for a balance in parental control. Overprotection can lead to doubt and uncertainty. Yet there is clearly a need to continue to protect; the young preschooler cannot be permitted unsupervised and unlimited freedom to explore. Although there are few saber-toothed tigers or meat-eating dinosaurs out there, there are cars and trucks and trains and other things that can be just as deadly.

The third stage, *initiative versus guilt,* spans the remaining preschool years. The new sense of competence required of the child involves a sense of initiative, a sense of personal agency. But there still lingers a desire to retain the comfort and security that come from allowing other people—especially parents—to maintain control and responsibility.

According to Erikson's theory, then, much of "growing up" during the preschool period involves developing a sense of an autonomous self—a self that is capable of forming intentions and of behaving in ways that are effective. The underlying competencies are greatly facilitated by infants' physical exploration of the environment, as well as by mushrooming language skills that make it possible to explore in other ways—as, for example, when the 4 year old bombards caregivers with questions. The development of social competence through the preschool period also requires achieving progressive independence from parents. Overprotective parents who do not easily

t able 8.1		
Erikson's psychosocial stages: 18 months to 6 years		
STAGE	**APPROXIMATE AGE**	**PRINCIPAL DEVELOPMENTAL TASK**
Autonomy vs. shame and doubt	*18 months to 2 or 3 years*	*Developing a sense of control and mastery over actions; learning that one is autonomous, that intentions can be realized; overcoming the urge to return to the comfort of allowing parents, especially the mother, to do all important things*
Initiative vs. guilt	*2 or 3 to 6 years*	*Developing a sense of self, largely through identifying with parents; developing a greater sense of responsibility for own actions; achieving progressive independence from parents*

permit independence may make children's progression through Erikson's stages more difficult. (See Chapter 2 for more details; see also Table 8.1.)

social imitation

Erikson (1968) believed that *imitation* is one of the important means by which preschool children become socialized, especially in the first two or three years of life. Later, *identification* (a process whereby children do not merely imitate models, but adopt their values and beliefs— in a sense, become like them) gains importance.

As we saw in Chapter 2, an important theory of social learning based on imitation has been proposed by Albert Bandura. To summarize briefly, Bandura's theory has behavioristic roots. It explains the complex effects of modeling partly in terms of rewards and punishments. But it is also a cognitive theory: It gives a tremendously important role to the informative function of models and to observers' understanding and interpretation of that information. It is what the observer imagines and expects that is important in learning through imitation.

Bandura describes three separate effects of imitation: the *modeling effect,* evident in learning new behavior; the *inhibitory and disinhibitory effects,* in which

the rewards or punishment a model receives serve to bring about (disinhibit) some previously suppressed behavior or, alternately, to inhibit current behavior; and the *eliciting effect,* in which the model's behavior serves to evoke a related behavior in the observer.

Imitation-based theories of social learning are especially useful for explaining how children in nontechnological societies learn to do things like set snares and traps or wield brooms or use corngrinding stones. But most of us no longer need to learn how to operate a corngrinding stone or lay out a trap. So what do we learn by social imitation? Among other things, perhaps we learn important social tendencies such as cooperation and competition.

COOPERATION AND COMPETITION

There is considerable research to support the belief that children are socialized to be cooperative or competitive by the predominant way of life—the mores and traditions—of their immediate social environment (Madsen, 1971). Children from different ethnic groups can be remarkably different in terms of cooperation and competition.

Studies of cooperation and competition often use the four-person cooperation board (Madsen, 1971), an 18-inch paper square covered with a piece of pa-

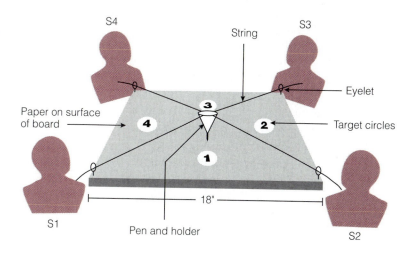

Cooperation board. Source: Madsen & Lancy (1981), p. 397.

per that may be marked with target circles as in Figure 8.1. Near the center of the paper a heavy Plexiglas cone that serves as a pen holder is moved over the paper by means of four strings that pass through eyelets at each of the four corners of the board. As it moves, the pen traces a line on the paper. In a typical experiment, subjects may be asked to draw a line through each of the target circles in numbered sequence, or they may be required to draw a line through their assigned circle (the one to the left or right of their particular corner). Note that this can be accomplished only if subjects cooperate; that is, no one subject, by pulling his or her string alone, can cause the pen to pass over an assigned circle.

In a variation of this procedure, target circles might be drawn under the strings at each of the four corners. Now it is possible for a subject to draw a line through a corner circle simply by pulling harder than anybody else—that is, by competing and winning. Of course, if one subject is strong enough to win by competing, it is also possible for that subject to prevent all the others from drawing lines through their circles.

A CROSS-CULTURAL ILLUSTRATION

Madsen and Lancy (1981) used the cooperation board to look at competition

and cooperation among two groups of Papua New Guinea children: the Imbonggu, a highly intact tribal group whose traditional way of life is based on cooperation, and the Kila-Kila, a more heterogeneous group heavily influenced by rapid modernization and living in an urbanized setting characterized by violence and crime.

First, groups of four children were simply instructed to draw a line through the numbered circles, in order, and were rewarded as a group for being successful (each child was given a coin). The researchers' objective was simply to determine whether children were able to cooperate when so instructed and when rewarded for doing so.

After three one-minute trials under this "group reward" condition, subjects were then asked to write their names next to one of the circles (either to their right or left) and were told they would receive a coin each time a line was drawn through their circle. Now, in order to be successful, subjects had to cooperate. If they did not, the most competitive and aggressive subject would succeed in pulling the pen over to his or her corner. Subjects were then given three additional one-minute trials.

The results of the study are striking. There were no differences between the

Imbonggu and Kila-Kila on the first three trials. Each of the groups improved on every trial, and by the third trial, each succeeded in crossing an average of slightly more than 12 circles. But the results on the fourth, fifth, and sixth trials, when subjects were being rewarded individually rather than as a group, are intriguing. Whereas the Imbonggu continued to improve on each of the trials—a clear sign that they continued to cooperate—the performance of the Kila-Kila foursomes deteriorated dramatically. In fact, two-thirds of the Kila-Kila groups did not cross a single circle on the fourth trial; in contrast, the Imbonggu group that cooperated the least still managed to cross six circles (see Figure 8.2).

There appears to be little doubt that competitive and cooperative tendencies are markedly different between these groups. Madsen and Lancy (1981) attribute this difference to their "primary group" affiliations—that is, to the cultural groups in which the children have been socialized. Similar research has found the same sorts of patterns among various other groups when the cultures are different in terms of cooperation and competition. Thus rural Mexican children have been found to be more cooperative (less competitive) than urban Mexican children, as have Israeli kibbutz children compared with urban Israeli children; Blackfoot Indians compared with urban caucasians in Canada; urban and rural Colombians; urban and rural Maoris in New Zealand; and various other groups (Madsen & Lancy, 1981).

OBSERVATIONAL LEARNING IN COMPLEX SOCIETIES

It seems reasonable to suppose that observational learning—social imitation—is involved in learning important cultural values and tendencies (reflected, for example, in competition and cooperation), even in heterogeneous societies such as ours. Most of the Imbonggu are cooperative because their immediate families and friends—their primary groups—are mostly cooperative. And most of the Kila-Kila belong to more competitive primary groups. But we are not so homogeneous. Some of us are gentle and cooperative, others fiercely competitive. And still others, of course, are both, depending on the situation.

Still, we too are socialized. Observational learning is also prevalent in our

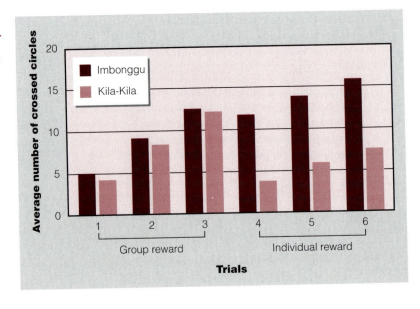

f i g u r e   8 . 2

Differences in cooperation and competition be-tween Imbonggu and Kila-Kila children. Source: Adapted from Madsen & Lancy (1981), p. 399.

culture. But our models are perhaps not as simple, not as obvious, as they might be in a more homogeneous society. A model need not be a real person whose behavior is copied by another. Anything that serves as a pattern for behavior may be considered a model: characters in literature, movies, and television programs; oral and written instructions; religious beliefs; or folk heroes (such as musicians or athletes). Bandura calls these **symbolic models**. Symbolic models are the most common models in a technological society. Their effects are displayed in a variety of ways in the behavior of adults and children—and one of the most powerful transmitters of these symbolic models may well be your television set (about which we say more in Chapter 10).

Another very powerful source of social influence are young children's playmates, for in play there is both competition and cooperation.

play

lay is activity that has no long-range goal, although it might have some immediate objectives (to hop from here to there; to make a sand hill; to fly a kite). **Play** is what children (and grown-ups) do for the fun of it. But that play has no ultimate purpose does not mean it is unimportant and useless. In fact, it is important for all aspects of children's development: social, physical, and intellectual (Varga, 1991). "Play," notes Weininger (1990), "has to do with exploration, curiosity, sensory-motor activity, social activity, verbal imitation . . ." (p. 15).

functions of play

Ethologists argue that play among animals is useful in developing and exercising physical skills that might be important in hunting or escaping from predators (Aldis, 1975). Play also serves to establish social position and to teach acceptable behaviors, as in the mock-fighting, rough-and-tumble play of lion cubs or chimpanzees.

Some of the functions of play among children are, in some respects, not very different from those among animals. Practice play is useful in developing and exercising physical skills and might also contribute to social adaptation. In addition, play involving physical exploration is closely linked to attention and learning (Ruff & Saltarelli, 1993).

Various forms of *imaginative* play have quite different functions. Imagining involves important cognitive abilities related to symbolizing, imitating, anticipating, and problem solving. Children's growing awareness of self and of others, and their gradual realization that we are all *thinking* beings, has its roots in play, claims McCune (1993). Not surprisingly, research reports positive correlations between play and level of cognitive development (Trawick-Smith, 1989).

PLAY IN PIAGET'S AND VYGOTSKY'S THEORIES

Children's play has a central role in cognitive theories such as those of Piaget and Vygotsky. For Piaget, children's play reflects level of intellectual development. Thus children progress from *practice play* (corresponding to sensorimotor development) to symbolic play (the preoperational period) to play with rules (concrete operations). Piaget (1951) claimed that play primarily involves *assimilation*, the exercising of previously learned activities. He contrasted play with imitation, which, according to his theory, consists mainly of *accommodation*—modifying activities. In a sense, play is "assimilation for the sake of assim-

table 8.2

Types of play

TYPE	EXAMPLE
Practice (sensorimotor) play	
Solitary	*Bouncing a ball up, down, up, down…*
Social	*Playing baseball*
Pretend (imaginative) play	
Solitary	*Giving a doll pretend tea*
Social	*Dramatizing monsters in a group*

ilation" (Nicolopoulou, 1993). Its main function according to Piaget is *satisfaction*.

In contrast, Vygotsky doesn't see play as simply reflecting children's level of intellectual development but as actively contributing to it (Nicolopoulou, 1993). According to Vygotsky (1967), play is always a *social* activity, even if it appears to be completely solitary. Play is always social in the sense that the themes and stories that children enact while playing reflect their understanding of roles and activities in their societies. Play is one of the ways in which children learn cultural practices and ideas and develop what he calls "higher psychological functions."

And quite apart from whatever larger purpose play might serve, much of it is simply fun. Why else play?

types of play

There are two broad forms of play in which young children engage: practice play and pretend play. **Practice play** (also called **sensorimotor play**) is mainly physical activity and is evident among the young of many animals (for example, a kitten chasing a ball; Vandenberg, 1987). **Pretend play** (sometimes called **imaginative play**) involves imag-

ining that the player, other people, activities, or objects are something other than what they really are. Both practice play and pretend play can be either solitary (a single player) or social (at least two players) (see Table 8.2).

Note that these simple categories of play are not mutually exclusive. A single "game" or play session might involve elements of both practice and pretend games and might be solitary in some respects and social in others. And, as we will see, there are different types of social play.

PRACTICE PLAY

Practice (or sensorimotor) play involves manipulating objects or performing activities simply for the sensations that result. It is often the only type of play that infants are capable of during the early stages of development. Practice play may consist of motor activities such as creeping, crawling, walking, running, skipping, hopping, or waving a hand, a foot, or anything else wavable. It also includes manipulating objects, people, parts of one's own anatomy, or anything else manipulatable. We see it in countless solitary games of young children, such as moving the hand along the steep precipice of the table edge and roaring "rrrrrrrr" deep in the throat in the manner of a well-tuned motorcycle; running around a room with arms spread wide, sputtering like a badly tuned airplane— "ahrahrahrahrahr"; or jumping up and down on the bed repeating rhythmically "upupupupupupup . . ." But these last activities are not simply sensorimotor; they are also pretend play.

PRETEND PLAY

Pretend play includes the multitude of make-believe games that are made possible when, around the age of 2, children can make objects, people, and activities be things they actually are not. In pretend play, boys are often superheroes such as Superman (or super antiheroes such as dragons or monsters); girls are often mothers or nurses (Paley,1984).

Fenson (1987) reports that children as young as 1 year old can pretend. At that age, pretending most often takes the form of simulating common activities—for example, pretending to eat or pretending to sleep.

REALITY AND FANTASY

Preschoolers are sometimes uncertain about the difference between reality and fantasy. Three-year-old Mollie wants to play a pretend game with the other nursery school children, but she knows some pretend bad thing is going to happen. But, as Paley (1986) puts it, "what if the bad thing doesn't know it's pretend?" (p. 45).

> *"Go to sleep, Mollie," Libbie orders. "There might be something dangerous. You won't like it."*
>
> *"I know it," Mollie says. "But I got a bunk bed at home and I sleep there."*
>
> *"Bunk beds are too scary," Amelia says.*
>
> *"Why are they?" Mollie looks worried.*
>
> *"It's a monster, Mollie. Hide!" (Paley, 1986, p. 45).*

But Mollie protests that there are no monsters in her house today. Still, she is unwilling to take any chances:

> *"I'm going to be a statue," Mollie whispers. "So he won't see me." (p. 45).*

Now Frederick comes roaring in on all fours. "I'm a lion. I'm roaring," he says.

> *"Is he scaring you, Mollie?"*
>
> *"No."*
>
> *"Is anyone scaring you?"*

Pretend play feeds children's imagination and contributes a great deal to the development of the mind. It also allows them to practice important language and social skills, even if only with stuffed bears.

> *"The bunk bed," she answers solemnly. (p. 45).*

Mollie, like many other 3 year olds, can create her own ghosts and monsters, and she has developed her own ways of dealing with them. If they threaten too frighteningly, she can become a statue so they won't see her, or she can hide by the teacher—or she can, ultimately, resort to her knowledge that the monsters are pretend monsters.

But when others create monsters, Mollie can never be quite certain that they are truly *pretend pretend*. Perhaps, just perhaps, one of them might be real pretend.

We, of course, do not suffer from the same limitations as does Mollie (nor do most of us enjoy quite as boundless an imagination). We have somehow learned to tell the difference between fantasy and reality; we can dismiss our monsters if they frighten us. Can't we?

DiLalla and Watson (1988) looked at the progression of children's ability to differentiate between fantasy and reality by having children play monster and superhero pretend games with an experimenter. They found that at the youngest ages (3 and 4 years in this study), subjects did not readily differentiate between fantasy and reality. If, while playing, they were brought back to reality by some interruption, they could not easily return to the fantasy again. Older subjects (ages 5 and 6), however, could go in and out of a fantasy character, invent new characters, or transform old ones at will. When younger subjects were asked about the meaning of pretend, they could not answer but typically simply ignored the question. In contrast, older subjects were able to discuss the meaning of real and pretend.

DAYDREAMING

Another type of imaginative play that becomes increasingly prevalent as preschoolers age is daydreaming. Unlike other types of imaginative play in which children actively engage in fantasy, daydreaming is imagining without the activity. Greenacre (1959) reports that daydreaming increases when children reach school age. Before that time their activity-oriented behavior does not lend itself to unlimited daydreaming.

IMAGINARY PLAYMATES

Yet another type of imaginative play, related to daydreaming, makes use of the imaginary playmate, a constant companion and friend to approximately half of all preschool children (Pines, 1978). These imaginary friends, complete with names and relatively stable personality characteristics, are spoken to, played with, teased, and loved by their creators. They are given names, forms, and places—and

young preschoolers will seldom admit their imaginary nature.

In one study, Taylor, Cartwright, and Carlson (1993) interviewed a dozen 4 year olds who had imaginary playmates, asking them to describe their imaginary friends, which they did quite readily. The remarkable thing is that when these children were interviewed again seven months later, their descriptions of their imaginary playmates had scarcely changed; they were every bit as stable as descriptions of real friends.

There is little information about the role imaginary companions might play in preschoolers' development. However, it seems clear that although most children who have imaginary companions act as though they are *real,* most realize they are *imaginary* (Singer & Singer, 1990). And one of the few variables that successfully predict subsequent creativity is the presence of an imaginary playmate in childhood (Schaefer, 1969). College students who recall an imaginary playmate tend to be more creative than those who do not.

The imaginary playmate is associated with other characteristics as well. In a study of 141 children ages 3 and 4, approximately half of whom had imaginary playmates, Singer (1973) and his associates found that children with imaginary playmates watched less television (and selected fewer violent programs when they did), were less aggressive, smiled more, were less bored, and were more advanced in their language development. Other studies show a relationship between very low predispositions to fantasy play and antisocial behavior or susceptibility to delinquency (see Singer, 1973).

the implications of imagination

In the play behavior of young children we find the first manifestations of imagination—manifestations that occur largely in the realm of the fantastic, the unreal.

IS FANTASY DANGEROUS?

Fantasy has not always been encouraged by students of childhood or by grandparents. In a less enlightened age, fairy tales were thought to be harmful to young children (Wertham, 1954). And daydreaming—including belief in imaginary playmates—was seen as indicating a lack of contact with reality. Children who daydream excessively suffer physically from the resulting inactivity, claimed Hurlock (1964). Furthermore, they also suffer psychologically from an eventual overreliance on daydreams to romanticize a self with which they are not happy.

Research and theory should do much to relieve any leftover fears of imagining and pretending that we might have. Theorists today believe that pretend play has a very constructive role in the development of cognitive and social skills. Piaget (1951), for example, views symbolic (pretend) play as one of the means by which children progress to more advanced forms of thought. Pretend play, along with deferred imitation and language, is one of the surest signs of mental representation. Cobb (1977) describes the "genius of childhood" in terms of imagination. He says it is "the imagination of childhood from which all later creative activities evolve" (p. 18).

CONTRIBUTIONS TO A THEORY OF MIND

Pretend play, says Leslie (1988), contributes to one of the cognitive capacities that sets us apart from other species. Specifically, it eventually enables us to think about ourselves and about others as thinkers, as organisms capable of having different states of mind. When mother puts a banana in her ear and says "Hello,"

4-year-old Nancy recognizes at once that the banana is a pretend telephone. But there is no confusion here between reality and fantasy; she still knows very clearly that it is a banana. What is also clear to Nancy, however, is that mother can have different states of mind, and that she can too. Nancy has begun to develop a "theory of mind," says Leslie (1988). And one important aspect of this theory is the recognition of others and of self as thinkers capable of deliberately selecting and manipulating ideas—even pretend ideas. Here, in the preschool period, is the dawning of what psychologists label *metacognition*—knowing about knowing.

If pretending, daydreaming, and creating imaginary playmates serve as some sort of compensation for an unhappy or disturbed childhood, as Freud believed, then we might expect pretend play to be more common among unhappy, disturbed, and perhaps lonely children. In fact, however, imaginative play is more common among children whose biological and psychological needs are reasonably well satisfied (Freyberg, 1973).

CULTURAL DIFFERENCES IN PLAY BEHAVIOR

It should not be surprising that there are some cultural and social differences in preschoolers' play behavior in spite of the fact that play appears to be universal among all cultures (Hughes, 1990). For example, in societies in which children must assume work responsibilities at very early ages, there is less childhood play, an observation that is also often true of children who are economically and socially disadvantaged (Schwartzman, 1987).

Children learn many of their first play behaviors in interaction with principal caregivers, note O'Reilly and Bornstein (1993). One might therefore expect that among the poor, many mothers would be preoccupied or busy and would devote less time to interacting with infants. Bowman (1993) reports that this expectation has been corroborated in the finding that the play of poor children is sometimes less complex and involves less advanced usage of language.

Farver and Howes (1993) analyzed videotapes of interactions between American and Mexican mother-preschooler pairs, looking specifically at instances of pretend and social play. They conclude that there are important cultural differences in preschoolers' play between these two cultures. "In the American setting," they write, "play activity is valued for its educational benefits" (p. 354). Accordingly, mothers spend more time organizing play activities and providing objects and ideas. In contrast, mother-child play is less common in the Mexican community. Thus when Mexican mothers were asked to play with their children, they were more likely to engage in shared-work activity rather than in the more child-centered, pretend play than the American mothers favored.

The fact that play activity is different in these cultures does not mean that one is better than the other for children's development. When Farver (1992) analyzed play dialogues used by American and Mexican preschoolers, she found no important differences. Both used dialogue to share meaning, whether real or pretend, and both played collaboratively, following story lines, cooperating, and practicing social skills.

social play

Children's developing motor skills owe a great deal to sensorimotor play; and cognitive development owes much to imaginative play. By the same token, some of the roots of children's personality and interpersonal skills lie in social play.

Social play is any type of play that involves interaction among two or more children. Accordingly, either practice or pretend play is social when it involves more than one child. Skipping rope alone in the darkness of one's basement is a solitary sensorimotor activity; skipping rope out on the playground with others turning the rope and chanting "pepper, pepper, salt and . . ." is a cooperative or social activity. Similarly, creating elaborate and

Social play provides important opportunities for acquiring and practicing behaviors involved in social interaction, for developing cooperative behaviors, for learning how to resolve conflict, for making friends, and for fostering imagination and creativity.

fantastic daydreams in the solitude of one's bedroom is private imaginative play, but playing "let's pretend—you be the veterinaman and I'll be the dog" is social imaginative play.

Parten (1932) observed the play behavior of groups of nursery school children and identified five different kinds of social play distinguishable in terms of the type and amount of peer interaction involved. Although these develop sequentially, they also overlap (see Table 8.3).

PRIMITIVE SOCIAL PLAY

Most of children's play before the age of 2 appears to be solitary (Piaget, 1923). In **solitary play**, children play alone with toys or engage in some solitary motor activity, paying little attention to other children. Nevertheless, there are some forms of **primitive social play** that sometimes occur even before the age of 6 months (Brenner & Mueller, 1982). "Peek-a-boo" games, as well as games that include tickling, tossing, and related activities, are clear examples, although these typically occur with parents or older children, rather than with peers.

But there are examples of nonsolitary play among peers before the age of 2 (Ross, 1982). Such play usually involves what Brenner and Mueller refer to as shared meaning (rather than shared rules) and is illustrated in the "chase" games of toddlers or in the "touch me and I'll touch you" game.

ONLOOKER PLAY

As the label implies, **onlooker play** consists of a child watching others play, but not participating actively. Onlooker play occurs throughout childhood. Often, the onlooker may talk with the players, perhaps even giving them advice or asking questions.

PARALLEL PLAY

In **parallel play**, children play side by side, often with similar toys, but do not interact, do not share the activities involved in the game, and do not use any mutually accepted rules. Parallel play is nevertheless social play of a primitive sort because it involves two or more children who apparently prefer to play together even if they do not interact. Some research indicates that the presence of toys often detracts from social interaction and leads to parallel or perhaps solitary play, particularly among very young children (Vandell, Wilson, & Buchanan, 1980). Not surprisingly, in the absence of toys, children are more likely to interact with each other.

ASSOCIATIVE PLAY

With advancing age, children become more interested in interacting with peers and are more likely to include toys in what is termed **associative play**. This type of play involves interaction among children, even though they continue to play separately. In associative play, children sometimes share toys, but each child plays independently without mutually accepted goals or rules.

t a b l e 8 . 3

Classifications and examples of children's social play

CLASSIFICATION	POSSIBLE ACTIVITY
Primitive social play	"Peek-a-boo."
Onlooker play	Child watches others play "tag" but does not join in.
Parallel play	Two children play with trucks in sandbox, but do not interact; they play beside each other, but not together.
Associative play	Two children play with dolls, talk with each other about their dolls, lend each other diapers and dishes, but play independently, sharing neither purpose nor rules.
Cooperative play	"Let's pretend. You be a monster and I'll be the guy with the magic sword and…."

COOPERATIVE PLAY

Children who play cooperatively help one another in activities that require shared goals and perhaps even a division of roles. Although most research on preschoolers' play behavior indicates that associative and cooperative play are not common before the age of 4 or 5, there is sometimes evidence of cooperation in the play of much younger children. Rubin and colleagues (1976) report that preschoolers who have had considerable experience with similar-aged peers (in childcare facilities, for example) are far more likely to play cooperatively whenever they can than are children reared in more solitary circumstances (see Figure 8.3 for older children's choices of favorite play places).

It is largely through cooperative social play that preschoolers form friendships. Not surprisingly, the best liked children appear to be those who are most cooperative (as well as least aggressive and least difficult) (Denham & Holt, 1993). Patterns of interactions in preschool friend-

figure 8.3

A map of children's favorite places. When 48 boys and 48 girls ages 9 through 12 were asked to draw their favorite places, these are the places depicted most often in their drawings. Figures indicate the percentage of children including a given item in their drawings. Source: Moore (1986).

LAWNS .71
PLAYGROUNDS
PLAY EQUIPMENT
SCHOOLYARDS .65
CHILD'S OWN HOME .51
LOCAL PARKS .40
SINGLE TREES .36
THROUGH STREETS .34
PAVEMENTS .30
OTHER DWELLINGS .29
FENCES .28
FRIEND'S HOMES .25
FOOTPATHS .24
SWIMMING POOLS .19
SPORTS FIELDS .18
FLOWERS/MISC. STRUCTURES .17
PONDS & LAKES .16
SHRUBS .15
CHILD'S SCHOOL/CHILD'S FRIENDS .13
TRAFFIC/BRIDGES .11
SELF PORTRAIT/TOPOGRAPHY/DIRT & SAND .10

★ ★ ★ ★ ★ ★

TREE CLUSTERS/YARDS & GARDENS .09
HILLS/ASPHALT & CONCRETE/CLIMATIC CONDITIONS .08
CAR PARKS/CLIMBING TREES/WOODLAND/ABANDONED BUILDINGS .06
WILD BIRDS & INSECTS/CUL DE SACS/CULVERTED STREAMS/LOCAL SHOPS/TALL GRASS, LEAVES & WEEDS/CATS & DOGS/BUILDING INTERIORS/SHOPPING CENTERS/COMMUNITY BUILDINGS/VEGETABLE GARDENS/ROCKS/STREAMS/WILD ANIMALS/CHILD'S RELATIVES & OTHER ADULTS/RAILWAY LINES/BUS STOPS/FORTS, CLUBHOUSES & CAMPS/SPORTS COURTS/VACANT BUILDING SITES/FRUITING TREES/NEIGHBOR'S & BABYSITTER'S HOUSES/SECRET, HIDING PLACES/TREE HOUSES/TREE SWINGS/FISH & AQUATIC LIFE/CHILD'S SIBLINGS/CHURCHES——.05 and less.

ships appear to be quite stable (Park, Lay, & Ramsay, 1993).

An important example of cooperative social play is found in the drama that children sometimes enact in their pretend play:

"You be the baby."

"I be the baby."

"I be the mother."

"You be the mother. I be the baby."

"If you're bad . . . if you wee-wee your diaper, well, you know . . ." (making an abrupt spanking gesture, but smiling broadly all the while.)

Garvey (1977) found that the most common interactions in dramatic play were mother-infant, mother-child, or mother-father. She found too that children often reveal their fears and worries, their hopes and aspirations, in their dramatic play. Social play of this kind is more than just fun; it provides an important opportunity for acquiring and practicing behaviors involved in social interaction, for developing cooperative behaviors, for learning how to resolve conflict, for making friends, and for fostering imagination and creativity.

And as Paley (1984) points out, the roles that children adopt for their pretend dramas—monster or mother, baby or father, superhero or witch—reveal much about the gender roles with which they are comfortable.

gender roles in early childhood

Gender is one of those visually conspicuous characteristics on which we base our judgments of people and our reactions to them, says Fiske (1993); others are age, race, and physical appearance.

In most cultures, including ours, there are usually marked differences between the ways in which males and females are expected to think, act, and feel. The range of behaviors considered appropriate for males and females—that are considered *masculine* or *feminine*—together with the attitudes and personality characteristics associated with each, define **gender roles**. The learning of sex-appropriate behavior is **gender typing**.

The toys that are selected for children, and the games and toys that they select for themselves, reveal much about the roles that parents and society consider appropriate for each gender. Gender typing begins in infancy and becomes increasingly clear through the preschool period.

In Chapter 6 we saw that gender typing begins from the very earliest moment, when the mere fact that a child is male or female determines much of what a parent's reactions to the infant will be. Thus parents unabashedly describe their newborn sons as strong, lusty, vigorous, and alert, and their newborn daughters as fine-featured, delicate, and pretty (Rubin, Provenzano, & Luria, 1974).

gender schemas

"One of the first social dimensions that children notice is sex," claim Serbin, Powlishta, and Gulko (1993, p. 1). Very early in life they begin to develop what researchers label **gender schemas** (also sometimes labeled *gender scripts*). Gender schemas are children's knowledge about characteristics associated with being male and female (Levy, 1993). Much of this knowledge consists of stereotypes such as those associated with common occupations or with predominant personality characteristics. Children use their gender schemas both as guides for interpreting and understanding the behavior of others and for directing their own behavior.

Infants begin to develop gender schemas very early in life. Even at the age of 5 months they can already discriminate between photographs of males and females (Leinbach & Fagot, 1986). And by the age of 2 or 3 years they can correctly label people as man or woman (or boy or girl). By then they can also make predictions of the sorts of activities or occupations that would be most likely for specific individuals, knowing nothing about them other than their gender (Gelman, Collman, & Maccoby, 1986).

Gender schemas are complex and multifaceted. Although the processes by which they are acquired are not completely understood, Levy and Fivush

(1993) suggest that they are learned much as other things are learned: through experiencing, observing, doing, and thinking.

assuming gender identity

Infants and preschoolers not only learn what it means to be male or female, they also begin to adopt the roles associated with their sex.

Although children begin to discriminate between male and female very early in life—that is, they begin to develop gender schemas early—it isn't until later in the preschool period that they finally understand that gender is a permanent category that can't easily be changed (Serbin, Powlishta, & Gulko, 1993). At the same time, children assume the role they associate with their sex. And their understanding of this role, claim Levine, Resnick, and Higgins (1993), determines and constrains much of their behavior. Because boys are not *supposed* to cry, then Johnny tries hard not to. And because girls aren't supposed to be truck drivers, Sarah ignores the dump truck in the sand box.

TWO THEORIES OF GENDER TYPING

Freud suggested that boys learn to behave as "boys" and girls as "girls" at least partly through identifying with their parents and with other males and females. In his terms, the values, behaviors, beliefs, and attitudes of each sex become the children's as they are *introjected* (in a sense borrowed) from significant people in the children's environment.

A more cognitive explanation suggests the gender typing results from preschoolers' understanding of the meaning of gender. Kohlberg (1966) describes three stages or levels of understanding.

The play of childhood

Play, in its countless forms, is the essence of childhood. It is not only its magic and its joy; it is also its teacher. For in the sensorimotor play of childhood, children develop and practice physical skills; in imaginative play, they stretch their minds; and in social play, they learn the many rules and roles of a more serious life.

In the pouring of the tea the child practices not only the act of pouring, but also the act of giving; in the mad scramble to the beach, there are new friendships found, old ones confirmed; in the settling of the rules, there are leaders made, and followers too.

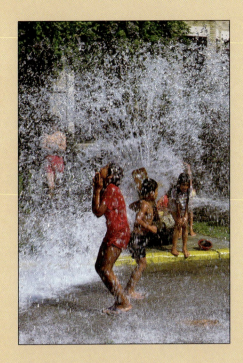

Not all the play of childhood is social. Much of it is solitary—sometimes even when others are near. But even solitary play, such as with television or computers, or with books and written words, often involves interacting with the feelings and thoughts of others.

At one extreme, there is the truly solitary play of the daydream—the imagining without the acting, the thinking without the doing. Then there is play that is shared—a melding of action and imagination. Ultimately, the play of childhood is not only its magic, its joy, and its teacher; it is also a confirmation of thinking and feeling—a confirmation of being.

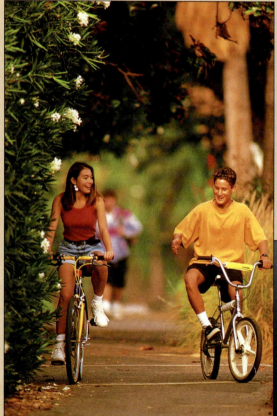

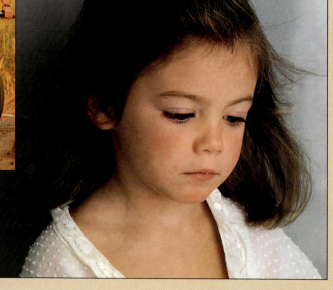

These stages reflect children's increasing awareness of gender:

- *Stage 1. Basic gender identity* describes the initial stage in which an infant recognizes simply that he is a boy or she is a girl.

- *Stage 2. Gender stability* refers to the realization that gender is permanent and unchangeable.

- *Stage 3. Gender constancy* reflects children's eventual understanding that superficial changes (in ways of behaving or dressing, for example) are irrelevant to basic gender.

Kohlberg argues that once children become aware of their gender identity and its meaning, they actively participate in organizing their behaviors and their environments to conform to sex-appropriate patterns. Thus, having decided that she is a female, a girl selects feminine toys and behaviors. And having decided that he is a male, a boy leaves the "doll corner," except when he raids it with his phasers and missiles or haunts it as a pretend monster. Not surprisingly, the most widely used indicators of gender typing at the preschool level are based on selection of toys and activities. In the elementary school years, more abstract measures of self-perception are possible (Boldizar, 1991).

gender differences

There are obvious biological differences between the sexes; that there are also psychological differences is less obvious and certainly far more controversial. Nevertheless, as is shown in Chapter 12, there are some small (and diminishing) differences between males and females in some areas, perhaps most notably in aggressiveness.

In the later preschool period there is already evidence of gender differences in the play of boys and girls. When they are only 3, boys will gladly pretend to be babies, mothers, fathers, or monsters. Most are as comfortable wearing the discarded apron and the nursery school teacher's high-heeled shoes as the fire fighter's hat or the ranch hand's boots. They play in the doll corner as easily as do the girls.

But when they are 5, Paley (1984) informs us, the atmosphere in the doll corner changes dramatically. Now when there are pretend games, the boys are monsters and superheroes, and the girls are princesses and sisters. But these are not the only changes that come with age. In Paley's (1984) words:

> In the [kindergarten] class described in this book, for example, you hop to get your milk if you are a boy and skip to the paper shelf if you are a girl. Boys clap out the rhythm of certain songs; girls sing louder. Boys draw furniture inside four-story haunted houses; girls put flowers in the doorways of cottages. Boys get tired of drawing pictures and begin to poke and shove; girls continue to draw. (p. xi)

Several consistent findings have emerged from studies that have examined sex differences in play behavior. To begin with, there is little evidence of any greater predisposition toward fantasy (imaginative play) in either girls or boys (Singer, 1973), but there is repeated evidence of sex typing, not only in the toys that boys and girls are given but also in the toys they choose. Rheingold and Cook (1975) looked at the rooms of 96 children and found, not surprisingly, that boys are given what we consider to be male-typed toys: trucks, airplanes, boats, soldiers, and guns. Girls are given dolls, plastic dishes, cooking utensils, and doll houses.

Among additional sex differences in play behavior are that boys use more physical space in their play, play outdoors more, and are more interested in "rough and tumble," noisy play. Girls are more interested in "nurturant" play (helping, caring for). Boys tease, wrestle, push, run, and engage in sex-typed role-playing games in which they are fire fighters, builders, warriors, and so on; girls often play house, cooking, cleaning, looking after children, and helping each other with aprons, hats, and other items of clothing (Pitcher & Schultz, 1983).

These sex differences are less apparent among 2 year olds, who engage in a great deal of cross-sex play, than among 5 year olds, who tend to play more often with children of the same sex. Pitcher and Schultz note that societies, and consequently parents, have traditionally attempted to maximize sex differences in the play (and other interests) of young children, sometimes even punishing and ridiculing children whose games seemed less appropriate for their sex. More recently, there have been concerted social efforts toward understanding and reducing these differences. As Christopherson (1988) puts it, "the learning of gender roles . . . reflects one of the earliest and most profound focuses in the family socialization process" (p. 129).

But are gender differences entirely a matter of social learning? Or are there basic biological differences between the sexes that make some gender differences inevitable?

GENETIC INFLUENCES ON GENDER

There is evidence that genes do influence *some* gender-role differences. If a difference is genetically based, argues Lynn (1974), it would (1) be displayed at a very young age, before other environmental forces could have influenced it; (2) be evident in a wide variety of cultures; (3) be seen among nonhuman primates; and (4) be related to the effects of hormones on masculinity and femininity.

All these criteria hold with respect to the greater aggressiveness of males than females. Males are more aggressive than females at an early age, a finding that is consistent in most cultures and also for nonhuman primates; and the injection of male hormones into pregnant mothers affects the subsequent aggressiveness of female children who were in utero at the time (Maccoby & Jacklin, 1980; Jacklin, 1989).

SOCIOCULTURAL MODELS AND GENDER EXPECTATIONS

We should not conclude, however, that the greater aggressiveness of males in our culture is inevitable given probable genetic differences in aggression. The influence of cultural factors cannot be discounted. For example, many occupations requiring physical aggression and strength have traditionally been restricted to males, whereas those requiring nonaggressive, passive, nurturant behavior have been considered more appropriate for women. Hence the models society provides for children are clear. Children encounter them everywhere: on television, in books, in schools, on the playground. The message clearly is that certain behaviors, attitudes, and interests are appropriate—and inappropriate—for one's sex (Askew & Ross, 1988). And, as Connell (1985) notes, almost all the soldiers, police officers, wardens, admirals, bureaucrats, and politicians who control the machinery of collective violence are men—as are most murderers, rapists, muggers, and scoundrels.

Studies of the role of television in sex typing have found that children who are exposed to conventional, stereotyped portrayals of male-female roles tend to have more stereotyped conceptions of what these roles are and should be. By the same token, when researchers have presented children with programs designed to reduce gender-role stereotypes, results have been encouraging (Roberts & Bachan, 1981). Tremendous strides have been made in the past several decades in removing sexual biases in books, films, television, and thus in our attitudes—which is not to say that we have yet gone as far as we should.

PARENTAL ATTITUDES TOWARD GENDER ROLES

Parents treat displays of aggression in children differently according to their sex; they are likely to encourage it in boys and punish it in girls. Similarly, parents typically reinforce daughters less for independence and problem solving, and are more protective of daughters than of sons (Block, 1983). When mothers are asked at what ages they would allow their children to play alone outside, to cut with scissors, and so on, ages are almost always higher for girls than for boys. It appears that gender-role training begins very early in life.

Are these sociocultural facts a result of innate biological differences, or do sociocultural expectations simply exaggerate these differences? In other words, do basic, genetic sex differences cause parents and societies to ascribe different roles to the sexes, or do these different roles cause the sex differences? Is this a chicken-and-egg problem?

the contemporary family

From the beginning of life," writes Stratton (1988), "it is overwhelmingly the family that mediates cultural and social values and presents them to the child" (p. 5). The family's importance can hardly be overstated.

The **nuclear family** was once North America's most prevalent family; only a few years ago, more than 85 percent of all children lived in families consisting of a mother, a father, and approximately 1¼ siblings—this latter phenomenon made possible solely through those statistical manipulations that calculate the average family size to be about 3.23 people (U.S. Bureau of the Census, 1992). In contrast, a majority of the world's societies have traditionally been characterized by **extended families**: parents and their children, grandparents, uncles, aunts,

The traditional definition of the typical North American family has been turned on its ear. It is no longer the once common white, two-parent-plus-children, nuclear family. Today's family might be white, African-American, Hispanic, or some other mix; it might be one- or two-parent; it might be an intact family or a blended family ("stepfamily"); or it might, as is shown here, be a gay or a lesbian family.

cousins, and various other assorted relatives.

Our vision of the "typical" North American family is still most often that of a nuclear family—mother, father, and one or two children—with father as breadwinner, although mother might also work. This view is a myth, argue Lamanna and Riedmann (1994). They point out that at present, fewer than 30 percent of all families conform to this vision. Of the remainder, a large and growing proportion are single-parent families. About 85 percent of single-parent families are headed by a mother (U.S. Bureau of the Census, 1992).

The traditional "white, two parents and children" definition of the North American family is no longer correct. "There is no single correct definition of what a *family* is," Fine (1993, p. 235) writes. It might be white, African-American, Hispanic, Asian, or some mix; it might have one or two parents; it might be an intact family or a blended family ("stepfamily"); or it might be a gay or lesbian family.

Not only is the family difficult to define, but it is also very private and highly dynamic rather than static. The family is dynamic in that it changes with the addition of new members (and sometimes the loss of old ones), as well as in response to both external and internal pressures.

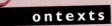

in other ontexts   Baruch, a kibbutz child

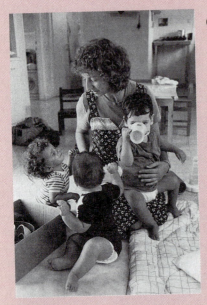

wo days after he was born, Baruch and his mother returned from the hospital to the kibbutz (based on Lieblich, 1982, and Rabin & Beit-Hallahmi, 1982). His mother went to the quarters she shared with her husband; little Baruch was put into the "infant house."

For the first six weeks, Baruch's mother was available to nurse him "on demand." After that, he was put on a four-hour schedule, although his mother continued to look after him at intervals during the day, with the help of his metapelet, an unrelated woman assigned to look after him.

At the age of 9 months, Baruch, like all other like-aged kibbutz infants, was given over almost entirely to the care of his metapelet who, with the help of an assistant, looked after five other children as well, playing with, washing, dressing, feeding, and talking to them. In short, these women, and often other children's metaplot (which is the plural of metapelet), did all the things a mother might do.

At the age of 15 months, Baruch was moved to the "toddler's house." A metapelet and her assistants continued to be responsible for all aspects of his care, interrupted only by short daily visits to his parent's home and by somewhat longer visits on Saturdays and Sundays.

At age 4, Baruch became a member of the kindergarten group. A teacher, along with two assistants, began to familiarize him and some 15

Given the family's privacy, researchers seldom have access to the most intimate aspects of its functioning. And given its dynamic nature, the relationships and influences within it do not expose themselves clearly and simply to the scrutiny of social scientists. Hence the family is difficult to research; there is much about which we can only speculate. (See "In Other Contexts: Baruch, A Kibbutz Child.")

parenting young children

According to Westman (1991a), the family serves three principal functions in North American societies: (1) It has a *sustenance* function (to provide food, shelter, and clothing); (2) it has *developmental* functions (through caregiving and parenting); and (3) it has *advocacy* functions (through ensuring children's access to education, health care, a safe environment, and so on).

In Chapter 6 we saw that for infants the most important features of caregiving are *attentiveness, physical contact, verbal stimulation, material stimulation, responsive care,* and *absence of restrictiveness.* As infants age and as their verbal, motor, and intellectual abilities blossom, important dimensions of parenting begin to change. But parenting is no less important for older children than it is for preschoolers.

other students with the activities and chores of the kibbutz. The emphasis was on cooperation, group activities, and discipline.

For elementary school, Baruch was moved to a combined school/dormitory serving about 20 students. With three others he moved into a bedroom, acquired a new metapelet (responsible primarily for his physical care), and began to study in a clearly cooperative, noncompetitive setting.

Through all of this, Baruch was always a member of a group, although its composition changed from time to time. Until puberty, groups remained completely coeducational, with boys and girls sharing classrooms, bedrooms, even showers (although taboos prohibiting sexual exploration were always clear and strict).

Had Baruch been born more recently, his upbringing in the kibbutz might have been very different. There have been dramatic changes, note Rabin and Beit-Hallahmi (1982), in communal childrearing in the kibbutz. There is now much closer contact between parents and children; in fact, they often sleep in the same quarters (sometimes until adolescence). In some cases, parents have become principle caregivers and socializers. In these circumstances, "children's houses" serve more as day-care facilities than as the "multiple mothering" and socializing centers they traditionally were. In addition, many families have television sets, their own dining areas, even their own kitchens and refrigerators. Thus, the family is taking over many of the roles once given over to the commune.

To Think About: Historically, kibbutzim de-emphasized the nuclear family at a time when most Western societies held it up as the childrearing ideal. Now children in Western societies are increasingly exposed to aspects of "multiple caregiving" (through nonparental childcare and through changing family structures); at the same time kibbutzim appear to be reemphasizing the role of the nuclear family. What do you think are the best features of each of these systems? Can they be combined? How do you suppose Baruch might turn out in a traditional kibbutz system? In one less traditional?

To Read: Rabin, A. I., & Beit-Hallahmi, B. (1982). Twenty years later: Kibbutz children grown up. New York: Springer.
Lieblich, A. (1982). Kibbutz Makom: Report from an Israeli kibbutz. London: André Deutsch.

PARENTING STYLES

Baumrind (1967) looked at the kinds of parenting associated with three distinct groups of children. One group consisted of buoyant, friendly, self-controlled, and self-reliant children; another, of discontented and withdrawn children; and a third, of children who lacked self-reliance and self-control.

Baumrind found some consistent and striking differences among the parenting styles of the mothers and fathers of these children. Parents of the friendly, self-controlled, self-reliant children were significantly more controlling, demanding, and loving than parents of either of the other groups. Parents of the discontented and withdrawn children also exercised much control but were detached rather than warm and loving. And parents of the children low in self-esteem were warm but highly permissive.

On the basis of studies such as these, Baumrind (1989) identifies three different styles of parenting, each of which is characterized by different types of parental control: permissive, authoritarian, and authoritative (see Table 8.4).

Permissive parenting is a nonpunitive, nondirective, and nondemanding form of parental control. Permissive parents allow children to make their own decisions and to govern their own activities. They don't try to control through the exercise of the power that comes from authority, physical strength, status, or the ability to grant or withhold rewards; but they might, on occasion, try to appeal to children's reason.

Authoritarian parenting is grounded on firm and usually clearly identified standards of conduct, often based on religious or political beliefs. Authoritarian parents value obedience above all and exercise whatever power is necessary to make children conform. Children in authoritarian homes are neither given responsibility for personal decisions nor involved in rational discussion of the family's standards.

Authoritative parenting falls somewhere between permissive and authoritarian control. It uses firm control but allows rational discussion of standards and expectations; it values obedience but tries to promote independence. Authoritative parents, in contrast with authoritarian parents, have standards derived more from reason than from religious or political beliefs.

table 8.4

Parenting styles

STYLE	CHARACTERISTICS	EXAMPLES
Permissive	*Laissez-faire; nonpunitive; children responsible for own actions and decisions; autonomy more important than obedience; non-demanding.*	*"Okay. I mean sure. Whatever you want. You decide."*
Authoritarian	*Dogmatic; very controlling; obedience highly valued; self-control and autonomy limited; little recourse to reasoning.*	*"You're going to darn well study for 40 minutes right now. Then you say your prayers and go right to bed. Or else!"*
Authoritative	*Based on reason; permits independence but values obedience; imposes regulations, but allows discussion.*	*"Don't you think you should study for a while before you go to bed? We'd like you to get good grades. But you know we can't let you stay up that late. It isn't good for you."*

Interestingly, the parenting styles of mothers and fathers within families tend to be more alike than different. Bentley and Fox (1991) compared the responses of 52 pairs of mothers and fathers of children ages 1 through 4 years to the Fox Parenting Inventory (Fox, 1990). The scale measures three areas of parenting: *expectations* ("My child should use the toilet without help"); *discipline* ("I yell at my child for whining"); and *nurturance* ("I read to my child at bedtime.") Although mothers received higher nurturance scores than fathers, mothers and fathers did not differ on expectations or discipline.

NOVICE AND EXPERT PARENTS

Some parents are probably better at parenting than others. In Cooke's (1991) terms, some are *novices* and some are *experts*. How are the two different? Among other things, experts are better at sensing children's needs and goals, especially in problem-solving situations; they have better general knowledge of child development and childrearing; they have consciously thought about their roles and their goals; and they foster activity that provides their children with opportunities to be self-directive.

These characteristics of *expert* parents are most evident in *competent* children—that is, children whose measured achievement compares favorably with that of other children. Other dimensions of effective parenting do not have outcomes as clearly measurable but may be even more important. For example, Dix (1991) suggests that parents' emotions can be used as an indication of the quality of parenting. Parenting is an emotional experience, says Dix, "because children are vital to parents' daily concerns and life goals. Emotions are barometers for relationships because they reflect parents' assessments of how well interactions are

proceeding . . ." (p. 19). Even competent parents report frustration and occasional anger with their children, but most parents report far more positive than negative emotions—except in dysfunctional families.

---

do parents make a measurable difference?

Which parenting style is best, and will it be best under all circumstances? How much do parents really matter?

The Freudian model says yes, parents matter a great deal because children are extremely sensitive to the emotional experiences of their early lives, especially to their relationships with their parents. And the behavioristic model says yes, too, because children are highly responsive to the rewards and punishments of their environments.

CONFLICTING FINDINGS

But the results of research are not entirely clear. For example, retrospective studies (looking backward in time, often using interviews or questionnaires) with delinquent and otherwise disturbed adolescents and adults have generally found that their childhoods were marked by a variety of traumas sometimes associated with alcoholic or abusive parents, poverty, authoritarianism, rejection, and a variety of other factors. In one such study, women whose partners were alcohol-dependent reported significantly more problem behaviors among their children (Tubman, 1993). But when researchers try to predict which of a group of children will be maladjusted and which will be happy and well-adjusted, they are unsuccessful about two-thirds of the time (Skolnick, 1978). Indeed, some very successful, well-adjusted individuals have home environments that should

Which parenting style is best? Should parents be authoritarian, making and enforcing all important decisions? Should they be "laissez-faire," allowing children to make their own decisions? Or should they be more authoritative, seeking to guide and protect, but allowing the child input as well? Experts don't always agree; nor is parenting style always a good predictor of child-rearing outcomes.

place them at high risk. It seems that predicting the effects of childrearing practices is far more difficult than explaining these effects after the fact. What this indicates most clearly is that our after-the-fact explanations might have been entirely wrong in the first place.

THE SEARS STUDY OF PARENTING PRACTICES

In the early 1950s, Sears and his associates (Sears, Maccoby, & Lewin, 1957; Sears, 1984) interviewed 379 mothers of kindergarten children, rated each on more than 100 childrearing practices, and looked at the relationships between these practices and the personalities of their children. In general, the observed relationships were unimpressive and the findings ambiguous.

McClelland and his associates (1978) later tracked down 78 subjects from the original Sears study—subjects who had been children at the time of the original interviews but who were now 31 years old. These subjects were interviewed in depth, and 47 of them were brought into a clinical setting for a battery of psychological tests. The researchers' conclusion: "Wide variations in the way parents

reared their children didn't seem to matter much in the long run. Adult interests and beliefs were by and large not determined by the duration of breast-feeding, the age and severity of toilet-training, strictness about bedtimes, or indeed any of these things" (p. 46).

BAUMRIND'S ADVICE FOR PARENTS

Following extensive investigations of the relationships between behavior and characteristics of parents and the personalities of their children, Baumrind (1977) concludes that there is no one best way of rearing children. Like McClelland, she argues that there are no specific childrearing practices (breast-feeding, toilet training, and bed times, for example) that should be recommended over others, but there are some general characteristics of parents, reflected in their behaviors and attitudes toward their children, that might have highly positive effects—and negative ones, too. She found, for example, that parents who were firm and directive were more likely to have children who would be responsible (as opposed to socially disruptive and intolerant of others) and active (as opposed to passive). But what she advocates is not authoritarian but authoritative parenting— parenting that is firm, but reasonable; demanding, but warm, nurturing, and loving.

Baumrind also argues against the permissiveness that was ushered in by what is sometimes termed the Spock era of child-rearing (in reference to Dr. Benjamin Spock, not Mr. Spock of "Star Trek"). She suggests that permissiveness is based on a number of false assumptions, especially that firm feeding habits, toilet training, spanking, and other forms of punishment are unquestionably bad and that unconditional love is good. She points out that punishment is effective and does not rupture attachment bonds between parents and children, provided it is reasonable punishment by an authoritative and loving parent; that unconditional love is likely to lead to the development of selfish and obnoxious children; and that there is virtually no good research evidence to support a belief that toilet training or insisting on regular feeding habits is inadvisable.

There is evidence that Baumrind's advice is sound. Bronstein et al. (1993) report a number of studies that have found a link between authoritative parenting and positive child outcomes—and between lax parenting and poorer child adjustment.

CHILDCARE ADVICE

Parents do make a difference, but our recommendations concerning the best parenting styles must be tentative. As McCartney and Jordan (1990) note, the conclusions of parenting research have not always been clear because researchers have tended to use simple models that were not adequate for the complexity of the interactions involved. If the conclusions are to be valid and useful, they argue, researchers must adopt ecological models such as that proposed by Bronfenbrenner (see Chapter 2). These mod-

els not only emphasize the complexity of parenting, but suggest as well the possibility that parenting styles that are excellent for certain children in given circumstances may be quite disastrous for other children or under different circumstances.

There are nevertheless some recognizably good—and bad—ways of parenting. "At the most simple level," says Christopherson (1988), "if the children are basically happy, the parents are probably not doing too much that is wrong" (p. 133). At a more detailed level, he offers seven guidelines for childrearing practices (pp. 133–136):

- Behavior and relationships with others depend on the extent to which children's basic needs are met.

- Parents need to recognize each child as a unique individual.

- The faith, honesty, confidence, and affection between parent and child affects the quality of the parent-child relationship.

- Parents should separate the worth of children from their behavior.

- Children should be allowed as much freedom as possible to make mistakes and discoveries, but to do so with safety and respect for the rights of others and for social convention.

- Parents should arrange the environment to encourage prosocial behavior.

- Parents should be ready to lend support directly or indirectly through physical or verbal guidance.

learning to parent

How do parents learn to care for children? In many close-knit and so-called "primitive" societies, the old ones show the young ones what must be done. And there is evidence that, at least to some extent, the same thing happens in our more complex contemporary societies. Ijzendoorn (1993) surveyed a large number of parenting studies and found a significant amount of what is termed *intergenerational transmission of parenting styles*. It seems that we have a tendency to parent the way our own parents did.

SOURCES OF CHILDCARE ADVICE

Not all parents simply rely on their own intuition, common sense, and intelligence, or on the transmitted wisdom of their parents and grandparents. Many turn to one or more of three major groups of commercial childcare advisors: (1) the medical profession, whose personnel readily provide advice relating to psychological and physical health; (2) books, which are the preferred source of advice for the majority of parents (Abram and Dowling, 1979); and (3) parenting courses.

There are a handful of well-known and widely established parent-education courses, including Gordon's parent effectiveness training (PET), Adler's systematic training for effective parenting (STEP), and Berne's transactional analysis (TA) (Gordon, 1975, 1976; Dinkmeyer & McKay, 1976; Harris, 1973; Berne, 1964).

Parent-education courses usually require relatively lengthy training and practice sessions. They are almost invariably based on a recognition of the rights of children and take into consideration their needs and desires. They treat children as important human beings and discourage punitive approaches to parental control (such as shouting, threatening, physical punishment, and anger-based behaviors). Instead, they encourage reasoning (Brooks, 1981). The ultimate aim of most of these courses is to foster a warm, loving, and nurturant relationship between parent and child. And the principal method by which each of the various techniques operates involves communication.

To summarize, what most parent education programs have in common is that: (1) they encourage parents to be authoritative (firm, democratic, reasonable, respectful) rather than either authoritarian (harsh, controlling, demanding, dogmatic, powerful) or permissive (laissez-faire, noncontrolling, weak); and (2) they teach specific techniques to help parents become authoritative.

Parent education programs also share some major weaknesses: The solutions they provide are often too simple for the complexity of the problems with which parents must occasionally deal. In addition, they typically do not take into account important differences among children of different sexes and ages. And finally, they sometimes mislead parents into thinking that all the answers can be found in a single method (Brooks, 1981).

family composition

Parenting styles are one feature of the family; there are, of course, others. The family, says Hoffman (1991), is a dynamic (changing) and interactive social unit. The experiences of siblings in the same family can be very different depending not only on characteristics of the parents and the siblings, but also on factors such as birth order and family size.

birth order

Galton (1896) was among the first to note the effects of **birth order** when he observed that among the great scientists that Great Britain had produced there was a preponderance of firstborn children. Since then, research has attributed a number of advantages to being firstborn (or an only child). Among them are more rapid and more articulate language development, higher scores on measures of intellectual performance, higher scores on measures of achievement motivation, better academic performance, more curiosity, and a higher probability of going to college (see Melican & Feldt, 1980; Page & Grandon, 1979; Ernst & Angst, 1983). And, for what it's worth, the probability of a firstborn child going into space seems considerably higher than that of a laterborn child. *Newsweek* (1969) reported that of the seven original U.S. astronauts, two were only children and the remaining five were firstborns; of the first 23 astronauts to travel in space, 21 were either only children or firstborns. Of the remaining men, one had an older brother who died as an infant, and the other was 13 years younger than his older brother.

There are a number of plausible explanations for the observed effects of birth order. Certainly, these effects are due not simply to being firstborn, a middle child, or lastborn, but more likely to the fact that the interactions and relationships to which children are exposed are partly determined by position in the family. As Zajonc and Markus (1975) point out, a firstborn child enjoys a close relationship with two adult models. It is hardly surprising that language development should be more accelerated under these conditions than it might be if the child had been a laterborn child or had been one member of a multiple birth. In these latter cases, not only do the parents have less time to interact with the child, but other, nonadult models are now an important part of the family environment.

Before we go running off bragging that we're firstborns or only children—or complaining that we're not—we should note that the contribution of birth order to intelligence and academic achievement may, after all, be negligible. Following a massive investigation of 9,000 high school students and their brothers and sisters (a total of more than 30,000 subjects), Hauser and Sewell (1985) found that the importance of birth order was quite trivial. What appears to be important is not whether you are first- or laterborn, but the size of your family.

family size

Although in general things may be cheaper by the dozen, the larger the family, the more limited the advantages to the children. As Hernandez and Myers (1993) note, although having many brothers and sisters allows for the development of more family relationships, it also means that more children compete for parental time and resources. In the Hauser and Sewell (1985) study, for example, large family size had a significantly negative effect on schooling. In addition, some investigators have found consistent evidence of lower intelligence test scores among members of larger families (Grotevant, Scarr, & Weinberg, 1977; Zajonc, 1976). In explaining these findings, Zajonc argues that the intellectual climate in homes with large families is, on the average, less conducive to cognitive development than the climate characteristic of homes with smaller families.

social class and related factors

Family size *per se* may not be that important, claim Page and Grandon (1979). Not only are the relationships among birth order, family size, and achievement (or intelligence) not very high, but they may be due primarily to socioeconomic factors. Unfortunately, much of the research on family size has not considered the fact that large families are far more common among the poor, the culturally deprived, and certain ethnic minorities.

When these factors are taken into account, it becomes clear that socio-economic status is a more important predictor of intelligence and academic achievement than are family size or birth order (Page & Grandon, 1979; Doby, 1980).

We should always bear in mind that the conclusions of social scientists are usually based on the average performance of large groups of people. Within these groups are individuals whose behavior does not even come close to matching the predictions that social scientists might make. Thus there are saints and geniuses whose siblings numbered in the tens and twenties, and there are poltroons and oafs who were the firstborn in tiny little families.

one-parent families

Close to half of all American children are spending (or will spend) an average of six years in a family with only one parent. The majority of these one-parent families result from separation or divorce; a smaller number result from death of the mother or father or bearing children out of wedlock. Amato and Keith (1991) cite projections that parents of 38 percent of white children and 75 percent of black children in the United States will divorce before the children are 16. Most one-parent families are headed by mothers rather than fathers (see Figure 8.4 in "At a Glance: Family Living Arrangements of U.S. and Canadian Children").

general effects of loss of a parent

There is considerable evidence that separation and divorce, or the death of one parent, is a difficult—sometimes traumatic—experience for most children. Allison and Furstenberg's (1989) investi-

gation of 1,197 children found that marital breakup had widespread and lasting effects evident in higher incidence of problem behavior, psychological distress, and poorer academic performance. Similarly, Amato and Keith's (1991) summary of 92 individual studies (termed a *meta-analysis*) of the impact of divorce found significant negative effects on school achievement, behavior, adjustment, self-concept, and relations with both the remaining and the departed parent. In Bronstein et al.'s (1993) words: "Children from divorced families are more likely to experience behavioral, social, emotional, or academic problems" (p. 268). These effects vary considerably depending on such factors as the child's age, the relationship of the child to the departed as well as the remaining parent, and parental relationships following breakup of the marriage. We look at each of these factors next.

developmental effects of divorce

Almost all investigations indicate that the most serious effects are experienced by children in the middle age groups, mainly elementary and high school students; the least apparent effects are on college students or very young infants (Amato and Keith, 1991).

An ongoing investigation of 60 families in which divorce occurred provides more specific information about how children of different ages react to their parents' divorce (Wallerstein & Kelly, 1974, 1975, 1976, 1980). The early effects of parental separation for the youngest group in this study (2 to 3 year olds) included regression displayed in loss of toilet habits, bewilderment, and clinging behavior in the presence of strangers. In some cases, development was still retarded one year later.

only their mothers. Between 1970 and 1988, divorce rates increased dramatically, and the percentage of children living only with mothers doubled. During the same period, the percentage living with fathers tripled—although percentage of children living with fathers only is still one-seventh of that living with mothers. The proportion of children living with neither parent has remained constant at about 3 percent. In Canada, 12.9 percent of all families were one-parent families in 1987.

f igure 8.4

Living arrangements of U.S. and Canadian children. Source: Adapted from U.S. Bureau of the Census (1992), p. 55; Minister of Supply and Services Canada (1989), pp. 2–31.

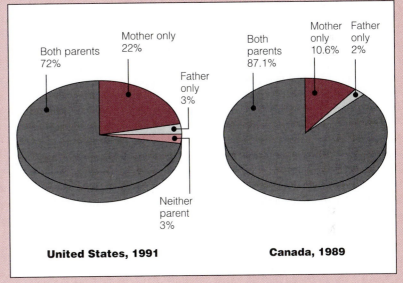

Both parents 72% — Mother only 22% — Father only 3% — Neither parent 3%

United States, 1991

Both parents 87.1% — Mother only 10.6% — Father only 2%

Canada, 1989

Three- and 4-year-old preschoolers exhibited loss of confidence and self-esteem and were prone to blame themselves for the departure of the father. As Neal (1983) observes, preschoolers typically understand divorce as a question of one parent leaving them, rather than of parents leaving each other. They are likely to think they have done something "bad" to cause the parent to leave.

The 5- and 6 year olds were less affected developmentally, although there was a tendency for some of the daughters to deny the reality of the situation and to continue expecting that their fathers would return.

The 7 and 8 year olds were understandably frightened by the divorce and intensely saddened, many of them missing their fathers constantly. Many of these children also lived in fear of making their mothers angry, perhaps imagining that she too might leave them.

Nine and 10 year olds initially reacted with apparent acceptance, many of them trying to understand why the divorce had occurred. But their outward calm covered feelings of anger, sometimes intense hostility toward one parent or the other (or both) and shame (Wallerstein & Kelly, 1976). A year later, half of these children seemed to have adjusted, with resignation and some lingering sadness, to their new situation. Significantly, however, half suffered from varying degrees of depression, low self-esteem, poorer school performance, and poorer relationships with peers.

Interviews of young adolescents (ages 12 to 14) revealed a much deeper understanding of their parents' divorce (Springer & Wallerstein, 1983). Most of these adolescents had become keen observers and analyzers of interactions between their parents, and many were able to evaluate the situation objectively and arrive at plausible psychological explanations for their parents' divorce. Unlike younger children, they were much less likely to harbor feelings of guilt about the divorce or hostility toward their parents. However, some of these children, who initially seemed to have coped well with the divorce, later manifested varying degrees of anger, resentment, and maladjustment. These children are examples of what Wallerstein (1989) labeled the "sleeper" effect.

sex-related effects of divorce

Some researchers have suggested that boys are more adversely affected by divorce than are girls (Hetherington, Cox,

& Cox, 1979; Guidubaldi & Cleminshaw, 1985). This is especially true if loss of the father occurs before the age of 5 (Warshak & Santrock, 1983). However, the Amato and Keith (1991) meta-analysis indicates that sex differences are not very pronounced. Other than for the fact that boys have more difficulty adjusting to the divorce than do girls, there is no consistent pattern of greater negative effects for boys than for girls. In short, there is no greater incidence of behavior problems, of difficulty in school, of lowered self-esteem, or of problems with parent-child relationships.

contextual effects of divorce

One of the remarkable findings of the Amato and Keith (1991) meta-analysis of 92 studies was that the year the study was conducted appeared to be related to its outcome: In general, more recent investigations found *fewer negative* effects on children. It seems clear that the impact of divorce was far stronger in the 1950s and 1960s than is now the case. Why? Perhaps because divorces were less common, less acceptable, and more difficult to arrange. Consequently, both children and parents would be more likely to have to cope with disapproval and would be provided with less support. It is perhaps for these same reasons that the consequences of divorce are less severe in the United States than they are in many other countries (Amato & Keith, 1991).

why divorce has negative effects

There are at least three different reasons why divorce might affect children negatively.

ABSENCE OF THE FATHER (OR MOTHER)

Much of the research in this area has focused on the father's absence and has attributed negative consequences to this lack. We might expect that fathers' absence could have an effect on children either because the roles traditionally fulfilled by the father would no longer be fulfilled (or might be fulfilled less adequately by the mother, who must also continue to carry out her own roles), or because the absence of the father has an effect on the mother, who then interacts with her children in a different way. These traditional fatherly roles are, on the one hand, economic and, on the other, psychological. Freudian theory suggests, for example, that the presence of both parents is especially crucial during the phallic phase of development (ages 4 to 6), when children resolve their Oedipus or Electra complexes, identify with the same-sex parent, and begin to develop appropriate sex roles. Accordingly, the presence of a father is especially important for young boys. But it is also highly important for girls, not only because a father's behavior indicates to a daughter what men should be like when she begins to date, but also because of the role a loving and accepting father plays in the development of a daughter's self-esteem. Similarly, the absence of a mother, an increasingly common situation, might be expected to have different effects on boys than on girls.

ECONOMIC IMPACT

Some of the effects of one-parent families may be due to changes that occur in the family itself after the father is gone, rather than to the lack of a father as a source of psychological influence. Children must cope not only with the absence of the father but also with a husbandless mother. In addition, the economic conditions of one-parent homes are, on the average, considerably poorer than those of two-parent families—especially if the mother is the single parent. Average income in mother-headed homes is less than half that of two-parent families and more than a third less than that of father-headed homes (U.S. Bureau of the Census, 1992) (see Figures 8.5 and 8.6 in "At a Glance: Economic Characteristics of Mother-Only Families"). The not-infrequent change from relative affluence to poverty can be especially difficult for children whose peers are more advantaged, and is associated with a higher probability of difficulties with school or with the law.

FAMILY CONFLICT AND EMOTIONAL UPHEAVAL

In addition to the economic impact of divorce or separation and the psychological impact of the loss of a male or a female model are the immediate (and sometimes long-term) effects of rupturing or altering the emotional bonds that link parent and child, as well as the consequences of conflict between parents both before and during the process of separation. One of the most striking findings revealed in the research summarized by Amato and Keith (1991) is that children living in high-conflict but *intact* families fared less well than children whose parents had divorced; they manifested more adjustment problems, lower self-esteem, and more conduct problems. This is strong evidence, conclude Amato and Keith, that family conflict is an important explanation for the negative effects of divorce.

---

some conclusions

Marital disruption and its effect on children is a complex and difficult subject. There are too many variables involved for us to identify them easily, lay them flat on the tables of our reason, see their interrelatedness, and understand them clearly. Even our simplest summaries remain in need of further summarizing and simplification.

I n 1991, nearly three-fourths of U.S. children under 18 lived with both parents. Of these, nearly 47 million children (71.8 percent) lived in families that owned rather than rented their homes. Of the 2 million children who lived with their fathers only, more than half (51.4 percent) lived in owned homes. In contrast, only about one-third (32.8 percent) of the 14.6 million children living with mothers only were living in owned homes. Moreover, income in these mother-only homes was dramatically lower than in two-parent or father-only homes.

f **igure 8.5**

(bottom left) Median income of two-parent, father-only, and mother-only U.S. families, 1991. The median is the midpoint; half the families in each category earn more than the median and half earn less. Source: Adapted from U.S. Bureau of the Census (1992), p. 452.

f **igure 8.6**

(bottom right) Percentage of two-parent and mother-only U.S. families in various income brackets, 1991. Source: Adapted from U.S. Bureau of the Census (1992), p. 54.

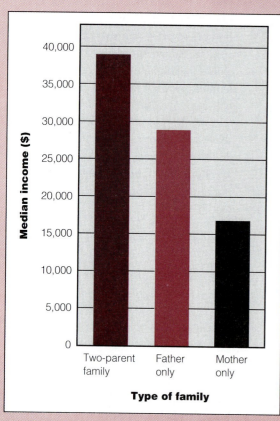

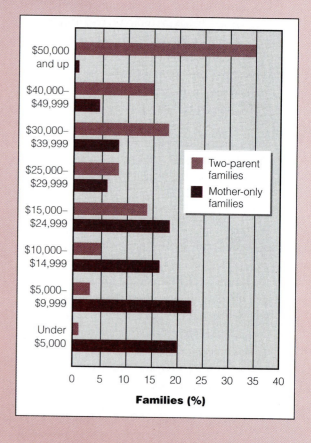

Peterson, Leigh, and Day (1984) provide an approach that separates the variables involved and underlines their interaction. It is an approach that looks at the relationship between degree of parental disengagement and children's social competence. Degree of parental disengagement ranges from varying levels of marital discord through temporary separation, long-term separation, divorce, and death; children's social competence is defined in terms of their ability "to engage in social relationships and possess adaptive psychological qualities" (Peterson, Leigh, & Day, 1984, p. 4).

In examining the relationship of these two variables—parental disengagement and children's social competence—Peterson and colleagues (1984) take into account much of the wealth of research in this area and reduce its conclusions to the following (summarized) series of propositions (statements):

- The higher the degree of disengagement, the greater the impact on children. In other words, divorce is generally more stressful than temporary separation. By the same token, a situation in which one of the parents breaks all ties with the child is more stressful than one where both parents continue to maintain close ties with the child.

- The severity of the immediate crisis brought about by the divorce is closely related to the negative impact of divorce. Children who have been abused or neglected by a parent are less likely to view the divorce as a very serious calamity and are likely to experience a lower degree of stress.

- The more accurate the child's perception of the parents' relationship before marital breakup, the less negative the consequences. Children who incorrectly view their parents' relationship as "happy" immediately before separation or divorce suffer the greatest stress.

- The more positive and amicable the parents' relationship following the marriage breakup, the less negative the effect on the child.

- The closer the relationship between the leaving parent and the child before marital breakup, the more serious the effect on the child.

- Age is related to the severity of consequences in a curvilinear fashion, with the most serious consequences occurring for children between the ages of 3 and 9 and the least severe occurring before and after those ages.

- When fathers are the ones who disengage (move out of the home), consequences are usually more serious for boys than for girls.

a final word

Research on the consequences of marital dissolution has clearly focused on the problems faced by parents and children in one-parent families and has tended to emphasize the extent to which the one-parent family is an inadequate childrearing environment. As a result, there is a danger that the negative aspects of divorce have been exaggerated. Although divorce is almost invariably a trying time for children, living in conflict (and sometimes with physical and mental abuse) can also be very trying. We must be careful not to mistakenly assume that what might be generally true for groups must also be true for all individuals. We should not conclude that divorce is always detrimental to the welfare of children and that intact families are always good because this is clearly not the case. Lowery and

Settle (1985) review several studies that suggest that there is a point at which family conflict in the intact home has greater negative effects on children than the potentially negative effects of divorce. When that point is reached, divorce is the best solution, both for parents and for their children.

It bears repeating that there are expert and loving single parents who can effectively overcome whatever trauma might be associated with the loss of one parent and that there are countless two-parent families in which parenting is inadequate and love is seldom if ever shown.

Most children (and parents) adapt to life in a single-parent home within two or three years of the initial disruption (Hetherington, Stanley-Hagen, & Anderson, 1989). Richards and Schmiege (1993) interviewed 71 single parents and found that money was the number one problem for mothers; problems with the ex-spouse was a greater problem for men. Both men and women reported that parenting became easier over time. However, at about the time that adjustment to life in a one-parent family seems almost complete, remarriage often occurs. And that, too, can require major readjustments.

children in stepfamilies

About 60 percent of all first marriages now end in divorce; and the majority of those who divorce remarry. Thus about half of all American children spend at least some time in a one-parent family, and many of them also eventually become members of stepfamilies (also called blended families) (Pasley, Dollahite, & Ihinger-Tallman, 1993).

A stepfamily is the family grouping that results from the remarriage of a widowed or divorced parent; consequently, only one of the two married adults in the family is the child's biological parent. Almost one in every five American families with children under 18 is a stepfamily (Glick, 1989), and projections are that this proportion may reach 50 percent by the year 2000.

Interestingly, stepfamilies are no more enduring than first marriages, with about 60 percent ending in divorce (Pill, 1990). In addition, remarriages in which there are stepchildren are more likely to dissolve than if there are no children, especially if the children are older than 9 (Visher & Visher, 1988).

possible problems in stepfamilies

Does this mean that parenting is more difficult in stepfamilies?

Perhaps. Clearly, the number and complexity of relationships that can exist within a stepfamily are much greater. For example, the marriage of a man and woman who have both been married previously and who both have children can create a staggering number of new relationships involving the biological relatives of each of the stepparents, not to mention previous spouses and their parents, siblings, uncles, aunts, and cousins.

Loss of a parent through separation, divorce, or death can be a difficult and sometimes a traumatic experience for children. Unfortunately, the remarriage of the parent in a one-parent family does not automatically do away with the difficulties or the trauma. Instead, it often brings a whole new set of problems. Children who have had to cope with the initial disruption of the family through death or divorce must now cope with another reorganization of the family. And whereas remarriage is almost invariably seen as a highly positive gain for the child's parent because it reestablishes an important relationship, it is often seen as a loss by the child because it implies a change in the relationship between child and parent. Many children experience feelings of abandonment following the remarriage of a parent because much of the time and attention that the parent had previously given them is now given to the stepparent (Visher and Visher, 1982).

In addition to the loss, real or imagined, of some of the biological parent's attention and perhaps affection, children must now also deal with the establishing of new relationships with the stepparent, with stepsiblings if there are any, and perhaps with a new set of grandparents and other relatives. Furthermore, children's role in the family often changes. This can be particularly difficult for adolescent children, whose newly developed adult roles, sometimes accelerated by the absence of one parent (for example, the boy has become "man of the house" following his biological father's departure), can be severely disrupted by the appearance of a new stepparent (Duberman, 1975). Similarly, the creation of a new stepfamily can disrupt established patterns of control and discipline and sometimes lead to serious problems ("You're not my dad! I don't have to listen to you!").

Other problems sometimes associated with the stepfamily include sexual fantasies and inclinations between stepsiblings and between children and their stepparents (and resulting feelings of guilt and confusion); stepsibling rivalry and competition; ambivalence about children's role in the new family; confusion or conflict over whether and how the departed parent should continue to fit into children's lives; and the need for children to abandon the fantasy or wish that the divorced parents might one day be reunited (Chilman, 1983).

the positive side of stepfamilies

Fortunately, the effects of stepfamilies on children are often positive. Pasley et al. (1993) report that well-functioning stepfamilies are no different from well-functioning intact families, although it's true that initially there is a sometimes difficult period of adjustment. Interestingly, stepparents who have previously been parents tend to adjust more easily to the stepparenting role. Also, those who ease more slowly into the new stepparenting roles fare better than those who try to assume the role too quickly, especially with respect to control and discipline.

The fairy-tale stereotype of the stepfather or stepmother as the wicked wielder of terrible powers is, in fact, a fairy tale. Clearly, many stepparents are kind and considerate people who want to love and be loved by their stepchildren. Once the initial adjustments have been made, stepchildren, in a great many cases, can be as fortunate as many children in intact nuclear families.

childcare outside the home

At one time most North American children spent their preschool years in intimate contact with their mothers, a situation that Bowlby (1982), Klaus and Kennell (1983), and others consider an ideal childrearing arrangement. Today, an increasing number of children are cared for during the day by others. In fact, childcare by someone other than a parent is now the norm for more than 50 percent of all American preschool children—a percentage that is climbing (Browne Miller, 1990). About 75 percent of mothers of preschoolers now work outside the home, and it is becoming increasingly common for many mothers to go back to work within weeks of childbirth. Gamble and Zigler (1986) report that *infant* childcare is the fastest growing type of supplemental care in the United States.

Nonparental childcare takes a variety of forms, ranging from situations in which families can afford to hire a private, in-the-child's-home caregiver, to institutionalized centers for large numbers of children with many caregivers. Most common, however, are private homes that look after perhaps a half dozen youngsters and are referred to as *family childcare*. About half of all children are cared for by grandparents or other relatives (Hofferth, 1992). Although family childcare is the most common form of early childcare, most of the research in this area has focused on institutional centers (Goelman, Shapiro, & Pence, 1990).

In addition to arranged care for children, there are self-supervised or *latchkey* children, so called because their parents sometimes hang keys around their necks so they can let themselves into their homes after school (Long & Long, 1983). Self-supervision is sometimes associated with more behavior problems (Vandell & Ramanan, 1991).

general effects of childcare

Given the proliferation of nonparental childcare, it's very important to ask whether it's as good for infants and preschoolers as parental care, and what the characteristics of good childcare are. There is no lack of research (see, for example, Scarr & Eisenberg, 1993; Hayes, Palmer, & Zaslow, 1990).

CHILDCARE VERSUS HOME CARE

An early emphasis in this research was an attempt to determine whether infants and preschoolers cared for by someone other than their mother might suffer harmful consequences relating to difficulties in forming affectional bonds with their mother. For example, Bronfenbrenner, Belsky, and Steinberg (1977) reviewed several dozen studies comparing childcare and home-care children in so-

cial, intellectual, and motor development. Cognitive differences were seldom significant. A number of studies found a slightly greater tendency for childcare children to interact with others (both peers and adults), and a number reported somewhat more aggressiveness among childcare children. Similarly, Kagan, Kearsley, and Zelazo (1977) found few important differences between a group of 33 infants who attended a childcare center and comparable children who were kept at home by their mothers. On a battery of measures administered on eight occasions—including assessments of attentiveness, language development, confidence, memory, and maternal attachment—childcare and home-care infants performed equally well.

More recent research has generally corroborated these findings. As Bowman (1993) puts it, "In general, nonfamily care and education have not been found to jeopardize the development of young children" (p. 109).

SPECIFIC EFFECTS OF CHILDCARE

More recently, childcare research has focused on the characteristics of childcare programs that seem to have the most positive effects on children, as well as on the characteristics of children for whom nonparental care is most likely to be a positive or negative experience.

It appears that high-quality childcare can have measurable positive effects on the social and cognitive development of children, especially of disadvantaged children (Scarr & Eisenberg, 1993). For more advantaged children, however, the effects of nonparental childcare seem to depend on a variety of factors. For example, poor-quality care has sometimes been associated with poorer adjustment and social/emotional problems, especially among boys (particularly if they are temperamentally difficult) (Mott, 1991).

Two things should be noted: The occasional negative effects of childcare are not very general, and they are almost invariably associated with *poorer-quality* childcare.

research on the quality of childcare

Quality of the care provided in childcare facilities is closely related to children's social development, to the quality of parent-child interaction, and to children's general cognitive development (Phillips, McCartney, & Scarr, 1987; Peterson & Peterson, 1986). In the Phillips, McCartney, and Scarr study involving 166 childcare children, a significant relationship was found between indicators of childcare quality (such as staff to child ratio, caregiver-child interaction, equipment and supplies, and so on) and children's social development as revealed in measures of intelligence, considerateness, sociability, task orientation, and dependence. In the Peterson and Peterson study, childcare quality was assessed in terms of three components: variety of equipment available; degree of caregiver involvement with children; and evaluation of setting, activities, curriculum, and teacher behavior. The study looked at the relationship between quality of childcare and parent-infant interaction. Children from lower-quality centers had more difficulty following instructions and had less-sustained dialogues with their mothers (they tended to use more single-statement utterances). In contrast, children who attended higher-quality centers tended to engage in sustained dialogues with their mothers and to display more maturity in following instructions. The authors suggest that children learn patterns of adult-infant interaction in childcare facilities. In lower-quality centers that are characterized by a high ratio of children to caregivers, interactions tend to be briefer and less frequent.

finding quality childcare

How can parents determine what is likely to be good or bad childcare?

In a highly practical book, Endsley and Bradbard (1981) advise parents on this question. They suggest that although it is difficult to evaluate different childcare programs, those that are very bad may have a number of characteristics in common, and those that are excellent might also. Among programs to avoid are those characterized by the following:

- Unsanitary and unhealthy physical surroundings

- Obvious physical hazards

- Excessive overcrowding both in terms of available space and the number of young children per available supervising adult (for example, adult-child ratios that exceed 1 to 20 or, in the case of infants, 1 to 10)

- Lack of activities and materials that are interesting and challenging to young children

- Staff (usually untrained) who are at best thoughtless and insensitive and at worst rejecting of and abusive to young children

- Disregard for parent's feelings about childrearing (p. 32)

In contrast, characteristics associated with high-quality programs include:

- The financial resources to design and equip a special environment for children

- The time, freedom, motivation, and physical energy to work only with children for 6 to 10 hours each day

■ The training necessary to organize experiences and activities to develop optimally children's understanding of themselves and the world around them (p. 33)

Kagan (1978) too emphasizes that what appears to be important in childcare is that the ratio of staff to children be kept high, that staff be reasonably knowledgeable about child development, and that children be given ample opportunity to exercise social, cognitive, and language skills.

Licensing requirements for establishing childcare facilities vary tremendously throughout North America and are usually nonexistent for smaller, family-based centers (Hernandez & Myers, 1993). As a result, although there are many high-quality facilities available, others have environments that are of far lower quality.

How can a parent assess the quality of childcare facilities? Endsley and Bradbard (1981) suggest that parents should obtain personal references and, perhaps most important, visit the centers, observe them in operation, and talk with the people in charge. Sadly, however, most of us are likely to spend more time looking, comparing, and obtaining references when buying a car than we are when finding someone to care for our children.

main points

THE SOCIALIZATION OF EMOTIONS

1. By the age of 9 months, infants can interpret emotions in others and are capable of self- and other-directed regulatory behaviors. Later in the preschool period they attempt to control their emotional displays, but not always very successfully.

THEORIES OF SOCIAL DEVELOPMENT

2. Erikson's stage theory of social development describes the resolution of psychosocial conflicts through the development of competence. In the preschool stage, *initiative versus guilt,* children develop a sense of control and responsibility for their actions. Bandura explains social learning through imitation of models, many of which are *symbolic.* Imitation may account for our tendency to cooperate or to compete, which is highly influenced by our immediate culture.

PLAY

3. The two broad categories of children's play are practice (or sensorimotor) play (mainly physical activity, useful in developing and exercising important physical skills) and pretend play (or imaginative play, such as daydreaming or imaginary playmates, importantly related to cognitive development). These can be social, in which two or more children interact, or solitary. Social play underlies personality development and the development of social skills. It may be *onlooker play* (watching without joining in), *parallel play* (play side by side but not together), *associative play* (children play together physically but do not share rules or goals), or *cooperative play* (children share rules and roles).

GENDER ROLES IN EARLY CHILDHOOD

4. *Gender roles* are the range of behaviors considered appropriate for males and females and the personality characteristics that define masculinity and femininity. *Gender schemas* are children's knowledge about gender roles.

Gender typing is the learning of sex-appropriate behavior. A three-stage cognitive explanation for gender typing involves (1) recognizing basic gender identity (maleness or femaleness); (2) realizing that gender is stable, permanent, and unchangeable; and (3) realizing that superficial changes (such as in dress or behavior) do not change gender.

5. Genetic influences on gender differences are especially evident in the greater aggressiveness of males. Family-based influences are reflected in the fact that most parents treat boys and girls differently, rewarding aggression, independence, and boisterousness in boys and rewarding nurturant, affective, compliant behavior in girls.

THE CONTEMPORARY FAMILY

6. A nuclear family consists of mother, father, and children; extended families also include a variety of other blood relatives. The family has sustenance, developmental, and advocacy functions. Baumrind's three parenting styles are *permissive* (nonpunitive, noncontrolling, nondemanding), *authoritarian* (dogmatic, controlling, obedience-oriented), and *authoritative* (firm but based on reason, nondogmatic, geared toward promoting independence but encouraging adherence to standards). Some parents are more *expert*, others more *novice*.

7. It is difficult to predict future adjustment and personality characteristics of children on the basis of what might be known about the childrearing practices of their parents. However, in North American societies an authoritative parenting style may be preferable to either a permissive or

authoritarian style. Three important sources of childcare advice are the medical profession, books, and parenting courses.

FAMILY COMPOSITION

8. There is a tendency for firstborn and only children to achieve better in school, score higher on tests of intellectual performance, and develop language facility sooner. Children from larger families do less well on average than children from smaller families on measures of intellectual performance (primarily because of interactions in the family and socioeconomic factors).

ONE-PARENT FAMILIES

9. Some of the effects of one-parent families on children may be due to the lack of a parent; they may also be due to altered economic conditions, changed interaction with the remaining parent, and other factors. Recent research finds less negative effect than did earlier research.

10. Divorce sometimes affects children's social competence (adjustment and relationships). The severity of the effect relates to children's sex (more severe for males), children's age (more severe between ages 3 and 9 than before and after that period), the accuracy of children's perception of the parent's previous relationship, the severity of the immediate crisis, and the parents' relationship following marital breakup (the more positive the relationship, the less serious the consequences).

CHILDREN IN STEPFAMILIES

11. Stepchildren sometimes face problems relating to loss (real or imag-

ined) of some of the biological parent's time and affection; establishing new relationships with the stepparent, stepsiblings, and others; coping with stepsibling rivalry; dealing with new sexual inclinations and fantasies; and abandoning the fantasy that the biological parents might one day be reunited.

CHILDCARE OUTSIDE THE HOME

12. About 50 percent of North American preschoolers spend time in childcare facilities. In general, childcare does not have detrimental effects on the social, emotional, and intellectual development of children, especially with high-quality childcare (characterized by high staff-children ratios, adequate equipment and materials, trained and caring staff, and adequate financial resources).

focus questions: applications

■ What do preschoolers understand of what others feel?

1. Can you explain why it is that young children are so easily moved to tears? And to laughter?

■ Of what importance is play in childhood?

2. Observe children playing in a park or playground. Categorize the play you observe as practice or pretend, solitary or social. Can you make even more detailed analyses of the types of imaginary or social play you observed?

■ To what extent are masculinity and femininity determined by our genes?

3. Identify two or three arguments for and against the proposition that gender is largely biologically determined.

■ What differences does parenting make? Family size? Position in the family?

4. What is your position in your family? Was that important to who you are? Why?

■ How significant is the loss of a parent?

5. Using library resources, write a paper on the effects of parental death on children of different ages.

■ Is out-of-home childcare as good as at-home care by parents?

6. Develop a checklist of the most important dimensions of *quality* childcare—the sorts of things a parent might find useful when choosing a childcare facility.

study terms

emotions 345
socialization 348
symbolic models 353
play 353
practice play 354
sensorimotor play 354
pretend play 354
imaginative play 354
social play 358
solitary play 359
primitive social play 359
onlooker play 359
parallel play 359
associative play 359
gender roles 361
gender typing 361
gender schemas 362
nuclear family 365
extended family 365
permissive parenting 368
authoritarian parenting 368
authoritative parenting 368
birth order 372

further readings

Paley's books offer fascinating, often delightful, descriptions of life in the preschool period. The first of these short books follows 3-year-old Mollie through a year of nursery school, revealing her excitement and her fears in the little dramas that are an intrinsic part of Paley's classes. The second follows the lives of a kindergarten class, providing insights into how children struggle to arrive at their own understanding of what it means to be a boy or a girl.

Paley, V. G. (1986). *Mollie is three: Growing up in school.* Chicago: University of Chicago Press.

Paley, V. G. (1984). *Boys and girls: Superheroes in the doll corner.* Chicago: University of Chicago Press.

The first of the following two books presents a brief but detailed analysis of the games children play and of the role of play in development; the second is a collection of articles dealing with the significance of social pretend play:

Hughes, F. P. (1990). *Children, play, and development.* Boston: Allyn & Bacon.

Howes, C., Unger, O., & Matheson, C. C. (Eds.). (1992). *The collaborative construction of pretend: Social pretend play functions.* New York: State University of New York Press.

For an intelligent discussion of sexism in education and in everyday life, and for suggestions about measures that can be taken to counter it, see:

Askew, S., & Ross, C. (1988). *Boys don't cry: Boys and sexism in education.* Philadelphia: Open University Press.

A practical approach to shared custody following marital dissolution is:

Coulter, L. (1990). *Two homes: A parent's guide to joint custody in Canada.* Toronto: Harper Collins.

The Hernandez and Myers book presents a detailed analysis of recent changes in North America that are having an important impact on childcare. The Endsley and Bradbard book is a useful guide for parents attempting to evaluate childcare facilities:

Hernandez, D. J., & Myers, D. E. (1993). *America's children: Resources from family, government, and the economy.* New York: Russell Sage.

Endsley, R. C., & Bradbard, M. R. (1981). *Quality day care: A handbook of choices for parents and caregivers.* Englewood Cliffs, N.J.: Prentice-Hall.

five

Middle Childhood

---

*Sweet childish days, that were as long
As twenty days are now.
William Wordsworth, To a Butterfly*

Do you recollect those "sweet childish days"? Do you remember how summer vacation stretched so far you could barely imagine its end? Do you remember too that in those childish days, trees were giants and butterflies wore shimmering coats of dazzling colors and birds warbled startling songs we can no longer hear?

It is a sadness to see the days shrink so, to find the seasons whirling mindlessly on each other's heels, to sense the years slip away. To think there was once time to kill.

"Time to kill"—such a senseless phrase. Even children have better things to do with time than to try to kill it—things like learning about the fine, concrete logic that explains the world; about elegant strategies for remembering important things, and trivial ones too; about how valuable the self is and how important friends are. If there is any time still left, there is little need to kill it; it can always be spent watching television.

These are the subjects of the next two chapters. As you read them, it might be worthwhile to stop and wonder whether the trees that crowd 12 year olds' forests are as tall as those that tower in the forests of 6 year olds, the butterflies as brilliant, the birds' songs as stunning.

And is there some way we too, like a child, can put 20 days between the coming and the going of our suns?

9

Physical and Cognitive Development in Middle Childhood

Give me a firm place to stand, and I will move the earth.
Archimedes, Collectio, Papus Alexander

focus questions

ARE NORTH AMERICAN CHILDREN IN GOOD PHYSICAL SHAPE? WHAT ARE THE CAUSES AND IMPLICATIONS OF CHILDHOOD OBESITY?

WHAT IS PIAGET'S VIEW OF IMPORTANT COGNITIVE CHANGES IN MIDDLE CHILDHOOD?

WHAT MODEL OF HUMAN MEMORY IS BASIC TO CURRENT VIEWS OF INFORMATION PROCESSING?

WHAT IS INTELLIGENCE? HOW DO WE MEASURE IT? HOW IMPORTANT IS IT?

WHAT ARE THE DIMENSIONS OF INTELLECTUAL EXCEPTIONALITY?

outline

MIDDLE CHILDHOOD DEFINED

PHYSICAL DEVELOPMENT

Growth
Nutrition and Health
Motor Development
Some Physical and Sensory Problems
The Physically Gifted

INTELLECTUAL DEVELOPMENT: PIAGET'S VIEW

The Conservations
Can Conservation Be Accelerated?
Classes, Seriation, and Number
Summary of Concrete Operations

CHILDREN AS INFORMATION PROCESSORS

Types of Memory
Memory Processes
Schemata and Scripts: A Model of Long-Term Memory
Developmental Changes in Memory

METACOGNITION AND METAMEMORY

Motivation and Self-Efficacy in Learning
Cultural Differences in Learning Strategies
The Use of Cognitive Strategies

INTELLIGENCE

What Is Intelligence?
Measuring Intelligence
Developmental Changes in IQ
Misconceptions About and Misuses of IQ
The Usefulness of Intelligence Tests

INTELLECTUAL EXCEPTIONALITY

Mental Retardation
Learning Disabilities
Intellectual Giftedness
Creativity
Trends and Controversies in Special Education

THE MAGICAL CHILD

MAIN POINTS

FOCUS QUESTIONS: APPLICATIONS

STUDY TERMS

FURTHER READINGS

t was an X-rated movie. Of course, I didn't see it; I was told about it afterward. The plot is irrelevant; the behavior of the viewers is not.

In one apparently moving scene, the camera zoomed in on the upper portions of several actors engaged in activities below the camera's lower limit. It was then that my friend had to stand on his seat to look over the heads of the people in front of him, who had risen in an attempt to see what was happening below the heads of the actors. My friend was able to rise high enough to see over the heads in front of him, but he could not see the action below the camera's limits.

In this sense, and in one other, studying children is very much like watching a movie. In writing this text, I find myself vainly stretching my intellectual and intuitive neck in an attempt to see below and beyond the work of Piaget, Skinner, Freud, Bronfenbrenner, and a thousand others. At the same time, I can sometimes sense you peering over my shoulder trying to see what might be between the lines that come out of my computer, and I want to say to you, "Can you see?" It's a frustrating business because we both know there is much more there than is apparent. Within the limitations of words on printed pages, it is absolutely impossible to convey the complete story of children and childhood—just as it was impossible for my friend to see below the screen. We can only imagine and hope that our imagination is not too desperately far from the truth.

There is yet another sense in which studying children is like watching a motion picture—and, at the same time, quite unlike it.

Even though a movie gives the illusion of continual motion, it can be halted at any point to reveal that it actually consists of isolated pictures, of static representations. The development of a child can also be stopped and examined in much the same way as it is possible to examine the individual pictures that make up a movie. That is really what happens when we talk about stages, ages, and phases. But there is a fundamental difference between the development of a child and the progression of a movie. The static pictures that define a motion picture are its reality, and their movement is an illusion. The static stages that define child development are illusory; the reality of human development is its continuous movement.

middle childhood defined

The movement that concerns us in this chapter occurs during middle childhood—approximately ages 6 to 12. Because this stage ends with the onset of pubescence (changes leading to sexual maturity) and because pubescence occurs at different ages for different people, its upper boundary is more indefinite.

physical development

The physical development of many of the world's children is neither normal nor optimal, sometimes because of inadequate diet and sometimes simply because of lack of exercise. Estimates are that as many as 30 percent of all North American children may be obese (Cusack, 1984); and as we saw in Chapter 1, vast numbers of the Third World's children are undernourished. These observations underline the importance of knowledge about the normal course of physical development and about the contributions of nutrition and exercise to physical and mental well-being.

growth

Although girls tend to be slightly shorter and lighter than boys from birth until the end of the preschool period, the shapes of the growth curves for each are almost identical; that is, both sexes gain at approximately the same rate. This pattern changes in middle childhood. Although the average girl is three-quarters of an inch (2 cm) shorter at age 6, she has caught up with and surpassed the average boy by the age of 11 and is still slightly taller at the age of 12 (see Figure 9.1). In weight, girls are close to 2 pounds (1 kg) lighter at age 6 and do not catch up with boys until the age of 11 (see Figure 9.2).

*Height at 50th percentile for U.S. children.
Source: Health Department, Milwaukee, Wisconsin; based on data by H. C. Stuart and H. V. Meredith, prepared for use in Children's Medical Center, Boston. Used by permission of the Milwaukee Health Department.*

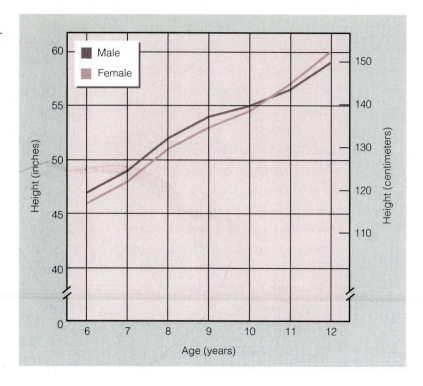

*Weight at 50th percentile for U.S. children.
Source: Health Department, Milwaukee, Wisconsin; based on data by H. C. Stuart and H. V. Meredith, prepared for use in Children's Medical Center, Boston. Used by permission of the Milwaukee Health Department.*

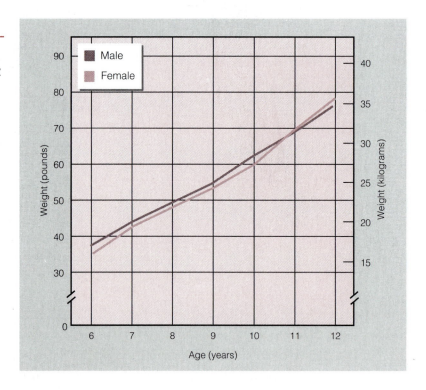

Between ages 11 and 12, however, there is a sudden spurt in weight gain for girls that puts them 3 pounds (1.4 kg) ahead of boys in the course of a single year. Chapter 11 points out that not until the age of 14½ do boys overtake girls in weight, and not until age 14 do they exceed girls in height. From then on, the weight and height of average men exceeds that of women—until death renders us all equally short and light.

Another trend of physical growth that continues throughout middle childhood is a gradual decrease in the growth of fatty tissue, coupled with increased bone and muscle development. Muscle development is generally more rapid in boys, whereas girls tend to retain a higher percentage of body fat (Smoll & Schutz, 1990).

THE GROWTH SPURT

Toward the end of childhood there is a dramatic growth spurt in height and weight. On average, it occurs about two years earlier for girls than for boys. And for some children, it occurs months (or even years) earlier or later. As a result, there are sometimes striking height and weight differences among like-aged children. These differences are sometimes a source of acute embarrassment or worry for children. At a time when peer approval has become among the most important things in life, it may be a great misfortune—or sometimes a great fortune—to be either precocious or retarded in physical development. It may be humiliating for a boy to suddenly find that his younger sister has become taller than he. It can be equally uncomfortable to be the tallest boy or the tallest girl in the class and to live with the secret fear of being a tall, skinny freak.

Nature sometimes compensates for initial discrepancies. When Doris Doré was 9 or 10, we called her "chimney" (or another less kind name), so tall was she—and so cruel were we. But when she was 15, most were as tall as she was. And when I was 14 or 15, there were some who dared call me *Bûche*—which means "stump"—so late was I in starting to grow. But now, as the French saying goes, "*Je mange de la tarte sur leures têtes*"—meaning "I eat pie off their heads."

However, nature does not always make up for early differences. The early bloomer does not invariably stop growing while later developers catch up; we are not all destined to reach the same end. Clearly, some end up short and others tall; some are light and others heavy. Our hypothetical average child hides these individual differences. (See Chapter 11 for a discussion of the psychological effects of early and late maturation.)

nutrition and health

If they are well nourished, between the ages of 6 and 12 children grow 2 to 3 inches (5 to 7.5 cm) and gain about 5 to 7 pounds (about 2.25 to 3 kg) each year. Normal gains in height are a better indicator of the long-term adequacy of children's nutrition than are weight gains; gains in weight often reflect the shorter-term effects of nutrition (Pipes, Bumbals, & Pritkin, 1985).

During middle childhood there is a high requirement for protein in children's diet, as well as a great need for vitamins and minerals (especially calcium, because of the rapid development of the skeleton). Unfortunately, many of the world's children are not well nourished, and many millions die of starvation each year. And although starvation is uncommon in North America, malnutrition is not. Malnutrition takes one of two forms: *overnutrition*, often leading to obesity, and *undernutrition*, often reflected in the intake of foods low in protein and in essential vitamins and minerals.

OBESITY

The most common nutritional problem among children in North America is obesity, which may affect as many as 30 percent of all children (Cusack, 1984). Unfortunately, obese children are likely to become obese adults.

Obesity is a serious condition that is difficult to rectify. Its relationship to cardiovascular and other health problems is well known; its implications for children's social and emotional well-being are perhaps less obvious but no less real. Not only do severely obese children often find it difficult to participate in the games and activities that are a fundamental part of the lives of many children, but such children may also be subjected to the ridicule and ostracism that is reflected in the countless derogatory nicknames children invent ("Tubs," "Piggy," "Fatslob," and others less kind).

Obesity in children is linked to a number of factors; overeating is clearly the most important. Some children simply take in more than they expend in growth and activity. This, of course, does not mean that obese children eat excessively all the time. In fact, many obese children might only eat slightly more than they require each day; still, the cumulative long-term effect is obesity.

Also important is the child's genetic background. Some children are clearly more susceptible to obesity than others. Those whose parents are themselves obese are far more likely also to become obese than are children of slim parents (Brownell & Wadden, 1984). Similarly, when one member of a pair of identical twins is obese, the other is also more likely to be. Interestingly, however, studies of identical twins indicate that those

who are genetically predisposed to being thin are much less likely to show the consequences of overeating. It's as if their bodies are programmed to burn more calories (Bouchard et al., 1990).

A third very important factor in childhood obesity is inactivity. Children who lead sedentary lives, who spend much of their day watching television, are more likely to gain excess weight. Watching television is especially important in contributing to weight gain, not only because it is physically passive, but also because it encourages indulging in a variety of high-calorie snacks and drinks.

Although obesity is difficult to reverse, it can be prevented in most children, even when genetic background predisposes the child to gaining weight. Two factors need to be controlled: diet and exercise. Children need to be encouraged to develop good eating habits. Care must be taken to ensure that they consume adequate amounts of protein, vitamins, minerals, and fiber—and also that they resist the ever-present temptation of junk foods. Meals should be leisurely, not a bite on the run. And food should not be a reward—or a punishment.

INFECTIOUS DISEASES

Although the development of vaccines has drastically reduced the incidence of many infectious diseases among children, most nevertheless suffer occasionally from a variety of problems. Most common are respiratory infections such as colds, although these are about half as common after age 5 as before. About 96 percent of children under 5 suffer from an upper respiratory infection at least once a year, but only 46 percent of those aged 5 to 17 do (U.S. Bureau of the Census, 1992).

Far less common than respiratory infections are communicable diseases such as chicken pox, mumps, mononucleosis, and measles. Very uncommon are vac-

Through middle childhood, children's muscular control continues to develop, manifesting remarkable increases in locomotor skills, agility, coordination, and physical strength. Some of these skills are especially important for participation in games, and relate in important ways to the child's acceptance and happiness.

cine-preventable diseases such as tetanus, poliomyelitis, pertussis (whooping cough), and smallpox. Rabies, too, is uncommon.

motor development

Children's muscular control continues to develop through middle childhood. Early in this period their control of large muscles is considerably better than their control over smaller muscles, which explains the inelegant writing of first- and second-grade children. By the end of middle childhood, control of the large muscles has become nearly perfect, and control over the small muscles is much improved.

SEX-DIFFERENCES IN MOTOR SKILLS

Changes in locomotor skills, agility, coordination, and physical strength are particularly interesting, not only because they demonstrate consistent differences between sexes, but also because they explain some of children's interests. For example, throughout middle childhood

boys' physical strength (measured in terms of grip strength) is superior to girls', even though the average girl is taller and heavier than the average boy (Corbin, 1980). Similarly, boys consistently outjump girls after the age of 7, and do better in tests of kicking, throwing, catching, running, broad jumping, and batting (Johnson, 1962). Girls surpass boys in motor skills that are more dependent on muscular flexibility, balance, or rhythmic movements, such as those in hopscotch and rope skipping and some forms of gymnastics (Cratty, 1978).

Not surprisingly, these differences are consistent with the gender typing of these activities; that is, rope skipping and hopscotch have traditionally been more feminine than masculine, and throwing balls, catching, running, and jumping are considered more masculine. In addition, the differences between boys and girls—when there are differences—are seldom very great. There is typically a great deal of overlap so that in activities in which boys are better than girls, some girls are better than some boys; conversely, when girls are, on the average, better than boys, some boys are better than some girls (Lockhart, 1980).

Although sex differences in motor skills are typically very small during middle childhood, after adolescence the disparity increases dramatically, generally in favor of males (Smoll & Schutz, 1990). As noted, however, this is not the case for some skills, such as those requiring balance, which girls perform better than boys (Laszlo, 1986).

EXPLANATIONS FOR SEX DIFFERENCES IN MOTOR SKILLS

What is not clear is the extent to which sex-related differences in motor skills, both in childhood and later in adolescence, result from innate biological differences between the sexes, and the extent to which cultural norms, expectations, and experience are involved. We do know, however, that at least for some activities, proportion of adipose (fatty) tissue is closely related to performance for both boys and girls. In a comparison of the motor performance of more than 2,000 children ages 9 to 17, Smoll and Schutz (1990) found that fatness alone accounted for as much as 50 percent of the variance between males and females. Because females on average retain significantly more adipose tissue than boys from early childhood on, some of the observed male-female differences in motor performance are probably related to this biological difference.

With advancing age, note Smoll and Schutz (1990), sex differences in motor activity and skills are increasingly influenced by environmental factors reflected in social expectations and opportunities. For example, there are far more opportunities for boys to participate in a variety of sports considered "masculine" (hockey, basketball, baseball, to name a few),

which explains in part why they become more proficient at them.

---

some physical and sensory problems

Not all children are born with normal sensory abilities or physical skills; nor do all have the same potential to develop these capabilities. Those who differ markedly from the average are termed *exceptional.*

Exceptionality is seen in all areas of human development: physical and motor, intellectual, and socioemotional. It might be manifested in extraordinary talents and skills, or it may be apparent in deficits and disorders. Later in this chapter we look at intellectual exceptionality in middle childhood. Here we look briefly at physical and sensory problems.

VISUAL IMPAIRMENT

People who can see at 20 feet what a "normal" person can see at 20 feet are said to have 20/20 vision (or normal vision); those who see at 20 feet what normal people can see at 200 feet are said to have 20/200 vision. People are classified as legally blind if their corrected vision in their better eye is no better than 20/200. Accordingly, most individuals who are classified as legally blind can in fact see, which is one reason why the term *visually impaired* is highly preferable to the term *blind.* About half of all legally blind children can read large type or print with the help of magnification. The number of legally blind people in the United States is estimated at between 1 and 5 per 1,000 (Hallahan & Kauffman, 1991).

For the special needs teacher, it is especially important to determine whether a child is capable of learning to read by sight or will have to learn to read by touch. For those who can read visually, the "special" qualities of education might not need to go beyond providing magnifying equipment or large type, unless other problems are involved. Multiple handicaps are not uncommon (Donovan, 1980).

Special classrooms and special teachers for visually impaired children are much less common today than they once were. Many of these children are now educated in regular classrooms, a practice termed *mainstreaming* (or *inclusive education*), about which more is said in a later section of this chapter. Those who must learn to read Braille, however, require special equipment and teachers (Donovan, 1980).

HEARING IMPAIRMENT

Deafness is the inability to hear sounds clearly enough for the ordinary purposes of life. The *hard of hearing* are those who suffer from some hearing loss but who can function with a hearing aid (and sometimes without). Estimates of hearing impairment indicate that approximately 17 out of 1,000 school-age children have hearing problems (U.S. Department of Education, 1991).

A useful way of describing deafness is to distinguish between loss of hearing that occurs before learning a language (*prelinguistic deafness*) and that which occurs later (*postlinguistic deafness*). Unfortunately, loss of hearing is most often congenital (present at birth) or occurs within the first two years of life, often from *otitis media*, an inflammation of the middle ear that typically results from an infection (Erickson, 1987). Fewer than 1 child in 10 who is deaf lost hearing after the age of 2.

In terms of cognitive development, deafness generally presents a far more serious handicap for children than does visual impairment, largely because of the severe difficulties children have learning

to understand and to speak—hence the outdated expression "deaf and dumb" or "deaf-mute." There is little evidence that the visually impaired are intellectually handicapped as a result of their blindness, but the same is not true of those who are hearing impaired.

Although there is considerable controversy over whether deaf children are as intelligent as "normals" (see Berdine & Blackhurst, 1985), investigators generally agree that their academic achievement often lags behind, a fact that can be attributed largely to language deficiencies. Only a very small percentage of deaf individuals ever progress far enough in their development of language skills that they can read a college-level text with understanding. This, of course, applies to the prelinguistically deaf, not to those whose loss of hearing occurred after they had already learned a language.

In addition to academic problems associated with deafness, there are often emotional and social problems. Hallahan and Kauffman (1991) note that deaf children often grow up in relative isolation, largely because of difficulties in communicating with hearing children. As a result, they sometimes have difficulty making friends.

The education of the deaf generally requires specially trained teachers and most often occurs in institutions. Understandably, the principal emphasis is on the acquisition of language, usually one or a combination of American Sign Language (ASL), finger spelling, and speechreading (lipreading).

The education of children with only a partial hearing loss may also require special instruction, especially if the loss is evident in speech disorders. Although many children with partial hearing are able to follow conversations at close range or if they are sufficiently loud, they often have difficulty distinguishing among consonants for which there are no visual clues (for example, between p and b, t and d, and f and v). Their speech may consequently be affected. The special educational needs of these children can often be met without removing them from regular classrooms. Itinerant teachers (who travel from class to class or school to school) are often used for this purpose.

OTHER PHYSICAL PROBLEMS

A number of other physical problems in middle childhood sometimes require special education or services. These include diseases and conditions such as muscular dystrophy, cancer, asthma, diabetes, the absence of one or more limbs, and paralysis. Some are congenital, some are caused by infections, and others result from accidents of various kinds. In many cases, serious emotional and social problems are associated with them; many of these problems are related to difficulties the child experiences in being accepted by others and in developing a positive self-concept. Hence, a great deal of what special needs programs, parents, and therapists can do for physically exceptional children relates to their emotional and social well-being.

the physically gifted

Our cultural (hence political and educational) emphases in the matter of exceptionality have long focused on disadvantaged individuals. But there are exceptional individuals at the other end of the spectrum as well. And although some attention is paid to cognitive giftedness, we focus less often and less systematically on identifying those who possess exceptional physical skills and on providing special programs so that these children might "develop their full human potential." Indeed, there is an increasingly noticeable lack of research on the emotional, social, and intellectual characteristics of the physically gifted and on the ways their development might be enhanced. One of the few ways that we recognize physical giftedness is to furnish scholarships for those who are inclined toward competitive athletics.

intellectual development: Piaget's view

When we left our discussion of children's minds in Chapter 7, it was not because their minds had stopped growing while they continued to advance physically and socially, but because considering all aspects of development at once is too complex and confusing. We pick up the thread of intellectual development once more, keeping in mind that as their intellect is developing, children are also growing in other ways. For the moment, our guide is Jean Piaget, and the period through which we are moving is *concrete operations*. Children approach this period by way of the sensorimotor period (birth to 2 years) and two preoperational subperiods: preconceptual thought (2–4 years) and intuitive thinking (4–7 years) (see Table 9.1).

According to Piaget, children's thinking toward the end of the intuitive stage is egocentric, perception-dominated, and intuitive. Thus it abounds in contradictions and errors of logic. But during middle childhood, many of these deficiencies disappear and are replaced by more logical thinking.

Recall that although Piaget's descriptions highlight some of the important features of preschool thinking, they are sometimes criticized because they emphasize weaknesses and deficiencies in children's thinking. As a result, they don't

table 9.1

Piaget's stages of cognitive development

STAGE	APPROXIMATE AGE	SOME MAJOR CHARACTERISTICS
Sensorimotor	0–2 years	Motoric intelligence; world of the here and now; no language, no thought in early stages; no notion of objective reality
Preoperational	2–7 years	Egocentric thought
Preconceptual	2–4 years	Reason dominated by perception
Intuitive	4–7 years	Intuitive rather than logical solutions; inability to conserve
Concrete operations	7 to 11 or 12 years	Ability to conserve; logic of classes and relations; understanding of numbers; thinking bound to the concrete; development of reversibility in thought
Formal operations	11 or 12 to 14 or 15 years	Complete generality of thought; propositional thinking; ability to deal with the hypothetical; development of strong idealism

do justice to the child's cognitive achievements. It is worth noting as well that Piaget's concept of stages as major, sequential, and universal developmental milestones no longer seems as useful as it once did. There are two main reasons for this: One is the discovery that there are tremendous individual variations in the performances of same-aged children on the various Piagetian tasks; the other is that very minor changes in the tasks can sometimes lead to very different responses. Accordingly, a number of neo-Piagetians have suggested different and usually less specific developmental milestones sometimes labeled *levels* rather than stages (Fischer & Silvern, 1985).

In spite of the recognition that Piaget's stages are not universal and that they fail to account for some important features of development (such as aspects of *metacognition* and *social cognition*, with which we deal later), his description of *concrete operations* illustrates important differences between the thinking of preschoolers and that of older children. These differences are most clearly illustrated in the *conservations*.

the conservations

Conservation refers to the fact that the quantitative aspects of objects do not change unless something has been added to or taken away from them, despite other changes in the objects. In Chapter 7, for example, we described a situation in which a child is presented with two equal balls of modeling clay and asked whether there is still as much clay in each after one has been rolled into something like a snake. The preoperational child's belief that there is more clay in the snake than in the ball (because it is now longer and therefore *looks* as though it has more) is an example of the inability to conserve. The eventual realization that the transformed object does not have more or less substance than it previously had marks not only the acquisition of concepts of conservation but also the transition between preoperational thought and concrete operations.

MEANING-MAKING

The significance of the acquisition of conservation is not so much that children

Piaget describes the preschooler's thinking as abounding in contradictions and errors of logic. During middle childhood, a new logic begins to guide thinking. But there are major cognitive achievements yet to come; and tremendous individual differences in the ease with which they will be mastered.

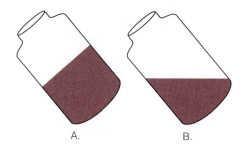

A.   B.

figure 9.3

When asked to draw the fluid level in a tilted jar, young children typically draw the figure shown in (A) rather than (B)—not because they have ever seen anything like (A) in the real world, but because the logic they use in their attempts to make meaning out of their experiences is not always appropriate.

are no longer deceived by a problem, but rather that they have now learned some basic logical rules that become evident in much of their thinking. That is, in the course of what Kuhn (1984) calls "meaning-making" (or what Piaget called "constructing" knowledge), the child has discovered that there is a logic that governs things and relationships—that the game of knowing has rules. These rules make it possible for children to overcome many of the errors that characterized their thinking during the preoperational period. They can now rely on **operations** (thought processes governed by rules of logic) rather than on **preoperations** (thinking based on perception and intuition).

That children attempt to use logic and "make meaning" does not mean that they will always respond correctly. In fact, one of the clearest illustrations of meaning-making occurs during the preoperational period *and leads to an incorrect answer.*

When a preschooler is asked to draw the water level in a tilted jar, the most common response is (A) in Figure 9.3, rather than the correct response, (B). Since the child has never actually seen anything like (A), the drawing does not reflect actual experience so much as an attempt to make sense of experience (Kuhn, 1984).

IDENTITY, REVERSIBILITY, AND COMPENSATION

Part of the meaning that young schoolchildren invent involves a gradual recognition of the logic that governs things. Three rules of logic that are discovered (or invented) during this period are particularly important for the acquisition of conservation: **identity, reversibility**, and **compensation**. Each can be illustrated by the conservation of quantity problem in which children are asked whether a deformed object still contains the same amount of clay as an unchanged object. Children who answer correctly (who conserve) may be reasoning in one of three ways: nothing has been added to or taken away, so the deformed object must be identical to what it was (identity); the deformed objected can be reformed into what it was and so must contain the same amount (reversibility); or the deformed object appears to have more material because it is longer, but its thinness makes up for its length (compensation).

Once a child has learned about identity, compensation, and reversibility, do these rules apply to all thinking? The answer is no. There are as many different kinds of conservation as there are characteristics of objects that can vary in quantity (for example, mass, number, weight, area, volume, and so on). If the rules of logic that make these conservations possible were completely general, they would all be acquired at the same time. When children realize that the amount of clay does not change when a ball is flattened, they should also realize that the amount of water does not change when it is poured from a tall thin vase into a shallow wide bowl. But, as Figure 9.4 shows, the approximate ages at which the various conservations are acquired span a number of years.

Additional evidence from *extinction studies* indicates that children's rules of logic at the concrete operations stage are not completely general. In these studies, children who have already acquired a specific conservation are given evidence that their reasoning is incorrect. The argument is that if a conserver truly believes that conservation is a logical and necessary consequence, there should be strong resistance to extinction of that logic.

In a typical extinction experiment in conservation of weight, subjects agree that two balls weigh the same, and then continue to maintain that this is the case even after one or both of the balls have been deformed or broken into little pieces. At this point, however, the experimenter asks subjects to verify their conservation response by using a balance scale. But it's a trick! The scale is rigged so that one of the balls now seems to weigh more than the other!

Miller (1981) reviewed more than 25 extinction experiments. In a majority of them, subjects believed evidence that contradicted their original conservation response and that, by the same token, contradicted the logical rules that led to that response. Young conservers (and sometimes older ones) do not always behave as though they believe these rules of logic to be necessarily true in all relevant cases. However, further questioning of subjects in extinction studies often reveals that they don't doubt the certainty of the logical rule, but rather that they are simply not always clear about when to apply the rule. Even young children realize that social rules are arbitrary and uncertain, says Miller (1981); but they also know that Piagetian rules of logic are more universal. However, the rigged balance scale presents a real-life problem rather than a problem in logic. In this situation, children are not deciding whether the logical rule is correct (they know it is), but whether the scale is correct.

In a similar series of experiments, Winer and McGlone (1993) asked children *and college students* misleading conservation questions such as: "When do you weigh more, when you are walking or running?" Or, after presenting two equal rows of checkers in a conservation of number problem and then spreading one out, they asked "Who has more, you or I?" Strikingly, some college students show lack of conservation in these circumstances—as do even more third- and sixth-grade students. Why? Perhaps, though not likely, because we are acquiescent, suggest Winer and McGlone. Or maybe because subjects are responding to what they think the experimenter *means* rather than *says* ("She probably means 'Who *looks* like they have more?' rather

Some simple tests for conservation, with approximate ages of attainment.

1. Conservation of substance (6–7 years)

A.

The experimenter presents two identical modeling clay balls. The subject admits that they have equal amounts of clay.

B.

One of the balls is deformed. The subject is asked whether they still contain equal amounts.

2. Conservation of length (6–7 years)

A.

Two sticks are aligned in front of the subject. The subject admits their equality.

B.

One of the sticks is moved to the right. The subject is asked whether they are still the same length.

3. Conservation of number (6–7 years)

A.

Two rows of counters are placed in one-to-one correspondence. Subject admits their equality.

B.

One of the rows is elongated (or contracted). Subject is asked whether each row still contains the same number.

4. Conservation of liquids (6–7 years)

A.

Two beakers are filled to the same level with water. The subject sees that they are equal.

B.

The liquid of one container is poured into a tall tube (or a flat dish). The subject is asked whether each still contains the same amount.

5. Conservation of area (9–10 years)

A.

The subject and the experimenter each have identical sheets of cardboard. Wooden blocks are placed on these in identical positions. The subject agrees that each cardboard has the same amount of space remaining.

B.

The experimenter scatters the blocks on one of the cardboards. The subject is asked whether each cardboard still has the same amount of space remaining.

than 'Who actually has more?' "). Or, most likely, this simply illustrates that both children and adults are capable of thinking at various levels of sophistication, and that even after we have learned a dozen elegant rules of logic, we don't always behave as though we had.

can conservation be accelerated?

American researchers and educators were fond of asking Piaget questions like: "If we can accurately describe some of the important capabilities that children develop and the sequence in which these appear, might it not also be possible to accelerate their appearance by providing children with appropriate experiences? And could we not, by so doing, speed up the developmental process, increase children's cognitive capabilities, and perhaps even make them more intelligent?"

But Piaget did not answer such questions directly. He had always been more concerned with describing and explaining cognitive development than with trying to change its course. However, an impressive number of other researchers have attempted an answer. Many (including *moi* in quest of a Ph.D.; see Lefrançois, 1968) have looked at the possibility of accelerating the development of concepts of conservation—concepts that are simply defined, easy to measure, and important in cognitive development. The reasoning is that if important cognitive achievements can be accelerated through training, then we can probably design school programs that would be far more beneficial for cognitive growth than those presently used.

Many of the early studies designed to teach conservation to young children before they would be expected to acquire it naturally were unsuccessful or only partly successful. Investigators have tried a variety of approaches. Rosenthal and Zim-

merman (1972) used a conserving child as a model. Many nonconserving subjects later demonstrated knowledge of conservation on related but not identical tasks. But when these investigators tried giving instruction in relevant rules, they were unsuccessful. In contrast, Siegler and Liebert (1972) accelerated acquisition of liquid conservation by giving children rules and information about the accuracy of their responses. But Kuhn (1972), who used a modeling procedure, failed to increase conservation behavior appreciably in subjects.

In summary, there is no evidence that development can be altered easily and significantly through short-term training programs in conservation. Although conservation can be accelerated, training programs need to be detailed and systematic, especially if children are still some distance from acquiring conservation naturally (see Furth, 1980; Gelman & Gallistel, 1978). And whether such efforts, when successful, contribute significantly to intellectual development—or to happiness and self-esteem—remains unclear.

classes, seriation, and number

In addition to acquiring various conservations, children gain or improve three other abilities as they enter concrete operations.

CLASSES

First, they learn to deal with classes, achieving the capacity to understand class inclusion and to reason about the combination and the decomposition of classes. An 8 year old, for example, would be unlikely to make a mistake when asked to decide whether there are more roses or more flowers in a bouquet consisting of 15 roses and 5 tulips. At this level, children typically understand that roses make up a subclass of the larger class of flowers.

Similarly, they would have little difficulty answering the question "If there are red balls and gray balls, and some are large whereas others are small, how many different kinds of balls are there?" by multiplying the number of colors by the number of sizes (see Figure 9.5). Recall from Chapter 7 that preschool children too have some ability to deal with class-inclusion problems. Many can correctly answer questions in the form: "A Siamese is a cat, but not an alley cat. Is a Siamese an animal?" However, they typically cannot respond correctly to the flowers problem.

SERIATION

A second achievement of the period of concrete operations is the understanding of **seriation** (ordering in sequence). Piaget's seriation task presents children with a series of objects (for example, dolls), each a different height, so they can easily be arranged from tallest to shortest. The bottom row of Figure 9.6 illustrates the correct arrangement, quickly produced by concrete-operations children. However, intuitive-stage children are ordinarily incapable of responding cor-

rectly. A typical response is to place several of the dolls in order while ignoring the fact that others may fit in between those that have already been positioned (top row). If the next doll the child selects is too short to be placed where the child intended it to be (at the upper end), it is placed without hesitation at the other end, even though it might be taller or shorter than the adjacent doll. The child does not yet understand that if A is greater than B, and B is greater than C, then A must also be greater than C. Understanding this concept eliminates the necessity of making all the comparisons that would otherwise be necessary.

NUMBER

Understanding this concept also makes it possible to understand the concept of number more completely, because the ordinal properties of numbers (their ordered sequence: first, second, third, . . .) depend on a knowledge of seriation. Similarly, their cardinal properties (their quantitative properties, the fact that they represent collections of different magnitude) depend on classification. As we saw in Chapter 7, however, many preschool

f igure 9.5

The use of multiplication to answer the question "If there are red balls and gray balls, and some are large whereas others are small, how many different kinds of balls are there?" illustrates the classification abilities of children during the period of concrete operations.

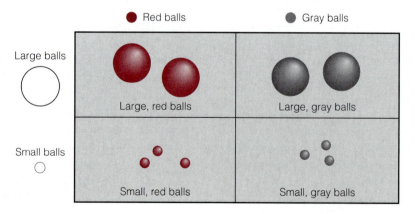

children already have an impressive knowledge of number, a fact that Piaget largely overlooked as he searched for the limitations of preoperational versus operational thought.

summary of concrete operations

An operation is a thought that is characterized by rules of logic. Because children acquire conservations early in this period and because these concepts are manifestations of operational thinking, the period is called operational. It is also termed concrete because children's thinking deals with real objects or those they can easily imagine. Children in the concrete operations stage are bound to the real world; they do not yet have the freedom made possible by the more advanced logic of the formal operations stage—freedom to contemplate the hypothetical, to compare the ideal with the actual, to be profoundly unhappy and concerned about the discrepancy between this world and that which they imagine possible.

children as information processors

Piaget's view of the growth of mind is one approach to understanding the intellectual development of children; there are others. Some are concerned with exploring the accuracy and usefulness of Piaget's system and with elaborating on it. These approaches have informed us that Piaget's stages are perhaps not entirely universal, that the transitions between them are not abrupt, and that there are sometimes marked variations in the responses of a single child to problems that appear to require the same underlying logical competence. Still, Piaget's system continues to be the most widely known and widely researched of cognitive developmental theories.

figure 9.6

A test of a child's understanding of seriation. The elements of the series are presented in random order and the child is asked to arrange them in sequence of height. The top row was arranged by a 3½ year old; the bottom, by an 8 year old.

But there is another view of the cognitive development of children, one that complements rather than contradicts Piaget's. It begins, as all views of developing children must, with the observation that a newborn infant is, as my grandmother so poetically put it, "pretty doggoned ignorant" (this is a rough translation of what might be viewed as somewhat impolite French). The expression is not at all derogatory when applied to an infant, although it was when she applied it to Frank. The difference, you see, is that infants are supposed to be ignorant. They are not expected to know that day follows night, which itself follows day; that butterflies whisper to each other when they perch on buttercups in the sunshine; or that tigers have tails. In fact, they are strangers to their very own hands and feet, strangers to the world. And, as Rheingold (1985) points out, the process of development is a process of becoming familiar with the world.

The difference between newborns—who are almost totally unfamiliar with everything around them—and older children—who have learned about tigers, tautologies, and tarantulas—can be described in a number of ways. We can say, with Piaget, that the developing child, through the processes of assimilation and accommodation, has constructed a sort of reality that conforms, more or less, to certain logical rules that, in turn, define a sequence of orderly stages.

Or we can say that the developing child begins with no knowledge base, few strategies for dealing with cognitive material, and no awareness of the self as a knower or as a processor of information. This approach permits us to view development as the business of acquiring a knowledge base, developing **cognitive strategies**, and gradually gaining an awareness of self as a knower. This is an **information-processing approach** to cognitive development.

There are then three important things that the information-processing approach looks at: the knowledge base and its creation; the processes and strategies by which information becomes part of the knowledge base or is retrieved from it;

The knowledge base that the teacher brings to her embroidery consists of skills and information of which her young charges have not yet dreamed—although with the right experiences and a little help, they too will get there. Information processing theorists look not only at the content of the knowledge base but also at the processes and strategies that allow it to grow and to be used, as well as at the emergence of the child's awareness of the self as a knower and processor of information.

and the emergence of the child's awareness of self as a player of what Flavell
(1985) calls the "game of cognition." The
first two of these relate to human memory: The individual's knowledge base is
made up of what is in memory, and the
strategies that enable the child to develop
and use a knowledge base are those that
permit adding or retrieving things from
memory. The third component of the
information-processing approach—the
recognition of self as a knower capable of
using and evaluating strategies—involves
what is termed **metacognition**, which
refers to knowing about knowing.

types of memory

The information-processing model
views children as consumers and processors of information—as little organisms
that shed their ignorance as they build
up a store of memories. The most common model is based on Atkinson and
Shiffrin's (1971) description of information-processing in terms of three types of
information storage: sensory memory
(also called *sensory register*), short-term
memory (also called *working memory*), and
long-term memory (see Figure 9.7).
Each is defined mainly in terms of the
amount and nature of processing that it
involves. Processing refers to mental activities such as sorting, analyzing, rehearsing, and summarizing.

SENSORY MEMORY

Our sensory systems (vision, hearing,
taste, smell, and touch) are sensitive to a
tremendous range of stimulation that
constantly bombards them. But the bulk
of this stimulation is not attended to. You
are never *aware* of all the sights, sounds,
tastes, smells, and tactile sensations that
are immediately possible. Most of this
stimulation has only a fleeting (less than
one second) and unconscious effect on
memory. These momentary impressions
associated with sensory stimulation define **sensory memory**. Sensory memory requires virtually no cognitive
processing.

One of the most important characteristics of sensory memory is that although
the stimulation is not attended to or
processed, it is nevertheless available for
processing. A series of experiments in
which different messages are fed to each

---

f **igure 9.7**

The three components of memory. Sensory information first enters sensory memory and is forgotten almost immediately unless it is rehearsed. If rehearsed, it becomes part of short-term memory and remains available (as a name or word, for example) so long as it is being rehearsed. Much of the material in short-term memory will also be forgotten as soon as it is no longer being used (rehearsed); some, however, may be coded for storage in long-term memory, in which it takes the form of meanings and concepts. It is important to note that these three components of memory do not refer to three different locations in the brain or other parts of the nervous system, but to how we remember—or, more precisely, to how we study memory.

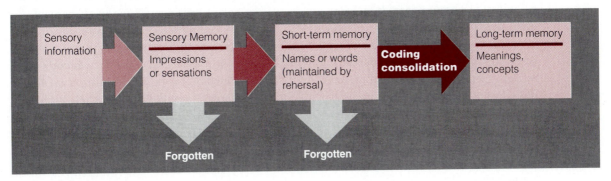

of a subject's ears by means of head-phones serves to illustrate this. In some of these experiments subjects are instructed to pay attention to the message being broadcast into one ear while other unrelated messages are fed to the other ear (Cherry, 1953). Subsequent questioning typically shows that subjects have no memory whatsoever of what has transpired in the unattended ear. In fact, they don't even notice changes from one language to another (Broadbent, 1952) and cannot recall the message even when it consists of only a single word repeated as many as 35 times (Moray, 1959). But when the subject's name is mentioned a single time in the unattended ear, attention shifts immediately. This phenomenon is sometimes called the *cocktail-party phenomenon* because it can often be observed in crowded rooms when individuals busily engaged in one conversation will turn immediately when their name is spoken by someone else across the room.

SHORT-TERM MEMORY

Our ability to recall the beginning of a sentence as we read it illustrates **short-term memory** (or working memory). If we can't remember the beginning of the sentence, it's usually because we're not paying attention. The consequence of not paying attention is that the stimulation being ignored (not being attended to) flits through sensory memory but never makes it to short-term memory.

In a sense, short-term memory is equivalent to attention span. It includes everything of which we are immediately conscious (everything that is now being attended to). As Calfee (1981) puts it, it is sort of a "scratch pad" for thinking. But this scratch pad has two important limitations: Its capacity is limited, and it lasts only for seconds rather than minutes.

Short-term memory is limited to around seven items (plus or minus two) (Miller, 1956). We can glance casually at

a flock of geese drifting through an autumn sky and see (without having to count one, two, three . . .) that there are exactly four or six or even seven geese. But if there were 13, our immediate estimate would be just that—an estimate or a guess. We cannot instantaneously enumerate 13 separate geese on the screens of our short-term memories.

The storage limitations of short-term memory are often expanded through a process called **chunking**. Chunking is nothing more complex than grouping items into related units; three groups of four geese and a stubborn loner. Miller (1956) illustrates the process by referring to a change purse that can hold only seven coins. If you put seven pennies into this purse, then its full capacity is seven cents. But if you fill it with seven groupings (chunks) of pennies—such as nickels, dimes, or quarters—its total capacity increases dramatically.

One common measure of short-term memory is to have subjects try to repeat a sequence of unrelated numbers they have just heard, a task that is used on a number of intelligence tests. Average adolescents and adults are able to repeat correctly six or seven (or sometimes even nine) digits. In contrast, 6 year olds will typically succeed in repeating only two or so.

Children's limited *working* memory may be extremely important in explaining some aspects of cognitive development. Siegler (1989), for example, suggests that children are often unable to solve certain problems simply because they cannot keep in mind all relevant information simultaneously. Put another way, the ways in which they **encode** (represent in memory) information are different. Case (1991), in his neo-Piagetian theory of cognitive development, claims that the most important constraint on children's use of schemes to understand and to solve problems is simply a limitation on short-term storage space.

Sensory memory, as we saw, does not involve cognitive processing, but is simply a fleeting impression almost like an echo. In contrast, short-term memory is highly dependent on rehearsal or repetition. Without this type of processing, the material fades and is forgotten within seconds. When I look up a telephone number and dial it immediately, I need only repeat the number for as long as it takes to dial it. Typically, by the time I have finished dialing I will no longer remember the number. It resided in short-term memory for only that brief period during which it was rehearsed, and then it disappeared again.

LONG-TERM MEMORY

But if I think I might need the number again tomorrow, there are several things I can do. The easiest from a cognitive point of view would be to write it down so that I would not have to remember it; that would impose little cognitive strain. I would not have to use any of the strategies required to move material from short-term to long-term storage. But it would still require the use of long-term memory; tomorrow I would have to remember not only that I made a note of the necessary number, but also where that note is. And I would have to remember a tremendous range of other information as well, including how to translate telephone numbers into the orderly and sequential act of dialing, how to speak and listen with a telephone, and so on. Put another way, even as habitual a behavior as using a telephone requires quite a large knowledge base. And our knowledge base is, in effect, our **long-term memory**. It includes everything we know—about ourselves, about the world, about knowing.

Our contemporary models or metaphors for long-term memory are **associationistic**; they are based on the notion that all items of information in

The complex skills involved in learning to ride a horse cannot easily be put into words and retrieved from long-term memory so that they can be analyzed and discussed. But the details of putting bridle and saddle even on a reluctant horse might be made more explicit. All complex activities require a stable knowledge base—which is, in effect long-term memory.

our memories are connected in various ways. It is precisely because of these connections that we are able to remember so impressively.

memory processes

There are three basic processes involved in remembering: *rehearsing, elaborating,* and *organizing*. In addition, there are a number of specific strategies that can be used with each of these processes (Horton & Mills, 1984).

REHEARSING

Rehearsing involves repetition and has an important role both in maintaining information in short-term memory and in transferring material from short- to long-term storage. The simplest rehearsal strategy is to name the material (five, five, five, one, two, one, two) over and over until it seems unlikely that it will escape. Most children younger than 5 do not spontaneously rehearse and cannot easily be taught to do so (Wellman, 1988).

ELABORATING

To elaborate is to extend material or add something to it in order to make it more memorable. For example, **elaborating** might consist of forming associations between new material and existing knowledge, or of creating mental images that go beyond (elaborate on) the actual material (Higbee, 1977). Elaboration that relates to the *meaning* of what is being learned seems most effective. Bradshaw and Anderson (1982) had subjects try to recall sentences such as "The fat man read the sign." Those who elaborated this sentence to something like "The fat man read the sign warning of thin ice" significantly improved their ability to remember that the man in question was fat. Again, younger children do not spontaneously elaborate to improve recall. By age 12, memory strategies of this kind are more common (Justice, 1985).

ORGANIZING

Organizing involves arranging items or concepts in terms of relationships. Assume, for example, that you have been asked to memorize this list: pencil, horse, pen, house, barn, cat, apartment, bear, typewriter. You might have noticed that the list can easily be organized into three groups of related items (animals, dwellings, writing instruments) and you can use this organization to help remember the items. Young children will not usually notice these relationships and will not organize material the way you would. Their use of strategies is more limited than yours; they know less about knowing.

schemata and scripts: a model of long-term memory

The main function of these three memory processes is to help establish *associations* among related items of information to facilitate remembering.

The associationistic view of human memory has led to a number of abstract models to describe what it is that is stored in long-term memory over periods of minutes, weeks, or years. These cognitive models are based on *meaning*; they make use of various terms, including *nodes, schemas, scripts, frames, networks, categories,* and *coding systems*. These labels are metaphors and not literal descriptions. They don't say that long-term memory *is* such and such, but rather that long-term memory is *like* such and such or might be compared to such and such (Bransford, 1979).

REMEMBERING MEANINGS

In most real-life situations, we remember *meanings* rather than specific occurrences (Smith & Graesser, 1981). When someone tells you a funny story, you remember its gist and perhaps the wording of the punch line, but seldom the exact wording of the entire story, the pauses, the intonations, and the facial expressions of the speaker. In the current jargon, what you remember are **schemata**, which are like clusters of knowledge that define concepts. They are what we know about this or that. Our schemata relating to wild cows might include items of knowledge relating to size, color, characteristic sounds, foods, and habitat. Our schemata might also include some affective (emotional) reactions having to do with the taste of these creatures or their smell. If someone tells me a story about wild cows, what I remember of the story will be profoundly influenced by my wild cow schema.

One aspect of schemata that is particularly important in remembering real-life information (such as what goes with what, the gist of stories, or even such mundane things as whether desserts come before or after soups and salads) is called a **script**. Scripts are the part of cognitive structure (of knowledge, hence of schemata) that deals with routines and sequences. We all know the script for going into a restaurant, eating, and ordering . . . which is why the first part of this sentence is jarring. Our scripts say ordering and then eating, not vice versa.

Children's memories for things like stories are highly dependent on their relevant schemata and scripts. For example, when they are told stories, they tend to fill in gaps according to their personal scripts. In one study, Johnson, Bransford, and Solomon (1973) presented subjects with the following short passage:

> *John was trying to fix the birdhouse. He was pounding the nail when his father came out to watch him and to help him do the work.*

When subjects were later shown these sentences along with others, one of which was

> *John was using the hammer to fix the birdhouse when his father came out to watch and to help him do the work.*

they overwhelmingly agreed that they had seen the last sentence rather than the two that they had actually seen. Note that the hammer was not even mentioned in the original text. It seems clear that subjects recalled the central ideas of the two sentences and "generated" the hammer because hammers are what we use to pound nails. Their birdhouse-building scripts, like yours and mine, include the use of hammers.

One of the implications of the fact that we often "generate" things when we're trying to remember is that understanding should facilitate memory. Paris and Lindauer (1976) asked children to remember the simple sentence "The workman dug a hole in the ground," adding "with a shovel" for half their subjects. One of the recall procedures was to present subjects with cue words (in this case, "shovel"). Significantly, the word "shovel" served equally well as a cue for children who had not seen the word in the original sentence. Clearly, the cue word would have been totally meaningless for children who did not initially understand that holes can be dug with shovels.

---

developmental changes in memory

An information-processing model of memory leads to a number of predictions about infants' and children's memory that can be tested directly. For example, we would expect that for the stages of memory that involve little cognitive processing, young children might not perform very differently from older children or adults, but that when processing strategies are necessary, there should be greater differences between younger and older children.

SENSORY AND SHORT-TERM MEMORY

In general, these predictions have been supported by research. Memory that does not depend on processing strategies does not appear to change very much as children develop. For example, recognition memory, a task that does not ordinarily involve complex strategies, is highly accurate from early childhood on (Paris & Lindauer, 1982). Similarly, comparisons between adults and children with respect to sensory and short-term memories—neither of which requires any strategy more elaborate than simple repetition—have found few significant differences. It appears that short-term memory and sensory memory change little from childhood to adulthood because they do not require the use of elaborate or cognitively demanding strategies.

LONGER-TERM MEMORY

Memory that is highly dependent on the use of processing strategies should improve as children's recognition and understanding of strategies improve. This prediction too is supported by the evidence. It appears that very young children do not rehearse and organize as systematically as older children (Gitomer & Pellegrino, 1985). Paris and Lindauer (1982) note that research has found significant developmental changes in memory under at least four sets of circumstances: when the memory tasks require intentional memorization, when the material is unfamiliar, when specific organizational strategies are required, and when the task requires a change in the learner's strategies.

Liberty and Ornstein (1973) presented fourth-graders and college students (average ages 10 and 19, respectively) with 28 words, each printed on a separate card. Subjects were asked to sort the cards, face up, into bins on the table in front of them so the words would be easier to learn. The sorting procedure was repeated six times, or until the subject sorted consistently. At this point, subjects were tested for recall.

There are two important findings: The first is that older subjects consistently remembered more words than did the younger subjects, which is not surprising given that the task is essentially one of long-term recall. The second is that younger subjects were far more idiosyn-

cratic in how they chose to group the words. It seems that processing strategies are less adequate in young children.

It seems that the most important developmental changes in children's memories have to do with the use of the three basic processes involved in remembering (and especially in long-term memory): rehearsal, elaboration, and organization. Preschoolers apparently seldom use these strategies to learn and remember. Appel et al. (1972) showed pictures to children ages 4, 7, and 11 under one of two sets of instructions: "Look at these pictures" or "Remember these pictures." When the 7- and 11 year olds were asked to remember, they deliberately used strategies to aid their recall. In contrast, 4 year olds behaved exactly the same way under both sets of instructions, relying on recognition rather than on strategies.

metacognition and metamemory

Not only are younger children less capable of organizing material, but they also seem less aware of the importance of doing so. They are not reflective about themselves as knowers and seem not to have recognized the special skills that allow them to know and remember. In other words, they seem to know less about knowing, to understand less about understanding (Flavell, 1982).

Knowledge about knowing is termed **metacognition**. Metacognitive skills are what allow us to monitor our own progress, to estimate the effects of our efforts to learn, and to predict our likelihood of success in remembering. They tell us that there are ways in which to organize material so that it will be easier to learn and remember, that there are rehearsal and review strategies that are more effective for one kind of learning than another, and that some kinds of learning require the deliberate application of cognitive strategies whereas others do not. In other words, metacognition refers to knowing about knowing rather than simply to the content of what is known. And because memory is inseparably linked with cognition, it includes what is sometimes labeled **metamemory**—knowing about remembering.

Metacognitive skills seem to be largely absent in young children. This does not mean that they use no memory or learning strategies; it simply means that they are not aware of them, that they do not consciously apply them. When Moynahan (1973) asked young children whether it would be easier to learn a categorized list of words or a random list, children below third grade selected either list; children in third grade were more likely to select the categorized list. Paradoxically, even when children are capable of engaging in useful memory strategies, they often do not.

Borkowski, Milstead, and Hale (1988) point out that among children there is a greater spread between memory behavior and memory knowledge (metamemory) than there is among adults. They suggest that the explanation for this is that metamemory consists of different components, not all of which are learned and used at the same time. One of the components of metamemory is knowledge of specific strategies—knowing, for instance, that grouping items might facilitate recall. Specific strategies such as this are sometimes understood by young children or can be taught to them (Pressley, Forrest-Pressley, & Elliott-Faust, 1988). Another component has to do with knowing how and when to use a specific strategy—a component that Borkowski et al. (1988) label *metamemory acquisition procedures*. Teachers are not often very systematic about teaching memory skills,

There is still considerable conflict and disagreement about what constitutes intelligence. Special aptitudes—such as musical, numerical, verbal, or even scholastic—are somewhat easier to define and measure. But playing an instrument well probably represents more than just an innate aptitude; it might also reflect a combination of motivation, persistence, practice, and determined parents.

say Borkowski and associates. As a result, children are usually left to decide on their own whether a strategy should be used and, if so, what strategy, when, and how. It should come as little surprise, then, that they often know about a strategy but do not spontaneously use it.

motivation and self-efficacy in learning

Knowing about strategies and their usefulness is only one of the factors involved in learning and remembering; motivation is another.

MOTIVATION

Motives are the *whys* of behavior; they are what account for the fact that behavior occurs in the first place. They also serve to direct it, and they explain its termination. At a biological level, for example, the need for food—that is, *hunger*—accounts for food-related behaviors such as buying a hamburger or making a stew. The eventual satisfaction of our hunger explains why we stop eating.

But even at this level, our behavior isn't quite so simple. Other factors, such as the availability of a restaurant or of sufficient funds, or the wish to maintain a trim figure, also have a lot to do with our actions. But perhaps most important, it is our knowledge about the relationship between restaurants, money, food, and hunger that drives our actions. We can imagine the hamburger; we can taste it in our minds. Ultimately, it is our anticipations, our cognitions, that move us.

SELF-EFFICACY

Cognitions motivate our behaviors, says Bandura (1989a), in the sense that they allow us to preview the consequences of our actions and thus to establish goals. This process is closely linked with how competent and capable we think we are. As we saw in Chapter 2, people who have high estimates of their own personal competence—what Bandura labels high **self-efficacy**—are most likely to accept difficult challenges and set high goals. Those who see themselves as less effective (who lack confidence) set lower goals and give up rapidly when they begin to fail.

The best learners—those who are best at using memory strategies—are typically individuals who have positive beliefs about the efficacy of their memories. As we noted, simply knowing about memory strategies is not enough. When Rebok and Balcerak (1989) taught a specific memory strategy for remembering words, subjects later used the strategy only if they believed it made them better memorizers. Those whose perceived memory-efficacy was unaffected by the

training did not spontaneously use the strategy. Bandura (1989a) concludes: "Training in cognitive skills can produce more generalized and lasting effects if it raises self-beliefs of efficacy as well as imparts skills." In addition to awareness of specific strategies, children's metacognitive and metamemory skills must include notions of themselves as competent, skillful knowers and rememberers.

cultural differences in learning strategies

Cognitive strategies are learned; accordingly, they reflect the effects of schooling and of culture. For example, memory strategies such as categorization appear to be more common among German children than among children in the United States (Schneider et al., 1986). Similarly, studies have demonstrated that in the absence of schooling, children (and adults) do not perform as well on many cognitive and memory tasks (Das & Dash, 1990). Not only does schooling add to the child's knowledge base, claim Das and Dash, but it also enhances cognitive skills. And the single factor that is perhaps most intimately involved in increasing cognitive skills and knowledge base is literacy. As Olson (1986) puts it, "Language makes us human; literacy makes us civilized . . . " (p. 109).

Reading requires the exercising of what Kirby and Das (1990) describe as among the most important cognitive processes: planning, attending, and processing. It is inevitable that it should also lead to advances in other cognitive skills and strategies.

the use of cognitive strategies

Metacognition and metamemory deal with our knowledge about how we know, with our awareness of ourselves as players of what Flavell (1985) calls the "game of cognition." The object of the game of cognition is to pay attention, to learn, to remember, to retrieve from memory, and to do a variety of things such as sorting, analyzing, synthesizing, evaluating, creating, and so on.

There is more than one way to play the game of cognition. Some people play it very badly. They learn slowly, remember inaccurately, and seem lost and clumsy when faced with tasks requiring evaluation, synthesis, or creation. Others play it very well. Their responses are quick and accurate, their syntheses elegant, their creations startling.

One of the differences between those who play the game of cognition well and those who play less well—but by no means the only difference—is that the better players have better tools with which to play. Put another way, their cognitive strategies are better.

Simply defined, cognitive strategies are what control cognitive behavior. It is a cognitive strategy that tells one person to rehearse a list of the aardvark's characteristics and another person to create bizarre mental images of the creature. The strategy itself has nothing to do with the content of what is learned, remembered, or retrieved, but deals only with the processes involved in these activities. In Gagné and Briggs's (1983) words, it is "contentless." In this sense, cognitive strategies are related to what we call intelligence—and perhaps to creativity as well.

TEACHING STRATEGIES

Cognitive strategies have traditionally not been taught systematically in schools. Instead, we simply assume that students will learn them incidentally as they need them. Recently, however, a number of programs have been designed deliberately to teach children cognitive strategies (see

Royer, Cisero, & Carlo, 1993). For example, Mulcahy (1991) uses a *Socratic dialogue* question-and-answer teaching method to lead students to a recognition of their own cognitive strategies. Similarly, Collins, Brown, and Newman (1989) suggest a *cognitive apprenticeship* approach in which mentors (parents, teachers, peers, siblings) serve as both models and teachers. The object is to provide learners with cognitive strategies so that they are equipped to explore, organize, discover, and learn on their own. Research makes it plain, claim Perkins, Jay, and Tishman (1993), that instruction in the skills that define metacognition can significantly improve learning and memory.

intelligence

ntelligence is what the tests test," Boring (1923, p. 35) informs us. This simple definition of what is not a simple concept is a useful and not entirely tongue-in-cheek definition. Weight is not a simple concept, either, yet to say that weight is what a scale measures is both useful and accurate. A butcher doesn't have to know the scientific definition of weight to use a scale properly. Perhaps a psychologist or a teacher need not know what intelligence is to make use of the results of intelligence tests.

Then again, maybe we do need to know, because there is an important difference between measuring weight and measuring intelligence. We agree about what weight is; we define it precisely and objectively. Our scales measure weight with marvelous accuracy. They measure exactly what they're supposed to measure, and nothing else—that is, they are **valid**. And they measure consistently, yielding the same weights for the same objects over and over again—that is, they are **reliable**.

But we don't know exactly what intelligence is. Some theorists have assumed that it is a quality of human functioning that depends on some basic, general capacity or trait in a person—that if you have a lot of this general something (popularly referred to as g), then your behavior will be intelligent in all areas. If this supposition is correct, then those who are highly intelligent (have high g) should do well in all tasks: mathematical, verbal, spatial, reasoning, memory, and so on. This **general factor theory**, as it is known, originated with Spearman (1927).

A second approach to defining intelligence, **special abilities theory**, assumes that rather than depending on a common underlying factor, intelligence consists of separate abilities.

THURSTONE'S APPROACH

One example of a special abilities approach is provided by Thurstone (1938), who identified seven "primary mental abilities" on the basis of test results and who defined intelligence in terms of the following abilities:

- S (space): visualization of geometric figures from different angles

- N (number): speed of computational skills

- P (perceptual speed): speed of perceiving details

- V (verbal meanings): grasp of meanings of words

- W (word fluency): speed of manipulating single words

- M (rote memory): facility in memorizing simple material

- I (induction): logical reasoning ability

Thurstone believed that these abilities were relatively independent—that a person could be very good at all of them, at none of them, or at just some of them. The most intelligent people, of course, would be those who did well in all of them.

GARDNER'S APPROACH

Gardner (1983), like Thurstone, rejects the notion of a single, global capacity underlying intelligence. But unlike Thurstone, he does not speak of separate intellectual abilities, but of separate and distinct intelligences—of, in his words, multiple intelligences. There are six kinds of these intelligences: linguistic, musical, logical-mathematical, spatial, bodily-kinesthetic, and personal (having to do with interpersonal skills and self-knowledge). In any given society, some of these intelligences will be considered more important than others. In ours, for example, linguistic and logical-mathematical skills are clearly most important; accordingly, these are the skills that are taught in our schools—and they are also the skills that are most often measured by our intelligence tests.

CATTELL'S APPROACH

Cattell's (1971) approach distinguishes between two kinds of intelligence. On the one hand there are certain abilities, labeled **fluid abilities** (or sometimes *fluid intelligence*), that seem to underlie much of our intelligent behavior. These abilities are not learned and are therefore relatively unaffected by cultural and environmental influences. Fluid abilities are manifested in individuals' ability to solve abstract problems and are evident in measures of general reasoning, memory, attention span, and analysis of figures.

In contrast to these basic fluid abilities is a grouping of intellectual abilities that are primarily verbal and are highly influenced by culture, experience, and education. These abilities, labeled **crystallized abilities** (or *crystallized intelligence*), are reflected in measures of vocabulary, general information, and arithmetic skills.

Several developmental predictions can be based on the notion of fluid and crystallized intelligence. First, because fluid intelligence is independent of experience, it should remain constant throughout most of development, increasing slightly perhaps as the nervous system matures through childhood and adolescence, and maybe decreasing somewhat in old age as the nervous system ages. Second, because crystallized intelligence is highly dependent on experience, it should grow with increasing age, perhaps right through old age.

These predictions have been extensively investigated by Horn and Donaldson (Horn, 1976; Horn & Donaldson, 1980), who report that crystallized abilities do increase, sometimes into very old age, and that fluid abilities show some slight declines during old age. Other researchers argue that decline with age has been exaggerated and is neither inevitable nor irreversible.

STERNBERG'S APPROACH

Intelligence, Sternberg (1984) informs us, is a quality of human functioning that is best defined in terms of the context in which it occurs. In this **contextual theory of intelligence**, intelligence is what makes adaptation possible, and adaptation occurs in specific contexts. In Sternberg's (1984) words, intelligence is the "purposive selection and shaping of and adaptation to real-world environments relevant to one's life" (p. 312). Thus certain behaviors may be highly intelligent in one context but quite unintelligent in others.

How do we find out what intelligence is in a particular context? One way, according to Sternberg, is to ask people. If

you ask enough people, you might arrive at a pretty clear definition. In North American cultures, we define intelligent people as those who can solve practical problems, who have high verbal ability, and who are socially competent. Elsewhere the definition might be somewhat different.

Sternberg (1985) suggests that adaptation to the real world (in other words, *intelligence*) involves the interaction of three different components of intelligence: metacomponents, performance components, and knowledge-acquisition components.

Metacomponents are the cognitive strategies of which we spoke earlier. They include skills related to problem identification, allocation of resources, monitoring of ongoing cognitive processes, and use of feedback to change or modify strategies. This component of intelligence includes what we have been discussing as metacognition or metamemory (Gardner, 1985).

Performance components relate to actually doing—in contrast to the metacomponents, which are involved in selecting problems and procedures, responding to feedback, changing procedures, and so on. Put another way, the metacomponents of intellectual functioning define its executive functions, its decision-making functions. Performance refers simply to the execution of decisions made at the metacomponent level.

Knowledge-acquisition components are what is actually achieved in the process of learning. Because this component has to do with adaptation, it relates directly to Sternberg's contextualist view of intelligence (see Figure 9.8).

measuring intelligence

The principal use of intelligence tests is for prediction. An intelligence test score is, in effect, a prediction that an individual will do well (or not do well) on tasks that require intelligence. It says, "so-and-so has an aptitude for doing well on things that require intelligence."

Among the most widely used and respected intelligence tests are the Stanford-Binet and the Wechsler. These are *individual intelligence tests*; that is, they can be administered only to one child at a time and only by a trained tester. They yield a richer picture of intellectual functioning than do *group tests*—tests that can be administered to a large group at one time and are commonly of a paper-and-pencil variety.

REVISED STANFORD-BINET

The revised Stanford-Binet (4th edition; Thorndike, Hagen, & Sattler, 1985) consists of a wide range of different types of questions. At the youngest age levels, for example, it requires children to identify parts of the body on a large paper doll; to build a tower with blocks; to recognize objects in terms of their functions ("show me the one that we drink out of; can cut with; use to iron clothes"); to string beads; to copy simple geometric designs. At higher age levels it asks subjects to repeat digits (in order and reversed); to answer questions based on a story; to define words; to name the days of the week; to identify synonyms and antonyms. And at adult levels, it requires the solution of arithmetic problems; the explanation of proverbs; discrimination between abstract words; and the solution of complex problems. And these are only a few of the more than 100 different tests that make up the Stanford-Binet.

The Stanford-Binet yields scores in four separate areas: verbal reasoning, quantitative reasoning, abstract/visual reasoning, and short-term memory. It also provides a composite score described as a measure of "adaptive ability." This

---

Intelligence is adaptation to real-world environments and involves selecting and shaping the environment.

Metacomponents

Executive skills involved in planning, monitoring, and evaluating cognitive activity

Performance components

Processes actually used in carrying out tasks, such as encoding, inductive reasoning, remembering

Knowledge acquisition components

Processes used in acquiring new information, such as separating important from unimportant information (selective encoding); relating items of information (selective combination); and comparing new information with old (selective comparison)

f i g u r e   9 . 8

The three components of intelligence in Sternberg's contextual theory of intelligence.

---

composite score is an **intelligence quotient** (IQ). The IQ derives its significance from the fact that we know that the average IQ of large, unselected populations is around 100, and that IQ is distributed as shown in Figure 9.9. Note that approximately two-thirds of all individuals have measured IQs that range between 85 and 115. Fewer than 2.5 percent score above 130 or below 70.

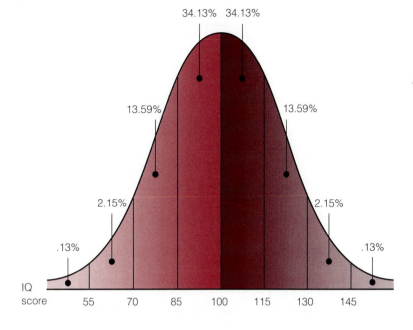

f igure 9.9

A normal curve depicting the theoretical distribution of IQ scores. Note that the average score is 100 and that 68.26 percent of the population scores between 85 and 115. Only 2.28 percent scores above 130.

THE WECHSLER

The Wechsler Intelligence Scale for Children (3rd ed., 1991), also called the WISC-III, yields a composite IQ score comparable to that obtained with the Stanford-Binet. The tests differ in several important respects, however. Most notably, the WISC-III also yields separate standardized scores for various subjects, as well as a verbal IQ and a performance IQ (in addition to the composite IQ). Deficiencies in language background are sometimes evident in disparities between verbal and performance scores.

Wechsler tests are also available for adults (WAIS-R: Wechsler Adult Intelligence Scale Revised, ages 16 to 75) and for preschool children (WPPSI: Wechsler Preschool and Primary Scale of Intelligence, ages 4 to 6½). The various subtests of the WISC-III are described in Table 9.2.

developmental changes in IQ

A normal 6-year-old child can correctly repeat two or three digits if they are presented clearly and distinctly at a rate of approximately one per second, but would not be expected to repeat four digits in reverse order. An average 3 year old can quickly identify legs, arms, hands, nose, and mouth on a doll, but might hesitate if asked to point to the infranasal depression. Clearly, there is a marked improvement in children's problem solving, memory, language, reasoning, and so on. Does that mean that intelligence improves?

Of course, the answer depends on how intelligence is defined. If it is defined in terms of being able to do those things we consider examples of intelligent behavior (like remembering, reasoning accurately, and expressing oneself clearly), then the answer is yes, children become more intelligent with age. But if intelligence is defined psychometrically (that is, in terms of how we measure it), the answer is no. Measured IQ is not an absolute indicator of how much or what a child can do; instead, it is a measure of what a child can do *compared with* what other children of similar ages and experi-

table 9.2

The Wechsler Intelligence Scale for Children (WISC-III)

VERBAL SCALE

1. General information. *Questions relating to information most children have the opportunity to acquire (M)**

2. General comprehension. *Questions designed to assess child's understanding of why certain things are done as they are (M)*

3. Arithmetic. *Oral arithmetic problems (M)*

4. Similarities. *Child indicates how certain things are alike (M)*

5. Vocabulary. *Child gives meaning of words of increasing difficulty (M)*

6. Digit span. *Child repeats orally presented sequence of numbers, in order and reversed (S)**

PERFORMANCE SCALE

1. Picture completion. *Child indicates what is missing from pictures (M)*

2. Picture arrangement. *Child must arrange series of pictures to tell a story (M)*

3. Block design. *Child is required to copy exactly a design with colored blocks (M)*

4. Object assembly. *Child must assemble puzzles (M)*

5. Coding. *Child follows a key to pair symbols with digits (M)*

6. Mazes. *Child traces way out of mazes with a pencil (S)*

7. Symbol Search. *Child performs symbol location task that measures mental processing speed and visual search skills (S)*

*(M) Mandatory
(S) Supplementary

ence can do. And because children improve in similar ways, the "average child's" measured intelligence does not change from year to year. By definition, it stays right around 100.

But, as we have said more than once, there is no "average child"; average is merely a mathematical invention. What about the individual?

The individual, research informs us, may display many different developmental patterns. As a result, measured differences between two individuals do not necessarily remain constant. For some children, measured IQ may increase over a period of years; or it may decrease; or it might go up and down like a bouncing ball (McCall, Applebaum & Hogarty, 1973). For the majority, however, measured IQ is relatively stable; it fluctuates within a range that would be expected given the precision of the tests. This indicates, claim Gustafsson and Undheim (1992), that the factors that underlie intelligence are relatively stable.

misconceptions about and misuses of IQ

The IQ is not always clearly understood; nor is it always used intelligently. A number of misconceptions are still common.

MISCONCEPTION 1

IQ is a mysterious thing that everybody has in different quantities. In fact, the IQ is simply a number based on a person's ability to perform in prescribed circumstances. It does not reveal mystical, hidden qualities that would otherwise be known only by clever psychologists who have dedicated their lives to the pursuit of the hidden truth.

MISCONCEPTION 2

IQ is a constant. I have x amount, you have y, and that's that. Not so, claim Salomon, Perkins, and Globerson (1991). There is evidence that interaction with new technologies like computers and tel-

It is a misconception that intelligence tests measure all the important things. Among other things, they don't measure a large number of personality characteristics such as motivation, persistence, creativity, and the ability to influence others. Nor do they measure adjustment—or physical strength.

evision may be *increasing* measured intelligence. And there is also striking evidence that schooling increases intelligence (Husén & Tuijnman, 1991).

But even if intelligence does not change, *measures* of IQ are not constant; they can vary tremendously from one testing time to another (McCall, Applebaum, & Hogarty, 1973). Measures taken in infancy are the least reliable (Thorndike & Hagen, 1977). This, of course, does not necessarily mean that whatever underlies intelligent behavior is highly unstable. It might simply reflect the questionable validity and reliability of intelligence tests.

MISCONCEPTION 3

IQ tests measure all the important things. Not so. As Weinberg (1989) notes, IQ tests tell us nothing about social intelligence or about adaptation, motivation, or emotion. Nor do they reveal anything about athletic ability, creativity, self-concept, or a host of other important personality variables.

MISCONCEPTION 4

IQ tests are fair. Many IQ tests are culturally biased; they penalized children whose backgrounds are different from the dominant white, middle-class majority. They are culturally biased because many were constructed for use with white, middle-class children and because they were usually standardized on samples comprising middle-class children. Not surprisingly, children from minority groups often do less well on these tests than their like-aged, middle-class, white counterparts. However, the most recent revisions of the Wechsler and the Stanford-Binet have taken this weakness into account and have used more representative norming samples. Accordingly, they are much fairer to minorities.

the usefulness of intelligence tests

IQ is related to success, particularly in school, but also in later life. In an important article, McClelland (1973) argues that intelligence tests bear very little relationship to success in life or in careers; furthermore, he claims, such tests are generally unfair to minorities. Hence they should be abandoned in favor of other tests that would measure *competence* rather than intelligence.

This article has had a profound influence on psychologists (as well as on popular thinking) and quickly led to widespread skepticism about intelligence testing. In fact, formal intelligence testing has been abandoned in many school jurisdictions, often at the insistence of parents.

But McClelland's conclusions are wrong, claim Barrett and Depinet (1991) following a detailed review of relevant research. "The evidence from these varied scientific studies leads again and again to the same conclusion: Intelligence and aptitude tests are positively related to job performance" (p. 1016).

The controversy over the use and usefulness of intelligence tests will not be quickly resolved. They have weaknesses and limitations, but they can be very useful. Unfortunately, although they are widely used, they are not always widely understood—hence the need to urge that information derived from tests be used in a restrained and intelligent way. This means that no important decisions should be based on a single test and without considering information from all other important sources. And perhaps nowhere is this admonition truer than when we are dealing with exceptional children.

intellectual exceptionality

*xceptionality* refers to mental, physical, or socioemotional functioning that departs significantly from the norm in either direction. Thus, there are those who are exceptionally gifted, who possess extraordinary talents, and there are those to whom nature and nurture have been less kind. In the remaining pages of this chapter we discuss both dimensions of intellectual exceptionality: mental retardation on the one hand and intellectual giftedness or very high creativity on the other.

mental retardation

Mental retardation is a complex exceptionality that can vary tremendously in severity.

DEFINITION

The American Association on Mental Retardation (AAMR) defines **mental retardation** as " . . . significantly subaverage general intellectual functioning existing concurrently with deficits in adaptive behavior, and manifested during the developmental period" (Grossman, 1983, p. 12). The AAMR definition of mental retardation is essentially the definition now adopted by the American Psychiatric Association (1987) as well.

The meaning of mental retardation is clarified by Grossman's (1983) analysis of the key terms involved. First, *general intellectual functioning* is defined in terms of test scores on one or more of the well-known individual intelligence tests—for example, the Stanford-Binet or the Wechsler Scales. An IQ of 70 is the accepted (and admittedly inexact) cutoff between normalcy and mild mental retardation.

Second, *deficits in adaptive behavior* are described as significant maturational deficits, most often apparent in inability to learn or in inability to reach the levels of independence, social responsibility, or social effectiveness that would normally be expected. Failure to learn to dress oneself or to become toilet trained during the preschool period might be indications of an impairment in adaptive behavior.

Finally, the definition specifies that the deficits must be manifested during the developmental period, which extends from conception to age 18.

IDENTIFICATION

In practice, mental retardation is most often identified and defined by performance on intelligence tests, with some occasional (though limited) attention given to adaptive behavior, a characteristic that is difficult to measure or define (Landesman & Ramey, 1989). This excessive reliance on measured intelligence is sometimes unfortunate for at least two reasons: First, measures at the lower levels of mental retardation are extremely unreliable because almost nobody in the norming samples ever scores below 50

(Reschly, 1992); and second, intelligence may be reflected more accurately—and more usefully—in individuals' level of adaptation than in more abstract measures of IQ, especially for those from different cultural or language backgrounds.

The AAMR provides a detailed discussion of what is meant by adaptive behavior and how it might be assessed. For example, adaptation during infancy and early childhood is evident in children's development of sensory motor skills, ability to communicate, progressive socialization, and in the appearance of self-help skills. During later childhood, children would also be expected to learn and apply basic academic skills, develop age-appropriate reasoning and judgment, and develop social skills evident in participation in group activities. During adolescence, in addition to the continued age-appropriate development in all these areas, individuals would also be expected to assume more adult roles reflected in work and social responsibilities. Various standardized inventories are available for assessing level of adaptive behaviors (see Reschly, 1990).

Feuerstein (1979) suggests that one way of taking adaptive skills into account is to stop basing assessments of mental retardation solely on measures of intelligence such as the Stanford Binet and the Wechsler. These, he argues, simply reflect how children have benefited from experience until now. What we need instead is an indication of the child's capacities for benefiting from experience in the future. In short, what is needed is a *dynamic* rather than a *static* assessment of intellectual potential. To this end he developed a *learning potential assessment device* (LPAD), which focuses on intellectual functioning—on intellectual processes—rather than simply on whether or not the child is capable of responding correctly. The instrument (actually a modification of several existing tests) permits the examiner to teach the child, to offer hints and clues, to direct and aid. In the end, it may give a much more useful picture of the child's potential, as well as of possible remediation.

PREVALENCE

Estimates of the prevalence of mental retardation vary. The normal distribution of intelligence in the general population suggests that 2.68 percent of the population should score below IQ 70 (Reschly, 1992). But if level of adaptation is taken into account, the figure is closer to 1 percent (Patton & Polloway, 1990).

As we noted in Chapter 6, the existence of multiple developmental problems is not uncommon (Hooper, 1992). Thus many children who are mentally retarded also manifest other developmental disorders. For example, Coulter (1993b) reports that many mentally retarded children also have cerebral palsy. And of these, about half also suffer from epileptic seizures.

CAUSES

The causes of mental retardation are so varied that it is almost always classified in terms of severity rather than cause. Still, researchers identify two main groups of causes: the *organic* and the *familial* (Zigler & Hodapp, 1991). Organic causes can be either *prenatal* or *postnatal* and include chromosomal aberrations such as Down syndrome (see Chapter 3); maternal conditions such as rubella, malnutrition, or diabetes; drugs or chemicals; and radiation. Familial causes include unstimulating environments, inadequate genetic endowment, or a combination of both.

Although identifying causes may be very important, particularly for medicine and genetics, it is much less important for special educators and clinicians. Hence mentally retarded children are ordinarily described in terms of degree rather than cause of exceptionality.

CATEGORIES AND CHARACTERISTICS

The American Association on Mental Retardation distinguishes among four categories of retardation: mild, moderate, severe, and profound (Figure 9.10). The American Psychiatric Association makes exactly the same distinctions but allows for more overlap between categories. The categories are defined in terms of scores on intelligence tests. Overlapping categories that are of more practical use for special-needs educators distinguish among educable, trainable, and custodial retardation.

The largest proportion of intellectually handicapped children (approximately 75 percent) are only *mildly retarded*. Most of these children are not identified as being retarded until they have been in school for some time. They ordinarily develop social and language skills and experience relatively normal motor development. The majority are capable of acceptable academic achievement in elementary school. This group roughly corresponds to the group described as educable mentally retarded (EMR).

Children classified as *moderately retarded* compose another 20 percent of the retarded group and, along with some of the severely retarded, are often described as trainable. These children can learn to talk during the preschool period; most will also learn to walk, although their verbal and motor skills may be inferior to those of normal children. Many moderately retarded children are mainstreamed—that is, educated in regular schools, though often with special teachers and equipment.

Severe mental retardation is usually associated with poor motor development, few communication skills (although these skills sometimes develop slightly later in life), and a high degree of dependence throughout life. Children who are *profoundly* mentally retarded may not learn toilet or dressing habits; in addition, many do not learn to walk.

learning disabilities

There are a significant number of children in schools who, in the absence of apparent emotional or physical disturbances and without being mentally retarded, experience serious learning difficulties in one or more areas. Such

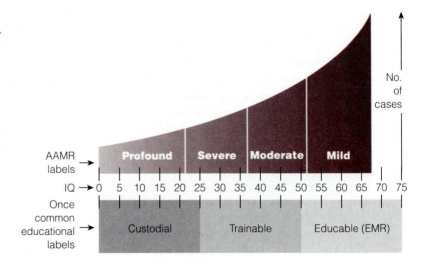

figure 9.10

Two common classification schemes for mental retardation, both based entirely on measured IQ; in practice, adaptive skills would also be taken into account. The American Association on Mental Retardation classifications shown here are based on the Stanford-Binet or Cattell tests. The Wechsler Scales (not shown) have a different distribution and therefore different IQ ranges: 55–69 (mild), 40–54 (moderate), 25–39 (severe), and 0–24 (profound).

children have sometimes been described as suffering from hyperactivity, learning dysfunction, cerebral dysfunction, minimal brain damage, perceptual handicaps, dyslexia, or perceptual disability, or simply as being slow learners. Each of these terms is relatively nonspecific, often confusing, and sometimes meaningless. In 1963, Samuel Kirk proposed a new term—**learning disability**—that would, in effect, include all the conditions previously described by these and other labels. This term neither carries the stigma attached to such terms as brain damage or cerebral dysfunction nor complicates our understanding with excessive categorization (see Kirk, 1979).

DEFINITION

The term *learning disability* is now widely used to describe a variety of conditions that are not always easily defined or identified. U.S. Public Law 94-142, which provides funding programs for children with special needs, includes a definition of learning disabilities that serves as a guideline for the allocation of funds. However, the definition is open to a number of interpretations and has led to the use of different definitions in different jurisdictions. None of these definitions actually says what a learning disability is; each simply describes behaviors and conditions considered symptomatic of learning disabilities (Kavale, Forness, & Lorsbach, 1991).

In spite of the considerable disagreement that still exists concerning what learning disabilities are—and what they are not—most definitions concur with respect to four general characteristics of any condition so labeled (Morsink, 1985):

- *Discrepancy.* There is a marked discrepancy between the child's actual and expected behavior. This discrepancy is most often evident in an uneven pattern of academic achievement.

- *Deficit.* The learning disabled child has a specific performance deficit. Such a child may do reasonably well in most subjects but will be unable to do certain things that other children do easily.

- *Focus.* The learning disabled child's deficits typically center on one of the basic psychological processes involved

Many exceptional children are not noticeably different from other children in their social and personality characteristics or in their needs.

in language, and sometimes in arithmetic. Hence the condition is often manifested in disorders of listening, thinking, talking, reading, writing, spelling, or arithmetic.

■ *Exclusions.* The problems associated with learning disabilities are not the result of other problems relating to hearing, vision, or general mental retardation.

SYMPTOMS AND IDENTIFICATION

Initial indications of learning disabilities are typically vague. The characteristic most likely to be noticed by parents and teachers is general academic retardation. Note, however, that academic retardation does not define a learning disability, although it often occurs as a result of the child's problems with reading, writing, and other aspects of the language arts.

Other general symptoms that are sometimes associated with learning disability include inattentiveness, mood shifts, hyperactivity, and impulsiveness (see Table 9.3).

The various tests used in identifying the learning disabled are designed to pro-

table 9.3

Some symptoms associated with learning disabilities

Inattentiveness (short attention span)

Impulsiveness

Hyperactivity

Frequent shifts in emotional mood

Impaired visual memory (difficulty in recalling shapes or words)

Motor problems (difficulty in running, hitting a ball, cutting, writing)

Disorders of speech and hearing

Specific academic difficulties (reading, writing, spelling, arithmetic)

Source: Based in part on Clements (1966) and the Edmonton (Alberta) Public School Board (1978).

vide information concerning three aspects of the student's characteristics and functioning (Morsink, 1985). The tests measure general intelligence, examine basic psychological processes involved in learning and remembering, and look at the possibility that other factors, such as visual problems, hearing deficits, physical or health handicaps, low intelligence, or environmental disadvantages, might be involved. Whereas the first and third of these (measuring intelligence and eliminating other deficits) are relatively straightforward, the second (assessing basic psychological processes) is not. One of the problems is that there is no general agreement on what these processes are. Certain tests, such as the Detroit Tests of Learning Aptitude, attempt to look at processes involved in activities such as reading and are sometimes useful for identifying specific weaknesses.

Given these problems of definition and identification, it is not surprising that faulty categorization is highly common. Following a survey of 800 children classified as "learning disabled," Shepard, Smith, and Vojir (1983) found that more than half of this sample had characteristics that did not conform to government regulations for meeting the definition criteria. Many had emotional disorders, mild retardation, or specific language problems.

Faulty categorization of this kind might partly account for the fact that the number of children classed as learning disabled more than doubled between 1978 and 1983 (Kavale & Forness, 1985). The learning disabled now make up about two-thirds of all special needs students in the United States (Myers & Hammill, 1990).

CATEGORIES

Relatively little is known about the origins and causes of specific learning disabilities, although brain damage or some other neurological impairment is suspected in many cases (Mercer, 1990). Various diseases and infections, malnutrition, and other environmental or genetic factors might also be involved.

Learning disabilities are most often classified according to the specific type of disability and are labeled according to whether they involve oral or written language, comprehension or production of speech, or particular problems in spelling or arithmetic. By far the most frequently diagnosed learning disabilities are those that have to do with language, and more specifically with reading.

A common learning disability manifested in reading problems is **developmental reading disorder**—also called **dyslexia** or *specific reading disability* (Stanovich, 1992). The main feature of developmental reading disorder, according to the American Psychiatric Association, is impairment in recognizing words and in understanding what is read. These difficulties are not related to mental retardation, physical problems such as deafness, or inadequate schooling (American Psychiatric Association, 1987). Developmental reading disorder is usually first manifested in problems associated with learning to read and may later be evident in spelling difficulties (erratic rather than consistent errors) (Hargrove & Poteet, 1984). Individuals with *developmental reading disorder* are typically of average measured intelligence but, in spite of ample opportunity to learn to read, are usually several years behind in reading skills. Remedial teaching can sometimes be highly effective in overcoming some of the effects of dyslexia.

Other reading-related learning disabilities are sometimes evident in any of the following problems: attention difficulty, perceptual problems, poor motivation or attitude, poor sound-symbol association, memory problems, language deficits, and transfer difficulties (Morsink, 1985).

The American Psychiatric Association also recognizes what is labeled **developmental arithmetic disorder** (American Psychiatric Association, 1987). Its essential feature is significant impairment in developing arithmetic skills in the absence of other problems such as mental retardation. Developmental arithmetic disorder may be linked directly with computational problems (difficulties in adding, subtracting, multiplying, or dividing) or may be related to problems in processing visual or auditory information. Accordingly, reading problems are sometimes associated with arithmetic disabilities (Semrud-Clikeman & Hynd, 1992).

In addition to reading and arithmetic disorders, learning disabilities also include what are referred to as process disorders; that is, they are sometimes labeled in terms of a deficit in a basic psychological process. Thus there are deficits relating to perception (some students are confused by words that sound or look alike), memory (sometimes evident in problems associated with remembering and generalizing what has been learned), and attention (a condition labeled "attention deficit disorder" is sometimes associated with restlessness, hyperactivity, low frustration tolerance, and distractibility). In practice, however, it is often difficult to separate a basic process disorder from a disorder that is manifested in a specific subject area.

Learning disabilities, as they are currently defined, are usually treated in the regular classroom. Alternately, learning disability specialists, many of whom specialize in reading or writing skills, may work with these children in the regular classroom. In a declining number of cases these children are given no special treatment.

intellectual giftedness

There are two related manifestations of giftedness in cognitive functioning: high intelligence and high creativity. Recall that mental retardation is typically defined not only in terms of much lower-than-average performance on an intelligence test, but also in terms of significant retardation in adaptive behavior. In much the same way, intellectual giftedness cannot easily be identified solely on the basis of high scores on measures of intelligence or creativity; evidence of superior development of apparent potential must also be considered. For this reason, Hallahan and Kauffman (1986) suggest that "gifted" individuals be defined in terms of a combination of three criteria: high ability (often measured by intelligence tests), high creativity, and high task commitment (defined in terms of motivation and persistence). They suggest, further, that to be truly gifted, individuals must surpass 85 percent of their peers on all three measures and 98 percent on at least one.

U.S. Public Law 91-230, defines giftedness as follows:

> *Gifted and talented children are those identified by professionally qualified persons who by virtue of outstanding abilities, are capable of high performance. These are children who require differentiated educational programs and/or services beyond those normally provided by the regular school programs in order to realize their contribution to society.*

The law goes on to state that capacity for high performance may involve demonstrated achievement or the potential for high achievement in one or more of the following areas: general intellectual ability, specific academic aptitude, creative thinking, leadership ability, visual and performing arts, and psychomotor ability.

A common estimate is that between 3 and 5 percent of the school population might be considered gifted (Hallahan & Kauffman, 1991). However, special education programs are provided for nowhere near this number. This is especially true of the gifted who are culturally disadvantaged (Patton, Prillaman, & Tassel-Baska, 1990). An observation made by Terman (1925) more than half a century ago might still be true today: When comparing potential and achievement, we find that the most "retarded" group in our schools is the highly gifted.

Among these highly gifted are the creative.

creativity

Stephen Winsten (1949), George Bernard Shaw's biographer, alluding to the "hair's breadth" separating genius and madness, said to Shaw one day: "The matter-of-fact man prefers to think of the creative man as defective, or at least akin to madness." And Shaw quickly replied, "Most of them are, most of them are. I am probably the only sane exception" (p. 103).

Not so; there are other exceptions. In fact, we have little evidence that many of the highly creative are mad—or that many of the mad are creative. (See "In Other Contexts: Ruth Duskin and Other Quiz Kids.")

SOME DEFINITIONS

Psychology offers us a creative assortment of definitions for **creativity**. For example, Guilford (1959) assures us that creativity involves responses or behaviors characterized by "fluency, flexibility, and originality." Parnes and Harding (1962) define creativity as a behavior that results

How can a parent, or teacher, determine whether a stunning self-portrait such as this one is a manifestation of outstanding creative talent? Or is it simply a matter of practice and luck? Psychology, which presents a creative assortment of definitions for creativity, provides no simple answer. Creativity is evident not only in novel, original, and useful products, but may also be apparent in children's personality or in the processes by which they solve problems.

in "a novel work that is accepted as tenable or useful or satisfying by a significant group of others at some point in time" (p. 86). Mednick (1962) argues that creativity is "the forming of associative elements into new combinations which either meet specified requirements or are in some ways useful. The more mutually remote the elements of the new combination, the more creative the process of solution" (p. 221). And Feldman (1989) claims that creativity is "the purposeful transformation of a body of knowledge, where that transformation is so significant that the body of knowledge is irrevocably changed from the way it was before" (p. 18).

Do these definitions mean anything clear and simple? Hoge (1988) suggests that perhaps they don't. One of the major problems in the area of giftedness, he asserts, has to do precisely with the definition of the qualities in question. In practice, these qualities are most often defined in terms of scores on tests: Intellectual giftedness is defined as a very high measured IQ; high creativity is defined in terms of an extraordinarily high score on a test designed to measure creativity. And the school administrator who must make a decision about who will be labeled "gifted" (and who, at least by implication, will be labeled "not gifted") also looks at test scores and perhaps asks teachers for their nominations. There are serious problems with this approach, claims Hoge. First, there is considerable ambiguity about the meaning of high IQ or high creativity scores; second, what is represented by these tests is often quite different from the definitions that government agencies or school jurisdictions have adopted; and third, the programs that are provided for children identified as gifted are not often matched to the specific strengths revealed by tests (nor are they designed to eliminate any of the relative weaknesses that might have been uncovered).

MEASURING CREATIVITY

Heinzen (1991) describes three approaches to measuring creativity: personality inventories, biographical and

Beginning in 1939 and lasting for more than a dozen years, "The Quiz Kids" radio (and, later, television) program captivated Sunday afternoon audiences. On this show, children as young as 7 competed against each other, answering mind-boggling questions. "Kids can't be that smart," some complained. "The show's fixed."

Not so, declares Ruth Duskin Feldman (1982), one of the dozen or so Quiz Kids who served as regulars on the show from age 7 to 16 (there were more than 600 occasional Quiz Kids who didn't earn enough points to continue). These were normal, bright children, she says. Terman (1925), a leading authority on giftedness, predicted tremendous future success for these children.

Not all share Terman's optimism. Some see the gifted child as a social

misfit doomed to misery and failure. One example to support this view is the case of William Siddis, whose father had deliberately raised him to be a genius. At 2, the boy could read; at 3, he knew four languages; at 11, he entered Harvard; and at 16 he graduated *cum laude* and began teaching

activity inventories, and behavioral measures. Personality inventories focus on what are considered to be the characteristics of creative people (for example, openness and flexibility). Biographical and activity inventories are based on the assumption that past creative activity is the best predictor of future creativity. They look at the extent to which individuals have already *been* creative. And behavioral measures try to predict future creativity by looking at specific behaviors

such as performance in school. With all of these approaches, there is, in Heinzen's (1991) words, tremendous "diversity and lack of coherence" (p. 8).

In studies of creativity, the most frequently used measures are open-ended tests, which require subjects to produce a variety of different responses. Wakefield (1991) labels these *production tests*. The intellectual ability required in a production test is *divergent thinking*. Individuals think divergently when they produce a number

at Rice University. But at 19, he had become a recluse, drifting from one job to another, finally dying in poverty and obscurity at age 46.

It wasn't until Ruth Duskin had married, had children, and lived a normal, productive life that she finally asked the question, What happend to the Quiz Kids? Here, briefly, are the stories of five of them:

Gerald Darrow: The youngest of the original quiz kids, Gerald Darrow was on the cover of Life magazine at age 9. His knowledge of birds, his precise memory for everything he read, his ability to recite entire Greek myths, were astounding. But at 47 he died almost unnoticed, having spent many of the last years of his life on social assistance. He had never married. When he died, he had been living with a 91-year-old aunt.

Claude Brenner: A quiz kid at age 12, Claude Brenner reportedly already knew four languages and tons of facts. When Ruth Duskin tracked him down 40 years later, he had just lost both his job and his wife. When asked about his Quiz Kids experience, he confessed, "I think, on the whole, it was an exceedingly damaging experience" (Duskin Feldman, 1982, p. 126). He feels that in many ways he is still a Quiz Kid, almost desperately needing to compete and to win.

Jack Lucal: Jack Lucal holds the record for the greatest number of consecutive wins on "The Quiz Kids." He was an extremely popular boy who studied his school subjects only if they were exceptionally interesting, and who didn't get the highest marks in his class. High grades, said Jack, are not the point of studying. Jack had wanted to become an ambassador to China when he was 14; in the end, he became a Jesuit priest.

Margaret Merrick: A childhood polio victim (she walked with crutches), Margaret Merrick became a Quiz Kid at age 14. At 52, she had a Ph.D. and worked as an educational consultant. Happily married, she was a mother of four and grandmother of eight.

Smylla Brind: Smylla Brind's IQ of 169 propelled her onto "The Quiz Kids" for a handful of appearances before her good looks moved her to Hollywood and a new name: Vanessa Brown. Vanessa Brown starred in some 20 movies, made the cover of Look magazine at 16, and modeled for Life. At 53 she was a contented ex-actress, married for the second time, raising a 17-year-old daughter.

A Conclusion. The Quiz Kids have done better than average. One-third have Ph.D.s or M.D.s; one (James D. Watson) won a Nobel Prize; many of the women have successfully managed both childrearing and other careers.

To Think About: "Exceptional intelligence does not preclude ordinary happiness or worldly success," writes Duskin Feldman (1982). "But neither does it guarantee extraordinary accomplishment" (p. 348). How important do you think intelligence is for happiness? Why?

of different solutions for a single problem. In contrast, measures of intelligence typically present items that require *convergent thinking*—the production of a single correct response.

Most production measures of creativity are based on Guilford's (1950) work, elaborated by Yamamoto (1964) and Torrance (1966, 1974). The *Torrance Tests of Creative Thinking* continue to be widely used in research (see Diaz, 1983). These tests are based on Guilford's assumption that the most important factors involved in creative ability are *fluency, flexibility,* and *originality*. Accordingly, the open-ended tasks require the production of a variety of different responses that can then be scored in terms of these factors. For example, one item asks subjects to think of as many uses as they can for a brick. Counting the total number of responses gives a measure of fluency. Flexibility is revealed in the number of shifts from one class of uses to another (for example, shifting from responses in which bricks are used for building purposes to ones in which they are used for holding objects down). Originality is revealed in the number of unusual or rare responses. Table 9.4 gives another example of a creativity item and how it might be scored. (You might want to test your creativity with the problems in "At A Glance: Creative Problems" on page 436. Their solutions are given on page 438.)

Interestingly, when children are given tests of divergent (creative) thinking and told to be creative, their scores typically increase (Runco, 1986a). This finding has sometimes been used as a basis for arguing that children who normally score high on creativity tests simply perceive the test differently. It is significant, however, that children who improve most on measures of originality when they are asked to be creative also score highest on measures of giftedness in the first place.

Runco (1986b) makes the important point that although measures of creativity reflect creative potential, they do not reflect creative performance. The greatest achievers—those who eventually attain eminence in the world—are characterized by more than just high scores on measures of intelligence and creativity. We'll say more about eminence shortly.

t able 9.4		
Sample answers and scoring procedure for one item from a creativity test		
Item:	How many uses can you think of for a nylon stocking?	
Answers:	*	Wear on feet
	§*	Wear over face
	*	Wear on hands when it's cold
	†*	Make rugs
	*	Make clothes
	§†*	Make upholstery
	†*	Hang flower pots
	*	Hang mobiles
	§†*	Make Christmas decorations
	†*	Use as a sling
	†*	Tie up robbers
	§†*	Cover broken window panes
	§†*	Use as ballast in a dirigible
	†*	Make a fishing net
Scoring:	*	Fluency: 14 (total number of different responses)
	†	Flexibility: 9 (number of shifts from one class to another)
	§	Originality: 5 (number of unusual responses—responses that occurred less than 5 percent of the time in the entire sample)

SOME CHARACTERISTICS OF CREATIVE CHILDREN

Creativity appears to be a relatively stable personality characteristic. Children who are creative as preschoolers tend to continue to be creative throughout their childhood and into adulthood (Magnusson & Backteman, 1978). However, correlations between childhood and adult creativity scores are typically considerably lower than those for intelligence (Kogan, 1983). It is not clear to what extent this is due to the greater unreliability of mea-

sures of creativity, and to what extent it might be due to greater fluctuations in creativity itself.

Getzels and Jackson (1962) looked at the relationship between creativity and intelligence among children in a private Chicago high school. They found that the most creative students were often not the most intelligent. Interestingly, although many of the highly creative students achieved as well as those with higher measured intelligence (but lower measured creativity), they were typically

figure 9.11

Characteristics of children who have combinations of high or low scores on measures of intelligence and of divergent thinking. Source: Based on studies reported by Wallach and Kogan (1965).

Measured intelligence

	High control over their own behavior; capable of adultlike and childlike behavior	High internal conflict; frustration with school; feelings of inadequacy; can perform well in stress-free environment
High Divergent thinking (creativity)	High control over their own behavior; capable of adultlike and childlike behavior	High internal conflict; frustration with school; feelings of inadequacy; can perform well in stress-free environment
Low	Addicted to school; strive desperately for academic success; well liked by teachers	Somewhat bewildered by environment; defense mechanisms include intensive social or athletic activity; occasional maladjustment

not as well liked by teachers. Getzels and Jackson suggest this might be due to highly creative individuals' greater independence and lower willingness to conform.

Another study attempted to discover whether the personality characteristics of the highly creative or highly intelligent were consistently different from those of students low in measured creativity or intelligence (Wallach & Kogan, 1965). Results of this study, summarized in Figure 9.11, indicated that highly intelligent but less creative students tended to be addicted to school and were well liked by teachers. In contrast, highly creative but less intelligent students were most frustrated with school and suffered most from feelings of inadequacy. The most favored group, not surprisingly, consisted of those who had high scores on both intelligence and creativity. Wallach and Kogan report that these students were most in control of their behaviors and were capable of both adultlike and childlike behaviors. Related to this, other studies have found a close relationship among playfulness, fantasy, and creativity (see, for example, Dansky, 1980; Kogan, 1983).

A review by McCabe (1991) suggests that IQ is a better predictor of achievement than is creativity. The highest achievers are those who are both highly creative and highly intelligent.

A CONTEXT FOR EMINENCE

For practical purposes, there is seldom a need to separate high intelligence and high creativity. Not only are the two closely related, but programs for gifted and talented children are not tailored for one or the other. And studies of eminent individuals—that is, of those who have achieved fame and recognition on the basis of outstanding performance in any area—typically find that these individuals are both highly intelligent and specially gifted in a creative sense (Albert & Runco, 1986).

But truly eminent individuals are not just highly intelligent and specially gifted. There are countless individuals who score extremely high on all our measures of giftedness and intelligence but never approach eminence. A follow-up of the Terman studies of genius, for example, found that very few of the original sample ever attained eminence (Oden, 1968).

What is special about the few gifted individuals who achieve eminence? Perhaps a number of personality characteristics, say Runco and Albert (1986), such as high motivation and persistence—and,

Problems vary considerably in difficulty as well as in the strategies that might be used to solve them. For example, Greene (1975) describes six levels of problems:

Level 1: The solver already knows the solution. The problem is therefore simply one of retrieving from memory. (Example: What is the next-to-last phone number you had?)

Level 2: The solution is unknown, but rules and procedures that will lead to the solution are known (finding the square root of 1,244).

Level 3: The solution is learned in the course of dealing with the problem (finding a way out of a forest or a city).

Level 4: Different possible solutions must be selected and evaluated (doing a crossword puzzle).

Level 5: Problem needs to be reformulated and analyzed, and the required solution will be a novel one

---

perhaps most important, the right family context. It is no accident that there is a high correlation between parents' measures of divergent thinking and those of their children (Runco & Albert, 1986). Family background seems to have been an important factor in the lives of a majority of those who have achieved eminence.

Albert and Runco (1986) warn that perhaps we have taken too simple and too cognitive a view of giftedness and that, as a result, we have been guilty of neglecting important personality and family variables. They identify seven factors related to the development of eminence. First, if children are to become eminent in later life, they must be both intelligent and creative; second, they must develop the values, motivation, and abilities that allow them to undertake im-

portant or highly unusual work; third, their family context must be such that it encourages the development of these values and drives; fourth, there must be a proper "fit" between talents and career demands, such that the demands of the career are sufficiently challenging to lead to eminence; fifth, the family must provide the right combination of experiences (that is, musical, athletic, academic, and so on); sixth, the family history must be consistent with appropriate experiences and values (that is, grandparents, who were influenced by their parents, also influenced their children, who now influence the children of whom we speak); and seventh, the immediate direction provided by the family should also be consistent with the development of the gifted child's talents (rather than unrealistic, overly demanding, or uncaring).

(inventing a new fuel-saving carbu-
retion device).

Level 6: Solver first needs to realize
that a problem exists and is then
required to generate new solutions
or new procedures for arriving at solutions (identifying a new medical
problem and discovering a cure
for it).

It is likely that the lives of ordinary
people are filled largely with lower-level
problems. But you, whose life is more
extraordinary, might want to consider
the following "creative" problems (answers appear on the following page):

1. Suppose that one day you walk
from Pascal to Shell River. You leave at
8 A.M., stop four or five times to rest,
fish off the bridge for almost an hour at
lunch time, and finally arrive at Shell
River at 4 P.M. Having spent the night in
Shell River, you return to Pascal the
next day following exactly the same
route, again leaving at 8 A.M., but this
time you walk faster and reach Pascal
by noon. Is it true that at some point
on your return trip you will necessarily
be at one place at exactly the same
time that you were at that place the
day before?

2. Using only six matches of equal
length, make four equal-sized triangles
in which the length of each side is
equal to the length of one match.

3. Two fathers and two sons went fishing and caught only three trout. Each
took one home. How can that be?

4. Two trains hurtle toward each other,
one traveling 100 miles per hour, the
other going only 50 miles per hour.
When the trains are only 75 miles
apart, a deranged hummingbird flies
from the front of one train directly toward the other at an incredible speed
of 90 miles per hour. And when it
reaches the other train, it turns immediately and flies back to the first again.
Again it turns...and again...and
again, flying back and forth between
the two trains, always at 90 miles per
hour, slowing down not a whit every
time it turns. How far will this deranged hummingbird have flown by the
time the two trains collide?

Among these factors there are important implications for the nurturing of
giftedness.

trends and controversies in special education

There are a number of related trends
in implementing special services for exceptional children; there are also a number of controversies associated with these
trends. Some of these have been touched
on in the preceding pages of this chapter
and are summarized briefly here.

MAINSTREAMING

A recent trend in providing for the
needs of exceptional children has been a
gradual shifting of responsibility from
special organizations and institutions to
the public school systems. In part, this
trend reflects a growing recognition that
disadvantaged children should have an
opportunity to lead lives as nearly normal
as possible. Deinstitutionalization and
nonsegregation are the natural consequences of this trend, and perhaps nowhere is this more obvious than in the
mainstreaming movement.

To mainstream is to place in regular
classrooms children who might once
have been placed in "special" classrooms
or even in institutions. The mainstreaming movement in the United States followed the passage of U.S. Public Law
94-142 in 1975. Specifically, this law requires, among other things, that school
jurisdictions provide special services for
exceptional children in "the least restrictive environment" possible. Subsequently,
various court decisions interpreted "the
least restrictive environment" to mean the

regular classroom. In California, for example, between 14,000 and 22,000 children previously classified as educable mentally retarded were moved into regular classrooms following the implementation of new legislation (Bancroft, 1976). Among other things, the effectiveness of special classrooms for mildly retarded children had been called into question, and a consensus seemed to be growing that mildly retarded children would do better in regular classrooms.

Mainstreaming remains highly controversial for several reasons (Chester, 1992). First, the inclusion of special-needs students in regular classrooms is expensive and difficult for school administrators, particularly because the law stipulates a need for extensive, *unbiased* testing. Second, caring for special needs students sometimes presents a difficult burden for classroom teachers, who are not always trained for this responsibility. Third, there is evidence that some exceptional children might fare better in segregated classrooms—or, alternatively, children in regular classrooms might fare better without these students. For example, Simon

(1992) argues that behaviorally disruptive children with serious aggressive tendencies might function better in segregated classrooms with specially trained teachers.

The bulk of the research indicates, however, that inclusive education can meet the needs of exceptional children and that the self-concepts of mainstreamed students are typically better than those of segregated students (Macmillan, Keogh, & Jones, 1986). As Sobsey (1993) puts it, "the majority of the research to date shows both educational and social advantages for integrated settings over segregated alternatives" (p. 1). However, he advises that in many cases, the needs of exceptional children can best be served through *adaptive education*—that is, by providing intensive, individualized, "special" programs for these children within the regular classroom.

LABELING

A second controversy concerns the use of labels. Critics of the use of labels argue that they are unfair because (1) a disproportionate number of minority-group

Solutions to "Creative Problems"

1. Yes, you will be at exactly the same place and time once on your way back from Shell River. This is easy to explain (and understand) if you consider what would happen if one person left Shell River and the other Pascal at the same time and on the same day. It makes no difference how fast each goes; providing they follow the same route, they must meet (that is, they must be at the same place and time on one occasion). The problem is identical to this situation; you are simply "meeting" yourself on a different day.

2. If you had trouble with this one, it is probably because of "set"—the predisposition to respond in certain ways. You likely tried to

lay the matches flat on some horizontal surface. The solution (below) requires a shift from horizontal to vertical.

3. This problem is a bit of a "trick." Two fathers and two sons need not be four people;

they might be only three: a grandfather with his son and his grandson. Hence two fathers and two sons!

4. This problem sounds far more complex than it is. The two trains, because their speeds are constant, will collide in exactly 30 minutes—because the two combined cover 150 miles in one hour (one travels 100 miles, and the other, 50), and they start out 75 miles apart. The crazed hummingbird, no matter that it turns back and forth more and more often as the trains approach each other, can only travel 45 miles in 30 minutes because it is always going 90 miles per hour.

children are labeled (and perhaps mislabeled, owing to the biased nature of many of our tests); (2) the imposition of a label changes children's environments by affecting their self-concept; and (3) there is a growing tendency to view exceptional children as quantitatively rather than qualitatively different from normal children.

In spite of these objections, labeling has definitely not been abandoned, although there has been a concerted attempt to use less stigmatizing labels, to use them more judiciously, and to avoid making labels serve as explanations. It has never been very useful to label Johnny dyslexic and then to say that he can't read because he's dyslexic. Here, as elsewhere, labels name and classify; they do not explain.

the magical child

"The parents of the magical child lead him into the world by example," Pearce (1977, p. 213) tells us. "At seven, he is open to suggestion, able to construct the abstractions needed for moving into the world. . . . [H]e is fascinated with the world and becomes analytic. He wants to take the world apart and see what makes it tick."

In Piaget's terms, the children of which we have spoken in this chapter are ready to construct a knowledge system that will lead to a mounting understanding of the world.

Or, in the language of information-processing theory, children seek to create a knowledge base, to discover processes and strategies for dealing with knowledge, and to develop a sense of self as perceivers, knowers, and rememberers.

As we noted, infants are not expected to know that day follows night; that butterflies whisper to each other when they perch on buttercups in the sunshine; and that there is a smooth, cold logic that can be invented to explain the mysteries of numbers and classes and series, though perhaps not the whispers of butterflies. Those are among the discoveries of later childhood.

But happily, the grand mysteries of cognition are not all solved in middle childhood. There is yet a concreteness to the child's logic, a limit to the reaches of imagination. We continue the story in Chapter 11.

main points

PHYSICAL DEVELOPMENT

1. Boys are heavier and taller than girls throughout their lives, except for a brief period late in middle childhood. (Girls undergo their adolescent growth spurt about two years earlier than boys.) Height is a good indicator of the long-term effects of nutrition; weight sometimes reflects effects that are more short term. Obesity (linked to overeating and underexercising, as well as to genetic background) is the most common childhood nutritional problem. Sex differences in motor abilities are usually very small during childhood and are consistent with the gender typing of the skills measured.

2. Physical and motor problems that sometimes cause children to require special services include cerebral palsy, epilepsy, various diseases, congenital physical problems, physical problems resulting from accidents, and deafness and blindness. Hearing impairments often have more socioemotional and

academic problems associated with them than do visual impairments because of the crucial role that hearing plays in the acquisition of language.

INTELLECTUAL DEVELOPMENT: PIAGET'S VIEW

3. Piaget describes middle childhood in terms of concrete operations, which is well illustrated by *conservation*—the realization that certain transformations do not change the quantitative features of objects. In addition to the conservations, children acquire abilities relating to classification, seriation, and number during this period.

CHILDREN AS INFORMATION PROCESSORS

4. The information-processing model looks at how developing children develop a knowledge base, strategies for dealing with cognitive material, and awareness of the self as a processor of information. A basic information-processing model describes memory in terms of three components: sensory memory (momentary effect of sense impressions; no cognitive processing); short-term memory (attention span; lasts a few seconds; involves rehearsing; limited to 7 plus or minus 2 items); and long-term memory (longer-term retention involving cognitive processing—rehearsal, elaboration, and organizing). Sensory and short-term memory do not appear to be substantially different in younger children and adults, but long-term memory improves.

METACOGNITION AND METAMEMORY

5. Metacognition refers in part to our awareness of ourselves as players of the game of cognition. We play this game with rules called cognitive strategies and are influenced by our estimates of how good we are (how optimistic our estimates of self-efficacy).

INTELLIGENCE

6. Spearman is associated with the general factor theory (*g*) of intelligence. Cattell describes two classes of abilities: fluid (abstract, unaffected by culture) and crystallized (learned, highly influenced by culture). Thurstone proposes a special abilities theory that describes seven separate abilities. Gardner suggests we have multiple intelligences (linguistic, musical, logical-mathematical, spatial, bodily knowledge, and personal knowledge). Sternberg describes the components of intelligence: meta-components (metacognition and metamemory), performance components (intellectual skills such as analyzing, sorting, elaborating), and knowledge-acquisition components (relate to what is achieved in the process of learning).

7. Two widely used individual (one person at a time) intelligence tests are the Stanford-Binet (ages 2 to adulthood; widely used with young children; highly verbal) and the Wechsler Scales (ages 4½ to adult; yield separate performance and verbal scores, as well as a composite IQ). Defined psychometrically (in terms of its measurement), average IQ does not change from year to year, but an individual's measured intelligence may increase or decrease. Measured IQ is not a mystical, fixed, unchanging, and unmodifiable something. Intelligence tests often do not measure a variety of important things (interpersonal skills, motivation, creativity, athletic and musical ability) and are

sometimes culturally biased. Measured IQ *is* related to success, especially in school.

8. Mental retardation is characterized by a general depression in ability to learn and is defined as subnormal performance on measures of intelligence and impairments in adaptive behavior. Classified in terms of severity, it may be mild, moderate, severe, or profound. (Educationally relevant labels are educable, trainable, and custodial.) Those who are mildly retarded are typically capable of acceptable achievement in ordinary elementary school classrooms.

9. *Learning disability* includes a wide range of specific learning problems not associated with mental retardation or other physical or emotional disturbance—for example *developmental reading disorder* (dyslexia) and *developmental arithmetic disorder*.

10. Intellectual giftedness is manifested in exceptional intelligence, exceptional creativity, and high motivation. Creativity is often defined in terms of innovation or originality and appears to be a relatively stable personality characteristic very highly related to intelligence.

11. Recent trends in special education include deinstitutionalization, mainstreaming, and an antilabeling movement.

focus questions: applications

■ Are North american children in good physical shape? What are the causes and implications of childhood obesity?

1. Plan the sort of physical activity program you think would be ideal in an elementary classroom.

■ What is Piaget's view of important cognitive changes in middle childhood?

2. Replicate one or more of Piaget's conservation problems (Figure 9.4) with children several years below and above the approximate normal age of attainment.

■ What model of human memory is basic to current views of information processing?

3. Provide your own examples of sensory, short-term, and long-term memory.

■ What is intelligence? How do we measure it? How important is it?

4. If intelligence is the capacity to adapt, how might children's intelligence be measured?

■ What are the dimensions of intellectual exceptionality?

5. Using library resources, write a reasoned and well-documented argument against (or for) mainstreaming exceptional children.

study terms

conservation 401
operations 402
preoperations 402
identity 402
reversibility 402
compensation 402
seriation 406
cognitive strategies 408
information-processing approach 408
metacognition 409
sensory memory 409
short-term memory 410
chunking 410

encode 410
long-term memory 411
associationistic 411
rehearsing 412
elaborating 412
organizing 412
schemata 412
script 412
metacognition 414
metamemory 415
motivation 415
self-efficacy 416
intelligence 417
valid 417
reliable 417
general factor theory 418
special abilities theory 418
fluid abilities 418
crystallized abilities 419
contextual theory of intelligence 419
intelligence quotient 420
mental retardation 424
learning disability 427
developmental reading disorder 429
dyslexia 429
developmental arithmetic disorder 429
creativity 430
mainstreaming 437

further readings

The first of the following two books is a highly readable and excellent analysis of cognitive development. It looks in detail both at Piaget's theory and at current work in information processing and metacognition. The second is a more complex collection of articles dealing with neo-Piagetian approaches:

Flavell, J. H. (1985). *Cognitive development*. Englewood Cliffs, N.J.: Prentice-Hall.

Case, R. (Ed.). (1991). *The mind's staircase: Exploring the conceptual underpinnings of children's thought and knowledge.* Hillsdale, N.J.: Lawrence Erlbaum.

A clear and useful account of developmental disorders in infancy and childhood is:

Hooper, S. R., Hynd, G. W., & Mattison, R. E. (Eds.). (1992). *Developmental disorders: Diagnostic criteria and clinical assessment.* Hillsdale, N.J.: Lawrence Erlbaum.

Aylward presents the basics of psychological testing of children and provides useful descriptions of a variety of tests in:

Aylward, E. H. (1991). *Understanding children's testing: Psychological testing.* Austin, Tex.: Pro-Ed.

A provocative and practical book dealing with the development of creativity, critical thinking, and problem-solving skills is:

Fischer, R. (1990). *Teaching children to think.* Oxford: Basil Blackwell.

For a sensitive look at giftedness and numerous practical suggestions for fostering excellence in the home and in the school, see:

Clark, B. (1983). *Growing up gifted: Developing the potential of children at home and at school* (2nd ed.). Columbus, Ohio: Charles E. Merrill.

10

Social Development in Middle Childhood

You should not take a fellow eight years old
And make him swear to never kiss the girls.
Robert Browning, Fra Lippo Lippi

focus questions

ARE CHILDREN AS SENSITIVE AS ADULTS TO OTHERS' EMOTIONAL STATES?

HOW MANY FRIENDS DOES A TYPICAL CHILD HAVE? HOW CLOSE AND IMPORTANT ARE THEY?

DOES VIOLENCE ON TELEVISION TRANSLATE INTO VIOLENCE ON THE STREET AND IN THE HOME?

HOW PREVALENT IS PHYSICAL, PSYCHOLOGICAL, AND SEXUAL ABUSE OF CHILDREN?

WHAT ARE SOME OF THE MOST PROBLEMATIC FORMS OF SOCIOEMOTIONAL EXCEPTIONALITY FOR ELEMENTARY SCHOOL TEACHERS?

outline

SOCIAL COGNITION
The Development of Social Cognition
Theories of Mind

SELF-WORTH
Some Definitions
Theoretical Approaches To Self-Worth
Measuring and Investigating Self-Worth

THE INFLUENCE OF FRIENDS AND PEERS
Children's Views of Friendship
Dimensions of Childhood Friendships
Peer Groups
Parents and Peers
Sociometric Status
Functions of Peers

THE ROLE OF THE SCHOOL
Schooling and IQ
Teachers' Expectations
Self-Expectations

THE EFFECTS OF TELEVISION
Children's Viewing Patterns
What Children Comprehend
Violence and Aggression
Positive Effects
Why Is Television Influential?
Rock Videos, VCRs, and Video Games
A Summary of Television Issues

VIOLENCE IN THE FAMILY
The Case Against Punishment
The Case for Punishment
Kinds of Punishment
Child Maltreatment
The Nature of Child Abuse and Neglect
The Consequences of Maltreatment
The Abusive Family Context
What Can Be Done?

SOCIOEMOTIONAL EXCEPTIONALITY
Prevalence and Causes
Attention-Deficit Hyperactivity Disorder
Other Behavior Disorders
Stress in Childhood
Socioemotional Giftedness

MAIN POINTS

FOCUS QUESTIONS: APPLICATIONS

STUDY TERMS

FURTHER READINGS

M y young daughter's imaginary playmate, Horton, began to live with us when she was 4. We paid little attention at first; he didn't take much room at the dinner table, usually just wanting to sit on her lap. And he ate only small tidbits from his mistress's plate. Later he sometimes required his own chair. And one night we had to place a large turkey drumstick on his plate. There it sat, sadly becoming colder while we ate our meal. "He doesn't really like turkey," our daughter informed us, "and I don't either."

But generally Horton was no great bother. He spent most of his time sitting in a chair, always close to his mistress where she could talk to him, which she did at great length and sometimes with breathless intimacy. And whenever we went anywhere, he always came with us. Often we had to wait for him; he had the annoying habit of not being ready on time. Whenever this happened, his mistress would rush back to get him from her bedroom or sometimes from the bathroom, for he too occasionally needed to use that facility. She would drag him out then, complaining and scolding so severely that I sometimes felt sorry to see him so humiliated in front of his family.

Near her seventh birthday I asked her about Horton. "What do you mean?" she said. I told her what I thought I meant. "He likes chocolate and he wears different clothes," she answered. "Is he real?" I inquired. She looked up rather sadly. "No, he isn't. He's imaginary."

social cognition

My daughter's sense of reality had changed; the line between fantasy and reality had become clearer. Still, at age 6 or 7 life has not yet drawn the thick, black line that we adults see so clearly between the real and the unreal. Our frames of reference are quite different from those of childhood. Our worldviews are more scientific, more reasonable. And our cognitions do not so readily admit magic.

Cognition refers to knowing, *metacognition* is knowing about knowing, and **social cognition** refers to an awareness of others as selves that, like our own selves, are also capable of feelings, motives, intentions, and so on. As Showers and Cantor (1985) note, social cognitions help us make sense of situations.

the development of social cognition

Social cognitions start to develop in early infancy when infants begin to differentiate between the self and others and begin to recognize that some things out there are persons, and others are nonpersons (Wellman & Gelman, 1992). At about the same time, infants begin to form strong attachments, usually to their caregivers. Thus begins the process of socialization.

But infants' social cognitions unfold slowly and reflect many of the limitations that characterize nonsocial cognitions. Recall how young infants and even preschoolers have difficulty adopting another person's point of view, as is illustrated by Piaget's mountain problem (in which children view a three-dimensional "mountain" display from one angle and are asked to describe what it would look like from a different angle). Piaget, and other researchers such as Shantz (1983) and Selman (1981), believed that, in much the same way, infants and preschoolers cannot easily make inferences about what other people are thinking or feeling. If this is true, infants and children are also unlikely to empathize with another's feelings. However, recent research suggests that preschoolers may be far better social thinkers than had been thought.

theories of mind

"Current research," write Wellman and Gelman (1992), "reveals sophisticated reasoning about the mental states of self and others in 3- to 5-year-olds" (p. 351). What this research indicates is that preschoolers have already begun to develop an implicit **theory of mind** based on an understanding that other people have mental states describable in terms of thoughts, emotions, wishes, and beliefs. It is absolutely essential that children have a theory of mind if they are to understand others and interact intelligently with them. If 4-year-old Sammy does not have a theory of mind—that is, does not understand that his mother has her own thoughts and beliefs—then it might not occur to him to lie to her when she asks, "Did you poke that hole in your bedsheet, Sammy?"

Intentional deception, claim Ruffman et al. (1993), requires that children understand not only that people can believe different things, but also that it is possible to make people believe things that are false. Recall from Chapter 8 that 3 year olds have considerable difficulty deceiving others or understanding deception. But 4 year olds have no such problem—strong evidence, claim Ruffman et al. (1993), of the beginning of a theory of mind.

The roots of a theory of mind are found in the behavior of even younger

Eight year olds have no difficulty interpreting the pain that a hurt child might feel. Their understanding of others' minds and feelings, what psychologists refer to as their theories of mind, allows them to recognize feelings in others, and to feel empathy—as is clear from their expressions in this scene.

children. Dunn (1988) observed 2- and 3 year olds in their homes; she found considerable evidence of their awareness of other's mental states in their conversations, their play, and their fighting. Two year olds would tease a sibling, steal a favorite toy, call each other names. They acted as if they *knew* the likely effects of their behaviors. Similarly, in their pretend games they could become babies or mothers, changing their behaviors to conform with their notions of how mothers and babies think and act.

"Children as young as 2 years old are, in some respects, quite competent social reasoners, and so they must have some kind of 'theory of mind,'" writes Perner (1991). But he goes on to acknowledge that it isn't until 4 that children finally understand that others can entertain false beliefs. And although a 2 year old might appear to empathize by crying when an-

other child cries, this might have nothing to do with the ability to understand or to represent what the other child is feeling (Flavell, 1985). In the same way, a 4 year old lying to her mother does not prove she understands that this might affect her mother's beliefs. It's possible that she has simply learned that certain behaviors are less likely to be punished or more likely to be considered funny.

ROLE-TAKING AND EMPATHY

Early investigations of the development of empathy (the ability to recognize and share the feelings of others) often asked children to recognize the emotion that would accurately reflect the reaction of a person in a story. Many of these investigations relied heavily on Piaget's interviewing techniques (the *méthode clinique*). In one study, for example, Selman (1980) told children the following story:

> *Holly is an 8-year-old girl who likes to climb trees. She is the best tree climber in the neighborhood. One day while climbing down from a tall tree, she falls off the bottom branch but does not hurt herself. Her father sees her fall. He is upset and asks her to promise not to climb trees anymore. Holly promises.*
>
> *Later that day, Holly and her friends meet Shawn. Shawn's kitten is caught up in a tree and can't get down. Something has to be done right away, or the kitten may fall. Holly is the only one who climbs trees well enough to reach the kitten and get it down, but she remembers her promise to her father. (p. 36)*

Children were then asked whether Holly knows how Shawn feels about the kitten; what Holly thinks her father will do if she climbs the tree; how Holly's father will feel if he knows she has climbed the tree; and what the child being questioned would do in the same situation.

Selman (1980) describes the development of children's ability to understand and verbalize another person's point of view in five stages, labeled 0 to 4 (see Table 10.1). Illustrated by reference to the kitten story, the stages are:

- **Stage 0: *The egocentric viewpoint*.** Until perhaps the age of 6 or so, children are largely unaware of the existence of any perspective—of any role—other than their own, very personal view. When asked how someone else is likely to feel in a certain situation, their responses usually reflect the feelings they would themselves experience: "Her daddy will be happy 'cause he likes the kitten."

- **Stage 1: *Social-informational role-taking*.** Between ages 6 and 8, children become aware that others have different points of view, different perspectives. But they have little understanding of the reasons for these different points of view and are likely to assume that anybody who knew what they know would think and feel as they do: "He'd let her climb if he understood how she felt!"

- **Stage 2: *Self-reflective role-taking*.** Eight- to 10-year-old children have gradually become aware that the feelings and thoughts of others, as well as their own personal feelings, can be inferred by others. But they respond only in terms of one or the other of the individuals involved: "He'll be mad 'cause he doesn't want her to climb trees."

- **Stage 3: *Mutual role-taking*.** Between 10 and 12, children can switch effortlessly from one point of view to another and can interpret and respond as might an objective onlooker: "Holly and her father can talk to each other. They will understand each other. They can work it out."

t a b l e 1 0 . 1	
Selman's developmental progression in social cognition	
STAGES	**EXAMPLES**
0. Egocentric (to 6 years)	*There is no perspective but mine. People feel the way I would in that situation.*
1. Social-informational (6–8)	*Okay, so others have a point of view too, but they would feel the way I do if they had the same information.*
2. Self-reflective (8–10)	*Actually, we can have different points of view. There's hers and there's mine. I can see mine; she can see hers.*
3. Mutual (10–12)	*Well, maybe I can see hers and she can see mine. We can even talk about our different points of view.*
4. Social and conventional (12–15+)	*Given her limited resources and taking into consideration the ethical problems involved, her decision is enlightened. On the other hand...*

Note: These stages reflect children's ability to *verbalize* their perspectives and their understanding of other perspectives; their actual behavior reflects more advanced understanding of other people's thoughts, beliefs, and feelings during the preschool period.

- **Stage 4: *Social and conventional role-taking*.** From ages 12 to 15 and beyond, adolescents can use the principles and ideals of their social systems, political ideologies, or religions to analyze and evaluate their perspectives, as well as those of others: "It depends on whether her father thinks the cat's life or Shawn's feelings are more important than obedience. Besides, . . ."

A CONCLUSION

One possible conclusion from studies such as Selman's is that infants and preschoolers are largely ignorant of others' states of minds until the age of 6 or 7 (Hoffman, 1975, 1978). As Moore and Frye (1991) put it, children have not yet learned to see the world through other eyes. However, as we saw, preschoolers' ability to deceive, and their apparent anticipation of the consequences of their behavior, indicate that they do have some understanding of others' mental states. But preschoolers' understanding remains limited. They cannot easily imagine themselves in someone else's mental state or verbally explain another person's behavior. For example, Bruchkowsky (1991) showed children a video in which a girl's (Mary's) dog dies. Children were later asked "What made Mary feel sad?" A typical 4 year old answered, "Because Harry died." "Why did that make Mary sad?" asked the experimenter. Silence.

In contrast, 6 year olds responded immediately: "Because her dog died, and she misses him." And 10 year olds elaborated even more: "Because her dog died, and she really loved him, and still really misses him 'cause he was her best friend" (p. 160).

Clearly, preschoolers' theory of mind is less sophisticated than that of older children. But just as clearly, important developments have occurred in preschoolers' growing capacity to understand belief, intention, and other aspects of mind.

self-worth

The child's theory of mind, says Astington (1991), "is the understanding children have of their own and others' minds. . . . [T]his understanding enables children to predict and explain actions by ascribing mental states . . . to themselves and to other people" (p. 158). Thus theory of mind implies an awareness of self and of others as distinct selves.

Put another way, it implies a concept of the self, a **self-concept**. Concepts such as self-worth, **self-esteem**, or self-concept are all aspects of what we refer to in Chapter 2 as *self-referent* thought— thought that has to do with our selves. It is in that sense, say Wells and Stryker (1988), that the self is *reflexive* (Involves reflection). In addition, a sense of self implies *intention* or willfulness and is the result of a *social* process (Schneider, 1991).

some definitions

In common usage, the term *self-concept* is an evaluative term that refers primarily to how we evaluate our selves. People have *positive* self-concepts when they think well of themselves, and *negative* self-concepts when they do not think much of themselves. In fact, however, *self-esteem, self-worth,* or *self-appraisal* are better expressions for this meaning because they are clearly evaluative (Yost, Strube, & Bailey, 1992).

There are aspects of the self-concept that are not evaluative. They have to do with abstract, cognitive notions of what the self is rather than with whether the self is good or bad, worthwhile or worthless, lovable or detestable, moral or immoral.

theoretical approaches to self-worth

There are two major (and very old) approaches to explaining self-worth (or self-esteem): those of William James and Charles Horton Cooley.

JAMES'S APPROACH

James's approach (1892) says: My self-worth is a direct function of the difference between what I would like to be and what I think I am. The closer my actual self (as I perceive my *self*) to my ideal

Strong, positive feelings that we are worthwhile contribute to mental health, happiness, confidence, and high achievement. What we think of ourselves is related to two things: how competent we think we are in important areas (James's competence/aspiration theory) and what we think important others think of us (Cooley's looking-glass theory). Having the very best goose is the boy's proof that he is competent and that others think so too. It's almost enough to make him smile.

self (the way I would like to be), the more I will like myself, and hence, the higher my self-esteem.

COOLEY'S APPROACH

Cooley (1902) says: My self-worth is a direct function of what I think others think of me; my worth is reflected in their behavior toward me. (Hence Cooley's phrase *looking-glass self*.) If people avoid me, that is evidence that I am not very worthy; if they seek me out, the evidence is more positive. Those who are most important in serving as mirrors in whose behavior I can view my *self* are people who are important to me—part of the microsystem in Bronfenbrenner's terms. Hence for preschoolers, parents and siblings are most important; for ele-

table 10.2

Two theories of the basis of self-worth

THEORY	EXAMPLE OF REASONING PROCESS
James: Discrepancy between actual and ideal self (What I would like to be versus what I think I am)	"I'm a blonde, which is what I would want to be if I had a choice. My skin is clear, and I like my eyes—nice blue. Physically, I know I'm, well, pretty attractive. But I've just been pulling C's in school, which is the pits. I want at least B's."
Cooley: Looking-glass self (What I think important others think of me)	"Willie asked me to his house. Billy asked me to his cabin. People always pick me when we're choosing sides. I must be fun to be with."

mentary school children, peers and teachers also become important—and perhaps also coaches, mentors, tutors, religious leaders, and so on. (See Table 10.2.)

measuring and investigating self-worth

Harter (1985a, 1985b, 1987, 1988) has developed an instrument for measuring self-worth based directly on James's *discrepancy* theory and Cooley's looking-glass approach: the *Self-Perception Profile for Children*. It asks children questions relating to how well they think they perform in each of the five areas considered important for developing notions of self-worth: athletic, scholastic, social, physical, and moral. In some studies, children are also asked how important they think it is to do well in these areas; this provides investigators with a basis for computing the difference between actual performance (competence) and the child's wishes, and thus arrive at a measure relating to James's approach.

In addition to answering questions relating to actual competence and to importance of competence, children might also be asked to what extent they feel their importance is recognized by others, how well others treat them, whether they think they are liked, admired, and respected. This line of questioning provides information relating to the regard in which others hold the child (Cooley's approach).

Finally, children might also be asked questions relating to a more global concept of self-worth—questions relating to how well they like themselves as people.

Use of questions such as these permits investigators to answer a number of important questions: Are competence/aspiration-based estimates of self-worth (James's theory) or "looking-glass" estimates (Cooley's theory) actually related to general concepts of self-worth? Are discrepancies between competence and the ideal more important in one area than another (for example, are athletics more important than scholastics)? Are there developmental changes in areas of importance? Is the source of approval and social regard important?

Harter (1987) provides answers for a number of these questions based on her investigations of children in grades three through eight (approximately 8 to 13 years of age). Before the age of 8, children do not seem to have a single, clearly defined, and measurable notion of self-worth; accordingly, younger children are not included in Harter's samples.

SOME IMPORTANT FINDINGS

First, although children have a general estimate of personal worth, they also make individual estimates of self-worth in at least five separate areas: *scholastic competence, athletic competence, social acceptance, behavioral conduct,* and *physical appearance.* (Table 10.3). In other words, even though some children may see themselves as athletically competent (good and

table 10.3

Areas in which children evaluate their self-worth

AREA	DESCRIPTION
1. Scholastic competence	How competent, smart, the child feels with regard to schoolwork
2. Athletic competence	How competent the child feels at sports and games requiring physical skill, athletic ability
3. Social acceptance	How popular or socially accepted the child feels with peers
4. Behavioral conduct	How adequate the child feels with regard to behaving in the way one is supposed to behave
5. Physical appearance	How good-looking the child feels, how much the child likes such characteristics as height, weight, face, hair

Note: Children's estimates of self-worth are based on (1) what significant other people (the microsystem) think of the child's capabilities and worth (Cooley's looking-glass theory) and (2) the extent to which the child lives up to personal ideals and aspirations (James's discrepancy between aspirations and competence theory). Both kinds of evaluations occur in the five areas described here.
Source: From Harter, 1987.

worthwhile), these same children may have decided that they were not "good" in a moral sense, or that they are not as worthwhile scholastically.

Second, Harter's studies indicate that children's judgments of self-worth reflect both major sources described by James and Cooley; that is, the difference between competencies (in each of the five important areas) and the child's aspirations and desires is reflected in estimates of self-worth. At the same time, how others regard the child also has an important influence on self-esteem.

Third, not all five areas are equally important to every child. High or low competence in important areas will have a more powerful influence than competence or incompetence in less important areas. If athletics are more important than being good (behavior conduct), not being a good athlete will be more damaging to self-esteem than behaving immorally. In Harter's studies, physical appearance is the most important area in determining self-worth, both for younger (grades three to six) and older (grades six to eight) children. Children who see themselves as attractive are most likely to like themselves. For both these age groups, behavioral conduct (goodness of behavior in a moral sense) was least important (see Table 10.4).

Fourth, as we noted, some sources of social regard and support are more important than others. For example, it might not matter very much that some nameless fan yells disparaging remarks while 10-year-old Willie stands at the plate waiting for the pitch, but it might matter a great deal if his coach later makes the same remarks. In Harter's (1987) studies, the most important sources of support in determining self-worth, for both the younger and older children, are parents and classmates, rather than friends or teachers. It is noteworthy that parents retain their importance through these years, because this contradicts a popular belief that as peers become more important, parents must become less important. It is also significant that classmates are typically more important than are friends. This may well be because classmates' opinions may be seen as more objective; the evaluations of friends, on the other hand, may be more biased.

Fifth, estimates of self-worth are closely linked with affect (emotion or mood), which, in turn, has much to do with motivation. As Harter (1988) comments, elementary school children who like themselves (who have high self-

t a b l e   1 0 . 4

Correlations between children's self-worth and perceived inadequacies in specific areas

	ELEMENTARY SCHOOL: GRADES 3–5	MIDDLE SCHOOL: GRADES 6–8
Physical appearance	.66	.57
Social acceptance	.36	.45
Scholastic competence	.35	.36
Athletic competence	.33	.24
Behavioral conduct	.30	.26

Source: S. Harter, 1987. "The Determinants and Mediational Role of Global Self-Worth in Children." In *Contemporary Topics in Developmental Psychology* (p. 229), N. Eisenberg (Ed.), New York: John Wiley. © 1987 John Wiley & Sons, Inc. Used by permission of the publisher.

esteem) are the happiest; in contrast, those who do not think very highly of themselves are more likely to feel sad or even depressed. Also, children who are happy are most likely to feel motivated to do things; those who are sad are least likely to want to do things. Figure 10.1 depicts the relationship between mood and self-worth scores for three groups of children from grades three through eight. Note that for all three groups, very low affect scores (sadness bordering on depression) are associated with very low self-worth scores; conversely, high affect is associated with high measures of self-worth.

SOME IMPLICATIONS OF SELF-WORTH

Some of the practical implications of self-worth are clear. To the extent that positive self-esteem is closely related to happiness and to high motivation—and, by the same token, to social adjustment and general well-being—parents, teachers, and others who share responsibility for rearing youngsters must be concerned

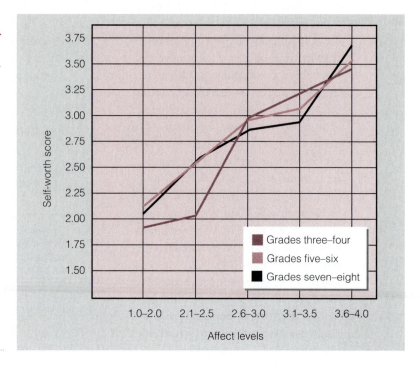

f i g u r e   1 0 . 1

The relationship between mood and self-concept. In Harter's study, children who were sad (low affect level) had the lowest opinions of themselves. Lowest scores indicate lowest estimates of self-worth and least positive moods.

with far more than their cognitive development or their physical well-being. They must do what they can to ensure that the evaluation that every child places on the *self* is positive judgment.

Unfortunately, the causes of self-worth are not simple. They include factors over which we have limited control, such as scholastic competence or physical appearance. But they also include things over which we have more control, such as our personal estimates of children and our communication of love and support.

We are not alone in determining children's self-worth. Friends, classmates, teachers, and parents are all important.

the influence of friends and peers

riendships of children," writes Berndt (1989), "appear to exist in a kind of never-never-land, a world of fun and adventure that adults rarely if ever enter and cannot fully understand" (p. 332). But science, in its careful and analytic way,

asks questions whose answers might increase understanding—questions like "How do children view friendship?"

children's views of friendship

For the 3- to 5 year old, claims Selman (1980, 1981), a friend is merely a playmate, and friendship is nothing more complex than "playing together." A friend is someone who happens to be present and who plays with the child. At this stage, children have no concept of friendship as an enduring kind of relationship. And if they are asked how friendships are formed, they are likely to say, "By playing together." If asked to describe a friend, they will speak of activities, but not of traits or characteristics ("He plays with me" or "He doesn't hit me").

Even in the preschool period, however, patterns of interactions among pairs of friends appear to be relatively stable over time. Park, Lay, and Ramsay (1993) studied 24 pairs of preschool friends (average age: 46 months) and found high correlations between observations made one year apart. Pair interactions tended to be highly consistent in terms of characteristics such as how happily the children played together, what strategies were used for resolving conflicts, and how well children shared.

By the age of 11 or 12, children understand that friendships develop over time and that they involve a reciprocal sharing of thoughts and feelings and a high degree of mutual trust. When asked to describe friends, they are likely to speak of qualities ("She understands people; she's so sincere") and of mutual interests ("We like a lot of the same things"). Whereas younger children assume that the best friends are those who live close by and who want to play, older children realize that the best friends are those who share interests, who are mutually supportive, who like each other. A 5 year old assumes that to become friends it is only necessary to play together; a 12 year old believes that to become friends it is necessary to get to know one another.

The pattern in the development of friendships is highly similar to that which characterizes the development of role-taking skills, or the ability to empathize—which is not surprising because these are all aspects of social cognition, tied in with children's elaboration of a theory of mind. In the beginning, infants do not separate self from world or even people from nonpeople, but with time there develops an increasing ability to understand the emotional and cognitive perspective of others. At the same time, there is a growing tendency to view others as social beings rather than as physical entities. And ultimately children shift from the view that social interaction consists only of momentary encounters to an appreciation of the lasting and mutual nature of relationships.

Friendships are of paramount importance in children's lives. Not only do they provide intimacy, encouragement, and support, but they also contribute to the capacity to form meaningful and lasting emotional relationships in adulthood. Friendships are extremely important factors in the socialization of children (Hartup, 1989).

BEST FRIENDS

Strictly speaking, only one of our friends can be *best* friend; none of the others can be more than second best. However, in common usage *best friend* refers not to the one very best friend, but to a particularly close type of friendship in which several people can be best friends all at the same time.

It seems that most 6- to 12-year-old youngsters have more than one best friend, although that is not always apparent in research. Berndt (1988) points out that if children are asked to name their best friend, they will obligingly name only one person. But if they are asked to name their best *friends*, they gladly name a number of people. And if the question is changed only slightly and they are asked instead to indicate whether each child in their class is a best friend, a friend, or not a friend, some children will name most of the class as best friends.

For children, there is not as clear and important a distinction between best friends and other friends. But by adulthood, says Berndt (1988), we have learned to make fine distinctions between a best friend, close friend, good friends, and other friends.

SEX DIFFERENCES

Most children have a number of close friends who are most often of the same age, race, and grade, who share common

One gender difference in patterns of play behavior is that boys in middle childhood tend to have more friends than girls and to play in larger groups. Another is that they play more aggressively and more competitively at all ages.

interests, and who are almost invariably of the same sex. Both boys and girls usually have two or three close friends rather than just one "best" friend. Berndt's (1989) investigations of friendship and helping among schoolchildren found that girls often have fewer friendships than boys but that these are generally more intimate; that is, they involve more self-revelation and more close sharing. The pattern in elementary school, notes Erwin (1993), is for boys to have more friends than girls and to play in larger groups. Also, as we noted in Chapter 8, boys play more aggressively and more competitively at all ages.

For most children from kindergarten to eighth grade, friendship patterns appear to be highly mutual. If one child indicates that a second is a best friend, the second child will very likely also have chosen the first as a best friend. As Hartup (1983) notes, reciprocity is a prominent characteristic of all childhood friendships.

COOPERATION AND COMPETITION AMONG FRIENDS

Friendships are typically *cooperative* socializing contexts, says Hartup (1989). In many situations, friends are more likely to cooperate and help each other than to compete. Strangely, however, there are situations in which friends are more competitive than one might expect. In one of Berndt's experiments, for example, pairs of friends were given a timed coloring task for which each would be rewarded on the basis of the number of squares colored correctly on a pattern but for which only one crayon of the appropriate color was provided. In one experimental condition, the child who first has the crayon need not share with the friend but may do so. Although experiments such as these tend to show that friends will compete under these circumstances (some "friends" never share the crayon), there is generally less competition (more cooperation) among girls than boys—a finding that probably reflects the effects of social learning.

Berndt (1988) suggests that one possible explanation for the fact that children sometimes compete rather than cooperate has to do with the implicit understanding that friends should be equal. Thus children may not cooperate if cooperating means that the friend will be more successful and more rewarded, but may choose to compete instead.

IMPORTANCE OF FRIENDS

There is little doubt that having friends is extremely important to all normal children. More than half the children referred for emotional or behavioral problems have no friends or have difficulty in peer interactions (Oden, 1988).

Rubin (1980) suggests that, among other things, friendships contribute significantly to the development of social skills (such as being sensitive to other people's points of view, learning the rules of conversation, and learning sex- and age-appropriate behaviors). In addition, interactions with friends are involved in developing notions of self and self-worth. Friendships may also be important in developing feelings of belonging to a group and may therefore play a crucial role in the development of notions of cultural identity.

In addition to these general and somewhat speculative functions served by friendships, there is strong evidence that friends have powerful influences on each other. Berndt (1988) summarizes research that has found that a child's academic performance can be positively or negatively influenced by choice of friends. Similarly, friends may serve to encourage or discourage deviant behaviors (such as delinquency or drug use).

Close friends are only one source of influence on the developing child; peers are another.

peer groups

A **peer group** is a group of equals. Most individuals in our society have a peer group—excluding hermits, whose peers, by definition, are also isolated and therefore of little consequence to their development.

The peer group is both a product of culture and one of its major transmitters, particularly during middle childhood and adolescence. During the years of middle childhood (Freud's latency period), the peer group typically consists of same-sex children. In addition, because of the different abilities, capacity for understanding, and interests among the different ages spanning this period, the peer group usually consists of peers close in age.

During adolescence the peer group may be enlarged to include members of both sexes and a wider range of ages (Hartup, 1983).

parents and peers

In fancy and early childhood, parents have traditionally been the center of children's lives—although with increasing numbers of children in day-care facilities, the importance of peer groups during the preschool period has increased significantly in recent decades. By the beginning of middle childhood, peers have assumed tremendous significance. And as children's interests and allegiances shift gradually toward peers, there are important changes in the ways in which they interact with and conform to their parents.

In early childhood, parental authority is largely unquestioned. This does not mean that all children always obey their parents; sometimes temptation or impulse are just too overwhelming. And sometimes, too, parents overstep the unwritten but clearly understood boundaries of authority. As Braine et al. (1991) note, parental authority does not extend to immoral acts; nor can it be permitted to infringe on important areas of personal jurisdiction such as choice of friends.

In later childhood and adolescence, parental authority is subjected to more constraints, and a child's area of control increases. Berndt (1979) asked 251 children in grades three, six, nine, and eleven and twelve to respond to hypothetical situations in which parents or peers urged them to do something antisocial, something prosocial, or something neutral. As expected, Berndt found that conformity to parents decreased with age—and so did conformity to peers, except with re-

f **i g u r e** **1 0 . 2**

Changes in average conformity scores as a function of age and source of pressure. The situations in this study were hypothetical ("What would you do if . . . ") and may not always reflect what participants would actually have done. Source: From T. J. Berndt, "Developmental changes in conformity to peers and parents." Developmental Psychology, 1979, 15, 608–616. © 1979 by the American Psychological Association. Reprinted by permission of the author.

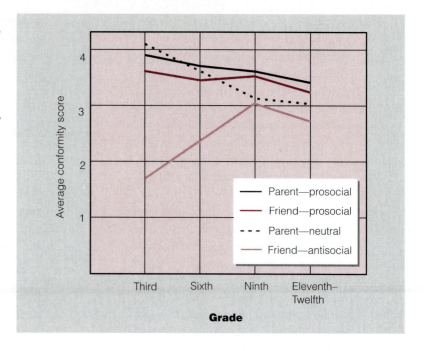

gard to antisocial influences, which increased until about grade nine (age 14) before declining again (see Figure 10.2).

Prado (1958) studied the shift in allegiance from family to peers during late childhood and adolescence. Participants in this study were two groups of boys, one aged 8 to 11 and the other, 14 to 17. These boys and their fathers, along with each boy's "best" friend, were brought to a laboratory, where the friends and the fathers were asked to throw darts at a target. The target was arranged so that the boy could not see the exact scores made by either his father or his friend. His task was to estimate their performance.

The results of the study reveal that both the younger boys and the adolescents were almost equally accurate in their estimates. However, the younger boys consistently *overestimated* the scores made by their fathers and *underestimated* those made by their friends. In contrast, adolescents tended to underestimate their fathers' scores and overestimate their friends' scores. The evidence strongly

suggests that from middle childhood to adolescence there is a marked decline in the importance of parents and a corresponding increase in the importance of peers.

We should be cautious in interpreting studies such as these, however. That at some age children conform more to peers and somewhat less to parents or that they overestimate how peers will perform in a trivial task does not mean that peers are more important than parents in the lives of children. That is clearly not the case, as forcing children to select between parents and peers would quickly prove. Furthermore, as we saw earlier, the approval and regard of parents continues to be as important as that of peers, and more important than that of friends in influencing self-worth.

Here, as in other areas of human development, relationships and interactions are complex and influence each other. Accordingly, it is misleading and overly simplistic to consider parent-child relations on the one hand, and child-peer re-

Through middle childhood, the approval of parents is at least as important as that of peers in determining feelings of self-worth. In addition, it is misleading to compare and contrast parents and peers because relationships with each are so closely related.

lations on the other, and to compare and contrast them as though they were completely isolated and unrelated. There is evidence, for example, that the kind of relationship a child has with parents is very closely related to later relationships with peers. For example, Fuligni and Eccles (1993) found that children who felt that their parents did not relax their power and provide them with more opportunities for decision making as they neared adolescence were more likely to be extremely peer-oriented.

There is considerable evidence that supportive parenting leads to good peer relationships. Thus, securely attached infants (see Chapter 6) are more likely to subsequently have good relationships with peers. Similarly, the most socially competent preschool children often have the most positive and playful relationships with parents (Parke et al., 1989).

PEER ACCEPTANCE

Peer acceptance or rejection (**sociometric status**) is typically assessed using one of two methods: *peer ratings* or *peer nominations* (Terry & Coie, 1991). In a peer rating study, each member of a group

(for example, a classroom) might be asked to rate all other members of the group in terms of how well they like them, whether they would like to play with them, how smart they are, how popular, and so on. A study using peer nominations might ask participants to name the three individuals they like best, the three they like least, the three smartest kids, the three dumbest, and the like. Data gathered in this way can then be analyzed to provide an index of sociometric acceptance or rejection and can sometimes be depicted pictorially in a **sociogram** (Figure 10.3). Information of this kind is sometimes useful in research that seeks to identify the qualities associated with popularity or social isolation.

QUALITIES RELATED TO PEER ACCEPTANCE AND REJECTION

In general, children who are friendly and sociable are more easily accepted than those who are hostile, unsociable, withdrawn, or indifferent (Putallaz & Gottman, 1981). Similarly, children who are intelligent and creative are more acceptable than those who are slow learners or retarded (Green et al., 1980). Size,

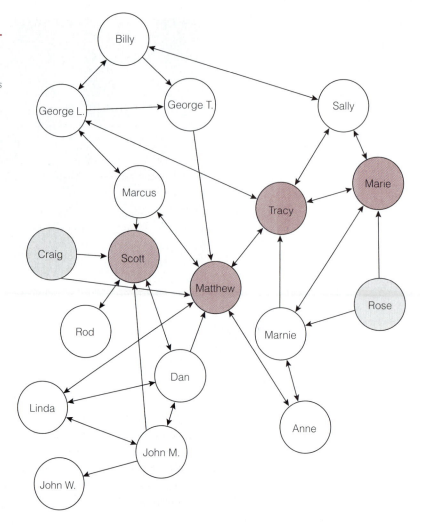

A sociogram of a fourth-grade classroom. Children were asked with whom they would most like to play. The popular children are Scott, Matthew, Tracy, and Marie. The unpopular ones and Rose and Craig.

strength, athletic prowess, and daring are particularly important characteristics for membership in boys' peer groups; maturity and social skills are more important for girls, especially as they approach adolescence (Langlois & Stephen, 1981). Attractiveness is important for both (Hartup, 1983).

Among characteristics often associated with peer rejection are those that make the child different or that are perceived as undesirable. In a study of 362 8- to 11 year olds, Pope, Bierman, and Mumma (1991) found that aggressive, hyperactive, and immature boys were likely to be re-

jected. Similarly, Juvonen (1991) reports that children who engage in behaviors others consider deviant (rule-breaking, for example) are more likely to be rejected.

SOCIAL COMPETENCE

The observation that friendly, socially competent children have more friends (have higher *status*, as sociologists put it) raises an interesting and important question: Are the characteristics of high-status (accepted) and low-status (rejected) children the cause or the result of their status? Does a friendly child have many friends because she is friendly, or is she friendly because she has many friends? Similarly, does social rejection lead to socially incompetent behavior, or is the socially incompetent behavior present to begin with and lead to social rejection?

A review of a large number of studies strongly suggests that popular children are popular because they are more competent socially and that unpopular children lack social skills (Newcomb, Bukowski, & Pattee, 1993). In other words, how a child interacts with others is a primary cause of social status. Not surprisingly, when children interact with new peers, they tend to very quickly achieve the same sort of status they enjoyed with more familiar peers (Asher, 1983).

Certain characteristics of the interaction styles of the high-status children are readily apparent. According to Asher (1983), these characteristics reflect three important qualities of social competence. First, socially competent children quickly sense what is happening in an unfamiliar social situation and are able to modify their behaviors accordingly. Thus they are less likely to engage in behaviors that are inappropriate or unexpected than are socially incompetent children. Second, socially competent children are able to respond to what others initiate, rather than always initiating. And third, the socially competent are more patient with social relationships. They realize that relationships develop slowly over time; they do not insist on becoming leaders or best friends immediately.

In addition to these characteristics of social competence, Bryant (1992) found that the most socially preferred children are those most likely to use calm approaches to resolve conflicts. In contrast, children most likely to be rejected by peers are those who react to conflict either with anger and retaliation or with avoidance.

We are not equally loved and sought after by our friends. Indeed, not all of us have friends. Some of us are *social isolates*.

TWO DEFINITIONS OF SOCIAL ISOLATION

Two definitions of social isolation are often used. The first looks at frequency of interaction: The socially isolated are those who do not often interact with peers. The second looks at the nature and extent of peer acceptance: The socially isolated are those who are seldom selected as "best friend" by anyone and who might often be chosen as "someone I don't really like very much." These two definitions are different, says Gottman (1977). Some children are liked and accepted but do not interact much with their peers; at the same time, some children are very low on everybody's list of "my best friends" or "who I would most like to be with" or "who I would most like to be like," but they nevertheless interact frequently with peers.

FIVE LEVELS OF SOCIAL STATUS

In an attempt to explore these definitions and clarify the nature of social isolation, Gottman studied 113 children in depth. His observations suggest five distinct categories of children (see Table 10.5). *Sociometric stars* are those who are consistently "especially liked." *Teacher negatives* are usually in conflict with teachers and might be either high or low on measures of peer acceptance. *Mixers* are those who interact often with peers; they too might be either high or low on measures of acceptance. The *tuned out* are those who are usually not involved with what is going on—those who are tuned "out" rather than "in." The tuned out, rather than being strongly rejected, are simply ignored. And, finally, *rejectees* are

t a b l e   1 0 . 5

Five categories of social status

CATEGORY	CHARACTERISTICS
Sociometric Stars	Especially well-liked by most.
Teacher negatives	Typically in conflict with teachers. Some are liked; others not.
Mixers	High peer interaction. Some well liked; others not.
Tuned out	Not involved; are ignored rather than rejected.
Sociometric rejectees	Not liked very much. Rejected rather than simply ignored.

Source: Based on Gottman (1977).

those who are not only disliked by their peers, but are actively rejected by everyone. These are the children who, in childhood, are the butts of all the cruel jokes and taunts.

ACCEPTANCE, FRIENDSHIP, AND ADJUSTMENT

Research indicates that the quality of children's relationships with their peers is very important for their happiness and adjustment (La Greca & Stone, 1993). However, although peer rejection may be associated with poorer adjustment, that is certainly not always the case. In a study of 881 children in grades three through five, Parker and Asher (1993) found that many children who are *not* very popular nevertheless have very close and very satisfying friendships. There are wide individual differences in the *sociability* of different children. Not all are outgoing, talkative, expansive; many appear withdrawn and shy. We should not make the mistake of assuming that children who appear shy are also lonely and friendless. Nor should we assume that all are likely to be rejected by their peers or socially *tuned out*. Some of these children are extraordinarily socially competent; many

have a large number of close friendships. Some might, in fact, be among Gottman's *sociometric stars*.

INFLUENCES ON SOCIOMETRIC STATUS

There is some evidence that sociability is partly genetic. Identical twins are highly similar to each other—even at very young ages, before personality would have been greatly affected by environmental influences (Goldsmith, 1983). That environmental influences are also involved is clear as well. Ainsworth's research (reviewed in Chapter 6) provides evidence that the nature of the attachment between caregiver and child influences the child's relationships with others. Specifically, securely attached infants are more likely to be highly sociable. Similarly, Baumrind's research (reviewed in Chapter 8) indicates that warm, supportive, and authoritative parents are more likely to raise well-adjusted, sociable children.

functions of peers

Children's peer groups have several important functions. One of these, discussed earlier in this chapter, has to do with the development of feelings of self-worth. As we saw, if children believe others think highly of them, they are more likely to think highly of themselves (France-Kaatrude & Smith, 1985).

A second function of peer groups is what is termed *normative*; that is, the peer group serves to teach and reinforce important cultural norms. Thus peer groups are important for the formation of values and attitudes. In one study, for example, Lamb, Easterbrooks, and Holden (1980) found that children as young as 3 reinforce their peers for sex-appropriate behavior but are quick to criticize what they perceive to be inappropriate cross-sex behavior. Not surprisingly, children who are reinforced tend to continue the behavior for which they received reinforcement. In contrast, most of those who are not reinforced (or who are criticized) abandon their old behavior and go to some new activity within a minute or less.

Studies such as this leave little doubt that peers are extremely powerful sources of punishment and reinforcement. In addition, they are an important source of information about sex- and age-appropriate and inappropriate behaviors, as well as about how to do things, what one should look and sound like, what music is good and bad, and on and on.

But peers are not the only source of influence on children. The family, as we saw in Chapter 8, is another. So is the school.

School experiences are essential for imparting important new skills and knowledge. They also play a vital role in helping children develop a public personality that will characterize them throughout life.

the role of the school

utside of the family, say Asp and Garbarino (1988), the school is the most pervasive socializing influence in the life of a child. When children leave home and enter school, they leave behind much of their "play" and begin the serious "work" of childhood. Now the process of socializing for adulthood takes on a new urgency—a new seriousness—as the child is called upon to learn new rules and adopt new roles. In Bronfenbrenner's terms, the transition from home to school is a transition from the microsystem of the family to that of teachers and peers. The implications for the continued development of social, cognitive, and physical competence, as well as for the development of the child's sense of self and of worth, can hardly be overestimated.

Schools are centrally involved in teaching children much that is necessary for their effective interaction in our increasingly complex world. They are our fundamentally important, formal, monolithic disseminators of culture. To simplify greatly, children acquire essential language and cognitive skills in schools, as well as the social skills and public personality that will characterize them throughout life. In fact, note Stevenson et al. (1991), the influence of the school is so pervasive and so general in our society that much of what developmental psychologists view as "normal" development is, in fact, a reflection of what children learn in schools.

schooling and IQ

Schools do more than socialize children and teach them important information and skills; there is evidence that they also increase measured intelligence. For example, there has been a massive increase in IQ scores in the Netherlands since the 1950s. This increase, argue Husén and Tuijnman (1991), is due to changes in context, the most important of which may be formal schooling. Similarly, Flynn (1987) found that in 14 industrialized countries there has been an increase of about 15 IQ points in one generation.

There is additional evidence that formal schooling is closely tied to measured intelligence. For example, Ceci (1991) reviews studies that show a relationship between level of schooling (grade attained) and IQ; between missing school and declines in IQ; between delayed school entrance and lower IQ; and between increasing school attendance in a locale and general increases in measured IQ. And Stevenson et al. (1991) found significant differences in cognitive development between Peruvian children who attended school and those who didn't. Perhaps more striking, they found remarkable similarities in the cognitive functioning of first-graders from such diverse cultural backgrounds as Peru, Taiwan, Japan, and the United States—almost as though the experiences of first grade had already begun to wipe out what would otherwise have been highly noticeable differences.

The evidence, claim Husén and Tuijnman (1991), supports the conclusion "that not only does child IQ have an effect on schooling outcomes, but also that schooling per se has a substantial effect on IQ test scores" (p. 22).

teachers' expectations

One illustration of how schools can affect children is found in Rosenthal and Jacobsen's (1968a, 1968b) classical study of how teachers' expectations can become *self-fulfilling prophecies*. The study involved administering students an intelligence test in the spring of the school year, telling teachers this was a test designed to identify academic "bloomers" (students *expected* to blossom next year), and then later "accidentally" allowing teachers to see a list of likely bloomers. In fact, these bloomers were a randomly chosen group of about 20 percent of the school's population. No other treatment was involved in the study.

THE SELF-FULFILLING PROPHECY

Significantly, many teachers observed exactly what they expected to see. The experimental group not only scored higher on measures of achievement than a comparable control group, but also scored higher on a general measure of intelligence.

Hundreds of replication studies have been undertaken since the original studies (see Meyer, 1985). Brophy and Good (1974) reviewed 60 of these and concluded that many are confusing and inconclusive. However, many of these studies do show patterns of teachers' expectations that appear to be linked with student self-concept as well as achievement. Similarly, Braun's (1976) review supports the conclusion that many teachers develop predictable patterns of expectations that are often more positive for students who are from more advantaged socioeconomic backgrounds, who are more attractive, who are more articulate, and who sit close to the teacher and speak clearly. Teachers also develop more positive expectations for students given more positive labels: "learning disabled" rather than "mentally retarded" (Rolison & Medway, 1985) and "excellent" rather than "weak" (Babad, 1985). Thus the effects of teachers' expectations have sometimes been used as a partial explanation for the poorer school performance of some minority-group children.

Unfortunately, a quick overview of the results of studies such as these makes them seem far more dramatic and important than they actually are. In addition, there is a tendency to assume that negative expectations are more potent and more pervasive than are positive expectations. This is not the case.

OPPOSITE EFFECTS OF EXPECTATIONS

Strange as it might seem, sometimes expectations can have an opposite effect. For example, in one study reported by Goldenberg (1992), two first-grade Hispanic girls were given a reading readiness test, and both scored very low. Hence both would be expected to do poorly in first-grade reading achievement. For intuitive reasons, and without any awareness of their nearly identical reading readiness scores, the teacher had very high expectations for one of the girls, but very low expectations for the other.

She was wrong. The girl of whom the teacher expected much did very poorly; the other did remarkably well. Amazing? No, says Goldenberg. What happened was that the teacher provided more assistance and more attention to the girl she thought needed more help. What matters most, argues Goldenberg, is not what the teacher *expects* but rather what the teacher *does*. Negative expectations might lead one teacher to give up on a student, to pay little attention, to provide no help, perhaps even to stop interacting with that student—and the self-fulfilling effects of the expectation may seem clear. But another teacher might react as did the Hispanic girl's teacher, with additional assistance and attention, and the final results might be in direct opposition to expectations.

self-expectations

Teachers' expectations, it seems, might affect the performance of some students. Can the student's own expectations also have an effect? Attribution theory suggests yes.

ATTRIBUTION THEORY

An **attribution** is an assignment of cause or blame for the outcomes of our

---

t able 10.6

Why did you fail or succeed? internally oriented versus externally oriented attributions

EXTERNAL	INTERNAL
Difficulty (task too easy or too difficult)	Ability (intelligence, skill, or the lack thereof)
Luck (bad or good)	Effort (hard work, industriousness, self-discipline; or laziness, distractions, lack of time)

---

behaviors. If I think I am stupid because I hit my head on a low branch when I was 10, then I attribute my stupidity to that event. Attribution theories look for predictable regularities in the ways we attribute causes to the things that happen around us (or to us) (see Weiner, 1980a).

Recall from Chapter 2 that children are different in how they typically assign responsibility for their successes or failures. Those who accept personal responsibility for the consequences of their behavior are said to have an *internal locus of control* (or to be **mastery-oriented** or persistent) (Dweck, 1986). Others are more likely to attribute successes and failures to circumstances or events over which they have no control and are described as having an *external locus of control* (in Dweck's terms, characterized by **learned helplessness** rather than by persistence). Thus mastery-oriented children are most likely to attribute their successes to ability or effort, factors that are personal or over which they at least have personal control; in contrast, helpless children are more likely to attribute their successes or failures to luck or the difficulty of the task, factors over which they have no personal control (Table 10.6).

DIFFERENCES BETWEEN MASTERY-ORIENTED AND HELPLESS CHILDREN

Differences between mastery-oriented and helpless children are often highly ap-

Mastery-oriented children tend to be more highly achievement-oriented, and are more likely to attribute their successes and failures to causes for which they are personally responsible. They are also more likely to undertake tasks that are more challenging, like tutoring younger children.

parent. First, mastery-oriented children tend to be much more highly achievement-oriented. They undertake tasks that are more challenging and strive harder to do well in them (Thomas, 1980).

Second, mastery-oriented and helpless children react very differently to successes and failures. When Diener and Dweck (1980) arranged a situation so that all children would experience an unbroken sequence of eight successes, helpless children still predicted they would not do very well if they had to repeat the eight tasks. These children found it difficult to interpret success as indicating they are capable. Even after succeeding they continue to underestimate future successes and to overestimate future failures. In contrast, mastery-oriented children were confident they would continue to perform as well. And even when they were given a series of failure experiences, they continued to see themselves as capable and to predict future success experiences. They have higher expectations of themselves.

CHANGING EXPECTATIONS AND ATTRIBUTIONS

Can expectations and attributions be changed, and will these changes be re-

flected in behavior? Perhaps. In one study, Dweck and Reppucci (1973) identified a group of *learned helpless* children—children who attributed failure to lack of ability or other factors they could not control and who typically gave up after a single failure. Dweck (1975) later trained these children to take personal responsibility for failure and to attribute it to insufficient effort rather than to lack of ability. Subsequently, contrary to their earlier behavior, many of these children began to persist following failure.

A related study conducted by De Charms (1972) involves what the author terms "personal causation training." De Charms describes two broad categories of people: *Pawns*, who characteristically see themselves as "pushed around," are *learned helpless*; in contrast, *origins*, who see themselves as the originators of their own behaviors, are *mastery-oriented*. De Charms attempted to make pawns more like origins by training teachers to encourage self-study, to foster the evaluation of personal motives, to bring about an understanding of the value of realistic goals and proper planning, and to highlight the importance of the distinction between origins and pawns. Subsequently, teachers helped develop a series of *personal causation training* classroom exercises for their sixth- and seventh-grade classes. Final results showed an increase both in teacher and student motivation, as well as a significant increase in the academic achievement of students.

What attribution-change programs have in common, Wittrock (1986) notes, is that they attempt to move the student in the direction of *effort* attributions. There is increasing evidence that they can be successful, at least in the short term. Still, a number of crucial questions remain to be answered, perhaps the most important of which concerns the origins of helplessness. Although most researchers think it is learned (Tzuriel, 1989) and that it can therefore be unlearned, the issue is still not resolved. In addition, helplessness has been implicated in physical and psychological disorders, as well as in achievement and adjustment problems, but its precise contribution to these is not clear (Seligman, 1975).

the effects of television

There is a fear in the hearts of some that the mass media will taint the still tender and highly corruptible young. First they feared **fairy tales**, few of which have happy endings and even fewer of which are without violence. Next they went after **comic books**, whose primary characteristics have been described as "violence in content, ugliness in form and deception in presentation" (Wertham, 1954, p. 90). Now there is television.

For some time now, prophets of doom have been predicting that television will have highly negative effects on children. Their main claims are that television is producing a generation of passive people or, alternatively, that the violence pervading many television programs will produce a generation of violent people. Furthermore, claim the critics, television

transmits the message that immorality is often rewarded; thus it exercises a corrupting influence. And, given the amount of a child's time it consumes, it has a harmful effect on family relationships, on the social development of children, and on sports, reading, and playing. Although the research evidence is incomplete, we have enough answers to partially respond to these criticisms and to present a more balanced impression of the actual influence of television on the lives of children.

children's viewing patterns

In 1950 there were about 100,000 television sets in North American homes; one year later there were more than 1 million. Now it is no easy thing to find any home without at least one set (Gunter & McAleer, 1990).

A 1984 Nielsen report (*Nielsen Television Index*, 1984) indicates that preschool children spend an average of 27.9 hours per week watching television. Figures for the 6- to 11-year-old group are very similar: 24.5 hours per week. A conservative estimate, Winn (1985) tells us, is that preschoolers spend more than a third of their waking time watching television. Singer and Singer (1983) point out that many young children spend more time watching television than they spend in conversation with adults or siblings. By the age of 18, many children will have spent about 50 percent more time watching television than going to school and doing schoolwork combined (Luke, 1988). Only sleeping will have taken more time than watching television (Huston et al., 1990).

Preschoolers tend to prefer cartoons. As they get older, preferences shift to situation comedies and to action/adventure programs. During the school years boys prefer "mechanical" themes (science and action); nurturant themes (mothering, caring for) appeal more to girls (Mielke,

1983). These sex differences are not apparent in the preschool years (Anderson & Bryant, 1983).

---

what children comprehend

What children see and understand from television might be quite different from what you or I might see. As Winn (1985) points out, children do not have the same backlog of experiences and understanding that we do; their conceptual bases are more fragmented, less complete. We can evaluate television in terms of things we know and have experienced. Television, in a very real sense, reminds us of life. In contrast, children are less able to relate television offerings to their knowledge about the world. Perhaps when this television-reared generation has finally grown up, real life will occasionally remind them of television. They might be a little like Jerzy Kosinski's character in the novel (and movie) *Being There*—a man who had spent all his life in front of a television set and who, when he was finally forced into the real world, thought he would really rather watch. It was somehow better than *being there*.

Collins et al. (1978) report that preschoolers understand very little of motives, characters, or plots—hardly surprising given their social cognitions. They are still learning that others have private emotions, motives, beliefs. Accordingly, preschoolers respond to the most salient features of what is actually happening: the sights, the sounds, the action. What they don't understand, notes Evra (1990), they simply ignore. But even at the age of 5 or 6, children use fairly sophisticated cognitive skills to understand television's messages. And those with the most advanced verbal skills have a much higher level of comprehension (Jacobvitz, Wood, & Albin, 1991).

Through elementary school, children become progressively more sensitive to motives and more attentive to implications of actions for the characters involved. They pay attention to why things happen and to the consequences of their happening, rather than simply to what happened.

Commercial programs for young children seem to be based on the assumption that the best way of capturing and holding the viewer's attention is through rapid action, constant change, high noise level, and slapstick violence (Huston & Wright, 1983). One very important question concerns the effects of this violence on children.

---

violence and aggression

In the great body of literature that looks at the influence of television on children, the terms *violence* and *aggression* are used not only as though they mean exactly the same thing, but also as though it is clear that everybody knows exactly what they do mean. Not so. They mean slightly different things, and they are not understood in the same way by everybody.

AGGRESSION

The more general of these two terms is **aggression**, which is defined as "hostile or forceful action intended to dominate or violate" (Lefrançois, 1983, p. 504). It includes a wide range of behaviors beginning with insistence, assertiveness, or perhaps intrusion and culminating in anger and violence. Thus violence is simply an extreme form of aggressiveness. **Violence** implies physical action or movement and possible or actual harm to people or objects. It is well illustrated in television episodes in which people are kicked, beaten, shot, or knifed, or in which rocks and other objects are dropped on their heads from great heights. It is also evident when dogs are kicked or cars are smashed.

Clearly, aggression is not always undesirable or unavoidable. The totally nonaggressive are unlikely to achieve as many of their desires as are the more aggressive. In fact, our survival as a species, as well as that of many other animals, is very likely related to aggressiveness. That, of course, does not necessarily mean that we still need to be as aggressive as many of us now are.

Many—perhaps most—television programs contain violence in one form or another: sometimes verbal, frequently physical, and occasionally symbolic. The U.S. Surgeon General's report on television concludes that violence, defined as "the overt expression of physical force against others or self, or the compelling of action against one's will on pain of being hurt or killed," is the dominant theme of television, and especially of children's television. One study reports that over 98 percent of all cartoons contain violent episodes, the frequency of violence in children's programs being six times greater than that in adult programs (Gerbner, 1972). The critical question concerns the effects of this violence on children. (See Figure 10.4 in "At A Glance: Gender Differences in Criminal Behavior" for an indication of sex differences in aggression.)

EARLY LABORATORY RESEARCH

In an early series of studies, Bandura and his associates (Bandura, Ross, & Ross, 1963; Bandura, 1969) exposed children to violent models that were either live actors, real people in films, or animated cartoon characters. Following exposure to a violent model (typically, the model was aggressive toward an inflated rubber clown), children were given objects similar to those toward which the model had been aggressive and were observed at play through a one-way mirror. In most studies of this kind, a majority of the children who have been exposed to models of violence behave aggressively; in contrast, those who have not been exposed to violent models most often respond nonaggressively.

Although these studies have been widely interpreted as evidence that

TV—a beneficial force increasing literacy, language sophistication, and moral reasoning? Or an antisocial agent robbing children of imagination, creativity, and social skills?

lmost all forms of hu-
man aggression are
more common among
males than females.
Of 29 categories of crime tracked by
the F.B.I., there were only two for which
there were more females than males
arrested in 1990: (1) prostitution and
commercialized vice and (2) juvenile
running away (both "nonserious
crimes").

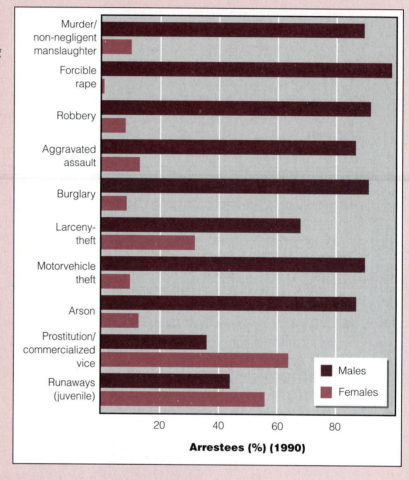

f **igure 10.4**

Sex distribution with respect to the more than
11.2 million criminal arrests in the United
States in 1990. Source: Adapted from U.S. Bureau of the Census (1992), p. 187.

violence on television would lead
to violence in real life, this kind of
generalization is probably unrealistic.
First, the aggression displayed in an
ordinary television program is directed
against people rather than against inanimate objects, and children learn early in
life, through socialization, that aggression
against people is normally punished.

Next, the experimental situation generally exposed children to objects identical
to those aggressed upon by the model,
and usually immediately afterward. But a
child who watches a violent scene on television is rarely presented immediately
with an object (or person) similar to the
one on whom the televised violence was
inflicted. Finally, striking a rubber clown

with a mallet, kicking it, or punching it after seeing a model do so may not be a manifestation of aggression at all. The child may have simply learned that these are appropriate and expected behaviors with this inanimate object.

NATURALISTIC RESEARCH

Studies of television viewing under more natural circumstances may provide clearer information about its impact. Unfortunately, it is difficult to find children who have not been exposed to television and who can therefore serve as control groups for these studies; hence there are few such studies.

One conducted by Joy, Kimball, and Zabrack (1977), spanned a two-year period and involved several small towns. When the study began, television was just being introduced in one of the towns, whereas another still remained without television. Residents of these towns were highly comparable socially, educationally, and economically, and children in each of these towns appeared to be equally aggressive at the beginning of the study. Two years later, however, children in the town into which television had been brought manifested a measurable increase in aggressive behavior.

As Liebert and Schwartzberg (1977) note, although these studies demonstrate some short-term, although rather undramatic, effects of television violence, few studies have looked at its long-term effects. One longitudinal study reported by Lefkowitz et al. (1972) examined the relationship between children's preferences for violent television programs and their aggressive behavior, and attempted to relate these variables to the same children's preferences and aggressive behavior 10 years later. Results indicate that preferences for violent programs are significantly related to aggressive and

delinquent behavior 10 years later (at age 18), especially for boys.

Similar results have also been reported in Sweden, where researchers found high positive correlations between television viewing and aggressiveness (Rosengren & Windahl, 1989). Note, however, that these studies do not *prove* that viewing violent television programs causes aggression. It may be that children who initially preferred violent programs would have been more aggressive and more prone to delinquency than other children even if they had not been exposed to these programs.

CROSS-CULTURAL COMPARISONS

A series of studies examined the effects of television violence on aggressiveness in children from five countries: the United States, Finland, Israel, Poland, and Australia (Huesmann & Eron, 1986b). Not only are some of these cultures very different, but television accessibility and the nature of television programming varied tremendously. For example, in the Israeli kibbutz, children watched TV for only one or two hours a week and were almost never exposed to television violence. In contrast, American children watched 20 or more hours of television, most of it characterized by violent themes and violent acts.

The main conclusion advanced by Huesmann and Eron is essentially the same as the conclusion reached by the Surgeon General's Report on Television and Social Behavior more than a decade earlier: Television violence does have an adverse effect on some children. Second, television viewing and aggression appear to be interdependent—that is, the most aggressive children tend to select the more violent television programs and to view more of them; at the same time, those who watch more violent programs tend to be more aggressive.

Finally, although some of the research linking television violence with aggressiveness in children has dealt with what might appear to be short-term and perhaps trivial manifestations of aggressiveness, there is now evidence of a link between aggressiveness in childhood and subsequent criminality. A study conducted by Huesmann and his associates (1984) found significant correlations between measures of aggression at the age of 8 and indications of antisocial aggression at the age of 30 (for example, spouse abuse, criminal convictions, physical punishment of children, and self-ratings of physical aggression).

A CONCLUSION

Most summaries of research that has looked at the relationship between aggression and television viewing reach similar conclusions: As Rosenkoetter, Huston, and Wright (1990) put it, "Most professional reviews . . . have concluded that the weight of evidence indicates that television violence does increase viewer aggression" (p. 125). But, as Evra (1990) emphasizes, the most recent studies indicate that the *long-term* impact of television violence may, in fact, be negligible.

It may be that the negative effects of television have less to do with violence and aggression on television than with some of its more general influences. As Singer (1982) suggests, "the problem with heavy television viewing is not so much that it may or may not stimulate aggression, but that it may interfere with the development of the social skills and mental capacities that children need to acquire the socially approved, successful behaviors they need to get what they want without resorting to aggression" (p. 60). He also points out that television viewing robs many children of what would otherwise be "play" time and may

do a great deal to impede creativity (Singer & Singer, 1983). For example, some studies have found a high negative correlation between watching fantasy and violence, and enthusiasm for school work (Zuckerman, Singer, & Singer, 1980). Similarly, Meline (1976) reports that television may have a negative influence on the amount of imagination and creativity that children display in their problem-solving behavior. And Winn (1985), whose criticism of television is extensive, argues that it serves as a narcotic—that parents deliberately use it to pacify and control their children.

OTHER POSSIBLE NEGATIVE EFFECTS

Another possible negative effect of violence on television is the instillation of *fear* in some children, an effect that, for some, may be more serious than increased aggressiveness (Gerbner & Gross, 1980). In fact, a survey conducted by Ridley-Johnson, Surdy, and O'Laughlin (1991) found that parents are as concerned about fear-related influences of television as about aggression-related effects.

There is controversial evidence, too, that television may have a negative influence on the development of reading and writing skills (Winn, 1985). For example, a California survey of sixth-graders found a relationship between television viewing and lower scores on statewide achievement tests (California Assessment Program, 1982). Specifically, students who watched the most television performed most poorly. The availability of television sets in children's bedrooms was also associated with lower achievement. Interestingly, however, the negative relationship between achievement and television viewing was mainly for students who watched five or six (or more) hours of television per day.

Some researchers suggest that the main problem with heavy television viewing is it interferes with other activities that are important to the child's development—like social play or reading. Perhaps it helps to have someone with whom to read.

---

positive effects

Clearly, however, the potential effects of television are not all negative.

ACADEMIC EFFECTS

In the California study just described, for example, children from lower socioeconomic classes who watched two or three hours of television per day actually achieved *better* than those who watched little or no television. For many children, insists Rice (1983), television contributes to the acquisition of language and of a wealth of information and concepts.

Evidence that this might be so is found in a series of studies of the effects of *Sesame Street* on the cognitive development of children (Lesser, 1977). In general, most of these studies report highly positive findings, which can be summarized as follows: (1) Most viewers gain significantly on a variety of measures, including recognizing and naming letters, sorting different objects, naming body parts, and recognizing and labeling geometric forms; (2) children who view more programs make the highest gains; and (3) adult supervision and encouragement of viewing, although helpful, are not necessary. As Cook et al. (1975) observe, these findings strongly suggest that "Sesame Street" does lead to positive cognitive changes. Interestingly, there is also some indication that middle-class children might have benefited more from educational television than less advantaged children, perhaps because they appear to watch more of it (Cook et al., 1975).

PROSOCIAL EFFECTS

In the same way that television might be instrumental in undermining such values as nonviolence, family stability, cooperation, altruism, and gender equality, so too might it serve to bring about and strengthen these values. Unfortunately, the most popular area of television research—particularly in the early 1970s, when such research was at its height—was concerned primarily with television's potential antisocial effects, especially with its contribution to aggression. At present there are still only relatively few studies concerned with the benefits of television. Their results are mostly encouraging.

Baran, Chase, and Courtright (1979) found that cooperation could be increased in young children after exposure to an episode of "The Waltons" that dealt with cooperation in problem solving. Similarly, research with episodes of "Mister Rogers' Neighborhood" and with a number of other deliberately prosocial programs found clear evidence of improvement in prosocial behaviors such as friendliness, generosity, cooperation, creativity, empathy, racial tolerance, and others (Rosenkoetter, Huston, & Wright, 1990).

WHAT TO BELIEVE?

"Television," writes Neuman (1991), "is a wonderful nemesis for those inclined to fret over the education of the young. It has been accused of robbing youngsters of childhood, reducing attention spans, and impairing children's ability to think clearly" (p. 158). She goes on to describe how television has been blamed for poor achievement, aggression, illiteracy, and so on. But following a review of the research she concludes, ". . . the charges against the medium have been unwarranted" (p. 158).

This does not mean, of course, that television never harms anybody. Excessive viewing and excessive violence can clearly have negative effects.

why is television influential?

Explanations of the effects of television typically rely on one or more of several explanations.

Theories of imitation (observational learning) suggest that children learn aggressive behaviors from observing televi-

sion models performing aggressive acts (Bandura & Walters, 1963).

An *attitude-change* model suggests that constant exposure to violence might serve to desensitize children, leaving them with the impression that the aggressive acts so common on television are, in fact, trivial and socially acceptable.

The Freudian *cathartic model* claims that television might serve as a *catharsis* (release) for pent-up emotions. For some individuals, painting might be a catharsis for aggressive impulses that cannot be acted on for moral reasons; others might try to kick their cats. In the same way, exposure to television violence may be a release for pent-up hostility, aggressive urges, and other antisocial tendencies. If this model is valid, it follows that television violence might result in a decrease in violent behavior. Similarly, prosocial themes on television might occasionally result in a decrease in prosocial behavior. Huesmann and Eron (1986a) suggest that there is no evidence whatsoever that viewing violence prevents aggression by serving as a catharsis.

Another explanation of the effects of television violence is the cognitive, *information-processing theory* advanced by Huesmann and Eron (1986b). The theory is based on the notion that much of our social behavior is controlled by schemas (also called schemata) and scripts (described in Chapter 9). Schemata are metaphors for mental representations of what we know. Scripts are one aspect of schemata; they are metaphors for our knowledge of sequences and routines—of what should follow what. According to this model, learning aggression from television violence requires that children encode (represent mentally) this violence; encoding involves processes such as rehearsing and elaborating. Huesmann and Eron suggest that whenever a child fantasizes a violent sequence, rehearsing occurs. And whenever violence is seen in a new context, or whenever a slightly different form of violence is seen in an old context, elaboration may be occurring. The result is that the imaginative and aggressive child who views a great deal of television violence ends up with a wealth of *violence schemata*. In addition, such a child also learns and rehearses a variety of scripts that detail when violence is appropriate and the precise sequence in which it is to be manifested. All that is left is for the child to retrieve these schemata and their related scripts as required.

A pair of spectators sitting close to me at a hockey game recently engaged in a very brief (albeit heated) discussion about the maternal origin of one of the players. One of these individuals, anxious to settle this important question, kept urging his reluctant adversary by using a not very original, but widely known script: "Go ahead! Hit me, you @#★$%★! Come on! *Make my day!*"

rock videos, VCRs, and video games

Television-related technology now provides us with new sources of potential influence on children.

ROCK VIDEOS

Close to the cutting edge of television technology, and sometimes very close as well to the edge of what society's changing tastes and morals find acceptable, are rock videos. Basically, they are very simple: Take a popular, avant-garde, rock-type song; create images to accompany the lyrics; and combine the two in a frenetic, jarring, surprising, evocative, and sometimes bizarre way. The result? A dazzling, seductive, intriguing audiovisual experience that has rapidly transformed

the music industry—and that has alarmed some parents and educators as well. Why? Because, as one commentator put it, "some of them are sending messages that are questionable, to say the least: antiwork, anti-marriage, anti-family, pro-violence, pro-casual sex, pro-woman-as-victim" (*Television & your children,* 1985, p. 52).

Rock videos, says Luke (1988), have much the same faults that are found in commercial television: They are racist, sexist, violent, and highly commercialized. Although research on their effects is still rare, it is likely that they will be at least as influential as more ordinary television programs. Indeed, they might even be more influential, given their technological slickness, the addictive quality of their lyrics and their rhythms, and their popularity with a teen and preteen generation that has increasingly easy access to home videocassette players and to cable television.

VCRs

The rapid proliferation of VCRs brings an additional worry for those concerned with the potentially harmful effects of television. Rosengren and Windahl (1989) point out that parents and society either do not have, or often don't exercise, significant control over children's selections of the video recordings that they rent for home viewing. In most areas it is possible for children to rent videos that depict aggression and standards of morality that would not be considered acceptable on commercial television. Similarly, the increasing availability of quasi-private channels through home satellite systems means that increasing numbers of children may be exposed to extreme forms of violence and pornography at very young ages. There is clearly a need for more research to ascertain the probable effects of this exposure and to identify the parameters that might interact to make some children more vulnerable than others.

VIDEO GAMES

Video games have been a source of concern for some parents as well, particularly in view of their quasi-addictive qualities and their overwhelmingly violent themes. However, Griffiths's (1991) review of relevant studies indicates that frequent players are no more maladjusted, conduct disordered, or likely to use drugs than infrequent players or nonplayers. Although some studies report greater incidence of aggressiveness among frequent players, at least half do not.

a summary of television issues

There is little doubt that television can have both beneficial and harmful effects. That it has had more of one than the other is still unclear and will be difficult to ascertain. Further clarification depends on longitudinal, carefully controlled studies in which the characteristics of viewers and programs are carefully identified and for which adequate control groups are available. We already have some indication that not all portrayals of violence have the same effects. Collins (1983), for example, suggests that comedies with slapstick violence and violent cartoons are too unrealistic to serve as powerful models of violence. In contrast, realistic portrayals of violence, violence perpetrated by "good guys" in their attacks upon "bad guys," and violence that appears randomly and unrelated to the plot produce more real-life violence among viewers (Singer, 1982).

An increasing number of researchers are now arguing that schools should teach children the basic skills of television literacy—skills relating to distinguishing be-

tween reality and fantasy, making wise choices among available programming, and limiting viewing and engaging in other important social and intellectual activities such as conversation, reading, and playing (see Anderson, 1983).

Following a review of television and its effects on children, Huston, Watkins, and Kunkel (1989) recommend federal guidelines that would ensure a minimum amount of quality children's programming and that would protect children from commercial exploitation. The long-range goal, these authors argue, should be to eliminate advertising directed at children. This, they believe, would have a significant effect on programming. And ultimately, it might serve to reduce violence in the contemporary family.

violence in the family

Even very conservative estimates of child abuse, spouse abuse, and child sexual abuse are startling, says Emery (1989). He quotes surveys that have found that 20 percent of all murderers are members of the victim's family, and that between 2 and 3 percent of a random sample of women had been coerced into having sex with a father, stepfather, or brother before the age of 18. In addition, more than 2 million instances of child abuse and neglect are reported each year in the United States (U.S. Bureau of the Census, 1992).

Children are surrounded by violence—in the home, on television, in school. Boulton (1993) surveyed more than 100 elementary school boys and girls. More than half reported they had engaged in at least one physical fight during the preceding year, with boys engaging in more fights than girls. The main reasons for these fights were retaliation for teasing and disagreements over the way games were being played.

Some argue that much of the violence in our society begins with violence in the home, and that much of the violence in the home begins with cultural values that, at least implicitly, have maintained that it is acceptable for parents to use physical force to control and punish their children.

the case against punishment

There is a fine line, claims Sabatino (1991), between discipline and child abuse. But that is only one of the reasons for discouraging the use of punishment. Another is the fact that punishment does not ordinarily illustrate desirable behavior, but rather draws attention to that which is undesirable, thus contributing little (if anything) to the learning of socially acceptable behavior. Also, it is often accompanied by negative emotional side effects that can become associated with the punisher perhaps as easily as with the behavior for which the child is being punished (Clarizio & Yelon, 1974).

Another reason for discouraging the use of punishment is that it sometimes has effects opposite to those intended. Children whose parents punish them for aggressive behavior are more likely to be aggressive; children whose mothers punish them to toilet train them are more likely to wet their beds subsequently (Sears, Maccoby, & Lewin, 1957). And some habitual mischief-makers whose misbehavior earns them an otherwise preoccupied parent's or teacher's punishment may misbehave even more. The attention that accompanies the act of punishing sometimes serves as reinforcement for the behavior punished.

the case for punishment

There is a case to be made for the use of punishment, however, especially when

Punishment may have effects opposite to those intended. Children whose parents punish them for aggressive behavior are more likely to become aggressive.

the punished behavior is dangerous to the child or to others—such as touching matches to the family drapes or shooting neighborhood cats with big brother's air rifle. Under certain circumstances, punishment can be effective in suppressing undesirable behavior (Parke, 1970). The important variables in its use appear to be timing, intensity, consistency, and the relationship between the punisher and the punished. Delayed punishment is much less effective than punishment that immediately follows a transgression. Also, very intense physical punishment is more effective than mild punishment when effectiveness is determined in terms of number of recurrences of the punished behavior. In fact, intense punishment appears to be very effective even when it is delayed.

Punishment by a parent who is ordinarily warm and loving is significantly more effective than punishment by a usually cold and distant parent (Aronfreed, 1968). Parental consistency is also an important variable, with inconsistent parents being less effective than consistent parents. Reassuringly, there is no evidence that punishment administered by a loving parent decreases the affection between parent and child (Walters & Grusec, 1977). However, in considering the effects of physical punishment on children we should realize that any desirable changes that occur in children's behavior as a result reinforce the parents' punitive behavior and may lead to child abuse (Mulhern & Passman, 1979).

kinds of punishment

Objections to the use of punishment apply mainly to physical punishment. There are at least three other kinds of punishment that parents and teachers often use and to which those objections are not as relevant. These include *reprimands* and the use of *time-out* and *response-cost* procedures.

REPRIMANDS

Reprimands are simply verbal or nonverbal indications of disapproval. They can be mild (a gentle headshake) or harsh (a shout). They are, in a sense, the opposite of praise. Praise says "I like . . . "; reprimands say "I do not like . . . " Research clearly indicates that reprimands can be very effective in suppressing undesirable behavior and in bringing about more desirable responses. It also points out that the most effective reprimands not only identify the undesirable behavior but also provide specific rationales for doing something (or for not doing the opposite) (Van Houten & Doleys, 1983). Studies on the use of reprimands in the classroom also suggest that reprimands that are given at a closer distance are often more effective than those that are given from farther away (Van Houten et al., 1982).

TIME-OUT PROCEDURES

In a **time-out** procedure children are removed from a situation they enjoy, such as watching television. Brantner and Doherty (1983) describe several time-out procedures that can be used in a classroom. *Isolation* involves removing a student from the classroom. A less severe time-out procedure, *exclusion*, does not remove students from the classroom but simply prevents them from participating in ongoing activities.

RESPONSE-COST PROCEDURES

Response-cost is a form of punishment in which the penalty for bad behavior is the loss of rewards that have been awarded for good behavior. For example, in a school-based response-cost system, children earn tokens for certain behaviors but also run the risk of losing them for misbehaviors. Research reported by Pazulinec, Meyerrose, and Sajwaj (1983) indicates that response-cost procedures can bring about significant increases in classroom achievement and marked reductions in disruptive behavior. One of the advantages they have over time-out procedures is that they do not remove the child from ongoing activities. In addition, they are usually combined with reinforcement programs, making it easier for parents and teachers to use them to bring about desirable behavior as well as to eliminate less desirable behavior.

child maltreatment

Most of the objections to the use of punishment relate to physical punishment and not to other methods of control. The line between acceptable physical punishment—if, indeed, any form of physical punishment is acceptable—and physical abuse is very thin, claims Sabatino (1991). Yet physical punishment is still very much a part of contemporary childrearing. Indeed, physical violence, often an outgrowth of a parent's attempt to punish physically, is appallingly prevalent. A shocking one out of every seven murder victims is a child (Henderson & Henderson, 1984).

PREVALENCE

Reported cases of child maltreatment continue to increase—from 3.5 per 1,000 population in 1980 to 8.3 per 1,000 in 1987 (U.S. Bureau of the Census, 1992). However, as Straus and Gelles (1986) point out, it is not clear whether this means that child maltreatment is actually increasing or whether reporting and detection are more thorough. A large-scale survey of 2,143 families in 1975 and 3,520 families in 1985 found, in fact, that child and wife abuse declined appreciably during that 10-year period. Although incidence of the more minor forms of child abuse had not changed appreciably, the more severe forms of abuse (kicking, beating up, using a knife or a gun), which conform to the public's general understanding of what abuse is, had declined by 47 percent (Table 10.7). Still, more than 2 million cases of child maltreatment were reported in 1987. Given the difficulty of obtaining information from parents and even from doctors in cases of child abuse, this figure probably represents a very conservative estimate. Murray, Henjum, and Freeze (1992) surveyed a sample of 110 college students and found that a shocking 22 percent of the women had been sexually abused as children (6 percent of the men); about three-fourths had experienced physical punishment (spanking, slapping, hitting).

table 10.7

Violence against children in the United States, 1985.

TYPE OF VIOLENCE	RATE PER 1,000 CHILDREN AGES 3 THROUGH 17*
Minor violent acts	
Threw something	27
Pushed, grabbed, shoved	309
Slapped or spanked	549
Severe violent acts	
Kicked, bit, hit with fist	13
Hit, tried to hit with something	97
Beat up	6
Threatened with gun or knife	2
Used gun or knife	2
Violence indexes (cases)	
Overall violence	620
Severe violence	107
Very severe violence	19

*For two-caregiver households with at least one child ages 3 to 17 at home.
Source: Adapted from "Societal Change and Change in Family Violence from 1975 to 1985 as Revealed by Two National Surveys" by M. A. Straus and R. Gelles, 1986, *Journal of Marriage and the Family*, 48, 465–479. Copyright 1986 by the National Council on Family Relations, 3989 Central Ave., N.E., Suite 550, Minneapolis, MN 55421. Reprinted by permission.

In a survey of child abuse in the United States, Gelles (1979) found that 58 percent of a sample of 1,146 parents had used some form of physical violence on a child at least once during the past year. An astounding 2.9 percent admitted to having used a knife or a gun on one of their children at least once in their lifetimes—small wonder that one out of every five murders in the United States is committed among immediate family members in their own home. (See Figures 10.5 and 10.6 in "At A Glance: Abused Children.")

Reported instances of child abuse and neglect have risen dramatically in recent decades—from 10.1 cases per 1,000 children in 1976 to 32.8 cases in 1986. It is unclear to what extent rising rates represent an actual increase in maltreatment and to what extent they reflect increased awareness and reporting on the part of people such as teachers, physicians, relatives, and family acquaintances.

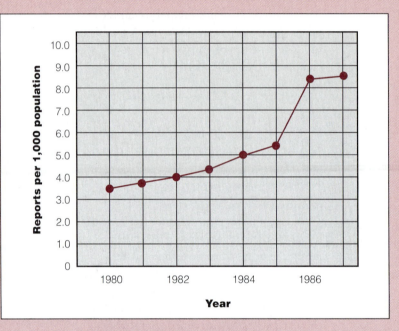

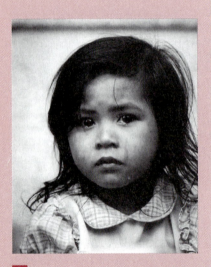

Changing our society's attitude toward corporal punishment may be the only truly effective means of preventing child abuse.

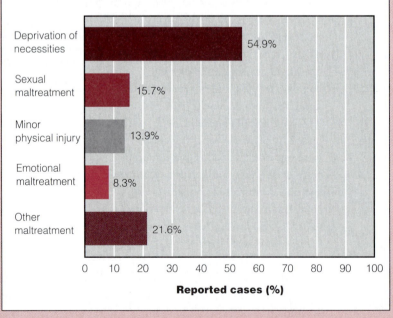

f i g u r e   10.5

(top) Reported cases of child neglect and abuse per 1,000 population, 1980 to 1987. (Note that these figures would be much higher per 1,000 children.) Source: Adapted from U.S. Bureau of the Census (1990), p. 176.

f i g u r e   10.6

(bottom) Child maltreatment cases, with type of maltreatment as a percentage of the nearly 2.1 million cases reported in the United States in 1986. (Note that some children are classified more than one way; hence percentages total more than 100). Source: Adapted from U.S. Bureau of the Census (1990), p. 176.

The term *child abuse* includes a tremendous variety of behaviors inflected on children. Chase (1975) categorizes these behaviors in terms of physical and emotional abuse and physical neglect. In addition, there is sexual abuse.

PHYSICAL ABUSE

Physical injury to children is the main criterion of physical abuse. In a survey by Gil (1970), the majority of children who were victims of abuse suffered from bruises and welts (67.1 percent). Others had abrasions, contusions, and lacerations (32.3 percent); bone fractures and skull fractures (10.4 and 4.6 percent, respectively); burns and scaldings (10.1 percent); and wounds, cuts, and punctures (7.9 percent).

PHYSICAL NEGLECT

Physical neglect involves acts of *omission* rather than *commission* and is usually evident in parents' failure to ensure that children have adequate nourishment, shelter, clothing, and health care. Physical neglect is somewhat more difficult to detect than physical abuse but nevertheless makes up a relatively large proportion of reported abuse cases.

EMOTIONAL ABUSE

Emotional abuse consists of parental behaviors that cause emotional and psychological harm to the child but are not instances of physical abuse or neglect— for example, continually shaming or ridiculing children, isolating them, depriving them of emotional contact and comfort, blaming, yelling, and other behaviors that might be classified as involving mental cruelty. The effects of emotional abuse, unlike those of physical abuse or neglect, are often invisible. Consequently, instances of emotional abuse are seldom reported. However, the long-term effects of emotional abuse and neglect are sometimes more serious than those of physical abuse. They may come to light years later and often involve serious adjustment and emotional problems (Wolock & Horowitz, 1984). (See "At A Glance: Humiliation as Child Abuse" for illustrations of different forms of emotional abuse.)

SEXUAL ABUSE

Sexual abuse is a form of child maltreatment in which sexual behaviors are forced upon a child. Victims of sexual abuse are primarily female and are often very young; in fact, they are sometimes still infants. Incest is often but not always involved in the sexual abuse of children.

Estimates of the prevalence of sexual abuse vary considerably for two reasons. One is the problem of definition. Sexual abuse may be defined as an unwanted sexual act involving physical contact; it may also be defined as any of a number of actions that do not involve physical contact (for example, a proposition or suggestion, verbal enticements, or exhibitionism). Estimates vary depending on the researcher's definition.

A second problem in arriving at accurate estimates has to do with the extreme social taboos that surround all forms of incest, especially father-daughter incest. Estimates of the prevalence of these acts have typically been based on cases reported to courts or other legal jurisdictions or that come to light in the course of mental health treatment, and are probably gross underestimates.

Because of these problems, estimates of sexual abuse are largely meaningless, although they're extremely common. Finkelhor et al.'s (1986) survey of 10 recent studies found prevalence rates ranging from a low of 6 percent of the sample to 62 percent. This review indicates that

There were more than 2 million reported cases of child maltreatment (deprivation of necessities, physical injury, sexual maltreatment, emotional maltreatment, and other forms of maltreatment) in the United States in 1986 (U.S. Bureau of the Census, 1992). Slightly more than half of maltreated children were female (52.5 percent); about the same percentage of the perpetrators were females (55.9 percent).

Emotional maltreatment, which may have more disastrous long-term consequences than physical maltreat-ment, often goes unreported because it is usually subtle and not easily noticed. Yet more than 8.3 million cases of emotional maltreatment were reported in the United States in 1986.

Humiliation, claims Battachi (1993) is one of the ways in which children are emotionally maltreated.

f i g u r e 10.7

Four common ways of humiliating children.

there are some broad characteristics that might serve to identify situations in which the risk of sexual abuse is higher than normal. To begin with, girls are at considerably higher risk than are boys, although boys too are at some risk. Those who live alone with their fathers are at higher risk, as are those whose mothers are employed outside the home or who are ill, disabled, alcoholic, or battered. Girls living with a stepfather are also at higher risk. A review by Powell (1991) also found that marital dissatisfaction, poor mother-daughter relationship, social isolation of the family, a history of child abuse in the family, and violence in the home all increased the likelihood that a daughter would be sexually abused. Note, however, that these are extremely broad categories that include so many individual exceptions that their predictive value is severely limited.

the consequences of maltreatment

Apart from the physical consequences of child abuse—which may even include death—there are serious emotional and psychological consequences. These can result perhaps as readily from physical abuse and neglect as from emotional or sexual abuse. (See "In Other Contexts: Mash, An Ixil Indian.")

GENERAL EFFECTS OF MALTREATMENT

Abused children are often frightened. Their behaviors may range from complete social withdrawal, uncontrolled aggression, and regression to behaviors characteristic of younger children: crying, truancy, and delinquency. Reyome (1993) also reports that the school achievement of sexually abused and neglected children, on average, is significantly poorer than that of those who are not maltreated.

Emery (1989) makes the point that the long-term effects of child maltreatment are highly varied and often unpredictable. They include an increased probability of greater aggression, problems with peer relationships, impaired social development, lack of empathy, depression, and poorer performance on cognitive tasks. Studies of adults with behavioral and emotional problems (delinquency and criminality or mental disorders, for example) have often found that these adults were abused as children. Fischer and Pipp (1984) report, for instance, that child abuse seems to be related to the development of multiple personality, a mental disorder in which the patient develops two or more highly distinct personalities (the classical "split" personality, often confused with schizophrenia, which is a different disorder). They found that most individuals suffering from this disorder seem to have been subjected to severe abuse as young children.

EFFECTS OF SEXUAL ABUSE

Among adolescents who have been victims of sexual abuse there is a higher than normal incidence of running away, attempted suicide, emotional disorders, and adolescent pregnancies—particularly if the father was the abuser. One investigation of 41 rural mothers who had been pregnant as teenagers found that an astounding 54 percent had been sexually abused before the age of 18 (Butler & Burton, 1990).

Kendall-Tackett, Williams, and Finkelhor (1993) reviewed 45 studies that examined the consequences of sexual abuse on children ages 18 or younger. About one-third of the victims of abuse appeared to have no symptoms; a full two-thirds did. The most commonly studied childhood symptom of sexual abuse—and perhaps one of the most common effects of sexual abuse—is *sexu-*

The reporter found Mash polishing the major's boots in an army camp in Guatemala. He is perhaps 7 or 8; no one knows for sure. Nor does anyone know his full name. He speaks to no one.

Mash has already been a guerilla. He can load and fire a rifle faster than most of the major's soldiers; he can hide like a snake in the jungle and strike like a panther.

But that was before the soldiers came. Before his very eyes, they shot his mother and father. Then they dragged him away, kicking and screaming. Now that he has gotten used to them, they keep him around like a little mascot, strangely proud of their 7- or 8-year-old little ex-guerilla. But still he refuses to speak, or smile, or laugh, or even cry; he only stares with his black eyes.

The reporter, Alison Acker (1986), arranges to take him away to a children's home. The boy fights his would-be rescuers and tries to bite them. For a long time they hold him tightly in the back of the station wagon as they bounce through the jungle and over the dry river beds until, after seven hours, they reach the children's home. Mash has refused to eat. He would take neither peanuts nor Coca Cola and still will not speak. The children's home accepts him, but when they try to fill out the identification form, all they know to write is Tomás, the Spanish form of

Mash; every other blank is filled with the word desconocido—unknown.

"Will Mash eventually start to talk," Acker asks the doctor who runs the home (Acker, 1986, p. 23).

"Sure," the doctor answers, pointing as an example to a 5-year-old girl in the next room. "She was raped so many times her vagina and anus are now fused into one passage. She'll recover. So will he" (p. 24).

When Acker returns to see Mash three weeks later, he still trusts no one. But there is now hope, reports his house mother. When she heard him crying one night and asked him why, at first he would say nothing; but when she asked whether it was because of his mum and dad, he said "Yes."

And the next day, when he again climbed the big tree he has been climbing every day, he finally explained why he does so.

"They're coming for me," he said. "My mum and dad" (p. 25).

More Facts: Guatemala is one of some 30 countries in the world classified as having high mortality rates for children under 5. (Another 38 have very high mortality rates.) Under 5 mortality rate (abbreviated U5MR) is a widely accepted index of how a nation treats its children. Canada and the United States have U5MRs under 20 per 1,000; Guatemala's is above 71. Other important differences? Adult literacy rate in Guatemala is about 55

percent; in North America, it's about 99 percent. Some 36 percent of Guatemalans who enroll in primary school later enroll in high school; 98 or 99 percent of Americans and Canadians do so. Life expectancy is about 15 years longer in the United States and Canada than in Guatemala. And in Guatemala, 17 percent of the urban population and 51 percent of the rural population is below absolute poverty level (meaning that adequate nourishment is simply not available); comparable figures for North America are negligible (Grant, 1992).

To Think About: What do you think Mash's chances for a normal life are? Why?

alized behavior. Sexualized behavior includes sexual play with dolls, inserting objects in vaginas and anuses, excessive masturbation, seductive behavior, asking for sexual stimulation from others, and more advanced sexual knowledge than expected. Other effects of sexual abuse include anxiety, depression, fear, poor self-esteem, and behavior problems.

EFFECTS ON OTHER FAMILY MEMBERS

Theories such as Bronfenbrenner's emphasize the importance of looking at the ecology—that is, at the interactions—within which the abused child and parent find themselves. From this perspective, child abuse may be seen as a symptom of a dysfunctional family. Membership in this family system would be expected to have negative effects not only on the victims of abuse, but on other family members as well. Accordingly, it is perhaps not surprising that when Jean-Gilles and Crittenden (1990) compared reported abuse victims to their siblings, they found remarkable similarities between the two. Siblings were also frequently subjected to abuse (often not reported) and manifested similar behavior problems. The common view that one child in a family serves as a scapegoat and that the others are spared is largely inaccurate and misleading, claim Jean-Gilles and Crittenden. Hence attempts to understand, to prevent, and to treat child abuse and neglect must take into consideration the entire family as a dynamic, functioning system.

the abusive family context

Child maltreatment sometimes appears to be a lower-class phenomenon because parents of abused children tend to be from lower socioeconomic levels and have lower educational achievements. They are also more likely to be unemployed and on social assistance (Trickett et al., 1991). However, higher-class parents may simply be better at hiding child maltreatment. When the poor and uneducated need help, they go to the police; when the well-to-do need help, they hire professional counselors.

CHARACTERISTICS OF ABUSIVE PARENTS

Many abusive parents have themselves suffered abuse as children (Kempe & Kempe, 1984), but only a small number of child abusers may be classified as psychotic or as suffering from some other personality disorder (Emery, 1989). However, many abusive parents share one or more of the following traits: limited knowledge of childrearing; low tolerance for common infant behaviors such as crying; and misinterpretations of children's motivations for crying (Emery, 1989). An investigation of 28 abusive families found that parents in these families were less satisfied with their children, found childrearing difficult and unsatisfying, lived with more anger and conflict, and were less likely to reason with their children than simply to forbid certain behaviors (Trickett & Susman, 1988). Probably because they carry the major responsibility of childcare, mothers tend to abuse more often than fathers, although they are not often as extreme in their abuse (Blumberg, 1974; Gelles, 1979).

CAN PUNISHMENT LEAD TO ABUSE?

Although most parents are not abusive, research indicates that many parents might become abusive under certain circumstances. In a series of investigations, Passman and his associates have systematically studied how parental punishment and rewards are affected by their children's behavior and gender. In one typical experiment (Mulhern & Passman, 1981), a parent is seated at a table on which there sits a piece of equipment labeled *Parental Judgment*, and on which there are 10 buttons numbered 0 to 9. The child is ostensibly in a separate room engaged in a puzzle assembly task. Experimenters explain to the parent that the object of the study is to investigate how parents teach their children using rewards and punishments. They are to reward their children by pressing one of the buttons to indicate how many candies (from zero to nine) are to be added to or taken from the child's collection. A tone signals children's successes, a buzzer indicates failures, and an error counter keeps track of points added or subtracted. Parents are told that the only information children have about their successes and failures results from the parent pressing a button other than zero—that is, from the parent adding or taking away candy (rewarding or punishing, in other words). In reality, however, the children are simply playing in another room, and indications of successes and failures are manipulated by the experimenters to discover how parents react.

Of particular interest is the finding that under these circumstances, as children make more errors, parents tend to administer more punishment. In one study, Mulhern and Passman (1979) found that when punishing a child leads to increases in desirable behavior, parents might subsequently tend to use even more punishment. It is also significant that mothers tend to be more punitive than fathers and tend to punish boys more than girls (Mulhern & Passman, 1981). And with increasing stress, mothers become even more punitive (Mulhern & Passman 1979).

These findings support two hypotheses: First, in some cases children's responses to parental punishment may influence parents' behavior and lead to even more punishment, and perhaps even

to physical abuse; second, the findings provide experimental corroboration for the hypothesis that parental stress is sometimes directly implicated in child abuse (Knutson, 1978).

In an effort to clarify some of the factors involved in child maltreatment, Belsky (1980) presents an ecological model that takes into consideration the entire family system. He suggests that certain influences on interactions in this system contribute to the likelihood of family dysfunction and child maltreatment. These influences include characteristics of the abused child (such as the child's sex); discord between husband and wife; economic problems sometimes associated with unemployment; social isolation; alcohol and drug abuse; and a macrosystem that condones the use of physical violence in the family and that, in addition, is reluctant to question the autonomy of the family or to invade its privacy.

WHO IS MALTREATED?

As might be expected, infants are often victims of child abuse, and more of those abused are boys than girls. Hamner and Turner (1985) report that some 25 percent of all bone fractures in the United States occur in the first two years of life; many of these are related to physical abuse. Among the factors that contribute to the likelihood of an infant's being abused are prematurity, the presence of deformities, being a twin, being born to a mother who has often been pregnant, and being born to a very busy or depressed mother (Klein & Stern, 1971; Carey, Miller, & Widlak, 1975).

In the United States there is an overrepresentation of nonwhite children among those abused. This higher incidence appears to be related to a variety of socioeconomic factors, including poverty, lower educational levels of parents, larger families, and a higher likelihood of having a father substitute in the home (Garbarino & Crouter, 1977).

It would be misleading to suggest that the probability of being an abused child is linked solely to social and economic characteristics of the home, sex of the child, and personality characteristics of the parents. There is some evidence that certain children are much more likely than others to be victims of abuse (Martin, 1976). Such children are frequently the products of difficult births or cesarean delivery, are often premature, and sometimes suffer from postnatal complications, facts that might contribute to the absence of a strong parent-infant bond, particularly if the child is hospitalized for some time following birth. In addition, children who are abused are sometimes characterized by extreme irritability, feeding problems, excessive crying, and other behaviors that are annoying to parents. Sadly, many of these maltreated children continue to be abused when placed in foster homes.

what can be done?

Even though it is unlikely that child abuse can be completely eliminated, particularly because physical force is a widely accepted childrearing technique in contemporary societies, a number of things can be done. Gil (1970) suggests three separate approaches that might reduce the frequency and severity of child abuse. First, systematic educational efforts should be directed toward changing our current permissive attitudes toward the use of physical punishment. Second, because poverty and its related ills appear to be related to the incidence of child abuse, efforts to relieve poverty should be greatly increased. Finally, preventive and therapeutic agencies should address themselves directly to problems of child abuse.

Some prevention strategies have been designed to discover ways of predicting which parents or children are most likely to be involved in child abuse so that something can be done before the problem occurs. Unfortunately, although abused children have a number of characteristics in common, many of these characteristics are also found among nonabused children (Starr, Dietrich, & Fischhoff, 1981). Similarly, although we know that certain racial, economic, and social factors are involved in child abuse, we cannot reliably predict who is most likely to be abused (or abusive). Prevention based on prediction remains difficult, costly, and susceptible to the error of false identification (Starr, 1982).

Other preventive strategies that might be highly effective in the long term include Gil's (1970) suggestion that we change contemporary society's attitudes concerning corporal punishment and Starr's (1979) suggestion that we make wider use of parent training programs. However, dramatic changes in parental attitudes are likely to be difficult to achieve. Nor can social agencies attempt to identify and label potential abusers without running the risk of unfair and discriminatory practices and invasion of privacy.

Emery (1989) describes two types of intervention currently used. The first is apprehension and punishment of abusers; the second includes social programs and therapy, often involving the entire family. Baxter and Beer (1990) suggest that school personnel also need to be involved. In particular, they need assistance in dealing with immediate problems relating to child maltreatment, and they need training in identifying instances of abuse and neglect and in understanding the legal and psychological implications of their involvement. There is a need, too, argues Moriarty (1990), for screening procedures and preemployment testing to ensure that potential child molesters and abusers are not employed in situations in which children are easy victims. Unfortunately, this is very difficult because there is no clear personality profile that easily identifies potential child maltreaters—other than perhaps criminal conviction or psychiatric diagnosis in the case of pedophiles.

Neither the problem nor its solution is simple.

socioemotional exceptionality

Among the possible consequences of child maltreatment are a variety of adjustment and behavioral problems that tend to be both varied and highly individualistic; they are not easily classified or even defined. Many of these problems result from the interactions of a variety of other factors.

Terms that are frequently used synonymously to refer to children with such problems are *behavior-disordered, emotionally disturbed*, and *socially maladjusted*. Each of these terms describes children who are troubled and who may also cause trouble for parents, teachers, peers, and others (Kovacs, 1989). Note that the labels describing social and emotional problems are only descriptions, not explanations. Children who are diagnosed as having *attention deficits* are so labeled because they display a common set of behavioral and emotional symptoms; but the label *attention deficit* serves in no way to explain these behaviors and symptoms.

Problems associated with defining and identifying socioemotional maladjustment are far more difficult than those relating to physical exceptionality. Whereas reasonably competent individuals can usually arrive at some consensus diagnosis of visual or hearing impairments, the same does not hold for common socioemotional problems (autism, childhood depression and anxiety disorders, and attention disorders such as hyperactivity, for example).

prevalence and causes

Estimates of the prevalence of behavior disorders vary considerably depending on the criteria used for identification and on whether estimates include mild as well as severe instances of disturbance. Balow (1980) reports that these estimates range from 0.5 to 40 percent of the school population. Tuma (1989) reports data indicating that about 15 to 19 percent of U.S. children and adolescents suffer from problems requiring some form of mental health services.

CLASSIFICATIONS

Classifying emotional disturbances in childhood presents a number of difficulties. Kazdin (1989) points out that because of some important characteristics of childhood behaviors, models of adult affective disorders are not always appropriate. First, a number of behaviors that might be symptoms of underlying disorders in adults are relatively common in younger children. Uncontrollable laughter or temper tantrums are common and expected in childhood; but among adults, these behaviors might seem bizarre and might be a symptom of some underlying disorder.

Second, there are often developmental changes in problem behaviors that must be taken into account. The most common pattern is one in which apparent problems become less frequent and less severe with increasing maturity. Lying, for example, is quite common among 6-year-old boys but becomes far more infrequent by adolescence.

Third, over the course of development, some behavioral and emotional problems may be manifested in different symptoms. Kazdin (1989) illustrates this by reference to the youngster who initially threatens and shoves other children who are in his way, but whose aggressive behavior will later take other forms more typical for his age—for example, fighting or using weapons.

Finally, some disorders are primarily childhood problems; others are more common in adulthood. For example, hyperactivity (discussed in the next section) appears to be primarily a childhood disorder, although there is now evidence that many children do not "outgrow" it (Henker & Whalen, 1989). In contrast, serious affective (emotional) disorders such as depression and mania were long thought to be adult rather than childhood disorders. We now know, however, that although children rarely suffer the manic disorders, they do suffer depression (Kovacs, 1989).

CONTRIBUTING FACTORS

The factors that contribute to the development of behavior disorders vary a great deal as well. These are often classified in one of two ways: genetic/congenital and social/psychological. Possible genetic and congenital causes include chromosome abnormalities, maternal malnutrition, maternal infections, and birth injury. Social/psychological contributing factors include neglect, maltreatment, malnutrition, head injuries, and diseases and illnesses, as well as conditions within the family such as stress associated with conflict. In addition, poverty, parental abuse, parental rejection, physical handicaps, age, sex, and racial and religious discrimination have been implicated (Kazdin, 1989). There is also evidence that cognitive problems such as mental retardation or learning disabilities are sometimes related to behavior problems (Cole, Usher, & Cargo, 1993).

RISK

Given adequate knowledge of their biological history and environment, it is sometimes possible to identify children who may be described as being at greater psychiatric risk than others. Anthony and his associates (1975; Anthony & Koupernik, 1974) have undertaken longitudinal research designed not only to identify factors that might be useful for predicting the probability of emotional disturbance in later childhood (or even in adulthood), but to prevent disorders as well. If we can accurately identify contributing factors, then it might also be possible to modify the environment to reduce the incidence of emotional disturbances. However, we need considerably more research to identify the forces that are associated with emotional disorders, and those that might be associated with healthy development as well.

attention-deficit hyperactivity disorder

Estimates are that as many as 3 percent of current elementary schoolchildren suffer from varying degrees of hyperactivity (American Psychiatric Association, 1987). Of these, a significant number also suffer from attention problems and are classified as having **attention deficit hyperactivity disorder (ADHD)**. Attention problems can also exist without hyperactivity. Many ADHD children experience considerable difficulty adjusting to school and at home and are considered to be relatively serious problems.

In general, ADHD is marked by excessive general activity for the child's age (often taking the form of incessant and haphazard climbing, crawling, or running), difficulty in sustaining attention and apparent forgetfulness, and impulsivity (tendency to react quickly, difficulty taking turns, low frustration tolerance). The criteria described by the APA also stipulate that the duration of the child's hyperactivity be at least six months.

DIAGNOSIS

Diagnoses of hyperactivity (or hyperkinesis) are sometimes—perhaps even often—made inappropriately by parents and teachers who are confronted by children who are restless and who find it difficult to do the quiet things that adults sometimes demand. Strictly speaking, diagnosis of ADHD as defined by the American Psychiatric Association (1987) requires the presence of at least 8 of the 14 criteria presented in Table 10.8. The onset of the disorder must be before the age of 7 to differentiate it from disorders that might arise as reactions to stressful events or illness.

Clearly, not all children suffering from this disorder display the same combination and severity of symptoms. However, given the fact that the condition appears to be easy to diagnose (it is defined largely in terms of observable behaviors) and that it can therefore easily be overdiagnosed, extreme caution should be exercised before applying the label to any child.

TREATMENT

The most common treatment for a child diagnosed as having an attention deficit disorder with hyperactivity involves the use of stimulant drugs such as dextroamphetamine (Dexadrine) and methylphenidate (Ritalin). This might seem strange, given that stimulants ordinarily increase activity and that the ADHD child already suffers from excessive activity. However, these drugs appear

---

t a b l e 10.8

DSM-III-R diagnostic criteria for attention-deficit hyperactivity disorder

A. A disturbance of at least six months duration during which at least eight of the following are present:

1. Often fidgets with hands or feet or squirms in seat (in adolescents, may be limited to subjective feelings of restlessness)

2. Has difficulty remaining seated when required to do so

3. Is easily distracted by extraneous stimuli

4. Has difficulty awaiting turn in games or group situations

5. Often blurts out answers to questions before they have been completed

6. Has difficulty following through on instructions from others (not due to oppositional behavior or failure of comprehension); for example, fails to finish chores

7. Has difficulty sustaining attention in tasks or play activities

8. Often shifts from one uncompleted activity to another

9. Has difficulty playing quietly

10. Often talks excessively

11. Often interrupts or intrudes on others; for example, butts into other children's games

12. Often does not seem to listen to what is being said to him or her

13. Often loses things necessary for tasks or activities at school or at home (such as toys, pencils, books, assignments)

14. Often engages in physically dangerous activities without considering possible consequences (not for the purpose of thrill seeking); for example, runs into street without looking

B. Onset before the age of 7.

C. Does not meet the criteria for a Pervasive Developmental Disorder.

Note: A criterion is considered to be met only if the behavior is considerably more frequent than that of most people of the same mental age. The items are listed in descending order of discriminating power based on data from a national field trial of the DSM-III-R criteria for Disruptive Behavior Disorders.
Source: Adapted from *Diagnostic and Statistical Manual of Mental Disorders* (3rd ed., revised) (pp. 53–54), 1987. Copyright © 1987 American Psychiatric Association. Reprinted with permission.

to have what is termed a *paradoxical effect* on children; that is, they appear to sedate rather than stimulate (Erickson, 1992). Considerable evidence suggests that they are effective in controlling problem behavior in many ADHD children. There is also tentative evidence that they increase the child's ability to focus (Tannock, Schachar, & Logan, 1993) and that they might be associated with preventing continued achievement declines in school (Weber, Frankenberger, & Heilman, 1992). But they can also have some side effects such as weight loss, growth retardation, and mood changes (Roche et al., 1979). Henker and Whalen (1989) note that the use of stimulants with hyperactive children is the most prevalent and controversial of child therapies.

CAUSES

The causes of ADHD are unclear, although research with twins indicates that it has a genetic component. If one member of a pair of identical twins is hyperactive, the other is much more likely to be (Willerman, 1973). In addition, between 80 and 90 percent more males than females are hyperactive, a fact that also supports the genetic hypothesis (Wesley & Wesley, 1977).

There is evidence that ADHD is to a large extent a maturational problem involving the central nervous system. Not only is the activity level of hyperactive children often similar to that typical for children aged 4 or 5 years, but many hyperactive children (though not all) seem to outgrow their symptoms after adolescence (Henker & Whalen, 1989).

Other explanations for hyperactivity have sometimes implicated neurological impairment or brain damage and dietary or vitamin-linked causes. However, the evidence for either of these causes is weak (Erickson, 1992). There is some evidence, however, that between 5 and 10 percent

of hyperactive children react badly to certain food dyes and that these children might therefore be helped through dietary means (Ross, 1980).

other behavior disorders

There are a number of sometimes serious behavior disorders of childhood and adolescence, not all of which can easily be classified. Many of these are problems of socialization manifested in aggressive, hostile, and essentially antisocial behavior—as in, for example, extreme noncompliance (labeled *oppositional defiant disorder* by the APA). Alternatively, conduct disorders might be evident in withdrawal, social isolation, or extreme shyness. Not surprisingly, aggressive and hostile behaviors (delinquency, vandalism, and so on) are likely to be dealt with (or at least punished); social isolation and extreme shyness are much more likely to be ignored.

Other social disorders may be seen in lying, stealing, inability to form close relationships with others, temper tantrums, disobedience and insolence, extremely negative self-concepts, and related behaviors and attitudes.

Anorexia nervosa is another disorder that might be classified as a conduct or behavior disorder. It involves drastic changes in eating habits leading to serious—sometimes fatal—weight loss. Because it affects adolescents far more often than any other age group, it is discussed in Chapter 11.

Treatment of children exhibiting conduct and personality disorders largely depends on the severity of the disturbance. In cases of moderate or mild disturbance, teachers and parents can often cope adequately; with the occasional help of professional personnel, they can sometimes do much more than cope. More severe disturbances may require therapeutic and sometimes judicial intervention.

stress in childhood

Many of the emotional and behavioral problems of childhood, and perhaps a number of the physical problems as well, are related to something we call stress—a difficult concept that everybody understands at least intuitively.

STRESS DEFINED

In the physical sciences, stress is a force that is exerted on a body, sometimes causing deformation or breakage. In psychology, **stress** is a nonphysical force that is exerted on an individual, sometimes causing negative change. Johnson (1986) suggests that there are two approaches to defining stress: One is concerned with stimuli; the other with responses. Stimuli are said to be stressful when they make excessive demands on the individual; responses are stressful when they are accompanied by the physiological changes of high arousal such as increased heart rate, perspiration, trembling, and so on.

THE EFFECTS OF STRESS

Lazarus (1993) classifies stress in terms of the severity of its effects. Thus there is *harm*, which implies actual damage; *threat*, which implies the possibility of damage; and *challenge*, which implies demands that can be met.

This classification recognizes that stress is clearly not always negative. Challenge, even threat, may lead to what are essentially adaptive physiological responses. In such cases, argues Selye (1974), stress prepares the individual for action. The sudden shot of adrenaline and the acceleration of heart rate when we are threatened or challenged increase the effectiveness of our running, our fighting, or our speech making.

But under other circumstances we may have an overload of stress and suffer *harm*. The implications of this overload vary from one individual to another but

are clearly not limited to adults. As we saw in Chapter 6, infants and preschoolers can suffer profound distress at the loss of a parent, or sometimes even as a result of temporary separation from a parent. The effects are sometimes apparent in sleeping or eating disturbances, or in a general listlessness sometimes bordering on depression (Field, 1987).

Among children, the effects of stress might include physical complaints (such as stomach pains, sometimes caused by ulcers; or asthma) or emotional problems (such as persistent fears, high anxiety, or even depression) (Johnson, 1986).

ASSESSING STRESS IN CHILDHOOD

Elkind (1981a) describes several sources of childhood stress, many of which are more common to this generation of children than they were to earlier generations. These sources of stress relate to *stimulus* or *demand* overloads. There is, for example, *responsibility overload*, in which young children whose parents work are made responsible for tasks such as looking after younger siblings, buying groceries, preparing meals, cleaning the house, and so on. There is *change overload*, in which children from mobile families are shunted rapidly from one community to another, transferred from school to school, and left with a sequence of caregivers. *Emotional overload* may result when children are exposed to emotion-laden situations that directly affect their lives, but over which they have little control (parents quarrelling, for example). Finally, there is *information overload* resulting largely from the tremendous amount of information to which television exposes the child. Add to all these potential sources of stress the sometimes exorbitant achievement demands that are placed on the child by school, parents, and society. "Hurry," they all say to Elkind's (1981a) hurried child. "Hurry! Grow up! There isn't much time!"

Clearly, not all children are exposed to the same stressful situations; nor will all react the same way. Some children remain unperturbed in the face of events that might prove disastrous for others. Nevertheless, psychology provides a number of ways of assessing stress in the lives of children, or at least of determining potential for stress. Many of these are based on the assumption that all major changes in a person's life are potentially stressful and that, although most individuals can cope with a limited number of changes, there eventually comes a breaking point. Accordingly, these stress scales simply ask individuals to identify all ma-

t able 10.9

*Stressful events in children's lives**

LIFE-CHANGE EVENT	POINTS	LIFE-CHANGE EVENT	POINTS
Parent dies	100	Older brother or sister leaves home	29
Parents divorce	73	Trouble with grandparents	29
Parents separate	65	Outstanding personal achievement	28
Parent travels as part of job	63	Move to another city	26
Close family member dies	63	Move to another part of town	26
Personal illness or injury	53	Receives or loses a pet	25
Parent remarries	50	Changes personal habits	24
Parent fired from job	47	Trouble with teacher	24
Parents reconcile	45	Change in hours with baby-sitter or at day-care center	20
Mother goes to work	45	Moves to a new house	20
Change in health of a family member	44	Changes schools	20
Mother becomes pregnant	40	Changes play habits	19
School difficulties	39	Vacations with family	19
Birth of a sibling	39	Changes friends	18
School readjustment (new teacher or class)	39	Attends summer camp	17
Change in family's financial condition	38	Changes sleeping habits	16
Injury or illness of a close friend	37	Change in number of family get-togethers	15
Starts a new (or changes) an extracurricular activity (music lessons, Brownies, and so forth)	36	Changes eating habits	15
Change in number of fights with siblings	35	Changes amount of TV viewing	13
Threatened by violence at school	31	Birthday party	12
Theft of personal possessions	30	Punished for not "telling the truth"	11
Changes responsibilities at home	29		

*If scores for a one-year period total ≤150, stress exposure is average; if between 150 and 300, there is a higher probability of stress-related symptoms; above 300, serious consequences are highly probable.
Source: From *The Hurried Child* (pp. 162–163) by David Elkind. © 1988. Reading, MA: Addison-Wesley Publishing Co., Inc. Adapted with permission of the publisher.

jor changes in their lives. Some changes are clearly more important than others (the death of a parent compared with changing schools, for example). Values are assigned accordingly. Table 10.9 (see p. 491) is one example of this approach for children. Holmes and Rahe (1967) present a similar scale for adults.

socioemotional giftedness

Here, as elsewhere, exceptionality has two dimensions: the disadvantaged, among whom are the autistic, the depressed, the hyperactive, and those exhibiting personality and conduct disorders; and the advantaged, to whom we have paid little special attention. Nevertheless, it is possible to identify two groups of gifted children. One group, variously labeled "superkids" or "invulnerables" (see Pines, 1975, 1979), has been identified in research originally designed to investigate psychiatric risk among children. One of the observations that intrigued researchers was that a significant number of children whose biological and environmental histories were such that the likelihood of emotional disorder was extremely high did not become psychological casualties. Quite the contrary: Not only did some of these children appear to be invulnerable to the emotional disorders that would surely claim a large number of other children in the same circumstances, but also they seemed to thrive on early adversity and to emerge unscathed and in some ways superior (Werner & Smith, 1982). Garmezy (1976) describes these invulnerables as exceptionally competent and at ease in social situations, highly capable in social interaction with adults, characterized by feelings of personal powerfulness (as opposed to helplessness or powerlessness), highly autonomous, and achievement-oriented.

The importance of understanding why some children survive and even thrive in high-risk situations and why others do not is related directly to the possibility of "inoculating" children against risk or of ameliorating risk for those who are most vulnerable. Anthony (1975) suggests, for example, that exposure to a certain amount of adversity may be crucial for the development of resistance to disturbance. At the same time, exposure to too many stresses may have just the opposite effect. It may be that there is a particular combination of personality characteristics or genetic predispositions that, in interaction with a stressful environment, produces a highly adjusted, healthy person. The critical problem is to identify this combination of characteristics and environment in an effort to maximize the development of human potential. The emphasis is dramatically different from that which focuses on identifying and treating disorders.

Exceptional social and emotional competence may be seen not only in those who survive high risk but also in exceptional individuals whose early lives and biological history present no unusual psychological threats. Walker (1978) suggests that among the socially gifted may well be found the leaders of tomorrow, and perhaps the leaders of today were yesterday's socially gifted children.

Should we not provide "special education" for the socially gifted?

main points

SOCIAL COGNITION

1. Social cognition refers to an awareness of ourselves and of others as being capable of feelings, motives, intentions. Even in infancy, children begin to de-

velop this awareness, manifested in their intuitive *theories of mind*. Selman describes five stages in children's ability to adopt the point of view of others (perspective-taking): *egocentric* (to age 6; don't realize there might be other views); *social-informational* (6–8; are aware of but don't understand other views); self-reflective (8–10; begin to infer other views); mutual (10–12; can switch perspectives); social and conventional (12–15+; can analyze perspectives in abstract terms).

SELF-WORTH

2. *Self-worth* refers to self-appraisal. Self-worth, said James, reflects the discrepancy between the individual's actual performance and ideal competence. Cooley believed we evaluate our selves on the basis of how we think others evaluate us (the *looking-glass self*). After the age of 8, children can assess their worth in general terms as well as in five areas: scholastic, athletic, physical appearance (most important in elementary grades), social acceptance, and morality. High self-worth is associated with happiness; low self-worth, with sadness and depression.

THE INFLUENCE OF FRIENDS AND PEERS

3. During the preschool period, children see friendship as simply a matter of playing together; later they realize friendships are enduring and reciprocal relationships based more on similarity, trust, and affection. Most children tend to have more than one "best friend," to want positive outcomes for their friends, but to compete with them at the same time. Girls have fewer but more intimate best friends.

4. A peer group is a group of equals. Social competence—reflected in children's ability to sense what is happening in social groups, in a high degree of responsiveness to others, and in an understanding that relationships develop slowly over time—is important for peer acceptance. Gottman's five categories of social status are: *sociometric stars* (especially well liked); *mixers* (high interaction); *teacher negatives* (conflict with teachers; some high status, others not); *tuned out* (uninvolved; ignored rather than rejected); and *sociometric rejectees* (not liked; rejected). Being accepted, and especially having friends, is important for happiness and adjustment.

THE ROLE OF THE SCHOOL

5. The school is a powerful socializing influence and also affects IQ and cognitive development. Teachers' expectations sometimes serve as self-fulfilling prophecies. Students' self-expectations and related *attributions* are also important. Some children are mastery-oriented (attribute outcomes to personal factors like intelligence or effort) and are encouraged by success but not overly discouraged by failure. Others are helpless (attribute outcomes to uncontrollable factors like luck or task difficulty) and tend not to change their estimates of their capabilities when presented with success. Attributions can sometimes be changed.

THE EFFECTS OF TELEVISION

6. Young children watch TV about one-third of their waking hours. Older children are more sensitive to motives, more attuned to why things happen and to the consequences of program events. There is some evi-

dence of at least a short-term relationship between television viewing and aggression—perhaps due as much to the activities it prevents or discourages (reading, socializing, developing hobbies) as to any direct influence. There are also fears that the anti-work, anti-family, pro-violence, pro-casual sex, anti-establishment messages of rock videos may have negative influences on children. Television can also have prosocial effects.

7. The influence of television may be due to *imitation* (observational learning); *attitude-change* (exposure to violence desensitizes); *catharsis* (viewing provides a release); or *cognitive information-processing* changes (children learn violence *schema*, fantasize them, and then retrieve relevant scripts when they are moved to aggression).

VIOLENCE IN THE FAMILY

8. Violence in the family reflects cultural values that condone physical punishment and family privacy. Punishment often does not work, emphasizes undesirable behavior, provides undesirable models, and may have emotional side effects. For dangerous, self-injurious behavior, it may be the only effective alternative. Reprimands, time-outs, and response-cost procedures do not have the same drawbacks as physical punishment.

9. Child abuse may be *physical abuse* (punching, kicking, beating), *physical neglect* (failure to provide food, clothing, shelter, health care), *emotional abuse* (habitual ridicule, scolding, ostracism), or *sexual abuse* (sexual behaviors forced upon the child). Any of these forms of abuse can have serious and long-lasting physical and psychological consequences.

10. Infants are more often abused than older children (more probable if the infant is premature, deformed, or irritable, or if the mother is overworked, often pregnant, or depressed). Nonwhites are overrepresented among this group in the United States. Abusers are sometimes disturbed in a clinical sense, although they often are not; many of those who abuse their children were themselves abused as children.

SOCIOEMOTIONAL EXCEPTIONALITY

11. Causes of behavior disorders may be genetic/congenital (chromosome abnormalities, maternal malnutrition or infections, birth injuries) or social/psychological (poverty, parental abuse, rejection, physical handicaps, ethnic discrimination, illnesses, trauma).

12. Attention-deficit hyperactivity disorder, is characterized by excessive activity and deficits in attention span without evidence of brain damage or neurological dysfunction (sometimes treated with stimulant drugs such as Ritalin). Other behavior disorders are sometimes seen in socialization problems; extreme defiance (oppositional defiance disorder); misbehaviors such as lying, stealing, delinquency, aggression; social withdrawal and excessive shyness; and eating disorders.

13. Stress can cause *harm*, or might simply pose a *threat* or a *challenge*. Among children, it can result from responsibility overload, change overload, emotional overload, school-related stress, and information overload. Scales that look at major life-change events sometimes identify the possibility of stress-related prob-

lems. Some children are more "in-vulnerable" than others to risk of emotional disorder.

focus questions: applications

- Are children as sensitive as adults to others' emotional states?
1. Pretend you're a 7 year old, and write down the most important details of your middle-childhood "theory of mind." Include in it your beliefs about how others think, imagine, feel, and so on.

- How many friends does the typical child have? How close and important are they?
2. Write a short essay recalling the role your "best" friend played in your life at some point in middle childhood.

- Does violence on television translate into violence on the street and in the home?
3. Using library resources, support what you think is the best conclusion to the following question: Does television violence cause violence in society?

- How prevalent is child physical, psychological, and sexual abuse?
4. Outline what you think should be done with respect to child abuse.

- What are some of the most problematic forms of socioemotional exceptionality for elementary school teachers?
5. Consult the latest revision of the *Diagnostic and Statistical Manual* of the American Psychological Association and review operational definitions for one or two childhood disorders, including ADHD.

study terms

social cognition 445
theory of mind 445
self-concept 448
self-esteem 448
peer group 455
sociometry 457
sociogram 457
attribution 463
mastery-oriented 463
learned helplessness 463
fairy tales 465
comic books 465
aggression 466
violence 466
reprimands 476
time-out 476
response-cost 476
sexual abuse 479
attention–deficit hyperactivity
   disorder 487
stress 490

further readings

The first of the following two books presents an intriguing account of children's development of intuitive theories of mind; the second looks at the development of social cognition:

Frye, D. & Moore, C. (Eds.). (1991). *Children's theories of mind: Mental states and social understanding.* Hillsdale, N.J.: Lawrence Erlbaum.

Selman, R. L. (1980). *The growth of interpersonal understanding.* New York: Academic Press.

A detailed analysis of the dimensions and importance of childhood friendships is:

Erwin, P. (1993). *Friendship and peer relations in children.* New York: John Wiley.

The powerful effects of social pressure are dramatized in Golding's fictional account of the lives of a group of school boys marooned on an island. Is fact stranger than fiction?

Golding, W. (1962). *Lord of the flies.* New York: Coward, McCann & Geoghegan.

A brief, simple, and useful analysis of child-rearing practices that contribute to child mal-treatment is:

Sabatino, D. A. (1991). *A fine line: When discipline becomes child abuse.* Blue Ridge Summit, Pa.: TAB Books.

The much-studied impact of television on the lives of children is reviewed in:

Gunter, B., & McAleer, J. L. (1990). *Children and television: The one-eyed monster?* New York: Routledge.

Evra, J. V. (1990). *Television and child de-velopment.* Hillsdale, N.J.: Lawrence Erlbaum.

Neuman, S. B. (1991). *Literacy in the tele-vision age: The myth of the TV effect.* Norwood, N.J.: Ablex.

The following books are useful sources of infor-mation on stress. The first is a detailed collec-tion of articles that look at the physiology of stress and its effects at all age levels: the second is a short book concerned specifically with the effects of major changes in the lives of children and adolescents.

Field, T. M., McCabe, P. M., & Schnei-derman, N. (Eds.). (1987). *Stress and coping.* Hillsdale, N.J.: Lawrence Erlbaum.

Johnson, J. H. (1986). *Life events as stres-sors in childhood and adolescence.* Beverly Hills, Calif.: Sage.

A clear but comprehensive look at childhood behavior disorders is presented in:

Erickson, M. T. (1992). *Behavior disorders of children and adolescents* (2nd ed.). En-glewood Cliffs, N.J.: Prentice Hall.

six

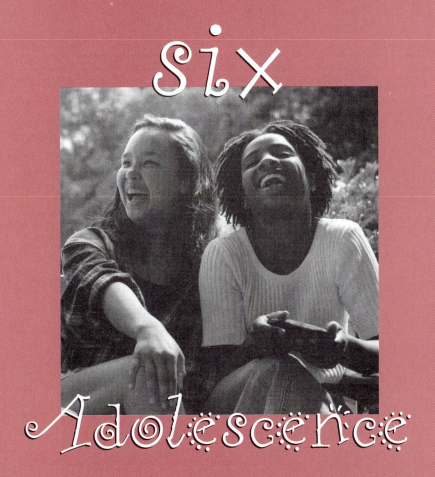

Adolescence

Life can only be understood backwards;
But it must be lived forwards.
Sören Kierkegaard, Life

*i*nfants do not look backward. They would see little, in any case, in the gloom from which they came.

Older children could look backward a short distance; but for most, the living of life fills the days too full to leave much time for peering into the past. Besides, in the cemented-in-reality stage of "concrete operations," the questions that drive us to seek the meaning of life don't suggest themselves.

But they do suggest themselves to adolescents. "What is the meaning of life?" they ask. "What ought?" "What should?" "Why?" That they now ask these questions reflects some of the changes that bridge the gulf between childhood and adulthood: physiological changes that lead to sexual maturity; intellectual changes that result in a more ideal logic; social changes that reflect new needs and sometimes new sources of conflict and turbulence. These are the changes we look at in the next two chapters.

Look backward to your own adolescence—if you have finished it. Try to remember what it was like. Looking backwards, Kierkegaard insists, is the way to understand life.

11

Physical and Cognitive Development in Adolescence

Miss Nancy Ellicot smoked
And danced all the modern dances;
And her aunts were not quite sure how they felt about it.
But they knew that it was modern.
Thomas Stearns Eliot, Cousin Nancy

focus questions

IS ADOLESCENCE A UNIVERSAL PSYCHOLOGICAL PHENOMENON, OR IS IT LARGELY CULTURAL?

WHAT ARE THE MOST IMPORTANT BIOLOGICAL CHANGES OF ADOLESCENCE?

WHAT ARE THE DEFINING CHARACTERISTICS OF ANOREXIA? OF BULIMIA?

HOW IS FORMAL OPERATIONS DIFFERENT FROM CONCRETE OPERATIONS?

IN WHAT WAYS ARE ADOLESCENTS EGOCENTRIC?

IS BEING GOOD OR BAD AN INESCAPABLE PART OF OUR PERSONALITIES?

outline

A PERIOD OF TRANSITIONS
Transitions in Preindustrial Societies
Transitions in Industrialized Societies

PHYSICAL CHANGES OF ADOLESCENCE
Puberty
Pubescence
Physical Changes
Early and Late Maturation
Physical Concerns of Adolescents

NUTRITION DURING ADOLESCENCE
Obesity
Anorexia Nervosa
Bulimia Nervosa

INTELLECTUAL DEVELOPMENT IN ADOLESCENCE
Piaget's View: Formal Operations
An Information-Processing View

ADOLESCENT EGOCENTRISM
The Imaginary Audience
The Personal Fable
Reckless Behavior

MORAL DEVELOPMENT IN ADOLESCENCE
Behaving Morally
Morality as an Understanding of Justice
Piaget's Approach to Morality
Kohlberg's Stages of Morality
The Generality of Kohlberg's Stages
Gilligan's Approach: Gender Differences in Morality
Implications of Research on Moral Development

MAIN POINTS

FOCUS QUESTIONS: APPLICATIONS

STUDY TERMS

FURTHER READINGS

H ere is another true story. One night after I had been working for my uncle for most of the summer, my father brought our parish priest, Father Paradis, to see me. They come out into the black dirt of my uncle's field where I had been working all day, pulling the cultivator back and forth with the ancient, knock-kneed John Deere. When I saw my father and the priest standing in the newly turned dirt, I shut off the tractor. And in the painful silence that followed, I wished for a moment that I had pretended not to see them, that I had continued, "chug … chug … chuck a chuck …" down the field.

Father Paradis stopped in front of me, shuffling his foot absently in the dust, as if uncertain where to begin. My dad beat him to it.

"You know why we're here?" It was more statement than question.

"No, I said, trying to smile while I scrambled for something clever and disarming to say.

"What is your … How … What kind of explanation …" I couldn't be certain whether it was anger, humiliation, or great disappointment that made my father struggle so with his questions.

"Let me …" the priest offered, sweeping his left arm out in the terrible gesture that always punctuated his sermons on the Great Sins. "Maybe he can just confess quietly and you can take him away from temptation."

"Confess?" I blurted.

"Maybe he doesn't know!" the priest said.

"Know what?"

"Why your uncle's fired you?" my dad said, his tone sounding both angry and embarrassed.

"Fired?" I said. My uncle liked me! How could he possibly fire me?

"Fired," the priest said.

"Fired," my dad echoed.

"Fired?" I said again.

"Fired. You know why. You and Syl ... You and Sylvia."

"We never did anything! Nothing!"

"Perhaps a short confession," Father Paradis offered.

"There's nothing to confess," I insisted. My father looked terribly discouraged.

"Your uncle saw you," he said. "He's seen you talking and how you always sit next to each other and ... Well, she's your cousin."

"Your cousin," Father Paradis repeated. "Dangerous. A mortal sin," he added by way of explanation.

"So he thought it would be better if you left now before you ... you know. And I brought Father Paradis in case you ... well ..."

"I didn't. I don't."

"A confession ..." Father Paradis seemed disappointed. "Just take a minute. Right here. Get it over with right now."

"But I never," I insisted.

"Well, maybe ... did you think about it?" the priest suggested helpfully. "Were you tempted? That's where it starts."

"And she's your cousin, too," my father added significantly. "And neither of you is even grown up yet!"

a period of transitions

Would it have been different if I had been grown up? Should I have confessed?

Maybe I *was* grown up and my dad and the priest didn't know it yet. Or was I still in transition—in adolescence?

Simply defined, **adolescence** is the transition between childhood and adulthood, the period during which children have achieved sexual maturity but have not yet taken on the roles and responsibilities—or the rights—that accompany full adult status.

In contemporary industrialized countries, adolescence is easily defined, say Schlegel and Barry (1991): It spans the period of the teen years. But in preindustrial societies, it is not always clear that the period even exists.

transitions in preindustrial societies

In many preindustrial societies, passage from childhood to adulthood is clearly marked by ritual and ceremony, collectively termed **rites of passage**. Interestingly, even in totally unrelated societies, these rites often share some common features evident in the four typical steps of the process. First, the children are separated from the group. Among some tribes (the Navahos and Pueblos, for instance) young boys are sent to live in buildings constructed for this purpose (Cohen, 1964). A common **taboo** (socially forbidden behavior) during this period is that of brother-sister or mother-son contact.

Second, children are trained in the behaviors expected of adults—and the sorts of childish behaviors adults are expected to leave behind.

The third step is that of the *initiation* itself: the actual rituals that mark passage from childhood to adulthood. They are a time of celebration, but they are also usually a time of pain and suffering. Thus, many initiation ceremonies include one or more of the following: fasting, scarification (the inflicting of wounds with resulting scars), and circumcision (Bloch & Niederhoffer, 1958).

The final step of the passage rite is *induction* (absorption into the tribe). Inductees now know, without any doubt, that they are full-fledged, adult members of their social group.

Rites of passage serve a number of useful functions. They impart a sense of adult responsibility to children, and they lessen the ambiguity that might otherwise exist concerning the transition between childhood and adulthood. In addition, many primitive rites reinforce certain important taboos, such as those having to do with incest. Bloch and Niederhoffer (1958) suggest this may be the main reason for separating boys and girls, as well as parents and their opposite-sex children, before initiation.

Another important function of a passage rite is that it creates a strong psychological bond between the initiate and the tribe, and among initiates as well. At the same time it helps to weaken bonds that might otherwise exist between the child and the immediate family. It is as though initiates are being told that they belong to the tribe and not the family, that they can look to the tribe for support and strength, but that they must also defend and protect it. (See "In Other Contexts: Byoto's Superincision.")

transitions in industrialized societies

These "primitive" societies have no adolescence as we commonly know it. There is only childhood, the passage, and adulthood.

We, on the other hand, have no rites of passage. Our young ones are exempted from the separation, the training, the initiation, and the induction. Instead, they are put through a period labeled adolescence, a period of life sometimes described as the most troubled, the most stressful, and the most difficult of all stages of development. The individual most responsible for this description of adolescence is G. Stanley Hall (1916), who believed that all adolescents go through a period marked primarily by *Sturm und Drang* (storm and stress). He believed that because this period of upheaval and turmoil is biologically based, it is therefore largely inevitable, and that it must also be common to all cultures. We now know that this view is fundamentally incorrect and misleading, that adolescence is not tumultuous for the majority of adolescents—although it is for some (Petersen, 1988).

In contemporary Western cultures there are no formal rites of passage (excluding perhaps the Bar or Bat Mitzvah, in which Jewish boys or girls become adults at the age of 13 through a religious ceremony, and the "coming-out" or debutant party in certain social groups). No one tells the child, "Today you are an adult, although yesterday you were a child." Our "rites" of passage are less definite, more confusing. They vary from one place to another and from one decade to the next. They might include, among other things, getting a driver's license, being old enough to vote or to drink, losing virginity, beginning work, growing (or trying to grow) a mustache, starting to date, graduating from high school, and so on. These events can span a wide range of ages, and none of them alone is certain evidence that adulthood has been reached.

There are writers who claim that secondary schools now serve as *rites de pas-*

Byoto struggled not to cry out; it would have embarrassed him. He knew that in the olden days—even in the days of the uncle, the tuatina who was about to cut into his penis—it had been common for boys to cry out when it happened to them. In those days, the tuatina used shells and often they had to slash many times before the cutting was done. Now the uncle had a razor and, unless he were terribly unlucky, there would only be a single slash.

Preparations had begun many days earlier. The first indication that he would be made a man had come the night the men took him on the mataki ramanga, the torch-fishing expedition, even though all he had been allowed to do was to paddle.

In the days that followed, he had been invited to visit all the houses and villages of his relatives. And in each, his body had been smeared with tumeric mixed with coconut oil. All the other boys his age, those who were to become men with him, had also walked about the village smeared with tumeric, as though covered with the fresh blood of many wounds—a sign of the bloodletting yet to come. Meanwhile, huge mounds of coconuts, bananas, taro, and breadfruit had been piled in front of his parents' house in preparation for the feasting, and his relatives had written new songs and rehearsed old ones that would be sung in his

honor. And yesterday both the men and women had taken nets out in the boats and filled many baskets with fish. All the mats had been made, the gifts prepared.

But first the razor. Byoto stood rigid with fear, held tightly by the tangata me, the man who would cover his eyes just before the superincision. The entire village, all his relatives and all the other boys' relatives, had assembled. Throughout the morning, each group had taken turns moaning and scratching at their faces or even nicking them with knives so that, as Byoto stared wildly around, he saw nothing but bloodied faces and saddened eyes. Suddenly, the tangata me covered Byoto's eyes, as Byoto knew he would. He felt his foreskin being drawn forward by the tuatina; involuntarily, his penis withdrew, but the tuatina pulled it firmly, laid the razor on the top of the foreskin, about two inches from the tip, and slashed straight through to the end. . . .

"Aaaaargh! . . ."

To Think About: What purposes might be served by a ritual such as that among Byoto's people? How universally valid do you think our conceptions of adolescence are?

*Based in part on an account of rituals among the Tikopian, a Polynesian culture living on islands southeast of Taiwan, given by Fried, M. N., & Fried, M. H. (1980). Four rituals in eight cultures. New York: W. W. Norton.

sage very similar to the traditional rites of many nonindustrialized societies. They have all the same characteristics, Fasick (1988) claims. They exemplify *separation* (children are segregated into schools) and *training* (adolescents are formally socialized for the responsibilities of adult life); and there is something like *initiation* and *induction* in the high school graduation ceremony. Fasick suggests that this ceremony is almost universal for much of the middle and working class; for many adolescents it clearly marks passage from the world of childhood to a world of adult responsibilities.

In general, however, our society is *continuous* rather than *discontinuous*; it does not clearly demarcate passage from one stage to the next. Accordingly, there is no easy way to determine the end of adolescence, but its beginnings are somewhat more definite.

physical changes of adolescence

Although adolescence as a *psychological* phenomenon does not appear to be universal, clear, predictable biological change is the one universal feature of adolescence in all cultures (Montemayor & Flannery, 1990). Biologically, adolescence is the period from the onset of puberty to adulthood. **Puberty** signifies sexual maturity; **pubescence** refers to the changes that result in sexual maturity. These changes occur in late childhood or early adolescence and terminate with adulthood. Adulthood cannot easily be defined but may arbitrarily be considered to begin at the age of 20. It would be convenient to say that adolescence begins at 12, because we have included the earlier ages in preceding developmental periods. But the beginning of adolescence is variable, and age 12 is simply an approximation.

puberty

Puberty defines sexual maturity, the ability to make babies. As Jersild (1963) has observed, before puberty individuals are children; afterward they can have children. The problem is that it is almost impossible to determine exactly when a person becomes fertile. Past research has relied on information about girls' first menstrual period (**menarche**) to discover the age at which puberty begins. Actually, however, a girl is frequently in-

In Western cultures, the age of menarche dropped from around 17 one hundred or so years ago, to about 12 today. It remains much higher in most less-developed countries, which suggests that improved health care, nutrition, and living conditions may be part of the explanation for this secular trend. One of the results of delayed sexual maturation is that childrearing begins somewhat later than it otherwise might.

fertile for about a year after her first menstruation, so that the menarche is not an accurate index of puberty (Tanner, 1970); nevertheless, it is a useful indication of impending sexual maturity (Malina, 1990).

It is almost impossible to arrive at a clear index of sexual maturity for boys, although first ejaculation (**spermarche**) is sometimes taken as a sign comparable to menarche. However, the probability that a boy can become a father immediately after first ejaculation is low, although not zero. The reason for this is that the concentration of sperm in the semen remains very low for the first year or so.

AGE AT PUBERTY

The average age for puberty in North America is about 12 for girls and 14 for boys, which is immediately following the period of most rapid growth (the growth spurt). Consequently, age at puberty may be established by determining the period during which the person grew rapidly. The period of rapid growth may begin as young as 8.7 years for girls compared with 10.3 years for boys (Malina, 1990). However, there is a wide age range. Some girls may not reach sexual maturity until age 16; some boys, not until age 18 (Tanner, 1975).

THE SECULAR TREND

Age of menarche in Western cultures, claims Tanner (1955), has dropped from an average close to 17 to an average closer to 12 in the past 100 or so years. That is a drop of as much as one-third to one-half year per decade since 1850. In addition, adolescents are often taller and heavier than they were several generations ago. This trend is labeled the **secular trend**.

There is evidence that the secular trend has slowed or stopped in most de-veloped countries (Frisch & Revelle, 1970). And there is also evidence that it was perhaps not as dramatic as Tanner assumed. Bullough (1981) reports that Tanner based his estimate of the age of menarche in 1850 on a single source, and that a more accurate figure would have been closer to 14.

Reasons for the secular trend are unknown. However, it is not evident in a number of less developed parts of the world. For example, in New Guinea, menarche still occurs at ages ranging from an average of 15.5 to 18.4 years (Eveleth & Tanner, 1976). Similarly, among a large sample of Nigerian boys, spermarche occurred at an average age of 14.3 (Adegoke, 1993); average age of spermarche in North America in a similar study was 12.4 (Gaddis & Brooks-Gunn, 1985). These observations, coupled with the fact that the secular trend seems to be a phenomenon of the last century or so, suggests that improved health care, improved nutrition, and generally improved living conditions may be part of the explanation (Chumlea, 1982).

---

pubescence

Pubescence refers to all the changes that lead to sexual maturity. These changes, which are universal, are linked to a dramatic increase in hormones (Inoff-Germain et al., 1988). Most signs of pubescence are well known. Among the first in both boys and girls is the appearance of pigmented pubic hair, which is straight initially but becomes characteristically kinky during the later stages of pubescence. At about the same time as pubic hair begins to appear, boys' testes begin to enlarge, as do girls' breasts. Girls then experience rapid physical growth, the first menstrual period, the growth of axillary (armpit) hair, the continued enlargement of the breasts, and a slight lowering of the voice. Boys' voices change much more dramatically; boys too grow rapidly, particularly in height and length of limbs; they acquire the capacity to ejaculate semen; they grow axillary hair and eventually develop a beard.

The changes of pubescence that relate directly to the production of offspring involve **primary sexual characteristics**. These include changes in the ovaries (organs that produce ova in the girl) and the testes (organs that produce sperm in the boy) so that these organs are now capable of producing mature ova and sperm.

Changes that accompany the maturation of the sex organs but that are not directly related to reproduction are said to involve **secondary sexual characteristics**. The appearance of facial hair in the boy and the development of breasts in the girl, voice changes, and the growth of

axillary and pubic hair are all secondary sexual characteristics.

Although the ages at which primary and secondary sexual characteristics develop vary a great deal, the sequence of their appearance is more predictable, though not entirely fixed. Tables 11.1 and 11.2 summarize that sequence.

physical changes

Adolescence is a period of significant physical change.

HEIGHT AND WEIGHT

The rapid changes in height and weight characteristic of pubescence begin before the age of 12 and are charted in Figures 9.1 and 9.2 (on page 394). Figures 11.1 and 11.2 contain average height and weight data for boys and girls ages 12

table 11.1

Normal sequence of sexual maturation for North American girls

SEQUENCE	PHYSIOLOGICAL EVENT
1	Beginning of adolescent growth spurt
2	Appearance of unpigmented pubic down
3	Breast elevation ("bud" stage)
4	Appearance of pigmented, kinky pubic hair
5	Increase in size of vagina, clitoris, and uterus
6	Decline in rate of physical growth
7	Menarche
8	Development of axillary (armpit) hair; continued enlargement of breasts; slight lowering of the voice
9	Increase in production of oil; increased perspiration; possible acne

Note: The first of these changes may occur as young as age 7¼; the last may not be completed before age 16. Menarche generally occurs between ages 11 and 13.

table 11.2

Normal sequence of sexual maturation for North American boys

SEQUENCE	PHYSIOLOGICAL EVENT
1	Appearance of unpigmented public down; growth of testes and scrotum (sac containing testes)
2	Beginning of adolescent growth spurt
3	Enlargement of penis
4	Appearance of pigmented, kinky pubic hair
5	Lowering of voice; appearance of "down" on upper lip
6	First ejaculations occur
7	Decline in rate of physical growth
8	Development of axillary (armpit) hair; growth of facial hair
9	Increase in production of oil; increased perspiration; possible acne
10	Growth of chest hair

Note: The first of these changes may occur as young as age 9½; the last may not be completed before age 18. First ejaculation generally occurs between ages 12 and 14.

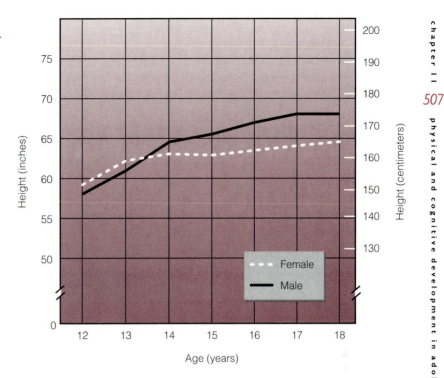

figure 11.1

Height at 50th percentile for U.S. children.
Source: *Health Department, Milwaukee, Wisconsin; based on data by H. C. Stuart and H. V. Meredith, prepared for use in Children's Medical Center, Boston. Used by permission of the Milwaukee Health Department.*

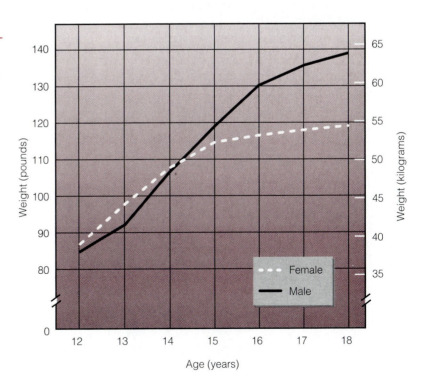

figure 11.2

Weight at 50th percentile for U.S. children.
Source: *Health Department, Milwaukee, Wisconsin; based on data by H. C. Stuart and H. V. Meredith, prepared for use in Children's Medical Center, Boston. Used by permission of the Milwaukee Health Department.*

to 18. On average, by the age of 11½ girls surpass boys in height and maintain a slight advantage until 13½. Girls outweigh boys at approximately 11, but by 14½ boys catch up to and surpass girls.

An additional physical change, of particular significance to boys, is a rapid increase in the length of limbs. As a result, many boys acquire the gangling appearance often associated with early adolescence, exaggerated by the fact that their rate of clothes purchasing often lags considerably behind the rate at which they outgrow them.

BODY COMPOSITION

The body composition of boys and girls is different throughout childhood, with boys having relatively more of what is termed *fat-free mass* and less *fat mass*; the two, taken together, determine body weight (Malina & Bouchard, 1988). During the adolescent growth spurt, boys' proportion of fat decreases even more because fat-free mass grows at a faster rate than does fat mass. This is not the case for girls, however, so that average sex differences in proportion of body weight due to fat mass are magnified.

STRENGTH AND MOTOR PERFORMANCE

Changes in muscular strength, aerobic performance, and motor capacity also reflect the physical growth spurt, especially in boys. As a result, sex differences in many aspects of motor performance increase in favor of males (Beunen & Malina, 1988). This is especially evident in competitive athletics, in which male records almost invariably surpass those of girls.

early and late maturation

The "average adolescent," whose growth is depicted in Figures 11.1 and 11.2, is no more real than the "average child"; both are abstractions, inventions designed to bring some semblance of order to our understanding of a very complex subject. Hence, although the "average adolescent" matures at about 12 or 14 depending on sex, some mature considerably earlier and some considerably later. Given that maturity tends to be judged in terms of physical appearance, the age at which the physical changes of adolescence take place are very important to children.

The adolescent growth spurt among boys results in dramatic changes in muscular strength and motor capacity—and, frequently, corresponding changes in their interests and responsibilities. Changes in motor performance are not as dramatic for girls, and are reflected in greater male-female differences in motor performance after adolescence.

EFFECTS FOR BOYS

In general, early-maturing boys suffer fewer psychological problems than those who mature later, probably largely because they often excel in activities and abilities that are highly prized in the adolescent peer culture. Not only are they larger and stronger and therefore more likely to be better athletes, but they are also more socially mature and hence are more likely to lead in heterosexual activities.

Detailed longitudinal studies of early and late maturation in boys have provided consistent findings (Jones, 1957, 1965; Crockett & Petersen, 1987). Early-maturing boys are typically better adjusted, more popular, more confident, more aggressive, and more successful in heterosexual relationships. In addition, they appear to have more positive self-concepts (about which more is said in Chapter 12). In contrast, adolescent boys who mature later than average are, as a group, more restless, more attention-seeking, less confident, and have less positive self-concepts.

Note that the apparent advantages of early maturation among boys are most evident *during* adolescence and apply mainly to social areas (adjustment, popularity, and leadership). In later life the advantages of early maturation are not nearly so apparent (Clausen, 1975; Peskin, 1973).

EFFECTS FOR GIRLS

Findings are somewhat more inconsistent for girls. However, a number of studies indicate that early-maturing girls are initially at a disadvantage, a finding that directly contradicts the results of similar studies conducted with boys (Siegel, 1982). Stattin and Magnusson (1990) found higher incidence of sexually precocious behavior and violations of social norms among early-maturing girls. Similarly, Simmons and Blyth (1987) report more conduct problems in school and lower academic success among early maturers. In later adolescence, however, these disadvantages have often disappeared. Thus it appears that the effects of early and late maturation in girls depends on their ages. Early maturation is a disadvantage in the very early grades, when most girls have not yet begun to mature and when the early-maturing girl is likely to find herself excluded from peer-group activities. Also, given the fact also that girls are on the average two years in advance of boys in physical maturation, the early-maturing girl may well be four or more years in advance of like-aged boys—which might not contribute positively to her social life. At a later age, however, when most of her age-grade mates have also begun to mature, the early-maturing girl may suddenly find herself in a more advantageous position. Her greater maturity is now something to be admired.

AN ECOLOGICAL INTERPRETATION

As Petersen (1988) notes, pubertal change is most stressful when it puts adolescents out of step with peers, especially if the change is not interpreted as desirable. And the consequences of maturational timing are most clearly understood in terms of their effects on relationships and interactions that are important to adolescents. Thus, early maturation may enhance peer relations for boys but is less likely to do so for girls. Furthermore, evidence suggests that relations with parents are better for early-maturing boys and for late-maturing girls (Savin-Williams & Small, 1986).

From an ecological perspective, what we know of the implications of maturational timetables presents an excellent example of the child's characteristics interacting with each other (specifically, degree of sexual maturity interacting with age) to determine important elements of the child's ecology (namely, the nature of interaction with parents and peers). But we should note that the child's ecology is individualistic, that every child-other interaction creates a unique microsystem. Thus although there may be some general advantages or disadvantages associated with the timing of pubescence, there are many individual exceptions to our generalizations. Not all early-maturing boys and girls are characterized by the same advantages or disadvantages of early maturation; nor are all those who mature later affected in the same way.

table 11.3

t a b l e   1 1 . 3

Personal concerns of contemporary adolescents

CONCERN	PERCENTAGE INDICATING "A GREAT DEAL" OR "QUITE A BIT" OF CONCERN
What am I going to do when I finish school?	68
Finances	54
School concerns	50
Time (not enough time to do the things I want)	48
Appearance	44
What is the purpose of life?	44
Boredom	43
Height or weight	43
Loneliness	35
Feelings of inferiority (poor self-image)	29
Sex	28
Parents' marriage	20

Source: Adapted from Bibby, R. W., & Posterski, D. C. (1985). *The emerging generation: An inside look at Canada's teenagers*, Table 4.1, p. 60. Toronto: Irwin Publishing. Reprinted with permission of Stoddart Publishing Co., Ltd.

physical concerns of adolescents

Frazier and Lisonbee (1950) asked tenth-grade adolescents to list the problems that concerned them and the degree to which they were worried about each. Items most frequently listed as the greatest worry for boys included the presence of blackheads or pimples, irregular teeth, oily skin, glasses, and other slight physical abnormalities such as noses that were too thin or too long, skin that was too dark, heavy lips, protruding chins, and so on.

Girls, like boys, were most concerned about the presence of blackheads or pimples ("zits"). In addition, they were particularly concerned about freckles. Scars, birthmarks, and moles were also a source of worry, as were the dangers of being too homely, having oily skin, and wearing glasses.

Physical concerns of today's adolescents have changed little. In a survey of 3,600 Canadian adolescents from 150 different schools, almost half indicated that their physical appearance is a matter of considerable concern, and almost the same proportion were worried about their height or weight (Bibby & Posterski, 1985). In this survey, the adolescent's greatest worry concerned life beyond graduation—"What am I going to do after high school?"—a problem that affected approximately two-thirds of all respondents. Other important concerns had to do with such things as money, achievement in school, boredom, loneliness, and the parents' marriage (see Table 11.3).

CONCERNS ABOUT MENARCHE AND SPERMARCHE

Interestingly, adolescents' worries about physical changes typically do not include concerns about menarche or spermarche, especially if they are prepared for the event. Gaddis and Brooks-Gunn (1985) interviewed 13 young adolescent boys and found that of the 11 who had experienced ejaculation, most had strong positive feelings about the event and none had been upset or ashamed. However, two of the boys had been unprepared for the event (usually nocturnal upon first occurrence, and referred to as a "wet dream") and had been frightened.

In a replication of Gaddis and Brooks-Gunn's study in Nigeria, Adegoke (1993) surveyed 188 boys and found that an overwhelming majority felt positively about spermarche. They described their feelings as "happy" and "proud" and only occasionally as "scared." Although 60 percent of the boys in this sample had not been prepared beforehand for the event, there was no difference in the reactions of prepared and unprepared boys.

Girls' recollections of their menarche are often not as positive, perhaps because of the lingering remnants of cultural attitudes that led to menstruation being labeled "the curse" (Morrison et al., 1980). However, menstruation is not a source of worry for most girls.

The adolescent's concern with the body is to be expected given the importance of physical appearance to psychological adjustment—an importance related not only to the role that appearance plays in peer acceptance but also to the way perception of the body affects self-concept. In fact, physical appearance is one of the most important influences on adolescents' self-worth (Harter, 1990). Accordingly, it is not surprising that the preferred body type for adolescent males is athletic—neither obese nor thin (Lerner & Korn, 1972). Nor is it surprising to find that the desire of some young adolescent girls to be slim is sometimes so overwhelming that it can be reflected in serious eating disorders.

nutrition during adolescence

Most adolescents, especially if they are very active physically, expend a large number of calories each day. In addition, during the rapid skeletal and muscular growth of pubescence—the growth spurt—their bodies require a high intake of protein and minerals, and especially of calcium, for normal growth. Calcium deficiencies, especially in women, sometimes become apparent in later life in the form of *osteoporosis* (a thinning and weakening of the bones). So we should not be alarmed to see our adolescents consuming great mounds of hamburgers, devouring bowls of spinach and lentils and wonderful lettuces, and drinking gallons of milk.

But we should be concerned if they eat snacks of mostly empty calories and sugar-laden drinks, or if they eat too little of anything at all, or if they eat only in binges—because any of these might be a sign of a serious problem.

obesity

As we saw in Chapter 9, obesity is the most common nutritional problem among North American children. Unfortunately, obese children often grow up to be obese adolescents; and they, in turn, have a high probability of growing up to be obese adults. Not surprisingly, obesity is also the most common nutritional problem among adolescents, affecting up to one-quarter of all North American teenagers (Whitney & Hamilton, 1984).

The consequences of obesity are serious and far-reaching, which is not surprising given that physical appearance is probably the most important influence on the adolescent's self-worth (Harter, 1990). In addition to its negative effects on health, obesity contributes to rejec-

The rapid physical and hormonal changes of adolescence—sometimes reflected in skin eruptions, changing body shape, obesity, awkwardness, or the wearing of glasses—are occasionally sources of concern for adolescents. Often, however, these changes are sources of pride and of increasing feelings of worth.

tion by peers, to negative peer interactions, to low self-esteem, and to unhappiness (Baum & Forehand, 1984). It is also associated with poorer performance in school, although it isn't clear whether this is because obese adolescents are subject to discrimination, because they are expected to do less well, because they avoid participation, because teachers involve them less, because they lack self-esteem or independence, or for other reasons (Morrill et al., 1991).

At a superficial level, the causes and cures of obesity seem simple. Other than for rare glandular and metabolic problems, and in spite of genetic contributions, obesity in adolescents—and in others—is caused by taking in more calories than are expended. Weight reduction can therefore be achieved by consuming fewer calories and by expending more.

Unfortunately, the problem is not so simple. Its alleviation requires nutritional information that not all adolescents have or are interested enough to accept; and it requires that adolescents change habits that are not only self-rewarding, but that also are encouraged by the media and consequently extraordinarily persistent. As a result, obesity continues to be a very significant North American problem, and its alleviation a major industry.

Strangely, in spite of the prevalence of obesity, contemporary Western societies place tremendous emphasis on physical attractiveness which, especially among girls, is clearly defined as *thin*.

anorexia nervosa

Karen Carpenter, a well-known pop singer of the 1970s, died at the age of 32. Cause of death: heart failure due to a chemical imbalance that, in turn, was probably related to a medical condition for which the singer had been undergoing treatment. The medical condition? Anorexia nervosa.

DEFINITION

Translated literally, **anorexia nervosa** means loss of appetite as a result of nerves. It describes a complex and only partly understood condition that may be increasing in frequency. Anorexia is defined medically as involving a loss of at least 15 to 25 percent of "ideal" body weight, this loss not being due to any detectable illness. The American Psychiatric Association's (1987) definition includes intense fear of gaining weight, distortion of body image, and significant weight loss as criteria (Wilson & Walsh, 1991).

Anorexia nervosa almost always begins with a deliberate desire to be thin and consequent dieting, and it ends in a condition in which the patient seems unwilling or unable to eat normally. Many affected females cease menstruating relatively early following initial dieting, and many become excessively active and continue to engage in strenuous exercise programs even after their physical conditions have deteriorated significantly. In the absence of medical intervention, anorexia nervosa is sometimes fatal. Baker and Lyen (1982) report that estimates of anorexia-related death range from 0 to 19 percent.

PREVALENCE

Estimates of the prevalence of anorexia vary considerably depending on the criteria used. Pope and associates (1984) conducted a survey of 544 female college and secondary school students and found that the proportion that could be described as anorexic was somewhere between 1 and 4.2 percent, depending on the definitions used. Similarly, using very strict criteria for diagnosis of anorexia, Crisp, Palmer, and Kalucy (1976) found that 1 percent of the girls in nine London schools were *severely* anorexic.

When estimates of anorexia are based on eating attitudes and habits, estimates are much higher. For example, in a study of 191 athletes, Stoutjesdyk and Jevne (1993) found that 10.6 percent of the females and 4.6 percent of the males scored in the "anorexic" range on a test of eating attitudes. Similarly, in a study of more than 1,250 adolescents ages 13 to 19, Lachenmeyer and Muni-Brander (1988) found that a full 13 percent of the girls reported significantly restricting their diets and scored very high on measures of eating attitudes and behaviors linked with

Among the American Psychiatric Association's criteria for anorexia nervosa are significant weight loss, an intense fear of gaining weight, and distortion of body image. Many very thin anorexic women consistently overestimate their body size.

anorexia. Although not every one of these "restricters" meets strict criteria for a diagnosis of anorexia, each is at risk (see Figure 11.3 in "At A Glance: Eating Disorders Among Adolescents").

Although anorexia continues to be far more common among girls than boys, there are indications that eating disorders are now much more frequent among adolescent boys than had previously been suspected. Significantly, in the Lachenmeyer and Muni-Brander survey, 6.3 percent of the males in a lower-socioeconomic (SES) sample (primarily black and Hispanic students) and 3.4 percent of a higher-SES sample (primarily white) were also "restricters." These rates for males are much higher than have traditionally been reported.

n investigation by Penner, Thompson, and Coovert (1991) indicates that very thin, anorexic women consistently over-estimate their body size, whereas average-size, nonanorexic women do not. Anorexia, severely restricted eat-ing, is just one of the eating disorders that relates to our current cultural em-phasis on being thin. Bulimia—alternat-ing food binges with severe dieting and self-induced vomiting and diarrhea—is perhaps three or four times more com-mon than anorexia (Figure 11.3).

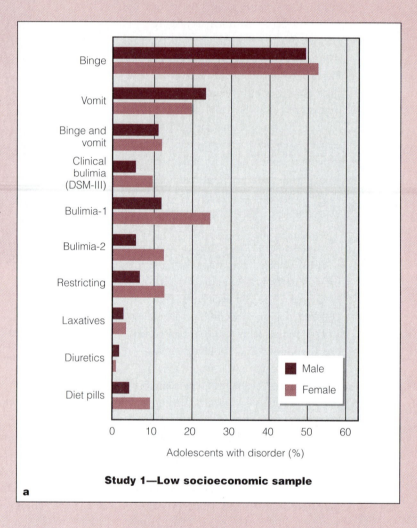

Study 1—Low socioeconomic sample

a

CAUSES

The causes of anorexia nervosa are neither simple nor well understood. As Walsh (1982) notes: "In anorexia nervosa, there are multiple psychological, behav-ioral, and physiological aberrations, suggesting that the central regulatory mechanisms which govern an individual's emotional and physical equilibrium are grossly disturbed" (p. 85). Although there is some evidence of endocrine imbal-ances in anorexia (Walsh, 1982), as well as some indication that the disease may be genetically linked (Holland et al., 1984), the condition is thought to be primarily psychological.

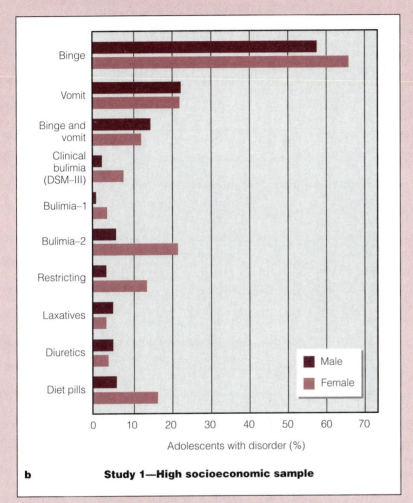

f **i g u r e** **1 1 . 3**

Prevalence rates for eating disorders among adolescents. (a) The low-socioeconomic sample consisted of 328 females and 384 males; (b) the high-socioeconomic sample consisted of 314 females and 235 males. Note that clinical bulimics meet all DSM-III criteria for bulimia; Bulimia-1 individuals meet all criteria except one; and Bulimia-2 individuals meet all criteria except two. Source: Data from Lachenmeyer and Muni-Brander (1988).

Some speculate that anorexic individuals typically do not feel that they are in control of their lives but discover that they can control their body weight; in the end, control becomes an obsession.

Others suggest that lack of positive self-image coupled with the emphasis that society places on thinness (particularly among females) may be manifested in anorexia in people who attempt to obtain parental and societal approval by dieting.

Another hypothesis argues that physical activity may be implicated in as many as 38 to 75 percent of all cases of anorexia (Epling, Pierce, & Stefan, 1983). One of the common observations about anorexics is that many of them continue to engage in strenuous physical activity even after they have become grossly emaciated. In this connection, it is interesting to note that mice and rats who are exposed to restricted feeding (unlimited food, but only for 60 minutes per day) and unlimited exercise (free access to a "running wheel") will sometimes starve themselves to death (Epling, Pierce, & Stefan, 1983). It seems that it is possible to develop something like anorexia among these animals through exercise and dieting. However, when rats and mice are exposed only to the diet (60 minutes per day of food access) but not to the exercise wheel, their body weight stabilizes and is maintained.

Are some anorexics like these rats? Epling and associates suggest that yes, at least part of the time anorexia is related to activity. They cite evidence that indicates that under some circumstances humans, like rats, eat less when they exercise.

TREATMENT

Anorexia nervosa is a particularly frightening and baffling condition for parents. It is frightening because it can be fatal, and it is baffling and frustrating because it may seem to parents that the anorexic adolescent deliberately and totally unreasonably refuses to eat. And neither pleas nor threats are likely to work. What is?

Because anorexia nervosa is not, in most instances, primarily a biological or organic disorder, its treatment is often complex and difficult. There are no drugs or simple surgical procedures that can easily cure it. In some instances, patients respond favorably to antidepressant drugs such as chlorpromazine (Walsh, 1982); at other times it is necessary to force-feed anorexic individuals to save their lives. Generally, however, successful treatments have typically involved one of several forms of psychotherapy. Among these, behavior therapy—the use of reinforcement and/or punishment in attempts to change behavior—has sometimes been dramatically effective, as have approaches that treat the entire family as a system that affects each of its individual members (Griffin, 1985). In addition, group therapies have sometimes been effective (Kline, 1985).

bulimia nervosa

Whereas anorexia nervosa is characterized by not eating (in spite of the fact that some anorexics occasionally go on infrequent eating binges), **bulimia nervosa** (or simply bulimia) involves recurrent episodes of binge eating.

DEFINITION

The American Psychiatric Association (1987) describes bulimia nervosa in terms of recurrent episodes of binge eating (rapid consumption of large amounts of food in a short time). Other criteria for a diagnosis of bulimia nervosa include a feeling of lack of control over eating behavior; regular indulgence in self-induced vomiting, use of laxatives or diuretics, strict dieting or fasting, or vigorous exercise; a minimum average of two binge eating episodes per week; and persistent overconcern with body shape and weight.

Typically, foods consumed during a binge are high in calories and eaten inconspicuously. Abdominal pain is a common result, as are frequent weight fluctuations. Other possible medical consequences of bulimia nervosa are listed in Table 11.4. Unlike anorexia, bulimia does not usually present an immediate threat to life—although its eventual medical consequences can be quite serious.

PREVALENCE

Bulimia is a more common eating disorder than anorexia. In the Pope et al. (1984) study of 544 female college students, between 1 and 4.2 percent of the sample could be classified as anorexic; a frightening 6.5 to 18 percent were bulimic. In another study, this one of a sample of 500 students who had gone to a university psychiatric clinic, 4.4 percent met all the criteria for an eating disorder (according to the American Psychiatric Association's Diagnostic and Statistical Manual—DSM-III) (Strangler & Printz, 1980). Of these, an astounding 86.4 percent were bulimic. Similarly, in the Lachenmeyer and Muni-Brander survey mentioned earlier, 7.6 percent of the total nonclinical lower-SES sample, and 4.7 percent of the higher-SES sample, met all the criteria for a clinical diagnosis of bulimia. The proportion of males who are clinically bulimic is higher than expected: 5.7 percent of the males in the lower-SES group, compared with 9.7 percent of the females; and 2.1 percent of the males in the higher-SES group, compared with 7.6 percent of the females. Percentages of the sample who occasionally binged or induced vomiting (or both) and who used laxatives, diuretics, and diet pills were also very high.

CAUSES

One important contributing factor in the increasing incidence of bulimia nervosa is the tremendous emphasis that our society places on thinness. Not surprisingly, among the characteristics that most clearly differentiate bulimic girls from those who are nonbulimic are a greater desire to be thin, a higher degree of dissatisfaction with their bodies, and chronic dieting. In addition, bulimic females are more likely to see themselves as being overweight and tend to be significantly more depressed (Ledoux, Choquet, &

---

t a b l e 11.4

Possible medical consequences of bulimia nervosa

Dehydration

Constipation

Abnormal heartbeat, atrial flutter, fibrillation

Increased susceptibility to cold

Menstrual irregularities

Abdominal distention

Excessive weight fluctuations

Dehydration and fluid shifts, sometimes resulting in headaches and fainting; problem more serious if diuretics are used or if bulimia follows prolonged fasting

Electrolyte imbalance, aggravated by laxative or diuretic use and by repeated vomiting

Hypoglycemic symptoms

Malnutrition-related problems (might include cardiovascular, kidney, gastrointestinal, or blood problems, as well as insomnia)

Dental/oral problems sometimes associated with loss of enamel as a result of frequent exposure to stomach acidity during vomiting episodes; other possible gum, salivary duct, and tongue problems associated with emesis (vomiting).

Specific gastrointestinal difficulties, sometimes associated with ipecac abuse, prolonged use of which can lead to cardiac problems and death

Laxative-related problems, which vary depending on the nature of the laxative abused

Insomnia resulting from malnutrition, nocturnal binges, or underlying depression

Various neurological and endocrine problems

Source: Based on Goode (1985) and Brown (1991).

Manfredi, 1993). Marston et al. (1988) report that adolescents who are most at risk are those whose parents have the highest frequency of addictive problems (alcoholism, drug use, overeating, and gambling).

Polivy and Herman (1985) suggest that part of the explanation for bulimia may lie in the fact that dieting promotes the adoption of cognitive rather than physiological controls over eating. Put another way, whereas food intake would normally be regulated by the physiological mechanisms related to hunger, the dieter deliberately takes conscious control of food intake and ignores physiological indicators of hunger. And perhaps the binges that follow dieting are partly facilitated by the awareness (cognition) that the individual can control the effects of the binge through a purge and through continued dieting, as well as by the fact that the individual has learned to ignore the physiological signals that ordinarily control food intake.

TREATMENT

The precise causes of bulimia, like those of anorexia nervosa, remain unknown, although the incidence of both conditions appears to be rising (Schumer, 1983). Nor is there a simple and universally effective cure for either condition. Bulimia, like anorexia, is sometimes responsive to group therapies, and to various individual psychotherapies including hypnosis and relaxation training (Brown, 1991). And there are those, like Polivy and Herman (1985), who argue that one of bulimia's main causes is dieting, and that to treat it effectively requires controlling dieting. And perhaps to control dieting it is necessary to change the social and cultural conditions that have placed such a tremendous value on thinness.

intellectual development in adolescence

We have traced, sketchily to be sure, the development of the child's mind from birth to the beginning of adolescence, using as our guides both the theory of Jean Piaget and information-processing theories. Through Piaget's eyes we saw infants assimilating aspects of the environment, accommodating to others, equilibrating (balancing) the two processes, and constructing progressively more advanced

views of reality. In time infants succeeded in separating self from world, in representing aspects of the world symbolically, and in dealing with knowledge in increasingly logical ways. And by the end of concrete operations, children understood the logical necessity of conservation, could solve a variety of problems, and could classify, seriate, and deal with numbers at a surprisingly sophisticated level.

We also examined information-processing theories that did not always agree with Piaget's notion of a stage-bound developmental progression and that often described a more capable child than the one described by Piaget. Thus we saw that preschoolers are not always prelogical or preconceptual, but possess impressive classification and number skills. Information-processing descriptions of school-aged children describe people with a rapidly expanding knowledge base, increasingly sophisticated and appropriate strategies for processing information, a mounting awareness of the dimensions and processes of knowing, and increasing recognition of the characteristics of the self as a knower (metacognition).

In the following sections we continue our examination of intellectual development, looking first at Piaget's contributions (see Table 11.5) and then at information-processing approaches.

Piaget's view: formal operations

Some of the important distinctions between concrete and **formal operations** are illustrated in children's responses to the following problem posed by Inhelder and Piaget (1958).

A PIAGETIAN PROBLEM

Subjects are presented with five test tubes that contain different unidentified

t able 11.5

Piaget's stages of cognitive development

STAGE	APPROXIMATE AGE	SOME MAJOR CHARACTERISTICS
Sensorimotor	0–2 years	Motoric intelligence; world of the here and now; no language, no thought in early stages; no notion of objective reality
Preoperational	2–7 years	Egocentric thought
Preconceptual	2–4 years	Reason dominated by perception
Intuitive	4–7 years	Intuitive rather than logical solutions; inability to conserve
Concrete operations	7 to 11 or 12 years	Ability to conserve; logic of classes and relations; understanding of numbers; thinking bound to the concrete; development of reversibility in thought
Formal operations	11 or 12 to 14 or 15 years	Complete generality of thought; propositional thinking; ability to deal with the hypothetical; development of strong idealism

chemicals; certain combinations of these chemicals will result in a yellow liquid. This phenomenon is demonstrated for subjects so they know that one special tube, which is kept apart, is the catalyst for the desired reaction. What they do not know is which combination(s) of the other four tubes is correct. They are asked to discover this for themselves and are allowed to experiment as necessary to solve the problem.

Typical 10 year olds begin by combining two of the chemicals. If this combination does not provide any positive information, they then combine another two chemicals, or perhaps they combine one of the first two test tubes with a third. They continue in this manner until, by chance, they arrive at a correct solution, whereupon they exclaim, "There, those two! That's the solution." If the experimenter then says, "Are there any other solutions—any other combinations that will also make a yellow liquid?" subjects will be forced to admit they do not know yet, but that they can try to find out. Their strategy changes little. They continue to combine pairs of liquids;

they may even combine several groups of three or perhaps all four, and to these they add liquid from the fifth tube. Their approach is unsystematic, and if they are unlucky or not persistent enough, they may not discover even a single correct combination.

Intelligent 14 year olds behave in quite a different manner. As illustrated in Figure 11.4, they solve the problem by systematically combining the tubes by twos, threes, and finally all four, yielding 15 possible combinations (16 including the combination in which nothing is combined). There is no doubt in their minds that they have found all correct combinations.

FORMAL VERSUS CONCRETE THINKING

This experiment illustrates some of the main differences between thinking during the stage of concrete operations and thinking characterized by formal operations.

First, 10 year olds approach the problem by attempting actual combinations; their hypotheses are real behaviors. In

figure 11.4

All possible combinations of the four test tubes to which the fifth can be added. The experiment requires the subject to discover the combination(s) that yields a yellow liquid when potassium iodide is added. The correct solutions have a light gray background.

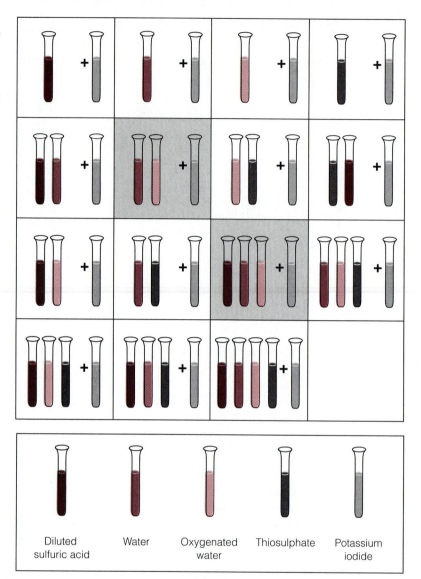

| Diluted sulfuric acid | Water | Oxygenated water | Thiosulphate | Potassium iodide |

contrast, bright 14 year olds begin by *imagining* all the possibilities and then trying them. There is a fundamental difference in the orientations: The first reflects the *concrete* nature of the child's thought; the second reflects the *hypothetical* and *deductive* capacities of adolescent thinking.

Second, the experiment illustrates the *combinatorial* capacity of the adolescent's thinking. Because 10 year olds consider every combination as a separate and unrelated hypothesis and because they arrive

at these combinations in a haphazard way, they are likely to overlook possibilities in the process. In contrast, the adolescent first considers the range of all possible combinations. The concrete logic that was sufficient to deal with classes and seriation is replaced by what Piaget terms the "logic of propositions." This form of logic is a much more powerful tool for dealing with the hypothetical—with statements that need not relate to reality but are simply characterized by the possi-

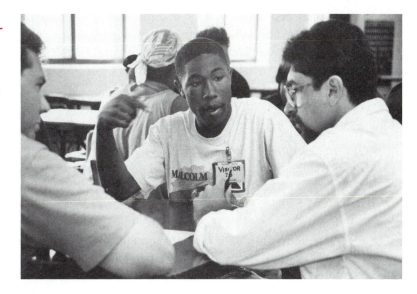

Piaget's formal operations thinking of adolescence is apparent not only in the ability to apply tough rules of logic to complex problems, but also in a sometimes intense new idealism—which may be manifested in activities aimed at protecting and saving the planet, its resources, or, as in this case, its people.

bility that they can be true or untrue. (In fact, this is the definition of a proposition: a verbal statement that can be true or false.)

IMPLICATIONS OF FORMAL THINKING

Adolescents' newly acquired capability to deal with the hypothetical might not be very obvious, or perhaps even very important, if it were manifested only in problems of chemistry and physics. But formal operations extend well beyond the realms of science. They are apparent in new preoccupations with understanding the self as an abstraction (Harter, 1990), in an egocentric reliance on logic (Lapsley, 1990), and in an intense new idealism. Children can now contemplate states of affairs that do not exist; they can compare the ideal to the actual; they can become profoundly distressed at the failure of preceding generations to avoid the confusion that they now observe around them; and they can be perplexed by some of the profound questions that have always puzzled philosophers. It is precisely adolescents' ability to deal with the hypothetical that made it possible for 44 percent of the subjects in Bibby and

Posterski's (1985) study to claim that they were very concerned about the purpose and meaning of life. Such questions do not often suggest themselves to 10 year olds.

With the idealism of formal operations there also comes a belief in the omnipotence of thought. The egocentrism of adolescence (which we discuss later in this chapter) can be seen in the belief that reason and logic provide all the answers and in an apparent inability to adopt the point of view that admits that we do not have all the answers—and that even if we did, social, political, and other human realities sometimes oppose their implementation. It is this unshakable belief in the power of thought that may underlie adolescents' absolutely insistent political, social, and religious arguments with parents and others.

an information-processing view

Piaget's stage-bound description of intellectual development, although it provides many important insights into cognitive functioning, is not always an accurate description of children's capabilities. The irony is that whereas Piaget seems to have *underestimated* the cognitive achievements of infants and preschoolers, he may have *overestimated* those of adolescents. There is evidence, for example, that the abstract and logical thinking defined by formal operations, which is not ordinarily present at the beginning of formal operations (at age 11 or 12), is often absent even among adults.

A complementary approach to understanding intellectual development falls under the general heading of information processing. As we saw in Chapter 9, information-processing theories are concerned with three important aspects of cognition: the acquisition of what Chi and Glaser (1980) label a knowledge base, the development of information-processing strategies, and the development of metacognitive skills.

To review briefly, the knowledge base consists of concepts, ideas, information, and so on. Infants begin life with very little knowledge base, which derives from the individual's experience. Schools do a great deal to expand and organize the knowledge base.

Information-processing strategies are the procedures involved in learning and remembering. They include strategies such as organizing and rehearsing.

Metacognitive skills relate to information the knower has about knowing and remembering and to awareness of the self as an information processor and, consequently, as a player of Flavell's (1985) game of cognition. As metacognitive skills increase, so too do children's ability to analyze performance, to predict the likelihood of success, to change strategies, and to evaluate and monitor.

An information-processing view of development describes how each of these three aspects of information processing (knowledge base, processing skills, and metacognitive skills) changes with age and experience.

CHANGES IN KNOWLEDGE BASE

Knowledge base grows with increasing experience and exposure to schooling. Anderson (1980) describes how children progress from being novices in all areas to being experts in at least some areas—most especially in certain games, in aspects of social interaction, in certain levels and classes of school subjects, and perhaps in hobby-related or cultural pursuits. One of the important differences between experts and novices has to do with knowledge base. But the difference is not simply that experts know more (have more content in their knowledge structures), but also that they have formed more associations among the things they know. Their knowledge is richer in the sense that it suggests more relationships. The artist who is an expert in color does not understand the color blue in the same way as a novice such as I might. My pitiful understanding permits me to relate blue to robin eggs and morning skies; the expert might relate it to these as well but might also break it down into a dozen hues whose subtlety and associations have no meaning for me. More than this, the expert might well understand blue as a wavelength, might understand its relationships to other waves of different lengths, and might have a sense of its crispness or fragility that quite escapes me.

CHANGES IN PROCESSING

Development, then, is a process of shedding some of the novice's ignorance and acquiring increasing expertise, but expertise involves more than changes in knowledge base; it also involves changes in information-processing capacity. Among other things, information-processing capacity depends on the availability of appropriate strategies; and it depends on attention span.

That attention span increases with age is clear. Intelligence tests such as the Stanford-Binet, for example, require that subjects try to recall sequences of digits presented at one-second intervals. Whereas a preschool child might correctly recall a string of two or three digits, an adolescent might easily recall six or seven.

Changes in the availability of appropriate strategies are not as readily investigated, partly because it is not always easy to identify a strategy and determine whether or not it is present. However, Piaget's investigations of concrete and formal operations suggest that the strategies available to older adolescents are substantially different, and considerably more powerful, than those available to younger children. First, the adolescent is more systematic, plans more carefully, considers more options. Second, the adolescent has more ready-made solutions. For example, there are many Piagetian tasks that present real problems for a younger child, but that can be solved almost from memory by an older child. A 6 year old might need to "figure out" whether there is still the same amount of material in a deformed object; the adolescent need not "figure."

METACOGNITIVE CHANGES

One additional important area of developmental change in information processing involves children's understanding of the self as a processor of information and an increasing understanding of the processes of cognition. As we saw in Chapter 9, metacognitive skills seem to be largely absent in young children, but are clearly present in older children and adolescents.

In summary, information-processing views of cognitive development describe changes in three areas: content (knowledge base increases in terms of specific knowledge and of relations and associations among items of information); processing capacities (increases in memory and attention capacities and increases in the availability of more sophisticated strategies); and metacognitive changes (increasing awareness of self as information-processor and increasing ability to monitor, evaluate, and control ongoing cognitive activities). These changes make more of an expert of adolescents. But they do not eliminate adolescents' egocentrism.

adolescent egocentrism

I n Piagetian theory, egocentrism is not the derogatory term it might be in ordinary usage. It refers less to a *selfishness* than to a cognitive and emotional *self-centeredness* and is apparent in children's inability to be completely objective in their understanding of the world and in their interactions with others. Recall, for example, that during sensorimotor development, egocentrism marks infants' ability to differentiate between self and the physical world: Objects exist only when they are being looked at, tasted, felt, or smelled—a rather extreme egocentrism. And in the preschool period there is evidence of egocentricism in children's centeredness on the perceptual features of objects in their incorrect responses to conservation problems.

The egocentrism of adolescents is not as extreme or naive as that of infants. It is characterized by an inability to differentiate between objects and events of concern to others and those of concern to the adolescent. This egocentrism is sometimes apparent in behaviors that seem to be motivated by the adolescent's belief that everybody is watching and is terribly concerned.

Adolescents' great concern with hair and dress may have much to do with the imaginary audience that constantly judges them.

Elkind (1967) clarifies the concept of adolescent egocentrism by examining two separate notions that adolescents create through egocentrism. These notions, the imaginary audience and the personal fable, may be extremely useful in understanding some aspects of adolescent behavior and experience.

the imaginary audience

The **imaginary audience** is a collection of all who might be concerned with the adolescent's self and behavior. It is the "they" in expressions such as "they say . . . " or "they predict . . . " Social psychologists inform us that each of us behaves as though "they" are watching and care. But the imaginary audiences of adults are much smaller, much less pervasive, and far less important than those of

adolescents. According to Elkind, it is because of this imaginary audience to which adolescents are continually reacting that young adolescents are often very self-conscious. It is also because of this same audience that many become so concerned with their hair, clothing, and other aspects of their physical appearance. It is as though adolescents believe that others are as deeply concerned about them as they themselves are, and that these others constantly judge them. As Jahnke and Blanchard-Fields (1993) note, the imaginary audience reflects adolescents' failure to differentiate between their thoughts and those of others.

MEASURING THE IMAGINARY AUDIENCE

How does research investigate beliefs such as these? How can psychology locate an imaginary audience?

With an instrument appropriately called the Imaginary Audience Scale (IAS), developed by Elkind and Bowen (1979). The IAS is based on the assumption that individuals who act as though an imaginary audience is watching them will be self-conscious. Accordingly, the scale attempts to measure two aspects of self-consciousness: abiding or relatively permanent aspects (labeled AS, for abiding self), and temporary or transient aspects (labeled TS, for transient self). One example of an abiding aspect of self is intelligence; a more transient characteristic is hairstyle or clothing.

Items for the IAS scale were selected from a pool of suggestions given by students who were asked to describe situations they might find embarrassing. The final scale consists of 12 items, the first four of which are reproduced in Table 11.6.

Elkind and Bowen administered the IAS to 697 students in grades four, six, eight, and twelve. They found that young adolescents (eighth-grade students) were more reluctant to reveal themselves to an audience than were younger children or older adolescents, and that girls were more self-conscious than boys on the test. However, these findings have not always been replicated. A number of investigations using Elkind and Bowen's IAS or the Adolescent Egocentrism Scale (Enright et al., 1980) found considerable variability in the ages at which children become egocentric (Buis & Thompson, 1989). Lapsley (1990) concludes that more often than not, egocentrism is manifested in adolescence. But we don't yet understand its origins, and our instruments for measuring it need improvement.

Clarification of adolescent egocentrism might have a number of practical implications, quite apart from what it might contribute to the elaboration of theory. In the first place, it might do a great deal to clarify adolescents' experi-

---

t a b l e 11.6

The imaginary audience scale (IAS)

Instructions: *Please read the following stories carefully and assume that the events actually happened to you. Place a check next to the answer that best describes what you would do or feel in the real situation.*

TS scale	1. You have looked forward to the most exciting dress-up party of the year. You arrive after an hour's drive from home. Just as the party is beginning, you notice a grease spot on your trousers or skirt. (There is no way to borrow clothes from anyone.) Would you stay or go home?

___ Go home.

___ Stay, even though I'd feel uncomfortable.

___ Stay, because the grease spot wouldn't bother me.

AS scale	2. Let's say some adult visitors came to your school and you were asked to tell them a little bit about yourself.

___ I would like that.

___ I would not like that.

___ I wouldn't care.

TS scale	3. It is Friday afternoon and you have just had your hair cut in preparation for the wedding of a relative that weekend. The barber or hairdresser did a terrible job and your hair looks awful. To make it worse, that night is the most important basketball game of the season and you really want to see it, but there is no way you can keep your head covered without people asking questions. Would you stay home or go to the game anyway?

___ Go to the game and not worry about my hair.

___ Go to the game and sit where people won't notice me very much.

___ Stay home.

AS scale	4. If you went to a party where you did not know most of the kids, would you wonder what they were thinking about you?

___ I wouldn't think about it.

___ I would wonder about that a lot.

___ I would wonder about that a little.

Source: From D. Elkind & R. Bowen (1979). Imaginary audience behavior in children and adolescents. *Developmental Psychology,* 15(1), 38–44, p. 40. Copyright 1979 by the American Psychological Association. Reprinted by permission of the authors.

ences for us. Second, as Elkind (1981b) suggests, it might contribute in important ways to our understanding of vandalism, teenage pregnancy, drug abuse, and other related behaviors. One of the important motives that might underlie these behaviors may relate directly to what adolescents expect the reaction of the imaginary audience to be. Teachers, parents, counselors, and friends are all members of that audience.

the personal fable

Adolescent egocentrism is reflected not only in the creation of an imaginary audience, but also in the elaboration of fantasies, the hero of which is, not surprisingly, the adolescent. These fantasies, labeled **personal fables**, have a number of identifying themes, the most common of which are "I am special," "I will not get pregnant," "I will not become addicted to these drugs I take only for recreation," "Mom, you just don't understand what real love is," and "nor do you, Dad!"

One of the characteristics of the personal fable is a sense of invulnerability. Unfortunately, it is often sadly inappropriate, as is evident in the fact that adolescents—especially males—have the highest accident rate of all age groups except those over 65 (U.S. Bureau of the Census, 1992).

Elements of the personal fable run through the lives of most of us. Most of us believe that we are somewhat unique, just a little special. But these beliefs appear to be greatly exaggerated in adolescence and may account in part for the casualness with which adolescents will take risks that they know cognitively to be horrendous.

reckless behavior

Adolescents—especially males—engage in a variety of reckless behaviors, many of which have potentially devastating consequences (see Table 11.7 in "At A Glance: Adolescents' Risks and Violent Death").

MANIFESTATIONS OF ADOLESCENT RECKLESSNESS

Where I live, automobile insurance rates for 16-year-old male drivers are about four times higher than they are for *moi*. Why? Not because I am a technically better driver than they are, but simply because more of them drive at high speed when sober—and even more of them drive at high speed when drunk. Over one-third of all drunk drivers involved in fatal accidents are ages 16 to 24, even though this age group represents fewer than one-fifth of all licensed drivers (U.S. Bureau of the Census, 1992).

About 50 percent more sexually active teenage girls than sexually active women ages 25 to 44 do not use contraception. And over one million unmarried teenagers become pregnant in the United States each year (U.S. Bureau of the Census, 1992).

Adolescents have the highest rate of illegal drug use of any age group (Arnett, 1992). In 1990, 28 percent of all serious crimes in the United States were committed by people under 18 (U.S. Bureau of the Census, 1992).

Adolescent recklessness is seldom manifested in only one form of high-risk behavior. Teenagers who drink are also more likely to take illegal drugs, to be involved in automobile accidents, or to commit crimes (Elster, Lamb & Tavare, 1987).

The risk-taking behavior of adolescents, especially of adolescent males, may be due in part to what Elkind labels the personal fable—the feeling that the adolescent is special and somehow invulnerable, that bad things happen only to other people. Risk-taking behavior is manifested in drug abuse, dangerous hobbies, and automobile and other accidents and is especially evident in the incidence of violent death among white adolescent males. Violent death among blacks is more common than among whites and does not reveal the same pattern of higher incidence in adolescence, perhaps because it involves a higher proportion of homicides, which continue at a high rate after adolescence, and perhaps because of more limited access to automobiles. For both blacks and whites, violent death is considerably lower for females than for males.

table 11.7

1989 U.S. death rates (per 100,000 population) by age for accidents, suicides, and homicides combined

| | WHITE | | BLACK | |
AGE	MALE	FEMALE	MALE	FEMALE
15–24	107.1	32.7	188.0	33.9
25–34	96.0	26.6	205.9	47.4
35–44	80.4	24.7	184.9	40.8
45–54	73.8	25.5	144.0	30.8
55–64	80.1	28.7	130.6	37.3
65 and older	151.9	81.4	187.1	87.8

Source: U.S. Bureau of the Census (1992)

WHY ADOLESCENTS TAKE RISKS

Adolescents' reckless behaviors, explains Arnett (1992), involve doing things that they recognize as dangerous, but the danger is deliberately underestimated and precautions that could be taken are ignored. When Beyth-Marom et al. (1993) asked adult and adolescent subjects to describe the possible consequences of high-risk behaviors such as drinking and driving, their responses were remarkably similar. Adolescents *know* the risks involved in their behaviors; they can anticipate their possible outcomes as clearly as can adults. But they consistently underestimate risks associated with activities in which they themselves engage. Benthin, Slovic, and Severson (1993) had adolescents rate perceived risks and benefits of 30 high-risk activities such as smoking, drug use, drinking, and sex. Not only did participants perceive lower risks for their own high-risk behaviors, but they also perceived greater benefits. And, strikingly, they consistently overestimated the extent to which their peers engaged in the same activities.

Adolescents' tendency to underestimate the probability of bad outcomes for themselves is one factor that explains risk taking, claims Arnett (1992). Another is their personal fable of invulnerability—their frequently expressed belief that "It won't happen to me." A third is a personality trait labeled *sensation seeking*, which may be related to levels of sex hormones. Sensation seeking implies a desire to take risks for the sensations involved. Driving motorcycles, water skiing, and using drugs have all been shown to be related to high scores on the Sensation Seeking Scale (Zuckerman, Eysenck, & Eysenck, 1978). Finally, a wealth of research suggests that peer influences contribute to the likelihood of reckless behavior (see Arnett, 1992).

THE CAUTIOUS ADOLESCENT

Although adolescence is a period of greater apparent recklessness than any other period of life, it would be misleading not to emphasize that the majority of adolescents are not reckless. In 1991, more than 5.6 million Americans ages 16 to 19 worked, and more than 14 million were in school—and that, too, for a lot of them, is serious, nonreckless, work. It is also worth noting that in a 1991 survey, 87 percent of all adolescents ages 12 to 17 had *never* used marijuana, 97.6 percent had never used cocaine or stimulants, and more than half had never used alcohol (U.S. Bureau of the Census, 1992).

Clearly, not all adolescents are totally unrestrained, reckless, and immoral.

moral development in adolescence

Morality involves interactions between people in which questions of trust, ethics, values, and rights are involved. In this sense, learning to be "moral" is quite different from learning social convention (Nucci and Turiel, 1978). Learning social conventions involves learning behaviors that are accepted or not accepted but that are essentially arbitrary. Thus in Western cultures, conventions relating to eating tell us we should use knives and forks, sit at tables, eat off plates and out of bowls, and try to refrain from belching and doing other things unmentionable in polite textbooks. Elsewhere, we might learn to eat with sticks while squatting on the ground, lapping food off rocks, belching, and making other fine noises with great gusto. These behaviors are arbitrary, and thus if different behaviors were substituted for them, we would not likely be judged evil—foolish and disgusting, perhaps, but not truly evil. Morality, in contrast, is far less arbitrary. It refers to behaviors and judgments relating to broad issues of human justice, such as the value of human life, the ethics of causing harm to others or to their property, and the placement of trust and responsibility.

Most of us believe implicitly that some people are good and others less good, that goodness or evil is an intrinsic part of what we are—of our selves. Are we really good or bad, or do we simply behave well some of the time and badly at other times? If we are really good or bad, are we born that way, or do we later become one or the other? Further, is being good in a moral sense the same thing as conforming to accepted social rules, or are the two separate?

When we judge people morally "good" or "bad," says Kohlberg (1964), we might be referring to any one of three things: their ability to resist temptation, the amount of guilt that accompanies failure to resist temptation, or our evaluation of the morality of a given act based on some personal standard of good or evil.

Clearly, these dimensions of morality are not necessarily very closely related. A person may repeatedly violate some accepted code of conduct—behave immorally, in other words—and yet feel a great deal of guilt; a second may engage in exactly the same behavior and feel no guilt. Despite these differences, both may judge the act equally evil. Who is the more moral?

behaving morally

Carroll and Rest (1982) suggest that four steps are involved in behaving morally. First, moral behavior requires recognizing a moral problem and being sensitive to the fact that someone's welfare is involved. Second, it is necessary to make a judgment about what is right and wrong—about what ought to be done in a given situation. Third, the individual needs to make a plan of action that takes into account relevant ideals and **values**. Finally, the plan must be put into action.

It is entirely possible, Carroll and Rest argue, to fail to act morally because of a deficiency in only one of these components. Research on bystander intervention, stimulated by the now-famous murder of Kitty Genovese, is a case in point (Latané & Darley, 1970). Genovese was a New Yorker who, returning home from work at three o'clock one morning, was set upon by a maniac. At least 38 of her neighbors in fashionable Kew Gardens were awakened by her screams and came to their windows. And watched. No one tried to help her; no one yelled at the murderer; no one even called the police. They simply watched for a full half hour as Kitty was being slowly murdered below them.

How can their behavior be interpreted in light of Carroll and Rest's analysis of what is required for moral behavior?

First, some of the bystanders who failed to respond might not have initially recognized the seriousness of the situation ("It's only a lover's quarrel"). Some might have been unable to devise a plan of behavior compatible with their ideals and values ("How can I save her life without endangering mine?"). Still others might have felt incapable of implementing the plan they might have devised ("I should restrain the attacker physically, but I am not strong enough"). Finally, there is the chilling possibility that some among the spectators might have developed values that run counter to helping someone in this situation ("If he wants to kill her, hey, it's up to him").

To summarize, the four components of moral behavior are:

- Moral sensitivity (recognition of a moral problem)

- Moral judgment (deciding what ought to be done)

- Moral values (conscience; ideals; that which guides moral action)

- Moral action (moral or immoral behavior)

morality as an understanding of justice

Most of the research on moral development has dealt with what Eisenberg (1990) refers to as prohibition- or justice-oriented moral reasoning, rather than with prosocial morality. With some exceptions, researchers have not been especially concerned with changes in children's prosocial behavior or with their motives for and understanding of this behavior. Instead, they have looked at children's understanding of right and wrong primarily as this understanding is reflected in their awareness that "wrong" things are prohibited and that certain outcomes and punishments are fair (therefore moral) and others less fair.

Darley and Schultz (1990) speak of three different kinds of justice that might be considered when investigating moral development. *Retributive justice* relates to punishment; *distributive justice* has to do with fairness in the allocation of rewards; and *procedural justice* relates to the impartiality and fairness of the methods by which moral decisions are reached.

Piaget's approach to morality

There is, notes Piaget, a close relationship between playing games that have rules and the development of morality. In a sense, morality is the internalization of rules. Whereas the rules that govern game playing relate specifically to each game, the rules of morality govern all of life. And that too may be considered a game—not play, but a game nevertheless.

GAMES WITH RULES

There are two aspects to children's understanding of the rules of games, says Piaget (1932), and the two are often contradictory. On the one hand there is their verbalized belief about the nature, origins, and permanence of rules; on the other is their actual behavior when playing games with rules.

When Piaget observed children actually playing, he identified four broad stages. In the first, lasting until about age 3, they do not follow any rules. In the second, they imitate rules but don't really understand them and consequently change them to conform to their inter-

pretation of the game (ages 3 to 7 or so). In the third, they have begun to play in a genuinely social manner, with rules that are mutually accepted by all players and that are rigidly adhered to (until about age 10 or so). But it is not until the age of 11 or 12 that children realize that rules exist to make games possible and that they can be changed by mutual agreement.

But when Piaget questioned children about rules, their responses suggested a surprisingly different sequence of understanding. Before age 3 children don't understand rules—which is reflected in their actual behavior as well. In the second stage, they believe that rules come from some external source (such as God), that they are timeless and permanent, and that children should not take it upon themselves to change them. But during this stage they constantly break rules. During the next stage, they never change rules when they play, even though they now believe that rules are made by people and can be changed by the players if they so wish. And in the final stage, when they understand rules more fully, they change them by mutual consent (Table 11.8).

MORAL RULES

Piaget (1932) investigated children's morality by telling them stories and asking them to judge how good or bad the characters were. In one story, a child accidentally breaks 15 cups; another deliberately breaks a single cup. Is one worse than the other?

Based on children's responses to these stories, Piaget identified two broad stages in the development of beliefs about guilt. In the first, children judge guilt by the apparent consequences of the act: The child who has broken the largest number of cups or who has stolen the greatest quantity of goods or the largest amount

table 11.8

Piaget's description of children's understanding and use of rules

APPROXIMATE AGE	DEGREE OF UNDERSTANDING	ADHERENCE TO RULES
Before 3	No understanding of rules	Do not play according to rules
To 7 or 8	Believe rules come from God (or some other high authority) and cannot be changed	Break and change rules constantly
To 11 or 12	Understand social nature of rules and that they can be changed	Do not change rules; adhere to them rigidly
After 11 or 12	Complete understanding of rules	Change rules by mutual consent

of money is considered more evil than the one who deliberately broke only one cup, or stole just a few things or just a little money. Following this stage, children's judgment becomes more adultlike; they are more likely to consider the intentions and motives behind the act.

PIAGET'S TWO STAGES OF MORALITY

Young children, claims Piaget (1932), do not respond in terms of abstract conceptions of right and wrong as might adolescents. Instead, they respond more in terms of the immediate consequences of behavior. Thus, a young child's morality is governed by the principles of pain and pleasure. Good behaviors are those that have pleasant consequences; bad actions have unpleasant consequences. Accordingly, children respond primarily to outside authority because authority is the main source of reinforcement and punishment. Piaget labels this first stage of moral development *heteronomy*.

In the second stage, morality comes to be governed more and more by principles and ideals. As a result, moral judgments become more individual and more autonomous; hence Piaget's label, *autonomy*, for the second stage.

OTHER RESEARCH

Piaget thought that the transition between heteronomy and autonomy likely happened by the age of 9 or 10. However, subsequent research indicates that children as young as 6 or 7 are likely to consider the actor's intentions in judging the severity of an act (Darley & Shultz, 1990). Also, they often take into account other factors, such as whether an authority permits the act to occur (Tisak, 1993). Thus children will judge an act more harshly if it intentionally causes harm than if the harm is unintentional. Similarly, they will judge an actor more punishable if the harm should have been foreseen, even if it was unintentional (Darley & Zanna, 1982). Also, children at this age have begun to consider other mitigating circumstances in their judgments of culpability. Thus various justifications such as necessity, provocation, or the fact that the transgressor has attempted restitution serve to reduce the degree to which children think a transgressor should be punished.

In some ways, then, the moral judgments of children are somewhat similar to those of adolescents and adults. But, as Kohlberg's (1980) research shows, in other ways children think quite differently.

Kohlberg's stages of morality

Kohlberg (1969, 1980), whose research closely follows Piaget's pioneering investigations, studied moral development by posing moral dilemmas to groups of children, adolescents, and adults. These dilemmas took the form of stories, among the best known of which is the story of Heinz (Kohlberg, 1969), paraphrased here:

Heinz's wife was dying of cancer. One special drug recently discovered by a local druggist might save her. The druggist could make the drug for about $200 but was selling it for 10 times that amount. So Heinz went to everyone he knew to try to borrow the $2,000 he needed, but he could only scrape together $1,000. "My wife's dying," he told the druggist, asking him to sell the drug cheaper or to let him pay later. But the druggist refused. Desperate, Heinz broke into the drugstore and stole the drug for his wife. Should Heinz have done that? Why? (p. 379)

Children's responses suggest three levels in the development of moral judgments, each consisting of two stages of moral orientation (shown in Table 11.9). The three levels are sequential, although

---

t a b l e   1 1 . 9

Kohlberg's levels of morality

Kohlberg identified levels of moral judgment in children by describing to them situations involving a moral dilemma. One example is the story of Heinz (described above) whose wife is dying but who might be saved if given a drug that was discovered by a local pharmacist, who charges such an exorbitant price that the husband can't pay. Should he steal the drug?

Level I Preconventional	Stage 1: Punishment and obedience orientation	"If he steals the drug, he might go to jail." (Punishment)
	Stage 2: Naive instrumental hedonism	"He can steal the drug and save his wife, and he'll be with her when he gets out of jail." (Act motivated by its hedonistic consequences for the actor)
Level II Conventional	Stage 3: "Good-boy, nice-girl" morality	"People will understand if you steal the drug to save your wife, but they'll think you're cruel and a coward if you don't." (Reactions of others and the effects of the act on social relationships become important.)
	Stage 4: Law-and-order orientation	"It is the husband's duty to save his wife even if he feels guilty afterwards for stealing the drug." (Institutions, law, duty, honor, and guilt motivate behavior.)
Level III Postconventional	Stage 5: Morality of social contract	"The husband has a right to the drug even if he can't pay now. If the druggist won't charge it, the government should look after it." (Democratic laws guarantee individual rights; contracts are mutually beneficial.)
	Stage 6: Universal ethical*	"Although it is legally wrong to steal, the husband would be morally wrong not to steal to save his wife. A life is more precious than financial gain." (Conscience is individual. Laws are socially useful but not sacrosanct.)

*None of Kohlberg's subjects ever reached Stage 6. However, it is still described as a "potential" stage. Kohlberg suggests that moral martyrs such as Jesus or Martin Luther King, Jr. exemplify this level.

Source: Based on Kohlberg (1969, 1980).

succeeding levels never entirely replace preceding ones, making it almost impossible to assign ages to them.

PRECONVENTIONAL LEVEL

At the **preconventional level**, children's judgment of right and wrong takes one of two orientations. In the first (Stage 1), children believe that evil behavior is that which is likely to be punished, and that good behavior is based on obedience or the avoidance of the evil of disobedience. Thus, children do not evaluate right or wrong in terms of the objective consequences of the behavior or the intentions of the actor; judgment is based solely on the consequences to the child.

The second preconventional moral orientation (Stage 2) is a **hedonistic** one in which children interpret good as that which is pleasant, and evil as that which has undesirable consequences. At this level begins the reciprocity that characterizes morality at the second level; but it is a practical reciprocity. Children will go out of their way to do something good for someone if they themselves will gain by the deed.

CONVENTIONAL LEVEL

The second level, a morality of **conventional** role conformity, reflects the increasing importance of peer and social relations. Stage 3 is defined as morality designed to maintain good relations. Hence moral behavior is behavior that receives wide approval from significant people: parents, teachers, peers, and society at large. Stage 4, conformity to rules and laws, is also related to children's desire to maintain a friendly status quo. Thus conforming to law becomes important for maintaining adults' approval.

POSTCONVENTIONAL LEVEL

At the highest level, the **postconventional level**, individuals begin to view morality in terms of individual rights and as ideals and principles that have value as rules or laws apart from their influence on approval (Stage 5). As we noted, however, Stage 5 moral judgments are rare even among adults, and Stage 6 judgments, based on fundamental ethical principles, are even rarer. Colby and Kohlberg (1984) suggest that there is some doubt as to whether or not Stage 6 should even be included as a stage in moral development.

A SEVENTH STAGE?

But Kohlberg (1984) also spoke of the possibility of a seventh stage; a mystical, contemplative, religious stage—a metaphorical stage in which, through the "logic of contemplation and mystical logic . . . we all know that the deepest feeling is love and the ultimate reality is life" (Hague, 1991, p. 283).

---

the generality of Kohlberg's stages

Kohlberg's early research suggests that children progress through the stages of moral development in predictable sequence and at roughly the same ages. Theoretically, this makes a lot of sense because moral judgments are essentially cognitive and would therefore be expected to reflect level of cognitive development. As Walker (1988) explains, preoperational thought parallels Stage 1 moral reasoning (physical consequences and authority determine morality); concrete operations makes Stage 2 morality possible (morality is instrumental and self-serving); and the beginning of formal operations is necessary for Stage 3 morality (emphasis on being a "good" person;

what is approved of is moral). Successively higher stages of moral judgment are made possible by the elaboration and consolidation of formal operations.

Note that the higher stages of moral development do not necessarily accompany advances in intellectual development. What Kohlberg and his followers maintain is that certain levels of cognitive performance are essential for corresponding levels of moral reasoning but are not sufficient. This is, in fact, the principle that underlies the relationship between intellectual and moral development.

SOME CRITICISMS

Some researchers have criticized aspects of Kohlberg's concept of stages of moral development and have contradicted his belief that these stages parallel cognitive development and are universal. For example, Holstein (1976) found that many subjects skipped stages, reverted to earlier levels of moral reasoning, or were so inconsistent in their responses to moral dilemmas that they could not easily be classified in any stage. Similarly, Kurtines and Grief (1974) and Fishkin, Keniston, and MacKinnon (1973) found few advances in moral reasoning among older children and found that subjects often operated at different stages depending on the specifics of the moral questions to which they were responding. And cross-cultural studies using Kohlberg's theory illustrate that the stages are not universal (Snarey, 1985).

KOHLBERG'S RESPONSE

Following these criticisms, Kohlberg (1980) de-emphasized Stage 6 (no one ever reached it) and revised the scoring methods for the moral dilemma questions. He then reanalyzed his original data using the new scoring procedures (Colby & Kohlberg, 1984). What the

reanalysis indicated was that progression through the stages takes much longer than first had been thought and that post-conventional morality is the exception rather than the rule, even among adults. Specifically, 10 year olds were typically either in Stage 2 or still in transition between Stages 1 and 2; young adolescents (ages 13–14) were primarily still in transition between Stages 2 and 3; and late adolescents and young adults were mainly in Stage 3. Only one of every eight adults in this sample operated at a postconventional level.

Although Kohlberg's reanalysis indicates that the stages span wide age spreads, it also strengthens his contention that these are legitimate stages in that they conform to the three common criteria for stages: (1) progression is forward (not backward); (2) there is no skipping of stages; and (3) the thinking characteristic of a stage is generally applied to all content areas while the individual is at that stage.

Walker (1988) subsequently analyzed and summarized a large number of studies that have examined Kohlberg's findings. He also concludes that there is little skipping of stages or regression to earlier stages.

Most of the research agrees, however, that although progress through the higher stages may be possible with the development of formal operational thinking in adolescence, it typically remains potential rather than actual. As Lapsley (1990) notes, adolescence is not marked by principled moral reasoning, as we might expect given adolescents' newly developed ability to deal with abstractions and principles. Most young adolescents reason at a preconventional, Stage 2 level (a self-serving, hedonistic morality) or at a conventional, Stage 3 level (emphasis on conforming, being good, doing the expected). In fact, Stage 3 reasoning is not very general until the ages of 16 to 18 and is common into adulthood.

MORE CRITICISMS

Researchers who are concerned with the information-processing, rule-governed aspects of moral development, rather than with Kohlberg-type stages, suggest that Kohlberg's moral dilemmas are perhaps too verbal and too abstract for children. They require that children understand and keep in mind very complex situations involving a number of actors, and they require the manipulation of a variety of factors and circumstances. Frequently, they do not provide sufficient information; but if they did, they would be even more complex. As a result, it is possible that the Kohlberg dilemmas underestimate children's moral reasoning. When questions are made simpler, or when children and adolescents are observed in naturalistic settings, researchers sometimes find evidence of very sophisticated moral reasoning at very young ages (see Darley & Shultz, 1990; Lapsley, 1990).

There is now mounting evidence that moral judgments are related not only to the age of subjects but also to a host of other variables, including the intentions of the transgressor; personal characteristics such as kindness and cruelty; social, material, or personal consequences; and interpersonal relationships (see, for example, Damon & Colby, 1987; Tisak, 1993).

Gilligan's approach: gender differences in morality

In addition to the criticism that progression through Kohlberg's stages may not be quite as predictable or systematic as Kohlberg had thought, Gilligan (1982) suggests that Kohlberg's research suffered

from at least two other important weaknesses. One is that all his subjects were male—and there is evidence of important male-female differences in morality. The other is that the moral dilemmas he used in his investigations were typically totally irrelevant to the lives of his subjects. A person's response to an abstract or hypothetical moral dilemma ("What would you do if you had to choose between letting your partner die or spending the rest of your life in jail?") might be quite different from that person's actual behavior in the case of a real (rather than hypothetical) dilemma.

FEMALE MORALITY

Gilligan reasoned that subjects' apparent stages of moral reasoning might seem *higher* in the case of an abstract and impersonal moral dilemma like Heinz's problem (Table 11.9) than they would be in the case of a more immediate and perhaps more realistic dilemma. Following this line of reasoning, she examined morality in women by interviewing them while they were caught up in an actual moral dilemma. Her subjects were 29 women who had been referred to a counseling clinic for pregnant women and who were currently facing the need to make a decision about having an abortion.

Based on her analysis of the women's reasons for having or not having an abortion, Gilligan describes three stages in female moral development. In the first stage, women are moved primarily by selfish concerns ("This is what I want . . . what I need . . . what I should do . . . what would be best for me"). In the second stage, women progress through a period of increasing recognition of responsibility to others. And the final stage reflects a morality of "nonviolence." At this stage, women's decisions are based

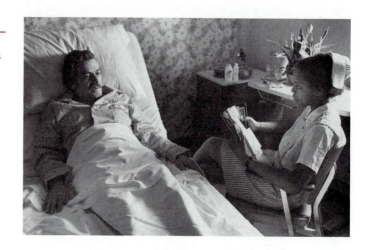

Gilligan suggests that female morality is more concerned with empathy than is male morality, that it responds more to social responsibility.

on their desire to do the greatest good both for self and for others.

GILLIGAN'S VIEW OF MALE-FEMALE DIFFERENCES

If Gilligan's description of female moral development is accurate, it reflects a number of important differences between male and female morality. In contrast with Kohlberg's description of male moral progression from what are initially hedonistic (pain-pleasure) concerns toward a conventional, rule-regulated morality, Gilligan describes female morality as a progression from initial selfishness toward a recognition of social responsibility. Boys are perhaps more concerned with law and order than the personally meaningful dimensions of morality. Women's morality is a morality of *caring* rather than of *abstract justice* (Stander & Jensen, 1993).

Nunner-Winkler (1984) elaborates Gilligan's position by reference to Kant's (1797) distinction between *negative* and *positive* moral duties. Negative duties are illustrated in rules such as "Do not kill" and "Do not steal." These rules are absolute and clear; you follow them, or you do not. In contrast, positive duties are open-ended, as reflected in rules such

as "Be kind" and "Be compassionate." There are no boundaries or limits on positive duties. They don't specify how kind, to whom, how often, or when.

Negative duties, says Nunner-Winkler, reflect the justice orientation of males; females feel more obliged than males to fulfill positive duties, which relate more closely to caring and compassion.

OTHER RESEARCH ON MALE-FEMALE DIFFERENCES

Do women and men see the world differently and make different moral judgments? Some research says yes. Stimpson et al. (1991) asked college students to rate 18 adjectives having to do with "interpersonal sensitivity" and "caring." Females consistently rated these adjectives higher in terms of goodness than did males. Similarly, Eisenberg et al. (1991) found that girls' prosocial reasoning was higher than boys' in late childhood and adolescence.

But other research finds less clear evidence of sex differences in morality. Muuss (1988) reviewed a number of studies and concluded that the distinctions between male and female morality are not very clear. He reasons that if Gilligan's descriptions are correct, it follows that females should, on average, be more altruistic, more empathetic, more concerned with human relations; in contrast, males should be less altruistic. But research on altruism, cooperation, and other forms of prosocial behavior has not found such differences. Note, however, that these findings do not invalidate Gilligan's basic conclusions. It may well be that males and females are equally altruistic, but their altruism might stem from fundamentally different orientations reflecting very different moralities. Females may, as Gilligan suggests, be altruistic because of their concern for humanity; males may be just as altruistic because of their adherence to principles and ideals that emphasize the injustice of being unkind.

One of the important contributions of Gilligan's approach is that it underlines the need to be aware of the possibility that many of our theories and conclusions in human development are not equally applicable to males and females. In Gilligan's (1982) words, the sexes speak *in a different voice*. Neither voice is louder or better; they are simply different.

implications of research on moral development

Some of the most important implications of research on morality relate to the observation that individuals who operate at the lowest (hedonistic) levels are more likely to be delinquent than those who operate at higher levels. As Gibbs (1987) notes, delinquents' behavior generally reflects immature moral reasoning and egocentricity. Individuals who operate at higher levels of morality are more likely to be honest and to behave in a generally

moral way (Kohlberg & Candee, 1984). Similarly, altruism in children is highly related to level of moral development. Children who are still at a hedonistic level (good things are those that lead to pleasant consequences) typically engage in less prosocial behavior (share less, for example) than children at more advanced stages (Eisenberg-Berg & Hand, 1979).

Can moral reasoning and behavior be improved?

THE MORAL INFLUENCES OF SCHOOLS

There is considerable evidence that moral judgments and behaviors can be influenced. Kohlberg (1978) reports that simply discussing moral dilemmas in the classroom typically leads to an increase in level of moral judgment (approximately one-third of a stage). Similarly, Berkowitz, Oser, and Althof (1987) provide evidence that discussing moral problems and evaluating the ethical implications of behavior in groups can do much to elevate moral judgment and behavior. Arbuthnot (1975) found that older adolescents displayed higher levels of moral reasoning after role-playing situations involving specific moral dilemmas. In the Arbuthnot investigation, subjects role-played with a partner (opponent) who used arguments at a level higher than that at which the subject had been assessed. Modeling procedures have also been used to increase morality (Damon & Colby, 1987).

A comprehensive program designed to increase prosocial behavior among elementary schoolchildren is described by Battistich et al. (1991). This program included activities in the school and in the home. Activities were intended to develop prosocial values and interpersonal understanding and made extensive use of cooperative learning and discussion of ra-

The development of morality is an important social and family responsibility. Some evidence suggests that children who are exposed to trials and hardships, or who are placed in situations where they must care for others who are in need, are more likely to develop altruistic, caring behavior.

tionales for rules and reasons underlying moral behaviors. The authors report that after five years, program children engage in more spontaneous prosocial behavior in the classroom, have better perspective taking skills, and are more skilled at resolving conflicts. They caution, however, that differences between program children and other comparable children are slight and often inconsistent. However, it isn't always easy to measure the short-term (let alone the long-term) effects of programs such as this.

SUGGESTIONS FOR ENHANCING MORAL GROWTH

Clearly, the development of morality is an important social and family responsibility. Hoffman (1976) suggests four different types of activity that might be conducive to the development of altruistic, caring behavior:

- Situations in which children are allowed to experience unpleasantness rather than being overprotected

- Role-taking experiences in which children are responsible for the care of others

- Role-playing experiences in which children imagine themselves in the plight of others

- Exposure to altruistic models

THE MORAL INFLUENCES OF THE FAMILY

In addition to what schools and educators might attempt to do, the values and behaviors of parents are highly instrumental in determining those of their children. Indeed, the values of adolescents typically resemble their parents' values rather than those of their peers (Reiss, 1966), and parents' social class is also closely related to children's understanding of rules and social conventions (Johnson & McGillicuddy-Delisi, 1983).

Research reveals a clear relationship between parenting styles and children's morality. Specifically, the internalization of moral rules is fostered by two things: the frequent use of discipline that points out the harmful consequences of the child's behavior for others, and frequent expression of parental affection (Hoffman, 1979). Most forms of parental discipline, Hoffman argues, contain elements of "power assertion" and "love-withdrawal"; that is, discipline usually involves at least the suggestion of the possibility of loss of parental love as well as something like deprivation of privileges, threats, or physical punishment. The main purpose of this "power assertion," according to Hoffman, is to get the child to stop misbehaving and pay attention. From the point of view of children's developing morality, however, what is most important is that there now be an accompanying verbal component. The purpose of this verbal component is to influence children cognitively and emotionally—perhaps by bringing about feelings of guilt or of empathy and by enabling children to foresee consequences. The verbal component might simply admonish ("Don't do that"); ideally, however, it should go beyond simply admonishing ("Don't do that because . . . " or "If you do that, the cat might . . . ").

The future of this world depends on the morality of our children.

main points

TRANSITIONS

1. In many nonindustrialized societies, progress from childhood to adulthood is marked by ritual and ceremony collectively known as rites of passage, often characterized by separation, training, initiation, and induction. Initiation procedures sometimes involve scarification and circumcision. Some writers claim that secondary schools serve as rites of passage.

PHYSICAL CHANGES OF ADOLESCENCE

2. Puberty is sexual maturity, which results from pubescence. The changes of pubescence that make reproduction possible involve *primary sexual characteristics* (menstruation and the capacity to ejaculate semen). Other changes that are not directly linked to reproducing involve *secondary sexual characteristics* (axillary hair, breasts, and voice changes, for example). For a time in late childhood and early adolescence, girls are taller and heavier than boys. From childhood through adulthood, boys have relatively more fat-free mass than girls.

3. Early maturation appears to be advantageous for boys but less so for girls. Pubertal change is most stressful when it puts adolescents out of step with peers, especially if the change is not seen as an advantage. Menarche (first menstruation) and spermarche (first ejaculation) are positive, nonworrisome events for most adolescents. Common adolescent concerns include worries about the future, finances, school, appearance, feelings of inferiority, loneliness, the purpose of life, sex, the stability of the parents' marriage, and lack of time.

NUTRITION DURING ADOLESCENCE

4. Although obesity is the most common nutritional problem of adolescents in North America, concerns over appearance and weight are sometimes apparent in eating disorders such as anorexia nervosa (significant weight loss, refusal to maintain weight, distorted body image) and bulimia nervosa (recurrent eating binges, use of laxatives and diuretics, self-induced vomiting; is more common than anorexia).

INTELLECTUAL DEVELOPMENT IN ADOLESCENCE

5. The intellectual development of adolescents may culminate in thought

that is potentially completely logical, that is inferential, that deals with the hypothetical as well as with the concrete, that is systematic, and that results in the potential for being idealistic. Among other things, formal operations make possible a type of intense idealism that may be reflected in adolescents' frustration or rebellion, as well as in more advanced levels of moral orientation.

6. Information-processing views of development are concerned with three aspects of cognition: the acquisition of a knowledge base (grows with schooling and experience); the development of information-processing strategies (develop by increasing memory capacity and by acquiring better and more appropriate processing strategies); and the development of metacognitive skills (relate to awareness of what is involved in knowing and remembering).

ADOLESCENT EGOCENTRISM

7. Adolescent egocentrism describes a self-centeredness that often leads adolescents to believe that all others in the immediate vicinity are highly concerned with their thoughts and behaviors. It may be manifested in the creation of the *imaginary audience* (a hypothetical collection of people assumed to be highly concerned about the adolescent's behavior) and the *personal fable* (a fantasy whose themes stress the individual's invulnerability and uniqueness).

8. Adolescents' reckless behavior may be linked to a tendency to underestimate the probability of unpleasant outcomes; sensation-seeking drives, perhaps related to changing hormone levels; and the influence of the

peer culture. Some adolescents remain cautious.

MORAL DEVELOPMENT IN ADOLESCENCE

9. Carroll and Rest describe four components of moral behavior: recognizing a moral problem (moral sensitivity), deciding what ought to be done (moral judgment), devising a plan of action according to ideals (moral values), and implementing the plan (moral action). Failure to act morally may be due to a deficiency in any one of these four components.

10. Piaget draws a parallel between understanding the rules governing games and moral development (from no understanding of rules, to a final stage in which rules are understood as being arbitrary, useful, and changeable). Kohlberg describes morality as a decision-making process that progresses through three levels: *preconventional* (concerned with self: pain, pleasure, obedience, punishment), *conventional* (concerned with the group, with being liked, with conforming), and *postconventional* (concerned with abstract principles, ethics, social contracts). Each level consists of two stages.

11. The evidence indicates that cognitive advances are necessary, but not sufficient, for advances in moral judgment. Most young adolescents reason at a preconventional Stage 2 level (concerned with self); Stage 3 morality (emphasis on conforming) does not become common until ages 16 to 18. Principled morality (based on abstract ideals) is rare, even among adults. Gilligan suggests that males become progressively more concerned with law and order (a moral-

ity of *justice*); in contrast, women respond more to social relationships and to the social consequences of behavior (a morality of *caring*).

12. Various programs using indoctrination, role playing, moral discourse, cooperative learning, and modeling have been successful in increasing levels of moral judgment (and sometimes behavior). Parental discipline that points out the harmful consequences of a child's behavior for others, and the frequent expression of parental affection, are also important.

focus questions: applications

■ Is adolescence as we know it a universal psychological phenomenon, or is it largely cultural?

1. Using anthropological studies of primitive rites in other cultures, address the question: Is adolescence a universal phenomenon?

■ What are the most important biological changes of adolescence?

2. Did you mature early or late? Was the timing important? Why?

■ What are the defining characteristics of anorexia? Of bulimia?

3. Starvation is a serious third-world problem; the reasons for this are clear. Overeating, anorexia, and bulimia are serious problems of the developed world. List several explanations for each of these problems.

■ How is formal operations different from concrete operations?

4. Try to find at least one example of formal operations in your own thinking.

■ In what ways are adolescents egocentric?

5. How does adolescents' willingness to take risks relate to egocentricity?

■ Is being good or bad an inescapable part of our personalities?

6. Invent a moral dilemma, and ask several people what they think the *best* resolution for it might be. Analyze their responses in terms of Kohlberg's levels of morality.

study terms

adolescence 501
rites of passage 501
taboo 501
puberty 504
pubescence 504
menarche 504
spermarche 505
secular trend 505
primary sexual characteristics 506
secondary sexual characteristics 506
anorexia nervosa 512
bulimia nervosa 516
formal operations 518
imaginary audience 524
personal fables 526
morality 528
values 529
preconventional level 533
hedonistic 533
conventional 533
postconventional level 533

further readings

The following is an excellent collection of chapters dealing with the transition from childhood to early adolescence. Especially pertinent to this chapter are Malina's chapter on physical growth and performance, Eisenberg's chapter on morality and prosocial development, and Lapsley's account of social/cognitive development.

Montemayor, R., Adams, G. R., & Gullotta, T. P. (Eds.). (1990). *From childhood to adolescence: A transitional period? (Advances in adolescent development, Vol. 2).* Newbury Park, Calif.: Sage.

An excellent account of adolescence today, viewed against the backdrop of historical changes in adolescence, is provided by:

Kett, J. F. (1977). *Rites of passage: Adolescence in America, 1790 to the present.* New York: Basic Books.

A useful collection of articles that describes various approaches and programs for fostering moral development is:

Kurtines, W. M., & Gewirtz, J. L. (Eds.). (1991). *Handbook of moral behavior and development: Vol. 3: Application.* Hillsdale, N.J.: Lawrence Erlbaum.

12

Social Development in Adolescence

I would that there were no age between ten and three-and-twenty, or that youth would sleep out the rest; for there is nothing in between but getting wenches with child, wronging the ancientry, stealing, fighting . . .
William Shakespeare, The Winter's Tale, Act III, Scene 3

focus questions

IS ADOLESCENCE GENERALLY A TIME OF STRIFE, TYPICALLY MARKED BY PARENT-ADOLESCENT CONFLICT?

HOW FREE OF GENDER DISCRIMINATION ARE THE LIVES OF ADOLESCENTS?

WHAT ARE THE PRINCIPAL SEXUAL BELIEFS AND BEHAVIORS OF TYPICAL ADOLESCENTS?

HOW COMMON AND SERIOUS ARE TEENAGE DELINQUENCY, DRUG ABUSE, AND SUICIDE?

outline

THE SELF
The Self in Adolescence
A Measure of Self-Image
Sturm und Drang?
Developmental Changes in Notions of Self
Some Origins of Self-Worth
Identity

SOCIAL DEVELOPMENT IN CONTEXT
Parenting Adolescents
Peer Groups

GENDER ROLES IN ADOLESCENCE
Gender-Role Stereotypes
Gender Differences

SEX
Sexual Beliefs and Behavior
Adolescent Pregnancy
Homosexuality
Sexually Transmitted Diseases

THE TURMOIL TOPICS
Delinquency
Adolescent Gangs
Drugs
Suicide

ANOTHER NOTE

MAIN POINTS

FOCUS QUESTIONS: APPLICATIONS

STUDY TERMS

FURTHER READINGS

W

hen I was setting out to write the first of these books, I often visited my grandmother. She had a way of putting things in perspective—and me in my place.

Like one night when I was about to start a chapter on social development in adolescence. The old lady was sitting on her porch soaking her feet when I arrived. "Wards off the arthritis," she said, insisting I put my feet next to hers in the hot brine, and adding, with hardly a pause, "Beats scrubbing floors in the convent."

She was often like that, my grandmother. Mischievous. She was trying to get my goat by bringing up an old transgression of which I was far more innocent than might have seemed at the time—a transgression that almost ruined my already feeble high school career.

I admit that we weren't supposed to be in the girls' convent at any time, and especially not in the dormitory. But my behavior was, on the whole, quite exemplary. First, it was not my idea (I won't rat and say whose it was; besides, it doesn't really matter anymore). Second, I was not the one who tied the rope to one of the doorknobs, then across the hall to another, then back to another, and back again until all the doorknobs had been tied and the rope zig-zagged like a long snake all the way down the hall. Nor was it I who turned on the fire alarm. If I had, as I tried to explain at the time, I would clearly have left the building with all the others. The fact that I was the only one caught inside should have been proof enough of my innocence.

Also, the only reason I stayed as long as I did—in Céline's room, that is—was because she seemed more panicked than the others in the confusion that followed the alarm, what with girls frantically tugging at their doorknobs and screaming, some of them even breaking their windows. I was in Céline's room to comfort her, I explained. But nobody paid much attention, especially since my reputation was not totally unsullied in those years, a result more of bad luck than anything else.

So the choice was to accept expulsion from school or to scrub the convent's dining room floor every Saturday night (at which time, I might add, all of the girls would be out for their Saturday evening stroll). I decided accepting the expulsion might be the better of the two choices, but my father thought differently.

"Beats scrubbing the convent floor," my grandmother repeated, wriggling her ancient toes.

the self

Maybe. But scrubbing the convent floor wasn't all that bad. It sort of made me the center of attention, which, I confess, I didn't mind. Frankly, I was often lonely as an adolescent.

Hodapp and Mueller (1982) observe that infancy is perhaps the least lonely period of the entire life span. At no other time are we more likely to be surrounded by others intimately concerned with our comfort and well-being: mothers, fathers, sisters and brothers, grandparents, medical personnel, and assorted relatives.

In contrast, adolescence is perhaps the beginning of the loneliest period of our lives, for it is then, Sartre insists, that we first begin to sense our terrible aloneness, our abandonment (see Chapter 13). As we are cast adrift from our parents, there is a fear that we will find nothing else upon which to anchor.

Maybe it is this realization, this fear, that drives us so strongly to seek the company of others—this and one other thing: our sexual drives. (That is *not* why I was in the convent that night!) Because among the most important aspects of social adaptation are those that are directed by the hormonal changes of adolescence, those that have to do with the mounting urges of sexual maturation. Recognition of our aloneness and of our sexuality— these two, taken together, might do much to clarify our understanding of adolescence and of humanity.

Lerner and Shea (1982) argue that all human behavior is basically social. Even biological adaptation requires adjusting to a world filled with others of our own species. In their words, "biological adaptation is, in essence, social behavior" (p. 503). The social adaptation that occurs during adolescence has much to do with the continued discovery and invention of self.

The concept of the **self** is crucially important to a study of adolescence. It is a difficult and complex concept, not easily defined.

In one sense, the self is the *essence* of a person—that which makes the person unique. Thus *personality*, which consists of all our traits and characteristics, is the external manifestation of self.

The term **identity** is often used synonymously with *self*. For example, in Erikson's writings on adolescence, *identity* is used to mean individuals' own notions about who they are—their *self-definition*. One of the important tasks of adolescence is to develop a strong sense of identity—that is, of *self*.

Carl Rogers (1951) and other humanistic psychologists maintain that an individual's self can be understood only from the individual's unique point of view, that because one's self is necessarily private and alone, it can never be completely known by any outsider. And perhaps it cannot be known very well by the individual, either.

the self in adolescence

As we saw in Chapter 10, self includes evaluative aspects sometimes referred to as self-worth, self-appraisal, or self-esteem. In a global sense, my self-esteem (or self-worth, or self-appraisal) is a reflection of how well I like myself.

In childhood, self-evaluation is possible in a variety of areas, each of which is more or less important in determining evaluations of self-worth. For example, Harter (1983) studied children's evaluations of athletic, scholastic, social, physical, and behavioral self-worth. And Marsh, Holmes, and MacDonald (1990) developed a self-description questionnaire that looks at the individual's assess-

ments of physical ability and appearance, peer relations, and academic performance in specific school subjects. For those who think being a good athlete is most important for being liked, evaluations of their worth as athletes contribute significantly in determining global self-worth.

In adolescence, the evaluation of self becomes more cognitive, say Byrne and Shavelson (1987). It is based on a more objective (as opposed to emotional) understanding of who and what the self is, rather than mainly on how well adolescents like themselves or how competent they think they are in important areas. According to Byrne and Shavelson, adolescents make cognitive inferences about the *self* in specific activities (playing ball; writing English compositions; solving arithmetic problems; playing the harpsichord; carrying on conversations) as they evaluate their behaviors in these areas. Inferences in specific areas lead, in turn, to inferences about the self in general areas (for example, athletics or academics). All these inferences lead ultimately to a global self-concept. And although this global self-concept is arrived at through a series of cognitive inferences, it is clearly evaluative. It is difficult to make judgments about what the self is without also at least implicitly deciding whether that is good or bad, desirable or undesirable. Our notions of self-identity are always evaluative.

a measure of self-image

The term **self-image** is used extensively in adolescent research. It is essentially an evaluative concept; as such, it means something very much like what we have taken self-esteem or self-worth to mean. Thus, the Offer Self-Image Questionnaire, a widely used instrument for assessing self-image, has teenagers report on their attitudes and feelings about themselves in a number of different areas (Offer, Ostrov, & Howard, 1981).

OFFER'S FACETS OF SELF

Offer, like Harter (see Chapter 10), based his questionnaire on the assumption that the adolescent has a multiplicity of selves that can be considered and evaluated separately: the *psychological* self, the *social* self, the *sexual* self, the *familial* self, and the *coping* self:

- *Psychological self.* Composed of adolescents' concerns, feelings, wishes, and fantasies. This self reflects adolescents' emotions, their conceptions of their bodies, their ability to control impulses. Examples of items relating to this facet of self are "I am proud of my body" or "I frequently feel ugly and unattractive." (Each descriptor in the Offer questionnaire is worded both positively and negatively.)

- *Social self.* Consists of adolescents' perceptions of their relationships with others, their morals, and their goals and aspirations. An item related to the social self is "I prefer being alone to being with kids my age."

- *Sexual self.* Reflects attitudes and feelings about sexual experiences and behavior; for example, "Sexual experiences give me pleasure" or "Thinking or talking about sex frightens me."

- *Familial self.* Consists of adolescents' feelings and attitudes toward parents and other members of their family; for example, "I can count on my parents most of the time" or "I try to stay away from home most of the time."

- *Coping self.* Mirrors psychological adjustment and emotional well-being and taps, as well, how effectively adolescents function in the outside world. Items designed to assess this aspect of the self deal with mastery of the external world (for example, "When I decide to do something, I do it"), psychopathology ("I am confused most of the time"), and indications of superior adjustment ("Dealing with new intellectual subjects is a challenge for me").

The Offer questionnaire investigates each of these five facets of self by presenting adolescents with a series of statements, such as in the previous examples, and having them select one of six alternatives relating to how well the statement describes the respondent (ranging from "Describes me very well" to "Does not describe me at all") (see Table 12.1).

The Offer questionnaire was developed more than 20 years ago (scoring procedures have changed since then) and has been given to tens of thousands of adolescents. The results of the many studies that have used this questionnaire are especially useful for our purposes. They not only reflect *self-image* but also provide important data concerning adolescent relationships with parents and peers, attitudes toward sexual matters, changes in values and morals, aspirations and goals, and so on. Thus there is a great deal in these studies that can clarify the nature of adolescents' experiences for us.

In a massive study, appropriate translations of the Offer Self-Image Questionnaire were administered to 5,938 adolescents in 10 different countries (Australia, Bangladesh, Hungary, Israel, Italy, Japan, Taiwan, Turkey, the United States, and West Germany) (Offer et al., 1988). One of the objectives was to compare adolescents' self-images in each country to arrive at a closer understanding of what might be universal about adolescence in today's world, as well as what might be specific to given cultural contexts. Adolescents included in the

table 12.1

Facets of self in the Offer self-image questionnaire

IMPORTANT ASPECTS OF SELF*	RELEVANT SELF-EVALUATIVE QUESTIONS
Psychological self	Do I like my body? Am I in control of myself? What are my wishes? My feelings? My fantasies?
Social self	Am I friendly? Outgoing? Do people like me? What kind of morals do I have? What are my aspirations? Am I a loner?
Sexual self	How do I feel about sex? What do I think of pornography? Am I sexually attracted to others? Sexually attractive to them? Comfortable with my sexuality?
Familial self	How do I feel about my parents? Home? Siblings? Other relatives? Do I prefer to stay home? Do people at home like me? Need me? Want me?
Coping self	How effective am I? How well do I cope with what others demand? What school demands? What I demand? Am I well adjusted? Reasonably happy? How decisive am I?

*Note: What adolescents feel about each of these multiple selves has important implications for adjustment and happiness.

study were both male and female, classified into two age groups: younger (ages 13 to 15) and older (ages 16 to 19).

THE "UNIVERSAL ADOLESCENT"

Adolescents in these 10 countries resembled each other in a striking number of ways. The "universal adolescent," to use Offer et al.'s phrase, shares common characteristics with respect to each of the major facets of self-image:

Psychological. The universal adolescent is usually happy and optimistic and enjoys being alive.

Social. These adolescents also enjoy the company of others. They are caring and compassionate. They place great value on school, education, and preparation for adult work.

Sexual. The universal adolescent is confident about the sexual self and willing to talk and think about sex.

Familial. A large majority of adolescents in all 10 cultures express strongly positive feelings toward parents, a high degree of satisfaction with their home lives, and good feelings about their relationships at home.

Coping. Finally, adolescents across these cultures express confidence in their ability to deal with life. They feel talented and able to make decisions.

CONTEXT-BOUND ADOLESCENTS

But there are differences, too, across these cultures. Adolescents from Bangladesh were consistently lower on impulse control. Forty-two percent of the Bengali (Bangladesh) adolescents reported that they were constantly afraid; many admitted feeling inferior to other people; they felt sadder, lonelier, more vulnerable. Why? Context seems the most plausible explanation. This was the poorest of the

Research informs us that the universal adolescent is happy and optimistic, enjoys the company of others, is caring and compassionate, is confident about sex, has strongly positive feelings toward parents, and feels effective and able to make decisions. There are exceptions.

countries sampled. Lack of economic opportunities and of adequate medical care, coupled with widespread disease and starvation, might well lead to feelings of vulnerability and fear.

Other cross-national differences included the very high value placed on vocational and educational goals by American adolescents, and the very low value placed on them by Hungarian and Israeli teenagers—probably because vocational choice is a complex and important developmental task for American adolescents. For most Israeli and Hungarian adolescents, choices are more limited or are largely predetermined by society.

Not surprisingly, there were marked differences in the sexual attitudes of adolescents from some countries. In particular, Turkish and Taiwanese adolescents reported extremely conservative sexual attitudes and behaviors (see Table 12.2)—clear evidence of the extent to which such attitudes are influenced by cultures. Similarly, Israeli adolescents reported the

most positive family relationships, again not very surprising given the emphasis on family and community in their society.

Sturm und Drang?

G. Stanley Hall believed that adolescence is a period of storm and stress for most adolescents in *all* cultures because he thought the mood changes, the irritability, and the conflict of this period are related directly to a dramatic increase in sex hormones. But when Buchanan, Eccles, and Becker (1992) examined the research, they found this supposition to be untrue. Adolescents are not victims of raging hormones, they claim; in fact, nonbiological, contextual factors are more important influences on adolescents' moods and behavior than are hormones. Not surprisingly, if the Offer et al. (1988) cross-national study were to be summarized in a single paragraph, it might read something like this: Contrary to what has been a popular view of adolescence since Hall's pronouncements about the storm and stress of this period, adolescence throughout the world is predominantly a positive, nonturbulent, energetic, growth-filled period.

At the same time, approximately 15 percent of North American adolescents describe themselves as anxious, depressed, confused, and emotionally empty (Offer, Ostrov, & Howard, 1984). This percentage is, in fact, significantly higher than for pre-adolescents.

table 12.2

Sexual self: sample items showing consistent intercountry differences across age and gender

PERCENT ENDORSEMENT

ITEM	AUSTRALIA	BANGLADESH	HUNGARY	ISRAEL	ITALY	TAIWAN	TURKEY	UNITED STATES	WEST GERMANY
Dirty jokes are fun at times.	82	33	39	78	69	43	19	78	69
I think that girls/boys find me attractive.	53	63	58	68	55	41	59	73	63
Sexually I am way behind	20	26	11	10	7	33	19	24	11
Thinking or talking about sex scares me.	7	50	13	6	7	27	22	10	6
Sexual experiences give me pleasure.	67	44	65	72	67	22	49	74	67
Having a girl-/boyfriend is important to me.	69	77	68	75	76	52	74	73	82

Note: Items presented (1) were on a scale on which at least one country was consistently high (or low) in all four age-by-gender cells and (2) were consistently high (or low) for that country for that scale. Consistently high (or low) was defined in terms of being in the upper (or lower) third of nine countries in all four age-by-gender cells. Percentages shown are the average percent endorsement for that item for the country across four age-by-gender cells.
Source: From The Teenage World: Adolescents' Self-Image in Ten Countries by D. Offer, E. Ostrov, K. Howard, and R. Atkinson, 1988, New York: Plenum. Reprinted by permission of the publisher.

STRESS AND LIFE CHANGE

A number of researchers have suggested that one of the main reasons for higher stress during this period is that adolescents experience more significant changes in their lives than do younger children. Both frequency of life change events (such as parental divorce, change of schools, adjusting to work, losing old or establishing new interpersonal relationships) *and* their intensity have important influences on stress, claim Mullis et al. (1993).

To investigate this belief, Larson and Ham (1993) gave questionnaires to 483 fifth- to ninth-graders and their parents to obtain a measure of life events. They also obtained a measure of students' emotions by having them rate their moods at various times. There were two especially important findings: (1) Young adolescents experienced significantly more life-change events than pre-adolescents. The most common of these events include some that were family-based (getting along worse with parents; someone going to the hospital; someone in the family being in trouble with the law), school-based (disciplinary action; changing schools; being suspended), relationship-based (breaking up with a girl- or boyfriend), and other events such as being sick or being cut from a sports team. And (2) young adolescents reported significantly more *negative* affect than pre-adolescents. Larson and Ham also found a close relationship between the occurrence of negative events and an increase in negative moods. Their conclusion is that: " . . . higher rates of daily distress experienced in adolescence may be partly attributed to the greater number of negative life events encountered" (p. 130).

This pattern of negative affect in response to negative life experiences, they add, "is not the universal storm and stress described by early theorists" (p. 138).

"But it is experienced by a substantial minority and it does suggest that for some early adolescence is a pivotal point in the development of positive versus negative adjustment to daily life" (p. 138).

This "substantial minority" includes adolescents whose notions of self-worth are largely negative but whose lives are only moderately unhappy; it includes, as well, those who are profoundly unhappy, who are delinquents and criminals, who seek out and instigate violence, who abuse drugs, who are depressed and prone to suicide. We speak again of these turmoil topics in the final section of this chapter.

developmental changes in notions of self

My self is my *me*. It includes what I think of me, what I think I am capable of, what I think others think of me.

My notions of what I am—my self-concept—are not the same today as they were when, at the age of 6, I stole molasses cookies in Aunt Lucy's kitchen. The self-concept develops, as does the rest of the child. In general, it becomes more abstract, less concrete. When Montemayor and Eisen (1977) had 262 boys and girls from grades four, six, eight, ten, and twelve give 20 answers to the question "Who am I?" they found a progressive increase in the number of responses relating to basic beliefs, values, personal style, self-determination, and other abstract personal qualities. At the same time, there was a dramatic reduction in the number of responses relating to geographic area, citizenship, possessions, and physical attributes. For example, a typical 9-year-old boy's responses included: "I have brown eyes; I have brown hair; I have seven people in my family; I live on 1923 Pinecrest Drive." An 11½-year-old girl offers somewhat less concrete notions of self: "I'm a human being; I'm a girl; I'm a truthful person; I'm a very good pianist," and a 17-year old girl presents a highly abstract self-concept, based largely on interpersonal style and emotional states: "I am a human being; I am an individual; I don't know who I am; I am a loner; I am an indecisive person; I am an atheist" (pp. 317, 318).

Indications of other changes that occur in self-concepts with advancing age are found in the Offer et al. (1988) survey of self-image in 10 countries. Among other things, this study found that older adolescents (ages 16 to 19) compared with the younger group (ages 13 to 15) were typically more self-confident, more expressive, and more open to the opinions of others. Younger adolescents also report more self-consciousness, a feeling that is probably closely linked with their lower self-confidence. Not surprisingly, more of the younger than the older group reported that thinking or talking about sex frightened them.

some origins of self-worth

Children spend the first seven years of their lives trying to determine *where* they are, we're told. Then they spend another seven wondering *who* they are, and yet another seven pondering the question of *why* they are.

There is a fourth, equally important question dealing not with where, who, or why, but simply with whether the self is worthwhile, lovable, and other good things that most of us want to believe we are. What I think of me—my self-worth or self-esteem—is fundamentally important to my behavior and to my happiness.

COOPERSMITH'S STUDY

The classic study in this area is Coopersmith's (1967) intensive investigation of self-esteem among 85 boys. These boys were divided into groups according to their self-esteem, a concept defined in Coopersmith's words as the "extent to which the individual believes himself to be capable, significant, successful, and worthy. In short, self-esteem is a personal judgment of worthiness that is expressed in attitudes the individual holds toward himself" (p. 5).★

Among Coopersmith's most important findings were that individuals with higher self-esteem were more likely to be selected as friends; found it easier to make friends; were more likely to assume an active rather than a listening role in group discussions; were less likely to be highly conformist; scored higher on measures of creativity; and were more outspoken, less sensitive to criticism, and less self-conscious. Supporting this, Elliott (1982) reports that adolescents low on self-esteem are more likely to present a false front (lie or deceive to make themselves look good).

FACTORS CONTRIBUTING TO SELF-ESTEEM

The major goal of Coopersmith's investigation was to identify factors related to the development of high or low **self-esteem**. Especially important is his finding of significant relationships between parents' characteristics and childrearing modes and their children's self-esteem. Parents with high self-esteem tended to have children who also thought highly of themselves. These families were characterized by closer relationships and less discord and were more democratic in their decision making. Perhaps most striking, families of boys high in self-esteem were significantly less permissive, more demanding, stricter, more consis-

★Or, of course, "herself."

tent in the enforcement of rules, but more prone to reinforcing good behavior. In Baumrind's (1977) terms, they were more authoritative than authoritarian or permissive (see Chapter 8).

Other interesting findings from this study are that boys high in self-esteem tend to be more intelligent, to appear happier to their mothers, to develop more rapidly in locomotor areas, and to achieve better in school.

In summary, the Coopersmith study indicates that self-esteem is closely related to adjustment and behavior, that an individual's chances for success increase with self-esteem. What is not clear is the extent to which high self-esteem determines success and happiness and the extent to which happiness and success contribute to the development of self-esteem.

INSIGHTS FROM A CROSS-CULTURAL COMPARISON

A large number of studies indicate that Chinese children have lower self-esteem than American children (see, for example, Stigler, Smith, & Mao, 1985). At first glance this might seem strange because we know that self-esteem is closely related to feelings of competence. The higher one's self-assessment of competence, typically the higher will be self-esteem (Statman, 1993; Nesbitt, 1993). But even Chinese students who do very well nevertheless have lower self-concepts.

One possible explanation for this, Stigler et al. (1985) suggest, is the high desirability of self-effacement in Chinese society—and an opposing tendency to reinforce confidence and aggressiveness in American society. But this may be only part of the explanation.

Chiu (1993) looked at self-esteem among more than 800 Taiwanese and American children using the Cooper-

smith Self-Esteem Inventory. He, too, found significantly higher self-esteem scores for American students. But, claims Chiu, an analysis of teacher ratings as well as of student responses indicates that the Taiwanese students did not minimize their estimates of self-worth out of a need for self-effacement. He suggests that their general tendency to consider themselves unworthy—that is, to lack self-respect—may be due largely to the fact that they have far fewer opportunities for success than do American students. Chinese classrooms, notes Chiu, are unidimensional; all students work on the same tasks at the same pace and mostly with similar success. And both in the school and in the home, children tend to be treated with less respect and to be praised less for success. In Chiu's (1993) words, "the socialization process emphasizes modesty and humility. Chinese children tend to blame themselves when they fail and to give the credit to others when they succeed . . ." (p. 313). It should not be surprising that Chinese children do not evaluate themselves as positively.

What cross-cultural research such as this emphasizes is the extent to which different socializing experiences are reflected in different developmental outcomes—and the extent to which we must be cautious when generalizing our theories and findings.

identity

The notion that one of the most fundamental aspects of all development is the development of self (and of self-esteem) is shared by a large number of psychologists. Erikson's (1988) work is probably the best example of a theoretical position devoted to clarifying the importance of self or *identity* (see Chapter 2). By the term *identity*, Erikson (1968) means a sense of *wholeness* that derives from the

past but that also includes future goals and plans. As Waterman (1984) puts it, identity means:

> having a clearly delineated self-definition [comprising] those goals, values, and beliefs to which the person is unequivocally committed. These commitments evolve over time and are made because the chosen goals, values and beliefs are judged worthy of giving a direction, purpose, and meaning to life. (p. 331)

THE ADOLESCENT DEVELOPMENTAL CRISIS

According to Erikson, the development of strong feelings of identity—of clear feelings of who one is—is the most important developmental task facing adolescents. Accordingly, the main developmental crisis of adolescence is the conflict between accepting, choosing, or discovering an identity and diffusion of adolescents' energies resulting from conflict and doubt about choice of identities. Recall that the fifth of Erikson's eight developmental stages is labeled *identity versus identity diffusion*.

Resolution of adolescents' identity crises can take a variety of forms, the most common of which is the selection of an identity that conforms to social norms and to the individual's expectations. Erikson points out that one of the major social functions of prolonged adolescence is that it serves as a period during which adolescents can experiment with different roles in their quest for identity. He is not particularly alarmed that some of these roles constitute negative identities (delinquency and other forms of rebellion, for example) because in most cases they are temporary, eventually giving way to more acceptable and happier identities.

Waterman (1988) points out that even when adolescents appear to have achieved an identity—that is, to have made firm commitments to career and life-style plans—further changes often occur. For example, some college students move in and out of identity crises before finally making a final commitment. And there are those among us who, like Peter Pan, never really grow up.

Erikson's description of this developmental stage has been clarified by Marcia's investigations of the development of identity in adolescence (Marcia, 1966; Marcia & Friedman, 1970). Marcia describes adolescents in terms of the extent to which a positive, stable identity has been achieved—what is called *identity status*. There are four distinct types of identity status, claims Marcia, easily distinguished in terms of whether the adolescent has undergone (or is currently undergoing) a crisis and whether a commitment has been made to a specific identity. The key concepts are *crisis* and *commitment*.

IDENTITY DIFFUSION

Adolescents in this state are characterized by a total lack of commitment, and they have not yet experienced an identity crisis. These are individuals whose political, social, and religious beliefs are ambiguous or nonexistent and who have no vocational aspirations. Muuss (1975) suggests that whereas **identity diffusion** is common and normal in early adolescence, it is less normal in late adolescence. Individuals who have not developed a mature sense of identity by late adolescence are sometimes recognizable as what Marcia calls *playboys*, or as disturbed individuals characterized by high anxiety, low self-esteem, and lack of self-confidence (Marcia, 1980). Waterman (1988) also reports that these individuals are likely to be at the preconventional level of moral reasoning and are often social isolates.

FORECLOSURE

Foreclosure is a strong commitment to an identity without having experienced a crisis. It is clearly illustrated in situations in which political, religious, and vocational decisions have been made for an adolescent and are accepted without question, as might be the case in close-knit religious or political communities in which the roles of each individual (as well as their beliefs) are determined by others. It is also the case when adolescents simply allow parents (or sometimes peers) to make important

identity-related decisions for them. These adolescents do not go through an identity crisis. Their most striking characteristics appear to be high adherence to authoritarian values (obedience, respect for authority) (Marcia, 1980).

Côté and Levine (1988) point out that the negative aspects of adopting a "ready-made" identity have been unfairly emphasized. On the positive side, some of the "foreclosed" choices that adolescents adopt are admirable. In addition, such individuals often manifest better adjustment, lower anxiety, and better relations with their parents.

MORATORIUM INDIVIDUALS

A large group of adolescents actively explore a variety of roles and experiment with different commitments for various periods of time termed *moratoria*. The moratoria of adolescence, says Erikson, serve as periods during which it is not essential to be fully committed to one life-style, one vocation, or one set of beliefs—periods when adolescents can explore available alternatives. During the **moratorium** stage, adolescents have vague, changing commitments. In this sense, they are in a crisis. But it is a useful crisis for most adolescents, because in the absence of a moratorium during which they can explore, they are in danger of premature commitment (as in the case of foreclosure) or of continuing lack of commitment (as in identity diffusion).

IDENTITY-ACHIEVED INDIVIDUALS

Adolescents who have experienced the moratorium (have, in other words, experienced a crisis of lesser or greater severity) and who have arrived at a choice—a commitment—may be described as *identity-achieved*. Marcia reports that these adolescents are more independent, respond better to stress, have more realistic goals, and have higher self-esteem than adolescents in any of the other three categories. However, he also emphasizes that identities are never completely static and absolutely permanent.

Marcia's descriptions of the development of identity status are summarized in Table 12.3.

COMMON PATTERN OF IDENTITY DEVELOPMENT

Researchers usually ascertain adolescents' identity status either through interviews or using measures such as Grotevant and Adams's (1984) *Extended Objective Measure of Ego Identity Status*. This 64-item questionnaire looks at adolescents' religious, occupational, political, philosophical, and social commitments.

Findings from studies using these approaches indicate that most adolescents progress through some or all of these identity statuses in similar ways. Thus early adolescence is generally characterized by *identity diffusion* (no crisis; no commitment). This period is followed by the *moratorium* (a period of crisis; exploration of alternatives). Finally, adolescents achieve identity (crisis finished; commitment made).

Of course, there are exceptions to this pattern, most notably with respect to *foreclosure* individuals who bypass the identity crises of adolescence by adopting a ready-made identity.

GENDER DIFFERENCES IN IDENTITY DEVELOPMENT

Gilligan (1982; Gilligan et al., 1988) also suggests there might be some important exceptions relating to gender differences. She argues that Erikson's stages are based on a masculine model, and that the process of identity development for females is quite different. Whereas males are oriented toward defining themselves in terms of occupations and careers, females are more oriented toward defining themselves in terms of relationships.

t a b l e 12.3

Marcia's descriptions of identity status in terms of crisis and commitment*

STATUS	CHARACTERISTICS
Identity diffusion	No crisis; no commitment (ambiguous belief systems; no vocational commitment)
Foreclosure	No crisis; strong commitment (commitment predetermined by political, social, or religious affiliation)
Moratorium	Crisis; no commitment (period of exploration of alternatives)
Identity achieved	Crisis finished; commitment made

*A *crisis* is defined as a period of active and conscious decision making during which various alternatives are examined and evaluated. *Commitment* is acceptance of a combination of political, social, religious, or vocational alternatives.

Streitmatter (1993) investigated the possibility of gender differences in identity development by comparing responses of male and female students assessed in early adolescence (seventh and eighth grades) and again three years later. Not only did she find that these students progressed very much as predicted on the basis of Erikson's theory, but she also found *no* significant differences between males and females. In her words: "The identity development process does not appear to be differentiated by gender" (p. 64). However, Streitmatter is quick to point out that our measures of identity development are not very complete, and that identity development may be more complex for females.

social development in context

The development of self does not occur in a vacuum, as our cross-cultural research so dramatically emphasizes. It occurs in a specific ecological context, a niche characterized by a wealth of in-

t a b l e 1 2 . 4

Three stages of socialization

STAGES	TIME FRAME	CONFLICT
High dependence on parents	Early childhood	Low
Decreasing dependence on parents and increasing independence	Late childhood Early adolescence	Increasing Increasing
High independence	Late adolescence Early adulthood	Decreasing Decreasing

teractions and influences. In Bronfenbrenner's (1989) terms, face-to-face
interactions define adolescents' *microsystem*, perhaps the single most important
source of influence on the developing
person. As we saw earlier, peers and parents are a fundamental part of the microsystem at every age through childhood.

***

parenting adolescents

At the risk of oversimplifying, we can
describe the socialization of adolescents
in terms of three general stages based on
the changing roles of friends and parents
(Table 12.4). The first, a pre-adolescent
phase, is marked by children's continuing
physical, social, and emotional dependence on the family and by low conflict.
The second, spanning early adolescence,
involves increasing independence and
greater conflict. The third stage, beginning in later adolescence, is marked by
declining conflict and the achievement of
relative independence from parents. Independence does not imply that children
break all bonds with their family and tie
themselves irrevocably to groups of
peers. In fact, as Offer et al.'s (1988) study
of adolescent self-image showed, the
majority of teenagers have very good
relations with their parents. There is a
mutual interdependence between parents
and their children that continues well beyond adolescence (Collins, 1991).

ROLES OF PARENTS

Alvy (1987) proposes that parents of
adolescents have several important responsibilities: providing basic resources
and care (food, medical and dental care,
shelter, clothing), protecting adolescents
(monitoring activities, teaching self-
protection skills, safeguarding from
threats of all kinds), guiding and supporting development (providing opportunities for intellectual, social, emotional, and
spiritual growth; fostering self-esteem),
and advocacy (supporting and helping
adolescents in relation to groups such as
schools, employers, and various experts
and institutions involved with their care).

Much of parenting involves protecting
children from their own immaturity. For
young children, whose immaturity is
clearly reflected in their dependence, this
role poses little conflict. But parenting
adolescents, whose immaturity is less
(and who, in most cases, do not recognize their immaturity), is a far more difficult function.

There are several reasons, suggest
Small and Eastman (1991), why rearing
adolescents in contemporary society
might be more difficult and might lead to
more conflict. First, the period of adolescence has lengthened significantly in all
industrialized countries. Hurrelmann
(1990) notes that most adolescents attend
schools and post-secondary institutions
through their teen years and beyond, and

many remain economically dependent on their family for all or much of that time. This has led to greater uncertainty about the responsibilities of parents. Parents have also become confused about how best to prepare adolescents for entry into an increasingly complicated and rapidly changing world with competing sources of information and values. There are also more dangers about which to worry—high-risk and potentially harmful activities, and substances and influences such as drugs or radical cults. Finally, increases in family breakup and increased mobility of family members have led to an erosion of the family so that parents of adolescents have fewer sources of advice or support.

Partly because of the responsibilities and difficulties of parenting adolescents, and partly because of the changing roles and relationships of parents and adolescents, this period frequently involves conflict.

PARENT-ADOLESCENT CONFLICT

"The irrevocable giving-up of the love relationships of childhood," says Kaplan (1984), "entails an extended and painful emotional struggle" (p. 141). It is a period often characterized by varying degrees of conflict between parents and child. The current view is that conflict typically arises because the changing needs and interests of adolescents require a readjustment in the family system. Paikoff and Brooks-Gunn (1991) note that the greatest conflict occurs in early adolescence (during puberty), before adjustments in the family. Conflict typically declines in later adolescence.

Part of the "turbulence on the home front," say Bibby and Posterski (1992), relates to adolescents' increasing allegiance to peers. In their survey of nearly 4,000 adolescents, freedom and friendship ranked first and second in terms of im-

portance; family life was a distant ninth (Figure 12.1). Early in adolescence, children find themselves torn between two forces: On the one hand is their former allegiance to their parents, their continued love for them, and their economic dependence on them; on the other is a newfound allegiance to friends and a need to be accepted by peers. Adolescents often list the following as causes of strife: parental interference with social life, lack of adequate financial assistance, parental intrusion about schoolwork or criticism of grades, and parental criticism of friends (Sebald, 1984).

Petersen (1988) reports that areas of conflict have apparently not changed appreciably in the past 50 years, and that they still concern the more "mundane" things in life: chores, curfews, acceptable dress, homework, and so on. Potentially more explosive matters such as those relating to sex and drugs are not usually discussed.

peer groups

"Adolescents have an urgent need to belong," says Drummond (1991, p. 283). Not only do the **peer group** and friends satisfy emotional needs, but they are an important source of information and opportunity for socialization. The adolescent peer group is, in many ways, like a separate culture that eases the transition from childhood to adulthood.

Adolescent peer groups vary in size, interests, social backgrounds, and structure. They might consist of two or three same-sex people (buddies, pals, best friends), larger groups of same-sex individuals, or couples who currently find themselves in the throes of romantic love. Yet another type of peer group includes people of both sexes who "hang out" together. In addition, there are gangs,

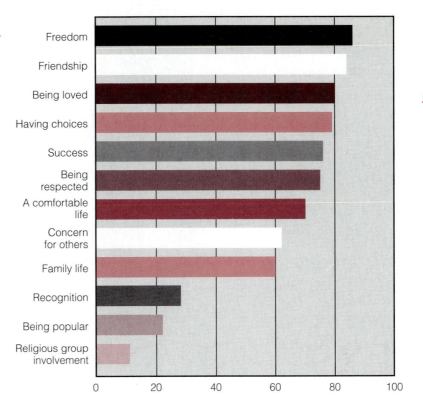

f **igure 12.1**

Percentage of Canadian adolescents selecting each value as "very important." Values were presented as "terminal" or "end-state"—as something desirable and worth striving for, for the future. Source: R. W. Bibby and D. C. Posterski, Teen Trends: A nation in motion, Toronto: Stoddart Publishing Co., 1992, p. 15. Reprinted by permission of Stoddart Publishing Co., Ltd.

about which we say more in a later section. Most adolescents belong to several groups at the same time. Indeed, friends (who are typically part of the peer group) are adolescents' most common source of enjoyment (music is second; dating, third) (Bibby & Posterski, 1992).

DEVELOPMENTAL CHANGES IN PEER GROUPS

Research indicates that peer groups change in predictable ways through adolescence, becoming both larger and more complex (Crockett et al., 1984). At the same time, adolescents spend increasing amounts of time with peers whom they have chosen as friends, rather than simply with classmates. The intimacy of friendships also increases, with adolescents sharing more thoughts and feelings, rather than simply engaging in activities together (Gottman & Mettetal, 1987).

Figure 12.2 illustrates the development of groups in adolescence as they progress from small groups of same-sex members to interaction between groups of different sexes, leading eventually to the formation of what Dunphy (1963) calls the "crowd"—a large heterosexual group that has formed from the smaller single-sex groups. In later stages of adolescence there is a gradual disintegration of the earlier cohesiveness of the groups, brought about by the pairing of boys and girls into couples

AGE SEGREGATION OF PEER GROUPS

Adolescent peer groups tend to consist of people of similar ages. Montemayor and Van Komen (1980) observed 403 adolescents in natural settings (parks, shopping centers, schools, playgrounds, and so on) and questioned them about their relationships with the people with them

f **igure 12.2**

*Stages in peer group development during ado-
lescence. (Based on D. C. Dunphy, "The Social
Structure of Urban Adolescent Peer Groups,"
Sociometry, 26, p. 236. Copyright 1963 by
The American Sociological Association. Used by
permission.)*

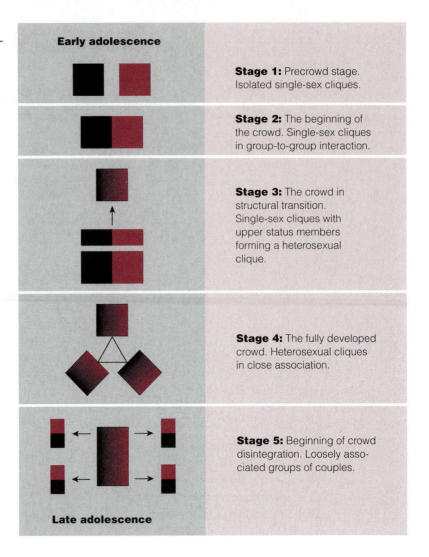

Early adolescence

Stage 1: Precrowd stage.
Isolated single-sex cliques.

Stage 2: The beginning of
the crowd. Single-sex cliques
in group-to-group interaction.

Stage 3: The crowd in
structural transition.
Single-sex cliques with
upper status members
forming a heterosexual
clique.

Stage 4: The fully developed
crowd. Heterosexual cliques
in close association.

Stage 5: Beginning of crowd
disintegration. Loosely associated groups of couples.

Late adolescence

(for example, were they parents, friends,
relatives?). These researchers found considerable evidence of age segregation,
particularly in schools. Older adolescents
were most likely to be found with same-
sex, same-age peers; younger adolescents
were sometimes found with people of
different ages, most of these being relatives. In general, adolescents were found
most often with other adolescents, rarely
with younger children, and also rarely
with parents (especially fathers).

Age segregation of peer groups appears to be general throughout childhood, claims Hartup (1978). When

children have a choice, they are most
likely to select friends similar to them
in age (as well as in ability and interests,
both of which are related to age). Hartup
suggests that age segregation is not necessarily a good thing, a point also argued by
Bronfenbrenner (1970) and others. These
researchers maintain that it is important
for children to have contact with individuals of a variety of ages. Contact with
young children might help prepare adolescents for parenthood; by the same
token, contact with older people is important for the socialization of children
and adolescents.

THE IMPORTANCE OF PEER ACCEPTANCE

The importance of being accepted by peers is highlighted in a large-scale study reported by Gronlund and Holmlund (1958). A group of 1,073 sixth-grade children were asked to select five people with whom they would like to sit, work, or play. Based on these sociometric data, the investigators divided the entire sample into two groups, designated the high-status group and the low-status group. The high-status children were those selected more often: 27 or more times; low-status children were those selected fewer than three times. Seven years later the records of some of the children in these groups were examined to determine how many had graduated from high school. It is significant that 82 percent of the high-status group compared with 45 percent of the low-status group had graduated, particularly because observed differences in intelligence between the two groups were too small to account for the higher dropout rate of the low-status children.

Studies like this are not certain evidence that peer rejection is the causal factor in school dropouts, delinquency, or other forms of social maladjustment. It is equally plausible to suppose that those factors responsible for maladjustment are the very factors that cause children to be rejected by peers in the first place.

The characteristics of adolescents who are well liked by their peers are similar to the qualities of well-liked school-age children described in Chapter 10. Children who are friendly, sociable, and outgoing as opposed to hostile, withdrawn, and unsociable are most liked by their peers. In addition, adolescents tend to emphasize personality characteristics associated with happiness. The person who is sociable, cheerful, active, and fun loving is typically the most popular.

gender roles in adolescence

n Chapter 8 we pointed out some of the typical differences in the play behavior of young boys and girls. Not only is the play of boys frequently more boisterous, aggressive, and physical than that of girls, but the toys they select (and that parents select for them) tend also to be "sex-typed."

Differences between the sexes go far beyond the toys with which they play and their physical movements while playing. They include as well the sometimes dramatic (and sometimes very subtle) differences in the behaviors that are expected of males and females—hence that are considered *masculine* or *feminine*. These differences in behavior, together with the attitudes and personality characteristics associated with them, are what define **gender roles**, (sex roles). *Gender* refers specifically to the psychological characteristics typically associated with biological sex. Thus there are two sexes, male and female, and two corresponding genders, masculine and feminine. Bem (1974) also argues that there are individuals who share relatively equally the characteristics of both genders, and labels these individuals "androgynous." The learning of sex-appropriate behavior (of gender roles) is referred to as **gender-typing**. Explanations of gender-typing are presented in Chapter 8.

gender-role stereotypes

Very early in life, children begin to learn about the behaviors their culture finds acceptable and desirable for members of their sex. What do they learn in North America? Traditionally, males learn that it is masculine to walk without excessive buttock movement, to run fiercely with arms swinging free, to sit with legs sprawled, to throw a ball with an extended arm and a flexed wrist, to wrestle and fight (or at least to be playfully aggressive), to love sports, and to be interested in science and mathematics. Females learn that it is feminine to walk with a more exaggerated buttock movement, to run with elbows tucked into the rib cage and with limp-wristed hands, to sit with legs crossed properly at the knee and hands held neatly in the lap, to throw a ball with a stiff-wristed motion, to sit quietly and demurely, to play the piano, to be interested in arts and books, and to learn to cook and sew.

These sexual stereotypes are in some cases superficial and trivial; in others they are more fundamental. Some might reflect basic anatomical differences; others are influenced more by context. In general, North American gender roles associate the male figure with active, work-oriented, and positively evaluated activities and the female figure with more passive, home-oriented, and less positively evaluated roles (Long, 1991). Boys and girls still have little difficulty in identifying personality characteristics that are stereotypically masculine or feminine. In fact, not only do they agree about what boys and girls should be like, but also they agree that masculine characteristics are more desirable (Shepherd-Look, 1982). It is perhaps partly for this reason that research indicates that masculine (and androgynous) sex-role orientations in women are associated with positive self-concepts (Long, 1991).

SEX-ROLE PREFERENCE

"If you woke up tomorrow and discovered that you were a girl, how would your life be different?" Tavris and Baumgartner (1983) asked a group of American boys. "Terrible . . . ," "a catastrophe . . . ," "I would immediately commit suicide . . . ," were some typical answers.

But when girls were posed the same question—that is, what would happen if you discovered you had become a boy?—they responded quite differently: "Great . . . ," "now I can do what I want . . . ," "now I can be happy. . . ."

Patterns of responses were clear: Girls often responded positively to the "change-sex" question; boys did so extremely rarely. This difference was evident in children as young as age 8 and as old as age 17. These sexual stereotypes appeared to be learned very young and to be very pervasive.

Five years later, Intons-Peterson (1988) asked the same question of 11-, 14-, and 18-year-old Swedish and American adolescents to see if there had been any measurable changes in the intervening years. In addition, she used other measurements to uncover predominant beliefs about differences between males and females. She selected Sweden because, since 1968, the Swedish government has had an explicit, family-based social program aimed at equalizing the sexes. As a result, Intons-Peterson expected that gender stereotypes would not be as marked in Sweden as in the United States and that male and female reactions to the sex-change question would not reflect as decided a preference for the male sex.

Some of her predictions are borne out by the results of the study. As expected, personality characteristics thought to be most descriptive of males in the United States reflect the "hard-driving, macho image of lore" (Intons-Peterson, 1988); females are seen as less aggressive, as gentler. And although these differences are also apparent in the Swedish samples, they are not as extreme. Swedes in the study were more likely to see women as capable and effective and men as being emotional and tender.

Responses to the "sex-change" question were essentially identical to what they had been in 1983. Although a majority of females were content with their gender, most responded in terms of the positive aspects of becoming male. They wrote that they would now enjoy athletics more, that they would travel and stay out later at night, that they would study less but think more about a career. They also felt they would be more aggressive and less emotional, that they would be less concerned about their appearance, and that they would need to become interested in fighting and in "showing off."

Most males still responded very negatively to the thought of becoming female. They saw themselves as becoming burdened by menstruation and more concerned with contraception and becoming pregnant. They expected to be more passive, weaker, and restricted more to indoor activities. They thought, too, that they would become more interested in permanent sexual relationships and more emotional.

Interestingly, these gender differences are more apparent for the 18-year-olds than for the younger group, especially in Sweden. This might be evidence that attempts to eradicate sex stereotypes and to achieve greater gender equality are beginning to have an effect.

These evaluations reflect some of our culture's widely held beliefs about gender; in other words, they reveal our prevalent sexual stereotypes. Stereotypes are sometimes partly valid, sometimes not. Rarely are they entirely one or the other. Gender stereotypes are no exception. What are some of the real differences between males and females?

gender differences

There are obvious biological and physical differences related to anatomical sex; psychological differences are less clear.

BIOLOGICAL DIFFERENCES

We know that males are taller and heavier than females (except for a brief period in late childhood) and that females mature approximately two years earlier than males. Other biological differences include the fact that, beginning in puberty, male blood pressure is higher than that of females; female heart rate is between two and six beats higher than that of males; metabolic rate of males is higher than that of females; physical energy is greater, recuperative time is less, and muscle fatigue occurs more slowly (Shepherd-Look, 1982).

In many ways, however, males are the weaker sex—even from the very beginning. Males produce perhaps 50 percent more sperm bearing the male (Y) sex chromosome than the female sex chromosome, but there aren't 150 male infants born for every 100 females because male sperm are more fragile. And so it continues throughout life. At birth there are about 105 males for every 100 females, but males are more vulnerable to mortality from most infections and diseases, so that by adolescence, numbers of males and females surviving are approximately equal; by age 65, there are almost 150 females living for every 100 males!

Nor only are males more fragile and less long-lived, but they are also more prone to learning, speech, and behavior disorders, are greatly overrepresented among the retarded and the mentally disordered, and are more prone to bed-wetting, night-terrors, and hyperactivity (Shepherd-Look, 1982).

PSYCHOLOGICAL DIFFERENCES

Apart from these primarily physiological differences between the sexes, are there psychological differences?

The answer is yes; but it is not a simple yes, and it is not without controversy.

In an earlier review and summary of much of the important research in this area, Maccoby and Jacklin (1974) concluded that there are clear differences between the sexes in four areas: verbal ability (favoring females); visual/spatial ability (favoring males); mathematical ability (favoring males); and aggressiveness (lower among females).

But at least some of these gender differences no longer seem as clear in the 1990s as they did in 1974—evidence perhaps that because they resulted mainly from socialization processes, they reflected a cultural context that has changed dramatically in the past several decades. Let's look briefly at research in each of these four areas.

The Maccoby and Jacklin (1974) summary indicated that females had greater verbal ability than males. However, subsequent research has found that whereas the difference sometimes exists, it is not very general, it is usually very small, and it is not apparent at early ages (Shepherd-Look, 1982). In a large-scale survey of performance in high school (and beyond), Marsh (1989) found no significant differences between boys and girls on measures of verbal performance. Girls in this sample were somewhat more likely than boys to take additional English courses, but they were no less likely to take mathematics courses. And Feingold (1992) also failed to find significant male-female differences in verbal ability.

Males often do better than females in tests of visual-spatial ability after early adolescence (see Hyde & Linn, 1986). Tests of spatial ability require that the subject visualize three-dimensional objects and be able to rotate or otherwise manipulate them mentally. As Chipman (1988) notes, there isn't a great deal of information about the importance of spatial ability, although some researchers argue that this gender difference may be related to differences in mathematics achievement (Pearson & Ferguson, 1989).

There is some evidence that males perform better than females in mathematical skills *from adolescence onward* (Randhawa, 1991), as well as in science (Erickson & Farkas, 1991). Differences are most evident at the highest levels of mathematics achievement, at which males consistently outnumber females. Hedges and Friedman (1993) report that there are about twice as many males as females in the top 5 percent in tests of mathematical ability—and about six times more in the top 1 percent.

Interestingly, gender differences in mathematics and science are negligible in the earlier years. That females do not continue to do as well may be explained by culturally determined interest and motivational factors. Eccles and Jacobs (1986) found, for example, that students' anxiety about math, its perceived value for students, and parents' stereotyped views of how boys and girls typically perform in math—especially mothers' beliefs about how difficult math is—account for most of the observed gender differences in mathematics achievement.

Significantly, in the same way that gender differences in verbal performance have declined (and, in many instances, completely disappeared), so too have differences in mathematics performance. Hyde, Fennema, and Lamon (1990) did a meta-analysis of 100 studies in this area, involving more than 3 million subjects. Their conclusion? Girls actually show a slight superiority in mathematical computation in elementary and junior high school, but differences in favor of males emerge in high school and are most evident in problem solving. Becker (1990) reports very similar findings based on student performance on the SAT (Scholastic Aptitude Test); only at the higher age levels do differences favor males. And, as

Friedman (1989) concludes following a meta-analysis of research done between 1974 and 1987, differences in both mathematics and verbal ability are very small and are declining.

As we saw in Chapter 8, males are *generally* more aggressive than females. Following yet another meta-analysis (there has been a great deal of interest, and consequently of research, in this area), Hyde and Linn (1986) conclude that males are, *on average*, more aggressive both physically and verbally. This gender difference is assumed to have both a biological and a cultural basis. But even if aggressiveness is related to anatomy and to hormones (hence to genes), it does not follow that observed gender differences would continue to exist in the same form in different sociocultural contexts.

A CONCLUSION

Studies of gender differences reveal very small *average* differences—when there are any differences at all. They do not provide data that would be sufficient for making inferences about specific individuals. As Linn and Hyde (1989) point out, gender differences in height and strength are far more significant and far more stable. Interestingly, so are gender differences in career accessibility and in earning power. Other than perhaps for aggressiveness, not only are psychological gender differences very small, but they have been declining (Jacklin, 1989; Friedman, 1989). It is likely that important social changes are involved here; gender differences may become even smaller in coming decades, and may even disappear completely in some areas. And perhaps, as Chipman (1988) argues, these small average sex differences are not very important in any case. Perhaps it would be far more useful to try to understand how interests and abilities develop and interact.

sex

ex is an area of profound preoccupation for many adolescents, an area that consumes a great deal of their time and energy and to which they sometimes devote themselves with rarely equaled ardor. To begin with, sex is simply a category—male or female—that is usually easily defined by some obvious biological differences.

Sex is also a psychoanalytic term referring to thumb sucking, defecation, masturbation, fantasies, repressions, and indeed to all of living. According to Freud, sex is the source of energy that motivates all of us from birth to death, whether by way of the "normal" psychosexual stages or through the labyrinth of neuroses and psychoses springing from the constant warring between our ids and superegos. Needless to say, not all theorists agree with this Freudian notion.

Sex is also more than a psychoanalytic term or a biological dichotomy. It can mean (as it does in this section) nothing more or less complicated than the physical union between male and female, or variations thereof, or the wish thereto, or the fantasy thereof.

There have been some major changes in sexual attitudes and behavior in recent decades. These are reflected in three areas, says Zani (1991): standards, attitudes toward sexual behavior, and age of sexual initiation.

THE DOUBLE STANDARD

First, the old *sexual double standard* has largely crumbled. This standard said, basically, "Boys will be boys, but girls, well, they should behave." In the 1950s, when Kinsey and his associates (1948, 1953) first began to study sexual activity, the standard was in full force. At that time, most males reported experiencing orgasm before marriage, but only 30 percent of females report_ loing so. By the mid-1960s, incidence of premarital intercourse among girls had risen to about 40 percent—still shy of males' reported 60 percent (Packard, 1968). By the 1980s, however, percentages were about equal at around 75 or 80 (Darling, Kallen, Van Dusen, 1984) (See Figure 12.3).

ATTITUDES TOWARD SEXUALITY

Second, there have been important changes in *attitudes* toward sexuality, re-

f i g u r e 12.3

One manifestation of the sexual revolution: the decline in percentage of people who claim to be virgins at the time of marriage—a more dramatic revolution for women than for men.

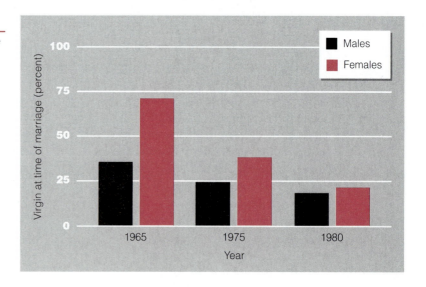

flected not only in the demise of the double standard, but also in an increased openness about sexuality and in a wider acceptance of premarital sex. This does not mean that sex has become totally casual and matter-of-fact among today's adolescents. In fact, the vast majority of teenagers do not think it appropriate to have intercourse when dating casually, but more than half believe it is proper when in love and dating only one person (Roche & Ramsbey, 1993) (Figure 12.4). For the majority of adolescents, the critical factor is whether the partners have a caring and committed relationship. The new standard holds that sexual activity is permitted for both sexes providing there is affection between partners (Table 12.5).

AGE OF SEXUAL INITIATION

Third, average age of sexual initiation has declined in recent decades. A study of more than 600 Italian adolescents found that about one-third of the girls and one-quarter of the boys had had sexual intercourse before age 15 (Zani, 1991). Brooks-Gunn and Furstenberg (1989) report similar findings for the United States but note that it is not uncommon for teenagers to have sex at 14 or 15 and then not to repeat the activity for another year or more.

Among the most obvious antecedents of sexual activity are the biological changes of pubescence. Changes in hormone levels affect sexual arousal directly. In addition, changes in secondary sexual characteristics, such as breast enlargement in girls or lowering of boys' voices, may serve as important sexually linked stimuli. Parental influences are also considered important factors in the sexual behavior of adolescents, although there isn't a great deal of research on the link between the two (Brooks-Gunn & Furstenberg, 1989). Similarly, peers probably influence whether or not an adolescent is likely to engage in sexual intercourse. In this connection, it is perhaps significant that adolescents typically overestimate the

figure 12.4

Percent of a sample of 238 mainly Roman Catholic adolescents who considered sexual intercourse proper, according to intimacy of relationship. Based on data reported by Roche, J. P., & Ramsbey, T. W. (1993). Premarital sexuality: A five-year follow-up study of attitudes and behavior by dating stage. Adolescence, 28, 67–80.

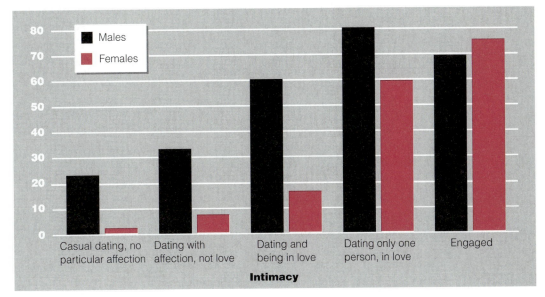

t able 12.5

What adolescents consider appropriate dating behavior. Responses to the question: "If two people on a date like each other, do you think it is all right for them to?":

	MALE	FEMALE	TOTAL
Hold hands			
Yes, first date	92	91	92
Yes, after a few dates	7	9	8
No	1	0	0
Kiss			
Yes, first date	84	80	82
Yes, after a few dates	16	19	18
No	0	1	0
Neck			
Yes, first date	59	42	50
Yes, after a few dates	38	52	45
No	3	6	5
Pet			
Yes, first date	42	16	28
Yes, after a few dates	50	63	56
No	8	20	15
Have sexual relations			
Yes, first date	19	3	11
Yes, after a few dates	51	33	42
No	29	59	44
If they love each other	1	5	3

Source: Based on Bibby, R. W., & Posterski, D. C. *The emerging generation: An inside look at Canada's teenagers,* Table 5.1, p. 76. Toronto: Irwin Publishing, 1985. Reprinted by permission of Stoddart Publishing Co., Ltd. *Note:* Based on a survey of 3,600 high school students ages 15 to 19.

amount of sexual activity engaged in by their peers and underestimate the age at first intercourse (Zani, 1991; Roche & Ramsbey, 1993) (see Figure 12.5).

MASTURBATION

The most common form of sexual outlet for adolescent males and females is **masturbation**. Sorensen (1973) reports that 49 percent of all adolescents ages 13 to 19 have masturbated at least once. Males masturbate more frequently than females, reaching their peak sexual activity (peak is defined as frequency of orgasm, regardless of its cause) between

ages 16 and 17. Among some adolescents, the practice may still be accompanied by totally unfounded fears of impotence, mental retardation, or some other dire consequences. Early writers such as G. Stanley Hall (1916) treated masturbation as abnormal, debilitating, and sinful and provided parents with a number of suggestions for its avoidance or cure.

For males, first ejaculation (spermarche)—sometimes through a nocturnal emission, or through masturbation or intercourse—is usually the first sign of pubescence. But unlike females' menarche, it is often a secretive affair. In Adegoke's (1993) sample of Nigerian boys, only half told someone—usually a friend—about their first ejaculation. Sixty percent of these boys were not prepared for the

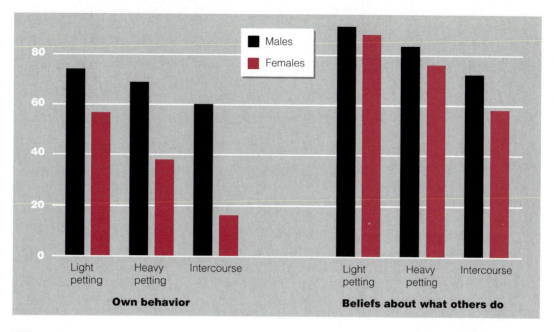

Own behavior **Beliefs about what others do**

figure 12.5

Teenagers' (ages 18 or 19) reported sexual behavior and their beliefs about what others do when dating and in love. Based on data reported by Roche, J. P., & Ramsbey, T. W. (1993). Premarital sexuality: A five-year follow-up study of attitudes and behavior by dating stage. Adolescence, 28, 67–80.

event. Zani (1991) notes that because of males' reluctance to admit ignorance or innocence in sexual matters, most do not seek information.

Although current attitudes toward masturbation are that it is normal, pleasurable, and harmless, some adolescents continue to feel guilty and ashamed about masturbating, this being more the case among younger than older adolescents (Hass, 1979).

adolescent pregnancy

Estimates suggest that there are as many as 12 million sexually active teenagers in the United States—7 million male and 5 million female. Of the 5 million or so sexually active females, approximately 1 million become pregnant each year (see Figures 12.6 and 12.7 in "At A Glance: Births to Unmarried Teen-

agers"). The teenage birthrate in the United States accounts for 12.5 percent of all births (U.S. Bureau of the Census, 1992). It is now among the highest in the world, approximately 17 times higher than in Japan, 3 times higher than in the former Soviet Union, and about twice as high as that in Canada (Jones and associates, 1986). Who gets pregnant? Why? What are the outcomes and implications of teenage pregnancy?

WHO GETS PREGNANT

Teenage pregnancies are not restricted to any particular social, economic, religious, or ethnic group. However, in the United States, teenage pregnancies are more common among blacks than among whites. In 1989, 23.1 percent of all births to black mothers were to teenagers; 10.7 of white births were to teenagers. For mothers of Hispanic origin, 16.7 percent of births were to teenage

chapter 12   569   social development in adolescence

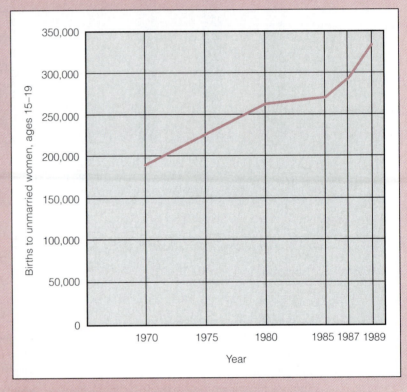

f igure 12.6

Births to unmarried mothers ages 15–19, 1970–1989. Although about a million U.S. teenagers get pregnant each year, many of them are either married or do not give birth. Source: Data from U.S. Bureau of the Census (1992), p. 69.

n the United States, the number of infants being born to unmarried women is steadily increasing. In 1970, about 1 in 10 births (10.7 percent) was to an unmarried mother; by 1989 the proportion was more than 1 in 4 (27 percent), with unmarried teen mothers (ages 15–19) accounting for nearly a third of such births. The birthrate among unmarried women of all ages is likewise going up. In 1989, there were 41.8 births per 1,000 unmarried women, up from 26.4 in 1970. For young women age 15–19, the birthrate per 1,000 unmarried women increased by more than half, from 22.4 in 1970 to 40.6 in 1989.

mothers (U.S. Bureau of the Census, 1992).

Teenage pregnancies are also more common in economically depressed areas (Donnelly & Voydanoff, 1991). Compared with married mothers of the same age, socioeconomic status, and religious background, unmarried teenage mothers often have lower educational and occupational status, more often come from broken homes, and have more difficulty

with opposite-sex relationships (Danilewitz & Skuy, 1990).

REASONS FOR TEENAGE PREGNANCY

The vast majority of teenage pregnancies are unplanned. Black and DeBlassie (1985) suggest that there are a number of plausible reasons for increasing rates of teenage pregnancy. First, social attitudes toward sexual activity and toward preg-

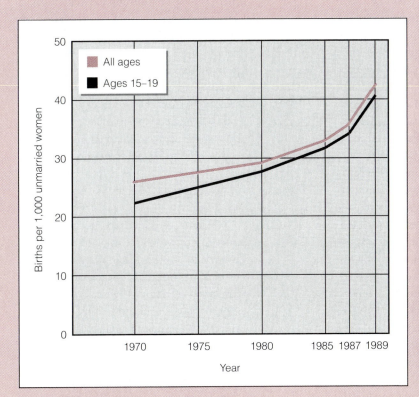

figure **12.7**

Birthrate among unmarried women, 1970–
1989. Source: Data from U.S. Bureau of the
Census (1992), p. 69.

nancy have changed dramatically in recent decades. Pregnancy no longer brings
with it shame and humiliation. Accordingly, there is less pressure, both on boys
and girls, to prevent conception.

Second, there are a raft of psychological factors that might motivate sexual
intercourse. These might include the
loneliness and alienation that are often
part of life in socially and economically
depressed surroundings and that might

sometimes lead girls to grant sexual favors
in an attempt to obtain commitment and
friendship. They might also include girls'
wish to "get back" at overprotective parents or boys' wish to establish the "macho"
image that some male-dominated societies still reinforce. There is some evidence, for example, that teenagers from
more rigid, authoritarian families are
more likely to become pregnant (Romig
& Bakken, 1990). And at times teenagers

may be motivated by a genuine desire to have a baby, someone to love.

Third, there is adolescents' egocentrism, the personal fable that stresses the special invulnerability of teenagers and that is premised on the belief that "It won't happen to me." Arnett (1990) found a close relationship between contraception use among high school students and two measures often highly descriptive of adolescents' experience. One was a measure of adolescent egocentrism; the other, not surprisingly, a measure of sensation-seeking—of the urge to confront danger and take risks. Similarly, Johnson and Green (1993) found that the more mature (cognitively, as well as in terms of age and grade) and the less egocentric the teenage girl, the more likely she was to use contraceptives.

Fourth, and perhaps most important, the majority of pregnancies occur accidentally and as a consequence of ignorance or misinformation concerning sex and contraception. More than half of all teenagers do not use contraception at the time of first intercourse, and perhaps a third continue to use none later (Arnett, 1990). Significantly, approximately half of all pregnancies occur within six months of first intercourse. Many teenagers do not know where to get birth control information, and of those who have adequate information, many are only intermittently sexually active. For them, the cost of the safest birth control methods makes their use prohibitive. In addition, use of an IUD (intrauterine device), oral contraceptives, or a diaphragm requires the cooperation of a physician. As a result, of those who do use contraception, many are forced to use the least reliable methods: withdrawal, rhythm (attempting to time intercourse to coincide with the woman's cyclical periods of infertility), and condoms. Brooks-Gunn and Furstenberg (1989) argue that we

need to know much more about teenage sexual activity and attitudes toward condoms in order to encourage their use.

More cynically, some researchers report that in many (although not all) cases there is little relationship between what adolescents know about contraception or conception and the likelihood of their using contraception. Arnett (1992) suggests that adolescents' behavior is often a result of a tendency toward sensation-seeking, reckless behavior, explained in part by an egocentricity that insists that they are special and invulnerable.

Sadly, they are not invulnerable.

IMPLICATIONS OF TEENAGE PREGNANCY

The effects of teenage pregnancies, the majority of which are unplanned and unwanted, often include a dramatic disruption in the mother's educational and career plans (Kuziel-Perri & Snarey, 1991). There are also much higher health risks with teenage pregnancy and delivery, both for mother and infant (Anastasiow, 1984)—risks that seem to be worse for the second or third teenage pregnancy than for the first (Smith, Weinman, & Malinak, 1984). Moreover, the economic and social conditions under which the majority of teenage mothers are forced to live, and the emotional stresses associated with these conditions and with childrearing, can be a heavy burden. Grindstaff (1988) surveyed a group of 30-year-old women, almost a third of whom had borne children in adolescence. Not surprisingly, he found that those who had no children or who had waited until the age of 25 before having them were better off educationally and economically.

Donnelly and Voydanoff (1991) summarize the findings as follows: "Children [of unmarried adolescent mothers] are more likely than those of older mothers to experience a number of difficulties as they grow and develop. These difficulties include poverty and its associated problems, physical problems, lower educational attainments, problem behaviors, maltreatment and the increased likelihood of becoming adolescent parents" (p. 404).

Although the economic disadvantages of teenage childbearing often disappear over time, as Furstenberg, Brooks-Gunn, and Chase-Lansdale (1989) put it, "The children of teenage mothers, however, are distinctly worse off throughout childhood than the offspring of older childbearers" (p. 313).

The implications of teenage parenthood are clearly more direct and more applicable for mothers and children than for fathers, a great many of whom are not involved in any pregnancy-related decisions or in subsequent childrearing. However, school dropout rates are higher for teenage fathers, even when they do not marry the mother (Marsiglio, 1986). A survey by Redmond (1985) involving 74 white males indicates that most unwed fathers would like to be told if a pregnancy occurs. Most would also like to be involved, along with the girl and their parents, in making decisions related to the outcome of the pregnancy. Interestingly, however, they are unlikely to involve peers in this process.

Divorce rates for teenage marriages are much higher than for marriages that occur later. In addition, some research indicates that these marriages are sometimes associated with suicide, depression, and child mortality. Teenage parents, note Passino et al. (1993), tend to be socially less competent than their nonpregnant peers. They also manifest higher levels of stress and are less sensitive to the needs of their infants. Following a three-year investigation of 48 teenage couples between 15 and 19 years of age, DeLissovoy (1973) concluded: "In general, I found

the young parents in this study to be, with a few notable exceptions, an intolerant group—impatient, insensitive, irritable and prone to use physical punishment with their children" (p. 22).

Clearly, however, these observations and conclusions do not apply to all teenage parents. Many are sensitive, caring, and competent parents. Sadly, however, the probability that this will be the case, given their relative immaturity and lack of experience and information, is not overwhelmingly high.

WHAT TO DO?

Not all teenage mothers are economically disadvantaged, have inadequate job skills, and have children who experience developmental problems (Furstenberg, Brooks-Gunn, & Chase-Lansdale, 1989). Still, as Roosa (1991) notes, most adolescent mothers and their children would benefit by postponing early pregnancies.

Given what Jorgensen (1991) describes as the "staggering" economic, psychological, and social costs of adolescent parenthood, the U.S. Public Health Service has, since 1981, funded a variety of pregnancy prevention programs. The majority of these are offered in junior high schools through sex and family life education programs. Their objective is to decrease adolescent pregnancy by changing sexual attitudes and sexual behavior. For legal (and sometimes moral) reasons, many are *abstinence* programs that do not permit discussion of contraception or abortion (Jorgensen, 1991).

Many of these programs have not been based on systematic research or knowledge about the antecedents of pregnancy, and most have not involved adolescents' family and peer systems. Perhaps it should not be surprising that evaluations of their effectiveness have yielded mixed results (Jorgensen, 1991; Roosa, 1991; Chase-Lansdale, Brooks-Gunn, &

Paikoff, 1991). However, indications are that with more sensitive and careful program development and evaluation, and with further refinement of preventive strategies, program results will be positive (Miller & Dyk, 1991).

Brooks-Gunn and Furstenberg (1989) list a number of preventive strategies that might be implemented by schools and communities. These include offering free access to contraception, providing information about sexuality and contraception, influencing sexual attitudes, and expanding adolescents' life options.

Sex education and pregnancy prevention programs in schools remain controversial; even more controversial is the decision by a number of school jurisdictions to provide condom dispensers for students. Some parents fear that sex education and easy access to contraception may serve to increase adolescent sexual behavior and to foster values that run counter to those of the family and the community. Because of this, and because of the danger of sexually transmitted diseases, many parents advocate sexual-abstinence programs (see Hess, 1990). However, adolescents are not always highly motivated to participate in such courses, especially when what the programs teach contradicts their values and their behaviors. When Christopher and Roosa (1990) investigated the effects of an adolescent pregnancy-prevention program that focused on self-esteem and resisting peer pressure and that taught that sex should occur only after marriage, program dropout rates were very high. Nor was there any evidence that the program was effective in reducing sexual activity. However, Christopher and Roosa point out that the most successful programs are not typically based on abstinence alone, but also provide the alternative of effective contraception.

Brooks-Gunn and Furstenberg (1989) report that sex-education programs are rare in elementary school, although the vast majority of parents and school jurisdictions support them in high school. They report, as well, that the fear that these programs might increase sexual activity does not appear to be warranted.

homosexuality

Homosexual experiences during adolescence do not appear to be especially common. Evidence suggests that approximately one out of every ten adolescent boys, and perhaps half that proportion of girls, have isolated sexual experiences with someone of the same sex, usually during early adolescence (Dreyer, 1982). Estimates of the number of these who subsequently adopt a homosexual or bisexual life-style are extremely unreliable, but are probably considerably less than the 8 or 9 percent who have had adolescent homosexual experiences. That homosexual groups have become more visible and more outspoken in recent decades may account for the popular perception that their numbers have increased. Hyde (1986) reviews evidence that suggests that numbers have remained stable and that incidence of homosexuality is very similar in a number of cultures.

Causes of homosexuality are not known, although there are a variety of theories: genetic, social learning, hormonal. And it is extremely difficult—in most cases impossible—to alter sexual preference.

sexually transmitted diseases

There are more than two dozen known **sexually transmitted diseases (STDs)**, also known as *venereal* diseases. Among the most common are chlamydia, gonorrhea, and herpes; less common are syphilis and AIDS.

CHLAMYDIA

Chlamydia is currently the most common of the STDs ("Sleeping with the enemy," 1991). It was rarely seen until very recent years and still goes largely undetected. Estimates are that as many as 1 of every 10 sexually active women has chlamydia—twice as many·as have gonorrhea. It is now one of the leading causes of infertility among women and is especially widespread in North Africa, the Far East, Great Britain, and the Scandinavian countries ("Chlamydia—More common than gonorrhea," 1988). In the majority of women (approximately 80 percent), chlamydia presents no symptoms in its early stages; this is also the case for about 20 percent of infected men. In later stages, abdominal pain may send the victim for medical help, but by then the woman is often infertile. Chlamydia can be treated easily and effectively with antibiotics.

GONORRHEA

Gonorrhea declined dramatically during the 1980s but is still a highly common STD, at about 1.4 million cases per year in the United States ("Sleeping with the enemy," 1991). Symptoms in males usually include a discharge from the penis and pain during urination. Symptoms in females are more subtle and often go unnoticed. The disease can usually be treated simply and effectively with penicillin and related drugs. Like some other sexually transmitted diseases, it can sometimes be prevented through the use of a condom or simply by washing the genitals thoroughly after intercourse.

GENITAL HERPES

Herpes is caused by a virus and remains incurable; the virus can remain inactive for long periods of time. An estimated 500,000 new cases are reported each year. The disease is believed to be contagious only when lesions are present (like tiny cold sores, commonly found on the penis and scrotum in males and on the vulva, vagina, and cervix in females).

AIDS

AIDS (Acquired Immune Deficiency Syndrome) is a sexually transmitted disease caused by the human immunodeficiency virus (HIV), an organism that appears to mutate rapidly, thereby increasing the difficulty of treating it ("AIDS virus strain beats pill," 1989). At present it is incurable and fatal. It is transmitted through the exchange of body fluids, principally blood and semen. Largely for that reason, AIDS has been found primarily among four high-risk groups: intravenous drug users who often share needles; homosexual males who engage in anal intercourse; hemophiliacs who have been exposed to the virus through blood transfusions; and certain groups of Haitians who engage in rituals involving blood exchange. As of 1991, 199,516 cases had been reported in the United States (U.S. Bureau of the Census, 1992). But because there may be as much as a 10-year lag between exposure to the virus and development of symptoms, reported cases may reflect what was happening 10 years ago. The World Health Organization predicts that worldwide, 4 million women will have died of AIDS by the year 2000 ("AIDS will kill 4M. . . ," 1993). At present, there are about seven times more male than female cases of AIDS in the United States, and homosexual as well as drug-related transmission are most common. However, heterosexual transmission is the norm throughout most of the world and is expected to become more common in North America as well ("Sleeping with the enemy," 1991).

The fact that total numbers suffering from the disease seem small, coupled with the observation that AIDS is still relatively uncommon outside the four

AIDS is sometimes thought to have boundaries defined largely by homosexuality, drug use, and hemophilia. But because of a long lag between infection and symptoms, current manifestations tend to reflect conditions that existed 8 or 10 years ago. Through much of the world, AIDS is a heterosexual disease; some expect it to become that in North America as well.

high-risk groups, has been a source of reassurance for many. However, there are indications that our complacency may be misplaced and that the numbers are higher than expected ("The AIDS threat," 1988). What is perhaps even more alarming is Masters, Johnson, and Kolodny's (1988) assertion that AIDS is spreading rapidly in the heterosexual community. They argue that far more individuals are currently infected than official reports indicate; that transmission can occur from male to female or from female to male in either vaginal or anal intercourse, and even through oral sex; and that because of a time lag of up to seven months between exposure to the AIDS virus and the ability to detect antibodies, some of the blood supply used for transfusions is contaminated.

There has been some speculation that incidence of casual and extramarital sexual encounters and sexual activity among homosexual males would decline signifi-

cantly or change in other ways in the wake of widespread accounts of increases in the incidence of AIDS and other STDs. Stall, Coates, and Hoff (1988) and Morin (1988) report that a number of programs aimed at homosexual males have resulted in dramatic declines in casual sexual encounters and especially in unprotected sexual activity among this group.

Adolescents appear to be well informed about AIDS and how it is transmitted, say Roscoe and Kruger (1990), and as many as one-third claim they have changed their sexual behavior because of fear of AIDS. That means, however, that two-thirds have not.

OTHER STDS

Other STDs include *pelvic inflammatory disease*, a complication that can result from diseases such as gonorrhea or chlamydia. Resulting inflammation of the cervix and fallopian tubes can lead to infertility or tubal pregnancies. Genital warts are also sexually transmitted. They are caused by a virus and affect about 1 million people in the United States each year. They are not usually dangerous and can be removed. Sexual transmission is also the leading cause of hepatitis B, which accounts for about 5,000 deaths in the United States each year ("Sleeping with the enemy," 1991).

the turmoil topics

Adolescence is undoubtedly a time of turmoil for many. At the same time, it is quite the opposite for a number of adolescents, who pass exuberantly through their teen years. These individuals discover the joys of their increased powers of mind and body and are successful in overcoming or avoiding the turmoil that besets their less fortunate peers.

Offer and Offer (1975), following extensive analysis of data derived from administering their self-image questionnaire to groups of adolescent boys, describe three routes male adolescent development can take. *Continuous growth* describes a positive pattern of steady growth; *surgent growth* describes a pattern in which positive growth alternates with brief periods of turmoil and strife; and *tumultuous growth* is characterized by the turmoil that Hall (1916) claimed was the major characteristic of this period. Interestingly, fewer than one-quarter of these samples could be classified as tumultuous. And as we saw earlier, typically only 15 percent of all adolescents describe themselves as anxious or confused or depressed (Offer, Ostrov, & Howard, 1984). Clearly, then, the turmoil topics—delinquency, drugs, suicide—relate only to the minority.

But they are an important minority. And these are important topics.

delinquency

Delinquency is a legal rather than a scientific category. A delinquent is a juvenile who has been apprehended and convicted for transgression of established legal rather than moral laws. Adults in similar situations are termed criminals rather than delinquents.

When delinquency is defined in this manner, surveys of its prevalence can be based directly on police and legal records. These records indicate a tremendous increase in the delinquency rate in recent decades. There are now more crimes committed by adolescents and younger children than by people over 25 (U.S. Bureau of the Census, 1992). However, many of the offenses for which juveniles are apprehended and brought to court are status offenses such as truancy, running away, sexual promiscuity, under-age drinking, or driving without a license (see Table 12.6 in "At A Glance: Juvenile Delinquency and Violence").

When delinquency is defined simply in terms of transgression alone, rather than in terms of transgression, apprehension, and conviction, the picture changes dramatically. In self-report questionnaires, approximately 80 percent of all adolescents admit to having broken one or more laws (Hindelang, 1981), but fewer than 10 percent are ever arrested.

A number of factors appear to be related to delinquency, but because most of the studies that have investigated delinquency simply indicate correlations, it is impossible to identify its specific causes. Age, for example, is related to delinquency; we have no evidence that it causes delinquency. Other related but not necessarily causal factors include social class, intelligence, peers, parents, personality, and sex.

SOCIAL CLASS

Literature on the relationship between social class and delinquency is ambiguous and inconclusive. Although the lower classes, as well as some racial subgroups, are greatly overrepresented among delinquent groups, it is by no means clear that there are in fact many more delinquents

Random and unprovoked violence, sometimes perpetrated by gangs and sometimes by individuals, is as frightening as it is unpredictable. Violence that is not random, but that is based instead on allegiance to ideology and on hatred of identifiable groups (as is the case for some racist groups), is no less terrifying. Although the number of delinquency cases dealt with by North American courts has not changed very much in recent years (in the United States, 1.050 million cases in 1975 and 1.189 million in 1989; in Canada, 77,350 cases in 1987), incidence of violent offenses in the United States increased from 57,000 cases in 1982 to 77,000 cases in 1989. Male juvenile delinquents still outnumber females by a factor of more than 4 to 1; with respect to violent offenses, males outnumber females by approximately 7 to 1.

t a b l e   1 2 . 6

Number (in 1,000s) and types of delinquency cases disposed of by American juvenile courts in 1989

REASON FOR REFERRAL	CASES (THOUSANDS)
All delinquency offenses	1,189
Violent offenses	77
Criminal homicide	2
Forcible rape	4
Robbery	23
Aggravated assault	28
Property offenses	514
Burglary	131
Larceny	309
Motor vehicle theft	67
Arson	7
Delinquency offenses	599
Simple assault	108
Vandalism	83
Drug law violations	78
Obstruction of justice	82
Other*	248

*Includes such offenses as stolen property offenses, trespassing, weapons offenses, other sex offenses, liquor law violations, disorderly conduct, and miscellaneous offenses.
Source: Adapted from U.S. Bureau of the Census (1992), p. 196.

among these groups. Because of the nature of current law-enforcement systems, the often unconscious prejudices of the systems, and their consequently greater likelihood of recognizing and apprehending delinquents among minority and lower-class groups, it is hardly surprising that more of these adolescents are classified as delinquents. At the same time, to the extent that delinquency is a form of rebellion that is sometimes motivated by the desire for material possession, it is reasonable to expect that more of the poorer adolescents would be delinquent. Furthermore, lower-class parents tend to look to the police for help with their children; middle-class parents go to therapists.

INTELLIGENCE

There is a large body of evidence linking delinquency with lower-than-average measured intelligence (see Binder, 1988, for a review of some of these studies). The evidence indicates, in fact, that the difference between average IQs of delinquent and nondelinquent groups may be in the order of approximately eight IQ points (Quay, 1987). However, this should not be taken as direct evidence that lower intelligence causes delinquency. Quay notes that much of this difference in measured intelligence may be accounted for in terms of lower verbal ability. This puts children at a disadvantage in social interaction and in school. Consequently, they are more likely to get into trouble with teachers, school administrators, and parents, and perhaps with friends as well.

PEERS

The influence of peer groups is related to delinquent behavior and has been extensively investigated, particularly in the study of gangs. Like other peer groups, delinquent gangs reinforce their domi-

nant values and also serve as a model for translating these values into actual behaviors. Examples of the importance of peer groups in establishing values and in encouraging certain kinds of behavior are prevalent in television programs. They are also prevalent in various detention centers and other correctional institutions. Because correctional institutions comprise primarily delinquent peer groups, it is not particularly surprising that some 60 percent of all admissions are, in fact, readmissions (Stuart, 1969).

A study reported by Claes and Simard (1992) indicates that delinquent adolescents are more likely to make friends outside of school than are nondelinquents. Not surprisingly, they are also more likely to commit antisocial acts with their friends.

PARENTS

The father is perhaps the most influential parent with respect to delinquency (Biller, 1982). Fathers of delinquent boys are, on the average, more severe, more punitive, more prone to alcoholism, more rejecting, and more likely to have engaged in delinquent behavior themselves. Herzog and Sudia (1970) report as well a higher probability of delinquency among boys from fatherless homes. They speculate that fathers' absence may contribute to delinquency in sons, perhaps by failure to provide adequate male models, perhaps as a function of protest against female domination, or simply because of inadequate supervision. Girls too appear to be more prone to delinquency in father-absent homes (Lynn, 1979) or when the mother is viewed as cold and rejecting (Kroupa, 1988).

PERSONALITY

Many studies have looked at the possibility that delinquency is at least partly a function of an individual's personality characteristics. In one study, for example, Monachesi and Hathaway (1969) administered the MMPI (Minnesota Multiphasic Personality Inventory, a widely used, very detailed, and comprehensive personality test) to more than 15,000 ninth-grade students. Police and court records were checked routinely later for the names of these students. As have a number of other researchers, Monachesi and Hathaway reported that several personality variables appeared to correlate most highly with later delinquency—namely, those having to do with psychopathic tendencies (evident in amorality and rebelliousness) and emotional instability (high scores on what is labeled "neurotisism," manifested in high anxiety and mood fluctuations).

There is evidence as well that high impulsivity (low impulse control), high need for stimulation (danger-seeking orientation), and low self-esteem are related to delinquency (Binder, 1988). With respect to low self-esteem, we noted earlier that delinquents typically think less well of themselves than do nondelinquent adolescents.

SEX

The incidence of delinquency is about four times higher among boys than girls. This may be partly explained by males' greater aggressiveness. Traditionally, delinquency among males has involved more aggressive transgressions, whereas girls were apprehended more often for sexually promiscuous behavior, shoplifting, and related activities. Evidence indicates that this pattern is now changing as more girls become involved in aggressive delinquent acts, including breaking and entering, car theft, and even assault. Drug-related offenses also account for an increasing number of detentions. Interestingly, in a study of female delinquency, Caspi et al. (1993) found highest risk for delinquency among girls who matured earliest. Early maturing girls were far more likely to know—and be friends with—delinquent boys than was the case for girls who matured later.

In summary, it appears that a complex of psychological and social forces impinges on the potential delinquent, although no single factor can reliably predict delinquent behavior. Social class, age, sex, home background, intelligence, personality, relationship with the father, and peer influences are all implicated, but none of these, alone or in combination, can give a complete picture. Clearly, many adolescents from the most deprived backgrounds are not delinquents, and many from apparently superior environments are.

adolescent gangs

Sociologists define a gang as a group that forms spontaneously, that interacts on a face-to-face basis, and that becomes aware of its group membership through conflict with some other group or, perhaps more often, with some representatives of established society (Cartwright, Tomson, & Schwartz, 1975). A gang may consist of different numbers of individuals from a wide variety of backgrounds and locales, although it typically includes a fairly homogeneous group of people who at least live close to one another and who often attend the same school. But most important, a group does not become a gang until it comes into conflict with something external. It is hardly surprising, then, that the word *gang* has always been closely associated with juvenile delinquency, truancy, rebelliousness, and other disturbing behaviors.

Of special current interest are gangs whose members engage in violent behaviors, sometimes simply because of an apparent taste for violence and mayhem.

Some British soccer riots and the occasional school-holiday violence seen in some North American resort areas are examples of this kind of violence. At other times, gang violence is premised on fundamental beliefs and principles that express themselves in strong feelings against certain groups or institutions. In Edmonton, for example, two members of a group identifying themselves as neo-Nazi skinheads beat up and blinded a 60-year-old man who had, more than a decade earlier, expressed anti-Nazi views ("The 'scene' and the skinheads, 1990"). Their admitted philosophy is clearly racist; their dream is of an all-white society; their music is counterculture, frenetic, anarchist; their dress, hairstyles, and makeup intended to shock and outrage; and violence is their *modus operandi*.

They are only one faction of one subgroup; there are many other gangs, most of them small. Some of them are determinedly nonviolent; others are anything but. Some call themselves by such names as skaters, punks, thrashers, headbangers, and death rockers. In California, where the neo-Nazi skinhead movement originated, there are other groups and other labels (for example, SHARP, a counterculture group that claims to be antiracist and that has also been involved in violent incidents).

Fagan, Piper, and Moore (1986) argue that violence among delinquent gangs is often an expression of a new identity that gang members adopt. Adolescents who join small, highly cohesive, counterculture groups are provided with a set of beliefs and principles that are sometimes very well articulated. Their allegiance to the gang is not only a rejection of family, school, and larger cultural values, but is also an embracing of the values and of the individuals in a new community.

But not all adolescents who are dissatisfied, disillusioned, or in need of the community of groups join them in protest. A significant number of the severely dissatisfied drop out of society. Lest another stereotype be fostered, we must point out that the methods of dropping out described here are undertaken by the adventurous and the timid, by the weak and the strong, and by the deluded and the rational—and frequently they are not attempts to drop out but merely attempts to intensify the experience of living.

drugs

Drug use is a fact of life. Drugs are with us constantly in the guise of coffee, tea, headache tablets, cocktails, beer, tobacco, and in thousands of other forms. People have been familiar with drugs for centuries, although they have not always known the chemical components of the substances that they ate, drank, chewed, applied to wounds, inhaled, put in ears, or otherwise used on their persons. But the label is much less important than the effect and sometimes the availability.

The most commonly abused drugs are classified in Table 12.7. The U.S. Bureau of the Census (1992) reports declines between 1974 and 1991 in use of hallucinogens, tranquilizers, marijuana, opiates—and even cigarettes (see "In Other Contexts: Born-With-Two-Teeth and Bobby Thom Have a Smoke"). However there are some indications that alcohol use and abuse has increased during this time, and evidence as well that use of cocaine has increased (see Figure 12.8 in "At A Glance: Changing Patterns of Drug Use"). The United States has the highest rates of illegal drug use among industrialized nations (Newcomb & Bentler, 1989).

SOME DEFINITIONS

The American Psychiatric Association (1987) distinguishes among a number of

table 12.7

Classification of the most frequently abused drugs

CLASS	EXAMPLES
Narcotics	Opium
	Morphine
	Heroin
	Codeine
	Methadone
Sedatives (downers)	Barbiturates (Phenobarbital, Seconal, Nembutal)
	Tranquilizers (Valium, Librium, Vivol)
	Alcohol
Stimulants (uppers)	Cocaine
	Crack
	Amphetamines (Benzedrine, Dexedrine, Methedrine)
Hallucinogens (psychoactive, psychotropic, psychedelic, psychomimetic)	LSD
	PCP
	Mescaline
	Psilocybin
	Marijuana
Inhalants	Glue
	Paint thinner
	Aerosol sprays
	Solvents
Unclassified (or sometimes classified as stimulant)	Nicotine
"Designer" drugs	Any of a combination of chemicals and drugs, often manufactured by amateur chemists

drug-use terms. **Drug abuse** refers primarily to the *recreational* use of drugs and is not considered a disorder unless it impairs social or occupational functioning. **Drug dependence**, a disorder ordinarily resulting from the repeated use of drugs, is manifested in a strong desire to continue taking the drug, either for the pleasant sensations that might result or to escape feelings of withdrawal.

The APA distinguishes between **physiological dependence**, commonly called *addiction*, in which the desire to continue taking the drug is at least partly organically based (for example, not taking it will lead to unpleasant physiological reactions), and **psychological dependence**, sometimes called *habituation*, in which the desire to continue taking the drug has to do mainly with its psychological rather than its physiological effects. **Drug tolerance** refers to changes that occur in the user so that with the passage of time, more and more of the drug is required to produce the desired effect.

Newcomb and Bentler (1989) make the important point that whether or not drug use is *abuse* depends on the drug, the organism, and the context. Thus, use of certain drugs that are toxic or that are likely to have serious adverse consequences is probably abuse; use of drugs by young children or adolescents may be abuse because of the possibility that drug use will interfere with important aspects of development and adjustment; and use of drugs in inappropriate contexts (at work, in school) is also more likely to be abuse.

WHO USES DRUGS?

Researchers have sometimes assumed that there is a drug-use continuum that reflects psychological health and adjustment. At the most positive extreme is the drug abstainer; at the most negative extreme, the frequent drug user or the addict; and in between are infrequent users who occasionally experiment with drugs. However, a longitudinal study conducted by Shedler and Block (1990) indicates that this view is inaccurate. The study looked at psychological characteristics of children from preschool through age 18.

When Bobby Thom wants a smoke, he reaches into the left sleeve of his T-shirt, where he keeps his pack of cigarettes. He saw Marlon Brando do that once in a movie. He thinks it's cool.

Bobby Thom then shakes a cigarette loose from the pack, lights it with his disposable lighter, and sucks the Virginia blend deep into his lungs. Now, cigarette dangling from his lips, he bends over the table, lines up the shot, and smoothly strokes the cue ball.

When Born-With-Two-Teeth wants a smoke... well, it isn't really a question of wanting a smoke. You see, Born-With-Two-Teeth is a medicine man, a shaman of the Stoneys. Tobacco is not just something you burn and inhale like you might chew on the stalk of a meadow plant or suck on a wild hazelnut. Tobacco is something to enrich a man's dreams, to give him visions, to move him to trances. Tobacco smoked jointly by those who are angry makes them peaceful. The sick and diseased can sometimes be cured when smoke is wafted over them. Gods who are offered tobacco will send rain or fish. Sometimes they will even send infants to those who are barren. And tobacco smoked by a shaman when the moon is full may bring visions of the future so clear they seem like yesterday.

Tobacco is holy. One has to be careful with its use.

Tobacco, says Dobkin de Rios (1984), served as a hallucinogenic drug in the New World long before European contact. It was used extensively by the Mayans, the Aztecs, and the Incas, as well as by many other native tribes in what is now Mexico and by the Plains Indians of North America. But it was not used as a pastime or as recreation—as rapidly became common among Europeans once the drug had been introduced there.

Some botanists speculate that the tobacco smoked by native North and South Americans was far more powerful than the blends in common use today (see, for example, Heiser, 1969). There is evidence, nevertheless, that traces of certain hallucinogenic substances are still present in today's commercial tobaccos (see Dobkin de Rios, 1984).

To Think About: To what extent are people's reactions to drugs shaped by cultures? What factors are involved in determining the acceptability, the availability, and the legality of drugs? What sorts of changes in acceptability, availability, and legality might be desirable? How could they be brought about?

n the 1960s, social prophets loudly trumpeted their fears that drugs were taking over the lives of adolescents, that coming decades would witness drug-related social upheavals and political catastrophes that could scarcely be imagined. But recent decades have seen a decline in the use of drugs in most categories.

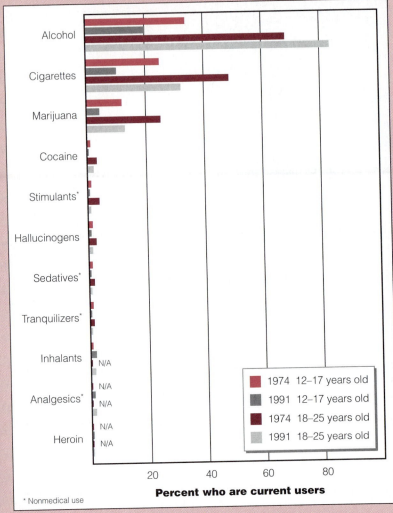

f **igure** **12.8**

Changing patterns of drug use in the United States, 1974–1991. (Based on U.S. Bureau of the Census, 1992, p. 127.)

At age 18, children were identified as drug abstainers, drug experimenters, and drug users. As expected, drug users were found to be the least well adjusted, the most impulsive, and the most likely to suffer from emotional problems. But the abstainers were not the best adjusted of the three groups; the drug-experimenters were. In Shedler and Block's (1990) words, " . . . the picture of the abstainer that emerges is of a relatively tense, over-controlled, emotionally constricted individual who is somewhat socially isolated and lacking in interpersonal skills" (p. 618).

In the Shedler and Block study, children who later became frequent drug users were often identifiable by a complex of common characteristics, even as young as age 7. Often these children did not get along as well with their peers, were less advanced in moral judgments, were more impulsive, displayed less self-reliance, had lower self-esteem, and were more prone to emotional distress. At age 11 these children continued to be more emotional, less attentive, and less cooperative, and they reacted poorly to stressful situations. In short, frequent drug users frequently appear to be relatively malad-justed as children. Low self-esteem is perhaps the single personality variable that is most often implicated in drug abuse (Franklin, 1985).

There also appear to be gender differences in drug user characteristics. Male drug users are often more aggressive or shier as children; females are more likely to show symptoms of emotional disorders such as depression, to have attempted suicide, to have been abused as children, and to have a family history of drug abuse (Toray et al., 1991). For both males and females, alcoholism in one's father is also a strong predictor of drug abuse (Chassin, Rogosch, & Barrera, 1991).

REASONS FOR DRUG USE

When teenagers are asked about their decisions to use or not to use drugs, they seldom refer to morality, social convention, or even parents or the law. Even abstainers claim that the decision is a matter of personal choice dictated by prudence and not by morality. And perhaps the most important factor in making that personal decision is the individual's perception of dangers associated with a drug. Heavy drug users are most likely to discount a drug's harmfulness (Nucci, Guerra, & Lee, 1991).

Franklin (1985) notes that the reasons for drug use are many and complex and are not to be found solely in the personality characteristics of the frequent drug user. Also, the reasons why drug use becomes drug dependence or abuse in some, but not in others, are many. As we saw, personality characteristics and environmental factors such as the father's alcoholism or maltreatment as a child may be implicated. The fact that children of alcoholics may be as much as four times more likely to become alcoholics than children of nonalcoholics also suggests the possibility of a genetic contribution (Marlatt et al., 1988). However, the meaning of this relationship is not entirely clear. It might mean that there are genetically determined physiological (chemical-hormonal-metabolic) characteristics that make one person more susceptible than another to alcoholism; it might also mean that the social and economic implications of being raised in the home of an alcoholic parent are conducive to alcoholism; or both.

One of the most important influences in adolescents' decision to use drugs relates to the influence of peers. Dinges and Oetting (1993) surveyed more than 100,000 junior and high school students. Among other things, they found that adolescents who used a specific drug almost invariably had friends who also used the same drug. In their words, "drug-using friends are a necessary condition in the evolution of drug use" (p. 263). Swaim et al. (1993) report similar results with samples of Native American adolescents.

Reasons for first *using* (and not necessarily eventually *abusing*) drugs often have to do with a simple urge to experiment (Pearl, Bryan, & Herzog, 1990). Newcomb (1987) argues that there is little evidence to support the belief that experimentation with drugs presents a significant danger to subsequent health and psychological well-being. In fact, research indicates that the majority of adolescents who drink heavily will moderate their use of alcohol as adults (Kandel & Logan, 1984).

Use of drugs is most likely to become misuse, Franklin (1985) suggests, among individuals with poor self-esteem who also experience the strong pressures of a peer drug culture, and who are not reared in a growth-fostering environment (parental neglect, abuse, alcoholism; poverty; inadequate schooling; and so on). The type of drugs experimented with is also very important. Some drugs have a higher potential for physiological and psychological dependence than others (heroin and free-base cocaine (crack), for example). In addition, genetics may well be involved in the nature and intensity of an individual's reaction.

The fact that there are genetic, social, and personality variables that appear to be related to the likelihood of drug use and abuse should be interpreted with caution. The evidence does not warrant the conclusion that these inevitably *cause* drug abuse. Nor, as experience clearly shows, does the apparent absence of these factors guarantee that a given adolescent is safe. As Polson and Newton (1984) point out, one of the most common refrains heard when parents are first con-

fronted with the fact of their child's drug use is: "Not my kid, couldn't happen to my kid."

Sadly, perhaps it could.

IMPLICATIONS OF TEENAGE DRUG USE

It is clearly unrealistic to expect that adolescents will not experiment with drugs. As Newcomb and Bentler (1989) note, the vast majority will have puffed on a cigarette or sipped somebody's alcoholic drink well before adolescence. In adolescence, not to drink occasionally—and perhaps not to smoke cigarettes or try marijuana—would, in many instances, not be socially *normal*. Society's focus, these authors claim, should be on *delaying* drug experimentation as long as possible to allow for the development of social and intellectual adaptive skills. The emphasis should perhaps be less on preventing *use* as on preventing *abuse*.

The short-term implications of drug abuse among adolescents are sometimes painfully obvious. Alcohol, for example, is implicated in a staggering number of fatal automobile accidents involving teenagers. Less dramatic but no less real, drug abuse may be reflected in poorer school achievement, dropping out of school, failure to adjust to the career and social demands required for transition to young adulthood, deviance, and criminality. Watts and Wright (1990) report very high correlations between use of alcohol, tobacco, and marijuana and other illegal drugs and the occurrence of delinquency. In their study of black, white, and Mexican-American adolescents, frequent drug use was the best predictor of both minor and violent delinquency.

The long-term implications of teenage drug abuse have been examined by Newcomb and Bentler (1988), who looked at seven different aspects of the lives of young adults (including family formation, stability, criminality, mental health, and social integration). They found that teenagers who had used high levels of drugs were more likely to have left school early and to have consolidated family and career plans earlier. Those who had used a variety of drugs had often adopted adult roles less successfully; their attempted careers and marriages were more likely to have failed.

The long-term medical consequences of the use of drugs such as nicotine and alcohol have also been extensively researched and are well known. In the following sections we look at these and at some other commonly used drugs.

MARIJUANA

Marijuana is derived from hemp, a tall annual plant appearing in male and female forms. The specific chemical that accounts for its effects is *tetrahydrocannabinol* (THC). This drug is variously known as dawamesc, hashish, bhang, grass, ganja, charas, marijuana, muta, grefa, muggles, pot, reefer, guage, stick, Acapulco Gold, Panama Red, Panama Gold, Thai stick, jive, Indian, Jamaican, tea, dope . . . and more.

Marijuana is ordinarily smoked, although it can also be eaten or drunk. Its main psychological effect is a pleasant emotional state. If taken in sufficient doses and in sufficiently pure forms, it may evoke the same types of hallucinogenic reactions sometimes associated with stronger drugs such as LSD (Cox et al., 1983).

Whether marijuana is physically addictive remains controversial. Gold (1989) suggests that it may be addictive following prolonged use; others believe it has not been shown to be addictive or especially harmful (Royal College of Psychiatrists, 1987).

The physiological effects of marijuana use depend largely on the dosages and frequency of use. Cox et al. (1983) report that minor cardiovascular changes (increased heart rate, for example) are common even with very low doses. The respiratory system may be adversely affected with prolonged use and with heavier doses (marijuana produces more tars than tobacco, and these contain a higher concentration of certain cancer-causing agents) (Cox et al., 1983).

The fear that marijuana is the first step toward heroin addiction has generally been discounted. There is no evidence that marijuana users develop tolerance to marijuana, as users do to some other drugs such as heroin. Hence the marijuana user does not need to go to more powerful drugs to continue to achieve the same "high." Nor is there any evidence that using marijuana leads to a psychological craving for heroin.

LSD

LSD-25 (d-lysergic acid diethylamide tartrate) is the most powerful hallucinogen known. Because it is a synthetic chemical, it can be made by anyone who has the materials, the equipment, and the knowledge. The most common street name for LSD-25 is acid; others are barrels, California sunshine, blotters, cubes, domes, flats, wedges, purple haze, jellybeans, bluecaps, frogs, microdots, and window panes. Its use appears to have declined (Bell & Battjes, 1985).

LSD-25 (ordinarily referred to simply as LSD) is usually taken orally, commonly in the form of a white, odorless, and tasteless powder. Its effects vary widely from one person to another, as well as from one occasion to another for the same person. The predominant characteristic of an LSD experience (called an "acid trip") is the augmented intensity of sensory perceptions. Color, sound, taste, and vision are particularly susceptible. On occasion, acid trips are accompanied by

Alcohol is clearly the drug of choice among adolescents, the vast majority of whom drink at least "sometimes."

hallucinations, some of which may be mild, whereas others can be sufficiently frightening to lead to serious mental disturbance in the subject even after the immediate effects of the drug have worn off (Cox et al., 1983).

ALCOHOL

Alcohol, the most commonly used and abused drug in contemporary society, is a central nervous system depressant. In relatively moderate doses, its primary effect is to suppress inhibition, which is why many individuals who have consumed alcohol behave as though they had taken a stimulant. In less moderate doses, the individual progresses from being "high" or "tipsy" to intoxication. Literally, to be intoxicated is to be poisoned. Behavioral symptoms of various degrees of intoxication may include impaired muscular control, delayed reflexive reactions, loss of coordination and balance, impaired vision, uncertain speech, faintness, nausea, amnesia (blackouts), and, in extreme cases, paralysis of heart and lung muscles sometimes leading to death (Reid & Carpenter, 1990).

Alcohol is physiologically addictive, although prolonged or excessive consumption is generally required before symptoms of physical addiction are present. Signs of psychological dependency (a strong desire to continue taking the drug) may appear considerably sooner (Cox et al., 1983). One of the major physiological effects of alcohol is its contribution to cirrhosis of the liver, one of the 10 leading causes of death in the United States. In addition, it is implicated in more than half of all motor-vehicle deaths, a large number of which involve adolescents (Beatty, 1991).

Alcohol consumption among adolescents is widespread. Most surveys report that extremely few teenagers have not tried alcohol at least once (Newcomb & Bentler, 1989). Close to 20 percent of adolescents ages 14 to 17 are considered problem drinkers (see Table 12.8).

Why do adolescents drink? There are clearly many reasons, including social pressure, experimentation, insecurity and other personal problems, as well as simply for the sensation of being "tipsy," "high," or "drunk." Why do adolescents want to get drunk? To feel good, have fun, celebrate, let off steam, cheer up, forget worries, feel less shy, and impress friends, they claim (Brown & Finn, 1982). But when they are asked what their actual be-

ota b l e 1 2 . 8

Percentages of students reporting drinking with friends

AGE	NEVER	SOMETIMES	USUALLY	ALWAYS	AT LEAST SOMETIMES*	TOTAL NUMBER OF STUDENTS
12	72	24	2	2	28	163
13	62	29	6	3	38	142
14	34	37	23	6	66	242
15	20	42	28	10	80	208
16	13	35	35	17	87	249
17	12	41	33	14	88	219

Source: Brown and Finn, 1982, p. 15

*This column gives the sum of the previous three columns.

haviors and feelings are when they are drunk, although a large number do "feel good" and "laugh a lot," a significant number fall asleep, feel unhappy, cry, damage property, and get into fights—and approximately one-third at all age levels occasionally get sick.

When is alcohol consumption by adolescents deviant or a problem? Is it a problem only when the adolescent gets into trouble? Does it become a problem with alcohol consumption becomes habitual or excessive or when it interferes with normal social or physical functioning? Or is it always a problem because the behavior is generally illegal? There are no easy answers.

COCAINE

Cocaine is ordinarily a white powder derived from coca leaves. Also known as coke, big "C," snow, gold dust, star dust, flake, Bernice, or Corine, it is most commonly inhaled vigorously through the nostrils, although it can also be injected. Cocaine is sometimes purified to produce "free-base" cocaine, which, when inhaled, has a more profound effect on the user. Some users mix it with heroin and inject it intravenously (called a "speedball").

In moderate doses, the primary effect of cocaine, like that of other stimulants, is one of euphoria and high energy. In higher doses it can lead to hallucinations and sometimes convulsions. For some decades it was widely believed that cocaine was nonaddictive and largely harmless. It is now considered to be extremely dangerous (Cheung, Erickson, & Landau, 1991). Indications are that it may be as addictive as heroin (Ringwalt & Palmer, 1989).

Cocaine use has increased dramatically among high school populations, especially in its free-base ("crack" or "rock") form (U.S. Bureau of the Census, 1992). Next to marijuana, it is the most widely used *illegal* drug in North America.

Crack appears to be particularly attractive to adolescents for several reasons. First, it is far cheaper than cocaine. Second, its effects are almost instantaneous and intensely euphoric. And third, so much glamour and misinformation has surrounded the so-called "recreational" use of cocaine that many adolescents think there is nothing to fear.

Crack is easily and quickly manufactured by cooking down ordinary powdered cocaine with bicarbonate of soda. Small pieces of the resulting solid are then smoked, usually in a waterpipe. The euphoric effect or "rush" occurs within 10 seconds and is far more intense than that associated with inhaling ordinary cocaine because the concentrations of cocaine that reach the brain are many times higher than is the case with inhalation. Consequently, there is a far higher risk of overdosing with crack, of experiencing convulsions, or even of dying. Many crack users experience an overwhelming compulsion to use it again as soon as possible, even after using it only once. The use of crack is also associated with psychological changes, the most common of which involve strong feelings of paranoia. Many users also become violent (Washton, 1989), and some commit suicide.

OTHER DRUGS

Other drugs used by some adolescents include various other hallucinogens such as STP and MDA (methyl amphetamines), PCP (phencyclidene), inhalants, various barbiturates and other milder tranquilizers, and a range of new molecular variations of these and other chemicals, sometimes collectively labeled "designer drugs." Of these, alcohol is still the drug of choice among both adolescents and adults (see Table 12.9 for some symptoms of drug use and abuse).

suicide

Suicide, the deliberate taking of one's own life, is final—an end that is sought when individuals can see only two choices: life as it is now or death. Evidently, they prefer to die.

Suicide is not a pleasant topic; it so violently contradicts our implicit belief in the goodness of life. Consequently, a powerful social stigma is associated with the act, and the event is often covered over both by the information media and by the attending physician. As a result, we know only of suicides of people whom we have known (and sometimes not even then), or of particularly prominent people (not always those either), or of people who commit the act so flagrantly that it compels attention.

There are relatively few scientific investigations of suicide, its causes, and the personalities of those who deliberately choose their time and method of departure. Do children commit suicide? How often? How about adolescents, disillusioned idealists that they are, caught up in the stress and turmoil of the transition to adulthood? Here are some facts.

RATE

The suicide rate in the United States is about 12 per 100,000. Few children under the age of 15 commit suicide. Suicide rates increase slowly from adolescence, peaking at above age 65 for white males and at around ages 45 to 55 for white females; peaks are at younger ages for African-Americans and are also lower (U.S. Bureau of the Census, 1992). The most dramatic recent increase in suicide rates is among those ages 15 to 19, for whom suicide rates nearly doubled between 1970 and 1988 (U.S. Bureau of the Census, 1992; see Figure 12.9 in "At A Glance: Suicide Rates").

SEX DIFFERENCES

Among adolescents, far more girls than boys attempt suicide, but a higher percentage of the boys are successful. Some have argued that this is because the boys who attempt suicide are more seri-

t able 12.9

Symptoms of drug use and/or abuse

DRUG	SIGNS AND EARLY SYMPTOMS	LONG-TERM SYMPTOMS
Narcotics	Medicinal breath Traces of white powder around nostrils (heroin is sometimes inhaled) Red or raw nostrils Needle marks or scars on arms Long sleeves (or other clothing) at inappropriate times Physical evidence may include cough syrup bottles, syringes, cotton swabs, and spoon or cap for heating heroin	Loss of appetite Constipation
Sedatives	Symptoms of alcohol consumption with or without odor Poor coordination and speech Drowsiness Loss of interest in activity	Withdrawal symptoms when discontinued Possible convulsions
Stimulants	Excessive activity Irascibility Argumentativeness Nervousness Pupil dilation Dry mouth and nose with bad breath Chapped, dry lips Scratching or rubbing of nose Long periods without sleep Loss of appetite Mood shifts Changes in friends "Hangover" symptoms	Loss of appetite Possible hallucinations and psychotic reactions
Hallucinogens, marijuana	Odor on breath and clothing Animated behavior or its opposite	None definite
LSD, PCP, MDA, STP	Bizarre behavior Panic Disorientation	Possible contribution to psychoses Recurrence of experiences after immediate effects of drug
Inhalants	Odor of glue, solvent, or related substance Redness and watering of eyes Appearance of alcoholic intoxication Physical evidence of plastic bags, rags, glue, or solvent containers	Disorientation Brain damage

ous about wanting to die than are the girls. It may also be because the more violent and instantaneous methods used by males do not provide much opportunity for help. In contrast, the slower and more passive methods most often attempted by females often allow time for rescue. Male adolescents are most likely to shoot them-selves; females are more likely to use poisoning or asphyxiation (Ladame & Jeanneret, 1982). Obviously, many other methods are available, but some of these result in a death that appears accidental (drowning, a car accident) and is difficult to identity as suicide unless the person has left a note, a letter, or a book that can

Adolescent suicide rates have risen dramatically in the past several decades. In the United States, the rise reflects an enormous increase for males but not for females. Males typically use more violent methods such as guns (65.0 percent of all male suicides compared with 40.8 percent of female suicides); female methods are more passive and protracted and sometimes less successful (for example, poison: 36.4 percent of female suicides compared with 13.3 percent of male suicides).

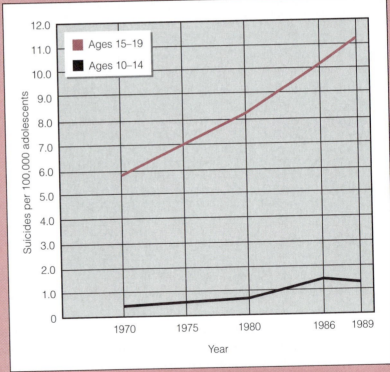

f **igure 12.9**

Changes in suicide rates for U.S. adolescents, 1970 to 1986. Source: Adapted from U.S. Bureau of the Census (1992), p. 90.

be interpreted as a message of intention to end it all. Because a suicide note appears in only 15 percent of all reported suicides, many apparent accidents are probably in fact unidentified suicides.

PSYCHOLOGICAL EXPLANATIONS

There are a raft of psychological explanations for suicide. For example there are *biological theories* (suicide is due to bad genes, psychiatric disorders, biochemical changes of adolescence, and the like), *psychoanalytic theories* (suicidal adolescents are those whose unconscious death wish is exaggerated by deficient ego development during this critical period), *psychological stress theory* (suicide results from a perceived inability to cope with stress associated with rapid and demanding life changes), *sociological theories* (social norms sometimes sanction suicide by providing adolescents with the opportunity to die for the group; alternately, groups sometimes exclude adolescents, thus causing depression and leading to suicide), *social learning theories* (suicidal behavior is suggested by the behaviors and attitudes of friends, family, or other important people, and *ecological theory* (individual, environmental, and social factors contribute to suicidal tendencies).

Henry et al. (1993) suggest that of these, the most useful may be the ecological approach. Not only does it take into account most of the explanations included in other theories, but it provides a way to understand how suicide might result from the combined effects of a variety of factors. Thus reasons for adolescent suicide can include a range of family-based problems (Bronfenbrenner's *microsystem*) such as death in the family, parental abuse or alcohol use, suicide by other family members, or inability to satisfy parental expectation. They can also include wider social problems (*meso-, exo-* or *macro-* systems). For example, Henry et al. (1993) report that suicide rates are about 10 times higher among Native American youths, perhaps partly because of economic, social, and even cultural factors associated with *hopelessness.* In the same way, certain characteristics of contemporary societies, such as high mobility, family instability, lack of inter-generational cohesiveness, poor economic conditions, high unemployment, and expensive and sometimes inaccessible post-secondary education, might all contribute to a greater likelihood of suicide.

INDIVIDUAL EXPLANATIONS

Although adolescent suicide might result from the combined effects of these various factors, it is often precipitated by a single event such as the death of a parent or friend, fear of pregnancy, rejection by a close friend, or arrest. Meneese, Yutrzenka, and Vitale (1992) found that the best predictors of adolescent suicide for males are depression and lack of family cohesiveness; for females, the best predictors are depression and level of anxiety (as a personality characteristic). In a study by Neiger and Hopkins (1988), depression and family relationships were also found to be good predictors of suicide, as were alcohol and drug use, failure in school, and a recent serious loss. Shreve and Kunkel (1991) suggest that the *shame* that accompanies these conditions may be the determining motive.

Adolescent suicide, like most adult suicides, rarely occurs without advance warning. The most common warning is one or more unsuccessful attempts at suicide. Ladame and Jeanneret (1982) report that as many as four out of five adolescents who succeed in committing suicide have previously attempted to kill themselves at least once. Other warning signs include statements such as "I wish I were dead," "Nobody would miss me if I weren't here," and "I wish I'd never been born."

Suicide is still the solution of an isolated few. Most of us choose to wait for death and hope that it will be a long time in coming. And for most adolescents, life is only occasionally turbulent and stressful; for most, it abounds with joy and excitement.

another note

uicide would not have been a very pleasant note upon which to end this chapter. Nor would it have been very realistic. Indeed, closing the chapter with the "turmoil topics," as we have, is misleading.

It bears repeating that the adolescents whose lives are described among these last pages are not our "average" adolescents. Our "average" adolescents are more joyful than sad, more exuberant than depressed, more confident than self-deprecating. They like order more than chaos, purpose more than dissipation—and junk food more than drugs.

And they laugh and smile a lot more than they cry. That's a better note upon which to end.

main points

THE SELF

1. Responses to questionnaires like the Offer Self-Image Questionnaire reflect self-appraisal (self-image) in different areas and reveal that adolescents in different countries share characteristics such as general happiness and optimism, caring and concern for others, confidence and openness about sexual matters, positive feelings toward the family, and

confidence in their ability to deal with life. However, they are also different in predictable ways with regard to things such as confidence, feelings of vulnerability, values placed on educational and vocational goals, and sexual attitudes. Contrary to Hall's belief, adolescence is not a period of storm and stress for the majority of the world's adolescents.

IDENTITY

2. According to Erikson, the major developmental task of adolescence is to develop a sense of identity (a notion of self reflected in commitments). Marcia describes four possible identity statuses of adolescents, including *identity diffusion* (no commitment and no identity crisis), *foreclosure* (strong commitment to parent- or religion-determined identity), *moratorium* individuals (active exploration of alternatives, sometimes negative); and *identity achieved* (commitment following the crises of the moratorium).

SOCIAL DEVELOPMENT IN CONTEXT

3. Adolescent social development generally involves increasing independence from parents and increasing allegiance to peers, although most teenagers have good relations with their parents. Peer groups begin as small single-sex groups and progress through four more stages: single-sex groups that interact but remain intact, a "crowd" stage consisting of single-sex groups interacting in a closer fashion, large heterosexual groups, and less cohesive groups of couples.

4. Peers' acceptance is profoundly important for social and psychological well-being. Friendships tend to be

highly age-segregated and to involve similar rather than dissimilar individuals. High-status (well-liked) children tend to be happier, more cheerful, more active, and more successful.

GENDER ROLES IN ADOLESCENCE

5. The "sex-change question"—What if you were a boy (girl)?—reveals predominantly positive evaluations of the male role and negative evaluations of the female role by both males and females. Our gender stereotypes see the male role as more active, more aggressive, more rational, more powerful; the female role is seen as more passive, more emotional, more nurturant, less aggressive.

6. Males are physically more fragile (higher mortality rates and much lower life expectancies). They have traditionally been more aggressive, and females have been more submissive and nurturant. Gender differences in verbal and mathematical ability are small and inconsistent and are better explained in terms of culturally determined interests and opportunities rather than in terms of basic genetically ordained differences. More males score at the extreme ends of most measures of ability.

SEXUAL BEHAVIOR

7. The sexual revolution among adolescents is reflected in an increase in the number of adolescents reporting sexual intercourse before marriage and a much greater increase in sexual activity among females than among males. Teenage parents are more likely to divorce than are people who marry later. Also, their marriages are more often associated with depression, sui-

cide, infant mortality, child neglect, and other signs of inadequate parenting.

8. The most common sexually transmitted diseases (STDs) are gonorrhea, herpes, and chlamydia. Syphilis and AIDS are rarer. Gonorrhea, chlamydia, and syphilis can be cured with drugs; herpes can be controlled but not cured; AIDS, which is most common among homosexual males, intravenous drug users, and hemophiliacs, is fatal.

DELINQUENCY, DRUGS, AND SUICIDE

9. Delinquency is a legal category defined by juvenile apprehension and conviction of a legal transgression. Related factors include social class, sex, intelligence, self-esteem, family background, and peer influences. A small minority of adolescents become members of countercultural and sometimes violent gangs.

10. "Drug abuse" refers to the recreational use of drugs. "Drug dependence" is manifested in a strong desire to continue taking a drug. It may be physiological (desire to take the drug is partly organically based; also termed *addiction*) or it may be psychological (the urge to continue taking the drug is related mainly to its psychological effects; termed *habituation*). Predictors of the likelihood of drug abuse among teenagers include earlier maladjustment; drug use among peers or parents; delinquency; stressful life changes; parental neglect, abuse, or abandonment; and low self-esteem.

11. Marijuana smoking, which has potentially harmful effects on the respiratory system, does not appear to be

physiologically addictive, although it may lead to psychological dependence. LSD-25, a synthetic hallucinogenic drug, can cause psychoticlike reactions. Alcohol is a highly addictive central nervous system depressant. Cocaine, especially in free-base form, creates feelings of euphoria and is potent, potentially dangerous, and highly addictive.

12. Suicide is an uncommon end, although its frequency among adolescents has more than doubled in recent decades. More girls than boys attempt suicide, but fewer are successful. Although adolescent suicides are often precipitated by a single event (such as the death of a friend, pregnancy, parental divorce, arrest), few occur without warning. Depression, family and relationship problems, or serious loss or failure are predictive of suicide.

focus questions: applications

■ Is adolescence generally a time of strife, typically marked by parent-adolescent conflict?

1. Using library resources and illustrating your arguments with personal experience, examine the proposition that adolescence is a period of "*Sturm und Drang.*"

■ How free of gender discrimination are the lives of adolescents?

2. Answer the sex-change question (honestly): "If you woke up tomorrow and discovered that you were a girl (boy), how would your life be different?"

Now examine your answer for evidence of sexual stereotypes and gender biases.

■ What are the principal sexual beliefs and behaviors of typical adolescents?

3. Debate the following proposition: Teenagers should not be discouraged from having sex, but should be provided with sex education and contraception.

■ How common and serious are teenage delinquency, drug abuse, and suicide?

4. Outline a drug abuse prevention program that takes into consideration each of the principal factors potentially involved in drug abuse.

study terms

self 546
identity 546
self-image 546
self-esteem 552
identity diffusion 555
foreclosure 555
moratorium 555
peer group 558
gender roles 562
gender-typing 562
sex 566
masturbation 568
sexually transmitted diseases (STDs) 574
delinquency 577
drug abuse 582
drug dependence 582
physiological dependence 582
psychological dependence 582
drug tolerance 582
marijuana 587
LSD-25 587
cocaine 589
suicide 590

further readings

Offer and associates presented a self-image questionnaire to nearly 6,000 teenagers in 10 different countries. The result is a fascinating look at the thoughts and attitudes of teenagers around the world:

Offer, D. O., Ostrov, E., Howard, K., & Atkinson, R. (1988). *The teenage world: Adolescents' self-image in ten countries.* New York: Plenum Press.

A highly readable and insightful look into the world of early adolescence is:

Schave, D., & Schave, B. (1989). *Early adolescence and the search for self: A developmental perspective.* New York: Praeger.

Gender stereotypes are widely held beliefs about male-female characteristics and differences. The first of the following two references examines the typical stereotypes and prejudices of American and Swedish adolescents; the second presents a balanced view of the gender differences psychology has actually found.

Intons-Peterson, M. J. (1988). *Gender concepts of Swedish and American youth.* Hillsdale, N.J.: Lawrence Erlbaum.

Halpern, D. F. (1986). *Sex differences in cognitive abilities.* Hillsdale, N.J.: Lawrence Erlbaum.

The following book is a fascinating account of the lives of street children—runaways, delinquents, drug addicts, or simply the lost and homeless:

Webber, M. (1991). *Street kids: The tragedy of Canada's runaways.* Toronto: University of Toronto Press.

Perkins and McMurtrie-Perkins present down-to-earth advice for parents concerned about drug use by their children:

Perkins, W. M., & McMurtrie-Perkins, N. (1986). *Raising drug-free kids in a drug-filled world.* Austin, Tex.: Hazelden.

seven

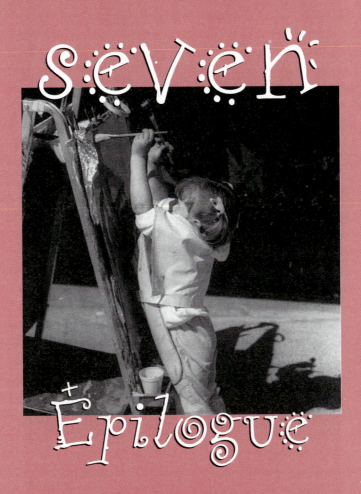

Epilogue

"Begin at the beginning," the King said, very gravely,
"and go on till you come to the end: then stop."
Lewis Carroll, Alice in Wonderland

*B*egin at the beginning," the King said...."

We began close to the beginning, and in the many pages between there and here we probed and pulled and tugged at the secrets of the life of developing children, as though we might unravel its fabric, uncover its mysteries, understand its profoundest truths.

We have seen much, and understood much, of the processes and products of development.

But if we have uncovered the profoundest truth of all, it's simply that we've recognized more clearly the wonderful complexity of human development.

To recognize complexity is not to understand it all.

Our painting of children is not yet done. Sadly, there are forms we have not yet learned to draw, colors we have yet to invent.

"...and go on till you come to the end: then stop."

But there is no end, no real end. Our subjects keep changing....

Still, only one more short chapter, one more stroke of the brush.

Let's call it The End.

13

The End

When I am dead, I hope it may be said
"His sins were scarlet, but his books were read."
Hilaire Belloc, On His Books

o u t l i n e

A SUMMARY

Chapter 1
Chapter 2
Chapter 3
Chapter 4
Chapters 5 and 6
Chapters 7 and 8
Chapters 9 and 10
Chapters 11 and 12
*Of "Average Children" and of
    Other Children*

OTHER VIEWS

Humanism
Existentialism

H ad you been standing behind me these past months, looking over my shoulder, you would surely have thought I was writing this book. But it is not really so, for books are only partly from the minds and guts of their authors. A large part of them comes from somewhere else, and we, the authors, sit at our keyboards waiting for them to happen. Not until a book has set itself down on paper does it really exist. Before that time it could have taken any number of forms. But from the moment it is recorded it has its own definite shape and substance.

The life of a child is something like a book. It too can take any number of shapes and directions, and no one knows precisely what that form will be until it happens. But quite unlike a book, as the life of a child unfolds and takes form and substance, it never irrevocably possesses that form. It changes constantly. That is the undeniable truth of human development.

Sometimes we forget that. One night not very long ago, as I staggered through a dimly lit hallway in our house, I met a tall stranger who, it seemed, grumbled something mean under his breath. I jumped back in sudden fright, curling my toes and raising my fingers in some unconscious and thoroughly primitive defensive gesture.

But it was only my 14-year-old son who had muttered a greeting and who now lurched toward his bedroom, all arms and legs and long, scrawny neck. I had forgotten that he has become taller than I am and that his voice now rumbles from hidden places in his chest.

He is not a stranger at all, this son. Nor are my other two children, but sometimes I wonder who they will become, even who they are.

It is easy for me to sit here in this booklined workplace and keyboard such humanistic phrases as "There is no average child," "It is the whole infant with whom we are concerned," and "A child is an incredibly complex little organism." But it is something else to be faced with the whole infant, the nonaverage child, and the incredibly complex organism all at once and in the flesh—and not just for a brief passing glance but for an uninterrupted period of years.

As I look at my children, I cannot help thinking that they are what I have undertaken to describe in this book. And I now know so much more clearly than before that there is no average child, that the whole process of attempting to set down in static words a thing that is at once as dynamic and as elusive as a child "in progress" necessarily robs both the child and the process of their dynamism.

To repeat again that this is so makes it no less so. But perhaps it does make us more aware of what concerns us: that a child, like an adult, is never what will be but is always becoming. The small insight I have gained from trying to relate what I have written to my children is this: When all the layers that make up the chapters and sections of this book have been bound together and the painting of children finally rendered, it will still bear only a faint resemblance to its subjects. For the subjects of the process of becoming do not stop and pose; by their very nature they continue to move forever.

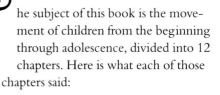

a summary

The subject of this book is the movement of children from the beginning through adolescence, divided into 12 chapters. Here is what each of those chapters said:

chapter 1

Child development studies the progressive adaptation of mythical "average children," although we know that children are neither average nor mythical; they are real and individual. Our beliefs about children reflect our social/cultural contexts; our methods are those of science.

chapter 2

Theories direct our investigations and shape our beliefs about what is important. What is important, you ask? Early emotional experiences and especially child/parent relationships, says Freud. Social competence, insists Erikson. Consequences, the behaviorists inform us. The ability to symbolize and to anticipate the outcomes of our behavior, says Bandura. Language, culture, and social/historical context, Vygotsky asserts. The ecology of human interaction, thinks Bronfenbrenner.

chapter 3

The fact that there is a you or a me is largely a matter of fortune. It could have been another ovum; it could have been any one of several million other sperm cells. In each case, the result would have been someone else. Or would it?

What you and I are continually becoming is not solely a function of the intricate arrangement of DNA molecules that our parents passed on to us (that they, in turn, got from their parents, and so on, so that there exists in a remote sense a common pool of genes for all of us). What we are is also a matter of where we have been at different times in our lives, and of who the people around us have been—of our contexts, the ecologies of our micro-, meso-, exo-, and macrosystems.

chapter 4

We begin as a microscopic speck in one of our mother's fallopian tubes. Through the next 266 days, this indistinct glob of cells changes into the form and functions that make up newborns. And although these changes are ordered, systematic, and highly predictable, they are nevertheless subject to external influences such as drugs, illnesses, malnutrition, and other stressors.

And then we are born. And just about everybody loves us!

chapters 5 and 6

As infants, we discover our hands, our feet, and our parents; and we learn that blankets are for chewing. Later, we are initiated into the wonderful secrets of language, and we learn that there are things to cry and laugh about of which we could never have dreamed. And if we continue to be lucky, just about everybody still loves us a lot. We mean something!

chapters 7 and 8

In early childhood, we learn mystical, magical things that dazzle our senses and our minds. A new logic invades our thinking—egocentric, perception-dominated, and intuitive, but never-

theless the germ of a finer, more advanced logic. As preschoolers, our world enlarges; the microsystems of our ecology are no longer defined only by parents and siblings, but also include peers and playmates and caregivers and teachers. Sometimes we have to struggle a little to be loved. Some of us pretend we don't care all that much. But deep down, we do.

chapters 9 and 10

Through middle childhood, we expand our powers of mind and body, refining our thinking, expanding our knowledge base, honing our language and social skills. And perhaps as our construction of reality becomes more sophisticated, we begin to forget a little of the magic and the mystery that filled our younger lives. But not all of it, for we are still in those sweet childish days, when every day is like 20. Now our lives are filled with buddies, and love is a remote abstraction. Being really liked is enough.

chapters 11 and 12

Finally we become adolescents, newly aware of the power of our logic, egocentric and full of our selves, smitten with a sense of competence and invulnerability, imbued with a wonderful conviction that we are very special. Then Bang! puberty strikes, sending hormones raging through our veins, and we are driven even further from our childish games as we struggle to invent the many meanings of love. We teeter uncertainly on the brink of adulthood—sometimes torn and confused, sometimes angry and rebellious, sometimes hungry to try everything that life has to offer before it's too late, desperate to gather our rosebuds while we may. And sometimes, as adolescents we just sleep in for a surprisingly long time.

A child in the process of becoming is a dynamic and elusive thing, not easily captured and reduced to printed words on textbook pages. The subject does not stop and pose; it moves forever.

of ''average children'' and of other children

At every step in the chronology that composes this text, something was said of the physical, cognitive, and social development of the "average child." Even the *exceptional* children of whom we spoke were sometimes treated as averages too. But at every step, you were urged to keep in mind that the average of which we spoke is an invention. To emphasize this, in boxes scattered here and there in *Of Children*, we spoke as well of children in other contexts, whose lives are sometimes dramatically different from yours or mine. But sadly, we couldn't reveal much of the detail of these other lives. Still, we have tried hard not to rob children of their individuality, not to strip the dynamism and the magic from the processes and the outcomes of development.

That part of the story has now been told. There remains only the attempt to bring the various layers and pieces into a cohesive whole to provide a richer, more accurate, more complete, and more human picture of children in the process of becoming.

other views

Who am I? Is the "I" who is sitting here thinking about who he is different from the "I" who questioned my grandmother's fertile theories? Was I the same me when, as an adolescent, I let my fantasies shine in my eyes, causing my uncle to fire me? Was the "I" who went to school as a freshly scrubbed 6 year old the same person who graduated from college many years later? Who is my self and what is it; how did it become what it is?

Perhaps we still can't answer the question of personal identity, a question that has plagued philosophers, psychologists, theologians, grandmothers, and all manner of thinkers since thinking began. But there are two useful answers that are often given—both intuitive, highly subjective, but no less meaningful. The first asserts there is an unidentifiable something about the self that continues from the dawning awareness of a personal identity until the oblivion of psychotic disorder, memory loss, or death destroys all sense of existence. The other answer does not contradict the first but simply extends it: The self is continually developing, despite the individual's feeling of a single and unique personal identity throughout life.

As we saw in Chapter 2, the self and its development have been a primary concern of humanistic psychology; it is also a major concern of existential philosophy. Each of these two orientations can add to our understanding and appreciation of the phenomena of development. Although a complete discussion of their contributions is beyond the scope of this text, a summary of humanism and an introduction to existentialism are presented here. These are intended partly as an alternative to the somewhat unreal picture that results from attempting to examine children in objective psychological detail, and partly as a finishing touch for the painting that has been attempted in this text.

humanism

Recall that humanism is a concern for humans, for humanity, for the development of humanness, and for its expression. It exalts the individual and glorifies the self. Thus the concepts of paramount concern to the humanistic psychologist include notions such as self-structure, self-concept, self-image, self-understanding, self-acceptance, self-enhancement, self-realization, and self-actualization. Humanism is concerned with that which is most clearly human; accordingly, it sees the development of self (self-actualization) as the goal toward which humans should strive.

The process of self-actualization is the act of becoming whatever one has the potential to become through one's own efforts; it is the process of actualizing—of making actual or real that potential. But it is not a static goal toward which individuals consciously or unconsciously strive; it is a process, an ongoing activity. Self-actualization is, in fact, the process of development. We could have substituted different terms in this text to make this relationship more apparent. For example, instead of speaking of development, we might have spoken of self-actualization or of the development of self; instead of referring to the frustrations of adolescents, who cannot easily determine whether they are child or adult, we could have referred to the difficulty of establishing the identity of the self during the transition from childhood to adulthood; and instead of discussing forces that impede or accelerate development, we could have discussed self-enhancement or changing self-structure or contributions to self-esteem. The picture that would have emerged might have been a more integrated one, for we would constantly have been speaking of the self. It would also have been a more realistic picture that dealt more with real children than with a hypothetical "average child"—for the self belongs solely to the individual; there is no "average" self. To speak of the "average self" is to distort the concept miserably. At the same time, our portrait would probably have been a more global, less precise, and less informative study of the child. (See "In Other Contexts: Yeo-hsien Han, a Pious Child.")

Yeo-hsien Han, a Chinese boy, desperately wanted to be a good son, so he read the ancient stories of children who serve as the best examples of filial piety. These stories are found in dozens of official historical books, in biographies, in local papers, throughout China (see Wu, 1981). He read, for example, of a son who mourned, in costume, the death of his father for 30 years and then dedicated the rest of his years to being a vegetarian bachelor. He studied the life of Wu Meng who, at the age of 8, so loved his parents that when the mosquitoes were especially bad at night, he would remove his clothes and lie naked next to them to attract the insects. He heard of Wang Xiang, who lay on the frozen river to melt the ice with his body so that his stepmother might have fresh fish. This same Wang Xiang, when asked to guard the fruit on his stepmother's tree, spent an entire windy night sleeplessly holding the trunk so that the branches would not sway and the fruit fall to the ground. But the story that moved Yeo-hsien Han most was that of the son who, when his father had committed a capital crime, offered to die in his place, so impressing the emperor that he forgave the father.

To Think About: Among important cultural values reflected in stories of filial devotion, says Wu (1981), are the beliefs that (1) from the earliest age, children should show great devotion to their parents; (2) parents' welfare comes before that of children; and (3) children should be obedient and try to make their parents' lives pleasant and comfortable no matter what.

Are there similar values in your culture? Are cultural values important? How? Why?

existentialism

To complete our description of children, we might consider the concepts of existential psychology, which are similar to those of humanistic psychology. From Jean-Paul Sartre we borrow a description of the human condition—cynical and pessimistic, but one that enables us to understand better the direction of development, particularly in its nearly adult stages. From Martin Buber we borrow ideas from a philosophy of personalism, which is only a short distance from humanism.

Jean-Paul Sartre's existential picture of people and of the forces that move them can be described by three words: anguish, abandonment, and despair. These words summarize the human condition: they are both the facts of existence and its consequences. We are forever in anguish because we are constantly forced to make decisions and yet have no guides for these

Does the old person ever know that the child within has grown and is gone forever? Does self-actualization ever become self-realization?

decisions. There is no guarantee that anything we do is correct, for there is no God, Sartre informs us; and without a God all action must be justified in terms of its effects on others. Such resolution is a tremendous and terrible responsibility, and its consequence is deep and undying anguish.

We have also been abandoned, and abandonment is an indescribably lonely feeling. We have not been abandoned simply by others but in a general sense, without purpose and with no *a priori* values—abandoned and not only free to make choices but also required to make them. So we despair because we are free but without hope, because to will something is not necessarily to achieve it, and because when we die all our efforts may have been in vain.

This is *atheistic existentialism*, and we describe it here to give a perspective through contrast to the more optimistic reflections of Martin Buber. Buber (1958, 1965) tells us that there are four main evils in the modern world, and that the effect of these evils is to highlight the importance of the human self. The first of these evils is our terrible loneliness,

and loneliness has long been recognized by existentialists as a concept of extreme importance. Existence as a self is essentially a lonely experience because the self always belongs only to the individual; it can never be shared completely. Therefore, we are always alone.

Buber's second evil is the never-ending drive for technological progress, the individual's worth lessening with the increasing importance of machines and science. The third evil stems from human duality, the good-versus-evil dichotomy—the id warring with the superego. Finally, Buber contends that the individual is being degraded by the state; the conglomerate, impersonal, and faceless entities that define states are incompatible with the uniqueness and personal worth of the individual.

The result of these evils is summarized in a single existentialist (and humanistic) term: alienation. To be alienated is to be separated from, to be a stranger to. We are alienated from ourselves, from others, and from our environment. In short, we have been uprooted from the relationships that we should have with all three: our private self, those who surround us, and our environment. Accordingly, the greatest evil that besets us, social animals that we are, is alienation; and the greatest good is love—love of self and love of others. Buber's philosophy is seldom pessimistic, for it asserts strongly that our salvation, our happiness, and our consequent self-actualization can be achieved through love.

Love, says Buber, is a question of relationships—what he terms the *I-Thou* relationship. In the I-Thou relationship the object or person being related to is not being used selfishly; the relationship is mutual, there is dialogue as opposed to monologue, and people say and do what they honestly mean rather than what is merely convenient or socially appropriate.

If the process of human development has a goal—if it ever ceases to be a process of becoming—then its goal must surely be a capacity to feel great love, and the reward for having reached that state must surely be great happiness.

Does self-actualization ever become self-realization? Does the adolescent ever know that the child has grown up? Does the adult? The old person?

This glossary defines the most important terms and expressions used in this text. In each case the meaning given corresponds to the usage in the text. For more complete definitions, consult a standard psychological dictionary. ★

Abandonment The existential dilemma. An atheistic-existential concept referring to an intense feeling that results from the realization that we have been abandoned on earth with no purpose, no knowledge of where we come from or where we are going. (See *alienation*.)

Abortion A miscarriage occurring usually before the twentieth week of pregnancy when the fetus ordinarily weighs less than 1 pound.

Accommodation The modification of an activity or an ability that a child has already learned, to conform to environmental demands. Piaget's description of development holds that assimilation and accommodation are the means by which an individual interacts with the world and adapts to it. (See *assimilation*.)

Acquired immune deficiency syndrome (AIDS) An incurable and fatal sexually transmitted disease, transmitted through the exchange of body fluids.

★Some of these definitions are taken from the glossary in Guy R. Lefrançois, *Psychology for teaching: A bear . . .* (8th ed.). Belmont, Calif.: Wadsworth, 1994. Used by permission.

Adaptation The process whereby an organism changes in response to the environment. Such changes are assumed to facilitate interaction with that environment. Adaptation plays a central role in Piaget's theory. (See *accommodation, assimilation*.)

Adolescence A general term signifying the period from the onset of puberty to adulthood, typically including the teen years (13 to 19). (See *puberty*.)

AFP test A screening test designed to detect the likelihood of a fetal neural tube defect by revealing the presence of *alphafetoprotein* in the mother's blood.

Afterbirth The placenta and other membranes that are expelled from the uterus following the birth of a child.

Aggression Forceful action intended to dominate or intimidate, including actions such as insisting, asserting, intruding, or being angry or even violent. (See *violence*.)

Alienation In existential philosophy and psychology, an individual's feeling of separation from people and things that are important to that individual. (See *existential psychology*.)

Alzheimer's disease A disease associated with old age (but also occurring as young as 40), marked by progressive loss of memory and of brain function and eventual death.

Ambivalent infants Infants who are profoundly upset when their princi-

pal caregiver leaves and who are often angry when that person returns.

Amniocentesis A procedure whereby amniotic fluid is removed from a pregnant woman by means of a hollow needle. Subsequent analysis of this fluid may reveal chromosomal aberrations (Down syndrome, for example) and other fetal problems.

Amniotic sac A sac filled with a dark fluid (amniotic fluid) in which the fetus develops in the uterus.

Anal stage The second of Freud's psychosexual stages of development, beginning at approximately 8 months and lasting until around 18 months. It is characterized by children's preoccupation with physical anal activities.

Anorexia nervosa A medical condition not due to any detectable illness, primarily affecting adolescent girls and involving a loss of 15 to 25 percent of ideal body weight. It usually begins with dieting and ends when the patient is unwilling or unable to eat normally.

Anoxia A condition in which there is an insufficient supply of oxygen to the brain.

Apnea A temporary paralysis or collapse of throat muscles during sleep. Victims typically awaken at once and again breathe normally. Apnea is involved in about 5 percent of all insomnia complaints. Severe apnea can endanger life.

Arousal As a physiological concept, arousal refers to changes in functions such as heart rate, respiration rate, electrical activity in the cortex, and electrical conductivity of the skin. As a psychological concept, arousal refers to degree of alertness, awareness, vigilance, or wakefulness. Arousal varies from very low (coma or sleep) to very high (panic or high anxiety).

Artificial insemination An artificial breeding procedure often used in animal husbandry and sometimes with humans. This procedure eliminates the necessity for a physical union between a pair of opposite-sex individuals.

Assimilation The act of incorporating objects or aspects of objects to previously learned activities. To assimilate is, in a sense, to ingest or to use for something that is previously learned; more simply, the exercising of previously learned responses. (See *accommodation.*)

Association Refers to links or bonds among stimuli and responses. (See *associationistic.*)

Associationistic A term often used synonymously with stimulus-response explanations of learning. Also used to describe a memory model premised on the assumption that items of information in memory are *associated* in various ways in terms of their meanings.

Associative play A form of social play in which children sometimes share toys, but each child plays independently without mutually accepted goals or rules.

Attention deficit hyperactivity disorder (ADHD) A disorder marked by excessive general activity for the child's age, attention problems, high impulsivity, and low frustration tolerance.

Attribution An assignment of cause or blame for the outcomes of our behaviors. Our attributions are important influences on our behavior.

Attribution theory Theory that looks for regularities in the ways we attribute things that happen to certain causes, either internal or external.

Authoritarian parenting A highly controlling, dogmatic, obedience-oriented parenting style in which there is little recourse to reasoning and no acceptance of children's autonomy.

Authoritative parenting A moderately controlling parenting style in which value is placed on independence and reasoning, but in which parents impose some regulations and controls.

Autistic disorder A serious childhood mental disorder usually apparent by 30 months, characterized by social unresponsiveness, poor or nonexistent communication skills, and bizarre behavior.

Autosomes All chromosomes in mature sperm and ova other than the sex chromosome. Each of these cells therefore contains 22 autosomes.

Avoidant infants Infants who are *anxiously* attached to a caregiver, who show little signs of distress when that person leaves, and who initially *avoid* re-establishing contact when the person returns.

Babbling The relatively meaningless, repetitive sounds that young infants repeat.

Babinski reflex A reflex present in newborn children but disappearing later in life. The toes fan out as a result of being tickled in the center of the soles of the feet. Normal adults curl their toes inward rather than fanning them outward.

Baby tossing The medieval practice of tossing infants from one player to another in a bizarre sort of game in which the object was to throw accurately and *not* to drop the baby. Someone usually lost.

Basic needs Unlearned physiological requirements of the human organism; specifically, the needs for food, drink, and sex.

Behavior modification A general term for the application of behavioristic principles (primarily principles of operant conditioning) in systematic and deliberate attempts to change behavior.

Behavioristic theory A general term for those theories of learning concerned primarily with the observable components of behavior (stimuli and responses). Such theories are labeled *S-R learning theories* and are exemplified in classical and operant conditioning.

Birth The process whereby the fetus, the placenta, and other membranes are separated from the mother's body and expelled. (See *labor.*)

Birth order The position a child occupies in a family (for example, first, second, or third born).

Blind procedure An experimental procedure in which subjects or experimenters are not aware of who are members of experimental and control groups. When only one of these is unaware, the procedure is termed *single-blind*; when both are unaware, the procedure is *double-blind*.

Breech birth An abnormal presentation of the fetus at birth: buttocks first rather than head first.

Bulimia Nervosa Significant overconcern over body shape and weight manifested in recurrent episodes of binge eating often accompanied by self-induced vomiting, use of laxatives or diuretics, strict fasting, or vigorous exercise.

Canalization Waddington's term to describe the extent to which genetically determined characteristics are resistant to environmental influences. A highly canalized trait (such as hair color) remains unchanged in the face of most environmental influences; less highly canalized characteristics (such as manifested intelligence) are highly influenced by the environment.

Cephalocaudal Referring to the direction of development beginning with the head and proceeding outward toward the tail. Early infant development is cephalocaudal because children acquire control over their heads before acquiring control over their limbs.

Cervix The small circular opening to the womb (uterus) that dilates considerably during birth to permit passage of the baby.

Chorion villus sampling (CVS) A procedure in which samples of the membrane lining the uterus are used to permit prenatal diagnosis of potential birth defects.

Chromosomal disorders Chromosomal errors sometimes evident in the presence or absence of extra chromosomes or portions thereof.

Chromosome A microscopic body in the nucleus of all human and plant cells containing the genes—the carriers of heredity. Each mature human sex cell (sperm or ovum) contains 23 chromosomes, each containing countless numbers of genes. (See *genes*.)

Chunking A memory strategy that involves grouping related items of information in an attempt to make them easier to remember.

Classical conditioning Also called learning through stimulus substitution because it involves the repeated pairing of two stimuli so that a previously neutral (conditioned) stimulus eventually comes to elicit the same response (conditioned response) that was previously evoked by the first stimulus (unconditioned stimulus). This type of conditioning was first described by Pavlov.

Cocaine A stimulant drug, ordinarily inhaled as a white powder, the primary effects of which are feelings of euphoria. Possible effects also include hallucinations. In some forms (freebase or as what is called "crack" or "rock"), its effects are more immediate and more intense, and its use leads more readily to psychological dependence.

Cognition Mental processes such as thinking, knowing, and remembering. Theories of cognition attempt to explain intellectual development and functioning.

Cognitive strategies Procedures, knowledge, and information that relate to the processes involved in learning and remembering rather than to the content of what is learned. Cognitive strategies have to do with identifying problems, selecting approaches to their solution, monitoring progress, and using feedback. They are closely related to metacognition and metamemory.

Cohort A group of individuals who have in common the fact that they were born within the same range of time.

Comic book A collection of cartoon stories, most of which are not comic and many of which are characterized by violence.

Communication The transmission of messages. Communication does not require language, although it is greatly facilitated by it. Lower animals communicate even though they do not possess language.

Compensation A logical rule relating to the fact that certain changes can compensate for opposing changes, thereby negating their effect. For example, as a square object becomes longer, it also becomes thinner. Increases in length compensate for decreases in width. These changes combine to negate any actual changes in mass.

Concept A collection of perceptual experiences or ideas related by virtue of their possessing common properties.

Conception The beginning of life. Also called *fertilization*, conception occurs with the union of a sperm cell with an egg cell.

Conceptualization The forming of concepts (ideas or meanings); an intellectual process leading to thinking and understanding.

Concrete operations The third of Piaget's four major developmental stages, lasting from age 7 or 8 to approximately 11 or 12, characterized primarily by children's ability to deal with concrete problems and objects or objects and problems easily imagined in a concrete sense.

Conditioned response A response that is elicited by a conditioned stimulus. A conditioned response resembles its corresponding unconditioned response. The two are not identical, however.

Conditioned stimulus A stimulus that does not elicit any response or elicits a global response initially, but as a result of being paired with an unconditioned stimulus and its response acquires the capability of eliciting that same response. For example, a stimulus that is always present at the time of a fear reaction may become a conditioned stimulus for fear.

Conditioning A term used to describe a simple type of learning whereby certain behaviors are determined by the environment. (See also *classical conditioning, operant conditioning.*)

Conservation A Piagetian term implying that certain quantitative attributes of objects remain unchanged unless something is added to or taken away from them. Such characteristics of objects as mass, number, area, and volume are capable of being conserved.

Contextual model A developmental model that emphasizes the importance of the individual's interaction with environmental *context*. It looks at the historical period in which individuals are raised, as well as at the unique experiences they have.

Contextual theory of intelligence Sternberg's model based on the belief that intelligence involves adaptation in real-life contexts, in contrast with the view that intelligence is best measured by means of abstract, timed questions and problems.

Control group Consists of subjects who are not experimented with but who are used as comparisons to the experimental group to ascertain whether the outcomes were affected by the experimental procedure.

Conventional Kohlberg's second level of morality, reflecting a desire to establish and maintain good relations with others (law and order; obedience).

Correlation A mathematical measure of a relationship among variables. It is usually expressed as a number ranging from +1.00 (a perfect positive relationship) through 0 (no relationship) to −1.00 (a perfect inverse relationship).

Correlational studies Studies that attempt to determine the extent to which two or more variables covary. Correlational research cannot establish cause-and-effect relationships.

Creativity Generally refers to the capacity of individuals to produce novel or original answers or products. The term *creative* is an adjective that may be used to describe people, products, or processes.

Critical period The period during which an appropriate stimulus must be presented to an organism for imprinting to occur.

Cross-sectional study A technique in the investigation of child development that involves observing and comparing different subjects at different age levels. A cross-sectional study would compare 4- and 6 year olds by observing two groups of children at the same time, one group consisting of 6-year-old children and the other of 4-year-old children. A longitudinal study would require that the same children be examined at the age of 4 and again at age 6.

Crystallized abilities Cattell's term for intellectual abilities that are highly dependent on experience (verbal and computational skills and general information, for example). These abilities may continue to improve well into old age. (See *fluid abilities.*)

Culture-fair tests Psychological tests designed to measure accurately among individuals whose cultures are different. Although no test is absolutely free from cultural bias, some are fairer than others to disadvantaged groups.

Cytomegalovirus A herpes virus that affects the salivary glands and that can be transmitted from mother to infant during the birth. An important cause of mental retardation and deafness.

Defense mechanism A relatively irrational and sometimes unhealthy method used by people to compensate for their inability to satisfy their basic desires and to overcome the anxiety accompanying this inability.

Deferred imitation Imitating people or events in their absence. Deferred imitation is assumed by Piaget to be critical to developing language abilities.

Delinquency A legal category defined as the apprehension and conviction of a juvenile for some legal transgression.

Delivery The second stage of labor, beginning with the baby's head emerging (in a normal delivery) at the cervical opening and terminating with the birth of the child.

Deoxyribonucleic acid (DNA) A substance assumed to be the basis of all life, consisting of four chemical bases arranged in an extremely large number of combinations. The two strands of the DNA molecule that compose genes are arranged in the form of a double spiral (helix). These double strands are capable of replicating themselves as well as crossing over from one strand of the spiral to the other and forming new combinations of their genetic material. The nuclei of all cells contain DNA molecules.

Dependent variable The variable that may or may not be affected by manipulations of the independent variable in an experimental situation. (See *independent variable, variable.*)

Development The total process whereby individuals adapt to their environment. Development includes growth, maturation, and learning.

Developmental arithmetic disorder Significant impairment in developing arithmetic skills in the absence of other problems such as mental retardation; sometimes associated with reading problems.

Developmental psychology That aspect of psychology concerned with the development of individuals.

Developmental reading disorder A learning disability manifested in reading problems of varying severity; sometimes evident in spelling difficulties. Also labeled *dyslexia* or *specific reading disability*.

Diabetes An insulin deficiency disease, some forms of which are associated with a recessive gene.

Diary description A method of child study that records sequential descriptions of a child's behavior at predetermined intervals (daily or weekly, for example). Sometimes useful for arriving at a better understanding of general developmental patterns.

Diethylstilbestrol (DES) A drug once widely prescribed to lessen the probability of miscarriages. It has been linked with medical problems in offspring.

Dilation and curettage (D&C) A surgical procedure that involves scraping the walls of the uterus. It is occasionally necessary after birth if all of the placenta has not been expelled.

Disinhibitory effect The appearance of previously suppressed deviant behavior as a function of observing a model.

Dominant gene The gene (carrier of heredity) that takes precedence over all other related genes in genetically determined traits. Because all genes in the fertilized egg occur in pairs (one from the male and one from the female), the presence of a dominant gene as one member of the pair of genes means that the hereditary characteristic that it controls will be present in the individual. (See *recessive gene*.)

Double-blind procedure An experimental method in which neither subjects nor experimenters involved in data collection or analysis are aware of which subjects are members of experimental groups and which are not. Double-blind procedures are used as a safeguard against experimenter and subject bias.

Double helix The natural state of DNA molecules; essentially, two spiralling, intertwining chains of corresponding molecules.

Down syndrome The most common chromosomal birth defect, related to the presence of an extra twenty-first chromosome (technically labeled *trisomy 21*) and sometimes evident in mild to severe mental retardation.

Drug abuse The continued use of drugs in spite of persistent physical, social, psychological, or occupational problems that result.

Drug dependence Drug dependence is marked by a preoccupation with obtaining a drug, a compulsion to use it, and relapse following attempts to cease using it.

Drugs Chemical substances that have marked physiological effects on living organisms.

Drug tolerance Physiological changes following drug use that lead to higher doses of the drug being required to achieve the same effect.

Dyad A group of two people in interaction. A *triad* consists of three people.

Dyslexia A form of learning disability manifested in reading problems of varying severity. Dyslexia may be evident in spelling errors that are erratic rather than consistent.

Ecological validity An expression sometimes used to refer to the fact that psychological phenomena are highly dependent on environmental factors. For example, cultural, social, and other systems affect our behavior. More precisely, a generalization is said to be ecologically valid to the extent that it takes environmental circumstances into account.

Egg cell (See *ovum*.)

Ego The second stage of the human personality, according to Freud. It is the rational, reality-oriented level of human personality, which develops as children become aware of what the environment makes possible and impossible and therefore serves as a damper to the id. The id tends toward immediate gratification of impulses as they are felt, whereas the ego imposes restrictions that are based on environmental reality. (See *id, superego*.)

Egocentric Adjective based on Latin words for *self (ego)* and *center*. Literally, it describes a self-centered behavior, attitude, or personality characteristic. Although egocentrism often has negative connotations of selfishness, it is simply descriptive rather than evaluative when applied to childrens' perception of the world. For example, egocentric perception is characterized by an inability to assume an objective point of view.

Egocentric speech Vygotsky's intermediate stage of language development, common between ages 3 and 7, during which children often talk to themselves in an apparent effort to control their own behavior. (See *inner speech, social speech*.)

Elaborated language code A phrase used by Bernstein to describe the language of middle- and upper-class children. Elaborated language codes are grammatically correct, complex, and precise. (See *restricted language code*.)

Elaborating A long-term memory process involving changing or adding to material or making associations to make remembering easier. (See *organizing, rehearsing.*)

Electra complex A Freudian stage occurring around the age of 4 or 5 years, when a girl's sexual feelings lead her to desire her father and to become jealous of her mother. (See *Oedipus complex.*)

Elicited response A response brought about by a stimulus. The expression is synonymous with the term *respondent.*

Eliciting effect That type of imitative behavior in which the observer does not copy the model's responses but simply behaves in a related manner. (See *inhibitory effect, disinhibitory effect, modeling effect.*)

Embryo stage The second stage of prenatal development, beginning at the end of the second week after conception and terminating at the end of the eighth week.

Emitted response A response not elicited by a known stimulus but simply emitted by the organism. An emitted response is an operant.

Emotions The *feeling* or *affective* component of human behavior; an individual's responses to the occurrence of events relating to important goals.

Encode Change into a form that can be represented in memory.

Environment The significant aspects of an individual's surroundings. Includes all experiences and events that influence a child's development.

Epigenesis The developmental unfolding of genetically influenced characteristics.

Episiotomy A small cut made in the vaginal opening to facilitate the birth of a child. An episiotomy prevents the tearing of membranes and ensures that once the cut has been sutured healing will be rapid and complete.

Equilibration A Piagetian term for the process by which we maintain a balance between assimilation (using old learning) and accommodation (changing behavior; learning new things). Equilibration is essential for adaptation and cognitive growth.

Ethology The science concerned with the study of behavior in natural settings.

Eugenics A form of genetic engineering that selects specific individuals for reproduction. Applying eugenics to humans raises a number of serious moral and ethical questions. It is widely accepted and practiced with animals, however.

Event sampling A method of child study in which specific behaviors are observed and recorded and unrelated behaviors are ignored.

Exceptionality A category used to describe physical, social, or intellectual abilities and performance that are significantly above or below average.

Existential psychology A philosophical-psychological movement characterized by a preoccupation with existence. Existential philosophers describe the human condition in such terms as abandonment, loneliness, despair, and alienation. These feelings are purported to result from individuals' lack of knowledge about their origin and eventual end. Hence the term *existentialism*, because the only knowable reality is existence.

Exosystem Interactions between a system in which a child is involved (microsystem) and another system that does not ordinarily include the child (father's relationships with employers, for example).

Experiment A procedure for scientific investigation requiring manipulation of some aspects of the environment to determine what the effects of this manipulation will be.

Experimental group A group of subjects who undergo experimental manipulation. The group to which something is done in order to observe its effects. (See *control group.*)

Extended family A large family group consisting of parents, children, grandparents, and occasionally uncles, aunts, cousins, and so on. (See *nuclear family.*)

Extinction In operant conditioning, the cessation of a response as a function of the withdrawal of reinforcement.

Failure To Thrive (FTT) Infants' failure to gain weight at a normal rate (within the bottom 3 percent of the population) for no apparent organic reason. Also called *maternal deprivation syndrome* because maternal absence or neglect may be implicated.

Fairy tales Stories, many of which have very ancient origins, frequently told to young children. Fairy tales are only infrequently about fairies, although many end with "and they lived happily ever after." Many are characterized by violence and by the description of fear-inducing situations.

Fallopian tube One of two tubes that link the ovaries and the uterus. Fertilization (conception) ordinarily occurs in the Fallopian tubes. From there the fertilized egg cell moves into the uterus and attaches to the uterine wall.

Feral children Wild children; children allegedly abandoned by their parents and raised by wild animals.

Fertilization The union of sperm and ovum; the beginning of life.

Fertilized ovum stage (also **germinal stage**) The first stage of prenatal development, beginning with fertilization and ending at the end of the second week of intrauterine development.

Fetal alcohol syndrome A collection of symptoms in newborns associated with maternal alcohol consumption during pregnancy and sometimes evident in varying degrees of neurological, mental, and physical problems.

Fetoscopy A surgical procedure that allows the physician to see the fetus while obtaining samples of tissue for determining its status.

Fetus An immature child in the uterus. Fetal development begins eight weeks after conception and lasts until the birth of the baby.

Fluid abilities Cattell's term for intellectual abilities that seem to underlie much of our intelligent behavior and that are not highly affected by experience (general reasoning, attention span, memory for numbers). Fluid abilities are more likely to decline in old age than are crystallized abilities. (See *crystallized abilities*.)

Forceps Clamplike instruments that sometimes assist in the delivery of a baby.

Foreclosure Marcia's term for the adoption of a ready-made identity.

Formal operations The last of Piaget's four major developmental stages. It begins around the age of 11 or 12 and lasts until about 14 or 15. It is characterized by children's increasing ability to use logical thought processes.

Fragile X syndrome A sex-linked primarily male disorder that increases with the mother's age and that is often manifested in mental retardation.

Fraternal (dizygotic) twins Twins whose genetic origins are two different eggs. Such twins are as genetically dissimilar as average siblings. (See *identical twins*.)

Frustration An affective (emotional) reaction to the inability to gratify one's desires.

Gametes Mature sex cells. In humans, the egg cell (ovum) and the sperm cell.

Gender roles The particular combination of attitudes, behaviors, and personality characteristics that a culture considers appropriate for the individual's anatomical sex—what is considered masculine or feminine. Also termed *sex roles*.

Gender schemas Knowledge about the characteristics associated with being male and female.

Gender typing Learning behavior according to the sex of the individual. The term refers specifically to the acquisition of masculine behavior for a boy and feminine behavior for a girl.

General factor theory A theory of intelligence based on the assumption that there is a basic, underlying quality of intellectual functioning that determines *intelligence* in all areas. This quality is sometimes labeled *g*. (See *special abilities theory*.)

Generalizability The extent to which conclusions can be applied (generalized) from one situation to others; the generality of conclusions.

Generalized reinforcer A stimulus that, through learning, is reinforcing for a wide variety of behaviors. Such consequences of behavior as praise, social prestige, money, and power are important generalized reinforcers for human behavior.

Generation gap A cliché referring generally to the conflict that exists between the established generation and the one still growing.

Genes The carriers of heredity. Each of the 23 chromosomes contributed by the sperm cell and the ovum at conception is believed to contain between 40,000 and 60,000 genes. (See *dominant gene, recessive gene*.)

Genetics The science that studies heredity.

Genital stage The last of Freud's stages of psychosexual development, beginning around the age of 11 and lasting until around 18. It is characterized by involvement with normal adult modes of sexual gratification.

Genitalia A term referring generally to sex organs.

Genome The complete set of genetic instructions contained in our genes.

Genotype Our inherited chromosomal or genetic makeup.

Germinal stage (See *fertilized ovum stage*.)

Gestation period The period of time between conception and birth (typically 266 days for humans).

Growth Ordinarily, such physical changes as increasing height or weight.

Hawthorne effect The observation that members of experimental groups sometimes seem to improve their performance simply because they know they are participating in an experiment.

Head-turning reflex A reflex elicited in infants by stroking the cheek or the corner of the mouth. Infants turn their heads toward the side being stimulated.

Hedonistic Relating to the pain-pleasure principle, to the tendency to seek pleasure and avoid pain.

Heredity The transmission of physical and personality characteristics and predispositions from parent to offspring.

Heterozygous Refers to the presence of different genes with respect to a given trait. One of these genes is dominant and the other recessive. (See *homozygous*.)

Homozygous Refers to an individual's genetic makeup. Individuals are homozygous with respect to a particular trait if they possess identical genes for the trait. (See *heterozygous*.)

Humanist A person with a philosophical and psychological orientation primarily concerned with the worth of humans as individuals and processes that augment their human qualities.

Huntington's disease An inherited neurological disorder characterized by neural degeneration, typically beginning between the ages of 20 and 40 and usually leading to death.

Hypothesis An assumption, prediction, or tentative conclusion that may be tested through the application of the scientific method.

Id One of the three levels of the human personality, according to Freudian theory. The id is defined as all the instinctual urges to which humans are heir and is the source of all human motives. A newborn child's personality, according to Freud, is all id.

Identical (monozygotic) twins Twins whose genetic origin is a single egg. Such twins are genetically identical (See *fraternal twins*.)

Identification A general term referring to the process of assuming the goals, ambitions, mannerisms, and so on of another person—of identifying with that person. (See *imitation*.)

Identity A logical rule specifying that certain activities leave objects or situations unchanged. (See *reversibility*.)

Identity In Erikson's theory, a term closely related to *self*. To achieve identity is to arrive at a clear notion of who one is. It includes the goals, values, and beliefs to which the individual is committed. One of the important tasks of adolescence is to select and develop a strong sense of identity.

Identity diffusion Marcia's term for an adolescent state devoid of commitment or identity crisis; common in early adolescence.

Imaginary audience An expression of adolescent egocentrism; an imagined collection of all who might be concerned with the adolescent's self and behavior.

Imaginative play (also called *pretend play*) Activities that include make-believe games, daydreaming, imaginary playmates, and other forms of pretending; highly prevalent during the preschool years. (See also *play, sensorimotor play*.)

Imitation The complex process of learning through observation of a model.

Immature birth A miscarriage occurring sometime between the twentieth and the twenty-eighth weeks of pregnancy and resulting in the birth of a fetus weighing between 1 and 2 pounds.

Imprinting An instinctlike type of learning that occurs shortly after birth in certain species and that is seen in the "following" behavior of young ducks or geese.

Incidental mnemonics Nonsystematic, *incidental* approaches to remembering sometimes used by young children, such as paying attention.

Independent variable The variable in an experiment that can be manipulated to observe its effect on other variables. (See *dependent variable, variable*.)

Individuation The recognition of one's own individuality.

Infancy A period of development that begins a few weeks after birth and lasts until approximately 2 years of age.

Infant state Describes the general, current condition of an infant—for example, sleeping, crying, drowsy, or alert.

Infanticide The murder of an infant.

Information-processing approach Psychological theories that attempt to explain cognitive processes such as remembering, decision making, or problem solving. They are concerned primarily with how information is processed (organized, rehearsed) and stored.

Inhibitory effect The suppression of deviant behavior as a result of observing a model.

Inner speech Vygotsky's final stage in the development of speech, attained at around age 7, and characterized by silent "self-talk," the *stream-of-consciousness* flow of verbalizations that give direction and substance to our thinking and behavior. Inner speech is involved in all higher mental functioning. (See *egocentric speech, social speech*.)

Intelligence A property measured by intelligence tests. Seems to refer primarily to the capacity of individuals to adjust to their environment.

Intelligence Quotient (IQ) A way of describing intelligence by assigning it a number. May be arrived at by giving tests to estimate mental age, and then multiplying the ratio of mental to chronological age by 100. Average IQ is therefore 100.

Interaction A condition that exists when two or more forces influence each other, sometimes in very complex ways; also relates to how two or more forces act together (*coact*) to affect certain outcomes.

Intrauterine Within the uterus.

Intuitive thinking Thought in children from ages 4 to 7 based on immediate comprehension rather than logical processes. Also characterized by difficulties in class inclusion, egocentricity, and marked reliance on perception.

In utero A common medical term meaning "in the uterus."

Klinefelter's syndrome Results from the presence of an extra X chromosome in a male child; marked by the presence of both male and female secondary sexual characteristics.

Labor The process during which the fetus, the placenta, and other membranes are separated from the woman's body and expelled. The termination of labor is usually birth.

Language Complex arrangements of arbitrary sounds that have accepted referents and can therefore be used for communication among humans.

Lanugo Downy, soft hair that covers the fetus. Lanugo grows over most of a fetus's body sometime after the fifth month of pregnancy and is usually shed during the seventh month. However, some lanugo is often present at birth, especially on the infant's back.

Latency stage The fourth of Freud's stages of psychosexual development, characterized by the development of the superego (conscience) and by loss of interest in sexual gratification. This stage is assumed to last from the age of 6 to 11 years.

Learned helplessness Personality characteristic evident in a tendency to attribute outcomes to causes over which the person has no control. (See *mastery-oriented.*)

Learning Includes all changes in behavior that are due to experience. Does not include temporary changes brought about by drugs or fatigue or changes in behavior resulting simply from maturation or growth.

Learning disability Significant impairment in a specific skill or ability in the absence of a general depression in ability to learn (mental retardation).

Libido A general Freudian term denoting sexual urges. The libido is assumed to be the source of energy for sexual urges. Freud considered these urges the most important force in human motivation.

Longitudinal study A research technique in the study of child development that observes the same subjects over a long period of time. (See *cross-sectional study.*)

Long-term memory Memory that lasts from minutes to years and that involves rehearsal and organization.

LSD-25 (d-lysergic acid diethyl-amide tartrate) A particularly powerful hallucinogenic drug; an inexpensive, easily made, synthetic chemical that can sometimes have profound influences on human perception. In everyday parlance it is often referred to as "acid."

Macrosystem All interactive social systems that define a culture or subculture.

Mainstreaming The practice of placing students in need of special services in regular classrooms rather than segregating them. Also called *inclusive education.*

Marijuana A substance derived from the hemp plant. When smoked, it ordinarily induces a pleasant emotional state.

Marker genes Genes whose presence on a chromosome is associated with a known characteristic.

Mastery-oriented Personality characteristic marked by a tendency to attribute the outcomes of behavior to factors under personal control. (See *learned helplessness.*)

Masturbation Sexual self-stimulation.

Maturation A developmental process defined by changes that are relatively independent of a child's environment. Although the nature and timing of maturational changes are assumed to result from genetic predispositions, their manifestation is at least partly a function of the environment.

Mature birth The birth of an infant between the thirty-seventh and the forty-second weeks of pregnancy.

Meaning A large term whose meaning is *meaning.* Relates to the significance or sense of a thing.

Mechanistic model A model in human developmental psychology based on the belief that it is useful to view human beings in terms of their reactive, *machinelike* characteristics.

Meiosis The division of a single sex cell into two separate cells, each consisting of 23 chromosomes rather than 23 pairs of chromosomes. Meiosis therefore results in cells that are completely different, whereas mitosis results in identical cells.

Menarche A girl's first menstrual period, an event that transpires during pubescence.

Mendelian genetics The study of heredity through an examination of the characteristics of parents and offspring. (See *molecular genetics.*)

Menses A monthly discharge of blood and tissue from the womb of a mature female. The term refers to menstruation.

Mental retardation A global term referring to the mental state of individuals whose intellectual development is significantly slower than that of normal children and whose ability to adapt to their environment is consequently limited.

Mesosystem Interactions among two or more microsystems (for example, family and school).

Metacognition Knowledge about knowing. As we grow and learn, we develop notions of ourselves as learners. Accordingly, we develop strategies that recognize our limitations and that allow us to monitor our progress and to take advantage of our efforts.

Metamemory The knowledge that we develop about our own memory processes—knowledge about *how* to remember rather than simply about our memories.

Metaneeds Maslow's term for higher needs. In contrast to basic needs, metaneeds are concerned not with physiological but with psychological functions. They include the need to know truth, beauty, justice, and to self-actualize. Also termed *growth needs*.

Microsystem Defined by immediate, face-to-face interactions in which everybody affects everybody (for example, child and parent.)

Middle childhood An arbitrary division in the sequence of development beginning somewhere near the age of 6 and ending at approximately 12.

Mitosis The division of a cell into two identical cells. Occurs in body cells as opposed to sex cells.

Model A pattern for behavior that can be copied by someone else.

Modeling effect Imitative behavior involving the learning of a novel response. (See *eliciting effect, inhibitory effect, disinhibitory effect*.)

Molecular genetics The study of genetics based on the structure of chromosomes. (See *Mendelian genetics*.)

Morality The ethical aspect of human behavior. Morality is intimately bound to the development of an awareness of acceptable and unacceptable behaviors. It is therefore linked to what is often called conscience.

Moratorium Marcia's term for an adolescent stage marked by crisis and by vague, changing commitments; a time of exploration before commitment.

Moro reflex The generalized startle reaction of a newborn infant. It characteristically involves throwing out the arms and feet symmetrically and then bringing them back in toward the center of the body.

Morphemes Combinations of phonemes that make up the meaningful units of a language. (See *phonology*.)

Motherese Term for alterations in a mother's speech vis-a-vis her child.

Mother–infant bonding The emotional bond that exists between mother and infant.

Motivation Our reasons for behaving. What initiates, directs, and accounts for the cessation of behavior.

Motor development The development of such physical capabilities as walking, climbing, creeping, grasping, and handling objects.

Muscular dystrophy (MD) A degenerative muscular disorder, most forms of which are genetic, usually manifested in an inability to walk and sometimes fatal.

Mutagen Substance capable of causing changes in genetic material. (See *teratogen*.)

Natural childbirth Childbirth with little or no use of drugs such as pain killers.

Naturalistic observation The study of children in natural settings; an investigation in which the observation has little effect on the behavior of those observed. (See *nonnaturalistic observation*.)

Nature–nurture controversy A very old argument in psychology about whether genetics (nature) or environment (nurture) is more responsible for determining development. Also called *heredity-environment question*.

Need Ordinarily, a lack or deficiency in the organism. Needs may be unlearned (for example, the need for food and water) or learned (the need for money or prestige).

Negative reinforcement A stimulus that, when it is removed from the situation, increases the probability of occurrence of the response that precedes it. A negative reinforcer is usually an unpleasant or noxious stimulus that is removed when the desired response occurs.

Neonatal abstinence syndrome Neonatal symptoms associated with narcotics use by the mother that has resulted in the newborn also being addicted. Severe cases may be fatal.

Neonate A newborn infant. The neonatal period terminates when birthweight is regained.

Neural tube defects Spinal cord defects often linked with recessive genes, sometimes evident in failure of the spine to close (spina bifida) or in the absence of portions of the brain.

Nonnaturalistic observation The study of children using questionnaires or interviews (clinical investigations) or when the environment is manipulated or changed (experimental investigations). (See *naturalistic observation*.)

Nonstandard language A variation (different dialect) of the dominant *standard* language. Nonstandard dialects are often ungrammatical and local.

Norm An average or standard way of behaving. Cultural norms, for example, refer to the behaviors expected of individuals who are members of that culture.

Normal curve A mathematical function represented in the form of a symmetrical bell-shaped curve that illustrates how a large number of naturally occurring or chance events are distributed.

Nuclear family A family consisting of a mother, a father, and their offspring. (See *extended family*.)

Object concept Piaget's expression for a child's understanding that the world is composed of objects that continue to exist quite apart from the child's immediate perception of them.

Observational learning Learning through imitation.

Obstetrics A sophisticated medical term for midwifery; the medical art and science of assisting women who are pregnant, both during pregnancy and at birth.

Oedipus complex A Freudian concept denoting the developmental stage (around 4 years) when a boy's increasing awareness of sexual feelings leads him to desire his mother and envy his father. (See *Electra complex*.)

Onlooker play Consists of child watching others play but not actively participating.

Open systems A theory that recognizes the interactive nature of biological, psychological, and social systems, and the impossibility of predicting final outcomes with absolute confidence (in contrast with a *closed* system, which is completely predictable).

Operant The label used by Skinner to describe a response not elicited by any known or obvious stimulus. Most significant human behaviors appear to be operant. Such behaviors as writing a letter or going for a walk are operants, if no known specific stimulus elicits them.

Operant conditioning A type of learning in which the probability of a response changes as a result of reinforcement. Much of the experimental work of B. F. Skinner investigates the principles of operant conditioning.

Operational thought A Piagetian developmental stage beginning around the age of 7 or 8. Specifically, an operation is a thought that is governed by certain rules of logic.

Oral stage The first stage of psychosexual development, lasting from birth to approximately 8 months of age. The oral stage is characterized by preoccupation with the immediate gratification of desires. This is accomplished primarily through the oral regions, by sucking, biting, swallowing, playing with the lips, and so on.

Organismic model This model in human development assumes that people are active rather than simply reactive and that they are therefore more like biological organisms than like machines.

Organizing A memory strategy involving grouping and relating material to maintain it in long-term memory. (See *elaborating, rehearsing*.)

Orienting response The initial response of humans and other animals to novel stimulation. Also called the orienting reflex or orientation reaction. Components of the orienting response include changes in EEG patterns, respiration rate, heart rate, and galvanic skin response.

Ovary A female organ (most women have two of them) that produces ova (egg cells).

Ovum (plural, **ova**) The sex cell produced by a mature female approximately once every 28 days. When mature it consists of 23 chromosomes, as opposed to all other human body cells (somatoplasm), which consist of 23 pairs of chromosomes. It is often referred to as an egg cell. (See *sperm cell*.)

Palmar reflex The grasping reflex that newborn infants exhibit when an object is placed in their hand.

Parallel play A form of play in which children play side by side but individually, sharing neither activities nor rules.

Peer group A group of equals. Peer groups may be social groups, age groups, intellectual groups, or work groups. Young children's peer groups are usually age and grade mates.

Perception Reaction to and interpretation of physical stimulation (sensation). A conceptual process, dependent on activity of the brain.

Permissive parenting A parenting style that may be characterized as "laissez-faire." Permissive parents are nonpunitive and undemanding. Their children are autonomous rather than obedient and, as such, are responsible for their own decisions and actions.

Personal fable An expression of adolescent egocentrism marked by the elaboration of fantasies, the hero of which is the adolescent.

Phallic stage The third stage of Freud's theory of psychosexual development. It begins at about the age of 18 months and lasts to the age of approximately 6 years. During this stage children become concerned with their genitals and may show evidence of the much-discussed complexes labeled *Oedipus* and *Electra*. (See *Electra complex, Oedipus complex.*)

Phenomenology An approach concerned primarily with how individuals view their own world. Its basic assumption is that each individual perceives and reacts to the world in a unique manner, and that it is this phenomenological worldview that is important in understanding an individual's behavior.

Phenotype Manifest characteristics related to genetic makeup.

Phenylketonuria (PKU) A genetic disorder associated with the presence of two recessive genes.

Phoneme The simplest unit of language, consisting of a single sound such as a vowel.

Phonology The phonemes or sounds of a language.

Phrase structure rules The implicit (or explicit) rules that govern the formation of correct phrases. For example, a phrase structure rule might specify that correct noun phrases may consist of a noun; an article and a noun; an article, an adjective, and a noun; a pronoun; and so on.

Physiological dependence Commonly called *addiction*; refers to physiological changes following drug use such that stopping use leads to withdrawal symptoms.

Placenta A flat, thick membrane attached to the inside of the uterus during pregnancy and to the developing fetus. The placenta connects the mother and the fetus by means of the umbilical cord, through which the fetus receives nourishment.

Play Activities that have no goal other than the enjoyment derived from them.

Populations Collections of individuals (or objects or situations) with similar characteristics.

Positive reinforcement A stimulus that increases the probability of a response recurring as a result of being added to a situation after the response has occurred. It usually takes the form of a pleasant stimulus (*reward*) that results from a specific response.

Positive symptoms Symptoms of pregnancy that determine positively that the woman is bearing a child. These include fetal heartbeat, the ability to feel the fetus by palpating the woman's stomach, X rays, and ultrasound.

Postconventional Kohlberg's third level of morality, reflecting an understanding of social contract and more individualistic principles of morality.

Postmature birth The birth of an infant after the forty-second week of pregnancy.

Postpartum depression A form of depression that affects about 10 percent of all women beginning shortly after childbirth. In some cases, postpartum depression can be serious and dangerous, but it usually ameliorates and disappears with time.

Practice play (See *sensorimotor play*.)

Pragmatics In reference to language development, implicit rules that tell children when and how to speak.

Preconcept The label given to a preconceptual child's incomplete understanding of concepts, resulting from an inability to reason correctly about related classes. (See *preconceptual thought*.)

Preconceptual thought The first substage of the period of preoperational thought, beginning around 2 and lasting until 4. It is so called because children have not yet developed the ability to classify and therefore have an incomplete understanding of concepts. (See *preconcept*.)

Preconventional The first of Kohlberg's three levels of moral development, based on hedonistic or obedience-oriented judgments.

Pregnancy The condition of a woman who has had an ovum (egg cell) fertilized and who, nature willing, will eventually give birth.

Premature birth The birth of a baby between the twenty-ninth and thirty-sixth weeks of pregnancy. A premature baby weighs somewhere between 2 and 5½ pounds and is less likely to survive if less than 2 pounds.

Prenatal development The period of development beginning at conception and ending at birth. That period lasts approximately nine calendar months in the human female (266 days).

Preoperational thought The second of Piaget's four major stages, lasting from about 2 to 7 or 8 years. It consists of two substages: intuitive thinking and preconceptual thinking. (See *intuitive thinking, preconceptual thought*.)

Pretend play (See *imaginative play*.)

Primary circular reaction An expression used by Piaget to describe a simple reflex activity (such as thumb-sucking) that serves as a stimulus for its own repetition. (See *secondary circular reaction, tertiary circular reaction*.)

Primary reinforcer A stimulus that is reinforcing in the absence of any learning. Such stimuli as food and drink are primary reinforcers because presumably an organism does not have to learn that they are pleasurable.

Primary sexual characteristics Changes of sexual maturation involved in the production of offspring (for example, the ability of the testes to produce sperm and of the ovaries to produce ova).

Primitive social play An early form of social play involving "shared meaning" rather than shared rules; for example, infant "peek-a-boo" games or toddler "chase" games.

Productiveness The quality of language that allows its users to *produce* an almost unlimited range of meanings simply by combining words and using pauses, intonations, and so on, in different ways.

Prolapsed cord A condition that sometimes occurs during birth when the umbilical cord becomes lodged between the infant's body and the birth canal, cutting off the infant's supply of oxygen. The effect may be brain damage of varying severity, depending on the length of time until delivery following prolapsing of the cord.

Proteins A molecule made up of chains of one or more amino acids. In a sense, proteins are the basis of organic life.

Proximodistal Literally, from near to far. Refers to a developmental progression in which central organs develop before external limbs and in which the infant acquires control over muscles closer to the center of the body before acquiring control over those more peripheral.

Psycholinguists People who study the relationship between language (linguistics) and development, thinking, learning, and behaving (psychology).

Psychological dependence Sometimes called *habituation*; refers to a strong desire to continue using a drug.

Psychology The science that examines human behavior (and that of animals as well).

Psychosexual development A Freudian term describing child development as a series of stages that are sexually based. (See *anal stage, genital stage, latency stage, oral stage, phallic stage*.)

Psychosocial development A term used by Erikson to describe human development as a sequence of stages involving the resolution of crises that are primarily social.

Puberty Sexual maturity following pubescence.

Pubescence Changes of adolescence leading to sexual maturity.

Punishment Involves either the presentation of an unpleasant stimulus or the withdrawal of a pleasant stimulus as a consequence of behavior. Punishment should not be confused with negative reinforcement because punishment does not increase the probability of a response occurring; rather, it is intended to have the opposite effect.

Pupillary reflex An involuntary change in the size of the pupil as a function of brightness or darkness. The pupillary reflex is present in neonates.

Quickening The name given to the first movements of the fetus in utero. Quickening does not occur until after the fifth month of pregnancy.

Rabbit test A once-common test for pregnancy that required sacrificing a virgin rabbit or mouse. It has been replaced by highly reliable, inexpensive, easily performed chemical tests that can be conducted much earlier than could the rabbit test.

Radiography The use of X rays; occasionally used as a tool in prenatal diagnosis.

Rapid eye movement (REM) sleep A stage of sleep characterized by rapid eye movements. Most of our dreaming occurs during REM sleep, which accounts for approximately 25 percent of an adult's sleep time and as much as 50 percent of an infant's.

Reaction range All the possible outcomes for a particular characteristic given variations in the nature and timing of environmental influences.

Recessive gene A gene whose characteristics are not manifest in the offspring unless it happens to be paired with another recessive gene. When a recessive gene is paired with a dominant gene, the characteristics of the dominant gene will be manifest.

Rehearsing A memory process involving repetition, important in maintaining information in short-term memory and in transferring it to long-term memory. (See *elaborating, organizing*.)

Reinforcement The effect of a reinforcer—an increase in the probability of a response recurring. (See *negative reinforcement, positive reinforcement, reinforcer, reward*.)

Reinforcer A reinforcing stimulus.

Reliable A measure is reliable to the extent that it measures accurately whatever it measures.

Replicability A crucial quality of valid scientific or experimental procedures. A procedure is said to be replicable when it can be repeated and the results of so doing are identical (or highly similar) with each repetition.

Reprimands Indications of disapproval that are usually verbal; a form of punishment.

Respondent A term used by Skinner in contrast to the term *operant* (also synonymous with *elicited response*). A respondent is a response elicited by a known specific stimulus. Unconditioned responses of the type referred to in classical conditioning are examples of respondents.

Response cost A form of punishment involving the loss of a previously earned reward.

Restricted language code A term used by Bernstein to describe the language typical of the lower-class child. Restricted language codes are characterized by short and simple sentences, general and relatively imprecise terms, idiom and colloquialism, and incorrect grammar. (See *elaborated language code*.)

Reversibility A logical property manifested in the ability to reverse or undo activity either empirically or conceptually. An idea is said to be reversible when a child can imagine its opposite, and realize that certain logical consequences follow from doing so.

Reward An object, stimulus, event, or outcome that is perceived as pleasant and may therefore be reinforcing.

Rite of passage Ritualistic ceremony marking the passage from childhood to adulthood in many primitive societies.

Schemata In information-processing theory, a global term used as a metaphor for concepts. Schemata are what we know about things.

Scheme (also **schema** or **schemata**) The label used by Piaget to describe a unit in cognitive structure. A scheme is, in one sense, an activity together with its structural connotations. In another sense, scheme may be thought of as an idea or a concept. It usually labels a specific activity: the looking scheme, the grasping scheme, the sucking scheme.

Script A term used to describe our knowledge of what goes with what and in what sequence. Scripts are that part of cognitive structure that deals with the routine and the predictable.

Secondary circular reaction Infant responses that are circular in the sense that the response serves as a stimulus for its own repetition and secondary because the responses do not center on the child's body, as do primary circular reactions. (See *primary circular reaction, tertiary circular reaction*.)

Secondary sexual characteristics Changes of pubescence that accompany maturation of the sexual organs (for example, growth of facial hair, development of breasts, voice changes).

Secular trend The trend toward earlier maturation.

Securely attached infants Infants who are strongly and positively attached to a caregiver, who are distressed when that person leaves, and who quickly reestablish contact when the person returns.

Self The concept that an individual has of himself or herself. Notions of the self are often closely allied with individuals' beliefs about how others perceive them.

Self-actualization The process or act of becoming oneself, developing one's potentiality, achieving an awareness of one's identity, fulfilling oneself. The term *actualization* is central to humanistic psychology.

Self-concept The ideas an individual has of him- or herself. Notions of the self reflect what we think others think of us, our own estimates of what we are relative to what we would like to be, and our estimates of our competence and "goodness" in various important areas.

Self-efficacy Describes our estimates of our personal effectiveness. The most *efficacious* individuals are those who deal most effectively with a variety of situations, especially those that are ambiguous or stressful.

Self-esteem An individual's opinion of his or her own behavior and person.

Self-image Often used interchangeably with *self-esteem* or *self-worth*; denotes an individual's personal evaluations of the self.

Self-referent thought Ideas or thoughts that have to do with the self and, specifically, with self-knowledge. Self-referent thoughts are often evaluative; they deal with our personal estimates of how effective we are in our dealings with the world and with others. (See *self-efficacy*.)

Semantics The component of language that relates to meaning or significance of sounds.

Sensation The physical effect of stimulation; a physiological process dependent on activity of the senses.

Sensitive period A period during which specific experiences have their most pronounced effects—for example, the first six months of life during which an infant forms strong attachment bonds to the mother or caregiver.

Sensorimotor period The first stage of development in Piaget's classification. It lasts from birth to approximately age 2 and is so called because children understand their world primarily through their activities toward it and sensations of it.

Sensorimotor play (also called *practice-play*) Activity involving the manipulation of objects or execution of activities simply for the sensations that are produced. (See also *play, imaginative play, social play.*)

Sensory memory The simple sensory recognition of stimuli (also called short-term sensory memory). Sensory memory requires no cognitive processing and does not involve conscious awareness.

Seriation The ordering of objects according to one or more empirical properties. To seriate is essentially to place in order.

Sex cells Sperm and ovum. Mature sex cells each contain 23 chromosomes rather than 23 pairs and are different from each other. (See *somatic cells.*)

Sex chromosome A chromosome contained in sperm cells and ova responsible for determining the sex of the offspring. Sex chromosomes produced by the female are of one variety (X); those produced by the male may be either X or Y. At fertilization (the union of sperm and ovum), an XX pairing will result in a girl; and XY pairing will result in a boy. Hence the sperm cell is essentially responsible for determining the sex of the offspring.

Sexual abuse A form of maltreatment in which the victim is forced—physically or by virtue of the abuser's status and power—to submit to sexual behaviors.

Sexually transmitted disease (STD) Also called *venereal diseases*; any of several dozen diseases transmitted primarily through sexual intercourse (for example, gonorrhea, herpes, chlamydia, and AIDS).

Short-term memory Information that lasts from a few seconds to a minute, requiring limited cognitive processing.

Siblings Offspring whose parents are the same. Siblings simply are brothers and sisters.

Social cognition The realization that others have feelings, motives, intentions, and so on; knowledge of the emotions of others.

Social play Activity that involves interaction between two or more children and that frequently takes the form of games with more or less clearly defined rules. (See also *play, sensorimotor play, imaginative play.*)

Social speech In Vygotsky's theorizing, the most primitive stage of language development, evident before the age of 3, during which a child expresses simple thoughts and emotions out loud. The function of social speech is to control the behavior of others. (See *egocentric speech, inner speech.*)

Socialization The complex process of learning those behaviors that are appropriate within a given culture as well as those that are less appropriate. The primary agents of socialization are home, school, and peer groups.

Sociobiology A science founded on the assumption that many social behaviors are genetically based.

Sociogram A pictorial or graphic representation of the social structure of a group.

Sociometry A measurement procedure used extensively in sociological studies to determine patterns of likes and dislikes in groups and to plot group structure.

Solitary play Nonsocial child play that a child undertakes alone. It is the most common form of play before age 2.

Somatic cells Also called *body* cells; all cells in our body other than sex cells. Normal somatic cells each contain 23 *pairs* of chromosomes. All our body cells normally contain identical genetic information. (See *sex cells.*)

Special abilities theory A theory of intelligence based on the assumption that intelligence consists of a number of separate factors (for example, numerical, verbal, memory) rather than a single underlying factor common to performance in all areas. (See *general factor theory.*)

Specimen description A method of child study in which detailed specific instances of a child's behavior are recorded. Useful for in-depth studies of individual children.

Spermarche A boy's first ejaculation, often a nocturnal event. (See *menarche.*)

Sperm cell The sex cell produced by a mature male. Like egg cells (ova), sperm cells consist of 23 chromosomes rather than 23 pairs of chromosomes.

Stages Identifiable phases in the development of human beings. Such developmental theories as Jean Piaget's are referred to as stage theories because they describe behavior at different developmental levels.

Standard language The correct (hence standard) form of a society's dominant language; the form that is taught in schools and against which other dialects are judged for correctness.

STD (See *sexually transmitted disease.*)

Stress A force exerted on an individual, often related to change or to high environmental demands; sometimes associated with high arousal.

Sucking reflex The automatic sucking response of a newborn child when the oral regions are stimulated. Nipples are particularly appropriate for eliciting the sucking reflex.

Sudden infant death syndrome (SIDS) Unexplained and unexpected infant death. The leading cause of infant death between the ages of 1 month and 1 year (not really a *cause*, because the cause remains unknown; rather, a *label*).

Suicide The deliberate taking of one's life.

Superego The third level of personality according to Freud. It defines the moral or ethical aspects of personality and is in constant conflict with the id. (See *ego, id*.)

Symbolic The final stage in the development of a child's representation of the world. The term is used by Bruner to describe a representation of the world through arbitrary symbols. Symbolic representation includes language, as well as theoretical or hypothetical systems.

Symbolic models Nonhuman models such as movies, television programs, oral and written instructions, or religious, literary, musical, or folk heroes.

Syncretic reasoning A type of semilogical reasoning characteristic of the classification behavior of very young preschoolers. In syncretic reasoning, objects are grouped according to egocentric criteria, which are subject to change from one object to the next. In other words, children do not classify on the basis of a single dimension but change dimensions as they classify.

Syntax The grammar of a language, consisting of the set of implicit or explicit rules that govern the combinations of words composing a language.

Taboo A prohibition imposed by social custom; a behavior widely accepted as forbidden and inappropriate by a culture.

Tay-Sachs disease A fatal genetic enzyme disorder that can be detected before birth, but that cannot yet be prevented or cured.

Temperament The biological basis of personality—its hereditary components. The expression *infant temperament* refers to infants' characteristic emotional responses.

Teratogens Drugs and other substances that cause fetal defects.

Teratology The study of birth defects.

Tertiary circular reaction An infant's response is circular in the sense that the response serves as the stimulus for its own repetition, but the repeated response is not identical to the first response. This last characteristic, the altered response, distinguishes a tertiary circular reaction from a secondary circular reaction. (See *primary circular reaction, secondary circular reaction*.)

Theory An organized, systematic explanation of observations useful for explaining and for predicting.

Theory of mind The intuitive notions children have about the existence and characteristics of their own and others' minds. A theory of mind allows a child to predict and explain behavior by relating it to mental states like beliefs and intentions.

Time-lag study A developmental study in which subjects of one age are compared to other groups who are also the same age, but at a different point in time (for example, comparing 12 year olds in 1995 with 12 year olds in 1990 and in 1985).

Time-out A form of punishment in which the transgressor is removed from ongoing (and presumably rewarding) activities.

Time sampling A method of child observation in which behavior is observed during specific time intervals, frequently with the aim of recording instances or frequency of specific behaviors.

Toddler A label sometimes used to describe a child between the ages of 18 months and 2½ years.

Transductive reasoning The type of semilogical reasoning that proceeds from particular to particular, rather than from particular to general or from general to particular. One example of transductive reasoning is the following: (1) Cows give milk. (2) Goats give milk. (3) Therefore, goats are cows.

Transformational rules Implicit (or explicit) grammatical rules that govern the alteration of expressions and their resulting meanings. For example, there is a transformational rule specifying that a declarative sentence may be transformed into a question by altering the order of the words (as in transforming "I can go" to "Can I go?").

Transitional objects Blankets, teddy bears, or other objects that children focus affection and attention on while in transition between a state of high parental dependency and the development of a more independent self.

Transverse presentation A crosswise presentation of the fetus at birth.

Trauma An injury or nervous shock. Traumatic experiences are usually intense and unpleasant.

Triarchic theory Sternberg's label for his description of intelligence. The three *arches* of human intelligence are metacomponents (cognitive strategies that have to do with identifying problems, solving them, monitoring progress, and other aspects of meta-cognition and metamemory); performance components (the actual execution of procedures selected at the metacomponential level); and knowledge-acquisition components (what is actually achieved in the process of learning and behaving).

Trisomy 21 (See *Down syndrome*.)

Turner's syndrome A chromosomal abnormality in which a female child is born with a missing sex chromosome (one rather than two X's); characterized by underdeveloped secondary sexual characteristics that can sometimes be improved with injections of estrogen before puberty.

Ultrasound A diagnostic technique in medicine whereby high-frequency sound waves are used to provide images of internal body structures. Ultrasound recordings are used extensively to evaluate the condition of the fetus.

Umbilical cord A long, thick cord attached to what will be the child's navel at one end and to the placenta at the other. It transmits nourishment and oxygen to the growing fetus from the mother.

Unconditioned response A response elicited by an unconditioned stimulus.

Unconditioned stimulus A stimulus that elicits a response before learning. All stimuli capable of eliciting reflexive behaviors are examples of unconditioned stimuli. For example, food is an unconditioned stimulus for the response of salivation.

Uterus A relatively sophisticated term for the womb.

Valid A measure is said to be valid to the extent that it measures what it is intended to measure. (See *reliable*.)

Values Judgments or beliefs about the desirability of certain behaviors or goals.

Variable A property, measurement, or characteristic that is susceptible to variation. In psychological experimentation, such qualities of human beings as intelligence and creativity are referred to as variables. (See *dependent variable, independent variable*.)

Vegetative reflexes Reflexes pertaining to the intake of food (for example, swallowing and sucking).

Version Turning; in obstetrics, refers to turning the child in the uterus to facilitate birth.

Violence An extreme form of aggressiveness, implying physical action and real or possible physical harm to people or objects.

Visual acuity Sharpness and clarity of vision. Visual acuity is often expressed in terms of Snellen ratings in which 20/20 vision is considered average (the individual can see as well at 20 feet as individuals with normal vision). Vision can be poorer than 20/20 (for example, 20/40 when the individual sees as clearly at 20 feet as people with normal vision see at 40) or better (for example, 20/15, when the individual sees as well at 20 feet as average people do at 15).

Work Activities engaged in, not primarily for the pleasure derived from them, but rather for what may be gained as a result of the activities. (See *play*.)

Zone of proximal development Vygotsky's phrase for the individual's current potential for further intellectual development, a capacity not ordinarily measured by conventional intelligence tests. He suggests that hints and questions might help in assessing this *zone*.

Zygote A fertilized egg cell (ovum). A zygote is formed from the union of a sperm cell and an egg cell; it contains 46 chromosomes (a full complement).

Abecassis, J. (1993). De Henri Wallon à Jérome Bruner, continuité ou discontinuité? *Enfance, 47*, 47–57.

Abel, E. L. (1984). *Fetal alcohol syndrome and fetal alcohol effects.* New York: Plenum Press.

Abram, M. J., & Dowling, W. D. (1979). How readable are parenting books? *The Family Coordinator, 28*, 365–368.

Abramson, L. (1991). Facial expressivity in failure to thrive and normal infants: Implications for their capacity to engage in the world. *Merrill-Palmer Quarterly, 37*, 159–182.

Abroms, I. F., & Panagakos, P. G. (1980). The child with significant developmental motor disability (cerebal palsy). In A. P. Scheiner & I. F. Abroms (Eds.), *The practical management of the developmentally disabled child.* St. Louis: C. V. Mosby, 145–166.

Acker, A. (1986). *Children of the volcano.* Toronto: Between the Lines.

ACOG Technical Bulletin. (1988). *Human Immune Deficiency Virus Infections.* Number 123. Washington, D.C., December.

Acredolo, L. P., & Hake, J. L. (1982). Infant perception. In B. B. Wolman (Ed.), *Handbook of developmental psychology.* Englewood Cliffs, N.J.: Prentice-Hall.

Adair, J. G., Sharpe, D., & Huynh, C. (1989). Hawthorne control procedures in educational experiments: A reconsideration of their use and effectiveness. *Review of Educational Research, 59*, 215–228.

Adams, R. E., Jr., & Passman, R. H. (1979). Effects of visual and auditory aspects of mothers and strangers on the play and exploration of children. *Developmental Psychology, 15*, 269–274.

Adams, R. E., Jr., & Passman, R. H. (1981). The effects of preparing two-year-olds for brief separations from their mothers. *Child Development, 52*, 1068–1070.

Adams, R. E., Jr., & Passman, R. H. (1983). Explaining to young children about an upcoming separation from their mother: When do I tell them? *Journal of Applied Developmental Psychology, 4*, 35–42.

Adegoke, A. A. (1993). The experience of spermarche (The age of onset of sperm emission) among selected adolescent boys in Nigeria. *Journal of Youth and Adolescence, 22*, 201–209.

AIDS kids beat odds against survival. (1994). *Edmonton Journal*, April 17, C7.

The AIDS threat: Who's at risk? (1988). *Newsweek*, March 14, pp. 42–52.

AIDS virus strain beats pill; scientists scramble for new cure. (1989). *Edmonton Journal*, March 15, A2.

AIDS will kill 4M women by 2000: WHO. (1993). *Edmonton Journal*, September 8, p. A12.

Ainsworth, L. L. (1984). Contact comfort: A reconsideration of the original work. *Psychological Reports, 55*, 943–949.

Ainsworth, M. D. S. (1973). The development of infant-mother attachment. In B. M. Caldwell & H. N. Ricciuti (Eds.), *Review of child development research* (Vol. 3). Chicago: University of Chicago Press.

Ainsworth, M. D. S. (1979). Infant-mother attachment. *American Psychologist, 34*, 932–937.

Ainsworth, M. D. S., Blehar, M. C., Waters, E., & Wall, S. (1978). *Patterns of attachment.* Hillsdale, N.J.: Lawrence Erlbaum.

Albert, R. S., & Runco, M. A. (1986). The achievement of eminence: A model based on a longitudinal study of exceptionally gifted boys and their families. In R. J. Sternberg & J. E. Davidson (Eds.), *Conceptions of giftedness.* New York: Cambridge University Press.

Alcock, J. (1984). *Animal behavior: An evolutionary approach* (3rd ed.). Sunderland, Mass.: Sinauer.

Aldis, O. (1975). *Play fighting.* New York: Academic Press.

Allen, R. E., & Oliver, J. M. (1982). The effects of child maltreatment on language development. *Child Abuse and Neglect, 6*, 299–305.

Allen, R. E., & Wasserman, G. A. (1985). Origins of language delay in abused infants. *Child Abuse and Neglect, 9*, 335–340.

Allison, P. D., & Furstenberg, F. F., Jr. (1989). How marital dissolution affects children: Variations by age and sex. *Developmental Psychology, 25*, 540–549.

Als, H., Tronick, E., Lester, B. M., & Brazelton, T. B. (1979). Specific neonatal measures: The Brazelton Neonatal Behavior Assessment Scale. In J. D. Osofsky (Ed.), *Handbook of infant development.* New York: John Wiley.

Alvy, K. T. (1987). *Parent training: A social necessity.* Studio City, Calif.: Center for the Improvement of Child Caring.

Amato, P. R., & Keith, B. (1991). Parental divorce and the well-being of children: A meta-analysis. *Psychological Bulletin, 110,* 26–46.

American Psychiatric Association. (1987). *Diagnostic and statistical manual of mental disorders* (3rd ed., revised). Washington, D.C.: American Psychiatric Association.

Anastasiow, N. (1984). Preparing adolescents in child bearing: Before and after pregnancy. In M. Sugar (Ed.), *Adolescent parenthood.* New York: SP Medical and Scientific Books, 141–158.

Anderson, D. R., & Bryant, J. (1983). Research on children's television viewing: The state of the art. In J. Bryant & D. R. Anderson (Eds.), *Children's understanding of television: Research on attention and comprehension.* New York: Academic Press, 331–355.

Anderson, J. A. (1983). Television literacy and the critical viewer. In J. Bryant & D. R. Anderson (Eds.), *Children's understanding of television: Research on attention and comprehension.* New York: Academic Press, 297–327.

Anderson, J. R. (1980). *Cognitive psychology and its applications.* San Francisco: W. H. Freeman.

Anthony, E. J. (Ed.). (1975). *Exploration in child psychiatry.* New York: Plenum Press.

Anthony, E. J., & Koupernik, C. (Eds.). (1974). *The child in his family: Children at psychiatric risk* (Vol. 3). New York: John Wiley.

Appel, L. F., Cooper, R. G., McCarrell, N., Sims-Knight, Y., Yussen, S. R., & Flavell, J. H. (1972). The development of the distinction between perceiving and memorizing. *Child Development, 43,* 1365–1381.

Arbuthnot, J. (1975). Modification of moral judgment through role playing. *Developmental Psychology, 11,* 319–324.

Aries, P. (1962). *Centuries of childhood: A social history of family life* (R. Baldick, trans.). New York: Alfred A. Knopf. (Originally published 1960.)

Arlin, P. K. (1975). Cognitive development in adulthood: A fifth stage? *Developmental Psychology, 11,* 602–606.

Arnett, J. (1990). Contraceptive use, sensation seeking, and adolescent egocentrism. *Journal of Youth and Adolescence, 19,* 171–182.

Arnett, J. (1992). Reckless behavior in adolescence: A developmental perspective. *Developmental Review, 12,* 339–373.

Aronfreed, J. (1968). *Conduct and conscience.* New York: Academic Press.

Asher, S. R. (1983). Social competence and peer status: Recent advances and future directions. *Child Development, 54,* 1427–1434.

Askew, S., & Ross, C. (1988). *Boys don't cry: Boys and sexism in education.* Philadelphia, Penn.: Open University Press.

Aslin, R. N., Pisoni, D. P., & Jusczyk, P. W. (1983). Auditory development and speech perception in infancy. In M. H. Haith & J. J. Campos (Eds.), *Handbook of child psychology* (2nd ed.): *Infancy and developmental psychology.* New York: John Wiley.

Aslin, R. N., & Smith, L. B. (1988). Perceptual development. *Annual Review of Psychology, 39,* 435–473.

Asp, E., & Garbarino, J. (1988). Integrative processes at school and in the community. In T. D. Yawkey & J. E. Johnson (Eds.), *Integrative processes and socialization: Early to middle childhood.* Hillsdale, N.J.: Lawrence Erlbaum.

Astington, J. W., (1991). Intention in the child's theory of mind. In D. Frye & C. Moore (Eds.), *Children's theories of mind: Mental states and social understanding.* Hillsdale N.J.: Lawrence Erlbaum.

Atkinson, R. C., & Shiffrin, R. M. (1972). The control of short-term memory. *Scientific American, 225,* 82–90.

Aubrey, C. (1993). An investigation of the mathematical knowledge and competencies which young children bring into school. *British Educational Research Journal, 19,* 27–41.

Babad, E. Y. (1985). Some correlates of teachers' expectancy bias. *American Educational Research Journal, 22,* 175–183.

Aubrey, C. (1993). An investigation of the mathematical knowledge and competencies which young children bring into school. *British Educational Research Journal, 19,* 27–41.

Babson, S. G., Pernoll, M. L., Benda, G. I., & Simpson, K. (1980). *Diagnostics and management of the fetus and neonate at risk: A guide for team care* (4th ed.). St. Louis: C. V. Mosby.

Bäckström, K. (1992). Children's rights and early childhood education. *International Journal of Early Childhood, 24,* 22–27.

Baillargeon, R. (1987). Object permanence in 3½- and 4½-month-old infants. *Developmental Psychology, 23,* 655–664.

Baillargeon, R. (1992). The object concept revisited. In *Visual Perception and Cognition in Infancy: Carnegie-Mellon Symposia on Cognition,* Vol. 23. Hillsdale, N.J.: Lawrence Erlbaum.

Baker, D. P. (1993). Compared to Japan, the U.S. is a low achiever . . . really: New evidence and comment on Westbury. *Educational Researcher, 22,* 18–20.

Baker, L., & Lyen, K. (1982). Anorexia nervosa. *Current Concepts in Nutrition, 11,* 139–149.

Baker, R. L., & Mednick, B. R. (1984). *Influences on human development: A longitudinal perspective.* Boston: Kluwer-Nijhoff Publishing.

Bakwin, H. (1949). Psychologic aspects of pediatrics. *Journal of Pediatrics, 35,* 512–521.

Balke, E. (1992). Children's rights and the world summit for children. *International Journal of Early Childhood, 24,* 2–7.

Balow, B. (1980). Definitional and prevalence problems in behavior disorders of children. *School Psychology, 8,* 348–354.

Bancroft, R. (1976). Special education: Legal aspects. In P. A. O'Donnell & R. H. Bradfield (Eds.), *Mainstreaming: Controversy and consensus.* San Rafael, Calif.: Academic Therapy Publications.

Bandura, A. (1969). *Principles of behavior modification.* New York: Holt, Reinhart & Winston.

Bandura, A. (1977). *Social learning theory.* Englewood Cliffs, N.J.: Prentice-Hall.

Bandura, A. (1981). Self-referent thought: A developmental analysis of self-efficacy. In J. H. Flavell & L. Ross (Eds.), *Social cognitive development: Frontiers and possible futures.* Cambridge: Cambridge University Press.

Bandura, A. (1986). *Social foundations of thought and action: A social cognitive theory.* Englewood Cliffs, N.J.: Prentice-Hall.

Bandura, A. (1989a). Regulation of cognitive processes through perceived self-efficacy. *Developmental Psychology, 25,* 729–735.

Bandura, A. (1993). Perceived self-efficacy in cognitive development and functioning. *Educational Psychologist, 28,* 117–148.

Bandura, A., Ross, D., & Ross, S. A. (1963). Vicarious reinforcement and imitative learning. *Journal of Abnormal and Social Psychology, 67,* 601–607.

Bandura, A., & Walters, R. (1963). *Social learning and personality development.* New York: Holt, Rinehart & Winston.

Banks, M. S. (1980). The development of visual accommodation during early infancy. *Child Development, 51,* 646–666.

Baran, S. J., Chase, L. J., & Courtright, J. A. (1979). Television drama as a facilitator of prosocial behavior: "The Waltons." *Journal of Broadcasting, 23,* 277–285.

Barrett, G. V., & Depinet, R. L. (1991). A reconsideration of testing for competence rather than for intelligence. *American Psychologist, 46,* 1012–1024.

Basseches, M. (1984). *Dialectical thinking and adult development.* Norwood, N.J.: Ablex.

Bates, E. (1976). *The emergence of symbols.* New York: Academic Press.

Bates, E., Bretherton, I., Shore, D., & McNew, S. (1981). Names, gestures, and objects: The role of context in the emergence of symbols. In K. E. Nelson (Ed.), *Children's language* (Vol. 3), New York: Gardner Press.

Bates, E., Thal, D., Whitesell, K., Fenson, L., & Oakes, L. (1989). Integrating language and gesture in infancy. *Developmental Psychology, 25,* 1004–1019.

Bates, J. E. (1989). Concepts and measures of temperament. In G. A. Kohnstamm, J. E. Bates, & M. K.

Rothbart (Eds.), *Temperament in Childhood.* New York: John Wiley.

Battachi, M. W. (1993). Une contribution à la psychologie des émotions: L'enfant humilié. *Enfance, 47,* 21–26.

Battistich, V., Watson, M., Solomon, D. I., Schaps, E., & Solomon, J. (1991). The child development project: A comprehensive program for the development of prosocial character. In W. M. Kurtines & J. L. Gewirtz, (Eds.), *Handbook of moral behavior and development* (Vol 3: Application), Hillsdale, N.J.: Lawrence Erlbaum.

Baum, C. G., & Forehand, R. (1984). Social factors associated with adolescent obesity. *Journal of Pediatric Psychology, 9,* 293–302.

Baumrind, D. (1967). Child care practices anteceding three patterns of pre-school behavior. *Genetic Psychology Monographs, 75,* 43–88.

Baumrind, D. (1977). Some thoughts about childrearing. In S. Cohen & T. J. Comiskey (Eds.), *Child development: Contemporary perspectives.* Itasca, Ill.: F. E. Peacock.

Baumrind, D. (1989). Rearing competent children. In W. Damon (Ed.), *Child development today and tomorrow,* San Francisco: Jossey-Bass.

Baxter, G., & Beer, J. (1990). Educational needs of school personnel regarding child abuse and/or neglect. *Psychological Reports, 67,* 75–80.

Bayley, N. (1969). *Bayley scales of infant development.* New York: Psychological Corp.

Beatty, P. (1991). Forward. *The Journal of Drug Issues, 21,* 1–7.

Beckwith, L., & Rodning, C. (1991). Intellectual functioning in children born preterm: Recent research. In L. Okagaki & R. J. Sternberg (Eds.), *Directors of development: Influences on the development of children's thinking.* Hillsdale, N.J.: Lawrence Erlbaum.

Beckwith, R. T. (1991). The language of emotion, the emotions, and nominalist bootstrapping. In D. Frye & C. Moore (Eds.), *Children's theories of mind: Mental states and social understanding.* Hillsdale N.J.: Lawrence Erlbaum.

Bell, C. S., & Battjes, R. (1985). *Prevention research: Deterring drug abuse among children and adolescents.* NIDA Research Monograph 63. Rockville, Md.: National Institute on Drug Abuse.

Belsky, J. (1980). Child maltreatment: An ecological integration. *American Psychologist, 35,* 320–335.

Belsky, J. (1981). Early human experience: A family perspective. *Developmental Psychology, 17,* 3–23.

Belsky, J., Lerner, R. M., & Spanier, G. B. (1984). *The child in the family.* Reading, Mass.: Addison-Wesley.

Belsky, J., & Rovine, M. J. (1988). Nonmaternal care in the first year of life and the security of infant-parent attachment. *Child Development, 59,* 157–167.

Bem, S. L. (1974). The measurement of psychological androgyny. *Journal of Consulting and Clinical Psychology, 42,* 155–162.

Benthin, A., Slovic, P., & Severson, H. (1993). A psychometric study of adolescent risk perception. *Journal of Adolescence, 16,* 153–168.

Bentley, K. S., & Fox, R. A. (1991). Mothers and fathers of young children: Comparison of parenting styles. *Psychological Reports, 69,* 320–322.

Berdine, W. H., & Blackhurst, A. E. (Eds.). (1985). *An introduction to special education* (2nd ed.). Boston: Little, Brown.

Bereiter, C. (1991). Implications of connectionism for thinking about rules. *Educational Researcher, 20,* 10–16.

Bereiter, C., & Engelmann, S. (1966). *Teaching disadvantaged children in the preschool.* Englewood Cliffs, N.J.: Prentice-Hall.

Berg, W. K., & Berg, K. M. (1987). Psychophysiological development in infancy: State, startle, and attention. In J. D. Osofsky (Ed.), *Handbook of infant development.* New York: John Wiley.

Berkowitz, M. W., Oser, F., & Althof, W. (1987). The development of sociomoral discourse. In W. M. Kurtines & J. L. Gewirtz (Eds.), *Moral development through social interaction.* New York: John Wiley.

Berndt, T. J. (1979). Developmental changes in conformity to peer and parents. *Developmental Psychology, 15,* 608–616.

Berndt, T. J. (1988). The nature and significance of children's relationships. In R. Vasta (Ed.), *Annals of child development* (Vol. 5). Greenwich, Conn.: JAI Press.

Berndt, T. J. (1989). Friendships in childhood and adolescence. In W. Damon (Ed.), *Child development today and tomorrow.* San Francisco: Jossey-Bass.

Berndt, T. J., Cheung, P. C., Lau, S., Hau, K. T., & Lew, W. J. F. (1993). Perceptions of parenting in Mainland China, Taiwan, and Hong Kong: Sex differences and societal differences. *Developmental Psychology, 29,* 156–164.

Berne, E. (1964). *Games people play.* New York: Grove Press.

Bernstein, B. (1958). Social class and linguistic development: A theory of social learning. *British Journal of Sociology, 9,* 159–174.

Bernstein, B. (1961). Language and social class. *British Journal of Sociology, 11,* 271–276.

Bertalanffy, L. von. (1950). The theory of open systems in physics and biology. *Science, 111,* 23–29.

Bertenthal, B. I., & Campos, J. J. (1990). A systems approach to the organizing effects of self-produced locomotion during infancy. In C. Rovee-Collier & L. P. Lipsitt (Eds.), *Advances in infancy research* (Vol. 6), Norwood, N.J.: Ablex.

Beunen, G., & Malina, R. M. (1988). Growth and physical performance relative to the timing of the adolescent spurt. *Exercise and Sport Sciences Review, 16,* 503–540.

Beyth-Marom, R., Austin, L., Fischhoff, B., Palmgren, C., & Jacobs-Quadrel, M. (1993). Perceived consequences of risky behaviors: Adults and adolescents. *Developmental Psychology, 29,* 549–563.

Bibby, R. W., & Posterski, D. C. (1985). *The emerging generation: An inside look at Canada's teenagers.* Toronto: Irwin Publishing.

Bibby, R. W., & Posterski, D. C. (1992). *Teen trends: A nation in motion.* Toronto: Stoddart Publishing.

Bijou, S. W. (1989a). Behavior analysis. In R. Vasta (Ed.), *Annals of child development* (Vol. 6). Greenwich, Conn.: JAI Press.

Bijou, S. W. (1989b). Psychological linguistics: Implications for a theory of initial development and a method for research. In H. W. Reese (Ed.), *Advances in child development and behavior.* New York: Academic Press.

Bijou, S. W., & Sturges, P. S. (1959). Positive reinforcement for experimental studies with children—Consumables and manipulatables. *Child Development, 30,* 151–170.

Biller, H. B. (1982). Fatherhood: Implications for child and adult development. In B. B. Wolman and others

(Eds.), *Handbook of developmental psychology*. Englewood Cliffs, N.J.: Prentice-Hall.

Binder, A. (1988). Juvenile delinquency. *Annual Review of Psychology, 39*, 253–282.

Bishop, J. E., & Waldholz, M. (1990). *Genome: The story of the most astonishing scientific adventure of our time—the attempt to map all the genes in the human body*. New York: Simon & Schuster.

Black, C., & DeBlassie, R. R. (1985). Adolescent pregnancy: Contributing factors, consequences, treatment, and plausible solutions. *Adolescence, 78*, 281–290.

Bloch, H. A., & Niederhoffer, A. (1958). *The gang: A study in adolescent behavior*. New York: Philosophical Library.

Block, J. H. (1983). Differential premises arising from differential socialization of the sexes: Some conjectures. *Child Development, 54*, 1335–1354.

Bloom, L. (1973). *One word at a time: The use of single word utterances before syntax*. The Hague: Mouton.

Bloom, L., Beckwith, R., Capatides, J. B., & Hafitz, J. (1988). Expression through affect and words in the transition from infancy to language. In P. B. Baltes, D. L. Featherman, & R. M. Lerner (Eds.), *Life-span development and behavior* (Vol. 8), Hillsdale, N.J.: Lawrence Erlbaum.

Blum, K., Noble, E. P., Sheridan, P. J., Montgomery, A., Ritchie, T., Jagadeeswaran, P., Nogami, H., Briggs, A. H., & Cohn, J. B. (1990). Allelic association of human dopamine D$_2$ receptor gene in alcoholism. *Journal of the American Medical Association, 263*, 2055–2060.

Blumberg, M. L. (1974). Psychopathology of the abusing parent. *American Journal of Psychotherapy, 28*, 21–29.

Boldizar, J. P. (1991). Assessing sex typing and androgyny in children: The Children's Sex Role Inventory. *Developmental Psychology, 27*, 505–515.

Bolton, P. J. (1983). Drugs of abuse. In D. F. Hawkins (Ed.), *Drugs and pregnancy: Human teratogenesis and related problems*. London: Churchill Livingstone, 128–154.

Boring, E. G. (1923). Intelligence as the tests test it. *New Republic, 35*, 35–37.

Borkowski, J. G., Milstead, M., & Hale, C. (1988). Components of children's metamemory: Implications for strategy generalization. In F. E. Weinert & M. Perlmutter (Eds.), *Memory development: Universal changes and individual differences*. Hillsdale, N.J.: Lawrence Erlbaum.

Bornstein, M. H. (1979). Effects of habituation experience on posthabituation behavior in young infants: Discrimination and generalization among colors. *Developmental Psychology, 15*, 348–349.

Bornstein, M. H., & Marks, L. E. (1982, January). Color revisionism. *Psychology Today*, 64–72.

Bouchard, T. C., Tremblay, A., Despries, J. P., Nadeau, A., Lupien, P. J., Theriault, G., Dussault, J., Moorjani, S., Pinault, S., & Fournier, G. (1990). The response to longterm overfeeding in identical twins. *New England Journal of Medicine, 322*, 1477–1488.

Bouchard, T. J., Jr., & McGue, M. (1981). Familial studies of intelligence: A review. *Science, 212*, 1055–1059.

Boulton, M. J. (1993). Proximate causes of aggressive fighting in middle-school children. *British Journal of Educational Psychology, 63*, 231–244.

Bower, T. G. R. (1971). The object in the world of the infant. *Scientific American, 225*, 30–38.

Bower, T. G. R. (1977). *The perceptual world of the child*. Cambridge, Mass.: Harvard University Press.

Bower, T. G. R. (1989). *The rational infant: Learning in infancy*. New York: W. H. Freeman.

Bowlby, J. (1940). The influence of early environment. *International Journal of Psychoanalysis, 21*, 154–178.

Bowlby, J. (1953). Some pathological processes set in train by early mother-child separation. *Journal of Mental Science, 99*, 265–272.

Bowlby, J. (1958). The nature of the child's tie to his mother. *International Journal of Psychoanalysis, 39*, 350–373.

Bowlby, J. (1969). *Attachment and loss: Vol. 1. Attachment*. New York: Basic Books.

Bowlby, J. (1979). *The making and breaking of affectional bonds*. London: Tavistock Publications.

Bowlby, J. (1980). *Attachment and loss: Vol. 3. Loss, sadness and depression*. New York: Basic Books.

Bowlby, J. (1982). *Attachment and loss: Vol. 1. Attachment* (2nd ed.). London: Hogarth Press.

Bowman, B. (1993). Early childhood education. In L. Darling-Hammond (Ed.), *Review of Research in Education* (Vol. 19). Washington, D.C.: American Educational Research Association.

Bowman, J. M. (1990). Maternal blood group immunization. In R. D. Eden, F. H. Boehm, & M. Haire (Eds.), *Assessment and care of the fetus: Physiological, clinical, and medicolegal principles*. Norwalk, Conn.: Appleton & Lange.

Boyd, G. A. (1976). *Developmental processes in the child's acquisition of syntax: Linguistics in the elementary school*. Itasca, Ill.: F. E. Peacock.

Bradshaw, G. L., & Anderson, J. R. (1982). Elaborative encoding as an explanation of levels of processing. *Journal of Verbal Learning and Verbal Behavior, 21*, 165–174.

Braine, L. G., Pomerantz, E., Lorber, D., & Krantz, D. H. (1991). Conflicts with authority: Children's feelings, actions, and justifications. *Developmental Psychology, 27*, 829–840.

Bransford, J. D. (1979). *Human cognition: Learning, understanding and remembering*. Belmont, Calif.: Wadsworth.

Brantner, J. P., & Doherty, M. A. (1983). A review of time-out: A conceptual and methodological analysis. In S. Axelrod & J. Apsche (Eds.), *The effects of punishment on human behavior*. New York: Academic Press.

Braun, C. (1976). Teacher expectations: Sociopsychological dynamics. *Review of Educational Research, 46*, 185–213.

Brazelton, T. D. (1973). *Neonatal behavioral assessment scale*. Philadelphia: J. B. Lippincott.

Brazelton, T. B., Nugent, J. K., & Lester, B. M. (1987). Neonatal behavioral assessment scale. In J. D. Osofsky (Ed.), *Handbook of infant development*. New York: John Wiley.

Breast milk prevents disease. (1984). *Glimpse*, Vol. 6, No. 2.

Brendt, R. L., & Beckman, D. A. (1990). Teratology. In R. D. Eden, F. H. Boehm, & M. Haire (Eds.), *Assessment and care of the fetus: Physiological, clinical, and medicolegal principles*. Norwalk, Conn.: Appleton & Lange.

Brenner, J., & Mueller, E. (1982). Shared meaning in boy toddler's peer relations. *Child Development, 53*, 380–391.

Bretherton, I. (1991). Intentional communication and the development of an understanding of mind. In D. Frye & C. Moore (Eds.), *Children's theories of mind: Mental states and social understanding*. Hillsdale N.J.: Lawrence Erlbaum.

Brewin, C. R., Andrews, B., & Gotlib, I. H. (1993). Psychopathology and early experience: A reappraisal of retrospective reports. *Psychological Bulletin, 113*, 82–98.

Brisk, M. E. (1991). Toward multilingual and multicultural mainstream education. *Journal of Education, 173*, 114–129.

Broadbent, D. E. (1952). Speaking and listening simultaneously. *Journal of Experimental Psychology, 43*, 267–273.

Broderick, P. (1986). Perceptual motor development in children's drawing skill. In C. Pratt, A. F. Garton, W. E. Tunmer, & A. R. Nesdale (Eds.), *Research issues in child development*. Boston: Allen & Unwin.

Brody, J. (1988). Cocaine: Litany of fetal risks grows. *New York Times*, C1, C8.

Bronfenbrenner, U. (1970). *Two worlds of childhood: U.S. and U.S.S.R.* New York: Russell Sage Foundation.

Bronfenbrenner, U. (1977a, May). Nobody home: The erosion of the American family. *Psychology Today*, 41–47.

Bronfenbrenner, U. (1977b). Is early intervention effective? In S. Cohen & T. J. Comiskey (Eds.), *Child development: Contemporary perspectives*. Itasca, Ill.: F. E. Peacock.

Bronfenbrenner, U. (1979). *The ecology of human development*. Cambridge, Mass.: Harvard University Press.

Bronfenbrenner, U. (1989). Ecological systems theory. In R. Vasta (Ed.), *Annals of child development* (Vol. 6). Greenwich, Conn.: JAI Press.

Bronfenbrenner, U., Belsky, J., & Steinberg, L. (1977). Day care in context: An ecological perspective on research and public policy. In *Policy issues in daycare*. Washington, D.C.: U.S. Department of Health, Education, & Welfare.

Bronson, G. W. (1971). Fear of the unfamiliar in human infants. In H. R. Schaffer (Ed.), *The origins of human social relations*. London: Academic Press.

Bronson, G. W. (1972). Infants' reactions to unfamiliar persons and novel objects. *Monographs of the Society for Research in Child Development, 37*, No. 3.

Bronstein, P., Clauson, J., Stoll, M. F., & Abrams, C. L. (1993). Parenting behavior and children's social, psychological, and academic adjustment in diverse family structures. *Family Relations, 42*, 268–276.

Brooks, J. B. (1981). *The process of parenting*. Palo Alto, Calif.: Mayfield.

Brooks-Gunn, J., & Furstenberg, F. F., Jr. (1989). Adolescent sexual behavior. *American Psychologist, 44*, 249–257.

Brophy, J. E., & Good, T. L. (1974). *Teacher-student relationships: Causes and consequences*. New York: Holt, Rinehart & Winston.

Brown, J., & Finn, P. (1982). Drinking to get drunk: Findings of a survey of junior and senior high school students. *Journal of Alcohol and Drug Education, 27*, 13–25.

Brown, J. L. (1964). States in newborn infants. *Merrill-Palmer Quarterly, 10*, 313–327.

Brown, K., Covell, K., & Abramovitch, R. (1991). Time course and control of emotion: Age differences in understanding and recognition. *Merrill-Palmer Quarterly, 37*, 273–287.

Brown, M. H. (1991). Innovations in the treatment of bulimia: Transpersonal psychology, relaxation, imagination, hypnosis, myth, and ritual. *Journal of Humanistic Education and Development, 30*, 50–60.

Brown, R. (1973). *A first language: The early stages.* Cambridge, Mass.: Harvard University Press.

Browne Miller, A. (1990). *The day care dilemma.* New York: Plenum Press.

Brownell, K. D., & Wadden, T. A. (1984). Confronting obesity in children: Behavioral and psychological factors. *Pediatric Annals, 13,* 473–480.

Bruchkowsky, M. (1991). The development of empathic cognition in middle and early childhood. In R. Case et al., (Eds.), *The mind's staircase: Exploring the conceptual underpinnings of children's thought and knowledge.* Hillsdale, N.J.: Lawrence Erlbaum.

Bruner, J. S. (1977). Early social interaction and language acquistion. In H. R. Schaffer (Ed.), *Studies in mother-infant interaction.* London: Academic Press.

Bruner, J. S. (1978). Learning the mother tongue. *Human Nature,* September, 43–49.

Bruner, J. S. (1983). *Child's talk.* New York: W. W. Norton.

Bruner, J. S. (1985). Models of the learner. *Educational Researcher, 14,* 5–8.

Bryant, B. K. (1992). Conflict resolution strategies in relation to children's peer relations. *Journal of Applied Developmental Psychology, 13,* 35–50.

Buber, M. (1958). *I and thou.* New York: Charles Scribner's.

Buber, M. (1965). *The knowledge of man* (M. Friedman, Ed.). New York: Harper & Row.

Buchanan, C. M., Eccles, J. S., & Becker, J. B. (1992). Are adolescents the victims of raging hormones: Evidence for activational effects of hormones on moods and behavior at adolescence. *Psychological Bulletin, 111,* 62–107.

Buis, J. M., & Thompson, D. N. (1989). Imaginary audience and personal fable: A brief review. *Adolescence, 24,* 773–781.

Bullinger, A. (1985). The sensorimotor nature of the infant visual system: Cognitive problems. In V. L. Shulman, L. C. R. Restaino-Baumann & L. Butler (Eds.), *The future of Piagetian theory: The neo-Piagetians.* New York: Plenum Press.

Bullock, J. R. (1993). Children's loneliness and their relationships with family and peers. *Family Relations, 42,* 46–49.

Bullough, V. L. (1981). Age at menarche: A misunderstanding. *Science, 213,* 365–366.

Burns, B., & Lipsitt, L. P. (1991). Behavioral factors in crib death: Toward an understanding of the sudden infant death syndrome. *Journal of Applied Developmental Psychology, 12,* 159–184.

Bush calls for unprecedented increase in Head Start program. (1992). *The Monterey Herald,* January 22, p. 3A.

Buss, A. H., & Plomin, R. (1985). *Temperament: Early developing personality traits.* Hillsdale, N.J.: Lawrence Erlbaum.

Butler, J. R., & Burton, L. M. (1990). Rethinking teenage childbearing: Is sexual abuse a missing link? *Family Relations, 39,* 73–80.

Byrne, B. M., & Shavelson, R. J. (1987). Adolescent self-concept: Testing the assumption of equivalent structure across gender. *American Educational Research Journal, 24,* 365–385.

Cairns, R. B. (1983). The emergence of developmental psychology. In P. H. Mussen (Ed.), *Handbook of child psychology* (4th ed.) (Vol. 1): *History, theory, and methods* (W. Kessen, Ed.). New York: John Wiley, 41–102.

Cairns, R. B., Gariépy, J. L., & Hood, K. E. (1990). Development, microevolution, and social behavior. *Psychological Review, 97,* 49–65.

Cairns, R. B., & Valsiner, J. (1984). Child psychology. *Annual Review of Psychology, 35,* 553–577.

Caldwell, B. M. (1980). Balancing children's rights and parents' rights. In R. Haskins & J. J. Gallagher (Eds.), *Care and education of young children in America: Policy, politics and social science.* Norwood, N.J.: Ablex.

Caldwell, B. M. (1989). Achieving rights for children: Role of the early childhood profession. *Childhood Education, 66,* 4–7.

Caldwell, J. C. (1986). Routes to low mortality in poor countries. *Population and Development Review, 12,* 171–214.

Calfee, R. (1981). Cognitive psychology and educational practice. In D. C. Berliner (Ed.), *Review of Research in Education* (Vol. 9). Washington, D. C.: American Educational Research Association.

California Assessment Program. (1982). *Survey of sixth grade school achievement and television viewing habits.* Sacramento: California State Department of Education.

Campbell, S. B., & Cohn, J. F. (1991). Prevalence and correlates of postpartum depression in first-time mothers. *Journal of Abnormal Psychology, 100,* 594–599.

Canning, P. M., & Lyon, M. E. (1991). Misconceptions about early child care, education and intervention. *Journal of Child and Youth Care, 5,* 1–10.

Carey, E. J. B., Miller, C. L., & Widlak, F. W. (1975). Factors contributing to child abuse. *Nursing Research, 24,* 293–295.

Carey, S. T. (1987). Reading comprehension in first and second languages of immersion and Francophone students. *Canadian Journal for Exceptional Children, 3*, 103–108.

Carey, W. B. (1989). Introduction: Basic issues. In W. B. Carey & S. C. McDevitt (Eds.), *Clinical and educational applications of temperament research.* Berwyn, Penn.: Swets North America.

Carlson, P., & Anisfeld, M. (1969). Some observations on the linguistic competence of a two year old child. *Child Development, 40*, 572–574.

Carroll, D. W. (1986). *Psychology of language.* Monterey, Calif.: Brooks/ Cole.

Carroll, J. L., & Rest, J. R. (1982). Moral development. In B. B. Wolman and others (Eds.), *Handbook of developmental psychology.* Englewood Cliffs, N.J.: Prentice-Hall.

Cartwright, D. S., Tomson, B., & Schwartz, H. (1975). *Gang delinquency.* Monterey, Calif.: Brooks/ Cole.

Case, R. (1991). General and specific views of the mind, its structure and its development. In R. Case, et al., (Eds.), *The mind's staircase: Exploring the conceptual underpinnings of children's thought and knowledge.* Hillsdale, N.J.: Lawrence Erlbaum.

Casler, L. (1961). Maternal deprivation: A critical review of the literature. *Monograph of the Society for Research in Child Development, 26* (2).

Caspi, A., Lynam, D., Moffitt, T. E., & Silva, P. A. (1993). Unraveling girls' delinquency: Biological, dispositional, and contextual contributions to adolescent misbehavior. *Developmental Psychology, 29*, 19–30.

Cattell, R. B. (1971). *Abilities: Their structure, growth, and action.* Boston: Houghton Mifflin.

Ceci, S. J. (1991). How much does schooling influence general intelligence and its cognitive components? A reassessment of the evidence. *Developmental Psychology, 27*, 703–722.

Chase, N. F. (1975). *A child is being beaten.* New York: Holt, Rinehart & Winston.

Chase-Lansdale, P. L., Brooks-Gunn, J., & Paikoff, R. L. (1991). Research and programs for adolescent mothers: Missing links and future promises. *Family Relations, 40*, 396–403.

Chasnoff, I. J. (1986). Perinatal addiction: Consequences of intrauterine exposure to opiate and nonopiate drugs. In I. J. Chasnoff (Ed.), *Drug use in pregnancy: Mother and child.* Boston: MTP Press.

Chasnoff, I. J. (1986/1987). Cocaine and pregnancy. *Childbirth Educator,* 37–42.

Chasnoff, I. Burns, W., Schnoll, S., & Burns, K. (1985). Cocaine use in pregnancy. *New England Journal of Medicine, 313*, 666–669.

Chassin, L., Rogosch, F., & Barrera, M. (1991). Substance use and symptomatology among adolescent children of alcoholics. *Journal of Abnormal Psychology, 4*, 449–463.

Cherry, E. C. (1953). Some experiments on the recognition of speech with one and two ears. *Journal of the Acoustical Society of America, 25*, 975–979.

Chess, S., & Thomas, A. (1989a). Temperament and its functional significance. In S. I. Greenspan & G. H. Pollock (Eds.), *The course of life: Vol II. Early Childhood.* Madison, Conn.: International Universities Press.

Chess, S., & Thomas, A. (1989b). The practical application of temperament to psychiatry. In W. B. Carey & S. C. McDevitt (Eds.), *Clinical and educational applications of temperament research.* Berwyn, Penn.: Swets North America.

Chester, R. D. (1992). Views from the mainstream: Learning disabled students as perceived by regular education classroom teachers and by non-learning disabled secondary students. *Canadian Journal of School Psychology, 8*, 93–102.

Cheung, Y. W., Erickson, P. G., & Landau, T. C. (1991). Experience of crack use: Findings from a community-based sample in Toronto. *Journal of Drug Issues, 21*, 121–140.

Chez, R. A., & Chervenak, J. L. (1990). Nutrition in pregnancy. In R. D. Eden, F. H. Boehm, & M. Haire (Eds.), *Assessment and care of the fetus: Physiological, clinical, and medicolegal principles.* Norwalk, Conn.: Appleton & Lange.

Chi, M. T. H., & Glaser, R. (1980). The measurement of expertise: Analysis of the development of knowledge and skill as a basis for assessing achievement. In E. L. Baker & E. S. Quellmalz (Eds.), *Educational testing and evaluation: Design, analysis and policy.* Beverly Hills, Calif.: Sage.

Chilman, C. S. (1983). Remarriage and stepfamilies: Research results and implications. In E. D. Macklin & R. H. Rubin (Eds.), *Contemporary families and alternative lifestyles: Handbook on research and theory.* Beverly Hills, Calif.: Sage.

China fears sexual imbalance. (1983). *Edmonton Journal,* March 14, p. D-4.

Chipman, S. F. (1988). Far too sexy a topic. *Educational Researcher, 17*, 46–49.

Chiu, L. H. (1993). Self-esteem in American and Chinese (Taiwanese) children. *Current Psychology: Research & Reviews, 11*, 309–313.

Chlamydia—More common than gonorrhea. (1988). *Folio.* Edmonton, Alberta: University of Alberta, Nov. 24., p. 6.

Chomsky, N. (1957). *Syntactic structures.* The Hague: Mouton.

Chomsky, N. (1965). *Aspects of the theory of syntax.* Cambridge, Mass.: M.I.T. Press.

Christopher, F. S., & Roosa, M. W. (1990). An evaluation of an adolescent pregnancy prevention program: Is "Just say no" enough? *Family relations, 39,* 68–72.

Christopherson, V. A. (1988). The family as a socialization context. In T. D. Yawkey & J. E. Johnson (Eds.), *Integrative processes and socialization: Early to middle childhood.* Hillsdale, N.J.: Lawrence Erlbaum.

Chugani, H. T., & Phelps, M. E. (1986). Maturational changes in cerebral function in infants determined by FGG positron emission tomography. *Science, 231,* 840–843.

Chumlea, W. C. (1982). Physical growth in adolescence. In B. B. Wolman and others (Eds.), *Handbook of developmental psychology.* Englewood Cliffs, N.J.: Prentice-Hall.

Churchill, J. A. (1965). The relationship between intelligence and birth weight in twins. *Neurology, 15,* 341–347.

Claes, M., & Simard, R. (1992). Friendship characteristics of delinquent adolescents. *International Journal of Adolescence and Youth, 3,* 287–301.

Clarizio, H. F., & Yelon, S. L. (1974). Learning theory approaches to classroom management: Rationale and intervention techniques. In A. R. Brown & C. Avery (Eds.), *Modifying children's behavior: A book of readings.* Springfield, Ill.: Charles C. Thomas.

Clark, H. H., & Clark, E. V. (1977). *Psychology and language: An introduction to psycholinguistics.* New York: Harcourt Brace Jovanovich.

Clarke-Stewart, K. A. (1984). Day care: A new context for research and development. In M. Perlmutter (Ed.), *The Minnesota symposia on child psychology: Vol. 17. Parent-child interaction and parent-child relations in child development.* Hillsdale, N.J.: Lawrence Erlbaum.

Clarke-Stewart, K. A. (1989). Infant day care: Maligned or malignant. *American Psychologist, 44,* 266–273.

Clarkson, M. G., & Berg, W. K. (1983). Cardiac orienting and vowel discrimination in newborns: Crucial stimulus parameters. *Child Development, 54,* 162–171.

Clausen, J. A. (1975). The social meaning of differential physical and sexual maturation. In S. E. Ragastin & G. H. Elder (Eds.), *Adolescence in the life cycle: Psychological change and social context.* New York: John Wiley.

Clements, S. D. (1966). *Minimal brain dysfunction in children: Terminology and identification* (NINDB Monograph No. 3). Washington, D.C.: U.S. Department of Health, Education, & Welfare.

Cobb, E. (1977). *The ecology of imagination in childhood.* New York: Columbia University Press.

Cohen, Y. A. (1964). *The transition from childhood to adolescence.* Chicago: Aldine.

Colby, A., & Kohlberg, L. (1984). Invariant sequence and internal consistency in moral judgment stages. In W. M. Kertines & J. L. Gerwirtz (Eds.), *Morality, moral behavior, and moral development.* New York: John Wiley.

Cole, P. M. (1986). Children's spontaneous control of facial expression. *Child Development, 57,* 1309–1321.

Cole, P. M., Usher, B. A., & Cargo, A. P. (1993). Cognitive risk and its association with risk for disruptive behavior disorder in preschoolers. *Journal of Clinical Child Psychology, 22,* 154–164.

Collett, J., & Serrano, B. (1992). Stirring it up: The inclusive classroom. *New Directions for Teaching and Learning, 49,* 35–48.

Collins, A., Brown, J. S., & Newman, S. E. (1989). Cognitive apprenticeship: Teaching the craft of reading, writing, and mathematics. In L. B. Resnick (Ed.), *Knowing, learning, and instruction: Essays in honor of Robert Glaser.* Hillsdale, N.J.: Lawrence Erlbaum.

Collins, W. A. (1983). Interpretation and inference in children's television viewing. In J. Bryant & D. R. Anderson (Eds.), *Children's understanding of televison: Research on attention and comprehension.* New York: Academic Press, 125–150.

Collins, W. A. (1991). Shared views and parent-adolescent relationships. *New Directions for Child Development, 51,* 103–110.

Collins, W. A., & Gunnar, M. R. (1990). Social and personality development. *Annual Review of Psychology, 41,* 387–416.

Collins, W. A., & Russell, G. (1991). Mother-child and father-child relationships in middle childhood and adolescence: A developmental analysis. *Developmental Review, 11,* 99–136.

Collins, W. A., Wellman, H., Keniston, A. H., & Westby, S. D. (1978). Age-related aspects of comprehension and inference from a televised dramatic narrative. *Child Development, 49,* 389–399.

Condon, W. S., & Sander, L. W. (1974). Neonate movement is synchronized with adult speech: Interactional participation and language acquisition. *Science, 183,* 99–101.

Connell, B. (1985). A new man. In *The English Curriculum,* ILEA. London: English Centre Publication.

Cook, T. D., Appleton, H., Conner, R. F., Shaffer, A., Tamkin, G., & Weber, S. J. (1975). *"Sesame Street" revisited.* New York: Russell Sage Foundation.

Cooke, B. (1991). Family life education. *Family Relations, 40,* 3–13.

Cooley, C. H. (1902). *Human nature and the social order.* New York: Charles Scribner's.

Coopersmith, S. (1967). *The antecedents of self-esteem.* San Francisco: W. H. Freeman.

Corbin, C. B. (1980). The physical fitness of children: A discussion and point of view. In C. B. Corbin (Ed.), *A textbook of motor development.* Dubuque, Iowa: Wm. C. Brown.

Cortada, J. M., Milsark, I., & Richards, C. S. (1990). Genetic counseling issues in the use of DNA analysis for Duchenne/Becker muscular dystrophy. In B. A. Fine, E. Getting, K. Greendale, B. Leopold, & N. W. Paul (Eds.), *Strategies in genetic counseling: Reproductive genetics and new technologies,* White Plains, N.Y.: March of Dimes Birth Defects Foundation.

Côté, J. E., & Levine, C. (1988). A critical examination of the ego identity status paradigm. *Developmental Review, 8,* 147–184.

Coulter, D. (1993). Alberta students lag behind Asians in math: North American youths spend too much time on sports, socializing, study shows. *Edmonton Journal,* October 25, p. A5.

Coulter, D. L. (1993). Epilepsy and mental retardation: An overview. *American Journal on Mental Retardation, 98,* 1–11.

Coustan, D. R. (1990). Diabetes mellitus. In R. D. Eden, F. H. Boehm, & M. Haire (Eds.). *Assessment and care of the fetus: Physiological, clinical, and medicolegal principles.* Norwalk, Conn.: Appleton & Lange.

Cox, T. C., Jacobs, M. R., Leblanc, A. E., & Marshman, J. A. (1983). *Drugs and drug abuse: A reference text.* Toronto: Addiction Research Foundation.

Cratty, B. J. (1978). *Perceptual and motor development in infants and children* (2nd ed.). Englewood Cliffs, N.J.: Prentice-Hall.

Creasy, R. K. (1988). Preterm labor and delivery. In R. K. Creasy & R. Resnik (Eds.), *Maternal-fetal medicine; Principles and practice.* Philadelphia: W. B. Saunders.

Creasy, R. K. (1990). Preterm labor. In R. D. Eden, F. H. Boehm, & M. Haire (Eds.), *Assessment and care of the fetus: Physiological, clinical, and medicolegal principles.* Norwalk, Conn.: Appleton & Lange.

Crisp, A. H., Palmer, R. L., & Kalucy, R. S. (1976). How common is anorexia nervosa: A prevalence study. *British Journal of Psychiatry, 128,* 549–554.

Crockett, L. J., Losoff, M., & Petersen, A. C. (1984). Perceptions of the peer group and friendship in early adolescence. *Journal of Early Adolescence, 4,* 155–181.

Crockett, L. J., & Petersen, A. C. (1987). Pubertal status and psychosocial development: Findings from the Early Adolescence Study. In R. M. Lerner & T. T. Foch (Eds.), *Biological-psychosocial interactions in early adolescence: A life-span perspective.* Hillsdale, N.J.: Lawrence Erlbaum.

Crowell, J. A., & Feldman, S. S. (1991). Mothers' working models of attachment relationships and mother and child behavior during separation and reunion. *Developmental Psychology, 27,* 597–605.

Crowley, P. A. (1983). Premature labour. In D. F. Hawkins (Ed.), *Drugs and pregnancy: Human teratogenesis and re-

lated problems.* New York: Churchill Livingstone, 155–183.

Culbertson, J. L. (1991). Child advocacy and clinical child psychology. *Journal of Clinical Child Psychology, 20,* 7–10.

Cummins, J. (1986). Empowering minority students: A framework for intervention. *Harvard Educational Review, 56,* 18–36.

Cummins, J., & Swain, M. (1986). *Bilingualism in education: Aspects of theory, research and practice.* London: Taylor & Fry.

Curtiss, S. (1977). *Genie: A psycholinguistic study of a modern-day wild child.* New York: Academic Press.

Cusack, R. (1984). Dietary management of obese children and adolescents. *Pediatric Annals, 13,* 455–464.

Cziko, G. A. (1992). The evaluation of bilingual education. *Educational Researcher, 21,* 10–15.

Dalton, K. (1980). *Depression after childbirth.* Oxford: Oxford University Press.

Damon, W., & Colby, A. (1987). Social influence and moral change. In W. M. Kurtines & J. L. Gewirtz (Eds.), *Moral development through social interaction.* New York: John Wiley.

Danilewitz, D., & Skuy, M. (1990). A psychoeducational profile of the unmarried mother. *International Journal of Adolescence and Youth, 2,* 175–184.

Dansky, J. L. (1980). Make-believe: A mediator of the relationship between play and associative fluency. *Child Development, 51,* 576–579.

Darley, J. M., & Shultz, T. R. (1990). Moral rules: Their content and acquisition. *Annual Review of Psychology, 41,* 525–556.

Darley, J. M., & Zanna, M. P. (1982). Making moral judgments. *American Scientist, 70,* 515–521.

Darling, C. A., Kallen, D. J., & Van Dusen, J. E. (1984). Sex in transition, 1900–1980. *Journal of Youth and Adolescence, 13*, 385–394.

Darwin, D. (1877). A biographical sketch of an infant. *Mind, 2*, 285–294.

Das, J. P., & Dash, U. N. (1990). Schooling, literacy and cognitive development: A study in rural India. In C. K. Leong & B. S. Randhawa (Eds.), *Understanding literacy and cognition: Theory, research, and application.* New York: Plenum Press.

Dasen, P. R. (Ed.). (1977). *Piagetian psychology: Cross-cultural contributions.* New York: Gardner Press.

David, C. B., & David, P. H. (1984). Bottle feeding and malnutrition in a developing country: The "bottle-starved" baby. *Journal of Tropical Pediatrics*, Vol. 30.

Davis, S. M., & Harris, M. B. (1982). Sexual knowledge, sexual interests, and sources of sexual information of rural and urban adolescents from three cultures. *Adolescence, 17*, 471–492.

Dawkins, R. (1976). *The selfish gene.* New York: Oxford University Press.

DeCasper, A. J., & Fifer, W. P. (1980). Of human bonding: Newborns prefer their mother's voices. *Science, 208*, 1174–1175.

DeCharms, R. (1972). Personal causation training in the schools. *Journal of Applied Social Psychology, 2*, 95–113.

DeLissovoy, V. (1973). Child care by adolescent parents. *Children Today*, July, 22–25.

DeMause, L. (1974). The evolution of childhood. In L. deMause (Ed.), *The history of childhood.* New York: Psychohistory Press.

DeMause, L. (1975, April). Our forebears made childhood a nightmare. *Psychology Today*, 85–88.

Dement, W. C. (1974). *Some must watch while some must sleep.* San Francisco: Newman.

DeMyer, M. K., Barton, S., DeMyer, W. E., Norton, J., Allen, J., & Steele, R. (1973). Prognosis in autism: A follow-up study. *Journal of Autism and Childhood Schizophrenia, 3*, 199–246.

Denham, S. A., & Holt, R. W. (1993). Preschooler's likeability as cause or consequence of their social behavior. *Developmental Psychology, 29*, 271–275.

Dennis, W. (1941). The significance of feral man. *American Journal of Psychology, 54*, 425–432.

Dennis, W. (1951). A further analysis of reports of wild children. *Child Development, 22*, 153–158.

Denver Developmental Materials: *Catalog of screening and training materials.* (1990) P.O. Box 6919, Denver Colo., 80206–0919.

deRegt, R. H., Minkoff, H. L., Feldman, J., & Schwartz, R. H. (1986). Relation of private or clinic care to the Cesarean birth rate. *The New England Journal of Medicine, 315*, 619–625.

Desor, J. A., Maller, O., & Greene, L. S. (1978). Preference for sweet in humans: Infants, children and adults. In J. M. Weiffenbach (Ed.), *Taste and development: The genesis of sweet preference.* Bethesda, Md.: National Institute of Dental Research, DHEW Publication 77–1068.

Deuel, R. K. (1992). Motor skill disorders. In S. R. Hooper, G. W. Hynd, & R. E. Mattison, (Eds.), *Developmental disorders: Diagnostic criteria and clinical assessment.* Hillsdale, N.J.: Lawrence Erlbaum.

deVries, M. W. (1989). Difficult temperament: A universal and culturally embedded concept. In W. B. Carey & S. C. McDevitt (Eds.), *Clinical and educational applications of temperament research.* Berwyn, Penn.: Swets North America.

deVries, M. W., & Sameroff, A. J. (1984). Culture and temperament: Influences on infant temperament in three East African societies. *American Journal of Orthopsychiatry, 54*, 83–96.

Diaz, R. M. (1983). Thought and two languages: The impact of bilingualism on cognitive development. In E. W. Gordon (Ed.), *Review of Research in Education* (Vol. 10). Washington, D.C.: American Educational Research Association.

Dick-Read, G. (1972). *Childbirth without fear: The original approach to natural childbirth* (4th ed.) (H. Wessel & H. F. Ellis, Eds.). New York: Harper & Row.

Diener, C. I., & Dweck, C. S. (1980). An analysis of learned helplessness: II. The processing of success. *Journal of Personality and Social Psychology, 39*, 940–952.

DiLalla, L. F., & Watson, M. W. (1988). Differentiation of fantasy and reality: Preschoolers' reactions to interruptions in their play. *Developmental Psychology, 24*, 286–291.

Dill, F., & McGillivray, B. (1992). Chromosome anomolies. In J. M. Friedman, F. J. Dill, M. R. Hayden, & B. C. McGillivray (Eds.), *Genetics*, Baltimore: Williams & Wilkins.

Dinges, M. M. & Oetting, E. R. (1993). Similarity in drug use patterns between adolescents and their friends. *Adolescence, 28*, 253–266.

Dinkmeyer, D., & McKay, G. (1976). *Systematic training for effective parenting (S.T.E.P.).* Circle Pines, Minn.: American Guidance Service.

Dix, T. (1991). The affective organization of parenting: Adaptive and maladaptive processes. *Psychological Bulletin, 110,* 3–25.

Dobkin de Rios, M. (1984). *Hallucinogens: Cross-cultural perspectives.* Albuquerque: University of New Mexico Press.

Doby, J. (1980). Firstborn fallacies. *Science, 80,* 4–10.

Doman, G. J. (1984). *How to multiply your baby's intelligence.* Garden City, N.Y.: Doubleday.

Donaldson, M. (1978). *Children's minds.* London: Fontana/Croom Helm.

Donate-Bartfield, E., & Passman, R. H. (1985). Attentiveness of mothers and fathers to their baby's cries. *Infant behavior and development, 8,* 385–393.

Donnelly, B. W., & Voydanoff, P. (1991). Factors associated with releasing for adoption among adolescent mothers. *Family Relations, 40,* 404–410.

Donovan, C. M. (1980). Program planning for the visually impaired child. In A. P. Scheiner & I. F. Abroms (Eds.), *The practical management of the developmentally disabled child.* St. Louis: C. V. Mosby, 280–289.

Dreyer, P. H. (1982). Sexuality during adolescence. In B. B. Wolman (Ed.), *Handbook of developmental psychology.* Englewood Cliffs, N.J.: Prentice-Hall.

Drugan, A., Johnson, M. P., & Evans, M. I. (1990). Amniocentesis. In R. D. Eden, F. H. Boehm, & M. Haire (Eds.), *Assessment and care of the fetus: Physiological, clinical, and medicolegal principles.* Norwalk, Conn.: Appleton & Lange.

Drummond, W. J. (1991). Adolescent relationships in a period of change: A New Zealand perspective. *International Journal of Adolescence and Youth, 2,* 275–286.

Duberman, L. (1975). *The reconstituted family: A study of remarried couples and their children.* Chicago: Nelson-Hall.

Duffty, P., & Bryan, M. H. (1982). Home apnea monitoring in "near-miss" Sudden Infant Death Syndrome (SIDS) and in siblings of SIDS victims. *Pediatrics, 70,* 69–74.

Duncan, S., & Fiske, D. W. (1977). *Face-to-face interaction: Research methods and theory.* Hillsdale, N.J.: Erlbaum.

Dunn, J. (1988). *The beginnings of social understanding.* Cambridge, Mass.: Harvard University Press.

Dunphy, D. C. (1963). The social structure of urban adolescent peer groups. *Sociometry, 26,* 230–246.

Duskin Feldman, R. (1982). *Whatever happened to the quiz kids? Perils and profits of growing up gifted.* Chicago: Chicago Review Press.

Dweck, C. S. (1975). The role of expectations and attributions in the alleviation of learned helplessness. *Journal of Personality and Social Psychology, 31,* 674–685.

Dweck, C. S. (1986). Motivational processes affecting learning. *American Psychologist, 41,* 1040–1048.

Dweck, C. S., & Reppucci, N. D. (1973). Learned helplessness and reinforcement responsibility in children. *Journal of Personality and Social Psychology 25,* 109–116.

Eastman, P., & Barr, J. L. (1985). *Your child is smarter than you think.* London: Jonathan Cape.

Eccles, J. S., & Jacobs, J. E. (1986). Social forces shape math attitudes and performance. *Signs, 11,* 367–389.

Eckerman, C. O., & Whatley, J. L. (1975). Infants' reactions to unfamiliar adults varying in novelty. *Developmental Psychology, 11,* 562–566.

Eckland, B. K. (1977). Darwin rides again. *American Journal of Sociology, 82,* 693–697.

Eden, R. D., Blanco, J. D., Tomasi, A., & Gall, S. A. (1990). Maternal-fetal infection. In R. D. Eden, F. H. Boehm, & M. Haire (Eds.), *Assessment and care of the fetus: Physiological, clinical, and medicolegal principles.* Norwalk, Conn.: Appleton & Lange.

Edmonton (Alberta) Public School Board. (1978). *Learning disability,* Fall, No. 7.

Egeland, B., & Stroufe, L. (1981). Attachment and early maltreatment. *Child Development, 52,* 44–52.

Egeland, B., & Vaughn, B. (1981). Failure of "bond formation" as a cause of abuse, neglect, and maltreatment. *American Journal of Orthopsychiatry, 51,* 78–84.

Egeland, J. A., Gerhard, D. S., Pauls, D. L., Sussex, J. N., Kidd, K. K., et al. (1987). Bipolar affective disorders linked to DNA markers on chromosome 11. *Nature, 325,* 783–787.

Eiger, M. S., & Olds, S. W. (1987). *The complete book of breastfeeding.* New York: Workman.

Eilers, R. E., & Minifie, F. D. (1975). Fricative discrimination in early infancy. *Journal of Speech and Hearing Research, 18,* 158–167.

Eilers, R. E., & Oller, D. K. (1988). Precursors to speech. In R. Vasta (Ed.), *Annals of child development* (Vol. 5). Greenwich, Conn.: JAI Press.

Eisenberg, N. (1990). Prosocial development in early and mid-adolescence. In R. Montemayor, G. R. Adams, & T. P. Gullotta (Eds.), *Advances in adolescent development: Vol. 2. From childhood to adolescence: A transitional period?* Newbury Park, Calif.: Sage Publications.

Eisenberg, R. B. (1976). *Auditory competence in early life*. Baltimore: University Park Press.

Eisenberg-Berg, N., & Hand, M. (1979). The relationship of preschoolers' reasoning about prosocial moral conflicts to prosocial behavior. *Child Development, 50*, 356–360.

Eisenberg, N., Miller, P. A., Shell, R., McNalley, S., & Shea, C. (1991). Prosocial development in adolescence: A longitudinal study. *Developmental Psychology, 27*, 849–857.

Elder, G. H., Jr. (1974). *Children of the great depression*. Chicago: University of Chicago Press.

Elder, G. H., Jr. (1979). Historical change in life patterns and personality. In P. B. Baltes & O. G. Brim, Jr. (Eds.), *Life span development and behavior* (Vol. 2). New York: Academic Press.

Elder, G. H., Jr., Nguyen, T. Van, & Caspi, A. (1985). Linking family hardship to children's lives. *Child Development, 56*, 361–375.

Elkind, D. (1967). Egocentrism in adolescence. *Child Development, 38*, 1025–1034.

Elkind, D. (1981a). *The hurried child: Growing up too fast too soon*. Reading, Mass.: Addison-Wesley.

Elkind, D. (1981b). Understanding the young adolescent. In L. D. Steinberg (Ed.), *The life cycle: Readings in human development*. New York: Columbia University Press.

Elkind, D. (1987). *Miseducation: Preschoolers at risk*. New York: Alfred A. Knopf.

Elkind, D., & Bowen, R. (1979). Imaginary audience behavior in children and adolescents. *Developmental Psychology, 15*, 38–44.

Elkington, J. (1986). *The poisoned womb*. Harmondsworth, Middlesex, England: Penguin Books.

Elliott, G. C. (1982). Self-esteem and self-presentation among the young as a function of age and gender. *Journal of Youth and Adolescence, 11*, 135–142.

Elster, A. B., Lamb, M. E., & Tavare, J. (1987). Association between behavioral and school problems and fatherhood in a national sample of adolescent youths. *Journal of Pediatrics, 1211*, 932–936.

Emery, A. E. H. (1984). Introduction— The principles of genetic counseling. In A. E. H. Emery & I. Pullen (Eds.), *Psychological aspects of genetic counseling*. New York: Academic Press.

Emery, A. E., & Mueller, R. F. (1992). *Elements of medical genetics* (8th ed.). Edinburgh & London: Churchill Livingstone.

Emery, R. E. (1989). Family violence. *American Psychologist, 44*, 321–328.

Endsley, R. C., & Bradbard, M. R. (1981). *Quality day care: A handbook of choices for parents and caregivers*. Englewood Cliffs, N.J.: Prentice-Hall.

Enright, R., Shukla, D., & Lapsley, D. (1980). Adolescent egocentrism— sociocentrism in early and late adolescence. *Adolescence, 14*, 687–695.

Epling, W. F., Pierce, W. D., & Stefan, L. (1983). A theory of activity-based anorexia. *International Journal of Eating Disorders, 3*, 27–45.

Erickson, G., & Farkas, S. (1991). Prior experience and gender differences in science achievement. *Alberta Journal of Educational Research, 37*, 225–239.

Erickson, J. D., & Bjerkedal, T. (1981). Down's syndrome associated with father's age in Norway. *Journal of Medical Genetics, 18*, 22–28.

Erickson, M. T. (1987). *Behavior disorders of children and adolescents*. Englewood Cliffs, N.J.: Prentice-Hall.

Erickson, M. T. (1992). *Behavior disorders of children and adolescents* (2nd ed.).

Englewood Cliffs, N.J.: Prentice Hall.

Erikson, E. H. (1956). The problems of ego identity. *Journal of the American Psychoanalytic Association, 4*, 56–121.

Erikson, E. H. (1959). Identity and the life cycle: Selected papers. From *Psychological Issue Monograph Series*, 1. New York: International Universities Press.

Erikson, E. H. (1961). The roots of virtue. In J. Huxley (Ed.), *The humanist frame*. New York: Harper & Row.

Erikson, E. H. (1968). *Identity, youth and crisis*. New York: W. W. Norton.

Ernst, C., & Angst, J. (1983). *Birth order: Its influence on personality*. New York: Springer-Verlag.

Erwin, P. (1993). *Friendship and peer relationships in children*. New York: John Wiley.

Ethical standards for research with children. (1973). *SRCD Newsletter*, Winter, 3–4.

Evans, R. I. (1989). *Albert Bandura: The man and his ideas—a dialogue*. New York: Praeger.

Eveleth, P. B., & Tanner, J. M. (1976). *Worldwide variation in human growth*. Cambridge, England: Cambridge University Press.

Evra, J. V. (1990). *Television and child development*. Hillsdale, N.J.: Lawrence Erlbaum.

Eysenck, H. J., & Kamin, L. (1981). *Intelligence: The battle for the mind*. London: Macmillan.

Fagan, J., Piper, E., & Moore, M. (1986). Violent delinquents and urban youths. *Criminology, 24*, 439–468.

Fagan, J. F., III. (1974). Infant color perception. *Science, 183*, 973–975.

Fantz, R. L. (1963). Pattern vision in newborn infants. *Science, 140*, 296–297.

Fantz, R. L. (1965). Visual perception from birth as shown by pattern selectivity. *Annals of the New York Academy of Science, 118,* 793–814.

Farleger, D. (1977, July). The battle over children's rights. *Psychology Today,* 89–91.

Farver, J. M. (1992). An analysis of young American and Mexican children's play dialogues: Illustrative study #3. In C. Howes, O. Unger, & C. C. Matheson, (Eds.), *The collaborative construction of pretend: Social pretend play functions.* New York: State University of New York Press.

Farver, J. M., & Howes, C. (1993). Cultural differences in American and Mexican mother-child pretend play. *Merrill-Palmer Quarterly, 39,* 344–358.

Fasick, F. A. (1988). Patterns of formal education in high school as *rites de passage. Adolescence, 23,* 457–471.

Feingold, A. (1992). Sex differences in variability in intellectual abilities: A new look at an old controversy. *Review of Educational Research, 62,* 61–84.

Feldman, D. H. (1989). Creativity: Proof that development occurs. In W. Damon (Ed.), *Child development today and tomorrow.* San Francisco: Jossey-Bass.

Fenson, L. (1987). The developmental progression of play. In A. W. Gottfried & C. C. Brown (Eds.), *Play interactions: The contribution of play materials and parental involvement to children's development.* Lexington, Mass.: D. C. Heath.

Feuerstein, R. (1979). *The dynamic assessment of retarded performers: The learning potential assessment device, theory, instruments, and techniques.* Baltimore: University Park Press.

Field, T. M. (1987). Coping with separation stress by infants and young children. In T. M. Field, P. M. McCabe, & N. Schneiderman (Eds.), *Stress and coping.* Hillsdale, N.J.: Lawrence Erlbaum.

Field, T., Mai, W., Goldstein, S., Perry, S., & Parl, S. (1988). Infant day care facilitates preschool social behavior. *Early Childhood Research Quarterly, 3,* 341–359.

Fine, M. A. (1993). Current approaches to understanding family diversity: An overview of the special issue. *Family Relations, 42,* 235–237.

Finkelhor, D., and associates (Eds.). (1986). *A source-book on child sexual abuse.* Beverly Hills, Calif.: Sage.

Fischer, K. W., & Pipp, S. L. (1984). Development of the structures of unconscious thought. In K. Bowers & D. Meichenbaum (Eds.), *The unconscious reconsidered.* New York: John Wiley.

Fischer, K. W., & Silvern, L. (1985). Stages and individual differences in cognitive development. *Annual Review of Psychology, 36,* 613–648.

Fishkin, J., Keniston, K., & MacKinnon, C. (1973). Moral reasoning and political ideology. *Journal of Personality and Social Psychology, 27,* 109–119.

Fiske, S. T. (1993). Social cognition and social perception. *Annual Review of Psychology, 44,* 155–194.

Flavell, J. H. (1982). On cognitive development. *Child Development, 53,* 1–10.

Flavell, J. H. (1985). *Cognitive development* (2nd ed.). Englewood Cliffs, N.J.: Prentice-Hall.

Flynn, J. R. (1987). Massive IQ gains in 14 nations: What IQ tests really measure. *Psychological Bulletin, 17,* 171–191.

Fogel, A. (1984). *Infancy: Infant, family, and society.* St. Paul, Minn.: West.

Fogel, A., Toda, S., & Kawai, M. (1988). Mother-infant face-to-face interaction in Japan and the United States: A laboratory comparison using 3-month-old infants. *Developmental Psychology, 3,* 398–406.

Fong, L., & Wilgosh, L. (1992). Children with autism and their families: A literature review. *Canadian Journal of Special Education, 8,* 43–54.

Food and Nutrition Board. (1990). *Nutrition during pregnancy.* Washington, D.C.: National Academy Press.

Fouts, R. S. (1987). Chimpanzee signing and emergent levels. In G. Greenberg & E. Tobach (Eds.), *Cognition, language and consciousness: Integrative levels.* Hillsdale, N.J.: Lawrence Erlbaum.

Fox, R. A. (1990). *Assessing parenting of young children.* Bethesda, Md.: Center for Nursing Research of the National Institutes of Health. (Contract 1 RO1 NRO1609O1A1)

France-Kaatrude, A., & Smith, W. P. (1985). Social comparison, task motivation, and the development of self-evaluative standards in children. *Developmental Psychology, 21,* 1080–1089.

Frankenburg, W. K., Fandal, A. W., Sciarillo, W., & Burgess, D. (1981). The newly abbreviated and revised Denver Developmental Screening Test. *Journal of Pediatrics, 99,* 995–999.

Franklin, J. T. (1985). Alternative education as substance abuse prevention. *Journal of Alcohol and Drug Education, 30,* 12–23.

Frazier, A., & Lisonbee, L. K. (1950). Adolescent concerns with physique. *School Review, 58,* 397–405.

Freud, A. (1946). *The ego and the mechanisms of defense* (C. Baines, Trans.). New York: International Universities Press.

Freyberg, J. T. (1973). Increasing the imaginative play of urban disadvantaged kindergarten children through systematic training. In J. L. Singer (Ed.), *The child's world of make-believe.* New York: Academic Press.

Fried, M. N., & Fried, M. H. (1980). *Four rituals in eight cultures.* New York: W. W. Norton.

Fried, P. A. (1986). Marijuana and human pregnancy. In I. J. Chasnoff (Ed.), *Drug use in pregnancy: Mother and child.* Boston, Mass.: MTP Press.

Friedman, J. M. (1992). Teratogenesis and mutagenesis. In J. M. Friedman, F. J. Dill, M. R. Hayden, & B. C. McGillivray (Eds.), *Genetics.* Baltimore: Williams & Wilkins.

Friedman, J. M., & McGillivray, B. (1992). Genetic paradigms in human disease. In J. M. Friedman, F. J. Dill, M. R. Hayden, & B. C. McGillivray (Eds.), *Genetics.* Baltimore: Williams & Wilkins.

Friedman, J. M., Dill, F. J., Hayden, M. R., & McGillivray, B. C. (1992). *Genetics.* Baltimore: Williams & Wilkins.

Friedman, J. M., Dill, F. J., & Hayden, M. R. (1992). Nature of genetic material. In J. M. Friedman, F. J. Dill, M. R. Hayden, & B. C. McGillivray (Eds.), *Genetics.* Baltimore: Williams & Wilkins.

Friedman, L. (1989). Mathematics and the gender gap: A meta-analysis of recent studies on sex differences in mathematical tasks. *Review of Educational Research, 59,* 185–213.

Frisch, R. E., & Revelle, R. (1970). Height and weight at menarche and a hypothesis of critical body weights and adolescent events. *Science, 169,* 397–398.

Frye, D. (1991). The origins of intention in infancy. In D. Drye & C. Moore (Eds.), *Children's theories of mind:*

Mental states and social understanding. Hillsdale N.J.: Lawrence Erlbaum.

Fuligni, A. J., & Eccles, J. S. (1993). Perceived parent-child relationships and early adolescents' orientation toward peers. *Developmental Psychology, 29,* 622–632.

Furrow, D., Nelson, K., & Benedict, H. (1979). Mother's speech to children and syntactic development: Some simple relationships. *Journal of Child Language, 6,* 423–442.

Furth, H. (1980). Piagetian perspectives. In J. Sants (Eds.), *Developmental psychology and society.* London: Macmillan, 142–168.

Furstenberg, F. F., Jr., Brooks-Gunn, J., & Chase-Lansdale, L. (1989). Teenaged pregnancy and childbearing. *American Psychologist, 44,* 313–320.

Gaddis, A., & Brooks-Gunn, J. (1985). The male experience of pubertal change. *Journal of Youth and Adolescence, 14,* 61–72.

Gagné, R. M., & Briggs, L. J. (1983). *Principles of instruction design* (3rd ed.). New York: Holt, Rinehart & Winston.

Galler, J. R. (Ed.). (1984). *Human nutrition: A comprehensive treatise: Vol. 5. Nutrition and behavior.* New York: Plenum.

Galton, F. (1896). *Hereditary genius: An enquiry into its laws and consequences.* London: Macmillan.

Gamble, T. J., & Zigler, E. (1986). Effects of infant day care: Another look at the evidence. *American Journal of Orthopsychiatry 56,* 26–42.

Garbarino, J., & Crouter, A. (1977). The human ecology of child maltreatment: A conceptual model for research. *Journal of Marriage and the Family, 39,* 721–735.

Garcia, E. E. (1993). Language, culture, and education. In L. Darling-

Hammond (Ed.), *Review of Research in Education* (Vol. 19). Washington, D.C.: American Educational Research Association.

Gardner, H. (1983). *Frames of mind: The theory of multiple intelligences.* New York: Basic Books.

Gardner, M. K. (1985). Cognitive psychological approaches to instructional task analysis. In W. W. Gordon (Ed.), *Review of Research in Education* (Vol. 12), Washington, D. C.: American Educational Research Association, 157–196.

Garmezy, N. (1976). Vulnerable and invulnerable children: Theory, research, and intervention. Master lecture on developmental psychology. American Psychological Association.

Garvey, C. (1977). *Play.* Cambridge, Mass.: Harvard University Press.

Gelles, R. J. (1979). Violence toward children in the United States. In R. Bourne & E. H. Newberger (Eds.), *Critical perspectives on child abuse.* Lexington, Mass.: D. C. Heath.

Gelman, R. (1978). Cognitive development. *Annual Review of Psychology, 29,* 297–332.

Gelman, R., & Gallistel, C. R. (1978). *The young child's understanding of number.* Cambridge, Mass.: Harvard University Press.

Gelman, R. (1982). Basic numerical abilities. In R. J. Sternberg (Ed.), *Advances in the psychology of human intelligence* (Vol. 1). Hillsdale, N.J.: Lawrence Erlbaum.

Gelman, S., Collman, P., & Maccoby, E. (1986). Inferring properties from categories versus inferring categories from properties: The case of gender. *Child Development, 57,* 396–404.

Genesee, F (1985). Second language learning through immersion: A review of U.S. programs. *Review of Educational Research, 55,* 541–546.

Gerber, M. (1958). The psycho-motor development of African children in the first year and the influence of maternal behavior. *Journal of Social Psychology, 47*, 185–195.

Gerbner, G. (1972). Violence in television drama: Trends and symbolic functions. In G. A. Comstock & E. A. Rubenstein (Eds.), *Television and social behavior* (Vol. 1). Washington, D.C.: U.S. Government Printing Office.

Gerbner, G., & Gross, L. (1980). The violent face of television and its lessons. In E. L. Palmer & A. Dorr (Eds.), *Children and the faces of television*. New York: Academic Press.

Gesell, A. (1925). *The mental growth of the pre-school child*. New York: Macmillan.

Getzels, J. W., & Jackson, P. W. (1962). *Creativity and intelligence*. New York: John Wiley.

Gewirtz, J. L. (1965). The course of infant smiling in four child-rearing environments in Israel. In B. M. Foss (Ed.), *Determinants of infant behavior 3*. London: Methuen.

Gianino, A., & Tronick, E. Z. (1988). The mutual regulation model: The infant's self and interactive regulation coping and defense. In T. Field, P. McCabe, & N. Schneiderman (Eds.), *Stress and coping*. Hillsdale, N.J.: Lawrence Erlbaum.

Gibbs, J. C. (1987). Social processes in delinquency: The need to facilitate empathy as well as sociomoral reasoning. In W. M. Kurtines & J. L. Gewirtz (Eds.), *Moral development through social interaction*. New York: John Wiley.

Gibson, E. J., & Walk, R. D. (1960). The "visual cliff." Scientific American, 202, 64–71.

Gil, D. G. (1970). *Violence against children: Physical child abuse in the United States*. Cambridge, Mass.: Harvard University Press.

Gilligan, C. (1982). *In a different voice: Psychological theory and women's development*. Cambridge, Mass.: Harvard University Press.

Gilligan, C., Ward, J. V., Taylor, J. M., & Bardige, B. (1988). *Mapping the moral domain*. Cambridge, Mass.: Harvard University Press.

Gilmore, D. H., & Aitken, D. A. (1989). Specific diagnostic techniques. In M. J. Whittle & J. M. Connor (Eds.), *Prenatal diagnosis in obstetric practice*. Boston: Blackwell Scientific Publications.

Gitomer, D. H., & Pellegrino, J. W. (1985). Developmental and individual differences in long-term memory retrieval. In R. F. Dillon (Ed.), *Individual differences in cognition* (Vol. 2). New York: Academic Press.

Glick, P. C. (1989). Remarried families, stepfamilies, and stepchildren: A brief demographic profile. *Family Relations, 38*, 24–27.

Goelman, H., Shapiro, E., & Pence, A. R. (1990). Family environment and family day care. *Family Relations, 39*, 14–19.

Golbus, M. S. (1982). Future uses of fetoscopy. In H. Galjaard (Ed.), *The future of prenatal diagnosis*. London: Churchill Livingstone, 128–132.

Gold, M. S. (1989). *Drugs of abuse: A comprehensive series for clinicians* (Vol. 1). *Marijuana*. New York: Plenum Press.

Gold, R. (1986). Failure on Piagetian tasks: Misinterpretation of the question? In C. Pratt, A. F. Garton, W. E. Tunmer, & A. R. Nesdale (Eds.), *Research issues in child development*. Boston: Allen & Unwin.

Goldenberg, C. (1992). The limits of expectations: A case for case knowl-

edge about teacher expectancy effects. *American Educational Research Journal, 29*, 517–544.

Goldberg, S. (1983). Parent-infant bonding: Another look. *Child Development, 54*, 1355–1382.

Goldgaber, D., Lerman, M. I., McBride, O. W., Saffiotti, U., & Gajdusek, D. C. (1987). Characterization and chromosomal localization of a DNA encoding brain amyloid of Alzheimer's disease. *Science, 235*, 877–880.

Goldsmith, H. H. (1983). Genetic influences on personality from infancy to adulthood. *Child Development, 54*, 331–355.

Goldsmith, J. (1990a). *Childbirth wisdom: From the world's oldest societies*. Brookline, Mass.: East-West Health Books.

Goldsmith, J. P. (1990b). Neonatal morbidity. In R. D. Eden, F. H. Boehm, & M. Haire (Eds.), *Assessment and care of the fetus: Physiological, clinical, and medicolegal principles*. Norwalk, Conn.: Appleton & Lange.

Goode, E. T. (1985). Medical aspects of the bulimic syndrome and bulimarexia. *Transactional Analysis Journal, 15*, 4–11.

Goodwin, R. (1980). Two decades of research into early language. In J. Sants (Ed.), *Developmental psychology and society*. London: Macmillan, 169–218.

Gordon, E. W., & Armour-Thomas, E. (1991). Culture and cognitive development. In L. Okagaki & R. J. Sternberg (Eds.), *Directors of development: Influences on the development of children's thinking*. Hillsdale, N.J.: Lawrence Erlbaum.

Gordon, T. (1975). *P.E.T.: Parent effectiveness training*. New York: New American Library.

Gordon, T. (1976). *P.E.T. in action*. New York: Bantam Books.

Gottesman, I. I. (1974). Developmental genetics and ontogenetic psychology: Overdue detente and propositions from a matchmaker. In A. Pick (Ed.), *Minnesota symposia on child psychology,* 12, 55–80.

Gottesman, I. I., & Shields, J. (1982). *The schizophrenic puzzle.* New York: Cambridge University Press.

Gottlieb, G. (1992). *Individual development and evolution: The genesis of novel behavior.* Oxford: Oxford University Press.

Gottman, J. M. (1977). Toward a definition of social isolation in children. *Child Development,* 48, 513–517.

Gottman, J. M., & Mettetal, G. (1987). Speculations about social and affective development: Friendship and acquaintanceship through adolescence. In J. M. Gottman & J. Parker (Eds.), *Conversations of friends.* New York: Cambridge University Press.

Gould, S. J. (1981). *The mismeasure of man.* New York: W. W. Norton.

Graham, J. M., Jr. (1985). The effects of alcohol consumption during pregnancy. In M. Marois (Ed.), *Prevention of physical and mental congenital defects.* New York: Alan R. Liss.

Grant, J. P. (Executive Director of the United Nation's Children's Fund, UNICEF). (1986). *The state of the world's children: 1986.* New York: Oxford University Press.

Grant, J. P. (1992). *The state of the world's children: 1992.* New York: Oxford University Press.

Green, K. D., Forehand, R., Beck, S. J., & Vosk, B. (1980). An assessment of the relationship among measures of children's social competence and children's academic achievement. *Child Development,* 51, 1149–1156.

Greenacre, P. (1959). Play in relation to creative imagination. *Psychoanalytic Studies of the Child,* 14, 61–80.

Greene, J. (1975). *Thinking and language.* London: Methuen.

Greenfield, P. M., & Savage-Rumbaugh, E. S. (1993). Comparing communicative competence in child and chimp: The pragmatics of repetition. *Journal of Child Language,* 20, 1–26.

Greenspan, S. I., & Lieberman, A. F. (1989). A quantitative approach to the clinical assessment of representational elaboration and differentiation in children two to four. In S. I. Greenspan & G. H. Pollock (Eds.), *The course of life: Vol II. Early Childhood.* Madison, Conn.: International Universities Press.

Grieser, D. L., & Kuhl, P. K. (1988). Maternal speech to infants in a tonal language: Support for universal prosodic features in motherese. *Developmental Psychology,* 24, 14–20.

Griffin, S. (1985). Eating issues and fat issues. *Transactional Analysis Journal,* 15, 30–36.

Griffiths, M. D. (1991). Amusement machine playing in childhood and adolescence: A comparative analysis of video games and fruit machines. *Journal of Adolescence,* 14, 53–73.

Grindstaff, C. F. (1988). Adolescent marriage and childbearing: The long-term economic outcome, Canada in the 1980s. *Adolescence,* 23, 45–58.

Gronlund, N. E., & Holmlund, W. S. (1958). The value of elementary school sociometric status scores for predicting a pupil's adjustment in high school. *Educational Administration and Supervision,* 44, 255–260.

Grossman, J. J. (Ed.). (1983). *Manual on terminology and classification in mental retardation, 1983 revision.* Washington, D.C.: American Association on Mental Deficiency.

Grotevant, H. D., & Adams, G. R. (1984). Development of an objective measure to assess ego identity in adolescence: Validation and replication. *Journal of Youth and Adolescence,* 13, 419–438.

Grotevant, M. D., Scarr, S., & Weinberg, R. A. (1977). Intellectual development in family constellations with adopted and natural children: A test of the Zajonc and Markus model. Paper presented at a meeting of the Society for Research in Child Development, New Orleans.

Grow, L. J. (1979). *Early childbearing by young mothers: A research study.* New York: Child Welfare League of America.

Guidubaldi, J., & Cleminshaw, H. (1985). Divorce, family health, and child adjustment. *Family Relations,* 34, 35–41.

Guilford, J. P. (1950). Creativity. *American Psychologist,* 5, 444–454.

Guilford, J. P. (1959). Three faces of intellect. *American Psychologist,* 14, 469–479.

Gunter, B., & McAleer, J. L. (1990). *Children and television. The one-eyed monster?* New York: Routledge.

Gustafson, G. E., & Harris, K. L. (1990). Women's responses to young infants' cries. *Developmental Psychology, 26,* 144–152.

Gustafson, J. E., & Undheim, J. O. (1992). Stability and change in broad and narrow factors of intelligence from ages 12 to 15. *Journal of Educational Psychology, 84,* 141–149.

Hague, W. J. (1991). Kohlberg's legacy—More than ideas: An essay review. *The Alberta Journal of Educational Research, 37,* 277–294.

Haith, M. M. (1980). *Rules that babies look by: The organization of newborn visual activity.* Hillsdale, N.J.: Lawrence Erlbaum.

Haith, M. M. (1986). Sensory and perceptual processes in early infancy. *Journal of Pediatrics, 109,* 158–171.

Hakuta, K., & D'Andrea, D. (1992). Some properties of bilingual maintenance and loss in Mexican background high-school students. *Applied Linguistics, 13,* 72–99.

Hakuta, K., & Garcia, E. E. (1989). Bilingualism and education. *American Psychologist, 44,* 374–379.

Hall, G. S. (1891). The contents of children's minds on entering school. *Paediatric Seminars, 1,* 139–173.

Hall, G. S. (1916). *Adolescence* (2 vols.). New York: Appleton-Century-Crofts.

Hall, W. G., & Oppenheim, R. W. (1987). Developmental psychobiology: Prenatal, perinatal, and early postnatal aspects of behavioral development. *Annual Review of Psychology, 38,* 91–128.

Hallahan, D. P., & Kauffman, J. M. (1986). *Exceptional children: Introduction to special education* (3rd ed.). Englewood Cliffs, N.J.: Prentice-Hall.

Hallahan, D. P., & Kauffman, J. M. (1991). *Exceptional children: Introduction to special education* (4th ed.). Englewood Cliffs, N.J.: Prentice Hall.

Halonen, J. S., & Passman, R. H. (1978). Pacifiers' effects upon play and separations from the mother for the one-year-old in a novel environment. *Infant Behavior and Development, 1,* 70–78.

Hamner, T. J., & Turner, P. H. (1985). *Parenting in contemporary society.* Englewood Cliffs, N.J.: Prentice-Hall.

Hampson, J., & Nelson, K. (1993). The relation of maternal language to variation in rate and style of language acquisition. *Journal of Child Language, 20,* 313–342.

Hampsten, E. (1991). *Settler's children: Growing up on the Great Plains.* Norman: The University of Oklahoma Press.

Handyside, A. H. (1991). Preimplantation diagnosis by DNA amplification. In M. Chapman, G. Grudzinskas, & T. Chard (Eds.), *The embryo: Normal and abnormal development and growth.* New York: Springer-Verlag.

Hanna, E., & Meltzoff, A. N. (1993). Peer imitation by toddlers in laboratory, home, and day-care contexts: Implications for social learning and memory. *Developmental Psychology, 29,* 701–710.

Hare, J. W. (Ed.). (1989). *Diabetes complicating pregnancy: The Joslin Clinic Method.* New York: Alan R. Liss.

Hargrove, L. J., & Poteet, J. A. (1984). *Assessment in special education: The education evaluation.* Englewood Cliffs, NJ.: Prentice-Hall.

Harland, D. (Ed.). (1989). *Children on the front line: The impact of apartheid, destabilization and warfare on children in Southern and South Africa,* New York: United Nations Children's Fund.

Harlow, H. F. (1959). Love in infant monkeys. *Scientific American, 200,* 68–70.

Harris, P. L., & Gross, D. (1988). Children's understanding of real and apparent emotion. In J. W. Astington, P. L. Harris, & D. R. Olson (Eds.), *Developing theories of mind.* New York: Cambridge University Press.

Harris, T. (1972). *I'm ok—You're ok.* New York: Avon Books.

Harris, Y. R., & Hamidullah, J. (1993). Maternal and child utilization of memory strategies. *Current Psychology: Research and Reviews, 12,* 81–94.

Harrison, L. (1985). Effects of early supplemental stimulation programs for premature infants: Review of the literature. *Maternal-Child Nursing Journal, 14,* 69–90.

Harter, S. (1983). Developmental perspectives on the self-system. In P. H. Mussen (Ed.), *Handbook of child psychology* (4th ed.) (Vol. 4): *Socialization, personality, and social development* (E. M. Hetherington, Ed.). New York: John Wiley.

Harter, S. (1985a). Processes underlying the construct, maintenance and enhancement of the self-concept in children. In J. Suls & A. Greenwald (Eds.), *Psychological perspectives on the self* (Vol. 3). Hillsdale, N.J.: Lawrence Erlbaum.

Harter, S. (1985b). *The Self-Perception Profile for Children: Revision of the Perceived Competence Scale for Children, Manual.* Denver: University of Denver.

Harter, S. (1987). The determinants and mediational role of global self-worth in children. In N. Eisenberg (Ed.), *Contemporary topics in developmental psychology.* New York: Wiley.

Harter, S. (1988). Developmental processes in the construction of self. In T. D. Yawkey & J. E. Johnson (Eds.), *Integrative processes and socialization: Early to middle childhood.* Hillsdale, N.J.: Lawrence Erlbaum.

Harter, S. (1990). Processes underlying adolescent self-concept formation. In R. Montemayor, G. R. Adams, & T. P. Gullotta (Eds.), *Advances in adolescent development: Vol. 2. From childhood to adolescence: A transitional period?* Newbury Park, Calif.: Sage.

Hartup, W. W. (1978). Children and their friends. In H. McGurk (Ed.), *Issues in childhood social development.* London: Methuen.

Hartup, W. W. (1983). Peer relations. In P. H. Mussen (Ed.), *Handbook of child psychology* (4th ed.) (Vol. 4): *Socialization, personality, and social development* (E. M. Hetherington, Ed.). New York: John Wiley, 103–196.

Hartup, W. W. (1989). Social relationships and their developmental significance. *American Psychologist, 44*, 120–126.

Haskins, R. (1989). Beyond metaphor: The efficacy of early childhood education. *American Psychologist, 44*, 274–282.

Hass, A. (1979). *Teenage sexuality: A survey of teenage sexual behavior.* New York: Macmillan.

Hauser, R. M., & Sewell, W. H. (1985). Birth order and educational attainment in full sibships. *American Journal of Educational Research Journal, 22*, 1–23.

Havighurst, R. J. (1972). *Developmental tasks and education.* New York: D. McKay.

Havighurst, R. J. (1979). *Developmental tasks and education* (4th ed.). New York: D. McKay.

Havighurst, R. J. (1982). The world of work. In B. B. Wolman (Ed.), *Handbook of developmental psychology.* Englewood Cliffs, N.J.: Prentice-Hall.

Hay, D. F. (1981). Multiple functions of proximity-seeking in infancy. *Child Development, 51*, 636–645.

Hay, D. F., Stimson, C. A., & Castle, J. (1991). A meeting of minds in infancy: Imitation and desire. In D. Frye & C. Moore (Eds.), *Children's theories of mind: Mental states and social understanding.* Hillsdale N.J.: Lawrence Erlbaum.

Hayden, M. R. (1992). DNA diagnosis. In J. M. Friedman, F. J. Dill, M. R. Hayden, & B. C. McGillivray (Eds.), *Genetics.* Baltimore: Williams & Wilkins.

Hayes, C. D., Palmer, J. L., & Zaslow, M. J. (Eds.). (1990). *Who cares for America's children? Child care policy for the 1990's.* Washington, D.C.: National Academy Press.

Hayes, K. J., & Hayes, C. (1951). Intellectual development of a home-raised chimpanzee. *Proceedings of the American Philosophical Society, 95*, 105–109.

Hazen, N. L., & Lockman, J. J. (1989). Skill and context. In J. J. Lockman & N. L. Hazen (Eds.), *Action in social context: Perspectives on early development.* New York: Plenum Press.

Hebb, D. O. (1966). *A textbook of psychology* (2nd ed.). Philadelphia: W. B. Saunders.

Hedges, L. V., & Friedman, L. (1993). Gender differences in variability in intellectual abilities: A reanalysis of Feingold's results. *Review of Educational Research, 63*, 94–105.

Heinonen, O. P., Slone, D., & Shapiro, S. (1983). *Birth defects and drugs in pregnancy.* Boston: John Wright.

Heinzen, T. E. (1991). A paradigm for research in creativity. *The Creative Child and Adult Quarterly, 16*, 164–174.

Heisel, B. E., & Retter, K. (1981). Young children's storage behavior in a memory for location task. *Journal of Experimental Child Psychology, 31*, 250–364.

Heiser, C. B., Jr. (1969). *Nightshades: The paradoxical plants.* San Francisco: W. H. Freeman.

Henderson, G., & Henderson, B. B. (1984). *Mending broken children: A parent's manual.* Springfield, Ill.: Charles C. Thomas.

Henker, B., & Whalen, C. K. (1989). Hyperactivity and attention deficits. *American Psychologist, 44*, 216–223.

Henry, C. S., Stephenson, A. L., Hanson, M. F., & Hargett, W. (1993). Adolescent suicide and families: An ecological approach. *Adolescence, 28*, 291–308.

Hernandez, D. J. & Myers, D. E. (1993). *America's children: Resources from family, government, and the economy.* New York: Russell Sage Foundation.

Herzog, E., & Sudia, C. (1970). *Boys in fatherless homes.* Washington, D.C.: U.S. Department of Health, Education, & Welfare.

Hess, G. C. (1990). Sexual abstinence, a revived option for teenagers. *Modern Psychology, 1*, 19–21.

Hetherington, E. M., Cox, M., & Cox, R. (1979). Play and social interaction in children following divorce. *Journal of Social Issues, 35*, 26–49.

Hetherington, E. M., Stanley-Hagen, M., & Anderson, E. R. (1989). Marital transitions: A child's perspective. *American Psychologist, 44*, 303–312.

Higbee, K. L. (1977). *Your memory: How it works and how to improve it.* Englewood Cliffs, N.J.: Prentice-Hall.

Hillman, L. S. (1991). Theories and research. In C. A. Corr, H. Fuller, C. A. Barnickol, & D. M. Corr (Eds.), *Sudden infant death syndrome: Who can help and how.* New York: Springer.

Hinde, R. A. (1983). Ethology and child development. In P. H. Mussen (Ed.), *Handbook of child psychology* (4th ed.) (Vol. 2): *Infancy and developmental psychobiology* (M. M. Haith & J. J. Campos, Eds.). New York: John Wiley, 27–94.

Hinde, R. A. (1989). Ethological and relationship approaches. In R. Vasta (Ed.), *Annals of child development* (Vol. 6). Greenwich, Conn.: JAI Press.

Hindelang, M. J. (1981). Variations in sex-race-age-specific incidence of offending. *American Sociological Review, 46*, 461–474.

Ho, D. Y. F. (1987). Fatherhood in Chinese culture. In M. E. Lamb (Ed.). *The father's role: Cross-cultural perspectives.* Hillsdale, N.J.: Lawrence Erlbaum.

646

Hodapp, R. M., & Mueller, E. (1982). Early social development. In B. B. Wolman and others (Eds.), *Handbook of developmental psychology*. Englewood Cliffs, N.J.: Prentice-Hall.

Hofer, M. A. (1981). *The roots of human behavior: An introduction to the psychobiology of early development*. San Francisco: W. H. Freeman.

Hofferth, S. L. (1992). The demand for and supply of child care in the 1990s. In A. Booth (ed.), *Child care in the 1990's: Trends and consequences*. Hillsdale, N.J.: Lawrence Erlbaum.

Hoffman, L. W. (1991). The influence of the family environment on personality: Accounting for sibling differences. *Psychological Bulletin, 110*, 187–203.

Hoffman, M. L. (1975). Developmental synthesis of affect and cognition and its implications for altruistic motivation. *Developmental Psychology, 11*, 607–622.

Hoffman, M. L. (1976). Empathy, role-taking, guilt, and development of altruistic motives. In T. Likona (Ed.), *Moral development: Current theory and research*. New York: Holt, Rinehart & Winston.

Hoffman, M. L. (1978). Empathy: Its developmental and prosocial implications. In C. B. Keasey (Ed.), *Nebraska symposium on motivation* (Vol. 25). Lincoln: University of Nebraska Press.

Hoffman, M. L. (1979). Development of moral thought, feeling, and behavior. *American Psychologist, 34*, 958–966.

Hoge, R. D. (1988). Issues in the definition and measurement of the giftedness construct. *Educational Researcher, 17*, 12–66.

Holbrook, R. H., Jr.; Laros, R. K., Jr.; & Creasy, R. K. (1988), Evaluation of a risk-scoring system for prediction of preterm labor. *American Journal of Perinatology, 6*, 62.

Holland, A. J., Hall, A., Murray, R., Russell, G. F. M., & Crisp, A. H. (1984). Anorexia nervosa: A study of 34 twin pairs and one set of triplets. *British Journal of Psychiatry, 145*, 414–419.

Holmes, R. H., & Rahe, R. H. (1967). The social readjustment rating scale. *Journal of Psychosomatic Research, 11*, 213–218.

Holstein, C. B. (1976). Irreversible, step-wise sequence in the development of moral judgment: A longitudinal study of males and females. *Child Development, 47*, 51–61.

Hooper, S. R. (1992). The classification of developmental disorders: An overview. In S. R. Hooper, G. W. Hynd, & R. E. Mattison, (Eds.), *Developmental disorders: Diagnostic criteria and clinical assessment*. Hillsdale, N.J.: Lawrence Erlbaum.

Horn, J. (1983). The Texas Adoption Project. *Child Development, 54*, 268–275.

Horn, J. L. (1976). Human abilities: A review of research and theory in the early 1970's. In M. R. Rosenzweig & L. W. Porter (Eds.), *Annual review of psychology* (Vol. 27). Palo Alto, Calif.: Annual Reviews.

Horn, J. L., & Donaldson, G. (1980). Cognitive development in adulthood. In O. G. Brim, Jr., & J. Kagan (Eds.), *Constancy and change in human development*. Cambridge, Mass.: Harvard University Press.

Horton, D. L., & Mills, C. B. (1984). Human learning and memory. *Annual Review of Psychology, 35*, 361–394.

Howes, C., & Segal, J. (1993). Children's relationships with alternative caregivers: The special case of maltreated children removed from their homes. *Journal of Applied Developmental Psychology, 14*, 71–81.

Hsu, L. Y. F. (1986). Prenatal diagnosis of chromosome abnormalities. In A. Milunsky (Ed.), *Genetic disorders and the fetus* (2nd ed.). New York: Plenum Press.

Hubel, D. H., & Wiesel, T. N. (1970). The period of susceptibility to the physiological effects of unilateral eye closure in kittens. *Journal of Physiology, 206*, 419–436.

Huesmann, L. R., & Eron, L. D. (Eds.) (1986a). *Television and the aggressive child: A cross-national comparison*. Hillsdale, N.J.: Lawrence Erlbaum.

Huesmann, L. R., & Eron, L. D. (1986b). The development of aggression in children of different cultures: Psychological processes and exposure to violence. In L. R. Huesmann & L. D. Eron (Eds.), *Television and the aggressive child: A cross-national comparison*. Hillsdale, N.J.: Lawrence Erlbaum.

Huesmann, L. R., Eron, L. D., Lefkowitz, M. M., & Walder, L. O. (1984). The stability of aggression over time and generations. *Developmental Psychology, 20*, 1120–1134.

Hughes, F. P. (1990). *Children, play, and development*. Boston: Allyn & Bacon.

Hughes, R., Tingle, B. A., & Sawin, D. B. (1981). Development of empathic understanding in children. *Child Development, 52*, 122–128.

Hunt, C. E. (1991). Sudden infant death syndrome: The neurobehavioral perspective. *Journal of Applied Developmental Psychology, 12*, 185–188.

Hunt, E., & Agnoli, F. (1991). The Whorfian hypothesis: A cognitive psychology perspective. *Psychological Review, 98*, 377–389.

Hunt, J. McV. (1961). *Intelligence and experience*. New York: The Ronald Press.

Hurlock, E. B. (1964). *Child development* (4th ed.). New York: McGraw-Hill.

Hurrelman, K. (1990). Parents, peers, teachers and other significant partners in adolescence. *International Journal of Adolescence and Youth, 2,* 211–236.

Husén, T., & Tuijnman, A. (1991). The contribution of formal schooling to the increase in intellectual capital. *Educational Researcher, 20,* 17–25.

Huston, A. C., Watkins, B. Q., & Kunkel, D. (1989). Public policy and children's television. *American Psychologist, 44,* 424–433.

Huston, A. C., & Wright, J. C. (1983). Children's processing of television: The informative functions of formal features. In J. Bryant & D. R. Anderson (Eds.), *Children's understanding of television: Research on attention and comprehension.* New York: Academic Press, 35–68.

Huston, A. C., Wright, J. C., Rice, M. L., Kerkman, D., & St. Peters, M. (1990). Development of television viewing patterns in early childhood: A longitudinal investigation. *Developmental Psychology, 26,* 409–420.

Hutt, S. J., Lenard, H. G., & Prechtl, H. F. R. (1969). Psychophysiology of the newborn. In L. P. Lipsitt & H. W. Reese (Eds.), *Advances in child development and behavior.* New York: Academic Press.

Hyde, J. S. (1986). *Understanding human sexuality* (3rd ed.). New York: McGraw-Hill.

Hyde, J. S., Fennema, E., & Lamon, S. J. (1990). Gender differences in mathematics performance. A meta-analysis. *Psychological Bulletin, 107,* 139–155.

Hyde, S., & Linn, M. C. (1986). *The psychology of gender: Advances through meta-analysis.* Baltimore: Johns Hopkins University Press.

Iennarella, R. S., Chisum, G. M., & Bianchi, J. (1986). A comprehensive treatment model for pregnant chemical users, infants and families. In I. J. Chasnoff (Ed.), *Drug use in pregnancy: Mother and child.* Boston: MTP Press.

Ijzendoorn, M. H. Van (1993). Intergenerational transmission of parenting: A review of studies in nonclinical populations. *Developmental Review, 12,* 76–99.

Ingram, D. (1991). A historical observation on "Why 'Mama' and 'Papa'?" *Journal of Child Language, 18,* 711–713.

Inhelder, B., & Piaget, J. (1958). *The growth of logical thinking from childhood to adolescence.* New York: Basic Books.

Inoff-Germain, G.; Arnold, G. S.; Nottelmann, E. D.; Susman, E. J.; Cutler, G. B., Jr.; & Chrousos, G. P. (1988). Relations between hormone levels and observational measures of aggressive behavior of young adolescents in family interactions. *Developmental Psychology, 24,* 129–139.

Intons-Peterson, M. J. (1988). *Gender concepts of Swedish and American youth.* Hillsdale, N.J.: Lawrence Erlbaum.

Isabell, B. J., & McKee, L. (1980). Society's cradle: An anthropological perspective on the socialisation of cognition. In J. Sants (Ed.), *Developmental psychology and society.* London: Macmillan, 327–365.

Izard, C. E. (1977). *Human emotions.* New York: Plenum.

Izard, C. E., & Malatesta, C. Z. (1987). Perspectives on emotional development I: Differential emotions theory of early emotional development. In J. D. Osofsky (Ed.), *Handbook of infant development* (2nd ed.). New York: Wiley.

Jacklin, C. N. (1989). Female and male: Issues of gender. *American Psychologist, 44,* 127–133.

Jackson, J. F. (1993). Multiple caregiving among African Americans and infant attachment: The need for an emic approach. *Human Development, 36,* 87–102.

Jacobson, J. L., & Jacobson, S. W. (1990). Methodological issues in human behavioral teratology. In C. Rovee-Collier & L. P. Lipsitt (Eds.), *Advances in infancy research* (Vol. 6), Norwood, N.J.: Ablex.

Jacobson, J. L., & Wille, D. E. (1984). Influence of attachment and separation experience on separation distress at 18 months. *Developmental Psychology, 20,* 477–484.

Jacobson, S. W., Fein, G. G., Jacobson, J. L., Schwartz, P. M., & Dowler, J. K. (1985). Neonatal correlates of exposure to smoking, caffeine, and alcohol. *Infant and Behavior Development, 7,* 253–265.

Jacobson, S. W., & Kagan, J. (1979). Interpreting "imitative" responses in early infancy. *Science, 205,* 215–217.

Jacobvitz, R. S., Wood, M. R., & Albin, K. (1991). Cognitive skills and young children's comprehension of television. *Journal of Applied Developmental Psychology, 12,* 219–235.

Jacopini, G. A., D'Amico, R., Frontali, M., & Vivona, G. (1992). Attitudes of persons at risk and their partners toward predictive testing. In G. Evers-Kiebooms, J. P. Fryns, J. J. Cassiman, & H. Van den Berghe (Eds.), *Psychosocial aspects of genetic counseling.* New York: John Wiley.

Jahnke, H. C., & Blanchard-Fields, F. (1993). A test of two models of adolescent egocentrism. *Journal of Youth and Adolescence, 22,* 313–326.

James, W. (1890). *The principles of psychology*. New York: Holt, Rinehart & Winston.

James, W. (1892). *Psychology: The briefer course*. New York: Henry Holt.

Jean-Gilles, M., & Crittenden, P. M. (1990). Maltreating families: A look at siblings. *Family Relations, 39*, 323–329.

Jelliffe, D. B., & Jelliffe, E. F. (1990). *Growth monitoring and promotion in young children: Guidelines for the selection of methods and training techniques*. New York: Oxford University Press.

Jensen, A. R. (1968). Social class, race, and genetics: Implications for education. *American Educational Research Journal, 5*, 1–42.

Jensen, W. A., et al. (1979). *Biology*. Belmont, Calif.: Wadsworth.

Jersild, A. T. (1963). *The psychology of adolescence* (2nd ed.). New York: Macmillan.

Johnson, B., & Morse, H. (1968). Injured children and their parents. *Children, 15*, 147–152.

Johnson, H. R., Myhre, S. A., Ruvalcaba, R. H. A., Thuline, H. C., & Kelley, V. C. (1970). Effects of testosterone on body image and behavior in Klinefelter's syndrome: A pilot study. *Developmental Medicine and Child Neurology, 12*, 454–460.

Johnson, J. E., & McGillicuddy-Delisi, A. (1983). Family environment factors and children's knowledge of rules and conventions. *Child Development, 54*, 218–226.

Johnson, J. H. (1986). *Life events as stressors in childhood and adolescence*. Beverly Hills, Calif.: Sage.

Johnson, M. K., Bransford, J. D., & Solomon, S. (1973). Memory for tacit implications of sentences. *Journal of Experimental Psychology, 98*, 203–205.

Johnson, R. D. (1962). Measurements of achievement in fundamental skills of elementary school children. *Research Quarterly, 33*, 94–103.

Johnson, S. A., & Green, V. (1993). Female adolescent contraceptive decision making and risk taking. *Adolescence, 28*, 81–96.

Jones, E. F., and associates, (1986). *Teenage pregnancy in industrialized countries*. New Haven, Conn.: Yale University Press.

Jones, M. C. (1957). The later careers of boys who are early- or late-maturing. *Child Development, 28*, 113–128.

Jones, M. C. (1965). Psychological correlates of somatic development. *Child Development, 36*, 899–911.

Jones, M. C. (1974). Albert, Peter, and John B. Watson. *American Psychologist, 29*, 581–583.

Jorgensen, S. R. (1991). Project taking charge: An evaluation of an adolescent pregnancy prevention program. *Family Relations, 40*, 373–380.

Joy, L. A., Kimball, M., & Zabrack, M. L. (1977). *Television exposure and children's aggressive behavior*. Paper presented at the annual meeting of the Canadian Psychological Association, Vancouver, B.C.

Justice, E. (1985). Categorization as a preferred memory strategy: Developmental changes during elementary school. *Developmental Psychology, 21*, 1105–1110.

Juvonen, J. (1991). Deviance, perceived responsibility, and negative peer reactions. *Developmental Psychology, 27*, 672–681.

Kagan, J. (1976). Emergent themes in human development. *American Scientist, 64*, 186–196.

Kagan, J. (1978, August). The parental love trap. *Psychology Today*, 54–61, 91.

Kagan, J., Kearsley, R. B., & Zelazo, P. R. (1977). The effects of infant day care on psychological development. *Educational Quarterly, 1*, 109–142.

Kagan, J., & Snidman, N. (1991). Temperamental factors in human development. *American Psychologist, 46*, 856–862.

Kaitz, M., Meschulach-Sarfaty, O., Auerbach, J., & Eidelman, A. (1988). A reexamination of newborn's ability to imitate facial expressions. *Developmental Psychology, 24*, 3–7.

Kandel, D. B., & Logan, J. A. (1984). Patterns of drug use from adolescence to young adulthood: I. Period of risk for initiation, continued use, and discontinuation. *American Journal of Public Health, 74*, 660–666.

Kant, I. (1977; original in 1797). *Die Metaphysic der Sitten*. Frankfurt: Suhrkamp.

Kaplan, L. J. (1984). *Adolescence: The farewell to childhood*. New York: Simon & Schuster.

Kasof, J. (1993). Sex bias in the naming of stimulus persons. *Psychological Bulletin, 113*, 140–163.

Kato, T. (1970). Chromosome studies in pregnant rhesus monkeys macaque given LSD-25. *Diseases of the Nervous System, 31*, 245–250.

Kavale, K., & Forness, S. (1985). *The science of learning disabilities*. San Diego, Calif.: College-Hill Press.

Kavale, K. A., Forness, S. R., & Lorsbach, T. C. (1991). Definition for definitions of learning disabilities. *Journal of Learning Disabilities, 14*, 257–266.

Kaye, K. (1977). Toward the origin of dialogue. In H. R. Schaffer (Ed.), *Studies in mother-infant interaction*. London: Academic Press.

Kazdin, A. E. (1989). Developmental psychopathology: Current research, issues, and directions. *American Psychologist, 44*, 180–187.

Kegan, R. (1982). *The evolving self: Problem and process in human development.* Cambridge, Mass.: Harvard University Press.

Kelley, H. H. (1992). Common-sense psychology and scientific psychology. *Annual Review of Psychology, 43*, 1–23.

Kempe, R. S., & Kempe, C. H. (1984). *The common secret: Sexual abuse of children and adolescents.* New York: W. H. Freeman.

Kendall-Tackett, K. A., Williams, L. M., & Finkelhor, D. (1993). Impact of sexual abuse on children: A review and synthesis of recent empirical studies. *Psychological Bulletin, 113*, 164–180.

Kennell, J. H., Trause, M. A., & Klaus, M. H. (1975). Evidence for a sensitive period in the human mother. *Parent-Infant Interaction* (Ciba Foundation Symposium, new series) *33*, 87–102.

Kessen, W. (1965). *The child.* New York: John Wiley.

Kessen, W. (1975). *Childhood in China.* New Haven, Conn.: Yale University Press.

Kinsey, A. C., Pomeroy, W. B., & Martin, C. E. (1984). *Sexual behavior in the human male.* Philadelphia: W. B. Saunders.

Kinsey, A. C., Pomeroy, W. B., Martin, C. E., & Gebhard, P. H. (1953). *Sexual behavior in the human female.* Philadelphia: W. B. Saunders.

Kirby, J. R., & Das, J. P. (1990). A cognitive approach to intelligence: Attention, coding, and planning. *Canadian Psychology, 31*, 320–331.

Kirk, S. (1979). *Educating exceptional children* (3rd ed.). Boston: Houghton Mifflin.

Klaus, M. H., & Kennell, H. H. (1983). *The beginnings of parent-infant attachment.* St. Louis: C. V. Mosby. (Originally published as *Maternal-infant bonding*, 1980.)

Klaus, M. H., Kreger, N., McAlpine, W., Steffa, M., & Kennell, J. (1972). Maternal attachment: Importance of the first post-partum days. *New England Journal of Medicine, 286*, 460–463.

Klein, M., & Stern, L. (1971). Low birth weight and the battered child syndrome. *American Journal of Diseases 1, 22*, 15–18.

Kleinginna, P. R., Jr., & Kleinginna, A. M. (1988). Current trends toward convergence of the behavioristic, functional, and cognitive perspectives in experimental psychology. *The Psychological Record, 38*, 369–392.

Kline, S. M. (1985). Achieving weight gain with anorexia and bulimic clients in a group setting. *Transactional Analysis Journal, 15*, 62–67.

Kloza, E. M. (1990). Low MSAFP and new biochemical markers for Down syndrome: Implications for genetic counselors. In B. A. Fine, E. Gettig, K. Greendale, B. Leopold, & N. W. Paul (Eds.), *Strategies in genetic counseling: Reproductive genetics and new technologies*, White Plains, N.Y.: March of Dimes Birth Defects Foundation.

Knuppel, R. A., & Angel, J. L. (1990). Diagnosis of fetal-maternal hemorrhage. In R. D. Eden, F. H. Boehm, & M. Haire (Eds.), *Assessment and care of the fetus: Physiological, clinical, and medicolegal principles.* Norwalk Conn.: Appleton & Lange.

Knutson, J. F. (1978). Child abuse as an area of aggression research. *Journal of Pediatric Psychology, 3*, 20–27.

Kogan, N. (1983). Stylistic variation in childhood and adolescence: Creativity, metaphor, and cognitive style. In P. H. Mussen (Ed.), *Handbook of child psychology* (4th ed.) (Vol. 3): *Cognitive development* (J. H. Flavell & E. M. Markman, Eds.). New York: John Wiley, 630–706.

Kohlberg, L. A. (1964). Development of moral character and moral ideology. In M. L. Hoffman & L. W. Hoffman (Eds.), *Review of Child Development Research* (Vol. 1). New York: Russell Sage Foundation.

Kohlberg, L. A. (1966). Cognitive-development analysis of children's sex-role concepts and attitudes. In E. Maccoby (Ed.), *The development of sex differences.* Stanford, Calif.: Stanford University Press.

Kohlberg, L. A. (1969). Stage and sequence: The cognitive-developmental approach to socialization. In D. Gosslin (Ed.), *Handbook of socialization theory and research.* Chicago: Rand McNally.

Kohlberg, L. A. (1978). Revisions in the theory and practice of moral development. *New Directions for Child Development, 2*, 83–87.

Kohlberg, L. A. (1980). *The meaning and measurement of moral development.* Worcester, Mass.: Clark University Press.

Kohlberg, L. A., & Candee, D. (1984). The relationship of moral judgment to moral action. In W. M. Kurtines & J. L. Gewirtz (Eds.), *Morality, moral behavior, and moral development.* New York: John Wiley.

Kolata, G. B. (1978). Behavioral teratology: Birth defects of the mind. *Science, 202*, 732–734.

Konner, M. (1982). Biological aspects of the mother-infant bond. In C. Parks & J. Stevenson-Hinde (Eds.), *The place of attachment in human behavior.* New York: Basic Books.

Kopp, C. B., & Brownell, C. A. (1991). The development of self: The first 3 years. *Developmental Review, 11,* 195–196.

Kopp, C. B., & Kaler, S. R. (1989). Risk in infancy: Origins and implications. *American Psychologist, 44,* 224–230.

Kopp, C. B., & Parmelee, A. H. (1979). Prenatal and perinatal influences on infant behavior. In J. D. Osofsky (Ed.), *Handbook of infant development.* New York: John Wiley.

Korbin, J. E. (1981). "Very few cases": Child abuse and neglect in the People's Republic of China. In J. E. Korbin (Ed.), *Child abuse and neglect: Cross-cultural perspectives.* Berkeley: University of California Press.

Kotelchuck, M. (1976). The infant's relationship to the father: Experimental evidence. In M. Lamb (Ed.), *The role of the father in child development.* New York: John Wiley.

Kovacs, M. (1989). Affective disorders in children and adolescents. *American Psychologist, 44,* 209–215.

Kozulin, A. (1990). *Vygotsky's psychology: A biography of ideas.* New York: Harvester Wheatsheaf.

Kroupa, S. E. (1988). Perceived parental acceptance and female juvenile delinquency. *Adolescence, 23,* 143–155.

Kuhn, D. (1972). Mechanisms of change in the development of cognitive structures. *Child Development, 43,* 833–844.

Kuhn, D. (1984). Cognitive development. In M. H. Bornstein & M. E. Lamb (Eds.), *Developmental psychology: An advanced textbook.* Hillsdale, N.J.: Lawrence Erlbaum, 133–180.

Kurtines, W., & Grief, E. B. (1974). The development of moral thought: Review and evaluation of Kohlberg's approach. *Psychological Bulletin, 81,* 453–470.

Kuziel-Perri, P., & Snarey, J. (1991). Adolescent repeat pregnancies: An evaluation study of a comprehensive service program for pregnant and parenting black adolescents. *Family Relations, 40,* 381–385.

Kuzyk, B. (1993). Breast-feeding is best for babies. *Edmonton Sun,* September 2, p. 38.

Lachenmeyer, J. R., & Muni-Brander, P. (1988). Eating disorders in a nonclinical adolescent population: Implications for treatment. *Adolescence, 23* (90), 303–312.

Ladame, F., & Jeanneret, O. (1982). Suicide in adolescence: Some comments on epidemiology and prevention. *Journal of Adolescence, 5,* 355–366.

Lagercrantz, H., & Slotkin, T. A. (1986). The "stress" of being born. *Scientific American, 254,* 100–107.

La Greca, A. M., & Stone, W. L. (1993). Social anxiety scale for children-revised: Factor structure and concurrent validy. *Journal of Clinical Child Psychology, 22,* 17–27.

Lam, T. C. L. (1992). Review of practices and problems in the evaluation of bilingual education. *Review of Educational Research, 62,* 181–203.

Lamanna, M. A., & Reidmann, A. (1994). *Marriages and families: Making choices and facing change* (5th ed.). Belmont, Calif.: Wadsworth.

Lamaze, F. (1972). *Painless childbirth: The Lamaze method.* New York: Pocket Books.

Lamb, M. E. (1980). The development of parent-infant attachments in the first two years of life. In F. A. Pedersen (Ed.), *The father-infant relationship: Observational studies in the family setting.* New York: Praeger, 21–42.

Lamb, M. E., Easterbrooks, M. A., & Holden, G. W. (1980). Reinforcement and punishment among preschoolers: Characteristics, effects and correlates. *Child Development, 51,* 1230–1236.

Lamb, M. E., & Elster, A. B. (1985). Adolescent mother-infant-father relationships. *Developmental Psychology, 21,* 768–773.

Lamb, M. E., Frodi, M., Hwang, C., & Frodi, A. M. (1983). Effects of paternal involvement on infant preferences for mothers and fathers. *Child Development, 54,* 450–458.

Lambert, W. E. (1975). Culture and language as factors in learning and education. In A. Wolfgang (Ed.), *Education of immigrant students.* Toronto: Ontario Institute for Studies in Education.

Landesman, S., & Ramey, C. (1989). Developmental psychology and mental retardation: Integrating scientific principles with treatment practices. *American Psychologist, 44,* 409–415.

Landry, R. (1987). Additive bilingualism, schooling, and special education: A minority group perspective. *Canadian Journal for Exceptional Children, 3,* 109–114.

Langlois, J. H., & Roggman, L. A. (1990). Attractive faces are only average. *Psychological Science, 1,* 115–121.

Langlois, J. H., Roggman, L. A., & Rieser-Danner, L. A. (1990). Infants' differential social responses to attractive and unattractive faces. *Developmental Psychology, 26,* 153–159.

Langlois, J. H., Ritter, J. M., Roggman, L. A., & Vaughn, L. S., (1991). Facial diversity and infant preferences for attractive faces. *Developmental Psychology, 27,* 79–84.

Langlois, J. H., & Stephan, C. W. (1981). Beauty and the beast: The role of physical attractiveness in the development of peer relations and social behavior. In S. S. Brehm, S. M. Kassin, & F. X. Gibbons (Eds.), *Developmental social psychology.* New York: Oxford University Press.

Lapsley, D. K. (1990). Continuity and discontinuity in adolescent social cognitive development. In R. Montemayor, G. R. Adams, & T. P. Gullotta (Eds.), *Advances in adolescent development: Vol. 2. From childhood to adolescence: A transitional period?* Newbury Park, Calif.: Sage.

Larson, R., & Ham, M. (1993). Stress and "Storm and Stress" in early adolescence: The relationship of negative events with dysphoric affect. *Developmental Psychology, 29*, 130–140.

Laszlo, J. I. (1986). Development of perceptual motor abilities in children from 5 years to adults. In C. Pratt, A. F. Garton, W. E. Tunmer, & A. R. Nesdale (Eds.), *Research issues in child development.* Boston: Allen & Unwin.

Latané, R., & Darley, J. M. (1970). *The unresponsive bystander: Why doesn't he help?* New York: Appleton-Century-Crofts.

Lazar, I., Darlington, R., Murray, H., Royce, J., & Snipper, A. (1982). Lasting effects of early education: A report from the Consortium for Longitudinal Studies. *Monographs of the Society for Research in Child Development, 47*, no. 195.

Lazarus, R. S. (1993). From psychological stress to the emotions: A history of changing outlooks. *Annual Review of Psychology, 44*, 1–21.

Le monde au chevet de l'enfance menacée. (1990, September 29). *Le Monde,* p. 15.

Leboyer, F. (1975). *Birth without violence.* New York: Random House.

Ledoux, S., Choquet, M., & Manfredi, R. (1993). Associated factors for self-reported binge eating among male and female adolescents. *Journal of Adolescence, 16*, 75–91.

Lee, V. E., Brooks-Gunn, J., & Schnur, E. (1988). Does Head Start work? A 1-year follow-up comparison of disadvantaged children attending Head Start, no preschool, and other preschool programs. *Developmental Psychology, 24*, 210–222.

Lefkowitz, M., Eron, L., Walder, L., & Huesmann, L. R. (1972). Television violence and child aggression: A follow-up study. In G. A. Comstock & E. A. Rubinstein (Eds.), *Television and social behavior* (Vol. 3). Washington, D.C.: U.S. Government Printing Office.

Lefrançois, G. R. (1967). Jean Piaget's developmental model: Equilibration-through-adaptation. *Alberta Journal of Educational Research, 13*, 161–171.

Lefrançois, G. R. (1968). A treatment hierarchy for the acceleration of conservation of substance. *Canadian Journal of Psychology, 22*, 277–284.

Lefrançois, G. R. (1973). *Of children: An introduction to child development.* Belmont, Calif.: Wadsworth.

Lefrançois, G. R. (1983). *Psychology* (2nd ed.). Belmont, Calif.: Wadsworth.

Legerstee, M. (1991). Changes in the quality of infant sounds as a function of social and nonsocial stimulation. *First Language, 11*, 327–343.

Leinbach, M. D., & Fagot, B. I. (1986). Acquisition of gender labels: A test for toddlers. *Sex Roles, 15*, 655–667.

Lenneberg, E. H. (1969). On explaining language. *Science, 164*, 635–643.

Leon, M. (1992). The neurobiology of learning. *Annual Review of Psychology, 43*, 377–398.

Lerner, R. M. (1985). Individual and context in developmental psychology: Conceptual and theoretical issues. In J. R. Nesselroade & A. Von Eye (Eds.), *Individual development and social change: Explanatory analysis* (pp. 155–188). New York: Academic Press.

Lerner, R. M. (1987). The concept of plasticity in development. In J. J. Gallagher & C. T. Ramey (Eds.), *The malleability of children.* Baltimore: Brookes.

Lerner, R. M. (1991). Changing organism-context relations as the basic process of development: A developmental contextual perspective. *Developmental Psychology, 27*, 27–32.

Lerner, R. M., (1993). The demise of the nature-nurture dichotomy. *Human Development, 36*, 119–124.

Lerner, R. M., & Korn, S. J. (1972). The development of body-build stereotypes in males. *Child Development, 43*, 908–920.

Lerner, R. M., Lerner, J. V., Winelle, M., Hooker, K., Lenez, K., and others. (1986). Children and adolescents in their contexts: Tests of the goodness of fit model. In R. Plomin & J. Dunn (Eds.), *The study of temperament: Changes, continuities and challenges.* Hillsdale, N.J.: Lawrence Erlbaum.

Lerner, R. M., & Shea, J. A. (1982). Social behavior in adolescence. In B. B. Wolman and others (Eds.), *Handbook of developmental psychology.* Englewood Cliffs, N.J.: Prentice-Hall.

Leslie, A. M. (1988). Some implications of pretense for mechanisms underlying the child's theory of mind. In J. W. Astington, P. L. Harris, & D. R. Olson (Eds.), *Developing theories of mind.* New York: Cambridge University Press.

Lesser, H. (1977). *Television and the preschool child: A psychological theory of instruction and curriculum development.* New York: Academic Press.

Levine, J. M., Resnick, L. B., & Higgins, E. T. (1993). Social foundations of cognition. *Annual Review of Psychology, 44*, 585–612.

Levine, R. A. (1987). Women's schooling, patterns of fertility, and child survival. *Educational Researcher, 16,* 21–27.

Levitt, M. J., Guacci, N., & Coffman, S. (1993). Social network relations in infancy: An observational study. *Merrill-Palmer Quarterly, 39,* 233–251.

Levy, G. D. (1993). Introduction: An integrated collection on early gender-role development. *Developmental Review, 13,* 123–125.

Levy, G. D., & Fivush, R. (1993). Scripts and gender: A new approach for examining gender-role development. *Developmental Review, 13,* 126–146.

Lewin, R. (1975, September). Starved brains. *Psychology Today,* 29–33.

Lewis, M., & Lee-Painter, S. (1974). An interactional approach to the mother–infant dyad. In M. Lewis & L. A. Rosenblum (Eds.), *The effect of an infant on its caregiver.* New York: John Wiley.

Lewis, M., Sullivan, M. W., & Vasen, A. (1987). Making faces: Age and emotion differences in the posing of emotional expressions. *Developmental Psychology, 23,* 690–697.

Liben, L. (1975). *Perspective-taking skills in young children: Seeing the world through rose-colored glasses.* Paper presented at the meeting of the Society for Research in Child Development, Denver, April.

Liberty, C., & Ornstein, P. A. (1973). Age differences in organization and recall: The effects of training in categorization. *Journal of Experimental Child Psychology, 15,* 169–186.

Lieberman, A. B. (1987). *Giving birth.* New York: St. Martin's Press.

Liebert, R. M., & Schwartzberg, N. S. (1977). Effects of mass media. In M. R. Rosenzweig & L. W. Porter (Eds.), *Annual review of psychology*

(Vol. 28). Palo Alto, Calif: Annual Reviews.

Lieblich, A. (1982). *Kibbutz Makom: Report from an Israeli kibbutz.* London: André Deutsch.

Liggins, G. C. (1988). The onset of labor: An historical review. In C. T. Jones (Ed.), *Research in perinatal medicine (VII): Fetal and neonatal development.* Ithaca, N.Y.: Perinatology Press.

Liljeström, R. (1982). The family in China yesterday and today. In R. Liljeström, E. Norén-Björn, G. Schyl-Bjurman, B. Öhrn, L. H. Gustasfsson, & O. Löfgren (Eds.), *Young children in China.* Clevedon, Avon, England: Multilingual Matters Ltd.

Linn, M. C., & Hyde, J. S. (1989). Gender, mathematics, and science. *Educational Researcher, 18,* 17–27.

Lipsitt, L. P. (1982). Infant learning. In T. M. Field, A. Huston, H. C. Quay, L. Troll, & G. E. Finley (Eds.), *Review of human development.* New York: John Wiley.

Lipsitt, L. P., Engen, T., & Kaye, H. (1963). Developmental changes in the olfactory threshold of the neonate. *Child Development, 34,* 371–376.

Liu, D. T. (1991). Introduction and historical perspectives. In D. T. Liu (Ed.), *A practical guide to chorion villus sampling.* New York: Oxford University Press.

Lockhart, A. S. (1980). Motor learning and motor development during infancy and childhood. In C. B. Corbin (Ed.), *A textbook of motor development.* Dubuque, Iowa: Wm. C. Brown.

Loehlin, J. C. (1985). Fitting heredity-environment models jointly to twin and adoption data from the Califor-

nia Psychological Inventory. *Behavior Genetics, 15,* 199–221.

Loehlin, J. C., Willerman, L., & Horn, J. M. (1988). Human behavior genetics. *Annual Review of Psychology, 39,* 101–133.

Long, L., & Long, T. (1983). *The handbook for latchkey children and their parents.* New York: Arbor House.

Long, V. O. (1991). Gender role conditioning and women's self-concept. *Journal of Humanistic Education and Development, 30,* 19–29.

Lorenz, K. (1952). *King Solomon's ring.* London: Methuen.

Love, H., & Walthall, J. E. (1977). *A handbook of medical, educational, and psychological information for teachers of physically handicapped children.* Springfield, Ill.: Charles C. Thomas.

Lowery, C. R., & Settle, S. A. (1985). Effects of divorce on children: Differential impact of custody and visitation patterns. *Family Relations, 34,* 455–463.

Lozoff, B. (1989). Nutrition and behavior. *American Psychologist, 44,* 231–236.

Lynn, D. B. (1974). *The father: His role in child development.* Monterey, Calif.: Brooks/Cole.

Lynn, D. B. (1979). *Daughters and parents: Past, present and future.* Monterey, Calif.: Brooks/Cole.

Maccoby, E. E., & Jacklin, C. N. (1974). *The psychology of sex differences.* Stanford, Calif.: Stanford University Press.

Maccoby, E. E., & Jacklin, C. N. (1980). Sex differences in aggression: A rejoinder and reprise. *Child Development, 51,* 964–980.

Macfarlane, A. (1975). Olfaction in the development of social preferences in the human neonate. In Proceedings of CIBA Foundation Symposium, *Parent-infant interaction.* Amsterdam: Elsevier.

Macmillan, D. L., Keogh, B. K., & Jones, R. L. (1986). Special educational reasearch on mildly handicapped learners. In M. C. Wittrock (Ed.), *Handbook of research on teaching* (3rd ed.). New York: Macmillan.

Madsen, M. C. (1971). Developmental and cross-cultural differences in the cooperation and competitive behavior of young children. *Journal of Cross-Cultural Psychology, 2,* 365–371.

Madsen, M. C., & Lancy, D. F. (1981). Cooperative and competitive behavior: Experiments related to ethnic identity and urbanization in Papua, New Guinea. *Journal of Cross-Cultural Psychology, 12,* 389–409.

Magnusson, D., & Backteman, G. (1978). Longitudinal stability of person characteristics: Intelligence and creativity. *Applied Psychological Measurement, 2,* 481–490.

Malina, R. M. (1990). Physical growth and performance during the transitional years (9 to 16). In R. Montemayor, G. R. Adams, & T. P. Gullotta (Eds.), *Advances in adolescent development: Vol. 2. From childhood to adolescence: A transitional period?* Newbury Park, Calif.: Sage.

Malina, R. M., & Bouchard, C. (1988). Subcutaneous fat distribution during growth. In C. Bouchard & F. E. Johnston (Eds.), *Fat distribution during growth and later health outcomes.* New York: Liss.

Mandler, J. M. (1984). Representation and recall in infancy. In M. Moscovitch (Ed.), *Infant memory.* New York: Plenum Press.

Marcia, J. E. (1966). Development and validation of ego-identity status. *Journal of Personality and Social Psychology, 3,* 551–558.

Marcia, J. E. (1980). Identity in adolescence. In J. Adelson (Ed.), *Handbook of adolescent psychology.* New York: Wiley.

Marcia, J. E., & Friedman, M. L. (1970). Ego identity status in college women. *Journal of Personality, 39,* 249–269.

Marlatt, G. A., Baer, J. S., Donovan, D. M., & Kivlahan, D. R. (1988). Addictive behaviors: Etiology and treatment. *Annual Review of Psychology, 39,* 223–252.

Marsh, H. W. (1989). Sex differences in the development of verbal and mathematics constructs: The high school and beyond study. *American Educational Research Journal, 26,* 191–225.

Marsh, H. W., & Holmes, I. W. MacDonald (1990). Multidimensional self-concepts: Construct validation of responses by children. *American Educational Research Journal, 27,* 89–117.

Marsiglio, W. (1986). Teenage fatherhood: High school accreditation and educational attainment. In A. B. Elster & M. E. Lamb (Eds.), *Adolescent fatherhood.* Hillsdale, N.J.: Lawrence Erlbaum.

Marston, A. R., Jacobs, D. F., Singer, R. D., Widaman, K. F., & Little, T. D. (1988). Characteristics of adolescents at risk for compulsive overeating on a brief screening test. *Adolescence, 23,* 288–302.

Martin, H. (1976). *The abused child.* Cambridge, Mass.: Ballinger.

Martin, N., & Jardine, R. (1986). Eysenck's contributions to behaviour genetics. In S. Modgil & C. Modgil (Eds.), *Hans Eysenck: Consensus and controversy.* Philadelphia: Falmer.

Masi, W., & Scott, K. (1983). Preterm and full-term infants' visual responses. In T. F. Sostek & A. Sostek, (Eds.), *Infants born at risk: Physiological, perceptual and cognitive process.* New York: Grune and Stratton.

Maslow, A. H. (1970). *Motivation and personality (2nd ed.).* New York: Harper & Row.

Mason, W. A., & Kenney, M. D. (1974). Redirection of filial attachments in rhesus monkeys: Dogs as mother surrogates. *Science, 183,* 1209–1211.

Masters, J. C. (1979). Interpreting "imitative" responses in early infancy. *Science, 205,* 215.

Masters, W. H., Johnson, V. E., & Kolodny, R. C. (1988). *Crisis: Heterosexual behavior in the age of AIDS.* New York: Grove Press.

Mayer, N. K., & Tronick, E. Z. (1985). Mother's turn-giving signals and infant turn-taking in mother-infant interaction. In T. M. Field & N. A. Fox (Eds.), *Social perception in infants.* Norwood, N.J.: Ablex.

Maxim, G. W., (1993). *The very young* (4th ed.). Columbus, Ohio: Merrill.

Mazur, A. (1977). On Wilson's sociobiology. *American Journal of Sociology, 83,* 697–700.

McCabe, M. P. (1991). Influence of creativity and intelligence on academic performance. *The Journal of Creative Behavior, 25,* 116–122.

McCall, R. B., Applebaum, M. I., & Hogarty, F. S. (1973). Developmental changes in mental test performance. *Monographs of the Society for Research in Child Development, 38,* No. 150.

McCartney, K., Bernieri, F., & Harris, M. J. (1990). Growing up and growing apart. A developmental meta-analysis of twin studies. *Psychological Bulletin, 107,* 226–237.

McCartney, K., & Howley, E. (1992). Parents as instruments of intervention in home-based preschool programs. In L. Okagaki & R. J. Sternberg (Eds.), *Directors of development: Influences on the development of children's thinking.* Hillsdale, N.J.: Lawrence Erlbaum.

654

McCartney, K., & Jordan, E. (1990). Parallels between research on child care and research on school effects. *Educational Researcher, 19,* 21–27.

McClelland, D. C. (1973). Testing for competence rather than for "intelligence." *American Psychologist, 28,* 1–14.

McClelland, D., Constantian, C. S., Regalado, D., & Stone, C. (1978, June). Making it to maturity. *Psychology Today,* 42–53, 114.

McCormick, M., Shapiro, S., & Starfield, B. (1984). High-risk young mothers: Infant mortality and morbidity in four areas in the United States, 1973–1978. *American Journal of Public Health, 74,* 18–23.

McCune, L. (1993). The development of play as the development of consciousness. *New Directions for Child Development, 59,* 67–80.

McGillivray, B., & Hayden, M. R. (1992). Single gene alterations. In J. M. Friedman, F. J. Dill, M. R. Hayden, & B. C. McGillivray (Eds.), *Genetics.* Baltimore: Williams & Wilkins.

McGraw, M. B. (1943). *The neuromuscular maturation of the human infant.* New York: Columbia University Press.

McKay, J., Sinisterra, L., McKay, A., Gomez, H., & Lloreda, P. (1978). Improving cognitive ability in chronically deprived children. *Science, 200,* 270–278.

McGroarty, M. (1992). The societal context of bilingual education. *Educational Researcher, 21,* 7–9, 24.

McIlroy, A. (1993). Test can predict Alzheimer's victims. *Edmonton Journal,* September 18, p. B-1.

McNeil, D. (1970). *The acquisition of language: The study of developmental psycholinguistics.* New York: Harper & Row.

Mednick, S. A. (1962). The associative basis of the creative process. *Psychological Review, 69,* 220–232.

Melican, G. J., & Feldt, L. S. (1980). An empirical study of the Zajonc-Marcus hypothesis for achievement test scores declines. *American Educational Research Journal, 17,* 5–19.

Meline, C. W. (1976). Does the medium matter? *Journal of Communication, 26,* 81–89.

Meltzoff, A. N. (1988). Infant imitation after a 1-week delay: Long-term memory for novel acts and multiple stimuli. *Developmental Psychology, 24,* 470–476.

Meltzoff, A. N., & Moore, M. K. (1983). Newborn infants imitate adult facial gestures. *Child Development, 54,* 702–709.

Melzoff, A. N., & Moore, M. K. (1989). Imitation in newborn infants: Exploring the range of gestures imitated and the underlying mechanisms. *Developmental Psychology, 25,* 954–962.

Meneese, W. B., Yutrzenka, B. A., & Vitale, P. (1992). An analysis of adolescent suicidal ideation. *Current Psychology: Research & Reviews, 11,* 51–58.

Mercer, C. D. (1990). Learning disabilities. In N. G. Haring & L. McCormick (Eds.), *Exceptional children and youth* (5th ed.). Columbus, Ohio: Merrill.

Mesibov, G. B., & Van Bourgondien, M. E. (1992). Autism. In S. R. Hooper, G. W. Hynd, & R. E. Mattison, (Eds.), *Developmental disorders: Diagnostic criteria and clinical assessment.* Hillsdale, N.J.: Lawrence Erlbaum.

Meyer, W. J. (1985). Summary, integration, and prospective. In J. B. Dusek (Ed.), *Teacher expectancies.* Hillsdale, N.J.: Lawrence Erlbaum.

Mielke, K. W. (1983). Formative research on appeal and comprehension in 3-2-1 CONTACT. In J. Bryant & D. R. Anderson (Eds.), *Children's understanding of television: Research on attention and comprehension* (pp. 241–264). New York: Academic Press.

Miller, B. C., & Dyk, P. H. (1991). Community of caring effects on adolescent mothers: A program evaluation case study. *Family Relations, 40,* 386–395.

Miller, C. E., Edwards, J. G., Shipley, C. F., & Best, R. B. (1990). Assessment of routine amniocentesis for unexplained maternal serum alpha-fetoprotein elevations. In B. A. Fine, E. Getting, K. Greendale, B. Leopold, & N. W. Paul (Eds.), *Strategies in genetic counseling: Reproductive genetics and new technologies.* White Plains, N.Y.: March of Dimes Birth Defects Foundation.

Miller, G. A. (1956). The magical number seven, plus or minus two: Some limits on our capacity for processing information. *Psychological Review, 63,* 81–97.

Miller, L. B., & Bizzell, R. P. (1983). Long-term effects of four preschool programs: Sixth, seventh, and eighth grades. *Child Development, 54,* 727–741.

Miller, S. A. (1981). *Certainty and necessity in the understanding of Piagetian concepts.* Paper presented at the Society for Research in Child Development meetings, Boston, April.

Minister of Supply and Services Canada (1989). *Canada Yearbook (1990).* Ottawa: Statistic Canada.

Miyawaki, K., Strange, W., Verbrugge, R., Liberman, A. M., Jenkins, J. J., & Fujimura, O. (1975). An effect of linguistic experience: The discrimination of [r] and [l] by native speakers of Japanese and English. *Perception & Psychophysics, 18,* 331–340.

Moerk, E. L. (1991). Positive evidence for negative evidence. *First Language, 11*, 219–251.

Moffitt, A. R. (1971). Consonant cue perception by 20–24 week old infants. *Child Development, 42*, 717–731.

Monachesi, E. D., & Hathaway, S. R. (1969). The personality of delinquents. In J. N. Butcher (Ed.), *MMPI: Research developments and clinical applications.* New York: McGraw-Hill, 207–219.

Montemayor, R., & Eisen, M. (1977). The development of self-conceptions from childhood to adolescence. *Developmental Psychology, 13*, 314–319.

Montemayor, R., & Flannery, D. J. (1990). Making the transition from childhood to early adolescence. In R. Montemayor, G. R. Adams, & T. P. Gullotta (Eds.), *Advances in adolescent development: Vol. 2. From childhood to adolescence: A transitional period?* Newbury Park, Calif.: Sage.

Montemayor, R., & Van Komen, R. (1980). Age segregation of adolescents in and out of school. *Journal of Youth and Adolescence, 9*, 371–381.

Montessori, M. (1912). *The Montessori method.* New York: Frederick A. Stokes.

Moore, C., & Frye, D. (1991). The acquisition and utility of theories of mind. In D. Frye & C. Moore (Eds.), *Children's theories of mind: Mental states and social understanding.* Hillsdale N.J.: Lawrence Erlbaum.

Moore, R. C. (1986). *Childhood's domain: Play and place in child development.* London: Croom Helm.

Moray, N. (1959). Attention and dichotic listening: Affective cues and the influence of instruction. *Quarterly Journal of Experimental Psychology, 11*, 56–60.

Moriarty, A. (1990). Deterring the molester and abuser: Pre-employment testing for child and youth care workers. *Child and Youth Care Quarterly, 18*, 59–65.

Morrill, C. M., Leach, J. N., Shreeve, W. C., Radenaugh, M. R. & Linder, K. (1991). Teenage obesity: An academic issue. *International Journal of Adolescence and Youth, 2*, 245–250.

Morin, S. F. (1988). AIDS: The challenge to psychology. *American Psychologist, 43*, 838–842.

Morrison, E., Starks, K., Hyndman, C., & Ronzio, N. (1980). *Growing up sexual.* New York: Van Nostrand Reinhold.

Morsink, C. V. (1985). Learning disabilities. In W. H. Berdine & A. E. Blackhurst (Eds.), *An introduction to special education* (2nd ed.). Boston: Little, Brown.

Morton, J., & Johnson, M. H. (1991). CONSPEC and CONLERN: A two-process theory of infant face recognition. *Psychological Review, 98*, 164–181.

Moskowitz, B. A. (1978). The acquisition of language. *Scientific American, 239*, 92–108.

Mott, F. L. (1991). Developmental effects of infant care: The mediating role of gender and health. *Journal of Social Issues, 47*, 139–158.

Mowat, F. (1952). *People of the deer.* New York: Little, Brown.

Moynahan, E. D. (1973). The development of knowledge concerning the effect of categorization upon free recall. *Child Development, 44*, 238–245.

Mulcahy, B. F. (1991). Developing autonomous learners. *Alberta Journal of Educational Research, 37*, 385–397.

Mulhern, R. K., & Passman, R. H. (1979). The child's behavioral pattern as a determinant of maternal punitiveness. *Child Development, 15*, 417–423.

Mulhern, R. K., Jr., & Passman, R H. (1981). Parental discipline as affected by the sex of the parent, the sex of the child, and the child's apparent responsiveness to discipline. *Developmental Psychology, 17*, 604–613.

Mullin, J. B. (1992). Children prenatally exposed to cocaine and crack: Implications for schools. *B. C. Journal of Special Education, 16*, 282–289.

Mullis, R. L., Youngs, G. A., Jr., Mullis, A. K., & Rathge, R. W. (1993). Adolescent stress: Issues of measurement. *Adolescence, 28*, 280–290.

Murray, J., Henjum, R., & Freeze, R. (1992). Analysis of male and female experiences with abuse in family of origin. *Canadian Journal of Special Education, 8*, 90–100.

Muuss, R. E. (1975). *Theories of adolescence* (3rd ed.). New York: Random House.

Muuss, R. E. (1988). Carol Gilligan's theory of sex differences in the development of moral reasoning during adolescence. *Adolescence, 23*, 229–243.

Myers, P. I., & Hammill, D. D. (1990). *Learning disabilities: Basic concepts, assessment practices, and instructional strategies* (4th ed.). Austin, Tex.: Pro-Ed.

National Center for Health Statistics. (1987). *Advance report of final natality statistics, 1985.* Monthly vital statistics report (Vol. 36). Washington, D.C.: National Center for Health Statistics.

Neal, J. H. (1983). Children's understanding of their parents' divorces. In L. A. Kurdek (Ed.), *Children and divorce: New directions for child development.* San Francisco: Jossey-Bass, 3–14.

Nealis, J. T. (1983). Epilepsy. In J. Umbriet (Ed.), *Physical disabilities and health impairment: An introduction* (pp. 74–85). Columbus, Ohio: Charles E. Merrill.

Neiger, B. L., & Hopkins, R. W. (1988). Adolescent suicide: Character traits of high-risk teenagers. *Adolescence, 23*, 468–475.

Nelson, K. E. (1989). Strategies for first language teaching. In M. L. Rice & R. L. Schiefelbusch (Eds.), *Teachability of language*. Baltimore: Brookes.

Nesbitt, W. (1993). Self-esteem and moral virtue. *Journal of Moral Education, 22*, 51–54.

Neuman, S. B. (1991). *Literacy in the television age: The myth of the TV effect.* Norwood, N.J.: Ablex.

Newcomb, A. F., Bukowski, W. M., & Pattee, L. (1993). Children's peer relations: A meta-analytic review of popular, rejected, neglected, controversial, and average sociometric status. *Psychological Bulletin, 113*, 99–128.

Newcomb, M. D., & Bentler, P. M. (1988). *Consequences of adolescent drug use: Impact on the lives of young adults.* Newbury Park, Calif.: Sage.

Newcomb, M. D., & Bentler, P. M. (1989). Substance use and abuse among children and teenagers. *American Psychologist, 44*, 242–248.

Newsweek, January 6, 1969, p. 37.

Nicolopoulou, A. (1993). Play, cognitive development, and the social world: Piaget, Vygotsky, and beyond. *Human Development, 36*, 1–23.

Nielsen Television Index: Report on television usage. (1984). Hackensack, N.J.: A. C. Nielsen Co.

Norcia, A. M., & Tyler, C. W. (1985). Spatial frequency sweep VEP: Visual acuity during the first year of life. *Vision Research, 25*, 1399–1408.

Norén Björn, E. (1982). Welcome to the pre-school. In R. Liljeström, E. Norén-Björn, G. Schyl-Bjurman, B. Öhrn, L. H. Gustasfsson, & O. Löfgren (Eds.), *Young children in China.* Clevedon, Avon, England: Multilingual Matters Ltd.

Nucci, L., Guerra, N., & Lee, J. (1991). Adolescent judgments of the personal, prudential, and normative aspects of drug use. *Developmental Psychology, 27*, 841–848.

Nucci, L. P., & Turiel, E. (1978). Social interactions and the development of social concepts in preschool children. *Child Development, 49*, 400–407.

Nunner-Winkler, G. (1984). Two moralities? A critical discussion of an ethic of care and responsibility versus an ethic of rights and justice. In W. M. Kurtines & J. L. Gewirtz (Eds.), *Morality, moral behavior, and moral development.* New York: John Wiley.

O'Reilly, A. W., & Bornstein, M. H. (1993). Caregiver-child interaction in play. *New Directions for Child Development, 59*, 55–66.

Oatley, K. (1992). *Best laid schemes: The psychology of emotions.* New York: Cambridge University Press.

Oatley, K., & Jenkins, J. M. (1992). Human emotions: Function and dysfunction. *Annual Review of Psychology, 32*, 55–85.

Ohuche, R. O., & Otaalam, B. (Eds.). (1981). *The African child and his environment.* New York: Pergamon Press.

Oden, M. (1968). The fulfillment of promise: 40-year follow-up of the Terman gifted group. In R. S. Albert (Ed.), *Genius and eminence: The social psychology of creativity and exceptional achievement.* New York: Oxford University Press (1983).

Oden, S. (1988). Alternative perspectives on children's peer relationships. In

T. D. Yawkey & J. E. Johnson (Eds.), *Integrative processes and socialization: Early to middle childhood.* Hillsdale, N.J.: Lawrence Erlbaum.

Offer, D., & Offer, J. (1975). *From teenage to young manhood: A psychological study.* New York: Basic Books.

Offer, D. O., Ostrov, E., Howard, K. (1981). *The adolescent: A psychological self-portrait.* New York: Basic Books.

Offer, D. O., Ostrov, E., Howard, K. (1984). *Patterns of adolescent self-image.* San Francisco: Jossey-Bass.

Offer, D. O., Ostrov, E., Howard, K., & Atkinson, R. (1988). *The teenage world: Adolescents' self-image in ten countries.* New York: Plenum Press.

Olson, D. R. (1986). The cognitive consequences of literacy. *Canadian Psychology, 27*, 109–121.

Opper, S. (1977). Concept development in Thai urban and rural children. In P. R. Dasen (Ed.), *Piagetian psychology: Cross-cultural contributions.* New York: Gardner Press.

Ornstein, P. A., Baker-Ward, L., & Naus, M. J. (1988). The development of mnemonic skill. In F. E. Weinert & M. Perlmutter (Eds.), *Memory development: Universal changes and individual differences.* Hillsdale, N.J.: Lawrence Erlbaum.

Oster, H., Daily, L., & Goldenthal, P. (1989). Processing facial affect. In A. W. Young & H. D. Ellis (Eds.), *Handbook of research on face processing.* Amsterdam: North Holland.

Overton, W. F. (1973). On the assumptive base of the nature-nurture controversy: Additive versus interactive conceptions. *Human Development, 16*, 74–89.

Packard, V. (1968). *The sexual wilderness.* New York: Pocket Books.

Packard, V. (1983). *Our endangered children: Growing up in a changing world.* Boston: Little, Brown.

Padilla, A. M. (1991). English only vs. bilingual education: Ensuring a language-competent society. *Journal of Education, 173,* 38–51.

Page, E. B., & Grandon, G. M. (1979). Family configuration and mental ability. Two theories contrasted with U.S. data. *American Educational Research Journal, 16,* 257–272.

Paikoff, R. L., & Brooks-Gunn, J. (1991). Do parent-child relationships change during puberty? *Psychological Bulletin, 110,* 47–66.

Paley, V. G. (1984). *Boys and girls: Superheroes in the doll corner.* Chicago: University of Chicago Press.

Paley, V. G. (1986). *Mollie is three: Growing up in School.* Chicago: University of Chicago Press.

Pallas, A. M., Natriello, G., & McDill, E. L. (1989). The changing nature of the disadvantaged population: Current dimensions and future trends. *Educational Researcher, 18,* 16–22.

Paris, S. G., & Lindauer, B. K. (1976). The role of inference in children's comprehension and memory for sentences. *Cognitive Psychology, 8,* 217–227.

Paris, S. G., & Lindauer, B. K. (1982). Cognitive development in infancy. In B. B. Wolman and others (Eds.), *Handbook of developmental psychology.* Englewood Cliffs, N.J.: Prentice-Hall.

Park, K. A., Lay, K. L., & Ramsay, L. (1993). Individual differences and developmental changes in preschoolers' friendship. *Developmental Psychology, 29,* 264–270.

Parke, R. D. (1970). The role of punishment in the socialization process. In R. A. Hoppe, G. A. Milton, & E. C. Simmel (Eds.), *Early experiences and the process of socialization.* New York: Academic Press.

Parke, R. D. (1979). Perspectives on father-infant interaction. In J. D. Osofsky (Ed.), *Handbook of infant development.* New York: John Wiley.

Parke, R. D., MacDonald, K. B., Burks, V. M., Carson, J., Bhavnagri, N., et al. (1989). Family and peer systems: In search of linkages. In K. Kreppner & R. M. Lerner (Eds.), *Family systems of life span development.* Hillsdale, N.J.: Lawrence Erlbaum.

Parker, J. G., & Asher, S. R. (1993). Friendship and friendship quality in middle childhood: Links with peer group acceptance and feelings of loneliness and social dissatisfaction. *Developmental Psychology, 29,* 611–621.

Parnes, S. J., & Harding, H. E. (Eds.). (1961). *A source-book for creative thinking.* New York: Charles Scribner's.

Parten, M. B. (1932). Social participation among preschool children. *Journal of Abnormal Social Psychology, 27,* 243–270.

Pasley, K., Dollahite, D. C., & Ihinger-Tallman, M. (1993). Bridging the gap: Clinical applications of research findings on the spouse and stepparent roles in remarriage. *Family Relations, 42,* 315–322.

Passino, A. W., Whitman, T. L., Borkowski, J. G., Schellenbach, C. J., Maxwell, S. E., Keogh, D., & Rellinger, E. (1993). Personal adjustment during pregnancy and adolescent parenting. *Adolescence, 28,* 67–79.

Passman, R. H. (1974). *The effects of mothers and security blankets upon learning in children (Should Linus bring his blanket to school?).* Paper presented at the American Psychological Association Convention, New Orleans, September.

Passman, R. H. (1976). Arousal reducing properties of attachment objects: Testing the functional limits of the security blanket relative to the mother. *Developmental Psychology, 12,* 468–469.

Passman, R. H. (1977). Providing attachment objects to facilitate learning and reduce distress: Effects of mothers and security blankets. *Developmental Psychology, 12,* 25–28.

Passman, R. H. (1987). Attachments to inanimate objects: Are children who have security blankets insecure? *Journal of Consulting and Clinical Psychology, 55,* 825–830.

Passman, R. H., & Adams, R. E. (1982). Preferences for mothers and security blankets and their effectiveness as reinforcers for young children's behaviors. *Journal of Child Psychology and Psychiatry, 23,* 223–236.

Passman, R. H., & Erck, T. W. (1978). Permitting maternal contact through vision alone: Films of mothers for promoting play and locomotion. *Developmental Psychology, 14,* 512–516.

Passman, R. H., & Halonen, J. S. (1979). A developmental survey of young children's attachments to inanimate objects. *The Journal of Genetic Psychology, 134,* 165–178.

Passman, R. H., & Longeway, K. P. (1982). The role of vision in maternal attachment: Giving 2-year-olds a photograph of their mother during separation. *Developmental Psychology, 18,* 530–533.

Passman, R. H., & Weisberg, P. (1975). Mothers and blankets as agents for promoting play and exploration by young children in a novel environment: The effects of social and nonsocial attachment objects. *Development Psychology, 11,* 170–177.

Patton, J. M., Prillaman, D., & Tassel-Baska, J. V. (1990). The nature and extent of programs for the disadvantaged gifted in the United States and Territories. *Gifted Child Quarterly, 34,* 94–96.

Patton, J. R., & Polloway, E. A. (1990). Mild mental retardation. In N. G. Haring & L. McCormick (Eds.), *Exceptional children and youth* (5th ed.). Columbus, Ohio: Merrill.

Pavlov, I. P. (1927). *Conditioned reflexes.* London: Oxford University Press.

Pazulinec, R., Meyerrose, M., & Sajwaj, T. (1983). Punishment via response cost. In S. Axelrod & J. Apsche (Eds.), *The effects of punishment on human behavior.* New York: Academic Press.

Pearce, J. C. (1977). *Magical child: Rediscovering nature's plan for our children.* New York: Bantam Books.

Pearl, R., Bryan, T., & Herzog, A. (1990). Resisting or acquiescing to peer pressure to engage in misconduct: Adolescents' expectations of probable consequences. *Journal of Youth and Adolescence, 19.* 43–55.

Pearson, J. L., & Ferguson, L. R. (1989). Gender differences in patterns of spatial ability, environmental cognition, and math and English achievement in late adolescence. *Adolescence, 24,* 421–431.

Pease-Alvarez, L., & Hakuta, K. (1992). Enriching our views of bilingualism and bilingual education. *Educational Researcher, 2,* 4–6.

Penner, L. A., Thompson, J. K., & Coovert, D. L. (1991). Size overestimation among anorexics: Much ado about very little? *Journal of Abnormal Psychology, 100,* 90–93.

Pergament, E. (1990). Reproductive genetics in the 21st century: Fact and fantasy. In B. A. Fine, E. Getting, K. Greendale, B. Lepold, & N. W. Paul (Eds.), *Strategies in genetic counseling: Reproductive genetics and new technologies,* White Plains, N.Y.: March of Dimes Birth Defects Foundation.

Perkins, D., Jay, E., & Tishman, S. (1993). Introduction: New conceptions of thinking. *Educational Psychologist, 28,* 1–5.

Perlmutter, M. (1980). Development of memory in the preschool years. In R. Greene & T. D. Yawkey (Eds.), *Childhood development.* Westport, Conn.: Technomic Publishing.

Perner, J. (1991). On representing that: The asymmetry between belief and desire in children's theory of mind. In D. Frye & C. Moore (Eds.), *Children's theories of mind: Mental states and social understanding.* Hillsdale N.J.: Lawrence Erlbaum.

Peskin, H. (1973). Influence of the developmental schedule of puberty on learning and ego functioning. *Journal of Youth and Adolescence, 2,* 273–290.

Petersen, A. C. (1988). Adolescent development. *Annual Review of Psychology, 39,* 583–607.

Peterson, C., & Peterson, R. (1986). Parent-child interaction and daycare: Does quality of daycare matter? *Journal of Applied Developmental Psychology, 7,* 1–15.

Peterson, G. W., Leigh, G. K., & Day, R. D. (1984). Family stress theory and the impact of divorce on children. *Journal of Divorce, 7,* 1–20.

Phillips, D., McCartney, K., & Scarr, S. (1987). Childcare quality and children's social development. *Developmental Psychology, 23,* 537–543.

Piaget, J. (1923). *Le langage et la pensée chez l'enfant.* London: Kegan Paul.

Piaget, J. (1932). *The moral judgment of the child.* London: Kegan Paul.

Piaget, J. (1951). *Play, dreams and imitation in childhood.* New York: W. W. Norton.

Piaget, J. (1954). *The construction of reality in the child.* New York: Basic Books.

Piaget, J. (1961). The genetic approach to the psychology of thought. *Journal of Educational Psychology, 52,* 275–281.

Piaget, J., & Garcia, R. (1991). *Toward a logic of meanings.* Hillsdale N.J.: Lawrence Erlbaum.

Pianta, R. C., & Ball, R. M. (1993). Maternal social support as a predictor of child adjustment in kindergarten. *Journal of Applied Developmental Psychology, 14,* 107–120.

Pill, C. J. (1990). Stepfamilies: Redefining the family. *Family Relations, 39,* 186–193.

Pinchbeck, I., & Hewitt, M. (1973). *Children in English society* (Vol. II): *From the eighteenth century to the Children Act of 1948.* London: Routledge & Kegan Paul.

Pines, M. (1966). *Revolution in learning: The years from birth to six.* New York: Harper & Row.

Pines, M. (1975). In praise of the "invulnerables." *APA Monitor,* December, 7.

Pines, M. (1978, September). Invisible playmates. *Psychology Today,* 38–42, 106.

Pines, M. (1979, January). Superkids. *Psychology Today,* 53–63.

Pines, M. (1982, February). Baby, you're incredible. *Psychology Today,* 48–53.

Pipes, P. L., Bumbals, J., & Pritkin, R. (1985). Collecting and assessing food intake information. In P. L. Pipes (Ed.), *Nutrition in infancy and childhood.* St. Louis: Times-Mirror/Mosby.

Pipp, S., & Haith, M. M. (1984). Infant visual responses: Which metric predicts best? *Journal of Experimental Child Psychology, 38,* 373–399.

Pitcher, E. G., & Schultz, L. H. (1983). *Boys and girls at play: The development of sex roles.* New York: Praeger.

Plomin, R. (1987). Developmental behavioral genetics and infancy. In J. D. Osofsky (Ed.), *Handbook of infant development* (2nd ed.). New York: John Wiley.

Plomin, R. (1989). Environment and genes: Determinants of behavior. *American Psychologist, 44*, 105–111.

Pogrebin, L. C. (1980). *Growing up free: Raising your child in the 80's.* New York: McGraw-Hill.

Pogue-Geile, M. F., & Rose, R. J. (1985). Developmental genetic studies of adult personality. *Developmental Psychology, 21*, 547–557.

Polivy, J., & Herman, C. P. (1985). Dieting and binging. A causal analysis. *American Psychologist, 40*, 193–201.

Pollitt, E., Haas, J., & Levitsky, D. (Eds.). (1989). International conference on iron deficiency and behavioral development. *American Journal of Clinical Nutrition*, Vol. 50, No. 3.

Polson, B., & Newton, M. (1984). *Not my kid: A family's guide to kids and drugs.* New York: Arbor House.

Pope, A. W., Bierman, K. L., & Mumma, G. H. (1991). Aggression, hyperactivity, and inattention-immaturity: Behavior dimensions associated with peer rejection in elementary school boys. *Developmental Psychology, 27*, 663–671.

Pope, H. G., Hudson, J. I., Jurgelun-Todd, D., & Hudson, M. S. (1984). Prevalence of anorexia nervosa and bulimia in three student populations. *International Journal of Eating Disorders, 2*, 75–85.

Powell, M. B. (1991). Investigating and reporting child sexual abuse: Review and recommendations for clinical practice. *Australian Psychologist, 26*, 77–83.

Prado, W. (1958). *Appraisal of performance as a function of the relative-ego-involvement of children and adolescents.* Unpublished doctoral dissertation, University of Oklahoma.

Preemies' diet seen key to progress. (1988). *Edmonton Journal*, Feb. 1, p. C1.

Premack, A. J., & Premack, D. (1972). Teaching language to an ape. *Scientific American, 227*, 92–99.

Premack, D. (1965). Reinforcement theory. In D. Levine (Ed.), *Nebraska Symposium on Motivation* (Vol. 13). Lincoln: University of Nebraska Press.

Pressley, M., Forrest-Pressley, D., & Elliott-Faust, D. J. (1988). What is strategy instructional enrichment and how to study it: Illustrations from research on children's prose memory and comprehension. In F. E. Weinert & M. Perlmutter (Eds.), *Memory development: Universal changes and individual differences.* Hillsdale, N.J.: Lawrence Erlbaum.

Preyer, W. (1888–1889). *The mind of the child* (2 vols.). New York: Appleton Century. (First published in German, 1882.)

Provine, R. R., & Westerman, J. A. (1979). Crossing the midline: Limits of early eye-hand behavior. *Child Development, 50*, 804–814.

Putallaz, M., & Gottman, J. M. (1981). An interactional model of children's entry into peer groups. *Child Development, 52*, 986–994.

Quay, H. C. (1987). Intelligence. In H. C. Quay (Ed.), *Handbook of juvenile delinquency.* New York: John Wiley, 106–117.

Rabin, A. I., & Beit-Hallahmi, B. (1982). *Twenty years later: Kibbutz children grown up.* New York: Springer.

Randhawa, B. S. (1991). Gender differences in academic achievement: A closer look at mathematics. *Alberta Journal of Educational Research, 37*, 241–257.

Rank, O. (1929). *The trauma of birth.* New York: Harcourt Brace & World.

Ranney, M. D. (1991). SIDS and parents. In C. A. Corr, H. Fuller, C. A. Barnickol, & D. M. Corr (Eds.), *Sudden infant death syndrome: Who can help and how.* New York: Springer.

Ray, W. Z., & Ravizza, R. (1985). *Methods toward a science of behavior and experience* (2nd ed.). Belmont, Calif.: Wadsworth.

Rayburn, W., Wilson, G., Schreck, J., Louwsma, G., & Hamman, J. (1982). Prenatal counseling: A state-wide telephone service. *Obstetrics and Gynecology, 60*, 243–246.

Rayna, S., Sinclair, H., & Stambak, M. (1989). Infants and physics. In H. Sinclair, M. Stambak, I. Lézine, S. Rayna, & M. Verba (Eds.), *Infants and objects: The creativity of cognitive development.* New York: Academic Press.

Rebok, G. W., & Balcerak, L. J. (1989). Memory self-efficacy and performance differences in young and old adults: The effect of mnemonic training. *Developmental Psychology, 25*, 714–721.

Recommended Dietary Allowances (9th ed.). 1980. Washington, D.C.: National Academy of Sciences.

Redmond, M. (1985). Attitudes of adolescent males toward adolescent pregnancy and fatherhood. *Family Relations, 34*, 337–342.

Reid, L. D., & Carpenter, D. J. (1990). Alcohol-abuse and alcoholism. In L. D. Reid (Ed.), *Opioids, bulimia, and alcohol abuse & alcoholism.* New York: Springer-Verlag.

Reschly, D. J. (1990). Adaptive behavior. In A. Thomas & J. Grimes (Eds.), *Best practices in school psychology* (2nd ed.). Washington, D.C.: National Association of School Psychologists.

Reschly, D. J. (1992). Mental retardation: Conceptual foundations, definitional criteria, and diagnostic operations. In S. R. Hooper, G. W. Hynd, & R. E. Mattison, (Eds.), *Developmental disorders: Diagnostic criteria and clinical assessment.* Hillsdale, N.J.: Lawrence Erlbaum.

Reiss, I. L. (1966). *The social context of premarital sexual permissiveness.* New York: Holt, Rinehart & Winston.

Reissland, N. (1988). Neonatal imitation in the first hour of life: Observations in rural Nepal. *Developmental Psychology, 24,* 464–469.

Rescorla, L. (1991). Early academics: Introduction to the debate. *New Directions for Child Development, 53,* 5–11.

Reynolds, P. (1989). *Childhood in crossroads: Cognition and society in South Africa.* Grand Rapids, Mich.: Wm. B. Eerdmans.

Reyome, N. D. (1993). A comparison of the school performance of sexually abused, neglected and non-maltreated children. *Child Study Journal, 23,* 17–38.

Rheingold, H. L. (1985). Development as the acquisition of familiarity. *Annual Review of Psychology, 36,* 1–17.

Rheingold, H. L., & Cook, K. V. (1975). The contents of boys' and girls' rooms as an index of parents' behavior. *Child Development, 46,* 459–463.

Ricciuti, H. N. (1991). Malnutrition and cognitive development: Research-policy linkages and current research directions. In L. Okagaki & R. J. Sternberg (Eds.), *Directors of development: Influences on the development of children's thinking.* Hillsdale, N.J.: Lawrence Erlbaum.

Ricco, R. B. (1993). Revising the logic of operations as a relevance logic: From hypothesis testing to explana-

tion. *Human Development, 36,* 125–146.

Rice, B. (1982, February). The Hawthorne defect: Persistence of a flawed theory. *Psychology Today,* 71–74.

Rice, M. (1983). The role of television in language acquisition. *Developmental Review, 3,* 211–224.

Rice, M. L. (1989). Children's language acquisition. *American Psychologist, 44,* 149–156.

Richards, L. N., & Schmeige, C. J. (1993). Problems and strengths of single-parent families: Implications for practice and policy. *Family Relations, 42,* 277–285.

Ridley-Johnson, R., Surdy, T., & O'Laughlin, E. (1991). Parent survey on television violence viewing: Fear, aggression, and sex differences. *Journal of Applied Developmental Psychology, 12,* 63–71.

Ringler, N. M., Kennell, J. H., Jarvella, R., Navojosky, B. J., & Klaus, M. H. (1975). Mother to child speech at two years: Effects of early post-natal contact. *Journal of Pediatrics, 86,* 141–144.

Ringwalt, C. L., & Palmer, J. H. (1989). Cocaine and crack users compared. *Adolescence, 24,* 851–859.

Ritts, V., Patterson, M. L., & Tubbs, M. E. (1992). Expectations, impressions, and judgments of physically attractive students: A review. *Review of Educational Research, 62,* 413–426.

Roazen, P. (1975). *Freud and his followers.* New York: Alfred A. Knopf.

Roberts, D. F., & Bachan, C. M. (1981). Mass communication effects. *Annual Review of Psychology, 32,* 307–356.

Robinson, S. (1989). Caring for childbearing women: The interrelationship between midwifery and medical responsibilities. In S. Robinson &

A. M. Thomson (Eds.), *Midwives, research and childbirth* (Vol. 1). New York: Chapman and Hall.

Rochat, P. (1989). Object manipulation and exploration in 2- to 5-month-old infants. *Developmental Psychology, 25,* 871–884.

Roche, A. F., Lipman, R. S., Overall, J. E., & Hung, W. (1979). The effects of stimulant medication on the growth of hyperkinetic children. *Pediatrics, 63,* 847–850.

Roche, J. P., & Ramsbey, T. W. (1993). Premarital sexuality: A five-year follow-up study of attitudes and behavior by dating stage. *Adolescence, 28,* 67–80.

Rodeck, C. H. (1982). Fetal blood sampling. In H. Galjaard (Ed.), *The future of prenatal diagnosis.* London: Churchill Livingstone, 85–92.

Roethlisberger, S. J., & Dickson, W. J. (1939). *Management and the worker.* Cambridge, Mass.: Harvard University Press.

Roffwarg, H. P., Muzio, J. N., & Dement, W. C. (1966). Ontogenetic development of the human sleep-dream cycle. *Science, 152.* 604–619.

Rogers, C. R. (1951). *Client-centered therapy: Its current practice, implications, and theory.* Boston: Houghton Mifflin.

Rolison, M. A., & Medway, F. J. (1985). Teachers' expectations and attributions for student achievement: Effects of label, performance pattern, and special education intervention. *American Educational Research Journal, 22,* 561–573.

Romig, C. A., & Bakken, L. (1990). Teens at risk for pregnancy: The role of ego development and family processes. *Journal of Adolescents, 13,* 195–199.

Roosa, M. W. (1991). Adolescent pregnancy programs collection: An introduction. *Family Relations, 40*, 370–372.

Roscoe, B., & Kruger, T. L. (1990). AIDS: Late adolescents' knowledge and its influence on sexual behavior. *Adolescence, 25*, 39–48.

Rosenak, D., Diamant, Y. Z., Yaffe, H., & Hornstein, E. (1990). Cocaine: Maternal use during pregnancy and its effect on the mother, the fetus, and the infant. *Obstetrical and Gynecological Survey, 45*, 348–357.

Rosenblatt, R. (1984). *Children of war.* New York: Anchor Books.

Rosengren, K. E., & Windahl, S. (1989). *Media matter: TV use in childhood and adolescence.* Norwood, N.J.: Ablex.

Rosenkoetter, L. I., Huston, A. C., & Wright, J. C. (1990). Television and the moral judgment of the young child. *Journal of Applied Developmental Psychology, 11*, 123–137.

Rosenthal, R., & Jacobson, L. (1968a). *Pygmalion in the classroom: Teacher expectations and pupils' intellectual development.* New York: Holt, Rinehart & Winston.

Rosenthal, R., & Jacobson, L. (1968b). Teacher expectations for the disadvantaged. *Scientific American, 218*, 19–23.

Rosenthal, T. L., & Zimmerman, B. J. (1972). Modeling by exemplification and instruction in training conservation. *Developmental Psychology, 6*, 392–401.

Rosett, H. L., & Sander, L. W. (1979). Effects of maternal drinking on neonatal morphology and state regulation. In J. D. Osofsky (Ed.), *Handbook of infant development.* New York: John Wiley, 809–836.

Ross, A. O. (1980). *Psychological disorders of children: A behavioral approach to theory, research, and therapy* (2nd ed.). New York: McGraw-Hill.

Ross, H. S. (1982). Establishment of social games among toddlers. *Developmental Psychology, 18, 509–518.*

Rothstein, E. (1980). The scar of Sigmund Freud. *New York Review of Books*, October 9, 14–20.

Rousseau, J. J. (1911). *Emile, or on education* (Barbara Foxley, Trans.). London: Dent. (Originally published, 1762.)

Rovee-Collier, C. K. (1987). Learning and memory in infancy. In J. D. Osofsky (Ed.), *Handbook of infant development.* New York: John Wiley.

Rovee-Collier, C. K., Sullivan, M. W., Enright, M. L., Lucas, D., & Fagen, J. W. (1980). Reactivation of infant memory. *Science, 208*, 1159–1161.

Royal College of Psychiatrists. (1987). *Drug scenes: A report on drugs and drug dependence by the Royal College of Psychiatrists.* London: Gaskell Press.

Royer, J. M., Cisero, C. A., & Carlo, M. S. (1993). Techniques and procedures for assessing cognitive skills. *Review of Educational Research, 63*, 201–243.

Rubin, J. Z., Provenzano, J. J., & Luria, Z. (1974). The eye of the beholder: Parent's views on sex of newborns. *American Journal of Orthopsychiatry, 44*, 512–519.

Rubin, K. H., Maioni, T. L., & Hornung, M. (1976). Free play behaviors in middle- and lower-class preschoolers: Parten and Piaget revisited. *Child Development, 47*, 414–419.

Rubin, Z. (1980). *Children's friendships.* Cambridge, Mass.: Harvard University Press.

Ruff, H. A., & Saltarelli, L. M. (1993). Exploratory play with objects: Basic cognitive processes and individual differences. *New Directions for Child Development, 59*, 5–16.

Ruffman, T., Olson, D. R., Ash, T., & Keenan, T. (1993). The ABCs of deception: Do young children understand deception in the same way as adults? *Developmental Psychology, 29*, 74–87.

Runco, M. A. (1986a). Maximal performance on divergent thinking tests by gifted, talented, and nongifted children. *Psychology in the Schools, 23*, 308–315.

Runco, M. A. (1986b). Flexibility and originality in children's divergent thinking. *The Journal of Psychology, 120*, 345–352.

Runco, M. A., & Albert, R. S. (1986). Exceptional giftedness in early adolescence and intrafamilial divergent thinking. *Journal of Youth and Adolescence, 15*, 335–344.

Rymer, R. (1993). *Genie: A scientific tragedy.* New York: Harper Perennial.

Saarnio, D. A. (1993). Scene memory in young children. *Merrill-Palmer Quarterly, 39*, 196–212.

Sabatino, D. A. (1991). *A fine line: When discipline becomes child abuse.* Blue Ridge Summit, Pa.: TAB Books.

Sachs, M. (1984). *The fat girl.* New York: Dutton.

Sagan, C. (1977). *The dragons of Eden.* New York: Ballantine Books.

Sagi, A., Ijzendoorn, M. H. Van, & Koren-Karie, N. (1991). Primary appraisal of the strange situation: A cross-cultural analysis of preseparation episodes. *Developmental Psychology, 27*, 587–596.

Sagov, S. E., Feinbloom, R. I., Spindel, P., & Brodsky, A. (1984). *Home births: A practitioner's guide to birth outside the hospital.* Rockville, Md.: Aspen Systems Corporation.

Saidla, D. D. (1992). Children's rights regarding physical abuse. *Journal of Humanistic Education and Development, 31,* 73–83.

Salomon, G., Perkins, D. N., & Globerson, T. (1991). Partners in cognition: Extending human intelligence with intelligent technologies. *Educational Researcher, 20,* 2–9.

Sameroff, A. J. (1968). The components of sucking in the human newborn. *Journal of Experimental Child Psychology, 6,* 607–623.

Savin-Williams, R. C., & Small, S. A. (1986). The timing of puberty and its relationship to adolescent and parent perceptions of family interactions. *Developmental Psychology, 22,* 342–347.

Scarr, S. (1985). Constructing psychology: Making facts and fables for our times. *American Psychologist, 40,* 499–512.

Scarr, S., & Eisenberg, M. (1993). Child care research: Issues, perspectives, and results. *Annual Review of Psychology, 44,* 613–644.

Scarr, S., & Salapatek, P. (1970). Patterns of fear development during infancy. *Merrill-Palmer Quarterly, 16,* 56–90.

Scarr, S., & Weinberg, R. A. (1983). The Minnesota Adoption Studies: Genetic differences and malleability. *Child Development, 54,* 260–267.

Scarr-Salapatek, S., & Williams, M. L. (1973). The effects of early stimulation on low-birth weight infants. *Child Development, 44,* 94–101.

The "scene" and the skinheads. (1990). *Edmonton Journal,* Nov. 18, E1.

Schaefer, C. E. (1969). Imaginary companions and creative adolescents. *Developmental Psychology, 1,* 747–749.

Schaffer, H. R. (1966). The onset of fear of strangers and the incongruity hypothesis. *Journal of Child Psychology and Psychiatry, 7,* 95–106.

Schaffer, H. R. (1984). *The child's entry into a social world.* New York: Academic Press.

Schaffer, H. R., Collis, G. M., & Parsons, G. (1977). Vocal interchange and visual regard in verbal and preverbal children. In H. R. Schaffer (Ed.), *Studies in mother-infant interaction.* London: Academic Press.

Schaie, K. W. (1965). A general model for the study of developmental problems. *Psychological Bulletin, 64,* 92–107.

Schardein, J. L. (1985). *Chemical induced birth defects.* New York: Marcel Dekker.

Schave, D., & Schave, B. (1989). *Early adolescence and the search for self: A developmental perspective.* New York: Praeger.

Scher, J., & Dix, C. (1983). *Will my baby be normal? Everything you need to know about pregnancy.* New York: Dial Press.

Schiefelbusch, R. L., & McCormick, L. (1981). Language and speech disorders. In J. M. Kauffman & D. P. Hallahan (Eds.), *Handbook of Special Education.* Englewood Cliffs, N.J.: Prentice-Hall.

Schlegel, A., & Barry, H., III. (1991). *Adolescence: An anthropological inquiry.* New York: Free Press.

Schneider, D. J. (1991). Social cognition. *Annual Review of Psychology, 42,* 527–561.

Schneider, W., Borkowsky, J. G., Kurtz, B. E., & Kerwin, K. (1986). Metamemory and motivation: A comparison of strategy use in German and American children. *Journal of Cross-Cultural Psychology, 17,* 315–336.

Schneider-Rosen, K., Braunwald, K. G., Carlson, V., & Cicchetti, D. (1985). Current perspectives in attachment theory: Illustration from the study of maltreated infants. In I. Bretherton & E. Waters (Eds.), Growing points of attachment theory and research. *Monographs of the Society for Research in Child Development, 50,* No. 209.

Schumer, F. (1983). *Abnormal psychology.* Lexington, Mass.: D. C. Heath.

Schunk, D. H. (1984). Self-efficacy perspective on achievement behavior. *Educational Psychologist, 19,* 48–58.

Schwartzman, H. B. (1987). A cross-cultural perspective on child-structured play activities and materials. In A. W. Gottfried & C. C. Brown (eds.), *Play interactions: The contribution of play materials and parental involvement to children's development.* Lexington, Mass.: D. C. Heath.

Sears, R. R. (1984). Patterns of child rearing. In S. A. Mednick, M. Harway, & K. M. Finello (Eds.), *Handbook of longitudinal research* (Vol. 1): *Birth and childhood cohorts.* New York: Holt, Rinehart & Winston.

Sears, R. R., Maccoby, E. P., & Lewin, H. (1957). *Patterns of child rearing.* Evanston, Ill.: Row, Peterson.

Sebald, H. (1984). *Adolescence: A social psychological analysis* (3rd ed.). Englewood Cliffs, N.J.: Prentice-Hall.

Seligman, M. E. P. (1975). *Helplessness: On depression, development, and death.* San Francisco: W. H. Freeman.

Selman, R. L. (1980). *The growth of interpersonal understanding.* New York: Academic Press.

Selman, R. L. (1981). The child as friendship philosopher. In S. R. Asher & J. M. Gottman (Eds.), *The development of children's friendships.* New York: Cambridge University Press.

Selye, H. (1974). *Stress without distress.* Philadelphia: J. B. Lippincott.

Semrud-Clikeman, M., & Hynd, G. W. (1992). Developmental arithmetic disorder. In S. R. Hooper, G. W. Hynd, & R. E. Mattison, (Eds.), *Developmental disorders: Diagnostic criteria and clinical assessment*. Hillsdale, N.J.: Lawrence Erlbaum.

Serafini, S. (1991). Multiculturalism in the schools of Canada: Presentation to the fourth conference of CCMIE. *Multiculturalism, 14*, 12–14.

Serbin, L. A., Powlishta, K. K., & Gulko, J. (1993). The development of sex typing in middle childhood. *Monographs of the Society for Research in Child Development, 58*, No. 2.

Seymour, D. (1971). *Black children, black speech. Commonweal*, November, 19.

Shanklin, D. R., & Hodin, J. (1979). *Maternal nutrition and child health.* Springfield, Ill.: Charles C. Thomas.

Shantz, C. U. (1983). Social cognition. In P. H. Mussen (Ed.), *Handbook of child psychology* (Vol. 3): *Cognitive Development* (J. H. Flavell & E. M. Markman, Eds.). New York: John Wiley.

Shedler, J., & Block, J. (1990). Adolescent drug use and psychological health: A longitudinal inquiry. *American Psychologist, 45*, 612–630.

Shepard, L. A., Smith, M. L., & Vojir, C. P. (1983). Characteristics of pupils identified as learning disabled. *American Educational Research Journal, 20*, 309–331.

Shepherd-Look, D. L. (1982). Sex differentiation and the development of sex roles. In B. B. Wolman and others (Eds.), *Handbook of developmental psychology*. Englewood Cliffs, N.J.: Prentice-Hall.

Sherman, M., & Key, C. B. (1932). The intelligence of isolated mountain children. *Child Development, 3*, 279–290.

Sherman, M., & Sherman, I. C. (1929). *The process of human behavior.* New York: W. W. Norton.

Shortening the time between the bench and the bedside. (1993). *University of Alberta Folio*, November 21, p. 4.

Showers, C., & Cantor, N. (1985). Social cognition: A look at motivated strategies. *Annual Review of Psychology, 36*, 275–305.

Shreve, B. W., & Kunkel, M. A. (1991). Self-psychology, shame, and adolescent suicide: Theoretical and practical considerations. *Journal of Counseling and Development, 69*, 305–311.

Siegel, A. W., & White, S. H. (1982). The child study movement: Early growth and development of the symbolized child. In H. W. Reese (Ed.), *Advances in child development and behavior* (Vol. 17). New York: Academic Press.

Siegel, O. (1982). Personality development in adolescence. In B. B. Wolman and others (Eds.), *Handbook of developmental psychology*. Englewood Cliffs, N.J.: Prentice-Hall.

Siegler, R. S. (1989). Mechanisms of cognitive development. *Annual Review of Psychology, 40*, 353–379.

Siegler, R. S., & Liebert, R. M. (1972). Effects of presenting relevant rules and complete feedback on the conservation of liquid quantity task. *Developmental Psychology, 7*, 133–138.

Sigel, I. E. (1987). Does hothousing rob children of their childhood? *Early Childhood Research Quarterly, 2*, 211–225.

Silverstein, F. S., & Johnston, M. V. (1990). Neurological assessment of children: The damaged child. In R. D. Eden, F. H. Boehm, & M. Haire (Eds.), *Assessment and care of the fetus: Physiological, clinical, and medicolegal principles.* Norwalk, Conn.: Appleton & Lange.

Simmons, R. G., & Blyth, D. (1987). *Moving into adolescence: The impact of pubertal change and school context.* New York: Aldine & Gruyter.

Simon, L. (1992). Mainstreaming: Is it in the best interests of all children? *B.C. Journal of Special Education, 16*, 131–138.

Simpson, J. L. (1991). Aetiology of pregnancy failure. In M. Chapman, G. Grudzinskas, & T. Chard (Eds.), *The embryo: Normal and abnormal development and growth*. New York: Springer-Verlag.

Sinclair, H., Stambak, M., Lézine, I., Rayna, S., & Verba, M. (Eds.). (1989). *Infants and objects: The creativity of cognitive development*. New York: Academic Press.

Singer, D. G., & Singer, J. L. (1990). *The house of make-believe: Children's play and developing imagination*. Cambridge, Mass.: Harvard University Press.

Singer, J. L. (Ed.). (1973). *The child's world of make-believe: Experimental studies of imaginative play*. New York: Academic Press.

Singer, J. L., & Singer, D. G. (1983). Implications of childhood television viewing for cognition, imagination, and emotion. In J. Bryant & D. R. Anderson (Eds.), *Children's understanding of television: Research on attention and comprehension* (pp. 265–297). New York: Academic Press.

Singer, R. S. (1982). Childhood, aggression and television. *Television and Children, 5*, 57–63.

Singh, J. A., & Zingg, R. N. (1942). *Wolf-children and feral man*. New York: Harper.

Skinner, B. F. (1953). *Science and human behavior*. New York: Macmillan.

Skinner, B. F. (1957). *Verbal behavior.* New York: Appleton-Century-Crofts.

Skinner, B. F. (1961). *Cumulative record* (Rev. ed.). New York: Appleton-Century-Crofts.

Skolnick, A. (1978). The myth of the vulnerable child. *Psychology Today,* February, 56–60, 65.

Sleeping with the enemy. (1991). *Newsweek,* December 9, pp. 58–59.

Sloan, D., Shapiro, S., & Mitchell, A. A. (1980). Strategies for studying the effects of the antenatal chemical environment on the fetus. In R. H. Schwartz & S. J. Yaffe (Eds.), *Drug and chemical risks to the fetus and newborn.* New York: Alan R. Liss.

Small, S. A., & Eastman, G. (1991). Rearing adolescents in contemporary society: A conceptual framework for understanding the responsibilities and needs of parents. *Family Relations, 40,* 455–462.

Smith, C. L. (1979). Children's understanding of natural language hierarchies. *Journal of Experimental Child Psychology, 27,* 437–458.

Smith, D. A., & Graesser, A. C. (1981). Memory for actions in scripted activities as a function of typicality, retention interval, and retrieval task. *Memory and Cognition, 9,* 550–559.

Smith, P. B., Weinman, M., & Malinak, L. R. (1984). Adolescent mothers and fetal loss: What is learned from experience? *Psychological Reports, 55,* 775–778.

Smoll, F. L., & Schutz, R. W. (1990). Quantifying gender differences in physical performance: A developmental perspective. *Developmental Psychology, 26,* 360–369.

Snarey, J. R. (1985). Cross-cultural universality of social-moral development: A critical review of Kohl-

bergian research. *Psychological Bulletin, 97,* 202–232.

Snyder, L. A., Freifelder, D., & Hartl, D. L. (1985). *General genetics.* Boston: Jones & Bartlett.

Snyderman, M., & Rothman, S. (1987). Survey of expert opinion on intelligence and aptitude testing. *American Psychologist, 42,* 137–144.

Sobsey, D. (1993). Integration outcomes: Theoretical models and empirical investigations. *Developmental Disabilities Bulletin, 21,* 1–14.

Sodian, B. (1991). The development of deception in young children. *British Journal of Developmental Psychology, 9,* 173–188.

Sorensen, R. C. (1973). *Adolescent sexuality in contemporary America.* New York: World.

Sparkes, K. (1990). A visit to a rural preschool in China. *International Journal of Early Childhood, 22,* No. 2, 17–22.

Spearman, C. (1927). *The abilities of man.* New York: Macmillan.

Spellacy, W. N., Miller, S. J., & Winegar, A. (1986). Pregnancy after 40 years of age. *Obstetrics and Gynecology, 68,* 452–454.

Spezzano, C. (1981, May). Prenatal psychology: Pregnant with questions. *Psychology Today,* 49–57.

Spitz, R. A. (1945). Hospitalism: An inquiry into the genesis of psychiatric conditions in early childhood. Part 1. *Psychoanalytic Studies of the Child, 1,* 53–74.

Spitz, R. A. (1954). Unhappy and fatal outcomes of emotional deprivation and stress in infancy. In I. Galdston (Ed.), *Beyond the germ theory.* Washington, D.C.: Health Education Council.

Springer, C., & Wallerstein, J. S. (1983). Young adolescents' responses to their parents' divorces. In L. A. Kurdek

(Ed.), *Children and divorce: New directions for child development* (pp. 15–28). San Francisco: Jossey-Bass.

Sroufe, L., & Waters, E. (1976). The ontogenesis of smiling and laughter: A perspective on the organization of development in infancy. *Psychological Review, 83,* 173–189.

Sroufe, L., & Wunsch, J. (1972). The development of laughter in the first year of life. *Child Development, 43,* 1326–1344.

Stall, R. D., Coates, T. J., & Hoff, C. (1988). Behavioral risk reduction for HIV infection among gay and bisexual men. *American Psychologist, 43,* 878–885.

Stambak, M., Sinclair, H., Verba, M., Moreno, L., & Rayna, S. (1989). Infants and logic. In H. Sinclair. M. Stambak, I. Lézine, S. Rayna, & M. Verba (Eds.), *Infants and objects: The creativity of cognitive development.* New York: Academic Press.

Stander, V., & Jensen, L. (1993). The relationship of value orientation to moral cognition: Gender and cultural differences in the United States and China explored. *Journal of Cross-Cultural Psychology, 24,* 42–52.

Stanovich, K. E. (1992). Developmental reading disorder. In S. R. Hooper, G. W. Hynd, & R. E. Mattison, (Eds.), *Developmental disorders: Diagnostic criteria and clinical assessment.* Hillsdale, N.J.: Lawrence Erlbaum.

Stanton, W. R. (1993). A cognitive developmental framework. *Current Psychology: Research and Reviews, 12,* 26–45.

Starr, R. H. (1979). Child abuse. *American Psychologist, 34,* 872–878.

Starr, R. H. (1982). A research-based approach to the prediction of child abuse. In R. H. Starr, Jr. (Ed.), *Child abuse prediction: Policy implications.* Cambridge, Mass.: Ballinger.

Starr, R. H., Jr., Dietrich, K. N., & Fischoff, J. (1981). The contribution of children to their own abuse. Paper presented at a meeting of the Society for Research in Child Development, Boston, April.

Statman, D. (1993). Self-assessment, self-esteem and self-acceptance. *Journal of Moral Education, 22*, 55–62.

Stattin, H., & Magnusson, D. (1990). *Pubertal maturation in female development*. Hillsdale, N.J.: Lawrence Erlbaum.

Steenbarger, B. N. (1991). All the world is not a stage: Emerging contextualist themes in counseling and development. *Journal of Counseling and Development, 70*, 288–296.

Stein, Z., Susser, M., Saenger, G., & Marolla, F. (1975). *Famine and human development: The Dutch hunger winter of 1944–1945*. New York: Oxford University Press.

Steiner, J. E. (1979). Human facial expressions in response to taste and smell stimulation. In H. Reese & L. Lipsitt (Eds.), *Advances in child development and behavior* (Vol. 13). New York: Academic Press.

Stern, C. (1956). Hereditary factors affecting adoption. In *A Study of Adoption Practices* (Vol. 2). New York: Child Welfare League of America.

Stern, D. N., Spieker, S., Barnett, R. K., & MacKain, K. (1983). The prosody of maternal speech: Infant age and context related changes. *Journal of Child Language, 10*, 1–15.

Sternberg, R. J. (1984). A contextualist view of the nature of intelligence. *International Journal of Psychology, 19*, 307–334.

Sternberg, R. J. (1985). *Beyond IQ: A triarchic theory of intelligence*. New York: Cambridge University Press.

Sternberg, R. J. (1991). Directors of development: A play in an unknown number of acts. In L. Okagaki & R. J. Sternberg (Eds.), *Directors of development: Influences on the development of children's thinking*. Hillsdale, N.J.: Lawrence Erlbaum.

Stevenson, H. W., Chen, C., Lee, S. Y., & Fuligni, A. J. (1991). Schooling, culture, and cognitive development. In L. Okagaki & R. J. Sternberg (Eds.), *Directors of development: Influences on the development of children's thinking*. Hillsdale, N.J.: Lawrence Erlbaum.

Stifter, C. A., & Fox, N. A. (1990). Infant reactivity: Physiological correlates of newborn and 5-month temperament. *Developmental Psychology, 26*, 582–588.

Stigler, J. W., Smith, S., & Mao, L. W. (1985). The self-perception of competence by Chinese children. *Child Development, 56*, 1259–1270.

Stimpson, D., Neff, W., Jensen, L. C., & Newby, T. (1991). The caring morality and gender differences. *Psychological Reports, 69*, 407–414.

Stockman, J. A., III (1990). Fetal hematology. In R. D. Eden, F. H. Boehm, & M. Haire (Eds.), *Assessment and care of the fetus: Physiological, clinical, and medicolegal principles*. Norwalk, Conn.: Appleton & Lange.

Stoutjesdyk, D., & Jevne, R. (1993). Eating disorders among high performance athletes. *Journal of Youth and Adolescence, 22*, 271–279.

Strangler, R. S., & Printz, A. M. (1980). DSM-III: Psychiatric diagnosis in a university population. *American Journal of Psychiatry, 137*, 937–940.

Straus, M. A., and Gelles, R. (1986). Societal change and change in family violence from 1975 to 1985 as revealed by two national surveys. *Journal of Marriage and the Family, 48*, 465–479.

Stratton, P. (1988). Parents' conceptualization of children as the organizer of culturally structured environments. In J. Valsiner, (Ed.), *Child development within culturally structured environments* (Vol. 1), *Parental cognition and adult-child interaction*, Norwood N.J.: Ablex.

Streissguth, A. P., Barr, H. M., & Martin, D. C. (1983). Maternal alcohol use and neonatal habituation assessed with the Brazelton scale. *Child Development, 54*, 1109–1118.

Streissguth, A. P., Landesman-Dwyer, S., Martin, J. C., & Smith, D. W. (1980). Teratogen effects of alcohol in humans and laboratory animals. *Science, 209*, 353–361.

Streitmatter, J. (1993). Gender differences in identity development: An examination of longitudinal data. *Adolescence, 28*, 55–66.

Strelau, J. (1989). Temperament risk factors in children and adolescents as studied in Eastern Europe. In W. B. Carey & S. C. McDevitt (Eds.), *Clinical and educational applications of temperament research*. Berwyn, Penn.: Swets North America.

Stuart, R. B. (1969). Critical reappraisal and reformulation of selected "mental health" programs. In L. A. Hamerlynck, P. O. Davidson, & L. E. Acker (Eds.), *Behavior modification and mental health services*. Calgary, Alb.: University of Calgary Press.

Swaim, R. C., Oetting, E. R., Thurman, P. J., Beauvais, F., & Edwards, R. W. (1993). American Indian adolescent drug use and socialization characteristics: A cross-cultural comparison. *Journal of Cross-Cultural Psychology, 24*, 53–70.

Swain, I. U., Zelazo, P. R., & Clifton, R. K. (1993). Newborn infants' memory for speech sounds retained over 24 hours. *Developmental Psychology, 29*, 312–323.

Tanner, J. M. (1955). *Growth at adolescence*. Springfield, Ill.: Charles C. Thomas.

Tanner, J. M. (1970). Physical growth. In P. H. Mussen (Ed.), *Carmichael's manual of child psychology* (3rd ed.). New York: John Wiley.

Tanner, J. M. (1975). Sequence, tempo, and individual variation in the growth and development of boys and girls aged twelve to sixteen. In R. E. Grinder (Ed.), *Studies in adolescence*. New York: Macmillan.

Tannock, R., Schachar, R. J., & Logan, G. D. (1993). Does methylphenidate induce overfocusing in hyperactive children? *Journal of Clinical Child Psychology, 22*, 28–41.

Tavris, C., & Baumgartner, A. I. (1983). How would your life be different if you'd been born a boy? *Redbook*, February, 99.

Taylor, M., Cartwright, B. S., & Carlson, S. M. (1993). A developmental investigation of children's imaginary companions. *Developmental Psychology, 29*, 276–285.

Television & your children. (1985). Ontario: TV Ontario: The Ontario Educational Communications Authority.

Terman, L. M., assisted by B. T. Baldwin and others. (1925). *Genetic studies of genius* (Vol. 1). Stanford, Calif.: Stanford University Press.

Termine, N. T., & Izard, C. E. (1988). Infants' responses to their mother's expressions of joy and sadness. *Developmental Psychology, 24*, 223–229.

Terrace, H. S. (1985). In the beginning was the "Name." *American Psychologist, 40*, 1011–1028.

Terry, R., & Coie, J. D. (1991). A comparison of methods for defining sociometric status among children.

Developmental Psychology, 27, 867–880.

Thomas, A., & Chess, S. (1977). *Temperament and development*. New York: Brunner/Mazel.

Thomas, A., & Chess, S. (1981). The role of temperament in the contribution of individuals to their development. In R. M. Lerner & N. A. Busch-Rossnagel (Eds.), *Individual as producers of their development*. New York: Academic Press.

Thomas, A., Chess, S., & Birch, H. G. (1968). *Temperament and behavior disorders in children*. New York: New York University Press.

Thomas, A., Chess, S., & Birch, H. G. (1970). The origin of personality. *Scientific American, 223*, 102–109.

Thomas, A., Chess, S., & Korn, S. J. (1982). The reality of difficult temperament. *Merrill-Palmer Quarterly, 28*, 1–20.

Thomas, J. W. (1980). Agency and achievement: Self-management and self-regard. *Review of Educational Research, 50*, 213–240.

Thomas, R. M. (1992). *Comparing theories of child development* (3rd ed.). Belmont, Calif.: Wadsworth.

Thorndike, R. L., & Hagen, E. (1977). *Measurement and evaluation in psychology and education* (4th ed.). New York: John Wiley.

Thorndike, R. L., Hagen, E., & Sattler, J. M. (1985). *Revised Stanford-Binet intelligence scale* (4th ed.). Boston: Houghton Mifflin.

Thorpe, W. H. (1963). *Learning and instinct in animals* (2nd ed.). London: Methuen.

Thurstone, L. L. (1938). Primary mental abilities. *Psychometric Monographs*, No. 1. Chicago: University of Chicago Press.

Tierney, J. (1988). Not to worry. *Hippocrates*, January/February, pp. 29–36.

Tisak, M. S. (1993). Preschool children's judgments of moral and personal events involving physical harm and property damage. *Merrill-Palmer Quarterly, 39*, 375–390.

Toray, T., Coughlin, C., Vuchinich, S., & Patricelli, P. (1991). Gender differences associated with adolescent substance abuse: Comparisons and implications for treatment. *Family Relations, 40*, 338–344.

Torrance, E. P. (1966). Torrance's tests of creative thinking. *Norms technical manual*. Princeton, N.J.: Personnel Press.

Torrance, E. P. (1974). *Torrance tests of creative thinking*. Lexington, Mass.: Ginn.

Travis, L. D. (1992). Voice versus message: On the importance of B. F. Skinner. *Canadian Journal of Special Education, 8*, 151–162.

Trawick-Smith, J. (1989). Play is not learning: A critical review of the literature. *Child & Youth Care Quarterly, 18*, 161–170.

Trehub, S. E., Schneider, B. A., Thorpe, L. A., & Judge, P. (1991). Observational measures of auditory sensitivity in early infancy. *Developmental Psychology, 27*, 40–49.

Trickett, P. K., Aber, J. L., Carlson, V., & Cicchetti, D. (1991). Relationship of socioeconomic status to the etiology and developmental sequelae of physical child abuse. *Developmental Psychology, 27*, 148–158.

Trickett, P. K., & Susman, E. J. (1988). Parental perceptions of child-rearing practices in physically abusive and nonabusive families. *Developmental Psychology, 24*, 270–276.

Trofatter, K. F., Jr. (1990). Fetal immunology. In R. D. Eden, F. H. Boehm,

& M. Haire (Eds.), *Assessment and care of the fetus: Physiological, clinical, and medicolegal principles.* Norwalk, Conn.: Appleton & Lange.

Tronick, E. Z. (1989). Emotions and emotional communication in infants. *American Psychologist, 44,* 112–119.

Tryon, R. C. (1940). Genetic differences in maze learning in rats. *Yearbook of the National Society for the Study of Education, 39,* 111–119.

Tsang, M. C. (1988). Cost analysis for educational policymaking: A review of cost studies in education in developing countries. *Review of Educational Research, 58,* 181–230.

Tsuchiyama, B. (1992). Philippines OMEP kindergartens for poor children. *International Journal of Early Childhood Education, 24,* 56–64.

Tubman, J. G. (1993). Family risk factors, parental alcohol use, and problem behaviors among school-age children. *Family Relations, 42,* 81–86.

Tudge, J. R. H., & Winterhoff, P. A. (1993). Vygotsky, Piaget, and Bandura: Perspectives on the relations between the social world and cognitive development. *Human Development, 36,* 61–81.

Tuma, J. M., (1989). Mental health services for children. *American Psychologist, 44,* 188–195.

Turgi, P. A. (1992). Children's rights in America: The needs and actions. *Journal of Humanistic Education and Development, 31,* 53–63.

Turkheimer, E., & Gottesman, I. I. (1991). Individual and group differences in adoption studies of IQ. *Psychological Bulletin, 110,* 392–405.

Tzuriel, D. (1989). Development of motivational and cognitive-informational orientations from third to ninth grades. *Journal of Applied Developmental Psychology, 10,* 107–121.

U.S. Bureau of the Census. (1988). *Statistical abstracts of the United States 1987* (108th ed.). Washington, D.C.: U.S. Government Printing Office.

U.S. Bureau of the Census. (1990). *Statistical abstracts of the United States 1990* (110th ed.). Washington, D.C.: U.S. Government Printing Office.

U.S. Bureau of the Census. (1991). *Statistical Abstracts of the United States, 1991* (111th Ed.). Washington, D.C.: U.S. Government Printing Office.

U.S. Bureau of the Census. (1992). *Statistical Abstracts of the United States: 1992* (112th Ed.). Washington, D.C.: U.S. Government Printing Office.

U.S. Department of Education. (1991). *Thirteenth annual report to Congress on the implementation of the Handicapped Act,* Washington, D.C.: author.

U.S. Department of Health & Human Services. (1981). *The health consequences of smoking: The changing cigarette: A report of the Surgeon General.* Washington, D. C.: U.S. Government Printing Office.

U. S. Department of Health & Human Services. (1989). *Monthly Vital Statistics Report,* Vol. 37, No. 11, Feb. 1989. Public Health Service, Centers for Disease Control. Washington, D.C.: U.S. Government Printing Office.

Valdes-Dapena, M. A. (1991). The phenomenon of sudden infant death syndrome and its challenges. In C. A. Corr, H. Fuller, C. A. Barnickol, & D. M. Corr (Eds.), *Sudden infant death syndrome: Who can help and how.* New York: Springer.

Valsiner, J. (1987). *Culture and the development of children's action: A cultural-historical theory of developmental psychology.* New York: John Wiley.

Vandell, D. L., & Ramanan, J. (1991). Children of the National Longitudinal Survey of Youth: Choices in after-school care and child development. *Developmental Psychology, 27,* 637–643.

Van Houten, R., & Doleys, D. M. (1983). Are social reprimands effective? In S. Axelrod & J. Apsche (Eds.), *The effects of punishment on human behavior.* New York: Academic Press.

Van Houten, R., Nau, P. A., Mac-Kenzie-Keating, S., Sameoto, D., & Colavecchia, B. (1982). An analysis of some variables influencing the effectiveness of reprimands. *Journal of Applied Behavior Analysis, 15,* 65–83.

Vandell, D. L., Wilson, K. S., & Buchanan, N. R. (1980). Peer interaction in the first year of life: An examination of its structure, content, and sensitivity to toys. *Child Development, 51,* 481–488.

Vandenberg, B. R. (1987). Beyond the ethology of play. In A. W. Gottfried & C. C. Brown (Eds.), *Play interactions: The contribution of play materials and parental involvement to children's development.* Lexington, Mass.: D. C. Heath.

Vaughn, B., Gove, F., & Egeland, B. (1980). The relationship between out-of-home care and the quality of infant-mother attachment in an economically deprived population. *Child Development, 50,* 971–975.

Varga, D. (1991). The historical ordering of children's play as a developmental task. *Play and Culture, 4,* 322–333.

Verhaaren, P., & Connor, F. P. (1981). Physical disabilites. In J. M. Kauffman & D. P. Hallahan (Eds.), *Handbook of special education* (pp. 248–289). Englewood Cliffs, N.J.: Prentice-Hall.

Visher, E. B., & Visher, J. S. (1982). *How to win as a stepfamily.* New York: Dembner.

Visher, E. B., & Visher, J. S. (1988). *Old loyalties, new ties.* New York: Brunner/Mazel.

Volling, B. L., & Belsky, J. (1993). Maternal employment: Parent, infant, and contextual characteristics related to maternal employment decisions in the first year of infancy. *Family Relations, 42,* 4–12.

Von Hofsten, C., & Lindhagen, K. (1979). Observations on the development of reaching for moving objects. *Journal of Experimental Child Psychology, 28,* 158–173.

Vórhees, C. V., & Mollnow, E. (1987). Behavioral teratogenesis: Long-term influences on behavior from early exposure to environmental agents. In J. D. Osofsky (Ed.), *Handbook of infant development.* New York: John Wiley.

Vygotsky, L. (1978). *Mind in society: The development of higher psychological processes.* Cambridge, Mass.: Harvard University Press.

Vygotsky, L. S. (1967). Play and its role in the mental development of the child. *Soviet Psychology, 12,* 6–18.

Vygotsky, L. S. (1977). *Mind in society: The development of higher psychological processes.* Cambridge, Mass.: Harvard University Press.

Vygotsky, L. S. (1986). *Thought and language* (Translated and revised by A. Kozulin). Cambridge, Mass.: MIT Press.

Waddington, C. H. (1975). *The evolution of an evolutionist.* Edinburgh: Edinburgh University Press.

Wakefield, J. F. (1991). The outlook for creativity tests. *The Journal of Creative Behavior, 25,* 184–193.

Walker, J. J. (1978). The gifted and talented. In E. L. Meyen (Ed.), *Exceptional children and youth: An introduction.* Denver: Love.

Walker, L. J. (1988). The development of moral reasoning. In R. Vasta (Ed.), *Annals of child development* (Vol 5). Greenwich, Conn.: JAI Press.

Wallach, M. A., & Kogan, N. (1965). *Modes of thinking in young children: A study of the creativity-intelligence distinction.* New York: Holt, Rinehart & Winston.

Wallerstein, J. S. (1989). Children after divorce: Wounds that don't heal. *The New York Times Magazine,* January 23, 19–21, 41–44.

Wallerstein, J. S., & Kelly, J. B. (1974). The effects of parental divorce: The adolescent experience. In E. J. Anthony & C. Koupernik (Eds.), *The child in his family: Children at psychiatric risk* (Vol. 3). New York: John Wiley.

Wallerstein, J. S., & Kelley, J. B. (1975). The effects of parental divorce: Experiences of the preschool child. *Journal of the American Academy of Child Psychiatry, 14,* 600–616.

Wallerstein, J. S., & Kelly, J. B. (1976). The effects of parental divorce: Experiences of the child in later latency. *American Journal of Orthopsychiatry, 46,* 256–269.

Wallerstein, J. S., & Kelly, J. (1980). *Surviving the break-up: How children actually cope with divorce.* New York: Basic Books.

Walsh, B. T. (1982). Endocrine disturbance in anorexia nervosa and depression. *Psychosomatic Medicine, 44,* 85–91.

Walters, G. C., & Grusec, J. E. (1977). *Punishment.* San Francisco: W. H. Freeman.

War Crimes. (1994). *The Edmonton Sun,* February 13, p. 13.

Warshak, R. A., & Santrock, J. W. (1983). The impact of divorce in father-custody and mother-custody homes: The child's perspective. In L. A. Kurdek (Ed.), *Children and divorce: New directions for child development.* San Francisco: Jossey-Bass.

Washton, A. M. (1989). *Cocaine addiction: Treatment, recovery, and relapse prevention.* New York: W. W. Norton.

Wasserman, G. (1980). The nature and function of early mother-infant interaction. In B. L. Blum (Ed.), *Psychological aspects of pregnancy, birthing, and bonding.* New York: Human Sciences Press, 324–348.

Waterman, A. S. (1984). Identity formation: Discovery or creation? *Journal of Early Adolescence, 4,* 329–341.

Waterman, A. S. (1988). Identity status theory and Erikson's theory: Commonalities and differences. *Developmental Review, 8,* 185–208.

Waters, E. (1980). Traits, relationships, and behavioral systems: The attachment construct and the organization of behavior and development. In K. Immelman, E. Barlow, M. Main, & L. Petrinovich, (Eds.), *Development of behavior.* New York: Cambridge University Press.

Waters, E., Hay, D., & Richters, J. (1986). Infant-parent attachment and the origins of prosocial and antisocial behavior. In D. Olweus, J. Block, & M. Radke-Yarrow (Eds.), *Development of antisocial and prosocial behavior: Research, theories, and issues.* New York: Academic Press.

Watson, J. B. (1914). *Behavior: An introduction to comparative psychology.* New York: Holt, Rinehart & Winston.

Watson, J. B., & Rayner, R. (1920). Conditioned emotional reactions. *Journal of Experimental Psychology, 3,* 1–14.

Watts, W. D., & Wright, L. S. (1990). The relationship of alcohol, tobacco, marijuana, and other illegal drug use to delinquency among Mexican-American, black, and white adolescent males. *Adoléscence, 25*, 171–181.

Weber, K. S., Frankenberg, W., & Heilman, K. (1992). The effects of Ritalin on the academic achievement of children diagnosed with attention-deficit hyperactivity disorder. *Developmental Disabilities Bulletin, 20*, 49–68.

Wechsler, D. (1991). *Wechsler Intelligence Scale for Children—Third Edition: Manual.* New York: The Psychological Corporation.

Weinberg, R. (1989). Intelligence and IQ. *American Psychologist, 44*, 98–104.

Weininger, O. (1990). Play: For survival. In I. M. Doxey (Ed.), *Child care and education: Canadian dimensions.* Scarborough, Ont.: Nelson Canada.

Weiner, B. (1980a). *Human motivation.* New York: Holt, Rinehart & Winston.

Weiner, B. (1980b). The role of affect in rational (attributional) approaches to human motivation. *Educational Researcher, 9*, 4–11.

Weisfeld, G. E. (1982). The nature-nurture issue and the integrating concept of function. In B. B. Wolman and others (Eds.), *Handbook of developmental psychology.* Englewood Cliffs, N.J.: Prentice-Hall.

Weisskopf, M. (1987). Lead astray: The poisoning of America. *Discover, 8*, 76–77.

Wellman, H. M. (1988). The early development of memory strategies. In F. E. Weinert & M. Perlmutter (Eds.), *Memory development: Universal changes and individual differences.* Hillsdale, N.J.: Lawrence Erlbaum.

Wellman, H. M., & Gelman, S. A. (1992). Cognitive development:

Foundational theories of core domains. *Annual Review of Psychology, 43*, 337–375.

Wells, E., & Stryker, S. (1988). The early development of memory strategies. In F. E. Weinert & M. Perlmutter (Eds.), *Memory development: Universal changes and individual differences.* Hillsdale, N.J.: Lawrence Erlbaum.

Wells, G. (1985). *Language development in the pre-school years.* Cambridge: Cambridge University Press.

Werner, E. E., & Smith, R. S. (1982). *Vulnerable but invincible: A longitudinal study of resilient children and youth.* New York: McGraw-Hill.

Werry, J. S. (1972). The childhood psychoses. In H. C. Quay & J. S. Werry (Eds.), *Psychopathological disorders of childhood.* New York: John Wiley.

Wertham, F. (1954). *Seduction of the innocent.* New York: Rinehart.

Wertsch, J. V. (1985). *Vygotsky and the social formation of mind.* Cambridge, Mass.: Harvard University Press.

Wesley, F., & Wesley, C. (1977). *Sex-role psychology.* New York: Human Sciences Press.

Westbury, I. (1992). Comparing American and Japanese achievement: Is the United States really a low achiever? *Educational Researcher, 21*, 18–24.

Westbury, I., Ethington, C., Sosniak, L., & Baker, D. (Eds.). (1993). *In search of more effective mathematics education: Examining data from the IEA Second International Mathematics Study.* Norwood, N.J.: Ablex.

Westman, J. C. (1991a). Introduction. In J. C. Westman (Ed.), *Who speaks for the children?* Sarasota, Fla.: Professional Resource Exchange, Inc.

Westman, J. C. (1991b). The principles and techniques of individual child advocacy. In J. C. Westman (Ed.),

Who speaks for the children? Sarasota, Fla.: Professional Resource Exchange, Inc.

White, B. L. (1985). *The first three years of life* (Rev. ed.). Englewood Cliffs, N.J.: Prentice-Hall.

White, K. R., Taylor, M. J., & Moss, V. D. (1992). Does research support claims about the benefits of involving parents in early intervention programs? *Review of Educational Research, 62*, 91–125.

Whitney, E. N., & Hamilton, E. M. N. (1984). *Understanding nutrition* (3rd ed.). St. Paul, Minn.: West.

Whittle, M. J., & Rubin, P. C. (1989). Exposure to teratogens. In M. J. Whittle & J. M. Connor (Eds.), *Prenatal diagnosis in obstetric practice.* Boston: Blackwell Scientific Publications.

Whorf, B. L. (1941). The relation of habitual thought and behavior to language. In L. Spier (Ed.), *Language, culture and personality.* Salt Lake City: University of Utah Press.

Whorf, B. L. (1956). *Language, thought and reality.* New York: John Wiley.

Wiggins, J. S., & Pincus, A. L. (1992). Personality: Structure and assessment. *Annual Review of Psychology, 43*, 473–504.

Willerman, L. (1973). Activity level and hyperactivity in twins. *Child Development, 44*, 288–293.

Willerman, L. (1979). Effects of families on intellectual development. *American Psychologist, 34*, 923–929.

Wilson, E. O. (1975). *Sociobiology: The new synthesis.* Cambridge, Mass.: Belknap.

Wilson, G. T., & Walsh, B. T. (1991). Eating disorders in DSM-IV. *Journal of Developmental Psychology, 100*, 362–365.

Winer, G. A., & McGlone, C. (1993). On the uncertainty of conservation: Responses to misleading conservation questions. *Developmental Psychology, 29,* 760–769.

Wingerson, L. (1990). *Mapping our genes: The genome project and the future of medicine.* New York: Dutton.

Winn, M. (1985). *The plug-in drug* (Rev. ed.). New York: Viking Press.

Winnicott, O. (1971). *Playing and reality.* New York: Basic Books.

Winsten, S. (1949). *Days with Bernard Shaw.* New York: Vanguard.

Wittrock, M. C. (1986). Students' thought processes. In M. C. Wittrock (Ed.), *Handbook of research on teaching* (3rd ed.). New York: Macmillan.

Wolf-Schein, E. G. (1992). On the association between the Fragile X chromosome, mental handicap, and autistic disorder. *Developmental Disabilities Bulletin, 20,* 13–30.

Wolff, P. H. (1959). Observations on newborn infants. *Psychosomatic Medicine, 21,* 110–118.

Wolff, P. H. (1963). Observations of the early development of smiling. In B. M. Foss (Ed.), *Determinants of infant behavior 2.* London: Methuen.

Wolff, P. H. (1966). The causes, controls, and organization of behavior in the neonate. *Psychological Issues, 5.*

Wolff, P. H. (1969). The natural history of crying and other vocalizations in early infancy. In B. Foss (Ed.), *Determinants of infant behavior 4.* London: Methuen.

Wolock, I., & Horowitz, B. (1984). Child maltreatment as a social problem: The neglect of neglect. *American Journal of Orthopsychiatry, 54,* 530–543.

Wood, B. S. (1981). *Children and communication: Verbal and nonverbal language development* (2nd ed.). Englewood Cliffs, N.J.: Prentice-Hall.

Wright, H. F. (1960). Observational child study. In P. H. Mussen (Ed.), *Handbook of research methods in child development.* New York: John Wiley.

Wu, D. Y. H. (1981). Child abuse in Taiwan. In J. E. Korbin (Ed.), *Child abuse and neglect: Cross-cultural perspectives.* Berkeley: University of California Press.

Yamamoto, K. (1964). *Experimental scoring manual for Minnesota Tests of Creative Thinking and Writing.* Kent, Ohio: Bureau of Educational Research, Kent State University.

Yarrow, L. J., & Goodwin, M. S. (1973). The immediate impact of separation: Reactions of infants to a change in mother figures. In L. J. Stone, H. T. Smith, & L. B. Murphy (Eds.), *The competent infant: Research and commentary.* New York: Basic Books.

Yost, J. H., Strube, M. J., & Bailey, J. R. (1992). The construction of self: An evolutionary view. *Current Psychology: Research & Reviews, 11,* 110–121.

Young, I. D. (1991). Genetic counselling. In D. T. Liu (Ed.), *A practical guide to chorion villus sampling.* New York: Oxford University Press.

Zajonc, R. B. (1976). Family configuration and intelligence. *Science, 192,* 227–236.

Zajonc, R. B., & Markus, G. B. (1975). Birth order and intellectual development. *Psychological Review, 82,* 74–88.

Zani, B. (1991). Male and female patterns in the discovery of sexuality during adolescence. *Journal of Adolescence, 14,* 163–178.

Zigler, E., & Freedman, J. (1987). Early experience, malleability, and Head Start. In J. J. Gallagher & C. T. Ramey (Eds.), *The malleability of children.* Baltimore: Brookes.

Zigler, E., & Hodapp, R. M. (1991). Behavioral functioning in individuals with mental retardation. *Annual Review of Psychology, 42,* 29–50.

Zuckerman, D. M., Singer, D. G., & Singer, J. L. (1980). Television viewing and children's reading and related classroom behavior. *Journal of Communication, 30,* 166–174.

Zuckerman, M., Eysenck, S. B. G., & Eyenck, H. J. (1978). Sensation seeking in England and America: Cross-cultural, age, and sex comparisons. *Journal of Consulting and Clinical Psychology, 46,* 139–149.

acknowledgments

Page 1 Nubar Alexanian/Woodfin Camp & Associates; p. 8 The Coram Foundation/Bridgeman Art Library; p. 10 The Bettmann Archives; p. 16 J. Moore/The Image Works; p. 18 Nita Winter/The Image Works; p. 19 Ed Kashi; p. 21 Carol Palmer/The Picture Cube; p. 24 Robert Finken/The Picture Cube; p. 31 (left, right) Elizabeth Crews/The Image Works; p. 35 R. M. Collins/The Image Works; p. 41 McKay, Roby & Hertig/Photo Researchers Inc.; p. 47 Bill Aron/PhotoEdit; p. 50 The American Museum of Bath/Bridgeman Art Library; p. 56 Ken Karp/Omni-Photo Communications; p. 62 Elizabeth Crews/The Image Works; p. 68 Nita Winter; p. 74 Joel Simon; *Color insert 1 "Seven ages of human development": p. 1 Will & Deni McIntyre/AllStock; p. 2 (top) Bob Thomas/ Tony Stone Worldwide; p. 2 (middle) Momatiuk & Eastcott/Woodfin Camp & Associates; p. 2 (bottom) Roy Gumpel/Liaison; p. 3 (top left) Nicole Katano/Tony Stone Worldwide; p. 3 (top right) John Chiasson/ Liaison; p. 3 (middle) Roseanne Olson/ AllStock; p. 3 (bottom) Jim Pickerall/Tony Stone Worldwide; p. 4 (top) Momatiuk & Eastcott/Woodfin Camp & Associates; p. 4 (middle) David Swanson/Liaison; p. 4 (bottom) Jerry Howard/Stock, Boston Inc.; p. 76* Jean Boughton/The Picture Cube; p. 80 Nina Leen/Life Picture Service; p. 86 Nita Winter; p. 90 Bard Smith/Monkmeyer Press Photo; p. 101 Linda Ferrer/ Woodfin Camp & Associates; p. 104 The Bettmann Archives; p. 107 D. W. Fawcett/Photo Researchers Inc.; p. 111 Fred Bodin/OffShoot Stock; p. 116 The Bettmann Archive; p. 118 Science Library/Photo Researchers Inc.; p. 120 James Schaffer/PhotoEdit; p. 123 Gary Conner/PhotoEdit; p. 129 Michal Heron/Woodfin Camp & Associates; p. 136 Bob Kalman/The Image Works; p. 150 (left) Omikron/Photo Researchers Inc.; p. 150 (right) J. Stevenson/ Photo Researchers Inc.; p. 152 Robin Williams/Tony Stone Worldwide; p. 158 © 1990 Ted Wood/Picture Group; p. 162 Michael Okoniewski/Liaison; p. 166 Michael Siluk/The Image Works; p. 168 Philip & Karen Smith/Tony Stone Worldwide; p. 172 Anthrophoto File; p. 180 Arman Kachaturean/Liaison; p. 184 Ulrike Welsch/PhotoEdit; p. 196 Mitch Reardon/Photo Researchers Inc.; p. 199 Cleo/PhotoEdit; p. 203 Hank Morgan/Photo Researchers Inc.; p. 208 Suzanne Annus/The Image Works; p. 210 Linda Eber/The Image Works; p. 211 (left) Topham Collection/ The Image Works; p. 211 (right) Courtesy of Vandivert; p. 216 Michael Hayman/Tony Stone Worldwide; p. 229 Betty Press/Woodfin Camp & Associates; p. 230 Goodman/Monkmeyer Press Photo; p. 236 Barbara Griffith/ The Picture Cube; p. 238 Collins/ Monkmeyer Press Photo; p. 247 Suzanne Arms/The Image Works; p. 249 (left) Lilo Raymond/Woodfin Camp & Associates; p. 249 (right) Ken Karp/ Omni-Photo Communications; p. 260 Jason Laure/Woodfin Camp & Associates; p. 263 Stock, Boston Inc.; p. 267 D. Ogust/The Image Works; p. 271 Elizabeth Crews/The Image Works; p. 275 H. Gans/The Image Works; p. 277 Elizabeth Crews/The Image Works; p. 281 Anderson/Monkmeyer Press Photo; p. 284 B. Wells/The Image Works; p. 291 Dana Buckley/Liaison; p. 293 Nita Winter; p. 298 Nita Winter; p. 306 David Cupp/Woodfin Camp & Associates; p. 313 Elizabeth Crews/The Image Works; p. 315 Nita Winter; p. 321 The British Library/Bridgeman Art Library; p. 322 Nita Winter; p. 328 Kinda Clineff/The Image Works; p. 332 Elizabeth Crews/The Image Works; p. 338 Nita Winter; p. 348 Nita Winter; p. 349 Elizabeth Crews/Stock, Boston Inc.; p. 355 Elizabeth Crews/Stock, Boston Inc.; p. 358 J. Berndt/The Picture Cube; p. 361 James Shaffer/PhotoEdit; *Color insert 2 "The play of childhood": p. 1 (top left) Don Smetzer/Tony Stone Worldwide; p. 1 (top right) Kristin Finnegan/AllStock; p. 1 (bottom left) Terry Farmer/Tony Stone Worldwide; p. 1 (bottom right) Bob Krist/ Tony Stone Worldwide; p. 2 (top) Cathlyn Melloan/Tony Stone Worldwide; p. 2 (middle) Chuck Keeler/Tony Stone Worldwide; p. 2 (bottom) Peter Cade/Tony Stone Worldwide; p. 3 (top) Steve Leonard/Tony Stone Worldwide; p. 3 (middle) Sue Ann Miller; p. 3 (bottom) Richard Shock/Liaison; p. 4 (top) Barbara Campbell/AllStock; p. 4 (middle) Bob Torrerz/Tony Stone Worldwide; p. 4 (bottom) Barbara Campbell/AllStock;* p. 365 Elena Dorfman/OffShoot Stock; p. 366 Joel Fishman/Photo Researchers Inc.; p. 370 Nita Winter; p. 375 Michael Weisbrot/Stock, Boston Inc.; p. 378 Spencer Grant/Stock, Boston, Inc.; p. 389 Herbert Booth/Liaison; p. 397 Christopher Brown/Stock, Boston Inc.; p. 402 Nita Winter; p. 408 Anestis Diakopoulos/Stock, Boston Inc.; p. 411 Elizabeth Crews/Stock, Boston Inc.; p. 415 Frank Siteman/Stock, Boston Inc.;

acknowledgments

672

p. 423 Nita Winter; p. 427 Frank Siteman/Stock, Boston Inc.; p. 431 Jeffry Myers/Stock, Boston Inc.; p. 432 The Bettmann Archive; p. 437 Lauren Lantos/The Picture Cube; p. 446 Elizabeth Crews/Stock, Boston Inc.; p. 449 Jean-Claude LeJeune/Stock, Boston Inc.; p. 454 Nita Winter; p. 457 Bonnie Kamin; p. 461 Elizabeth Crews/Stock, Boston Inc.; p. 464 Nita Winter; p. 467 Rameshwar Das/Monkmeyer Press Photo; p. 471 Elizabeth Crews/Stock, Boston Inc.; p. 475 Sybil Shelton/Peter Arnold Inc.; p. 478 Nita Winter; p. 482 Victor Aleman/FPG; p. 503 Len & Des Bartlett/Photo Researchers Inc.; p. 504 Francene Kerry/Stock, Boston Inc.; p. 508 John Running/Stock, Boston Inc.; p. 512 Cleo/PhotoEdit; p. 513 Tony Freeman/PhotoEdit; p. 521 Nita Winter; p. 524 Spencer Grant/The Picture Cube; p. 527 Frank Siteman/Stock, Boston Inc.; p. 536 Alan Carey/The Image Works; p. 538 Photo Researchers Inc.; p. 549 Peter Menzel/Stock, Boston Inc.; p. 554 Peter Menzel/Stock, Boston Inc.; p. 561 Jean-Claude LeJeune/Stock, Boston Inc.; p. 578 Nita Winter; p. 583 Michal Heron/Monkmeyer Press Photo; p. 584 Frances Cox/Stock, Boston Inc.; p. 588 Judy Gelles/Stock, Boston Inc.; p. 592 Mark Richards/PhotoEdit; p. 597 Elizabeth Crews/Stock, Boston Inc.; p. 605 Roy Gumpel/Liaison; p. 607 Ik/Stock, Boston Inc.; p. 608 Marianne Gontarz.

Abecassis, J., 85
Abel, E. L., 157
Abram, M. J., 372
Abramson, L., 264
Abroms, I. F., 282, 283, 284
Acker, Alison, 482
Acredolo, L. P., 215
Adair, J. G., 36
Adams, G. R., 556
Adams, R. E., Jr., 273, 274
Adegoke, A. A., 505, 511
Adler, 372
Agnoli, F., 338
Ainsworth, L. L., 82, 262
Ainsworth, M. D. S., 267–268, 271, 278
Aitken, D. A., 124, 125
Albert, Peter, 64
Albert, R. S., 435, 436
Albin, K., 466
Alcock, J., 227
Aldis, O., 353
Allen, R. E., 329
Allison, P. D., 374
Als, H., 179
Althof, W., 537
Alvy, K. T., 557
Amato, P. R., 374, 376, 377
American College of Obstetrics and
    Gynecology, 148
American Psychiatric Association, 284, 285,
    429, 487, 488, 512, 516, 581
Anastasiow, N., 572
Anderson, D. R., 466
Anderson, E. R., 380
Anderson, J. A., 474
Anderson, J. R., 412, 522
Andrews, B., 35
Angel, J. L., 169
Angst, J., 134, 373
Anisfeld, M., 324
Anthony, E. J., 487, 492
Appel, L. F., 414
Applebaum, M. I., 422
Arbuthnot, J., 537
Aries, P., 8
Arlin, P. K., 79
Armour-Thomas, E., 86
Arnett, J., 526, 527, 528, 572
Aronfreed, J., 476
Asher, S. R., 459, 460
Askew, S., 364
Aslin, R. N., 209, 215, 216
Asp, E., 461
Astington, J. W., 448
Atkinson, R. C., 409
Aubrey, C., 312

Babad, E. Y., 462
Babson, S. G., 161
Bachan, C. M., 365
Bäckström, K., 14
Backteman, G., 434
Bailey, J. R., 448
Baillargeon, R., 222
Baker, D., 34
Baker, D. P., 34
Baker, L., 513
Baker, R. L., 168
Baker-Ward, L., 304
Bakken, L., 571
Bakwin, H., 9
Balcerak, L. J., 416
Balke, E., 14
Ball, R. M., 269
Bancroft, R., 438
Bandura, Albert, 21, 68–74, 350, 353, 416,
    467, 472
Banks, M. S., 209
Baran, S. J., 472
Barr, H. M., 157
Barr, J. L., 314
Barrera, M., 585
Barrett, G. V., 423
Barry, H., III, 501
Basseches, M., 79
Bates, E., 230, 231, 232
Bates, J. E., 257
Battachi, M. W., 480
Battistich, V., 537
Battjes, R., 587
Baum, C. G., 512
Baumgartner, A. I., 562
Baumrind, D., 368, 370–371, 460, 553
Baxter, G., 485
Bayley, N., 207
Beatty, P., 588
Becker, B. J., 565
Becker, J. B., 549
Beckman, D. A., 157, 158
Beckwith, L., 183, 250
Beer, J., 485
Beit-Hallahmi, B., 366
Bell, C. S., 587
Belsky, J., 247, 248, 278, 322, 382, 484
Bem, S. L., 562
Benedict, H., 328
Benthin, A., 527
Bentler, P. M., 581, 586, 588
Bentley, K. S., 369
Berdine, W. H., 399
Bereiter, C., 317, 326
Berg, K. M., 205
Berg, W. K., 205, 206

Berkowitz, M. W., 537
Berndt, T. J., 279, 452, 453, 454, 455
Berne, E., 372
Bernieri, F., 135
Bernstein, B., 335
Bertalanffy, L. von, 47
Bertenthal, B. I., 207, 210
Beunen, G., 508
Beyth-Marom, R., 527
Bianchi, J., 159
Bibby, R. W., 510, 521, 558, 559
Bierman, K. L., 458
Bijou, S. W., 62, 67, 234
Biller, H. B., 579
Binder, A., 579, 580
Birch, H. G., 256
Bishop, J. E., 115
Bizzell, R. P., 317
Bjerkedal, T., 121
Black, C., 570
Blackhurst, A. E., 399
Blanchard-Fields, F., 524
Bloch, H. A., 501
Block, J., 582, 585
Block, J. H., 365
Bloom, L., 236, 321
Blumberg, M. L., 483
Blyth, D., 509
Boldizar, J. P., 363
Bolton, P. J., 159
Boring, E. G., 417
Borkowski, J. G., 305, 415
Bornstein, M. H., 210, 357
Bouchard, C., 508
Bouchard, T. C., 396
Bouchard, T. J., Jr., 134
Boulton, M. J., 474
Bowen, R., 525
Bower, T. G. R., 217, 222
Bowlby, John, 79–82, 263, 264, 265, 266,
    267, 274, 381
Bowman, B., 358, 382
Bowman, J. M., 169, 278
Boyd, G. A., 234, 327
Bradbard, M. R., 383, 384
Bradshaw, G. L., 412
Braine, L. G., 455
Bransford, J. D., 412, 413
Brantner, J. P., 476
Braun, C., 462
Brazelton, T. D., 178–179, 181
Brendt, R. L., 157, 158
Brenner, J., 359
Bretherton, I., 232
Brewin, C. R., 35
Briggs, L. J., 417

Brisk, M. E., 334
Broadbent, D. E., 410
Broderick, P., 299, 300
Brody, J., 160
Bronfenbrenner, Urie, 47, 79, 84, 87–89, 91,
    107, 138, 245, 246, 247, 260, 316, 371,
    382, 461, 483, 557, 560, 593
Bronson, G. W., 253, 254, 255
Bronstein, P., 371, 374
Brooks, J. B., 372
Brooks-Gunn, J., 316, 505, 511, 558, 567,
    572, 573, 574
Brophy, J. E., 462
Brown, J., 588
Brown, J. L., 249
Brown, J. S., 417
Brown, M. H., 346, 347, 518
Brown, R., 236, 324
Brownell, C. A., 345
Brownell, K. D., 396
Browne Miller, A., 381
Bruchkowsky, M., 448
Bruner, J. S., 68, 232, 327
Bryan, M. H., 204
Bryan, T., 586
Bryant, B. K., 459
Bryant, I., 466
Buber, Martin, 607, 608–609
Buchanan, C. M., 549
Buchanan, N. R., 359
Buis, J. M., 525
Bukowski, W. M., 459
Bullinger, A., 79
Bullock, J. R., 13
Bullough, V. L., 505
Bumbals, J., 395
Burns, B., 204
Burns, K., 160
Burns, W., 160
Burton, L. M., 481
Buss, A. H., 256, 257
Butler, J. R., 481
Byrne, B. M., 546

Cairns, R. B., 21, 62
Caldwell, B. M., 15, 17, 20
Calfee, R., 410
California Assessment Program, 470
Campbell, S. B., 181
Campos, J. J., 207, 210
Candee, D., 537
Canning, P. M., 314
Cantor, N., 445
Carey, E. J. B., 484
Carey, S. T., 332
Carey, W. B., 256
Cargo, A. P., 487
Carlo, M. S., 417
Carlson, P., 324
Carlson, S. M., 356
Carpenter, D. J., 588
Carroll, J. L., 529
Cartwright, B. S., 356
Cartwright, D. S., 580
Case, R., 410
Casler, L., 275
Caspi, A., 138, 580
Castle, J., 227

Cattell, R. B., 418
Ceci, S. J., 462
Chase, L. J., 472
Chase, N. F., 479
Chase-Lansdale, L., 573
Chasnoff, I. J., 159, 160
Chassin, L., 585
Cherry, E. C., 410
Chervenak, J. L., 167, 168
Chess, S., 256, 258, 259
Chester, R. D., 438
Cheung, Y. W., 588
Chez, R. A., 167, 168
Chi, M. T. H., 522
Chilman, C. S., 381
Chipman, S. F., 564, 565
Chisum, G. M., 159
Chiu, L. H., 553
Chomsky, N., 329–330
Choquet, M., 517
Christopher, F. S., 574
Christopherson, V. A., 364, 371
Chugani, H. T., 200
Chumlea, W. C., 505
Churchill, J. A., 183
Cisero, C. A., 417
Claes, M., 579
Clarizio, H. F., 475
Clark, E. V., 236
Clark, H. H., 236
Clarke-Stewart, K. A., 82, 278, 316
Clarkson, W. G., 206
Clausen, J. A., 509
Cleminshaw, H., 376
Clifton, R. K., 218
Coates, T. J., 576
Cobb, E., 357
Coffman, S., 247
Cohen, Y. A., 501
Cohn, J. F., 181
Coie, J. D., 457
Colby, A., 533, 534, 535, 537
Cole, P. M., 347, 487
Collett, J., 335
Collins, A., 417
Collins, W. A., 250, 269, 270, 279, 466, 474,
    557
Collis, G. M., 328
Collman, P., 362
Comenius, J., 197
Condon, W. S., 266
Connell, B., 364
Connor, F. P., 282
Cook, K. V., 363
Cook, T. D., 470
Cooke, B., 369
Cooley, C. H., 449, 450
Coopersmith, S., 552–553
Coovert, D. L., 514
Corbin, C. B., 397
Corbin, S. B., 374
Cortada, J. M., 119
Côté, J. E., 555
Coulter, D., 34
Coulter, D. L., 425
Courtright, J. A., 472
Coustan, D. R., 160
Cox, M., 376

Cox, R., 376
Cox, T. C., 587, 588
Cratty, B. J., 397
Creasy, R. K., 182
Crisp, A. H., 513
Crittenden, P. M., 483
Crockett, L. J., 509, 559
Crouter, A., 485
Crowell, J. A., 273
Crowley, P. A., 182
Culbertson, J. L., 12–13
Cummins, J., 331, 334, 336
Curtiss, S., 105, 107
Cusack, R., 393, 396
Cziko, G. A., 334

Dalton, K., 181
Damon, W., 535, 537
D'Andrea, D., 330
Danilewitz, D., 570
Dansky, J. L., 435
Darley, J. M., 529, 530, 531, 535
Darling, C. A., 566
Darwin, Charles, 21
Das, J. P., 416
Dasen, P. R., 309
Dash, U. N., 416
David, C. B., 16
David, P. H., 16
Davis, 197
Davis, S. M., 165
Dawkins, R., 83
Day, R. D., 379
DeBlassie, R. R., 570
DeCasper, A. J., 216, 266
De Charms, R., 464
DeLissovoy, V., 573
deMause, L., 14, 22
Dement, W. C., 250
DeMyer, M. K., 285–286
Denham, S. A., 360
Dennis, W., 103
Denver Developmental Materials, 300
Depinet, R. L., 423
deRegt, R. H., 177
Desor, J. A., 217
de St. Marthe, S., 197
Deuel, R. K., 283
deVries, M. W., 260–261
Diamant, Y. Z., 160
Diaz, R. M., 330, 433
Dick-Read, Grantly, 179–180
Dickson, W. J., 35
Diener, C. I., 464
Dietrich, K. N., 485
DiLalla, L. F., 356
Dill, F., 123
Dill, F. J., 119, 120, 121, 122
Dinges, M. M., 585
Dinkmeyer, D., 372
Dix, C., 154
Dix, T., 369
Dobkin de Rios, M., 583
Doby, J., 374
Doherty, M. A., 476
Doleys, D. M., 476
Dollahite, D. C., 380
Doman, G. J., 314

Donaldson, G., 419
Donaldson, M., 311
Donate-Bartfield, E., 251
Donnelly, B. W., 570, 572–573
Donovan, C. M., 399
Dowling, W. D., 372
Dreyer, P. H., 574
Drugan, A., 165
Drummond, W. J., 558
Duberman, L., 381
Duffty, P., 204
Duncan, S., 232
Dunn, J., 446
Dunphy, D. C., 559
Duskin Feldman, Ruth, 432–433
Dweck, C. S., 72, 463, 464
Dyk, P. H., 574

Easterbrooks, M. A., 460
Eastman, G., 557
Eastman, P., 314
Eccles, J. S., 457, 549, 565
Eckerman, C. O., 272
Eckland, B. K., 83
Eden, R. D., 161
Egeland, B., 114, 265, 278
Eiger, M. S., 197
Eilers, R. E., 233, 234
Eilers, R. M., 329
Eisen, M., 551–552
Eisenberg, M., 382
Eisenberg, N., 529, 536
Eisenberg, R. B., 216
Eisenberg-Berg, N., 537
Elder, G. H., Jr., 138, 213
Elkind, D., 314, 319, 490, 524, 525, 526, 527
Elkington, J., 156
Elliott, G. C., 552
Elliott-Faust, D. J., 415
Elster, A. B., 165, 270, 526
Emery, A. E., 108, 114, 122, 123, 124, 125, 126
Emery, A. E. H., 121
Emery, R. E., 474, 481, 483, 485
Endsley, R. C., 383, 384
Engelmann, S., 317
Engen, T., 216
Enright, R., 525
Epling, W. F., 515, 516
Erck, T. W., 274
Erickson, G., 565
Erickson, J. D., 121
Erickson, M. T., 283, 285, 399, 489
Erickson, P. G., 589
Erikson, Erik, 56–59, 348–350, 553–554, 556
Ernst, C., 134, 373
Eron, L. D., 469, 472
Erwin, P., 454
Ethington, C., 34
Evans, M. I., 165
Eveleth, P. B., 505
Evra, J. V., 466
Eysenck, H. J., 137, 528
Eysenck, S. B. G., 528

Fagan, J., 581
Fagan, J. F., III, 210

Fagot, B. I., 362
Fantz, R. L., 210, 212
Farkas, S., 565
Farleger, D., 14
Farver, J. M., 358
Fasick, F. A., 504
Feingold, B. F., 564
Feldman, D. H., 431
Feldman, S. S., 273
Feldt, L. S., 373
Fennema, E., 565
Fenson, L., 355
Ferguson, L. R., 565
Feuerstein, R., 425
Field, T. M., 278, 490
Fifer, W. P., 216, 266
Fine, M. A., 366
Finkelhor, D., 479, 481
Finn, P., 588
Fischer, K. W., 46, 312, 401, 481
Fischhoff, J., 485
Fishkin, J., 534
Fiske, D. W., 232
Fiske, S. T., 361
Fivush, R., 362
Flannery, D., 504
Flavell, J. H., 196, 312, 409, 414, 416, 446, 522
Flynn, J. R., 461
Fogel, A., 216, 264
Fong, L., 285
Food and Nutrition Board, 157, 159, 160, 167
Forehand, R., 512
Forness, S. R., 427, 428
Forrest-Pressley, D., 415
Fouts, R. S., 321
Fox, N. A., 257
Fox, R. A., 369
France-Kaatrude, A., 460
Frankenberger, W., 489
Frankenburg, W. K., 300
Franklin, J. T., 585, 586
Frazier, A., 510
Freedman, J., 123, 133, 134
Freeze, R., 477
Freifelder, D., 117
Freud, A., 54, 362
Freud, Sigmund, 48–55
Freyberg, J. T., 357
Fried, M. H., 172
Fried, M. N., 172
Fried, P. A., 159
Friedman, J. M., 115, 118, 119, 123, 154, 155, 158, 159, 160
Friedman, L., 109, 565
Friedman, M. L., 554
Frisch, R. E., 505
Frye, D., 224, 448
Fuligni, A. J., 457
Furrow, D., 328
Furstenberg, F. F., 374
Furstenberg, F. F., Jr., 567, 572, 573, 574
Furth, H., 405

Gaddis, A., 505, 511
Gagné, R. M., 417
Galler, J. R., 202

Gallistel, C. R., 312, 405
Galton, F., 372
Galton, Francis, 130–131
Gamble, T. J., 275, 278, 381
Garbarino, J., 461, 485
Garcia, E. E., 330, 331, 333, 334, 335, 336
Garcia, R., 78
Gardner, H., 418
Gardner, M. K., 419
Garmezy, N., 492
Garvey, C., 361
Gelles, R., 477
Gelles, R. J., 477, 483
Gelman, R., 312, 313, 314, 405
Gelman, S., 362
Gelman, S. A., 78, 221, 264, 445
Genesee, F., 333
Gerber, M., 207
Gerbner, G., 467, 470
Gesell, A., 299
Getzels, J. W., 434
Gewirtz, J. L., 251–252
Gianino, A., 255, 347
Gibbs, J. C., 537
Gibson, E. J., 211
Gil, D. G., 479, 485
Gilligan, C., 49, 535–536, 537, 556
Gilmore, D. H., 124, 125
Gitomer, D. H., 414
Glaser, R., 522
Glick, P. C., 380
Globerson, T., 422
Goelman, H., 382
Golbus, M. S., 125
Gold, M. S., 587
Gold, R., 314
Goldberg, S., 265
Goldenberg, C., 463
Goldgaber, D., 122
Goldsmith, H. H., 460
Goldsmith, J., 171
Goldsmith, J. P., 183, 185
Good, T. L., 462
Goodwin, M. S., 275
Goodwin, R., 328
Gordon, E. W., 86
Gordon, T., 372
Gotlib, I. H., 35
Gottesman, I. I., 114, 130, 135, 139
Gottlieb, G., 105, 139
Gottman, J. M., 457, 459, 559
Gould, S. J., 134
Gove, F., 278
Graesser, A. C., 412
Graham, J. M., Jr., 158
Grandon, G. M., 373, 374
Grant, J. P., 10, 16, 19, 20, 129, 229, 281, 298, 315, 482
Green, K. D., 457
Green, V., 572
Greenacre, P., 356
Greene, J., 436
Greene, L. S., 217
Greenfield, P. M., 321
Greenspan, S. L., 261
Grief, E. B., 534
Grieser, D. L., 327
Griffin, S., 516

Griffiths, M. D., 474
Grindstaff, C. F., 572
Gronlund, N. E., 561
Gross, D., 346
Gross, L., 470
Grossman, J. J., 424
Grotevant, H. D., 556
Grotevant, M. D., 373
Grow, L. J., 166
Grusec, J. E., 476
Guacci, N., 247
Guerra, N., 585
Guidubaldi, J., 376
Guilford, J. P., 430, 433
Gulko, J., 362
Gunnar, M. R., 250, 269, 270
Gunter, B., 465
Gustafson, G. E., 251
Gustafsson, J. E., 422

Haas, J., 200
Hagen, E., 420, 423
Hague, W. J., 533
Haith, M. M., 211, 213, 214, 217
Hake, J. L., 215
Hakuta, K., 330, 331, 334
Haldane, John, 83
Hale, C., 305, 415
Hall, G. S., 577
Hall, G. Stanley, 21–22, 501
Hall, W. G., 206
Hallahan, D. P., 398, 399, 430
Halonen, J. S., 274
Ham, M., 551
Hamidullah, J., 304
Hamilton, E. M. N., 511
Hammill, D. D., 428
Hamner, T. J., 484
Hampson, J., 328
Hampsten, E., 7–8, 35
Hand, M., 537
Handyside, A. H., 149
Hanna, E., 69
Harding, H. E., 430
Hare, J. W., 160
Hargrove, L. J., 429
Harland, D., 19
Harlow, H. F., 262
Harris, K. L., 251
Harris, M. B., 165
Harris, M. J., 135
Harris, P. L., 346
Harris, T., 372
Harris, Y. R., 304
Harrison, L., 183, 186, 336
Harter, S., 274, 449, 450, 451, 511, 521, 546,
    547
Hartl, D. L., 117
Hartup, W. W., 453, 454, 455, 458, 560
Haskins, R., 316, 317
Hass, A., 569
Hathaway, S. R., 580
Hauser, R. M., 373
Havighurst, Robert, 59–61
Hay, D. F., 227, 268
Hayden, M. R., 117, 119
Hayes, Catherine, 320

Hayes, C. D., 275, 382
Hayes, Kevin, 320
Hazen, N. L., 207
Hebb, D. O., 255, 272
Hedges, L. V., 565
Heilman, K., 489
Heinonen, O. P., 154
Heinzen, T. E., 431, 432
Heisel, B., 303
Heiser, C. B., Jr., 583
Henderson, B. B., 477
Henderson, G., 477
Henjum, R., 477
Henker, B., 487, 489
Henry, C. S., 593
Herman, C. P., 517, 518
Hernandez, D. J., 373, 384
Herzog, A., 586
Herzog, E., 579
Hess, G. C., 574
Hetherington, E. M., 376, 380
Hewitt, M., 9
Higbee, K. L., 412
Higgins, E. T., 362
Hillman, L. S., 204
Hinde, R. A., 81, 84, 253
Hindelang, M. J., 577
Ho, D. Y. F., 270, 279
Hodapp, R. M., 123, 246, 252, 279, 425, 545
Hoden, J., 166
Hofer, M. A., 55, 83
Hoff, C., 576
Hofferth, S. L., 382
Hoffman, L. W., 372
Hoffman, M. L., 448, 538
Hogarty, F. S., 422
Hoge, R. D., 431
Holden, G. W., 460
Holland, A. J., 514
Holmes, I. W., 546
Holmes, R. H., 492
Holmlund, W. S., 561
Holstein, C. B., 534
Holt, R. W., 360
Hooper, S. R., 425
Hopkins, R. W., 593
Horn, J., 136
Horn, J. L., 419
Horn, J. M., 114, 135
Hornstein, E., 160
Horowitz, B., 479
Horton, D. L., 411
Howard, K., 547, 550, 577
Howes, C., 268, 358
Howley, E., 319
Hsu, L. Y. F., 165
Hubel, D. H., 200
Huesmann, L. R., 469, 470, 472
Hughes, 311
Hughes, F. P., 357
Hughes, R., 346
Hunt, E., 338
Hunt, J. McV., 45, 204
Hurlock, E. B., 357
Hurrelmann, K., 557
Husén, T., 423, 461
Huston, A. C., 465, 466, 470, 472, 474

Hutt, S. J., 249
Huynh, C., 36
Hyde, J. S., 565, 574
Hyde, S., 564, 565
Hynd, G. W., 429

Iennarella, R. S., 159
Ihinger-Tallman, M., 380
Ijzendoorn, M. H. van, 269, 372
Ingram, D., 234
Inhelder, B., 518
Inoff-Germain, G., 505
Intons-Peterson, M. J., 563
Isabell, B. J., 251
Izard, Carroll E., 27, 28, 250, 346

Jacklin, C. N., 364, 564, 565
Jackson, J. F., 272
Jackson, P. W., 434
Jacobs, J. E., 565
Jacobsen, L., 462
Jacobson, J. L., 156, 273
Jacobson, S. W., 156, 157, 226
Jacobvitz, R. S., 466
Jacopini, G. A., 117
Jahnke, H. C., 524
James, William, 85, 220–221, 448–449
Jardine, R., 135
Jay, E., 417
Jean-Gilles, M., 483
Jeanneret, O., 591, 593
Jelliffe, D. B., 202
Jelliffe, E. F., 202
Jenkins, J. M., 264–265
Jensen, A. R., 106
Jensen, L., 536
Jersild, A. T., 504
Jevne, R., 513
Johnson, B., 329
Johnson, H. R., 122
Johnson, J. E., 538
Johnson, J. H., 490
Johnson, M. H., 212
Johnson, M. K., 413
Johnson, M. P., 165
Johnson, S. A., 572
Johnson, V. E., 576
Johnston, M. V., 123
Jones, E. F., 569
Jones, M. C., 64, 509
Jones, R. L., 438
Jordan, E., 371
Jorgensen, S. R., 573
Jovonen, J., 458
Joy, L. A., 469
Jusczyk, P. W., 216
Justice, E., 412

Kagan, J., 226, 248, 257, 258, 259, 272, 382,
    384
Kaitz, M., 226
Kaler, S. R., 165
Kallen, D. J., 566
Kalucy, R. S., 513
Kamin, L., 137
Kandel, D. B., 586
Kant, Emmanuel, 536

Kaplan, L. J., 558
Kasof, J., 280
Kato, T., 159
Kauffman, J. M., 398, 399, 430
Kavale, K. A., 427, 428
Kawai, M., 264
Kaye, H., 216
Kaye, K., 264
Kazdin, A. E., 486, 487
Kearsley, R. B., 382
Kegan, R., 55, 73
Keith, B., 374, 376, 377
Kelley, H. H., 46
Kelly, J. B., 374, 376
Kempe, C. H., 483
Kempe, R. S., 483
Kendall-Tackett, K. A., 481
Keniston, K., 534
Kennell, H. H., 263, 265, 381
Kenney, M. D., 262
Keogh, B. K., 438
Kessen, W., 9, 197, 320
Key, C. B., 133
Kimball, M., 469
Kinsey, A. C., 566
Kirby, J. R., 416
Kirk, S., 427
Klaus, M. H., 263, 265, 381
Klein, M., 484
Kline, S. M., 516
Kloza, E. M., 125
Knuppel, R. A., 169
Knutson, J. F., 484
Kogan, N., 434, 435
Kohlberg, L. A., 362–363, 528, 531–535,
    536, 537
Kolata, G. B., 159
Kolodny, R. C., 576
Konner, M., 275
Kopp, C. B., 165, 168, 345
Korbin, J. E., 320, 321
Koren-Karie, N., 269
Korn, S. J., 259, 511
Kotelchuck, M., 271
Koupernik, C., 487
Kovacs, M., 486, 487
Kroupa, S. E., 579
Kruger, T. L., 576
Kuhl, P. K., 327
Kuhn, D., 402, 405
Kunkel, D., 474
Kunkel, M. A., 593
Kurtines, W., 534
Kuziel-Perri, P., 572
Kuzyk, B., 197
Kynn, D. B., 579

Lachenmeyer, J. R., 513, 517
Ladame, F., 591, 593
Lagercrantz, H., 177
La Greca, A. M., 460
Lam, T. C. L., 334
Lamanna, M. A., 366
Lamaze, F., 180
Lamb, M. E., 165, 246, 270, 460, 526
Lambert, W. E., 331
Lamon, S. J., 565

Lancy, D. F., 351, 352
Landau, T. C., 589
Landesman, S., 424
Landry, R., 331
Langlois, J. H., 213, 458
Lapsley, D. K., 521, 525, 534, 535
Larson, R., 551
Latané, R., 529
Lay, K. L., 361, 452
Lazar, I., 134
Leboyer, F., 180
Ledoux, S., 517
Lee, J., 585
Lee, V. E., 316
Lee-Painter, S., 252
Lefkowitz, M., 469
Lefrançois, G. R., 307, 338, 405, 466
Legerstee, M., 233
Leigh, G. K., 379
Leinbach, M. D., 362
Lenard, H. G., 249
Lenneberg, E. H., 329
Leon, M., 212, 262
Lerner, R. M., 47, 106, 130, 138, 139, 261,
    278, 511, 545
Leslie, A. M., 357
Lesser, H., 470
Lester, B. M., 181
Levine, C., 555
Levine, J. M., 362
Levine, R. A., 16, 20
Levitsky, D., 200
Levitt, M. J., 247
Levy, G. D., 362
Lewin, H., 370, 475
Lewin, R., 153, 167, 200
Lewis, J. M., 374
Lewis, M., 252, 347
Liben, L., 311
Liberty, C., 414
Lieberman, A. B., 177, 198
Lieberman, A. F., 261
Liebert, R. M., 405, 469
Lieblich, A., 366
Liggins, G. C., 173, 174
Liljeström, R., 129, 321
Lindauer, B. K., 413, 414
Lindhagen, K., 224
Linn, M. C., 564, 565
Lipsitt, L. P., 204, 216, 218
Lisonbee, L. K., 510
Liu, D. T., 125
Locke, John, 20, 23
Lockhart, A. S., 398
Lockman, J. J., 207
Loehlin, J. C., 114, 119, 135, 136
Logan, G. D., 489
Logan, J. A., 586
Long, L., 382
Long, R. E., 562
Long, T., 382
Long, V. O., 562
Longeway, K. P., 274
Lorenz, K., 80
Lorsbach, T. C., 427
Love, H., 284
Lowery, C. R., 379

Luke, C., 465, 473
Luria, Z., 279, 362
Lyen, K., 513
Lynn, D. B., 364
Lyon, M. E., 314

Maccoby, E., 362
Maccoby, E. E., 564
Maccoby, E. P., 370, 475
MacDonald, 546
Macfarlane, A., 218
MacKinnon, C., 534
Macmillan, D. L., 438
Madsen, M. C., 350, 351, 352
Magnusson, D., 434, 509
Malatesta, E. Z., 250
Malina, R. M., 505, 508
Malinak, L. R., 165, 572
Maller, O., 217
Mandler, J. M., 231
Manfredi, R., 517
Mao, L. W., 553
Marcia, J. E., 554–556
Marks, L. E., 210
Markus, G. B., 373
Marlatt, G. A., 585
Marsh, H. W., 546, 564
Marsiglio, W., 573
Marston, A. R., 517
Martin, D. C., 157
Martin, H., 485
Martin, N., 135
Masi, W., 212
Maslow, Abraham, 92–93
Mason, W. A., 262
Masters, J. C., 226
Masters, W. H., 576
Mayer, N. K., 232
Mayerrose, M., 476
Mazur, A., 83
McAleer, J. L., 465
McCabe, M. P., 435
McCall, R. B., 422
McCartney, K., 135, 319, 371, 383
McClelland, D., 370
McClelland, D. C., 423
McCormick, L., 336
McCormick, M., 166
McCune, L., 353
McDill, E. L., 330
McDonald, I. W., 438
McGillicuddy-Delisi, A., 538
McGillivray, B., 120, 121, 122, 123, 160
McGlone, C., 403
McGraw, M. B., 217
McGroarty, M., 335
McGue, M., 134
McKay, G., 372
McKay, J., 167
McKee, L., 251
McNeill, D., 235
Mednick, B. R., 168
Mednick, S. A., 431
Medway, F. J., 462
Melican, G. J., 373
Meline, C. W., 470
Meltzoff, A. N., 69, 210, 226, 227

Mendel, Gregor, 114
Meneese, W. B., 593
Mercer, C. D., 429
Mesibov, G. B., 285
Mettetal, G., 559
Meyer, W. J., 462
Mielke, K. W., 465–466
Miller, B. C., 574
Miller, C. E., 119
Miller, C. J., 484
Miller, G. A., 410
Miller, L. B., 317
Miller, S. A., 403
Miller, S. J., 165
Mills, C. B., 411
Milsark, I., 119
Milstead, M., 305, 415
Minifie, F. D., 233
Mitchell, A. A., 156
Miyawaki, K., 233
Moerk, E. L., 327
Moffitt, A. R., 206, 233
Mollnow, E., 154
Monachesi, E. D., 580
Montemayor, R., 504, 551–552, 559
Montessori, M., 317
Moore, C., 448
Moore, M., 581
Moore, M. K., 210, 226
Moray, N., 410
Moriarty, A., 485
Morin, S. F., 576
Morrill, C. M., 512
Morrison, E., 511
Morse, H., 329
Morsink, C. V., 248, 428, 429
Morton, J., 212
Moskowitz, B. A., 328
Moss, V. D., 319
Mott, F. L., 382
Mowat, F., 245
Moynahan, E. D., 415
Mueller, E., 246, 252, 279, 359, 545
Mueller, R. F., 108, 114, 122, 123, 124, 125,
    126
Mulcahy, B. F., 417
Mulhern, R. K., 476, 484
Mulhern, R. K., Jr., 483
Mullin, J. B., 160
Mullis, R. L., 551
Mumma, G. H., 458
Muni-Brander, P., 513, 517
Murray, J., 477
Muuss, R. E., 536, 555
Muzio, J. N., 250
Myers, D. E., 373, 384
Myers, P. I., 428

National Center for Health Statistics, 165
Natriello, G., 330
Naus, M. J., 304
Neal, J. H., 375
Nealis, J. T., 284
Neiger, B. L., 593
Nelson, K., 328
Nelson, K. E., 330
Nesbitt, W., 553
Neuman, S. B., 472

Newcomb, A. F., 459
Newcomb, M. D., 581, 586, 588
Newman, S. E., 417
Newton, M., 586
Nguyen, T. van, 138
Nicolopoulou, A., 354
Niederhoffer, A., 501
Norcia, A. M., 209
Norén Björn, E., 321
Norris, 222
Nucci, L., 585
Nucci, L. P., 528
Nugent, J. K., 181
Nunner-Winkler, G., 536

Oatley, K., 264–265, 345
Oden, M., 435
Oden, S., 454
Oetting, E. R., 585
Offer, D. O., 547, 550, 552, 557, 577
Offer, J., 577
Ohuche, R. O., 229
O'Laughlin, E., 470
Olds, S. W., 197
Oliver, J. M., 329
Oller, D. K., 233, 234, 329
Olson, David, 185
Olson, D. R., 416
Oppenheim, R. W., 206
Opper, S., 309
O'Reilly, A. W., 357
Ornstein, P. A., 304, 414
Oser, F., 537
Oster, H., 346
Ostrov, E., 547, 550, 577
Otaalam, B., 229
Overton, W. F., 105

Packard, V., 13, 566
Padilla, A. M., 335
Page, E. B., 373, 374
Paikoff, R. L., 558, 574
Paley, V. G., 355, 361, 363
Pallas, A. M., 330
Palmer, J. H., 589
Palmer, J. L., 382
Palmer, R. L., 513
Panagakos, P. G., 282, 283, 284
Paris, S. G., 413, 414
Park, K. A., 361, 452
Parke, R. D., 247, 457, 475
Parker, J. G., 460
Parmelee, A. H., 168
Parnes, S. J., 430
Parsons, G., 328
Parten, M. B., 359
Pasley, K., 380, 381
Passino, A. W., 573
Passman, R. H., 251, 273, 274, 476, 483, 484
Pattee, L., 459
Patterson, M. L., 138
Patton, J. M., 430
Patton, J. R., 425
Pavlov, Ivan, 62–63
Pazulinec, R., 476
Pearce, J. C., 237, 295, 439
Pearl, R., 586
Pearson, J. L., 565

Pease-Alvarez, L., 330, 331
Pellegrino, J. W., 414
Pence, A. R., 382
Penner, L. A., 514
Pergament, E., 128, 130
Perkins, D., 417
Perkins, D. N., 422
Perlmutter, M., 218
Perner, J., 446
Peskin, H., 509
Petersen, A. C., 502, 509, 558
Peterson, C., 383
Peterson, G. W., 379
Peterson, R., 383
Phelps, M. E., 200
Phillips, D., 383
Piaget, Jean, 21, 75–79, 86, 207, 219–220,
    221–222, 224, 225–226, 227, 301, 305,
    306, 308, 309, 311, 328, 337, 353–354,
    357, 359, 400–409, 445, 518–522, 530,
    531
Pianta, R. C., 269
Pierce, W. D., 515, 516
Pill, C. J., 380
Pinchbeck, L., 9
Pincus, A. L., 256
Pines, M., 356, 492
Pines, Maya, 217, 237
Piper, E., 581
Pipes, P. L., 395
Pipp, S., 211
Pipp, S. L., 481
Pisoni, D. P., 216
Pitcher, E. G., 364
Plomin, R., 84, 106, 130, 135, 138, 256, 257
Pogrebin, L. C., 280
Pogue-Geile, M. F., 135
Polivy, J., 517, 518
Pollitt, E., 200
Polloway, E. A., 425
Polson, B., 586
Pope, A. W., 458
Pope, H. G., 517
Posterski, D. C., 510, 521, 558, 559
Poteet, J. A., 429
Powell, M. B., 481
Powlishta, K. K., 362
Prado, W., 456
Prechtl, H. F. R., 249
Premack, A. J., 320–321
Premack, D., 320–321
Pressley, M., 415
Preyer, William, 21
Prillaman, D., 430
Printz, A. M., 517
Pritkin, R., 395
Provenzano, J. J., 279, 362
Provine, R. R., 224
Putallaz, M., 457

Quay, H. C., 579

Rabin, A. I., 366
Rahe, R. H., 492
Ramanan, J., 382
Ramey, C., 424
Ramsay, L., 361, 452
Ramsbey, T. W., 567, 568

Randhawa, B. S., 565
Rank, O., 182
Ranney, M. D., 205
Rayburn, W., 154
Rayna, S., 225
Rayner, R., 63–64, 253
Rebok, G. W., 416
Redmond, M., 573
Reid, L. D., 588
Reiss, I. L., 538
Reissland, N., 226
Reppucci, N. D., 464
Reschly, D. J., 425
Rescorlo, L., 315
Resnick, L. B., 362
Rest, J. R., 529
Retter, K., 303
Revelle, R., 505
Reynolds, P., 228
Reyome, N. D., 481
Rheingold, H. L., 363, 408
Ricciutti, H. N., 200
Ricco, R. B., 78
Rice, B., 36
Rice, M., 470
Rice, M. L., 232, 326, 328, 330, 337
Richards, C. S., 119
Richards, L. N., 380
Richters, J., 268
Ridley-Johnson, R., 470
Riedmann, A., 366
Rieser-Danner, L. A., 213
Ringler, N. M., 265
Ringwalt, C. L., 589
Ritts, V. I., 138
Roazen, P., 49
Roberts, D. F., 365
Robinson, S., 181
Rochat, P., 221
Roche, J. P., 567, 568
Rodeck, C. H., 125
Rodning, C., 183
Roethlisberger, S. J., 35
Roffwarg, H. P., 250
Rogers, Carl, 546
Rogers, C. R., 91
Roggman, L. A., 213
Rogosch, F., 585
Rolison, M. A., 462
Romig, C. A., 571
Roosa, M. W., 573, 574
Roscoe, B., 576
Rose, R. J., 135
Rosenak, D., 160
Rosenblatt, R., 19
Rosengren, K. E., 469, 473
Rosenkoetter, L. J., 470, 472
Rosenthal, R., 462
Rosenthal, T. L., 405
Rosett, H. L., 158
Ross, A. O., 489
Ross, C., 364
Ross, D., 467
Ross, H. S., 359
Ross, S. A., 467
Rothman, S., 139
Rothstein, E., 55
Rousseau, Jean-Jacques, 20–21, 23

Rovee-Collier, C. K., 218
Rovine, M. J., 278
Royal College of Psychiatrists, 587
Royer, J. M., 417
Rubin, J. Z., 362
Rubin, K. H., 279, 360
Rubin, Z., 454
Ruff, H. A., 353
Ruffman, T., 346, 445
Runco, M. A., 434, 435, 436
Russell, G., 279
Rymer, R., 105

Saarnio, D. A., 304
Sabatino, D. A., 475, 477
Sachs, M., 90
Sagan, C., 264
Sagi, A., 269
Sagov, S. E., 180
Saidla, D. D., 15
Sajwaj, T., 476
Salapatek, P., 253
Salomon, G., 422
Saltarelli, L. M., 353
Sameroff, A. J., 207, 260
Sander, L. W., 158, 266
Santrock, 376
Sartre, Jean-Paul, 545, 604, 607–608
Sattler, J. M., 420
Savage-Rumbaugh, E. S., 321
Savin-Williams, R. C., 509
Sawin, D. B., 346
Scarr, S., 45, 93, 137, 253, 373, 382, 383
Scarr-Salapatek, S., 185, 186
Schachar, R. J., 489
Schaefer, C. E., 356
Schaffer, H. R., 264, 265, 272, 328
Schaie, K. W., 33
Schardein, J. L., 154
Scher, J., 154
Schiefelbusch, R. L., 336
Schlegel, A., 501
Schmiege, C. J., 380
Schneider, D. J., 448
Schneider, W., 416
Schneider-Rosen, K., 268
Schnoll, S., 160
Schnur, E., 316
Schultz, L. H., 364
Schultz, T. R., 530, 531
Schumer, F., 518
Schunk, D. H., 71
Schutz, R. W., 395, 398
Schwartz, H., 580
Schwartzberg, N. S., 469
Schwartzman, H. B., 357
Scott, K., 212
Sears, R. R., 370, 475
Sebald, H., 558
Segal, J., 268
Seligman, M. E. P., 465
Selman, R. L., 445, 446, 447, 452
Selye, H., 490
Semrud-Clikeman, M., 429
Serafini, S., 335
Serbin, L. A., 362
Serrano, B., 335
Settle, S. A., 380

Severson, H., 527
Sewell, W. H., 373
Seymour, D., 336
Shanklin, D. R., 166
Shantz, C. U., 445
Shapiro, E., 382
Shapiro, S., 154, 156, 166
Sharpe, D., 36
Shavelson, R. J., 546
Shaw, George Bernard, 430
Shea, J. A., 545
Shedler, J., 582, 585
Shepard, L. A., 428
Shepherd-Look, D. L., 562, 564
Sherman, I. C., 250
Sherman, M., 133, 250
Shields, J., 135
Shiffrin, R. M., 409
Showers, C., 445
Shreve, B. W., 593
Shultz, T. R., 535
Siegel, A. W., 9
Siegel, O., 509
Siegler, R. S., 405, 410
Sigel, I. E., 314
Silvern, L., 46, 312, 401
Silverstein, F. S., 123
Simard, R., 579
Simmons, R. G., 509
Simon, L., 438
Simpson, J. L., 155
Sinclair, H., 221, 225
Singer, D. G., 356, 465, 470
Singer, J. L., 356, 363, 465, 470
Singer, R. S., 470, 474
Singh, J. A., 103
Skinner, B. F., 21, 64, 67–68
Skolnick, A., 369
Skuy, M., 570
Sloan, D., 156
Slone, D., 154
Slotkin, T. A., 177
Slovi, P., 527
Small, S. A., 509, 557
Smith, C. L., 312
Smith, D. A., 412
Smith, L. B., 209
Smith, M. L., 428
Smith, P. B., 165, 572
Smith, R. S., 492
Smith, S., 553
Smith, W. P., 460
Smoll, F. L., 395, 398
Snarey, J., 572
Snarey, J. R., 534
Snidman, N., 248, 257, 258, 259
Snyder, L. A., 117
Snyderman, M., 139
Sobsey, D., 438
Society for Research in Child Development,
    14
Sodian, B., 346
Solomon, S., 413
Sosniak, L., 34
Spanier, G. B., 278
Sparkes, K., 320
Spearman, C., 418
Spellacy, W. N., 165

Spezzano, C., 163
Spitz, R. A., 264, 274
Springer, C., 376
Sroufe, L., 252, 278
Stall, R. D., 576
Stambak, M., 221, 225
Stander, V., 536
Stanley-Hagen, M., 380
Stanovich, K. E., 429
Stanton, W. R., 75, 78
Starfield, B., 166
Starr, R. H., 485
Starr, R. H., Jr., 485
Statman, D., 553
Stattin, H., 509
Steenbarger, B. N., 47
Stefan, L., 515, 516
Stein, Z., 167
Steinberg, L., 382
Steiner, J. E., 216
Stephen, C. W., 458
Stern, C., 139–140
Stern, D. N., 327
Stern, L., 484
Sternberg, R. J., 105, 419
Stevenson, 34
Stevenson, H. W., 461, 462
Stifter, C. A., 257
Stigler, J. W., 553
Stimpson, D., 536
Stimson, C. A., 227
Stockman, J. A., III, 154
Stone, W. L., 460
Stoutjesdyk, D., 513
Strangler, R. S., 517
Stratton, P., 365
Straus, M. A., 477
Streissguth, A. P., 157, 158
Streitmatter, J., 556
Strelau, J., 257
Strube, M. J., 448
Stryker, S., 448
Stuart, R. B., 579
Sudia, S., 579
Sullivan, M. W., 347
Surdy, T., 470
Susman, E., 483
Swaim, R. C., 585
Swain, I. U., 218
Swain, M., 331, 334

Tanner, J. M., 505
Tannock, R., 489
Tassel-Baska, J. V., 430
Tavare, J., 526
Tavris, C., 562
Taylor, M., 356
Taylor, M. J., 319
Terman, L. M., 30, 430, 432
Termine, N. T., 27, 28, 250, 346
Terrace, H. S., 232, 321
Terry, R., 457
Thomas, A., 256, 258, 259
Thomas, J. W., 464
Thomas, R. M., 44, 46, 93
Thompson, D. N., 525
Thompson, J. K., 514

Thorndike, R. L., 420, 423
Thorpe, W. H., 81, 262
Thurstone, L. L., 418
Tierney, J., 157
Tingle, B. A., 346
Tisak, M. S., 531, 535
Tishman, S., 417
Toda, S., 264
Tomson, B., 580
Toray, T., 585
Torrance, E. P., 433
Trause, M. A., 265
Travis, L. D., 67
Trawick-Smith, J., 353
Trehub, S. E., 215
Trickett, P. K., 483
Trofatter, K. F., Jr., 161
Tronick, E. Z., 232, 255, 256, 347
Tryon, R. C., 132
Tsang, M. C., 20
Tsuchiyama, B., 315
Tubbs, M. E., 138
Tubman, J. G., 369
Tudge, J. R. H., 86
Tuijnman, A., 423, 461, 462
Tuma, J. M., 486
Turgi, P. A., 15
Turiel, E., 528
Turkheimer, 130
Turner, P. H., 484
Tyler, C. W., 209
Tzuriel, D., 465

Undheim, J. O., 422
U.S. Bureau of the Census, 10, 13, 109, 161,
    165, 322, 330, 365, 366, 377, 396, 526,
    569, 570, 575, 577, 581, 589, 590
U.S. Department of Education, 399
U.S. Department of Health & Human
    Services, 157, 173
Usher, B. A., 487

Valdes-Dapena, M. A., 204, 205
Valsiner, J., 21, 47, 85
Van Bourgondien, M. E., 285
Vandell, D. L., 359, 382
Vandenberg, B. R., 354
Van Dusen, J. E., 566
Van Houten, R., 476
Van Komen, R., 559
Varga, D., 353
Vasen, A., 347
Vaughn, B., 265, 278
Verhaaren, P., 282
Visher, E. B., 380
Visher, J. S., 380, 381
Vitale, P., 593
Vojir, C. P., 428
Volling, B. L., 322
Von Hofsten, C., 224
Vórhees, C. V., 154
Voydanoff, P., 570, 572–573
Vygotsky, L. S., 47, 84–87, 245, 304, 337,
    338, 353, 354

Wadden, T. A., 396
Waddington, C. H., 113

Wakefield, J. F., 432
Waldholz, M., 115
Walk, R. D., 211
Walker, L. J., 492, 533, 534
Wallach, M. A., 435
Wallerstein, J. S., 374, 376
Walsh, B. T., 513, 514, 516
Walters, G. C., 476
Walters, R., 69, 472
Walthall, J. E., 284
Warshak, R. A., 376
Washton, A. M., 590
Wasserman, G., 265
Wasserman, G. A., 329
Waterman, A. S., 554, 555
Waters, E., 252, 268
Watkins, B. Q., 474
Watson, John B., 22, 63–64, 67, 253
Watson, M. W., 356
Watts, W. D., 586
Weber, K. S., 489
Weinberg, R. A., 137, 373
Weiner, B., 71, 463
Weininger, O., 353
Weinman, M., 165, 572
Weisberg, P., 274
Weisfeld, G. E., 131, 132
Weisskopf, M., 156
Wellman, H. M., 78, 219, 221, 264, 303,
    412, 445
Wells, E., 448
Wells, G., 328
Werner, E. E., 492
Werry, J. S., 285
Wertham, F., 357, 465
Wertsch, J. V., 85, 338
Wesley, C., 489
Wesley, F., 489
Westbury, I., 34
Westerman, J. A., 224
Westman, J. C., 14, 367
Whalen, C. K., 487, 489
Whatley, J. L., 272
White, B. L., 206
White, K. R., 319
White, S. H., 9
Whitney, E. N., 511
Whorf, B. L., 337
Widlak, F. W., 484
Wiesel, T. N., 200
Wiggins, J. S., 256
Wilgosh, L., 285
Wille, D. E., 273
Willerman, L., 114, 135, 136, 489
Williams, L. M., 481
Williams, M. L., 185, 186
Wilson, E. O., 83
Wilson, G. T., 513
Wilson, K. S., 359
Windahl, S., 469, 473
Winegar, A., 165
Winer, G. A., 403
Wingerson, L., 114
Winn, M., 465, 466, 470
Winnicott, O., 274
Winsten, Stephen, 430
Winterhoff, P. A., 86

Wittrock, M. C., 465
Wolff, P. H., 248, 249, 251
Wolf-Schein, E. G., 123
Wolock, I., 479
Wood, B. S., 234, 322, 324
Wood, M. R., 466
Wright, H. F., 25
Wright, J. C., 466, 470, 472
Wright, L. S., 586
Wu, D. Y. H., 607
Wunsch, J., 252

Yaffe, H., 160
Yamamoto, K., 433
Yarrow, L. J., 275
Yelon, S. L., 475
Yost, J. H., 448
Young, I. D., 125
Yutrzenka, B. A., 593

Zabrack, M. L., 469
Zajonc, R. B., 373
Zani, B., 566, 567, 568, 569

Zanna, M. P., 531
Zaslow, M. J., 382
Zelazo, P. R., 218, 382
Zigler, E., 123, 133, 134, 275, 278, 381, 425
Zimmerman, B. J., 405
Zingg, R. N., 103
Zuckerman, D. M., 470
Zuckerman, M., 528

Abortion, 174
Abstraction principle, 313–314
Academic achievement. *See also* Education
gender differences, 564–565
and television, 470, 471
Accommodation, 75–76, 219, 353
Acquired immune deficiency syndrome. *See*
AIDS
Active experience, 220
Activity, 257
Adaptation, 75–76, 219, 419
Additive bilingualism, 331, 332–333
Additive model, 105–106
ADHD (Attention-deficit hyperactivity
disorder), 487–489
Adolescence
cognitive development, 518–528
definition of, 501
moral development, 528–539
physical development, 504–518
social development, 545–593
and transitions, 501–504
Adolescent cognitive development, 518–528
egocentricity, 523–526, 572
information-processing approach, 521–523
Piagetian theory, 518–521
reckless behavior, 526–528
Adolescent moral development, 528–539
and behavior, 529
gender differences, 535–537
and justice, 529–530, 536
Kohlberg's stages, 531–535
Piagetian theory, 530–531
research implications, 537–539
Adolescent physical development, 504–518
concerns, 510–511
maturation timing, 408–510
nutrition, 511–518
physical change, 506–508
puberty, 504–505
pubescence, 505–506
Adolescent social development, 545–593
delinquency, 577–580
gangs, 580–581
and gender differences, 563–565
gender typing, 562–563
identity, 553–556
and loneliness, 545–546
and parenting, 557–558
and peers, 558–561
self-image, 546–549, 550, 551–552
self-worth, 552–553
and sexuality, 566–576
and stress, 549, 551
suicide, 590–593
teenage pregnancy, 165–166, 569–574

Adoption studies, 136–138
Adults, Eriksonian theory, 58–59
Affiliative behaviors, 270–271
AFP test, 119
Afterbirth, 177
Agent Orange, 156
Aggression. *See* Violence
AIDS (Acquired immune deficiency
syndrome), 162, 163, 575–576
and prenatal development, 161, 162
Alcohol, 157–158, 588–589. *See also* Drug
use
Alcoholism, 585
Alpha-fetoprotein (AFP), 125
Altruism, 83, 537
Alzheimer's disease, 122
Ambivalent infants, 268
American Association on Mental Retardation
(AAMR), 424, 426
American Sign Language (ASL), 320–321,
399
Amniocentesis, 124–125, 165
Amyloid filaments, 122
Anal stage of psychosexual development, 53
Anesthetics, 154, 177, 181
Angry cry, 251
Animal studies, 131–132, 320–321
Anorexia nervosa, 489, 512–516
Anoxia, 182
Apgar scale, 178, 300
Apnea, 204–205
Arousal, 72
ASL (American Sign Language), 320–321,
399
Aspirin, 154
Assimilation, 75–76, 219, 353–354
Association, 62
Associationistic models, 411
Associative play, 359
Assortative mating, 130
Atheistic existentialism, 608
Attachment, 81–82, 261–271
bonding, 262–265
and daycare, 276, 278
and fathers, 270–271
implications of, 268–270
stages of, 265–267
types of, 267–268
Attachment in the making, 266
Attentional processes, 68
Attention-deficit hyperactivity disorder
(ADHD), 487–489
Attitude-change model, 472
Attribution, 71–72, 463–465
Authoritarian parenting, 368
Authoritative parenting, 368

Autistic disorder, 123, 285–286
Autonomy, 57, 349
Avoidant infants, 268

Babinski reflex, 151, 206
Baby talk, 236
Baby tossing, 14
Balanced bilinguals, 330
Barbiturates, 154
Basic needs, 92–93
Bayley Scales of Infant Development, 300
Behavior. *See* Emotional and behavior
problems
Behavioristic theories, 61–68. *See also* Social
cognitive theory
classical conditioning, 62–64
operant conditioning, 62, 64–66, 67
Behavior modification, 68
Best friends, 453
Bias, 35–36
Bilingualism, 330–336
and education, 330, 332, 334–335, 336
and nonstandard languages, 335–336
psychological effects of, 331–334
transitional, 330–331
Biological/ecological theories, 79–91
Bowlby's attachment theory, 81–82
Bronfenbrenner's ecological systems
theory, 87–89, 91, 107
ethology, 80–81
sociobiology, 83–84
Vygotsky's cultural-historical theory,
84–87
Biology. *See* Biological/ecological theories;
Gene-context interaction; Genetics
Birth order, 372–373
Black English, 335, 336
Blind procedure, 27–28
Body composition, 508
Bonding, 262–265
Bowlby's attachment theory, 81–82
Brain development, 200, 206
Brazelton Neonatal Behavioral Assessment
Scale (NBAS), 178–179, 217, 300
Breastfeeding, 16, 197–200
Breech birth, 176
Bronfenbrenner's ecological systems theory,
87–89, 91, 107
Bulimia nervosa, 516–518

Caffeine, 157
Canalization, 113–114
Cardinal prinicple, 313
Cathartic model, 472
Cephalocaudal development, 153, 208
Cerebral palsy, 282–283

Cervix, 175
Cesarean delivery, 177
Challenge, 490
Change overload, 490
Chemical exposure, 156–157
Child abuse, 474–486
    and attachment, 268
    consequences of, 481, 483
    family context, 483–485
    feral children, 104–105, 106–107
    and language development, 326, 329
    prevalence of, 477–478
    and punishment, 475–476, 483–484
    solutions, 485–486
    types of, 479–481
Childbirth, 170–182
    birth status classification, 174–175
    Cesarean delivery, 177
    child's experience, 181–182
    initiation of, 173–174
    maternal experience, 179–181
    and mortality, 172–173
    neonatal scales, 178–179
    stages of, 175–177
Child-directed language, 327–329
Child labor, 9–10
Children. See also specific topics
    historical treatment of, 7–13, 15
    observers of, 20–22
    rights of, 14–20
    uniqueness of, 13
Chlamydia, 575
Chorionic villus sampling (CVS), 125, 165
Chromosomes, 108–109. See also Genetics
    disorders, 120–122
    sex chromosome abnormalities, 122–124
Chunking, 410
Circumcision, 217
Classical conditioning, 62–64
Classification, 308, 309, 312, 405–406
Clear-cut attachment, 266–267
Clinical observations. See Nonnaturalistic
    observations
Cocaine, 159–160, 589–590
Cognition, 74–75
Cognitive development. See also Social
    cognitive theory
    adolescence, 518–528
    early childhood, 299–300, 301–314
    infancy, 77, 208, 217–227
    and language development, 337–338
    and motor development, 208, 299–300,
        301
    and play, 353–354, 357
    stages, 76–78
    theories, 74–79
Cognitive strategies, 408, 416–417
Cohorts, 31–33
Color, 209–210
Communication
    and emotions, 345–346
    and language, 227–228, 320–322,
        338–339
Compensation, 402–403
Competency, 369
Competition, 350–352, 454
Conception, 107, 147
Concepts, 306

Conceptualization, 209
Concrete operations period, 78, 400–408
Conditioned response (CR), 63
Conditioned stimulus (CS), 62–63
Conformity, 455–456
Conjunction, 324
Conservation, 77, 309, 401–405
Construction, 220
Context, 90. See also Cultural context;
        Family; Gene-context interaction
    ecological systems theory, 87–89
    and infant development, 228–229
    and motor development, 208
    and personality, 256
Contextual model, 47–48
Contextual theory of intelligence, 419
Control groups, 26
Conventional level of morality, 533
Convergent thinking, 433
Cooperation, 350–352, 454
Cooperative play, 360–361
Correlation, 28–30, 134
Crack. See Cocaine
Creativity, 430–437
    definitions of, 430–431
    measuring, 431–434
    and television, 470
Critical period, 80, 131, 265
Cross-cultural validity, 34–35
Cross-sectional research, 30–33
Crying, 251
Crystallized abilities, 419
Cultural context, 90. See also Context
    and attachment, 269, 276
    and childbirth, 172
    and cooperation/competition, 350–352
    and education, 315–316, 320–321
    and filial piety, 607
    and infant social development, 251
    and learning strategies, 416
    and parenting, 366–367
    and play, 357–358
    and research validity, 34–35
    and self-esteem, 553
    and self-image, 547–549, 550
    and separation anxiety, 272–273
    and social development, 245
    and temperament, 259–261
    and violence, 469–470
    Vygotsky's theory, 84–85, 86–87
CVS (Chorionic villus sampling), 125, 165
Cytomegalovirus, 161

D & C (Dilation and curettage), 177
Daycare. See also Education
    early childhood, 381–384
    infancy, 276–278
Daydreaming, 356, 357
Deafness, 399
Deception, 346–347
Defense mechanisms, 54, 55
Deferred imitation, 227
Deficiency needs, 92–93
Delinquency, 577–580
Delivery, 175–176
Denver Developmental Screening Test, 208,
    300
Denver II, 300–301

Deoxyribonucleic acid (DNA), 108, 114
Dependent variables, 26
Depth perception, 211–212
DES (Diethylstilbestrol), 154
Despair, 59
Detroit Test of Learning Aptitude, 428
Development. See also Theories of
        development; specific topics
    beliefs, 23–24
    definition of, 6–7
    ongoing questions, 22–23
Developmental arithmetic disorder, 429
Developmental coordination disorders,
    283–284
Developmental psychology, 6
Developmental reading disorder, 429
Diabetes, 119, 160
Diagnostic and Statistical Manual of Mental
    Disorders (DSM-III-R) (American
    Psychiatric Association), 284
Diary descriptions, 24
Diethylstilbestrol (DES), 154
Dilation, 175
Dilation and curettage (D & C), 177
Dioxin, 156
Direct instruction approach, 317
Discrepancy theory, 449
Disinhibitory effect, 70, 350
Displacement, 229
Display rules, 347–348
Divergent thinking, 432–433
Divorce, 374–380
Dizygotic twins, 134
DNA (Deoxyribonucleic acid), 108, 114
Dominant gene, 110
Double-blind procedure, 35
Double helix, 108
Doubt, 57, 349
Down syndrome, 120–121, 124–125, 165
Drug abuse, 582
Drug dependence, 582
Drug tolerance, 582
Drug use, 526, 581–589
    definitions, 582
    patterns of, 584
    and prenatal development, 154–155,
        158–160
    reasons for, 585–586
    symptoms of, 591
    types of drugs, 582, 587–590
Dyad, 27
Dyslexia, 429

Early childhood
    cognitive development, 299–300, 301–314
    education, 314–321
    language development, 323–338
    physical development, 295–301
    social development, 345–384
Early childhood cognitive development, 77,
    301–314
    achievements, 312–314
    intuitive thinking, 307–309
    memory, 301–305
    and motor development, 299–300, 301
    neo-Piagetian theory, 309–312
    preconceptual thought, 305–307

684

Early childhood language development, 323–338
  bilingualism, 330–336
  and cognitive development, 337–338
  explanations of, 326–330
  problems, 336–337
  stages of, 323–324, 326
Early childhood social development, 345–384
  and daycare, 381–384
  and definition of family, 365–367
  emotions, 345–348
  and family composition, 372–374
  gender roles, 361–365
  and parenting, 367–372
  play, 353–361
  and single-parent families, 374–380
  and stepfamilies, 380–381
  theories, 348–353
Eating disorders, 489, 512–518
Ecological approach, 87–89, 91, 107, 509–510, 593. See also Contextual model
Ecological validity, 34
Economics. See Social class
Education. See also Academic achievement; Daycare
  and bilingualism, 330, 332, 334–335, 336
  and cognitive development, 416
  early childhood, 314–321
  and exceptionality, 437–439
  and hearing impairment, 399–400
  and intelligence, 423, 461–462
  and middle childhood social development, 461–465
  and moral development, 537–538
  and rites of passage, 502, 504
Effort attributions, 465
Ego, 51, 53
Egocentricity, 308–312, 523–526, 572
Egocentric speech, 85, 337
Elaborated language codes, 335
Elaboration, 219, 412, 473
Electra complex, 53
Electrodermal response, 205
Elicited responses, 64
Eliciting effect, 70, 350
Embedding, 324
Embryo stage of prenatal development, 150–151
Emile (Rousseau), 20–21
Emitted responses, 64
Emotional abuse, 479, 480
Emotional and behavior problems, 486–491
  and genetics, 120
  and hearing impairment, 399
  and stress, 490–491
  and temperament, 258–259
Emotionality, 257
Emotional overload, 490
Emotions. See also Emotional and behavior problems
  definition of, 345–346
  early childhood, 345–348
  infancy, 250–256
Empathy, 446–447
Endogenous behaviors, 252

English-only advocates, 335
English Plus, 335
Environment. See Context; Gene-context interaction
Epigenesis, 114
Epigenetic landscape, 113
Epilepsy, 284
Episiotomy, 176
Equilibration, 220
Eriksonian theory, 56–59, 348–350
Ethology, 80–81
Eugenics, 131
Event sampling, 25
Evolution, 106
Exceptionality
  and education, 437–439
  infancy, 280, 282–286
  intellectual, 424–439
  physical, 398–400
  socioemotional, 486–492
Existentialism, 607–609
Exogenous behaviors, 252
Exosystem, 88–89
Expectations, 462–465
Experimental groups, 26
Experimenter bias, 35
Experiments, 26–28
Extended Objective Measure of Ego Identity Status (Grotevant & Grant), 556
External locus of control, 463
External speech, 85
Extinction, 65, 66
Extinction studies, 403

Faces, 212–213
Facial expressions, 346
Failure to thrive (FTT), 264, 274
Family. See also Child abuse; Parenting; *specific topics*
  birth order, 372–373
  definition of, 365–367
  and education, 319–320
  and infant social development, 247
  and moral development, 538–539
  single-parent, 374–380
  size, 373
  and social class, 373–374
  stepfamilies, 380–381
Family childcare, 382
Fantasy, 355–356, 357, 472–473
FAS (Fetal alcohol syndrome), 157–158
Fathers. See also Gender differences; Parenting
  absence of, 376–377
  and attachment, 270–271
  and delinquency, 579
  and drug use, 585
Fear
  infancy, 252–255
  and television, 470
Feral children, 103–105, 106–107
Fertility rate, 171
Fertilized ovum stage of prenatal development, 148–150
Fetal alcohol syndrome (FAS), 157–158
Fetal erythroblastosis, 169
Fetal period of prenatal development, 151–153

Fetoscopy, 125–126
Filial piety, 607
Flexibility, 433–434
Fluency, 433
Fluid abilities, 418–419
Forceps, 182
Foreclosure, 555, 556
Formal operations period, 78, 518–521
Fragile X syndrome, 123, 165
Fraternal twins, 134
Freudian theory, 48–55
  on father absence, 377
  on gender typing, 362
  on television, 472
Friendship, 452–455. See also Peers
FTT (Failure to thrive), 264, 274

Galvanic skin response (GSR), 205
Games, 530
Gametes, 107–108
Gangs, 580–581
Gender constancy, 363
Gender differences. See also Gender typing
  adolescence, 563–565
  child abuse risk, 481, 484
  delinquency, 580
  and divorce, 376
  drug use, 585
  early childhood, 363–365
  friendship, 453–454
  and gender typing, 279–280
  identity development, 556
  and infant behaviors, 254
  maturation timing, 509
  moral development, 535–537
  motor skills, 397–398, 508
  parenting, 246, 251, 271, 279–280, 484
  physical growth, 393, 395
  and sexuality, 566
  and SIDS, 204
  suicide, 590–591, 593
  television, 465–466
  violence, 468
Gender identity, 362–363
Gender schemas, 362
Gender stability, 363
Gender typing. See also Sexism
  adolescence, 562–563
  early childhood, 361–365
  infancy, 246, 279–280
  middle childhood, 397
Gene-context interaction, 105–107
  adoption studies, 136–138
  animal studies, 131–132
  and attachment, 265–266
  historical family studies, 130–131
  illustration, 138–139
  intervention studies, 133–134
  and language development, 326–330
  nature-nurture controversy, 23
  and plasticity, 139–140
  and sociometric status, 460
  twin studies, 134–138
General factor theory, 418
Generalizability, 33
Generativity, 59
Genes, 109–111. See also Genetics

Genetic counseling, 126–128
Genetic defects, 115–120
Genetics. *See also* Biological/ecological
    theories; Nature-nurture controversy
    chromosomal disorders, 120–122
    and context, 105
    definition of, 108
    and feral children, 103–105, 106–107
    and gender differences, 364
    genetic defects, 115–120
    heredity, 107–115
    and language development, 329–330
    prenatal diagnosis, 124–130
    sex chromosome abnormalities, 122–124
    and sociometric status, 460
    and temperament, 256
Genital stage of psychosexual development,
    54
Genotype, 111–112
Germinal stage of prenatal development,
    148–150
Gesell Developmental Schedules, 300
Gestures, 232–233
Giftedness
    intellectual, 430–437
    physical, 400
    socioemotional, 491–492
Goal-corrected attachment, 267
Gonorrhea, 575
Goodness-of-fit, 261
Grouping, 219
Group intelligence tests, 420
Growth, 6
Growth needs, 93
Guilt, 57–58, 349

Habituation, 206
Hall, G. Stanley, 21–22
Hard of hearing, 399
Harm, 490
Havighurst's developmental tasks, 59–61
Hawthorne effect, 36
Hearing
    development of, 214–216
    impairment, 399–400
Hedonistic level of morality, 533
Helplessness, 72
Hemophilia, 116
Heredity, 107–115
    canalization, 113–114
    chromosomes, 108–109
    genes, 109–111
    genotype/phenotype, 111–112
    molecular genetics, 114–115
Herpes, 160–161, 575
Historical family studies, 130–131
Holophrases, 235, 236
Homeostasis, 261
Homosexuality, 574
Humanism, 91–93, 606
Hunger cry, 251
Huntington's disease, 117
Hypothesis, 26

Id, 51, 53
Identical twins, 134
Identification, 51, 53, 350

Identity (number concept), 402–403
Identity (self), 56, 58, 546
    adolescence, 553–556
    mystery of, 605–606
Identity-achieved stage, 555–556
Identity diffusion, 58, 555, 556
Imaginary audience, 524–526
Imaginary Audience Scale (IAS), 525
Imaginary playmates, 356, 357
Imagination, 354–355, 356–358
Imitation, 226–227, 350–353
Immature birth, 174
Immunization, 169
Imprinting, 80–81
Incidental mnemonics, 302–303, 304
Incongruity hypothesis, 272
Independent variables, 26
Individual intelligence tests, 420–421
Individuation, 273–274
Induction, 502
Industry, 58
Infancy
    behavior, 205–207, 250–256, 258–259
    cognitive development, 77, 217–227,
        237–238
    Eriksonian theory, 56
    exceptionality, 280, 282–286
    Freudian theory, 51
    language development, 231–237, 322–323
    motor development, 207–208
    neonate, 195–197
    nutrition, 197–200
    perceptual development, 209–217
    physical growth, 200–202
    prematurity, 182–186
    research on, 210
    social development, 245–280
    sudden infant death syndrome (SIDS),
        202–205
Infant cognitive development, 77, 217–227
    imitation, 226–227
    memory, 217–219
    object concept, 220–222
    sensorimotor period, 77, 222–226
Infant mortality
    historical, 9, 171, 172, 173
    rates of, 11, 12, 203
    Third World, 16, 20, 198–199
Infant perceptual development, 209–217
    hearing, 214–216
    vision, 209–214
Infant social development, 245–280
    attachment, 261–271
    autistic disorder, 285–286
    and behaviors, 250–251
    and daycare, 276–278
    gender typing, 246, 279–280
    infant states, 248–250
    as interactional process, 245–246
    and parenting, 278–280
    and personal characteristics, 246–247
    separation/stranger anxiety, 252, 253,
        271–276
    temperament, 248, 256–261
    triadic model, 247–248
Infant states, 248–250
Inferiority, 58

Information overload, 490
Information-processing approach, 408–409,
    472–473, 521–523. *See also* Memory
Inhibitory effect, 70, 350
Initiations, 501–502
Initiative, 57–58, 349
Inner speech, 85, 337–338
Integrity, 59
Intellectual development. *See* Cognitive
    development
Intellectual exceptionality, 424–439
    and education, 437–439
    giftedness, 430–437
    learning disabilities, 426–430
    mental retardation, 120, 123, 424–426
Intelligence, 417–424. *See also* Intellectual
    exceptionality
    adoption studies, 136–138
    definitions of, 418–419
    and delinquency, 579
    developmental changes in, 421–422
    and education, 423, 461–462
    exceptionality, 424–439
    measuring, 419–424
    misconceptions, 422–423
    twin studies, 134–135
Interactive model, 105–107
Internal locus of control, 463
Intervention studies, 133–134
Intimacy, 58–59
Introjection, 362
Intuitive thinking, 307–309
In-vitro fertilization, 126, 128
IQ. *See* Intelligence
Isolation, 58–59, 459

Justice, 529–530

Kindergartens, 317, 319
Klinefelter's syndrome, 122–123, 165
Knowledge-acquisition components, 419
Knowledge base, 522

Labeling, 438–439
Labor, 174. *See also* Childbirth
LAD (Language acquisition device), 329–330
Lamaze method, 180
Language. *See also* Language development
    and communication, 227–228, 320–322,
        338–339
    definition of, 228–230
    development stages, 235
    and Down syndrome, 120
    elements of, 230–231
    infant development, 231–237
    and nature-nurture controversy, 106–107
    Vygotsky's theory, 85
Language acquisition device (LAD), 329–330
Language development
    early childhood, 323–338
    and hearing impairment, 399
    infancy, 231–237, 322–323
Lanugo, 151
Latency stage of psychosexual development,
    53–54
Laughter, 252
Lead, 156

Learned helplessness, 463–465
Learning, 6. *See also specific topics*
Learning disabilities, 426–430
Learning potential assessment device (LPAD), 425
Leboyer method, 180
Libido, 50
Limitation, 472
Locke, John, 20
Locus of control, 463
Longitudinal research, 30–33
Long-term memory, 411, 414
Love, 609
LSD, 159, 587–588

Macrosystem, 89, 260
Mainstreaming, 437–438
Malnutrition, 166–167, 200, 202, 395–396
Marijuana, 159, 587
Marital relationship, 247, 248, 377. *See also* Divorce; Family
Marker genes, 114, 120
Maslow's need theory, 92–93
Mastery orientation, 71–72, 463–465
Masturbation, 568–569
Maturation, 6, 220
Maturation timing, 408–510
Mature birth, 174–175
MD (Muscular dystrophy), 119
Meaning, 229
Mechanistic model, 46–47
Meiosis, 109, 120
Memory
    early childhood, 301–305
    infancy, 217–219
    middle childhood, 409–414, 415
    and research validity, 35
Menarche, 504–505, 510–511
Mendelian genetics, 114
Mental representation, 225–226
Mental retardation, 120, 123, 424–426
Mercury, 156
Mesosystem, 88
Metacognition, 409, 414–415, 522, 523
Metacomponents, 419
Metamemory, 305, 415
Metaneeds, 92
Méthode clinique, 446–447
Microsystem, 88, 260
Middle childhood
    cognitive development, 305, 400–439
    definition of, 393
    physical development, 393–400
    social development, 444–492
Middle childhood cognitive development, 305, 400–439
    cognitive strategies, 416–417
    intelligence, 417–424
    memory, 409–414
    metacognition, 414–415
    motivation, 415–416
    Piagetian theory, 400–408
    self-efficacy, 416
Middle childhood social development, 444–492
    and education, 461–465
    and family violence, 474–486
    peers, 452–461

self-worth, 448–452
social cognition, 445
socioemotional exceptionality, 486–492
and television, 465–474
theories of mind, 445–448
Midwives, 180–181
Miscarriage, 174
Mixers, 459
Mnemonics, 302–303
Modeling effect, 69, 350
Molecular genetics, 114–115
Monozygotic twins, 134
Montessori method, 317, 318
Moral development, 528–539
Moratorium stage, 555, 556
Moro reflex, 206
Morphemes, 230, 324
Motherese, 327–329
Mothers. *See also* Family; Gender differences; Parenting; Prenatal development
    age of, 121
    and attachment, 262–265
    education of, 16, 20
    teenage, 165–166
    work outside home, 277
Motivation, 415–416
Motivational processes, 69
Motor development
    and cognitive development, 208, 299–300, 301
    disorders, 282–284
    early childhood, 298–301
    infancy, 207–208
    middle childhood, 397–398
Motor reproduction processes, 69
Multicultural education, 335
Multiple caregiving, 272
Multiple personality disorder, 481
Multiple-word sentences, 323–324
Muscular dystrophy (MD), 119
Mutagens, 153, 156–157

Narcotics, 159
Natural childbirth, 179–180
Naturalistic observations, 24–25
Nature-nurture controversy, 23. *See also* Gene-context interaction
Negative reinforcement, 64
Neonatal abstinence syndrome, 159
Neonatal scales, 178–179
Neonate, 195–197. *See also* Infancy
Neo-Piagetian theory, 309–312
Neural tube defects, 119
New York Longitudinal Study, 256–258
Nicotine, 157
Nondisjunction, 120–121
Nonnaturalistic observations, 25–26
Normal curve, 112
Norms, 208
Nuclear family, 365, 366
Number concepts, 312–314, 406–407
Nursery schools, 316
Nutrition
    adolescence, 511–518
    infancy, 197–200
    middle childhood, 395–397
    and premature infants, 185
    and prenatal development, 166–168

Obesity, 396, 511–512
Object concept, 220–222
Observational learning, 68–70, 352–353, 472. *See also* Imitation
Observations, 24–26
Oedipus complex, 53
Offer Self-Image Questionnaire, 546–548
One-on-one principle, 313
Onlooker play, 359
Open systems, 47
Operant, 64
Operant conditioning, 62, 64–66, 67
Oral rehydration therapy (ORT), 16
Oral stage of psychosexual development, 53
Order irrelevance principle, 314
Organismic model, 46–47
Organization, 219, 412
Orienting response, 205–206
Originality, 433
Origins, 464
ORT (Oral rehydration therapy), 16
Other-directed regulatory behaviors, 255–256
Otitis media, 399
Overnutrition, 395
Ovum, 107–108. *See also* Prenatal development

Pain, 217
Pain cry, 251
Palmar reflex, 206–207
Paradoxical effect, 489
Parallel play, 359
Parenting. *See also* Child abuse; Family
    and adolescent social development, 557–558
    attachment theory, 81–82
    and breast-bottle controversy, 199–200
    discipline, 475–476
    and early childhood social development, 367–372
    and gender typing, 246, 279–280
    and infant behaviors, 252, 254
    and infant social development, 278–279
    and language development, 326–329
    and moral development, 538–539
    and peers, 455–459
    and separation anxiety, 272
    and temperament, 259
Pawns, 464
PCBs, 156
Peer groups, 455, 558–561
Peers
    adolescence, 558–561, 579, 585–586
    middle childhood, 452–461
Pelvic inflammatory disease, 576
Perception, 79, 209
Perceptual development, 209–217
Performance components, 419
Permissive parenting, 368, 371
Permutation, 324
Personal causation training, 464–465
Personal fable, 526
Personality
    definition of, 256
    and delinquency, 579–580
    twin studies, 135
Phallic stage, 53

Phenomenology, 91
Phenotype, 111–112
Phenylketonuria (PKU), 118–119
Phonemes, 230
Phonology, 230
Physical abuse, 479
Physical appearance, 138, 246, 511. *See also* Eating disorders
Physical development
  adolescence, 504–518
  early childhood, 295–301
  exceptionality, 398–400
  infancy, 200–202, 207–208
  middle childhood, 393–400
Physical growth
  early childhood, 295–298
  infancy, 200–202
  middle childhood, 393–395
Physical neglect, 479
Physiological dependence, 582
Piagetian theory, 75–79
  adolescence, 518–521
  early childhood, 305–312, 353–354, 357, 359
  infancy, 207, 219–227
  middle childhood, 400–408
  moral development, 530–531
  on motor development, 208, 299, 301
PKU (Phenylketonuria), 118–119
Placenta, 150
Plasticity, 139–140
Play, 353–361
  and cognitive development, 353–354, 357
  gender differences, 363–364
  and imagination, 354–355, 356–358
  social, 358–361
  types of, 354–356
Population control, 129
Positive reinforcement, 64
Postconventional level of morality, 533
Postlinguistic deafness, 399
Postmature birth, 175
Postpartum depression, 181
Poverty. *See* Social class
Practice play, 354
Pragmatics, 230–231
Preattachment, 266
Preconcepts, 307–308
Preconceptual thinking, 305–307
Preconventional level of morality, 533
Pregnancy detection, 147–148
Prelinguistic deafness, 399
Premack principle, 67
Prematurity, 174, 182–186, 484, 485
Prenatal development, 147–170
  and alcohol use, 157–158
  and caffeine consumption, 157
  and chemical exposure, 156–157
  conception, 147
  embryo stage, 150–151
  fertilized ovum stage, 148–150
  fetal period, 151–153
  and maternal age, 165–166
  and maternal emotions, 161, 163–164
  and maternal health, 160–161, 162
  and maternal nutrition, 166–168
  and nicotine intake, 157
  pregnancy detection, 147–148
  and prescription drug use, 154–155

Rh(D) immunization, 168–170
  and substance abuse, 158–160
Prenatal diagnosis, 124–130
Preoperational period, 77, 305–312
Preschool age. *See* Early childhood
Prescription drugs. *See* Drug use
Prespeech stage of language development, 231–232, 234–235
Pretend play, 354–355, 357
Primary circular reactions, 224
Primary sexual characteristics, 506
Primitive social play, 359
Production tests, 432
Productiveness, 229–230
Project Head Start, 133–134, 316
Prolapsed cord, 182
Proteins, 108
Proximodistal development, 153, 208
Psychoanalytic theory, 48–59
  Eriksonian, 56–59
  Freudian, 48–55, 362, 377, 472
Psycholinguists, 229
Psychological dependence, 582
Psychology, 6
Psychosexual development, 52–54
Psychosocial development, 56–59, 348–350
Puberty, 504–505
Pubescence, 505–506
Public Law 94-142, 427, 437–438
Punishment, 65, 66
Pupillary reflexes, 210
Purposeful coordinations, 224–225

Quinine, 154

Race/ethnicity. *See also* Bilingualism; Racism
  and eating disorders, 513
  and infant mortality, 203
  and low birthweight, 184
Racism, 473
Radiation, 156–157
Radiography, 126
Rapid eye movement (REM) sleep, 250
Reaction range, 113–114, 139
Reading, 416, 470
Recessive gene, 110
Reckless behavior, 526–528
Reflexes, 206–207, 222, 224
Rehearsing, 411–412, 472–473
Reinforcement, 64–65, 66
Reinforcers, 64, 66
Rejectees, 459–460
Reliability, 417
RELM (Rare event learning mechanism), 330
Replicability, 44
Replication, 27
Reprimands, 476
Reproductive technologies, 128, 130
Research methods, 24–37
  correlation, 28–30, 134
  evaluating, 33–37
  experiments, 26–28
  longitudinal and cross-sectional research, 30–33
  observations, 24–26
Respondent, 64
Response-cost procedure, 65
Response-cost procedures, 476

Responsibility overload, 490
Restricted language codes, 335
Retentional processes, 69
Reversibility, 305, 402–403
Rh(D) immunization, 168–170
Rhogam, 169
Rhythmic cry, 251
Rites of passage, 501–502
Rock videos, 473
Rousseau, Jean-Jacques, 20–21

Sampling, 33–34
Satisfaction, 354
Schemata, 75, 219–220, 412–413, 472–473
Schizophrenia, 122–123, 135
Schooling. *See* Education
Scripts, 413, 472
Secondary circular reactions, 224
Secondary sexual characteristics, 506
Second-order effects, 247
Secular trend, 505
Securely attached infants, 268
Selective social smiling, 252
Self, 546
Self-absorption, 59
Self-actualization, 92, 93
Self-concept, 448
Self-directed regulatory behaviors, 255
Self-efficacy, 70–74, 416
Self-esteem, 448, 552–553, 585
Self-fulfilling prophecies, 462–463
Self-image, 546–549, 550, 551–552
Self-referent thought, 71
Self-worth
  adolescence, 511, 552–553
  middle childhood, 448–452
Semantics, 230
Sensation, 209
Sensation seeking, 528, 572
Sensorimotor period, 77, 222–226
Sensorimotor play, 354
Sensory memory, 409–410, 413–414
Sentencelike word, 235
Separation protest, 271
Separation/stranger anxiety, 252, 253, 271–276
Sequential designs, 33
Seriation, 406
Sesame Street, 471
Sex cells, 108
Sex chromosomes, 109, 122–124
Sex differences. *See* Gender differences
Sexism. *See also* Gender typing
  and abortion/infanticide, 129, 281
  and Freudian theory, 48–49
  and language, 338
  and television, 473
Sexual abuse, 479, 481, 483
Sexuality, 566–576
  age of initiation, 567–568
  attitudes toward, 566–567
  and delinquency, 580
  double standard, 566
  in Freudian theory, 50
  homosexuality, 574
  masturbation, 568–569
  sexually transmitted diseases, 574–576
  and teenage pregnancy, 569–574

Sexualized behavior, 481, 483
Sexually transmitted diseases (STDs), 574–576
Shame, 57, 349
SHARP, 581
Short-term memory, 410–411, 413–414
Siblings, 134
Sickle-cell anemia, 117–118
SIDS (Sudden infant death syndrome), 202–205
Simple representation, 231
Single-parent families, 366, 374–380
Smell, 216–217
Smiling, 251–252
Smoking, 157
Sociability, 257, 460
Social class
    and child abuse, 483, 484–485
    and children's rights, 18, 20
    and delinquency, 577–579
    and eating disorders, 513, 514
    and family composition, 373–374
    and infant physical growth, 202
    and prenatal development, 168
    and single-parent families, 377, 378
Social cognition, 445
Social cognitive theory, 68–74
Social competence, 458–459
Social development
    adolescence, 545–593
    early childhood, 345–384
    infancy, 245–280
    middle childhood, 444–492
Social interaction, 220
Socialization, 348, 461
Social play, 358–361
Social smiling, 251
Social speech, 85, 337
Sociobiology, 83–84
Sociometric stars, 459
Sociometric status, 457–460, 561
Solitary play, 359
Sound discrimination, 233
Sound production, 233–235
Special abilities theory, 418
Specific reading disability, 429
Specimen descriptions, 25
Spermarche, 505, 510–511, 568–569
Sperm cell, 107
Spontaneous smiling, 251
Stable order principle, 313
Stages, 23
Standard language, 335
Stanford-Binet intelligence test, 420
STDs (Sexually transmitted diseases), 574–576
Stepfamilies, 380–381
Stepping reflex, 207
Stimulus overload, 490
Strange situation procedure, 267–268
Stress, 490–491, 549, 551
Subject bias, 35–36

Subject honesty, 35
Substance abuse. See Drug use
Subtractive bilingualism, 331–332
Sucking reflex, 151, 197, 207
Sudden infant death syndrome (SIDS), 202–205
Suicide, 590–593
Superego, 51–52, 53
Surgeon General's Report on Television and Social Behavior, 467, 469
Swimming reflex, 207
Symbolic models, 69, 353
Symbolic representation, 231–232, 312
Syncretic reasoning, 307
Syntax, 230, 324

Taboo, 501, 502
Taste, 216–217
Tay-Sachs disease, 119
Teacher negatives, 459
Teenage pregnancy, 165–166, 569–574
Television, 364–365
    influence of, 472–473
    positive effects, 471–472
    related technology, 473–474
    and violence, 465, 466–470, 472–473
Temperament, 248, 256–261
Teratogens, 153–155
Tertiary circular reactions, 225
Texas Adoption Project, 136–137
Thalidomide, 154
Theories of development, 44–94
    behavioristic, 61–68
    biological/ecological, 79–91
    cognitive, 74–79
    developing, 44–45
    evaluating, 45–46
    and expectations, 45
    functions of, 44
    Havighurst's developmental tasks, 59–61
    humanistic, 91–93
    models, 46–48, 49
    psychoanalytic, 48–59
    social cognitive, 68–74
    social development, 348–353
Theories of mind, 445–448
Third World, 10, 202
    infant mortality, 16, 20, 198–199
Threat, 490
Time-lag study, 33
Time-out procedure, 65
Time-out procedures, 476
Time sampling, 25
Tobacco, 157
Torrance Tests of Creative Thinking, 433
Total parenteral nutrition (TPN), 185
Touch, 217
Traits, 256
Transductive reasoning, 307
Transitional objects, 273–274
Translocation, 121
Transplacental hemorrhage, 169

Transverse birth, 176
Trauma, 182
Triadic model, 247–248
Trisomy 21. See Down syndrome
Trust, 56, 349
Tuned out, 459
Turner's syndrome, 122
Turn-taking, 232
Twin studies, 134–138
Two-word sentences, 235–237

Ultrasound, 125
Umbilical cord, 150
Unconditioned response (UR), 63
Unconditioned stimulus (US), 62
Undernutrition, 396
United Nations Charter of Children's Rights, 14–15, 18
U.S. National Committee for the Rights of the Child, 15
U.S. Public Law 94-142, 427, 437–438

Validity, 417
Variables, 26
VCRs, 473–474
Vegetative reflexes, 206
Venereal diseases. See Sexually transmitted diseases
Version, 176
Video games, 474
Violence
    and adolescent risks, 527
    and delinquency, 578
    family, 474–486
    and gangs, 580–581
    gender differences, 468
    and television, 465, 466–470, 472–473
Vision
    development, 209–214
    impairment, 398–399
Visual cliff studies, 211–212
Visual preferences, 212–213
Visual-vestibular sense, 212
Vitamins, 154
Voice discrimination, 216
Vygotsky's cultural-historical theory, 84–87

War, 19, 482
Watson, John B., 22
Wechsler Intelligence Scale for Children (WISC-III), 421
Weight
    and adolescence, 506–508
    newborn, 175, 184
    and pregnancy, 167–168
Working memory. See Short-term memory
World Bank, 20
World Health Organization, 198–199, 202

XYY males, 123

Zone of proximal development, 85–86